MAIN CURRENTS
IN
MODERN ECONOMICS

MAIN CURRENTS IN MODERN ECONOMICS

Ben Seligman

With a New Introduction by
E. Ray Canterbery

Routledge
Taylor & Francis Group

LONDON AND NEW YORK

Originally published in 1962 by The Free Press of Glencoe.

Published 1990 by Transaction Publishers

Published 2019 by Routledge
2 Park Square, Milton Park, Abingdon, Oxon OX14 4RN
52 Vanderbilt Avenue, New York, NY 10017

Routledge is an imprint of the Taylor & Francis Group, an informa business

Library of Congress Catalog Number: 89-5220

Library of Congress Cataloging-in-Publication Data

Seligman, Ben B.
    Main currents in modern economics: economic thought since 1870 / by Ben B.
Seligman; with a new introduction by E. Ray Canterbery.
        p.   cm.
    Originally published: New York: Fress Press of Glencoe, 1962.
    Includes bibliographical references.
    ISBN 0-88738-811-6
    1. Economic history — 20th century.   2. Economic history — 1750–1918.   3.
Economists — History.   I. Title.
HB171.S48   1989
330.1–dc20
                                                                                89-5220
                                                                                  CIP

ISBN 13: 978-0-88738-811-8 (pbk)
ISBN 13: 978-1-138-52741-6 (hbk)

For Libby, Robert, and Ruth

The purpose of studying economics is not to acquire a set of ready made answers to economic questions, but to learn how to avoid being deceived by economists.

—Joan Robinson

The ideas of economists and political philosophers, both when they are right and when they are wrong, are more powerful than is commonly understood. Indeed the world is ruled by little else.

—John Maynard Keynes

Mere inventories of our inheritance of ideas are not enough; we need to analyze them instead of merely describing if we are truly to reckon them among our permanent possessions.

—Lewis A. Coser

Contents

Part One
The Revolt Against Formalism

Part Two
The Reaffirmation of Tradition

Part Three
The Thrust Toward Technique

Contents x

Foreword

THE IDEA for a book of this nature dates back to my student and teaching days at Brooklyn College. It was Professor Edwin H. Spengler, now Director of the School of General Studies at Brooklyn, who first introduced me to the field of doctrinal history with his superbly organized courses in the evolution of economic thought and contemporary economic theory. In those days, almost three decades ago, few texts attempted to cover the entire range of economic thinking. And when it came to the contemporary phase, expository material was almost entirely lacking: the situation was exacerbated by the absence of translations of some of the major European works such as Schumpeter's *Theory of Economic Development* and Walras' *Elements of Pure Economics*. Wicksell was virtually unknown, while some of the more interesting theories had yet to be offered to a world distraught and puzzled by the economic collapse of the strongest nation on the globe.

Matters had not improved very much when I returned to Brooklyn College in 1947 to teach courses in economic analysis and the history of economic thought. Students in the School of General Studies were severely limited in time and there seemed to be some need for an adequate exposition of contemporary aspects in the development of economic theory which might provide guide lines in unraveling the numerous strands lying about. Some materials were available, but these were generally organized along topical lines. An intelligible thread in terms of men and ideas still was difficult to discern. However, an idea or a project often needs a catalyst. This was provided by Mr. Jeremiah Kaplan of The Free Press, who suggested a more integrated treatment of contemporary economic thought. For several years, I had been writing on economics and economists in various journals: essays on Keynes, Marx, and Schumpeter had appeared in *Dissent;* comments on game theory were published in *Commentary* and *Labor and Nation;* and a long exposition of the theory of economic growth was printed in *Diogenes.*

These modest articles were the beginnings of the present book. The nature of my bias or, more politely perhaps, my personal value system, was evident in those pieces, and pervades, I believe, this work. Having been "trained" as an institutionalist, I have never been overly sympathetic with efforts to make economics a matter of pure analytical technique. However, this does not mean that technical competence is not a requirement for effective economic reasoning. One walks before running. The sharpening of ideas and concepts afforded by the technical side of economic thought is clearly essential and invaluable. But for years my complaint has been that the profession has bogged itself down in technical refinements and, in the main, has failed to go beyond them.

Economics is primarily a social science, a study of human action in a complex environment. Models may help discern certain features of this complexity, but to be meaningful it would appear essential that they point toward policy decisions that may help unravel unsolved socio-economic questions. Problem-solving is important, but then the solution needs to be applied. For one thing, this suggests that more attention be paid to economics as a study of the relationships between men: the overwhelming stress on the man-goods and goods-goods relationships may have provided the foundation for the development of certain kinds of technical analysis, but it fails to tell us much about the economic manifestations of social behavior. There are, of course, some economists who have undertaken to join pure theory to questions of policy, and, in virtually all of these instances, they have had an eminently practical objective in mind. One thinks of the studies issuing from the Scandinavian nations and from the Netherlands as cases in point. In this country, on the other hand, one is often hard put to visualize how policy statements might stem from the kind of theoretical formulations that now dominate the field.

Yet it would seem that the fusion of theory and policy is not an unattainable goal. It requires a vision of society as a kind of complex totality, with theory to be employed as a tool rather than as an end in itself. Technique alone becomes a form of engineering ill-suited for a solution of the great problems which agitate us all.

Our story begins in the 1870's with the revolt of the German historical writers against the seeming rigidity of classical doctrine. There were, of course, earlier rebels, but this period seems a natural starting point for a history of contemporary theory. In essence, the history of economics today is tripartite in character: at first, there was the rejection of formalism and the attempt to construct a humanistic purview. The awareness of human consciousness as a potent factor in social science clearly motivated such writers as Schmoller, Sombart, Weber, and Tawney. The spirit of rebellion also was pursued in other directions by the socialists and institutionalists. All this is surveyed in Part One.

Part Two sets forth the reaffirmation of tradition in economics. This began with the discovery, or perhaps rediscovery, of marginalist ideas by Jevons, the Austrians, and J. B. Clark. True, the marginalists also rejected classical doctrine, but not so much to upend tradition as to place it on firmer footing. And an important aspect of this development was the libertarian trend exemplified by Ludwig von Mises and Friedrich A. von Hayek. Here, underlying philosophic preconcepions, coupled with a particular version of marginalism, issued in a conservative whig-like doctrine of society. But a more neutral theory of economic action had been supplied by the Lausanne School of Léon Walras and Vilfredo Pareto. This current of thought was continued and refined in the work of John R. Hicks, Paul A. Samuelson, and Wassily Leontief, insofar as each sought to create a kind of unified field theory of economics.

The chief characteristic of modern doctrine, however, has been the thrust toward technique for its own sake. Some of the roots of this development could be traced to the Swedish writers, although, as already noted, a greater awareness of the intimate relation of theory to practice could be found among them than was the case with many another economist. To the Swedes, problem-solving without regard to policy was a futile exercise in logic. Pure theory has been a favorite pastime too of some of the leading American writers, most notably in the work of Irving Fisher, Frank H. Knight, and Milton Friedman. Finally, one must account for those theorists who sought to deal with realistic matters—Schumpeter, Keynes, Robinson, and Chamberlin. Throughout, an attempt has been made to deal with both men and ideas. The book closes with a summary of the ultimate in economic technique—game theory and linear programming.

The reader will quickly discern that my approach is fundamentally historical, in the sense of exploring more than the inherent elements of a theory. A determined and calculated effort has been made to view the evolution of recent doctrine in terms of the responses required to face the challenge of an ever-shifting environment. Yet the kinds of theories that were elucidated need to be met on their own ground as well, so that this work could not help but issue in critical as well as historical observations. Thus, as George Lichtheim has so well put it, theory must be examined functionally, that is, one must uncover what a set of ideas reveals for the particular time to which it relates. To undertake this effort means simply enough that one seeks to establish the genetic relevance of a theory and the nature of its intellectual growth and to weigh its truth or falsity against this complex background. The age of science and sociology has made such an approach somewhat unpopular, but when shifts in theory depend ultimately on a perpetually altering climate of economic, political, and intellectual currents, the attempt always seems worthwhile.

I am grateful to several friends for a close reading of various chapters. My thanks go to Harvey Swados, Abraham Brumberg, Professor Harold Wolozin of American University, Professor Horace Komm of Howard University, and Professor Jack Barbash of the University of Wisconsin for their comments. The late C. Wright Mills was also helpful. Professor Herbert Marcuse of Brandeis University kindly located several Hegel citations for me. I should like to express my particular gratitude to Professor Lewis Coser of Brandeis University for his careful reading of a bulky manuscript and for his many cogent questions and observations. His was a task accomplished beyond the ordinary call of professional fraternity. The late Sidney Kramer, an extraordinary bibliophile, and his capable staff, as well as Augustus Kelley, were most uninhibited in their search on my behalf for numerous rare books that now fill my study. Their persistence in directing me to out-of-print items in the literature was as helpful as it was costly. A half-dozen contemporary theorists who remain anonymous only in this foreword were kind enough to supply me with the complete bibliographies of their articles. Several went so far as to read the sections on their work, but they bear no responsibility for what I have said about them. My publisher, Jeremiah Kaplan, is to be commended for exercising the patience of a Job. But even more important was his continuing moral support during the years the book took shape. Martin Kessler, editor for The Free Press, was critical, perceptive, and frequently sympathetic. And, as usual, the last word is reserved for the writer's wife. Her virtues were fully displayed by the most heroic task of all—reading a crabbed handwriting and whipping it into a readable typescript. No reward is great enough for that.

BEN B. SELIGMAN

Silver Spring, Md.
January, 1962

Introduction to the Transaction Edition

E. Ray Canterbery

Seligman and the Economics of Dissent

THROUGHOUT HIS RELATIVELY SHORT but remarkably busy life Ben Seligman (1912–1970) practiced the economics of dissent.[1] It is an art that went into swift but temporary decline at that magic moment when David Stockman, then-President Ronald Reagan's budget director, trundled a Trojan horse called tax reform (a Derby winner in 1981) into the U.S. Congress. Inside the horse, as Stockman himself relates, was good old-fashioned trickle-down economics under the catchy label of *Reaganomics*. Ever since, the Trojan horse has lost its good name.

Seligman, the son of a Jewish carpenter, would have unmasked the deceit for what it was, a blatant attempt to redistribute income and wealth to the few in the hallowed names of "economic growth" and "federal budget balancing." What would have been worse from the view of Seligman, once director of research and education for the Retail Clerks International Association (AFL-CIO), was the outcome. It worked; the poor and the middle class are worse off, and the rich are richer.

Wasn't Reaganomics an economics of dissent? True, certain elements were attacked by once-influential Keynesians such as Nobelist James Tobin. (Tobin explained to the decimal point how the Trojan horse would result in the devastating minidepression of 1981-1982, with its legacy in trillions of dollars of private and public debt.) To the extent modern monetarism, Nobelist Milton Friedman's creation, had become the professional orthodoxy and to the extent that laissez faire and analytical technique for its own sake were inseparable, Reaganomics surely could not have been repulsive to the economic priesthood. No, the dissenting economists failed during the 1980s. Orthodox economics also failed by every measure except the one that counts the most, ideological inertia.

Seligman's double life as scholar and participant gave his economics of dissent two ingredients: dissatisfaction with economic scholasticism, such as the counting of the number of extra pinheads required to produce an extra pin, and a strong distaste for economic injustice. The orthodox economist would counter that *he* is too busy counting pins and pinheads to bother with the imprecision of "injustice," something best left to sociologists and philosophers (a preemptive expression intended to discredit these specialties as "soft").

Seligman, a one-time editor of the journal *Labor and Nation* and frequent contributor to such magazines as *Commentary, Dissent,* and *Challenge,* nonetheless could perceive the connection between priesthoodedness and economic injustice; the economist cannot be both humane and ethically neutral. Economic models cannot be segregated from their higher purposes or uses, nor did Seligman consider the rationalization of the status quo as a "higher purpose." Higher purpose and the ability to imagine alternative futures are the characteristics separating humans from the lower primates and from some of their own models.

As to the problem of defining "economic injustices," Seligman would say that he never had any trouble doing it. Like the problem of defining an elephant, he knew injustice when he saw it. This is not a unique trait: Don't most humans recognize injustice for what it is? Does one have to be the director of the community services for the Jewish Labor Committee in New York City (as Seligman was in 1953) or director of the American Jewish Committee office in Washington, D.C. (as Seligman was in 1955) in order to identify injustices? Should academic economics somehow be excluded from those studies known to be sensitive to human needs and fairness? Yes, if technique is presumed to guarantee immunity from the impurities introduced by cognition of the real world. After all, this is the connection between economic scholasticism and amoral/ahistorical purity.

In this respect, perhaps Seligman was unique. He played an active role in the most vital social and economic controversies of his day, ranging from the economic bias of the Constitution to the price-fixing conspiracy in the electrical industry and the role of unions in the needle trades. Not every scholar has the breadth much less the desire to live such a double life. No doubt, however, real world experience led him as a founding member of the Association for Evolutionary Economics and as its president (1970). Moreover, his writing, including *Main Currents,* belongs in this school of thought, one that ignores neither history nor ethics. This is a bias that the reigning positivist school of thought religiously avoids.

The difference between what Seligman considered human significance in economics and what (became) the orthodox or positivist school view can be highlighted by the now-famous exchange with Milton Friedman in *Challenge*. Ben Seligman summarizes the human importance of Friedman's work by stating:

I shall not go into the technicalities involved, but merely observe that in his view poverty is simply a matter of choice made by the poor, since they are so utterly unwilling to undertake risk. Observations of this character are so outlandish in the light of contemporary sociological knowledge that they must be rejected out of hand.

Milton Friedman was furious with this characterization of his scientific views and demanded that a letter be published in the most prominent possible place. In Friedman's restatement of the disputed point, Seligman's folly was to attribute to Friedman the supposition that non-risk takers are the *only* unfortunates. There are, said Friedman, also "people who were willing to take risks, did so, and lost." In other words, Friedman's theory of poverty is much broader than Seligman thought! What became the orthodox—in contrast to Seligman's—view of poverty was only slightly elevated during the 1980s when poverty represented the failure of the individual to acquire a brokerage license.

I suspect that Seligman was on the right track. He notes in *Main Currents* how economics was narrowed to choice with constraints (mathematical, not real constraints). The focus always has been on the choice part and not on the "constraints," those nice little mathematical "side conditions" required to gain constrained optimal solutions. In turn, the optima were embraced as the "best" rather than the "best possible" within a set of horrible outcomes for many people. *Free to Choose* is a drama in which the poor guy chooses the used 1967 Chevy and the Yuppie stockbroker chooses the new BMW. Why the Chevy? It was a matter of preference. How do we know? Because he bought it (Paul A. Samuelson, Q.E.D.). If the truth be known and the mathematical problem properly stated, it is not a constrained optimum for the poor guy and not a matter of meaningful choice. The poor man is cornered by a corner solution, something that Samuelson realizes as a principles textbook author and as one of the humane economists.

Main Currents:
The Book

From this background comes *Main Currents in Modern Economics*. It deserves to be the classic it is. At the time of its publication, Seligman had immersed himself in the development of economic thought since 1870. This product of his efforts, a history of modern economic doctrines, is timeless—as befits a classic—even though the history ends with a chapter on ''technique'' that itself ends with a discussion of game theory and linear programming. Why is *Main Currents* still modern and surprisingly up to date?

Certainly the past is the past, and our understanding of it does not change all that much despite the work of new scholars. After taking classical economics through John Stuart Mill (characterized as a humane economist whose analysis is wrong), Seligman organizes his account around a central perspective that begins with an examination of the revolt against the formalism of the Classical School. The classicals were attacked on three fronts. Seligman's story really begins with the revolt of the German historical writers against the ''rigidity'' of classical doctrine, a natural starting point for contemporary theory. This spirit of rebellion was pursued in other ways by the socialists and institutionalists. Marxism, for example, was a non-nuclear fusion of economics, politics, and ideology. Institutionalism, with which Seligman was allied, takes us from the world of Thorstein Veblen to Galbraith's theory of countervailing power and affluent society—worlds that he makes us understand are not so much apart.

Seligman also shows us how the doctrines begin to repeat themselves. Tradition is reaffirmed with the rediscovery of marginalism by Jevons, the Austrians, and J. B. Clark. A more neutral version of ''equilibrium economics'' is supplied by Léon Walras and Vilfredo Pareto, a main current of thought extended by Nobelists John R. Hicks and the aforementioned Paul Samuelson. Seligman characterizes the principal trait of modern doctrine as the use of technique for its own sake. Dismissing G. L. S. Shackle's writing on uncertainty, he criticizes Shackle's use of continuous rather than discontinuous functions.

In some respects, *Main Currents* may have been published too soon to be fully appreciated. Seligman's focus on the thrust toward technique now has a ring of truth that can no longer be ignored. Pure theory without policy relevance has been a favorite pastime of some Nobel Prize-winning economists, such as Milton Friedman, who chose not to deal with the reality of market imperfections that had been highlighted by Schumpeter, Keynes, Sraffa, J. Robinson, and Chamberlin. In more recent times, the New Classicals has emerged as a school that not only does models for their own sake but considers their irrelevance to be their major (sole?) virtue. The formalism of the classicals has returned with a vengeance.

In some respects, only the names of the players have changed, and *Main Current*'s pertinence to today's issues is self-evident. Economics has moved so deeply into technique that the next generation may have to rediscover the past in order to find its way out. Seligman's book is a good place to begin the journey.

Where Do Modern Currents Next Flow?

The road traveled since the appearance of Seligman's book is that of high theory. The road less traveled is institutionalism, economic history, and an appreciation for economic doctrines. The outcome is much as Seligman had feared. If anything, Seligman underestimated the depth to which we would retreat into our own minds, always to emerge with higher order hypotheticals. The low (or high) point was reached with rational expectations and the New Classicals.

Rational expectations imputes to individual "agents" in the economy what before the Classicals were willing to grant only to economists. These workers and employers understand government actions, know the values of all kinds of variables, and solve complicated econometric models to calculate optimal predictions. This remarkable extension of the optimal solutions means that the government cannot influence real output or employment unless it can fool these brilliant balancers in pure auction markets, something the New Classical economists find impossible except in the short run.

The outcome was predicted by Seligman. By 1968 he believed that the technicist impulse would do away with such problems as poverty, income distribution, wealth distribution, economic power, business cycles, and states of consciousness beyond pure self-interest. Virtually everyone else knows about these problems but not the well-trained economic theorist of the 1980s.

Poverty and the distributional issues had long since been lost to the purity of Pareto optimality. If a dollar is transferred from the rich man to the poor man, no scientific judgment can be made as to whether the degree to which the poor man is marginally better off is as great as the marginal loss to the rich man. Beginning as early as the 1950s the prudent economist has been silent on this welfare issue lest his scientific credentials be lifted. Seligman would have said that one look in the face of the person sipping soup in a New York soup kitchen should have settled the issue.

I can recall a period during the 1980s when the mere mention of poverty in a room filled with economists would arch eyebrows. The message was clear; if you thought poverty was a problem, you simply did not understand market incentives in which poverty is part of the solution. If you didn't understand that, you didn't understand scientific economics. I sense this era is over. Even some youthful economists at Harvard are daring to speak the unspeakable, saying in public places that one out of every five American children lives in poverty. Countering this, other economists are complaining about the reduction of the poverty rate among the elderly through Social Security (bad because the transfer payments reduce savings rates).

The poverty intolerance is being replaced by a new form of nonsense. I shall call this the view that capitalism is sound because "socialism has collapsed." The socialist economies are in serious trouble; their people and governments not only know this, they are trying to do something about it. "The Cold War is over, the Capitalists have won! Perfectly competitive markets win over state planning." I do hope that the Cold War is over, and if it took "surrender" by the Soviets to pull it off, that's fine. This does not mean, however, that an economist finding markets quite imperfect rather than perfect in the American economy should be labeled a *Stalinist*. If the truth be known, Western Europe has been in an economic depression, and the U.S. economy is teetering atop a mountain of debt, off which a mudslide might happen anytime. For the first time in post-World War II history, the U.S. economy will be unable to sustain a recession. The difference is clear: Capitalism is in trouble but doesn't know it.

Which brings us to the mysterious disappearance of the business cycle in economic theory, another victim of the thrust of technique. The New Classicals have discovered that the real business cycle does not exist. By this, we might say that the ups and downs in the rate of growth in real GNP, used by the NBER to mark turning points in the cycle, if properly analyzed, do not exist. Whatever variation real GNP has is attributed to "white noise," a statistical term meaning that the variations are random and therefore not cyclical after all.

Can we imagine the kind of physical danger the academic economist would face if he told an unemployed GM blue-collar worker that his unemployment is simply "white noise"? More importantly, would the worker accept the notion that nothing can or should be done about the unemployment? I am not sure about the worker, but Ben Seligman would not accept the idea. To be fair, the New Classicals see the 25 percent unemployment rates of the Great Depression as a challenge to their ideas, but they are quite sure that the Keynesian explanation for the Great Depression is wrong because it is not *their* explanation. Besides, they are quite unfamiliar with Keynes anyway. It would seem that the rational expectations focus upon price alone, neglecting quantity information, would lead "rational" individuals into horrific errors, perhaps unemployment.

And Ben Seligman is correct about the loss of the idea of power in economics. Imperfect competition cannot coexist with general equilibrium and perfectly competitive markets. In the paradigm only the market has power: It has power because no person does. The wonderful thing about the system is that everyone is powerless. You might think that alienation would spring up, and everyone, but especially the capitalists, would revolt against the market.

General equilibrium theory can explain only what it purports because of the logic of Gödel's theorem. The formal mathematics cannot be both fully complete and fully consistent. The use of power would make the model "complete," even convincing, but not consistent. If the economic actors are truly self-interested, they avoid competition (and the constraints of the competitive model) at all costs. Giant corporations and labor unions (lately weakened) conspire to make prices and quantities inconsistent with general equilibrium. They exercise power *because* of self-interest. But, do the economic actors use "passion with reason" in a way that redefines self-interest? If they do, we are more likely to find the reason in the writings of Ben Seligman rather than in general equilibrium theory.

Note

1. Ben Baruch Seligman was born in Newark, New Jersey on November 20, 1912, the son of Reuben and Toby (Katz) Seligman. Ben Seligman died October 23, 1970, in Amherst, Massachusetts, where he had been professor of economics and director of the Labor Relations and Research Center for five years. Between those years Ben B. Seligman was an active participant in economic affairs and a prolific author.

Other Books
by Ben Seligman

Most Notorious Victory: Man in an Age of Automation (1966)

Permanent Poverty, An American Syndrome (1968)

The Potentates: A History of the American Businessman (1971)

Editor of: *Poverty as a Public Issue* (1965), *Aspects of Poverty* (1968), *Economics of Dissent* (1968), and *Molder of Modern Thought* (1970).

Part ONE

The Revolt Against Formalism

1

Protest from

the Historicists

"Geisteswissenschaft und Verstehen": The Awareness of Man

HISTORICAL ECONOMICS was a rebellion against classicism. The latter, after winning the field in the nineteenth century with astounding rapidity, at least in Great Britain, seemed to have solved problems common to the West with a theoretical finality that brooked no refutation. Yet within a few decades after John Stuart Mill, voices of criticism and objection were raised, if not in Britain itself, then on the Continent, and particularly in Germany. As might have been expected, these objections were nationalist in tone and intellectual in content. There was a similarity of view among the dissenters that could be explained only by a common heritage and shared viewpoint. The writers on the Continent had a feeling that the old society was somehow undergoing important changes which demanded a new kind of social science. To meet this demand, some of them built all-inclusive systems of thought, while others concentrated on specific problems in a way that soon created a peculiar kind of narrowness.

Yet what was most significant about them was their intense consciousness of the human factor which made them wonder if the mere imitation of physics was really sufficient to create a useful social science.[1] Economic institutions were said to be different, and it was to be expected that the concepts and attitudes utilized to explain developments in commerce and transportation would not be the same as those in England. At any rate, this seemed to be the case for Germany, where the late growth of the nation-state suggested a need for neomercantilist practice. The German state took part in economic affairs to a much greater extent than was customary across the Channel. As Wesley C. Mitchell has said of this period in German history: "Economic life was stabilized, crystallized according to certain forms and procedures which were dictated in good measure by political institutions and practices which had lasted for a very long while." [2]

Economic questions were political questions as well, so that the concept of a political or national economy, as the Germans were wont to say, had a genuine meaning soon lost to the Anglo-Saxon nations. For the Germans, the emphasis on the political suggested rules of public administration more than it did the pricing techniques of the market place. And German economic thinking not only was content with government intervention, it even encouraged it. The attitude toward free trade, for example, was conditioned by a feeling that this was a policy suited only to a nation that had gotten the economic jump on everyone else: it was of no use to a country working diligently to catch up. The state was an integral part of the equations of economic science, for it was a factor that transcended a mere collective gathering of individuals.

These notions were not alien to the Germans, for they had been reared in a transcendental tradition that made it easy to digest such a philosophy. There was little in their make-up to suggest the self-conscious individualism of British utilitarianism. In addition to the long standing bureaucracy, which had created the basic mental receptivity, there was the powerful influence of the noted philosopher, G. W. F. Hegel.[3] For Hegel, reason, as contrasted with understanding, was a kind of communication with the world spirit. In an effort to achieve the goal he deemed desirable, Hegel posited that the spirit moved forward via a dialectical process. This was no simple movement of forces, but rather a complex of thesis, antithesis, and synthesis with the latter always an entirely new phenomenon. Implicit in this idea was a sense of time and change.[4] Human development was essentially a revelation of the spirit of a people. But in this process the state always was morally superior to both individual and family.

Such were the philosophic preconceptions that underlay the historical approach. Culture was defined by Hegel in his *Phenomenology of Spirit* as the study of the history of the human spirit. Reform through the application of abstract reasoning was to be distrusted, Hegel insisted, for only the historical unfolding of the spirit could reveal the true course of human events. German intellectuals were profoundly affected by Hegel's views as they sought to relate human nature to institutions. The dialectic, although now dismissed as useless, shored up the notion of historical stages and helped strengthen the genetic method in social science. (Yet Hegel expressed admiration for Adam Smith and David Ricardo whose economics set the pattern for classical abstraction, so sharply rejected by the Germans!) The cultural process, therefore, could be recapitulated by a review of the past, and, through the exfoliation of spiritual forces, would in effect reveal a history of the future. History's basic function, said the Hegelian, was to determine the laws of such a cultural development. Only in this way could insight be gained into the relevant natural laws that governed society.[5]

The famous legal scholar, Friedrich Karl von Savigny, who taught at Berlin during the first half of the nineteenth century, also exerted a powerful influence on historical economics. He had stressed a species of historical jurisprudence in which law, language, and custom were all rooted in the experience of peoples. He sought to prove that law was part of culture and that it grew "naturally" if it were not arbitrarily tampered with. The courts and the jurists, he averred, who in higher civilizations helped nurture this law, acted as the representatives of the spirit of the people. This was an organic process which had to be studied closely. Although rejected by some of the historical economists, Savigny's influence was unquestionably profound.

Some writers have noted a resemblance between certain elements in historical economics and the notions of August Comte, the great French sociologist, who had argued that economic data must be related to other social phenomena and rooted in historical research if a genuine social science were to be built. Such a method, he predicted, would reveal prognostic capabilities. To Comte there were no qualitative distinctions between nature and society and hence the same sort of laws necessarily applied to both. This made his ideas less influential than they were in France and frequently generated sharp criticism. An attempt was made, notably by the followers of Wilhelm Dilthey, to distinguish clearly between the natural and social sciences, something that was obscured by Comte's positivism. They implied that there was a uniqueness in human history which had to be uncovered, and that it was necessary to impose organizing concepts on the data of history. This, it seemed to them, was a more effective way to integrate theory and history. Those who adopted this view were taking their lead not only from Dilthey, but from the older historian Leopold von Ranke (1795-1886), as well, whose outlook was in direct opposition to that of Hegel, in that he did not search for transcendental forces behind historical appearance, but rather for the general tendencies exhibited in a given epoch. He wanted to grasp phenomena as they were without any superimposed preconceptions.[6]

One of the greatest philosophic impacts on historical and economic thinking in Germany stemmed from Wilhelm Dilthey (1833-1911). He insisted that history dealt with concrete individuals while natural science was concerned with abstractions. The latter had to describe and explain; what was essential to the social sciences was *verstehen*—understanding. Explanation sought causal relationships, said Dilthey, but understanding explored the motives of the human beings who brought about an event. Consequently, the historian imparted to the materials with which he dealt a sense of vitality that came from within. He made the past alive through his experience and what he reconstructed was really a facet of his personality. In this way, Dilthey responded to the threat of a thoroughgoing positivism. He had no complaint about "scientific method," but, he averred, the study of man required a different kind of science from that found in the study of things. Since truth was to be attained in the cultural field through internal comprehension, historical meaning therefore changed in time with the writer's culture and the actions undertaken. But this position, virtually a problem in psychology, would make historical knowledge per se almost unknowable.[7] History is not experience but rather knowledge of the past from the vantage point of the present. Certainly Dilthey's own inability in his *Introduction to the Sciences of Mind* to integrate effectively the notion of the past with historical growth indicated a certain failure on his part.

He had set forth three basic approaches: the first dealt directly with real events; the second consisted of abstractions drawn from ordinary history and constituted the basis of social science; the third comprised the whole host of value judgments men were wont to make. The second type, illustrated by the propositions of economics and psychology, was most important, for it could heighten our understanding of historical phenomena. Yet this could be done but infrequently since most of the time the historian had to depend on his artistic capabilities. Above all else, Dilthey wanted to establish useful relationships between the concepts of experience and understanding so that it would be possible to construct a meaningful history. He was not entirely successful in this venture.[8] Yet his ideas were markedly influential, leading to the *Geisteswissenschaft* movement which focused attention on cultural forms rather than pure administration. Despite their differences, Werner Sombart and Arthur Spiethoff were both affected by Dilthey's *verstehende* philosophy. And a line can be drawn easily from it to the notions of economic systems, economic styles, and even the ideal types of Max Weber.

Under such influences the Germans could not help but reject the classicist's outlook. They found a doctrine reduced by its epigones to delicately refined abstractions about rent, profits, and wages—a body of theory which to them seemed to have only the most tenuous of connections with what went on in the world of reality. There was implicit in it a concept of human nature that in no way jibed with their own observations. The powerful tradition of historical investigation in Germany looked at British economic theory and found it wanting. Thus theoretical analysis never developed strong roots: in German academic circles advanced and rigorous training in theory for economists was simply unheard of.[9]

German reaction to classical doctrine may be traced as far back as Adam Müller (1779-1829) and Friedrich List (1789-1846). Müller's romanticism and List's nationalism were powerful models for later historical criticism which mounted a persistent attack employing mountains of empirical data to submerge the abstractions of classical economics.[10] The early representatives of this school, Wilhelm Roscher (1817-1894), Bruno Hildebrand (1812-1878), and Karl Knies (1821-1898), stressed the need to inquire into the growth and development of economic institutions. They wanted to gather all the relevant data they could, covering past and present, before attempting any generalizations. This method, they were certain, would make their conclusions much more pertinent than the cold, inhumane deductions of the British. "Instead of being a set of speculations about what would happen under certain imaginary conditions that correspond but imperfectly to the real conditions in life, this program would give them conclusions which were drawn from life itself." [11] Fundamentally, this, it seemed to the Germans, was the better way to gather information to guide public policy—a perfectly valid Cameralist objective.

Roscher urged a return to empiricism to overcome the deleterious impact of the classicists; Hildebrand wanted to transform political economy into a science whose concern would be economic growth; and Knies denied entirely the validity of economic law. Monographs in profusion were written and collected in an effort not so much to supplement theory as to displace it. As Roscher put it, the approach was to be practical as well as scientific. The ultimate objective was a total science of culture to which economics would contribute its modicum, and the knowledge that would be gained from historical developments would reinvigorate economic study. The final outcome of this trend was the assertion of the complete relativity of economic doctrine. Concepts, attitudes, and theories, said these writers, changed in consonance with institutional change. And while they frequently expressed sharp differences amongst themselves, they agreed on one thing: the classical approach with its implication of natural law in economics could not go unchallenged. Economic life, they argued, determined the nature of its theoretical expression, which was always provisional. New facts always arose to question the supposed perennial validity of any doctrine. While there was some merit to this argument, the historical economists, at least the early forebears, were tossing out baby and bath. To many the deductive approach still seemed useful, and when we come to later historical economists, we find somewhat less intransigence and hostility.

ii

Gustav von Schmoller and His "Grundriss"

Gustav von Schmoller (1838-1917) did not look with equanimity on purely theoretical discourse. When Karl Menger, the noted Austrian theorist, insisted that the historical method yielded only holistic generalizations that blurred the distinction between economics, law, and politics, Schmoller's heated response was that abstract dogma could not show the way to a fruitful development of economic science: only the rigorous application of descriptive, historical, and statistical data could assure that high aim.[12] The debate quickly degenerated into the famous and arid *Methodenstreit*.[13]

Schmoller must be acknowledged, however, as one of Germany's great economists. He taught briefly at the University of Berlin, to which many American students came for postgraduate study. He helped found the *Verein für Sozialpolitik,* a society for social reform; edited the *Jahrbuch für Gesetzgebung, Verwaltung und Volkswirtschaft*—the famous *Schmoller's Jahrbuch;* and, after several important studies of German small industry and industrial policy, authored the huge *Grundriss der Allgemeinen Volkswirtschaftslehre,* (1900-1914).[14] During the early part of his career, his skeptical attitude toward classicism was quickly made evident with the contention that reasoning from a few premises was unrealistic. A favorite remark to students was: "But gentlemen, it is so very complicated." Yet the procedure of his predecessors in the historical school, he intimated, was equally unreal, for the habit of establishing uniform sequences of economic change could not be supported by the vast conglomeration of empirical data. Theory had to flow from historical and statistical research, and he thought that he had finally developed in the *Grundriss* a genuine genetic approach which at last would adequately explain the structure and functioning of economic society.[15]

According to this method, the varying behavior of different groups was to be compared and carefully studied. Ecological and geographic distinctions were to be noted and ethnic features taken into account. Although hardly a master in all fields, Schmoller exhibited an extraordinary capacity for weaving together materials from psychology, ethnology, anthropology, biology, and geology in evaluating economic and social problems. There was a striking resemblance in his work to later criticism of economic theory, especially in its concern with social institutions, the concept of relativity, its emphasis on change, the demand for realism, and in its vehement attack on abstract deductive techniques.[16] Schmoller disliked the Austrians intensely and thought that Marshall's work, though well written, was quite inadequate. The social sciences, he insisted, had no room for mathematics, for man's reactions were too complex for the infinitesimal calculus. Statistical data, of course, were acceptable but they were viewed with some measure of detachment.

If economics could successfully establish the necessary scientific ties with ethics, history, sociology, and political science, it would really convert itself into the dominant social science. As a normative inquiry, that is, one able to set down prescriptive statements, it would deal not merely with the relationships of men to goods, but of men to men. But the way to derive causal explanations from these connections, said Schmoller, was through observation, definition, classification, and development. Certainly there seemed to be some gain in this: at least, more facts were now gathered about economic policy, medieval economy, the growth of cities, and the spread of industry, even if its cost was to turn the economist into an historian. Yet, in retrospect, it would appear that the historical school was not all sure that it was headed in the right direction. After two decades of painstaking scholarship, the reforms that they had promised for economic science had been barely formulated. Even in the classroom they found it necessary to teach the fundamentals of the theory they despised, for they were charged with the responsibility of preparing students for examinations.[17]

Schmoller and other members of the historical group were deeply concerned with social questions, and in 1872 they helped found the *Verein für Sozialpolitik,* an association that fostered the view that economists should participate in reform programs. Most members of the *Verein* were quite conservative, and they all agreed that liberal and socialist solutions for the economic problems of the day were Utopian, rationalistic simplifications. They presumed theirs to be vastly superior. They came to be known, ironically, as "Socialists of the Chair," a sardonic reference to their academic status. Their advocacy of practical reform was intended to strengthen the monarchy, for to them the crown always was above mundane class interest. Government intervention was not merely approved; it was urged as the sole way of assuring effective operation of the economy.

Yet it was possible to see some parallel between Schmoller's ideas and those of Marx. He admitted the existence of class conflict and conceded that at times the state did in fact behave as though it were the protector of the interests of the ruling class. This he deplored, for it inevitably led to abuse and was essentially a degenerate application of sovereign power. It was really in the interest of the state to protect the lower classes, he said. This could be accomplished by a vigilant civil service imbued with a sense of public responsibility strong enough to enable it to stand above the class struggle. In this way, social legislation and the guarantee of collective bargaining would wean workers away from revolutionary ideas. It was easy to see why Bismarck embraced the program of the *Verein für Sozialpolitik*. While Schmoller rejected Marx's economic diagnosis of capitalism, he accepted socialism's inevitability. The latter would come about, however, only through the joint efforts of the monarchy and the more sophisticated workers, not as a product of proletarian revolution.

The acme of Schmoller's work was his *Grundriss*. He wrote it with some reluctance, for he felt that it was only a provisional synthesis of the mass of empirical, historical data he and his colleagues had collected. Although based on lecture notes and previously published papers, it remains in many ways a fascinating monument to the art of fact-grubbing.[18] As a study of general economic history it had some illustrious predecessors in the historical investigations of Adam Smith and Thomas Malthus.[19] But in these writers the theoretical portions overshadowed the historical and empirical. The work of a Richard Jones made virtually no impression.[20] Schmoller, however, was not overly distressed at the state of affairs. He felt certain that economics could be rooted without difficulty in the rich earth of historical experience. His concept of political economy, however, was quite ordinary: it was, he said, the study of the want-satisfying activities of man. There was a distinction between free goods and economic goods, and the frightfully banal preference for a plentitude of the latter was posited. For all Schmoller's stress on the totality of the economy and its integrated and interconnected character, there was precious little in his work which could be described as analysis.

The *Grundriss* began with a study of the psychological, ethical, and legal foundations of communication. Then the origins of economics itself were traced, and the concepts of family, social groups, and community were related to notions of property, class, and the various forms of business. Finally, after traversing much historical and sociological ground, the more usual subject matter was reached: market, trade, value, rent, credit, labor, and economic crises. Such a vast framework made it virtually impossible to develop an incisive analytic approach. Schmoller's philosophic preconceptions required that he stress the notion of a social organism and the moral and ethical aspects of the economy rather than operational analytics. Social goals were thought of in terms of sex ties and a community of interest. Reflected through this were custom, morality, religion, and law.

Consciousness and communication were preliminary to an analysis of human drives, which emphasized status and the "competitive instinct." As a result, acquisitiveness became essential in the evolution of institutions. Ethical controls were necessary to limit and control such drives which, if unrestrained, could be damaging to the fabric of society. If effectively sublimated, the drives might be converted into industriousness and thrift. Throughout this exposition, which appeared in the first two parts of the *Grundriss,* the stress was on ethical qualities. Man's development, felt Schmoller, was generally toward the good life and a heightening of ethical habits of thought, although he conceded that there was ample evidence of rivalry and hostility as major modes of action. The discussion of enterprise had an organismic quality to it: it was the enterprise per se which struggled for a central position in the market, not those who promoted, organized, and operated it. The enterprise had an existence apart from people, and its growth stemmed from inherited modes of social grouping. And it was the spirit of an age that determined how a society would make use of its material resources.

When Schmoller spoke of natural factors as the determining elements in the economic order, he did not mean the extreme materialist view which stressed geography, topography, and technology, nor did he have in mind the idealistic approach which derided any sensible connection between thought and environment. He conceived rather of a reciprocating relationship .in which the complex interconnections between man and man and the mutual dependence of man and nature all had a role to play. Man, he said, could not separate himself from the forces of nature but united with them in effecting changes on the face of the globe. Yet, whenever the story impinged on matters of theory, as in the section on technology, Schmoller stumbled and had to rest himself on the sort of analysis offered by the Austrians. Egalitarian notions were rebuffed and class distinctions exhalted as essential instruments for genuine social progress. Again, only the monarchy could reduce social stress. One could detect in Schmoller's presentation a kind of Hegelian drive toward perfection of the spirit. Economics was basic to an understanding of cultural change, and its study would reveal helpful insights for a comprehension of the future. Whenever Schmoller offered some prescription or advocated some change in the institution he was describing, he did so in terms of his version of what "ought to be," and whenever he spoke of the latest stage of development there was the inescapable impression that he thought it to be the best. How else could one make progress? Such vulgarized Hegelianisms were not unexpected among scholars who gave expression to some sort of mission that Germany was supposed to fulfill.

The psychological underpinnings are not very impressive by modern standards. Based as they were on pleasures and pains, they differed little from Benthamist hedonism. Some effort was made to sketch a theory of instinct or drives, which at least had the virtue of raising the question of what a proper psychology for economics ought to be. The other discussions in the *Grundriss* also were, on reflection, not overly perceptive. Resource use required an understanding of technology. Price determination was based on ordinary supply and demand, except for government fees and similar regulated prices, which should be based on just price, as in medieval days. Each problem was discussed genetically, statistically, \and theoretically, and an effort was made to relate them to economic policy. That is, Schmoller was interested also in prescription. He defended the Reich's program of social legislation as essential to stability. Yet he could be as harsh with the captains of industry as he was with the trade unions: the major need for social strength was always a powerful government.

The *Grundriss* revealed an encyclopedic intelligence at work. Schmoller wanted to see economic study whole and in the round, and for this he brought history and statistics and all the other sciences—social and physical—to bear on his subject. Unfortunately, the attempt to integrate all this was fairly primitive, but the emphasis on broad perspectives was a healthy one. That Schmoller was less influential than he might have been stems perhaps from his continued support of the monarchy. After World War I such views were not entirely popular.

He minimized the individualist approach, urging, for example, that the "labor problem" could be solved only on a social-ethical plane. Traditional doctrine was theorizing this question out of existence, he said, yet it remained as a pressing matter to which society had to address itself. If social ruin was not to ensue, the lower classes would have to be accorded a larger share in the fruits of social gain. He hoped for a better distribution of income than was currently evident. The expression of these views led to his famous debate with the historian, Heinrich von Treitschke, in which Schmoller reiterated his position that psychological and ethical factors were as important as economic ones.[21] The pure economic theorist could not forgive Schmoller his historical view or his participation in social reform movements. When Schmoller thought it possible to attain a general economic theory through historical research, he was encroaching on their position. The only difference was the direction from which each of these schools of thought would come in reaching the goal of pure economic generalization.[22] Yet it must be said that the historical school did create a sense of the completeness of economic and social life which the more theoretically-minded economists often lost sight of.

The absence of valid universal rules for economic policy and behavior highlighted the historical school's concept of relativity. Since motives, they said, stemmed from multiple causes, pure logic as a tool for investigating human action was inadequate. Theory could not be entirely independent of motivation; once this proposition was accepted, the essential unity of the social sciences could be demonstrated through the evolution of social causation itself. Society was a totality, and isolated phenomena could supply but a truncated view of the nature of an economy. Interrelationships had to be supported by concepts of genetic cause and effect.

However, Schmoller himself was not so overwhelmingly historicist as some other members of the school. He frequently made reference to "regularities" rather than "laws"—a notion explored most brilliantly by his leading pupil, Arthur Spiethoff, of business cycle fame. Economics, it was felt, had not yet advanced sufficiently to allow for the formulation of "laws." Although Schmoller sought to gather all the detailed facts that were required in the field of theory, he deferred to orthodoxy and even to some of the newer approaches of the Austrians. He never tired of urging that research called for both the deductive and the inductive approaches, just as good walking needs two sturdy legs. Practically, many of the monographs and statistical studies, which the members of the school produced, provided the basis for much of the legislative action in Germany. But Schmoller's endless preaching frequently prevented him from pursuing some trenchant insights, as in his discussion of labor and business enterprise.[23]

Encyclopedic works such as the *Grundriss* are easy to attack. And despite Schmoller's really extensive knowledge, specialists were able to find many flaws in it. The theoretical material was ill-digested: supply, for example, was defined as a flow of goods, that is, objectively, while demand was treated entirely in subjective terms. Much of the statistical and sociological data seem to have been gathered in a somewhat haphazard fashion. The tendency to substitute Hegelian drives to ultimate goals for actual empirical explanation pervaded the entire work. Ethics and politics were confounded with scientific investigation. Moreover, the failure to seek out a *pattern* of change made the vast accumulation of data virtually pointless. Whatever theoretical apparatus there was among the historical economists soon deteriorated. As Knut Wicksell once said, the description of trade practices in the shoe peg industry in the sixteenth century was deemed the essence of economic inquiry.[24] In effect, the inhibition of theoretical analysis enforced by historical economics made the economist a kind of genetic sociologist who feared to make any broad statements whatever since this might occasion less contact with reality. The many layers of description that were piled up, with monograph upon monograph, were little more than preliminaries to the construction of a tentative hypothesis which might serve as a prolegomenon to economic inquiry. The decline of the historical school was sharp, perhaps unnecessarily so, and by the 1920's it was *de rigeur* to poke fun at its pretensions.

The historians could not displace the theoreticians. At best, they could merely offer some counterweight to the latter's own exaggerations. Yet the growth of corporate wealth, nationalism, social awareness, and the new evolutionary doctrine were all sufficient reason for the existence of the school. But the theoreticians did not stay penned up for long in the Ricardian framework. While the historical school could produce only minor histories of still minor industries, theoretical economics began to explore new and unheard of vistas.

Werner Sombart: History as Economics

The extremes to which the historical method could be pushed were to be illustrated in the work of Werner Sombart (1863-1941). After preparing himself in law and political economy at Berlin, Sombart worked for a while with the Dresden Chamber of Commerce before receiving an appointment at Breslau. In 1917 he returned to Berlin as successor to Adolph Wagner. For twenty years he described himself as an ardent admirer of Marx, writing several works on scientific socialism and its founders.[25] Despite his acknowledged success as a lecturer, he was kept at a rather low professional rank for almost fifteen years, as a result, it was said, of his radical outlook. His break with Marxian socialism, signaled by a work on the proletariat, was evidently motivated by some measure of self-interest.[26]

Sombart, who had been influenced by Schmoller as well as Marx, combined in many ways the excesses of each. He rejected the idea of universal laws, insisting that economic institutions were relative to time and place. Although he was anxious to work out the deductive generalizations that Schmoller had not been able to reach, he failed miserably in his attempt to combine history and theory. Certainly he could not approach Marx's achievement. And in his desire to attain reputation and scholarly acclaim, he was not averse to engaging in the wildest sort of speculation, so much so that a good portion of his work must be rejected finally as patently worthless.[27] He may have been something of an artist, as one commentator has described him, "combining reason with imagination in an eminent degree," but his was hardly a critical or perceptive imagination.[28] He was ". . . often indifferent to the quality of his sources. He had the capacity to integrate ideas drawn from a wide variety of social relations, and then to present them persuasively, but his logic was sometimes superficial and his reasoning based on intuition rather than strict evidence." [29] The best that might be said of Sombart is that his work was suggestive. His book on the Jews as a creative force in modern capitalism was intended to be an objective, scholarly work, but it was attacked by Jews as anti-semitic and by Jew-baiters as insufficiently so. But though his work was often overburdened with exaggerations, it did exert some influence, at least by stimulating a not inconsiderable amount of research into economic history. One noted economic historian, Frederick L. Nussbaum, has even gone so far as to frankly model a quite competent text on Sombartian lines.[30]

For Sombart, the life of the spirit was at the root of any useful conception of capitalism. History was essentially a reconstruction of the fragmentary experience of the past, which implied the need for criteria to select and abstract factual data. In this sense, history was a creative act. Man had to be recreated in his social, political, and economic framework. For economic history, the necessary data stemmed from the requirements imposed on men to earn a livelihood. But this situation also was a social one, for social relationships perforce were established through the cooperative nature of production and distribution. And the existence of law and property rights introduced political and legal facts. Social scientists were apt to adopt one or another viewpoint, calling forth a history dominated by either legalistic or sociological elements. When the latter approach was adopted by a Max Weber or Karl Bücher, the outcome was a history of human experience in terms of generalizations which reflected the common elements of different peoples.

Sombart thought this to be most inadequate, for in his "cultural" approach he wanted to discover the distinctive aims and objectives of each society. For him, there was no such thing as an economy in the abstract, but only certain economies, and the task of the historian and economist was to ascertain the nature of each system in its singularity.[31] This required a "formative concept not derived from empirical observation," thus making possible the construction of the "systems" Sombart had in mind. In this way economics could develop the conceptual apparatus needed to classify the main factors of the economy at any given time. But the theoretical technique used in such an analysis had to be based on the economic "spirit," the form or organization of economic life, and the state of the technological arts.

Economic activity was conditioned, consequently, by the various factors which could be encompassed in the institutions through which the unique quality of economic experience might be distilled. This was the basic approach of his *Der Moderne Kapitalismus*.[32] Dilthey's notion of understanding was an important element in it, for in addition to organization and technology, factors stressed by Marx and Schmoller, Sombart added the idea of *Wirtschaftsgeist*—supposedly a real force embodying the creative drives of a culture and inspiring the whole life of an era. Inevitably, what was created was a *system* in which the total pattern of an economy was revealed in all its uniqueness. Although Sombart readily conceded that all this was a mental construct, he frequently wrote as if it were genuine reality. The basic notion was that capitalism (the only evidence for which was taken from Europe) developed out of the states of mind and behavior which facilitated those forms characteristic of the modern world. These could be comprehended solely through *Verstehen*.

It was necessary therefore to distinguish between economic stages, economic systems, and economic activity. Unfortunately, in his own work, Sombart employed these concepts rather carelessly. Certainly, his notion of social interaction at the several levels of economy was not much of an advance over earlier descriptions. All that he could do was to indicate the existence of economic relationships between people in the individual, transitional, or social economies. In the first stage, there was little connection between economic units. Relationships were broadened somewhat in the transitional stage, which now witnessed the evolution of exchange transactions. In the social economy, division of labor became sufficiently widespread to demand the kind of interdependence characteristic of a well-shaped capitalist order. Sombart's evidence for his scheme was drawn from many historical periods, so that the social economy encompassed both slavery and capitalism, while tribal economics and self-sufficient farming both could be placed into the individual stage. All this was a most dubious sort of classification, for surely many tribal systems have exhibited intricate connections with economies outside themselves. At least anthropologists have noted the complexities and numerous forms of intertribal exchange, all of which escaped Sombart.

In a deeper sense, an economic stage to Sombart was an expression of a certain kind of activity, or, as Spiethoff was to say later, a particular *style* of economic existence. Economic behavior, therefore, had to be viewed in the light of the drives which were most apt to characterize a given society. Thus the rise of capitalism had to be explained in terms of the hidden urges which impelled the bourgeois to undertake the creation of a new world. This was a spirit supposedly compounded of equal parts of restlessness, unbounded striving, acquisition, competition, and rationality. The main purpose of economic activity, said Sombart, was acquisition, specifically in terms of money. Prior to the development of capitalism, goods had been produced for their use values, but under the regime of the acquisitive drives it was the amassing of a stock of material goods that became important. The aim under capitalism was to increase the fund of exchange values. Up to this point, the influence of Marx was self-evident. But the emphasis on the nature of the capitalist spirit heralded a departure from the socialist analysis. The competitive drive became a purely personal factor in which economic agents sought success by any possible legal means. The ultimate aim was the ingathering of profit and the more the better. Human energy was transformed into labor power to be sold for a price; nature was converted into resources; and existence was registered in double-entry books of account. Acquisition degenerated into ruthlessness, and whatever moral standards survived from olden days withered under the heat of unremitting toil. But economic rationality and calculation were also necessary if money was to be accumulated in sizeable quantities. Capitalism had to utilize roundabout methods of production and advanced technology, and for this calculated planning was in order. Thus rationality came to represent the intelligence of capitalism and soon permeated the whole culture. Yet, paradoxically, as a system, it remained irrational despite all the individual calculation, leading to tensions that were endemic to the capitalist economic order.

Capitalist organization, said Sombart, was based on the principles of individualism and liberalism, which enforced a certain set of rights as reflected in law and the accepted precepts of morality. He also observed that its structure was essentially authoritarian: the word he used was "aristocratic." The number of economic agents, Sombart observed, was small compared to the number of persons in the system, so that the majority was controlled and directed by a few. This demanded a high standard of organizational skill and technical knowledge. He noted also that coordination was attained through the decentralized market so characteristic of capitalism.

Now, high profits presumably required high productivity. But if wages were kept at the level of subsistence, as in classical doctrine, high production in the short run would yield a large mass of profit. That this might be due to a kind of intensified exploitation along the lines of a Bedaux or Taylor system escaped Sombart. He did note, however, that technological advances could bring about greater profit through expanded markets and capital accumulation. The entrepreneur, in his search for new ways of overcoming competitors, would not be averse to improved techniques; this demonstrated the way in which technological improvements conformed to the demands of rationality and the capitalist spirit.

Sombart, however, confused legal and economic aspects in a not uncharacteristic way. A capitalist enterprise, he insisted, acquired a life of its own, quite apart from the persons who constituted it. For example, he looked at the system of relationships as treated in the law and thought that an enterprise set its own tasks and chose its own means of reaching a predetermined goal. The enterprise ". . . is an intellectual construct which acts as a material monster," he said.[33] But from the standpoint of economics, Sombart's concept was not entirely acceptable, for an enterprise was bound to founder without the active participation of its principals, who set the goals and choose the means for arriving at them. In short, the decision-making process functions through human beings rather than analytical entities. The enterprise alone cannot function, despite all the legal decisions that once stemmed from such formulations as the Fourteenth Amendment. While an "enterprise" is a useful device for economic or sociological discourse, in Sombart's hands, it acquired curious mystical attributes.

Sombart conceded that capitalism without the entrepreneur was unthinkable. He was inventor, discoverer, organizer, merchant, and conquerer. He developed new modes of organization, new forms of production, new ways of marketing. He opened up new territories and united diverse peoples in one great effort to wrest ". . . from them the maximum productivity of which they are capable." [34] Sombart's description of the entrepreneur was a panegyric to the capitalist function: the entrepreneur is an organiser of remarkable resourcefulness; he cleverly selects the proper men to do his bidding; shrewdly chooses the best merchandise; rapidly calculates his chances for success; forcefully negotiates with suppliers; sees with a thousand eyes, hears with a thousand ears, feels with a thousand antennae.[35]

But in the early years of the twentieth century, changes could be observed in the operation of this capitalist function. With the new corporate development, management and ownership began to be severed one from the other. Various facets of entrepreneurial work were taken over by specialists: efficiency experts, marketing specialists, advertising men, bankers. No longer was the entrepreneur a well-rounded adventurer. He now had to deal with the technician whose sole concern was production; with the merchandiser whose interest was marketing; with the financier who supplied the wherewithal through a complex system of credit institutions. This was the situation in the period of "late" capitalism, the phase that ensued with World War I.[36]

The strains that stemmed from the conflict of rationality and irrationality, speculation and calculation, and capitalist adventure and bourgeois caution seemed to relax as the more rational outlook displaced the daring capitalist view. As systemized knowledge overcame instinctive reactions and intuition in business, production was budgeted and sales campaigns were carefully planned. Enterprise began to lose its capitalist spirit and became in fact a kind of public undertaking based on ordered information. The entrepreneur became a chancellor of the exchequer, parceling out fixed expenses as his experts did all that had to be done. The old flexibility of the capitalist system vanished as restrictive practices increased, either internally through cartels or externally through government regulations. The rhythmic oscillations once characteristic of true capitalism were no longer evident. Price exhibited an uncomfortable rigidity. Yet this whole logical, neat structure that Sombart had diligently built up was much too facile to be true. His generalizations were brilliantly irresponsible and based on little more than high order guesswork. There was no genuine empirical basis in it, and, like the proverbial pack of cards, it fell apart, as when he sought to make the Jews responsible for the origin of capitalism.[37]

Sombart had been moved by Max Weber's thesis concerning the impact of Protestantism on capitalism to offer an alternative. The question was: why did the center of capitalism in the sixteenth century move from the Mediterranean to the North Sea? That the New World discoveries might have had something to do with the problem seemed to him an inadequate answer.

The solution, he excitedly proclaimed, lay in the fact that the Jews, expelled from Spain and Portugal, settled in Antwerp and Amsterdam and brought with them the spirit of capitalism. This was, of course, an attempt to relate economic, social, and religious elements, but it was not even an heroic failure. Sombart selected the Jews as the carriers of capitalism because they ostensibly exhibited the perfect capitalist virtues: intelligence, thrift, rationality, and the pursuit of money. Moreover, they supposedly had the experience, for medieval commerce purportedly had been in their control. They were better prepared for capitalism than the Protestants because their religious precepts made poverty a virtue, upheld rationality long before Christianity did, fostered the control of nature, and imposed no restraints in such matters as interest taking and trading on the exchange.[38]

That Sombart had a lively, uncontrolled imagination was quite patent. He had had no training in theology and knew little, if anything, of Jewish religious philosophy. He was familiar with only the more common sources— the Bible, the Talmud, Maimonides, Joseph Karo—and could not check whatever secondary material he used for lack of Hebrew. From a few facts, he proceeded glibly to gigantic generalizations with the extraordinary foolhardiness of one determined to exploit a fascinating topic. The assumption that Judaism exhibited only rationalistic tendencies and was eminently suited, therefore, to the needs of capitalism and industrialism is exposed as the wild guess it really is when one recalls the Kabbala or the Chassidic movement.[39] Sombart's resort to the notion of an accounting of sins through the rabbinate suggested a belief that the rabbi was really a priest—a complete misunderstanding of the role of the rabbi, who was above all a teacher. In the *millet* type of society that existed in Eastern Europe he was required to know many things in order to be of help to the community. The Talmud—the source of knowledge, wisdom, and philosophy that guided the few—helped the adjustment to an alien world without violating the spirit of the Law. As Bert Hoselitz remarks, Sombart confounded cause and effect, for it was not the Jew who made capitalism, but capitalism that made the Jew what he was.[40]

Sombart's study was replete with guesses and conjectures as to what might have happened. That some Jewish financiers rendered services to a few rising centralized states was true, but they at no point, for example, approached the role of the Fuggers. Miriam Beard has conclusively demonstrated, in controverting Sombart, that from the thirteenth to the seventeenth centuries the primary figures in high international finance were Christians.[41] The Jew was at best subordinate. Whatever power he may have had in Spain was broken by a fanatical crown in the fifteenth century. Church finance predominated in Florence. Those who lent to the kings—the Fuggers, Imhofs, Welsers—were not Jews. In fact, it was not until the nineteenth century, when capitalism had already achieved a measure of maturity, that a Jewish name, that of the Rothschilds, appeared in high finance. By this time the pattern and style of capitalism had been fixed.[42] As to Sombart's contention that Jews were major participants in Dutch colonial ventures and in the Levant trade, the evidence is simply nonexistent. He looked at portraits of directors of trading companies and said that they appeared to be Jews or found that a man who used the name of "Coen" wanted to escape being "Cohen." [43] That there were better explanations did not trouble Sombart: if facts did not exist he invented them, as in the assertion that a Jew financed Cromwell.[44] He preferred a racial explanation, carrying German romanticism to the border of madness. The use of racist theories was to have a terrible future, and Sombart's contribution was to be no little one.[45]

The religious traits that Sombart spoke of were for him fixed; from them he derived his version of the capitalist spirit. As his views became known, a veritable critical storm arose but with little impact on the author. Few competent authorities took him seriously. Yet the sad fact must be recorded that Sombart's influence was pervasive.[46] Religions are hardly as rigid as Sombart thought, as the history of the Reformation and Counterreformation has amply testified. The capitalists of Antwerp were as receptive to Calvinism as were the peasants of Zeeland. Early Christianity's proscriptions on usury were sharply modified centuries later by St. Antoninus.[47] Judaism, which was originally the philosophy of a primitive agrarian society, was also altered as its followers were dispersed throughout all the nations. But Sombart either did not care to know or was entirely ignorant of all the changes that had taken place in Judaic thinking. He had an axe to grind.

Although Sombart sought to explore the unique qualities of an economic system, the technique he employed frequently resulted in pushing back the borders of capitalism so that monetary transactions in medieval days were deemed to show "capitalistic" traits. On this basis, capitalism could be revealed in ancient Greece and Rome as well. The broad concept that developed seemed to some to be an inadequate way of ascertaining the distinctive nature of modern economic institutions. Furthermore, it has been argued, the fusion of rationality and enterprise represented an inadequate substitute for an analysis in terms of the social relations which grow out of the basic needs to sustain a livelihood.[48]

After 1914 Sombart's work was suffused with a violent nationalism, a most blatant example of which was his *Händler und Helden* (1915), wherein Great Britain was cast in the role of the foul trader and Germany as hero. But this was to be expected, for Sombart's basic preconceptions and methodology, given the situation in Germany after World War I, led almost inevitably to a sharp and violent rejection of Western ideology. Sombart revealed a crude romanticism in his preference for the "hero" role. Consequently, it is not difficult to understand his praise for the adventurous capitalist, his disdain for the plodding bourgeois, and his regret at the growing bureaucratization of economic life. That he preferred syndicalists to social-democrats in his younger days reflects the same curious pattern. As Leo Rogin has said, there was in Sombart's last work a "threat of fanaticism and intolerance." [49]

The latent totalitarianism in Sombart was revealed in full dress in his last book, *Deutscher Sozialismus*.[50] The new socialism was strikingly different from the proletarian variety he had espoused as a young man. The totalitarian, activist, heroic, and nationalistic attributes of German National Socialism now were taken as basic truths. German socialism, said Sombart in his dotage, had an "historico-realistic" nature which made Germany's will to greatness the ultimate aim of all human existence. Its organization must be appropriate to the German soul. Quite obviously, inequality was a primary principle. Status and rank imposed by the high echelons of the new corporate body would keep everyone in his proper social place. This would establish the will of the whole. In this new caste structure the State and its military masters were to be supreme. Society would be planned and organized by "estates," and economics made subservient to political needs. Obviously, the *Fuehrer prinzip* was an integral element. Technology was to be harnessed to the demands of the state, while the individual desire for commodities was to be tamed. A new élite would guide taste. Economic institutions, credit, productive facilities, and transport would be put at the service of the military. The profit principle would be removed from the fabric of society, and factory operations made stable and continuous. All this would release finally the true German *Volksgeist* as the only effective antithesis to the Jewish capitalist spirit. Although he may not have been a party member, Sombart was a thoroughgoing Nazi. The mythology of his last work, married to the destructive power of the Third Reich, bore fruit in the crematoria of Treblinka and Maidenek.

His earlier works in economic history and the sociology of capitalism may have contained some elements of truth, although it would not be difficult to demonstrate that these had come from Marx. But when they were raised from the level of social philosophy and analysis to a generalized unifying principle, a vicious mythology was called forth, capable of generating the unbelievable mischief and destruction that only totalitarians are capable of achieving.

iv

Max Weber and the
Capitalist Spirit

Many of the writers who contributed to the historical stream were essentially conservative. Some, as in the case of Sombart, were virtual romantics incorporating into their views the worst excesses of that style of thought. In many ways a reaction to the French Revolution, conservatism in Germany was geared to the prevention of revolution. It was a kind of intellectual countermovement which had its inspiration in Edmund Burke.[51] That it was able to make any advance at all in Germany can be attributed to the absence of the kind of middle class that had given British thought a liberal perspective. Romanticism became a reaction to the middle class's rationalistic tendencies; the community was opposed to society and intuition to reason.

Max Weber (1864-1920), the next important figure in modern historicism, was a good deal more liberal than either Schmoller or Sombart, and his appeal was to reason and society. While he too sought evidence for his generalizations in historic materials, he did not by any means imitate his predecessors. Schmoller, for example, was something of a traditionalist and a staunch supporter of the German monarchy; Weber detested the Kaiser. Sombart spoke of History and Nation as though these concepts were autochthonous forces; Weber preferred human rationality. The historicists suggested that society was an organism anterior as well as superior to the individual; Weber and the liberals viewed society in terms of autonomous individuals conditioned by social forces. History to the conservative was something transcendental; to their opponents it was but a stream of events which could be comprehended through the application of reason. Thus, though Weber's intellectual antecedents may be found in the camp of the historicists, he rejected the idea of the uniqueness of history and refused to believe that it exhibited in any way the sort of undefined transcendentalism so characteristic of Sombart. Weber has come to be as intellectually important as Marx, exhibiting a similar quality of rebellion against received theory. Unquestionably, he was an important source of many ideas which highlighted obscure regions in social science. Economics, however, he tended to put to one side, preferring rather a broader and more general range of problems.

A powerful personality, who exerted a profound and lasting influence on students and other scholars as well, Weber managed, at least among sociologists, to create a kind of school. Although he wrote many works which impinged on the subject matter of economics, he was not really an economist in the analytical sense.[52] His main interest was economic sociology, through which he could view characteristic institutions. While he developed an institutional framework for economic action, he seldom inquired into what an economist would consider to be the really substantive issues. In his analysis of capitalism, for example, there is not much that one can find on business cycles. Whatever theory he used he took from the Austrians. He was essentially a polyhistor, a universal scholar who wanted to observe human beings through the science of sociology. The immediately practical did not concern him: he could easily pursue an idea that was quite distant from the pragmatic needs of the day. Consequently, he did not hesitate to investigate urbanism, music, art history, world religions, economic motivations, and other recondite matters.

Although he was a nationalist and a sometime believer in the notion of the *Herrenvolk,* he oddly enough stressed the importance of individual freedom, rejecting racism as a completely false ideology. As a student at Heidelberg he was deemed to be a nonconformist, rigid and stuffy in his ideals, and something of an annoying hypochondriac. In his studies of ancient Judaic society, Weber identified himself with the prophet Jeremiah and—irony of ironies—Germany, pariah among nations, was likened to the Jews. Although an intellectual, he nevertheless did not shun politics. In fact, he was somewhat ambivalent about it, often thinking he ought to follow politics as a full-time occupation. He despised the Kaiser because he felt that imperial policies were leading to unavoidable catastrophe through inefficiency and mismanagement. The Kaiser's behavior he thought disastrous, particularly in foreign policy, and the attitude of the Junker ruling class he described as idiotic. Although Weber had started as a conservative, he quickly moved to oppose the régime.

Weber was born in Erfurt in 1864 into a family quite active in civic affairs, and his father was a fairly well-known politician. But through the years the parents became more and more estranged, which had a disturbing impact on young Weber, who as a child was quite sickly. Intellectually precocious, his world was one of books rather than sports. He went to Heidelberg to study law, and there his penchant for rebelling against the authority of his elders soon manifested itself. Yet he could not escape student life and soon had his share of traditional dueling. Although influenced somewhat by the writings of William Ellery Channing, he could not abide the latter's pacifism. After completing his legal studies, Weber went on to economic history, writing a quite competent thesis on trading companies in the Middle Ages—it was a traditional study, combining characteristic German erudition and a nationalistic outlook. Little in it presaged the fiercely independent intellect that he was to demonstrate in later years.

In 1893 he married a distant cousin and accepted a professorship at Freiburg. In his initial lecture, imperialism, *real-politik,* and the Hohenzollerns were accepted as the touchstones of political wisdom. In 1896 he succeeded Knies at Heidelberg, only to suffer an emotional and mental collapse two years later. In fact, the state of his mental health was to plague him for the rest of his life: periods of depression, during which he could scarcely look at print, were followed by outbursts of the most intense intellectual activity. His recovery was slow and it was not until 1902 that he could return to Heidelberg.[53] As if to make up for all the lost time, Weber literally plunged headlong into studies of economic history, politics, and law. Frequent travel helped overcome the dread sense of anxiety that haunted him. In 1904, he visited the United States to lecture at St. Louis, and, in contrast to many distinguished visitors, Weber found this country fascinating. He was enthusiastic about the Brooklyn Bridge, mass transportation, Niagara Falls, and itinerant shoe-shine boys. Yet the tremendous waste of resources impressed him with equal force. Labor, immigration, the Negro problem, politicians—these were the things that caught his interest. When he returned to Germany, he did so with the conviction that professional machine politics were essential for modern mass democracy if a countervailing power to a bureaucratic mandarin class of civil servants was to be created.[54] Upon his return to Heidelberg, Weber joined as stimulating a group of individuals as could be found anywhere on the continent—his brother Alfred, Wilhelm Windelband, Georg Jellinek, Robert Michels, Sombart, Hugo Münsterberg, and Georg Lukacs were frequent visitors. Slowly he moved to the democratic view, not as a body of viable political ideas in the Anglo-Saxon tradition, but rather as a practical means of operating society. After World War I, Weber shifted his loyalties to the Republic. In 1919 he went to Munich to succeed Brentano. His last lectures were published posthumously in 1923 as the *General Economic History.*

Weber's approach to historical problems was a good deal more careful than Sombart's. Concerned as he was with methodological questions, he began with a demolition of the preconceptions of the earlier historical economists, particularly Roscher and Knies, and this essay, together with his other methodological writings, exerted a lasting influence on the social sciences.[55] In it Weber began his intellectual struggle against the banalities of a purely naturalistic approach as well as against the idealistic assertion that scientific work was not possible in the social sciences. His aim was to develop a rigorous conceptual structure that would order factual data more sensibly than was hitherto possible. Consequently, it was necessary to shed the heritage of the historical economists who were fusing in their work a curiously perverted

Marxism with the romantic, idealistic view of "spirit" and thus smuggling into the study of society an intuitive but irrational methodology. Weber's purpose rather was to establish law, calculability, and rationality as the basis of social science. In no other way would it be possible to establish causality and provide a satisfactory explanation of human behavior.

This led Weber to his Ideal Type, one of the most famous tools in modern social science.[55] Explanation, he said, was not merely a matter of description, but encompassed also interpretation of one's findings, so that the meaning of a culture might be comprehended more fully. This was his Interpretive Sociology. He accepted fully the concept of *Verstehen,* but he gave it a meaning somewhat at variance with the one employed by his predecessors. Whereas they had talked in terms of genetic categories, understanding for Weber had to be grounded in certain theoretical structures which might be used to establish the necessary causal relationships. Knowledge, he said, was always abstract. This was true even of empirical data, for the only facts one really knew were those of immediate concern to the inquirer. Consequently, social phenomena were described against a particular conceptual backdrop, the construction of which was prior to the attempt to generalize.[56] Four types of action, said Weber, encompassed the whole gamut of social actions: first, the type that fused numerous means to attain one's ends—*zweckrational;* second, that which was rational in means but nonrational in ends—*wertrational;* third, that which was guided primarily by emotional sentiments—*affektual;* and fourth, that which was based on habit and established patterns—*traditional*. This four-fold structure was directly related to Weber's Ideal Type concept and provided the basis for a description of society as a whole.[57]

In this way, argued Weber, the social scientist created an abstraction, albeit for his own convenience, but one which nevertheless revealed the essential features of the situation he had before him. To grasp how this Ideal Type methodology functioned it appeared essential to understand the meaning that the individual or actor himself gave to social action.[58] The Ideal Type was admittedly an artificial construct, but it contained elements of reality which became logical concepts when used as analytical tools. Illustrations were "economic man" or "feudalism." It described historical data in a comparative way: in fact, many Ideal Types could be constructed out of the materials of history that would enable one to comprehend much more easily the regularities of social and economic phenomena. It was a limiting concept, said Weber, to which the real situation was compared in order to extract certain significant components. In studying capitalism, for example, it was important to find out why it had failed to crop up in societies other than those of the west. The Ideal Type thus became a way of exploring the unique aspects of an historical situation. Insofar as it succeeded, it was related in some ways to Sombart's notion of "system." Although Weber could not escape the idea of understanding so popular in his day, he did give it a rationalistic twist. His constructions—society and community—did not exhibit the transcendentalism that was characteristic of Sombart and most of German social science at the time. Rather they were used to explain the behavior of the individual, and neither materialistic nor idealistic elements were allowed to predominate: both were viewed as particular types in a total milieu.

Much of Weber's investigative technique reflected the Marxian method, although he did quarrel frequently with the philosophy of historical materialism. Yet as Gerth and Mills remark, Weber's work in large part was an attempt to round out Marxian materialism with a political and military materialism.[59] While Marx thought that he had discovered the keys to social reality in the relationships that were revealed through the mode of production, Weber concentrated on the control of weapons and political administration, for he was interested mainly in the numerous ways in which the material instrumentalities of political power were established. Marx's alienation from the means of production was matched by Weber's bureaucratization of political and social life. While in Marx political and economic powers were intimately related, Weber kept these realms quite distinct. He insisted that religious and political ideas exhibited a force of their own to which man was answerable. Ideas were no mere superstructure; they could generate conflict and tension just as readily as material self-interest. In short, Weber agreed with Marx that the state was the locus of political power. They differed only on the nature of the approaches. Ideology and material interests also were intertwined through the technique of "rationalization," a process that could be extended even to "proletarian" systems, as we have come to know in the history of the Soviet Union. As Stuart Hughes has said, both had essentially a radical analysis of society.[60]

For Weber, capitalism was the epitome of rationality. To Marx, on the other hand, this would have been an intolerable concept simply because the forces of production were bound and restricted by existing social relationships. Weber insisted that the class struggle was not really central, being due merely to differences in property holdings and the varying success of participants in the market place. Socialism, said Weber, would merely extend the bureaucratization of economic life, something that he abhorred. While bureaucracy itself was rationalistic, the process enforced a deadly routine on its participants and depersonalized them. Alienation became a universal phenomenon that affected everyone.

Although none of this necessarily ruled out analytical economic theory, in Weber's hands an attitude of indifference seems to have been cultivated. In the main he accepted the findings of others, passing on to what appeared to him to be more critical matters. One of these was the relation of religious ideas to economic organization. A good part of his work in this area was incorporated in his *Economy and Society* in which he sought to outline the institutional framework of economic activity as well as the way in which this framework could be altered.[61] The latter implied, of course, that the "natural order" of the classicists was to be discarded. The existence of deep tensions in society made it doubtful that stability could be maintained. Yet Weber insisted that the economic system was one in which participants based their decisions on a rational comparison of utilities and costs. This process, he said, was integral to the spirit of capitalism, stemming mainly from a favorable psychological attitude. A rational state and impartial legal system were also elements of the same economy.

Whatever economic analysis entered into Weber's presentation centered on money and its uses. He also expressed an interest in the structure of markets and the relation of economic units to them. Obviously, money was very important in this milieu, for it made possible an extension of exchange relationships and helped the development of indirect exchange. Moreover, it not only heightened the acquisitive orientation implicit in capitalist behavior, but also made planning possible by facilitating the comparison of transactions. Since the existence of limited resources required allocation, behavior patterns developed which employed choice as a major factor. Nevertheless, self-interest did not necessarily bring about a social benefit, as in Adam Smith's "unseen hand of Providence." In fact, Weber recognized the existence of strain between individual and social objectives, which he described, somewhat ponderously, as tension between formal and substantive rationality. Attainment of the latter—the social aims—might be defined as the way in which an economy could be operated to meet the needs of a population and still conform to some agreed upon ethical norm. Formal rationality, or the way in which the economy carried through individual acts of exchange, depended on capital accounting and a continuous extension of the market. Weber did not think that socialism was an effective solution to the problem: here he accepted the Mises' argument, but he did acknowledge that market equilibria were not sufficiently stable to prevent the development of alternative solutions.[62] Still, the market theory of orthodox economics appeared to him to be the only rational answer—an answer which clashed harshly with his recognition of "approbation," whereby individuals were closed off from access to certain sectors of the economy. Monopoly was a case in point. Although Weber sought to escape the difficulty by relating appropriation to rights rather than things, it was quite evident that he was simply uninterested in the abstractions which formal economic analysis had to offer.

Weber's long discussion of labor-management relations yielded little in the way of fresh insights.[63] He recognized that in large-scale production the worker had to be separated from the means of production and that centralized control based on private property rights was essential to its effective functioning. Yet with the growth of large organizations and a widening of the market, the economy tended to become increasingly more rigid, he said. Even the workers began to think in terms of a "property right" to a job, thereby adding to the rigidity of the system. According to Weber, the "formal rationality," the pattern of transactions, had to function in a context of laissez faire. This implied private ownership, alienation of workers from tools, profit maximization, calculability, enforcement of contracts, and a rational money system.[64] However, much of Weber's discussion of economic problems was fragmentary, albeit quite suggestive, as in his section on economic motivation.[65] But to an economist it contained little that was original, particularly after one had met up with Veblen or Marx. Centering one's attention on market relationships and expressing a concern with the problem of calculation through the money economy can lead to some useful observations, but Weber evidently was not overly interested in these possibilities. He focused his sights rather on questions which were in the main sociological and noneconomic.

In his *Protestant Ethic and the Spirit of Capitalism,* however, Weber made a major contribution to the theory of capitalism's origins. In it he stressed the independent functioning of ideas as a significant basis for economic growth. Capitalism, he argued, required for its effective functioning a personality to whom spiritual and material asceticism were values in themselves. This he found in the Calvinist who sought to prove his worth as one of the chosen by making the success of an enterprise the prime objective. The Calvinist's theology dictated unremitting toil; he was not permitted the pleasurable ways of life. Gains could be reinvested only in business and from this ascetic behavior there stemmed capital accumulation. Rationality, unceasing labor, precise accounting to reveal what was happening at any given point in time, and peaceful trade were the only things that complied with such an ethos. Weber also illustrated the effect of religion on economics in an essay on the Protestant sects in the United States,[66] in which he observed that acceptance of one's business status was closely related to church membership. Sect membership, he said, was a certificate of moral qualification and business rectitude. Exclusion from a sect for a moral offense often meant a loss of economic position, while association with religion meant success in entrepreneurial endeavors. By stressing external factors in this way, Weber was saying that the economy could be explained not through internal elements alone: it was necessary to incorporate significant exogenous forces into the theoretical structure as well. Weber was not trying to say that Protestantism had caused capitalism: he was merely seeking to determine the extent to which religious forces exerted an influence on economic development. The rationalistic form of capitalism known to the west had not manifested itself in India or China, and this, Weber felt, was because only in Europe had certain spiritual drives and material concerns coincided at a given point in history to create the economy with which we are familiar. Weber's point was that in the case of occidental capitalism religion helped form an effective instrument for the creation of wealth.[67] Yet the more he became embittered with German politics, the more he realized how much material interest weighed in the success of an idea.[68] He was beginning to approach the Marxist view in spite of himself.

Certain aspects of capitalism could be visualized more clearly, said Weber, if a distinction were made between different "types." In political capitalism, profit stemmed from war and conquest. Adventure, the drive for colonial power, and booty were outstanding characteristics of this form. Pariah capitalism embodied the actions of certain marginal economic groups, such as the Jews or Parsees. Imperialist capitalism accompanied political expansionism, as in the case of the British Empire. Fiscal capitalism, typical of some older societies, was based usually on tax farming, as in ancient Rome and the Ancien Régime in France. The significant form today, however, was industrial capitalism, in which emphasis was placed on factory production utilizing free labor (already alienated from the tools of production) and which was based upon a considerable investment in fixed capital. In this form, particularly, all the elements were neatly balanced via double-entry books of account.

Contemporary capitalism, said Weber, was actually a highly rational form. It was rather the religious elements and the unceasing drive to work that appeared irrational. Yet the system's very rationality enforced a compelling routine that often spelled a loss of freedom for the mass of men. Freedom was available only to the wealthy who could purchase escape from toil, and, warned Weber, a growing impersonality and routinization threatened mankind. Men of genuine culture had become fewer and were displaced by experts and devotees of organization. In this description Weber was able to link the notions of *charisma* and the growing bureaucratic organization of society. The general processes of rationalization made a bureaucratic structure inevitable, and this indubitably represented a threat to genuine personal freedom—as we have come to know in the modern organization man.[69] Such a bleak prospect might be overcome, said Weber, by the charismatic personality who exhibited extraordinary qualities of leadership and authority in terms of the *specific* person. Out of the charismatic situation might come a new institution and thus a way out of the bureaucratic condition that threatened to engulf industrial man.[70]

With this theory Weber denied that population growth or the infusion of precious metal from the New World were sufficient conditions for the rise of capitalism. His was essentially a theory of the psychological factors underlying the growth of capitalism. While geographic factors, military needs, and the demand for luxury goods were contributing elements, the main drive stemmed from the particular ethos about which he wrote. Although it resembled Sombart's theory, Weber rejected the idea that the Jews were the carriers of capitalism. They did not, commented Weber, invent bills of exchange, shares of stock, or the corporation. They were a "guest" folk standing outside political society and entirely without influence.[71] The modern creator of capitalism was a Christian who did not fear innovation and who was willing to cast tradition aside. The spiritual quality, the necessary ethos, said Weber, was to be found in Calvinism—a theology that told the businessman that he was essentially an administrator for what God had given him. Capitalism became a "calling" and rational work the fulfillment of a God-given assignment. Thus, the pursuit of profit could be maintained without fear or guilt: the capitalist conscience was clear. The Calvinist entrepreneur ". . . gave to his employees as the wages of their ascetic devotion to the calling and of cooperation in his ruthless exploitation of them through capitalism the prospect of eternal salvation. . . ." [72] It would be many decades before this ethic would be stripped of its religious garb.

What merit was there in this thesis? Calvin had had some broad views of business practice which he had absorbed from the commercial thinking of the north Italian cities. He had always been close to business and businessmen and had often been consulted by merchants whose souls were troubled by their practices. After all, Luther had not altered the medieval view with regard to commerce.[73] But the basic historical problem still remains. Did this new creed sustain the independent action of business and lead men to the new ways of the Kingdom of Heaven on earth, or did the enterprising middle class simply reach out to the new theology to justify whatever it was doing? Weber's own views evidently came from some Puritan forebears: it was not too difficult for him to base bourgeois virtue on Calvinist theology. But the early Puritans had displayed few of the ascetic attributes which Weber said were essential. The Dutch Calvinists, English Puritans, and French Huguenots had not required religion as a spur. Nor had freebooting, fat monopolies, song, wine, and games been unknown to them.[74] What was really common to their ethos had been a rejection of absolutism, an intransigent individualism, and a stubborn protest against the overreaching authority of the new national state.

Neither Weber nor his chief opponent Lujo Brentano, who stressed political thought as the catalyst, had a complete explanation for capitalism's success. Surely the requirements of the state for an ever-increasing production were as significant as religious drives, if perhaps not more so. Even output for larger national armies and the hungry demands of royalty for luxuries to give their courtesans, something to which Sombart called attention, may have had some effect. Capitalism may have been, as he said, the "child of illegitimate love." Miriam Beard has suggested that Weber's and Sombart's ideas might be fused so that the old Calvinists might be considered ". . . the ideal purveyors of cannon for the King's fleets and silk stockings for his mistresses." She continued: "It is possible, and at any rate it would be a pity to exclude altogether what is the only hilarious theory in the entire depressing range of the 'dismal science' of economics." [75]

Be that as it may, Weber's excessive emphasis on the quality of rationality agreed at few points with the evidence. His approach seemed a limited one for grasping the nature of political or economic experience. Capitalism's rationality is deceptive: on this point Veblen's analysis of business ritual and the patent lack of genuine functionalism was much more relevant. Furthermore, the thesis of religious influence was a strained one. The commercial centers in southern Germany and Florence in the fifteenth century had been just as capitalistic as Geneva, yet they had been Catholic! It is even possible to prove that Catholicism was capitalism's driving force, as was attempted, in fact, by H. M. Robertson.[76] Nor can one dismiss so easily as Weber does the impact of the age of discovery and the tremendous influx of gold and silver from America. Traces of capitalist enterprise existed prior to the religious changes he spoke of. And there were secular influences on capitalism which he seems to have overlooked, as for example, in the writings of businessmen on money and prices. Nor were the English Puritans precisely the kind of Calvinists that Weber believed them to be. The individualism of late Puritanism would have been anathema to the Geneva Synod. And, as for the British, the Protestant ethic hardly would have encompassed aristocrat, Leveller, merchant, and artisan. The capitalist spirit was a much more complex affair than Weber was willing to concede.

v

Brentano, Bücher, Wagner, and Knapp

Weber's thesis concerning Calvinist influence was sharply disputed by Ludwig Joseph (Lujo) Brentano (1844-1931), who quite properly pointed out that the lust for power and the grasp for money did not need John Calvin's encouragement, as the history of the Renaissance amply demonstrated. Brentano, one of the great teachers of his day, had a flair for presenting his lectures in a brilliant and dramatic fashion. But he was more than just a teacher; an important activist in the world peace movement, he was one of the most famous of European pacifists. His output of books was prodigious, and many of them still merit close attention.[77] Brentano, who rejected the notion that the state was superior to the individual, felt rather keenly that those who controlled the state were often apt to abuse their power. It is evident that Brentano was a good deal more liberal in his views than the other historical economists. Free trade was accepted as an important ideal, but economic reforms, he felt, could not be imposed without reason and the exercise of intelligence. In his work on the economic history of England, still a useful study, he traced the origins of the trade unions, early labor regulations, and the relations of unions to medieval guilds. In his discussion of labor as a commodity, he argued that the trade unions were quite able to protect their own interests without state aid. Theoretical economics was employed more skillfully than in the case of Schmoller, and a much broader perspective was exhibited. Brentano was not a stiff-necked advocate of laissez faire: he conceded that some legislation might be necessary, but in moderation. His pacifist views stemmed from the same impulse as did his deep-felt concern for the downtrodden.

Brentano observed that economic units were always hostile to each other and sought to acquire all that they possibly could. However, the members of the unit itself were bound by sentiments of fraternity. In time, unfortunately, the economic unit degenerated so that its members, as in the primitive family, were infected with the same ethos that governed its relations with other units. The search for gain then became the essence of economic dealings between all persons. The possibilities of this thesis were quite interesting and Brentano explored them more than adequately. Certainly, he was one of the finer products of the German historical movement. Not only did he want to make sciences of history and economics, but he recognized at the same time that they were also arts, for only in this way could they become vibrant and lifesize disciplines.

Karl Bücher (1847-1930), well known for his interesting if somewhat mechanistic work on national economy,[78] began his analysis of capitalism with a good deal of rich ethnic and anthropological material but soon resorted to the use of "stages." Growth, said Bücher, proceeded through household, town, and nation. And while this was admittedly schematic, Bücher did manage to weave in a number of useful insights concerning the uses of capital and income. In the earliest stage, the household, production was for the group itself; the town economy was broader, envisaging the start of a product flow from producer to consumer; and in the national economy commodities moved through many hands. This was essentially an explanation of capitalism in terms of market structure. Actually, said Bücher, true capitalism was not achieved until the last stage had been reached.[79] It was in this phase that such categories as interest and capital were fully realized.

Bücher acknowledged that these stages encompassed long periods of time. Thus the latter phases of the Roman Empire and the many decades of the Middle Ages comprised a domestic economy that simply failed to change. In the town economy, which began to develop during the late periods of the earlier domestic stage, the gradual increase in exchange provided the impetus for the evolution of a newer economic form, which in effect distinguished its bearers, the trading classes, from the manor-oriented populace around them. A new institutional structure was created which by its impressive economic performance provided the thrust toward the next stage in economic development. And once the production of goods began to reach out beyond the walls of the city itself, a beginning was made toward the establishment of the broader markets required for a national economy. But intermingled with these economic forces, said Bücher, were potent political drives: just as the city offered a political and institutional framework for economic expansion, so on a national level, the rise of the territorial state extended a protective umbrella for advancing the interests of new economic groups. Unfortunately, there was implicit in Bücher's work a kind of Hegelian evolution toward more perfect forms of existence. His rigid approach elicited a vigorous attack by Sombart, who called the analysis mechanistic, unreal, and evasive of the multiplicity of elements exhibited by capitalism. Yet Bücher did exert a certain influence, notably on some important labor historians such as John R. Commons.[80] At any rate, it was evident that Commons' penchant for comparing relationships at various stages of economic development had been derived from Bücher.

Adolph Wagner (1835-1917), another member of the historical school, had a more widespread influence. A specialist in public finance, he may be placed somewhere between Menger, the analytical economist par excellence, and Schmoller. Wagner, who had been trained in classical economics, was as aware as any of the historicists of the infinite complexity of economic reality. In his work on public finance he successfully escaped the cameralistic and administrative approach, making taxation part of the general science of economics. He recognized that public finance could be an effective instrument for social justice, and thought that the unearned increment derived from increased urban land values ought to go to the public. Although basically a conservative in his political outlook, he acknowledged the need for social reform if society were to survive. Wagner employed juridical elements in his conception of economic development more extensively than did the other historical economists, but he rejected the notion of natural rights as conceived by the classicists, on the ground that rights were societal creations. Wagner was close to Bismarck and it seems possible that his attitude toward reform was conditioned by the political requirements of the monarchy.

Another outstanding member of the group was G. F. Knapp (1842-1926), of monetary theory fame. Starting his career as a statistician, he developed into a theorist and historical writer, sharing the faults and virtues of the historicists. He was head of the Leipzig statistical bureau at the age of twenty-five, making some notable contributions in the field of mortality measurement. His historical work began with a study of rural workers in Prussia in which the large estates were viewed as a capitalistic form of agriculture. In 1895 Knapp turned to monetary theory, publishing his *State Theory of Money*.[81]

The book had a remarkable success if one is to judge by the number of enemies it created. He argued that paper money was actually a better form than metal, for in this way its value could be based on the strength of the issuing agent, the state. Most economists, however, felt that this was completely wrong-headed and inadequate,[82] for it violated their faith in the independent action of economic law.

vi

Arthur Spiethoff: Economics as Style

The last of the great figures in the historical tradition was Arthur Spiethoff (1873-1957) who had been Schmoller's assistant from 1899 to 1908 and editor of the *Jahrbuch* after Schmoller's death in 1917. Spiethoff, one of the world's most renowned experts on business cycles, studied economics and politics at Berlin, completing his doctoral work on economic crises in 1905. He lectured at Berlin and Prague and then went to Bonn where he came to know Joseph A. Schumpeter. Although he wrote extensively for the *Jahrbuch* on numerous topics, his great interest remained economic crises.[83] Spiethoff acquired an international reputation as a result of his work in this field, but he always insisted that his contribution was much less analytical than historical.

Although Spiethoff was not fundamentally an historian, he did employ a kind of conceptual framework in his empirical investigations which was quite similar to that of the historicists. With this as a backdrop he gathered what seemed to be the relevant facts and used them to test the theory further. His approach was a direct one, and, contrary to Schmoller's universalistic penchant, he did not seek to embrace the entire social order. In a new preface to the reprint of his long study on business cycles, Spiethoff asserted that there were two sorts of theory—the "pure" kind of a Ricardo, von Thünen, or Menger and the empirical, observational (*anschauliche*) theory of a Schmoller or Weber. Although both approaches engaged in abstraction, he did not think that one could be transformed into the other. Pure theory, he said, starts with selected data, yet seldom is able to depict reality adequately, while "observational" theory takes its information from the real world but abstracts from unique events in order to arrive at the regular features of economic affairs. In other words, the repetitive aspects of economic phenomena had to be isolated and studied: historical accidents, said Spiethoff, were to be removed from any analysis so that only the essential regularities might be displayed. Consequently, observational theory could yield a description of a genuinely theoretical nature and ought not be confused with the data incorporated into pure theory.

Spiethoff felt that his crisis analysis conformed to this methodological approach. But it was valid, he insisted, solely for "an age which is marked by the prevalence of the highly developed capitalistic economy with a market system which is, in the main, free." [84] His analysis of cycles, therefore, was limited to capitalism's meridian, the period from 1822 to 1913. He felt that the period since then had witnessed the introduction of factors that made it no mere continuation of earlier history, but rather an entirely new one. In this regard, Spiethoff was indubitably right, even though cycles were still evident in the latter period as much as in pre-war days. The outcome of Spiethoff's theoretical views was a search for the uniqueness of certain economic actions without having to dispense with analytical techniques. Yet the patently time-conditioned quality of economic phenomena made it a dubious business to try to apply universally valid logical categories to them. The best that could be said was that different types of economic behavior might be characterized as "styles," each calling for its own conceptual posture. As Spiethoff put it: "Economic theory is an 'historical' category to the extent to which its applicability depends on the existence and dominance of a certain economic style, elements of which are embodied in the theoretical structure." [85] There were many historical styles of economics, but each exhibited its own theory in addition to a shared body of concepts belonging to pure theory. Rooted as they were in the conditions of their time, these theories were inspired by the practical problems with which their authors wrestled.[86] A theorist, implied Spiethoff, began with the institutions that he knew, and it was an error to assert that analytical findings circumscribed in time and place possessed universal validity.

What Spiethoff then did was to categorize economic theory into three broad groups: (1) nonhistorical, pure theory, seemingly universal in nature, employing constructions known as models, but much of it of doubtful relevance; (2) historical theory, which may employ either ideal types of Weberian character as tools or "real" types of Spiethoff's gestalt-like observational analysis; and (3) economic history of the ordinary kind. Spiethoff preferred the observational approach because it operated ostensibly from a framework of meaning and then, through induction, isolated significant phenomena in order to relate them back to the initial hypothesis. The purpose, he said, was to work out generalizations that would effectively describe observed uniformities. Observational theory, therefore, was thoroughly analytical, for it dealt with unique economic events and was also entirely historical because these were recurring uniformities. Philosophically, there would appear to be a connection in Spiethoff's conceptual structure to phenomenological notions as well as to Gestalt psychology.

In this framework, the concepts of "style" were central—the term Spiethoff used to describe certain institutional arrangements as well as the theoretical models themselves. He preferred, however, to restrict the notion to institutional patterns. The generalizations a theorist offered to describe the various uniformities with which he dealt set the tone of an economic style. There were differences, he felt, between his concept and Max Weber's; nor did he mean the same thing as Sombart's "system." A "style," averred Spiethoff, had a kind of inner coherence and unity which had to be sensed. It was essentially the form or shape that economic activity assumed in a given historical era, and to make it "specific" it was necessary to reveal the uniformities that characterized an economy.

For business cycle theory this meant that each crisis was historically and sociologically conditioned. In fact, the analysis that Spiethoff engaged in clearly reflected his philosophic preconceptions. Cycles were not a separate phenomenon but part of an economic *gestalt* which contained historical and empirical elements as well as theoretical ones. Whatever deductions one might make were rooted in historically inductive material. At the culmination of the analysis, a theoretical model should stand revealed which would exhibit all the stages of a typical cycle in a fully developed capitalism.

Spiethoff's objection to the exclusive use of pure theory was based on his contention that it was able to explore only single phenomena in isolation. The absence of empirical criteria make it difficult to establish controls over the various deductions. The ultimate worthwhileness of the method, he said, depended on the way in which problems were posed and the usefulness of the initial assumptions. If only for these reasons the observational method was deemed to be closer to reality. By the use of induction, its conclusions could be related to the data that were employed, which might, of course, encompass the uniform relations of a given economic situation. In this sense, observational theory dealt with patterns of economic life—or rather with styles. These were to be distinguished from economic history per se, for the latter was concerned with the uniqueness of events in sequence. Spiethoff, did concede, however, that the difference was frequently a matter of emphasis rather than of substance.[87] Nor did he want to suggest that induction alone was sufficient, for in making a distinction between objective and motivational causality, one established links between individual phenomena with the former, while the latter, being more complex, required intuitive perceptions. He was therefore admitting the need for deductive techniques as well.

The technical analysis of the business cycle began in the upswing which originated in spurts of profitable investments. These were due either to new discoveries or to opportunities left over from the previous depression. In the second stage of the process, new plants were installed which, while absorbing capital materials, did not expand consumption. When the latter did begin to expand, prices would have already advanced, so that a collapse could not be avoided. The unequal distribution of income also contributed to the downswing. This was all part of the capitalistic process in which the palpable lack of foresight and the inability of the individual to adjust quickly to general movements stood out as significant elements. But above all, the difficulty could be traced to the shortage of certain materials for capital, certain complementary goods required in production. In the final stage, the shortage of capital goods was rooted in misdirected production.

This framework made the cycle not merely a question of overproduction, but rather an endemic feature of the economy. The crisis stemmed from the new technology and the vast expansion of markets that took place under capitalism. What was overproduced, said Spiethoff, was capital equipment as well as the materials from which such equipment was made. As the capital goods industries developed, they concomitantly drew with them the industries producing their materials, such as coal, machine tools, rubber, and glass. When capacity in the latter became redundant, profits were depressed, upsetting the delicate balance between the flow of income from capital and the growth of the capital goods industries themselves.

Spiethoff's conception evidently had been very much influenced by Tugan-Baranovsky, the noted Russian economist who sought to solve the riddle of the cycle in the disproportions between producers' and consumers' goods.[88] The latter's notion that disproportionate investment was a major cause of depression impressed Spiethoff with its empirical possibilities and was hailed as the first important modern investigation of the business cycle.[89] In his article on "Overproduction," written for the *Encyclopaedia of the Social Sciences,* Spiethoff tried to distinguish between purely business overproduction and that which might be attributed to socio-economic factors. The former meant a lack of profit in ordinary production; in the latter, output exceeded consumption. The dichotomy, he conceded, was a formal one, for the business crisis generally was subsumed in the socio-economic type of cycle. Since profitless production is something businessmen avoid, it was difficult to discover empirical material that would illustrate a pure case of business overproduction. The businessman would sooner cut prices or alter his output schedule than operate at zero profit. But this raised a host of other problems of a basically sociological character and made it clear that the cycle was an historically conditioned phenomenon.

It was during the latter part of the upswing, said Spiethoff, that economic activity exhausted itself and capital became scarce. Overproduction in the widest sense became inescapable and was manifested by idle equipment, unemployment, low output, dumping, cost cutting, and the like. Spiethoff acknowledged that this was no simple phenomenon but an intricate complex of changes pervading the whole economy. This was not to be confused with a sudden obsolescence of goods or a temporary lack of demand resulting from excessively high prices or low income. The outstanding feature, however, was the overproduction of materials for the capital goods industries, often accompanied by a collapse of credit as well as a financial panic. Company promotions ceased and speculative activity ground to a halt.[90]

Spiethoff emphasized that anticipations rather than current profit were the significant investment determinants, a noteworthy observation at that time. The rate of interest, he said, indicated the cost of loan capital and acted as a rough guide for the capital market. Theoretically, both pure interest and a premium for risk were involved, although Spiethoff's treatment of these concepts was not particularly analytical. However, he illustrated the problem of interest rate changes with a wealth of data drawn from the price history of consols and other securities. But despite monetary shifts and the influence of interest rates, the expansion of investment remained the effective cause of the upswing. It was the purchase of iron, coal, and building materials used in the construction of factories that exerted the greatest impact on the course of the business cycle. The boom itself was marked by a considerable movement between the capital and money markets which tended to obscure the basic fact of overproduction of materials for capital equipment, or, as Spiethoff called them, "indirect consumption goods." The tremendous use of these goods during the upswing of a cycle was, of course, a direct reflection of the investment process, but nevertheless the key to the crisis lay in the production of capital materials. The changes and shifts might be irregular, and it was possible that crop alterations might have some slight influence, but in the final analysis it was the real factors of disproportionate investment that bore most heavily on the matter.[91] It seemed impossible to keep the production of investment goods exactly in step with capital formation and the expansion of demand.

This theoretical formulation was followed by a long history of business cycles, of interest mainly to specialists. But the data in it effectively illustrated the main stream of his thesis. The sudden shift of the ultimate cause of cyclical movements from "real" to "psychological" factors could be explained by his desire to encompass all relevant elements.[92] While plant extension and increased output might result in unabsorbed goods, the special expectations that ensued led to a sense of exhilaration and "mass psychology does the rest." [93] The main attraction was the favorable yield on capital. When the rate of interest was far below profit, then expectations acted as further stimuli. The development of new industry, new markets, new technology enhanced the prospect of new profits. Even price reductions could add to the catalogue of stimuli. But a sufficient quantity of labor had to be available, for otherwise the more roundabout methods of production that were bound to crop up would be of little use.[94] And all this had to be triggered by the availability of credit. The only way in which equilibrium might be maintained, suggested Spiethoff, would be through a perfect balance of the production of indirect consumption goods and their purchase by capital goods producers. But since these were different groups, disequilibrium and disproportion were not easily avoided. The capital goods materials, or indirect consumption goods area, responded quickly to demand, and in the fashion of the famous cobweb theorem, could easily outstrip requirements.[95] According to Spiethoff, this implied a need for capitalism to keep expanding and to perpetually seek new uses for goods and create new demands. Capitalism, he said, must ". . . rely on conquest, whether of fields of space or of fields of activities." [96] In this respect, the advertising agencies and modern automobile manufacturers evidently have taken Spiethoff's lessons to heart.

Spiethoff's theory was based essentially on the pulling power of new investment opportunity. But there was a point of saturation in the upswing phase, for at any given level of technology only a given amount of capital could be employed. Said Spiethoff: "The demand for productive equipment and for durable consumers goods is not continuous; and when an economy has been fully supplied with such goods, the plant and machines which produced them are thrown out of work." [97] There was an inelastic demand for capital at the cycle's upper phase but as prospective profits declined expansion was halted, the demand for capital dropped, and the collapse followed. A pessimistic outlook was engendered throughout the economy as production slowly ground to a halt. Income declined and underconsumption spread as the depression became a general phenomenon. The new upturn would come only as new investment possibilities were revealed. It seems evident that Spiethoff's conception of cyclical change was rooted not only in Tugan-Baranovsky, but in the somewhat related notions of Clément Juglar, the noted French business cycle analyst, and Joseph A. Schumpeter.

Business cycles, consequently, are striking illustrations of Spiethoff's basic vision of economic behavior. Different personalities react to change in different ways. The alternation of upswings and downswings create a type of individual who awaits opportunities to enrich himself. He lies in wait for the main chance afforded by cyclical change. Even the formation of social classes can be affected by the cycle. Society is dominated by a constant striving for wealth. "The rule of the acquisitive economic instinct over the soul of man goes together with the rule of the business cycle over the course of a nation's economy." [98] Spiethoff expressed no regret or sorrow that such a phenomenon as the business cycle should persist, for it was, he said, the life blood of the economic order. According to Spiethoff, once the cycle had been eliminated, the power of the West and its ability to increase wealth would become things of the past! There seems to be just a touch of romantic nonsense in this panegyric to economic bloodletting, but in the light of the tradition in which Spiethoff worked it is completely understandable.

vii
Simiand, Toynbee, Cunningham, and Ashley

The historical tradition was not limited to Germany. Its devotees could be found in France and Great Britain as well. An outstanding French practitioner was François Simiand (1873-1935), economist and statistician, who did notable work in the area of wage analysis.[99] From 1910 on he taught economic history, statistics, and the history of economics at the École Pratique des Hautes Études. Simiand, squarely within the tradition of positivism, felt that it was necessary to discover similarities in historical phenomena. He was not interested in "systems" and "styles" of economics, but rather in the cultural character of economic action, a notion akin to that employed by anthropologists. The student of economics, he said, had to stand outside the events he was studying in order to dissemble the whole pattern of economic behavior into its component elements. His famous study of wages was meant as an illustration of this thesis in that the measurable aspects of the wage structure were at least ascertained.[100] The caution implicit in this approach calls to mind that exercised by Wesley C. Mitchell and his followers. Simiand analyzed wage fluctuations and explored the various economic and social factors that might explain them. To him this was a valid experimental method which meant gathering and categorizing a vast quantity of empirical data before drawing any conclusions. Alternative analyses might be made to check the final observations, which were deemed in any case to be provisional. In this way statistical relationships hopefully could be reduced to a single causal nexus. That such a monistic approach had its difficulties appears fairly evident. Nor was Simiand any more successful with such external factors as changes in monetary conditions.

Simiand concluded that money rewards were more important than real ones. What seemed important to workers, he said, was a steady level of consumption. But he refused to generalize on the basis of these discoveries, for he felt that the psychological outlook they implied was essentially time-bound. Consequently, it may be said that Simiand's work was rooted in the same sociological factors as was the theory of the German historicists, although their preconceptions were set forth more explicitly.

The British historical school was not so well known, perhaps because it did not engage in strenuous polemics, but its representatives were easily the equals of the Germans. Somewhat more empirical, they eschewed the philosophic asides of which the Germans were so fond. Their erudition, however, was just as vast. J. K. Ingram, (1823-1907), for example, was a man of wide cultural accomplishment who, in addition to his interest in economics, was a poet who had served as professor of Greek at Dublin. His *History of Political Economy*,[101] written initially as an article for the *Encyclopaedia Britannica* in 1888, followed the methodology of the German historical school. His knowledge of history and philosophy was as great as the inadequacy of his technical economics. Ingram urged that economics should not be separated from the social sciences, for fear that this would intensify the trend to ahistorical emphases. More attention, he felt, ought to be paid to empirical research, at least in Britain. When these views were presented to the British Association in 1878, they were hailed by the historical economists in Germany. But Ingram was basically a Comtean in outlook, with a strong taste for social amelioration, as was revealed by the subject matter of his books: religion, morals, and the history of serfdom.

A brilliant member of the group was Arnold Toynbee (1852-1883), whose influence was widely felt, although his was a tragically short life. His ability to fuse his interest in social reform with admirable researches into economic history was revealed by the posthumously published *Lectures on the Industrial Revolution in England,* which added a new expression to the language.[102] Had he been given more years he undoubtedly would have written important works in economic history. In addition to a respect for facts, he demonstrated a genuine sense of the relevant. In his *Industrial Revolution* he set out to show that the outburst of energy in the eighteenth century was a single historical event. This was the framework on which all subsequent investigations were based.

Coordination of history and economics, said Toynbee, would enhance both disciplines: history could be more readily comprehended with a background of economic fact while economics could be illuminated with historical experience. By combining the two ". . . abstract propositions are seen in a new light . . ."[103] while history is understood better by virtue of the need to search for the right kind of facts. Although Toynbee rejected attacks on the deductive method, feeling that it had a rightful place in research techniques, he believed that the historical method had revealed the essential relativity of economic law.[104]

Other important British historicists included William Cunningham (1849-1919), whose major work, *The Growth of English Industry and Commerce in Modern Times*,[105] was a genuine landmark, and William J. Ashley (1860-

1927), an Englishman who occupied the first chair in economic history at Harvard. Cunningham, the first of a long line of great economic historians, gave expression to the evolutionary viewpoint perhaps more effectively than anyone else. But this was directed toward enhancing the position of the state much after the fashion of Schmoller and his school. Cunningham was born in Edinburgh and after studying at the University there he entered Cambridge in 1869. Attracted to the Anglican outlook, he was ordained as a minister in the Church of England in 1871. A short stay at Tübingen imbued him with a desire for order in social and economic affairs. When Cunningham began to teach economic history at Cambridge in 1878, he found no texts on the subject and so wrote one himself. He then held a number of academic posts, notably at Kings College and Harvard, prior to assuming religious duties.[106]

Cunningham's work in economics and economic history clearly reflected a rejection of the principles adumbrated by classicism. His views, like those of his German counterparts, were nationalistic in emphasis, so much so that the policy of free trade was attacked as one apt to inhibit the advancement of the basic interests of the British state. In his later years Cunningham was a forthright protectionist, although he recognized that the repeal of the Corn Laws had met the needs of the time.[107] But in the last decades of the nineteenth century, this was not the case, for Britain's trade position could no longer be sustained in a free market. The interests of the state, said Cunningham, were in opposition also to the demands of the socialists, who were simply creating hostility between classes rather than encouraging cooperation.[108] Such views did not lessen Cunningham's interest in social questions. He was deeply concerned with the human costs of industrialization and uninhibited competition, but again amelioration was to be directed toward strengthening the British national state. In short, for Cunningham, historicism became a variety of social imperialism.[109]

These ideas were echoed by William Ashley, who had been influenced by Toynbee as well as the German historicists. Ashley began his studies at Oxford in 1878 and, after a short stay at Toronto and Harvard, returned to Britain in 1901 to accept a chair at the University of Birmingham. He quickly became an ardent exponent of protectionism and wrote extensively on wages, tariffs, and related problems. His major opus was the *Introduction to English Economic History and Theory*.[110] Ashley, who was very close to the German historical economists, frequently exchanging views with Schmoller and Brentano,[111] never failed to call attention to the work being done on the continent. Like the other historical writers, he disagreed with the Marxists, preferring gradual reform to useless and harmful revolutionary activity. Nevertheless, he saw some merits to the socialist analysis of capitalism: concentration and accumulation did press disadvantageously on small producers, and there was a visible tendency toward socialized forms as expressed in the creation of large firms and the passage of social legislation.[112] One of the most effective instruments for reform, said Ashley, was the trade union, which provided a sound basis for industrial peace.

For Ashley, economic history was a joint discipline which encompassed historical criticism and theoretical analysis. There was no prejudice in his approach to problems: all issues and problems were weighed dispassionately. Economic theory, however, was not a body of absolute doctrine but a collection rather of useful generalizations. Man, said Ashley, had always speculated about his economic condition and so spawned theoretical constructs. But these were formulated under conditions that were true only for a given time and place; consequently, theories of the past had to be evaluated in terms of the economic facts that had been prevalent in the past. Modern theories, intimated Ashley, could not be universal. They were true neither for the past when conditions were different, nor for the future, for society underwent perpetual change.

viii

R. H. Tawney: Ethics in Economics

The moral qualities so patent in the writings of many of the historical economists acquired a special lustre in the work of R. H. Tawney (1880-1962). The social criticism implicit in his major opus, *Religion and the Rise of Capitalism*,[113] was even more sharply etched in his other volumes, *Equality* and *The Acquisitive Society*.[114] The point of view was boldly stated: the system of inherited rights stemming from an agrarian society was utterly useless and even harmful in an economy founded on the principles of industrialism. Tawney, born in Calcutta, the son of a British civil servant, was educated at Oxford, and spent his entire lifetime in teaching and writing. It is said that Tawney did not accept his M. A. at Oxford (although he did have many honorary degrees) because the main consideration was the payment of a fee and therefore not completely equalitarian. Professor of economic history at the University of London from 1931 to 1949, he also served on numerous government commissions. His influence on the British Labor Party and particularly on the Fabians was profound. A remarkable personality, who was apt to put a still lit pipe into his pocket as he lectured, his radical standpoint motivated much that went into British reform in the twentieth century. But most important, he was an impeccable scholar given to meticulous attention to details and deeply versed in sixteenth and seventeenth century historical documents. There were few writers who brought to their subject so intense a concern with ethical precepts and it was this quality that lent to his economic studies an extraordinary moral thrust. Yet the scholar was always supreme, the preachments secondary, as evidenced by his *Tudor Economic Documents* (1925) and his biography of Lionel Cranfield, Lord Treasurer under James I.

Tawney agreed with Max Weber that theology had had a powerful impact on economics, citing the medieval Schoolmen's usury notions and Calvinism's conversion of business into a "calling" as cases in point. Religion simply could not keep its hand off business. Of course, economic and social change reacted on religion also, but Tawney's objective was to investigate the Weberian thesis. He conceded that many of the regulations found in business were rooted in religious and moral concerns. In medieval days, economic interests admittedly had been subordinate to the main business of salvation. But as society had changed, the various segments of intellectual life had begun to separate one form from the other. Thus, said Tawney, social theory as distinct from morals began to develop a naturalistic flavor, enabling capitalism to acquire secular justification. That medieval asceticism was no longer sufficient for the conduct of affairs was plainly evident in the modifications introduced by St. Antoninus.[115] Theory and practice went their separate ways: while the Church might castigate usurers, it was not averse to engaging in high finance itself.

In the fifteenth century, wrote Tawney, an economic as well as intellectual revolution took place. Venice declined in importance as the center of European commerce moved northward; mining and textiles became major foci of capitalist activity; trading companies grew apace as they employed "massed" capital to dominate their assigned areas, and the state became the major political force as medieval society collapsed in the agony of peasant wars. The symbol of the new age was Antwerp. Yet throughout the period, said Tawney, religious principles continued to be asserted as superior to economic ideas. The Lutherans had no intention of relaxing their rigid precepts, and, if capitalism was affected by a change in outlook, this had not been the intention of the Protestant reformers.[116] In fact, said Tawney, the avarice of the north Italian cities was a prime factor in stiffening the attitude of the Swiss and Germans.

Had the social theory of the Reformation been applied strictly, it would have hampered capitalism as Luther might have wanted, for he considered commerce to be a relapse into paganism. But there was a reluctance to draw the practical implications from these attacks on trade, so that the consequent ambivalence that developed "sowed the seeds from which new freedoms, abhorrent to Luther, were to spring." [117] Calvin, on the other hand, wanted to reconstruct society completely, and make it thoroughly urban. Calvinism frankly acknowledged the facts of economic life. A commercial civilization no longer seemed alien to the life of the spirit and all economic virtues were applauded. Action brought salvation by sanctifying the world through strife and labor. Thrift, diligence, sobriety, and frugality became Christian virtues. Economic success seemed hand tailored to the needs of theological virtue. The Swiss Calvinists, seeking not social reforms but moral regeneration, seized upon ". . . the aptitudes cultivated by the life of business and affairs, stamped on them a new sanctification and used them as the warp of a society in which a more than Roman discipline should perpetuate a character the exact antithesis of that fostered by obedience to Rome." [118] Since this was not merely a question of convenience, but the new will of God, the bourgeoisie was welded into a powerful social force. Discipline and asceticism became the spearheads of the economic revolution. The world of business was welcomed into the Calvinist fold, but as suppliant rather than conqueror.[119]

Meanwhile, wrote Tawney, foreign trade and capitalist ways of doing business developed apace in Holland and Britain. The discussions on economics that took place in those nations were patent efforts to rationalize current practice. Locke's concept of property eventually became the basis for economic freedom, and economics as an objective science began its "disillusioning career." [120] As more and more writers thought that economics and ethics ought to be distinct fields of inquiry, the conception of social theory based on religion was being discredited. The church abandoned its function of social criticism and acquiesced to the new individualism, at least in commercial affairs. To the Puritan, religion and trade became the same thing: religion hailed the triumph of the spirit of capitalism. Personal responsibility and character were the end-all of existence, circumstance meant nothing, and poverty became a moral failing to be condemned rather than pitied.[121] The Puritan-Capitalist became a votary of a profitable God and compensated himself for a shop-worn idealism by plunging recklessly into the business of making and losing money. It was not long before social vices were transmuted into moral virtues. The practical side of life was given a firm foundation by the new religion.[122] Morality was not so much displaced as a factor in private actions, Tawney wrote with much justice, as it was ousted by the increasing force of profit and greed. To this day, religion has had to justify economics or remain on the periphery of the affairs of men. Thus Weber, Sombart, and virtually all the historians of capitalism whom we have surveyed were stood on their heads.

For Tawney, those who had hailed the rise of capitalism had not been vulgar materialists but rather advocates of a new freedom from tyranny. On the other hand, nineteenth-century liberalism was a philosophy of a different order. Lacking a critical spirit, it had become mere dogma for justifying the absolutism of property rights. It was precisely such dogma that was subjected to merciless exposure in *The Acquisitive Society*. As Raymond Williams has emphasized, Tawney had much in common with such social critics as John Ruskin and Matthew Arnold.[123] An increase in purchasing power, said Tawney, was not enough to raise the quality of life for the mass of mankind. A vast expansion of the public realm was needed to provide hospitals, schools, roads, parks, and a host of services which could not be supplied by private industry. Quite simply, surplus private income had to be converted into social income. And such measures had to be supported by the creation of an industrial democracy in which human rights were paramount. This was not a matter solely of politics or economics: to Tawney, the construction of a better society was a moral issue. The choice was between false gods and true ones. Otherwise, he argued, we should merely stumble from one crisis to the next.

2

The Socialist Attack

Marxian Economics Revisited

MARXISM, as a unified organon, had its roots in German philosophy, French utopian socialism, and English economics. As such, it became not only an economic theory, but a philosophy of history, a sociology, and a prescription for politics. Marxism was, above all, a *weltanschauung*, a world outlook, which recognized change, not as the progressive blandness of the Victorian era, but rather change through strife, according to the Hegelian dialectic. The truth of the Marxist cosmogony has been argued for decades; but it must, of course, be tested by the realities of time. Whether Marxism may be described as "science" is also moot, for it has taken on a coloration of a state religion with a prescribed theology, a hierarchy, Gospels, and a collection of heretics.

Marx was a wide-ranging writer and a complex personality. As a political agitator, he was of no small interest, but it is not this Marx who is our present subject. Let us abstract from all the diverse characteristics of his milieu and look for a moment at Marx *qua* economist. If we do this, we shall discover a serious thinker who dealt with problems that most of his contemporaries refused to touch. His was a most devastating critique of the capitalism of his day and a forecast also of the coming socialist millennium. Yet his technical apparatus did not examine the functioning of socialism; indeed, it is paradoxical that while his theory was one of capitalism, it was classical economics that in a sense best described an ideal socialist state! [1]

Only when standard economics began to acknowledge the growth of monopoly and the possibility of such disturbing phenomena as unemployment (this was far back in the 1920's) did the attitude of contempt for Marx begin to dissolve. More and more, social scientists began to acknowledge that his effort to look at the economic system in its totality was relevant to the problems at hand. They noted that Marx had tried to work out carefully and analytically the relationships between the various social and economic components. He even set up "models," so dear to the hearts of modern theorists. But above all, he dealt with technology, underconsumption, unemployment, and the concentration of capital. These were big questions and Marx sought to supply the big answer. That he was not always able to come up with the right one is beside the point.[2] The fact is that he was a serious thinker who dealt with serious problems. That so many of his supposed intellectual descendants assert all the Marxian phrases as absolute truth is merely sad, for this reveals them to be precisely the sort of fools that Marx abhorred.

Orthodox economists have evolved through the years some fairly elegant analytical structures from which, as Joan Robinson has said, it has been possible to derive with great accuracy the value of a cup of tea. This, however, was a little question, not a big one. Marx, although possessing much cruder tools, exhibited a far deeper sense of the meaningful: his formulations of economic problems towered over most of the works of this time "in rough and gloomy grandeur."[3] For Marx, capitalism was in a sense to be admired, for it had an historic mission, to wit, spreading its productive power over the face of the globe. It enforced the accumulation of capital and thereby increased the wealth of nations. Marx wanted to demonstrate, however, that the major benefits of this inexorable process would accrue to the few, and that it was because of this fundamental "inner contradiction" that capitalism was bound to stumble.

Unfortunately his demonstration was obscured by a penchant for fuzzy Hegelian language. Often employing tendentious arguments, Marx frightened away many readers who might have learned much from his analysis of economic affairs. They did not realize that this passionate agitator was at heart a scholar who, as Joseph A. Schumpeter remarked, wrestled with every fact and every idea and frequently came up with really useful generalizations on the manner in which men lived. Marx was interested, said Schumpeter, ". . . in the problem as a problem [and] was primarily concerned with sharpening the tools of analysis proffered by the science of his day, with straightening out logical difficulties, and with building . . . a theory that in nature and intent was truly scientific whatever its shortcomings." [4] The historical method employed by him was remarkably effective, and the interrelations of social change with given modes of production could not be denied.

Marx was an important economist, if for no other reason but that his challenge to standard doctrine could not be ignored.[5] We do not hesitate to elevate Adam Smith and David Ricardo to the high status of great thinkers, although many of their notions now seem to us quaint and naive. Marx was as keen an analyst as they, and while we may expose his most egregious errors with great glee, it must be underscored that in his own day he had few peers. His use of the labor theory of value illustrated his analytical approach. Those who preceded Marx—Robert Owen, Thomas Hodgskin, John Bray, William Thompson—placed the theory into a hard moralistic shell: labor, they said, was being robbed of its own fruit. Marx pointedly denied this by arguing that in reality workers received full value, but that labor's problem was due to the fact that it was a peculiar commodity —it always created a value greater than itself, and it was this situation, a built-in imperative of the capitalist system, that remained the basic reality of the economic order.

In a wonderful series of talks to students a few years back, Joan Robinson put Marx in the same basket with Marshall and Keynes.[6] This must have appeared outrageous to the orthodox on both sides, but there is much merit in her argument. The only substantial difference between these gentlemen, she said, was the color of the glasses through which they looked at economic reality—Marshall's were blue, Keynes' slightly pink, and Marx's a bit on the red side. For example, all three agreed that revenue minus wages, materials cost, and depreciation yielded profit. However, they did not agree on the definition of the elements to be deducted from revenue. As to the remainder, they simply had different names for what the reasonable person called profit. Marshall considered this a great driving force, Marx scorned it, and Keynes was indifferent, believing it fine so long as it did not impede the proper functioning of the economic system.

Still, most economists did not bother to find out what it was that Marx was talking about. It was necessary to await the arrival of monopoly, imperfect competition, and cycles to discuss once again exploitation, accumulation, and economic growth.[7] One difference is that today we use a more esoteric terminology. For example, Sir Roy Harrod, the biographer of Keynes, developed a theory of "warranted growth" in which it was shown that when an economy moved away from equilibrium it was rather hard to get it back.[8] This was nothing less than what Marx had called capitalism's "law of motion."

Of course, die-hard followers of the pure Marxian doctrine find it extraordinarily difficult to accept the belief that someone other than Marx could have come across the same ideas, nor are they willing to accept the notion that certain details of the master's analysis might be incorrect or inconsistent. As Joan Robinson has said, when a Marxist is asked whether capital is to be defined as a stock or a flow he is apt to reply that Marx was a genius. This, usually known as the Moscow subway argument, has been of no help in solving an economic, or for that matter, any other kind of problem.

Marx had the capacity to take the long view of historical developments. He would not release the results of his investigations merely for the sake of publication, which explains why only the first part of *Das Kapital* was issued in his own lifetime. He was able to relate a vast body of empirical data to an abstract model of the economy in a way that few economists in the nineteenth century had been able to match. He knew that he could not escape making value judgments, but at least they were explicitly set forth and not obscured by long lines of deduction.[9] He began with an essentially sociological vision of society which sought to discover how its usufruct was distributed. The method was not different substantially from that employed by Ricardo and was no more arbitrary than any Robinson Crusoe economics.

Economic questions were approached with an enormous command over the relevant factual data which he hammered into shape with some rather interesting analytical tools. One of these was the "economic interpretation of history," a concept which contrary to what most commentators have said did not mean that men are motivated by purely economic or material considerations. Marx's early writings, notably the *German Ideology* and the *Holy Family*, clearly showed that noneconomic factors and the way in which social reality reflected itself in individual behavior were important facets of the Marxian view. Marx did not say—and here the burden of proof is on those who insist he did—that art and ethics and religion were reducible to materialistic elements.[10] What he did maintain was that economic situations markedly shaped the institutions and ideas of men, and in so saying he tried to prove that it was necessary to explore the ideology of the moment. The various forms of production known to history, said Marx, deeply affected social relationships, and these in turn conditioned men's attitudes.[11] While engaged in this investigation, Marx was not averse to pouring slop over the heads of his hapless opponents, who in his eyes confounded verbal formulations with actual behavior. Such polemics did not make the Marxian viewpoint any the more palatable.

Yet, as has been noted by other writers, his economic interpretation remains but a brilliant approximation. Its very facility makes it a dubious device, for social behavior is infinitely more complex and more devious than its implications would suggest. Even if we grant that the "modes of production" exhibit a kind of internal logic in the course of their exfoliation, during which succeeding modes of production are evolved, we must allow for numerous exceptions that can be explained only by admitting a good deal more interaction between the economic and noneconomic than Marx might have agreed to.

It is in the pure economics of his social science (aside from the labor theory of value) that the most useful parts of Marx's system may be identified. Unfortunately, most of them are obscured by the Hegelian elements in the early sections of *Das Kapital*. Here Marx tried to demonstrate that value was derived from the socio-economic relationships entered into by men for the purpose of producing means of subsistence. Economics, he said, was concerned with those relationships which are set in an employer-employee context. The labor theory of value, which was wrapped in Hegelianisms, was where Marx began. The theory, stemming mainly from Ricardo, proclaimed that the value of a commodity was proportional to the quantity of socially necessary labor time included in it. Obviously this held, even in Marx's framework, only under conditions of perfect competition. Nothing in the Marxian model accounted for the existence of monopoly or other imperfections. The essential point, however, is that from this definition there flowed surplus value, the excess created by labor over its own worth. It should be noted, especially for analytical purposes, that labor power, the term preferred by Marx, acted only on part of the equipment committed to production. The value creating process affected only that portion of the means of production which entered into the final product. Thus only circulating capital and depreciation were involved rather than the total stock of capital. This has caused no end of confusion, for it is generally customary to consider total capital in computing the rate of profit, a procedure rejected by Marx.[12]

The theory, however, had a logical function. Marx clearly intended to use these concepts for establishing conditions of economic equilibrium in the broad, macroeconomic sense, since the idea of a rate of surplus value applied to a single enterprise was clearly little more than an heroic abstraction. Yet it was possible to argue in favor of the Marxian definition of the profit rate when the concept was extended to the entire economic system. Despite this, the theory was as static as anything developed by the marginal economists with their Robinson Crusoe doctrines. It must be recognized that prices and production according to Marxian categories can be explained only through a number of restrictive assumptions which are most unlikely to exist in a dynamic economy. Moreover, the labor theory of value cannot really operate as a measuring device, surely an important function for such a theory. Try to explain price level changes via the labor theory and one comes up against the skilled versus unskilled worker problem; or again, consider the famous question of the transformation of value into prices, over which a furious debate has raged through the years. (Joan Robinson contends that the whole problem was unreal, for the very values which need to be explained are obtained by first transforming price into value!) Another problem was the distinction between productive and nonproductive labor. According to Marx, packaging and bookkeeping did not add surplus value to goods, which in accordance with the ratio of constant to variable capital (capital's organic composition or the degree of mechanization) would differ in different industries. How then are we to account for wages and profits in commercial enterprise? Marx's answer was that these were obtained from the surplus value created in industry. Just how this was done was not clear, but there was the admission that from the "commercial capitalists" viewpoint bookkeepers are productive.[13]

The fact is that the labor theory of value had a metaphysical rather than a genuinely economic base. Labor was divided into concrete and abstract; the latter supposedly represented the common quality of work *qua* work. While this was never defined precisely, it seemed to be the average of abstract labor that provided the standard of measure for value. But this approach simply ignored the question of effective demand. Marx's objective was to make labor value the foundation of his exploitation theory, which in accordance with the organic composition of capital, or the degree of mechanization, would differ in different industries. The rate of profit, however, would tend toward equality in all lines because of competition between capitalists. But Marx got into difficulties when he said that prices corresponded to values, for this implied that the rate of exploitation tended toward the same level in all industries. This was a problem that not even the ingenious revision of von Bortkiewicz had been able to solve convincingly.[14]

More specifically, the labor theory of value is nonoperational, for not only does it fail to measure changes in the prices of goods or in productivity, but it is impossible to fit empirical material into its framework. Output has risen over the years despite a reduction in man-hours, and even recourse to the famous "socially necessary labor time" phrase fails to rescue the theory, which is unverifiable and simply describes a general tendency easily countervailed. In that sense it is merely a pure concept. We must conclude that the labor theory of value fails as an analytical tool. If it works at all, it can do so only under conditions of perfect competition and under the assumption that labor is the sole factor of production. The glaring unreality of such a premise is self-evident.[15]

One is tempted to agree with Joan Robinson when she says that ". . . no point of substance in Marx's argument depends on the labor theory of value."

Yet despite this unnecessary appendage, many parts of the Marxian economic corpus can still stand. It is a remarkable body of doctrine which incorporates numerous effective devices for explaining the internal drive of the capitalist economy. With its emphasis on the long view, the Marxian system has been fairly useful in sketching the direction in which we have at times moved. While ordinary economics has proved superior in such matters as the price of tea and other little things, Marxian economics has been generally concerned with questions in the round.

This characterization may be demonstrated more clearly when we leave behind the metaphysics in the early sections of Volume I and go on to the problems of circulation and accumulation which were more fully explored later on. These were perhaps the most spectacular parts of his doctrine, for they represented in a fundamental way a theory of economic development. Here the fact was underscored that the central theme of *Das Kapital* was precisely what the title implied—man-made means of production and the social relations that governed their use. Since the latter were rooted in the wage relationship, capital had to be defined by alienation from tools and ownership of property. Workers not only were legally free but also free from the means of production. And because of this, capital had begun to assume a monopolistic aspect, for it was the capitalist who, upon hiring the means of production, came into possession of the entire product which he then distributed to the different factors.

Here was the nub of the circulation and reproduction process. Industries were divided into those supplying new means of production, those which provided workers with the means of subsistence, and the ones whose output consisted of luxury goods to satisfy the consumption of capitalists. The production of each was divisible into variable capital, constant capital, and surplus value. In all three groups the latter might be consumed or reinvested. If investment was the course to be followed, surplus value again became either variable or constant capital, in which case part of the output was to be exchanged against goods of the other sectors. For example, capitalists making the means of production might, if they wished, directly reinvest part of their output to replace that depleted in the manufacturing process. Other portions would be exchanged for wage goods and luxury items produced in the remaining sectors of the economy.[16]

The foregoing is a rather simplified version of what appears to be the most useful element in the Marxian apparatus. At this stage it was but a first approximation. Nevertheless, it did lead eventually to what Veblen called the "climax of [Marx's] great work," the law of accumulation. In the beginning there was no accumulation, no ingathering of capital, but merely replacement, as in the stationary state of the bourgeois economist. This was the simple reproduction of Volume I. Consumer goods, fixed and circulating capital were put back as used, so that the value created during a given period was equal to the claims on consumption. The Marxian schema here may be visualized as a flow analysis of income, one of the most analytically effective ones in the history of economics. Output represented what Keynes called aggregate supply, while income comprised expenditure on both means of production and consumption. Thus, each component in the circulation process was expressed as a supply and a demand. So far no serious problems were encountered, for in this model there was no technical progress and the ratio of capital to labor was unaltered. In fact, the labor theory of value almost came into its own in such an "economy" since the unit product value was also constant.

But to Marx accumulation and growth were central, for this was the locus of all the fundamental contradictions of the capitalist order. Involved in this process was the fall in the rate of profit and the periodic eruption of economic crisis. And superimposed on all this was group conflict, class consciousness, and the whole sociology of revolution—the political elements in the story which have served, unfortunately, to obscure the economic analysis. Basically, the economic problem was to discover how the continuous reduction of labor requirements affected accumulation and the changing structure of capitalism. English history provided Marx with many striking illustrations of this inexorable process. The industrial revolution offered the first occasion where fixed rather than circulating capital was accumulated. Against this backdrop, wealth could be measured by buildings and machinery rather than by stocks of goods in warehouses. The small farmer was forced off the land; cottage industries were violently disrupted; native economies in colonial regions were torn asunder; the worker irrevocably lost control of his tools; and heavy, fixed equipment became the hallmark of a new order. Accumulation was associated with a "rising organic composition of capital."

These dynamic changes demonstrated to Marx the need for a more complex model of circulation. This he built in the "expanded reproduction" scheme which revealed how capital was augmented. We know that not all of the surplus value available to capitalists was consumed: some portion was invested for the express purpose of enlarging the total stock of capital. This implied the need to create more means of production than what was necessary to replace used up constant capital. More wage goods were also needed for the workers. The analysis of expanded reproduction then went on to break down the value categories in a way that accounted for their different combinations. Surplus value was now distributed to additional variable capital, to more constant capital, and to ordinary consumption for the capitalist. However, what happened was that the constant capital in the producers' goods industries increased faster than the output of consumers' goods, and the disproportion in the economic structure became more and more evident. Equilibrium could be maintained only if both the producers' and consumers' goods industries were able to expand jointly. According to Marx, this was quite unlikely.

Another way of looking at this question is to say that in the case of an ever-increasing stock of capital, investment can occur only when the market itself keeps expanding. If savings are less than what is required for ordinary investment, capital is apt to become scarce with pressure on resources as the likely result. Of course, the situation is somewhat more complicated than this, since new capital might be unused or merely substituted for earlier, older capital, in which case the economy must face a possible waste of resources.

In an expanding economy, productive capacity increases in consonance with income. The required ratio for stable economic growth is established when the rate of increase in capacity equals the rate of increase in income. Simple offsets to savings are not enough to maintain a "growing equilibrium," for, in fact, investment must always exceed saving. The economy must behave like an Einsteinian universe, constantly expanding at an accelerated rate. But should investment fail to meet these conditions, excess capacity would soon ensue, giving rise to deflationary conditions. Add to this situation leakages in income flow and it will appear unlikely that a continual expansion is indefinitely sustainable.

The foregoing seems to express the matter in Keynesian rather than Marxian language. But Marx was not unaware of the savings-investment problem; his analysis of disequilibrium in simple reproduction demonstrated a fairly clear grasp of the question. For example, he pointed to an accumulation of depreciation reserves unmatched by demand offsets as a cause of economic crisis. In his view, equilibrium required renewals of fixed capital in sufficient quantity to balance "amortization." And this was not the only parallel with Keynesian thinking. Marx, like Keynes, rejected automatism in economics. Shift a few terms about and the Marxian decline in the rate of profit becomes a nineteenth-century cousin of the Keynesian marginal efficiency of capital. Keynes also believed, as did Marx, that accumulation was not merely a passive phenomenon, but an active, often creative, often disturbing process penetrating all the interstices of the economic system. But above all, to both Marx and Keynes, economic breakdown resulted from internal insufficiencies. At this point the major distinction between the two writers was their use of aggregates: Marx talked about surplus value, while Keynes spoke of income flow and effective demand.

Surplus value was for Marx the instrument of accumulation. It was the rate of saving out of surplus value that governed investment; the pace, however, was set by the competitive drive to defeat one's rivals in the market place. It is easy to understand why such factors as the rate of exploitation and labor productivity were viewed by Marx as important, for these were the very elements that swelled the available total of surplus value.

Now, accumulation meant an increased demand for labor, despite the fact that the value theory adopted by Marx would suggest otherwise. But, if the demand for labor in a dynamic capitalist order was increasing, how could one account for misery and unemployment? Here Marx dragged in the *deus ex machina* of the industrial reserve army, unemployed surplus labor, which presumably kept growing as the proportion of labor utilized in production declined. Wages in the long run were supposed to be determined by the size and effectiveness of the reserve army. But under the most favorable conditions, the increase in capital equipment might take place without changing the technical input factors. Accordingly, the division of the national income became a matter of haggling and bargaining, and on this point Marx's answer was no better than that of the "bourgeois" economist.

Under these conditions Marx admitted the possibility of a rise in the absolute level of wages. But he did suggest that the relative share would decline. For though real wages might rise, they were unlikely to rise proportionately with productivity. Yet modern experience has indicated a contrary trend, for the possibility of wages increasing in consonance with productivity has been demonstrated much too often to make the Marxian proposition a valid one. For example, J. Steindl showed in his *Maturity and Stagnation in American Capitalism* that labor's share in national output over the long run has not fallen.[17] In many industries the drop in the wage proportion that might have been occasioned by technological change was overcome by increases in productivity. Kuznets has offered data to show that the share of wages in net income moves in ways that Marx would not have thought possible—downward in an upswing and upward in a depression.[18] That is to say, wages are sticky. Marx's reasoning on this score was entirely classical, for he thought that capitalists got themselves out of the rough by cutting wages. Yet Keynes showed that this only worsened matters.

Even contemporary die-hard followers of Marx have had their hitherto staunch belief shaken on this point. Shortly after the Hungarian Revolution in 1956, a dispute among French Marxists revolved around the question of potential versus actual remuneration. It was grudgingly conceded that some improvement in wages and living standards had occurred, but still, it was insisted, the restricted opportunities of the working class must prove Marx's theory of increasing misery. The evidence offered was the case of a worker who once walked to work but who now drove a Renault while his employer, who once used an ancient horse and buggy, now drove a Cadillac. A further indication of "increasing misery," said the French Marxists, was the great amount of time workers had to spend travelling to and from the job. It is obvious that the notion of immiseration—whether relative or absolute—is no longer defensible.[19]

Another major argument in the Marxian system related to the rate of profit.[20] Here Marx looked to the structural organization of capitalism; that is, he did not stress the lack of sales or falling demand as the cause of profit decline, but pointed rather to the rising organic composition of capital. It was really a matter of simple arithmetic: if the rate of exploitation was constant, with an increasing ratio of capital to labor, the rate of profit was bound to fall. Only through a greater degree of exploitation, more intense work, speed-up, depressing wages below the value of labor power, or through foreign trade could declining profit rates be halted. Marx conceded that these countervailing forces might be quite potent, but he supplied no definite answer as to the general tendency over the long run, feeling that the specific circumstances in a given era would determine the actual movement of profits.

Marx seems to have had some difficulty in relating the falling profit rate theme to accumulation, for it is obvious that the latter would soon grind to a halt with declining profit ratios. Marxists have responded to this question by happily underscoring it as one of capitalism's "contradictions." If, however, the significant relationships had been redefined in a way that permitted a decline in constant capital while productivity was maintained, Marx would have discovered quite another aspect to the problem. The assumption underlying the declining rate of profit was an increasing ratio of constant to variable capital, so that the proportion of surplus value to the totality of constant plus variable capital always had to fall. This implied that the only conceivable technological improvements were solely labor-saving in character. But if investment were of the capital-saving variety, a larger surplus value could be extracted without reducing the rate of profit, for now surplus value could be maintained at a constant or even larger proportion to the sum of constant and variable capitals. Such an experience has not been unknown in western capitalism, as was shown by David Weintraub in his study of capital formation and technology.[21] Moreover, it would appear to be quite reasonable to relate profit to the sale of output and thus ultimately to effective demand. With the latter kept steady on a fairly even keel, one would think that the rate of profit could be maintained without this particular internal contradiction. Marx did in fact recognize capital saving as a countervailing force, but he thought it quite unimportant. In short, the Marxist theory of the falling rate of profit is too constricted and too limited to be fully useful for analytical purposes.

To Marx, falling profit and accumulation could not be separated from the problem of economic crises. Continuous, uninterrupted accumulation under capitalism seemed unlikely, and in fact, upon close inspection, it was impossible. The realization of surplus value would require an expansion of demand, an unlikely development in the face of limited purchasing power made available to the mass of the population. "The last cause of all real crises," he said, "always remains the poverty and restricted consumption of the masses as compared to the tendency of capitalist production to develop the productive forces in such a way that the absolute power of consumption of the entire society would be their limit." [22] This was to him a fundamental "contradiction" caused by the tendency toward disproportionate growth in the producers' and consumers' goods industries. Further complications arose from such factors as the excessive resort to credit, the relationships of interest to profit, speculative activities, monetary inflation, and errors in planning. The increasing inability to realize surplus value impeded further investment while paradoxically stimulating laborsaving devices. In all this there was revealed an inherent tendency to disequilibrium, for, according to the Marxian model, the value of the replacement goods failed to match accumulated depreciation reserves. In Keynesian terms, there was an insufficiency of investment.

Much in Marx's analysis of economic upset anticipated modern thinking. Certainly his comments on the impact of speculation and overselling and on the compulsion to produce beyond the limits of reasonable demand are not unrelated to the contemporary problem of inventory stockpiling. Here Marx approached what present-day economists call acceleration, or the way in which demand affects investment. His distinction between industrial and financial circulation is a reminder of depression talk about hoarding. Also implicit in his analysis was recognition of the role of money as a store of value as well as a means of payment. But in contradistinction to others, notably Keynes, Marx did not believe that it was possible to shore-up the economy by schemes designed to bolster consumer demand. There was a clear implication in his theory that capitalism could not sustain for long any built-in stabilizers.

As one commentator has written: "Marx developed a comprehensive analysis of the category of capital and of capitalist accumulation in relation to the complicated and highly differentiated set of institutions which were provoked by this accumulation and which in turn accelerated. . . . It is this which makes *Capital* such a rich mine of suggestions for the interpretation of capitalism, even to those who are not in sympathy with [Marx]." [23] The process of accumulation and growth was internal to the economic order and did not require any outside stimulus to get it going. This is the basic message of Marxian theory, one frequently overlooked by other economists.

The values of Marx may be seen in his emphasis upon technology and the central role of the capitalist. Investment and accumulation were at the heart of what he called capitalist motion. Yet stability could be attained only if economic growth was properly balanced between the producers' and consumers' sectors of the economy—an unlikely contingency by virtue of capitalism's essential nature. The relation of the accumulation or investment process to the distribution of income and mass consumption was clearly delineated. One of Marx's great failings, however, was his refusal to take account of population growth and its palpable pressure on resources. Marxian theory, for example, could not explain, in purely economic terms, the perpetual stagnation of the so-called underdeveloped regions. Nevertheless, the underscoring of political factors and imperial power was an element that other economists might have acknowledged a good deal sooner than they did.[24]

Certainly we must agree with Schumpeter when he said that Marx's economic ideas could not be easily dismissed. Despite the enormous handicaps under which Marx worked, he was able to carve out a significant body of theory. He was, said Schumpeter, ". . . a born analyst, a man who felt impelled to do analytic work, whether he wanted to or not. . . ." The errors and false trails notwithstanding, his theory cannot be blithely ignored, as is all too often done, for its numerous insights can provide useful leads to an understanding of the real functioning of the economy. But to grasp these ideas requires more than a casual perusal of Volume I. We must again agree with Schumpeter when he said that an understanding of Marx demanded not only a grasp of the economics of his day (that is, Ricardo's) but resigning oneself to a careful reading of the whole of *Das Kapital* and the *Theorien über den Mehrwert*, the so-called "fourth volume" (a brilliant study of the history of economic thought) as well.[25]

ii

Early Critiques of Marxism:
The Transformation Problem

A few economists in Marx's own day were curious enough at least to try to understand what it was that he was saying. One such was Philip Wicksteed, the noted English theologian-economist, whose review of Volume I in 1884 was one of the first serious critical evaluations of *Das Kapital*.[26] Wicksteed's major contention was that Marx had undertaken a logically illegitimate transition from the notion of usefulness to that of labor value. In actuality, said Wicksteed in rather telling fashion, socially necessary labor does not count in the concept of "value" unless it is useful. Thus Marx could not really dispose of utility as blithely as he did. Commodities were alike not because they partook of abstract labor, but because they all embodied an abstract *usefulness*. Exchange value, therefore, stemmed from utility, not from labor. "The exchanged articles differ from each other in the *specific desires* which they satisfy. They resemble each other in the *degree of satisfaction* which they confer." [27] That is to say, while the specific utility is not an element in ordinary transactions, there can be little doubt but that abstract utility is basic to exchange.

In order to measure value, Wicksteed resorted to the Jevonian notion of diminishing utility, defining exchange value for any two transacted commodities merely as the point at which an equivalence of utility resulted. Here he countered Marx's use of Robinson Crusoe by arguing that such an isolated person would surely have to measure the worthwhileness of a given endeavor in terms of the satisfactions rendered by his individual output. Equilibrium for Robinson would be attained when the desire for more food, clothing, or shelter would be proportional to the time required to produce the specific goods, for at that point equal applications of labor would yield equal utilities. For a community, equilibrium in the output of any two commodities was attained when the point of indifference between them was reached, since at that point the utility for each was the same. Prices, said Wicksteed, were set by "the force of demand at the margin of supply." When this concept was applied to improvements in labor productivity, Wicksteed demonstrated that the value of goods fell not because less labor was embodied in them, but because output produced with redundant labor was less useful. As might be expected, Wicksteed rejected the whole Marxian labor value apparatus. The value of labor, he said, bore no logical relation to the value of other commodities because labor power could not be directed to any specific purpose. As a generalized concept, it could not be related analytically to the amount of labor embodied in it. If this were so, then the notion of surplus value had no genuine meaning.[28]

Wicksteed was no hard-bitten opponent of socialism. He was friendly enough to its meliorist ideas and even spoke at times to labor groups. His review of Marx, however, stirred some discussion, particularly among the Fabians, one of whose leading writers, George Bernard Shaw, responded with a rather pointless attack. Wicksteed replied in kindly fashion, and it was not long before Shaw conceded the victory to the minister-economist.

The marginalist approach to value, which was rapidly displacing the older cost of production theories, became a powerful intellectual weapon in combatting socialist ideas. Value theory began to be examined from the microscopic view; the individual businessman operating in a market that he could not control now became the subject of economics, and his exchanges with equally impotent consumers became the origins for a new subjective theory of value. Production and distribution were essentially market phenomena, and an evaluation of Marxian ideas had to start there.

Perhaps the most elaborate critique of Marxism was Eugen von Böhm-Bawerk's, which provided leads for virtually all subsequent evaluations. Böhm-Bawerk observed that there was a transformation problem implicit in the Marxian doctrine. That is, values had to be changed in some way into prices.

But he did not feel that Marx would be able to offer a solution. When Volume III of *Das Kapital* appeared, Böhm-Bawerk contended that his suspicion had been vindicated. Nevertheless, he stated that Marx was important enough an economist to be studied carefully. He was merely surprised that such a keen mind should have pursued so many false paths, simply because his mentors, Adam Smith and David Ricardo, were held in such high esteem. But neither they nor Marx, said Böhm-Bawerk, were able to supply self-consistent proofs of the labor theory of value.[29]

Marx had argued that surplus value was created in proportion to investment in labor rather than in proportion to the total investment. Since profit, however, was computed in relation to total capital, commodities would not exchange in accordance with the labor embodied in them. This, said Böhm-Bawerk, was the source of the great contradiction. But more basic, perhaps, was the fact that Marx had limited himself to the study of *commodities*, that is, the products of labor destined for market exchange. These goods— and they represented but a part of the total spectrum—did have a common factor, namely, abstract labor. And the oscillations in their market prices might be averaged so that the original law of value remained unchanged. Now, Marx's argument suggested that the same rate of surplus value could be related to varying rates of profit, since the latter depended solely on the organic composition of capital. Thus, with a larger variable capital component, the rate of profit would be greater. However, the structure of industries varied, so that profit rates patently were different even though the rate of surplus value might be the same. Consequently, Marxian theory seemed to demand that capitals of equal size but of different organic compositions should have different profits. Yet Marx, said Böhm-Bawerk, could not escape the observation that in the real world investments of equal amount yielded similar profits. This was the contradiction that Volume III had set out to reconcile. Up to this point in the Marxian model commodities had sold at their *values*. But with different profit rates, the economy was no longer in equilibrium, for movement between the sectors had been stimulated by the ensuing disequilibrium. The Marxian argument posited that for the economy as a whole capitalists shared in society's pool of surplus value in proportion to their total investment. Prices now were based on expended capital plus a share of the total surplus value. By doing this Marx had shifted his focus from the individual capitalist to the system as a whole, thus presumably allowing for differences in prices and values and enabling individual transactions to be labeled prices of production.

But as Paul Sweezy conceded,[30] this was a logically weak solution, for it required that new assumptions, not part of the model itself, be introduced. Böhm-Bawerk called the procedure illegitimate and merely the Ricardian cost of production theory in new dress. The averaging of profits implied that some capitalists obtained gains derived from someone else's surplus value. That is to say, competition was the force which averaged profits and converted values into prices. But, asked Böhm-Bawerk, if in this revised garb commodities no longer exchanged in proportion to embodied labor, what then happened to the labor theory of value? [31] The argument was advanced with great skill and clarity, and, despite the debater's tone, it was difficult to counter. "Marx's third volume," concluded the Austrian, "contradicts the first. The theory of the average rates of profit and of the prices of production cannot be reconciled with the theory of value." [32]

When Marxists responded that total prices were equal to total values despite individual fluctuations, or that prices were rooted in values by virtue of changes in socially necessary labor time, or that value governed exchange in the primary stages of production, or that value determined prices indirectly and in some ultimate sense, they were merely evading the basic logical issue, said Böhm-Bawerk. [33] They simply could not have it both ways, he argued, for either value governed the exchange of individual commodities or it did not. Furthermore, to assert that prices equal values as a totality did not explain component changes, since an average of permanent differences was not quite the same as an average of fluctuations. Marx had tried to convert the former into the latter, an arbitrary and inadmissible procedure. He also had overlooked the time factor in production, an egregious omission to the Austrian school. As for the argument based on the historical priority of value, this, said Böhm-Bawerk, was a mere assumption without proof.

In Volume III of *Das Kapital* the price of production was defined as the cost of the means of production entering into the commodity plus an average profit on capital. The Marxian argument was that value affected price through surplus value, which was distributed over total capital, thereby providing for an average rate of profit. This then was applied to a single unit of output and so presumably solved the transformation problem. But Böhm-Bawerk argued that there was no true connection between the individual and the aggregate concept; [34] and that, in fact, the notion of an aggregate such as surplus value was not subject to the laws of exchange. There were many other difficulties with the labor theory, said the Austrian professor, notably the fact that wages can deviate from the rate equivalent to labor embodied in the means of subsistence and that elements other than labor can influence ratios of exchange.

Marx went astray, averred Böhm-Bawerk, because he rejected the supply and demand analysis rooted in market forces. In addition, he excluded from his model those goods which were not commodities in the peculiar Marxian sense. Böhm-Bawerk thought this to be an especially serious error, for many things in nature, he argued, were subject to commercial transactions and property rights which did not stem from labor. At this point, Böhm-Bawerk clearly was injecting the element of scarcity. However, Marx would have dismissed this as a mere derivative of natural monopoly. Böhm-Bawerk also caught Marx up on his rather tenuous distinction between skilled and un-skilled labor, whereby one is made a simple multiple of the other.[35] Time and again, Böhm-Bawerk ticked off telling arguments against his victim, very much like a skillful attorney conducting an embarrassing cross-examination. Yet he conceded that the middle portion of *Das Kapital* was a remarkable per-formance. "These parts of the system," he said, "by their extraordinary logical consistency permanently establish the reputation of the author as an intellectual force of the first rank. . . . This long middle part of his work . . . is really essentially faultless." [36] What Böhm-Bawerk rejected were the early chapters of Volume I of *Das Kapital* and particularly chapter ten in the third volume.

Yet one wonders whether Marx would have grasped the Austrian's stric-tures, or whether Böhm-Bawerk really understood Marx. The latter sought to discover the social relationships arising from capitalist methods of produc-tion, while to the former economic reality consisted virtually entirely of psychic relations rooted in demand and the consumption of goods.

Pareto's criticism of Marxism, set forth in his *Les Systèmes Socialistes,*[37] was somewhat broader in scope than Böhm-Bawerk's, dealing as it did with sociological implications as well as value theory. Much of Pareto's attack was rooted, of course, in his own conception of social reality. If the senti-ments that socialism created were useful, he said, it was not particularly im-portant if its economic theory was false.[38] For example, when socialism stimu-lated labor to form trade unions in order to protect workers' rights, an important service was being performed. Pareto was quick to concede the ef-fectiveness of socialism as a political myth, but beyond this he dealt with Marxism very much along Böhm-Bawerk's lines. He questioned the reduction of skilled labor to units of unskilled labor; he observed that the labor theory of value was restricted to reproducible goods; and he noted that the theory could not account for changes in consumer taste and income or for the impact of shifts in the conditions of production. Marx's theory, he insisted, was un-able to deal with alterations in productivity, for if the latter should increase, thereby reducing the value embodied in a good, what incentive would cap-italists have to introduce new equipment?

The reply was obvious enough: the lag between the introduction of new capital equipment and the establishment of a new equilibrium was sufficient to enable the capitalist to extract an additional gain over and above the con-stant capital transferred to the commodity. Pareto replied rather testily that if such a lag yielded a surplus to capital before equilibrium was estab-lished, it ought to do so at all times since in real life equilibrium was never attained. Aside from these remarks, Pareto's arguments paralleled those of Böhm-Bawerk—the historical basis of value was unproven; there were factors other than labor in exchange; the transformation of values into prices ran afoul of simple logic.[39]

The Marxists did not fail to meet the Austrian challenge. Rudolf Hilferding, a leading socialist theorist, whose other contributions we shall discuss below, responded with a scathing rebuttal in 1904, *Böhm-Bawerk's Criticism of Marx*.[40] Despite the polemics, Böhm-Bawerk remained unconvinced. Hilferding's assertion that commodity analysis in the Marxian sense vividly revealed capitalist social relationships made no impression whatsoever on the Austrians. They could not see why *all* social relationships should be subject to critical economic examination. Hilferding, on the other hand, insisted that labor in its socialized form provided the measure of value, thus establishing economics as a social and historical science.[41] Böhm-Bawerk's exchange relationships were unhistorical in character, said the young Marxist, and implied that we must surrender all prospects of discovering capitalism's law of motion. "Private labor acquires validity only insofar as they are social labors. *Society has, as it were, assigned to each of its members the quota of labor necessary to society; has specified to each individual how much labor he must expend. And these individuals have forgotten what their quota was, and rediscover it only in the process of social life*." [42] Of course, this sort of Hegelianism did not really answer Böhm-Bawerk, whose insistent query of why elements other than labor were excluded from the analysis went unanswered.

Hilferding argued that the scarcity concept could be derived from the cost of labor; that skilled labor must be a multiple of unskilled labor as demonstrated again and again by human experience; and that Böhm-Bawerk erroneously wanted Marx to solve the problem of absolute prices. If the last point had been true, Böhm-Bawerk could have been charged with having asked the wrong question. Unfortunately for Hilferding, this was not the case, since the Austrian professor was concerned with *relative* values. Finally, Hilferding was forced to admit that the analysis of skilled labor as somewhat more complex units of unskilled labor was possible only in a theoretical, not in any operational sense.[43] What irritated Hilferding and all the Marxists who came after him was the Austrian focus on the subjective evaluation of exchange ratios. Labor was related to disutility and value converted into a psychic phenomenon. On such foundations, the objective view of society became untenable and made Marxian macroeconomics incomprehensible. This was all well and good, but when Hilferding sought to employ analytic techniques, as in his discussion of supply and demand, he was able to come up only with some rather crude and unconvincing tautologies.[44]

Nevertheless, Marxians continued to employ arguments similar to those advanced by Hilferding. They asserted that the charge of a contradiction between Volume I and Volume III stemmed from a thoroughgoing misapprehension of Marxian method and purpose. In the famous letter to Kugelmann [45] Marx had argued that individual labor was transformed into social labor through the private exchange of commodities. The individual coincidence of value and price was rare, occurring only when the organic composition of capital in a given industry was the same as for the social average. Otherwise, Marx implied, one could speak only of a tendency toward coincidence. Thus, as is the case with all economic models, the Marxian theory did not have to be an exact copy of reality; it was an abstraction which by its essentially simple construction highlighted the critical forces in actual economic life.[46]

In his third volume, Marx was merely trying to demonstrate the forms of movement in capitalist production as a whole.[47] This was his frame of reference for realizing profit from surplus value. For Marx the macroeconomic picture required that the total surplus value in the economy be distributed amongst the firms not in proportion to the wages bill but in accordance with total investment. Firms whose organic composition differed from the social average sold their output at prices of production, not at their values. To the non-Marxian observer, however, this was little more than the classical cost of production which in the long run was "a prerequisite of supply, of the reproduction of commodities in every individual sphere." [48] Marx insisted that the prices of production were derived from values and that the rates of profit in specific lines were related to surplus values originating in the area of production. For most Marxists this was but a modification of the basic argument. The total amount of surplus value and the average rate of profit and the dispersion of prices from values were determined as in Volume I of *Das Kapital*. The Volume III problem occurred only because commodities exchanged as "products of capital which claim equal shares of the total amount of surplus value." [49]

However, some Marxists, notably Ronald Meek of the University of Glasgow, admitted that the transformation of inputs and outputs into prices would, as traditionally stated, fail to maintain the Marxian equilibrium.[50] It would be normally impossible to effect a transformation whereby total profit would equal total surplus value at the same time that total prices equalled total values, said Meek. Despite this difficulty, die-hard Marxists have averred that such a discrepancy does not vitiate the analysis in Volume I. Marx, they say, was aware of the problem, for his analysis pointed the way to a consideration of interdependent production. The value-price transformation could be made more realistic if both inputs as well as outputs had their values changed into prices. In modern terminology, the question was whether the relations between producers' goods and consumers' goods industries in the Marxian model could be expressed as a set of self-consistent equations.

It was Ladislaus von Bortkiewicz (1868-1932), an eminent German statistician and quite competent critic of both Marx and Böhm-Bawerk, who first showed how this might be done.[57] He exhibited a deep critical faculty, particularly when examining details of an economic model. In fact, Schumpeter remarked that he overdid this, making himself something of a comma hunter. Basically an orthodox Ricardian, Bortkiewicz went to great lengths to defend the classical system and was thus drawn to what was, to all intents and purposes, a defense of Marxian economics, which he felt was anyway a variant of Ricardianism.[52]

The values of commodities, said Bortkiewicz, while admittedly ratios of exchange, should bear the "same proportion to each other as their absolute values." And if the latter were defined in terms of labor, then values would be in proportion to embodied labor. But in trying to solve the transformation problem of Volume III, Marx showed a confusion between values and prices by carrying over certain data from the value category without altering them. In present-day language, some of the input data were retained as values. Instead of starting over again, Marx had excused the odd mixture by asserting that price deviations were self-compensatory. But such countervailing adjustments, argued Bortkiewicz, resulted from the peculiar Marxian method and would be totally unnecessary if the equality of price and value were not initially assumed. The whole trouble had started in Volume III with the calculation of used-up raw material and constant capital at prices corresponding to values. But all this ran the risk of becoming a circular argument since the values utilized in the beginning were arrived at through prices. Not even Bortkiewicz observed that if the whole business were set forth in money terms, the labor theory would become redundant.

Bortkiewicz noted that the Marxian aim was to locate the origin of profit in the production sphere rather than in circulation where commercial mark-ups could seemingly be made to account for surplus value. After developing many tedious mathematical equations, his model settled down to a product-price system in which there were four price-value factors with but three equations. Equating the relationship for the capitalists' own consumption with gold, it became possible to state the value schema in terms of money and to eliminate one of the four unknowns, thus making the model capable of solution.[53] When one takes a close look at the Bortkiewicz model, the realization that value has been dropped is inescapable. Obviously it was the relationships between wages, prices, and the rate of profit that were important, rather than the origin of value.[54] In fact, as Sweezy virtually conceded, price calculation could tell us all that we need to know about the economic order and its functioning.[55] Yet there was no denying the fact that Marx seemed to be on the right track, for he was seeking to delineate these identical relationships. The difficulty, averred Bortkiewicz, was in his insistence on utilizing a value framework for what essentially should have been a set of operational equations.

The transformation problem has continued to disturb Marxists down to the present day.[56] Maurice Dobb has insisted that it poses no real logical difficulty, for a solution is feasible if the basic Marxian equations are stated in terms of wage goods and capital goods industries only. If real wages and the labor force do not change, then output in the wage goods industry can be constant. If capital in that industry represented advances to workers then the rate of profit would also be constant. But once constant capital was introduced into the Dobb's model, the flow of output from producers' goods industries to consumers' goods altered the profit-value-price relationships. The former, with a higher organic composition of capital, would have an initially lower rate of profit. A flow of capital, induced by differential profit ratios, would start between the two sectors. This, said Dobb, demonstrated how the averaging of profit rates was attained. But the fact remained that the *transformation* of values into prices was no more satisfactory in this sophisticated version than it had been in Marx's original. Again, prices were introduced as the element that formally satisfied the equational system. As in the Seton version,[57] where an input-output matrix was developed, it was merely demonstrated that the substitution of prices for values made the problem amenable to solution. But in no instance did it answer the original Böhm-Bawerk complaint.

The Marxian economist, who interpreted the transformation problem in its historical sense, asserted that in industries with a high organic composition of capital prices would on the average exceed values. This presumably explains why early capitalists preferred consumer goods manufacturing to commercial enterprise, thus stressing light goods to the detriment of a really rapid growth of industry. Not until the transformation process had equalized the rate of profit for all did the economy begin to witness an expansion of steel, railroads, and the like. Thus, as Seton said, the mass of people were cheated out of the fruits of genuine productive possibilities. By implication, of course, this offers about as neat a justification for the Soviet crash program of industrialization as could be imagined. But neither the conclusion nor its implications are warranted, for the Marxians are here confusing an analytical problem with a structural one. To say that light industries grew up first is an admission of the fact that under conditions of ordinary competition (another word for transformation?) heavy industries developed in response to market demand. One might note what has happened in underdeveloped countries which have sought to build heavy industry in a low demand economy. After all is said and done, one must again agree with Joan Robinson when she called the transformation problem a purely formal exercise with no real significance.[58] She further contended that the price theory of Volume III was little more than a Marshallian long run cost of production proposition—a theory of normal price in which the equality of prices and values held only in special situations. Although Marxists have offered the argument that their master developed a macroeconomic approach in which the ratio of capital to labor was held constant so that changes in capital, labor, and productivity could be observed, there is no escaping the gnawing realization that Marx did after all think of values as an inherent quality of a good. Despite all the debates and heated arguments and appeals to history, the basic difficulty still rests in Marx's insistence on an embodied labor theory of value.

iii

The Rise of German Revisionism

When the Paris Commune was liquidated in 1871, socialists in Europe went entirely onto the defensive. Within a few years, the proletariat, allegedly the vanguard class, had all but forgotten the goals for which earlier generations of socialists had fought. Even the old slogans were unknown. In Great Britain, the tradition of the Chartists became merely a legend, while in Germany the revolution of 1848 was relegated to the history texts. The intellectuals and the radical elements of the middle class no longer expressed sentiments of revolution. The workers, although honoring the memory of those who had been slaughtered defending the barricades of the Palatinate, did so mainly as a kind of ritual. Socialism as a viable movement seemed utterly exhausted. After 1870 conservative forces were in the ascendant as the German Empire and Russian Czarism joined hands to impose a reactionary axis over most of Europe. Austria, no longer the power center it had been in 1815, followed suit. Italy, although now unified, brought no improved living standards to its peasants. Democratic movements in general, and socialism in particular, were at a low ebb.[59]

Yet the radical tradition and the movement to which it gave birth somehow survived. German Social-Democracy managed to hold its own in the struggle against Bismarck's persecution and even provided leadership to the embryo socialist parties in other West European countries. Still, no new international ties could be created for the socialists. Despite several efforts, the general feeling, even in 1881, was that circumstances were not yet ripe for a formal organization of socialist parties.[60] But the gathering impetus for an eight-hour day led to more discussions between European and American socialists, and by 1889 the foundations for the Second International had been laid. The two socialist groups that met in Paris that year (one of which was thoroughly Marxist) were the core for a new organization. The eight-hour day program was soon displaced by the need for a union of parties devoted to political action. Of course, demonstrations for a shorter work day continued, for to many socialists these were essential actions against a hostile state. But it was not deemed possible to formulate a parliamentary program for the nationalization of industry, as in later British experience. The Germans especially expressed the view that state control of industry would merely strengthen the bourgeoisie, since the latter dominated the state. Only when power could be captured could the cause of the working class be furthered.

The French socialists developed contrary views. They came to feel that the state might have to be defended against ambitious would-be dictators. While a good number of French Marxists agreed with their German counterparts, there was nevertheless a greater willingness in France to cooperate with the liberal bourgeoisie. The famous case of Alexander Millerand, a leading French socialist (and later president of the Republic) who entered a Radical Socialist cabinet in 1899, illustrated the attitude of many French Marxists. Millerand, a gradualist, scoffed at the notion that socialists could reach their objectives without first winning a constitutional majority. As the new century opened, the reformist coloration in the socialist movement became more and more pronounced. And its revolutionary élan began to disappear.[61]

The German Social-Democrats suddenly discovered that they were winning votes. This posed a problem for their Marxist political science. They had long been accustomed to a virtual underground existence: the Bismarckian restrictions under which they had operated enforced a highly centralized organization, placing policy matters in the hands of a few, albeit capable leaders, notably Wilhelm Liebknecht, August Bebel, Karl Kautsky, and Eduard Bernstein. Their history, prior to the Gotha Program of 1875, had taught them to abjure parliamentary action as an illusory path to victory. But by the 1890's a new tune was being played, for the increasing share of the electorate going to the Social-Democrats seemed to forecast an eventual majority of parliamentary seats.

This was the background for the growth of a practical reformist spirit. There developed a desire to evolve a socialism via reform rather than revolution. The changing structure of the Social-Democratic party itself enforced the milder viewpoint, for with posts in provincial legislatures and local communities a firebrand outlook suggested irresponsibility. In 1891 the Erfurt Congress demanded popular elections. This appeared good strategy with which to greet the new Emperor. The theory was that a large Social-Democratic vote would make the reimposition of Bismarckian legislation unlikely. But even more significant was the inescapable fact that both economic and social situations had altered, so much so that the original Marxian analysis seemed quite out of date. Large-scale organization of business and industrial concentration was welcomed on the ground that such developments would make it all the easier for socialists to take over. Small businessmen and the farmers, however, were viewed with distaste bordering on contempt. The socialists promised the peasantry a future of utter extinction, simply as a matter of the inexorable logic of capitalist change. The peasants, however, were stubborn enough to resist this logic and not only refused to fade away but even multiplied. In many areas of Europe large-scale agriculture did not displace the small farmer, and even if the latter was getting himself into debt he displayed a remarkable tenacity in holding on to his little plot of land. Thus, the more realistic Marxist felt it necessary to tailor doctrine to reality if parliamentary gains were to be made; without the farmers there was little prospect of winning enough seats in the Reichstag. This was particularly recognized in Southern Germany where socialists went out of their way to woo the peasants.

In the meantime, the German nation was becoming ever more prosperous. The new unified government had pursued a policy of economic expansion through direct support for public works as well as military needs. Industrialization developed apace, for the Germans knew that they had to work rapidly to catch up to England. Borrowing the new technology with alacrity they absorbed quickly what other nations had to offer, and, blessed with an ample domestic supply of coal and iron, they were able to construct a thriving home industry. Starting in the 1890's a boom developed which began to weaken the orthodox Marxist strength. Cartels and concentrated industry grew; from 1882 to 1895 large enterprises employing more than eleven persons jumped 82 per cent, while small enterprises with less than five employees increased 24 per cent. During the same time the German population advanced about 13 per cent: the expansion of output was faster than the increase in the number of people.[62] Marxists gritted their teeth as prosperity spread its euphoria over the entire economy. This was not what Marx had foretold! Yet the general sense of optimism which pervaded popular feeling obscured the slums and poverty in the industrial areas. As the trade unions gained in membership and strength, they became placid and conservative and anxious to preserve their hard won material gains.[63] In time, the pragmatism of the trade unionists influenced the thinking of the party leadership itself. Revisionism became the ideology of the trade unions long before it won out in the Social-Democratic party, for it accorded them a meaningful role in the slow road to the socialist commonwealth. As revisionist ideas became general currency, the Social-Democratic party began to change and develop into an institution of means, with its own press, bureaucracy, and corps of settled elder statesmen.[64]

In this social and political milieu Eduard Bernstein (1850-1932), chief protagonist of the revisionist posture, developed his main ideas. Bernstein, born in Berlin, had as a young man worked in a bank. But attracted to socialist aims he went off to Switzerland to edit a journal for his friends. When the German authorities prevailed on the Swiss government to expel him in 1888, Bernstein went to England where he remained until 1901. There he came to know the Fabians and learned at first hand of their moderate variety of socialism. Although he had worked closely with Karl Kautsky, German Socialism's major pundit, and was something of a protegé of Engels', he began to stray from the fold. In 1896 he started his famous *Neue Zeit* article series, "Die Voraussetzungen des Sozialismus und die Aufgaben der Sozialdemocratie" (issued later in English as *Evolutionary Socialism)*, which actually initiated the revisionist debate.[65] As might be expected, Karl Kautsky reacted sharply, as did Rosa Luxemburg, whose rejoinder was venomous. Yet Bernstein remained in the Social-Democratic party and soon after the turn of the century was even elected to the Reichstag.

Despite his lack of formal academic training, Bernstein was one of Social-Democracy's outstanding minds. Although early in his career he had been influenced by Eugen Dühring, the blind radical philosopher, Engels' devastating attack, the *Anti-Dühring,* convinced the younger man that it was pure Marxism that formed the answer to civilization's ills. While in Great Britain he published a volume on Cromwell in which the Civil War was interpreted as an economic and social revolution of great significance. His emphasis on the role of Gerald Winstanley, leader of the Digger sect, was a contribution of no small importance.

Bernstein began his reevaluation of socialist doctrine by questioning the proposition that capitalism was in imminent danger of collapse. If this were not to be the case, should not the worker concern himself with immediate needs rather than some distant utopia? In fact, said Bernstein, irritating party leadership no end, the final aims of socialism meant nothing, for it was the movement that was everything.[66] He was, of course, implying that the socialist state would emerge gradually from an accumulation of piecemeal change. Philosophically, he rejected the Hegelian leap so dear to the Marxians—the sudden transformation of quantity into quality—and substituted for it a kind of hard-headed empiricism which he must have absorbed during his prolonged stay in Britain. Bernstein manifested a predilection for plain fact, an approach that made him close kin to the Fabians, and his was a linear concept of progress in which struggle and conflict played little part. As Herbert Marcuse has said, Bernstein put common sense where the dialectic should have ruled and replaced the revolutionary interest with a secure and stable flow of events moving inexorably toward the socialist ideal.[67] Dialectical materialism, said Bernstein, was too one-sided, since it suggested a far smaller role for the human spirit than a valid reading of history would allow. Not surprisingly, he sought to bring Kant forward once more as the philosopher to whom socialists should pay attention, for it was the latter's critical realism rather than Hegelian mysticism with which Bernstein felt most comfortable.[68]

The rejection of dialectical conflict meant that the class struggle was not a meaningful concept. Nor for that matter was the concept of economic determinism, which, despite frequent disclaimers, still seemed essential to the Marxian eschatology. The theory of value as worked out finally in the third volume of *Das Kapital* was a deep disappointment to Bernstein, and the failure to solve the "great contradiction" led him to doubt the validity of the entire labor theory of value. It was, he felt, much too abstract and did not seem to have any special advantage over the utility approach of the Austrian economists. He even intimated that socialism might just as well get along without any theory of value at all![69]

Bernstein conceded that there was a tendency in capitalism to develop centers of concentration, but he argued that the continual prosperity of small business was a significant countervailing force. He denied vehemently that the little entrepreneur was being declassed, citing much statistical evidence to sustain his point. Furthermore, he continued, the development of large aggregations of capital always called forth new firms as auxiliaries.[70] In addition to these considerations, ownership of corporate shares was becoming widespread and consequently making business itself more democratic. Bernstein failed to realize, however, that the meaningful element was not ownership but control, and that the separation of these two aspects of corporate institutions was growing with industrialism itself. His observation that the middle class was not disappearing into the ranks of the proletariat was much more valid. He noted that the class structure was becoming more complex, so that the idea of proletariat versus capitalist was essentially simplistic. Nor was it possible to assert that the fate of the worker was one of increasing misery, as had been predicted by Marx. Not only were the fruits of capitalism's increasing productivity being distributed more widely, but the working class itself was developing ameliorating pressure through cooperatives, collective bargaining, and social legislation. Marx's theory of crisis was rejected rather sharply, for, said Bernstein, economic disturbances were actually becoming milder.[71] If it were true that excessive credit encouraged speculation, this was mainly characteristic of new industries, for as firms matured there was less need for speculative adventures to build capital. The fact was, argued Bernstein, that the growth of world trade, improved means of transportation, and an expanded credit system, together with the growth of cartels, had produced a moderating effect on economic gyrations.

As the revisionist case developed, particularly in its economic phase, it became more and more vague. Some commentators have been uncharitable enough to suggest that the very fuzziness of the argument allowed an escape clause should actual developments have been otherwise.[72] It was clear that Bernstein was taking his inspiration from the prosperity enjoyed for so long in Western Europe, where a general sentiment existed that the depression of the 1870's would never be repeated. Actually, Bernstein was urging that the Social Democratic party change its tactics. It was possible, after all, for the state to do some good for the workers, whose everyday needs simply had to be met. Only through practical experience in handling mundane daily business would the workers learn to conduct the affairs of society; no amount of revolutionary theory and action could teach the proletariat how to run steel mills as going concerns. It was in this sense, thought Bernstein, that consumers' cooperatives performed a highly useful function, since they could become genuine training grounds for the socialist commonwealth.

But Bernstein permitted his enthusiasm for a new moderate, basically middle-class socialism to run away from him. He came to defend nationalism in its nineteenth-century garb, arguing that the colonial policy of the big nations was justifiable because it represented a civilization "higher" than that existing in backward regions. These thoughts, together with those described above, were sufficient for his opponents to say that Bernstein did not so much modify Marx as cast him overboard, bag and baggage. All this was quite offensive to the Social-Democratic leadership and it was voted down again and again at party congresses. Yet as one looks back upon the history of European socialism one wonders whether it was not Bernstein, rather than Marx, who won out after all.

Bernstein, of course, did not go unanswered. Karl Kautsky (1854-1938), the party's chief theoretician, hastened to reply to the revisionist attack. Educated in Vienna and a onetime journalist, Kautsky had made his journal, *Neue Zeit*, founded the year Marx died, the leading forum of its kind. In its pages he defended what he thought to be true Marxism against both Bernstein's rightist attack and Lenin's onslaught from the left. Kautskian orthodoxy was exemplified in his *Economic Doctrines of Karl Marx*, a pedestrian introduction to Volume I of *Das Kapital*.[73] The notion of unproductive labor, the doctrine of increasing misery, and surplus value were uncritically displayed as the last word in analytical economics. The state was an instrument of class oppression and socialists would have to do all they could to weaken it. But improvements would come about only when the workers will have come to power. Despite all the talk about revolution, Kautsky persistently believed that power could be obtained only by parliamentary means. The abolition of capitalism, he insisted, would be brought about through the ballot box. This made him basically a man of the center and explained his antipathy for Leninist *coup d'état*. Russia wasn't ready for the Socialist revolution, he said, because there weren't enough workers there. On the other hand, he opposed social legislation because it would strengthen the bourgeois state. By insisting on a pristine purity, Kautsky succeeded in making Marxism more sterile than was necessary. It was no wonder that his debate with Bernstein soon degenerated into dry arguments over barren ground.

One of Kautsky's early pedagogic efforts was his gloss on the 1891 Erfurt program of the Social-Democratic party. This statement, on which Bernstein also worked, was advanced on the premise that concentration and the growth of trusts were characteristic of contemporary capitalism. Accompanying this development, asserted the document, was the elimination of the farmer. Socialism was the only solution to the dire calamities that would ensue. But the Erfurt program avoided appeals to revolution, proposing rather to reach the desired objectives via constitutional reform. A whole set of requirements were set forth: tax reform, social legislation, free education, equal rights for women, factory regulation, and all the measures advocated today as conducive to the general welfare. There was also evident in the Kautskian formulations a bias toward large-scale industry with socialism defined in terms of state control of the means of production. But all of these reforms would come about when the workers will have won the reins of government.

Kautsky's services to the German Socialist movement were prodigious. He popularized Marxian economics; he issued Marx's *Theorien über den Mehrwert,* the so-called fourth volume of *Das Kapital;* and he wrote numerous historical studies, including works on Sir Thomas More, the peasant wars in Germany, and the origins of Christianity. His *Materialistic Conception of History* (1927) was a well-ordered analysis which recognized the complexity of historical forces and conceded that human will had a role to play in social action. But in true Marxist fashion, the emphasis was on the palpable economic basis of human behavior. Granting that institutions in various societies differed, Kautsky nevertheless pointed to economic factors as those which accounted for significant distinctions. Socialists, he cautioned, had to be "historically mature," implying that they should move with history rather than express an impatience with the impersonal unfolding of social change. That, thought Kautsky, would be self-defeating. Socialism was inevitable, and we would have to await its arrival. This did not mean that Social-Democracy was not revolutionary: it was simply not a maker of revolutions. These great upheavals must come as a consequence of subterranean social and economic processes. They could not be hastened, for to do so would be to make socialism a conspiracy. In the meantime, socialists could prepare themselves for the future by struggling to extend and further democracy.

The concept of the proletariat was carefully defined. Kautsky accepted the Marxian designation of proletarian destiny, but insisted that the political power workers might secure was related not only to their role in production, but also to the discipline and intelligence they could exercise. The working class as a whole, he insisted, comprised not only the politically alert proletariat but the *lumpen,* together with the labor aristocracy and the great mass of workers who accepted capitalism as the only system they understood. The labor aristocracy, those highly-skilled workers who enjoyed a kind of monopoly in their particular trade and drew benefits from this favored position, were objects of Kautsky's special scorn, for they were entirely *verburgerlicht.* Obviously, political leadership could stem only from the politically alert.

When Kautsky wrote on agriculture he was as dogmatic as the most orthodox of Marxians. He was outraged that the small farmer did not pass from the economic scene in accordance with the Marxian timetable. Finally, he begrudgingly conceded that small farm holdings would persist, even in Russia. On this point it was Bernstein who had the last word.

Others who jumped into the revisionist fray were Rosa Luxemburg, a brilliant Pole,[74] and the American, Louis B. Boudin. Luxemburg emphasized the rise of finance capital as a new feature in the economy and insisted that Bernstein was overlooking the factor of imperialist conflict. The standard Marxian argument had been that economic and social breakdown would inevitably come about from a plethora of capital goods, revealing in no uncertain ways the inability of the economy to absorb its own output. Here Luxemburg was beginning a new line of thought, foreshadowing her later *The Accumulation of Capital*. Capitalism's problems, she said, were momentarily solved through colonialism and the export of capital.

Her attack on Bernstein in her *Sozialreform oder Revolution* [75] was a most effective one. With biting sarcasm she hit her adversary at his weakest point, the question of power. She charged him with abandoning the real aim of Social-Democracy and substituting for it idealism and bourgeois reform. Capitalism's present prosperity, she insisted, was a false one and there was little doubt in her mind that severe crises were on history's agenda. Yet half of Luxemburg's sarcasm was pointless since she frequently was unable to respond to revisionist statistics and revisionist empiricism.

Boudin's participation in the debate was interesting, for his was the only effective American voice in it. He had come to the United States from Russia at the age of fifteen and by the time he was twenty-five had become a lawyer. As a young man he was an ardent socialist, ready to defend pure Marxism against its critics.[76] In 1907 he published *The Theoretical System of Karl Marx,* one of the better exegetical treatises of its kind.[77] In it he denied that the law of value was useless, offering the standard Marxian defense. He went so far as to urge that value did not have to be transformed into prices, for it was not, he said, a quantitative principle, but rather an abstraction which was prior to the formation of prices.[78] His reply to Bernstein's middle class argument was more effective, for all the latter had demonstrated was that incomes were increasing. The important question, the source and derivation of income, was ignored by Bernstein. It was Boudin's contention that income figures were meaningful solely in regard to their relationships to economic control. Such an approach, he urged, would show the "new" middle class to be in reality but a new white collar proletariat, a rather prescient argument for so early in the century. This new middle class exercised no genuine control over industrial affairs, despite all the shares of stock it might own.[79] On other points, Boudin's arguments paralleled those of Luxemburg.

The debate dragged on for years. Officially, the decision at party congresses repeatedly went to orthodox Marxism, particularly since Bebel and Kautsky were staunch opponents of Bernstein. Yet their characteristically middle position, taken again and again to avoid an open break in the party ranks, evaded the real issue. The result was a distinct dichotomy between theory and policy. The actual party posture was one of reform and revision: the demands were for shorter hours, higher wages, and universal suffrage, all stemming mainly from the practical but conservative trade unions.

What was the significance of the revisionist debate? For one thing, it was obvious that the major tenets of the gradualist philosophy emanated from a supposed reevaluation of the nature of capitalism. In Sombart's words, the shoals of ice cream and apple pie were playing havoc with the underpinnings of socialist doctrine, and it was necessary to explore new channels for steaming ahead to the new paradise. Yet, as Schumpeter remarked, the whole controversy had a salutary effect on Marxism, for it impelled its practitioners to become more critical of statements made in the name of the master and to do more thinking than was required by the mere citation of appropriate extracts from original gospel. But in the main, revisionism reflected a deep-rooted mood of quiescence among the socialists, who with prosperity and age felt it the better part of valor to practice some discretion. When in later years they were faced with the dynamic challenge of the totalitarians of both right and left, they were at an utter loss as to how to react.

iv

The Fabians and Guild Socialists

Althought Marx lived and worked in London for many years, his direct influence upon British socialism was negligible. His only followers were the members of Hyndman's Social Democratic Federation, an organization whose futility was soon apparent. The British temper, disillusioned with liberalism, was not yet prepared for the heavy dose of theoretical study demanded by Marxism. The whole tangle of imperialism, the Irish question, and Egypt had irritated the already strained relations between the middle class and the rest of the population. Classical political economy came under attack by a new group of thinkers who viewed society not as eternally fixed, but as a viable, ever-changing organism. William Morris, John Ruskin, William Cunningham, and Arnold Toynbee all reflected the new outlook, which implicitly set forth the proposition that social relations were the outcome, not of uncontrollable natural forces, but of the interaction of *people*. Within such a framework, the study of social problems demanded the elevation of ethical standards as guides to action. This meant that social legislation should be used, if necessary, to raise the weak and to prevent society from being torn asunder by conflict. It was amelioration in scientific garb.

New studies of society and history were stimulated as exemplified by Cunningham's *Growth of English Industry and Commerce* and Toynbee's *Industrial Revolution.* The leaders of this new intellectual movement insisted, as did Cliffe Leslie, that the ". . . whole economy of every nation is the result of a long evaluation in which there has been both continuity and change and of which the economic side is only a particular aspect or phase. And the laws of which, it is the result, must be sought in history." [80] David Syme remarked that if the individual is to be motivated by self-interest, then society also should be allowed to guide itself in this manner. This implied, of course, substituting cooperation for competition.

Such was the intellectual backdrop against which the Fabian movement developed. Spiritual blood brothers of the German revisionists, the Fabians also rejected Marxian revolutionary eschatology.[81] They were really leaders of a sector of British middle-class intelligentsia, and, while primarily interested in ideas, they did not hesitate to immerse themselves in "sewage, gas and municipal politics." [82] Nor did they remain aloof from practical affairs but worked closely with the trade unions, as well as with the somewhat utopian Independent Labor Party. They were genuine highbrows, with a vague yen toward moral uplift, less concerned with destroying capitalism in the immediate present than with reforming it.

Their beginnings went back to 1882 when several young intellectuals began to meet together to discuss social problems. The vague concept of an ethical fellowship was urged upon them by Thomas Davidson, a visiting American professor. After several sessions, a number of the participants felt that socialism could be advanced more effectively through legislation rather than group discussion. In 1884 they formed a permanent society to accomplish precisely these aims, taking the name of the Roman general who opposed Hannibal. Like Fabius they would wait for the right moment to strike hard. (H. G. Wells later asked just when it was that Fabius had struck). At any rate, what these young, enthusiastic reformers meant to underscore was their belief in socialism by gradual accretion.

The Society was fortunate in attracting several brilliant individuals, among them George Bernard Shaw, Sidney Webb, Graham Wallas, Edward Pease, Frank Podmore, H. G. Wells, and Beatrice Potter, later Mrs. Webb. Shaw, who had come to London from Dublin at the age of twenty, became a brilliant book reviewer, art and drama critic, and music specialist. He soon joined the Fabians, writing numerous political and economic tracts and then gave posterity his famous dramas and prefaces. During the Boer War, Shaw supported the Empire position, arguing that the South African republics were reactionary. Furthermore, he said, both sides had ignored the welfare of the natives, and, since there was no international caretaker body in existence, the British Empire might just as well take possession. This came as a shock to British Radicals, but Shaw, who delighted in needling his audiences, complained that since the highest objective was to raise the general welfare, this could be achieved best through Empire supremacy.[83] In fact, before World War I the Fabians espoused a kind of social imperialism in their pronouncements on international affairs. They were thoroughgoing nationalists and firm believers in the promotion of the Empire, especially to meet the challenge of Germany.[84]

Sidney Webb, born in London in 1859 (died 1947), was educated on the continent. An active member of the London County Council for many years, he served on dozens of government commissions. Between 1894 and 1925 over twenty volumes on trade unionism and social problems came from his pen. His wife, Beatrice Potter (1858-1943), co-authored many of them. A tense woman with an alert mind, she could not abide those she thought fools, yet despite her impatience she was in many ways a more attractive spirit than her bureaucratically minded husband. Less certain than he that administration would solve everything, she wanted to explore nongovernmental ways of achieving socialist aims. Coming from a rather well-to-do background, she saw in the rise of capitalism the history of her own family. It was a visit to Lancashire that finally aroused her social sentiments. Sidney Webb, on the other hand, arrived at socialism via Thomas Huxley and John Stuart Mill. To him it was all a pure intellectual construct. The new society was to be built slowly, with knowledge, technical skill, method, and above all with due regard to the prejudices of the average man.

The Fabians read Marx, Lassalle, and the other socialists of the day. But they did not neglect the English classicists and this was to have a pervading influence on their thinking. Indefatigable as pamphleteers and careful researchers, they churned out tract after tract, seeking all available data to sustain their arguments. The fundamental Fabian view was set forth in an interesting document called the "Basis." This declared them to be socialists and affirmed their belief in community control of capital and in the abolition of private property. They set forth the argument that rent should be socialized and monopoly abolished.[85] An early pamphlet which set the tone for the Fabian posture was *Facts for Socialists,* a statistical analysis of the extremes of riches and poverty. In it, socialism was portrayed as the inescapable outcome of the inherent tendencies of capitalism. Socialism was the fulfillment of what now existed, although the Fabian goal would be attained through change by bits-and-pieces reform. Then in 1888, after several other tracts, came Sydney Olivier's *Capital and Land,* the first of the so-called theoretical studies. Olivier sought to demonstrate that capital was as much of a monopoly as land, the latter to be understood in the Ricardian sense. And this brings us to the kernel of Fabian economics, its theory of rent.

This theory, most explicitly stated in Webb's *Problems of Modern Industry* (London, 1898), visualized the law of rent as the central feature of modern capitalism. It was not meant solely for landed property, but for capital goods as well. The Fabians reasoned that if a given commodity came upon the market with a different cost structure for each producer, while all units sold at the same price, a surplus, after the fashion of the Ricardian differential, necessarily would exist for the more favorably situated producers. But since the economic order was set in a social context, it was reasonable, they said, for the state to appropriate this surplus. The similarity not only to Ricardo, but to Henry George, was obvious. If society required that all the units of the given commodity be produced, then the price must be such as to enable the last or least important producer to make ends meet. The surplus, however, was appropriated by the landlord as his price for permitting workers to be employed. And as society advanced, rents increased, since the pressure of progress brought into the economy poorer sites and marginal operations. The Fabians did not hesitate to apply the theory to differences in personal ability and skills, although it wasn't clear whether the State was to appropriate rents as well.

The main point was that the differential gains of favorably situated establishments were really industrial rents, the major part of which were largely unearned. Moreover, they stemmed from social development and general economic growth rather than the special efforts or services of capitalists. The implication was virtually self-evident: the gain of the capitalist was excessive and should be curtailed. The unearned increment ought to be turned over to society. The class struggle was not between capitalist and worker but between rentiers in agriculture and industry and those who did the actual work. Differential rent was due to community effort and should be returned to the community.

To accomplish this objective, said the Fabians, land should be owned by local councils, and indeed this ought to be the case with all industry, except for such natural monopolies as railroads. The latter might be turned over to the national state. New enterprises should be established out of tax proceeds derived from the acquisition of the industrial surplus: these would become "yardstick" enterprises and gradually would displace the private entrepreneur. Industry then would become "the property and business of the whole body of citizens." [86] From these notions came the basic policy views of the Fabians. In the *Fabian Essays,* a series of popular articles frequently reprinted, an attempt was made to show how obvious and inevitable their kind of socialism was. The evidence was all around them: the decline of small business, the rise of the trusts, and the continued centralization all were preparing the ground for an easy transition from capitalism to the new society. The only requisite for the coming victory was an electorate as intelligent as the Fabians.

The Fabian arguments were characteristically British. Socialism, they believed, would be brought about through rational analysis and a native impulse for social justice. It was an informed public opinion that would bring power to the socialists, not the catastrophe prophesied by Marx. The Fabians directed their appeal to all classes in society, thereby rejecting out of hand Marxian class struggle. As Beer said, they combined an ounce of theory with a ton of practice.[87] They wanted to foster ethical behavior by education and suasion. In the final analysis, they were a compound of utilitarianism distilled through John Stuart Mill via Sidney Webb with Darwin, Jevons, and just a pinch of historical materialism added for flavor.

The Fabians were probably the most prolific of socialist writers. Their many books [88] reflected mainly the consumer's point of view: it was no accident that they had kind words for the consumers' cooperative movement. They did not urge that the workers should run their own industries in a full functioning socialism. Rather, said the Fabians, it would be incumbent upon the socialist state to govern the realm of economics. In this setup the trade unions would be well-disciplined institutions helping in the task of keeping a smooth flow of goods and incomes. The Fabian view can be described as nationalization with a heavy overlay of bureaucratic management. Essentially it was a form of state socialism. Perhaps this explains the Webbs' later attraction to Soviet communism.

When one looks carefully at the Fabian output, one realizes that ultimately there is no Fabian theory. Basically, their doctrine was little more than a set of policies to be advanced through "permeation," or as it might be called today, infiltration.[89] Members of the Fabian Society were expected to join other groups and parties in order to influence their views and policies. They were quite willing to extend their cooperation on various public matters, but nevertheless they preferred to try to move single individuals and small groups rather than propagandize large organizations such as the trade unions. Even their belated recognition of the importance of the latter did not alter their approach.

Modern experience reveals how naive was the view that socialism had to be made coterminus with the all-powerful state. After the Soviet experiment (all the awful facts of which, except the administrative structure and techniques, escaped the Webbs), the vision of a ubiquitous, benevolent state as the sole employer of labor and arbiter of the affairs of men has become a harrowing one. The admiration of the state and their somewhat childish belief in its omnipotence was rooted in the Fabian's worship of the efficiency expert. That the individual spirit might be irrevocably distorted in the process of building the perfect state did not occur to either Shaw or the Webbs. They had infinite faith in the ability of their socialism to raise up a model ruling class, which on further thought was little more than a reflection of their own image. They were not egalitarians by any means: their administrative socialist society would make *lebensraum* for the sort of excellence that they alone represented. The Fabians believed in themselves, with an uncomfortable sense of self-assurance. Yet despite the arrogance of absolute certainty that permeated their writing, they were able to make the socialist idea quite palatable— palatable enough for Her Majesty's Socialist Government to carry on.

Guild Socialism in Britain was in one sense an attempt to countervail the influence of the Fabians. It was a kind of parallel to France's syndicalist movement, for it sought to make an approach to socialism via the producer.[90] Guild Socialism's discussion of trade unionism suggested that the latter would become the instrument of social and economic salvation. This was coupled with the notion that state-chartered guilds would assume the management of industry and thus free the workers from the bonds of capitalist wage slavery. These ideas were imbedded in A. J. Penty's *Restoration of the Guild System* (London, 1906), and in the pages of the *New Age,* a journal founded by O. R. Orage. G. D. H. Cole (1890-1959), also an active participant, for a while tried to interest the Fabians in Guild Socialism, but he finally broke away from the Webbs and Shaw in 1915 when the National Guilds League was set up.

The Guild Socialists were interesting on several counts, not the least of which was their insistence that the worker had to be freed from the capitalist "wage system" which was converting him into a "wage slave." The kind of state socialism implied in the Fabian system was equally outrageous, for, said Cole and his colleagues with considerable prescience, a state would be just as harsh to its wage slaves as the private capitalist. The only suitable balance, delicate as it might be, was a system of self-governing guilds rooted in the trade union movement which could successfully counterpose itself to a state, whose powers should be markedly curtailed. This would put producers on one side and consumers on the other, each carefully watching the other.

The notion that power could be attained through an enlightened electorate seemed otiose to the Guild Socialists. So far as they were concerned ballot-box oratory obscured the fact of class struggle. This attitude, together with their hostility to state ownership, sharply distinguished them from the Fabians, for whom they reserved their best vituperation. The Guild Socialists were incredibly violent polemicists, attacking their opponents as knaves, fools, and bureaucratic idiots.[91] But invective aside, they earnestly wanted the workers to assume mastery of the means of production, for only this would abolish poverty and replace the deviltry of the wage system. Working for wages, the laborer, they said, was subjected to the law of profit and entirely alienated from the work process. Separation from production and control of output gave the worker a degraded status. But once they had made these observations, the Guild Socialists could only suggest that "pay" take the place of "wages."

Cole insisted that Guild Socialism was basically an ethical system in that it opposed the concept of state socialism and was concerned with "the vital importance of individual and group liberty." [92] The twin plagues destroying the workers' lives were wage slavery and insecurity. But industrial democracy would have to precede political democracy in order to attain fundamental freedom: the worker first had to feel free in the shop. Parliament ought to be conceived as but one of several power centers, all carefully counterbalanced by an assembly representing the various industries. In this sense, the medieval guilds were models worthy of duplication, for they had been genuine foci of service. The most likely candidate to do a similar job in the present day was the trade union, the members of which unfortunately were too easily gulled by the bourgeoisie. A real trade union spirit had to be rekindled. Structurally, this mean an emphasis on industrial unionism as opposed to organization on craft lines. Only thus could the social system be reorganized.

British society, however, was never in dire peril, for trade union leadership did not relish the idea of revolutionary turnover, nor did it seem likely that the economy prior to World War I would collapse. Had the workers attempted a putsch, they would have been easily crushed by a government only too anxious to delimit and restrict trade unionism. Still, the Guild Socialists insisted that class war was inevitable [93] and that parliamentary action by the working class represented nothing less than vile class collaboration. Cole rejected the identity of the community and the state [94] and urged representation based on social function in order to achieve the common purpose. He argued that power had to be distributed in a diffuse way since no single body could effectively represent all the people—as curious a mixture of William Morris, Kropotkin, and downright Leninism as could be imagined.

Despite such romanticism, there was a hard core of reality in the Guild Socialist approach. In the case of Cole particularly, there was a rebellion against the omnipotent state and its bureaucracy, which was threatening to become an instrument of oppression. The Soviet experience revealed how right Cole was. His numerous books and articles urged a need for direct control by workers. Functionalism, through which consumers, producers, and workers would find a voice, was for him a genuinely meaningful concept.

Cole was one of the more attractive personalities in the history of socialism. From 1925 to 1957 he was at Oxford, teaching and writing on political and economic theory, labor history, and economic institutions. His dislike of the orthodox economics of the nineteenth century reflected just the sort of outlook that would reject apologies for industrial exploitation. He capped his long writing and teaching career with an immense multivolumed *History of Socialist Thought,* one of the best source books on the subject ever written. It is an encyclopedic production which takes the story of socialism from the French Revolution down to the early 1930's, covering virtually every nation on the globe. Although he acknowledged the historic importance of the Russian upheaval of 1917, Cole rejected the Communist version of Marxism as much as he rejected early Fabianism. The old approach to socialism he thought excessively rational and therefore dull and mechanistic. Nor was he inclined to follow the programs of any of the larger Social Democratic parties, distrusting as he did big organizations. Cole was more kindly disposed toward the Mensheviks and Independent Labor Party than he was toward the Bolsheviks and other large groups. For all the vituperation and seeming bitterness in it, Cole's vision was an optimistic one. Whatever ills there were in capitalism, and he recognized a fair number of them, would have to be dealt with by constitutional parliamentary methods. This departure from earlier views reflected a new faith in a decentralized socialism which, above all, would be democratic.[95]

The Guild Socialists were useful irritants. While their hope seemed bootless that the state might eventually dissolve and fade away, their insistence on a greater measure of worker control than most socialists were prepared to accept for nationalized industries was important. They underlined the need to make socialization something more than a mere exchange of one employer for another. The workers, they said, had to be given a real sense of participation if the alienation enforced by two hundred years of capitalism was to be remedied. To suggest that there was no escaping the state merely because we were born into it [96] was to surrender to a Leviathan that would one day swallow us all.

v

Analyses of Capitalist Maturity: Hilferding, Luxemburg, and Bauer

Other socialistic movements, such as the Anarchists and Syndicalists, shall not be discussed at length here, for they were in the main philosophical or sociological in nature and provided essentially the rationale for a particular form of political action. The Syndicalists in France stressed class struggle through the trade unions as the one way to socialist salvation. Girding themselves to meet the bourgeois enemy they made the general strike their supreme weapon. Most Marxists, including the moderate Jules Guèsde, thought the notion somewhat ludicrous. And there was little economics or economic analysis in these movements, Furthermore, gradualism became an increasingly popular idea even as the French socialists kept separating into more and more splinter groups. Soon they virtually all were to settle down to the smooth course of ordinary parliamentarianism.

An outstanding personality among the French was Jules Guèsde, who founded the Workers' Party in imitation of German Social-Democracy. An orthodox Marxist, believing in a centralized party, he felt that socialism would be the inevitable result of capitalist economics. The really great figure, however, was Jean Jaurès (1859-1914), a superb orator, who performed the revisionist role for French socialism. While he accepted the philosophy of historical materialism, he sought to modify its patently harsh implications by appealing to spiritual factors in human society. He was particularly concerned that centralist tendencies be modified. His shrewd parliamentarianism held together diverse factions, and had he been labeled an opportunist he would not have objected. In many ways Jaurès was more practical and realistic than either Kautsky or Bernstein. Socialism, he said, stemmed simply from man's right as a person, indicating a basically humanistic approach. And in this context he had no objection to exploring in greater detail the nature of the future society—more than what most socialists were willing to do. Measures would be taken to make incomes more equal through public ownership of productive resources, although Jaurès was aware that wage differentials might still be required to assure labor mobility. He ran into difficulty in trying to use the labor theory of value as a basis for economic calculation, yet he knew instinctively that a mode of price determination was as essential to socialism as it was to capitalism. The *raison d'être* of the new society would be the socialization of its surplus value.[97] Jaurès was assassinated on the eve of World War I by a fanatical nationalist.

The Germans and Austrians did the best analytical work in socialist economics prior to and just after World War I and one of the most important of these studies was Rudolf Hilferding's *Das Finanzkapital*.[98] The author, born in 1877 in Vienna, had been caught up in socialist circles while a student of medicine. He came to Kautsky's attention and began to write for the *Neue Zeit* in 1902 and in 1907 became foreign editor for *Vorwarts*, the Social Democratic newspaper. Earlier he had written a vigorous reply to Böhm-Bawerk's attack on Marx. In 1910 he produced his *magnum opus*, the work on finance capitalism. This gave Hilferding a wide reputation and the book has been cited as a model of Marxian analysis and scholarship ever since. One person on whom it had an unquestioned influence, even though it was largely unacknowledged, was Lenin. For the rest of his life, Hilferding remained a journalist and socialist politician, serving twice as Minister of Finance under the Weimar Republic. Although he flirted briefly with the left socialists, Hilferding was mainly identified with the more moderate and cautious wing of Social Democracy When Hitler came to power in 1933, he fled to Switzerland and then went to Paris. In 1941, the Vichy government police turned him over to the Gestapo just as he was about to board ship at Marseilles. He died a few days later.

Das Finanzkapital was an attempt to bring Marx up to date. In Hilferding's milieu the dominant figures were no longer the industrialists but the financiers whose interests pervaded the entire economy. Their aim was to produce no particular commodity, but rather to extract generalized surplus value through monopolistic control of the sources of funds. His early chapters on monetary theory appear somewhat archaic today, based virtually in their entirety on German experience. The usual Marxian habit of punctuating the argument with copious quotations from the master was once again in evidence.

The main thesis was that finance capital was not independent of the sphere of production. Capital became money when the C-M-C sequence was broken. On the other hand, money could not be viewed as capital unless it was applied to production. Now, since the turnover of money seldom coincided with the turnover of production, some part of money funds were held idle, and the proportion so held would have a significant impact on the economic order. The period of turnover also affected the amount going into idle balances. Capitalists preferred a shorter turnover period since it made possible an increase in the mass of surplus value. When there was a shortage of funds for production, the capitalist went to the banks, which utilized idle money as a basis for extending credit. Finance capital, said Hilferding, transformed international economic relations so much so that the flow of capital tended to displace commodity movements in international trade. It was against such a backdrop that financiers frequently appealed to the state for aid.

Yet Hilferding's money theory was somewhat crude, as exemplified by his contention that credit replaced metallic money, rather than being an extension of the money system. At another point he argued that credit had no influence on the supply and demand of productive capital, although most economists have since acknowledged the impact of variations in money supply and credit availability.[99] When he insisted that the labor theory of value would reveal the true nature of paper money, he became entirely obscure. Interest was again, as with all Marxists, a portion of surplus value, although the rate, he agreed, was determined by the supply and demand for loans. Nevertheless, the interest rate tended to be stable due to the strength of the financial interests who placed the burden of economic adjustment on profit takers whenever a tight situation developed.[100] With his ability to extend credit, based on fractional reserves, the financier was able to win domination over the industrialist. The financier created new business forms and by virtue of his central position on boards of directors he was able to exercise infinitely more power than was ever enjoyed by the capitalist. Further, he could encourage the creation of cartels and monopolies in order to make certain that a free price system would not upset all the carefully designed schemes of economic control.

In this way, Hilferding sought to connect finance capital with the astounding development of the corporate form of business. He shrewdly observed that the separation of ownership and control, a feature that would become even more distinct in later decades, made it possible for the banker to inject himself quite actively into operational economics. However, the many interesting hints and comments were seldom developed: his remarks on corporate bureaucracy and the capital gathering function of enterprises were extremely interesting but unfortunately never went beyond the level of suggestion. His trenchant analysis of stock market speculation foreshadowed Keynes' description. And there was even some anticipation of the later theory of monopolistic competition in his remark that monopoly price was set at a level which would allow a volume of sales such that the scale of output would not raise costs enough to endanger profit per unit of output.[101]

A major point in the book was the contention that finance capital facilitated the tendency toward the equalization of the rate of profit.[102] The tendency toward concentration was a result of the competitive process and was encouraged by the banks which, in the interest of guaranteeing their own share of surplus value, sought to reduce conflict among capitalists. But despite these efforts, said Hilferding, rivalry nevertheless developed from time to time between different sectors of the capitalist class, especially between "commercial" and "industrial" groups.[103] These quarrels had to be arbitrated by the financial interests. Thus, by careful application of the credit system and by maintaining an air of impartiality in the interest of the system itself, finance capital had penetrated successfully the protected fastness of industrial and commercial capital and so had attained absolute control and power.[104]

Economic crises occurred, said Hilferding, because production was separated from consumption. He did not mean to suggest by this an underconsumption theory: lack of purchasing power was a factor, he argued, but not the sole one. Basically, the roots of economic collapse were to be found in disturbance of the circulation process. Here Hilferding, who based himself on Marx's second volume, argued that when the proportions governing the structure of producers' goods and consumers' goods industries were disturbed, a break was caused in the reproduction flow. Consequently, the major cause of economic crisis was a tendency for the economy to develop a disproportionate structure. The crisis was in effect "structural." Ultimately, said Hilferding, the problem could be traced to the decline in profit stemming from changes in the organic composition of capital. The downward spin was accentuated by capitalism's new emphasis on heavy fixed investment, for this impeded mobility and a quick adjustment to new situations. Although panic might ensue, finance capital was able to weather the storm quite easily because it had initially diversified its holdings. And it was precisely through the crisis that financial capital's grip on the system was strengthened.[105] Reformist implications were obvious in this analysis, for it could be argued that maintenance of the proper proportions between the key sectors of the economy, a thesis developed by Tugan-Baranovsky, allowed capitalism to continue the even tenor of its ways. Applied to international affairs, for example, it implied that imperialism was not an immanent development of capitalism, but rather a matter of policy.[106]

The Marxian profit equalization theory then was extended to international trade, for capital export took place only when rates of profit varied among nations. This led Hilferding into the analysis of imperialism which so impressed Lenin. The leading industrial nations had begun to struggle for control of colonies, and finance capital exhibited a direct concern with the power position of the nation.[107] Finance capital was so pervasive an influence that it had even affected agriculture, said Hilferding. But here the revisionists were closer to the truth, for they had clearly demonstrated that, for their time at least, the small farmer was holding his own. Yet Hilferding seemed to feel that finance capital had its objective usefulness, since continued concentration of industry would create the basic forms for a socialist society. All that remained was the seizure of power.

In 1927 Hilferding was saying much the same as he had in 1910. Capitalism was no longer a free economy, he told the Social Democrats at their Kiel Conference, but a highly organized system, dominated by cartels and trusts. The problem was again a mere matter of achieving a satisfactory transition to the new society, in which, however, democracy would have to be safeguarded if totalitarianism were to be avoided. Six years later Hitler came to power and European socialists were scattered to all parts of the globe.

In many ways Rosa Luxemburg (1870-1919) was the most interesting personality of prewar European socialism. A genuine cosmopolitan, coming from a middle-class, Polish-Jewish family, she quickly demonstrated superior intelligence and a deep-rooted sense of social justice. Possessed of keen sensibilities, she went through the gamut of human experience. Like many students of the time, she became involved in revolutionary activities and was compelled to complete her education in Switzerland. Speaking for the Polish socialists at the 1893 International Socialist Congress in Zurich, Luxemburg urged a democratic socialist movement that would call attention to the grievances of the masses through strike action, but which would nevertheless struggle for the advancement of democratic rights and freedom. This made excellent sense in the context of Czarist oppression, but at the same time she sought to distinguish the workers' movement from nationalistic impulses, no small problem for a Pole. Completing her doctoral work in 1898 with a study of the growth of industry in Poland, she migrated to Germany where she acquired citizenship through a not-unusual revolutionary marriage of convenience. She became active in the German Social Democratic party and began to write for Kautsky's *Neue Zeit*. In 1899, she reacted sharply to Bernstein's reform thinking.[108] The experience of the 1905 revolution in Russia, in which she took part, provided the basis for her comments on the general strike.[109] She advocated the use of the strike as a revolutionary instrument and not as a mere political club with which to extract concessions from the authorities.[110] With the advance of these views she became a leader of the left wing in the Social Democratic party and began to dispute Kautsky's theoretical leadership, insisting that the party had to prepare for revolution, not talk about it.

In 1908 she was back in Germany to teach political economy at the party school and from these lectures came the first volume of her *The Accumulation of Capital*, published in 1913.[111] Her strong internationalist position on World War I resulted in her sitting out the conflict in protective custody (on charges of having incited troops to mutiny). Meanwhile, her political views had moved further to the left of Kautsky and the other Social Democrats; but while she agreed with Lenin on some points, she rejected entirely his advocacy of a dictatorship by the party,[112] for, she said, it could not provide real leadership unless it was itself democratic. Party chieftains had to be genuinely responsible to the rank and file. Liberated from prison at the war's end, she quickly joined with Karl Liebknecht in heading Germany's left socialist forces. When these groups, centered in the Spartacus Bund, revolted, contrary to her counsel, she was arrested and then brutally murdered by rightist soldiers in January, 1919. Her body was later found in a canal.

Rosa Luxemburg's evaluation of the Russian Revolution was friendly but critical. Written while in prison and based on newspaper accounts and other materials smuggled into her cell by friends, her comments were at times so sharp that, ". . . zealous young communists were taught that it was some sort of sin and danger to the soul to be found reading it. . . ." [113] She denied that the Russian experience would be the final word in socialist history and reiterated the view that democracy was an essential ingredient of the proletarian revolution. Dictatorship of any kind, even that of the proletariat, was nothing more than a degeneration of ancient ideals. She opposed the Bolsheviks, therefore, only on the way they seized and held power. She knew full well that revolutions often issued in violence, but she felt that the elimination of this undesirable aspect and of corruption and bureaucracy could be countered by the active participation of the masses. No revolution was ideal, she averred, if it were carried through by putschists who were uncertain as to the basic sentiments of the people—a telling blow at Lenin and his Bolsheviks. Although accused of "underestimating the role of the party," she prophetically warned that the dictatorship of the proletariat would degenerate into a dictatorship of a few politicos.[114]

But our major interest here is Luxemburg's contribution to socialist economic analysis. This was centered almost wholly in her *The Accumulation of Capital*, which attempted to develop further the argument of the second volume of *Das Kapital*. It will be recalled that Marx had tried to demonstrate how the capitalist circular flow would eventually grind to a halt of its own accord. The circulation of individual capital, he had said, would require a careful dovetailing of the various stages of production and circulation, while at the same time permitting the expansion process to go on. Marx's analysis was intended to demonstrate how such growth could take place, how the demands of the various sectors of the capitalist economy could be met and satisfied, or, failing this, how a crisis would develop. The difficulty was compounded when it was realized that new investment goods were always being created, the output of which constantly searched for an ever-broadening market. In one sense, therefore, a capitalist crisis was simply a matter of failing to dispose of surplus goods derived from an internal inability to maintain equilibrium. However, both Marx and Luxemburg assumed constant real wages and in this way closed off one of the actual possibilities for achieving the necessary balance.

Luxemburg felt that Marx's formulation implied a virtually limitless process of accumulation, a notion she held to be incorrect. The original Marxian formulation had suggested that accumulation in the consumers' goods industries would be adjusted to that in the producers' goods sector. But the fact was, argued Luxemburg, that the latter developed more rapidly, so that their greater demand led to gluts in the output of consumers' goods. She observed that more and more capitalists found it necessary to penetrate noncapitalist areas in order to realize surplus value and make accumulation effective. The solution seemed to lie in overseas markets. This, she insisted, explained why crises had not worsened and why real wages in actuality had gone up. In the fifty years or so since Marx had set down his theory, the capitalists had been able to maintain and even improve their situation because they were exploiting the underdeveloped, backward regions of the earth. But in the long run, she said, this would solve few basic problems for capitalism, for this had merely postponed a resolution of the fundamental contradiction. More technically, Luxemburg was saying that in the phase of expanded reproduction some part of the surplus value could not be realized through the C-M-C nexus unless the capitalist went outside the original closed Marxian model. Thus it was inevitable that capitalist expansion would draw the backward areas into its orbit. The implication was clear: the system ultimately would collapse with the absorption of the new areas.

Although Marx had touched briefly on the question of imperialism in the first volume of *Das Kapital*, he had thought, perhaps with the American experience in mind, that new lands would give workers an opportunity to escape the rigors of capitalist existence. A more technical analysis of imperialism undertaken by his followers had served to explain new business forms, relations between entrepreneurs and the state, increased living standards, and why the labor movement had become more docile, more reformist.

Luxemburg's analysis started with the simple reproduction scheme describing an economy in which the stock of capital and flows of income were unchanged through time. There was no expansion. By the familiar Marxian equations, the output of the capital goods industries was equal to the replacement of capital in the consumers' goods industries. The system was static and there was no mobility, no movement of capitalists from one sector to the other. After considerable arithmetical manipulation of the Marxian equations, Luxemburg came to the conclusion that it was the producers' goods industries which initiated economic flows. Capitalists in the consumers' goods industries simply followed suit.[115] While this sounds like a Keynesian formulation, she did not really concern herself with what we should call the savings-investment relationship. She was concerned rather with the way in which the stock of capital was increased, and on this question she insisted that accumulation continued only if the capitalist was assured a market for his commodities.[116] And at no time did she concede that population growth or a Malthusian-type luxury program would resolve the dilemma.

The central part of the book was a long, discursive, and sometimes interesting and exciting polemic against Sismondi, Malthus, Ricardo, Rodbertus, and Tugan-Baranovsky, most of whom she dismissed as useless. The best reading by far, reminiscent of many of the burning pages of *Das Kapital*, was the third section, in which she described capitalist absorption of the noncapitalist world.[117] As capitalism penetrated the primitive world, she related, mass-produced commodities disrupted the centuries-old village economy, and in the train of agony and hardship a market was hammered out for the goods of capitalist nations.[118] Export industries in the metropolitan centers developed and stimulated further investment among producers' goods industries, expanding their capacity to spill forth an ever-increasing cornucopia of goods and services. Overseas investment became a profitable venture, for more surplus value could be extracted from either the native population or incoming migrants.[119] Since the latter's standard of living was low to begin with, the rate of surplus value was much higher than back home. This, exclaimed Rosa Luxemburg, was how capitalism was able to overcome its own contradictions. The political implication seemed clear: socialists had to accept the patent fact that this most-despised system would not collapse as easily as hoped for.

There were, however, several weaknesses in her economic argument. For one thing, the assumption of constant real wages, which she took from the simple reproduction schemata and installed in her version of expanded reproduction, ignored one way in which capitalism, within the Marxian model itself, could partially overcome the accumulation dilemma, to wit, increased real wages. Furthermore, technological advances provided an internal motive, as it were, for investment. But as Luxemburg's argument implicitly rejected this possibility, only imperialist expansion was able to explain the continued growth of capital.

Some critics have characterized Luxemburg's chief argument as irrelevant on the ground that imperialism merely changed the form of surplus value rather than facilitating its realization. This contention might be valid if the commodity flow between countries in international trade were always in equilibrium. Since metropolitan centers generally had a favorable merchandise balance *vis-à-vis* their colonial empires, it would seem that Rosa Luxemburg had the better part of the argument.[120] In fact, as Joan Robinson has pointed out, the factor of imperialism may have been a significant item in capitalism's vast secular boom. Luxemburg indeed may have woefully underestimated the impact of an explosive birth rate in Western nations, but the gnawing questions she raised still remain: what will happen when each of the underdeveloped countries has finally built all the steel mills, textile factories, shipyards, and auto assembly plants they want or need? Surplus value will then be realized neither at home nor abroad. Capitalism's contradictions remained intact and it was this lesson that Rosa Luxemburg sought to drive home in her polemics.[121]

Socialist thinking in Austria in the early twentieth century was an offspring of German Social-Democracy. Yet in many ways the young Viennese radicals were more attractive than the assorted collection of labor politicians to the north. Displaying keen minds, the Austrians tried to apply the general propositions of Marxian economics and sociology to specific problem areas. Otto Bauer wrote on the nationalities question, Karl Renner on law, Max Adler on philosophy, Hilferding on economics, Gustav Eckstein on sociology. With such a distinguished roster, it seemed inescapable that Vienna should become an important center for Marxian science, matching Amsterdam and Berlin. The most important of the group was undoubtedly Otto Bauer (1881-1938), who worked on the problem of coexistence between nationalities in a multinational state such as the Austro-Hungarian monarchy. His theory, in actuality a well-rounded statement of Austrian socialist party views, was intended to prevent the empire from disintegrating into a multiplicity of independent parochial states. He consequently emphasized the cultural rather than the economic or political aspects of nationality. He insisted that nationality had to be conceived of in terms of tradition rather than race or language, although he did not deny the role of the latter. It was on these grounds that he favored *Anschluss* with Germany. Bauer's notions on socialization led him to oppose direct state management of industries, advocating rather a commission form of control, whereby representatives of producers, consumers, and the workers would have a direct voice in the affairs of the particular firms.

Bauer also took issue with Luxemburg's accumulation thesis. He reworked the reproduction schemata to make them consistent and introduced population growth as an element which could give resilience to capitalism. Equilibrium was possible, said he, because surplus value moved from one sector to the other, mainly as a result of banking operations. He sought to demonstrate at least the possibility of equilibrium, for, given capital shifts, it was immaterial where surplus value was accumulated so long as there was an adjustment to demand. Essentially this was a debate over the nature of capital and whether it was possible to shift embodied values from goods to funds. Assuming such mobility and transference, capitalist balance could be maintained so long as increases in the rates of population growth, variable capital, constant capital, and surplus value were constant. Only a change in these relationships could lead to a crisis, said Bauer. In illustrating the argument Bauer assumed that constant capital increased at twice the rate of variable capital. However, he failed to work out his equations for a sufficiently long period. The whole system was bound to collapse since surplus value, which stemmed from variable capital, eventually would be exhausted. In this framework, imperialism became a search for an ever-increasing volume of surplus value.

It was Fritz Sternberg who most effectively took up the theme of capitalist growth and change after Rosa Luxemburg. Sternberg, born in Breslau in 1895, was educated at the university in that city. After teaching at Berlin, Breslau, Frankfort, and several other universities, he left Germany during the early Nazi days, coming to the United States in 1939 by way of Switzerland and England. Sternberg has a long list of works to his credit, all incisive studies of current problems from the socialist standpoint. In an early book, *Der Imperialismus*,[122] he amplified Luxemburg's argument regarding the final impasse between the producers' and consumers' goods industries, while contending at the same time that it was not impossible for the output of capital goods to continue for its own sake.[123] Yet the Luxemburg barrier was bound to arise. Consequently, imperialism could be described only as an economic and political policy with which capitalists bought time. Raw materials were drawn from colonial areas in exchange for goods from the metropolitan centers, but the latter represented only the unsold portion of home country output. The colony was not a dumping ground, as Luxemburg had contended, for it was necessary to share the gains of imperialism with workers in the dominating country. Again, the lower organic composition of capital in colonial territories provided a higher rate of profit and the motivation for political conquest.[124]

With some modification for contemporary circumstance, Sternberg successfully adapted this thesis to current affairs, mainly in *The Coming Crisis* and *Capitalism and Socialism on Trial*.[125] In these works Sternberg argued that open spaces were no longer available to capitalist nations after World War I, and that by the 1930's the old commercial imperialism had died. A large part of the globe had been eliminated from capitalist cultivation by the Soviets; the United States had hidden itself behind a high tariff rather than experiment with a revival of foreign trade; Central Europe had been absorbed into the *lebensraum* of a revived German imperialism; and Eastern Asia had become the exclusive domain of an industrialized feudal Japan. The capitalist nations, consequently, had to fall back on internal markets. By 1939 this effort had not succeeded: production remained low. Not until the gears of a huge war machine began to mesh had employment and incomes begun to rise. A high degree of economic activity was possible for the United States only if it helped other nations on a genuinely global scale. Yet, Sternberg argued, the problem was fundamentally insoluble. Foreign trade for the United States was too small to offer much promise; nor did Steinberg believe, as did the Keynesians, that it was possible to establish workable controls to guarantee adequate total purchasing power. Continued investment in capital goods industries provided no sure answer unless consumer spending also expanded. Economic decline still had to be explained by capitalism's internal contradictions. Sternberg's analysis was plain: capitalism faltered because inherently it was unable to keep purchasing power circulating in the proper fashion.

Few other post-World War I Marxists wrote effectively on economic questions. Most of them dealt mainly with political tactics: how to participate in a government coalition; or how to avoid the communists. In England, Maurice Dobb's shrewd, literate, and highly able essays sought to demonstrate that virtually everything the Russians did in economic planning was reasonable and proper.[126] In the United States, there were the brilliantly critical works of Lewis Corey, a remarkable autodidact who later taught economics at Antioch College.[127] John Strachey, a leading British Marxist, carried forward an intensive critique of capitalism in his *Coming Struggle for Power* and *The Nature of the Capitalist Crisis*.[128] In order for capitalists to survive, said Strachey, they would have to increase the volume of profit sufficient to overcome the tendency for the rate of profit to fall. But this implied a sharp restriction of wages and purchasing power, thereby inducing capitalism's classic contradiction. Years later Strachey was to modify his position, mainly as a result of a more critical view of what the Soviets had done. He was to discover that capitalist stability was indeed possible and that imperialism was not a necessary condition for its existence.[129] In Europe, Henryk Grossmann tried to prove in his *Accumulation and Breakdown of the Capitalist System* that capitalism simply had to collapse because it did not produce enough surplus value.[130] Starting with Otto Bauer's version of the reproduction scheme in which increments in constant capital grew faster than the creation of surplus value, Grossmann concluded that at the end of several decades a quantity of surplus value would be forthcoming that would be insufficient to meet the system's requirements. The average rate of profit on the monstrous sum of fixed investment would not allow for extended reproduction and might just be enough for simple reproduction. How close this was to the classical notion of the stationary state is obvious. Grossmann, furthermore, rejected the external trade solution, along the lines of Luxemburg's argument, contending that most nations, even those as heavily committed to foreign trade as England, depended primarily on their internal markets. He thought that his model possessed predictive value, a hope that was not verified in later years, for what Grossman omitted was the recognition of counteracting influences on the fall in the rate of profit. The difficulty with the Marxian model was the failure to face the possibility of population, constant capital, and variable capital all expanding together in almost explosive fashion, as in the 1950's. This was a contingency for which there seemed no sufficient explanation in ordinary socialist economics.

vi

Some Russians: Tugan-
Baranovsky and Investment;
Lenin and Imperialism

The first clues to adequate understanding of the nature of capital accumulation and investment were given by Mikhail Tugan-Baranovsky (1865-1919), a noted Russian economist, who, though not a Marxist, nevertheless considered himself a socialist. His work was of high quality and has proven to be quite influential, notably in the field of business cycles. Although influenced by Marx, he drew inspiration also from the English classicists and the Austrian economists, so that in the end his theoretical analysis was in many ways a fusion of marginal utility and the labor theory of value.[131] Tugan-Baranovsky's emphasis was mainly on cooperation and ethics, and, in association with Peter Struve's "Legal Marxist" group in St. Petersburg, he always expressed the viewpoint of the moderate. He did not believe that the growth of Russian capitalism would be a unique experience, a theory propounded by the "populist" groups. He also rejected the Marxist theory of exploitation and insisted that while profits stemmed from a complex of productive factors, their distribution was affected mainly by the relative bargaining strength of the different classes in society.

As a result of his study of Great Britain, Tugan-Baranovsky came to the conclusion that capitalism's basic problem was structural. Disproportion existed, he said, in the income flow of producers' goods and consumers' goods industries which was occasioned by the nature of accumulation and investment. Accumulation was a steady, slow, and regular process—what today we should call savings. Investment, on the other hand, was a discontinuous, erratic phenomenon, exhibiting sudden spurts and unpredictable contradictions. A boom situation developed whenever investment outran accumulation, but soon the failure to supply enough saving caused economic exhilaration to expire. Activity was renewed when the rate of interest, the price for investment funds, fell sufficiently to make satisfactory profits again possible. As Alvin H. Hansen has remarked, this was undoubtedly the first truly scientific work on business cycles in the modern sense.[132] In this approach, Tugan-Baranovsky rejected the notion that crises could be traced to a fall in the rate of profit per se or to the increasing misery of the masses. Crises, he insisted, stemmed from the periodic creation of fixed capital and the consequent structural disproportion between the two main sectors of the economy, the producers' goods and consumers' goods industries. The increased demand for investment goods in a period of rising activity was especially characteristic in such areas as iron production. Here the output of investment goods was quite volatile and affected other industries as well. An important distinction was made between accumulation of "free" capital, or loanable funds, and actual physical equipment. It was the growth of the first that Tugan called accumulation. In prosperity, there was not enough of it; in depression, too much, so that when loanable funds were exhausted a crisis occurred. The motive power in the economy, therefore, was unquestionably investment: when it moved up it tended to pull the entire economy with it and created a sense of general euphoria.

Keynes, whose main ideas can be traced to Tugan-Baranovsky, via Arthur Spiethoff and Knut Wicksell, later asked how accumulation could continue at a steady pace during a depression, implying thereby that its rate might not be as regular as Tugan suggested.[133] However, since Tugan may have had in mind actual money balances, the objection did not seem to be an especially weighty one, particularly in the light of unequal income distribution. Ultimately, the main causes of overproduction could be assigned to the clash of unplanned production and steady accumulation. The 1907 crisis in the United States appeared to Tugan as a classic illustration of his thesis. He conceded that capitalism's crises would become more intense and that only a socialist economy could achieve the required balance of forces for continued equilibrium.[134]

Around World War I the center of socialist thinking for many of its adherents moved eastward to Russia, where a long and interesting history of radicalism had roots dating back to the 1830's.[135] Some of its beginnings could be found in the writing of Alexander Herzen, who had thought that capitalism could be avoided in Russia if economic development were to stem from the peasant commune.[136] This had been deemed desirable, for then the value as well as the forms of precapitalist society could be retained. It was against this most romantic view that the Russian Marxists were to inveigh. N. G. Chernishevsky argued that a really rapid growth of mechanization would facilitate the growth of cooperative forms in agriculture and so permit an escape from the curse of capitalist ways. Others suggested that capitalism was impossible in Russia because its domestic market was too narrow, and because it could not at this late date secure a foothold in foreign markets, for all these had been captured by others.

Although officialdom did more than merely frown on populist notions, often persecuting its adherents, it was the Marxist camp that led the attack on them. Of course, Marx himself had believed that capitalism was inevitable in Russia, and Engels had remarked that the peasant commune could survive only within the framework of a socialist society. George Plekhanov, the founder of Russian Social-Democracy, sought to prove that the peasant commune was already dissolving in the 1880's as a result of capitalist developments. The Marixsts naturally enough were required to demonstrate the inevitability of their new society, and a corollary of their creed was the belief that capitalism would precede it.

But when this view was advanced by Peter Struve, he was sharply criticized by Vladimir Ilyich Ulyanov, otherwise known as Lenin. Struve, said Lenin, had been too "objective" and had not given adequate attention to capitalism's inherent contradictions. This had to be emphasized if the proletariat were to be assigned a meaningful role in the unfolding revolution. Curiously enough, it was Tugan-Baranovsky's work on the rise of the factory system in Russia that thoroughly demolished the populist position.[137] Lenin supported the attack with his *Development of Capitalism in Russia,* in which he argued that a market was developing and that this would provide the foundation for the advancement of capitalism.[138]

Lenin always tailored his theories to the strategic requirements of the moment.[139] And in that sense, his writing exhibited a distinct short-run quality. Prior to 1905, the orthodox Marxian view had been accepted by Lenin at face value, so that the course of history in Russia would necessarily have to comply with Marxist schemata. Influenced by Kautsky's conception of the agrarian problem, Lenin looked forward to large-scale capitalistic growth in the countryside as well as in the city.[140] Kautsky, in response to the revisionist attack, had argued in his *Die Agrarfrage* that the farming areas would have to conform to capitalist growth patterns, since agricultural enterprise was basically capitalist in nature. Private property, intensive use of equipment, and virtually all the forms of business enterprise were as visible in farming as in industry, said he. If the small farmer still made his presence felt, it was primarily because of government subsidy.

This thesis Lenin accepted as valid.[141] In practical terms, he preferred to see a free farming class organized somewhat along the lines of the legendary American "family farm," for by destroying the old feudal forms, the free farmers would facilitate the establishment of great socialist latifundia. Actual collectivization under Stalin in the early 1930's showed how tragically wrong he had been, for the small peasant resisted enforced socialization at a terrible cost to his person and to the economy. Yet for Lenin the "free farm" idea was a useful ideological weapon in winning the peasant to the side of the Bolsheviks.

Lenin was no scholar, nor was he a writer in the literary sense.[142] His style consisted of a dogged piling of fact upon fact, each hammered to the special thesis of the day, until the reader was convinced by the sheer compulsiveness of the argument. His study of Russian capitalism, an assemblage of statistics, was accompanied by appropriate remarks to highlight whatever trend they might suggest. "He is simply a man," said Edmund Wilson, "who wants to convince." [143] That this made for tedious reading is almost self-evident. As indicated above, the studies on capitalism were intended as rebuttals to the Narodniki or Populist groups who visualized a peasant socialism based on the traditional village commune. However, Lenin was shrewd enough to say that the peasants were an important group, even though their ancient ways were being displaced by capitalist forms, and to devise ways of reaching them with his revolutionary message.

What interests us now is his theory of Imperialism, which Lenin called the monopoly stage of capitalism. But even here there was little originality of thought. He borrowed his main ideas from John A. Hobson, Rosa Luxemburg, Rudolf Hilferding, and Nicholai Bukharin (a rising young star in the Bolshevik party, later a Stalinist purge victim in the 1930's) and transmuted them into a persistent attack on capitalism. With Hilferding, he observed that in the age of imperialism the industrialist capitalist was dependent on the banks. With Luxemburg, he noted the impulse to seek surplus value overseas. With Hobson, he saw the increasing penetration by metropolitan centers into backward areas. And with Bukharin, he found monopoly growing on a world-wide scale.[144] In this context World War I was nothing more than an imperialistic struggle for political domination of the world.

Lenin's peculiar formulation of the question, embodied in his short study, was later used, ironically enough, to club Bukharin into ideological recantations and submission to the official line. The latter was accused of having advanced a thesis of organized capitalism when he suggested that a single capitalistic trust would evolve in the imperialistic stage. This, of course, was also implicit in the Leninist thesis.[145] But Bukharin became a heretic because he deemed it possible for capitalistic national economies to join together for some mutual purpose. This was long before the day of common markets.

Basically, Lenin's theory of imperialism intended to explain, after the fashion of Rosa Luxemburg, why the revolution was not succeeding in Western nations. It was a theory of the solution of capitalist contradictions, when the dominant features of the economy would mature, and commercialization, monopoly, finance capital, and the power of the state would be fully displayed. According to Lenin, the extraordinary profits that the monopolies extracted from the colonial regions were used to buy off the proletariat in the metropolitan centers, thus giving some sections of the working class a vested interest in imperialism. Capitalist exploitation was girdling the globe, and the mass of surplus value was greater than ever. But conflict was inevitable: hence capitalism in its imperialist stage was moribund. But any suggestion that this structure would fall apart from its own weight was to be rejected, for in that case how could the proletariat be stirred to heroic effort? This demonstrated again that revolutionary tactics took precedence over political or economic theory, a characteristic discernible in all of Lenin's writings.

A case in point was Lenin's early venomous attack on those who advocated what was called "economism." [146] This was closely related to the trade union question. Lenin approved of unions so long as they served as schools to awaken the revolutionary ardor of the workers. But by 1897 he noticed that some Social Democrats expressed keener interest in short-run economic gains than in the coming revolution. They felt, simply enough, that the economic struggle through the trade unions was more important than the political one. Those who advocated such bits-and-pieces approaches were dubbed advocates of "economism." To Lenin this was a heinous error and was to be exorcised with all the vituperation at his command. He did not mean to suggest that economic gains were to be overlooked, but only that at no time should Social Democrats forget the ultimate goal. He did not oppose trade unions: it was merely that the political objective was the primary one. In one sense, by making politics the predominant element, Lenin stood Marx on his head. The latter had viewed economic forces as fundamental, but Lenin, in his determination to change the world, knew that politics had to be his primary instrument. In the nature of the case, the twentieth century was a political one, and in this conflict Lenin brilliantly expressed its dominant theme. The greatest crime of the "Economists" was their implication that conscious leadership was inessential and that the unfolding of the proper economic environment would provide an effective framework for the advancement of the working class. This Lenin could not abide, for to him conscious leadership was the key to revolutionary success.

The workers could not be permitted to develop their own ideology. The true nature of the revolution had to be explicitly demonstrated over and over again. The economic organizations of the workers, their trade unions, had to be mere fronts led by a few select revolutionaries.[147]

There was a good deal more in the Leninist corpus, such as the dictatorship of the proletariat and the eventual withering of the state. But before we take our leave of this most successful of revolutionists, let us examine briefly his thoughts on the shape of the new society he thought he was creating. Lenin visualized no serious problems in organizing the socialist successor to capitalism. In *State and Revolution* he said that the economy would be very much like the post office, with the workers merely employed by the state.[148] Nationalization was simply a matter of keeping accounts and anyone could be a bookkeeper. Of course, a banking system was necessary, he conceded. In 1921 the absurdity of all this came to a head when Lenin was compelled to retreat to his New Economic Policy, in which the attempt to create a closed economy was abandoned. Private capital was allowed into Soviet Russia; private stores were permitted to carry on trade; a money system was introduced; and production began to revive.

Lenin favored economic planning, but it had to be centralized with, ironically enough, full recognition of a system of status and authority.[149] The predilection toward an egalitarian society was merely theoretical: its realization presumably would have to await the withering of the state. As Barrington Moore, Jr. has said, there was a ". . . partial recognition of the social function of inequality, woven in with a strong strand of emotional equalitarianism. . . ."[150] The Leninists had hoped to take over a young economic concern. They did not want to destroy capitalism's industrial heritage, for considerable progress had been made in the later years of the Czarist régime.[151] Yet while they seemed aware of the complexities of operating an economic order, some of their comments and suggestions verged on the comic. All that was necessary was workers' control through accounting, and the registration and checking of managerial functions, whatever the latter might have meant.

vii

Socialism without Marx

The only document in which Marx developed any ideas on the nature of the future socialist society was the *Critique of the Gotha Programme,* which itself stemmed from political negotiations between the Lassalleans and Karl Liebknecht. Marx's irritation with the proposed single Social-Democratic party knew no bounds, and both he and Engels were quick to submit their criticisms.

In the critique Marx vigorously attacked the Lassallean view on the "iron law of wages," the related notion of the right of labor to the whole product, and his opponent's concept of the state. Marx insisted that nature was as much a source of wealth as labor and that the idea of an equitable distribution of the social product was to be rejected. Even a socialist society, argued Marx, would have to make certain deductions before distributing its economic output. Provision would have to be made for depreciation, contingencies, and capital growth or accumulation. No individual equity was concerned in these computations, said Marx, since they involved the unquestioned needs of the entire social order. There would also have to be deductions for public administration, schools, and health programs. The point that the Lassalleans had overlooked was a simple one: even these deductions belonged to the worker in a socialist state, for then there would be no separate product, no division into one part for the worker, another for the capitalist.

This is perhaps as much as one can find in the Marxian corpus concerning the future good society. Some notions on the nature of the socialist state were discussed by Jaurès and Kautsky. But most speculations on the shape of the future society were offered by writers on the periphery of Marxian socialism.[152] Any attempt to analyze the structure of the coming new civilization was deemed to be an exercise in utopianism. The refusal to take up these matters and to explore them as fully as possible was a costly aberration for the Marxists. Yet Marx had not been unaware of such problems as resource allocation under socialism. As Oskar Lange once showed, Marx's discussion of Robinson Crusoe's problem revealed a fairly clear grasp of the matter, particularly when he transferred this question to the social level, where the total product of the community was divided into one portion for productive goods and another for consumption.[153] Of course, it could not be expected that he would have visualized this outside the context of the labor theory of value. In the famous letter to Kugelmann in 1868, Marx had argued that it was necessary to distribute "social labor in definite proportions" which "cannot be done away with by the particular form of social production, but can only change the form it assumes . . . ," thereby implying that a socialist society too would function according to labor value theory.[154] But the problem of resource allocation, it turned out later, was virtually insoluble on the basis of the labor theory of value.

Resource allocation, according to some definitions, is precisely what economics is concerned with. Man-hours, raw material, and equipment must be assigned to alternative possibilities so that a maximum of "social satisfaction" will be attained. Under a capitalist order, this objective, assuming it is the general aim, is reached via the price system, which presumably balances costs and utilities. In technical language, when price equals minimum average cost, a producer has reached a position of least cost combination. Those who employ more resources than are required are inefficient, and, under the influence of competitive forces, they are apt to be eliminated. Marx, however, was convinced that the capitalist price system did not effectively allocate resources. In fact, all it did, he said, was to create chaos. Since the price system did not really function as well as the bourgeois economist said it did, profits were by no means a genuine measure of social utility. Certainly, some sort of allocation takes place, as evidenced by the distribution of labor power among the various industries, but the socialist method of allocation will be different and more effective. Unfortunately, Marx never suggested just how this key question would be solved under socialism.[155]

Marx was quite unaware of the marginalist method of analysis, although the works of Jevons and the Austrians were available in his lifetime. Whatever reservations one may have about this somewhat abstruse approach, it does play a basic role in contemporary thinking.[156] Concerned as it is with the behavior of individual firms rather than aggregate actions, marginalism has provided conduct models of the *firm,* not of the economic order as a whole.[157] In more modernistic terminology, it attempts to delineate a decision-making procedure. The behavior of firms is concerned fundamentally with three sets of actions: purchases of labor and other resources; conversion of these into products, and the sale of what is produced. Since these can be expressed as "schedules of quantitative relationships," it becomes logically feasible to subject these behavior patterns to a kind of mathematical treatment.

The relationships that are developed are really not complex. An average curve describes the variation of one factor over the entire range of another related factor. Average cost is simply the relation of total cost to total output. Marginal concepts, however, attempt to establish a functional relationship between one element and small changes in another. Marginal cost at a given level of output is the change in the total cost resulting from the most recent increase in output. It is the *increment* in cost to be attributed to the last unit produced. The mathematically minded will see that this concept lends itself to facile treatment via the calculus.

Once the economist makes the assumption that the businessman always wants to maximize his profit, marginalism seemingly becomes a rather powerful analytical tool. The process of finding a maximum is implicit in the concept of allocating scarce resources to alternative uses. The theory suggests, therefore, that economic behavior has a large and significant rational component which, revolving as it does about measurable pecuniary quantities, is subject to analysis. Cost, revenue, and productivity in their marginal form are said to simplify economic thinking. Decision-making can be founded on marginal concepts even though total or average figures are not known.[158]

Marginalism originated with the Austrian school of economists, who together with Jevons sought to create a sound psychological basis for their discipline. Among their many noteworthy ventures was a broadside attack on Marxism. Determined to root out this alien influence in Western economics, they chortled approvingly when Böhm-Bawerk announced the complete and utter demise of the Marxian heresy.[159] Yet ironically it was the very marginalism which stemmed from Austrian theory that provided the building blocks with which a non-Marxist socialist theory was constructed.

As shown above, Böhm-Bawerk derided socialism because the Marxian transformation of value into prices was supposedly a complete and utter logical mishmash. The implication of his argument was that the marginal subjectivist approach was logically superior to cost of production notions such as the labor theory of value. Moreover, marginalist theory was capable of much greater theoretical generality and even could be employed to evaluate extra-market phenomena. The Marxist response was that Böhm-Bawerk was asking the wrong question: the basic economic problem was to analyze the social process of production. Marginalist theory merely substituted psychology for the facts of economic life.[160]

From the subjectivism of the Austrians there came in time a rational, logical set of ideas that would be used to describe the proper functioning of a socialist society. The Austrians began their theorizing with the case of Robinson Crusoe in order to facilitate outlining certain fundamental patterns of economic behavior which were supposedly universal. Questions of value, cost, and returns were appropriate to any society, they said: in the long run neither history nor sociology was really necessary for economic analysis. In fact, the more one could abstract from an historically determined system, be it capitalism or socialism, the purer the economics.

Friedrich von Wieser, one of the first to suggest that a general economic theory could be evolved to describe a socialist régime, said that the problem of allocating scarce resources to alternative ends, in order to maximize satisfactions, was evident in any social order, whatever its political form.[161] Wieser had worked out the notion of opportunity cost, a concept which measured the *real* cost of a venture in terms of next best alternatives. This was, of course, an allocation problem and lent itself to analytic maximizing techniques. Incorporated into his treatment of economic calculation, (the key question in a non-Marxian socialist theory), his basic ideas were set in terms of the economics of the household, business enterprise, and government. From this it was easy to derive the notion that capitalist and socialist economies were governed by the same basic "economic laws." The legal and political superstructures were put to one side, on the supposition that these reflected the "ends of existence," and thereby were irrelevant to pure economics.

The argument was basically simple: those who controlled the socialist economy had to account for used-up resources, assuming that the labor theory of value was useless in this allocation task. It was rather in the market that the required economic calculation was established. Interestingly enough, Wieser had some doubts about the efficacy of capitalism's market. Competition, he thought, could be a risky affair, "where the stronger would too often find opportunities of mercilessly exploiting the weaker." [162] His preference was for a mixed economy.

The argument over a rational, socialist economics kept recurring without being resolved one way or another. N. G. Pierson, a Dutch economist, debated the matter with Kautsky in 1902, saying that even a socialist society would have to deal with problems of value.[163] His position was plausible: regardless of their political complexion, nations would have to make pecuniary value judgments if they were to engage in trade. If value were not the basis of trade, then relations between countries would degenerate into a kind of economic warfare in which some traders would have unwanted commodities forced upon them. Furthermore, without some valuation method, net income could not be properly calculated.

Albert Schäffle (1831-1903), an Austrian professor, whose organismic concept of society led him to insist that the community was anterior to the individual, argued that capitalism would eventually be transformed into socialism. Consequently, he went to some pains to provide a scheme for a central planning authority which would employ statistical analysis, taxes, and subsidies as controlling devices. The central authority, said Schäffle, could not use the labor theory of value as a guide in solving the problem of production, but would have to fix values in some way analogous to free-market methods. Only thus could it be possible to maintain an equilibrium between labor and consumption. Socialism's basic objective, he insisted, was to maintain the virtues of a liberal economy.

On the other hand, Lujo Brentano, the noted German economist, insisted that socialist planning was incompatible with real freedom because the aims of the planners would often diverge and even conflict with the aims of the common people. Inevitably this would impose on the socialist consumer a prison-like existence. Erwin Nasse, another participant in the unflagging debate, thought that a socialist central-planning authority could not function if free choice were allowed to the consumer. What remained was the collection of statistics and adjusting the output of goods via fiscal policy. But this might very well be beyond the limits of human intelligence, since estimating human needs was too gigantic a job for any administrative board.

The major attack on socialism as a practicable notion was leveled by Ludwig von Mises, for whom all the world's ills could be traced to a political disease called statism.[164] Mises' opus, *Socialism,* purported to be a massive sociological compendium on the subject.[165] In it, he spoke of chiliastic urges, collectivism, guild socialism, speculation, free love, and the distutilities of labor as well as economic calculation. The latter point was, of course, central to the Mises' position, and there was no doubt but that he raised the question more sharply than anyone else. In fact, he has made a career of it.

Mises' main point was that markets in which prices were set for land, labor, and capital, could not exist under socialism. But, economic calculation required pricing. How then, asked Mises, could calculation be carried on in the absence of markets? Economic activity would be absolutely chaotic, for without a pricing mechanism the central authority would have no data for allocating resources or determining consumer demand. Means of production would be applied to frivolous uses or entirely wasted.

This view was supported by F. A. von Hayek, whose name was frequently linked ideologically with Mises.[166] Hayek, however, interpreted the problem a bit more subtly. He too saw the choice between socialism and capitalism as one that revolved about the ability to distribute resources among alternative uses. Granting that a collective economy might approach a solution by ordering the community's needs in some preordained way, he did not believe, however, that it could account for the costing problem. Costs were "advantages to be derived from the use of given resources in other directions." [167] In capitalism, such a decision, which is in essence an opportunity cost, was brought to fruition in the market without any conscious action on the part of particular personalities. Decision-making stemmed from the way in which prices were structured, and this in turn was rooted in the many acts of many people. At the same time Hayek sought to reply to the welfare economists' approach whose views we shall shortly examine. The latter implied a calculus of utility and it was the validity of this that he rejected. Individual utility scales could not be added to create a kind of social utility, for there was no way, he said, in which interpersonal comparisons could be legitimately validated. Therefore, the only approach to a theory of resource allocation was through choice as reflected in the determination of market price under capitalism.

Hayek persisted in his view that a socialist solution to the problem of resource allocation was impracticable simply because complete knowledge of all the relevant data would be unavailable to the authorities.[168] This had to be so, since economic knowledge existed in but scattered parts, in a dispersed and incomplete form in the minds of many individuals. Such knowledge, he agreed, would have to be transferred to the central authorities under socialism. But it was not viable, communicable, scientific knowledge; it was, rather, knowledge of time and place—information incapable of testing and measurement by a single agency. Such knowledge—of a particular skill, of the existence of some surplus stocks, of a sudden need for roofing— could not enter into statistics and therefore could not be conveyed to the planners.

Yet Hayek had to admit that the capitalist market transmitted such information, since businessmen did react to bits-and-pieces knowledge in ways of which he would approve. He insisted that central planning could employ only scientific or statistical data and such information was mainly technological in nature. The conclusion was obvious: only knowledge of time and place, mysteriously entering the price system, provided the basis for economic decisions, something that central planning could not accomplish. Hayek's refusal to concede that planning might be an effective instrument for overcoming conditions of imperfect knowledge was odd, for businessmen increasingly have sought through such methods as market and motivation research to reduce scattered information to measurable form. In actuality, efforts have always been made to get behind the forces that influence prices, for no businessman has wished to consign his future to the realm of total ignorance. There seemed no logical reason why a central planning authority could not adopt similar devices.[169]

Hayek's approach was rooted in a concern with economic structure. He averred, for example, that a central planning authority would have to treat two similar machines located in different places as distinct means of production. Should the equipment have been installed during different time periods, there certainly would be no question as to the need to characterize these as dissimilar units, each of which would have to appear in the "equations" a central planning body must solve. This would make the problem of calculation seemingly insuperable. As Pareto once had remarked, if with 100 people and 700 commodities there would be 70,699 equations, what would happen when there were several million inhabitants and several thousand commodities? And when account was taken of goods in progress and those transported, it appeared that not all the relevant data could be made available to even formulate the necessary equations. Changes in climate, population, and the consumption package itself made it dubious that "rational ideal" planning was a practicable proposition.[170]

At the same time that Hayek was developing these seemingly devastating arguments against the collective society, Mises arrived at the further notion that socialism, by sundering distribution from production, would compound its inner difficulties. Said he: "It is irreconcilable with the nature of the communal ownership of productive goods that [socialism] should rely even for a part of its distribution upon the economic imputation of the yield to the particular factors of production." [171] Just why this should be so was not made clear, although it was evident that to Mises the problem lay in the inability, in the absence of a market, to relate the values of output to the rewards of factors: in technical terms, so the argument ran, imputed values could not be calculated without market prices. Mises, however, could only assert that "it is in the very nature" of socialist production that the shares of land, labor, and capital cannot be determined. Perhaps exchange of consumer goods under socialism was possible and perhaps money could be utilized as a kind of *numéraire*. But the important point, said Mises, was that production goods could not be evaluated, making genuine economic calculation impossible.[172] Yet when he admitted in the same breath the possibility of socialist productive requirements being affected by demand, one began to wonder whether his entire argument could really stand up! Clearly, if this were possible there had to be a more intimate economic value relationship between the various sectors of the economy, even in a socialist system.

It was obvious that the Mises-Hayek approach purported to make socialism a logical impossibility. When the Austrian utility analysis was adopted, valuation of the so-called higher-order and lower-order goods, that is, producer and consumer goods, took place through exchange value based on psychic entities. However, the transactions were entirely objective in themselves and were abstracted from any utility comparisons. In fact, the latter was anathema to many economists. But the economic calculations that came out of this process were short run, avoiding price variability over the long haul or considerations outside the cash nexus of the exchange equation. All that Mises and Hayek were interested in was the market itself and the wonderful job it did, for no human mind could encompass the "bewildering mass of intermediate products and potentialities of production." [173] Socialism could not work because under it there was no exchange of production goods. Therefore, socialism was not a real economic system, at least not in the Mises-Hayek meaning.

Curiously enough, the proper response to this seemingly devastating argument was available during the century's first decade in the writings of Vilfredo Pareto and some of his followers. Pareto had some rather sharp things to say about socialism in his *Les Systèmes Socialistes*.[174] Yet from his ideas came the notion that the general economic principles worked out for capitalism could apply equally as well to socialism. Every society, whether it was Crusoe's, Jefferson's, or Carnegie's, had but limited resources which needed to be distributed efficiently among competing needs. The economic problem was to do this in a way that would bring about maximum results in productivity, profits, taxes, sales, and satisfaction. The economic theorist was not concerned with ultimate social ends: that he left to the philosopher. His realm was resource decision-making, wherein the correct apportionment of limited resources was the major objective.

These were the clear implications of Pareto's thinking. No doubt he was convinced that laissez faire and free trade brought about better results, that it most effectively increased economic welfare. In principle, any small shift in the spectrum of economic relationships which benefited everyone was to be welcomed: this heightened welfare.[175] But changes in the economy which brought a gain for some and a loss for others were to be rejected, since maximum "ophelimity," or utility, was not enhanced thereby. There was no reason, said Pareto, why a collectivist society could not raise utility to a maximum, for it might sell goods at cost and cover losses through subsidies derived from taxation. This would enable the socialist authorities to increase production beyond the point at which private enterprise would call a halt. Of course, socialists would have to face the administrative problem, said Pareto, anticipating by several decades Karl Mannheim's question, "Who plans the planners?" [176] But this was a political question which did not necessarily weaken the economic argument for socialism.

Pareto's hint was developed further in a genuinely remarkably way by an Italian economist, Enrico Barone. An army colonel and later professor of political economy who also wrote film scripts, Barone was a "prodigy of speed in assimilation and simplification." [177] A superb mathematician, he developed in greater detail the Paretian optimum idea, especially as it might be applied to the planning of production in a collective society. His analysis, presented in an unfinished article, "The Ministry of Production in a Collectivist State," [178] developed socialist equilibrium equations somewhat analogous to Walras' general equilibrium system for a free enterprise economy. But while in the latter, the simultaneous answer for all the variables yielded a solution for both production and distribution, a socialist economy would have to decide on distribution in advance. Only then might the decisions regarding production be worked out. The purchasing power distributed by the Ministry would provide the basis for constructing the necessary supply and demand schedules, leading to the allocation of labor and savings. Investment decisions would have to be decided upon by the central authority.

The basic data essential for establishing the equilibrium conditions of the socialist equations would include information on available capital, productive capacity and coefficients, and consumer tastes. The last merely implied that with a given set of prices consumers would distribute their income between spending and saving in a certain way; it did not suggest an inquiry into utility or satisfaction. Four sets of equations were developed by Barone: the first related to the physical basis of production; the others, successively to new capital; the final cost of goods and services (which equaled the prices of the factors of production); and the cost of production, which equaled the prices of the final products plus the services of new capital. Given these equations as the basic economic model for production, Barone saw no reason why a socialist Ministry could not solve them as effectively as the free market. The basic precondition was simply that a pattern of income distribution be enforced which would maximize welfare in the Paretian sense. This suggested that in Barone's view production equilibrium in a socialist society depended on income distribution. Saving, interest, and net investment all had to be provided for. But to dictate what proportion of income should be saved might detract from welfare, hence it seemed preferable to employ a system of premiums in order to bring saving into balance with investment. By deducting a part of income, the authorities then could produce new capital in excess of amortization, that is, they could engage in economic expansion.

The significant point in Barone's model was that the individual was left free to make his own choices among consumption goods. The only guiding rule the Ministry had to observe was to "maximize welfare." This could be done by so adjusting production as to reduce the need for individual movement; that is, by ordering the economy in a way that would make everyone satisfied with his current situation. When cost of production was minimized and the value of the output corresponded to such minimum cost, then equilibrium would be achieved. Thus, quite subtly Barone reached a point where there was no distinction between the system of equations in a collective society and that of free enterprise. As Paul Samuelson said: "It is a tribute to his work that a third of a century after it was written there is no better statement of the problem in the English language to which the attention of students may be turned." [179]

Yet Barone felt that the equations could be tested only by an experimental approach, for they did not lend themselves to easy calculation. He thought that there were practical difficulties in establishing on paper the necessary numerical equivalents. However, should it be possible to process such data— and in the era of the electronic calculator, this is no wild notion—there would be no serious analytical problems to face. The only hesitation that Barone expressed involved the enormous variability of the economic factors, rather than the technical ones.[180] That is to say, as a theoretical matter, socialism was entirely within the realm of feasibility.[181]

The Barone model evidently weakened Hayek's position, even if it did not shake Mises' intransigent opposition. Hayek's retreat was heralded by the charge that the "competitive solution" was really a tacit admission of the superiority of free enterprise. But he could not deny that the proposed imitation of the market could work, at least in logic. Hayek's later strictures revolved around the question of solving the equations that the exchange situation produced.[182] If the solution of these equations was so difficult in the free market, how much more complex would it be in an administrative setting? The institutional feasibility of such an approach was nil, argued Hayek, for a central planning body could not possibly match the adjustment speed of a free market. Here Hayek began to shift his argument in quite subtle ways: the unwary reader suddenly discovered himself in the midst of the imputation argument—prices for capital goods could not be established under socialism because a market was lacking. That this was a costing problem and was amenable to solution, even in terms of his own theory, escaped Hayek. Then he returned to the "speed of adjustment" argument, saying that the lag in price adjustment by a central authority would prevent a socialist economy from taking account of differences in quality and differences in time and place.[183] Just why this should be so was not clarified, but it was asserted that plant managers would have no inducement to take advantage of special market opportunities because of the lag.

The definitive response to the Hayek-Mises attack was given in the modern welfare approach beginning with Fred M. Taylor's famous 1928 presidential address to the American Economic Association.[184] The principles of this new approach were relatively uncomplicated. In a socialist society the prices of finished goods, as well those of the factors of production, were to be set by a process of trial and error. Equilibrium was to be reached by adjusting the prices of these commodities so as to eliminate surpluses or deficits. Decisions on output and investment were to be made by plant managers on the assumption that resources would be utilized up to the point where marginal cost equaled price, that is, to the point at which the cost of producing an additional unit would just be covered by the prevailing unit return. The premise was that marginal cost would increase with further output, a seemingly reasonable surmise. Consequently, production beyond the equality of marginal cost to price would merely incur losses. This was, of course, the short-run view: in the long run, new investment would be undertaken if the return from the added output would be equal to or greater than the long period cost incurred.

The objective of the welfare approach was to avoid centralizing investment and output decisions. All the central planning board had to do was to decide on the total amount to be invested, while the managers guided the direction of investment and output in consonance with the principle just outlined. The demand and supply of capital could be adjusted by the central planning board by altering the rate of interest which, contrary to Marxist theory, would become part of long period cost.

Taylor's excellent essay again argued that production in a socialist state would be guided in quite the same way as under private enterprise. The state would give its citizens a money income and authorize them to spend it in any way they desired. This assured independence of consumer choice. Taylor, however, made no comment on the pattern of income distribution, merely assuming that the state, in the interest of maximizing welfare, would do so to the benefit of the entire citizenry. Purchases by citizens would in effect constitute a social judgment. Commodity prices would be based on cost, defined as the "drain on the economic resources of the community," which was unfortunately not a clear concept. It became even more obscure when Taylor hinted that what he had in mind was the drain on primary materials. Capital goods, however, were fully amenable to evaluation by imputation, or derivation from the value of consumer goods. The socialist authorities, said Taylor, should be able to devise "factor valuation tables" which should give satisfactory results in costing items, such as sewing machines or drill presses. Argued Taylor: "It would be necessary to multiply the valuation of each factor used in producing that machine by the quantity of that factor so used and add together these different products." The implication was that such a procedure could be stated easily in monetary terms.

An ideal socialism, said Taylor, would be impelled by its very nature to guide its actions in accordance with consumer decisions. If prices of output were set at levels higher than the cost of the resources absorbed in their manufacture, consumers would in effect suffer a diminution of income. Too low a price would lead to shortages. A trial-and-error solution of price determination would result in a clearing of the market (the economist's equilibrium) and at the same time solve the problem of imputed value for capital goods. Whatever knowledge was available could supply the information for the factor valuation tables; enterprises would conduct their affairs as if the tables were correct; they would observe carefully the results of their decisions and make adjustments as needed. Too high a valuation would induce sparse utilization and lead to factor surplus; a low valuation would create shortages. Taylor concluded confidently "that if the economic authorities of a socialist state would recognize the equality between cost of production on the one hand and the demand price of the buyer on the other as being . . . adequate proof that the commodity in question ought to be produced, they could . . . perform their duties . . . with well-founded confidence that they would never make any other than the right use of the economic resources placed at their disposal." [185]

Oskar Lange, a brilliant theoretical economist who spent some years in the United States before returning to post-war Poland, supported Taylor's argument with a persuasive series of articles in the *Review of Economic Studies* in 1936 and 1937.[186] Lange categorically rejected the contention that economic calculation was impossible in a socialist society. The fact was, said Lange, that Mises and Hayek had been confused by misreading the function of prices, which were not only ratios of exchange but also general propositions for judging the economic terms on which alternatives were offered. It was the latter concept that had meaning for a socialist society, for it was precisely this notion which was relevant to the problem of allocation. There was no reason why socialism could not provide the institutional setting for guiding choice and selecting alternatives. The latter would require information regarding how inputs related to outputs, or what is known as the production function, in order to judge alternatives, but this should not be difficult in a socialist state.

The argument that one would have to "solve" hundreds of equations was wrongheaded, said Lange, for Hayek and Mises solved these equations every time they bought a newspaper, as did millions of consumers. Yet there were few mathematicians among them. In actuality, said Lange, even under capitalism, trial and error underlies the business of satisfying consumer needs and allocating resources. In a theoretical sense, consumers maximized total utility by spending their income so that the marginal utility derived from all applications was equal. Producers maximized their profits through achieving an optimum scale of output, which was reached at the point where marginal cost equaled price. In the competitive situation price had to be regarded as a parameter, a variable constant, over which the individual producer had no direct influence. Since it was only in such circumstances that the textbook version of the market really came into existence, it could be said that perfect competition existed only in a socialist society.

If socialism began its economic functioning with free consumer choice in the selection of both goods and employment, the central planning board's "artificial" price system represented exactly the same sort of parameter to which producers and consumers would have to react under capitalism. Naturally, different behavior patterns would induce alterations in the parametric set. Producers, instead of pursuing a course which under capitalism was intended to maximize profit, would now follow the instructions of the planning board. The only rules they would have to obey were those which required proper combination of factors so that the scale of production set by the equality of marginal cost to price would be achieved. Furthermore, if the lowest average cost of production could be assured, the distribution of resources would be such as would make the marginal productivity of inputs equal in all possible uses. The prices of capital goods—again the inputation problem—could be arrived at by starting with the historical costs available to the planning board when it was created and subsequently by working out trial-and-error adjustments. Errors could be quickly corrected since they would be localized rather than distributed throughout the economy.

Lange conceded that arbitrary decisions regarding the rate of interest would be a disadvantage, since this would not necessarily reflect consumer wishes. The planning board, in other words, would have to decide for itself an appropriate rate of capital accumulation. Another thorny question stemmed from the apportionment of labor among the different occupations. Here, the need to balance rewards with "disutilities of work" would lead to unequal income, an outcome directly in conflict with the objective of equal income distribution. Lange would have overcome this anomaly by supplying suitable doses of free income—leisure, parks, social services, and the like—all of which would create the *effect* of equal income.

Insofar as the political framework was concerned, Lange thought at that time that the institutional changes he was advocating would not abolish private property. In small industry and farming, where competition was still effective, there would be no need to alter property relationships: a socialist economy merely had to assure at the very least a formal competitive system. Where competition already existed there would be no reason to disturb the situation. However, argued Lange, socialism could not be brought about by gradual means. It would have to be accomplished at once in those areas where it could operate most effectively, or else the "withdrawal of efficiency" by opponents would ensue.

Lange's views on these matters revealed a certain naiveté regarding the complexities involved in achieving a political and economic transformation. Certainly the admission that rationing might be employed to supplement the efforts of the central planning board vitiated the applicability of his rules for governing the economy, for this would necessitate the utilization of output quotas in order to achieve a given production goal. This gave his system an uncomfortable resemblance to the Soviet economic order. How such a society does function in fact was revealed all too clearly by Joseph Berliner in his *Factory and Manager in the USSR*,[187] a work highly recommended for its keen insight into what is actually planless socialism.

The central problem in the new society, said Lange, was the growth of bureaucracy, which could become ossified and inflexible in dealing with subtle matters of economic planning. But he was hopeful that no civilized people would tolerate such a situation—sadly underestimating the extreme limits to which the human being can be pushed. However, he did score a point in his debate with Mises-Hayek when he argued that to measure the efficiency of a socialist bureaucracy one ought to compare it with the work of corporation officials rather than a capitalist civil service. Socialism, he felt confident, could create a democratic administrative machinery if it developed an atmosphere of publicity and responsibility.

The theory of market socialism was attractive particularly to British writers who were anxious to avoid Marxian formulations. H. D. Dickinson especially made notable contributions to the discussion. Again trial and error was the point at which to start, and, beyond that, mathematical calculations by the central planning board would provide the required information for demand, supply, and production functions. The objective was to model the socialist society on the operations of an equilibrium system of simultaneous equations.[188] Money institutions were to be retained, as well as consumer choice and labor mobility. A socialist society organized in this manner, said Dickinson, could account easily for community gains and losses stemming from individual action. These ideas were derived in large part from the work of A. C. Pigou, who had demonstrated how total welfare was affected by private behavior.[189] Dickinson accepted Pigou's analysis of the point of optimum production, as well as his famous technique of applying subsidies and bounties. Socialism, said Dickinson, could carry out such policies of counterbalancing payments more easily than capitalism, thus demonstrating its innate superiority.

Other economists developed interesting variants of the market model, notably Abba P. Lerner. Lerner, however, disputed Lange's rule whereby average cost was to equal price, arguing that in a socialist economy prices should be proportional to marginal cost. What he was arguing for in this seeming quibble over technical minutiae was the application of some principle akin to opportunity cost rather than merely duplicating a competitive state.

At the time when Lerner responded to Lange's idea—in 1936—he still considered himself a socialist and was quite anxious to develop marginal analysis for the solution of economic problems in a socialist society.[190] He thought that prices should be so set that resources freed by reduced output would be sufficient to produce an equal sum of another good. That is, no commodity should be produced unless its importance was to be greater than the alternative which had been foregone.[191] While Lerner acknowledged that the techniques for achieving this aim were at best approximate, he doubted that this would represent any real impediment.

It was in his *Economics of Control* [192] that Lerner first put forth a complete statement of his views. (The earlier articles had been academic quarrels with other writers on definitions of overhead cost, prime cost, and which significant marginal concepts should apply in a socialist state.) The book was started as a treatise on socialist economics, but in the process of composition British Fabianism gave way to American New Dealism. Although the work discussed the economics of socialism, the major emphasis was on the theory of control in a capitalist society. Lerner's main objective became an attempt to reveal those operations of the price mechanism which would be applicable to laissez faire as well as collectivism.

Marginalist rules were devised to control both price and output. A basic prerequisite, as in all these systems of diffused control, was freedom of action and choice in both commodity and factor markets. The rule was a simple one: factory managers were to be instructed to increase output so long as the value of the marginal product of any factor was greater than its price. In actuality, the problem was a good deal more complicated than Lerner's rule suggested, for in putting the matter in this way the operational difficulties were simply pushed to one side. Furthermore, combining the factors of production and establishing rules for setting price policy were really distinct matters. In Lerner's guide book, however, these were subsumed in a single set of "instructions."

Lerner argued that his was a middle-of-the-road economics, quite neutral in its political implications. The economics of control suggested, however, that governments had the responsibility to see to it that all resources were properly employed, that monopoly was minimized, and that income was distributed in the most efficacious manner. And these were as much political as they were economic questions. Income distribution, he said, would be at an optimum when it was no longer possible to increase welfare or satisfactions by further shifting goods among the citizenry. At this point the marginal substitutability of goods would be equal for all. But it was not clear how goods would be exchanged in Lerner's scheme, although barter arose as a possibility. A money economy might be instituted through the distribution of a proper *numéraire*. Again, satisfactions might be increased by shifting incomes about from those whose usefulness for money was less to those whose utility was greater.

Now, doubtless the central planning board would discover how intricate was the task of comparing the values of marginal products, which presumably was necessary in order to judge relative efficiencies. The best way out of the dilemma would be simply to allow managers to price output according to ordinary market procedures. The planning board would still have enough work to do, said Lerner wryly, in supervising managerial operations. But the main point, he averred, was that individuals would be induced to pursue those economic measures that in themselves would result in social gains. This got uncomfortably close to Adam Smith's invisible hand. Said Lerner, ". . . every individual, in trying to minimize his own sacrifice of alternatives when he spends his money income to his own best advantage, is led automatically and even unconsciously to minimize the social sacrifice in producing what gives him most satisfaction." [193] Yet Lerner acknowledged that private enterprise as constituted today could not fulfill the requirements of "optimum allocation"; monopoly, advertising, and product differentiation all had set up barriers which impeded the attainment of welfare. The objective of the controlled economy, therefore, would be to work toward the conditions necessary for achieving an optimum. And this brought Lerner around to the very "competitive solution" from which he had originally demurred, for only by assuring that market impediments would not arise could the central planning board point toward a welfare goal.

All this implied, of course, that only under a competitive situation, or its reasonable facsimile, could the sum of society's total satisfactions be maximized. This necessarily suggested that interpersonal comparisons of utilities were at least logically feasible,[194] and that it would sometimes be quite legitimate to interfere with the results of market operations if the transfers resulting therefrom (such as tax measures to achieve some income redistribution) would be generally beneficial. As I. M. D. Little, an English economist, has demonstrated, these welfare propositions were all rooted in value judgments.[195] Granted that all the optimum conditions in the welfare system would create a socialist economy, the transfers and shifts contemplated by the equations still would result in hurting somebody.[196] Just who, implied Little, was so much a matter of political decision that the whole neutralist approach of the welfare economist was exposed as fallacious. (But as Samuelson has remarked, is there any reason why economists are absolved from studying the consequences of different value judgments?) Furthermore, said Little, it was "impossible to envisage a society in which all the optimum conditions presupposed by the idea that price ought to equal marginal cost, are fulfilled." [197] For example, taxation at the margin would demand that price be less than marginal cost. But above all, socialism was more than a simple matter of a price rule: the basic questions, at least insofar as economics was concerned, appeared to be matters of industrial technique and management. On these the welfare equations had very little to say.

Marginalist pricing was at best applicable to only a few items, said its critics. The practical difficulties for ordinary factory operations were enormous: the lack of uniform output, the discontinuities in input, the computational problems, the existence of joint products, all created serious administrative questions. In the case of transportation, on which there is a huge literature, it was said that the proposed pricing method would result in "overloading" at the margin. Other objections raised by Little stemmed from the proposed use of subsidies to achieve optimum output, for this, it was alleged, would encourage inefficiency.

An extreme form of marginalism *cum* socialism was to be found in the theories of Burnham P. Beckwith, who conceived of his theory as a prescriptive rule to direct planners in their decision-making.[198] Only by following the marginalist rule, insisted Beckwith, would the socialist economy attain the ideal level of output at the ideal price. Production would have to be pursued to the point where marginal cost equaled price. Any losses that single plants incurred could be counterbalanced by subsidies. Fundamentally, this was not much different from what Lange, Lerner, and other writers had said, although Beckwith, who polemicized with everyone who ever wrote a footnote on the subject, would probably disagree. His rule drove him inexorably to a set of "corollaries" which reflected a curiously rigid conception of socialist economics. Thus, Beckwith would make prices the same for all comers; optional services, such as delivery, would have to be priced separately; prices would be varied with seasonal and cyclical changes; no effort would be made to attain price stability; and the wage system would have to be based on piece rates. These proposals raised a host of interesting questions from which a socialist administration might never recover. The world of premium stamps and discounts would be replaced by daily price changes and laces in shoes would be paid for separately! Doubtlessly the multiplicity of goods on the market would be reduced drastically and central control vastly increased. All this would have to be accomplished within a framework of free consumer choice, but by the time Beckwith was through prescribing correct courses of action there was precious little left for freedom.[199] Production was to be supervised by a Bureau of Economic Co-ordination, so that each sector of the economy would be dovetailed with the other. This could be accomplished best by simply studying "consolidated" supply and demand schedules which would be constructed from past sales records![200] The Bureau would point out discrepancies in individual factory plans, and the managers presumably would adjust their output program accordingly. The one difficulty with Beckwith's scheme was the dead-level uniformity which it implied. Somehow, this did not accord with the image of a vital, socialist economy.

An interesting deviation from the marginalist position was E. F. M. Durbin's argument for socialist economic planning based on the average cost concept.[201] While he conceded that equalizing the marginal product in all possible uses might be desirable, he felt that price determination under socialism would at best be but roughly solved in this manner. Durbin questioned whether it would be possible to increase output until price was equal to marginal cost. In fact, where industries in a socialist society operated under conditions of increasing returns, the marginal cost pricing rule could not provide a suitable guide, since average cost would exceed marginal cost over a considerable output range. This could lead to a loss in income which would have to be covered by public subsidy. The best policy then would be to abandon marginal cost as the pricing rule and turn to average cost. Again, he argued, there was no clear distinction between maintenance cost and marginal prime cost. Additionally, a socialist pricing mechanism based on average cost could simplify matters considerably, for it would allow plant managers to react independently to changes in market conditions and would avoid the complex system of subsidies and taxes required by the marginalist approach.[202] Obviously, Durbin's solution was a matter of practicality, for while he conceded that the correct theoretical answer had been given by the marginalists, he felt that accounting along such lines would fail to show the proper responsibility since profits and losses would be determined by factors quite beyond a plant manager's control. Moreover, what really had to be taken into account was the anticipated future average cost. The relevant cost curves, both average and marginal, would have to be based on estimates of future costs, said Durbin. If the process of production was continuous, as it necessarily was in an advanced economy, all replacement costs would have to be met and accounted for in current costing procedures. But marginalist methods overlooked this element, argued Durbin, since the pricing technique that stemmed from its logic covered only the cost of hiring input factors which had alternative uses in the present. And this could lead to considerable price variation, an undesirable consequence. The fact was that all future payments were to be included in price estimates—long period, short period, fixed, variable, and replacement, as well as current. This implied that output would have to be varied to cover average costs.[203]

The notion that taxes and bounties could be employed to achieve an optimum level of production was developed at some length by Arthur C. Pigou.[204] However, said Pigou, the required data to work out the necessary balances would not be easy to come by, and there was no reason for asserting that a socialist system would have an easier time collecting the information than a competitive society. Consequently, a central planning board could, if it were deemed desirable, allocate goods by coercion and by merely telling each plant manager what and how much to produce. Work would be secured by fiat without free choice of occupation, and total consumption would be defined by the terms of the central plan. The major drawback in such a highly centralist approach was that it ignored welfare concepts, basing itself solely on the goals established by the society's governing group.

An alternative approach, according to Pigou, one that would establish a basis for a decentralized economy, would be to give citizens money with the proviso that it must be spent quickly. This would make consumption equal to total money income and allow adjustments in prices to become the major instrumentality for attaining a supply and demand equilibrium. Thus, Pigou's system at first glance was not much different from Lange's, although there were some variations in the definition of the critical marginalist point. Pigou suggested also that some of the adjustments could be made by shifting labor around rather than by changing prices. But with an arbitrary distribution of income, it would be necessary to set up an "accounting wage," so that the central planning board could function as if it really did have prices for factors. The board would know it had set a correct "accounting wage" when the total demand for labor at that price absorbed the available supply. All this, said Pigou, suggested the theoretical possibility of socialism but did not avoid the appalling practical difficulties that would have to be met.[205] In the last analysis, he concluded, there was no real way of judging whether socialism would create more welfare than capitalism, although the presumptive evidence pointed in that direction.[206]

Perhaps the final word on the kind of socialism we have been discussing was given by Joseph A. Schumpeter.[207] He began by asking, "Can socialism work?" and his answer was: "Of course it can." "No doubt is possible about that," he continued, "once we assume, first that the requisite stage of industrial development has been reached and second that transitional problems can be successfully resolved." [208] Schumpeter's institutional setup also included a central planning board, although there might be a parliament or other elective body to set basic policy. Further, he assumed that plant managers would need some degree of freedom to decide on production: in fact, a socialist economy could not function effectively until a *modus vivendi* had been established between managerial latitude and central control. Yet of all the writers on this problem, Schumpeter, whose abhorrence for socialism was well known, was the only one to realize that the new society would have to be more than a matter of the full stomach. Socialism, he held, implied a new kind of human being, toward the development of which economics was no great help. In fact, he said, reflecting his concept of economics as neutralist mechanics, the principles of a socialist economy could hold for any kind of society, so long as the marginalist rules were observed.

Technically speaking, the basic question was whether the economic data of socialism would make possible the formulation of equations which were consistent and sufficient in number to permit for a solution of all the unknowns.[209] To Schumpeter, there was no question but that this was entirely possible. Insofar as the Lange-Mises debate was concerned, it was the latter who had been in error. Schumpeter granted that under socialism political decisions would guide the initial distribution of income. In a completely egalitarian society income would be divided evenly; but a less than completely egalitarian socialism was also conceivable. Whatever the pattern was, the central planning board merely would have to see to it that all the vouchers distributed were equal to the total available consumer goods. [210] The central planning board would allocate basic resources to individual plants on condition that managers would pursue economic means and follow marginalist principles in their pricing policies. Enterprises would know what their production schedules should be as soon as prices and consumer demands were known. The central planning board had only to set prices at that level which would clear the market. Naturally, this would be in accordance with the marginalist rule, for "as long as this rule is being observed no element of productive resources can be devoted to any other line of production without causing destruction of as much consumer's values, expressed in terms of consumers dollars, as that element would add to its new employment." [211]

Schumpeter stressed the point, often voiced by nineteenth-century socialists, that a socialist society, to be successful, ought to inherit from its capitalist predecessor a full endowment of skills, experience, and techniques. That is to say, a socialist society should follow a mature capitalism. Schumpeter, as did Lange, saw bureaucracy as a major problem. It was inevitable that such a society would require a large number of administrators. But despite the serious administrative problems stemming from the unfolding of Parkinson's Law,[212] socialism still could function more effectively than capitalism, for uncertainty—the very element that absorbed the full energy of the capitalist —will have been abolished. No longer would plant operations have to be predicated on estimates of probabilities of rival operations, since these would be known through the central planning board. There would be no waste of resources or delays in timing, and the reserves for conducting economic warfare, so characteristic of a capitalist economy, would be eliminated. The central planning board also could adjust its investment program so that the trade cycle would become an archaic phenomenon.[213] In fact the ". . . socialist management could attain [its goal] with less disturbance and loss without necessarily incurring the disadvantages that would attend attempts at planning progress within the framework of capitalist institutions." [214] It was Schumpeter's contention that socialism could be as superior to big-business capitalism as the latter had been to the eighteenth-century competitive system.

Socialist rationality, continued Schumpeter, was superior to capitalist rationality: in a capitalist society, technological improvements had to simmer through the economy by gradual adoption on the part of individual firms, while under socialism such improvements could be adopted simultaneously by all enterprises. But above all, the saving in cost through the elimination of economic strife would be enormous. In fact, society might very well spare the work of some occupations, such as that of lawyers, for in the absence of private property and capitalism's typically complex tax structure, what would they have to do? There would be no demigods about, only ordinary citizens. The clerk would continue to look at a Sunday football game through socialist television, while experts, professionals, and politicians would abound. It was even possible that a socialist bureaucracy might develop useful incentives that would not hamper the proper functioning of the economy. But the chief merit of a socialism rooted in welfare concepts lay in its clear revelation of the true nature of economic phenomena, something much too obscure under capitalism.

viii
Contemporary Neo-Marxists

One might have thought that Schumpeter's approach would have met with the approval of even those for whom Marx has always had the last word. But this, unfortunately, has not been the case. Marginalism, opportunity cost, and consumer choice have always exemplified mere bourgeois prejudice to orthodox Marxists. Such writers as Maurice Dobb, Paul Baran, and Paul Sweezy, knowledgeable as they are in the ways of ordinary economics, have rejected welfare theorems as thoroughly unsuitable to a socialist economy. For them, the assumption of consumer sovereignty was somewhat silly, since lopsided distribution of income made "voting" in the market a patently uneven affair. Welfare socialism could not overcome this condition since some trades would be receiving more income by virtue of a higher social valuation of their output or because of greater relative scarcity. This, they said, would merely perpetuate uneven income distribution. In fact, equal incomes, continued these critics, would distort the cost structure unless a system of bounties and taxes were instituted. For these reasons, said Dobb, competitive socialism was an illusion.[215] The determination of priorities in production through marginalist analysis, he insisted, was unnecessary, since it might be essential for socialism to invest as heavily as possible in capital goods. Dobb suggested that the socialist economy forego present needs in the interest of building up future satisfactions; no other meaning could be given to his advice than that the planning authorities "violate the principle of equimarginal returns and apply a different time discount to different sections of an industry." [216]

It would appear that these precepts were economic arguments for political decisions. A "socialist," or an underdeveloped economy for that matter, with a large work force, might conceivably create difficult conditions for itself were it to shift suddenly to a capital intensive technique in an effort to displace ostensibly inferior methods of production. Considerable hardships could ensue until such time as there might be sufficient output. In the interim the total flow of consumer goods would have to be shared among the populace, enforcing lower real wages and depressing living standards. Total output was not the sole problem: the division of the social dividend as between new equipment and consumer goods was equally important. Obviously, the more rapid the rate of investment, the greater the human travail during the transition to a fully functioning socialist state. And from a political standpoint, it was difficult to say when the transition would end. That Dobb's approach was but a theoretical justification for Soviet experience was inescapable.

Paul Baran's reaction to welfare socialism was even sharper, if less subtle. He simply dismissed it as irrelevant.[217] It was an unwarranted assertion, he argued, to say that the kind of "welfare" stemming from capitalism was equivalent to that of a socialist state. To Baran, the values and aims which determined economic choice were conditioned by the features of a particular social system. Hence, no purpose could be served by establishing socialist optimums which were borrowed almost in their entirety from an individualistic economics.

In Baran's view, socialism could not be based on consumer sovereignty. Since he took the Soviet economy as a model, it was necessary to grant him his premise. One can question only whether sovietism is genuine socialism, for as Baran conceded, the state would have to mould consumer choice ". . . in the interest of the community as a whole." [218] Change, he insisted, required compulsion. Opportunity cost was of no aid in working up major decisions regarding the proper choice "among the few technological alternatives involving large indivisibilities and fixed coefficients." Unfortunately for Baran's thesis, some leading Russian economists have been doing just that in their stumbling toward opportunity cost notions. Unable to work out systems of priorities via the labor theory, they have had to devise techniques, as we shall see below, which can be described only as marginalist. The Baran-Dobb attitude merely explained why economic theory has progressed so little in the Soviet Union.

But Dobb was even more centralist in his views than Baran. In an early essay he insisted that socialist economics could be discussed only in terms of the Soviet scheme of things.[219] Since capitalist class relations had been done away with, the coordination of production had to be more direct than the market allowed. Welfare socialism meant a diffusion of decisions and consequently a diffusion of results, so that the old tendency to disequilibrium would be carried over. Why this should be so, Dobb seldom made clear. His obvious concern was to justify the Soviet crash program and to this end he developed his theory of investment saturation. Decisions had to be made centrally, for action by individual enterprises would lead only to uneven development. Ordinarily, saving, consumption, and income are the outcomes of disconnected acts, but with planning these would be "separate facets of a single decision." Thus, there was no need for the central planning board to follow the competitive solution, for this would only duplicate capitalist calamities. Consumer choice, argued Dobb, was not a reliable guide, for individual desire might easily conflict with social requirements. Moreover, he said, the presumption that consumer choice would be any more rational under welfare socialism than under capitalism was unwarranted. Choice under competitive conditions, said Dobb, revealed a bias toward a greater variety of goods than was necessary for the collective interest. And if allowed to govern, the result could be a kind of Gresham's law of taste in which the baser satisfactions would dominate the social outlook. Thus, he averred, consumer sovereignty did not necessarily imply the development of desirable goals.

As Abba Lerner later remarked, Dobb appeared to be searching for a transcendental optimum, in which an attempt would be made to create an ethic of social behavior based on some kind of undefined collective consensus.[220] Why such collective choices should be superior to individual action was not made clear. Nor was Dobb able to specify the nature of economic law in his centralist socialism, unless it was *diktat* from the top administrative body, as with Soviets. At best, one learned only that economic law was concerned with how man handled materials, a trite and none too informative proposition.[221] The analysis of the relation of wages income to the value of consumer goods was little more than a restatement of Marx's surplus value theory in the phraseology of receipts and costs. Dobb's main point was that production required a proper balance between component elements at different points of time, so that each stage of production was defined as part of the process of making a finished commodity in the distant future. Aside from the fact that this was basically a technological rather than an economic problem, it also offered a neat justification for a policy of applying as much as one-fourth or one-third of national output to gross investment. Needless to say, the kind of socialism which Dobb found so attractive before the war has hardly lived up to the expectation that it would also be humanistic.

Dobb's socialist scheme began with a set of equations in which wages would equal consumption goods and "profits" would be equal to the proportion spent by the state on new construction, all this multiplied by the wages bill. This formula indicated that a certain share of consumer goods would be absorbed into "profit." The central planning board would be concerned mainly with technological decisions: the size of plants, their number and location, the labor input, and the like. Investment, insisted Dobb, could be self-financing. When a price was set for investment goods, wages would tend to increase because of the resulting increased demand. As prices rose, the consequent "profit" could be used to finance further investment. Decisions on alternative investment possibilities could be made simply by inspection. The board merely had to determine the ratio of productivity to the cost of a project, and in this way work up a list of priorities which would enable it to plan investment over the long period.[222] This would eliminate uncertainty: control would be maintained over key decisions rather than diffused through the economy; high standards of production could be established; new plants would produce new goods rather than duplicate old ones; and "unnecessary" products would be forbidden.

Dobb's later views, to judge by a recent set of lectures, have been somewhat modified.[223] At least he has expressed a more willing flirtation with some of the concepts of market socialism. Whereas at one time the microeconomic details—which exist perforce in any system—were dismissed as of no great consequence, their presence now was acknowledged with the statement that central planning could handle "infrastructural" adjustments as well as the broader problems of the planned economy. There was a greater willingness to listen to the arguments of those who said that market relationships could be utilized as guides to socialist production.[224] Yet the preoccupation with massive investment in the early stages of socialist economic development was still evident in his thinking. Discussion of price parameters after the fashion of Lange and Taylor could not come about, he insisted, until "economic backwardness had been left behind." Yet he acknowledged that the policy of rapid growth had involved a good deal of waste. Price relationships would have to provide effective incentives to plant managers, and an *agio,* or premium, would have to be applied to capital in order to achieve proper rationing. Still, he continued, the demand for capital goods at the industry or plant level could not be controlled completely through such an allocation device. Moreover, the existing pattern of market prices was not an infallible guide to the future structure of investment. Implicitly, a preference remained for control from the top; otherwise individual enterprises might follow pathways that would distort the major objectives of the central plan.[225]

ix

The Soviets Discover Calculation

There were occasional admissions even in Dobb's writing, that the pricing of such "goods" as railway services and electricity could not be determined in accordance with the labor theory of value.[226] He finally conceded that even the Russians were moving hesitantly and tentatively in the direction of a kind of marginalist analysis—the clear import of the post-war Soviet debate on investment timing and project selection.[227] The problem was simple: allocation of scarce resources, even in the Soviet Union, demanded a logic that could not be met by Marxist theory. According to the latter, interest charges as a method for pricing capital equipment was a bourgeois prejudice which had no place in socialist theory. But even though the state gave enterprises their capital, the supply was not limitless, and, even if decisions on allocations were politically motivated, they had to take account of a certain measure of scarcity. In actuality, interest can be used to guide capital allocation, and as such is a measure of availability.

The USSR has had its own microeconomic problem, one concerned with decisions on specific projects and the kind of resources that would be absorbed by them. While this appeared to be solely an engineering question, it nevertheless had its economic aspects, particularly insofar as decisions had to be made regarding the relative share of capital to be applied to the project at hand.[228] The ensuing discussion among the Russians was, as Gregory Grossman has said, one of the greatest neglected debates in the history of economic thought.

The Russian dispute revolved around the problem of efficient capital investment. Some writers thought the guide to decision-making in this area should be similar to "profitability," while others rejected all objective cost considerations, since only the planners' wishes counted. Those who argued for "profitability" said that it could be an effective guide to investment. Moreover, they insisted, a relatively simple index was available by measuring the ratio of plant profit plus the turnover tax to invested funds which then could be related to price parameters. However, the "abolition" of the interest rate, which took place in the 1930's, had made capital in effect a free good and had led to useless and costly capital intensive projects. Allocation of resources had been done directly by the planners, who had followed the dictates of political leaders. In the late 1930's most of the participants in the debate disappeared and the argument ceased. But the problem of efficient project making still could not be purged out of existence, and engineers simply selected the technological "mix" which would yield the lowest operating cost. In some lines, however, such as railroad construction, it began to be questioned whether the omission of interest charges was wise, since without proper costing the most grandiose and uneconomic projects would have the semblance of being worthwhile. Thus, Russian economists began to flirt with notions dangerously similar to opportunity cost and even marginalism.[229] In order to control resource use in the timber industry, for example, a kind of differential rent was applied.[230] Planners began to discuss "minimum recoupment periods" which would provide additional capital, only if savings in current cost allowed them to recapture the added outlay in a given number of years. If this could be interpreted as the ratio of savings to additional capital, then there was in effect a rate of interest.[231] A. L. Luria, a well-known Soviet economist, developed a theory of investment choice in which he discussed the effects of interest rates on the ability of added capital units to "substitute" for future operating costs, virually arguing that capital should be allocated so as to equalize its marginal effectiveness in all uses!

Other Russian economists, notably V. V. Novozhilov and S. G. Strumilin, began to propose economic guides for project investment.[232] Novozhilov's problem was to determine the minimum labor input on the basis of a fixed plan of investment and final goods. Employing labor time as a *numéraire,* he worked out an equilibrium system somewhat reminiscent of Barone. Equilibrium prices were established for goods-in-process, rents, and interest; and, since output was predetermined by plan, the problem was to minimize some quantity—in this case labor—so that obeisance was made in the direction of Marx, too. Thus, with all the elements known, a choice could be made among possible alternatives.[233]

Socialist efficiency demanded that total cost be at a minimum. But because certain costs were "inversely related," it was possible that the criterion of minimum total cost might be incompatible with the cost pattern of a specific product. It was evident in this formulation that the Russians were reaching toward a concept of opportunity cost! Calculations for project making had to select those methods which yielded a minimum of all labor costs over the whole range of required tasks, said Novozhilov, suggesting the principle of minimizing costs at the margin.

Strumilin was concerned with working out time rates for input flows. His analysis could be reduced to the proposition that in weighing alternatives it was necessary to compare capital efficiencies in terms of their effects on future output. This actually raised the question of interest charges, something the Soviets officially dismissed as of no significance. But what Strumilin did was to "devalue" output proportionately as labor productivity increased, thus causing current cost to fall over time. At the same time, a "compensatory fund" was to be accumulated as a device for financing new investment, a category dangerously close to interest. Strumilin evidently felt that his formulation would make it possible to evaluate capital investment on the basis of its future annual additions to income as compared with the "interest" charge incurred. True, the author hastened to deny that his theory was akin to capitalist interest, but it was difficult to take his disavowal seriously, especially when he insisted that an investment project must make up losses through "devaluation" as well as allow for replacement.[234] In effect, more critical Soviet economists were beginning to bring Western economic ideas into play. They were beginning to struggle with the theoretical problems of investment and were even trying to work outside the closed system imposed by official notions.

These positions, however, could not be sustained for long. Officialdom soon hit at the Novozhilov-Strumilin ideas as improper, idealistic, bourgeois, scarcity notions divorced from Soviet reality. The usual recantations and self-criticisms followed. Once again, Stalin's banal formulations on the law of value became the final authority on economic theory.[235] Genuine economic problems were avoided, reducing the entire discussion to a simple gloss on the labor theory of value, and Strumilin strove heroically to bring pricing formulas into accord with Marxian dogma. Then in 1956 there were stirrings in the official journals, consisting mainly of criticisms of earlier ideas and the usual call for more creative work. Many of these rumblings were stimulated by the thaw initiated at the Twentieth Congress in February, 1956.[236] As late as 1958, Strumilin, still active at the age of eighty-one, was able to evaluate critically the capital investment programs of the government's economic plan. Interestingly, his discussion centered on broad categories rather than minute details, so that political implications were brought into clear focus. He felt that productivity would rise a good deal faster than the central planners had thought was feasible and, consequently, that it ought to have been possible to provide larger funds for educational and cultural needs. Continued emphasis on investment in capital equipment seemed to him a confession of the Soviet economy's disproportionate growth, a belief he was reluctant to accept. In fact, certain parts of the government's plan, said Strumilin, had indicated a sufficient basis for reallocating resources, although some heavy projects merited continued support.[237]

Thus, only in recent years have genuine theoretical discussions been forthcoming in the Soviet Union. Articles on obsolescence were written, hitherto a contemptible bourgeois notion; criticism of the turnover tax was made; a debate on costs and productivity in agriculture was staged; and the barest beginnings of a critical examination of value and pricing were discernible. In 1958, a huge forward step was taken when the Institute of Economics recommended the use of "recoupment periods" in investment planning. This signalled a virtual restoration of interest in Soviet economic thinking, although it is not yet clear that full economic rationality will be encompassed. The basic reason for this may very well be, as Grossman says, a desire for greater speed in industrialization.[238]

An interesting example of the demand for rationality in Socialist economic planning was an article on "Socialist Production and the Law of Value" by W. Brus, a Polish economist, published in 1955.[239] Brus, whom the Russians considered something of a "revisionist," admitted that in the early phases of the Communist order "commodity-money" relationships had to be used in conjunction with planned programs. While he did not explicitly say so, it was evident that a market sector was being conceded. This being the case, he advocated employing the "law of value" as an "objectively conditioned means of influencing production. . . ." The fact was that the planning authorities had to take account of the structure of demand and sales on "organized" or state markets as well as on nonorganized, free markets. Thus, the "law of value" was said to have a direct influence on the real wages of workers in state enterprises, and within certain limits, on the "accumulation plan" and the "achievement of the relative rates of increase of production." What clearer way was there of saying that prices, production, and profit were meaningful for a socialist economy? Brus bluntly remarked that the ". . . continued existence of the *commodity form* in socialist production is an objective necessity."

The prices that stemmed from such a market structure, said Brus, could not be decided arbitrarily, but would have to be determined in accordance with the "law of value." Unless this were done, improper value categories would develop, resulting in either overproduction or underproduction. The striking similarity between these ideas and those developed by Taylor, Lerner, and other Western writers was almost self-evident. Attempts to improve the central economic plan by administrative fiat rather than through economic means was no great virtue, said Brus, for these attempts would merely introduce further distortions and difficulties. A greater dependence on what might be described as market factors would not only reduce costs, it was argued, but would diminish the influence of the bureaucracy. The problem, of course, was to balance the material interests of the workers with those of the state, a task that might be accomplished by using value and price in the Western sense—important tools for maintaining a satisfactory equilibrium even for a socialist society.

The fact that improper costing has been endemic to Soviet industry has unquestionably resulted in immense waste. The Soviet price system has not fulfilled the job of effectively allocating resources: the entire stress has been on capital intensive projects, with the economy wrenched and distorted out of balance. This has not escaped Soviet economists willing to face the difficult facts. Western concepts and techniques in economic thinking have suggested ways of dealing with these problems, and, as Wassily Leontief reported several years ago, there has been some attempt to utilize once-forbidden methods.[240] An important change has been the Soviet willingness to plan capital investments by taking account of interest cost over the lifetime of the equipment. The failure to include interest as a legitimate cost, it has been acknowledged, had resulted in building larger and costlier projects than was necessary. It was discovered by Russian economists that electric power might be generated in more economical ways than by constructing gigantic dams and hydroelectric plants. They were even moved to take an inventory of industrial resources for the first time in thirty-four years, which was to include not only an enumeration of facilities, tools, and supplies but which would also list these in terms of cost and price. All this has clearly reflected a new, searching inquiry into the Soviet price system.[241]

Furthermore, a serious effort is being made to employ mathematics in Soviet economic calculations. Hitherto, the use of mathematics in economics was considered an anti-Marxist sin. Leontief has reported an awakened interest especially for input-output analysis and linear programming.[242] The usefulness of these techniques for economic planning has seemingly dawned upon the Russians, for through their application it can become possible to describe the operations of the whole economy with a series of equations which relate the output of industries to the resources that are required to produce that output. Every element going into a product can be identified, located, and evaluated and every output similarly analysed. L. V. Kantorovich, the Soviet discoverer of linear programming, courageously castigated his colleagues for failing to apply mathematical techniques to economic planning. As far back as 1938, Kantorovich had solved the basic problem of allocating limited resources to produce a certain output. There were two matters with which he dealt: one was the question of assigning certain machines to the task of producing a given product in various proportions, and the other was that of shipping goods from plants to different destinations. These were basically linear programming problems.[243] Moreover, the analysis of the various proportions to be produced with the given equipment implied a set of shadow prices which Kantorovich called "objective determined valuations." These shadow prices could be reflections of the efforts of socialist managers to maximize plant profits. In contrast, argued Kantorovich, officially decreed prices did not reveal relative scarcities in the same way, stemming as they did from the trial-and-error efforts of the central planners. These views did not go unchallenged; Kantorovich was attacked for smuggling in the pricing techniques of the capitalist market.[244] But, he charged, Marxian notions were useless in calculating the effectiveness of capital investments. His attack signalled a demand that Soviet planners should use all kinds of techniques in their thinking, including those which bourgeois economists were making available.[245]

All this has suggested that a socialist society may yet be able to solve the problem of pricing and allocation, perhaps even by resorting to market concepts. The attainment of economic rationality, that is, maximum results at a minimum cost, was clearly the prime objective. But what the factory manager and economic planner did had to be measurable.[246] The use of terror, however, did not achieve an optimum allocation of resources or maximum production. It only led to faked results, corruption, and the use of freewheeling expediters, known in the Soviet Union as *tolkachi*. In Russia, it became more important for factory managers to meet predetermined goals than to fulfill the needs of consumers. It is evident now, however, that the work of Western economists and of the heretics discussed above was having a serious impact on Soviet and East European economic thinking.

3

Institutionalism and

the Dissenting

Spirit

THE ENDURING APPEAL of Thorstein Veblen has been demonstrated again and again as new studies of this enigmatic character are added to the library shelves. From William Jaffé's Sorbonne thesis to Joseph Dorfman's enormous and definitive biography, to David Riesman's irrelevant psychoanalysis, and Lev Dobriansky's pretentious effort at philosophic criticism, evidence has accumulated on the seminal force of the Veblenesque vision of our contemporary existence.[1] It is an economics, nay, a whole social science, of rebellion against established habits of thought, and as such, it must always command the attention of thoughtful men.

Thorstein B. Veblen (1857-1929) was born to a season of revolt. All through the latter half of the nineteenth century western civilization had threatened to crack and come apart under the stress of a burgeoning industrial society. The climax came in World War I. Then, in the 1920's, there was a momentary recovery and a return to the normality of Veblen's predatory business tycoon. Of all the ironies that made up the life of Thorstein Veblen, the greatest was his inability to witness the débacle of Black Thursday on October 24, 1929. He had died the previous August.

Veblen's mature work came to fruition at a time when America seemed in utter turmoil. The farmer discovered at the turn of the century that he had to enter politics to defend himself against the rapacity of the monopolies. All too often his sallies came to nought. The railroads had fattened themselves on the public treasury and secured vast domains of public lands from Congress. Currency shifts had put an unconscionable burden on the small farmer as lenders were able to pry loose a greater value than they had given with the original mortgages.[2] The bankers and eastern businessmen, with their traditional insistence on a stable currency, had not been aware that increasing productivity and an explosive economic growth would mean price distortions in the absence of a larger supply of money. Goods became plentiful in relation to money, and as prices fell the farmer's reaction could be only one of anguish. In the meantime, the Rockefeller oil interests squeezed out their competitors with the leverage of railroad freight rebates, and the manufacturing classes sheltered their lusty, squalling infant industries in the swaddling clothes of a protective tariff.

These were not easy years. Society's wrongs against the common man were sufficient to give Johan Most and his anarchists some attentive audiences. These were years when the fears of intransigent industrialists, coupled with the anger of hungry workers, often flared into violence. Despite the collapse of the National Labor Union, strikes against wage cuts and other injustices were frequent. By the 1880's the Knights of Labor, a strange amalgam of fraternal mystery, middle-class reform, and genuine trade unionism, was able to force mighty railroad magnate Jay Gould to retreat. But the Knights disintegrated after the Haymarket affair, and the newer American Federation of Labor began to organize labor's élite.[3] The federal government, however, did not hesitate to help industry rebuff the unions, as in the great Pullman strike of 1894.[4] Meanwhile, the farmer, either as Greenbacker or Populist, watched prices drop, and as the currency became even more restricted than it had been, he began to add his own pressure to that of organized labor. Drought and snow in the Great Midwest contributed to the general torment. The Populist movement, despite its know-nothing temperament, began to express a native radical impulse.[5] The changes that both farmer and worker were demanding in the economic and social structure would have meant a substantial alteration in the American scheme of things.

The business world was a jungle in the eighties and nineties. Although the railroads bitterly attacked each other in areas where they were rivals, they unabashedly recouped their losses in sections where monopolies were enjoyed. The increasing pressure of fixed costs and heavy capital investment enforced consolidations and mergers, as consumers, farmers, and workers were made to foot the bill of industrial concentration. The farmer could not help but sell his products at low world prices, but the tariff system compelled him to pay high for the commodities he purchased. As with the Grangers in the 1860's and the Farmer's Alliance in the 1880's, agrarian political sorties represented organized counteractions to the politics of normality indulged in by the business community. For a while it appeared that these efforts would bear fruit: the Interstate Commerce Commission was established in 1887, and the Sherman Anti-Trust Act was passed in 1890. But these reforms came to nought as business fought back with dilatory tactics and legal obstruction. Curiously enough, organized labor expressed no hostility to trusts, so long as they could be regulated.[6]

Deep-seated changes were altering the American environment. As industry spread its tentacles over the land, urban existence became the characteristic setting for the human condition. In 1870, some 80 per cent of the population was still rural; by the turn of the century the movement had gone in the other direction, until, by the end of the third decade, virtually the whole span of Veblen's career, almost 60 per cent were gathered in cities. Urban culture displaced the rural outlook and new sources of political strength emerged in the wards of the big cities. A tidal flow of immigration began to change the American character. Tensions arose between the "old country" culture and the newly created marginal men, of whom Veblen perhaps was the classic paradigm. A sense of bewilderment and disillusion was common as society became fluid, rootless, even chaotic.[7] It seemed that only scientific fact could comprehend what was happening. Some optimism was generated by the naturalistic concepts implicit in the science and technology of the day. Change became an integral element of the scientists' view, but when this was carried into an analysis of society it was evident that coercion was a critical limiting factor. Freedom was truly the recognition of necessity.

Technology began to transform the nation with breath-taking advances in industry. The need for new capital and large-scale investment gave financiers an opportunity to exercise more stringent controls over the country's businessmen. The House of Morgan became a power in the land as stock promotions, mergers, and consolidations cartellized the economy. The Rockefellers were not to be outdone as their National City Bank cohorts and Harriman's railroads moved to join forces. The struggles on Wall Street were truly titanic.[8] In time, public opinion turned against the bankers and investment tycoons, who had been interested solely in the welfare of their companies, and, who, like the French kings of old, were wont to say, "Après moi, le déluge." Public sentiment was stirred by the muckrakers, a hardy band of journalists, who went after all the facts no matter how dirty they might be.[9] Ida Tarbell, Lincoln Steffens, Ray Stannard Baker, and others told millions through their syndicated magazine articles of the chicanery of the corporations. Congress had taken up the cudgels even earlier: the Industrial Commission of 1890 consumed nineteen volumes for a close look at the new society. They gave Veblen whatever empirical data he might have needed.

All this was the basis for the reforms demanded by the Progressive movement in the century's first two decades. Spearheaded by the General Federation of Women's Clubs, many legislative changes were brought about in municipal and state government. And virtually at all times, the business interests stood in staunch opposition to the demand for change. This was Veblen's world even if it did not penetrate the consciousness of other economists.[10] They, in turn, were writing about enterprise, thrift, production, and abstinence. For them, the realm of monopolies or the use of coercion was a *terra incognita*. If labor unions were mentioned it was only to lament their violation of the natural laws of the market. Economics in official places appeared mainly as a subtle apology for the boisterous captains of industry and their financier companions.

Thorstein Veblen was an alien in this world. The son of an immigrant Norwegian farmer, he was consumed by a life-long struggle to attain a sense of complete freedom. Yet he never really achieved such an exalted state, for that would have meant at least some acceptance and reconciliation with business values, something he could never abide. He was as alienated from the monied civilization of American capitalism as he had been from the Yankee farmers who surrounded the family homestead in his youth. He preferred to read Ibsen, approved of the Greenbackers, and shocked virtually everyone around him. The strains and stresses he was to describe in later life stemmed as much from his own inner tensions as they did from the society at which he looked with such acerbity. The status and prestige of academic honors were denied to him, and he suffered acute spiritual loneliness for his commitment to a strange set of values. His attack on capitalism called forth an almost personal hostility. His ideas were dangerous; he was unscholarly; he was not sound; he was a sociologist, not an economist; his grammar was poor and he did not write cleanly. The professors, shaken to their very core, and unable to meet him on his own grounds, had resorted to academic assassination. In actuality, Veblen had few peers with whom he could carry on a meaningful dialogue.

The Norwegian group in rural Wisconsin, where Veblen was born, had isolated itself more sharply from its neighbors than did others like them, so much so that English was a second language for the children, to be acquired well after the mother tongue.[11] At the age of seventeen, Veblen had ventured into the outside world. Urged by his older and more aggressive brother Thomas, he applied for admission to Carleton College. Thus began the process by which Veblen was to lose the preconceptions of his own, older culture without acquiring any of the new. He was to become like the emancipated Jew of his famous essay, "The Intellectual Pre-eminence of Jews in Modern Europe," [12] who, caught between two worlds, became a leader in "modern inquiry" and successfully employed just the kind of skepticism necessary to disturb the "intellectual peace." [13] The course of study at Carleton was calculated to make the alien, pecuniary culture palatable. The students were taught all the verities: man had a right to property, as well as to life and liberty; property rights had been established by God for the good of all men; leisure was the ultimate purpose of wealth; and rent meant ownership by natural right. Uncertain of himself in the use of English and angered by a denial of school awards, such an academic life was hardly one to enhance Veblen's receptivity. The only notable feature of his undergraduate career was his introduction to economics by John Bates Clark, who was Carleton's librarian and professor of political economy. Although Veblen's choice of topics for school essays were somewhat on the sardonic side, Clark instantly recognized him as a good deal better than the run-of-the-mill student.

From Carleton, Veblen went to Johns Hopkins in Baltimore, hoping to study philosophy, but the atmosphere in the eastern school was no better than at home. Before the term had ended he transferred to Yale to work with Noah Porter and William Graham Summer. This was a curious mixture, for Porter was determined to save Yale from Spencerian philosophy, while Sumner was equally insistent on the latter's merits. Long-time professor of political economy and anthropology, Sumner had fostered a naturalistic and evolutionary approach for the social sciences. He had made much of the Social Darwinism that stemmed from Malthus' population theory, hoping that social struggle and "survival of the fittest" would lead to a better civilization.[14] Ironically, his influence on Veblen and others was such as to eventually bring about the downfall of Social Darwinism. The original Spencerian version of this creed was a cruel one indeed; the poverty of the downtrodden was deemed to be the inevitable consequence of the struggle for perfection. And man, according to this argument, should not interfere with the process. Legislation to improve the human situation was bound to culminate in evil. Historically, such a philosophy could not help but become a source for the most rabid defense of special privilege. The successful captain of industry now had a ready-made justification for industrial concentration, monopoly, and plain, unalloyed greed.[15]

Undoubtedly, Veblen must have questioned this version of social evolution. He failed to see how social cooperation could stem from the sort of economic quarrels that tormented nineteenth-century America. Yet there was little doubt that Sumner's pessimism had found a mark in Veblen. Sumner had rejected the rationalistic psychology implicit in classical economic theory, for human beings, he insisted, exhibited irrational and even fatalistic behavior patterns. Although the competitive process might display certain meliorative features, by virtue of an improved standard of living, Sumner feared that the competitive struggle would crush the middle class between the Scylla of plutocracy and Charybdis of the proletariat.

Veblen obtained his doctoral degree at Yale in 1884 with a dissertation on Kantian ethics. Unable to secure a teaching post, he then returned to the family farm where he spent the next seven years puttering about, talking with his father, and getting in the way of his brothers. He read John Stuart Mill, Lassalle, and Harriet Martineau, and, observing what was going on in the world outside, he thought of writing a study of modern industry and offering some sort of socialism as an alternative.[16] Finally, in 1890, he went off to Cornell in search of a scholarship and took up work with none other than J. Laurence Laughlin, an arch conservative, for whom the new American Economic Association was much too radical an organization to join. Wearing a coonskin cap, Veblen laconically announced himself to Laughlin: "I am Thorstein Veblen." The older man was sufficiently impressed to obtain a special grant in order to keep Veblen at Cornell, and, when he went to the newly-established University of Chicago in 1892, he took Veblen with him. The latter was now thirty-five years old and still not a faculty member, merely a fellow. In addition to other duties he was assigned the task of editing the *Journal of Political Economy*. Given an opportunity to teach, he failed to hold many students, for they cared neither for the way he mumbled his words into his palm nor for the subtlety of his thought.

Contact with such luminaries as Jacques Loeb and John Dewey evidently gave more to Veblen than he was able to give to his own classes. In 1899, he published his first and in many ways most exciting book, *The Theory of the Leisure Class*,[17] which was taken up mainly by the literary set. William Dean Howells, the apostle of realism in American letters, wrote a review which helped make it famous. While the *Leisure Class* purported to describe the habits of the natives of the Pacific Islands and other distant places, it really dissected with quiet savagery and a curious prose style the Yerkes', Rockefellers, and Harpers. A solemn humor disguised an unalloyed contempt for capitalism, its manners, and its pecuniary vulgarity. Literary devices were exploited to highlight phenomena that others might overlook; the Veblenesque style frequently bordered on a parody of how some professors must have sounded. An extreme example, found in another essay, was: "If we are getting restless under the taxonomy of a monocotyledonous wage doctrine and cryptogamic theory of interest, with involute, loculicidal, tomentous and moniliform variants, what is the cytoplasm, centrosome or karyokinetic process to which we may turn, and in which we may find surcease from the metaphysics of normality and controlling principles? What are we going to do about it?"[18]

The main biographical facts are well known, thanks to Dorfman's monumental study. By 1900 Veblen was an assistant professor, although President

Harper thought he did not sufficiently advertise the university. After leaving Chicago, he went to Leland Stanford where he remained three years. A penchant for liaisons on which the authorities were bound to frown led to his resignation. Despite his careless dress and open disdain for household chores,[19] women were evidently attracted to him. He once complained to an associate: "What are you to do if the woman moves in on you?" In 1911 Veblen obtained another post at the University of Missouri, mainly through the good offices of Herbert J. Davenport, who had been one of his students. He did not stay long, and, after a short and fruitless effort at a government career, became an editor of the *Dial* in 1918. When the war ended he moved to the newly-established New School for Social Research. Here too he could not stay and after a halfhearted attempt to secure still another academic position he returned to California in 1927 where he passed the last two years of his life in utter poverty.

Veblen usually wrote with one eye on the objectives of his analysis and the other on his uncomfortable reader. As Wesley Mitchell has said, he practiced "vivisection upon his contemporaries" without benefit of anesthesia, and, instead of "seeking to facilitate the reception of his analysis by minimizing the reader's emotion, he artfully stimulates them for his own delectation." [20] It was said that he loved to play with the feelings of others not less than he loved to play with ideas. When asked by a professor of law during an examination at Yale what he thought of the nature of the state, he replied, "Why in hell do you want to know?" It was patent that this was to Veblen an important question.[21] He was a masterful phrase-maker whose superb constructions were as whiplashes across the skin: "conspicuous waste," "invidious comparisons," and "conscientious withdrawal of efficiency" are now so much a part of ordinary conversation that we are apt to forget how sharp their stings were fifty years ago. But when the pulpit is described as "an accredited vent for the exudation of effete matter from the cultural organism," we are still compelled to take notice. His humor, though unconventional, was nevertheless thoroughly American in its acerb quality, clothed in the solemn language of academic halls. It was a style which allowed him to select his victims, who remained quite unaware that, like the fabled Emperor, they were being displayed without dress. As Bernard Rosenberg has said, Veblen was an artist to whom words were to be used not only for their immediate sense but to evoke a host of images, suggestions, myths, and sagas. Yet he was a dreadful teacher. He usually mumbled his esoteric thoughts into his beard and often quite deliberately discouraged students from coming to class. Nor did he care very much, for he would have continued his widespreading speculations even though no one might be around. For the superior student, however, he presented an exciting, if disturbing vista. Wesley Mitchell, who had been one of his students at Chicago, remarked in a talk given in 1945, that Veblen

. . . did not controvert the classical doctrines. . . . Instead he explained why the classical masters believed what they did, and why our contemporaries thought as they did. What upset our intellectual complacency was that his explanation of current habits of thought applied to us personally. Not that Veblen ever made this application overtly; he was far too courteous for that. But a student had to be dull indeed not to see that he shared the pitiful respectabilities writhing under Veblen's scalpel. . . . To a well brought up scion of American culture, taking one of Veblen's courses meant undergoing vivisection without an anesthetic. Those who could stand the treatment, and not all could, came out with a much more critical attitude toward economic theory, and toward themselves. . . .[22]

No standard treatise for classroom use came from Veblen's pen. He produced books which were more like monographs. Yet what he said in each volume reflected a single point of view, so that any one of them can serve equally well as an introduction to his ideas. The major essays are collected in *The Place of Science in Modern Civilization* and *Essays in Our Changing Order*.[23] While a good portion of his subject matter appeared to be more properly the business of a sociologist, Veblen always wrote from the standpoint of an economist. The famous essays on why economics was not an evolutionary science may be found in the first of these collections. *The Theory of The Leisure Class* was followed by *The Theory of Business Enterprise*,[24] which exhibited a closer concern with purely economic questions than had the first book. *The Instinct of Workmanship,* published in 1914, stressed the idea that man's search for useful, serviceable activities stemmed from certain basic drives; in 1915, *Imperial Germany and the Industrial Revolution* analyzed the deadly effects of imposing the new machine technology on a society dominated by monarchy; *The Nature of the Peace,* issued in 1917, was as trenchant an analysis of the post-war settlements as was Keynes'; *Higher Learning in America* was a savage account of business domination in the colleges; in 1919 came *The Vested Interests and the Common Man;* and two years later *The Engineers and the Price System,* a very slight volume that was seized upon as a prophetic work by the Technocrats of the 1930's; finally, in 1924, there issued another biting attack on capitalism, *Absentee Ownership,* which was in essence a final summation of the Veblenian animus.

In the *Theory of the Leisure Class* Veblen said:

The life of man in society, just like the life of other species, is a struggle for existence, and therefore it is a process of selective adaptation. The evolution of social structure has been a process of natural selection of institutions. The progress which has been and is being made in human institutions and in human character may be set down, broadly, to a natural selection of the fittest habits of thoughts and to a process of enforced adaptation of individuals to an environment which has progressively changed with the growth of the community and with the changing institutions under which men have lived. Institutions are not only themselves the result of a selective and adaptive process which shapes the prevailing or dominant types of spiritual attitudes and aptitudes; they are at the same time special methods of life and of human relations, and are therefore in their turn efficient factors of selection.[25]

This passage clearly set forth the Veblenian method. It was evolutionary, but not in the Social Darwinist sense, for Veblen did not employ these concepts to apologize for the *status quo*. He was, in fact, sharply critical of the current passage of affairs. Institutions, attitudes, and personalities were both modes of existence and factors for change. With growth and shift in the social fabric, new individuals were brought to the center and new institutions created. As certain ethnic groups began to dominate, some stability finally was introduced into the community. Nature, however, proceeds by blind chance, insisted Veblen. The conflict inherent in the evolutionary process did not mean that the lowest strata in the populace would inevitably benefit, as suggested by the Marxian belief; it was quite possible that they would continue to suffer injury as the wealthy classes improved their status without hindrance.

Not until Veblen had worked out his concept of evolution was a full theory of social change incorporated into economic thought. True, Marx had proposed an economic theory which had successfully demonstrated change and motion, but it had been relegated to the academic underworld. In Veblen's formulation the brutal Spencerian concept of change, which had been so well-suited to the ideology of the gilded era, was obliterated. The plasticity of the human personality was acknowledged, and man became *the* creative factor in both the physical and social environments. A relationship of complete interpenetration between man, society, and environment was seen as the basis for change and growth. Process and activity was now the center of the social sciences. Of course, much of this had been derived from John Dewey's instrumentalist philosophy which had argued that ideas were plans of action in which human intelligence was the most useful tool. Oliver Wendell Holmes' concept of law as a living document written by judges in their courtrooms and Charles Beard's argument that attitudes in politics were conditioned by attitudes toward property [26] formed the new backdrop against which Veblen was to attempt his reconstruction of economic habits of thought.

The Veblenian analysis began with a critical evaluation of the accepted canons of economic doctrine.[27] He charged that economists, both past and present, had failed utterly to grasp the significance of the evolutionary approach.[28] They had unfortunately utilized concepts of natural, normal, and controlling principles—ideas that were alien to the genetic view. Classical economics had provided merely a convenient set of names for the industrial process and evaluated it in terms of pecuniary criteria. As a result, the formula substituted for the reality of economic life yielded nothing more than a set of logically consistent propositions. But logical consistency, argued Veblen, at least as exemplified in the classical system of economics, was not a special virtue. The classicists were good logicians, but the evaluation of a logical system had to rest in the relation of its propositions to the world of men. Quite simply, said Veblen, the premises of a system of logic had to have some roots in human reality.[29] He conceded that Adam Smith, David Ricardo, and Alfred Marshall tried to explore basic economic phenomena, but this had been done solely with the use of forces that drove inexorably to an equilibrium of normality. No room existed in such economics for the concept of change.[30] There was rather continual escape behind the unseen hand of Providence, natural wage, and normal value.

Veblen's attack on classical premises enforced a re-examination of assumptions that has not yet been equalled in economics. The economists, said Veblen, were ēnamored with the unchangeability of economic phenomena. This could stem only from the natural law and taxonomic methods utilized by orthodox economists. Their approach was static, exhibiting a concern with the perpetual restitution of what was supposedly normal. And although economics found itself falling far behind the requirements of the industrial order, the theory of value in its purely formal construction persisted. A pretense was made that consumption was the end product of industry, but the economists paid little attention, if any, to the way in which consumers really behaved or how they might be affected by the very goods they were required to ingest. Economists were asking the wrong questions, said Veblen. They were continually concerned with market price, whereas a proper social science would deal with cause and effect, with the genetic process.[31] Classical doctrine was attempting to order the "static state" when it should be investigating institutional growth, for he said, ". . . any science, such as economics, which has to do with human conduct, becomes a genetic inquiry into the human scheme of life; and where, as in economics, the subject of inquiry is the conduct of man in his dealings with the material means of life, the science is necessarily an inquiry into the life history of material civilization . . ."[32]

Notions of normality and taxomony involved the use of conjectural history, which eventually led to the concept of an ideal state.[33] Of course, Veblen himself could have been charged with recourse to conjectural history, for his descriptions of the simplistic nature of primitive life were as artificial as Marshall's "representative firm." Although he did concede that the British empirical tradition had created some sympathy for matter-of-fact precepts, Anglo-Saxon economics, in general, had not entirely escaped "animistic tendencies" and a belief in certain kinds of social superstition.[34] It was the metaphysic of amelioration implicit in the classical viewpoint that was distasteful to Veblen. Precepts of normality suggested that not only was there a purpose in existence, but that whatever transpired was right. In time, the normality of the market place became the normality of natural law.

Veblen found that the divine right of capital started when investment and its control were joined to the hedonic tradition. One consequence of this fusion was the failure to distinguish between capital as investment and capital as "appliances." [35] Economics was then reduced to a matter of valuation while the valuer himself was ignored: theory became a "pecuniary interaction of the facts valued." As the pecuniary interest was made congruent with economic interest, humans were omitted from economic situations.[36] The basic fault, said Veblen, was a failure to recognize that the proper subject matter of economics is human action, something manifestly more complex than the avowed normality of supply and demand equations. In reality, ordinary economics, with its concentration on pecuniary questions, was beyond the scope of those concerns that were related to the machine process, for it was with the latter that man in society was truly involved. The theory of utility overlooked the elements of prestige and status, while intangibles in exchange made the idea of specific productivity as developed by John Bates Clark quite useless.[37] Whereas productivity patently had a material basis, classical theory referred to something vendible or pecuniary.

Furthermore, went the Veblenian complaint, the older economists dealt with an outmoded conception of human psychology, for they persisted in resorting to hedonic motives. Man, said Veblen, was no ". . . lighting calculator of pleasures and pains, who oscillates like a homogeneous globule of desire. . . ." [38] There was no more futile concept in the social sciences than Bentham's felicific calculus, he said, for man was governed by instincts, propensities, and habit. In fact, habit affected ". . . the working out of any given line of endeavor in much the same way as if those habitual elements were of the nature of a native bias." [39] Yet despite the striking discoveries of the modern psychologist, economics persisted in retaining the pleasure-pain equation of an outmoded utilitarian philosophy.

Veblen made short shrift of John Bates Clark, his former teacher.[40] The latter's theory was described as thoroughly static, untenable, and suffused with a crude hedonism which reduced all existence to competitive acquisitiveness.[41] This, more than anything else, typified the pervading principles of a financial enterprise. The historical economists were treated no better.[42] Veblen could not abide the notion that history was a self-realizing process that unfolded itself by internal compulsion according to the dictates of an Hegelian godhead. This might yield a theory of development, but it could be only conjectural, without any sensible relation to the cause and effect of a genuine Darwinian process.

Veblen's method was not to meet logic with logic, but rather to examine premises and preconceptions. This extremely effective device stemmed, of course, from his philosophical training. He forced others to meet him on his own ground where he could bring his enormous erudition in noneconomic fields to bear on the economists' dream of everlasting normality. Yet implicit in Veblen's own thinking was a theory of value rooted in the idea of serviceability to the community and to the individual. Value might be imputed to a commodity so long as it contributed to the economy's ability to produce goods and services. This seemed to be tautological, but then so was the rest of economic theory. Value, for Veblen, was derived from the state of the industrial arts, population size, and the level of natural resources. Technology was given primacy of place.[43] Distribution and exchange were merely the pecuniary expressions of the industrial process, and it was through these flows that values were transformed into private gain. Without distribution in the pecuniary sense, value would unquestionably attain a true expression of its intent.[44] Given these concepts, marginal productivity was downright apologetics of the worst kind, for it submerged the industrial outlook into the pecuniary.

In essence then, Veblen's attack on "received" economics, a favorite term of opprobrium, centered on its factitious psychology and unwarranted teleology, the confusion between productive and pecuniary values, and the fantasy that normality reflected the facts of economic life. Veblen doubtless would have dealt just as harshly with some contemporary writers. He would have welcomed the fact that ordinary theory had at long last established diplomatic relations with the business cycle, but he would have observed that economists still were circumscribed by a narrow institutional purview. One interpreter of Veblen believes that he would have looked on the various saving-investment formulas and all the leads and lags which economists now talk about as so much taxonomy.[45] But he would have no more conducted a dialogue with the economists of the 1950's than he did with those of the 1890's. He would have simply cut to the heart of their doctrine and exposed it as a rather weak organ for a viable social science.[46]

Unlike some contemporary economists, Veblen went to the trouble of reading Marx. In fact, he had a considerable admiration for the latter [47] and was not above suggesting to students, in somewhat cryptic fashion, that Marx had all the answers. He was a rather close student of Das Kapital, so much so that some observers have detected as much a Marxian spirit in his evolutionism as a Darwinian one.[48] It was the emphasis on technology and habits of work that suggested an occupational basis for institutional change. Of course, Marx would have talked about the mode of production rather than selective adaptation in the discipline of work. But in his theory, social ties, perhaps more subtly delineated, were rooted in work, whereas for Veblen the relationships of one class to the other were not necessarily part of the work process. Yet the struggle for existence in the Veblenian mileu was as much a struggle for income and society's surplus product as it was in Marx. Only, to the former, socialism did not necessarily appear to be the final stage in history. Veblen was no Hegelian.

In his essay, "The Socialist Economics of Karl Marx and his Followers," [49] Veblen paid his respects to Marx as the serious thinker that he was.

But he insisted that theory, this time a socialist one, had to be viewed as a whole and examined in the light of its aims and postulates. Marx, he observed, was essentially a classicist who had ruthlessly worked out the logic of the system in an even more consistent fashion than his forbears. Unfortunately, it was also teleological, this time purporting to issue in a new socialist Arcadia. The labor theory of value was described as metaphysical mystique, while the idea of the reserve army was pronounced weak because it implied that population grew independently of resources. Consequently, the theory of accumulation did not appear to be very effective, said Veblen, since it was tied to both the reserve army and surplus value notions.

Exploitation theory in Veblen differed markedly from the socialist version, for cultural and pecuniary factors were given priority over the purely material ones derived from the use of capital.[50] On the other hand, Marx had not fussed so much over the notion of economic man. He obviously could not do this, since his own model of capitalism had made as powerful a use of self-interest as did Ricardo's, from which, of course, it stemmed. Veblen's rejection of hedonism impelled him to deal with instincts and motives in a way that was quite foreign to the Marxian system. The socialist theory considered psychological elements only insofar as they might enter into the analysis of classes. Marx's approach, of course, had been institutional in the sense that its abstractions had led to a critical examination of such questions as private property, the role of the state, and the relationships that were created by the production process. Veblen's institutions, however, were virtually psychological categories. Yet in many ways, Veblen's description of the functionless character of the capitalist leisure class was more incisive. Whereas in Marx psychology had been located within his system as an implicit element, in Veblen, problems of motives and economic behavior had to be treated separately.

Certain little things, such as walking sticks and women's high heeled shoes, were important to Veblen, as important as the categories of rent and interest. Precisely because motives were significant in the economic process, he needed to know about these and numerous other rituals that accompanied transactions. But where Marx appeared to have had a moral objective, Veblen avoided saying much about the future of civilization, other than that it was subject to an impersonal evolutionary process. Still, there were certain undeniable similarities. Both acknowledged change as relevant to an understanding of institutions and social relationships. Both despised the taxonomic habit of mind found among orthodox economists. Both recognized the existence of exploitation arising out of the desire to seize as large a part of the material surplus of society as was possible. And for both, the driving forces in economic and social change were material ones (although Veblen was wont to give more play to ideological and psychological elements).

In the Marxian system, the process of extracting surplus value suggested that there might be a point beyond which the economy could not function with any effectiveness, for consumption quite patently failed to keep pace with production.[51] This was the root of the class struggle. And at the turn of the century, there appeared to be some validity in it. Yet Veblen could not embrace the Hegelian elements implicit in Marxian class struggle, although he agreed that property and its yield were what the fighting was all about. Veblen's description of the current state of affairs hinted at the possibility of a peaceable transformation of society; he knew that this would be a more desirable eventuality than Marx's explosion of the capitalist integuments. And although Veblen fully accepted the economic drives inherent in Marx's vision of society, he interpreted them somewhat differently. For him, psychological and sociological elements were as meaningful, if not more so, as economic ones.

For Veblen, therefore, change was an inseparable part of the economic problem. The study of economics was a study of growth and emerging institutions in which the past was deeply embedded. Of course, this notion of process had been taken in liberal doses from the biological sciences.[52] But happily it lacked the rhythm and cycles of the Toynbean pattern, for Veblen would have argued that there was no revelation of a preconceived schematic arrangement in history. The opportunity for accident and chance was much too great to allow for an inner unfolding of historical process.[53] There were always alternative causes, and a supposed logic of development would have to exclude them. There was, of course, the need to establish relations and connections, but we should never forget, Veblen would have said, that the only active agent in history is man. He functions in a social matrix, and historical movement must take place in such a framework; action and economic activity have always been a manifestation of individuals in motion. The historical situation provides the objective condition for individual behavior, so that institutions and styles of thought arise from individual adaptation to the totality of social action.

Thus, while Veblen completely accepted the role of the individual in society, his emphasis was on function rather than structure. Whereas the latter resulted in taxonomy, mere classification, a functional analysis, incorporating historical and evolutionary perceptions, was both realistic and genuinely dynamic. Only in this way could such factors as institutional cumulation or augmented experience be explained.[54] How else was one to account for the way in which institutions imposed habitual patterns of behavior on individuals? Here Veblen shifted ground and indicated clearly the direction in which his interest was to go. Culture, he said, was formed by material factors, which, in turn, were hardened into customs and institutions.[55] What were these material factors? Clearly, they were nothing else but tools, vessels, land, buildings, machinery, and equipment; they comprised the single most important factor making for change. For Veblen, the major power drive in modern society had reduced itself to technology.[56]

Unfortunately, Veblen paid less attention to political factors than he might have. His stress on technological elements outweighed whatever consideration could be given to political forms and structures. In this respect, Marx was his superior: to the latter, political action was one of the major instrumentalities for achieving change. And the habits of mind stemming from the purely technological did not insure the good society, for there was more to human consciousness than mere technique. Ideals and passions do find distorted expressions in the machine, as the bitter and frightful lessons of Nazi Germany and Soviet Russia have taught us. This oversight was Veblen's one weak spot: it was most sharply highlighted when he sought to make the engineers the carriers of revolution.

Like some of the Europeans who wrote in a similar vein, Veblen conceived of history as several stages in man's way. There was early and late savagery, predatory and semi-peaceable barbarism, and the handicraft and business eras. The latter two represented the pecuniary culture of our time. Savagery had ended somewhere in the Middle Ages; the medieval period itself had been barbarian; while the modern temper was conditioned by the machine process. Veblen's analysis of these stages was filled with many erudite references, but the tone he adopted in his exposition suggested that the whole business was a gigantic spoof at the expense of the captains of industry.

He thought that the early stages had manifested cooperative activity. There had been purportedly no ownership, no exchange, no price mechanism in those halcyon days. Later on, however, when a surplus of material goods had been accumulated, it became worthwhile for the warlike and priestly elements to rule.[57] Thus the transition from simple savagery to barbarism had begun. As peaceful ways were displaced by warlike acts of predation, the instinct of workmanship was suppressed. Whereas man once had opposed nature, man now opposed man. Central to the whole new way of life was private property as a public demonstration of status and as a means of acquiring prestige. Settled agrarian groups were enslaved by predatory pastoral peoples. In later historical stages, the ostensibly peaceful forms of behavior merely masked the underlying barbaric habits of thought. Thus the origins of property could be traced to force and fraud, with all beneficial human proclivities completely submerged.[58] As a régime of status and hierarchy, with a leisure class ensconced on the apex of a social pyramid, had become mankind's common fate, conspicuous leisure and conspicuous consumption were converted into hallmarks of distinction. Though technological advances continued, enabling the later European culture to sustain itself, these advances and the spirit of workmanship had been contaminated as the populace expressed an unabashed preference for articles of display. Goods were desired not for their serviceability but rather to permit an invidious comparison with one's neighbors. The more one could reveal conspicuous waste, the greater the prestige one garnered. Thus the highest honors came to those who through the control of property had been able to extract a large flow of material goods from the industrial process without engaging in useful work.

Barbaric elements survived into our own time. According to Veblen, a fortuitous concatenation of race, science, technology, skepticism, and free institutions produced the pecuniary society we know. This had been preceded by a handicraft era in which there was a palpable respect for work.[59] And the materialistic proclivities that had been fostered were able to lend support to a changing technology. This was not to deny the presence of chicane and competition, for contemporary tendencies had to have roots in some pre-existing habits. Still there were genuine displays of workmanship; man as community member had been given an opportunity to function as he should.[60] The master craftsman, embodying the instinct of workmanship, was the characteristic figure of the period. But as the industrial system developed, he was separated from his tools; workmanship gave way to pecuniary drives, and the era of the businessman was ushered in. The material interests of society were made subservient to the profit-making requirements of the new order.[61] Thus began the dichotomy between business and industry.

The idea of historical stages running from barbarism to machine industry was endemic to the anthropology of the day. This sort of thinking could be found in Lewis H. Morgan's classic *Ancient Society,* from which Veblen adopted the unilinear scheme of development for leisure-class institutions. Related to this theory was a psychology based on certain instincts rooted in the biologic structure of man. These instincts were ostensibly creative forces, although they could be perverted by hostile institutions. The fact that it was quite difficult to explain history in terms of instincts of workmanship and idle curiosity did not disturb Veblen. What he now had was a theory of man far superior to the hedonic calculus of the orthodox writers and for him this was sufficient. Propensities and habits were more important than pleasures and pains. Metaphysics and theology especially were transformed into useless baggage; tropisms and reflexes, as well as deeply-rooted habit, sufficed to explain how man cheated man.

Veblen argued that although the instincts were virtually age-old they continually adapted themselves to institutional change. Instincts could be decomposed into various social elements, a fact that experimental psychology had long ago demonstrated.[62] Consequently they were not hereditary, but assumed the character of psychological reactions rooted in social experience. Yet they had to be stable enough to be useful as analytical devices. Veblen's instincts were much more akin to Freud's *treib* than to McDougall's specific list or Watson's rigid behaviorism.[63] This instinct psychology of Veblen's was derived from Jacques Loeb's physiological studies of tropismatic responses. However, to Veblen the instinct was no vegetative matter but a purposeful, active pattern which established a certain course for the individual. Moreover, it was always conditioned by an awareness of the situation in which it functioned and always displayed an ability to adapt to new conditions.[64] It contained a decided element of intelligence that was especially observable in its most highly developed form—the instinct of workmanship. From these biologic roots there issued a "body of derivative standards and canons of conduct." [65]

The chief instincts in Veblen's scheme were workmanship, parental bent, and idle curiosity. There were others, too—arrogance, the self-regarding instinct, as well as numerous proclivities, such as construction and pugnacity —all rather ill-defined. Workmanship and the parental bent supplied the drive for material well-being and survival. It was fortunate that they predominated, said Veblen, for in their absence society would indeed be grotesque. Yet they were frequently contaminated by hostile activities and the dead weight of custom, and their proper functioning was often distorted by residues from the earlier state of barbarism. With all the pressures and institutional restrictions, it was remarkable that they functioned as well as they did. Yet their biologic roots could not be overlooked. "For mankind, as for the higher animals, the life of the species is conditioned by the complement of instinctive proclivities and tropismatic attitudes with which the species is typically endowed." [66]

The parental bent was an altruistic instinct, leading to a sense of solicitude for the common good. It began with a concern for one's family which was later transmuted into a concern for all mankind. It was opposed by the self-regarding or acquisitive instinct which usually issued in self-aggrandizement. Idle curiosity, biologically related to play, was the basis for all inquiry, for it impelled men to investigate purely scientific problems, questions that seemed essentially pragmatic and even those that appeared irrelevant.[67] Explorations and innovations stemmed from this instinct. But the most important of all was workmanship. This was no single impulse but rather a complex of drives which provided for the manipulation of materials and led to efficiency in production. Essentially, it was the instinct of serviceability.[68] It involved creativity and the effective use of economic resources; it enhanced our technological inheritance and helped man mold the environment to his needs; and it was restrained only by a faith in the supernatural and religious ritual.

In the conflict between the parental bent and acquisitiveness one could observe a threat to the stability of human society. But this was primarily a psychological and cultural conflict, not one rooted in the relations of production, as in the Marxian scheme. Add to this the notion of cultural change sketched by Veblen, and it was not too difficult to see why he failed to share Marx's teleology. So far as Veblen could tell, anything might occur in the process of development. Change was a matter of cumulation for which the Hegelian thesis and antithesis posited much too rigid a formula. Culture, said Veblen, grew as a result of the "cumulative sequence of habituation," [69] which ultimately could be traced to the biological equipment of the individual. In this context everything was possible, for all institutions that grew out of the instinctual patterns of man were "natural." They constituted the culture in which both subject and environment affected each other at all times.[70] The theory of such a process, in which economic activity was to be observed, provided the basis for a genuine economics. A genetic study of the economy was essential to a comprehension of the path society had taken.

From one point of view, an institution could be described as a widely dispersed habitual custom. This was the meaning of Veblen's expression that institutions were habits of thought. A critical examination of the aetiology of an institution, he averred, would reveal nothing more than a habit of thought which had acquired a prescriptive sanction in establishing limits as well as direction for human behavior. Of course, those reared under the imprimatur of such institutions would invariably seek their perpetuation. In this analysis, Veblen was always concerned with function and process. Instinct and institutions were not fixed. They were subject to the stresses of social change; they represented inherited tendencies; they were always subject to the requirements of the individual; they blended and overlapped; and they always interfered with each other.[71]

In presenting this analysis Veblen roamed far afield from economics. He offered evidence from anthropology, philosophy, and cultural history, and was thus enabled to employ the idea of the instinct in its broadest sense.[72] The instincts became guiding principles to advance the state of material welfare. Although the impersonality of the evolutionary process might suggest that one instinct was just as life-enhancing as the next, it was evident that Veblen's preference was for the creative drives of workmanship and idle curiosity, thereby implying a moral judgment. He was on the side of the life-preserving forces.[73] Some criticized him for this on the ground that it undermined his biologic approach.[74] Other complaints were made that the instincts were imprecise, that because of their vague character they failed to carry the evolutionary changes that were imposed on them. Unfortunately, this stricture overlooked their essential sociological nature. With so broad a concept, man's psychology was by no means fixed, for changes and mutations were also part of nature.

An interesting problem arises when one thinks of how Veblen might have dealt with Freudian psychology. Little evidence indicates that he was aware of this newer science stemming from the Continent. Yet he doubtless would have accepted the Freudian concept of a distinct psychic realm. Surely there would have been no difficult transition from Veblen's specific instincts, especially the more salutary ones of workmanship and parental bent, to the powerful emotional drives that underpinned Freud's conception of man. Nor would there have been much questioning of the contention that Freudian instincts had their own vicissitudes and created conflicts with conscious ways of behavior in their search for expression. Like Dewey, Veblen might have preferred to emphasize more the responsibility of social institutions, but he would have modified, perhaps, Dewey's belief in the amorphous, neutral character of individual responses. The genetic analysis of character, implicit in the Freudian method, could have been incorporated quite easily into the Veblenian image. Indeed it might have lent a firmer biological basis to the various types which Veblen portrayed with such acerbity. Certainly, the alteration in basic habits occasioned by the evolution of particular dominant groups, the emulation of predatory habit, and conspicuous ways of consumption entailed discharges of human energy in ways that played havoc with the more wholesome instincts. This appears quite analogous to the Freudian process of repression and sublimation, albeit on a somewhat different level. But the major point in Freud's thinking would have been most meaningful for Veblen: that the very inadequacy of our social institutions was what circumscribed the areas in which the instinctual drives could function, and that this conflict posed the perpetual threat of an explosion in the human being.[75]

The evolutionary process, said Veblen, exhibited trends toward certain ethnic types which were well-adapted to the institutions that were being worked out. Unable to escape the quasi-racist thinking of his day, he spoke of long-headed blond Nordics, round-headed Alpines, and long-headed dark Mediterranean types. The Nordics were supposed to be the most recent mutation and also the most flexible and adaptable. In fact, modern culture reflected their domination. But since each race was itself a breed of impure stock, with individual specimens exhibiting a wide range of characteristics, it was therefore nonsensical to compare the different races. Each demonstrated ample capacity for growth and evolution. The institutional selection through the ages had tended toward a choice of two types—the peaceable and the predatory, with the latter predominant. Modern man, therefore, was in the main a barbarian for whom the institution of private property was a central habit of thought, effectuating control over society's surplus of material goods.[76] Veblen's final comment was that human beings in contemporary civilization were essentially savages or of such unstable character that an atavistic return to barbarism was an everpresent contingency.

According to Veblen, the proximate ends that guided the behavior of men stemmed from institutions, and when these coincided with the ultimate objectives established by the instincts, the social and economic environment was bound to be satisfactory. It was possible, of course, for idiotic institutions to subvert the instinctual patterns. The basic factor underlying institutional change was technology, for how man made a living affected his way of thinking. How close this was to the Marxian decalogue was patent. Yet the Veblenian conception of institutional growth and change was by no means mechanical: allowances were made for mutations, idle curiosity, hybrid races, and other nontechnological factors. But in modern society, economic elements appeared to have the upper hand,[77] although frequently there was manifested a kind of dialectical interplay between the technological and the psychological.[78] The important point was that institutions could change; they exhibited no permanent character as implied in orthodox economics. The modern framework placed great emphasis on factors of prestige, status, and emulation. But, said Veblen, with obvious relish, status and standards of emulation could be evaluated in accordance with criteria of wasteful consumption and the avoidance of serviceable work. The habits of the proper Bostonians and the last resorts of Long Island supplied him with sufficient evidence to sustain his point.

Capitalism consequently had created two basic viewpoints which established a deep-rooted dichotomy in society—the business outlook and that of industry. The latter was concerned with material production while business was interested in pecuniary gain. This was the basis for differentiating between the machine process and business enterprise, a distinction which was implicit in virtually all social conflicts. Industry made for serviceability: it led to a frame of mind that was related to usefulness and community gain rather than individual profit. It was an outlook that furthered the life process in an impersonal manner.[79] Serviceability was easily recognized, for it was the one way in which the instinct of workmanship was allowed full sway. The pecuniary outlook, on the other hand, stemmed from market forces. It was concerned with exchange values, which were, of course, mainly psychological in nature. Their basis was vendibility, which always could be enhanced by a deliberate restriction of the material supply of goods. Equipment and capital became useful only insofar as sales prices could be increased, thus allowing the business classes to appropriate the material surplus yielded by the application of technology and the instinct of workmanship. And the fact of mere ownership permitted the business classes to take the best of society's output.

This then was the struggle of the future, said Veblen. Those who were strategically situated always sought to divert the social surplus to their own private purposes. They developed attributes which were described as leisure-class.[80] On the other hand, those involved in the machine process were able to give thorough expression to the instinct of workmanship, and, as a matter of their own instinctual reaction, presumably developed a sense of class solidarity. Certainly, there was less of the economic man in this viewpoint than could be found in Marx. Veblen emphasized such notions as cultural lag and psychological reactions. And he was not so optimistic as some socialists that capitalist society would collapse of its own weight. Nor was there any warrant to assert that the workers would oppose the propertied classes in a time of crisis.[81]

The last of Veblen's works, *Absentee Ownership and Business Enterprise,* summarized these views in a bitter and unimaginably savage fashion—his final indictment of a society which he held in utter contempt. Yet he realized that little could be done to displace the captains of industry. It seemed likely that the "underlying population" would tolerate, without immediate abatement, a situation that merely continued to promise relief from their debased condition, even though little had been done to fulfill the promise. The concept of credit, developed in the earlier *Theory of Business Enterprise,* was employed in *Absentee Ownership* with telling effect, for in Veblen's view the modern version of this institution could not have arisen without corporate credit.[82] The right of the corporation to debauch the national wealth had now been accepted as a matter of national policy. This was exemplified by the way in which absentee ownership was able to function on a genuinely large scale. Teapot Dome, the notorious oil scandal of the Harding régime, could be cited as an illustration of the program of commercial sabotage. In a deeper sense, modern corporate finance represented a kind of feudal state of affairs, with the absentee captain of industry obtaining the largest share of the usufruct for himself. Turning to the arcane skills of bargaining, effrontery, salesmanship, and make-believe, the businessman was able to make gains at the cost of the community.[83] And, said Veblen wryly, as more of the community's wealth was appropriated, the greater the deference and imputation of merit that the businessman could garner.[84]

The simple fact of the matter, he said bluntly (he no longer had to disguise what he thought), was that the unhindered use of natural resources and the industrial arts was impeded by absentee ownership.[85] This now was the major capitalist institution through which the businessman could trade on a thin equity of ownership. Capitalization was increased in order to inflate pecuniary values, but these were then cancelled periodically via the mechanism of economic crisis, reducing at least half of the values on the books of business concerns. This sort of make-believe permeated farms and small town communities as much as it did the large centers of population. In *Absentee Ownership,* these facets of the Veblenian thesis were iterated again and again, but this time without the subtlety and playfulness of the earlier works. He had seen too much; there was a sense of impatience in the book which made it one of the harshest attacks with which the capitalist order has had to deal. The book reached a climax with a peroration on the art of selling, which Veblen found was unabashedly employing fear and shame as legitimate devices for insuring a higher curve of pecuniary income. The ultimate was reached with the salesmen of the faith who had attained the acme of perfection in this dubious art by promising everything and delivering nothing.[86]

Veblen was irritated by the fantastic waste and inefficiency which society was wont to approve in the interest of advancing the cult of the businessman. He doubted that the population would bring its habits up to date in consonance with material possibilities.[87] Much of this outlook stemmed, of course, from the earlier *Theory of Business Enterprise,* perhaps the most important of Veblen's works from a purely economic standpoint. At first glance, the several chapters in the latter appear as disconnected essays on the machine process, loan credit, capitalization, economic crisis, and the class structure of society. A tone of sober authority was lent to it by mathematical formulas which appeared on various pages; but it was likely that Veblen was indulging in private jokes, for, aside from the obscurity of the mathematics, the text displayed a remarkable forcefulness quite divorced from such legerdemain. The basic contention, one he was to repeat many times in his career, was that the machine process and the lust for profit were incompatible. Captains of industry, Veblen's title for businessmen, were less interested in economic efficiency than they were in extracting gains by transferring ownerships via the medium of saleable rights to property. The resulting disturbance of industry became quite normal; managers sought to enhance intangible assets rather than produce goods. Frequently, profitability was enhanced by curtailing serviceability. Vendibility was the key notion for the businessman. Here Veblen expounded the concept of the separation of ownership and control in the modern corporation in a way that made Berle and Means' later empirical proof relatively simple.[88] What was significant in the concept of vendibility was the obvious fact that overproduction and underproduction became business imperatives: nothing in the industrial process itself impelled the economy to go through periodic crises. The latter stemmed solely from interferences injected for reasons of profit.

Veblen contended that the drive for money had hampered the production of useful things. Since ours was a pecuniary culture, emulation was bound to be measured by monetary standards. Expensive, elegant objects, not necessarily required for the enhancement of life, were employed as devices for attaining the highest levels of prestige. The rich were admired because they were rich and even things of beauty were stamped with the dollar sign.[89] The business versus industry dichotomy was an exclusive feature of the machine technology, for in earlier periods profit-making had been a secondary phenomenon; the instinct of workmanship had full sway along with a recognizable unity of economic interest and purpose in society.[90] There was, unfortunately, no escape from the development of absentee ownership as a claim to income without work. Land ownership, money lending, and the separation of the technician from his tools literally enforced a change from solidarity to dichotomy. This was Marx's alienation written in new terms. Its highest expression could be found in the upper reaches of the corporation where the technique of manipulation was utilized solely for the creation of an ever-expanding universe of pecuniary values.[91]

Competition in the classic sense was no longer conceivable under the régime of the corporation. The incessant striving for success which impelled one businessman to outdo the others had become a moribund institution, as small firms were absorbed by larger ones. Without the modifying influences that might flow from such changes, the classical system could only provide price wars, depression, and stagnation, with public works and wartime preparation as the means by which continued economic activity could be sustained.[92] This, in a peculiar way, seemed to suggest Schumpeter's later notion of the stabilizing influence of the corporation, but Veblen extended his animus to both early and late capitalism. Corporations were as apt to be concerned with the "pacification of recalcitrant barbarians" as had been any of the conquistadores, only in contemporary times those who were to receive the blessings of peaceable ways were other businessmen. The imposition of peace was intended, of course, to make possible the extraction of income through a limitation of output. Veblen was not writing a wild tale; utilizing materials from the gigantic investigation of the Industrial Commission of 1898, he had been able to take close note of interlocking directorates, holding companies, and watered stock. It seemed obvious that production and output were entirely dependent on the pecuniary needs of the financiers. Their price policies, so different from what had been the case in the small firm of the Jeffersonian era, were geared to the maximization of profit through the enforcement of scarcity. Supply and demand could not be genuine foci of attention in economics, so long as it was possible for business to resort to a "conscientious withdrawal of efficiency." And the burden of economic movement, of course, was bound to fall on workers, small businessmen, and farmers, who were in no position to exercise controls of this nature.

Expanded credit was essential to the growth of the corporate milieu, for through it the values of physical assets could be inflated beyond the horizon of reality. Credit was a necessary device for the extraction of pecuniary gain. It was now possible for franchises, trademarks, and goodwill to be increased in value through capitalization.[93] The financing of these intangibles required borrowing, either from the banking system or the security markets. Credit was important, said Veblen, as a means of shortening turnover and increasing the expectation of profit. The outcome was a "syncopated process of expansion" in a way that always seemed to insure that capitalization would outrun the actual value of the physical assets.[94] Capitalization now meant the extraction of pecuniary gain. Thus, said Veblen, the corporate revolution had brought about profound changes in the economy, with ownership shifting from tangible goods to intangible rights, a notion that was to be explored later in all its complex ramifications by John R. Commons. What this did, remarked Veblen, was to foster an attitude of self-aggrandizement, coercion, and collusive control of industry.[95]

Credit, said Veblen, was not really essential for the production of goods per se, although its normal use was a legitimate way to improve industrial processes.[96] It was the abnormal application of credit that disturbed him. There was no doubt but that loans gave some firms a competitive market advantage. But their added purchasing power enabled them to indulge in certain speculative activities which had the effect of increasing prices rather than output. Moreover, credit was pyramided, one form piled on the other, particularly through capitalized prospective earning power. This became a kind of self-fulfilling process to which all the newly developed intangible assets were added for still more capitalization. Prospective profit, capitalized at the going rate of interest, became the prime mover in business cycles, for the economy was prosperous only when the rate of profit on capitalized values was accelerated. The process, said Veblen, became quite complex, so that the distinction between credit and the underlying tangible goods was obscured. Soon perceptible discrepancies developed between business values and the equipment they were supposed to represent. As the economy entered upon its anticipated state of euphoria, the growth of intangibles soon outsped the expansion in real goods.[97] A credit inflation ensued, which eventually turned into forced liquidation of assets.[98] Creditors feared that the discrepancy between business and real values had gone too far, and the demand for debt repayment initiated the economy's downward movement.

The basic cause seemed obvious enough: the market value of output could not keep up with capital inflation because incomes generally failed to expand proportionately. Were this not the case, then the inflated values would be absorbed by advances in costs, leaving the area of production as the sole source of value. But it was clear to Veblen that capitalism's distributive mechanism did not do this. The business cycle, therefore, was a pecuniary phenomenon related in the main to the institutions of credit and capitalization. In seeking an explanation of this, it would be necessary to look to the sphere of earnings and prices, rather than to production. The basic causes could be traced to society's fundamental dichotomy, the conflict between business and industry. The end product was a forced rerating of capital which placed the burden of deflation on the "normal owners of industrial equipment," with the lion's share of the gains going to "creditors and claimants outside the industrial process." [99] The resulting redistribution of property always seemed to inure to the benefit of the creditor class.

Yet the cycle was a normal feature of the economy, Veblen asserted. Upswings and downturns were part of the same process.[100] But as he viewed the situation, it appeared that depressions were outweighing and outnumbering the periods of economic exhilaration. This also seemed to explain the increasing pace of concentration. For after each series of forced liquidations and reratings, those firms that had been able to obtain access to the latest technological devices or to successfully reorganize or to rearrange their capital structures early in the upswing found themselves in sufficiently powerful competitive positions to be able to absorb their rivals.[101]

This sudden collapse in the prospective rate of return made Veblen's theory appear similar to the one that Keynes was to develop, in which overoptimism resulted in altering the relationship of the money rate of return to the marginal efficiency of capital.[102] In Keynes' theory, however, expectations played the key role, while in Veblen's the overcapitalization of embodied, historical cost was central. It was this approach that lent a more pessimistic outlook to Veblen's analysis. Moreover, he probably would have rejected the Keynesian contention that investment was identical with an increase in tangible equipment, for he insisted that intangible assets were precisely the most significant elements in the capital structure of a business concern. Through these rights, patents, trade marks, franchises, and good will, built up in costly ways through salesmanship and advertising, the business chieftain enjoyed advantages over his rivals. They gave him the leverage with which to restrict supply and control prices. The fact was, said Veblen, that the stock of capital did not alter much in a depression, although its valuation did shift sharply. The length of the cycle, therefore, was closely related to how long it would take to revise capitalizations. All this was a distinct part of the capitalist process of capturing an ever larger share of the market and swallowing one's competitors.

Monopoly, of course, was a central feature of the Veblenian vision. The corporate structure, he said, led to restrictionism, a policy that even the nascent trade union movement had found acceptable.[103] But such a policy could not continue without abatement, for it was incompatible with the machine process, and, for that matter, with the ultimate needs of the state. In *Imperial Germany and the Industrial Revolution,* Veblen advanced an ingenious explanation to account for the way in which capitalist society sought to solve internal difficulties through imperialist adventures. While the influence of John A. Hobson was patent, Veblen went further: aggressive national policies, he argued, were fostered in the backward areas in order to maintain the world economy on a war footing—a most prophetic comment, indeed. He then virtually forecast the course that Germany was to pursue in the twentieth century. Her economic capacity had been built up by borrowing a superior technology from Britain which she had imposed upon a "dynastic state" to create a new thrust toward world domination. The result was a fearful totalitarianism, just as Veblen had anticipated. Nor was he overly sanguine about the democracies, for he was only too well aware that the national spirit could be employed by the vested interests to perpetuate their own power. Patriotism was the handmaiden of pecuniary ambition. Moreover, by supporting policies of perpetual war-preparation, the democratic states were converting themselves into advocates of national integrity sustained by imperialism.[104] Eventually, even the business interests would be unable to escape the ultimate fate: they too were to be used in the interests of dynastic aims.[105] The end product of war was the domination of the authoritarian state.

Imperial Germany revealed more sharply than any of his other works how relevant to present-day affairs Veblen's analysis could really be. As Max Lerner has said, he has worn well and little in his writing has dated. Veblen described the nature of modern totalitarianism decades before it made its appearance: indeed many of the leaders of Nazi Germany, Imperial Japan, and Soviet Russia sounded as though they had taken their cues from this embittered but remarkably insightful American professor. Veblen contrasted the development of Germany with that of Britain, yet, so far as he could see, the predatory culture of modern times was characteristic of both. Insofar as the welfare of the people was concerned there was little to choose between them: coercion and exploitation were common features of their respective economic and social landscapes. In Germany, however, there had been no need to resort to the artful stratagems utilized by captains of industry to protect their pecuniary holdings. Industrial waste—the penalty of taking the lead—had been avoided by Germany, and so her economic growth had expanded at an accelerated rate.

The notion of escaping this penalty could be used not only to explain how the Kaiser's Germany and Imperial Japan were able to employ successfully Western technology, but to lend insight also into the nature of Soviet growth. For there too no restraining hand of business ownership was able to impose strange, intangible restrictions upon the flow of material goods. Once a nation had cast off the constraints of pecuniary requirements and the need to protect so-called funded wealth, it could push forth relentlessly toward building factories and machines. In the case of the totalitarian nations, the ultimate purpose had been power and domination. It might have been otherwise. Avoidance of the leader's penalty could be applied, for example, to the underdeveloped areas which today are seeking so desperately to raise their material standards. However, Veblen would have emphasized wryly that so long as the dead weight of tradition and pecuniary values continued to pervade the culture of such regions as Latin America, there was little likelihood that they would enjoy the full benefits accruing to newcomers to the industrial discipline.

What was so striking throughout this entire analysis, was Veblen's emphasis on coercion as the dominant principle in economic and social behavior. Since labor was a process whereby one created property for another, it was patent that income stemmed from certain pressures. In the present institutional arrangement, said Veblen, coercion was the rich man's prerogative. The distribution of material goods was secondary to that of creating a situation in which coercion could be employed to advantage. Since noneconomic methods were essential in developing conditions of profitability, appropriate pressures on legislative bodies, administrative agencies, and newspaper advertising departments had become instruments for assuring a suitable flow of business income. Acts of aggression and conflicts of interest were more common than orthodox textbooks were willing to concede.

Veblen's genetic approach to economics did not allow him to offer any prescriptions for a new society, but he did feel that more and more the state would come to dominate events. Dire consequences obviously would arise from the dominance of a military caste.[106] Yet always he harbored the hope that the "underlying population" might one day break away from old habits and seek to rebuild the social structure, "for better or worse."[107] One powerful barrier, however, was the continued attraction that business-as-usual held for Marx's proletariat. It was rather among technicians and intellectuals that Veblen thought he saw a glimmer of the kind of solidarity that was essential to the attainment of new modes of behavior. They had the practical and theoretical experience necessary to operate society on a new basis.[108] The problem of transferring power seemingly posed no real question, thought Veblen naively, for a general strike by the technicians could bring the country to its knees and enforce unconditional surrender on the business community.[109] Evidences of intangible assets, absentee ownership, and vested interests then would disappear as society would be reorganized along lines vaguely reminiscent of the Guild Socialists. Resources would be effectively and properly allocated, (just how was not made clear), and the industrial order at long last would be geared to the genuine needs of the consumer. A new discipline and new instinct would evolve, consonant with the new mode of getting things done. But sadly, this was only a utopian scheme and the kind of wishful thinking that Veblen would have ridiculed in his younger years. The implications that flowed from his basic thinking could lead him only to the point where he might posit, if he so desired, a coming stalemate between business and industry. The revolution of the engineers was a dream that he hoped wistfully would somehow come true. Yet he did not really believe it, for he was basically a pessimist who saw no real alternative to capitalism, as bad as it was. And this was his tragedy, for he espoused nothing after the harsh vision he had advanced. In the continual struggle between man and institutions, the odds were always against the individual. Veblen could never express the occasional admiration for capitalism that one finds, for example, in Marx. He was simply a visitor, examining the strange rituals of the society through which he was passing. The last words he had on the subject were:

In that strategy of businesslike curtailment of output, debilitation of industry, and capitalisation of overhead charges, which is entailed by the established system of ownership and bargaining, the constituted authorities in all the democratic nations may, therefore, be counted on to lend their unwavering support to all manoeuvres of business-as-usual, and to disallow any transgression of or departure from business principles. Nor should there seem any probability that the effectual run of popular sentiment touching these matters will undergo any appreciable change. . . . For the immediate future the prospect appears to offer a fuller confirmation in the faith that business principles answer all things.[110]

Veblen's profession of scholarly impartiality fooled no one. His tone and diction was but a brittle façade for a savage attack on the rapacity and vulgarity of his day. In this respect he was, as Bernard Rosenberg has said, an artist as well as social critic. His perception of the foibles of his fellow men was sharp enough to make them quite uncomfortable. He saw the leisure class as a functionless group, given to conspicuous display and invidious comparisons of status. The traits they exhibited and conserved were archaic as well as drains on industry. They were given to sports, dog breeding, gambling, and religious ritual, activities that did not foster the growth of material welfare. The tragedy, said Veblen, was that the middle class preferred to imitate these manners, thus forsaking whatever hold they might have on habits of frugality and industry. This, plus all the other elements of cultural lag, made the outlook a dubious one. Certainly change could not come from the proletariat, for their energies were exhausted in keeping themselves alive. The patterns of leisure-class life more and more dominated the whole of society, and its imbecile institutions triumphed over life and culture.[111]

In his perceptive study, Bernard Rosenberg has said that Veblen was so close to the truth that fear rather than outrage became a common reaction to his work.[112] For example, Veblen's observation of the low status of scholarly pursuits in America was unimpeachable. The primary concern in the colleges was material expediency, while true scholarship was not so much ignored as discomfited. Administrators of higher learning were more concerned with intrigue and extracurricular activities than they were with the pursuit of knowledge.[113] This may have stemmed, said Veblen, from the simple fact that the ruling group in the universities did not really qualify as scholars. As theologians or fund-raisers, they had to defer to the industrial magnates who sat on their governing boards. The university must ". . . make good both as a corporation of learning and as a business concern dealing in standardized erudition."[114] The president, Veblen continued, usually wrapped an unwholesome bulk in a decorous costume in order to achieve a mark of weight and responsibility and had to conform to a gentlemanly routing of conspicuous convivialities. This was frequently a matter of astute publicity. Were Veblen alive in this day of public and community relations, no doubt he would delight his readers with acid descriptions of the complex organs of bureaucracy that have been constructed to maintain suitable avenues for the laity to acquire esteem through appropriate "evidence of wasteful ability to pay." University donations have the character of an invest-ment in good fame: they are ". . . made by gentlemen and gentlewomen, to gentlemen, and the transactions begin and end within the circle of pecuniary respectability." [115] In time, the university is judged by criteria which have nothing to do with knowledge. Veblen's observations on life in the Academy, incorporated in his *Higher Learning in America,* was perhaps a personal work; but for those whose existence has all too often teetered on the pre-carious edge of the campus, his perceptions were suffused with the ineluctable aura of truth.[116]

These views on education reflected Veblen's conviction that economics was more than a study of prices and markets. Human action in all its facets was the proper province of the economist, he said,[117] for the social scientist had to concern himself with the relations of man to man. This involved not only the structure and organization of economic life, but all of social behavior. In the words of Allan Gruchy, Veblen was seeking a "holistic" ap-proach, one in which economics would evolve into a genuinely cultural science. It was the institutionalist contention that the market was not the sole arena for economic action. Moreover, the pattern of economics that held for one era did not necessarily apply to another. While this approach was a reasonable kind of relativism, it was suffused with the notion of growth and immanent change. Although perhaps less analytical than some thought desirable, it was nevertheless a brilliant attempt to grasp the mechanics of social development.

Although there may be few conscious institutionalists around today, quite a number of economists were able to trace their spiritual ancestry to Thorstein Veblen.[118] Of the older writers, Herbert J. Davenport, one of his students and a later benefactor, not only acknowledged the presence of the pecuniary in classical doctrine but tried to cleanse traditional theory of its apologetic underbrush. Robert F. Hoxie, a tragic figure in the history of American economics, developed an institutionalist theory of trade unionism which still exerts its force on our thinking; E. H. Downey used Veblenian arguments to defend the principle of workmen's compensation; W. W. Stewart employed the business-industry dichotomy in his study of banking; Carleton Parker developed a psychology of industrial relations that had a powerful effect on none other than John R. Commons, many of whose ideas paralleled Veblen's; John Maurice Clark sought a middle way between the economics of his father, John Bates Clark, and Veblen; Berle and Means, in their *Modern Corporation and Private Property,* were completely Veb-lenian; and above all, Wesley C. Mitchell, the great business cycle analyst, exemplified the application of empirical investigation to Veblenian concepts at its best. Even down to the present moment, Veblen's influence is at work: *vide* C. Wright Mills' enormous appetite for factual investigation and his perceptive and essentially Veblenesque insights into the character of American life or C. E. Ayres' work on economic progress, which stands virtually alone as a purely theoretical treatise in the institutionalist tradition.[119]

It can be fairly said that a Veblenian school of economics did in fact develop, but it did not last. The Veblenians were in their early thirties when the master died and they were soon caught up in day-to-day problems, particularly in New Deal affairs. With a depression and a war, they had to improvise policies after the fashion of their great political godfather—Franklin Delano Roosevelt. Each Veblenite took up a different facet of the many-sided institutionalist analysis. Some, as in the case of Walton Hamilton, became interested in legal matters, while others sought more empirical data, and after a while eschewed theory altogether. This, in a sense, was ironic, for Veblen himself had demonstrated that little could be gained by an everlasting ingathering of facts without theory. Yet Veblen's influence regrettably waned. The Keynesian revolution in economics and the explosive development of the mathematical approach in the forties and fifties shunted aside the genetic viewpoint. Lip service was paid to the problems of the group, as in game theory, but it was seldom done with the plasticity and variability that one finds in the real world. Industrial development frequently was treated as a question of the static comparative advantage of one region over the next without regard to such external factors as ordinary politics. Price theory became the be-all and end-all of much of economic analysis. Society was admittedly a highly complex affair, but its various components were said to be so closely and delicately knit that the slightest improper impulse would send convolutions gyrating in explosive (or dampened) fashion throughout the whole structure. The institutionalist, on the other hand, insisted that we live in a loosely integrated economy in which there was much give and play. A change in one part of the system did not necessarily transmit its impact with the directness or suddenness implied by received doctrine. The process of institutional growth and selection was also loose, accounting for the survival of many atavistic traits. Although the precision of a mathematical formula was indeed elegant, it also was deceptive.[120] To the institutionalist, the new economics appeared like a game of chess and just about as useful. Unfortunately, most economists today prefer the game of chess.

ii

John R. Commons:
Transactions and Going
Concerns

Of middle western origin, with an ancestry that went back to the reign of Queen Mary in the sixteenth century, John R. Commons (1862-1945), like his forebears, was rebellious and a purveyor of heresy. His father's family had migrated from North Carolina because they could not abide the institution of slavery, while his mother, who had come from Vermont, was an ardent abolitionist. The elder Commons, a devotee of Shakespeare and Darwin, eventually drifted away from Quakerism, the family faith. After several business ventures, all of which he obtained by swapping one for the next, he purchased a newspaper where the younger Commons learned the printers' trade, an occupation he was to pursue for a short while.[121] But even in this shop, Commons' father was unable to support the family, and his wife had to assume all the financial worries. A woman of remarkable character, she urged John to enter Oberlin in the hope that he would become a minister. In the meantime, she took in boarders to pay for his education.

At Oberlin, Commons demonstrated a forceful sense of independence. He refused to be subservient to others, especially in intellectual matters. Possessed by a desire to uncover his own facts and laboriously work out their relationships, he was, on the record at least, a poor student. Coupled with lengthy absences for health reasons, his undergraduate work took more than the normal length of time, with graduation finally attained in 1888. From Oberlin, Commons went to Johns Hopkins in Baltimore, taking with him an unabashed admiration for Henry George. This move eastward was a mark of the confidence that he inspired in others, for he had successfully borrowed $1,000 from an Oberlin trustee to help carry out his plans for an advanced degree. A major attraction at Hopkins was Richard T. Ely, whom Commons recognized as a kindred spirit. Ely, who had but recently returned from Germany, was imbued with the inspirational message of the historicists, and it was not long before Commons became his favorite student. The older man emphasized practical field investigation and Commons quickly discovered that there was a good deal more to economics than was to be found in the texts. But again he did poorly in class and in fact never did obtain his doctoral degree.

In 1890, Commons was appointed to a tutor's post at Wesleyan, but after a short stay was advised to go elsewhere. He was as poor a teacher as he had been a pupil. He then returned to Oberlin and finally went to Indiana University as professor of economics. While there he began to wonder whether religion might not be a suitable vehicle for social change, and these thoughts impelled him to organize an "American Institute of Christian Sociology," out of which came his *Social Reform and The Church*[122]—a discussion of temperance, political reform and proportional representation. Commons began to write also on money and related questions, but he advocated a point of view which soon labelled him a socialist. Yet radical ideology was actually unpalatable to Commons, for it seemed to overlook the importance of the individual. He said simply that social change would have to be achieved by stimulating the energies of people and that this must be done via government measures in order to guarantee equality of opportunity. The University hierarchy was apprehensive, however, despite his now acknowledged competence as an economic investigator. Commons did not help to solidify his position with his forthright opinions on sundry matters. He once wrote to Ely that he hoped he was learning to be somewhat cautious in his mode of expression.[123] When Syracuse University approached him with an offer, Commons tried to use it as a bargaining weapon with the Indiana president, who thereupon congratulated him and sent him on his way.

Commons now was beginning to develop some of the ideas that he was to set down in his *Distribution of Wealth*, his first major work.[124] He became engrossed in municipal reform, local government, and proportional representation, schemes that eventually were to find their way into the full fabric of his social theory. His penchant for getting into difficulty with university authorities stayed with him, however. Municipal reform, proportional representation, and unorthodox teaching methods were bad enough, but when he had the temerity to advocate Sunday baseball for workingmen, gifts to the university fell off. The authorities quietly abolished Commons' chair,[125] and he wryly observed that it was not religion but capitalism that governed Christian colleges.

Commons never again sought a university post on his own. After the loss of his job at Syracuse, he went to work for a friend, George Shibley, a bimetalist and an ardent supporter of William Jennings Bryan, the Democratic silver-tongued orator. Commons' assignment was to put together an index of wholesale prices, but when the index showed a price rise in July, 1900 —a disagreeable turn to the Democrats—Shibley cancelled the arrangement and Commons was again unemployed.[126] He then went to work for the Industrial Commission, and after that for the National Civic Federation, a group that sought to conciliate differences between labor and capital. By this time

Commons' views were fairly well set: he advocated compulsory arbitration in labor disputes; urged the eight-hour day; believed that increased wages brought added purchasing power to the masses; and was willing to accept concentration in industry as long as it provided serviceability. An assignment with the garment workers provided additional practical experience. For five years Commons wandered about the nonacademic world; then in 1904, Ely brought him into the University of Wisconsin. It was not a simple matter to bring Commons back onto the campus. He had irritated and alienated too many with his inquisitive ways, and he was now forty-two years old. The University agreed to Ely's demand only on condition that a private fund would pay half the salary. Yet the gamble that Ely took paid off. As Wesley C. Mitchell remarked, the man and the opportunity were well matched.[127] The chief purpose for which Commons went to Wisconsin was to help write a gigantic history of industrial democracy. He soon had full charge of the project, which was completely to his liking, and by 1911 there was published in ten volumes the massive *Documentary History of Industrial Society*.[128] Studies on labor history began to issue from the Commons group, the most notable of which was the classic *History of Labor in the United States*.[129]

There were many opportunities to observe political behavior at Wisconsin. Commons became an advisor to Robert La Follette, the State's exciting and forward-looking governor, who was anxious to undertake a wide variety of social reforms. Commons plunged into a mass of work. He helped draft a civil service bill in 1904; pushed public utility regulation in the municipal area; promoted a small-loan law which allowed a charge of 3½ per cent interest a month (for which he was attacked even though 42 per cent per annum was a good deal less than a 100 per cent interest charge); helped create the Wisconsin Industrial Commission; and in 1932 turned out one of the first state unemployment insurance measures in the country. He was also involved in studies of municipal ownership; the Pittsburgh Survey of 1906; the Federal Industrial Relations Commission of 1913; and the famous Pittsburgh plus-pricing case of 1923. He was America's closest challenge to the indefatigable Webbs.

Ultimately all this experience went into the creation of the peculiar system of thought exemplified in the *Legal Foundations of Capitalism* and *Institutional Economics*.[130] His unique ability for gaining the confidence of all sorts of people, from radical socialists to staid millionaires, enabled him to explore varying human situations. Despite personal tragedies—the loss of five children, and a sixth who suffered from paranoia, as well as his own poor health—he maintained a remarkable equanimity. Toward the end of his life, he felt that his last book, *The Economics of Collective Action*, finally had made clear to the profession what it was he had been trying to tell them for so many years.

Commons was not a quick worker. He admitted that he had to dig and dig; it took him twenty-five years to work out the transition from the concept of exchange to transactions.[131] Although his insatiable curiosity invariably set him off on tangents, they always ended in perceptive insights. His integration of personal experience with theoretical economics was one of his most striking characteristics. His work as a journeyman printer had impressed upon him the *collective* nature of a trade union and the way in which, as an *institution,* it guided and controlled individual behavior.[132] The kind of psychology Commons derived from his notion of collective action owed a good deal to Charles Peirce, the acknowledged founder of pragmatism, who had argued that clear thinking about an object required consideration of the practical effects which the object might conceivably involve. Implicit in Peirce's outlook was an emphasis on investigation, an approach to which Commons instinctively was attracted.[133]

Commons' social rebellion was expressed in odd ways, none of them especially calculated to help his status on the campus. If he did not approve of the hacks advanced by party politicians, he did not hesitate to vote for a Communist candidate. On occasion he brought a live radical into the classroom, if only to exhibit him as a political specimen. But he was a strong opponent of Marxian belief.[134] Two of Commons' most brilliant associates were Jewish refugees from Czarist oppression, Abraham Bisno and Selig Perlman. Both had begun as Marxists of sorts, but found their views changing under the influence of Commons and the American climate.

Although himself an intellectual, Commons felt that they really had no genuine role in the labor movement, for they were usually the sort of do-gooders who failed in practical affairs, and the labor movement was nothing if not practical.[135] His pragmatic experience aroused an abiding interest in the nature of bargaining transactions; it seemed to him that the patient, quiet investigation implicit in such arrangements, as a way of achieving what he called reasonable value, was much more fruitful than all the fiery dramatics of the class struggle.[136] This led him into the legal foundations of economic decisions, especially as they were revealed in public utility regulations. Added to this were the studies of municipal finances, organization, sanitation, and accounting, the object of which was to distill principles of economic efficiency. But these concepts had to be viewed against the backdrop of past economic theory before they could be incorporated into his own system.

Many economists today, both on campuses and off, owe a great intellectual debt to Commons. At first rejected by most of his colleagues, his ideas gradually penetrated the thinking of those who were willing to adopt concepts that were relevant to genuinely concrete historical possibilities. Going concern, bargaining strength, and transactions were recognized as fairly accurate descriptions of the course of economic behavior. It was acknowledged that intangible values were proper goals sought by businessmen. Market behavior reflected ways of economic action, and the limiting and strategic factors of which Commons spoke became meaningful analytic concepts. Moreover, with his insistence on the development of law as a reflection of social custom, he was able to stress the modifying impact of judicial decisions.[137]

Not only did he stimulate his students to work their utmost, but he was ever ready to help. His encouragement never flagged and he often conveyed to them a sense of having made a genuine contribution to economic science. Commons' graduate courses were true reflections of his personality; they were entirely devoid of formal organization, yet always challenging in their exploration of critical and unique problems. The important distinction he was to make between physical assets and the values they represented stemmed from his work in public utilities. Reflections on the nature of the corporation not only highlighted the relationship between taxes and intangibles, but also revealed that the center of activity was the "going concern." These activities could only give rise, according to the Commons lexicon, to reasonable value and futurity. And these were all pragmatic questions to be solved through the good offices of the law courts. Expectations were, of course, more significant than historical costs, since reasonable value looked to some settlement in the future. And an entire industrial order could be refracted through the prism of labor problems. In this way, an entire system of thought began to emerge out of the complex of the day-to-day problems with which Commons had chosen to contend.

In the early part of his career Commons had been something of a traditionalist. His *Distribution of Wealth,* published in 1893, had almost as much Austrian value theory in it as social reform. It was a curious mixture which revealed a sincere groping for a point of view. Böhm-Bawerk's value theory seemed to offer a solution for the problem of distribution, since the share of the social income going to the individual depended on the ratios in which the various products exchanged one for the other. A hint of Commons' later ideas cropped out in the notion of *customary* supply and demand.[138] Commons hoped that this concept would enable him to investigate the forces behind supply and demand in perhaps new ways. But this meant a study of property, and in fact, he criticized Böhm-Bawerk for failing to take account of it. From supply, Commons went on to a study of property and inevitably to legal problems, for property involved certain rights and duties without a clear definition of which society could not function. Rights changed with changing economic conditions, said Commons, and these included personal rights, which meant not only protection of the individual but a right to as high a portion of the national product as possible.[139] For this reason labor unions were legitimate organizations, for it was their function to raise the workers' marginal gains above the minimum. The remainder of this first slim volume was concerned with diminishing returns and rents. Commons concluded that diminishing returns was fundamentally a "potential" theoretical law which applied only in monopoly situations. Since the latter was on the increase, it was imperative to establish ways to protect the worker, who all too often became a victim of monopolistic pressures. Yet Commons, like Schumpeter after him, felt that the growth of trusts might have some beneficial effects insofar as depressions might be mitigated and production enhanced.[140] There was also a Ricardian quality to Commons' contention that a basic social conflict existed between capital and labor on one side and the "owners of opportunities" on the other.[141] The latter were essentially residual claimants of the social product, not unlike Ricardo's rentiers. This somewhat radical element in Commons' work explained the severe attacks leveled against it, a result that made his position at Indiana an uneasy one.

During the 1890's Commons was also interested in monetary questions. While he gave support to Bryan, his own views were not so "extreme." He thought that prices might be stabilized through the purchase and sale of silver, thus providing an elastic currency. Nevertheless, his preference was for a gold standard. The notion of a stable price level was similar to that advanced by Knut Wicksell, although Commons had not yet read the Swedish economist's writings.[142] Price fluctuations were analyzed by Commons, showing a long-run secular trend on which he imposed a shorter credit cycle which ostensibly worked its way through the economy every six to ten years. The analysis of credit was similar in many respects to that developed by Veblen. In later years, Commons renewed his interest in money. He wrote on monetary reform and was virtually economic advisor to the House of Representative's Committee on Banking and Currency, even arranging for Gustav Cassel, the noted Swedish economist, to give testimony before it. He "investigated" Federal Reserve operations and learned from Benjamin Strong, one of the key figures in the "Fed," how open-market operations could have a profound impact on price levels and the money market. One aspect that Commons was always interested in was the question of timeliness of action, a problem that has continued to plague the Federal Reserve System throughout the years.[143]

Commons was seldom disturbed that his notion of institutional economics did not jibe with what others thought it should be. Certainly it diverged sharply from Veblen's conception. For Commons it was the study of collective action in control of individual action. His experience in public affairs convinced him that collective action was the sole way of reconciling conflicts of interest.[144] And this brought him four-square into the center of legal issues, where he quickly concluded that it was through the courts that collective desires in economics were expressed. For example, intangible property was not only the right to an income but also the right to fix prices by withholding from others what they needed but did not own. The similarity between his view and Veblen's was readily conceded by Commons, but in contrast to the former's pessimism, he felt that the ways in which ideas of intangible property were crystallized could be resolved in a generally accepted settlement. This was Commons' reasonable value. That is, one could proceed from a conflict of interest through the courts toward a generally acceptable decision.

Now, said Commons, the whole process would have to be examined in terms of its historical roots. The idea of collective action had antecedents as far back as Marx, Proudhon, and Henry MacLeod, an English economist who had been one of the first to observe that banks manufactured credit. This made economics an evolutionary science which would require, to begin with, an examination of the court decisions of the past several hundred years in order to obtain a clear view of how collective action restrained individual action. Following this, said Commons, it would be essential to study the writings of economists to see how far these notions had been absorbed into their thinking.[145] The first task was accomplished in the *Legal Foundations of Capitalism,* and the second in the *Institutional Economics.* The latter book became a gigantic, chaotic study of raw intellectual power running to over nine-hundred pages. It roamed over the whole field of doctrinal history, always searching for the ways in which writers, from Hume to Veblen, had introduced "collective action" into their thought. Filled with many sharp insights, it represented, in the main, an inquiry into the methodological and philosophical preconceptions of economics. Yet everything in the end wound up in Commons' special viewpoint—the concept of collective action—so that a reconciliation between his institutional economics and the more individualistic outlook of his predecessors was always in the making. In fact, Commons did not think that he was working out anything especially new, for it was all there, said he, in the writings of the outstanding economists of the last two hundred years.[146]

The *Institutional Economics* began with John Locke and his *Essay Concerning Human Understanding,* since a central interest was the way in which ideas were organized by the mind. Commons wanted to demonstrate by exploring some of the odder pathways of philosophy that there was a concrete relationship between ideas and the external world. This was necessary in order to provide a solid base for the later concepts of scarcity and futurity.[147] Furthermore, such a philosophic exploration could give meaning to the notion of will, which underpinned all questions of decision-making in economics. This inquiry, so thoroughly characteristic of Commons, enabled him to say that his was "a theory of the joint activity and valuations of individuals in all transactions through which the participants mutually induce each other to a consensus of opinion and action." [148] For those to whom the unfolding of ideas is a fascinating pastime, Commons' explorations reveal a remarkable storehouse of thoughtful materials. David Hume, Richard Baxter, R. H. Tawney, Charles Peirce, Quesnay, Blackstone, Bentham, and MacLeod, as well as all the great figures in the history of economic thought, filed past the Commons' examination platform. His ultimate objective was to trace the

notions of interdependence, conflict of interest, and order as they might culminate in "reasonable value," something that Commons held was established,
in the last analysis, by the Supreme Court. The latter, said he, was the first
faculty of political economy in the United States.

Scarcity, an important facet of Commons' corpus, was found to have
been introduced into economics by Hume and refined by Malthus. These
writers had revealed their advanced thinking when they admitted that
rational behavior was not necessarily characteristic for the mass of mankind.
Stupidity and passion ruled all too often, and intense conflict arose over the
disposition of scarce goods. If rationality really did exist, then interdependence
would have been acknowledged and no third party would have been necessary
to help establish reasonable rules of behavior. One might hope that custom
would modify the deleterious effects of irrationality, for the habitual behavior
patterns stemming from custom could become a vehicle for reasonableness.[149]
If customs changed, as indeed they did, then the choice between old customs
and new might have created a conflict between reason and self-interest. Yet
custom tended to be unchangeable since it stemmed mainly from instinctual
behavior. It was found that certain repeated acts helped to preserve the
species, and this repetition from generation to generation made custom akin
to hereditary behavior.[150] Custom, however, issued in individual habit, said
Commons, reaching for as broad a perception of man as he could. He
related custom to collective action and to the shift from feudalism to a business economy, yet always he stressed the role of individual creativeness.[151]
People were not automatons, he said; they possessed the capacity to alter their
environment, thereby relaxing the normal rigidity of custom. But since this
capacity often resulted in conflict, it was incumbent on man to seek ways of
ameliorating tensions, especially when they were caused by property holdings.

Commons then discussed efficiency and scarcity at great length. These
notions suggested a clash between engineering and business concepts. Whereas
Veblen had been convinced that the two were essentially irreconcilable,
Commons thought that capitalism could attain a working balance between
these forces. Scarcity, however, had not been understood, said Commons,
until his great contemporary, Veblen, had shown how economic development
led to intangible property. Scarcity notions were also at the center of legal
decisions. The classical economists, of course, had spoken of scarcity at
great length. But they had seemingly taken wants for granted and had used
scarcity as a basis for fixing value, entirely overlooking value determination
through negotiation. Scarcity depended on labor pain or labor power. Then
the Austrian economists had come along and eliminated labor power by
adopting a purely hedonic structure.[152]

This long and sometimes tedious analysis of doctrinal history was intended to show how collective action evolved as a means of controlling individual action. Within this broad framework, men were related to each other

in the present through transactions, although they were also concerned with what might happen in the future. Complicating this analysis was the double-headed character of value itself, said Commons, for it was as both physical good and ownership that its meaning was revealed. That these were really two different aspects of property was proven by the capacity of ownership to change hands without any concomitant transfer of the objects involved. This required a more effective theory of incorporeal property and negotiable debt, without which the genuine significance of futurity could not be explained.[153] In the past, argued Commons, men had to live with unreleasable debt; liberty had been gained only insofar as debt became "releasable." This, essentially, had been the foundation of modern capitalism: political economy was really the study of the creation, negotiability, release and scarcity of debt. Promises to pay or to perform an action became saleable commodities. All this was reflected in past economic theory: MacLeod had seen an intimate relation between debt and commodity markets; Sidgwick had distinguished between the money and capital markets; Wicksell had spoken of a debt-paying community; Cassel had emphasized the scarcity of waiting as a basis for interest; Knapp had analysed debt release; Hawtrey had discussed debt creation; and Fisher had been concerned with overindebtedness. All these were facets of the same problem, said Commons.

This, then, was the Commons point of view—it was basically pragmatic and one seeking to avoid the purely abstract ideas of the nineteenth century. Yet though he gave the impression that his interests did not lie in generalization, his notions of transactions and the going concern were highly idealized and quite theoretical.[154] But in the main, there was an undeniable thrust toward the instrumentalist outlook, for economics to Commons was a practical business whose object was to restructure capitalism along "reasonable" lines. Moreover, the economist was ". . . himself a part of the purposeful subject matter of his science. This may not appear until he is forced by a crisis to choose between conflicting interests; then his pure theory is perhaps found to contain the assumptions which directed his choice."[155] A practical turn of mind would help economists to search out the meaningful questions and to approach their answers with techniques that were appropriate to the problem at hand. Commons clearly favored a "functionalist" rather than an abstractionist approach to particular questions. The world in which the economist worked was one ". . . of uncertain change, without foreordination or metaphysics, whether benevolent or non-benevolent, where we ourselves and the world about us are continually in a changing conflict of interests."[156] The economist's proper sphere, therefore, was the behavior of human beings, something he should be able to grasp readily because he was able to place himself in like situations and thus sense motives and purposes in action.[157]

Both the physical sciences and Darwinian natural selection were limited in their application to the social studies, argued Commons, since selection in human behavor was largely purposeful. In this respect, his institutionalism was again different from Veblen's. It was more self-conscious, more optimistic, and stressed adaptation by choice. Like Veblen's theory, it eschewed organismic thinking. But behavior did not exhibit the same sort of drift that one had found in Veblen; it was purposeful and expressed a general concern with future results.[158] This was the underlying preconception which explained the urgency implicit in Commons' demand for acceptable rules in going concerns. It gave him an opportunity to introduce the factor of human will and to reveal social action as completely voluntaristic. He did not deny that the deductive method had some usefulness in economic science, but, so far as he could see, the more complex character of banker capitalism and cartellization impelled the economist to employ psychological concepts such as power and coercion in order to grasp what was really happening.

All this implied that the human mind was no passive receptacle, no Lockean *tabula rasa*. Mind was for Commons a creative factor of great consequence. The purpose of social science—to convert the experience of external events and the perception that one had of them into a kind of order that would make possible useful generalizations—meant that the selection and refinement of thought was not a contemplative process, but rather an active one. From this posture, Commons was able to work up his "volitional" or negotiational psychology for which the idea of willingness was so important. Furthermore, negotiation was an integral element of the transaction, so that for the first time a system of economics was rooted in a social psychology. Commons' psychological outlook definitely had a *Gestalt* character; it was an attempt to examine social and economic situations in their totality. Action, conflict, purpose and achievement were all commingled in transactions and their negotiations.

The development of an economy of collective action had a long history which Commons was able to trace to the era of merchant capitalism in the seventeenth and eighteenth centuries. This later had evolved into employer-capitalism and finally had attained the mature stage of banker or financial capitalism.[159] The development of markets had provided the impetus for the first stage, while technology and credit had been responsible for subsequent changes. In this somewhat schematic and naive history, Commons was influenced by Bücher, the noted German historian. The shoe-making industry was used as a classic illustration: Commons showed how the journeyman had moved about with his hand tools from farmer to farmer, receiving wages largely in the form of board and lodging. Then, with the emergence of towns and urban life, shops had been established in which the functions of owner, merchant, skilled worker, and employer were joined together. Customers now came to the bootmaker, and the price was set before the work was done, on a custom basis. Frequently, the quality of work and the prices the master might charge were fixed by an association, after the fashion of the craft guilds. This was followed by the retail shop stage: the merchant-master now assembled a stock of shoes made in slack times. The price was set after the work had been done, facilitating a separation of the merchant from the master-worker function. Speculative markets began to emerge as the merchant assumed economic hegemony. He took orders from other dealers and became a nascent wholesaler-manufacturer. The journey-man, now on the threshold of the industrial order of the nineteenth century, worked for three markets—local retail, custom, and wholesale. Prices in the retail market might be less than the others because of special services and transportation costs. Differences in wages began to appear and journeymen began to organize themselves into trade unions for protection against the chill winds of competition. In turn, the masters established their own associations and brought the journeymen to court where they were convicted for conspiracy under the common law.[160]

The wholesale stage featured the merchant capitalist and the beginnings of commercial banking operations. The merchant capitalist, however, had not stemmed from the master workman. He was a dealer pure and simple who controlled a raw material supply and was able to employ the craftsmen to make the goods he wanted to sell. This was the sweatshop stage, Commons said, where profits were made from the deliberate exploitation of humans. The retail merchant now was deprived of his employer status. Industrialism began to develop, requiring both bank finance as well as equipment. European workers who had been caught in the new economic vise tried to break out with cooperatives. Such efforts failed when transplanted to the United States and so the workers had no recourse but to try trade unions. In the meantime, industry grew prodigiously: railroads and telegraphs broadened the network of markets and ever more complex machinery was introduced. The small contractor became a manufacturer; the laborer was alienated from his tools; and the middleman became a powerful mediator between factory and store. At this juncture, said Commons, Marx had been able to develop his powerful, analytical weapons.[161]

The manufacturer then sought to free himself from the middleman's grip by building an integrated industry and establishing absolute control of his product through patents, holding companies, and other monopolistic devices. As soon as this was initiated, the banker was brought in as an ally. During the periods of merchant and employer capitalism, banking had been essentially short term in character. But in the era of high industry, pecuniary capital had to be gathered in vast sums through the flotation of securities: this required the aid of the investment banker. It was not long, said Commons, before the latter came to dominate corporate boards of directors, helpfully reorganize enterprises, and cater to the goodwill of the investors—a rather pleasant picture that contrasted sharply with Veblen's acid portrayal of financiers and captains of industry. Millions of small investors were happy to have their savings transferred to the investment bankers, who, if difficulties ensued, could always ask the government to lend aid and comfort. "Meanwhile central banks, controlled by bankers, rise to a new importance and Banker capitalism comes into control of industries and nations." [162] The legal and physical control of commodities had been separated: businessmen had sought to enhance pecuniary values; and the banker era became one of "stabilized scarcity." The final stage was virtual cartellization with such collectives as corporations, unions, and trade associations exercising the most powerful control yet seen over individual behavior.

But again Commons returned to the idea of reasonableness. The problem was to domesticate the investment banker. Loan transactions, by creating additional money, had allowed the banker to become an active participant in the economy.[163] Banker capitalism, by sponsoring promotions, had facilitated an economic arrangement in which the corporation became a versatile and flexible institution.[164] The latter then influenced legislatures, employed lawyers to argue its cases in courts, and established elaborate public relations programs. And at the center was the banking system. The potential for harm was indeed enormous, but Commons was sure that a regenerated legislature could construct adequate restraints on banker capitalism.[165] A genuine and careful effort by the government to protect the rights of the individual could save the whole system.[166]

Commons' brand of optimistic institutionalism was enunciated with the publication of the *Legal Foundations of Capitalism*. It was now evident that he was groping for a genetic study after the fashion of the Webbs in Britain and Veblen in the United States, yet his style of thought was very much his own, as was the organization of his materials. It was not difficult for him to become an institutionalist writer, for he had always sought to expose the cultural and historical roots of the phenomena with which he dealt. But, as Allan Gruchy has said, Commons had to use the case method to make his point.[167] The bent toward grand abstraction, so native to Veblen, was absent in him. Every generalization was hammered home with mountains of examples and citations. The exploration of value, transactions, and working rules had to be rooted firmly in the legal decisions of the last three hundred years. A close study of the latter would reveal a shift in the meaning of property from a corporeal thing to anticipated exchange value. This also meant increased liberty and power in economic affairs. The courts simply had to take a forward position in this evolution, said Commons, because ordinary common law had been unable to deal effectively with intangibles. This argument met considerable resistance, however. Commons' critics said that intangibles were handled satisfactorily by common law, and they argued that tangibles had as much to do with futurity as intangibles. The contention was also made that Commons had read his own peculiar bias into the decisions of the courts.[168]

But this was to misunderstand Commons' intent, for the aim of institutional analysis was to observe how the legal elements were exhibited in going concerns.[169] Collectivities in banker capitalism were animated by a common purpose and governed by common regulations. They were perpetually involved in a flow of transactions along lines set down by their own working rules. These collectivities could be described as going concerns, for they were motivated and held together by a kind of self-interest, to wit, the expectation of receiving a gross income which was then to be distributed among the members. Working rules did not come about *de nuovo,* but were built up slowly through statutory and common law, court decisions, and government regulations. The analysis of these rules and their operation comprised a substantial part of the *Legal Foundations.*

Commons made an important distinction between going plants and going businesses, both of which constituted the concern. The former was deemed to be the technological organization whose objective was the attainment of efficiency and a proper proportioning of input.[170] A going business, on the other hand, was interested in pecuniary matters: it was, in fact, immersed in the production of money values. The transactions in which a going business was involved did not create new values; they merely resulted in their redistribution. Again, Commons realized that conflict was implied in this description, but, in accordance with his optimistic bent, he thought that the contending interests could be balanced. "The best going plant is one where the technological factors are rightly proportioned by managerial transactions; the best going business is one where the purchases and sales are rightly proportioned by bargaining transactions; the best going concern is one where technology and business are rightly proportioned." [171] Yet Commons was quite aware that profit-making emphasized pecuniary demands rather than efficiency. In his later years, overproduction and unemployment were to dampen his optimism. Still, he was unwilling to go as far as Veblen and to assert that in the end only business would prevail.

There was no reason to question that reasonable value in bargaining situations could not be reached through the willing cooperation of both employers and workers, said Commons.[172] This, at least, was the message of his posthumous book, *The Economics of Collective Action.* The last of his works, it is logically the first that should be studied to get at the core of Commons' economics, for it is a much more lucid presentation of his central ideas than either the *Legal Foundations* or *Institutional Economics.* In the *Collective Action,* the role of the three major institutions or collectivities—corporations, unions, and political parties—was clearly sketched. He iterated his position that greater freedom was possible only through collective action: this he illustrated with a charming story of his experience as a printer in which he had found greater latitude in a unionized establishment than in a nonunion shop.[173] Of course, for the participants there was always ". . . strategy, weighing of alternatives and reasoning about what they were up against if they did not agree." [174] The collective institutions that were involved were really "pressure groups," but Commons saw nothing wrong in that.[175] A choice had to be made between alternative opportunities, for the participants in a bargaining situation were always faced with certain limiting or complementary conditions which could lead to either routine or strategic transactions. Control and manipulation of the environment were related to the limiting factors, while proper selection of time and place illustrated the use of strategical elements. In this way collective behavior made economics a science of activity and, in fact, provided the ultimate unit of investigation, the "going concern." Once an action was defined, it could be described in terms of performance, forebearance, or avoidance.[176]

With the going concern established, Commons now paid attention to the basic equation of economic behavior, the transaction. This implied that the economy had developed far beyond the level of individual exchange, for now it was possible to introduce factors of intangibility. In business parlance, he was dealing with assets rather than physical property.[177] The transaction penetrated law, economics, and ethics, and in its broadest sense involved elements of conflict, dependence, and order.[178] There were three types of transactions: bargaining, managerial, and rationing. Bargaining transactions involved at least five parties: the buyer and seller, the potential buyer and seller, and the court, ever ready to adjudicate issues and to enforce the rules of the capitalist game. Thus the group nature of the relationships was revealed as had seldom been done before. Managerial transactions expressed relationships of superiors to inferiors, as with wage and salary earners. Here the central issues involved command and obedience, with future action representing plans for inputs and output. Rationing transactions were illustrated by decisions of corporate boards, taxation, budgets, and price fixing. Historically, managerial transactions were the oldest, bargaining transactions the newest; but in our society the latter were clearly more important, involving as they did negotiations, transfers of ownership, and a host of legal considerations. But it was the changing assets and liabilities of going concerns that were important, and these in turn involved inducements for future action.[179]

This meant that price had a two-fold aspect, said Commons, for money was paid not only for physical things but to acquire ownership as well. Our economy, consequently, had not been merely one in which production and acquisitiveness were characteristic, but one where ownership was perpetually undergoing alienation.[180] Therefore, in evaluating the nature of a transaction, the courts had to account for four economic factors: transfer of ownership, the money price, the obligation to perform, and the payment. A transaction encompassed all of these. From the standpoint of the time sequence, there were three steps in the process: negotiation, commitment, and performance. Seen in terms of duration, transactions were instantaneous or cash, short term, and long term. Finally, Commons was able to tie together many loose ends through the transaction: persuasion, commitments for future action, or futurity, and the more usual problems of prices and quantities were all wrapped into a single analytic concept.

Once it had been admitted that the courts took part in transactions, there was no escaping the influence of state sovereignty. This was defined as the kind of physical sanction that induced compliance with earlier commitments.[181] It was the process whereby force in human affairs was authorized or prohibited. Compliance, of course, might be obtained through propaganda or other means of moral suasion. These were influences that, by their address to human will, distinguished economics and politics from the other sciences, said Commons. It also explained why concepts of property were intertwined with all the other strands of the social fabric.[182] Commons then decomposed the concept of sovereignty into its three major sectors: the executive, legislative, and judicial, with the last, naturally enough, being most meaningful, because it was supposedly the field in which the ultimate struggles over value took place.

In this context, the state substituted its own power of coercion for that exercised by private persons. Fortunately, Commons reminded us, the development of state power in Western history had moved in the direction of the democratic ideal, so that sovereignty had been more and more applied to the public welfare. Yet he did not deny that private interests often sought to control the state as a means of guaranteeing acquired privileges. The conflict for the control of the state was a serious one, but it was not the Marxian class struggle, said Commons. It was rather a jockeying about for position among numerous groups that were themselves always undergoing shift and change. "The conflicts are . . . the conflicts of labor and capital, of buyers and sellers, of farmers and wholesalers, of borrowers and lenders, and different classes of tax payers."[183] Each group exerted as much pressure as it was able in furthering its own welfare. Commons thought that proportional representation might mitigate the struggle, but it was obvious that he had not taken into his reckoning the fact that political and economic power were unevenly distributed to start with. Fully aware that conflict and contending groups militated against his theory of economic harmony, he nevertheless refused to surrender his hope that in the end reasonable value and peaceful habits would rule the ways of men.

Sovereignty for Commons was one of the five basic principles of economic behavior. The others were efficiency, scarcity, futurity, and working rules.[184] Efficiency had to do with use values: it was, in fact, an engineering concept.[185] Its related transaction type was the managerial one, for its objective was to *produce* goods. Its key notions were output and increases in wealth. Commons devoted a long chapter in his *Institutional Economics* to the idea of efficiency in which every possible relationship to past doctrine was explored.

Yet economics could not avoid the issue of scarcity values. The businessman, said Commons, ". . . sees that . . . the greater the efficiency . . . the greater is the production of wealth. Yet he also sees, from the private standpoint of ownership, of income, of demand and supply . . . that the less is their proprietary value. . . ." [186] Redefining income and output against this backdrop, Commons found that income was the price received by the owner based on his legal right to withhold a service from others while engaged in the proprietary process of bargaining and that output was a service rendered to others regardless of price. A distinction had to be made, consequently, between use value and scarcity value. It was clear that modern business was interested primarily in the latter.[187] Yet use value and scarcity value were inseparable, for both stemmed from the same producing and bargaining situations, the same going concerns. However, they did underlie different visions of society and supplied outlooks that represented fundamental polarities: one was the " . . . proprietary economics of rights and liberties; the other is the engineering economics of input and output."[188]

In the case of futurity, the objective was to have the legal and economic order provide a secure basis for expectations. Contracts had to be fulfilled, for otherwise profits and investments were endangered. "Without this security of expectations, there would be little or no present value, present enterprise, present transactions or present employment. Value is present worth of future net income." [189] Thus the whole structure of debt and credit was encased in the concept of futurity. It now became possible to reinterpret all capitalist behavior as debt and the exchange of negotiable instruments.[190] This introduced time into transactions in a way that permitted the future to influence the present. It explained the whole process of valuation, for if expectations were unrealized then it was clear that values would evaporate. Since every transaction had elements of futurity in it, this implied that dynamic economic factors, and the whole framework of law, government, the credit system, banks, the money market—in fact, the whole economy—were reflected in the transaction.[191]

Commons' critics argued that his concept of reasonable value was incapable of being interpreted in objective ways. He had conceived of reasonableness as the highest degree of working conditions that an industry would reasonably permit.[192] This, he thought, was applying practicality to a seemingly idealistic conception, for it allowed him to investigate particular situations. "A collectivistic theory of value," he said, "derived from existing best practices, from custom, the common law, and the decisions of the courts, could make reasonableness 'objective' and therefore capable of investigation and testimony, leading to the formation of working rules for collective action in control of individual action." [193] The courts would play a stabilizing role, as they moved carefully and examined each conflict in the light of its consequences. The legal approach was pragmatic, said Commons, and inevitably had to lead to reasonableness. If this meant "muddling through," then that was what it was. He did not deny that reasonable value incorporated a large component of ". . . stupidity, passion and mistake . . . ," but such was the nature of human behavior.[194] This made reasonable value an institutional concept: it is not ". . . a rational state of society that determines action, it is a marvelously irrational and complex set of expectations that confronts the participants in transactions. And it is a situation that changes from day to day and century to century. . . . It is out of these complexities and uncertainties that the concepts of reasonable practices and reasonable values emerge and change the institutions themselves from day to day and age to age." [195]

Earlier definitions of value had employed historical cost or present pleasures as basic concepts, as in the case of the classicists and Austrian economists. But only with the evolution of banker capitalism had the notion of value as the future enforcement of contracts come to the fore.[196] This meant a negotiational theory of value and explained why its determination wound up so frequently in the courts. Now, valuation did take usefulness into account, but it was, insisted Commons, future usefulness that was important. Valuation became, in his hands, both a social and individual matter, in which the opportunities and alternatives available to individuals were determined by the collective framework.[197] Said he: "The measurement of value is influenced by all those activities of bankers, politicians and courts, as well as the mass behavior of millions of persons with their psychology of hope or fear, which influence the level of prices, the volume of purchasing power or general prosperity or depression in an economy." [198] Value, of course, would have to consider cost, which was defined as resistance to inducements to perform. It was possible to employ pain or sacrifice concepts, but these were essentially ethical appeals.[199] But when cost was interpreted as the proprietary principle of resistance to risk and hiring out under satisfactory terms, then the actual psychological basis, said Commons, was revealed, with reasonableness demonstrated as the aim of such resistance. Connecting these concepts with the notion of futurity, one discovered value to be the anticipated control of future services—an attempt to induce people to put their resources to work. Cost and value, therefore, became primary concepts in which habit, custom, and persuasion were all involved. Commons finally concluded that political economy was the study of this entire process of attaining reasonable value: it was fundamentally the business of proportioning inducements to use resources by means of certain working rules through certain going concerns. There was no division between utility, sympathy, and duty, and between economics, ethics, and law. Economics was a cultural science based upon transactions in which social valuations were the means of attaining a stable society.

Commons perhaps was best known for his contribution to our understanding of the labor movement. He defended the National Civic Federation against attacks by the socialists, pointing to several strike settlements in which the union had been the major beneficiary.[200] His experience with the 1901 steel strike accounted for his distrust of the labor intellectual, who, he felt, should be content with the role of advisor.[201] At Wisconsin, he set out with John Andrews and Helene Sumner to collect, organize, and classify all existing materials on labor. The search was indeed a fruitful one, as shown by the *Documentary History of Industrial Society.* Several of Commons' essays in this series—notably those on the shoemakers, idealism in American social history, and the effect of business cycles on the growth of trade unionism— provided the basis for what came to be known as the "Wisconsin School" of labor.[202] His approach to trade unionism did not differ in any way from what he did in other areas; every conceivable facet was explored and every conceivable fact was dug up. He wanted to make no judgments, for in this area, at least, he was describing merely the facts of social life. Certainly, conflict was inescapable in the field of industrial relations, but again the urgent thing was to develop appropriate working rules.

Class struggle in the Marxian sense was not essential to trade unionism, said Commons. Did not unions, he asked, antedate the industrial system when class consciousness was supposed to have originated? Actually, the labor movement began as a reaction to the rapacity of the merchant capitalist. The early factory system had been evidenced mainly in textiles, and unions had been virtually unknown in that industry. But the journeyman and the master craftsman had been reduced to a "common level of dependency" by the merchants' extension of the market.[203] The basic social conflict was not between worker and owner, but rather between poor and rich, producer and nonproducer. The worker's viewpoint was, in fact, a property viewpoint and in the growth of unionism this had been a fundamental force. Job rights rather than class interest was the predominant motivation. The problems that workers had to contend with did not stem from the class struggle but originated in such impersonal factors as market competition and monopoly. The conflict usually expressed itself in an antagonism between market price and wages.[204] This culminated in the efforts of trade unionists to protect themselves by advocating such measures as tariffs and the union label. With their interest in job possession the unions had become merely another pressure group striving to protect their rights.[205] But this had been a perfectly reasonable approach, so far as Commons was concerned, with its moral justification provided by its emphasis on free association and self-realization. This implied a kind of "public utility" approach to labor problems. The classicists had looked upon labor as just another commodity. Engineers and scientific management people valued labor only insofar as production was enhanced; the "public utility" view, on the other hand, accorded labor certain rights which had to be respected in the bargaining process, for without them severe conflict would most likely ensue. Goodwill and *esprit de corps* were deemed to be essential elements in establishing industrial harmony.

The key factors in comprehending the character of the American labor movement were pinpointed by Commons as the existence of free land, the growth of markets, popular government, and the influx of immigrants. Labor's reaction to the last especially had revealed its sense of exclusiveness and self-interest.[206] Thus, Commons' observation of labor groups tended to support his conception of contending interests, and his experience with them sustained his belief in the efficacy of conciliation. His was a gradualistic view of the labor movement, friendly to the "business unionism" of the old craft organizations in which the practical issues of wages and hours were given primacy of place. Solution to social problems would have to be piecemeal.[207] Not only did he reject the class struggle, but he looked at participation in political affairs with some doubt. Collective bargaining was essentially a way to maintain the social equilibrium.[208]

Commons, despite his youthful reputation as a radical, was in no way interested in altering basic capitalist relationships. He was really a conservative at heart, always trying to develop voluntary approaches to the solution of industrial relations. That this might require a labor union to match a corporation in size and resources seemed to him quite reasonable. Whatever disputes would arise would be settled by a government commission, anyway. It never occurred to Commons, however, that the latter might be not quite as impartial as his studies had suggested they ought to be.[209] In actuality, class interest frequently does rear its undesirable head and engenders the kind of conflict that Commons abhorred. Indeed, the industrial system has not always been a royal road to reasonable value. Commons became aware of this as a result of the disastrous experience of the depression. Not until the 1940's and 1950's was the placid organization man created in the image of Commons' going concern, for only then did the worker come to know his role as a cog in the wheel of industrial efficiency.[210] That he was happy about it was, as Harvey Swados has said, quite another matter.[211]

It was evident that Commons, while writing his own peculiar challenge to official economic doctrine, was by no means the harsh and sardonic critic that Veblen became. His optimism, rooted in midwestern mores, was entirely alien to the Veblenian or Marxian ethos. He was a rebel only in that he did not hesitate to state his opinions in direct and forthright manner. And this was enough to cause him much grief. Yet all he had wanted to do was to achieve a reasonable settlement of disputes. Actually, his unorthodoxy was merely one of method. Few economists would have done what he did in the *Legal Foundations* and *Institutional Economics;* to distill a theoretical structure through the complex apparatus of several hundred court decisions and dozens of volumes of economic theory was a task that most would have avoided. Nor did his technique make his ideas any the more accessible: the difficulties were compounded by metaphysical intrusions and philosophical explorations of the most obscure points. Jurisprudence, economics, history, psychology, ethics, and politics were mixed in one grand potpourri. And when one had gone through all the material with any measure of care, there was revealed a rather mildly conservative gentleman who was quite comfortable with the outlook and pragmatic approach of a Samuel Gompers.

If the facts that Commons had gathered in a long lifetime of social and economic investigation were set to one side, one would discover that for all his avowed distaste of abstraction, the residue represented perhaps the most abstract theoretical system ever concocted by a native American economist. For Commons, theory had to serve as a clarion call to action. In this he was doubtless part of the great tradition in political economy. Yet the way in which he handled his materials suggested that he was still ensnared by the American pragmatic myth that human intelligence, if only put on to the right track, could solve all the pressing issues at hand.

iii

Wesley C. Mitchell:
Empiricism without Theory

The empirical application of Veblen's institutionalism was achieved by his pupil, Wesley Clair Mitchell (1874-1948). Although known throughout the world primarily as a specialist in business cycle analysis, his contributions stemmed from a deep concern with the broader aspects of economic behavior. Mitchell had always felt that detailed studies of cyclical and secular movement would provide the necessary insights into qualitative change. Business cycle analysis was for him the method par excellence for grasping the nature of the money economy. Moreover, he insisted, the possibilities of social control could be revealed best by the acquisition of such knowledge.[212]

Mitchell, born in Rushville, Illinois, in 1874, was the son of a former Union army surgeon whose forebears had come to the Middle West from New England. As the elder Mitchell was always in poor health, young Wesley had to learn to care for himself and the other members of the family, and he acquired a facility with the mechanical arts that stayed with him for the rest of his life. Years later, when one of Wesley Mitchell's young sons was asked by a teacher what his father did, the boy answered, "He makes cabinets." The teacher inquired whether he did not really lecture at the university. Said the six-year old: "Oh, that's where he goes to talk, but he really makes cabinets." [213]

Mitchell's childhood had been a placid and happy one, contributing no doubt to his later attitude of complete equanimity.[214] While the family was never poor, they were always in financial difficulties, mainly because of Dr. Mitchell's frequent and dubious experiments. Wesley did well at high school and when he heard of the opening of the University of Chicago in 1892, he enrolled there after a year of special preparation at nearby Morgan Park. Since he had always been a good student, the Mitchell family made a special effort to see him through. At Chicago he found a world of thought: sports and fraternities did not interest him. President Harper, determined to build a great school and possessing an ample supply of Rockefeller grants, had been able to bring to Chicago famous scholars from all over the country. The munificent salaries were irresistible, and the professors pirated from other institutions were welcomed so long as they might "advertise" the University.

Here Mitchell met Henry Hatfield, Jacques Loeb, Robert F. Hoxie, John Cummings, and, above all, Thorstein Veblen and John Dewey. The latter were to exert on him the most profound and lasting influences.[215] Although Mitchell had thought of specializing in the Greek and Latin classics, he quickly changed his mind when he discovered economics and philosophy. These disciplines seemed to him kindred in spirit. The technical parts were easy and he found no difficulty in spinning out endless speculations from a single set of premises.[216] This was an exciting intellectual adventure.

Veblen and Dewey had both centered their attention on human behavior, an emphasis that led Mitchell into a study of ethnology, anthropology, and psychology as subjects ancillary to economics and philosophy. To Mitchell, Veblen was a disturbing genius who with great ease upset the complacency of the few students he was able to keep. Compared to the other economists at Chicago, said Mitchell, he was a giant.[217] Added to Veblen's incisive analysis was Dewey's instrumentalist theory, which Mitchell was able to absorb and apply to economics in a telling way. From Veblen he got the idea that the rise and spread of custom and convention was the proper field of economic investigation and that the various theories which purported to explain economic action were themselves conventions that needed explication. This essentially genetic emphasis was attractive to Mitchell, but he was no blind follower of the Veblenian thesis. Years later he expressed his regret that Veblen had not utilized statistical verification. But the distinction between business and industry—which formed the core of the Veblenian attack—struck Mitchell as an especially brilliant perception, and was to play a major role in his own distinction between variations in production and variations in prices. It was related also to the dichotomy between the pursuit of profit, a private activity, and society's general concern with the public welfare. Veblen's massive demolition of orthodox theory was later to be complemented by Mitchell's huge collection of quantitative data. Classical doctrine was no longer the last word in economic science.[218]

In the meantime, Dewey had been spreading the gospel of pragmatism and looking askance at those systems of philosophy that had only their internal logical consistency to recommend them. He was interested in the social roots of philosophy, so that a more suitable explanation of economic action than that provided by British utilitarianism might be made available. He rejected the notion that human beings were motivated solely by the thrust for profit or by the pleasure-pain calculus. It was possible, he said, to achieve a working balance between man's activity and his physical environment. But this demanded the exercise of social intelligence: it implied the broadest conceivable approach in the analysis of social problems, so that classical economics, with its abiding concern for the individual entrepreneur was seen as too narrow a doctrine to be genuinely serviceable. It was rather the complex matrix of social institutions which would have to be investigated if knowledge was to be garnered on the nature of man. Dewey rejected the notion of instincts, preferring to speak of human potentialities or impulses which came to fruition when activated by the social milieu.[219] Impulses, he said, were absorbed into cultural life through the process of integration, after which they were controlled by force of habit. This underpinned Dewey's belief that social conflict could be sublimated in a constructive way. It was all a matter of an effective organization of society so that human needs might be better served. When habits threatened to create conservative institutions, human impulses were bound to crash through the rising barriers. The idea of locating all difficulties in the human environment was quite suited to the American liberal temper and gave a marked impetus to the notion that all that was needed for progress was a high order of social intelligence. These were the intellectual influences that molded Mitchell's outlook.

While at Chicago, he also came under the tutelage of J. Laurence Laughlin, the noted monetary specialist. Laughlin was an effective teacher who required his students to justify their dissent from the received doctrine of John Stuart Mill, at least to themselves.[220] His no-nonsense point of view dispensed with Mill's social philosophy on the ground that it was mere sociology;[221] he also rejected the quantity theory because it unduly emphasized the role of money in price formation. Under Laughlin's guidance, Mitchell began to give his attention to the problem of money, which had become central to economic discussions. Free coinage, the silver question, and declining gold reserves had made it a popular topic in public debate, and Mitchell selected the Civil War Greenback issue for his doctoral thesis. He noted that the value of money shifted with the fortunes of war and government policy, rather than with the quantity of money in circulation. The thesis was later incorporated into his definitive study of the Greenbacks.[222]

In 1893, Mitchell visited Europe and after listening to Conrad and Menger, who made no impression on him, he returned to the United States and completed his doctoral work, receiving the degree *summa cum laude*. Although he had not been trained in statistics, quantitative analysis entered his investigations from the start. He was, as his wife said, ". . . a scientist by temperament and conviction, an economist by profession and . . . a statistician by necessity." [223] After a year's service in the Census Bureau, terminated by a distaste for the servility of Washington clerks, he returned to Chicago to teach and complete his inquiry into the Greenback question. His book, *History of the Greenbacks,* eminently readable and still the authoritative work on the subject, demonstrated such high skill in handling both the descriptive and statistical material as to make digestion of the latter almost painless. The first part was a history of the legal tender acts analyzing the financial situation in 1861, the suspension of specie payments, and Salmon Chase's predilection for Treasury notes. This was followed by a pioneer study of price movements which demonstrated how disparately and irregularly they shifted, enabling profit takers to gain at the expense of the rest of the community. Discovering that existing statistical techniques were inadequate, Mitchell devised new ones. Lacking an index of retail prices, he constructed one of his own. He observed that persons with fixed or lagging incomes resisted price changes that might require larger money outlays. This, plus the conflict between rising food prices and sluggish wages, revealed the institutional tension implicit in so seemingly dry a matter as price movement. Mitchell concluded that the relation of prices to money was a good deal less visible than orthodox theory suggested.[224]

In 1903, Mitchell transferred to the University of California at Berkeley where he met his future wife, Lucy Sprague, the attractive and competent Dean of Women. He was then twenty-eight years old, and when he left California almost a decade later he had attained a pre-eminent place in American economics. Working at an intense pace, he turned out within three years a large quarto volume, *Business Cycles,* published in 1913. Conceived as a preface to a study of the money economy it opened new vistas in statistical analysis. He was able to show how economic problems might be approached in fresh ways, arguing that ". . . figures may often be used to explain our problems, to discover causal relations, to correlate different parts of our knowledge, as well as to supply the material for analysis." [225] Index numbers, he said, could give insight into the nature of price shifts in different markets and at different times in the same market. Wholesale prices, retail prices, raw material, and manufactured goods prices achieved a new importance in economic analysis. So important was Mitchell's work on index numbers that even after World War II he was able to help settle a dispute between labor and industry over the Consumers' Price Index.

At California, Mitchell taught courses in economic institutions, business cycles, and the history of economic thought.[226] He gradually became aware that ". . . the important matter to understand about money is the money economy—that is, the cultural significance of the highly organized group of pecuniary institutions, how they have developed since the Middle Ages, how they have gained a quasi-independence, and how they have reacted upon the activity and minds of their makers." [227] The work of the pure theorists did not appear very helpful to Mitchell, for it seemed that they had no real grip on the nature of the money economy.[228] The price system might reflect business demand occasioned by prospective profit and the ability to meet costs, but behind this façade of sales transactions was the social habit of getting and spending money. This habit had stemmed from a venerable culture dating back several hundred years, and it had created a personality type that conflicted with "basic human nature." Mitchell did not deny that the money economy had contributed much to economic advancement, for, in conjunction with the machine process, it had added considerably to material advancement. In fact, the money economy was essential, since it provided an accounting mechanism and was a device for establishing interdependence and cooperation.

A second work on the Civil War experience, *Gold, Prices and Wages,* followed in 1908. Although Mitchell expressed reservations about both books, (he was always modest about his own output) they were received by fellow economists as important contributions. Once again he devised new statistical techniques in order to follow the movements of time series. What impressed him most was the way in which the prices of different classes of goods moved about, but he refused to look upon these shifts as deviations from some standard of normality.[229] At the same time Mitchell read widely in economic history. He began to evolve the idea that economic theories developed as responses to social problems.[230] This, of course, reflected Veblen's teaching, but it troubled him that the latter's critique had made so little impact on other economists.[231] This, he felt, may have been due to its lack of empirical data, and, in a sense, his own work on business cycles could be visualized as a verification of the Veblenian argument. Mitchell's thinking also began to acquire a sense of teleology. In a revealing letter written to his wife in October 1911, he said:

. . . in all matters of social organization we remain backward: we don't know how to recast our inherited ways of treating each other with anything like the success we have had in recasting our inherited ways of treating [physical and chemical] materials. It is not our will that impedes progress, but lack of knowledge. We putter with philanthropy and coquette with reform when we would fain find a definite method of realizing the demand for social justice which is so strong an element in human nature.[232]

Yet Mitchell never evolved a specific program to meet social ills: he campaigned rather for a method of studying specific problems which would provide the knowledge with which people might intelligently plan for action. Research and education, both concerned with human behavior, were really the only sound tools, he thought.[233]

In 1913, Mitchell moved to Columbia where he remained for the rest of his life. Although several large eastern universities had competed for his services, he preferred to be in New York where he might study and work in the very center of the money economy. An omnivorous reader, he had collected an imposing library, much like other economists before him, notably Stanley Jevons, H. S. Foxwell, and Edwin R. A. Seligman. When his wife once asked him in a pique of exasperation whether he really needed "all those books," he replied, "I might." [234] An excellent stylist, he wrote clearly and lucidly, a rare accomplishment among economists. He would often make corrections merely for form and would frequently read his manuscript aloud, as if to grasp the true cadence of the sentences.[235] It was at about this time that Mitchell began to write a book on the history of economic thought, a project that was never completed. Some of the chapters, published as separate articles, revealed a deep perception into the social origins of economic ideas.[236] But his overwhelming preoccupation with the details of economic life became an insurmountable block to his writing. Fragments which Mitchell left behind tell of his intention to review economic theory in relation to the cultural thought and economic needs of the day. He wanted to know how men in the past had come to believe in the efficacy of hedonism, natural law, and the principles of normality. Classical views would have to be examined from his own standpoint, and, to do this with any genuine historical sense, one would have to grasp the crucial economic and social problems of eighteenth and nineteenth-century England.

The classicists, he thought, had been misled by their failure to comprehend innate drives and irrational behavior.[237] Thus they could not help but overlook the basic fact in modern society—the deep-rooted dichotomy between the neutral logic of the price mechanism and the real motivations of human beings. The profound impact of money on the behavior of men had been forgotten. Hedonism, said Mitchell, which ostensibly reflected a kind of pecuniary logic, had not come to grips with fundamental issues, for it had failed utterly to penetrate the logic of the money system. Concerned as it was with the mechanical laws of supply and demand, classical theory could not explain the habits of men in their use of money.

When World War I exploded, Mitchell went to Washington as Chief of the Price Section of the War Industries Board. The lack of reliable data was a serious handicap, and he did what he could to remedy matters. After the Armistice, he stayed on in Washington to finish a history of prices during the war. This experience reinforced his belief in what he was doing, for once more he saw how valuable statistical information could be when supplied with some semblance of regularity.[238] Upon his return to New York in 1918, he joined with James Harvey Robinson, Charles Beard, and Alvin Johnson in creating the New School for Social Research. Beard had resigned from Columbia in protest against the posture of President Nicholas Murray Butler, and the quartet, together with Thorstein Veblen, formed the nucleus of what was to become a unique institution. Three years later Mitchell returned to Columbia, feeling that the latter's graduates would have a greater influence than those of the New School.[239]

More important for later decades was Mitchell's involvement in the National Bureau of Economic Research. The idea for the Bureau went back to 1917, when Malcolm Rorty, a telephone company statistician, had suggested the creation of an organization to conduct quantitative investigations along independent lines. Yet in a real sense, Wesley Mitchell was its creator, serving as director of research for a quarter of a century. The Bureau's Board of Directors was a true cross-section of American society, with representatives ranging from the American Bankers Association to the socialist-oriented League for Industrial Democracy. Mitchell's own work on business cycles was the prototype for the Bureau's program. Statistical techniques were improved, time series analyses were applied to prices, living costs, interest rates, output, crops, and the like. The result was an unparalleled outpouring of statistical data, some of it so highly refined that only the most esoteric of statisticians could follow the thin thread of analysis. The Bureau's work was truly cast in Mitchell's mode: it made no recommendations, offered no judgments on policy; it simply recorded the facts as they were. To Mitchell, the Bureau was an institution where empirical work might be undertaken on much broader lines than he himself had been able to do. Over the years, numerous projects were developed in such areas as national income, capital formation, banking, transportation, housing and consumer finance, all of which have proven their unquestionable worth as empirical investigations. An outstanding feature of the Bureau's work has been the powerful impetus given to research in national product and income, as exemplified by the studies of Simon Kuznets, Wilford King, and Solomon Fabricant.[240] Mitchell himself co-authored many of the Bureau studies, writing, as well, numerous reports and memoranda on diverse subjects. His 1927 study of cycles, *Business Cycles: the Problem and Its Setting,* was published by the Bureau, as was his posthumous *What Happens During Business Cycles* (1951).

Mitchell's influence was indeed profound. The institutionalist outlook was given new direction toward empirical verification. His courses on business cycles and economic theory were immensely popular, and, while he dealt mainly with social and political backgrounds, his students soon discovered that he was quite adept at handling the more recondite issues of technical theory.[241] He was a superb lecturer who usually spoke with little reference to his notes. Mitchell supposedly suffered from a heart murmur for the greater part of his life, but this seldom inhibited his many activities. At the age of seventy-three he suffered the first of a series of coronary attacks, and on October 29, 1948, he died.[242] His life had been full and indeed satisfying, illustrating an heroic effort to realize his favorite motto: "The Many in the One, the One in the Many."

Mitchell's 1913 *Business Cycles* was a huge tome of over six hundred pages. It reviewed earlier theories, economic organization, business annals, as well as statistical series on prices, wages, interest rates, currencies, and banking. Part III, the famous description of what happens in the upswings and downswings, was later reprinted separately.[243] Earlier theories of cyclical change, said Mitchell, had exhibited a certain measure of plausibility, but it was essential to check them by the "collection and analysis of elaborate records of business experience in quantitative form." [244] In the main, earlier writers, lacking detailed data, had selected some strategic factor as the leading causal element. Theories had been abundant, virtually one for each supposed cause. But Mitchell wanted his study to be a "tested explanation of experience instead of an exercise in logic." [245] He focused his attention on the search for profit, to which the ebb and flow of economic activity was inescapably tied. The governing factors during a crisis stemmed from a desire to maintain solvency and minimize losses. Since business fluctuations were so widespread, it appeared reasonable to suppose that they were endemic to our business dominated culture. Each phase of the cycle was found to pass into the next, as the economy was subjected to a process of cumulative change. Thus, the seeds of a recession always were to be found in the antecedent prosperity.

Yet more and ever more facts were needed, since each new cycle exhibited its own idiosyncracies. "Business history repeats itself," he said, "but always with a difference." Consequently, it was impossible to construct a completely generalized theory of cycles. Sometimes revivals did not pass into prosperity, but simply collapsed, as in 1895 and 1910. Sometimes a period of stress took place in the midst of prosperity, as in 1896. "Every business cycle, strictly speaking, is a unique series of events and has a unique explanation, because it is the outgrowth of a preceding series of events, likewise unique." [246] The matrix for Mitchell's problem was, of course, the money economy, in which corporate enterprise and the machine process conspired to create regular oscillations in activity. It seemed to him that the pursuit of profit and the impact that this was bound to have on prices was the nexus par excellence for ordering empirical data. Within this framework, wholesale and retail prices, transportation, manufacturing, banking, and finance could be examined in all their complexity. The very diversity of the material, however, was no occasion for despair; Mitchell was certain that by selecting even a few uniform series out of the maze of sequences, some suitable guides to policy could be evolved. Such a procedure would provide a sound basis for a "descriptive analysis" of the business cycle and all speculations could then be submitted to empirical tests.

Although it was possible to begin at any point in the business sequence,

Mitchell started with the revival. The "conspicuous agent" which could stir entrepreneurs from depression doldrums was some striking event, such as a favorable crop, new overseas markets, or a spurt in investment. In each case it was the widening opportunity for profit that set things moving. This meant that the important quantitative factors were business receipts and expense, sales volume, available currency, and bank credit. The way in which these acted on one another determined profitability. Revival's upward movement was initiated when disinvestment halted, inventories were replaced, new business opportunities were discovered, and consumers began to fulfill postponed needs. Such forces combined to impel an increase in demand, permitting prices and sales to move ahead of costs, thus enhancing profitability.[247] This was the beginning of Mitchell's famous lead and lag situation in which all the factors were interpreted as internal or endogenous elements.

Revival periods, once started, spread rapidly, he said. Impulses moved out from industries which felt the first stimulus back to raw materials and supplementary goods. Retailers began to benefit from the increased demand, and, as the revivalist forces became cumulative, an optimistic bias was imparted to businessmen in general. "As it spreads, the epidemic of optimism helps to produce conditions that both justify and intensify it." [248] Yet lags could occur at this time, as in the case of agriculture. Nevertheless, the general tendency was for prices to push upward. The cumulative impact of increased demand continued. Whatever lags were revealed could be attributed to the stickiness of retail prices relative to wholesale prices, the stickiness of wholesale prices as compared with goods-in-process, and the lag of the latter behind raw materials. Wholesale prices of consumer goods rose more quickly but "less considerably" than those of manufactured producers' goods, while mineral prices moved faster than agricultural prices.[249]

Mitchell then analyzed the causes for these rigidities and movements in a way that revealed in most striking fashion his perceptive view of the economy. Wage rate movements were examined and found not to move in the way commodity prices moved: here the strength of trade unions was a significant factor.[250] Yet wage rates often tended to lag behind selling prices, giving entrepreneurs an advantage during the upswing. This stimulated investment, although it was found that the ". . . growth of industrial equipment is . . . very uneven." [251] When business investment achieved sizeable proportions, an even sharper stimulus was relayed to business activity, and economic expansion was rendered still more intense. "The salient feature of the whole development," said Mitchell, "is that each successive effect reacts to strengthen the causes that produced it, so that the movement toward prosperity gathers momentum as it proceeds." [252] Seemingly, this process might go on forever, but the necessary balance could not be sustained. Maladjustment brought the whole business to a grinding halt, as prosperity turned into crisis. Increased costs and higher fixed charges contributed to the strain.

Competition for limited resources compounded the difficulty, as stringencies in capital markets began to manifest themselves. Businessmen discovered that they no longer could secure money at the old rates of interest. And the net effect of these movements was a decline in prospective profits. Again, the various sequences were unevenly distributed as the upper turning point was reached.[253]

It was at this juncture that some economists, notably Alvin Hansen, argued that Mitchell's analysis of price movement was not incisive enough. It failed, said Hansen, to explain the *causes* of cyclical change.[254] He contended that quite frequently profit peaks were reached early in an upswing and remained at high levels throughout the movement. Consequently, he continued, it was unwarranted to say that the turning point was traceable to a decline in prospective profit, for this was a result of cyclical change rather than a cause.[255] Furthermore, said Hansen, new investment was not a function of the current average rate of profit, but was related rather to the prospective return of additional increments of investment. Yet Mitchell had spoken of prospective profit, so that Hansen's charge was merely a complaint that the role of capital investment had been slighted and that a theory of oscillations could not tell the whole story.

A large part of Mitchell's analysis paralleled Veblen's, especially the description of pyramided credit found in *The Theory of Business Enterprise*.[256] The emphasis in Mitchell was on shifts in profitability occasioned by the forced liquidation of accumulated debt. The crisis itself might be initiated by the collapse of an important enterprise, a crop failure, or a political upset. The analysis was illustrated with a remarkably detailed description of the financial crisis of 1907. The cessation of the crisis had come when pressures for liquidation were halted and businessmen had successfully withstood everything.[257] Yet those revival forces that had appeared could often be abortive and when no mass of new orders was forthcoming, hopes for renewed prosperity could be blighted. In the usual order of things, a move into the depression phase was inevitable. Prices would begin to drop, but again in uneven fashion. Wholesale prices moved faster than those at retail, and raw materials reacted even more sharply.[258] Yet in the process of decline, readjustments developed which set the stage for recovery. Costs were reduced, fixed charges realigned, bad debts liquidated, and after two or three years the demand for goods began to pick up.[259] Once marginal firms were squeezed out, there was a renewed desire to assume risks and investment could be undertaken once more. Such actions were enhanced by the fall in interest rates, contributing to a restoration of favorable prospects for profit.[260]

While Mitchell's model exhibited an oscillatory character, he insisted that no two cycles had the same combination of elements.[261] The underlying factors were simply different, even though a regular waxing and waning of business activity could not be denied. This was deeply rooted in the nature of the business system: each new change became the basis for further change, all taking place in an inexorably cumulative manner.[262] Business cycles in the modern sense had not appeared prior to the advent of industrialism, and in earlier times economic upsets could have been traced to speculative activity or wars. But with the rise of the factory system, the growth of transportation, and the development of new ways of doing business, the phenomenon of cycles had made its appearance. "Business cycles appear at that stage of economic history when the process of making and distributing goods is organized chiefly in the form of business enterprises conducted for profit." [263]

The regularity with which cycles made their appearance, said Mitchell, suggested possibilities for their control through such devices as banking reform or the use of government spending as a balance wheel.[264] Here he was influenced by Beatrice and Sidney Webb, to whom he acknowledged his debt in a characteristically generous way. Mitchell was attracted to their work because they had successfully demonstrated how the economic process could be used as an analytical concept, as in their study of trade unionism. They had dealt with real motives, not a hypothetical economic man.[265] Even Irving Fisher's "stabilized dollar" plan was looked upon as a useful device.

The phenomenon of cycles, related as it was to the business of making money, was not necessarily an outgrowth of the production of goods. In fact, expansion and contraction in the making of goods was seldom as severe as in the "corresponding pecuniary values." Yet the money economy had become so pervasive that it was able to harness successfully the productive forces of society and stamp its own set of values on human activity.[266] Money also had established a pecuniary basis for status and distinction, giving rise to social classes. Mitchell's main concern, however, was to study how the "technical exigencies" of the money economy subjected economic activity to the perpetual oscillations of the business cycle. Obviously economic theory could no longer treat money as a mere symbol of some deeper reality, for money-making was the goal of human endeavor. And this was the essence of capitalism.

Although Mitchell's analysis was generally well received by the profession, some economists chided him with having failed to construct a complete theoretical tool kit. In their view, his study had remained on the surface of economic problems: it was primarily descriptive, they said, and failed to touch on the critical issues raised by such questions as the investment process.[267] Others, however, argued that it was possible, for example, to translate Mitchell's system into the Keynesian language of multipliers, propensities, and accelerators.[268] An interesting, and on the whole successful, attempt to do this was undertaken by Milton Friedman of the University of Chicago.[269] While Mitchell had grave reservations as to the usefulness of purely theoretical work, Friedman showed how a theory of relative price change could be distilled from the *Business Cycles*. The various leads and lags on which Mitchell had placed great emphasis suggested the later techniques of econometrics and difference equations. A theoretical basis was revealed by the stress on the rational nature of the money economy, by the way in which the quantity theory of money was employed, and by Mitchell's recognition of substantial differences between cycles. The lag of expenditures behind receipts, the variations in price responses, the advance of decisions to invest over actual commitments, all suggested the kind of theoretical formulations that have now entered the common parlance of economists. It may very well have been Mitchell's constitutional inability to bridge the gap between his descriptive analysis and the more elegant mathematics of the theoreticians that accounted for the apparent disparity. Yet, as Friedman remarked, virtually every element of present day cycle theory can be found imbedded in Mitchell's *Business Cycles*.[270]

In Mitchell's eyes, theory had to be an explanation of actual business experience rather than logical legerdemain. His analysis of business cycles had described certain fundamental sequences which, while exhibiting numerous leads and lags, nevertheless comprised a series of regular movements from prosperity to depression. There was no single, unique cause for this action, he said: the only outstanding feature was the existence of change. It was precisely this belief that subjected the analysis to a fair amount of criticism, for it was felt that Mitchell's pluralism had evaded the search for really basic factors.[271] This bias suggested extreme caution in any program of practical action. With so many details to be listed, in the end nothing really could be accomplished. And as applied by Mitchell's direct intellectual descendants, particularly, the pluralistic approach became just as evasive as those which explained economic movement by single causes.[272]

Several more works on business cycles came from Mitchell's pen. The 1913 study was updated in 1927; *Measuring Business Cycles* was produced jointly with Arthur F. Burns in 1946; and the posthumous *What Happens During Business Cycles* was issued in 1951. Mitchell had planned still another volume which was to have finally fused the economic theory implicit in the voluminous statistical data which had been collected through the years. This book was never written. The final irony of Mitchell's long career was his inability to produce such a work: it was to have been a carefully "balanced statement interpreting the data that . . . had already been analysed, built into a broad picture of the way our money economy works in present day culture." [273] The central theme undoubtedly would have been what one finds in all of Mitchell's studies: that the business cycle is a complex of oscillatory movements which differ throughout the economic system. The 1927 volume, essentially an expansion of the first three chapters of the earlier work, took advantage of the existence of additional information, but in no way altered the basic conception. The various theories that others offered were again looked upon as so many shots in the dark. Nor did the description of business oscillations tell much about *levels* of activity. It appeared that Mitchell's cyclical phases required a somewhat broader backdrop than he had been able to supply. What became important now were problems relating to the absolute amount of investment and employment. Nevertheless, the second chapter of the 1927 volume was a truly remarkable performance. It revealed Mitchell's deep understanding of the historical roots of business enterprise in a way that had been seldom equalled. The monetary basis of the capitalist economy was again emphasized, and evidence was offered, based on intensive studies of business annals, to demonstrate that cycles were a phenomenon peculiar only to the realm of business institutions.[274] One found here too the basic ideas for national product accounting. And, as Joseph Schumpeter observed, there was almost a Walrasian character in Mitchell's notion of interdependence.

This elaborate apparatus was sustained by a decidedly new concept of the nature of man—new for the science of economics. From the beginning Mitchell had questioned the usefulness of hedonic psychology, and by 1914 he had begun to wonder whether a new approach might not be made available by the other social sciences. In a perceptive article on the subject written for the *Quarterly Journal of Economics,* he said: "Human nature is in large measure a social product, and among the social activities that shape it, the most fundamental is the particular set of activities with which economists deal." [275] With this almost Marxian proposition, he thus set out to review the latest contributions of the psychologists and other social scientists. While most of this is but of historical interest now, it does underscore Mitchell's abiding concern with these matters. Thorndike's numerous propensities, for example, while looked upon with some doubt, seemed to provide a useful plastic frame for the concept of man in economics.[276] In addition, Graham Wallas' view that human nature in one generation was nurtured by the activities of the previous one seemed to be a helpful idea. Mitchell's close study of the newer psychology convinced him that his rejection of utilitarianism had been correct. Like Veblen before him, he found that instincts, in the sense that they strived toward certain ultimate goals, could be useful categories of analysis. The application of intelligence and pragmatic means to instincts helped meet the ends of human behavior. In fact, many of the instrumental means utilized in this process were also deemed to be instinctual in nature. For Mitchell, this was a psychology better suited than hedonism for grasping the genetic approach to social institutions.[277] It could also provide a meaningful basis for social reform, since it could be argued that variations in means made human nature genuinely malleable. Here the stress was placed on variations, for these enabled economics to become a study of behavior as it manifested itself in a set of evolving institutions.

This led Mitchell to the concept of institutions, which provided standards and norms of behavior rooted in habits of acting and thinking. However, this was only the matrix of behavior, for the individual had to exercise his intelligence while participating in social activity, a notion not very distant from Commons' view of human volition. Mitchell acknowledged that Marx perhaps was the first institutionalist, for he had wrestled with the problem of internal change in a genuinely serious way. But Marx had never severed his ties to the classical mode of thinking, and his Hegelian philosophy imposed a mechanical formula onto social forms. Veblen, thought Mitchell, was superior to Marx since his notion of change had not employed an unnecessary metaphysic. Sombart too seems to have influenced Mitchell, but unlike these writers he had not broadened the institutionalist vision beyond the search for profit. Money, said Mitchell, was no mere veil, no simple medium of exchange, but the vehicle of economic life, in which the making and spending of money was the preponderant feature. The production of goods under this régime was dependent largely on the prospect of making money.[278] This was *the* logic of contemporary existence, rather than the "real forces" disclosed by the economics of normality and equilibrium. In the latter, money served only as a *numéraire* or a device to facilitate exchange without special significance. Yet in our society, said Mitchell, the demand for money takes primacy of place, and it is this fact which underlies the kind of institutions we enjoy. Older economists had been quite mistaken when they held money to be but a superficial phenomenon.[279] The so-called psychological school of Fetter and Davenport was quite right, he said, in trying to get economics back on the track of the pecuniary logic, for from the pervasive use of money there was derived not only useful theoretical concepts but all the countinghouse attitudes that permeated society.[280] Money might not be the root of *all* evil, commented Mitchell wryly, but it certainly was the root of economic science.[281]

One essay which demonstrated perhaps more than any of the others Mitchell's institutional perception was the famous *Backward Art of Spending Money*.[282] In it he contrasted the arts of making and spending money. Our pecuniary culture placed great emphasis on the former, but the art of spending clearly failed to keep pace with it. This, said Mitchell, was not necessarily due to any spendthrift proclivities, but stemmed rather from conditions quite beyond the control of the individual. The family once had been the chief producing and consuming unit, but now only the latter function remained and even for this it was ill-fitted. Spending via the family unit was uneconomic and inefficient, and there was no way of computing true costs of household operation. Echoing the Veblenian thesis, Mitchell found that spending all too frequently was intended to advance the purposes of emulation and invidious comparison.[283] It became one of the chief avenues for status-seeking.

Nor did the process of making goods necessarily culminate in want satisfaction, as the classicists had supposed. It was rather the major mode of making money. Profit could be enhanced by a curtailment of productive activity. But want satisfaction, or welfare, had to be measured by increases in commodities and services.[284] Yet, unlike his mentor Veblen, Mitchell did not castigate the businessman for this attitude, since the latter had been compelled to pursue profit "by the system of which we are all parts." [285] Without profit, the entrepreneur could not make goods, and no blame should be assigned to anyone for a situation that "bristles with economic contradictions." In this respect, Mitchell was much closer to Commons than to Veblen, for, he said, despite its very serious limitations, the money economy had turned out to be the best form of economic organization that man had yet been able to construct.

Mitchell's attitude toward economic theory, consequently, could only be instrumentalist. Theory would have to delineate the relationship between pecuniary institutions and human behavior. There was little doubt but that the money economy had a profound impact on the way in which man obtained knowledge of himself and his environment. This meant that attention had to be paid to money institutions.[286] Traditional theory was in no position to accomplish the necessary job of investigating such problems because it lacked historical imagination. Mitchell made this point especially clear in his essay on Wieser. By maintaining an institutionalist view, he said, one can open

. . . vistas enticing to future exploration, instead of suggesting a closed system of knowledge. [One] does not delude himself into believing that anyone's personal experience is an adequate basis for theorizing about how men behave: rather is he eager to profit by any light shed upon his problem by any branch of learning— history, statistics, ethnology, psychology.[287]

Once the economist became aware of this, it could be shown that the cash nexus would provide a better approach than the calculus of utility. "Money is the most effective practical instrument for systematizing economic control . . . because its use enforces the strictest discipline upon vague and careless human nature." [288] This did not mean that the more common type of price theory found in Marshall and his epigones was to be disposed of entirely; rather, said Mitchell, it was to be removed from the center of economic interest.[289] Only then would economics become a full-fledged quantitative science and a useful instrument for social control.[290] The classical system was not the whole of theoretical analysis, he continued, for it had become a kind of pecuniary logic which masqueraded as an explanation of human behavior, failing to realize that money standardized wants and colored the vision of men.[291] Mitchell might have agreed with C. Wright Mills when the latter said that social science has evolved into "a set of bureaucratic techniques which inhibit social inquiry by 'methodological' pretensions, which congest such work by obscurantist conceptions, or which trivialized it by concern with minor problems unconnected with publicly relevant issues." [292] Above all else, Mitchell was no grand theorist.

The purpose of Mitchell's quantitative method then was to measure activity rather than utility. His essay on Bentham underscored the fruitlessness of attempts to calculate degrees of want satisfaction, which, he said, had been the source of most of the difficulties encountered by the theorists. The measurement of utility offered no precise index of economic activity per se, making the pleasure-pain calculus simply useless.[293] For this view, Mitchell was charged with having been guilty of overemphasis. Paul Homan once said that he had not been a complete spokesman for the institutionalist viewpoint. "He shrinks from the philosophical, the intangible, the incommensurable. And if such reticence is pardonable in the economist whose gaze is centered upon the marts of trade, it ill becomes one who thinks of economics as the study of human behavior and human institutions. . . ." [294]

This, of course, is incorrect. As any number of writers have noted, it is entirely possible to relate Mitchell's concepts to the more theoretical approaches. Indeed, Allan Gruchy has shown that one can work from pure theory to institutionalist economics and at the same time forward from empirical investigation to theoretical formulations.[295] Keynesian economics, for example, has revealed any number of propositions which could have been distilled from Mitchell's *Business Cycles*. But the Keynesians abstracted from the political and social background and did not relate adequately their deductions to those flowing from other social sciences. This Mitchell assuredly would have criticized sharply. As Morris Copeland has said, the only areas of agreement between theoretical model builders and institutionalists are to be found at two points: that hypotheses should fit available data, and that one should be able to fill theoretical equations with empirical conent, since otherwise they would lack objectivity.[296]

Mitchell most clearly revealed how he felt about economic theory in his *Lectures on Types of Economic Theory*.[297] These unauthorized notes, taken down verbatim by one of his students, demonstrated his conception of theoretical analysis as a cultural expression and statement of social attitudes. They also suggested that had Mitchell written the book on theory he had been promising himself all his life, it unquestionably would have been a major work, comparable to Schumpeter's *History of Economic Analysis*. In his lectures, Mitchell covered the classicists down through Marshall and followed with sections on Jevons, Walras, Sombart, Schmoller, Fetter, Davenport, and, of course, Thorstein Veblen. He reviewed the social background and political climate as well as the individual preconceptions of each writer. By doing so he was able to work out a truly genetic account of the growth of economic thought. He had certain rather clearly defined concepts to guide him—the need for a proper psychology of human action; a rejection of purely deductive equilibrium theories; the need for verifiable data; economics as a study of institutions; cooperation between the different social sciences; and acceptance of economic planning for the advancement of welfare. The *Lectures,* an admirable fusion of economics with the history of political and social thought, underscored these precepts perhaps more than anything else Mitchell produced. As Gruchy has remarked, he was explaining the economic theorists rather than the theories.[298] The theme of Mitchell's work was stated by his remark that "the economic theorists who have counted most in the development of thought have been men who have been deeply concerned with problems that troubled their generations. Their theories have been attempts to deal scientifically with these problems, to point out promising means of practical action." [299]

When the Depression and the New Deal came along, Mitchell was called upon to lend his aid in the crisis.[300] This experience strengthened his belief in the need for planning. This was the nation's most important and most difficult task. But whatever else it was, insisted Mitchell, it was not un-American. Planning, he reminded his readers, could be found in the Articles of Confederation, Hamilton's scheme for a new economic system, and in wartime programs for mobilization.[301] In a talk to the economics club at Columbia in 1941, he again stressed the importance of factual knowledge for planning.[302] While he did not dismiss theory, he expressed greater preference for the fact economist as against the word economist. "In formulating economic policies to meet the present emergency," he said, "we shall find the empirical knowledge acquired by our science of inestimable value." But, he continued, "to get the most out of this knowledge we must use it analytically. That is, we must work as theorists with the data at our disposal." [303]

Mitchell had always felt that civilization could be solidly based only on cooperation between men. Although Western culture had emphasized individual development, he knew that social evolution would mean the reshaping of institutions through common effort. This was a process rooted in interdependence and knowledge. If the goal of amelioration implied government participation in the economy, Mitchell was unconcerned. The fact was, he said, that planning by business alone had not been successful.[304] Nor was he upset because this might subordinate economic inquiry to the objectives of welfare standards. His conception of economics, consequently, was essentially a moral one, perhaps without the heated indignation of a Marx, but still one that sought a high social purpose. Yet he approached the whole area of planning with characteristic hesitancy. When he was awarded the first Francis A. Walker medal by the American Economic Association in 1947, he urged caution in giving advice. There was a marked responsibility in guiding policy, he said, which could be sustained only by the accumulation of factual knowledge.[305] His interest in planning clearly stemmed from his book on business cycles. As early as 1923 he had thought enough information had been gathered to alleviate economic crises. He advocated the establishment of unemployment insurance, a somewhat radical proposal for the period. During the New Deal days he helped set up the National Resources Board which was intended to be a kind of central planning agency. He was aware that such developments would create a mixed economy.[306] In the *Recent Economic Changes,* written for President Hoover's Committee on Social Trends, he observed that a kind of neo-Malthusian economics was becoming widespread as reflected in the idea of high wages for corporate executives. Yet mass markets for consumer goods could be assured only when wages kept pace with output. He deemed the standard solution for bad times—wage reductions—to be a positive barrier to economic revival, a proposition that was to be demonstrated over and over again during the depression.[307] He also viewed technological unemployment as a serious problem, for any substantial increase in new jobs at that time appeared moot. Economic planning therefore was a rational requirement for the solution of the problems then plaguing society. These views were presented by Mitchell through numerous lectures and talks as part of his wish to educate the public on the need for such a program, for planning was to him essential to an orderly economy.[308] Mitchell never faltered in his belief in progress through the exercise of intelligence. He never forgot the lesson of his teacher, John Dewey.

Yet an attack was to issue from those who otherwise might have sympathized with him. His colleague at Columbia, the noted sociologist, Robert S. Lynd, seriously questioned such notions and pretensions in his *Knowledge For What?* [309] Mitchell was taken to task for continuing to operate within a closed system of data collection, index numbers, bank clearings and time series. No genuine attempt, said Lynd, was made to study real human behavior. While examining price movements, for example, no investigation was made of the process of price determination. Although information on savings was gathered, people's motives for saving were not studied. Emphasis on profit overlooked the palpable fact that nonmonetary incentives might also be at work. But, Lynd charged, the most serious failure was the economist's rejection of the problem of economic power as a serious subject for examination.[310] As a result, the fact-gatherer developed a flat empiricism which had no relationship to a system of values. By ignoring the potentialities for good or evil implicit in certain institutions, only facts *qua* facts were accumulated. Such a view not only assumed that facts were self-serving, but, in effect, rejected the central role of hypothesis-making in science. Mitchell's procedure, implied Lynd, said nothing about the worthwhileness of an institution, for it simply accepted things as they were and thereby established a conservative bias in social science. It was an evaluation of the *function* of an institution that was needed, argued Lynd.[311]

Mitchell responded to this sharp criticism in his usual gentle manner.[312] He agreed with Lynd's general aim and reiterated his belief that the social sciences justified themselves only by making contributions to the advancement of human welfare. He acknowledged that contemporary culture was thwarting human personality. Yet Mitchell could reply to his colleague's sweeping indictment only with the remark that ". . . such progress as mankind has made is due chiefly to its acquisition of knowledge of the kind that can be applied practically to the achievement of its ends." [313] This mere restatement of the empiricist credo, however, did not seem forceful enough. Basically, Mitchell had no satisfactory reply to Lynd's well-grounded attack. More and more it came to be realized that, aside from the occasional broader pronunciamentos, the main body of Mitchell's work suffered from its extreme limitation to facts.

Yet Mitchell was not unaware of the broader vistas of social science. It was simply that the institutional and empirical facets of his outlook did not appear to be fully integrated. He realized that when economists began to deal with real problems they must cross swords with physiologists, psychologists, anthropologists, political scientists, ethnologists, linguistic experts, and historians. They must know that man has a biologic structure as well as emotions and habits which function in a culture. Man is a whole and must be seen in the round. Economic valuations are social valuations, economic facts are social facts. Of course, Mitchell knew all this. He also knew that such an integrated outlook would dispense with the infatuation with utilities, want satisfaction and the logic of choice. The instrumentalist philosophy which he had imbibed from Dewey seldom left him.[314] But it was never made clear how detailed quantitative analysis *alone* would achieve the common objective of all social scientists.[315]

The extreme empiricism of Mitchell's later outlook was exemplified in the work of the National Bureau of Economic Research upon which he had so indelibly placed his mark. The Bureau's study of business cycles began with so-called reference dates which it validated by studies of business annals and a variety of other tests.[316] In studying its collection of time series, seasonal effects were first removed, permitting a series to be marked off into various segments so that conformity with the previously determined reference dates might be ascertained. From this, a determination of leads and lags was then made. Thus the pattern of change repeated in each cycle could be established. This was the framework for observing the historical peaks and troughs of cyclical movement. It was found that the average duration of the reference cycle from 1854 to 1949 was 49 months, with an expansion averaging 29 months or 59 per cent of the cycle period, and that contractions averaged 20 months or 41 per cent of the cycle. The segmentation process was then intended to permit comparisons of the various series in a relatively easy manner.

The next step was to work out measures of conformity, of which there were said to be three—conformity to the expansion of general business, to contraction and to the full cycle. The indices that were prepared were supposed to reveal the direction and rate of change of the various movements. Supplementing these were measures of amplitude, timing, and duration, which were supposed to show the extent to which the various cycles exhibited common features. As Arthur F. Burns has said, the method was intended to show the "business cycle" as a consensus of specific cycles.[317] To Burns, this meant that in the whole complex of changes in the many series used in the calculations there was ". . . a continual transformation of the economic system . . . beneath the surface phenomenon of aggregate expansion and contraction. A business cycle expansion does not mean that nearly everything within the economy is moving upward, nor does a business cycle contraction mean that nearly everything is shrinking." [318] The "business cycle" consequently, emerged as an artificial construct which merely compressed a body of disparate data into various patterns, with the hope that some usable knowledge would be gleaned from the cleansing process. Interestingly enough, the Bureau found no confirmation of the Kitchin, Juglar, Kondratieff theory—short, medium, and long cycles—propounded by Schumpeter.[319] It seemed that in the United States, at least, the 40-month cycle was more characteristic, since the other variations were randomly distributed. This was said to confirm the Bureau's empirical approach.

The Bureau's method was adapted also to short-run forecasting purposes, notably in Geoffrey H. Moore's device of leading and lagging series.[320] Moore selected 21 series as being the most consistent in their lead-lag behavior when compared to the standard reference cycle. Among the leading series were new incorporations, business failures, residential building, common stock prices, average weekly hours worked, and new orders for durable goods. Lags were found in personal income, retail sales, inventories, and bank rates. There were also coincident series, such as corporate profits, employment, industrial production, wholesale prices, and freight-car loadings. Yet the method had some serious limitations. It was useful solely in the short run, for Moore could report leads for only about six months. Furthermore, the device indicated turning points only and said nothing about amplitude. Nor, as Alvin Hansen has shown, have they been entirely accurate.[321]

The Mitchell technique aroused criticism on other grounds as well. Joseph A. Schumpeter in a review of the 1927 volume charged that it seriously underestimated the value of theoretical discourse.[322] Theory, said Schumpeter, was not a matter of putting forth tentative suggestions and then checking them with a collection of statistical data. The validity of a theoretical argument could be ascertained just as well in analytical terms, argued

Schumpeter. While for Mitchell, theory was a body of rational hypotheses and generalizations to be derived from a set of ordered facts, Schumpeter held that

> . . . science cannot progress after a certain stage has been reached, without the construction of tools of thought different from those of every day life, growing up as the result of conscious effort: *id est,* without a theory, which has . . . little to do with metaphysical speculation or political doctrine . . . and which is not an unscientific or provisional substitute for facts, but an instrument . . . needed in order to discern the facts.

That is, theory was to be essentially a guide to research. Of course, it must always be constructed to permit numerical treatment and to allow for modifications in theory as new facts are brought to light. Schumpeter obviously objected to what the thought was a complete and unwarranted rejection of theory in Mitchell.

Nor did Schumpeter think that the distinction between money and a moneyless economy was very fruitful. Of course, said he, the impact of money was important, but he dismissed it as mere sociology. The concept of a business economy was more significant if rooted in the division of labor.[323] Furthermore, said Schumpeter, as if applying the *coup de grâce,* Mitchell's price system was nothing more than a verbal restatement of Walras' general equilibrium scheme, a translation that was to be explained by an inherent dislike of theoretical work. While Schumpeter applauded the effort to obtain more statistical information, he questioned whether calculating averages, indices, coefficients of correlation, trends, and deviations from trends were genuinely significant. These were what C. Wright Mills was later to call "abstracted empiricism," lacking relation to some basis for judgment. A trend analysis, for example, made sense when it was derived ". . . only from previous theoretical considerations, which must not only guide us in interpreting results, but also in choosing the method. Failing this, a trend is no more than a descriptive device summing up past history with which nothing can be done. It lacks economic connotations. It is, in fact, merely formal." [324] The trouble with a trend analysis, continued Schumpeter, is that it can be decomposed in a variety of ways which may not necessarily have any connection with each other. And the cause of this trouble, said the Austrian, rested in Mitchell's reluctance to employ theory not as hypothesis but as a tool of analysis.

Further blows were levelled at the Mitchell approach by Edward Ames and T. C. Koopmans.[325] Ames complained that Burns and Mitchell had failed to establish a genuine model of the business cycle despite their 1200-some-odd time series. The only approximation to a model was the statement that cycles are a "type of fluctuation," a rather inconclusive proposition. Nevertheless, matching specific cycles against the reference cycle suggested a belief that some pattern could be exposed by the process of averaging. Yet an inconsistency patently appeared in Mitchell's method, said Ames, since random elements seemed to dominate the systematic features revealed in the time series. There was, consequently, no genuine sense of periodic change in the Bureau approach and no real hypothesis of the nature of cycles as an independent factor in the business economy.[326] With long cycles excluded from the analysis and the reference cycle utilized as a device to detect similarities in movement only, interest focused entirely upon the short run. The only norm in Mitchell's study of cycles was the arbitrary average which failed to reveal the truly dynamic economic forces. How, for example, was one to interpret a lead or lag? Which was the cause and which the effect? What of cycles that did conform to the reference pattern? Did these get their impulses from independent forces or from the reference cycle as well? These questions remained unanswered, as the structure was revealed to be exclusively empirical and not all analytical.

Koopmans was even harsher, saying that the whole approach was essentially arid. He contended that the selection of certain time series, such as pig iron production as related to consumer durable goods output, could not be validated without an adequate theoretical framework. The brutal question he posed was: are the various series relevant? Yet this could be determined only by reference to some idea of how the particular series affected economic fluctuations.[327] Burns and Mitchell had been talking about the behavior of time series, said Koopmans, whereas the object of a complete analysis would have been to study the behavior of social groups. Consequently, the definition of the terms used by Burns and Mitchell stemmed from a mechanical application of conceptual material. What had emerged from the whole collection of statistics was a flat, one-dimensional portrayal of economic reality.

A proper theoretical analysis would have actually introduced observations of motions and habits and, even though possibly incomplete, would have at least provided *direction* to the analysis. Moreover, as a tool of research, theory offered standards for the selection of appropriate empirical data. In Burns and Mitchell, everything had been tossed into the statistical hopper, so that the possibility of identifying the really significant relationships had been obscured. "The movements of economic variables are studied as if they were the eruptions of a mysterious volcano whose boiling caldron can never be penetrated." [328] The characterization seemed an apt one, for, in its last stages, cyclical behavior in Mitchell's work was drowned by random variations. Koopmans pointed out that this could have been avoided if a set of structural equations had been utilized. This, he contended, would have yielded a good deal more information about dynamic change than all the facts gathered in the gigantic Burns and Mitchell opus. Koopmans seemed to regret that so much energy had gone into time series analysis when the empirical testing of a few macroeconomic aggregates might have been more fruitful.

Nevertheless, Mitchell's influence was so widespread as to assure him an honored place in the history of economics. Always able to present his views clearly and persuasively, his contributions to statistical technique could not be gainsaid. His criticism of standard economics was on the whole salutary. Too much of the usual type of model building had been grounded in assumptions of perfect competition, automatism, and an identification of private self-interest with the common weal. While the institutionalists were frequently fuzzy about the sort of model they would employ, their pragmatic quality was all to the good. They did not deny the role that value judgments played in economics—something the model builders were wont to avoid. Institutionalism implied a conscious attitude of reform: to traditionalists this was anathema. Nor did Mitchell and his followers believe that filling a theoretical model with computations was being empirical enough, for this did not provide a truly genetic, historical system. Economic aetiology was central to the analysis of economic pathology, said the institutionalists. And this meant that true man had to be studied—man as a frequently irrational animal, motivated by fears, unknown wants, ill-defined drives, fads, fashions, and the pressures of his society. Orthodox theory, with its false hedonic constructs, was otiose. And the cloak of formal mathematics with which contemporary economics was beginning to clothe itself struck the institutionalists as an arid method devoid of genuine content.[329]

iv

John Maurice Clark: Social Control in Moderation

John Maurice Clark's contribution to contemporary economic thinking has been aptly described as a "constructive synthesis."[330] Well-grounded in the kind of static theory espoused by his father, John Bates Clark, he nevertheless exhibited sufficient independence of mind to strike out on his own, doing notable work in such dynamic areas as overhead costs and business cycles. Yet, in his deep concern with ethics and the middle way, there was revealed a continuous thread leading all the way back to the elder Clark's *Philosophy of Wealth*.

Clark was born in Northampton, Massachusetts in 1884 and completed his undergraduate work at Amherst. He then went on to Columbia for further study, specializing in economics, with minors in sociology, history, and law. While immersed in the kind of economic "laws" which his father had done so much to establish, he learned at Columbia that in reality there were many exceptions, all characterized by extreme variability. He found that with economic change theory itself underwent change and that it was the task of the economist to explain the nature of this interacting process. Here he was in agreement with many of the ideas so forcefully expounded by Veblen and Mitchell.

He became aware that economic phenomena were so complex that many of the statements which sought to explain human action actually were restricted to small sectors of the real world. Yet the mere collection of a great mass of data did not remedy the situation either. Clark came to feel that a meaningful economics would rest somewhere between these extremes and could stem only from the practical issues of the day. Consequently, economics would have to become involved in social values and economic change. The quality of serene contentment he detected in standard economic theory troubled Clark, especially the assumptions of equality between supply and demand, full use of resources, and the continuation of production to the point of equilibrium between marginal cost and marginal revenue. Clark's examination of factual data revealed unemployment of men and machines, fluctuations in demand, and an absence of equality between supply and demand as evidenced by excess capacity. It thus seemed as if two distinct systems of economic thought were required. Clark believed, however, that it might be possible to bridge the gap between older theory and newer facts. But this implied accepting the limitations of classical doctrine, a view that not all economists were ready to adopt. To make his point, Clark suggested that the theory of demand might be taken as a provisional statement of consumer behavior, after which one would have to absorb into economic theory a genuinely useful theory of psychological behavior.

Furthermore, Clark found that ordinary theory's overriding concern with the principle of profit maximization was misplaced, for in practice there was no precise way in which a firm could attain its profit objectives. The search for gain was guided by trial and error and filled with just the sort of gaps described by the analyst as leads and lags. Competition went on continuously, Clark discovered, with undulating movements and clusters of change, with aggressive action initiated by some and defensive answers supplied by others. Standard competitive theory consequently suffered from a cultural lag: it may have been adequate for an economy of small units, but the latter had been long since displaced by congeries of large firms, which together with the enhanced role of government, had created an essentially mixed system. In fact, the determinate character of theory was misleading: even the sort of historical past it purported to describe was mythical. Empirical data suggested a multiplicity of forms, market structure and responses, and these had been simply assumed away by the theorists, who, said Clark, were now merely prisoners of their own models of precision. It was not possible to discover identical demand and cost curves; the dynamic aspects of competition were ignored by timeless mathematical functions; elasticities were bound to vary with the kind of action undertaken by a firm, i.e., whether aggressive or defensive; output reactions were not instantaneous, for excess capacity still had a role to play; product differentiation was not to be deplored, since it widened choice; and long run adjustments seemed more meaningful than those in the short run.

After completing his graduate studies in 1908, Clark went to Colorado College, but preferring the east, he returned to Amherst two years later. In 1915, he moved to Chicago, returning to Columbia in 1926 to assume the chair vacated by his father. Chicago had given him an opportunity to study at close hand the actualities of large-scale business. Shortly after arriving at the Illinois metropolis, he witnessed the great men's clothing strike which gave birth to the Amalgamated Clothing Workers Union—an industrial outburst which reinforced his belief in the need for more social cooperation.[331] Clark's career has been a long and fruitful one, not only as a teacher and writer, but also as a consultant to numerous government agencies, including the National Planning Board in the thirties and the Office of Price Administration during World War II.

The seeds of Clark's most significant contribution—overhead costs and social control—are to be found in his doctoral dissertation on local freight discrimination. Studies on war economics came from his pen in both world conflicts, notably the *Demobilization of Wartime Economic Controls*,[332] in which problems of reconversion from war to peace were discussed in a most incisive way. Clark always stressed his intellectual debt to his father: there was a warm relationship between them, expressed in such a joint work as the revised edition of *The Control of Trusts* (1912). There seems little doubt but that the ethical strain found in Clark's work was an intellectual inheritance derived from John Bates' thinking. The latter had created a system of static analysis which purported to be complete in its own right, but beneath it one could detect an urge to improve and expand the borders of economic inquiry. Bates Clark repeatedly asserted that the work of developing a dynamic economics would be the task of future generations. Certainly the contribution his son made toward that end was a most important one.

In an interesting and revealing note to Joseph Dorfman, Clark briefly outlined his own intellectual heritage: "Overhead costs came first, 1905-23," he wrote.

Next in time I'd put the working out of a position relative to Veblen's and Davenport's criticisms of JBC, centering on *"social productivity* vs. *private acquisition."* This pointed to examination of *premises.* . . . All this in the Amherst period. Criticisms of the psychological assumptions of utility theory remained a challenge, and led to the two 1918 articles on psychology, with Wm. James' *Psychology* the most obvious source; Cooley's *Human Nature and Social Organization* next, perhaps. Carleton Barker came later, I *think,* as did Cooley's *Social Progress.* "Inappropriables" formed a natural key concept, and Ely's *Property and Contract* (1914) put content into it, followed by Roscoe Pound and Ernest Freund. Meanwhile Pigou's *Wealth and Welfare* (1912) and Hobson's *Work and Wealth* (1914) put "Welfare Economics" on the map relative to social productivity vs. private acquisition. Mitchell's *Business Cycles* (1913) led to the acceleration article. . . . [333]

More specifically, Clark learned from William James that the notion of rational action was false, that human psychology was much too malleable to permit so static a concept. Marginalism, for example, made sense only if all action were habitual, and yet this would hardly suggest the conscious deliberation characteristic of classical economic man. Clark's attraction to the thinking of Charles H. Cooley, the noted sociologist, was equally powerful. Cooley had started his work as an economist but soon switched to sociology, which enabled him to look at received economic theory with a fresh view. Always skeptical of classical dogma, he had found it to be a purely short-range theory unable to offer genuine insights into the broader mechanisms of social behavior. He insisted that society had to be examined as a whole and that this enforced upon the social scientist a genetic approach. Men were not isolated individuals, he said, but members of a community whose ideas and actions were interrelated. As the individual worked through society, he thereby modified the behavior of others in a continuous process. Consequently, the ability to make proper choices was not enhanced by placing total responsibility on the individual. This was more than could be fairly expected. The proper question to ask was whether the individual had responsibilities that were within his capacities.[334]

From this standpoint, the economy was a complex of interrelationships which offered ample room for programs of social reform. Collective action had to be employed to influence and even control individual action, said Cooley. He looked upon the theory of the economists as short-range mechanics, quite elaborate, but devoid of insights into the real world of man. He compared economists to people examining the second hand of a watch, but who were unable to tell time. The trouble was that economists began with demands, and assumed that they were all equally justified, thereby validating the system in which they were expressed. It was forgotten that demand was an expression of economic power and as such was a result as well as a cause of economic action. All the evils of the economy were implicit in the kind of demand to which it gave vent, argued Cooley. As evidence he pointed to the presence of prostitution, child labor, and corruption. Economists spoke of competition without reference to monopoly and industrial combinations. Yet it was these problems, he insisted, that made public control an integral element of the economic order, and this meant that ethics had to be part and parcel of economic study. In the last analysis, the only thing in which economists had expertise was the operation of market valuations. Yet Cooley was cautious, a trait he transmitted to Clark. He urged a limited role for the state, only because it was so clumsy a mechanism, placing his hopes rather on the growth of social intelligence and the voluntaristic application of his principles of cooperation. Like Clark after him, he stood halfway between the purely theoretical and institutionalist position, so that he was not nearly so pessimistic about the outcome for social science as was Veblen.

Clark reflected these strictures in his own work. In his discussion of marginal utility, for example, he remarked that the theory was simply a way of saying that one buys what he buys.[335] He noted that wants were neither stable nor uninfluenced by the actions of producers. Business, he said, was deeply involved in the aims of men and guided their "general instincts" into particular channels toward particular goods. Since standard theory had failed to deal with such situations, it could say little about their outcome, efficiency, or inefficiency. By stressing only the theory of production, ordinary economics had demonstrated an exclusive interest in an increased quantity of goods, leaving no room for alterations in wants, except as a passive phenomenon. Clark pointed out that economic theory was not able to encompass mistaken actions; the decisions of the market place were always deemed to be correct and final. Because of this, theory had been converted into a set of abstractions which always rejected the role of economic guidance because to do otherwise would have contaminated its purity.[336] Certainly, Clark was seeking to impart an ethical content to economics, for to speak of guidance was to raise a question of what was good for society and the individual. He then proceeded to demonstrate that the classical economic man was not even a good hedonist, for the supposed calculation of pleasures kept him going beyond the point where the trouble taken to measure each action cost more than it was worth. A good hedonist presumably would strike a balance between getting the most out of expenditures and securing a greater income. It was precisely this sort of devastating criticism that other theorists sought to overcome by resorting to the indifference curve analysis.

Economics, if it was anything, said Clark, was a study of social efficiency. For Clark, this implied a process of "socialization" which could not stop just this side of morals and ethics.[337] This process did not by any means displace theoretical discourse; certain hypotheses were still necessary to summarize and generalize what was gathered through inductive investigation. These propositions, however, would have to be verifiable, a characteristic for which marginal utility theory was not especially noted, since statements stemming from the latter were essentially tautological. It was evident that economic man, once so confident, was now withdrawing into himself and telling the inquiring economist that the way in which he made his choices was his own business.[338] And as a result, he had become little more than a symbol.

The difficulty was that orthodox economics had failed to account for such matters as rights and obligations, or, for that matter, the state of industrial knowledge. Private consumption was not the sole objective of economic action: it was just possible that society's aims were also a factor. Furthermore, asked Clark, how did the intensity and quality of work affect the pursuit of wealth? [339] Ought not ethical standards be permitted to intrude on valuations of economic service? Can the quality of man really be taken for granted with full attention focused on output? Should not the qualitative impact of the productive system on human beings be the concern of the economist? Are not private interests infused with public issues? Indeed, these were embarrassing questions for contemporary economics.

As an illustration of the kind of problem he had in mind Clark could point to competitive theory. Competition was not a simple and self-regulating device. There was no tendency toward equilibrium, for what one observed in the various markets was an endless and intertwining concatenation of forces. And one could not really assert that only the market of small units was beneficial, for the so-called monopolistic features of the contemporary economy often did reveal noteworthy benefits. Fewness did not imply stagnation or the absence of any drive toward efficiency. The trouble with theoretical models, including the Robinson-Chamberlin construction, was their unstated assumption that deviations from perfect elasticity of demand meant defective competition. In fact, argued Clark, a somewhat less than perfectly elastic demand favored competitive activity by providing a greater diversity of goods. The important point was to tie competition to serviceability so that the advantages of progress might be diffused, high and stable employment provided, and maximum freedom attained within the bounds of institutional and legal requirements.

One of the major practical problems to which Clark addressed himself was that of overhead costs. He emphasized repeatedly that what the private entrepreneur might deem to be a variable item could, from a broad social perspective, be viewed as fixed overhead. Clark's most striking illustration was that of labor cost, one of his boldest ideas. The overhead cost involved in labor had always been shifted by private producers, without any sense of justice, to society. Problems such as this led Clark to reject the foresight and rationality which standard theory proclaimed. But, above all, he was perturbed by the way in which machine technology was imposing its severe and repressive discipline on modern man. The machine made a bargain for a flowing cornucopia of goods and, in return, bound man to perpetual servitude. The one consolation, Clark added wryly, was that ". . . machines have not forced their culture on us by armed violence." [340] Man, however, had been compelled to accept the machine's rigid controls and the violent alternations in activity were then reflected in business cycles.

How could one build a socialized economics employing a collective intelligence? Clark found the materials easily at hand: in Sidgwick, J. S. Mill, Adam Smith's work on taxation, J. B. Clark's *Philosophy of Wealth;* in Thomas N. Carver, Thorstein Veblen, and John A. Hobson. These were the sources for concepts that could provide a theory of social value and unpaid costs. Essentially, this proposed a study of economic welfare, quite similar to that which A. C. Pigou was working on in Britain. Clark asked, for example, how we might compare the social costs of two factories, one of which was built with an eye toward beauty and the other with unrelieved ugliness? What was society's cost in such a case, what the individual's cost?[341] Again, the rarified atmosphere of value and distribution had failed utterly to meet this problem. Social value and social cost could be related meaningfully only to the whole matrix of forces that flowed from individual decisions. A single exchange transaction, consequently, was in reality but a unit of a "great social joint product." [342] Clark was in no way upset by the contention that such a discussion would carry one beyond the common definition of economics. He welcomed it, in fact, for this would provide him an opportunity to bring psychology, sociology, and ethics to bear on economic matters. Economics, he insisted, could ill-afford a policy of nonintercourse with other sciences.

Clark practiced what he preached, for, like the other institutionalists, he was deeply concerned with the psychological underpinnings of economic theory. Orthodox theory, by making few attempts to break out of its static and price-governed assumptions, had only contrived a concept of behavior that was mechanistic.[343] As a result, its mode of inquiry had been severely limited and, in fact, pursued the wrong questions. While utility theory had analyzed hedonic reactions, it overlooked many other forms of behavior well within the province of the economist. Evading psychological questions by taking choice as given was egregious, for economics as a study of man presupposed an interest in these very matters. How man's wants were molded was indeed part of the business of earning a living, said Clark.[344] Industry dealt with people, not with pleasant or unpleasant states of mind. Surely this fact involved social costs which might be studied "in a way far more useful as a guide to public action than is the *a priori* doctrine of equality between marginal disutility and marginal reward." [345] This statement clearly implied that the economist need know what the psychologist had to say, for this would make it possible to work up a dynamic interpretation of consciousness in place of the static hedonic conception of behavior. Hedonism asserted that man sought things for the sake of pleasure; it might very well be that pleasure was gained from things simply because man sought them out. The economists' rational behavior was really but a small part of total behavior, insisted Clark. In a hedonic world, choice presumably would become so perfect that pleasure itself might be eliminated.

Man ". . . can make nothing out of the world that the world does not first make out of him." [346] Man is formed by the slum, farm, school, church, newspaper, advertisements, and a whole complex of community contacts. Certainly in such a world, the management of income according to the lights of marginal utility would not always be the most efficient. Actually, said Clark, the putative efficiency of the marginalist was nonexistent, for often men did not turn first to the most important needs or most important goods. Marginalism, consequently, would have to be examined as a mode of thought relative to the totality of stimuli to which men were subjected. As a measure of social efficiency, concluded Clark, marginal utility lacked conclusiveness.[347]

Genuine consciousness, on the other hand, was a dynamic force: within the actual social milieu demand was seldom given; it was created rather by numerous pressures which were all intended to establish little monopolies. Competition was thereby transformed into the substitutability of disparate goods, and was intended to chip away as much of the consumer's income as possible. Thus, in 1918, Clark had been talking of matters that would later be refined into the theory of monopolistic or imperfect competition. He called for ". . . the development of a theory which takes as its normal case the rivalry of slightly different commodities in a market where prices, even for the same commodity, may differ on account of distance, ignorance or suggestion." [348] The effect that this observation would have on economic theory was enormous, for it revealed the limited applicability of competitive price theory. Prices in the real market did not penetrate each other but remained rather on different levels for substantially long periods of time. Market price theory omitted far too much; it said nothing of the organization of budgets or the relation of expenditures to wants. This omission, inferred Clark, was the cost of employing a faulty psychology.

A useful psychology would, of course, have recognized the forcefulness of habit: this was nature's mechanism for giving to the lower brain tasks initiated by the higher nervous sytem. Habit was effective in binding people to certain goods and so provided something of a static character to economic behavior.[349] However, social production not only created goods with "utilities" but guided human impulses as well. It established ways of maintaining order so that the enjoyment of goods might be protected from interference. Thus demand had to be studied as it was formed. This meant, further, an inquiry into property rights and the relationships that flowed from them. The role of advertising and education, previously relegated to the periphery as exceptions, was now brought to the forefront of economic inquiry. Marginal utility was no longer the best way to organize consumption;

it was conceivable that the business of using goods might often be better organized through the "collective power of society." [350]

Clark's social psychology was presented in perhaps its most trenchant form in a long outline appended to his essay, "Economics and Modern Psychology." [351] Here he pointed out that deliberation stemmed from the ability to utilize alternative courses of action suggested by "centrally excited stimuli." Naturally, past experience as well as present conditioning acted on the mechanism of stimulus and response. In this way ideas became guides to choice and provided the basis for deliberative action.[352] This might take the form of calculation, provided there was sufficient information, time, and resources. Yet there was always habit, custom, imitation, and ingrained ways to take into account. Weight had to be given to differences in foresight, responsibility, and intelligence, as well as to differences in social and industrial roles.

The economist had to keep within constant view the fact that social interests were not always encompassed in individual reckoning. Clark then went on to outline the way in which these precepts affected entrepreneurial choice and business efficiency. Human motives as well as the calculus of price entered into this complex, all underlying the more visible problems of overhead cost, accounting practices, and industrial innovation. These factors also entered into his analysis of the role of professionals, investors, workers, and the consumers. Clark showed, for example, how the worker suffered disadvantages, how he might be affected by class bias, and how union organizations might enhance his bargaining status. His primary conclusion was indeed significant: the standard of maximum gratification of wants was meaningless as a guide to policy and social efficiency. A more useful set of criteria would be the fulfillment of innate tendencies, freedom, and individual and social health. And the controlling fact would be the paradoxical nature of man.

Clark continued to concern himself with the psychological and biological substructure of economic behavior in his 1947 Cook Foundation lectures, *Alternatives to Serfdom*.[353] He conceded that we did not know enough about the human material from which a community was constructed.[354] Man was now visualized as more than a collection of instincts or conditioned reflexes; he was now ". . . a sort of very incompetent god, and just now a very frightened one, making and destroying worlds without knowing what he is doing. And he has to live in the worlds he makes, and they in turn make him." [355] While one could continue to talk of instincts and drives, these were not specifics in the old sense of the word. Man was now viewed as a bundle of inborn impulses and capacities of a very general character, taking many shapes and forms. It was their very malleability that was important, leading to a power of intelligent discrimination. Man employed learning, language, and imitation as vehicles for increasing his sense of anticipation, and the consequences of any course of action could increase the capacity of the individual to attain his objectives. These considerations made choice a central fact in economic life, thereby introducing rationality and calculation.[356]

But this by no means could be interpreted as a return on Clark's part to older modes of thought. The psychological underpinnings had a completely contemporary ring. While habit and custom, admittedly large components in economic action, lent a conservative tone to behavior patterns, at no time was his social man the solitary figure of classical economic theory. Men were parts of groups and their actions were always refracted through them. Even Veblen's instinct of workmanship could become a sensible idea because activity frequently was an end in itself. Human malleability and flexibility made market economics a dubious construct, for the laws of the market failed to cover *all* action. At no time was it possible to ignore the social component. Thus, for Clark, the application of social intelligence in building "freedom and a progressive social morality" was a precept that no economist could afford to overlook.[357] In a sense, many of the foregoing concepts were efforts to fulfill the static analysis developed by the elder Clark in his *Philosophy of Wealth* and *Distribution of Wealth*. Bates Clark had worked out a self-contained theory which seemingly explained all the problems of production and distribution. He had been aware that dynamic changes were perhaps basic, but he had never successfully completed the transition from statics to dynamics. His discussion of the latter had all been ultimately reducible to static situations.[358] Maurice Clark tackled the problem with a good deal more success. But while he knew that a dynamic economics called for a fresh set of premises, he had been reluctant to do away entirely with the approach worked out by his father, for he felt that by modifying the old formulas one could gain some insight into dynamic change.[359] Facts frequently underwent such rapid change that economists were hard put to keep pace. For this reason, the dynamic picture was seldom a complete one, so that statics still could perform a useful function in such areas as price and distribution and in helping to interpret the vast quantity of data gathered by advocates of the inductive method.

Returning to the work of Adam Smith, Clark found six key problems for economists—the theory of national efficiency, the never-ending search for a natural level of prices, the way in which deviation from the norm took place, the relation of economic quantities to welfare, the origins of economic behavior, and the justification for underlying institutions. The last three properly posed dynamic questions, said Clark, and should be dealt with in a genetic manner. Exhibiting no special attributes of equilibrium, they covered the gamut of problems from business cycles to collective bargaining and to the motives for economic action. There was no scope here for the classical economic man.[360] One notes too the concern with transactions and the legal basis for economic behavior, somewhat after the fashion of John R. Commons. This was inevitable, for as long as law altered the framework of action it would be essential for the economists to give his attention to this field also. And once the collective aspects of behavior were admitted into economic discourse, it was difficult to exclude ethical precepts. The closer one got to the realities of competition, business cycles, and overhead costs, the more did classical economics seem inappropriate. Only dynamic modes of thought were able to supply satisfactory solutions to urgent problems. The discontinuous, lumpy character of capital, continued Clark, the element of time, the existence of cost differentials, the introduction of innovations, the inability of both capital and labor to move easily from one industry to another, and the practice of price cutting and discrimination were all problems that called for something beyond the static analysis.

One of the major dynamic problems to which Clark addressed himself was the business cycle. His principle of acceleration, which sought to explain the inner workings of cyclical movements, made a profound impact on economic thought. Much of the evidence for this had been drawn from Wesley C. Mitchell's pathbreaking study. Of course, the idea could be found in the work of a number of other economists, notably Albert Aftalion, Arthur Spiethoff, A. C. Pigou, and Roy Harrod; but it remained for Clark to make it central to the explanation of cycles, wherein it was pictured as the key element in a self-generating process. Clark had observed that raw materials and producers' goods varied more sharply in price and output than did consumers' goods. Moreover, the manufacture of equipment fluctuated more widely than was the case with other goods. An examination of the relevant data suggested a unified explanation which could be centered in the output of capital goods. Producers' goods industries were meeting not only the maintenance requirements of other producers, but in addition were expected to supply new equipment and an increased stock of goods. Maintenance and replacement seemed to vary with the demand for finished goods, while increases in the sale of the latter appeared as the final factor in the demand for new construction. When the demand for finished products increased, the derived demand for new equipment would also rise; no sooner did the former level off than the derived demand for the latter would drop precipitately. This was induced investment, as distinguished from autonomous investment or the kind usually stemming from population growth, territorial expansion, and innovation.[361] Induced investment involved such factors as the durability of goods and overhead costs, elements which were primarily technological in nature. Clark noted that construction had a greater amplitude of change than finished goods and also seemed to lead in point of time.[362] Acceleration affected intermediate goods as well as consumer goods and capital equipment, but the fluctuation was more violent in those stages of production furthest removed from consumption.[363] The main point, said Clark, was that increases in capital goods varied not necessarily with the volume of demand for the consumers' product but rather with the rate of change in demand.[364] Acceleration, or the rate of change, would have to be constant if output in the capital goods industry was not to fluctuate.

The argument was fully developed in the *Strategic Factors in Business Cycles,* an outgrowth of Herbert Hoover's Committee on Recent Economic Changes. Clark made extensive use of Mitchell's data and the material produced by the National Bureau of Economic Research. His objective was to isolate the key elements in cyclical change, particularly those which exerted a causal influence and which might be made amenable to social control. True to his basic predisposition, Clark steered a middle course between theory and empiricism. He was attracted to the theoretical feature of the acceleration principle because it seemed to suggest an explanation internal to the whole process of change. Like Pigou, he distinguished between originating forces and business response. War and new inventions illustrated the first category: these produced cycles by virtue of external shocks to the system. But it was the latter, business responses to internal forces, that appeared more significant to him,[365] for it was these that set the stage for recovery and prosperity after a depression. The similarity to Mitchell's notion of cycles was obvious. Unlike the Pigovian theory, however, business optimism or pessimism did not seem particularly important, although Clark's discussion of self-fulfilling prophecies came quite close to the Britisher's view.[366]

Clark's examination of Mitchell's later data confirmed his 1917 assertion that construction activity showed leading characteristics. He found in the case of automobiles, for example, that fluctuations in output depended mainly on changes in income.[367] The same was evidently true of housing. A most important conclusion, almost lost to view, was his statement that depressions stemmed in large part from society's failure to distribute its income as fast as the output of consumers' goods.[368] Yet changes in income distribution, he feared, could be effective only if pursued in conjunction with a policy of industrial stabilization.[369] Another striking feature of Clark's analysis was the approach to the notion of the multiplier. Said he: "If a reduction of production, and of income, is followed by a *smaller* reduction of expenditures, then the series of derived effects is a dwindling series of the type which should have a finite, not an infinite sum." [370]

How could these effects be controlled? Here Clark turned to the concept of balance, for cycles were essentially departures from balanced economic relationships. Motion in one part of the economy should call forth correlative adjustments elsewhere. Writing during the depression, Clark remarked that if one merely sought an equality of supply and demand, an intolerable amount of unemployment would ensue. This perfectly good Keynesian idea revealed a groping toward the kind of growth theory later developed by Roy Harrod and Evsey Domar. Balance, said Clark, involved ". . . the development of new standards of capital equipment adapted to changing proportions of capital to labor and the direction of the increased productive power into making those commodities which are going to be desired by a population with more money to spend." [371] This clearly pointed to the need for a proper balance between the rate of saving and investment in more productive forms of capital, accompanied by higher standards and higher earnings. Clark, however, was fully aware that growth in this sense was limited by technical methods of production and available equipment. There had to be avenues of investment sufficient to absorb savings without wasteful duplication of plants. Unfortunately, the attainment of this ideal was hampered by the tendency of businessmen to fulfill their own expectations and prophecies. Anticipating a depression, remarked Clark, they acted in ways that helped turn a prosperous era sour. For corrective measures, Clark suggested regularization of production, capital outlay budgeting, and a shelf of public works to be used when needed. The key device, however, was the stabilization of consumer spending power through what has come to be known as the "built-in stabilizer." To judge by more recent events, some writers believe that this goal has been finally achieved. [372]

A number of economists have argued, however, that the acceleration principle is a limited one. Ragnar Frisch has asserted that the disappearance of demand for new equipment would be counterbalanced by increases in replacement demand. [373] Others have charged that in its simple form the acceleration principle went too far in assuming a constant ratio of consumer goods to capital goods. [374] Replacement demand, for example, might stem from factors other than shifts in consumer demand and unquestionably would be influenced by durability and obsolescence. Furthermore, innovations could create sudden investment spurts quite unrelated to immediate consumer demand. This seemed especially the case over the long run, when worn-out equipment would most likely reflect quite a different character. At any rate, the assumption of a constant ratio between change in demand and investment failed to give full play to the role of excess capacity, for when demand moved upward after a depression, the immediate investment response by producers would most likely be a sluggish one. Nor did acceleration leave room for overtime and double shifts. The presence of these elements suggested a weakening of Clark's theory of derived demand. Haberler argued in his monumental study of business cycles that it was quite possible for acceleration in one industry to be offset by decreased demand elsewhere in the economy. This, of course, would be conditioned by the relative durability of equipment, the extent of excess capacity, and the degree to which fixed capital in one industry might be employed to produce goods made by other industries. [375] For acceleration to have a lasting impact, it was said, the increased demand would have to be a continuing one; no new expansion would be embarked upon if the acceleration was expected to be temporary.

One must acknowledge that some versions of the acceleration principle have been mechanistic in that little stress was placed on the role of excess capacity and variations in the rate of capital replacement. Nevertheless, Clark's formulation, while lacking the elegance of Ragnar Frisch's mathematical presentation, was quite realistic. It implied something less than complete omniscience on the part of the businessman. There seemed to be enough volatility in the producers' goods industries to suggest a fair measure of validity in Clark's thesis.[376] Some of his critics also felt that he had failed to give sufficient weight to the availability of credit, but this cannot be accepted. Clark did note that

. . . the elasticity of credit undoubtedly facilitates and speeds the process of capital accumulation by enabling business to secure and spend at any time larger amounts of capital funds than have been furnished for the purpose by prior savings. . . . If there were no possibility of expanding credit, increased purchases of automobiles and residences would be limited to such current income as the consumer chose to divert from the fulfillment of other desires, and increased expenditures on capital equipment would be limited to that fraction of current income which the consumer chose not to spend, or which the business unit chose not to distribute.[377]

Clark's interest in the impact of machine technology on society had been revealed early in his career with his book, *Studies in the Economics of Overhead Costs*.[378] This was undoubtedly his most significant contribution and is in fact one of the most incisive studies on the subject ever written. It is filled with insights and observations that are still viable, and the book amply repays careful reading. Clark had been impelled to examine the problem at close hand under the stimulus of Arthur T. Hadley, who discussed the subject in his economics text. Hadley, who had studied with Sumner at Yale, became president of the college in 1899 after a successful teaching career. His economics had been essentially traditional in its purview, even going so far as to exhibit a mild version of Social Darwinism. But his experience in railroad economics had confirmed a deep-rooted belief that industries with substantial fixed investment would have to maintain production regardless of price. Fixed capital was becoming so important an element in industry that it was difficult to define cost, for fixed charges were now spread over the total output in a way that raised serious question regarding cost standards. Firms tended to stay in business so long as wages and raw materials expenses could be recaptured. Hadley's discussion of these problems, involving cutthroat competition, monopoly, excess capacity, and price discrimination, had encouraged Clark to take them up in greater detail. He now felt that a dynamic economics would have to make room for overhead costs.

Generally, overhead costs were those costs which could not be attributed to specific units of a business: increases or decreases in output had no great effect on them. Such costs stemmed solely from the nature of modern business, which required a heavy investment in fixed capital. This was not the situation in precapitalist days when the major components of production were raw materials and labor. Expenses then had been easily allocated to specific units of output. The maintenance of fixed investment, however, became a burden that the capitalist could not avoid if he was to stay in business. There was no variation in what the machine did: it produced goods that were uniform, with continuous operation its religion.[379] Machine costs fell on industry as constant charges and were incapable of being translated into variable charges allocable to particular services. Such costs could be observed in many industries in addition to railroads, said Clark. With large commitments in fixed equipment, the capitalist could not shift about easily from one industry to the next, so that he had to take whatever the market could bring: "normal" returns on investment were no longer assured, as had been suggested by ordinary economics. What were the results? Excess capacity, business cycles, and the kind of cutthroat competition which eventually led to pools, cartels, and "gentlemen's agreements" to avoid "spoiling the market." [380]

At another level, problems of considerable importance stemmed from the divergence between the overhead costs of a single firm and those of the economy as a whole. For example, it was possible in certain instances to convert what were ordinary overhead costs into variable items, as in the case of shoe manufacture and repair. Here, Clark pointed out, the United States Machinery Company, by leasing its equipment, had helped its customers to transform overhead into variable costs. (A contemporary illustration is the case of the supermarket in which direct labor cost, a discretionary fixed item, is converted into a variable through the employment of part-time workers.) When prices dropped, it became feasible for such firms to cut back on production with ease, thus compounding the social difficulties that ensued. The social interest which required some output at any price, so long as it was worth the excess cost of working, was thereby countervailed. Yet this very social interest, by inviting an intense brand of competition, told the private businessman to contemplate going out of business.[381] Here, in the language of Marx, was a neat contradiction.

Clark carried on his discussion of overhead in terms of types of cost—absolute, incremental or marginal, financial, production, long run, and short run. He analysed in detail the nature of operating expense, variable and constant cost, direct and indirect cost, joint cost and selling costs. He looked at the phenomenon from the viewpoint of the engineer, accountant, statistician, and economist. The study was rich and subtle, suffused with a rare imagination, and concluded that there was no universal meaning for the term. The treatment of selling cost suggested many of the concepts later exploited by Edward H. Chamberlin. This was an aspect of cost ignored by most economists of the day. Selling costs, said Clark, had to be added to manufacturing costs, with both in the long run covered by prices.[382] How should they be allocated? A selling or advertising effort frequently was hit or miss, aimed toward an unknown public. In a multiproduct plant, moreover, selling costs were too general in character to be allocable to a specific output. They assumed the aspect of sunk costs, since they did not necessarily bring about immediate results. Their very variability made it difficult to determine whether a given effort had been worthwhile.

A basic consideration stemming from overhead costs was the palpable fact that certain economies could be gained from an increased use of productive equipment which might otherwise lie idle. Even increased output when capacity was full could bring about economies. More complex equipment could be installed, thereby reducing unit costs, and, should sales continue at high levels, the additional capital would have been paid for easily. Thus, the long-run and short-run efforts of overhead cost would be markedly different.

This introduced the laws of return, the indeterminate nature of prices and production, and the whole question of idle capacity. Clark felt that these problems had been overlooked in classical theory and merited careful investigation. The law of diminishing returns as usually propounded seemed to Clark to be misleading, for in the present day its technical basis appeared unwarranted. Situations did arise in which the application of additional equipment relative to other factors would raise output quite rapidly. Furthermore, one had to concede the possibility of constant returns, a condition often found in manufacturing enterprises.[383] In reality, economic efficiency, said Clark, called for a balance between productive factors. Involved in the total situation were elements of capacity, peak load, standardization, and the extent to which the firm was integrated. Manufacturing itself was subject to a variety of indivisibilities, quite unlike the purportedly easy proportioning in agriculture. Shifts in demand made factory operations irregular, with plants not always able to adapt themselves to new conditions in the way prescribed by economic theory. "Unlike the mathematician, the business man seldom concerns himself with infinitesimals—never, except as incidents to a policy that he deems important. And the economist can fairly follow his example." [384] This, argued Clark, imposed certain limits on plant size which the capitalist had to include in his calculations, such as they were.

The cost curves theorists talked about were intended to isolate the effects of shifts in output. But Clark found that the short run cost curve usually represented operations at varying percentages of capacity, so that it was necessary to imagine a zone of cost rather than a line. Operations at a stated level of output were bound to differ with the length of time a plant remained at a given capacity rate. That is, changes to new output levels involved costs that had not been explained in theory. One also had to consider capital attrition, particularly when prices changed as capital replacements became due. Further, the utilization of "standard" cost formulas raised the question of full cost pricing, under which prices were set to cover all costs. This, in effect, meant employing average rather than marginal cost as the major consideration, an approach which seemed quite characteristic of the business man's mode of thinking. It was at this point that variations between firms occurred, since overhead was distributed differently in different situations. As a consequence, the profit maximizing price could not be determined with any measure of accuracy. And in some industries, Clark pointed out, the product was governed by a previously selected price-line, as in the garment trades. Here, the full cost goal might meet the firm's notion of maximum profit. In fact, full cost pricing appeared fairly prevalent, particularly when a firm sought some "target return" on its investment or wanted to stabilize prices or improve its market position. Even product differentiation could take precedence over price. These were practices to be found throughout the economy, for large firms as well as small ones.

In large-scale production, efficiency did not necessarily increase proportionately with increased equipment. There was no "law" that decreed greater efficiency for big units as contrasted with small ones. Bigness in industry might bring advantages in bulk buying and financing, but these could be outweighed by disadvantages caused by complexity in organization, impersonal relations, divided responsibility, and a loss of initiative. All this reflected Clark's deep concern over the problems of economic giantism. Like his father before him, he was distressed by the growth of trusts and monopolies. Combinations, he said, did not flow from economies of scale, but from a "natural urge to cease competing." [385] This was the soil in which monopoly and combination flourished. In such industries producers were impelled to combine in order to forestall wild competitive drives. In addition, the need to invest on a huge scale presented an obstacle to newcomers and limited their entry, making it all the more simple to control potential competition.[386] Thus, in Clark's analysis, overhead cost, large-scale production, monopoly, and the problems of cutthroat competition were all inextricably bound together.

Overhead costs played an important role also in business cycles, said Clark. He noted that large businesses which exhibited the highest ratio of constant costs were precisely those subject to the most violent fluctuations.[387] Clark related this phenomenon to his acceleration principle. The fact that demand for the means of production shifted so violently, as contrasted with consumer goods, seemed to stress the overriding importance of overhead costs. There was also a kind of psychological element involved, Clark admitted, for the direction of demand increased expectations for a continuation of the movement. Acceleration was intensified by the desire to buy as cheaply as possible: when the rate of demand increased, there was a rush to add new equipment before prices generally rose. Prosperity ground to a halt simply because sales levelled off, even if they were at high levels. Sometimes the decline in the rate of growth of demand caused disinvestment, as firms rushed to dispose of excess equipment. Thus, with overhead costs as the initiating factor, the shifts in money values distributed production and consumption over the different phases of the business cycle in ways that blocked the most efficient timing of industrial output. "When a depression has paralysed industry and crippled demand, the value of materials is greater for present working up and sale than the market shows, while the value of holding them for future use is less than the market indicates." [388] From the social standpoint, scarce goods ought to bear a high price as a means of allocating them for future use, but a depression reversed this by putting a low price on fewer goods, thereby aggravating the ailment.

When costs were converted into variable items, argued Clark, the true ratio between fixed and genuine variable items was distorted. In actuality, most costs ought to be interpreted as fixed and constant in nature.[389] If this were done, businessmen would be impelled to search for stabilizing devices. Merely setting price at a steady level would not have the desired effect. What remedies, then, were available? Here Clark suggested a pluralistic approach, encompassing education, proper planning, scheduling of production to fill in troughs and cut-off peaks, a shelf of easily instituted public works, unemployment insurance, employment exchanges, and better statistical services. Today these devices do not appear particularly striking, but at the time that he wrote, such measures were considered bold indeed. He did not, however, raise the question of effective demand. It remained for the Keynesians to take this up a decade and half later.

The answer to overhead costs seemed to lie in price discrimination. This was, of course, nothing new: in fact, it was the single price system that appeared artificial. Price discrimination was a perfectly natural form of competition and represented a highly satisfactory way of overcoming the problems created by overhead costs. The idea was to levy the burden on those parts of a business able to sustain it, while the other parts charged whatever they were able to secure regardless of cost. This was a sensible approach and was practiced in meat packing, communications, railroads, electric power, and similar industries. There were two standards for price discrimination, said Clark. One, discriminatory pricing should call forth demand that might otherwise not be available, and two, it should bring resources into play which in other circumstances would lie fallow. Discrimination, therefore, was not necessarily a sign of monopoly as at first had been believed, but rather a phenomenon stemming from overhead costs. Nor could it be considered a market aberration, as older theory had believed. Yet, averred Clark, it did raise issues beyond the behavior of a single firm, for it was not unusual for discrimination to become a vehicle for extorting more than a proper share of the consumer's dollar. This, at any rate, had been the cry of America's farmers for more than a decade.

There was more to the practice of price discrimination than economics.

It could be an instrument of favoritism, but also a means toward ". . . the highest social justice." [390] Differences in quality and location frequently limited the scope of a producer's market. It was, therefore, easier to maintain higher prices in one's own market than in neutral ones. Price competition set in only with the development of rivalry in a single market. The consequence could be cutthroat competition, unless inhibited by a strong feeling against "spoiling the market." On the other hand, discrimination in local markets could be a way of stifling potential rivals. Clark's review of discriminatory practices was mainly descriptive. It covered supposed differences in quality, service, distinctions between transient and regular customers, and business conducted on the basis of cash versus credit. Although it was not couched in the analytical terms of a Walras or Edgeworth it nevertheless remained an incisive presentation of the problem.[391] The modern analytical presentation of price discrimination was left for such writers as Joan Robinson and A. C. Pigou.[392]

As Joseph Dorfman has remarked, the idea of labor as an overhead cost was indeed a daring one.[393] As a factor of production, labor was in many ways similar to the inanimate productive equipment employed in the productive process. It required maintenance, was subject to wear and tear, cost a certain amount of money, and exhibited a certain return on investment.[394] Underlying all these questions was the basic problem of a minimum standard of living, which represented labor's constant cost element. Insofar as society was concerned, the burden of supporting labor continued regardless of output. But a deterioration of society's investment in labor was bound to occur where workers were assigned the responsibility of maintaining themselves under conditions of low wages. In the long run it would cost a good deal less to provide proper maintenance than to permit deterioration to take place. Yet under existing social arrangements labor had been treated as a variable cost. The burden of overhead was placed on the worker, said Clark, who was expected to carry himself and his family through periods of slack. Thus society's investment in training workers was irretrievably lost. Since few elements in the final costs of labor varied in proportion to the amount of work done, labor was in reality an overhead cost. The implication Clark drew from this was a rejection of unemployment as a necessary feature of the industrial system. Clark concluded that ". . . the overhead cost of labor is a collective burden upon industry in general, but the market does not allocate to each employer the share for which his own enterprise is responsible." [395]

Clark's remedy for this situation approached what later came to be known as the guaranteed annual wage. He was concerned lest these measures reduce labor's incentive to work, but certainly wage cutting during a downswing held no attraction for him. He thought that wages might be divided into two parts: a flexible portion which might provide the necessary stimulus during off-peak periods, and a guaranteed share to cover labor's maintenance and overhead.[396] Whatever solution was to be worked out would have to assign costs properly. The distribution of labor's overhead costs could not be left to ordinary wage contracts. Such costs, said Clark, must be allocated ". . . in the light of essential justice, and of the principle of placing burdens and incentives where they can do the most good in bringing about action which community efficiency demands." [397]

Obviously, this would require social action and community control. Clark reviewed the consequences of overhead costs in his *Social Control of Business,* the arguments of which flowed logically out of the earlier work.[398] It was a classic example of the institutionalist perception of society, combining insights from the fields of law and sociology as well as economics. Specific and conscious controls, argued Clark, directed toward the welfare of all, were necessary to meet the problems created by society's investment in fixed equipment. Thus far, a mixed economy had been evolved. Yet all too many persons behaved and thought as though pure individual rights were still the central forms of life and that private rights were in no way related to community interests. A complete community encompassed a good deal more than individual rights: it could not be based solely on the transactions of free exchange.[399] This was Clark's basic view justifying the imposition of social controls to impel individuals to act in the interest of the entire group. Many changes had already taken place in ways that had served to increase rather than lessen social controls. Virtually all met Clark's approval. Beginning with the railroads and then passing on to electric power, telephones, irrigation projects, and corporate monopoly, society was extending its regulatory and controlling powers over significant sectors of the economy. All this was rooted in the nature of large-scale production, for without controls we should be at the mercy of those who would gladly utilize the industrial machinery for their own private whims. Controls were essential, said Clark, since individualism failed to provide the protection which society demanded. Of course, many controls already existed, stemming as they did from ordinary custom and group suasion. And although many of these were informal, they were frequently supplemented by judicial and legislative action.

A substantial portion of *Social Control of Business* was concerned with a detailed discussion of these techniques. The traditional theory of market price and individualism again was shown to be inadequate to meet the urgent problems of contemporary society. The market had failed utterly, for example, to meet the needs of workers, neither providing them with the kind of work they wanted to engage in, nor in sufficient quantity. Furthermore, the theory of the market had little meaning for a society plagued by idle capacity, where prices were established long before goods reached the buyer, where adjustments were made through production rather than price, and where shortages existed not in available goods but in overall demand. If these problems required some sort of government action, Clark was not perturbed. He advocated control of monopoly measures to prevent conflict between large organizations, to alleviate economic catastrophe, and above all, to maintain equality of opportunity.[400] Yet, true to his tradition, he preferred the voluntaristic approach to these matters, arguing that control would have to be exercised carefully with proper regard to the requirements of particular situations. Control for its own sake, he reminded his readers, could very well lead to perversion and fakery.

It was evident that Clark's objective was a "balanced society," one in which private action and government control together would achieve an equilibrium between individual freedom and social intervention, between self-interest and group interests.[401] He hoped that this could be accomplished without coercion. But in the absence of the proper balance it would be difficult to avoid compulsion. This was a problem that market economics was forever overlooking. Essentially, Clark's position was one of moderation and the middle way. Individual business liberties were not to be considered sacrosanct if they threatened the general welfare. These problems would have to be met patiently, however, so as to ". . . strike a sane balance between liberty and control, and to reduce our worst evils to tolerable proportions by a process of adjustment, using voluntary means to the utmost of their capacity, the whole being subject to free discussion, not directed by arbitrary fiat and suppression of dissent." [402] Undue pressures from any group could prove damaging to the social fabric, said Clark. Only a sensible balance between diverging interests could foster the desirable objectives of maximum employment, security, peace, and a sense of belonging. All this would require a conscious effort, involving the full energies of society, something that the market itself hardly could be expected to achieve.[403]

Inevitably social control and the mixed economy raised the question of ethics. Economics, in Clark's hands, came round to the viewpoint of the ancient philosophers for whom ethical and economic behavior had been bound together.[404] Free men, said Clark, would have to work together to establish the necessary attitudes of responsibility if the present system were to survive. It was inescapable that notions of welfare should intrude into economic thinking; but he doubted that what currently passed for welfare economics was very helpful, for this was a body of thought that ended in complete agnosticism. The belief that the national dividend could be justifiably increased only when no one was harmed acted as a veto on any scientific approval of policy.[405] Welfare would have to be conceived in a much broader framework, one that would bridge the gap between what we could produce and the ethical basis of a properly constituted civilization. Clark definitely would have little to do with those systems of economic thought which omitted ethics. Economics dealt with the actual value systems of people, and, insofar as it did, ethical criteria, distinct from those of the market, were integral elements of its thinking.[406] As a science, economics had an ethical thrust reaching toward conclusions implicit in the data with which it dealt. And this included the ethics of voluntary cooperation. Otherwise, society would have to resort to the most distasteful brands of compulsion. This might very well mean going beyond the present limits of economic science, but there seemed no other way to achieve an awareness of the individual's relation to his community—an awareness that could stem only from a sense of history and from all of mankind's contributions to the realm of intellect.[407]

v

John A. Hobson: A British Institutionalist

Although a British citizen and trained in Britain's universities, the outlook of John A. Hobson (1858-1940) was closely related to American institutionalism. Deeply concerned with the ethical aspects of economic behavior, he became a powerful dissenter from standard theory, very much in the tradition of Marx and Veblen. Hobson wrote no less than fifty-three books, virtually all of which were notable for their insistent stress on noneconomic factors. This alone would hardly be sufficient to accord him an honored place in the pantheon of great economists. It was rather his theory of underconsumption, or oversaving, plus the idea of the need for a correct proportion between production and consumption, that made his ideas so striking, enough to mark him as a heretic throughout his long life. The underconsumption theory aroused no little controversy, especially among members of the Liberal party, of which Hobson was a member. Reviewing one of his books in 1913, John Maynard Keynes remarked: "One comes to a new book by Mr. Hobson with mixed feelings, in hope of stimulating ideas and of some fruitful criticisms of orthodoxy from an independent and individual standpoint, but expectant also of much sophistry, misunderstanding and perverse thought." [408] Yet some two decades later, when Keynes published his *General Theory of Employment, Interest and Money,* he had only the highest praise for Hobson's pioneering efforts. He described Hobson's first work, *The Physiology of Industry,* as a book which had opened an epoch in economic thought.[409] Hobson can be rightly described as a forerunner of the "new" economics.

Rather modest and retiring, Hobson's participation in public affairs was limited. He joined the Labor party after World War I, and was in a sense its leading economic theoretician. Certainly he had as much claim to the title of prophet of the welfare state as did the Fabians. Today his economic thinking, enshrined in the technical apparatus of others, is standard coin.[410]

Hobson once observed that he had been favorably situated for a complacent acceptance of the existing social order.[411] He had been born in a middle-sized town in the industrial Midlands of Britain where progress and order, class distinction, respectability, and the righteousness of wealth were the accepted canons of life. Poverty was attributed to the shiftlessness of the poor. Yet its widespread existence stirred in Hobson a feeling that all was not quite right in the world. The cultural atmosphere of his home was one of pristine liberalism, laissez faire, and strict churchgoing. After a standard grammar school education, he broke with orthodox Christianity, and with a reading of Mill's *On Liberty* and Spencer's sociology, social problems began to intrude upon his outlook. Cambridge University extension courses further broadened Hobson's vision. He soon entered Oxford, where the classics reigned supreme; this, he said, had contributed a good deal to the rationalism and humanism he was later to apply to economics.[412] The spirit of reform which swept through British universities, stirred by the perorations of John Ruskin, had a profound influence on him. The younger generation could not help but become aware of the depressing effects of the great industrial expansion of the seventies and eighties. Laissez faire no longer offered a satisfactory explanation of the wide discrepancies between economic growth and increasing distress.

After leaving Oxford in 1880, where his academic success had been hardly overwhelming, Hobson taught in the public schools for seven years and for a decade after that he gave extension courses for workers, mainly on economic subjects. His interest in economic questions had been aroused not only by the state of society, which he thought deplorable, but by Henry George's attack on landed property. Yet Hobson was never a single-taxer, nor for that matter was he a socialist, although in later life his feelings did move toward identification with the democratic left.[413]

While teaching at Exeter, Hobson met A. F. Mummery, a businessman with ". . . a natural zest for a path of his own finding, and a sublime disregard of intellectual authority." [414] In a discussion with Mummery over the cause of business depression, Hobson resorted to all the standard arguments, but later was convinced that Mummery's oversaving thesis had considerable merit. In 1889, they jointly wrote *The Physiology of Industry,* in which the heresy that thrift was no great social virtue was presented to the world of economics: oversaving was undesirable, they said, because it invariably led to a failure in demand.[415] The book had some references to the role of inventories in economic crisis and an analysis of the flow of demand, investment, and production through industry sectors which was thoroughly modern in tone. The consequences of this first act of heresy were momentous for Hobson. At that time he had undertaken to give University extension courses in economics and literature, but shortly afterward, the London Extension Board refused to allow him to teach political economy. This action evidently stemmed from the intervention of Francis Y. Edgeworth, professor at King's College, London, whose review of *The Physiology of Industry* had been most hostile. As Hobson remarked years later, the economics professor ". . . considered it as equivalent in rationality to an attempt to prove the flatness of the earth." [416] Ironically, in later years, Edgeworth's editorial successors for the Royal Economic Society, Keynes and Harrod, would come to find Hobson's ideas "moderate, reasonable and full of wisdom." [417]

Fortunately, an independent income allowed Hobson to continue his long heretical career. And today, many of his ideas have become so ingrained a part of received doctrine that it seems unlikely, as T. W. Hutchison has said, that another Hobson ever will be produced again. From 1897 on, Hobson worked as a journalist, writing books, pamphlets, articles, and newspaper accounts on a variety of subjects.[418] The audience he sought was a much wider one than the world of academe. Like Commons, his writings ranged far and wide, encompassing abstract theory as well as current affairs. Thus he was able to bring a body of factual information to bear on economics that was as unusual as it was enormous. Of the fifty-odd books he wrote, in an almost equal number of years, many were hastily assembled, barely surviving the print shop before they were hustled off to the remainder shelves. But he wrote enough substantial and meritorious volumes to assure him a position of honor and influence in the history of economic thought. Among these one could count, in addition to *The Physiology of Industry, The Evolution of Modern Capitalism* (1894), *Economics of Distribution* (1900), *Imperialism* (1902), *The Industrial System* (1904), *Science of Wealth* (1911), *Work and Wealth* (1914), *Taxation in the New State* (1919), *Economics of Unemployment* (1922), *Free Thought in the Social Sciences* (1926), *Economics and Ethics* (1929), and his charming intellectual autobiography, *Confessions of an Economic Heretic* (1938). Hobsonian ideas were sources of inspiration for Fabians, Socialists, New Dealers, and Keynesians. That he was not as scholarly at times as academicians would have desired did not trouble him, for it was not they he sought to impress. At any rate, he had the courage to challenge ideas that had been hallowed for so long that they seemed unimpeachable.

Hobson's oversaving heresy threatened the foundations of laissez faire by undermining the one claim orthodoxy had to respectability. The only justification for the self-centered concept of the economic man had been the advancement of the general welfare, and it was this fundamental idea that Hobson was calling into question. This was followed by a rigorous analysis of capitalism which was to become standard textbook fare for students of economic history—the *Evolution of Modern Capitalism*.[419] Its main theme was an account of the role of modern machinery in enlarging productivity and broadening the function of the capitalist. Society paid little attention to what was happening to the worker, although it had acquiesced in the business of separating him from his tools.

In 1899 Hobson went to South Africa to report on the Boer War, and out of this experience came one of his great works, *Imperialism*,[420] a book from which Lenin drew extensively. Again, the theory of underconsumption played a central role, for it was the need for metropolitan centers to dispose of surplus goods that motivated imperialist drives. The Boer War was a turning point in Hobson's thinking. It was for him the clearest example of the interplay of political and economic forces in imperialism. As he interviewed all the leading figures—Kruger, Smuts, Herzog, Hofmyer, and Cecil Rhodes—he learned from them how a ". . . particularly crude form of capitalism [operated] in a mixed political field."[421] Gradually, Hobson brought his own ethical instincts to bear on the problems of economics and politics, becoming ever more convinced of the basic immorality of an economic order in which transactions were carried out by parties utterly at odds in bargaining strength.

Upon his return to Britain, Hobson pursued his career in journalism and adult education. He wrote extensively for the *Nation*, always searching for the ethical connotations of the political and economic matters on which he wrote.[422] A series of visits to Canada and the United States brought him face to face with a new blend of ruthless competition and ruthless monopoly. Hobson came to know Lincoln Steffens and Henry Demarest Lloyd of muckraking fame, as well as Professor E. A. Ross, the noted sociologist. He read the works of Veblen, whose caustic and bitter comments on conspicuous consumption and standards of invidious comparison were patently attractive. However, the chief influence in Hobson's work can be traced to John Ruskin (1819-1900), the noted critic, whose defense of the early nineteenth-century painter, William Turner, had become a landmark in art history. From art Ruskin turned to economics and for over two decades conducted a furious polemic against classical doctrine. Although rejected by academicians as a rank amateur, Ruskin's writing exerted a remarkable influence with its appeal to dignity and simplicity in the ordering of social and economic life. Ruskin himself had been influenced by Thomas Carlyle and William Morris, whose romanticism offered the perfect backdrop for a sharp critique of the injustice and poverty engendered by modern industrialism. Hobson studied the works of Ruskin very carefully during the 1890's, publishing a book on him in 1898. The Ruskin credo that "there is no wealth but life" struck a responsive chord in the young economic heretic. It led Hobson to the notion that all wealth and income ". . . must be estimated in relation to the vital cost of its production and the vital utility of its consumption." This seemed to be the only satisfactory basis for a human valuation of industry.[423] Ruskin's religious eloquence did not disturb Hobson: he was concerned only that Ruskin had demonstrated how current economic thought degraded the true meaning of such terms as wealth, value and profit.[424] This obviously implied that ethical overtones were implicit in all economic concepts. The economist could stop at no mere description of "what is," for his function included a prescription of what "ought to be." Hobson was determined to advance Ruskin's idea of value in terms of life goals. Standards of consumption, he felt, could be raised by elevating the capacity of the consumer to use goods in fruitful ways. The highest "effectual" value was the ability to appreciate the world's beauty, a theme that Hobson was to dwell on again and again. From Ruskin, he derived the need to go ". . . behind the current monetary estimates of wealth, cost and utility, to reach the body of human benefits and satisfactions which gave them a real meaning." [425] For Hobson, this was not at all a matter of metaphysics: while such values seemed outside the limits of economics, they were important because they sustained ideas of welfare generally.

L. T. Hobhouse, the noted British sociologist, also influenced Hobson. Central to Hobhouse's thinking was the idea of studying society as an evolving unitary system. This required scientific studies of comparative religion, mythology, law, and morality as a basis for understanding man in society. Hobhouse's sociology encompassed ethical standards and implied that individual and social motives were the key to a harmonious development of individual personality. This emphasis on individual growth made a profound impression on Hobson.[426] From this stemmed his proposition that anyone working in the social sciences could not be unaffected by his own personal history and makeup, an idea later developed by Hobson in his *Free Thought in the Social Sciences*.[427]

Graham Wallas, the third of the important influences on Hobson's thinking, was interested mainly in the psychology of politics and in the intimate relationship between the rational and irrational elements in political behavior. Wallas left the Fabian Society because it had refused to attack British imperialism in the Boer War. As a member of the faculty of the London School of Economics, he sought to maintain a broad perspective for social scientists who were threatening to go overboard in a sea of specialties. It was this stress on human values in both Hobhouse and Wallas that attracted Hobson.[428]

The first book Hobson wrote, with Mummery, was a notable one. Economic science may have very well lost a luminary in the latter, who was killed in a mountain climbing accident in 1895. He had been the senior author of *The Physiology of Industry* and probably had supplied its key ideas.[429] The theme of the book was boldly set forth in the preface: "Our purpose is to show that an undue exercise of the habit of saving is possible and that such undue exercise impoverishes the Community, throws labourers out of work, drives down wages and spreads that gloom and prostration through the commercial world which is known as Depression in Trade; that

in short, the effective love of money is the root of all economic evil." [430]
While saving increased the totality of capital, said the authors, it also reduced
available consumer goods, leading to an oversupply of capital goods or general overproduction. Others, of course, had advanced similar ideas. Sismondi,
Lauderdale, Malthus, Rodbertus, and Marx all had voiced the opinion that
a lack of consumer purchasing power caused capitalism to stumble periodically over its own feet. [431] But few had made it so integral an element
of their economic thinking as did Hobson. There was lacking only the modern
stress on investment, for in Hobson's theory there was an unstated premise
identifying saving and investment without the usual lags. As Keynes was later
to remark, only half the problem had been set forth. [432] Not only was the
notion of cumulative action missing, but lacking also was the idea that a weak
propensity to consume could be at the root of lagging increments to investment. Aside from this, the theory was a forceful one.

Production was visualized as a flow from one sector of the economy to
another, through which the laws of distribution accomplished their work.
The mechanism was said to be delicately balanced, for the amount of capital
required in each stage bore an exact and fixed relation to the amount of consumer goods: excesses or deficiencies would throw the whole business out of
gear. [433] While the idea of the "right ratio" made its appearance from time
to time in Hobson's writings, unfortunately not much attention was paid to it.
Yet it bears a striking similarity to the ideas that have been adumbrated in
more recent days by Harrod and Domar. [434] The concept was developed
further in *The Industrial System,* by far Hobson's best analytical work. [435] In
the latter he argued that if the rate at which raw materials entered the industrial stream were to slacken there was grave risk of a corresponding
decline in output and employment. A drop in the rate of consumption could
also cause production to slow down, thereby suggesting the acceleration
thesis. A fall in retail prices communicated itself along the industrial line;
declining sales led to reduced orders and lower production. [436] These statements revealed a concern with long-run adjustments to an ever increasing
stock of capital and with the fact that total capacity could outrun total consumption. This also implied a dynamic economy with capital accumulation
and growth as important elements. [437] Although the multiplier concept was
not well developed in Hobson's model, he quite understood, by virtue of the
analysis of replacement funds and surplus, the nature of what today is
described as autonomous investment. [438]

All this may have been less elegantly put, and in language that contemporary writers might disapprove, but nevertheless it cut through to the
heart of the economic problem in a way that few in Hobson's own time had
been able to grasp. Even the idea of excess capacity was touched upon
when Hobson distinguished between real and nominal capital, with the latter
defined as redundant equipment. The accumulation of capital stock was said

to have meaning only so long as it could supply a flow of consumable goods which were absorbed by the available purchasing power. This was the constraint imposed upon production. If thrift increased, there had to be increased consumption in the future as well. If not, then all that was accomplished was the creation of nominal capital, or excess capacity. Such an oversupply could pervade the entire economy. The conclusion was self-evident. "Only by first increasing the demand for commodities is it possible to increase the amount of real capital in the community." [439]

This analysis represented a clean break with traditional theory, including Say's Law.[440] It was no wonder that Edgeworth's ire was aroused. Saving, said Hobson, could be viewed as an exercise in demand only insofar as it led to new forms of capital. This impelled an analysis of intersectoral movement similar to Schumpeter's circular flow. The basis for a theory of capital was laid: capital goods, said Hobson, were not only specific in nature but also continuous because of perpetual renewal.[441] The circular flow was employed to attack the wages-fund theory, with Hobson arguing that advances were not made to workers out of capital, but rather that labor was purchased in much the same way as land or equipment. Workers were paid, consequently, out of the total product of the industrial system, not from some special fund.

Ultimately, it was consumption that determined the extent to which the means of production were to be employed.[442] Total demand was total income, so that a decline in prices meant falling demand relative to the quantity of goods offered for sale, with depression as the probable outcome. An undue exercise of thrift was the root cause of the evil.[443] Hobson's complaint was directed toward the over-all behavior of society, not the individual. The classicists, with their fallacy of composition, had failed to make this important distinction and had implied that what was good for the individual was *ipso facto* good for society. Hobson vehemently affirmed that this was not the case at all.[444] Oversaving, from the community standpoint, could come about through improvements in technology requiring less capital for the same rate of output. Or it could result from the competition of individuals, making the savings habit thoroughly ingrained.[445]

Hobson rejected the argument that a fall in the price level would stimulate real demand. There was no reason to expect this effect to take place, for aggregate income was reduced by a decline in prices. This reaction, known as the Pigou effect, had little relevance for an economy where adjustments were made through production rather than price. This implied a degree of monopoly power that had been ignored by the classicists. Furthermore, consumption itself was sticky, for a price decline merely resulted in a smaller money outlay for the same basket of goods and might thereby encourage further increased savings.[446] Falling prices, therefore, would merely accentuate the glut, with reduced saving coming about only as a result of reduced national income. Equilibrium would be restored by a process of economic bloodletting:

liquidation of inventories and disinvestment would be accompanied by considerable human suffering. As roughhewn as this analysis might have been, it should be remembered that it was written prior to World War I, years before other economists were willing to concede its general soundness.

The rate of interest could not have much effect on the outcome, argued Hobson, since it was not related to saving. Its effect was rather slow and then only on part of aggregate capital supply.[447] The fact was, said Hobson, that most saving was automatic and had no connection to what the level of the rate of interest might be. Where such a relationship did exist, as in the wish for a fixed future income, a fall in interest rates would stimulate the relevant portion of savings. Moreover, changes in interest rates were deemed to be a result rather than a cause of business action.

A masterly analysis of the impact of the Franco-Prussian War served to illustrate Hobson's analysis. He demonstrated how increased consumption for war needs, enforced saving, and the post-war deficiency of capital goods had provided for the flow of demand necessary to bolster production. Not that Mummery and Hobson approved of war as a means to prosperity; yet, in this age of missile production, it is well to note what they said on the matter: ". . . when there is a tendency towards an undue multiplication of forms of capital through an excessive desire to save . . . war perform[s] a real service to commerce by giving a temporary use to the otherwise useless and excessive forms of capital." [448]

As noted, there were obvious deficiencies in this early formulation of the underconsumptionist thesis. No consideration was given to the effects that interest rate changes might have on the investment process, and the premise that savings were almost instantaneously translated into capital goods seemed unwarranted. Expectations played no role in the analysis. The *Physiology of Industry* made no reference to the uneven distribution of income, which was later to become an important cog in the Hobsonian mechanism. The problem of income distribution became an important element in his notion of economic surplus, as first suggested in the *Problem of the Unemployed*,[449] and later developed more fully in *The Industrial System*. In the latter, Hobson added the concept of the wage lag, thus accounting for the increasing share of income which went to the capitalist. It was this lag that made it increasingly difficult for the mass of workers to purchase the required output necessary to keep the economy in balance. The propensity to consume, to use Keynes' phrase, was bound to decline—a situation due to the superior bargaining strength of the buyers of labor power which allowed them to depress the price of labor to the lower level of the range of wages applicable to each grade of labor.[450]

Hobson also used the underconsumption thesis to explain imperialist drives by modern national states. The idea that a surfeit of goods resulted in an expansion of capitalism beyond metropolitan centers was also employed by Marxists. In fact, Lenin appropriated Hobson's argument for his own uses with but little change.[451] Hobson's book, *Imperialism,* however, remains the classic work on the subject.[452] In it, he denounced capitalist expansion beyond its own borders as a perversion of the nationalist spirit. Colonialism, he said, was quite another matter; here at least actual migration to unpopulated areas was accompanied by the transplantation of a complex culture.[453] This was in the best sense a natural overflow of nationality. But under imperialism, metropolitan centers established islands of settlers as ruling groups among peoples whose cultures and customs were completely different. It was the latter sort of expansion that had developed in the closing decades of the nineteenth century, particularly in Asia and Africa—a predatory form of expansion in which the economic power of the dominant country allied itself with the ruling groups of the subject area for purposes of drawing out surplus values. Armament races and war threats were used to seal off spheres of influence. Further, imperialism by its very aggressiveness engendered a nationalist spirit among subject peoples.

This thesis was expanded by Hobson in several other books, notably in *International Trade: An Application of Economic Theory* and *An Economic Interpretation of Investment.*[454] The major arguments had been stated, however, in the earlier work. The core of Hobson's position was that an excess of products in the home market impelled a drive toward overseas expansion.[455] This was nothing less than underconsumption at home. It required ". . . the acquisition of foreign markets and areas of lucrative overseas investment." [456] The backward regions were also important as sources of raw material and imported foods, which in turn were paid for by exports of finished goods or earnings from foreign investments. But the chief motivation was derived from a chronic tendency to overproduce at home with the consequent need for more markets. This itself, said Hobson, was due to a lopsided distribution of income which placed an inadequate share of income into the hands of the working class. Within this whole milieu there had grown up tariff barriers, quotas, subsidies, and all the other paraphernalia of trade restriction—all intended to assure to the metropolitan center a closed colonial market.

Hobson's attack was indeed a powerful one. The benefits of this dubious policy flowed only to certain sectors of the capitalist class, he said, especially to those which produced tools of war. But a political democracy, he contended, ". . . in which the interests and will of the whole people wield the powers of the State, will actively oppose the whole process of imperialism. Such a democracy has not learnt the lesson that substantial economic equality in income and ownership of property is essential to its operation." [457] There existed, consequently, the ever present threat that capitalists would seek to counteract the growth of democracy in order to further their own interests. Written in the climate of the 1930's, this statement, from Hobson's preface to the revised edition of *Imperialism,* was not a wild one. That capitalism has appeared to sustain itself only by a program of heavy war expenditures seems fully warranted, even if the rest of the argument is now outmoded.[458]

John Strachey, the British socialist writer, has recently argued that Hobson, and particularly Lenin, overlooked the capacity of contemporary capitalism to utilize surplus resources for purely internal growth.[459] Given an improved standard of living and an expansion of markets within the borders of the metropolitan centers, there was seemingly no reason why investment could not be directed toward one's own people. Consequently, said Strachey, imperialism could be viewed as a time-bound, historical phase of capitalist development in which the concatenation of surpluses, a lopsided distribution of income at home, and high rate of overseas investment made it appear that foreign adventures were inevitable. Yet, Strachey observed, the imperialist grasp was being loosened. Why? Adequate reasons were found in the rise of native nationalisms, the impulse toward self-development, and the patent fact that imperialism was being displaced by more profitable and less harmful modes of conducting business at home. These newer developments, therefore, made it necessary to modify Hobson's original thesis.

Despite frequent lacunae and shifts in emphasis, it must be said that Hobson's underconsumption theory has a large measure of consistency. As Paul Homan conceded, it hangs together. But Hobson was trying to do more than construct a theory: he was a practical reformer who sought to uncover the reasons for inequality and exploitation before working up a program for change. He was firmly convinced that the existing economic relationships had not produced welfare and that the main reasons for this condition could be discovered in the realm of income distribution. The first exploration of the problem, *The Economics of Distribution* (1900), was conventional and not especially noteworthy, stemming largely from Marshallian theory; *The Industrial System* (1910) was by far the more incisive work. Hobson set forth his thesis immediately. He rejected the classical assertion that the whole product of industry was automatically absorbed by factor payments. The argument that distribution took place by means of minimum payments required to call out the necessary quantities of capital and labor (with rent as a residual payment) was deemed to be an evasion of the problem.

Hobson's own approach was based on a distinction between costs and surplus. Costs were those payments necessary to evoke and maintain existing productive capacities, and represented a "permanent harmony between capital, labour and ability." Where industry produced an output in excess of these costs, the surplus was divided among the several factors of production in accordance with their respective bargaining strengths, or, as Hobson put it, in accordance with the economic pull they were able to exercise.[460] Under monopoly, it was possible for the entire surplus to be appropriated. With the surplus divided into many fragments, depending on relative bargaining power, there could be no residual claimant. Part of the economic surplus was utilized for growth, that is, to provide more and better capital and to improve labor skills. This Hobson described as "productive surplus." No social waste was incurred when this took place. However, the surplus in excess of these two requirements was "unproductive." All of rent was included in the latter category, as well as excessive interest, profits, and wages. Unproductive surplus was an encroachment on the social fund, said Hobson, which could be employed for socially desirable needs. And inasmuch as it was an unearned income, it represented the only genuinely sound tax base from which revenues could be obtained to develop public services.

These concepts, although lacking in measurability, provided the heart of Hobson's teachings. He started with an analysis of the structural complexities of the economy and showed how trades and industries were grouped to make up a completely interdependent system. Goods moving back from the raw material toward the finished product stage were passed en route by money flowing in the opposite direction. At each point in the process, income was distributed to participants. The capitalist was at the center, organizing production, selling the output, and paying off the cooperating factors.[461] The goods and money flows were both horizontal and vertical; the steel industry, for example, served a variety of other industries and, in turn, was served by still others. To a contemporary, the striking similarity to a Leontief input-output table is inescapable.[462] Competitive as well as complementary goods entered into the complex, as did the principle of substitution.[463] "The industrial atmosphere is kept continually vibrating with waves passing in direct currents from one trade to another distant trade, or widening from some local centre in ever larger, weaker waves over general trade until they disappear." [464]

In a static state, the flows would have been automatic and no savings would have been required.[465] But in reality, the economic situation was dynamic, since provision had to be made for expansion and growth. It was at this point that savings and surplus played their role. Saving and investment were again made identical, without lags, both stemming from the economic surplus. Interest, wages, and profit comprised necessary payments for maintenance, a "productive" surplus to make room for improvement and an "unproductive" surplus.[466] The usual way of measuring distribution shares was inadequate, said Hobson, because it had failed to explain that what capitalists sought were "units of productive power." [467] They did not purchase land and equipment per se, but the ability to produce. Now, this was certainly a highly abstract concept, in some ways similar to that employed by Frank H. Knight; but Hobson felt that the common quality of productive capacity had permitted him to establish a "unitary" method that would explain more satisfactorily differential rent and interest. It could tell, he said, why one type of land or labor was to be preferred to another. For labor, it revealed that a minimum subsistence wage still existed[468]—at a level necessary merely for efficiency in work and to sustain a family. Of course, such a level could shift as the social outlook changed. Yet an expanding economy would have to provide something more to stimulate growth.[469] A proper wage, therefore, would have to include at least two payments: a subsistence wage to maintain labor unimpaired, and a wage of "progressive efficiency" to bring forth an increased supply of more effective labor power. A similar analysis was applied to capital, with the payments which it received comprising at least two parts as well.

Although this was somewhat reminiscent of the classical differential rent concept, it became something quite different in Hobson's hands.[470] Viewed as a group, the least efficient worker in each grade had to be paid the minimum wage; but this did not by any means, argued Hobson, determine the level of payments for the whole group. While bargaining weaknesses might depress wages toward the subsistence level, the fact remained that employers frequently had to purchase blocs of labor power units at higher wages for reasons of differences in efficiency. The productive surplus was clearly the source of these payments. In the case of rent, other complications set in, since payments for improvements on land were a form of capital income. But contrary to the classical argument, marginal land did yield rent, said Hobson, simply as a matter of scarcity uses.[471] Nor did land at the margin of cultivation determine rent, since it was merely a payment for the use of certain productive powers.[472] This was the only feature of rent that was analogous to other factor payments. In fact, said Hobson, the margin was determined by the price of the unit of productive power, so that movements in this price effectively determined the margin. Thus, Hobson turned the classical doctrine on its head, asserting that prices determined margins of use, rather than the other way around.

In defining the nature of productivity, Hobson argued that no separation could be made between the cooperating factors; all were essential to produce goods and no specific productivity could be attributed to any single factor. He rejected, consequently, the theory of marginal productivity. What seemed more important to him was the average productivity of the group input factor.

Adding doses of labour and noting the increase in the aggregate product throws no serviceable light upon the determination of wages. The so-called marginal dose with its separate product, is only intelligible when regarded as an average dose in a fully equipped farm, factory, shop or other business: no separate dose has any separate product, and the only method of assigning it to any product is to divide the whole product equally among the constituent units, as if it represented the mere addition of their individual productivity instead of their joint co-operative productivity.[473]

The more important concept was average productivity which varied with the efficiency of the group and should be imputed in equal proportions among the members. As applied to labor, such a division supplied the upper limit of payments, just as alternative work opportunities supplied the lower limit.

Hobson went further, attacking the preconception of marginal utility itself with its proposition of fluidity in capital and labor, full knowledge of the market, and the like. In a society of imperfect competition, marginalism provided a false theory, said he. Insofar as price was concerned, changes were due to alterations in the average expense of the entire complex of factors. It was average costs that determined supply prices.[474] Hobson continued his attack on marginalist notions in his *Free Thought in the Social Sciences*.[475] The "dosing" method, he argued here, implied that there was no profit at the margin of capital and that therefore profit did not affect price. Such an error, said Hobson, could stem only from the improper treatment of one factor as fixed and the others as variable, thus revealing an erroneous application of the law of diminishing returns. The latter was simply a technological relationship among the factors which explained maximum efficiency and productivity. Removing one unit of a factor would tell us nothing about that unit's productivity, since the latter was the result of the work of the entire group. What would happen, we can almost hear Hobson ask, if a key worker on a modern factory belt were removed? Certainly, the belt would not continue to move—an indication that production was a matter of group cooperation.

Marginalism implied a separatist treatment of input factors which ignored the essential gestalt character of modern production. Hobson harshly dismissed as a "great bluff" the infinitesimal and continuous character of economic change that had been stressed by the marginalist.[476] The actual material of economics consisted rather of discrete units of production, an argument rather difficult to rebut. Furthermore, said Hobson, changes in market price were seldom reflected in demand until they were of "sensible magnitudes," since shifts in consumption were generally sticky and slow. By their insistence on smooth change, the economists simply had revealed their lack of knowledge of consumer habits. Whatever changes did occur were not at the margin, but rather at the center of productive or consumer activity, affecting the whole area.[477] Marginalism may have had some meaning for an agricultural society, and in fact, many of its ideas had stemmed from the analysis of agrarian problems; but it was unlikely, insisted Hobson, that it had anything sensible to say about an industrial system.

What, then, determined the shares of the product going to the factors of production? Mainly, the process of bargaining within the limits set by the necessary minimum payments on the one hand and the total flow of income on the other. What the entrepreneur obtained as profit was governed by bargaining with the other factors and by competition with other entrepreneurs. His real power lay in what Hobson called the "area of progressive industry,"

—in his ability to seek out new markets, produce new goods, and explore new ways of getting things done.[478] This was, of course, Schumpeter's innovator and to Hobson his was an important social function. But wide dispersion and bureaucratization of entrepreneurial functions required that profit include payments to financiers, royalties to inventors, salaries to officers, and dividends to investors. A larger profit, therefore, far in excess of the expenses of production, had to be extracted from the flow of social income.

This constituted a bargaining theory of distribution in which the strength of economic "pulls" determined who received what. Much of the surplus product of society went into inessential overpayments, said Hobson, thereby inhibiting efficiency and progress. Like Veblen, he felt that property owners had been able to draw more than sufficient income to devote themselves to such useless endeavors as sports and festivals.[479] This unproductive surplus and the way in which it was appropriated tended to disrupt the proper balance between spending and saving and ultimately brought about depressions. Saving out of the unproductive surplus was seldom used to fulfill essential human needs; insofar as it did, asserted Hobson, it was only because the rich could not consume as much as they thought. The soundest way of stimulating industrial development would be to readjust the distribution of income.[480] Quite simply, both inequality and the roots of the business cycle were to be found in the kind of distribution system engendered by the industrial order. No remedies could be effective unless they first corrected the tendency for production to outrun consumption. The social surplus should be converted into consumer income either by raising wages or by siphoning it into public funds to raise the standards of public life.[481]

Despite the hortatory tone and the sense of dogmatism so often found in Hobson's writing, it contained some decidedly positive elements. The notion that there had to be a unique ratio of spending to saving antedated some of the contemporary theories of growth, and, if it lacked the precision of the present day, it nevertheless came close to the truth. Hobson's stress of the proportion of spending to saving, rather than its absolute level, also approached the idea of a function. Any number of other comments revealed a perception of capitalist dynamics that was rare for his day. There was a prescience in his work, as in Veblen's, which deserved a good deal more regard than was given to it at first.

It was obvious that Hobson did not believe in eternal truths in economics. He knew full well that economic theory, even in its most neutral form, was filled with bias and apologetics. Official doctrine appeared to him as a mass of loosely related concepts, passion laden opinions, and appeals to popular prejudice. Its perceptions were variable and mixed with the observer's own feelings.[482] Such objectivity as might be uncovered, he said, was notoriously susceptible to false reasoning and the intrusion of motives unrelated to the purposes of the science. Economists and other social scientists were unfortunately prone to tamper with intellectual processes, disguising their almost unconscious personal interests with an esoteric terminology designed to bluff the public into an acceptance of social science on their own terms.

Seldom had such a passionate attack been leveled at economic precept and practice. Yet in view of what had been happening in economics some of his charges were not unjustified. Property had become so sanctified in law and morals that to levy taxes appeared downright wicked. Intellectuals had been called on to defend existing institutions, and, before long, their sympathies were engaged in sustaining the good opinion of practical men.[483] Hobson acknowledged that such habits of thought were to be found in all circles: reform had its propaganda also, often quite as reckless as that of the conservatives. The intrusion of ideology was inescapable, said Hobson, a thesis he amply illustrated with an incisive review of classical economic doctrine.[484] Proponents of classicism had contended that their body of theory was scientific. This was false, argued Hobson, for economics, if it was anything, was an art addressed to the ordering of human material interests toward the attainment of maximum welfare. Economic wealth should be treated in terms of "vital utility," and once this was done the belief in precise measurement was bound to evaporate. The notion of precision itself was ideology for the classicists, who, in developing their "science," simply furnished the new capitalists with a seemingly authoritative doctrine to justify their own actions.[485] Supply and demand curves, identical units of capital and labor, and infinitesimal change requiring adjustments at the margin were just so much ideology, for the theory's ". . . immanent conservatism recommended it, not only to timid academic minds, but to the general body of the possessing classes. . . ."[486] The system of providential design had provided a convenient intellectual framework for financial and industrial policies. And the precision of the "felicific calculus" had justified cheap labor, cheap capital, and the exploitation of foreign lands. Hobson's prose on these issues had the cadence of a Biblical prophet: "The theory that capital puts industry into motion and supports labour was a nutritious intellectual food to the self-approval of the new industrial magnates who had sniffed in with their hard Puritan traditions that reconcilement, nay copartnership, of God and Mammon, which has furnished to British capitalism so much spiritual energy for successful money making."[487]

While political economy had much to say about production, it could offer little on problems of distribution or consumption that was meaningful in human terms. This was Hobson's main charge against received doctrine. It had failed to find methods for giving human expression to concrete goods and economic processes. While interpersonal comparisons of satisfaction were not feasible, he conceded, it was nevertheless important to compare the utilities of goods with the disutilities of making them. The failure to make such comparisons explained to Hobson, at least, why economists had avoided such questions as public health, education, art, and recreation in their calculations. Such persistent needling and criticism had no little effect on the increased attention that was later given to these broader areas.

The investigation of these matters involved the expression of human cost in terms of the quality and kind of human effort, the capacities of the persons who exerted effort, and the distribution of work. On the other hand, utility was to be measured by the quality and kind of satisfaction, the capacities of the consumer to enjoy such satisfactions, and the distribution of utility among the public. Productive work, consequently, was subject to a system of grading. According to Hobson, the highest form was the activity of the creative artist who engaged in work for its own sake and incurred no human cost. His performance was an enhancement of life, not a diminution. Next on the ladder of utility-creating activity was the process of discovery and invention, yielding a high human utility, almost on the level of works of art. For these pursuits, education and leisure were prerequisites. Just a bit lower came the skilled mental work of the professional and administrative classes. These too were deemed to be pleasurable, providing broad scope for high net human utility. The administrators, however, began to reveal somewhat greater cost due to their routine work and overweening concern with money-making. Yet all of these activities obtained high remuneration because of their generally high utility, said Hobson. But when the wage earners were taken into account, these qualities were conspicuous by their absence. Repetition, uninteresting work, fatigue, strain, liability to accidents, and industrial disease were indicative of heavy human costs. And one had to add to this the burdens that society incurred by virtue of child labor and women workers.[488]

How might these burdens be lessened, asked Hobson? The answer lay in furthering the individuality of consumers and opening up possibilities for a worker to express himself through the goods he made. A much larger share of demand would have to be directed to intellectual, aesthetic, and personal services. Enlightenment as to the real meaning of value and work, and the sense of social service that would follow, could help to reduce the irksomeness engendered by modern industrialism. Costs were also involved in the supply of capital, as evidenced by risk-taking and saving; but the latter process really meant little insofar as the wealthy were concerned. Only as one proceeded down the income scale did the human cost of saving increase. Interest earnings hardly sufficed to compensate for the human costs engendered by stinting on the necessities of life. When Hobson came to the human costs involved in consumption patterns, his prose was worthy of a Veblen. Not only were the arts of consumption undeveloped, but they reflected habits stemming from the existing mode of production and distribution. Producers, obviously anxious to control the ways in which consumers used their goods, fostered articles of "illth" rather than wealth.[489] Adulterated goods and poor housing became sources of profit. Imitation and convention governed what goods were to be consumed. Instead of rationality, prestige, tradition and putative standards of respectability determined patterns of consumption.[490] This was followed by the elevation of leisure-class pursuits to a position of priority. Sports and dilettantism became the ". . . characteristic products of mal-distribution seizing that surplus income which is the economic nutriment of social progress, and applying it to evolve a complicated life of futile frivolities for a small leisured class who damage by their contagious example and incitement the standards of the working members of the society in which they exercise domination." [491] The outcome of these habits of action was an increasing proportion of useless goods, resulting in a loss of utility throughout society. This was clearly a misapplication of productive energy and ultimately a loss of real income to the community.

What Hobson thus wanted was a humanist economics. An equitable economic system, he said, was one which would assign the lowest aggregate cost and highest aggregate utility to the products it provided. It would assure equal gains from market transactions to all participants. Yet this was not possible under pure capitalism because the market was the scene of unequal bargaining pulls. He was not averse to planning, but he was enough of a political moderate, despite his heated attacks on fellow economists, to recognize that the individual was the measure by which all actions were to be judged.

These then were the bases of economic welfare. But Hobson's concept of welfare was not often carefully defined. He frequently described it as the highest expression of the constructive propensities of man, a notion much too vague to meet the standards of academic economists. At other times, he spoke of it as collective efforts exerted toward attaining maximum satisfaction and fulfillment from an economic system. But this, he urged, had all too often been perverted by high mortality and disease, poor education, long working hours, shoddy goods, and a system of work that was uninteresting and tedious, suppressing man's innate sense of craftsmanship and art.[492]

Hobson's major statements on economic welfare were set forth in his *Work and Wealth* and *Economics and Ethics*.[493] In these books he urged that a human evaluation of industry should give clear expression to cost and utility in terms of human effort and satisfaction. His standard was "organic welfare," a rather vague notion which he conceded was merely synonymous with the good life. This naturally brought ethical considerations into economic discussion: this he thought would be all to the good. Even the concepts of economic surplus were relevant, for welfare could be enhanced only after a clear demarkation of the social surplus necessary to maintain and enrich the community.[494] Welfare, consequently, implied an ordered set of values which was to be sought not in the higher realms of philosophy but rather in the everyday instincts and appetites of men. The criteria that stemmed from these values were to be defined in terms of individual and social health. They implied the harmonious cooperation of interrelated physical and mental activities.[495]

Although individual values and individual welfare could not be dissociated from the social milieu, it was essential that such values be founded on the principles of voluntary participation, said Hobson, in order to allow the highest possible expression to individual personality. The community, he insisted, should not be permitted to invade those areas in which individuals could develop themselves fully. Such restraint would be necessary to encourage research, criticism, and reform.[496] If this appeared to the economist to be the proper concern of the sociologist or social philosopher, in making this distinction the economist had failed to concede that, even as positive statements, the propositions with which he dealt were forms of philosophy. Hobson simply was being a bit more explicit in deriving his economic precepts from a previously acknowledged social viewpoint.

All this for Hobson pointed to a critical need to reform society. But before such reform could be undertaken it was essential to grasp the inner workings of industrial society. Beyond this the ". . . substitution of direct social control for the private profit-seeking motive in the normal processes of our industries is essential to any sound scheme of social reconstruction. . . . The existing structure of ordinary business life inhibits the realization of its social meaning by the stress it lays on the discordant and separatist interests." [497] Social control of business was thus deemed to be essential. Artistic work should be given free scope, minimum wage laws were essential, profits ought to be subjected to high taxes, a high wage economy fostered, and monopolies rigidly controlled, if not socialized—in short, the good life could be attained only via the welfare state. It was little wonder that Hobson became the intellectual godfather of the British Labor party. Much of their program clearly owed its inspiration to his many writings. But above all he was able to put his finger on two chief defects in ordinary economic thinking—the failure to recognize that welfare was an organic entity, not the mere addition of marginal satisfactions, and the failure to explain the periodic paucity of purchasing power. If only for these observations, Hobson's work may be counted as one of the most important contributions to economic thought in the present century.[498]

vi

Ayres, Hoxie, Selig Perlman, and Gardiner Means

The need for a broader perspective in economics remained the *leitmotiv* of the American institutionalists. Again, it was John Dewey's influence that provided the main motivation. Instrumentalist philosophy was discernible in many quarters, but no one used it so forcefully as did Clarence E. Ayres, who successfully fused the insights of Veblen and Dewey into an effective and sensible format. Ayres rejected biology as a basis for an understanding of behavior, asserting that the way man acted could be explained solely in cultural terms. Like the anthropologist, he was interested in the impact that such social forms as taboos might have on economic behavior. Science as such was not deemed to be a primary factor, for, he insisted, it was material technology that exerted the major influence on behavior and social structure. (Here Ayres was quarrelling with the attempt of scientists to establish themselves as the final arbiters of civilization.) This view, which he developed in the 1920's, provided the underpinning for Ayres' *Theory of Economic Progress.*[499] In it he argued that a reconstruction of economics would have to start by disposing of the whole façade of orthodox price economics. When Adam Smith had written his great tome, said Ayres, the market had been a genuine reality in which problems of price had a meaning that could not be denied. But the world had moved on a good deal since 1776. Industrialism, tools, technology—ways of doing things—now overshadowed the merchant's concern with price, demanding a fresh approach to the perennial problems of social science. Price economics was not well suited for an intelligent appraisal of the ills of modern society, and the inordinate preoccupation with mathematical refinements said little about the nature of business enterprise. By making economics a science of price, the entire question of value had been shunted aside.

Yet, said Ayres, the economist, as a social scientist, could not avoid the human concern with values and thereby with ethics.[500] Man earned his living, not by imitating the actions of the broker, but by the manipulation of tools and machines and by the exercise of knowledge and skills. Unfortunately, the use of our complex technology, said Ayres, was overladen with cultural requirements and compulsions stemming from a host of ceremonial forms. Custom and law concealed the inhibitions engendered by ceremony, yet sooner or later these restrictions would be bound to cause social and political explosions. The history of man, according to Ayres, had been the history of conflict between technology and ceremony. While this was roughly analogous to the Marxian dichotomy, Ayres was primarily an evolutionist in outlook and an instrumentalist in philosophy. He had no need for a mysterious dialectic.[501]

The ambivalence that could arise when an economist trained in traditional ways seriously absorbed the institutionalist credo was tragically portrayed in the career of Robert F. Hoxie. A close friend of Veblen's, Hoxie tried to apply institutionalism as a theory in the field of labor economics, to which he contributed the notion of psychological types. As a student at Cornell and Chicago he had been influenced at first by Laughlin and Fetter, but it was Veblen's work that was to become the dominant force in his thinking. Hoxie taught for a while in midwestern schools, then went to Cornell in 1903, moving to Chicago in 1906, where he gave courses in trade unionism and socialism. Here Veblen imbued him with a passion for research and a respect for the environmental forces that shaped men's lives. Unlike Veblen, however, he wanted to be a good teacher, as emphasized in his posthumous *Trade Unions in the United States*.[502] He always was concerned with the relation of psychology to trade unionism, and, as something of a Christian socialist, there was a strong moral strain in his writings. He instinctively rejected the idea of an inevitable conflict which permeated the Veblenian corpus. Nor did he feel that the machine technology was bound to have the deleterious impact which Veblen said it would.

But he agreed that it was difficult to predict the course of economic events. In his own specialty—trade unionism—cross purposes and varying aims made it impossible to say what shape the future would reveal. He decried the lack of democracy in unions and the essentially conservative outlook of its leaders. The emphasis on "delivering the goods" had converted unions into vehicles of opportunism. Hoxie clearly had great sympathy for those unionists for whom some measure of idealism represented an important motivation, and in this view he was quite at odds with Commons and Perlman, whose theories stressed a "bread-and-butter" posture. Hoxie's analysis of unions was based on a distinction between these polar types. He cross-classified craft with functional forms, and, in the end, he produced an elaborate taxonomy of trade unions. Yet from this he was able to arrive at a theory: unions, said Hoxie, were personal reactions to external market stimuli rather than expressions of a desire to control the means of production, as with Marx. Given a particular market, he said, the kind of unions that would develop would depend largely on the personalities involved. One always had to look for individual idiosyncrasies as the basic explanation of union types.

The last chapter of *Trade Unions in the United States* revealed a break with Veblenian thinking, and Hoxie's innate interest in ethical concerns came to the fore. He rejected Veblen's reliance on economic motives, saying instead that man was influenced by total social development, which suggested to him a greater ability to alter social arrangements than Veblen would have thought possible. For Hoxie "progressive uplift" was entirely feasible. Class conflict occurred only because of misunderstanding: it could be reduced or even eliminated by the introduction of a third party to adjudicate disputes. These new views were diametrically opposed to Hoxie's earlier Veblenian belief that conciliation of the interest of labor and capital was impossible. Early in his career Hoxie had accepted Veblen's psychology as pertinent to contemporary social situations, but after some empirical investigations he felt that the whole instinct approach was inadequate. Personal differences with Veblen were also upsetting. Suddenly, Hoxie began to feel that he had been all wrong, that Veblen too had been wrong. In 1916, suffering from mental despair, he killed himself.

The concern with labor has remained one of the central interests of the institutionalists. Stemming from Commons' pioneering work at Wisconsin, a huge number of studies have sought to define the role of unions in American society. Selig Perlman, (1888-1959), one of Commons' disciples, produced some of the more important of these works during his forty years on the Wisconsin campus.[504] But this preoccupation with but one facet of social and economic behavior illustrated more sharply than anything else what was happening to institutionalism. The broad vision of a Veblen or Commons was being narrowed to the kind of specialism which lost sight of how society really functioned. Institutionalists became labor historians, statisticians, and demographers; the kind of economic theory that could provide a view of society in the round was cast into the dustbin. Hobson's influence in America was not wide enough to fill the gap, and those who knew better, such as Mitchell and Clark, could not stem the tide of specialization. Institutionalism became less a study of how society functioned and more a means of preparing students for a vocation.

Selig Perlman, who in Europe had been a confirmed Marxian of the Social Democratic variety, emigrated to the United States from Russia at the age of twenty. In 1909 he went to Wisconsin to complete his education, where his work impressed both Frederick Jackson Turner and Commons. Joining the latter's labor history project, he was given the task of studying the origins of the immigrant trade union movement. And it was not long before Commons' market theory of capitalism had supplanted Perlman's youthful Marxism. He supplemented Commons' stress on the unionists' bias toward small enterprise and easy money with a perceptive analysis of the role of the ex-socialist who, on these shores, discovered "bread-and-butter" unionism. It was the ex-socialist, men like Gompers and Strasser, said Perlman, who had worked up the foundations for a new kind of unionism, one that displaced the chiliastic urges of a native American millenarian spirit. This had been done by appealing to craft solidarity and job consciousness rather than to class consciousness. It was a kind of unionism that had no conflict with capitalism; it merely wanted a better share of its fruits. The instrument for accomplishing this was the collective bargaining agreement, a device that regularized the relations between union and employer. Bargaining, of course, assumed some sort of equality, a situation that was non-existent at the time. Corporate capitalism was growing apace and trade unions simply got in the way. Furthermore, the emphasis on the collective agreement and on economic issues had relegated political action to a secondary role in trade union strategy.

In *A Theory of the Labor Movement*[505] Perlman tried to develop a sociological framework for the "Wisconsin" viewpoint. The trade union movement was shown to possess a unique history of its own, thus giving real substance to the economists' abstraction of labor as a factor of production. Perlman was convinced that with a greater distribution of wealth, economic expansion, and democracy, trade unions tended to become less idealistic and less reform-minded. He sought to document his thesis with ample citations from trade union constitutions, proceedings, and by-laws; and he found that unions that had survived the vicissitudes of economic and social change were precisely those that focussed their attention on job problems. They had to develop a concept of property rights in the job, for with limited opportunities it was necessary to establish job rights and to regulate job conditions via the medium of the collective bargaining agreement. This, said Perlman, was a new approach. It departed from revolutionary goals and represented an adaptation of unionism to the pragmatic American environment. It had been successful because it had acknowledged the inherent conservatism of the American community. With respect for property a powerful motif in American life, unions had been able to advance the theory that jobs too reflected that regard. Perlman acknowledged that such an attitude, however, might lead to a sense of complacency, as subsequent events were to reveal all too eloquently. In a time of crisis, as in the 1930's when workers in the mass production industries sought to organize, the leaders of the official labor movement were unable to rise to the challenge.[506]

Perlman then inquired why the individual worker displayed the loyalty he did to his organization. He found that this could be explained by the limited opportunities available to the worker and by a fear of scarcity. The union helped him overcome these limitations and helped him also to attain a sense of status and prestige. Whatever idealism there was in unionism could be best expressed by the achievement of practical goals. The abstract idealism of the intellectual, concerned as it was with a transcendental vision, had failed to meet the needs of the workingman, said Perlman. This was Commons' view also, and Perlman was certainly a good disciple. As a handbook of the underlying philosophy of American trade unions, the *Theory of the Labor Movement* was outstanding. It reflected perhaps more than any other work of its kind that American trade unions were what American society wanted them to be.

The outstanding feature of the American economy, however, was not laborism, but rather the growth of the corporation. This was not a new theme for economists, since they had been deeply perturbed by its pervasive influence as far back as John Bates Clark. But in the hands of Gardiner C. Means, (1896-   ) it became the central organizing principle for economic science. Means was not an academician. He interspersed government service with practical business, so that he could not be charged with never having met a payroll, a complaint frequently voiced about theoreticians. As an undergraduate, Means had specialized in chemistry; after graduation he engaged in economic research for the Columbia Law School, where he was associated with James C. Bonbright, the utilities expert, and Adolph A. Berle. His government service included stints with the National Resources Committee and the Bureau of the Budget. Today he is a staid businessman serving suburbanites harassed by unruly garden lawns.[507]

Means' chief interest has been the corporate revolution in the American economy, a topic which served as his doctoral thesis. Aside from the path-breaking volume he co-authored with Berle, *The Modern Corporation and Private Property*,[508] and a book on the holding company he wrote with Bonbright, most of Means' ideas, which have had a marked influence on current day thinking, must be distilled from various papers and government reports. The best known of these is the *Structure of the American Economy,* prepared for the National Resources Committee in 1939. The central point in his argument was that the modern corporation undermined the foundations of classical theory.[509] It was necessary, said he, to restructure economics to conform with the factual realities of the times. Corporate enterprise was something new: it differed radically from the kind of business characteristic of the eighteenth and nineteenth centuries. Consequently, new premises and new preconceptions were essential. Moreover, legal institutions had also been changed, so that the concept of property itself needed redefining. The separation of ownership and control, enforced by modern corporate structures, demanded a fresh look at the nature of private property, for the relationships most characteristic of the economic order had been altered in the corporate milieu. The economy was now dominated, said Means, by large aggregations of capital in which neither the nominal owner, the stockholder, nor the worker had much voice. Perhaps this development explained the rise of large power blocs, such as labor organizations and farm groups. Perhaps this sort of balance was essential, Means seemed to suggest, in order to avoid the conflict that frequently stemmed from a disproportionate distribution of power. Economic theory simply would have to include these new developments if it was to remain viable. The theory we now possessed had failed to fit the facts of reality, and policies based on such theories would be bound to culminate in social tension.

Means recognized that there were as many different theories as there were economic systems. The subsistence model of a colonial plantation revealed each economic unit producing for its own consumption with no buying and selling. The market played little role in such economy and the consumer was actually in control, exercising virtually all decisions on what to produce. It was possible, of course, to extend this model to include the market, but producer and consumer were still a single unit, as in the cash crop farm. But once the market had been introduced, consumers' influence waned. The factory system represented a third model. Here production was coordinated in a single place, with the worker separated from control of his tools and the consumer no longer able to influence production. This was the world of Marx, the world of private entrepreneurial capitalism. The fourth model, the one Means was concerned with, was one in which production was carried on by corporate units comprising great aggregations of capital, with ownership widely dispersed through stock ownership, so that even the stockholders exercised no control over the instruments of production. Separation of ownership and control made it possible to organize huge corporate entities employing thousands of workers, using billions of dollars of capital, and selling to millions of consumers, all controlled by small management groups, often perpetuating themselves in power through oligarchic devices. Means labelled this form "collective capitalism." [510]

Classical economic theory, from Adam Smith to Alfred Marshall, had been appropriate for the atomistic economy of the single entrepreneur. The key problem in this system had been price and this applied to labor as well as to the other factors of production. Marx recognized that with the rise of the factory system new assumptions had to be introduced into economics. While this was quite correct, said Means, Marx's theory had been neither consistent nor adequate. For "collective capitalism" there was still no useful theory available to explain what was happening. A corporate economy was not merely a deviation from classical normality: it represented an entirely new set of relationships. While the corporation drew together great quantities of wealth, no check had appeared to assure that public interests would be served. Certainly the stockholder was not served, as proxies, nonvoting stock, and other devices were employed to weaken his position. Was this private enterprise, as it was once known, asked Means, or a new collective dominated by management oligarchy? Was the profit motive sufficient to explain how management functioned? Was it really profit maximization they were interested in? [511] Moreover, were corporations concerned with market forces when they disposed of their output? Were they really subject to the law of supply and demand; did offers and bids actually affect their decision-making processes? All but the first question were answered in the negative.

The analysis of market forces in an atomistic economy also had explained how resources were co-ordinated. But this was a function now carried on, said Means, without recourse to the market, for a good deal of coordination now took place "within enterprises as well as between enterprises." [512] This meant that administrative direction emanated from the group in control of the corporation. It was no longer a case of production and investment following the dictates of market price, but one rather in which there were few producers, an absence of *price* competition, and a tendency toward inflexibility. This was the economy of administered prices and controlled markets. Competition, therefore, had to be expressed in ways other than price. Means argued that a large slice of the American economy now exhibited such characteristics, and he questioned whether such an economy could by itself achieve full utilization of resources. Yet he was not condemning what was taking place, for these features seemed to be endemic to the modern economic order. But he was concerned lest resource allocation and coordination reveal serious deficiencies in a system of corporate administered prices, especially since adjustments to changed economic conditions seemed to take place through production rather than price. Consequently, when depressions occurred, the burden was heaviest for workers and farmers.

Administrative techniques could equate supply and demand only by chance; yet when excess supply resulted from too high a price, the latter was seldom altered. Means noted that although retailing, as well as a large sector of manufacturing, employed administered pricing, economic theory had failed to take these newer developments into account. It was necessary, urged Means, to have a theory that would be concerned with the discrepancies occasioned by administered prices and the magnitude of price revisions, if and when such adjustments were made. What was needed was a theory of

. . . short run equilibrium on the assumptions that some prices are the classical type and that some are administered. We have the Walrasian formulation for an economy of perfectly flexible prices. We have the Keynesian formulation with its ambiguity about price, but it is capable of stating an equilibrium with prices fixed. What we need is a Walrasian-like formulation which will state the conditions of equilibrium if some prices are administered and some prices flexible, and to indicate how changes in the equilibrium determining factors will alter the equilibrium result.[513]

However, the major emphasis, said Means, would have to be on the administrative sector. A study of management motives would have to be included also, for it was evident that profit maximization was not the clue to the corporate way of life. Enterprise theory would have to deal with essentially the same kind of problems found in government; in the corporate structure the political scientist and economist would join hands. By focusing on the administrative use of resources, economics, said Means, could ". . . create a new kind of allocation theory in which the unseen hand of Adam Smith is replaced by the invisible hand of business bureaucracy." [514]

The influence of Adolph Berle was clearly discernible when Means asserted that corporations were accepting a new kind of social responsibility. The former argued in his *The 20th Century Capitalist Revolution*[515] that corporations had developed a quasi-political status which impelled them to act in the public interest, particularly since public opinion and the threat of state intervention were such potent controls. Private and government property were becoming increasingly intermingled, so that a tangled web of rights and privileges was being evolved in modern times threatening the rights of the individual. But, said Berle, with Means evidently in agreement, appeals to a court of equity, *within the corporate structure,* should suffice to guarantee personal freedoms. Management will simply have to grasp the fact that this is a world of people, and in so doing create a conscience for the corporation! Doubtless Berle and Means have pointed up some important political and sociological facets of corporate reality; it would be difficult to explain otherwise how oligopoly hardened and congealed competitive capitalism. But the assertion that all is well because the corporation now seems to be acquiring a soul hardly faced up to the basic problems.

In earlier years Means had been a good deal less enchanted by the corporation. Aware that corporate price and production policies had been significant elements in deepening the depression of the 1930's, he sought to develop a program that would neutralize harmful price practices before they worked their way through the economy. His administrative economics, to use Allan Gruchy's apt phrase, was primarily intended to sustain the kind of planning that would insure a more effective use of resources than the corporation had been able to achieve. He did not suggest altering inflexible prices by fiat, but wanted rather to relate flexible prices to the rest of the economy in a more meaningful way.[516] If the inconsistency between traditional economics and current reality were to be removed, it would be necessary to bring about equilibrium by conscious design. This, of course, might require new tasks for government. There was really no other way to do the job: at the time—in the late 1930's—it had seemed unlikely that the corporation would acquire a soul.

But it was clear that Means had shifted ground since he had co-authored the *Modern Corporation and Private Property.* He now expressed enthusiasm for collective capitalism and the corporate way of life,[517] although he still felt that the modifying influences of government and trade union action were essential. This was the new milieu in which resources could be allocated properly, a more equitable distribution of income provided, and freedom given to the individual to develop his own capacities. Of course, the new economics that would supply the theoretical framework would take account of administered prices and countervailing power.

vii

Countervailing Power and Affluence: J. K. Galbraith

Institutionalism, as a vital force in economic thinking, was perceptibly diminished by the time of the 1940's and 1950's. Its major influence had been felt in the decades before the war. The Great Depression, which broke upon a bewildered America, gave them an opportunity to apply their thinking to public policy; but due to their naïveté in the ways of political life, they were bound to fail. Earlier, capitalism seemed to have evolved the greatest civilization yet seen: there was now enough affluence to permit a few reforms, such as social insurance of a most limited nature, and some changes in banking practices. Even these were adopted with some reluctance. At the same time there was a willingness to flirt with newer trends in sociology and psychology: economics, it was felt, needed some broadening. Yet more and more institutionalists turned themselves into narrow specialists. Thus, attempts at cross-fertilization of ideas in the social sciences were frustrated; ambivalence was avoided by sticking close to what one knew best.[518] With Roosevelt's New Deal, many leading institutionalists, including Means and Berle and Rexford Tugwell, were caught up in administrative tasks. As the more exciting job of revamping society was undertaken, the urge to expound the institutionalist credo was lessened. When the depression was just about over, war came and new problems were at hand. By the end of the war, the institutionalists had run out of steam. They no longer had much say, and, in the face of the newer mathematical economics, they were completely at a loss for words. Problems they had once thought important had become the domain of the sociologist.

Yet there were a few economists, who if not squarely in the institutionalist camp, had enough of their spirit to continue the struggle for a humanistic economics. One such writer was John K. Galbraith, a Canadian, born in 1909. With degrees from Toronto, California, and Harvard, he addressed himself not only to his academic colleagues (who seemed to frown on his literary

activity) but to a wider general public as well. Chief of price control operations for the United States Government during the war, he was able to bring
this experience to bear on his economics. A long sojourn as an editor of
Fortune added to his store of practical knowledge. When the Democrats
came to power in 1960, he was appointed Ambassador to India, temporarily
postponing his flow of writing. His ability to present ideas with admirable
clarity and a felicitous style have made his books best sellers—a rare experience for an economist.

Galbraith was one of the first of contemporary economists to analyse
the problems of the disequilibrium system in a war economy.[519] He pointed
out that the modern market, oligopolistic in nature, lent itself more readily
to price control than the so-called free market.[520] The market as an abstraction disappeared whenever the number of buyers and sellers was small. They
were no longer unknown to each other, and thus it was possible for sellers
to impose informal rules of allocation on buyers. Favored buyers could be
granted preference in stringent situations, while the imposition of price control became a virtual invitation to allocation by private concerns. The
tendency for such a market to exhibit inflexible prices also helped the price
maker. Since conventional patterns and markups were already built into the
economy, wartime price control was simply a matter of continuing the
business game. In addition, government policy to insure industrial expansion
at decreasing cost was helpful in maintaining price control, said Galbraith,
especially in industries in which excess capacity was still a significant factor.[521]

These were the key features of the "disequilibrium system," an economy
in which the incentives and motivations of an unplanned system were supplemented by both price control and the direct allocation of resources. It
was also characterized by a greater money demand than there were goods
available. The purpose of the disequilibrium system had been to mobilize the
economy for war. Control of resources was essential, since the oligopolistic
industries had not been especially anxious to shift to a wartime footing for
fear of weakening their peacetime markets. Thus excess demand had become
a device for offering rewards to labor and capital to move to new places and
to produce necessary items. Only when there was no desire to save, or when
the supply curve of labor began to bend backwards, had the disequilibrium
system worn out its welcome. Nevertheless, it had made it possible for
modern oligopolistic capitalism to meet the requirements of a war economy.
There was, of course, a certain margin of tolerance, measured by that volume
of demand in excess of current supply, which was consistent with additions
to total output. This margin had not been exhausted in the United States,
as it had in Germany.

Thus the basic assumption in Galbraith's analysis of a wartime economy
dealt with the central role of oligopoly markets in contemporary capitalism.
The theme was further explored in his *American Capitalism: The Concept*

of Countervailing Power.[522] Here he began with the contention that the economy was a good deal more resilient than had been suspected. Like Means, he felt that this strength stemmed in large part from the corporate structure of business. Yet everyone was fearful that the encroachments of those whom he disliked would undermine the foundations of the economy. The conservatives disliked government and the liberals abhorred business. Each constructed his own economic ideology, said Galbraith, to justify his antipathies. One wanted the free market; the other, economic planning. For one, Say's Law provided a touching nostalgia, the other resorted to socialism, cooperation, or, more recently, Keynes. Yet neither set of beliefs was able to yield an adequate comprehension of the way a modern economy really functioned, argued Galbraith. Both liberals and conservatives remained captives of ideas which caused them to look at the world with alarm.

For one thing, said Galbraith with some justice, economic theory had not yet struck a speaking acquaintanceship with political science. This was a serious oversight, for the key to the economic problem seemed to rest on questions of power. With oligopoly structures so pervasive a feature, it would seem obvious that this would have to be central to the game of economics. But competitive theory, unfortunately, had ignored all the problems stemming from power as allegedly noneconomic in nature. On the other hand, large aggregations of economic power could not be explained by a devil theory of history, for the causes of concentration were organic. Once an industry was established it was difficult for newcomers to enter with any measure of ease. Only with the historic studies of Joan Robinson and E. H. Chamberlin did economic theory begin to catch up with economic reality.[523] At any rate, the theory of oligopoly led one away from the world of competition to that of monopoly. In fact, price competition, as J. M. Clark had demonstrated, could be disastrous. Insofar as the impact on the market was concerned, oligopoly with its selling costs and product differentiation seemed to work out for this worst of all possible worlds.[524] A new power to predetermine prices had been established which all the antitrust action and waving of big sticks were unable to disperse. And in the climate of American opinion the liberal hope for public regulation came to nought.

Yet the economy was working satisfactorily, said Galbraith, and one reason for this was the unmatched technology on which it was based. Oligopoly seemed best able to utilize technical innovations in unrestrained fashion.[525] The oligopolist, thought Galbraith, could benefit from an advanced technology before some interloper tried to share in the gains. And this made the disappearance of the free market no great tragedy. Moreover, the economy's overwhelming affluence assured a certain measure of tolerance for the inefficient. Yet this argument, at least as it applied to inventions and innovation, seemed much too facile in the face of persistent fact. The implication that oligopoly had dominated the innovation process overlooked the many independent inventors still around.[526] And it has appeared more than likely that small or medium-sized enterprises are able to apply innovations at least as effectively as the giants of industry, uninhibited as they are by overhead and obsolescence. Oligopolies often have been quite reluctant to scrap still usable plant and equipment, and, in fact, much of their innovative efforts have been either held in suspense or utilized to protect positions previously attained. There is ample evidence to sustain these observations, from the steel industry—where most of the important technological changes have been introduced by small firms—to the development of the O-cel-o plastic sponge. Moreover, the seeming advantage that oligopolies have enjoyed in applying technical innovation has stemmed in large measure from the government's defense program. The evidence does suggest, consequently, that the bigness of an enterprise has been no assurance that innovation would be encouraged or employed.

Thus while Galbraith's argument exhibited a surface similarity to Schumpeter's famous thesis, which defended the viability of the large concern, it nevertheless ignored precisely the sort of sociology that made the latter so striking a system. For Schumpeter had paid particular attention to the dilution of the spirit of adventurousness in modern corporate capitalism. The organization man, functioning in a new kind of bureaucratic milieu, has been all too ready to apply cautionary brakes to an unrestrained application of technological change.

Be that as it may, the central theme in Galbraith's work was that oligopoly developed its own restraints which stemmed not from rivals, but from the other side of the market—customers and suppliers. This was countervailing power, a happy phrase which replaced the uglier technical expression, oligopoly.[527] Economic power begat countervailance; strong sellers were accompanied by strong buyers. While competition in an oligopolistic market tended to be passive, this was not the situation for a powerful buyer. Moreover, countervailance was not the bilateral monopoly of ordinary academic theory, for the latter had been an irregular, almost accidental situation which had failed to recognize the innate tendency of oligopoly to generate balancing powers. Galbraith illustrated his thesis with several cogent cases, particularly from trade unionism and the retail field. In one such situation a large supermarket chain forced down the price of corn flakes merely by threatening to engage in its own manufacturing. And it is well known that some large retailers are not at all hesitant in exerting extreme pressures on those from whom they buy. While countervailing power admittedly did not exist in all parts of the economy, Galbraith thought it would help economic growth if it did. Housebuilding was a case in point: where a few builders had been able to bypass the numerous restrictions stemming from traditional practices and exercise influence on the market, not inconsiderable progress had been made. Achieving this demanded an ability to organize resources through the corporate form of business. Thus, Galbraith's theory established the praiseworthiness of Means' collective capitalism. Yet this in no way implied that the new capitalism would function automatically. Galbraith knew, as did Keynes, that there was no device at hand to enforce "proper performance." There would still be some need for government policy.

Still, for all of Galbraith's persuasiveness, it could be questioned whether oligopoly really did generate countervailing power at all times. Nor was there anything in the process like the inevitability he suggested. Certainly, when demand was on the upswing the force of countervailance was immeasurably weakened. And the justification for oligopoly appeared a bit strained. In fact, it would seem that businessmen themselves were reluctant to utilize such rationalizations of the new corporate capitalism. It was much safer and more comfortable to rely on the ancient wisdom emanating from the Chamber of Commerce than to toy with a risky new ideology.[528] Although ample illustrations of the sophisticated conservative approach appeared in *Fortune* magazine and publications of the Committee for Economic Development, by and large, the business community preferred the old-fashioned, blunt claim to lordship over all creation and praise of the general beneficence of the profit motive and free competition. Insofar as this myth has continued to exert its attractive force, Galbraith's analysis, as cogent as it may be, has not faced up to a fundamental issue—the justification by businessmen of the role they perform. The simple fact seems to be that the older views have provided a direct and effective means for the legitimation of power, and it is this that has led to the kind of ideology which has enabled the corporate director to counteract the claims of persons outside his enterprise. Granted that price takers may on occasion exercise countervailance, there still seems to be ample evidence that price makers play the more meaningful role. The latter are able to fix their own prices and to administer them in accordance with the dictates of sales strategy. Apparently, more than ordinary power compulsion is behind modern market decisions than the theory of countervailance would allow.

Paradoxically enough, flowing logically out of the theory of countervailing power with its basis in oligopoly, came the proposals of *The Affluent Society,* which were quasi-socialist in implication, if not in intent.[529] This fabulously successful book set forth a series of proposals that spelled out the sort of society socialists had been talking about for years. Despite some drawbacks of detail, this was done thoughtfully and with discernment of the complexities involved. The outstanding fact in our society, said Galbraith, was that we possessed the unquestioned ability to produce whatever it was we cared to produce. Since this was the case, society ought to be able to meet all needs, both private as well as public. Yet the real situation was that our productive system had reached a point of doubtful return. It had become a well-stuffed cornucopia that poured out an endless flow of goods, all seeking to satisfy the craving of the average American to gorge himself on a bewildering array of commodities. These goods, privately produced and privately sold, had created the image of an affluent society. Yet, in reality, we were much less prosperous than we thought. The amount of deprivation in public services was depressing; schools were old and overcrowded; there was a lack of parks and playgrounds; cities were unable to clean their streets; and the ghastly exhaust of insolent chariots polluted the skies. Galbraith wondered whether the desire for a nontoxic supply of air would suggest a revolutionary dalliance with socialism.

Galbraith argued quite persuasively that this strange disparity stemmed from a lack of social balance. Our economy was one in which private commodities and public services were complementary—more automobiles demanded more places in which to put them and more roads on which to drive. In the past, it had not been uncommon for a community to provide horse rails for vehicles to pause. But this had become impossible today, despite our vaunted technological wisdom. The consumption of private goods obviously required some facility or protective steps by government. Without this, civic strangulation seemed to be the prospect for America. Essentially, what was needed was a balance between private goods and the supply of public services. And the latter included investment in humans through an improved educational plant.

The disparity between the private and public realm was traced to the ideology of unremitting production implicit in the thinking of the classical economists. Their theory, which Galbraith dubbed the "conventional wisdom," had suggested that poverty and inequality would always be mankind's lot. They had seen a limited national income and a conflict of classes over its distribution. Marx too had seen this as the central problem, but, unlike the classicists, he did not expect the system to survive. Somehow it did, and perhaps, Galbraith suggested, part of the reason might be traced to the new technology and its affluent flow of goods. Galbraith's criticism of the older economists, however, did not take into account the optimistic strain which could be found running from Adam Smith to J. B. Say. The "conventional wisdom" might have appeared to exhibit some measure of accuracy only because there was imbedded in it a sense of hope and harmony which gave everyone an "uncertain reassurance" that everything in the end would turn out well. Whenever riches did flow, the economic harmonies of Say and Bastiat comforted us that this was the best of all possible worlds. This ideology, however, contained a fatal flaw that dissenting economists from Veblen to Hobson had used to clobber the classicists with. This was the simple fact that the income generated by the economic order did not always move in ways that absorbed the whole product. Galbraith, in his last study, underestimated this condition. It was the same weakness that both Marx and Keynes saw in Say's Law. Galbraith, however, examined the economy only when it had produced a surfeit of private goods, so that all that could now happen was a bit of irritating unemployment. Nor could one accept his contention that genuine inequality no longer existed.[530]

Nevertheless, Galbraith dismissed the notion that economic insecurity was essential for progress. Security, he said, was within reach with our kind of affluence. America's vast output had made useless the conventional wisdom's image of the slothful workingman. We ought to cultivate the art of getting more for doing less: the economy was well able to achieve this objective. In fact, said Galbraith, it had already developed this aim, for, apart from the universities, ". . . where its practice had the standing of a scholarly rite, the art of genteel and elaborately concealed idleness" was in full flower in the higher executive reaches of the corporation.[531] The main point was that production was so great that society could easily afford a certain slackness. Yet the conventional wisdom insisted that productive efforts must be unceasing, for wants were supposedly insatiable, and there wasn't anything that couldn't be sold to a consumer if only he was made to desire it. Galbraith's comments on the theory of consumer demand were equally sharp.[532] He questioned the efficacy of marginal utility on the ground that it avoided entirely the problem of the diminishing urgency of consumption. Attention to this problem was diverted in received economics by shifting from cardinal to ordinal utility, thus reducing consumer desires simply to terms of the preference of one good over the other, and thereby excluding the possibility that needs which were present regardless of the situation might be fully satisfied in the calculable future.[533]

Thus, for Galbraith the problem of production had been solved, while distribution left something to be desired. This was the same problem that all dissenters had stressed. The sort of distribution Galbraith advocated clearly meant an expansion of public services and welfare: he urged more and better education and the use of resources to lessen hunger and discontent. He wanted to break the connection between production and income, so that if unemployment came about he would hold effective demand high with unemployment insurance close to the full wage. As one examines Galbraith's work thus far, there is the inescapable feeling that the tradition of dissent in American economics is still alive.[534]

Part TWO

The Reaffirmation of Tradition

4

From Marginalism

to Libertarianism

W. S. Jevons: The Discovery
of Marginalism

I N THE THIRD QUARTER of the nineteenth century British economics had been dominated by John Stuart Mill and his disciples. Others who might have sought another approach to the perennial problems of the economic order could get no real hearing for their ideas. Yet during the decade of the seventies there began a movement away from classical objectivism which, before long, seemed to have overcome all barriers.[1] A desire developed to base economic thinking on subjective notions and to analyse exchange in virtually total abstraction from the social setting.

Why was this so? Criticisms of capitalism, as we have seen, had been growing apace, and it seemed impossible to express views about the social order in genuinely neutral terms. The turn given to classical doctrine by

Karl Marx was distressing.[2] It appeared necessary to rebut such a tendency and it was perhaps toward this end that marginalist doctrine was directed. The real cost analysis of the classicists was abandoned, with preference expressed for psychological cost ideas. These ideas implied a particular conception of human behavior which could then become an anchor for a new view of value. If the psychology were inadequate, that really was not upsetting, for one might even keep the form of the theory without the psychic content. While the marginalist defense of the *status quo,* one of their primary objectives, might have been an unconscious one, it seemed evident that, as Harvey Peck once remarked, they "at least strengthened the weak links of the classical theory, and thus re-established a system on the basis of which business men and idle capitalists could find a social justification for their personal ambitions or their defense of their privileges." [3] If this were so, then marginalism was a kind of concealed apology for the power élite, to use C. Wright Mills' term.[4] Of course, if economics were to be defined as a study of wealth rather than welfare, there ought not have been any complaint.

The first to launch a successful rebellion against the dominant theories of the time was William Stanley Jevons (1835-1882). The ninth of eleven children, only three of whom lived into adulthood, Jevons grew up in a Dissenter family, whose everlasting financial difficulties made it necessary for him to forego an attempt at Oxford or Cambridge. Instead, he went to the University of London where he did quite well in scientific studies. When gold was discovered in Australia in the 1850's, the authorities there sent to England for an assayer to man the new mint. Jevons was recommended for the post, and, at the age of nineteen, he interrupted his studies and went off half way round the world to a new venture. He needed the £630 a year, a magnificent salary for that day, for he felt that he would now be able to assist his brother and sister toward their education.

Jevons remained in Australia for five years, husbanded his resources carefully, and continued to study on his own. He developed a passionate interest in meteorology and, characteristically enough, compiled considerable data on the temperature and weather conditions of the continent, leading to his first published paper, *The Climate of Australia and New Zealand.* In 1857, at the age of twenty-two, he turned to economics, with the thought that he might be able to apply mathematics to the subject in a fruitful way. He had been reading some materials on railway economics and the problem of rate-making. These were areas of monopolistic behavior where fixed costs were large and direct costs small, so that one began to be aware of a nascent kind of marginalist theory.

With a limitless faith in his mental powers and a kind of youthfully arrogant belief that his own insights into the foundations of knowledge would yield a deeper understanding of social principles, he set out to create a new theory in economics.[5] After his stay in Australia, where his main ideas were formed—especially those on business cycles and economic theory—Jevons returned to Britain. In accordance with earlier plans, he first traveled through Peru, Panama, the West Indies, and the United States, inspecting their economies and particularly their gold mines. He returned home in 1859 and resumed his studies.

Jevons' concepts in mathematical economics soon began to take shape. By 1860 the notion of diminishing marginal utility had been formulated and two years later his paper on the subject, "Brief Account of a General Mathematical Theory of Political Economy," was sent to the British Association for the Advancement of Science.[6] It was received without a word of acknowledgement, much less encouragement. The Association was also sent a second paper, "On the Study of Periodic Commercial Fluctuations, with Five Diagrams," an early attempt to measure seasonal variations, indicating Jevons' deep interest in statistical techniques. Later in his career he made significant contributions to index number and probability theory.

After his graduation, Jevons tried his hand at writing for magazines, even attempting a ghost-writing venture. Neither effort was much of a success. In 1863 he finally accepted a teaching position at a small college in Manchester where he lectured on logic, moral philosophy, and, interestingly enough, political economy according to the lights of John Stuart Mill. He took his responsibilities quite seriously, worked hard, and ruined his health. Since he had to teach courses in logic, Jevons became interested in George Boole's symbolic system. In 1863 he published a small work on the subject, *Pure Logic,* and announced that he had discovered the universal principle of reasoning which he called the "substitution of similars." *Elementary Lessons in Logic* followed in 1870 and his famous *Principles of Science* in 1874.

Jevons was gradually acquiring public and professional recognition, even though his early essays had been ignored and his new economic theory, announced in 1871, studiously rejected. His reputation as a logician was high; in fact, much of his distaste for Mill seems to have stemmed from a fundamental difference over formulations in logic rather than political economy.[7] More than half of Jevons' published works were in scientific method and for almost fifty years British students were raised on Jevonian logic. Jevons was accepted for membership in the Royal Society in 1872, the first economist since Sir William Petty to be so honored, and in 1874 he became a member of the Political Economy Club. After resigning his professorship at London in 1880 on grounds of ill health, he devoted his time to independent research, working on his odd theory of business cycles. When astronomers announced that sun spots also came in cycles, Jevons wondered whether their effect on climate and weather might not be such as to influence agricultural conditions and, through these, shifts in business. He tried to demonstrate his contention by correlating the average period of crises with the average length of sun spot cycles. The whole affair came to nought.

Unquestionably, Jevons was a man of probity, even to the point of managing his investments according to his own theory of business cycles.[8] Basically conservative in outlook, he nevertheless had occasional kind words for the liberal view. The emphasis in his own education on mathematics and the physical sciences had a marked influence on his approach to economics. Yet Jevons evidently had little impact on those around him; convinced as he was of his own intellectual prowess, he preferred to work alone. Possessed of a somewhat dyspeptic temperament, music was his sole relaxation. And oddly enough, his lectures were pure distilled Stuart Mill, dry and dull and poorly attended. Yet there is some evidence that he managed to affect the thinking of such major economists as Wicksteed and Edgeworth.[9]

Jevons' hostility to Mill bordered on the paranoiac. He felt that the predominance of the classical view was a serious impediment to progress in economics. In one of his letters he said: "I fear it is impossible to criticize Mr. Mill's writing without incurring the danger of rousing animosity. . . ." [10] He charged Mill with inconsistency and insisted that he could substantiate this on virtually every page of Mill's work. So poor was the latter's output, said Jevons, that he even had no idea of capital.[11] In fact, said Jevons, the proper line of development in economics was not from Ricardo to Mill, but from Smith to Malthus to Senior. But he made no impression on the followers of Stuart Mill who simply continued to teach classical cost of production as if marginal utility had never existed. Curiously enough, Jevons did the same. The classical influence was not to be rooted out until Jevons had been joined in his crusade by the subjective economists out of Austria. Jevons died by drowning at the age of forty-seven, a considerable loss to economics since he was still at the height of his intellectual powers.

Jevons' major work in economics was the *Theory of Political Economy,* published in 1871.

My theory [he had written] is purely mathematical in character. Nay, believing that the quantities with which we deal must be subject to continuous variation, I do not hesitate to use the appropriate branch of mathematical science, involving though it does the fearless consideration of infinitely small quantities. The theory consists in applying the differential calculus to the familiar notions of wealth, utility, value, demand, supply, capital, interest, labour, and all the quantitative notions belonging to the daily operations of industry.[12]

Jevons believed quite firmly that economics could become an exact science if only better data were available. Were this the case, he said, numerical calculation and predictability would be assured. There need be only better ways of collecting data, for quantities of production and prices are precise notions. However, while the immense energies that go into the basic definitions of a statistical survey require highly refined conceptual skills, such techniques can not solve all economic problems. Society comprises many elements that are not subject to quantitative manipulation: significant relationships exist between groups and individuals that must be grasped with other tools and without which economic reality may be very well incomplete.

Be that as it may, Jevons' theory sought to explore what he viewed as the calculus of utility. He began with a theory of consumer goods grounded in marginal utility which was then extended to the pricing of the factors of production in a way that was close to the notions of marginal productivity. Although in its rough outlines, his theory resembled Léon Walras', it was much less elegant and much less effective. As a result, there was no sense of the genuinely comprehensive in Jevons. His mathematical elaborations lacked the potency of the literary formulations of Carl Menger and Friedrich von Wieser. Yet it is to his credit that he was able to draw attention to the central role of subjective marginal utility in his models.

Jevons started his analysis with the case of two trading bodies or two individuals with a given stock of goods, who, once initiating an exchange, continued the business of higgling until equilibrium was attained. At this point he concluded that the ratio of exchange was equivalent to the reciprocal of the ratio of the *final degree* of utility of the commodities involved.[13] The model could be enlarged to encompass more exchangers and more goods. But the concept of trading bodies entailed some conceptual problems. As Wicksell observed, the Jevonian equations seemed to assume a kind of collective marginal utility for a group of exchanging persons, a notion which was patently obscure.[14] Further, the trading bodies suggested a situation of interminable bilateral higgling with the fact of generalized competition—a mainstay of the theory in its over-all application—completely lost. Of course, continuous divisibility of the goods involved, as well as continuous variation in the marginal utilities, was implicit in the Jevonian construct. But, it was argued, the theory was meant to be applied to large numbers also, so that the concept of continuity thereby could be given clear meaning. In this way, the trading body notion was applicable presumably to trading between nations in international trade as well.

The basic postulate asserted that value stemmed from marginal utility. That is to say, demand was the predominant factor in exchange value, not cost of production as with the classicists. Nevertheless, Jevons did add the proviso that behind value lay the final degree of utility, which in turn was affected by supply, and that this, in its turn, was rooted in cost of production.[15] Clearly, this meant that subjective considerations were the determining ones solely when the supply was fixed and given. This, of course, made the theory short run and static. It could be said that in the long run, when supply was variable, cost came into its own as an element in value.[16] Here Jevons was delineating the fundamentals of exchange and distribution, abstracted from changes in population, political institutions, consumer taste, and capital growth.

The theory of value, he intimated, might be put into a neutral setting, removed from historical time and human events. Thus the problems of value, resource allocation, and distribution could exhibit universal attributes, germane to all sorts of economic societies. Resource allocation, for example, was to be achieved by making the marginal utility of output reveal the same ratio to all the marginal disutilities of labor in all the endeavors to which resources would be distributed.[17] Not that Jevons was unaware of the nature of economic dynamics; he simply felt that his approach was more manageable than the "natural complexities" of real affairs.[18]

But basic to value was utility and this in turn was rooted in the Benthamite pleasure-pain psychology. Pleasure, said Jevons, had two dimensions, intensity and duration. One might even speak of gross pleasure, from which gross pain was to be deducted in arriving at net pleasure.[19] Pleasure diminished through time and was clearly related to be the available supply of the commodity which yielded the particular pleasure in question. Jevons exploited Bentham's felicific calculus as much as he could: it seemed to him that pleasures and pains represented the sole genuine basis for understanding human motives.[20] Whereas Bentham, however, thought he could actually measure the pleasure-pain syndrome, Jevons confessed that this was inconceivable, since a unit of pleasure or pain could not be constructed. In fact, measurement was pointless. All that the economist had to know was simply whether one pleasure was greater than the other or when pleasures were in equilibrium and when a pleasure exceeded a pain. This implied a direct comparison of quantities in an ordinal sense and a judgment of the relationships among pleasures and pains. The final or marginal degree of utility would involve comparisons for the buyer of different possible applications of his purchasing power. This would not require interpersonal comparisons of utility.

All this, of course, was a drastic simplification of Bentham's formulas and might have suggested that man, after all, was no lightning calculator of pleasures and pains. Jevons was concerned with the "lowest rank of feeling"; the calculus of utility merely involved the ordinary wants of man.[21] He needed utility per se as the foundation stone of exchange value, which was itself determined by its own final degree, that is, the last point in the scale of diminishing satisfaction. This notion was virtually the same as marginal utility. Nevertheless, the impression persisted that utility was intended by Jevons to serve a quantitative purpose. In this sense, as C. Reinold Noyes has demonstrated, pleasure and utility concepts were preposterous.[22] Pleasure at best might be an introspectively revealed experience which had to be accepted as part of human behavior, but it was not useful for economic calculation. Furthermore, real economic man was no rational animal but rather a wild guesser operating on hunches and unknown factors.

But for Jevons, the ordinal comparison of pleasures and pains was a simple enough way of reaching value. Like pleasure, utility—defined as the relation of a consumer to his good—declined as the amount of the good increased. This, however, could be understood solely as a snapshot picture of consumption, certainly not in terms of repetitive uses over given units of time. In the latter sense, there conceivably might be no problem of satiation and no decline in the utility of discrete units repeatedly consumed. This was an interpretation that the marginalists tended to dismiss, as in the case of Menger, who insisted that even in such cases satiation still was bound to occur. Jevons carefully stressed the distinction between total utility and the final degree of utility, defining the latter as the ratio of the increment in utility stemming from the last unit of the good to the increment in the total stock of the good. This precise concept, however, made no headway against Menger's and Wieser's simpler notion of marginal utility, despite the fact that the Jevonian idea, employing ratios as it did, suggested a greater mathematical flexibility in comparing the results of consuming different stocks of goods.

From this point, it was but a short step to the proposition that utility was maximized when a consumer's expenditures were such that the final degree of utility was the same in all instances. Assuming the possibility of satiation over time, the principle could be applied to future consumption of goods, even though this was usually a remote and uncertain affair. Jevons believed that the stock of goods would be consumed in the present at maximum levels, thus giving greater weight to immediate uses. This characteristic, which Jevons assumed to be universal, was attributed to man's impatience. The presentation of utility theory, however, was so replete with ambiguities and so patently hedonic in its presuppositions that later economists sought to escape the pleasure-pain calculus by utilizing the Jevonian technique shorn of its psychological underpinnings.

Although Jevons employed utility and scarcity as devices for demonstrating the cooperative character of value creation, he somehow retained emphasis on labor as "the first price, the original purchase" paid for all things, and the beginning of all processes with which economists supposedly were concerned.[23] However, he soon lost sight of "labor," and the original intention to make psychic drives the major economic force quickly resumed the upper hand. The impression was created that the individual operated alone, unaffected by the social relations implied by market situations. Now, individual reactions certainly had considerable influence on behavior, but—

as Maurice Dobb has argued—any attempt to derive aggregates from such a theory raised serious logical questions, for the individual as an atomistic unit was not the same as the individual in a social setting.[24] A person was subject to many complex social influences which determined such matters as consumer choice. This was no neutral matter, as implied in Jevonian theory, since a given pattern of income distribution, one of the more significant social-economic forces, had much to do with fixing consumer choice. Consequently, the problem of economic motivation had to be rooted in institutional data. Otherwise the theory would be merely formalistic and without content.

The theory of capital was an important component of Jevons' system, as it was for the Austrians. Generally, notions of capital were based on the concept of a stock of measureable wealth, although the idea of a fund of assets was sometimes discernible. While the fund idea was developed more fully later on, it was anticipated by Jevons. Although he tried to start his analysis with the classical version of capital, he soon became aware of the important distinction between equipment and wage-goods. The function of capital, said Jevons, was to support a given number of employees during the time it took them to complete a job.[25] Capital allowed for the expenditure of labor "in advance," and an adequate supply of wage-goods was essential for further improvement of the productive process. This very well might have been interpreted as an elimination of all capital transactions, except for the exchange of money for labor. If, with further abstraction, money itself was removed from the analysis, the relationship would become simply that of wage-goods to labor services. The rate of interest could then be said to be but part of the collection of wage-goods. Earnings from sunk capital or equipment—which in the Jevonian sense were not really capital—were, properly speaking, a kind of rent, thus suggesting Marshall's concept of quasi-rent.

A restricted supply of wage-goods, stemming mainly from an insufficiency of finance, could seriously limit the choice of alternative productive processes and ultimately affect the nature of the final product itself. Important to Jevons here was the concept of time, for there was a gap between the beginning of a project and the point at which its yield or services could be realized. There was, in other words, a period of construction that required financing. The present and the future somehow would have to be connected: it was here that the capitalist came into his own—he brought together not only production and consumption, but carefully intertwined the output of today with the economic hopes and anticipations of tomorrow.[26] It was obvious that part of the collection of wage-goods supplied by the capitalist would have to be employed to help produce future goods, that is, to provide the requisite labor to replace and expand capital equipment. The major beneficiary from this expansion process then would not be the capitalist but the laborer who received an ever increasing pool of equipment from which to help enhance investment!

At this point the rate of interest entered the somewhat complex story. Jevons rejected abstinence as an element in interest, limiting his analysis to free capital or the portion of capital responsible for wage-goods.[27] Related as it was to the time gap in production, it came fairly close to a marginal productivity theory. Since a lengthening of the production period increased output, interest could be measured by the ratio of added output to added free capital. At best this was a crude approach to marginal productivity, which merely added time to the classical period of production. Nevertheless, Jevons' interest theory was well received. It was further developed in non-mathematical form by Böhm-Bawerk, for whom the concept of capital meant the substitution of indirect for direct methods of production, thereby increasing output and efficiency.

However, Jevonian capital theory, while advancing the fund concept, did little to further the theory of money. Jevons, in fact, pushed money far into the background of economic analysis.[28] As Wesley Mitchell has said, the hedonic calculus offered a theory of exchange in which there was no role for money to play. Instead of pecuniary business motives, Jevons substituted the search for pleasure as the unifying principle in economics. Not that Jevons was unaware of monetary factors: his book on *Investigations in Currency and Finance* amply demonstrated his interest in the subject.[29] But this was a far cry from developing a well-rounded general theory of value which incorporated propositions on the value of money as well. Such an interpretation, suggested by Arthur W. Marget, whose disputatious reconstruction of Jevonian money theory is based on mere fragments, is unacceptable. One must conclude that Jevons was not a monetary theorist at all.[30]

However difficult it may have been to incorporate money into the corpus of his theory, Jevons did not have the same problem with labor. An expansion in total utility simply implied more goods requiring greater expenditure of labor. This was merely the other side of the pleasure coin. Labor represented the "pain" experienced in creating utility.[31] In fact, labor was negative utility, as it were—the disutility of work—and as such was actually the only basic cost element in production. Since pain accumulated as the period of work was lengthened, a rising curve representing the increase in cost could be derived from this fundamental fact. It was this that underpinned scarcity in supply, said Jevons. Work continued up to a point where the utility of the last unit of goods was just matched by the increased sacrifice. The theory was set forth in diagrammatic terms by employing a diminishing output curve superimposed on the same axis with the labor curve. As the latter rose above the horizontal axis, pleasure in work increased. With an increase in output along the horizontal, the labor curve continued to rise but then turned down and finally dropped below the x-axis, indicating increasing disutility. Labor pain became an increasing function of the amount of work.[32]

Of course, this sort of snapshot analysis, merely for a single period, did not take into account the manifold complexities of the work situation or the fact that work was a daily repetitive process in which the curve of disutility was repeated day after day with no attainment of Jevonian equilibrium. Daily work might follow roughly some sort of utility curve, but the total work load continued without end as demanded by the exigencies of living and the industrial process. Furthermore, Jevons' theory assumed that disutility would be carefully balanced and weighed by the worker, a rather fanciful conception. Nor did the worker have the freedom of movement that the theory implied: modern capitalism simply did not function in Jevons' way. His algebra of motivation was nonexistent and the Benthamite calculus seemed entirely otiose in the contemporary setting. Individuals did not usually estimate the worthwhileness of work as against the energy expended: this sort of calculation evaded the task of examining economic relationships in a society where propertyless workers confronted private property holders, particularly of the corporate variety. Moreover, it was quite possible to assert, as did Hobson later on, that for certain types of work no disutility could be discovered.

The worker, said Jevons, was required to pay interest to the capitalist because he himself had been unable to save out of income and could not, therefore, provide his own means of production.[33] High wages, he continued rather smugly, offered no solution, for the worker was intemperate and ignorant of opportunities. Trade unions were useless, really; if the worker was able to pay dues to unions why should he not save? Yet Jevons did not really oppose unions, for he acknowledged their importance as a means for equalizing the bargaining situation. But union leaders, he argued, did not seem to realize that industrial conflict was a case of labor fighting labor, for the worker's interests were identical with those of his employer. True to his basic philosophy and his theory of distribution, Jevons advocated profit-sharing schemes because they made the worker a little capitalist.[34] He had no conception of the palpable historical fact that alienation from the means of production was a permanent feature of the economic order. Suppose workers did save, as indeed they do, what capital equipment would they be able to acquire? Perhaps more than anything else this fact revealed the futility of Jevons' neutralist approach. His strictures on labor seemed as helpful as his basic psychology.

Jevons' theory of wages was a kind of residual claimant theory.[35] This was evident when he said that wages coincided with ". . . what [the worker] produces, after the deduction of rent, taxes, and the interest of capital." [36] From another viewpoint, payments to the other factors were to be made by labor, thus suggesting that the worker was the central element in distribution theory. It would seem that in this area, at least, Jevons had been unable to escape his classical heritage. Furthermore, Ricardian rent theory was accepted virtually *in toto,* while profit was decomposed into wages of superintendence, insurance against risk, and interest on capital. Rent stemmed from variations in land fertility and the presence of diminishing returns. Risk was the differential required to induce capital to attempt uncertain ventures. In the long run, with competition, this would be equalized for all lines of activity.

Several other odd but interesting facets appeared in Jevons' economic theory. He was, of course, well known for his sun-spot theory of business cycles, a notion frequently ridiculed. As early as 1875, Jevons had suggested the possibility of some correlation between weather and economic conditions. In 1878 he repeated the argument, utilizing additional data which seemed to indicate a closer fit between solar periods and economic crisis.[37] But when European harvest periods did not seem to suit his purpose he employed data from India, on the theory that there was a closer relation between British trade and the Indian situation. His "facts" revealed the solar period to be 10.5 years and the business cycle the same—a beautiful correlation, he thought. But the dating was poor and the argument not at all strong. As Keynes remarked, Jevons would have been able to tie his theory to more solid earth-bound matters had he examined fluctuations in investments in agricultural stocks. By demonstrating how total stocks were maintained through lean years and fat, with alternating deficits and investments, he would have been on much safer ground. In short, the Jevonian cycle theory was an interesting fiction.

Nevertheless, Jevons was an eminent statistician as well as a leading theoretical economist. An early paper, *Commercial Fluctuations,*[38] while offering little new in the application of statistics to graphical analysis, suggested that a more rigorous mathematical treatment of these phenomena was to be required. Jevons was concerned with uniformities and tendencies. Said Keynes:

He would spend hours arranging his charts, plotting them, sifting them, tinting them neatly with delicate pale colours like the slides of an anatomist, and all the time poring over them and brooding over them to discover their secret. It is remarkable, looking back, how few followers and imitators he had in the black arts of inductive economics in the fifty years after 1862. But today he can certainly claim an unnumbered progeny, though the scientific flair which can safely read the shifting sands of economic statistics is no commoner than it was.[39]

Jevons would look at seasonal changes in discounts, bankruptcies, and the price of Consols. He had observed an upward secular trend in prices and, thinking that perhaps the value of money might have declined, he went on to study the problem of gold. In the course of these investigations he worked out his ideas on index numbers, discussing at great length problems of weighting, averages, and the number of items that should be included in a basket of index commodities. Virtually all the major questions of index number construction were solved by him. Jevons' contributions to statistics were acknowledged by no less a master than Wesley C. Mitchell, who in his *Business Cycles* said: "It was left for W. Stanley Jevons to give the first powerful impetus to statistical work in economic theory." [40]

Jevons felt that a steady upward secular movement was helpful in that it had an exhilarating effect and stimulated economic health. In this he was at one with John Maynard Keynes, who also made much of Jevons' hint that cycles might be traced to a disproportionate investment in fixed capital. However, even here the psychological aspect was dominant. In the *Investigations in Currency and Finance,* Jevons spoke of economic collapse as being possibly ". . . mental in their nature, depending upon variations of despondency, hopefulness, excitement, disappointment and panic." [41]

The book that brought Jevons his first public success was *The Coal Question,* published in 1865. It was noticed by none other than William Gladstone to whom the publisher sent a copy; Mill mentioned it in Parliament; and its thesis was used as an argument in favor of national debt reduction. If it were true, as the *Coal Question* implied, that Britain was living on its economic capital, then would not the reduction of the debt make the burden easier? Jevons' case was a simple one: in years to come, Great Britain's continued industrial leadership would require a huge expansion in energy resources. The demand for coal, like population in Malthus' "law," would grow in a geometric progression. But coal production, like Malthusian food production, was subject to diminishing returns. With deeper shafts and no new mines to exploit, costs would mount and the nation's industrial system be put in jeopardy. Jevons did not mean, of course, that the coal mines would be entirely exhausted, but rather that Britain's pre-eminent position could not go on forever, since the newer industrial countries on the continent and in North America would be bound to catch up. Although he underestimated the potentialities of new sources of energy, Jevons' insistence on the temporary character of Britain's industrial hegemony was remarkably prescient.

Jevons' interest in matters of public policy was, at best, peripheral. The agitation for voting reform meant little to him, and he confessed to his brother that he failed to understand politics at all.[42] He was concerned solely, he said, with pure economics and would prefer to leave questions of application to others. Whatever interest he did manifest in history was really of an antiquarian nature: he could explore the antecedents of a particular theory, rediscover Richard Cantillon, and trace index numbers back to the eighteenth century; but this was a far cry from revealing the human implications of the data with which he dealt. Whatever historical interest he expressed was converted into a useful bibliomania and the collection of obscure fragments of economic literature. Jevons built a huge library of over three thousand volumes in economics and related subjects which, after his death, found its way to Japan.[43]

In contrast to Jevons' interest in pure economics, traditional economics in Britain had expressed, in true Ricardian fashion, a deep and abiding concern with the events of the day. Economists were really *political* economists, anxious to employ their science as a direct instrument of melioration. In this rich heritage the major exemplars included all the giants of the classical tradition—Smith, Ricardo, Mill, and, in Jevons' own day, Alfred Marshall. But the new approach fostered by Jevons and the Austrians converted economics into quite another sort of inquiry. It was no accident that when he died, Jevons left behind an unfinished volume called *Principles of Economics,* not Political Economy.[44] The questions to be answered were now different. Ricardo and Mill had spoken of production, distribution, value, taxation, and population. Jevons' purview was a much narrower one, limited in the main to value and exchange. However, he did not reject other areas entirely: he simply applied the principle of division of labor, thinking that he could make a richer contribution to economics as a theoretician of static exchange.

Maurice Dobb later argued rather forcefully that economics was not really the same subject as political economy.[45] The latter, he said, dealt with relations between classes and social groups, as had been demonstrated in the work of Smith, Ricardo, and Marx. Economics, however, was a subject in which competitive equilibrium, attained in an atomistic society, was the central focus. Emphasis had shifted from costs of production to utility. At the same time the concept of exchange at the margin was advanced, which facilitated the utilization of mathematics so that infinitesimal change in market relationships could be studied. Not only were notions of objective cost dismissed, but the very concept of a surplus was declared useless. The crucial questions in economics were now matters of market value and the equilibrium of subjective states of mind. Value no longer had a simple cause since it stemmed from relationships between market participants. It was now due entirely to an ever shifting utility function.

Consequently, marginalist analysis was more than just another way of looking at value: it was an alternative approach to economic analysis. The psychological context for economic decisions was firmly established. The economic law pertaining to a single individual could be summed up as the behavior of a group and ultimately aggregated into the transactions of a nation.[46] Meaningful relationships had become the ones between men and goods, not between men and men, as both the classicists and Marxists had insisted. The latter, of course, could give rise to a partisan ideology—an undesirable manifestation for the scientific economist whose ambition was to create a positive discipline, with propositions sufficiently neutral to encompass problems of resource allocation for both a complex industrial society and Robinson Crusoe as well. Utility theory accomplished all that and, as an added dividend, weakened the theoretical underpinnings of the labor and cost of production theories of value.[47] As Carl Brinkmann has said, "It is possible to interpret marginal economics as a reaction against the deadlock to which the classical theory of cost value had been brought by Karl Marx's powerful exposition of labor costs and the surplus of exploitation." [48]

Today, Jevons would be described in some circles as somewhat "reactionary." His approach to questions of morals and social reform was firmly grounded in Victorian individualism. As a young man he had visited working class neighborhoods and was moved by the evils and poverty he observed. Yet he assigned responsibility for the workingman's ills to labor itself and insisted that inequalities of wealth and income stemmed entirely from differences in personal ability. On no account should fiscal policy be employed as an instrument of social change; taxes, he averred, should be in proportion to income, with imposts retained on commodities so as not to overburden the wealthier classes.[49] Free hospital service and medical assistance to the poor undermined their character and only intensified the lower classes' attitudes of dependence. However, public education was deemed useful because it could be employed to improve the character of the poor.

Jevons' theory, unlike Smith's or Ricardo's, did not stem from a great social conflict. He wanted to create an original scientific economics modeled on physics. Economics was for him a "vague sort of mathematics which calculates the causes and effects of man's industry." Yet in much of his analytical apparatus, Jevons remained a classicist. This was certainly true of his distribution theory, in which the older notions of rent and population change were accepted virtually in their totality. The only original element was his theory of value.[50] Nevertheless, he hoped that his theory would mitigate the conflict between labor and capital and that some day trade unionists would cease their continual strife against their true ally, the employer.[51] Jevons' major theoretical opus attracted very little attention when it was published in 1871. Nor did Marshall's cool reception help matters. Jevons' disappointment was further exacerbated when he discovered that his ideas had been anticipated by Hermann Heinrich Gossen in 1854.[52] He wrote to his brother that he felt in the position of a man whose theory most people believed to be nonsense while others knew it was not original.[53] Yet had the theory been constructed more precisely, it might have exerted the influence Jevons so desired. But his notions had been set out essentially in rough form and were merely suggestive. When the Austrians put forth similar ideas, their greater precision of argument—even though they did not utilize mathematics—won the field. In fact, it may very well have been Menger's avoidance of mathematical formulation in his *Grundsätze* that made his work more attractive than Jevons'.[54]

But in point of fact, Jevons had accomplished only half a job. The

Austrians were able to extend psychic value theory not only to consumer goods, but to capital and intermediate goods as well. This gave their theory a greater sense of generality: in Menger's and Wieser's hands, value could be transferred through "imputation" to items in transit and even to raw materials, simply by virtue of the value inherent in the final goods. A few years later Walras' general equilibrium theory explored the problem of value and utility more incisively, and Walras, being a better mathematician, did even a better job of model building. Jevons further was unfortunate in his Benthamite inheritance; about the time he was evolving his new version of value, it began to be realized that the human animal weighs choice neither by the pleasure-pain scale nor in infinitesimal units. Ironically enough, Jevons' major influence was found among the Fabian Socialists who had absorbed utility theory from Wicksteed via George Bernard Shaw. They became his most active disciples.

ii

Menger, von Wieser and the Origins of Austrian Doctrine

It is generally agreed that Carl Menger's *Grundsätze der Volkswirtschafts-lehre,* published in 1871, turned economic theory on its head.[55] Despite the lasting effect the book has had, it at first commanded but a limited audience. Menger's views were spread mainly through the work of his chief disciples, Friedrich von Wieser and Eugen von Böhm-Bawerk. Although Jevons' ideas also appeared in 1871 and Léon Walras published his pure economics just three years later, the three writers—creators of the marginalist revolution—worked independently. Their theories, however, were strikingly alike, and it was not too difficult to reformulate Jevons' mathematical proposition into Menger's literary statements. However, Menger was more systematic; those whose preferences are for refined positive propositions count him rather than Jevons as their spiritual ancestor.

Menger (1840-1921), born in Galicia, then part of Austria, came from an old family of Austrian civil servants and army officers. His early years, spent in western Galicia, had enabled him to observe feudal conditions in the countryside. In 1867, after studying law at both the Universities of Prague and Vienna, he turned to economics. His brother, Anton, was a well-known writer on law who authored the famous *Right to the Whole Produce of Labor.*

Menger's *Grundsätze* obtained an appointment for him at Vienna, where he remained until 1903, at which time he retired to devote himself entirely to research and writing. His output in economics was not overly large: in addition to the *Grundsätze* and some lesser pieces, there was his noted article which set forth the view that money was but the most saleable commodity in the system of exchange,[56] and a study on methodology, *Investigations into the Methods of Social Science and Political Economy in Particular,* published in 1883. From 1876 to 1878 Menger served as tutor to Crown Prince Rudolf, travelling widely over the Continent. Resuming his teaching career in 1879, his reputation, spread by the enthusiastic Wieser and Böhm-Bawerk, grew apace. The Austrian school of economics began to take form.

Hostility to the new theory in the German universities was stubborn, not so much on substantive grounds as on methodological ones. The historical school, under Schmoller, then dominated the academic landscape; the major interests of the German economists were essentially practical ones and centered on questions of reform and administration. Whatever theory there was stemmed from economic history and the attempt to solve such problems as the determination of "stages" of economic development. There was no room for a pure theorist. In fact, most of the economists did not appreciate the virtues of abstract reasoning. It was not that they were hostile to theoretical propositions, but rather that they were simply unable to grasp the advantages of such discourse or put it to use in any sensible way. The theoretical economist had no audience and those who were willing to lend their ears had to be led along the paths of theory with care lest they be left far behind. In this milieu it took no little courage to defend the abstract principles of marginal utility economics.

Thus, Menger's accomplishment was in a sense extraordinary. Although others had preceded him,[57] it was his perception that colored the new economics of the day, just as Ricardo had placed his signature onto Anglo-Saxon economics in the nineteenth century.[58] But unlike Ricardo, Menger did not search for ways of solving practical problems. He was simply a theorist seeking a fresh approach. When he and his disciples were done, a new fashion in economics had been unveiled in which the fact of utility, or the usefulness of a good as a psychological foundation, was deemed sufficient to explain economic law in any society one might envisage. We must remember that Menger was only thirty-one when the *Grundsätze* was issued.

Yet once he had published his theory and had dispensed with methodological issues, Menger preferred to work in the fields of philosophy and ethnography. Even after 1903, when he had retired to do full time writing, little was forthcoming. A second edition of the *Grundsätze* (to be referred to hereafter as the *Principles)* was published in 1923, two years after Menger died, which included some of the extensive notes he had prepared in his later years, notably on the theory of "needs." Menger was reported to have been an inspiring teacher: it became a tradition for students at Vienna who planned to become economists to make a pilgrimage to the Menger home for a session with the Master.[59] As a lecturer he was evidently very lucid and his notes were sought for twenty years afterward as the best means of preparation for examinations, much as later generations in America went hunting for the notes of Wesley C. Mitchell. Menger, however, never completed the economic system he had initiated; and, as Leo Rogin reflected, the failure to do so perhaps was ultimately related to his refusal to direct theoretical analysis to some urgent social question.[60] For Menger the social framework of economic problems took second place to matters of pure logic.

By the time the critics were through, classical economics had been badly battered, particularly after J. S. Mill's recantation of several critical points. After the historical economists in Germany and their cohorts in Britain had finished their attack on theoretical discourse, there seemed little worthwhile to hold onto. Yet a tradition remained—stemming from Condillac, Hermann, and the Italians—which insisted that value and utility were significantly related concepts.[61] Menger was aware of most of the older discussions in this area, with the possible exceptions of Cournot and von Thünen.[62] However, he did not utilize the mathematical techniques of his predecessors in the vineyards of utility economics. He may very well have been acquainted with mathematical ideas (his son Karl was a mathematician), but he rather doubted its usefulness for economic discourse. His major concern was with the relationships between quantities rather than with their mathematical manipulation, and for this purpose logical analysis was more to the point. Menger once remarked that he had come to the heart of his theory by a study of market reports, an opportunity that was afforded him when he worked as a journalist. This experience had brought home to him the striking disparity between traditional price theory and the actual market situation.[63]

Menger leveled his attack against the anti-theorists in 1883 with his *Untersuchungen über die Methode der Sozialwissenschaften,* a powerful polemic directed toward Schmoller, the leader of the historical school. Menger wanted to demonstrate that his approach was just as valid as Schmoller's. While some of his followers were a bit disappointed and even wondered whether all the bother had been really worth the candle, it did clarify, at least from the Austrian viewpoint, the special nature of scientific inquiry in the social sciences. That it did have some lasting influence, may be seen in the work of such writers as Mises and Hayek.[64] Menger emphasized a purely atomistic approach in the analysis of economic problems. For him this was a methodological tool for reflecting the dominant role of subjective factors. Theoretical discourse in economics was to be founded on self-interest, a complete knowledge of the market, and perfect mobility of input factors. Collective notions, he implied, had no meaning until they were reduced to their individual components. This could be interpreted as an unconscious political pronouncement rather than an absolutely scientific statement, for Menger's quite conservative views were well known. Again, its influence on the Mises-Hayek duo was patent.

Menger said that several vantage points were available for the study of economic phenomena: the historical, theoretical, and practical. Whereas the historical and practical examined economics in its policy aspects, the theoretical observed the generalized nature of economic problems, an area in which abstraction was an essential device. Menger spoke of the *exact* method of analysis, whereby economics would be decomposed into its simplest elements, with history and sociology employed as assisting sciences—*Hilfswissenschaften*. Theory then was the predominant requirement in understanding the movement of social forces. Menger did not reject empirical data; he merely relegated them to a minor role in economic analysis. So far as he was concerned, the historical method was just so much description.

This somewhat gratuitous blast at the Schmoller group brought on an instantaneous reaction which appeared justified. The fact was that historical and empirical data could not be eliminated so blithely as the Austrians and their followers desired. Yet, as Schumpeter remarked, the quarrel appears pointless now, since there ought to be enough room for both approaches in a field that pretends to deal with human society in motion.[65] But Menger would have preferred Burke's formula for unplanned social change. He rejected the notion that economic affairs could be legislated. Alteration and improvements in social relationships were best when accomplished unconsciously. Yet, as the Austrians sometimes recognized, the appearance of the Industrial Revolution had impelled people to acquire a greater measure of self-awareness. When alienation from the forces of production threatened to destroy the human being for the sake of the commodity, it seemed imperative that countervailing measures be undertaken.[66] But this aspect of policy was anathema to the Austrians.

Gustav Schmoller replied to Menger's polemic with a blistering counterattack, and the *Methodenstreit* was on. Menger countered with a pamphlet, *Irrthümer des Historismus in der deutschen National ökonomie* (Errors of Historicism), which repeated the arguments of the *Investigations* plus a few choice invectives. The debate became a heated one and quickly degenerated into personal insult. Schmoller declared that followers of the "abstract" Austrian school were unfit to teach in German universities and his influence was enough to enforce the ban. However, from 1884 on, the publications of Menger's followers—von Wieser, Böhm-Bawerk, Emil Sax, Robert Zuckerkandl, and others—began to make their mark. Marginalist studies of taxation, profits, and income were added to pure theory. The Austrian influence crossed over into Italy and spread its gospel into Britain through the didactic efforts of William Smart and James Bonar.[67] In 1888 Menger published a small

work on capital, *Zur Theorie des Kapitals*. And in the meantime, the controversy with Schmoller collapsed.

Menger did not publish his *Principles* until it had been carefully and
completely developed beforehand, spelling out the central idea as clearly as he
could so that no one would mistake it. All the implications as they appeared
to the author were pursued to their ultimate resolution. Since the *Principles*
was intended to be but the first part of a larger study, it seemed worthwhile to
Menger to explore in detail ideas that differed so sharply from received opinion. He studied with extraordinary subtlety the subjects of value, price, and
money and evidently intended to follow this first volume with others on credit,
distribution, production, commerce, and economic reform. Unfortunately, this
never came about. Thus, the *Principles,* standing by itself, exhibited a rather
high degree of abstraction and had but a bare minimum of historical data.
Ironically enough, the book was dedicated to Wilhelm Roscher, founder of
German historical economics. Although Menger's verbal formulations had
some advantages, the essentially hypothetical character of the new theory
was not revealed as incisively as a mathematical presentation might have
done. Consequently, the possibilities of quantitative analysis were not explored as fully as they had been by Walras.

The basic idea was the principle of marginal utility, a concept destined
to play an heroic role in the history of modern economic thought. Menger's
use of the notion was a remarkable performance. As Schumpeter has said,
"He was a careful thinker who rarely slipped, if ever, and his genius stands
out only the more impressively because he lacked the appropriate mathematical tools." [68] Human needs were the real starting point for analysis,
averred Menger. They arose when the human organism adjusted itself to the
physical environment. Tension and disturbance occurred when the adjustments required for balance and equilibrium were lacking. These disturbances,
varying in intensity, were significant because they generated certain needs
which expressed an attempt to restore the balance. All this seemed analogous
to physiological homeostasis, a process whereby equilibrium was maintained
between organisms and their environment.[69]

Menger defined wants, therefore, as a species of unsatisfied desires or disagreeable sensations which stemmed from a kind of physiological imbalance.
He then argued that a want could be satisfied to a greater or smaller degree
by some good leaving part of the want unsatisfied. A want with a larger
unmet portion of satisfaction exhibited a larger "final intensity," while a
completely satisfied want had zero "final intensity." Consequently, with limited resources, the problem for the individual would be to distribute his means
so as to keep the "final intensities" of all wants as small as possible. Needs
implied consciousness and reasoning; but, argued Menger, while certain needs
arose from custom or individual idiosyncrasy, they were not arbitrary. On the

other hand, the needs of larger groups, such as states, were not to be included in the individual economy.[70] The latter was one of the preconditions for a "thing" to become a "good." There were three other prerequisites: the existence of qualities or properties that would relate the potential good to the satisfaction of the particular need; human knowledge of this relationship; and command over the thing, enabling the individual to direct it to the satisfaction of the need.[71] That is to say, while useful things were physically able to satisfy a want, it was awareness of that ability and the power to dispose of the item that made it an economic good. This analysis abstracted entirely from value judgments regarding needs and wants. The latter did not have to be rational, for even if the want-satisfying power of the good were absent but the individual merely thought it was present, as with fraudulent articles, the goods-character of the item would nevertheless exist. That these concepts were rooted entirely in a kind of individualistic psychology was obvious. The relationship was that of simple cause and effect: the good was the cause and satisfaction the effect. And with just a bit more logical extension the goods concept could do away with the classical distinction between productive and nonproductive labor, for satisfactions could be derived from both corporeal and noncorporeal things.

But what was one to do with productive resources which were not consumed directly? The Austrian answer to this question has since become classic: factors of production exhibited the character of goods because they derived their want-satisfying power from the consumer goods which they created. The latter were "first order" goods or those of the "lower order," while resources were second, third, or higher order goods depending on the number of steps or processes they were removed from consumption goods. Menger was also careful to make a distinction between complementary or cooperating goods and those which functioned independently.[72] But there were apparent complications in this approach, for some goods might be lower order in one situation and higher in another, as with milk destined for consumption and milk in a cheese factory. The answer to this objection rested in the purpose of Menger's theory: he was concerned with the relationships of goods to people, not with the goods themselves. The important consideration was the location of the thing in the hierarchy of want-satisfying powers. It was this that gave goods their specific qualities, not something inherent in them.

The attribution of want-satisfying ability to higher order goods was the start of the famous imputation theory, according to which producers' goods obtained their value from their related consumers' goods.[73] Menger emphasized this point by asking what would happen to the value of tobacco stocks and cigarette factories if people suddenly ceased to smoke. Obviously, he said, these would lose their goods-character.[74] Now, said Menger, goods of a higher order required time in order to be transformed into lower order shapes.

This introduced the notion of the period of production, a concept that later loomed large in Böhm-Bawerk's system. As the number of steps between the highest and the lowest order increased, the time of production was extended. Error and uncertainty entered into the process since it was impossible to know in advance the quality and character of the good that would be available in the future. The determining factor then became the anticipated want.

Menger next sought to outline the quantitative aspect of things which possessed goods-character.[75] Here the problem was matching the quantities needed *(Bedarf)* and what was available. He observed that although needs were capable of indefinite expansion, at any particular moment they were given (that is, simply postulated). Therefore, it was difficult to ascertain the quantity needed since the degree of intensity of wants and the extent of their satisfaction were solely anticipatory and could not be fixed in advance. This observation suggested that it was the available supply of lower goods and the current technique of production which were significant in transactions. Complications set in when account was taken of complementarity, a condition which implied that production was to be based on a certain mix of input factors. Therefore, economy in the real sense of the word *(Wirtschaft)* meant the disposition of resources in a way that would lead to the attainment of full satisfaction of wants. This implied a clear-cut distinction between objective and subjective elements in the economy. Now, should the quantity needed exceed the supply, as was the case with most goods, then immediate attention would have to be given to the most important needs. Such goods were "economic." [76] Noneconomic goods were those for which the supply was greater than the need. Of course, there might be alterations in the basic relationship, resulting in a shifting of goods from one category to the other. Generally, these changes were explained by such dynamic factors as population growth, consumer taste, the depletion of resources, or the acquisition of new want-satisfying powers by specific goods. But in each instance the quality of being an economic good clearly stemmed from the relationship between what was available and the number required to satisfy wants. This was the basic proposition in psychic value.[77]

From the foregoing Menger easily arrived at the proposition that the state of supply determined value; increasing or decreasing the quantity of goods altered satisfactions and, *ipso facto,* the value attached to those goods. As the quantity of a good increased, the additional units had less want-satisfying power. This was Menger's main contribution; it was nothing less than the principle of diminishing marginal utility, whereby the value of a homogeneous supply of a commodity was determined by the last or least important unit. However, Menger's discussion of this rather important point was at times obscure and seemed to conflict with the principle of complementarity.[78] In offering an example to illustrate his argument, Menger tried to equate the satisfactions stemming from two goods without relating them in any way to either labor or money. The result was an improper statement of the nature of the alternatives.[79] Nor did he make it clear how an individual would dispose of his goods in order to maximize the satisfaction of his wants.

Throughout his discussion Menger developed the theme of imputing value according to psychological judgments. Where goods differed in quality, a higher imputation was accorded to the better goods. The value of lower order goods was the basis for the value of complementary and higher order ones, and the task of the theorist was to trace the relationship between these different levels in order to follow the flow of value in the economy. Complementary goods might be evaluated by observing the effect on the value of the total mix when one good was removed. Now, this was an important statement, for it occasioned some difference of opinion between Menger and his pupil, Wieser.[80] Critics have argued that marginal utility could not apply to production since withdrawing a factor could impede the whole process of creating goods. Austrian theory, they said, had obscured the role of land, labor, and capital. But Menger insisted that the value of the contribution of any one factor could be ascertained by imagining the removal of a small quantity of that factor while holding the others at the previous level and then noting the loss of satisfaction suffered by consumers. This came quite close to the concept of marginal productivity.

Marginal utility also solved the famous paradox of utility: diamonds might not have a great need or utility, but it was their minute supply in relation to the demand for them that created a high value. Of course, the concept of the margin was utilized here; but Menger seemed to think in terms of discrete changes, albeit small ones, rather than the continuous spectrum of the infinitesimal calculus. On this point, there was a distinct departure from the Jevonian and Walrasian concept. With these basic ideas firmly fixed, exchange value was equated to subjective value. The economic significance of a good for an individual was weighed against what could be gained by exchanging it for something else. As Knut Wicksell has argued, exchange value became really a kind of indirect use value.[81] This was the fundamental notion in Menger's system, for it permitted him to establish a common root for virtually all economic phenomena.

There were no tripartite factors of production for Menger, only goods of higher order. The classical division of inputs into land, labor, and capital was rejected with the clear implication that all resources were essentially similar.[82] In short, distribution was to be effected through the basic principle of imputation which would allocate the total product among all the contributing input factors. In its later version, this adding-up theorem asserted that, with constant returns to scale, the whole product could be exhausted by paying to the input factors a sum equal to the marginal contribution of each. But this assumed perfect competition in both product and factor markets, and in an imperfect world how real could such logic be? There might have been some sense to the proposition eighty or ninety years ago, but today it must be seriously questioned. That this created the best of all possible worlds by simply doing away with the problem of a social surplus seemed self-evident. It was also the most scientific of all apologetics, for the entrepreneur, and all the other factors as well, received only what they would get if they had worked at the next best alternative.[83]

In addition, marginalism transmuted costs into psychological phenomena, since what a firm paid for its inputs was to be based on the vendor's marginal utility as determined in the process of exchange. Thus, supply too was rooted in the psychology of the economic man. And since payments by firms to inputs established the distribution of the product, this also was determined by the same pervading value principle, with the whole economy governed by marginal utility. The economic system consequently became a huge conglomeration of complementary goods, each depending for its value on other goods, at both earlier and later stages of production. Thus, both past and future were subsumed in the present.

Menger's idea of exchange came quite close to simple barter, for transactions occurred only when someone possessed goods worth less to him than to another and when the feeling was reciprocated. Both parties to the exchange obviously were in a position to gain.[84] The purpose of price theory, then, was not only to explain the terms of trade but, above all, to demonstrate that a purchase and sale were not mere transfers of equivalences, as in the labor theory of value. It was precisely because there was an absence of such equivalence that exchange took place, said Menger. The terms of trade, on the other hand, depended on the number of individuals and goods involved and the state of competition in the market. This then led to a comparison of isolated exchange and monopoly [85] in which merchandise changed hands because of the capacity that certain goods had for circulation. Such a discussion, though, was somewhat reminiscent of old-fashioned chemistry, which had explained the composition of compounds by "affinities." Theories of this character did not appear to be very fruitful.

The main point, however, was that the ultimate cause of exchange was marginal utility; this factor established the ratios at which goods shifted hands. Thus Menger achieved what Marx and the classicists had thought impossible: exchange was founded on the concept of use value. Menger examined the isolated exchange of two goods and argued that this situation set up a range within which the transaction could occur. With one seller and many buyers, the limits of the exchange converged, so that in a case of fixed supply or fixed price, either one was uniquely determined and the distribution of the good among the buyers clearly established.[86] It is interesting to note that Wicksell criticized Menger rather sharply for leaving the problem at this stage and failing to extend the analysis to the case of many buyers and many sellers. Had Menger done so, said Wicksell, he doubtlessly would have come closer to the Walrasian approach.[87] The Swedish economist, who was a worthy successor to the Austrians, observed that in actuality Menger had converted the seller, because of fixed supply, into a recipient of a quasi-rent. The fact was that Menger had not quite solved the problem of price determination through use value.

While it was Wieser who worked out the theory of resource allocation, strong hints of it also appeared in Menger's work. He noted that a problem arose when men sought to satisfy all their wants despite an inadequate supply of goods. He surmised that the important wants would be dealt with first. But if a good were capable of satisfying several wants, the procedure of applying economic goods would be such that ". . . the most important of the satisfactions that cannot be achieved have the same importance for every kind of need, and hence all needs are being satisfied up to an equal degree of importance. . . ."[88] This was a rather long-winded way of saying that a good would have to be applied to its various uses so that in each case the satisfactions at the margin would be equal.

Although a similar train of thought lay at the root of what seemed to be an alternative cost theory, Menger did not pursue the question further. Instead, he insisted that cost stemmed from the prospective value of goods of lower order in whose production the various input factors served. Embodied costs were not part of the picture.[89] He simply rejected the proposition that objective cost could have a significant role in the productive scheme; for Menger, subjective value and expectation were the prime elements in making economic decisions. As neo-classical theory demonstrated, it was only in the short run—when supply could not be expanded readily—that the significance of costs was limited. Once the possibility of adjusting the supply, either through greater production or the creation of new facilities, was admitted, there could be no escaping the influence of objective cost. Menger's theory, after all, had come down to a perpetual short-run proposition.

One also finds in it the notion of substitution—the idea that it was possible to vary the proportions of an industrial mix in order to achieve the same results[90]—a problem made especially famous in the contemporary theory of linear programming. But when one recalled that substitution had also been implicit in the classical laws of return, Menger's contribution was not nearly so startling. The significant point was that a theory of a variable mix offered a beginning for a marginal theory of productivity. Menger, however, did not explore the possibility of decreasing returns, without which marginal productivity was at best dubious.

There were also some sketchy discussions of the capital problem in Menger's *Principles*. Production was intended to meet future needs. But this took time, requiring command not only over the means of production, but the power to employ them at the proper moment. Such control was itself a good and called for the payment of interest. However, this concept was entirely devoid of any element of waiting, with the result that it incurred strong objection from Böhm-Bawerk, the Austrian School's foremost exponent of capital theory. In 1888, Menger wrote an article *On the Theory of Capital* which had been stimulated by Böhm's version to which Menger was evidently antipathetic. While he did not join in a polemical debate with so distinguished a pupil, Menger did want to dissociate himself from the notion of time which was so central in the Bawerkian corpus. To Menger, capital was the fluid fund typified by the money value of property. Moreover, it was important to make a clear-cut distinction between rent and interest, if clarity was to be introduced into the discussion. Yet Menger felt that goods provided by nature might also be capital, so long as the crucial condition of scarcity were met when such goods were put into the stream of production. However, he made no allusions to the contingency of monopolistic control of resources.[91] The notion of capital as a fund contrasted sharply with its usual definition as a collection of physical things. Menger, however, failed to differentiate adequately between goods and the services they render. In the main, capital did consist of goods of higher order held during a given production period, although there was some concession by Menger to the view that the services of capital would have to be paid for. But nowhere was there a hint of the saving-investment process.

Menger had always been interested in the theory of money.[92] In 1873 he had written in some detail on the work of John E. Cairnes concerning the impact of gold discoveries on the money system. The basis for Menger's theory was the concept of the saleability of commodities, a notion more fully explored later on by Ludwig von Mises. The approach was essentially a subjective one, so that any clash with the more basic theory of value itself was avoided. This was in sharp contrast with the traditional quantity theory which utilized aggregates in its analysis of price, production, and turnover. Menger's interest in money as a standard of value dovetailed with his marginalist approach in general theory, but it merely indicated that certain stages of economic development corresponded with particular forms of money. Curiously enough, this reflected the influence of the German historical school. Briefly, Menger opposed the state theory of money; distinguished between external and internal factors influencing money; differentiated between the transactions and precautionary motives for maintaining liquidity positions; urged that metals were more suitable for the preservation of values than was the case with other commodities; and suggested that the value of money might be stabilized by regulating the production of gold and the amount of notes in circulation.

This then was the substance of Menger's contribution. He had introduced a concept into economics that led to a major reconstruction of theoretical foundations. Marginalism suggested wide possibilities for a new treatment of all sorts of questions beyond value determination. Above all, it suggested a solution of the problem of distribution and resource allocation. Once the Austrian formulation of the marginalist approach was restated in mathematical terms, it became clear that economic behavior could be described as a problem in maximization. The infinitesimal calculus could be employed to maximize utility, price, profit, production, revenue—and to minimize cost.

But some troublesome elements were imbedded in this ingenious structure, not the least of which was the imputation of values to productive services. One had to assert, for example, that consumer valuations were somehow carried forward to the level of production where psychic satisfactions were also experienced. The Austrian solution lay in the operation of the market through which an optimum allocation of resources and optimum distribution were attained. However, Menger never demonstrated quite clearly just how such coordination was effected; [93] but in contrast to his latter-day disciple, Friedrich von Hayek, he did concede that businessmen sought full knowledge of market situations.[94] The significant question to ask was: if buyers and sellers reacted only to market price, then why was the whole subtle psychic apparatus necessary? All that seemed necessary was information on the structure of production and consumer wants, together with the assumptions of maximum gain and least cost.

Criticism was leveled at Menger's theory on the quite valid ground that his psychology was entirely irrelevant to the objective facts of the economic process. Although recent theory has accepted anticipations and *ex ante* propositions, a forceful case also has been made for the rejection of psychological explorations in economics. The argument has been offered that economics need deal only with economic fact, not with the behavioral framework. Yet even economic analysis must take into account the limits established for human action by the broader social structure. The universal theory sought by Menger and his disciples had much more relevance for a Robinson Crusoe economy than for the mixed private, monopolistic, communal enterprise system that we all know today. The exploration of such an economic order, however, was beyond the Austrians, nor were they really interested. Their whole theory seemed to embody the voice of an abstract, desiccated economic man separated from the world that presumably had made him. Nowhere did this strike the observer with such force as in their early and fundamental discussion of goods.[95]

There were no social issues in Menger. His theory was not only static but bare and cold and utterly devoid of the kind of human concerns that moved an Adam Smith or a Karl Marx. It was to set the tone for scientific economics for the next seventy-five years or so. Nor was Menger really concerned with price phenomena and exchange relationships: these seemed to be secondary matters and much less interesting than those discussed in the early sections of the *Principles*. The central focus was need and want satisfaction. Cost of production and labor were simply wrong-headed theories which had refused to acknowledge that value stemmed from want-satisfying capacities.[96] The individualistic viewpoint was sharply etched. National wealth, for example, was deemed a myth, for such a notion falsely suggested that property might be devoted to the general welfare.[97] The national economy, said Menger, was really a collection of single economic units, each concerned with its own objectives. This clearly evaded the question of social responsibility, obscured the dichotomy between individual interest and group interest, and underpinned the rather dubious assumption that the objectives of the individual were consonant with social progress. It was Adam Smith's unseen hand writ large.

Friedrich von Wieser (1851-1926) was the only one of the Austrians to produce a genuine treatise. This was his *Social Economics,* a volume highly praised by Wesley C. Mitchell.[98] Successor to Menger at the University of Vienna, a post he had assumed in 1903, Wieser developed a fairly flexible variant of Austrian doctrine. He came of an old family of Austrian Civil servants and, as was the usual situation in such cases, went from the gymnasium to the study of law. His was quite a productive career, with articles and books steadily issued from 1876 down to the year of his death in 1926, a half-century's span.

Wieser at first was much interested in history, but his deep concern with the political and social events of his day soon led him into other fields. It was Herbert Spencer's *First Principles* and Tolstoy's *War and Peace* that sowed inquisitive seeds in his mind. He began to search for the laws of social behavior, and it was not too long before he came to believe that economics was the most useful of the disciplines for this purpose, since the "most conspicuous social relationships" were economic ones. These, he felt, would have to be explained first. Yet none of his explorations satisfied him: classical views were inconsistent and Marxism merely carried Ricardo to an ultra-logical conclusion. In 1874 Wieser discovered Menger's *Grundsätze* and he now felt that he had come upon the essential prelude to the kind of history that should be writen, a history of the movement of anonymous masses.

Together with Böhm-Bawerk, a boyhood friend and later his brother-in-law, Wieser began to concentrate on economics according to the gospel of Carl Menger. The two friends traveled about for several years, studying with Knies, Roscher, and Hildebrand in Germany. For Knies' seminar, Wieser wrote a paper on cost and value which foreshadowed his later interests. Here he first interpreted cost as indirect or sacrificed utility, a concept which in modern dress has been called opportunity cost. Later on this came to be known as "Wieser's Law," eloquent testimony from his peers as to the strength and originality of his thinking. Wieser was never fully satisfied with the mere application of Menger's value concept to producers' goods. In this early essay he proceeded from the valuation of a single good to a comparison of the *total* needs for the output of producers' goods and the *total* quantity of the goods. Even at so early a stage one could observe an effort to reach a broader social vision than could be discovered in Menger. However, he was loyal to the new economics, for he thought that the value of producers' goods was determined by the value of the last product capable of being produced by the entire complex.[99] This was indeed a striking application of the Mengerian thesis, yet, curiously enough, the master evinced little interest in the version of subjective value theory that was being developed by his disciples. However, Wieser kept working at the new utility economics with great diligence, and, although burdened by civil service duties, he was able to bring forth his *Ursprung und Hauptgezetze des wirtschaftlichen Wertes* in 1884 and so obtain an appointment as a lecturer at the German University in Prague. The book was a genuine milestone in the history of marginal utility economics, and, in fact, the word *Grentznutzen* gave marginalism its name. Like Menger's before him, Wieser's approach was nonmathematical. But as the first of the Austrian formulations to deal effectively with resource allocation and economic organization, his theory acquired a social perception that was quite unique for that school. In 1903 Wieser returned to Vienna and continued his efforts to apply marginalist concepts to problems of money and taxation. His major works were written usually in response to some occasion, as was the case with his *Social Economics,* which was composed at the request of Max Weber who was editing a new series of social science publications, the *Grundriss der Sozialökonomik.* His final work, *Das Gesetz der Macht,* a sociological study of power, was published in 1926. Appointed to the Austro-Hungarian Upper House in 1917, he served as Minister of Commerce in the last two cabinets of the Dual Monarchy.

Wieser employed the same method of abstraction as did Menger, the same "as if" mode of argument, and the same definition of theoretical problems in terms of value essences rather than real human behavior. Nevertheless, there was a genuinely attractive quality in Wieser's work which was not present in Menger or Böhm-Bawerk. He seriously questioned Menger's methodological quarrels with the historical school, which he had thought somewhat arid. And soon his broader social perspective came to the fore. It was not at all surprising that he should have visualized his economics as preparation for historical and sociological work. The *Social Economics* was a huge economic and social study of the growth of modern capitalism and in his *Gesetz der Macht,* Wieser dropped economics entirely for the analysis of politics. The notion of the anonymous mass base for social science led him to seek a different approach to these fields than was suggested by the techniques of the physical sciences. Although he conceded some imprecision in his concept, he said that this was to be expected. Moreover, it might even prove to be an advantage, for it enabled the analyst (who, he said, was also part of the situation) to enter into social phenomena from within. Actually, economics, said Wieser, did pursue an empirical method, although at first glance it appeared entirely deductive. It was an empiricism that described *typical* phenomena. As such, it required that the most usual, most common aspects of behavior be isolated in order to construct a kind of "ideal" type. Wieser employed this approach without wavering, at least in his more technical theory; his economic man was practically an automaton, with a single-minded and relentless purpose that made him quite incapable of committing error. But Wieser knew this to be merely an abstraction suitable only for purposes of analysis.

While such an approach might have been effective in Wieser's hands, there were some risks in it; for without testing hypotheses and checking empirical data, the inner voice of the social scientist might not be completely accurate. Methodology as a general pursuit, however, was eschewed by Wieser. He did not believe that such inquiries per se could be separated from particular questions or that such procedures could do much to advance social science. Method, he suggested, could emerge only from the business of scientific investigation, and he thought it was a matter for deep regret that Menger had devoted so much energy to it.

The central idea in economics was utility, which permeated all phenomena, including money and, of course, private property. Ultimately Wieser showed, as in his *Social Economics,* how a balance of forces between the competitive drives and government regulation acted to modify the classical concepts of private property. In this way he developed his links between theory and policy; the analytical technique was to proceed from abstraction to practical economic behavior. However, Wieser was not entirely successful, and, try as he might, he could not transfer the concept of marginal utility to the social level with all the aplomb he might have wished for.

The *Ursprung,* which had been developed out of an earlier paper, represented a somewhat preliminary formulation of Wieser's main ideas. Menger had failed to apply utility theory to production and distribution in any genuinely effective manner. It was left to Wieser, therefore, to work out applications in the form of opportunity cost and imputation. Although the *Ursprung* provided the early statements, their final shape awaited the publication of *Natural Value* in 1889.[100] For the next twenty-five years this remained the definitive presentation of Wieser's theoretical views. In the *Ursprung* itself the theory of allocation was set forth in terms of a fixed quantity of resources and given wants. The best distribution of resources was said to be that which would equalize the return from the units of the input factors as they were applied to all possible uses. A large stock of resources could be spread over a number of needs, thus encompassing even unimportant ones as well.[101] If the ability to exact a return declined, it would be due therefore to the diminishing marginal utility of the total stock of goods. The productive contribution of all resources was what determined the value of the stock of goods. Utility established the value of the last unit of a stock; value, however, was the cost of producing a commodity on the basis of foregone utility. With this formulation in the *Ursprung,* Wieser was approaching the idea of opportunity cost. From this vantage point, it was no great leap to the theory of cognate goods—those products which had at least one common input factor. These, said Wieser, would exchange for each other "as the quantities of it requisite for their production." [102]

In *Natural Value* Wieser restated the utility basis of economic action, and also emphasized scarcity as a significant element by asserting that superfluous goods had no value. Satisfactions stemming from goods were to be ranked, leading to Gossen's law of diminishing utility. But here Wieser observed that both discrete and continuous scales were possible.[103] This was an important observation, for, aside from the fact that it emphasized his differences with Menger regarding the determination of imputed value, it was a much more realistic assumption to make than the smooth infinitesimal changes which had been implied by both Jevons and Menger. In Book One a welfare concept was evinced in the remark that: "The principle for the economic employment of goods of manifold usefulness is not, then, that we must, in every employment, obtain the same lowest possible marginal utility, but that in all employment as low a marginal utility be reached as is possible without necessitating the loss, in some other employment, of a higher utility." [104] In contrast to the *Ursprung,* however, Wieser here argued that the distribution of goods over various uses would be such as would satisfy important needs first, thus seemingly violating the equi-marginal principle.

With a good deal more insight than other marginalists displayed, Wieser made it clear that marginal utility could be applied to but a single application of a good. While food was consumed day after day on quite the same intake level, it was, he said, at any point of one day that the significance of a satisfaction was to be gauged via the effects of the last meal. Unfortunately, Wieser did not pursue this reasoning, for it might have suggested alternative developments in marginalist theory. Production, after all, is geared to a repetitive series of satisfactions, with needs in the immediate future pressing hard on present ones. Such a concept as this essentially underlay Böhm-Bawerk's theory. Marginal utility may answer the question of price determination, but, without Wieser's suggestion of repetitive consumption, it would be difficult to establish a theory of production.

In addition to utility, price was a matter also of balancing value in use against the exchange value of money. While there was some allusion to reservation prices, the point of equilibrium was that at which marginal buyers were just able to enter the market.[105] Wieser, however, did recognize the impact that income differences could have on this equilibrium point, an observation that later marginalists tended to obscure. Exchange value became that which was attached to a good because of an *anticipated* act of exchange, thus maintaining the psychological basis of theory.[106] When Wieser discussed "objective" value, he was talking of value concepts on two distinct levels. Subjective value was an atomistic notion which allowed the ordering of an individual "economy." But this meaning was altered when subjective value was involved in price relationships. It then became objective value—a definite price—and, although it did not reflect necessarily the estimate put on goods by society, it was, said Wieser, a social fact.[107] Price in this sense was to become the basis for the social economy of Wieser's later work, *Social Economics,* in which individuals were brought together through the mechanism of exchange.

Here Wieser barely touched on the concept of social relationships which Marx had employed with such overwhelming force. For a while, it seemed as if Wieser's concern with social questions would move him in the direction of a broader analysis of economic problems. But this was not to be the case, for in his analytical work he returned repeatedly to the subjectivist approach. He conceded that individualism left much to be desired and that it was possible for values to be raised through enforced scarcity. But he rejected any contention that this required a reorganization of society; he felt that the necessary corrective measures could be instituted through the existing government.[108] Yet this discussion demonstrated Wieser's social outlook and his concern with economic problems beyond utility theory—a facet of his thinking studiously ignored by most commentators.[109] He quite bluntly remarked that production could be ordered to enhance wealth. "Instead of things which would have the greatest utility," he said, "those things are produced for which the most will be paid." [110] Wieser observed further that for ordinary goods, such as bread, both the rich and the poor had an equal effect on price; but the greater the surplus funds of the rich, the greater their purchases of luxuries and the larger the distortion of production.[111] In a rational and organic community, natural value was easily discernible. But it was unfortunately all too readily dissipated by fraud, force, and chance.

It was in Book Three of *Natural Value* that Wieser worked out his famous idea of imputed value as the basis for establishing value for producers' goods. His approach was to view the productive set-up as a going concern, a decided advance over Menger's formulation. That producers' goods derived their value from the value of their output was a satisfactory point of view so long as the evaluation was made for the entire mix of inputs; but this failed to answer the question of how to evaluate the distinct, separate, individual factors. Involved in this problem, of course, was the concept of opportunity cost. This was not merely a question of definition, but rather a fundamental maximizing proposition. Naturally enough, it was necessary to posit a fixed stock of good and resources. An interesting sidelight was Wieser's statement that the value relation between products and the means of production could be distorted by alterations in the rankings of personal claims on output [112]—a cogent distinction between personal and functional distribution of income. The latter represented the theoretical aspect of distribution and was capable of being distorted and obscured by such factors as property relations, inheritance, and the like.

The theory of imputation, the *Zurechnung,* was in effect a theory of distribution, for it sought to explain how the various factors of production shared in the final product. Menger's principle of deduction—whereby the value of a unit was measured by what would be lost if that unit were withdrawn—was rejected, with the concept of a productive contribution substituted in its stead.[113] Wieser sought to make his approach more realistic by speaking of discrete changes. He argued that Menger's formulation would result in distributing a sum greater than the product. This error, he said, stemmed from Menger's failure to acknowledge that the withdrawal of a unit of input could adversely affect the productivity of the remaining factors. The assumption here that discontinuity must exist among inputs was a notion for which he was to be harshly criticized.[114] Yet it reflected a genuine effort to attain a level of reality which many of these same critics had not yet become aware of.

From the arithmetical point of view, however, there seemed to be little difference between Menger and Wieser, as Knut Wicksell has observed. Under conditions of free competition, said Wieser, the share in the proceeds of any set of productive means would have to be approximately the same for all possible transactions.[115] Wieser's "productive contribution" then could be interpreted as merely the ordinary rewards obtained by the various factors. But there was an implication in Wieser's theory that seems to have been lost —for any good or factor which functioned as part of a going concern would clearly have had a greater impact than it would in isolation. Invariably, the withdrawal of an input in a given production mix would result in a loss of some of the economic power of the other inputs.[116] Here was a facet of Wieser's doctrine, the implicit going concern concept, that had been long overlooked. It emphasized his awareness that individual economic behavior was not something that occurred separately from a framework of social interdependence.

The imputation problem inescapably led to the question of capital and interest. Capital was the one factor of production that was continually used up, with the consequence that its return had to be sufficient to restore the original sum as well as leave behind a net gain or surplus. This was conceived by Wieser as capital's gross return to which the physical productivity of capital, a concept that could not be demonstrated directly, was clearly related. In contrast to Jevons, the notion of capital excluded wage-goods.[117] The justification of a return to capital stemmed from its function as a cooperating element in the process of production. It was obvious to Wieser that lenders would demand not only the return of their capital but a bit of a surplus as well. The surplus, defined as a net return, was interest. All this hardly appeared to be much of an explanation of so complex a phenomenon. At any rate, Wieser did make obeisance to the discounting approach. In his view the present value of capital was derived from the discounted sum of the products which a given capital good would yield in the future. In this way time was introduced as a crucial factor. Wieser conceived investment to be instantaneous, with no time lags. But he failed to integrate time satisfactorily into the main body of his theory. Net returns on land were to be capitalized, especially when improvements on land were part of the valuation problem. Yet this represented neither an acceptance of Böhm-Bawerk's differentiation of present and future goods nor the abstinence theory.[118] Wieser insisted that both present and future needs would have to be evaluated on equal terms.

What does seem quite patent was his intention to rebut the Marxian exploitation theory. There were frequent attacks in Wieser's work on the labor theory of value, and time and again capital's contribution to the productive process was stressed. Attempts to reduce capital to labor through the well-known application of "remembrance of things past" were also rejected. Nevertheless Wieser's counterargument seemed rather ineffective.[119]

The shares of productive factors could also be fixed by capitalization. Labor, of course, was not to be capitalized since it was a free agent, at least in the theoretical model. However, its individual acts and products could be subjected to such a computational device. In this way a share of the product going to the specific service of labor could be determined. From the overall view, the value of each such service depended ultimately on its supply and demand, the support it secured from other goods required in producing its stream of utilities, and the current state of technology.[120] But the decisive element in setting the price of a service of labor and thereby its share of the product was the utilization of the marginal unit. Wieser proceeded on the assumption of fixed co-efficients in production, so that his solution of distribution implied infinite elasticity in the demand for the service. This was the perfect market. But there were a number of difficulties inherent in this approach [121] which could vitiate any suggestion that Wieser might have achieved a sufficiently general statement of the matter. Finally, Wieser, although a sharp critic of Ricardian theory, felt that it was feasible to employ classical differential theory to explain the returns to factors of production other than land.

When it came to the problem of cost, Wieser turned explicitly to utility in seeking an explanation. His reasoning started with the value of a factor of production as determined by marginal utility. When the factor entered into the process of production, it carried its value along with it, so that it entered into the asking price by virtue of the transformation which had been accomplished in production. In the final analysis, therefore, the cost of production stemmed from marginal utility. Without production there could be no cost.[122] Further evidence of this concept of cost could be adduced, he said, from the changes in price that were occasioned by any new calculations of goods entering into production. All this subtlety, however, reduced itself to the proposition that costs were derived from goods that went into production and that they transmitted their values as a matter of fulfilling their purpose. But costs first had to embody values. The latter were obtained from imputation through which producers' goods were given the value of the marginal product, thus making cost stem from some sort of social pool of utility. If this pool were employed wisely, it could enrich the community; if not, impoverishment might be the unwanted outcome. Throughout this rather difficult analysis, it was always marginal utility that fixed value and costs.

When Max Weber asked Wieser to contribute to his encyclopedic project in the social sciences, in which the leading scholars of the day were to take part, he produced his magnum opus, the *Social Economics*. This was the same series for which Schumpeter wrote his *Economic Doctrine and Method*.[123] Wieser's work was the only genuinely comprehensive system of economics that had come thus far from the Austrian marginalists, but unfortunately the outbreak of World War I in the same year of its publication shunted it aside and it was not until 1924 that real notice was taken of it. Its basic approach did not differ markedly from that found in the earlier *Natural Value,* particularly in the long first part wherein Wieser described the theory of a simple economy. The basic problem was again the determination of value in a kind of Robinson Crusoe economy. Again, one dealt with the economic man who did everything with perfect and frightening certainty. This approach, once again acknowledged as theoretical, Wieser described as psychological, ostensibly best for exploring the economy of a single subject.[124] "The current individualistic concept of the economic principle," he said, "is a theoretical idealization . . . it is well adapted . . . to a deduction of the elements of economics. From this idealization one must make a transition, by decreasing abstraction, to the social concept that is actually current, if one would understand the concrete phenomena of life." [125] Wieser's simple economy began to exhibit behavior characteristics of a broader national economy: it was as if the latter were guided by a single mind so that the laws of *social* economics might be explored more effectively. In such a framework, averred Wieser, one needed only to envisage a single flow of resources—from the realm of production to the final consumer. The structure in this first part of *Social Economics* did not differ appreciably from the earlier work. Gossen's law of diminishing utility was advanced; the problem of needs and wants was stated in virtually the same way; costs were still merely disguised marginal values; the productive contribution was continued as the basis of distribution theory; and imputation was restated with the identical analogies employed in *Natural Value*.[126]

The latter part of the *Social Economics,* however, displayed fresh interests. Unlike the other Austrians, Wieser made an heroic effort to integrate his pure economics with a theory of society. He wanted to show how the social economy was constituted through the process of exchange—the main mechanism whereby single individuals expressed their economic interest.[127] But he recognized that on the level of social relationships people did not meet to conduct dialogues: he acknowledged that in the arena of human social activity there were indeed clashes, oftentimes of great force.[128] On this level, it could not be asserted that self-interest always promoted the general welfare. Social conflict frequently led to the domination of one class by another. The bourgeoisie, for example, had performed a notable historic service when they broke the power of the feudal lords; but in time they had evolved an economic and political despotism of their own, based on financial control and the alienation of workers from the tools of production. Although these sociological observations were uncomfortably similar to those made by the socialists, Wieser acknowledged their validity.

Wieser revealed the marked influence of Tolstoy's concept of history made by the anonymous mass and at the same time exposed his own sociological bias.[129] Men were social beings, he said, bound together in a community by a powerful urge toward freedom but subject nevertheless to strong forces of compulsion. It was these forces that made history. In the economic realm, the principles of utility and cost—which functioned so beautifully in a simple economy—operated in the real world only in an approximate way. The outcome of market behavior was not always beneficial as the earlier theory might have suggested, for the weak were often dominated and controlled by the strong.[130] Furthermore, in a social economy, prices were often stratified, reflecting the growth of different categories of goods as they were related to the different classes of society. The irrationality and economic distortion that stemmed from such a development were virtually self-evident.[131] Here, Wieser, like Thorstein Veblen, noted the overwhelming impact that ostentation exerted on the market. Price now became a social institution, for it acted to bring different people together. It was no longer the pure analytical device that had been found in the *Natural Value*. Stratified marginal utility was easily distorted.[132] Economic values in the social economy were warped and soon failed to reflect genuine rationality. Three groups of goods were involved: the mass of commodities that everyone used, both rich and poor; luxury goods; and intermediate items. The first were evaluated by the marginal utility of the poor, the second by the marginal utility of the rich, the third by the valuations of the middle class. It was this process that had created an unwarranted stratification of demand.

Excessive competition could arise and so overstimulate production, thus exposing one of the roots of economic crisis.[133] Wieser rejected the classical notion of competition as the ideal state and was rather critical of attacks on monopoly. After reviewing the functioning of monopolies, he said, in anticipation of Schumpeter as it were, "The classical formula, unconditional approval of the social competition and absolute repudiation of the anti-social monopoly, can no longer do justice to the institutions of today." [134] Nor was it possible any longer to speak exclusively of competition or monopoly, he observed, for there were now many novel intermediate monopoloid forms. Insofar as market positions were concerned, while monopoly represented a favored position, not all such vantage point represented true monopoly. Although the intermediate forms might exhibit monopolistic traits, they still were subject to competitive pressures. These concepts, although not particularly advanced ones, were suggestive of the later doctrines of Edward H. Chamberlin and Joan Robinson.[135] However, Wieser was oblivious of the notions of product differentiation or the effect that differences in location might have on price and demand.

The economic sociology Wieser developed in his *Social Economics* was rather striking for his day. He pointed to the social degeneration engendered by rapid urbanization, the harmful impact of inequalities in wealth, and industrialism's deadening oppressiveness and utter sense of alienation. He thought that perhaps trade unions, if concerned exclusively with matters of collective bargaining, might effectuate improvements; [136] he was quite certain that the worker in modern capitalism could find genuine freedom only through unionism.[137] These were indeed refreshing statements, after the unalloyed individualism, bordering on the rugged, of Jevons and Menger. How salutary it might be for some contemporary theorists to reread Wieser on this subject.[138] Here too he sought to relate policy questions to theoretical principles: he insisted that the action of unions could only assure payment of labor's full marginal productivity. He consequently recommended that unions should avoid industrial strife and seek "an amicable determination of the wages that are economically demanded." Even this formulation, limited as it was and restricted to a marginalist framework, was superior to that of his contemporaries.

Wieser's preference appears to have been for what today would be called the "mixed economy." He did say, however, that centralized control could not be as effective in achieving satisfactory results as could the myriad actions of many individuals.[139] At no time, of course, did he countenance the socialist view on economic and social questions. Economic calculation, he insisted, would be best under a capitalist order; but he conceded that the growth of a socialized sector was unavoidable. Problems of calculation were essentially problems of maximizing utility, but this might not be consonant with the objectives of the social economy. Since methods and forms of achieving these maxima were said to be basically alike, the laws of economic calculation in capitalism and socialism were actually the same.[140]

The nature of the state economy was discussed in an abbreviated Book Three of *Social Economics.* The state's objective, said Wieser, should be the protection and development of social production rather than the satisfaction of wants. When the state operated ordinary enterprises, it became involved in the exchange process with the principle of maximum exchange value still the main guide to action. Progressive taxation, however, was to be rejected despite the feasibility of its defense in terms of utility theory. The final part of the book dealt with the world economy. Wieser's viewpoint here was typically continental in that he found the classical view of international trade unacceptable. List's scheme of nationalism, with its apparatus of protection, was found to be quite valid. Although international price equilibrium might never be obtained, it was important, felt Wieser, that technical knowledge continually be broadened. This could be more important than access to resources.[141]

There has been an unfortunate tendency to underestimate Wieser. Granted that the criticisms one levels at the Austrians make him part of the target, the fact nevertheless remains that he developed Menger's utility theory in more incisive ways and formed virtually independent theories of cost and distribution. The *Social Economics,* which summed up a life's thinking on economic problems, underscored the now obvious point that a rounded view demanded analysis beyond the bare principles of a simple economy. In short, Wieser exhibited a vision of society as a functioning organism that was patently lacking in the other Austrians and marginalists. Even as George Stigler has conceded, Wieser exerted some influence on later economists.[142] Fred M. Taylor was sufficiently impressed by the problem of limited variation in factors to consider fixed coefficients of some importance, and there are even traces of Wieser in such a writer as J. R. Hicks.[143] Although Wieser believed he had worked out a purely psychological theory of economics, what he actually offered in his technical apparatus was a normative system—a theory of economy as it ought to be. One sees this particularly in his social analysis which stressed deviations from proper standards of action, as in the discussions of inequality and reform. He did not want to create a static economics: how else are we to understand his careful plotting of economic motion from the utility calculus of the natural system to the exchange value of the social economy, where freedom of contract and private property permit men to pursue their own aims, on to the national and international economy? Obviously he had been concerned with something more than pure theory. In his *Gesetz der Macht,* which expanded the sociology of the *Social Economics,* the major questions now were monopoly, leadership, and rights.

This clearly was a serious effort to integrate theoretical work and practice. If only for that, Wieser deserves an honored place in the history of economic doctrine.

iii

Eugen von Böhm-Bawerk: The Bourgeois Marx

The new economics was meeting no easy response. Jevons had come up against a blank wall in Britain and Walras worked alone at Lausanne. The Austrian marginalists, however, were more fortunate; there a school was formed virtually at once, with Wieser and Eugen von Böhm-Bawerk (1851-1919) as extremely capable and vocal disciples for Menger. Böhm-Bawerk especially fought vigorously for the new doctrine; his writing was a continuous and frequently brilliant polemic against all who objected to the introduction of subjectivism into economics.

Böhm-Bawerk, who was born in Brunn, came of a family of civil servants. His father had been vice-governor of Moravia, and, despite his interest in the physical sciences, Böhm-Bawerk had been required to follow the family tradition of law. From the University of Vienna, he went to a government post in lower Austria and then entered the Ministry of Finance where his abilities soon made a deep impression. His interest in theoretical economics was aroused by the new Mengerian approach. He then travelled in Germany for two years, with Wieser, his future brother-in-law, studying at Heidelberg, Jena, and Leipzig. Most of Böhm-Bawerk's career was given to public service, with the result that much of his writing had a somewhat unfinished character. No doubt, had he had the leisure time of an academician he would have revised and polished a good deal of it. The larger part of his energies, however, went into a persistent defense of Menger's new economic theory. In 1889 he was recalled to the Ministry of Finance, after a few years at Innsbruck University, expressly to work out schemes for fiscal reform. His anxiety to get on with public service resulted in a rather hasty job on his *Positive Theory of Capital,* the second part of the *Kapital and Kapitalzins.* Many of the ideas in it were in but rough state, yet there seemed little doubt that given a second chance, Böhm-Bawerk would have revised it considerably.

A top civil service career that ran from 1889 to 1904 left little time for writing. Yet Böhm-Bawerk did manage to teach and was even able to publish his famous critique of Marx.[144] In 1905 he turned his back on public office and undertook a full time professorial post at Vienna, where his seminar became quite famous. As a polemicist, he was one of the best, quick to concede his opponents' good points, but ever ready to destroy with dazzling displays of irrefutable logic the house of error constructed by antagonists. Surely the controversial nature of Austrian theory demanded such a skill if it were to be firmly established.[145]

As finance minister for the Austrian monarchy, Böhm-Bawerk stood for "sound financial principles." He was cautious and conservative. His formidable talents as a debater stood him in good stead when it came to withstanding the pressure of public opinion. Schumpeter, who in an obituary described Böhm-Bawerk's life as "a work of art," [146] commented that he had exhibited ". . . single-minded devotion to duty, complete disinterestedness, high intellectual endeavor, wide cultural interests and genuine simplicity—all of which was entirely free from sanctimoniousness or any propensity to preach." [147] Böhm-Bawerk's starting point was Menger and he had no desire to deviate from the master. There was no wasted effort and no seeking for momentary success: the object was to advance the theory of utility beyond the point to which it had been brought by Menger.

A missing element in the latter's system had been the theory of interest or the net return to capital. For Böhm-Bawerk, interest was the key to the understanding of capitalism, just as surplus value had been the central problem for Marx. The particular view that one had of interest and profit, thought Böhm-Bawerk, was most significant, for it conditioned one's attitude toward capitalism. Doubtless this was the only point on which he could have secured agreement from Marx. But in contrast to the latter, Böhm-Bawerk's approach was that of the pure theorist. He did not seek explanations for social problems nor did he advocate measures of amelioration as did Marshall. He merely wanted to show that capitalism was an economy that not only functioned well, but exhibited an internal *raison d'être* entirely consistent with its objectives.

Although the major influence on Böhm-Bawerk was avowedly Menger, there were also traces of Jevons and John Rae in his work.[148] Rae, an early nineteenth-century American writer, had discussed the role of invention in economic growth and the effect that the underestimation of future wants had on the economy. But it was Menger whom Böhm-Bawerk followed on value and price as well as on the period of production and the discounting of future goods—ideas that he later brought to full flower in a masterful way. And with these notions, he was able to erect an ideological structure quite his own, despite his desire to be purely "scientific." The first part of his magnum opus, *Capital and Interest,* was a detailed history and criticism of earlier theories of capital and interest.[149] He did not fail, of course, to offer his own views on these subjects.

Böhm-Bawerk's basic ideas had been set forth in an early work, *Rechte und Verhältnisse vom Standpunkte der volkswirtschaftlichen Güterlehre.*[150] It was this work that obtained for him his teaching post at Vienna. Embedded in it were the seeds of the future analysis of the capitalist process. The *Rechte und Verhältnisse* had distinguished economic rights from goods, thus providing entrée into a realm where capital might be defined as an aggregate of goods and commodities. While claims to goods did exhibit a capitalized value, Böhm-Bawerk's starting point in utility and the want-satisfying power of goods led him to overlook the immediate significance of the capitalized value of rights. As Veblen was to show later, such values constituted a major portion of economic values in capitalism. The outcome for Böhm-Bawerk was the construction of a kind of barter across time, with future and present goods as the major items of exchange.

In 1886, Böhm-Bawerk published his *Grundzüge der Theorie des wirtschaftlichen Güterwertes* and with this he achieved a firm position as a leader of the Austrian school. For years he played the role of major advocate for the new theory, defending and expounding its virtues and attacking all those who doubted its verities. His reputation was firmly established with *Capital and Interest,* although he made no attempt to study the various theories that he had reviewed in their historical context or to examine their philosophical implications. Each was analyzed purely in terms of its inner logic. Each was found wanting and sent to its doom on the Bawerkian guillotine. This approach underscored Böhm-Bawerk's desire to discover the general laws of economics, laws that would apply in any system regardless of time and place. He felt that such laws followed logically and objectively from the essential nature of economic activity. Economic problems were for him basically analytical in character. He was a "pure" scientist *sans* history and sociology.

The basic question for economists, intimated Böhm-Bawerk, was not to gather more facts, but how to study, digest, and analyse those already known and how to pursue to their ultimate the implications that could be drawn from them. This was to be done by abstracting from the totality of experience in a way somewhat analogous to the methods of theoretical physics. Böhm-Bawerk, however, did not care much for methodological disputations, feeling that such quarrels could only become arid impediments to serious scientific work. Nor did he care for practical applications, since, in the context of the debates that would inevitably arise, the theory itself, he thought, would be lost. This was not for him, despite his long interest in practical affairs. As Schumpeter has said, Böhm was writing for future generations.[151]

Böhm-Bawerk was well aware of the role that capital and interest played in social situations. This was quite evident from the *Capital and Interest* which classified the different doctrines in terms of friendliness or hostility to interest as an economic category. Earlier theories, he said, had been concerned with simple debtor-creditor relations; later ones had taken into account the capital-labor dichotomy. The shift in focus implied a new concept of capital, which now had to be defined as a stock of goods to be used in production rather than as a fluid fund. However, this did not mean that capital was to be conceived in a real historical context; it was still to be considered a theoretical notion, in spite of its seeming embodiment in concrete goods. As an historical category, capital would have meant conflict between social classes, and this was an implication that Böhm-Bawerk had to avoid at all costs. Yet his effort to construct a pure theory in order to escape from history was self-defeating. He simply could not avoid an ideological position. His disclaimers notwithstanding, Böhm's economics remained class-oriented, for by seeking to demonstrate its eternal and everlasting validity he was exploiting a subtle justification of a particular pattern of economic behavior. The argument that capital was a theoretical rather than an historical concept was a not overly successful attempt to abolish class conflict. Doubtlessly Böhm-Bawerk's reply would have been that he was merely exploring the reasons for the existence of interest, its äetiology. A sociological inquiry, on the other hand, would have had to ask how interest affected relations between people and would have examined both means and ends. This was something he did not want. He was determined to employ only cause and effect. Interestingly enough, he rejected the idea of interdependence and equilibrium, perhaps because he found mathematical ideas to be alien. He thought that the latter would involve circular reasoning.[152]

These views were reflected mainly in the *Positive Theory,* a somewhat chaotic work. The second part of the book was written while the first was at the printer, and certain theoretical obscurities were never completely clarified. As both Wicksell and Stigler observed, the reader frequently had the feeling that distinct streams of thought ran through it which, on occasion, appeared to conflict. The numerous "excursuses" and long critical notes, each a monograph in itself, added to the apparent confusion. The virtually complete lack of integration made the *Positive Theory* seem little more than a collection of essays, each at odds with the other.

Yet its importance could not be exaggerated, for it did represent an advanced statement of the marginalist position. An economic order consisted solely of capitalists, workers, and landlords, each of which had a specific function to fulfill. Like Ricardo before him, Böhm-Bawerk was interested in the problem of functional rather than personal distribution. The latter was no concern of his; he did not, like Wieser, recognize that the political and social climate which influenced personal distribution might play havoc with the putative distribution of income according to functional theory.

As with Wieser, the theory of value Böhm-Bawerk developed in Books

Three and Four of the *Positive Theory,* stemmed from Menger, who had, however, applied the concept of utility primarily to goods which directly satisfied wants. While Menger did have a kernel of the imputation notion, it was but a mere suggestion and critics were quick to point out the gap. A reply had been worked up by Wieser and expanded even further by Böhm-Bawerk, notably in his early essay, the *Grundzüge.* But even as between Menger's two disciples there were differences of view, revolving about the concept of the valuation of stocks of goods. Wieser believed that the units of a stock ought to be evaluated on the basis of marginal utility, so that the total value of the stock would equal the number of units multiplied by marginal utility. Böhm-Bawerk held that since marginal utility diminished for a given stock, the total value was equal to the sum of the fractional values of the units. A considerable debate developed among the devotees of marginalism. Some thought Wieser's formulation more accurate because the actual satisfaction of wants took place over time, so that portions of a stock might be utilized when needed without regard to fractional values. The assumption here, of course, was that the different units of stock were uniform. Most of the marginalists, however, followed Böhm-Bawerk.[153]

Other differences arose between the two over the question of imputation. Wieser had insisted that the sum of the imputed shares of the yield of a given production mix should be no greater and no less than the product itself. The apportionment, in other words, was perfect, Böhm-Bawerk, on the other hand, argued that the advantages of modern production stemmed from the ability to control each input factor, so that the values going back to them were greater than the values put in. That is to say, the total value of a cooperating group of inputs was smaller than the sum of the values going to the factors. This was no contradiction, for in many creative situations the whole is greater than the sum of the parts, a concept that would be essential if Böhm-Bawerk were to establish his particular notion of surplus value.

The utility of a good was clearly related to its use value. Without the latter the satisfaction of wants would be impossible. However, argued Böhm-Bawerk, value in the sense of exchangeability did not arise until use value was subjected to a condition of scarcity. Following this, he distinguished between wants per se and their relative intensity, enabling him to work out the "law of decreasing marginal utility." Consequently, the value of a good was determined by its lowest marginal utility. A more elegant way of putting the argument was to say that goods were valued in proportion to the decrease in satisfaction that their loss occasioned. This, however, implied a theorem of substitutability, for the value of a good could be said to be determined by the utility of the commodity which was foregone in the marginal instance—a principle that Böhm-Bawerk applied to freely reproducible goods and to goods capable of being put to more than one use. The case of complementary goods was then examined for the purpose of discovering the value of each good in the group of complementary items. This was done by assigning to the replaceable elements their value prior to their inclusion in the group and imputing the remaining value to the non-replaceable items. The procedure, however, was not only quite arbitrary but assumed also a fixed quantity of input factors.[154] Yet Böhm-Bawerk's approach was basically like Wieser's: he adopted the idea of the productive contribution in determining the imputed value of the factors of production; he also denied that the "disutility" of labor had any effect on value or on the allocation of resources. The rejection of the role of cost was significant in Böhm-Bawerk's theory, for it entirely eliminated objective elements— something that his British critics especially could not abide. Nor could they accept his illustration that the higher price for skilled labor had ruled out its ability to determine value at the margin.

Price—the market expression of value—was both determined and limited, on the one hand, by the subjective evaluations of the last buyer admitted and by the first seller able to enter into the exchange transaction, and, on the other, by the valuations of the weakest seller and the first buyer excluded from the market situation. This concept of marginal pairs converted supply and demand equations into a matter of marginal utility.[155] Böhm-Bawerk preferred this approach because he found the concept of supply and demand somewhat ambiguous. The basic factors, he thought, were the intensity of demand and the utility of goods. Price theory was thereby rooted in subjective value, and costs simply had to be stated as prices.[156] Fluctuations in prices, costs, and values were all traceable to marginal utility. The causal claim, he said, ran from value and price to value and cost—from iron ware to iron ore. This was "simply the great law of marginal utility fulfilling itself. . . ." Böhm-Bawerk did concede, though, that in the short run supply was somewhat inflexible and consequently depended largely on price, which had to be high enough to overcome the reservation prices of those suppliers who participated in a given exchange situation. This clearly was the meaning of his "marginal pair" horse market illustration [157] where obviously supply was affected by that price sufficient to exclude alternative uses as well as possible applications by the supplier himself. The continuous market curves familiar to contemporary students were not utilized: the explanation of market phenomena was in terms of discontinuities and discrete units.

Value theory provided the basis for an understanding of wages, rent, and profit. All goods were reducible to land and labor, which were ultimately the sole factors of production.[158] The value of a product had to work its way back to these factors, whose services thus were given their value and their prices, otherwise known as wages and rent. As labor was now to be paid in accordance with its marginal contribution, the theory of marginal productivity was revealed in all its pristine vigor. Profit and interest, however, stemmed from extraneous elements, usually frictions which caused prices to deviate from the normal course of affairs established by costs. Profits arose because of market imperfections, while interest was traceable to the factor of time. Here at last was Böhm-Bawerk's unique contribution to economic thought [159] and the feature that was to give his doctrinal pronouncements their characteristic coloration.

The value of a worker was to be measured by the discounted value of his productivity. This was also the case for income from the services of land. Wages and rent were to be both price expressions of the marginal products of labor and land multiplied by the quantity, all discounted to the present. Böhm-Bawerk employed this same procedure for the valuation of durable goods, and through this concept it was discovered that interest permeated the entire economic order. This was the basis of his theory of distribution. He would have nothing to do with the idea that variations in input factors could be part of production and distribution. Every input in the production mix was essential; in fact, the mix was virtually a single input and the last factor required to complete the mix would carry its full value.

Although this seemed somewhat akin to Wieser's "going concern" idea, it was, on the whole, fairly muddled. An alternative approach assigned a kind of minimum reservation price to the factors of production in order to encourage their participation, with such price based on what they might receive elsewhere. With replaceable goods the problem was easy, for values could be related to what factors presumably obtained in alternative employments.[160] But the difficulty in this "opportunity cost" approach stemmed from Böhm-Bawerk's rejection of the idea of economic interdependence, so that he was unable to solve the problem in any genuinely satisfactory way.

With regard to consumption and saving, Böhm-Bawerk observed that means of subsistence would have to be stored in order to provide a future supply of goods for landlords and workers. This implied that consumption was to be based on previous production; it appeared as the reverse side of the coin representing his period of production. It would be the job of the capitalist to maintain the supply of subsistence goods in order to support landlords and workers. True saving, however, would be the assignment of production to distant and remote purposes rather than to immediate needs. But this process could not be entirely responsible for the creation of capital, since the latter also had roots in prior production.[161] In fact, said Böhm-Bawerk, it was the productive power of capital which was saved, not capital itself. Furthermore, the transfer of these powers from the immediate to the remote through the business of roundabout production was responsible for calling forth intermediate goods. Ultimately, the real creative force was roundabout production, rather than capital equipment. It was this characteristic feature of capitalism which created, maintained, and augmented capital; [162] it was an indirect force which lent its impulse to the productive powers. Essentially, capital was an intermediate product of nature and labor. But it was the consumer who actually decided on the direction that production would take, for, by making or withholding expenditure, he utilized the strength of effective demand to impose his wishes and choice on society.

This represented the starting point of the central part of Böhm-Bawerk's economics, the theory of capital. But clearly he had felt impelled to clear the ground first, which explains the long detailed history of doctrine in *Capital and Interest.* The nature of an economic good would have to be defined; this was done in the *Rechte und Verhältnisse,* where the subjective theory of value and the concept of utility became the core of economic theory. Then one could proceed to the analysis of profit and interest. But to do this would require a clear-cut definition of capital and here Böhm-Bawerk limited himself to material goods rather than rights and intangibles. He sought to distinguish between capital as the means of production and capital as net return. The latter notion he thought somewhat naive and consequently turned his attention to capital as a collection of productive implements. Now, it was necessary, he said, to start with a conception of production as the transformation of matter for the purpose of creating things necessary to satisfy wants. This objective could be obtained if labor was first expended on certain other means of production which could then be utilized to produce more consumer goods.[163] This was the famous roundabout process. While the idea was not especially novel, it became an integral element of general economic theory in Böhm-Bawerk's hands. Capitalistic production, therefore, was roundabout production and the more roundabout the better. Capital comprised all the intermediate goods that were created in the various stages of the indirect process. It was clear that what others had deemed to be essential elements of capitalism—market situations, private property, a wage system—were less meaningful than roundabout production. Any economic order which employed this indirect method of producing goods was "capitalistic" and a net return to capital would exist even in the kind of economic order described as socialist. Private capital was defined as the fund of subsistence goods advanced to workers, a concept quite similar to Jevons' definition.[164] This then was contrasted with social capital, machinery, and raw materials in the hands of businessmen. But it was not a very fruitful distinction; in fact, it served to obscure rather than clarify matters and was subjected to some fairly sharp criticism, notably by Wicksell and Veblen.[165]

One missed in Böhm-Bawerk the analysis of the relation between capitalists, landlords, and workers which was to be found among the more sociologically-minded economists. These relationships were reduced by him to the category of time, something that had not been of great consequence for either the classicists or Marx. With them time had been suppressed, except insofar as it was part of the turnover concept. Not until Marshall was the time factor explicitly introduced into economic models. But in Böhm-Bawerk's system, time played a central role; it pushed aside the predominant concern with distribution that was so evident, for example, in Ricardo. Time was basic to capital's net return for two reasons: first, because of the profound influence that roundabout production exerted on the increase in productivity; and second, because of the element of postponement (Böhm-Bawerk did not want to employ the word "abstinence"). The discounting to the present of future goods brought time forcefully into the heart of economic doctrine. But it was not possible to extend roundabout production too far into the future: that is, there was a limitation on time, established mainly by the onset of decreasing returns. What Böhm-Bawerk had done, consequently, was to suggest a two-fold theory of capital, and he was never quite certain which one he preferred. The fact that he made much of roundabout production with its offshoot, the "average period," suggested a predilection for the former.[166]

The "period of production" required that capital be eliminated as a factor; this was done, as we have seen, by converting all inputs into land and labor and by introducing past time in a somewhat surreptitious fashion; once capital was extended backwards it was really nothing more than the product of nature and labor. Yet, this point, of which Böhm-Bawerk made much, was really irrelevant; it was required merely as a forensic device in his disputes with other theorists.[167] Roundabout production would increase the output of a given production mix, he said. An increase in the amount of capital could be used only to extend the average period of production.[168] Experience itself, he insisted, had demonstrated the absolute validity of this proposition. But all this was little more than a circular argument. It implied the notion that additional capital would only extend the production period, which was precisely what the theory was intended to prove. Entirely new goods were excluded, as was the possibility of maintaining output or even increasing it with a shorter period of production. Yet nothing in the logic of technology really eliminated such contingencies. The fact was that both shorter and longer processes existed in a dynamic system. Accumulation did encourage the installation of all kinds of equipment. Böhm-Bawerk's argument that the period always had to be lengthened was simply not convincing. His insistence on the roundaboutness of capitalist production gave him a static approach which raised doubts that he had been able to solve the interest problem at all. Schumpeter tried to explain away Böhm's deficiency on this important aspect by suggesting that the shortening process had been limited to new inventions.[169] If this were done Böhm-Bawerk's argument would have made sense, for those inventions within the current technological ken of producers then could have been analysed according to production time theory. But this still separated the production period from the theory of interest, a point that generated considerable controversy.[170]

The one virtue of the period of production was that it did begin to approach the idea of a dynamic capitalism.[171] Of course, the suggestion that the economy had begun to grow when primitive peoples had invented the first tools with their bare hands was utterly useless for analytical purposes. The types of production time were listed as (1) the absolute time between the insertion of the first intermediate good and present economic goods, and (2) the absolute period of production or the interval required for the making of present goods. The first was an historical rather than an economic concept; it was the second that was relevant for the determination of interest, since it was the average period of production of present goods that affected the rate of interest. The *time* of production, on the other hand, was defined as the length of life of the most durable of the intermediate capital goods. Now, although interest was the result of the relationships between capitalists and workers, it was not the time spent by the particular worker in replacing the most durable capital that was relevant, but rather the average time spent by all labor inputs. In this way, Böhm-Bawerk finally arrived at his average period of production, a notion vaguely suggestive of Jevons' capitalization period.[172] The durability of a good, however, was but one element in a whole range of factors that affected interest and production. The whole business was fairly complicated: inputs would hope to be weighted according to their relative importance and dated in order to arrive at an "average," as in the construction of index numbers. In Böhm-Bawerk's version the average was an average rate of turnover for the entire economy, so that sight was lost of the individual enterprise—something that clashed sharply with the fundamental Austrian approach. What happened was that the average period of production was based on the average of all time periods of each of the outputs. It could have been argued that the turnover concept for the entire economy ought to have had some meaning for particular firms. But the major question was just what did all this have to do with the theory of interest, since Böhm-Bawerk specifically had said that the latter stemmed from an exchange relationship between worker and capitalist. All that one could say, after this long and recondite analysis, was that the period of production was merely a framework for the determination of interest.[173]

Interest was as important a part of Böhm-Bawerk's theory as was capital, if perhaps not more so. It was developed in a highly formal model in which the means of production were always fully employed, always replaced, and constantly accumulated. His sociological backdrop, if one might have been said to exist, was a capitalist society of absolute proprietors and propertyless workers. Yet the basic theoretical problem to be solved was the same to which Marx had sought an answer: why did capitalists, as mere owners of property, receive an endless surplus of goods? The question was to explain the nature of interest not only in terms of surplus value but as the very device by which that surplus was gathered. This was by no means to suggest the sort of analysis by which Marx had threaded his way through the economic labyrinth. Böhm-Bawerk looked upon the formation of interest as a matter of imputed pricing. The socialist approach was in error, he said, because it constituted an exploitation theory; and this was wrong because interest was a value category, a purely positive notion, to which normative concepts ought not be applied. Obviously, he had to say this in order to avoid considering interest as a facet of distribution theory, for this would have involved him quite deeply in the problem that fascinated both Marx and Veblen—how to judge the nature and operation of capitalism itself.

The income which interest provided was the economic basis for society's dominant class. Whatever explanation one offered would surely reflect the attitude of the theorist toward the economic order. Again, Böhm-Bawerk first had to clear the ground: the dozens of theories then extant were all unsatisfactory. And so he proceeded to apply ". . . an incredibly diligent and acute analysis of virtually all theories of interest which had been developed before his time." [174] Theories of interest, said Böhm-Bawerk, were to be judged by criteria which specified its origin and flow. This process led him to classify the various formulations as either "productivity," "use," "abstinence," "labor," or "exploitation" theories. The productivity theories (J. B. Say, Lauderdale, Carey, von Thünen) divided income flows into different streams in accordance with the factors of production. [175]

These theories failed, he said, because they confused value and product concepts. Capital might be productive, but it was not interest that it created. What capital made were forms and shapes of materials. Interest as a value category could arise only in exchange. Simply enough, productivity theories forgot that capital was not a factor of production in that sense. The use theory, stemming chiefly from Menger, foundered on the distinction between the use of capital and its using-up. That is to say, the belief that there was a difference between the value possessed by the use of a good and the value of the good itself was a false one. Use theories suggested that interest was a payment for capital. But this, he said, was merely a right of disposal or control and was not a source of value. The right to control intermediate goods did not create value. Böhm-Bawerk's argument at this point was not only unpersuasive but was irritating enough for Menger to reply with his own exposition. [176] Böhm, however, simply returned to the basic marginalist principle: value could be derived only from consumer goods which then, through imputation, imparted that value to intermediate ones.

Nor did abstinence explain interest, for it did not adequately account for the increase in the size of a loan as a result of interest. However, this theory was useful in defending interest as an economic category. [177] But

Böhm-Bawerk did not reject Nassau Senior too strenuously, for then he might have found himself in the same camp as the socialists. Interest, he said, was not a required payment to assure abstinence, since it was more like a rent than a cost. He did concede that high interest might accrue to the rich, who obviously suffered little abstinence, while low or no interest at all would be gained by the poor, whose sacrifices were genuine enough. However, he felt there was a kernel of truth in Senior's version insofar as capital formation demanded the postponement of satisfactions.[178] But Senior was guilty of technical errors, asserted Böhm; to include the disutility of labor and the sacrifice of present goods for future ones in the same valuation was essentially duplication. The error here emanated from an improper theory of value, said the Austrian.

The labor theories were quickly dismissed in order to reach the exploitation versions developed by Rodbertus and Marx. The former's notion that all goods were products of labor Böhm rejected as otiose, while Marx was chided for overlooking the element of time. The trouble with these theories was that they were caught in a sociological trap—most of what they had to say was outside the realm of economic analysis. And the result was confusion and incompleteness.

The proper approach, said Böhm, would have been to take account of the two basic factors of production which through economic cooperation had given rise to a single flow of income. The process of valuation, rooted in utility and scarcity, effectively distributed the undifferentiated flow into its proper components. The difficulty with most of the other interest theories stemmed from their failure to consider valuation as an integral element of the economic process. Those theories that ignored time were also false because they were totally incapable of explaining how the "agio"—Böhm-Bawerk's term for interest—was appropriated by the capitalist; for it was precisely this agio that arose from time. In a sense, the Bawerkian attack on all other theories was a remarkable performance. *Capital and Interest* was interesting also in its own right as a history of economic doctrine, and, though directed toward quite another purpose, took its rightful place next to Marx's *Theorien über den Mehrwert*.

There were suggestions of Böhm-Bawerk's interest theory in *Capital and Interest*, which he described as an exchange or "agio." [179] Basically, his theory stemmed from the assertion that present goods were valued somewhat higher than future ones, so that the surrender of present goods called for some remuneration. The point of common contact between present and future was, naturally enough, marginal utility. Interest itself was simply a measure of the difference between present and future. This emphasized the fact that for Böhm-Bawerk interest was a value category indigenous to the analysis of value itself. Although the present was valued more highly, man produced for the future because he knew that unmet needs would arise at various points in time yet to come. The calculation of the premium or "agio" required for the surrender of present goods was complicated by the fact that roundabout production enhanced future outputs and value.[180] Böhm attributed the fact that lenders could wait for future production to the existence of a subsistence fund of consumers' goods which had been accumulated from past production. This was a social fund which moved into those fields where the level of marginal utility was ostensibly most advantageous. The agio, drawn from this fund, was itself an exchange of present for future goods.[181] Those who felt that the future was worth less than the agio said it was, would have to work out their own adjustment. The agio itself behaved very much as any price would, with its level moving proportionately to the length of the period of production.

All this seemed fairly evident in the case of money loans, for these were clearly exchanges of present claims for future ones. In fact, the whole apparatus seemed ideally suited for explaining money interest. But the system was to be adapted also to land and labor, since the sources of these factors could be purchased at present values and their future output sold at prices prevailing at that time. The increment in value began to make itself felt just as soon as the present means of production grew toward future values. This was the basis of Böhm-Bawerk's net return. The agio made its appearance as a discount from the value of future marginal products of the original means of production. Workers and landlords who offered their services, usually in the market governing the means of subsistence, would do so naturally subject to certain reservation prices. But the capitalists would be willing to engage in trade even at a small agio. The workers too would be glad to pay a small premium on present goods, because presumably they were unwilling to wait for the ripening of their efforts at some future date. Since they could not abstain from present consumption, they would have to exchange future goods for present ones which were controlled by those who held the subsistence fund. The existence of the agio and its relation to the time of production would exist even in a socialist society: the interest rate would be part of the plans of any central authority. But Böhm-Bawerk dropped in a *deux ex machina* by introducing a scarcity external to the agio itself. This was the limited size of the subsistence fund which not only placed a ceiling on the agio, but, as we have noted, limited the period of production as well.

Böhm-Bawerk set forth several reasons for the existence of interest. These were his famous *drei Grunde:* the psychological as well as the actual difference between the present and future; the acknowledged tendency to underestimate future goods, mainly because of deficient imagination; and the technical superiority of present goods stemming from the roundaboutness of capitalist production which made future goods somewhat remote.[182] While the influence of time pervaded all three "grounds," it was the third that really gave rise to the surplus value known as interest. Scarcity was implicit in the first proposition: the continued stress on present rather than future goods would itself tend to increase demand and create an agio. The under-estimation of the future set forth in the second statement was said to be rooted in defects of will and the "shortness and uncertainty of life." These elements gave present goods a higher market price than might otherwise have been the case.[183] In the third ground, time established a connection not only between present and future but with the objective and subjective as well. The psychological agio of the first proposition and the technical ad-vantages of the third combined to create interest.

Now, what did Böhm-Bawerk do with this elaborate structure? His whole purpose was to justify interest in relation to the use of capital goods. Capitalists, he said, derived their income from exchange transactions. Viewed as a class, from the macroeconomic standpoint, capitalists' gains, in the form of interest, stemmed from their "trade" with workers. Interest, however, should not be confused with entrepreneurial profit or windfalls: it was rather the income obtained from the ownership of capital goods. When labor was applied to the fund of previously accumulated subsistence goods a surplus was created, due mainly to roundabout methods of production. But as labor could not wait for future production, it bartered its output-to-come for present goods held by capitalists. Here the exchange of present and future took place, and, in the course of securing a return of his gross outlay, the capitalist obtained interest. Böhm-Bawerk now felt that he had successfully rebutted Karl Marx, for not only had he employed the apparatus of "surplus value," but he had demonstrated that there was really nothing wrong with the way the system worked. In fact, as William Smart, Böhm's translator, remarked, the whole unique structure was quite moral: wealth was made the center of economic analysis, and it was wealth that permitted a freer and fuller life. Clearly, these could be fundamental grounds for granting the capitalist a surplus return.

Böhm-Bawerk's grounds, however, were little more than assumptions. It does seem possible to value future needs more highly than present ones: how else can one explain, for example, the Soviet program of industrializa-tion? The defective imagination of the second ground suggests that some people are irrational for demanding present as compared with future goods. Can not a demand moving the other way also be called irrational? Nor can one be so sure, as was Böhm-Bawerk, that the technically superior methods of roundabout production directly affect utility and value. As Knut Wicksell suggested in his *Value, Capital and Rent,* if roundabout production did in fact create more goods, then surely both the third and first grounds were virtually the same.[184] The supply of future goods was not predictable, nor was the period of consumption any the less indefinite. If these factors were admitted, then how would it be possible to develop an exchange transaction between present and future in which comparisons of marginal utilities were to be worked out?[185] Obviously, if this could not be done in a theoretically satisfactory way, the whole edifice that Böhm-Bawerk had labored so long to build would threaten to collapse. Gaps were also revealed in the third ground, ostensibly the strongest and most objective. Lengthening the period of production would require that returns increase in geometric ratio or more in order to make the whole business worthwhile. Wicksell illustrated the point by showing that if a one-year period brought returns of 100 units and a two-year period, 150 units, then clearly the shorter period would be preferred by virtue of its greater *rate* of increase.[186]

The foregoing theoretical structure provided the framework for a determination of the market rate of interest. This began with the situation where labor's demand for present subsistence was the only factor. Böhm abstracted from the demand of other classes. He discovered that labor had no subjective value as was the case with other goods; it was valued rather in accordance with its anticipated output and this varied somewhat, depending upon the length of the period of production.[187] The amount of output that the capitalist could obtain from labor was determined by the uses to which it was put. Equilibrium would prevail most likely in a long period, for then the subsistence fund would be enough to pay for the entire product of labor, and the supply of labor and present goods would "come to mutual exchange."[188] In the short period, unemployment might result and workers would have to accept reductions in wages in order to be given jobs.[189] Thus, a long period of production would be most effective in absorbing all workers and disposing of the subsistence fund.[190] Of course, the capitalist would select that combination of time and number of workers that would bring him the largest net return. Böhm-Bawerk had no fear but that competition would enforce the necessary equilibrium.

The level of interest was fixed by the additional yield of the last possible lengthening of the period of production.[191] But involved in this were the three basic elements which determined the interest rate: the size of the subsistence fund; the number of available workers; and the degree of productivity achieved by the given period.[192] The larger the subsistence fund, the lower would be the rate of interest; the larger the other two factors, the higher would interest become. Yet despite all this analytical material, no particular rules were given which would enable one to foretell the level at which the interest rate would settle. Numerous psychological and social factors and elements of uncertainty and habit were also at work. But all of them were submitted finally to the principle of marginal utility in which Böhm-Bawerk expressed his ultimate faith.[193] His gigantic work, replete with much detail and tedious analysis, had reduced itself to an heroic attempt to construct a marginal productivity theory for the entire economy. The effort simply failed.

Böhm-Bawerk's conception of interest as a surplus, in the sense of an excess of output over input, represented a departure from the individualistic outlook of his teacher, Menger. True, when interest was looked upon as a component in the cost structure of a single capitalist, no surplus seemed to appear, for price equaled cost. But when the economy as a whole was examined, it was patent to Böhm-Bawerk that the capitalist class made a net return. Yet the difference between his interest theory and those of his opponents appeared to be essentially verbal. There seemed, for example, little to choose between Nassau Senior's abstinence and Böhm's agio. Within the setting of a competitive economy, both raised interest to the level of a factor payment coordinate with rent and wages. Furthermore, Böhm's subsistence was little more than the wages-fund theory in new garb. He refused to admit that this was so, for his account of the matter, he said, had made the fund a variable proportion of the stock of goods accumulated by the community.[194] It was not a predetermined lump of wealth, as with the classicists, and its purpose, he insisted, was quite a different one. Yet for all his disclaimers, it was difficult to visualize this collection of subsistence goods as anything other than a wages-fund.

Böhm-Bawerk was so anxious to develop a perfectly neutral theory that he even was willing to abstract from the framework of private capital. Yet he could not escape institutional elements entirely, for private ownership was clearly implied in the analysis of interest. If the inability of the worker to await the ripening of his product plus his dependence on the capitalist's subsistence fund stemmed from private property and the uneven distribution of income, then clearly crucial social factors did exist in the economic situation to which Böhm had given no attention. Ricardo and Marx viewed interest as a factor payment coming out of production; Böhm-Bawerk insisted that it arose in exchange. When the surplus was discounted to the moment of the original exchange, its present value equalled the subsistence obtained by the worker. Since the bourgeoisie were the fortunate possessors of the subsistence fund, they were able to impose interest as a kind of usury extracted, in the final analysis, from all consumers.[195] Interest became an impost, with the capitalist replacing the medieval moneylender. That this fact had placed it four square into an historical context completely escaped Böhm-Bawerk. It was a surplus stemming from the concentration of the means of production in the hands of capitalists. The agio arose from basic class relationships, with capitalists exploiting the workers. The fact was that Böhm-Bawerk's own process of valuation had put the surplus into the coffers of the capitalists. It was, after all, the system that generated exploitation!

Böhm-Bawerk has been described by Schumpeter as the bourgeois Marx.[196] The description was an apt one, for both sought to develop a scheme of economic analysis that would embody their respective visions of society; both were concerned with the surplus generated by capitalism; and both based themselves on predecessors of note. "Both created something whose greatness is manifested by the fact that no counter argument, as successful as it may be with respect to a concrete point of attack, can detract from the significance of the whole." [197] But there were as many rough spots in Böhm-Bawerk's structure as there were in Marx's. Böhm failed to distinguish between functional relationships and cause and effect; he confused infinitesimal change with shifts in discrete quantities; his marginal utility lacked precision; and he failed to explore adequately the more formal features of his theory. He did not discuss foreign trade, population growth, monopoly, money, or economic crisis. His model was one that described an isolated static state. Moreover, his theory of roundabout production had been anticipated by Mountiford Longfield in the 1830's who had made this a central feature of his analysis.[198]

Although Böhm gathered a few disciples, his polemics alienated many who were then only too happy to grasp every chance to retaliate. Possessed of a debater's temperament, he was ever ready to seize an opponent's weak formulations, seldom stopping to probe the thought behind the words, wanting only to score a point. Yet he indulged in no brow-beating; he was respectful of his antagonists. He knew only that he was right.

In many ways, Böhm-Bawerk has emerged the victor. After the Austrians, there was no question but that economics was to be a micro-analytic science. Böhm's function was to provide answers to such questions as: is capital beneficial? is property just? does interest originate in exploitation? is class conflict endemic to capitalism? His emphasis on the element of time was a notable contribution, and his insistence that interest would exist even in a socialist society was a useful concept. This clarified, at least, the distinction between factor payments as cost and as distribution shares. Indeed, Böhm's influence was remarkable despite all the strictures leveled at him. This was especially evident in Knut Wicksell who tried to fuse Austrian capital theory with Walrasian equilibrium.[199] Even those who have disagreed most sharply with Böhm-Bawerk have had to agree that his was a most interesting, if not fully convincing, performance.

iv

John Bates Clark: American Marginalist

Marginalism was no foreign import to the United States. Although the Europeans could claim priority in point of time, this new-style economics had a native protagonist in John Bates Clark (1847-1938), esteemed by many as America's greatest theorist. Clark, who worked out his version of the new doctrine quite independently of Jevons and the Austrians, later acknowledged that they all had arrived at the same vision of the economic process. Born in Providence, Rhode Island, Clark came of a family of old Yankee stock. Most of his creative work, done around the turn of the century, quickly attained for him a wide international reputation. His writing was lucid and replete with seemingly forceful analogical arguments, all suffused with powerful ethical overtones which stemmed from an early interest in Christian socialism.

While he was still at school, Clark's family had moved westward for reasons of health, and he was required from time to time to help manage affairs. He withdrew from Amherst for a while to direct his father's plow firm, and this experience of trying to operate a business among hard-hit farmers forcibly exposed him to the rigors of competitive capitalism. When he returned to Amherst in 1871 to complete his education he was a mature person, much more knowing in the ways of the world than his fellow students. His independence was illustrated by a refusal to participate in a contest which would have required him to defend a special viewpoint; he said simply that he could think for himself.

Although Clark was especially interested in philosophy, he turned to economics at the suggestion of President Seelye. Amasa Walker's text was the standard diet but Clark felt this to be rather inadequate. He therefore began to work out his own thoughts on the subject and from the beginning sought to relate economics to a proper ethical basis. After graduation, Clark went to Germany to study with Karl Knies. However, he was not influenced by the historical school; about the only thing he brought back from the Germans was a penchant for their outrageous organismic thinking habits. He returned to the United States in 1875 and went to Carleton College in Minnesota, where, although officially the librarian and professor of political economy, he was, in his own words, professor of "odds and ends." [200] Here the ideas that later were to become part of the *Philosophy of Wealth*, the first of his books, began to take shape. One of his students at Carleton was a young intellectual maverick named Thorstein Veblen. Clark's generosity was exemplified by the pride he took in Veblen's later accomplishments, despite the fact that these were directed mainly against the sort of economic thinking typified by the *Philosophy of Wealth* and the *Distribution of Wealth*, Clark's major theoretical contributions.[201] Clark was, according to all reports, the sort of person who easily commanded the affection of others. He seldom indulged in polemical debate; his disputes with others, as with Böhm-Bawerk, were marked by kind expressions of mutual respect.

In 1881 Clark went to Smith College, where he imbibed Christian socialist notions, and after a short stay there and an equally short stint at Amherst, he was invited in 1895 to Columbia where he stayed for the remainder of his academic career. By the end of the first decade of the century, Clark had completed his work in the field of economics. He was now interested in other matters, notably the peace movement, and in 1911 he became director of economics and history of the Carnegie Endowment.

Clark's economic theory was in essence a rediscovery of marginal utility and an extension of this idea into the area of distribution as well as production. His formulations, however, were neither as incisive nor as elegant as those of Jevons, or for that matter, of the Austrians. The most curious aspect of his career was the patent fact that he lived and worked during one of America's most tumultuous periods—the age of the robber baron—when industry proliferated and literally tore asunder an old society while creating a new one, yet precious little of this turbulence appeared in his system. Society's suffering was for Clark but transitory since "the core was sound." [202]

Clark's writing career began in 1877 with several essays in the *New Englander,* which were later incorporated in his *Philosophy of Wealth.* He confidently proposed to do nothing less than expose the numerous errors that had crept into economics, particularly the notion that some labor was not productive. All labor, he said, was productive, delivering a palpable hit at the classical dichotomy between productive and unproductive work.[203] "All labor is indirectly paid for; its compensation is in the market value of its product, and, in so far as moral efforts are represented in an industrial product, they are paid for as truly as other activities of the laborer." [204] Clark's particular vision of society was clearly evident in these early essays: his later work merely shifted the emphasis, to use Joseph Dorfman's words, from sentiment to logic.[205] His technical analysis began, as in the Austrians, with utility, to which he added the idea of appropriability, the quality of a good that made possible its ownership.[206] This idea was rather hard to pin down in specific terms, and, on reflection, Clark's formulation did not appear overly profound. Said he: "The condition of appropriation is a relation between commodities, on the one hand, and persons, on the other, and implies, therefore, that both the commodity itself and the society where it exists should. be such that the relation may be established." This was little more than a general statement of the conditions of property rights. But Clark wanted to establish it firmly as a basis for the production of wealth.[207] Utility and appropriability, therefore, were set forth as necessary conditions in defining wealth.

The *Philosophy of Wealth,* however was not a cohesive work. Based as it was on a series of previously published articles, it simply did not hang together, and one could on occasion discover contradictory statements in it. Yet the work had some interest, for it seemed to promise a wholly new avenue of exploration for economists. The question that remained was whether that promise was to be fulfilled. On this, however, there was justifiable doubt. Clark began by urging a fresh view of man's nature; classical economics, he argued, had assumed merely a mechanistic and narrow psychology, the outcome of which could not help but be an improper theory of value.[208] Clark sought to relate man to society by underscoring the element of interdependence. Yet his romantic notion of a social organism obscured the analysis at this point.[209] While the division of labor established social differentiation, value in the broadest conceivable sense stemmed from society as a functioning organism. Society was the foundation of human wants, which were "infinitely expansive." [210] Clark did acknowledge that any account of economic behavior would have to make room for such factors as social ideals, personal esteem, and elements of fashion, (suggesting, paradoxically enough, a possible influence on Veblen's thinking).[211] At this point the ethical implications of Clark's "economic law" became most evident. He firmly believed in man's altruism; it was society rather that enforced egotistic modes of behavior. Nevertheless, "one man's effort gratifies another man through the medium of some specific product; the effort of society gratifies all its members through the medium of all products." [212] This was his philosophic bias.

It was this approach that ultimately enabled Clark to merge the distinct areas of economic discourse, so that production, consumption, and distribution were virtually one. In such a setting, market price became the expression of social value and the central device through which each producer's share in the output of industry was established. Moreover, this became the process by which the distribution of the product itself was fixed.[213] In this framework, exchanges were always fair ones and always equivalents: unequal exchanges were simply frauds. The motive force in this entire process was competition. By this Clark did not mean hostile strife, but a healthy rivalry that would keep the economy moving in a genuinely progressive manner and which eventually would lead to solidarity between capitalists and laborers. This, Clark thought, was all to the good.

Technical aspects, of course, were not lacking. He insisted that a product included both tangible and intangible services; that wealth was to be attributed to the want-satisfying power of goods and not simply to labor; and that the various forms of utility stemmed from specific services rendered by the factors of production. The particular types of utility were the usual ones—elementary, form, place, and time, with the latter especially important since it was that kind which was supplied through capital.

Of course, it was impossible to separate value from utility; the latter was to be measured by value, and price was to be its market expression. The significant thing, however, was "effective utility," which could be measured by assuming that the marginal or last unit had been removed and then noting the effect of its absence.[214] Clark did not neglect to include scarcity as an element in the situation. But the theory of value in his version was rooted in at least part of classical value doctrine. Time and again, Clark thought he was bursting through the confines of classical theory only to discover that he was employing practically the same ideas and schemata. He rejected classicism's theory of man but was himself compelled to resort to similar hedonic notions. Competition, he argued, could be self-destructive, for it facilitated monopoly. Nevertheless, it was the basic unifying force in a well-functioning society.

The attack on classical doctrine seemed especially bootless in the light of Clark's notion of supply and demand. There was still the old idea of normal price toward which the market tended to move. Normal price to Clark was that level which gave to workers their ordinary wages, to capitalists ordinary interest, and to the employer an average profit.[215] There was nothing extraordinary in these propositions; in fact they appeared as fairly rough and imprecise statements of tendency. Analytically, they were not very striking. Diminishing returns was noted to be a factor in price determination, and Ricardian rent theory was accepted virtually without change. At one point, one could have thought that even the Ricardian vision of social tension had reared its ugly head: said Clark, claims for a share in the product create conflict![216] But this came to nought, for the system, he insisted, was one of harmonious balance wherein production combined and synthesized the elements of the social product while distribution effected its separation and division among the classes and groups in society.[217]

Here Clark was at the central part of this theory—the defense of the economic order against the onslaught of Henry George. In fact, he credited George with having stimulated his search for the particular theoretical model he had worked up.[218] Henry George had contended that the marginal product of labor could be distinguished only at the extensive margin where wages were established. From this, Clark elaborated his own version, and, applying it to his own uses, introduced the intensive margin and the idea of a zone of indifference. Wages, insisted Clark, represented the workers' share in the social output and they were to receive precisely what they produced. He conceded that the level of real wages at one time had been distressingly low and that this stemmed from the unequal strength of capital and labor. He knew that collective action served to improve wage levels.[219] But, he argued, industrialism in the long run had benefited the workingman; now that the laborer had achieved a status commensurate with his social and economic role, he ought to settle his differences with capital through arbitration.[220] Strikes and boycotts were, of course, to be abhorred.

The spirit of solidarity was firm also among the capitalists, as mirrored in the form of monopoly, something thoroughly distasteful to Clark. Here his yen toward the higher morality appeared: competition without restraint was dangerous, although it did promise continued progress through "national development." The dualism evident in business behavior—conscience on the one hand and depravity on the other—was a tragic phenomenon, much to be deplored.[221] Fortunately, labor in the United States had been able to escape some of the burdens of the acquisitive economy because of free land and the countervailing pressures of the trade unions. But the only sound way to insure an increasing margin of economic benefit for all would be through greater cooperation.[222] Whatever he may have meant by this, it was not the Rochdale system, in which the employee was allegedly not considered a genuine member of the enterprise. Furthermore, Rochdale cooperatives were hostile to capitalism.[223] Thus, what Clark wanted was some sort of fusion of capitalists and workers in a vaguely imagined cooperative venture along Christian socialist lines. Finally, said Clark, ". . . arbitration, profit-sharing and full cooperation must be our . . . solution of the labor problem." [224]

The *Philosophy of Wealth* was well received, as one might have expected, for it fulfilled adequately the intellectual requirements of the dominant social group. Franklin Giddings, the eminent sociologist, thought that Clark had created a new law of distribution.[225] On the other hand, others said that his concept of marginal utility was a fuzzy one, as indeed it was at this stage. H. T. Hadley, however, averred that Clark's strictures on competitive evils bordered on radicalism. All the commentators underscored his strain of social reform and his desire to found the theory of value on a firm logical base.

In Clark's next book, the *Distribution of Wealth,* the impulse to social reform, albeit of a most limited kind, disappeared altogether and was displaced by the logic of value. No longer could the reader sense a vague drift toward justice; in Clark's later work, the ethical problem was solved automatically by the very functioning of the economic system. Value theory established social equity by approving, as it were, whatever distribution the economy worked out. Implicit in this newer theory was an answer not only to the heresy of the socialists but also to the more dangerous subversion stemming from Henry George's single tax. Clark thought that the reply to the attacks from the left could be discovered in the fundamental rules of the process and growth of economic society. And imbedded in this exploration was a high moral purpose that could not fail but appeal to the better sentiments of mankind.

Coming as it did, fourteen years after the *Philosophy of Wealth,* Clark's major work departed strikingly from the earlier concern with ethical postures, although he did return to these matters in his lesser-known *Essentials of Economic Theory.*[226] His central interest in the *Distribution* was to establish for all time the general laws of economic life. Here the theory appeared in a precise and elegant garb with all the great problems of economic life solved in one grand stroke. It was the first major American work in pure theory and for many years was deemed to be the greatest. However, it loses some of its brightness today. Time and again, Clark offered generalizations and theoretical formulations which he promised to prove beyond question, yet the promises were seldom redeemed. The book was very well written and quite persuasive, almost too much so. The unwary reader was apt to be caught up in the author's enthusiasm for his own theory.

Distribution to Clark was obviously a social problem. The product of society would have to be shared in some way by the various groups and sub-groups that participated in its creation. The central feature of this process, said Clark, was the fact that wages and interest were fixed quite early by virtue of the contribution labor and capital were bound to make. "The goods are really apportioned in the making," he said.[227] The price system, operating on a basis of perpetual normality, passed social income through the various groups involved in production. This was, of course, the system of natural law and "so far as [these] are unperverted, labor tends to get, as its share, what it separately produces; and capital does the same." [228] It was Clark's firm intention to demonstrate not only that distribution was governed by natural law but that it gave to every agent of production just the amount of wealth it created. Thus the wages of labor were equal to that part of the product attributable to it, and interest was equal to that part due to the efforts of capital. The law of distribution assigned to each precisely what he produced. This was the law of *specific* productivity which proved that the "share of income that attaches to any productive function is gauged by the actual product of it." [229] That there was a prescriptive quality to these notions was undeniable, and, in fact, it has been described as a species of apologetics.

After all, Marx had twisted classical doctrine into a theory of exploitation. And the *raison d'être* of the existing economy was now in question. The idea of utility had been imbedded also in Adam Smith and David Ricardo, and the willingness to accept a theory stemming from this vague psychological notion was clearly rooted in the distaste that most economists had for Marxian animadversions. Clark was fully aware of the issues involved. Said he: "The right of society to exist in its present form, and the probability that it will continue so to exist, are at stake." [230] His theory, therefore, was important, for it was both a moral and political justification of the pricing results of the market.

Clark's basic concepts were simple ones: a framework of private property and individual freedom; value based on utility; government participation limited solely to the enforcement of the rules of the game; and capital and labor conceived as easily transferable mobile units. These made up his institutional background. If one compared it, however, with the mainstream of nineteenth-century doctrine, there appeared to be precious little difference. Even if one were to add Clark's distinctive notions—the organismic conception of society and his special definition of statics and dynamics—the old-fashioned flavor would persist. The competitive forces which he saw as the prime motive power in society really signalled a return of the classical economic man, despite the ostensible search for a more realistic psychology. The logic was that of hedonism. Society was comprised of a collection of self-interested, rapidly calculating humans, each working like an electronic computer, weighing units of satisfaction one against the other. There was no need to prove that this was a real system; the economic results that could be obtained were plainly evident in the outcome of the market. All this was an adaptation of Adam Smith *cum* Herbert Spencer: the derivation of social values from market prices strained one's credulity, for all Clark had done was to add up individual reactions and call it a social theory.

The inherent failure of Clark's system of economic thought was best illustrated by his static and dynamic concepts. The static analysis was the familiar one in which economic laws were developed in a context where labor and capital were fixed elements, no alterations in technology or organization took place, capital growth was unknown, and consumer taste never changed. [231] He knew that these were unreal, but he felt that despite the disturbances of the actual world, wages and interest in the long run would conform to the "natural" rates given by the static condition. This suggested to him that the latter was no mere logical construct. It appeared as a genuinely basic element in society; for, underneath all the friction and upsets that characterized a dynamic world, there was, Clark insisted, a set of norms which constituted the underlying static level. These were real forces; they were simply obscured by the hurly-burly of everyday life and it was the task of the economist, said Clark, to work out just how they functioned and especially how they governed the area of distribution. This was not an impossible job and in fact was a good deal easier than uncovering the laws of dynamic behavior. His main precept was that natural, normal, and static were synonymous.[232] Again, Clark promised to demonstrate scientifically that all was going well with society and that distribution was no matter of "institutional robbery." And again it was doubtful that he succeeded.

As against the usual division of economic discourse into production, consumption, exchange, and distribution, Clark divided the field into the study of universal laws, static social economics, and the realm of the dynamic. Diminishing returns, diminishing utility, the guidance of production through marginal utility, and capital accumulation illustrated the first category, that of universal laws. Although such a breakdown had seemed to promise a fruitful development, it was all reduced in Clark's hands to a "science" of functional distribution.[233] The underlying problem was one of maximizing satisfactions through the weighing of alternative choices, as in the case of his solitary hunter balancing a canoe against a spade.[234] The law of diminishing returns in the static state was simply a proposition regarding proportionality, since inputs and outputs were fixed by definition. Clark, however, applied the law to all input factors, not only to land. The adjustment of capital, he said, to new inputs of labor depended upon its mobility. Diminishing returns stemmed from the loss of productivity, in a physical sense. However, at times Clark appeared to deny the possibility of diminishing returns in a static state, asserting that such changes were attributable to dynamic forces and should be excluded from the kind of analysis he was engaged in.

What were the dynamic changes of which Clark spoke? He thought that there were five significant ones: population growth, new technology, changes in business organization, capital accumulation, and consumer tastes.[235] None of these, however, displaced any of the static forces at work; they merely completed the operation of normal drives. Standards were set by the latter, while variations were accounted for by dynamic factors.[236] This implied, for example, that market prices fluctuated about some static norm. Clark did concede that it was entirely possible for such norms to rise over the long run and standards to go up.[237] In one sense, all industry was dynamic, for change was constant; but the mental construction of a static condition was necessary in order to reveal the true situation.[238] Since the forces that acted in a static society continued to do so in its dynamic phase, said Clark, the study of the static became merely an heroic abstraction and, as such, only a tool of analysis.[239] Yet, as one observed Clark's handling of this theoretical device, one had the inescapable impression that his imaginary world had become a real one and that the static society was the essence of economic reality so far as he was concerned. His frequent analogies to quiet bodies of water and other hydraulic images stressed almost entirely static elements. For him the latter were obviously the more significant and the more powerful. The static state dealt with ultimate reality.

When he came to the analysis of wages he insisted that whatever dynamic forces were involved would eventually come down to static levels.[240] Not one jot nor one tittle, insisted Clark, would be taken away from the efficacy of static forces by dynamic change. Even if competition were not perfect, there would still be a tendency to reach the more quiescent norms. The static world was not a "dead" one; it was simply the mode by which basic economic forces could be seen most clearly. The natural character of values was essentially Ricardian, but Clark gave these a new direction by asserting that everyone received precisely what he produced. As the argument became more and more labored, Clark finally resorted to the statement that the five dynamic forces cancelled each other in any case, leaving only the unchanging realm of quietude and serenity. Dynamic forces, he remarked, ". . . largely neutralize one another, so far as group arrangements are concerned and cause the actual form of society to hover much nearer to the theoretical static forms than would be possible if these influences worked separately." [241] And with this remark, the interest in the dynamic was virtually at an end, at least in the *Distribution.* As Veblen remarked in his shattering attack on Clark's economics, the dynamic condition finally appeared as merely a deranged static state.[242] Clark was determined not to leave the never-never land of his imaginary static world where such real fluctuations as engendered by the business cycle simply did not take place.[243]

Clark thought that a thoroughgoing development of dynamic laws would be a job for future economists. However, he did attempt in his *Essentials of Economic Theory* a discussion of specific areas in which change was evident. But these were merely schematic treatments of particular problems rather than a cohesive study of dynamics. Nor was the attempt to adumbrate a realistic outline of a theory of change in the *Distribution* any more successful.[244] The world was divided into two parts—the advanced industrial center and the remaining backward portion.[245] The first included Europe, North America, and other advanced areas where Clark's static order worked well because capital and labor operated in mobile fashion against a backdrop of free enterprise. Such obstructions as tariffs and nationalistic commercial policies were brushed aside as essentially inoperative. In the rest of the world the dead hand of custom made property immobile and served to restrict economic action. Clark did not realize that such a division made his theory limited in time and place and consequently incapable of exhibiting genuine universality. But he was an incorrigible optimist for whom even the attenuated laws of dynamics harbored an unalloyed faith in the justice of specific productivity.

The study of practical matters found in chapters 24 to 29 of the *Essentials* had curiously little connection with his general theory. The outstanding characteristic of this review of monopoly, railroads, and labor unions was the thought that government should enforce competition so that values might come as close as possible to the true static ones. Strange that the advocate of free competition should have turned to government, but then he did insist that this was one way to compel people to play according to the rules. Yet theory and practice were worlds apart. For all Clark's hopes, a genuine dynamic economics could not originate in his system. There was no sustained inquiry into the process of change itself or any consideration of how the specific problems of which he spoke were related to the five-fold apparatus of economic growth. The dynamics were little more than an investigation into how equilibrium might be reestablished should there be some departure from the static norm.[246]

The distribution of income in Clark's system was governed by laws which expressed themselves through price. The market was the medium for both the social evaluation of goods and the apportionment of society's output. At the root of all this was individual marginal utility, although the results were actually social ones. "The motives in [economic] movement are individualistic, but the resultant is collective," said Clark. "Each man pursues his own interest; but as the outcome of his activity, society acts as a solitary man would act under the influence of the law of diminishing utility."[247] Competition eliminated profit so that in the end there were only two shares in the total product, interest and wages. The theme of specific productivity was repeated again and again, until by sheer iteration, if not by logic, the reader was convinced that wages were the equivalent of labor's marginal effort.[248] By the end of the *Distribution of Wealth* the inescapable impression was built up of a single unifying principle governing the world of economics. This was the law of economic causation—or, in modern language, marginal productivity—which could be stated in either value or physical terms. But as a principle of distribution, it was clearly tautological. As Veblen remarked, it did not conduce to intelligibility to say that wages were just and fair because they were all that was paid.[249] The system of harmonies implicit in Clark's system did not suggest a really searching examination of economic questions.

How the harmonies functioned was illustrated by Clark's wage theory. A unit of labor was defined as the amount of work an employee of average ability could expend. Differentials in wages were to be explained largely by variations in efficiency. In the static state, wages were identical with labor's specific product, which could be identified and isolated through the final increments of labor. Since the units were alike and interchangeable, the withdrawal of the last one would reveal the impact on the whole product and the resulting difference would be labor's specific product. At this point, the employer operated in a kind of twilight zone; that is, he was quite indifferent as to the loss or addition of another unit of labor.[250] Within this margin of safety, competition would insure that wages would equal marginal output. But observe how useful the indifference zone was to the theory, for surely without it difficulties would ensue! Applied to all industries, the concept insisted that ". . . what is produced within the zone of indifference in one industrial group tends to equal what is produced in the corresponding group in another. . . ."[251] What Clark had done was to supply himself with a safe range within which the theory might operate without a hitch.[252]

Let us, however, return to some of the singular ideas in Clark's work. Basic to his thought was the notion of utility, as it was in the case of the Austrians. Goods had one fundamental quality—that of want-satisfying power. But they exhibited also the character of "effective" utility, which was that obtained from the satisfaction of the last unit of a good. Satisfactions, therefore, were measurable and cost became the obverse or the subjective pain of acquiring a good. As such, it was basically a hedonic concept.[253] At one point Clark thought that the cost of production was still a serviceable notion.[254] Whatever refinements he worked out in utility theory had more to do with terminological issues than substantive ones. Again, market values were determined by the utility of the final increments of a good, not by the utility of the entire stock.[255] This, however, overlooked the discrete character of many commodities. Also, it was the final utility of a good as determined by society that made value a social phenomenon.[256] Value was the basic principle governing distribution among groups, just as productivity determined functional distribution. One can almost detect a group mind in operation here, evaluating, purchasing, and consuming. The whole affair was patently shot through and through with nineteenth-century hedonism: it was virtually a universal law that pleasure would always outweigh pain.[257]

There was but a slight difference in this approach from that of Jevons' who had measured value by the satisfaction derived from the last increment consumed in a series of units of a good. In a letter to a Japanese professor, Clark remarked that, in contrast to Jevons, he "thought of the consumer as measuring the importance to himself of different articles already in his possession and adjusting his purchases in such a way that articles of the same cost have the same 'effective utility' to him. . . ." [258] This was closer to the equi-marginal principle than was Jevons', yet it was basically the same as that outlined by Menger in his *Principles*.[259] With many buyers engaged in delicately balancing pleasures and pains, it became theoretically feasible to work out market demand schedules. Production adjusted itself to such demands in a truly marvelous way, averred Clark, with goods delivered at cost and production geared to the rendering of maximum satisfactions.

A significant portion of Clark's theoretical discourse was given over to a careful distinction between capital and capital goods.[260] Capital was conceived to be a permanent fund, while capital goods were impermanent tangible things which "must be destroyed, if industry is to be successful; and they must do so, in order that capital may last." [261] Capital, said Clark, was mobile; capital goods were not. The ability of capital to express itself in terms of money made it possible for it to live on by a process of transmigration, as it were, from one form to the other. Capital was really the sum of active and productive wealth which was reflected as successive instruments of production.[262] In terms of distributive shares, capital earned interest; but capital goods obtained rent.[263] Yet interest depended on rent, for it was in the final analysis but the totality of rent. On the other hand, in an almost dialectic fashion, rent was influenced by interest, for what one capital good earned was conditioned by the number of all such capital goods currently in use.[264] Since capital as a fund was basically self-sustaining, it was unnecessary to call upon abstinence to explain its formation. In fact, abstinence played a role only at the point where the fund was initiated, and, perhaps, in net increases of capital. But otherwise elements of capital matured and had to be replaced, so that once started there was no need to call upon external aid to sustain it. Here Clark seemed to depart from Nassau Senior's famous dictum. He also rejected the notion of a period of production, which was fundamental to Böhm-Bawerk's analysis; the fund of capital, he argued, really exhibited no discernible periodicity. Since capital represented a continuous flow, the length of life of a specific good was a matter of indifference.

Here Clark seemed to be reaching for a macroeconomic concept. His illustration of the growth and utilization of forest resources strongly suggested the idea; but he never developed a broad approach in any real sense. The best he was able to accomplish was a rejection of Böhm-Bawerk's period of production [265] and a rather mild criticism of Senior. Abstinence still could be a fruitful idea for static analysis, for without it interest would be generated only when new capital was created. Consequently, Senior really could not be dispensed with; and interest, like rent, virtually had to be restated in classical terms. It was as if Clark had suddenly realized that the earlier assertion that interest stemmed from the productive creativity of capital was quite inadequate, as indeed it was. But, Clark, true to his original vision, made interest also a marginal category: it was defined ultimately as the ratio of return to that portion of capital responsible for its production. This was just as tautological as the rest of his distribution theory. Diminishing returns was a general rule, for additional units of capital were said to add less to the product than earlier units, and, as in the case of labor, the final unit was responsible for the level of the return.

Clark sought to differentiate between types of capital in terms of utilities rendered because he had wanted to dispense with the duality of circulating and fixed capital.[266] But his thinking became quite fuzzy at this point, and, overburdened with organismic trappings, it virtually collapsed. His attempt to show that these forms of capital were really aspects of his own fund theory was not successful. Even the Jevonian notion, that capital supplied subsistence, was found to be inacceptable; capital simply had to be a pure fund moving about with complete agility in response to profitable openings.[267] While it would always seek to attain a maximum gain, earnings in a competitive society eventually would be equalized in all lines of endeavor, so that the end result would be a profitless society.

It was uncertain whether Clark wanted to define his fund in an investment sense or simply as a kind of protoplasmic flow between industries. If he had the former in mind, as may very well have been the case, then he failed to account for the complex money institutions that grew up around it and for the ways in which its very movement influenced the economy. This could have been the basis for a vital theory of economic change. But Clark preferred the approach of the mystic.[268] Even labor was conceived as a fund of energy that renewed itself through population growth. Units of labor moved easily to more remunerative occupations in response to the need for higher earnings; seen from the long-run point of view, labor therefore was also a fund.[269] Although individual skills were fixed, said Clark, changes in occupation had occurred from generation to generation that made labor a fluid force.[270] The charge of mysticism did not seem unreasonable. In the case of capital, Clark failed to recognize that as a fund it was closely tied to specific capital goods. When business suffered failures, the fund itself was endangered, as in the case of forced liquidation. Capital had no inherent permanent quality, even in Clark's sense; it was a pecuniary category subject to the influences of a pecuniary society.

Clark contended that the form of capital was altered with shifts in the application of labor. This implied that each combination of capital and labor was unique and would therefore provide the technique for determining the specific productivity of a unit of labor. The method, however, did not deviate very much from Menger's. The concept of uniform units made labor a bloodless figment, without heritage or skills, suitable only for the imaginary world of analytical economics. It simply was not true that the production function was comprised of elements that could be shuffled about so easily and readily as Clark thought. He could not demonstrate that the employer would always search for greater productivity upon the withdrawal of labor. He could only assert that this was ". . . amply attested by experience, is confirmed by deductive reasoning and is one of the undisputed truths of economic science." [271] Capital, he insisted, actually was transmuted into the required form, and all this was done automatically through the beneficence of the competitive system. Each industry would receive its proper portion of the whole social capital.[272]

The distinction between capital as fund and capital as equipment illustrated the sharp disagreement between American and European marginalists. This was a debate that continued on into the 1930's.[273] From Clark's standpoint, the notion of capital as goods had failed to come to grips with the problem of functional distribution. Furthermore, the period of production was a technological matter. Theoretically, said Clark, the production period was of no social import since capital was a permanent fund through which production and consumption were synchronized. This gave American theorists what they needed to attack Böhm-Bawerk, especially on his "third ground."[274] Nevertheless, the latter persisted in his view and through his ideological successor, Friedrich Hayek, was able to provide the groundwork for one of the more recent theories of business cycles. Böhm-Bawerk's failure rested in his inability to see that rights to income implied something of a fund notion, at least in the investment sense. Clark's failure was rooted in his unnecessarily sharp dichotomy between fund and goods. Insofar as assets were transferable from one going concern to the next, capital retained its liquidity and its mobility; but there clearly were limits to this process. Moreover, specific goods could be dated to account for their aging and wearing away, thus establishing a connection between capital as thing and capital as fund. The arguments on both sides were quite skillful. Irving Fisher and Frank Fetter, among others, took part in the debate. Fetter's point was one that both major antagonists might have pondered with profit: a concrete good was capital insofar as it could be expressed in terms of the general unit of value. No one, unfortunately, paid much attention to Veblen's contention that capital was an expression of the relationship between human intelligence and material goods.[275]

As indicated above, land and capital had been virtually indistinguishable in Clark's system. For an American this was a perfectly reasonable idea, since the vast stretches of free open space made it somewhat difficult to accept with equanimity the classical notion of limitation and scarcity in land. Moreover, such property was a major form of investment and accumulation and gave rise to a not unimportant return. In an early essay, *Capital and its Earnings* (1888), Clark asserted that land was to all intents and purposes a free good. Conceivably, differences in location might generate a rent, but, aside from that, land exhibited all the qualities of other capital goods. Thus, Ricardian rent was useful only as a short-run theory of differential gain.[276] Market rent, consequently, was nothing more than an extension of Ricardian theory to all capital instruments; or, defined in another way, the total product less the wages and interest of the penultimate unit of capital (the last unit being the "no-rent" one), thus providing a formulation of the marginal productivity concept. However, normal long term rent was governed by cost of production.

The notion of mobile factors was applied to land as well as to capital and labor.[277] While there was admittedly a greater measure of stickiness in the ability of capitalists to move their land investment from one purpose to another, there was nevertheless, Clark believed, enough mobility at the margin to insure an exact parallel with the case of equipment, so that in the final analysis, the rate of return from land would be equalized in all possible applications. He admitted that there were some exceptions, leading to what we should call a frozen asset. He did not observe that this vitiated the basic argument. This line of analysis indicated Clark's main objective: to reduce all material goods to forms of capital so that he might establish a zone of indifference or a margin of transfer broad enough to make his theory universal.[278] Yet rent here was basically Ricardian. Said Clark:

We have set all the men in society working, we have measured the amount created by the last addition to the force, and we have measured the surplus that each earlier unit of labor creates above this amount. The surplus is, in each case, a true differential product; since it is not merely a remainder that is left after paying wages, but is a difference between one product and another· It is the difference between the product of aided labor and that of the labor that is virtually unaided, and the sum of all these differences is the rent of the social fund of capital.[279]

The income stemming from concrete capital goods was also rent, and, when all such goods were viewed in their totality, the net return was essentially the same as interest. While these two income forms might not match exactly, they would coincide in a situation of perfect static adjustment. At this point Clark attempted to apply the marginal productivity concept to rent as in the case of interest, but the notion became elusive and one was never certain whether a value or product meaning was intended. The transition to interest, however, was not difficult. The latter was that fraction of itself that capital earned; it was a portion of the permanent fund of capital [280] and was fixed by what the final increment of social capital would earn. Competition among entrepreneurs for capital simply required that interest be paid.[281] The "final increment" to which Clark referred were the qualities inherent in capital, its ability to provide services, rather than a unit of equipment itself. But as Clark described the competitive process, the concepts of "quality" and "equipment" became inextricably intertwined. Time, in Böhm-Bawerk's sense, was not a factor; while specific capital goods might entail postponement and waiting, this was not the case for capital as such. The fund of capital implied in fact a conquest of time, for it was through it that labor and output were coordinated.

To summarize, Clark subjected all input factors to the notion of marginal valuation. Labor and capital were fluid funds with interchangeable units in which returns were established by the final inputs.[282] Did this mean exploitation, since all units were paid only what the final one commanded? By no means, averred Clark, for the loss of any one unit of labor was really the loss of the marginal one, and with mobility there would be an adjustment in capital allocation so that each unit of labor would work with the same amount of capital as previously. The specific product of labor would always be the same for all units. Variations in the marginal product could stem only from variations in the amount of capital employed per worker. Thus exploitation was really impossible.[283] All this was demonstrated with great detail and fine logic, but at no point could one escape the sensation of reading an apologia for the economy as it was. In fact, Clark's entire theory was little more than a defense of the *status quo,* an observation transparent enough to make some of his sophisticated followers, such as Taussig and Fetter, somewhat uncomfortable. This was no superficial allegation, as Stigler has insisted, for apologetics was patently the dominant tone in Clark's work.[284] Its intention was admittedly to answer the question of equity in distribution. And the conclusion that all was well in the economy as it was could, in the light of known empirical data, be described as nothing short of a shrewd theoretical defense of capitalism.

The *Essentials of Economic Theory* covered much of the same ground as the *Distribution of Wealth*. The concepts of labor and capital as funds of mobile units were restated; utility was again the foundation of value; and more than ever the central unifying principle in economic life was marginal productivity.[285] However, the major purpose was to explore the nature of dynamic change. Clark did not propose to construct a dynamic model; he merely wanted ". . . to examine seriatim the effects of different changes, to gauge the probability of their continuance and to determine the resultant of all of them acting together." [286] A dynamic society still was one that hovered close to the laws of a static economy and its motive forces still were rooted in population, capital growth, technology, organization, and consumer wants.[287] The book, though, was not at all on a level with the *Distribution*. Not only did it lack the attraction of novelty; it was in many ways distinctly inferior to the earlier work. Couched in the polite terms of a reasonable concern for the future, it reflected nothing of the excitement of expansion and growth in a study purportedly dealing with dynamics. There were chapters on monopolies, railroads, and labor. Much of this, unfortunately, has little interest for the present. But they did reveal that Clark was capable of fulminating against the iniquities of big business in the best American tradition.[288] While he felt that in the normal situation self-interest could be a sufficient basis for the ethics of economic behavior, monopoly was offensive precisely because it suppressed self-interest. Trusts were useful only insofar as they promoted efficiency, but they too degenerated into monopoly. Hence, regulation based on a kind of "most favored nation" treatment would be essential to avoid the industrial strife that big business was bound to engender. And the holding company, Clark held, was a menace. As time went on, the problem of monopoly became for him the central practical problem; in this context recourse to sentiment was entirely out of place.[289]

This was one of the few areas in which Clark could rouse himself into a pitch of irritation and anger. Monopoly, he cried, was an evil force, for it impeded competition. Once monopoly dominated the economy, progress would end.[290] One was not certain, however, what his definition of monopoly was. True, his concept was couched in terms of absolute product control, but this was unrealistic even for the day of the burgeoning robber baron. After a while one realized that what Clark disliked was bigness; it was economic giantism to which he was so antipathetic. In addition to regulating pricing practices, Clark would have instituted measures to insure easy entry into an industry. Yet here too there were signs of ambivalence.[291]

Clark acknowledged that labor organizations were necessary to equalize the relative positions of workers and employers. He conceded that in the absence of unions, wages would soon be depressed to a level acceptable to the lowest strata of worker. Under collective bargaining, wages would come closer to the norm established by the rule of marginal productivity. This was a better outcome than would be possible in a régime of individual bargaining.[292] The implication was that unions were natural phenomena and should be welcomed. Yet these observations contained in them an admission of exploitation, for where there had been no unions the wage level must have been much below the "natural" one. Clark, however, was reluctant to concede this, since to do so would have cast doubt on the central point of his theoretical analysis. Trade unions, he said, almost in the spirit of the wages-fund, could not push rates beyond the margin of specific productivity; otherwise there would be a reduction in the number of jobs that employers would offer.

Strikes, boycotts, and violence were frowned upon. Job control, by which he must have meant the closed shop, was a form of monopoly and therefore quite undesirable, while the loss of mobility was deemed to be one of the defects of trade unionism. The only solution to the labor problem, thought Clark, was arbitration, so that wages might be set at their proper level. He was quite certain that by ". . . instinctive judgment the [arbitration] court will hit upon some level of wages which falls well within the limit of what the monopoly can pay and is above the amount which marginal social labor gets." [293] Such a remark seemed to evidence a rather dubious faith in the justice to be meted out by those whose political and economic interests were antipathetic to unionism.

Clark's influence was undoubtedly widespread. What he taught became a byword for devotees of the *status quo.* The sentiment of *fin de siècle* radicalism was silenced by the logic of the marginal unit. This had been the first native offering of an all-encompassing theory: its attractiveness for many was the promise that all economic problems would be solved in automatic fashion. It cannot be said, however, that this promise was redeemed. Clark left behind many gaps despite his repeated remarks that all propositions would be proved beyond controversy. Doubt as to the efficacy of marginalism still remained. One of its chief motivations—to rebut Marxism—raised a question as to its putative objectivity. Marx had sought to demonstrate the presence of exploitation in the distributive mechanism; Clark denied this and tried to reveal that equity did exist. But his theory and laws had to bear the same charges that had been leveled against Marx: they were pure concepts, unverifiable, and basically ideological elaborations. The static-dynamic dichotomy was questionable, particularly since the static was no mere analytical device but supposedly a realm of genuine reality.

On a more technical level, doubt remained as to whether the product would be sufficient to meet the demands of all the input factors, since the size of the units that were to be added or subtracted was never defined. Clark's reduction of all inputs to either capital or labor was a dubious business —and at times there was the hint that capital was perhaps the only real factor, as when he had sought to convert land into capital. The concepts of social labor and social capital, at least in his formulation, were mystical rather than analytical. Further, to separate the productivity of a single factor appeared somewhat unreal, particularly where output seemed to be the result of a certain mix of inputs which together created the product. Insofar as wages were concerned, marginal productivity was at best but one of many elements required for the explanation of going rates. The blatant hedonism and unwarranted organismic theory of social structure, the confusion of ethics and analysis, the supposed fluidity of the factors of production, the assumption of an identity of reward and productivity, and the absence of a really useful theory of growth and change were all disappointing to those who searched for realistic answers to economic questions.

v

Ludwig von Mises:
Libertarianism "in Extremis"

The most extreme form of the individualism implicit in the Austrian tradition was exemplified by the work of Ludwig von Mises (1881-   ). Inflexible and thoroughly opinionated, he has defended the last vestiges of laissez faire with an intransigence as admirable as it was wrong-headed. He has conducted polemics with all sorts of opponents, mainly historicists, socialists, and institutionalists, and has defended staunchly the *a priori* approach to economics, which he defined as a system of logic stemming from universal principles incapable of empirical verification. His writing has been filled with an exasperating arrogance and a dogmatism that would have been laughed out of court had it come from anyone else.

Born in Lemburg, Mises studied at Vienna, where he was to serve as professor from 1913 to 1934. He then went to Geneva where he was professor of international economic relations; since 1940 he has been in the United

States lecturing mainly at New York University. Generally associated with the extreme conservatives, he has produced a number of works unmatched in the history of economic thinking for the abuse of those with whom he has disagreed.[294] While not as abstruse as the work of F. A. von Hayek, Mises' economics can frequently become just as dense. Whatever theory it had was obscured by a lush growth of political and quasi-philosophical verbiage, and much effort and tedious work were required to extract and distinguish the basic economic ideas from the strange sociology with which it was immersed. The more one read of Mises, the less economics one found, until in the later works, such as *Omnipotent Government* or *Theory and History*, little remained beyond a strange philosophical apology for a pristine eighteenth century laissez faire.

The single book that best reflected the sort of system developed by Mises was his *Human Action* (1949), an expanded version of a work published about a decade earlier, *Nationaloekonomie: Theorie des Handelns und Wirtschaftens*. Its basic concept was the notion of "praxeology"—the science of human conduct. Mises, unfortunately, never defined this fundamental idea except in the broadest way, leaving it to the reader to discern from the general context what he was speaking about. Presumably it was a science, the subject matter of which was human behavior, although at times one had the vague impression that only the principles of logical choice were involved. The method stemmed from certain *a priori* bases, employing what Mises had described in *Theory and History* as discursive reasoning.[295] By this he meant the faculty of drawing inferences. Now, why this should yield *the* science of economics or of human choice more clearly than some other method was never ascertained, although the basic principles, such as they were, were said to be eternally true. Propositions rooted in historical experience, on the other hand, were but partially *a priori,* and therefore not fully "praxeological." They were not above environment or individual circumstance, and hence were not sufficiently general and formal in character.[296] Praxeological categories, however, were external, unchangeable, and uniquely determined by the structure of the human mind. One could not go beyond these limits: there was either action or nonaction.[297] This theory ultimately led to economics as that realm of praxeology in which calculation was possible.

Addressing himself in this manner to "praxeology," Mises believed that he was getting behind the mere act of choice and that he was constructing a universal economics that would withstand the outrageous onslaughts of irrationalism, polylogism, behaviorism, and historicism. From praxeology, he went on to catallactics, or the science of economic exchange—the area in which the actions of men were intended to diminish the sense of unease that developed in human behavior.[298] Such actions were always rational and implied an ability to choose among available alternatives. The resulting exchanges might be interpersonal or "autistic," that is, of the Robinson Crusoe variety. With the origin of exchange established in this manner, Mises reaffirmed in no uncertain terms the subjective character of economics. His self-assurance was unbounded: these principles were applicable to all forms of human action. Yet little was really said when all relevant behavior had been reduced to these modes; it was like suggesting that breathing was essential to continued human existence.[299] The simple epistemological fact was that *a priorism* could not solve problems quite so simply, despite Mises' insistence.[300] Methodology could not be limited to pure deduction, and few contemporary economists would have anything favorable to say on the strictures that Mises leveled at the empirical approach. He blithely cast out historical investigation of economic phenomena and reduced them to mere forms of economic history, not especially useful for the impartial art of discursive reasoning. He insisted that such approaches reflected only the personality and bias of the writer and consequently could not achieve unanimous assent.[301] Of course, his own bias was never acknowledged.

The truth of the matter would seem to be that historical approaches are valuable to economists as well as other social scientists. At least this much has been learned from such writers as Weber and Marx, both objects of Mises' scorn, incidentally. While praxeology was supposed to be a study of action, one never knew from Mises' presentation whether it was concerned with the ends-means question, human psychology, or perhaps ethics. And although he wrote at length on the epistemological problems of economics, there was little of a recognizable theory of knowledge in his work, for his universal principles had nothing to do with the understanding of propositions. The objective rather was a putative analysis of a vague area of action limited in the main to the laissez faire market. Most striking in this strange corpus was his contemptuous dismissal of the influence of history on man. Changes in social structure, economic upheaval, and cultural shifts were all relegated to the intellectual dustbin. Mises has fought heroically to keep time and history out of economics, but, like Cervantes' noble Don, he was bound to be upended.

No debate over ultimate ends was to be entertained, argued Mises, if the aim of action was to seek relief from "felt uneasiness." Further, praxeology was concerned with positive propositions: it could express no opinion on sybaritism or asceticism. Value, however, could be attached to ends, said Mises, thus contradicting himself in virtually the same breath, no small achievement indeed. If value was important, how was one to judge the matter if no debate over ends was possible? But quite evidently the substitution of words for genuine logic was much to be preferred, as in his assertion that praxeology could predict with "apodictic" certainty the outcome of various actions. Since "apodictic" literally means logical certainty, it was clear that Mises had explained very little about the nature of praxeology.

Marginal utility remained the basis of the valuation process. Action, however, was to be merely a selection among alternatives and did not imply the need to weigh which choice would bring greater utility.[302] Marginal utility was related solely, said Mises, to the stock of goods chosen and in this sense was concerned only with subjective use value. But in this long and devious presentation, Mises added little to what had gone on before and in fact confused marginalist analysis with gratuitous and inessential *obiter dicta*. There was a long-winded restatement of the law of diminishing returns and a rejection of the distinction between tangible goods and intangible services. This led him to the first of many excursions into idealistic metaphysics: only the human mind was productive, since the forces of production were spiritual ones. Felt uneasiness was removed by man through ratiocination.[303] Broader, more sociologically inclined interpretations were discarded as so much nonsense. Moreover, they were dangerous for they led to collectivism! Yet he conceded that man is a social being: seen from the standpoint of the individual, society is a means for the attainment of ends, and the preservation of society is an essential condition for any plans that one may want to realize.[304] And it was through society that the division of labor, or, as Mises put it, the "law of association," was expressed. Society was then directed by ideas, for a particular order of events was always the outcome of ideology, and existing states of affairs were products of previously developed ideologies.[305]

Mises' own ideology was virtually self-evident. The belief that democracy might be able to attain a better society had been an egregious error of humanitarians and philosophers. Democracy could not prevent majorities from falling victim to erroneous ideas and inappropriate policies. "Only if men are such that they will finally espouse policies reasonable and likely to attain the ultimate ends aimed at will civilization improve. . . ." [306] But, for Mises, this was not something that democracy could accomplish, since it was essentially a government of armed men, gendarmes, soldiers, and hangmen. In a discussion of the effect of education in Eastern Europe, he said: "The philanthropists and pedagogues of England who advocated public eduaction did not foresee what waves of hatred and resentment would rise out of this institution." [307] Education might have some use, provided it be limited to reading, writing, and arithmetic. Beyond this, education was indoctrination by the party in power. Speaking of intellectuals, he remarked: "The emergence of a numerous class of . . . frivolous intellectuals is one of the least welcome phenomena of the age of modern capitalism. Their obtrusive stir repels discriminating people. They are a nuisance." [308] But then, Professor Mises has always been known as something of an extremist.

Mises had little use for mathematics in economics, denying that it could be employed, even in a probabilistic sense, to predict the future. Quantitative elucidation was impossible, for events could be comprehended only through "understanding." [309] "The mathematical method must be rejected," he said, "not only on account of its barrenness. It is an entirely vicious method, starting from false assumptions and leading to fallacious inferences. Its syllogisms are not only sterile; they divert the mind from the study of the real problems and distort the relations between the various phenomena." [310] Empirical work in such a field as demand theory was not to be compared to "aprioristic knowledge that enables us to anticipate the conduct of an entrepreneur who is in a position to resort to economic calculation." [311] Statisticians were foolish to try to measure long waves of business cycles.[312] Mises even depreciated index number construction. Now, while the specific details of index numbers are subject to considerable debate among the experts, few have denied their usefulness in measuring changes in prices or production.[313] Mises did not think that change was measureable: index numbers, he insisted, could tell us little because the "market basket" itself changed, valuations were altered, and the weighting employed was arbitrary. But while all this is perfectly true, it merely reflects the character of the technical problem. Mises' charges that index number construction and measuring changes in the cost of living were "pretentious solemnity" would have to be rejected.[314] He contended that there was no such thing as a general level of prices: the market reflected only prices of specific commodities. This clearly contradicted his earlier notion that there were no local differences in the purchasing power of money or in the cost of living.[315] The latter phrase merely meant that the same individual could not obtain the same satisfaction from the same goods in different places. Insofar as the purchasing power of money was concerned, it too was always the same; only the commodities were different! Fortunately, not many statisticians or mathematical economists have entertained such notions, for surely they border on the ludicrous.

Yet there was some method to this seeming foolishness. The rejection of mathematical calculation would be essential if welfare socialism, or any other variety of socialism for that matter, was to be refuted.[316] And while mathematics, said Mises, might be of some aid to a monopolist in that it could help establish optimum price, here too there would be nothing but futility, for the shape of the demand curve would still be unknown.[317] None of the elements that conditioned monopoly—cost, demand, production—were pertinent, according to Professor Mises. The basic problem still remained— monopoly price stemmed essentially from a restriction of supply.

The central theoretical model in Mises' scheme was a kind of circular flow construction which he called the "evenly rotating economy." [318] This was derived from a "conceptual image of a sequence of events logically evolved from the elements of action employed in its formation." [319] But there was nothing really new here; it was little more than model building of the common garden variety in which division of labor and private ownership were the main features. The function of government was to be limited to setting the rules of the game. The tendency in such an economy would be toward a state of rest. This, said Mises, was implied in the elimination of "felt unease"—attained when there was no longer a desire to exchange, and all orders to buy and sell, all puts and calls, had been completed. Market price thus would achieve stability, and, though Mises strongly denied it, he had arrived merely at the static price of the equilibrium economists. Yet he insisted that this was not by any means Schumpeter's circular flow, but one in which market prices were the same as prices in the final state of rest. "The system is in perpetual flux, but it remains always at the same spot. It revolves evenly round a fixed center. The plain state of rest is disarranged again and again, but it is instantly reestablished at the previous level."[320] This fictitious construction, Mises promised, would reveal the genuine essence of the economy. This promise, however, was not to be kept.

At the core of the "evenly rotating economy" was the market in which each person, acting for himself, acted for everyone. Producers were told by the price system what to produce, how, and in what quantities.[321] In this strange world where fiction became fact, there was no advertising, no hidden persuader.[322] The consumer reigned as sovereign king; his market demand, like voting in a ballot box, compelled the entrepreneur to comply with his wishes. The difficulty was that such voting strength has been frequently unequal, and it has been possible for distortion to set in. Quite simply, some people have had more votes than others, a patent fact that Mises overlooked.

The market, of course, was the sole arena for economic calculation, and was defined by Mises in heuristic rather than computational fashion. His approach, rooted as it was in Böhm-Bawerk, sought to show how individual choice in the sphere of interpersonal exchange resulted in market price. Exchanges could occur only when the values of the respective commodities were unequal.[323] This was due to the fundamental consideration of value as an extrinsic and psychic quality, as something decidedly not inherent in the things themselves. Furthermore, values "are not susceptible to mental grasp by the application of cardinal numbers."[324] But this threatened to dissipate the entire science of catallactics, for we were now faced with the contingency that the point at which price was set was, after all, an indeterminate one. There could be no uniform cognition in a market because people possessed different degrees of awareness of shifts in information and would respond differently.[325] He who was shrewdest in the use of bits and pieces of information supplied by the market would profit most.

This, incidentally, set the stage for Hayek's later theory of economic knowledge.[326] Calculation in any precise sense could not really take place, and Mises had to concede that he dealt only "with analysis of the mental processes performed by acting man in applying quantitative distinctions when planning conduct."[327] This was essentially an estimate of anticipated future outcomes. Yet Mises had to employ some sort of quantitative yardstick, and what better measure did he have but exchanges against money? Market prices therefore became the ultimate bases for economic calculation. That all this had involved him in a grand tautology seemed to have escaped Mises entirely. Furthermore, once having limited calculation to market phenomena, he could say little about behavior in nonmarket situations. And since catallactics had become the only science, Mises was compelled to dismiss politics and sociology as unworthy subjects. Quite simply, without calculation beyond the market Mises had disqualified himself entirely as a commentator on broader social science questions.

Hairline distinctions were made between valuation and appraisement. The notion of imputation was developed, but in ways inferior to that of his predecessors. Finally, Mises arrived at the quite uninformative statement that pricing was a social process. But under no circumstances would he accept the idea that pricing also was a means of effecting distribution.[328] This, despite a later comment that "prices of consumer goods are by the interplay of the forces operating on the market apportioned to the various complementary factors cooperating in their production." [329] The contradiction and lack of clarity were not unusual. Although Mises did score a point in his urging that the general price level was merely an abstraction, it was difficult to follow his argument that income formation had little to do with prices, but came rather from the prudent use of resources. Income, he insisted, was not a flow, for it was a category of action derived from the proper and economical application of land and working power. There was nothing in the market economy to which the idea of distribution might be applied.[330] The sole function that prices discharged was to direct production into channels where the wishes of the consumer would be served. The grand vision of a unified economic model meant little or nothing to Mises.

Civilization and private property are inextricably linked, said Mises, thus, dismissing in dogmatic fashion all those societies in which private property in the Western sense was unknown. These were not civilizations. Only market capitalism could be so identified, even though it had been "sabotaged by government and labor union interference." [331] This illustrated Mises' technique of developing a private history in addition to his quite private economics. A good example of the former was his contention that Western Europe had been able to accumulate capital faster than the rest of the world because it not only had the advantage of reason but the ability to check predatory militarism.[332]

For Mises such an anomaly as the lopsided distribution of income and wealth was most welcome.[333] There were certain responsibilities, he remarked blandly, that individuals would have to assume in the "joint productive effort" and inequality was to be the way in which this was done. More bluntly, a low wage was a good way to get people to go to work. That the professor's views here would be most helpful to certain propagandistic approaches was quite evident.[334] He denied that the market economy, at least in his version, would create class or caste. "Each individual is free to become a promoter if he relies upon his own ability to anticipate future market conditions better than his fellow citizens and if his attempts to act at his own peril and on his own responsibility are approved by the consumers." [335] The market was merely an arena for men who acted "consciously and deliberately aiming at ends chosen." Business propaganda was intended to convey information to consumers, and any restrictions would limit the freedom of consumers to choose.

As with so many of his concepts, Mises' notion of capital in the technical sense was a curious amalgam of Austrian as well as other ideas. Initially, in the true Austrian tradition, he had rejected the concept of capital as a fund. But later he argued that the definition of capital as the totality of produced factors of production must be rejected, for it would suggest a list of commodities and this would be of no special use in "action." In an earlier work, *The Theory of Money and Capital,* Mises suggested that money was capital insofar as it was a means of obtaining capital goods. Thus, while rejecting Clark's theory of capital as a fund, he allowed the same concept to return via the rear door.[336] Capital productivity, too, is not a helpful concept, said Mises, for basically capital was a "category of acting within a market economy." [337] But later on, in *Human Action,* he rejoined his fellow Austrians and insisted that abstract capital could not exist apart from concrete goods. The distinction between circulating and fixed capital was dismissed in favor of the notion of convertibility—a concept that nevertheless came perilously close to the fund idea. Convertibility, furthermore, would require a classification of specific forms of capital based on usage and consequently did not appear to be much of an improvement over the older fixed-circulating capital dichotomy. Mises did observe that convertibility, or the shifting of capital from fixed to circulating forms, became more difficult as accumulation proceeded, for with an expanded technology in the modern sense, a large measure of fixed capital had become essential. This threatened to become a fruitful discussion, but Mises only wandered off into a curiously ambivalent review of the patent system, suggesting a defense of monopoly practices.[338] He observed that limited convertibility of capital did not necessarily bind the owner, for as an investor he could move his funds about easily enough. But once Mises admitted this, he had to concede that the fund notion of capital did have some validity.[339]

According to Mises, capital was derived from saving and restriction of consumption; what limited saving and its subsequent investment was time preference. At this point, Jevons' capital concept entered the analysis, for in order to provide for the future a fund of consumption goods was necessary to meet the requirements of the waiting period.[340] Mises' attempted reply to Frank Knight's argument on the capital concept was not very effective, for he was able to resort only to the "preparation of earlier generations." Progress, said Mises, would be impeded so long as there was a shortage of capital, a notion more fully developed later on by Hayek. In effect, a capital shortage was nothing more than a dearth of time.[341] These concepts, of course, did fit the praxeological scheme of things, for they involved choice with respect to future time periods. Provision for the future embraced various alternatives: accumulating a larger stock of consumer goods; producing goods that were more durable; producing goods that required a longer period of production; or employing more roundabout methods even if the goods might have been produced in shorter ways.[342] All this mixed Jevonian and Bawerkian concepts together in a most intractable way. The acting man who was to engage in these activities bore a more than striking resemblance to the economic man of the classicists. Clearly, the desire to eliminate felt uneasiness was but the obverse of maximizing pleasure. All that Mises had added was the period of production and the duration and serviceability of the commodity, and even these ideas were not particularly original with him.[343] It was doubtful that the notions of "sooner and later" had completed the time-preference picture, for this said little of the desire for a particular income flow. It was the latter concept that played so central a role in Hayek's system; in Mises', it became lost in a miasmic potpourri of astringent economics and even more tasteless politics.

Central to Mises' system was the concept of exchange. He rejected the thought that money could be a neutral element. However, changes in the quantity of money, he observed, did affect different prices in different ways. Consequently, the quantity theory of money as usually expressed became untenable, since it suggested a proportionality in the movement of money and prices that could not be supported by factual evidence.[344] Money, though, was to be solely a medium of exchange: all other functions, such as the standard of deferred payments or the measure of value, were reduced by Mises to the single basic function of the exchange medium. Leakages in the flow of money, such as hoarding, had no impact in any real sense, for this stemmed from a demand for money to do precisely such work. That is to say, money was valued for this purpose on the basis of the services one expected from cash holdings.[345] Mises, however, had little to say on the motives for holding cash in the Keynesian sense.[346] In fact, despite Mises' criticisms of the quantity theory, he himself could do little better than to declare that ". . . the relation between the demand for and supply of money uniquely determines the price structure as far as the reciprocal exchange ratio between money and the vendible commodities and services is concerned." [347]

For a full discussion of Mises' theory of money one must turn to *The Theory of Money and Credit*, the first of his major works. In this volume, a good deal less strident and tendentious than his other books, the argument was more effective and often bordered on the convincing. Evidently the inter-war period had witnessed an unhinging of Mises' economics: one has to look at the appendix in the most recent English edition of *Money and Credit* to see how far to the morbid right his views had moved.

Curiously enough, Mises was fairly successful in integrating his monetary theory with his general economics. The central theme was "forced saving," disparities between the equilibrium and money rate of interest, and the changing relationships between the prices of producers' and consumers' goods which stemmed from the instability of credit.[348] The basic function of money, to serve as a medium of exchange, was derived from the way in which men, in the process of indirect exchange, sought to dispose of less marketable goods for those which were more marketable. The result was that the most saleable of all commodities became money. Now, money cannot measure value, said Mises, since subjective valuations can be only graded or ordered. But an element of contradiction appeared here too, for if one was to thread his way through the numerous exchange ratios of the market with the help of money, which was "preeminently suitable for this," then it would appear that money must perform the task of measuring values. Mises would have preferred to say that it measured prices.[349]

A long and somewhat useful discussion ensued of the ways in which substitutes for money were developed. But Mises was quite adamant in insisting that the state could not create money per se. At best the state might influence, through legal and juridical decisions, the form that money would take, but it could not dictate its worth. The value of money was to be determined in the same way that the value of other commodities was fixed—in the market. The state was no different from other parties in economic transactions; it had to comply with the requirements of supply and demand. It was the subjective use value of products that people sought which underpinned the value of money,[350] a concept which brought the theory back to Menger and Böhm-Bawerk.

New injections of money were apt to be unevenly distributed, said Mises, anticipating the core of Hayek's doctrine. Those who secured the bulk of the new supply of funds would have their market positions strengthened and the prices of the goods they demanded would be apt to rise. The result of the uneven changes in prices was that the last recipients of new money, and those who failed to obtain any at all, would find their real income reduced. This was "forced saving."[351] If new money entered the economy only once, the distortions in price relationships would not be sustained for long, and a readjustment to older levels could occur. As a result, variations in the objective exchange value of money were not proportional to variations in its quantity. Fundamentally, new money did not do the economy much good, argued Mises, thus giving no thought to the possibility of underutilized resources and unemployed manpower. What he feared mainly was inflation, which, he insisted, led to consumption of capital through false hopes and improper economic calculation. Price increases stemming from new money were illusory, for since no real additional capital had been added to the economy, capital in actuality was depleted by the payment of dividends and higher wages.[352] As one examined the experience of the American economy in the 1950's, when prices and wages increased together with real physical capital, one had the distinct impression that Mises' economics would not be able to explain what had happened.

Mises' view implied, in a sense, that the businessman would immediately alter the structure of production as soon as interest rates fell below the marginal rates of return from real capital investment. However, it was possible to conceive of situations in which the same structural pattern would be maintained, with the difference between loan rates and real rates representing a windfall gain. Only in future periods would entrepreneurs undertake to extend their investments. Producers' goods industries would become relatively more profitable than those in consumers' goods and it would be an effect such as this that would encourage them to shift the structure of production. Under conditions of full employment, this would occasion increased payments to input factors, causing real wages and rents to rise. But this assumed no change in the price level, which obviously would rise, thus preventing real wages from increasing despite the greater competition for resources. Again, there would be no impelling motive to change the structure of production. Clearly, all these movements were more complex than Mises had imagined.

The phenomenon of "originary" interest arose with the introduction of time preference. In true Austrian fashion, interest was the manifestation of discounted future goods as contrasted with present goods. Since present goods were valued more than future ones of the same kind and quality, the sum apportioned through the market to future needs fell behind present prices. The difference Mises called "originary interest." [353] This was not the same as entrepreneurial profit, which stemmed rather from changes in market data, thus making profit a kind of accidental gain. Interest was essential in order to sustain a "current reiterated income," a notion similar to Hayek's later concept of constant income. But it seemed doubtful that Mises had escaped the productivity notion anymore than Böhm-Bawerk did. The difference between the sum of the prices of the factors of production and the products resulted ostensibly from the higher valuation for present goods. This higher valuation seemed to be related not merely to the future services of the factors but to a process of production as well: no mere passage of time was involved, but rather decisive elements of creativity and productivity.

Mises added to the confusion by insisting that "originary" interest was a ratio of commodity prices, not a price itself, and that there was, moreover, a tendency for this ratio to be the same for all commodities. In an evenly rotating economy this could be the only outcome. As a category of action, "originary" interest determined the demand and supply of capital and fixed the balance between satisfactions in near and distant time periods. (Schumpeter, argued Mises, was quite wrong in saying that interest disappeared in the circular flow.) Mises, however, evaded the question of the relation of saving to interest. He did not think it possible to develop any useful "praxeological theorems" on this point, for want-satisfaction in future periods was presumably determined by nonmeasurable value judgments. But if interest stemmed from a choice between present and future goods, this choice had to be related to the quantity of available capital. If this was the case then Mises quite patently had evaded a praxeological responsibility by refusing to explore the implications of savings and the supply of capital insofar as these affected interest. He could only assert that variations in property holdings affected saving and, in that way, the ratio between the value of present to future goods.[354]

Yet the rate of interest was influenced by the issuance of new money.[355] The flow of credit depressed the rate of interest on money loans below the rate that ought to apply if all the economic elements were to be accounted for. The latter could give us Wicksell's natural rate of interest based on the productivity of the marginal period of production. Mises defined this as the last period which might be justified in an economic sense. It had to be of sufficient length so that the subsistence fund would be able to meet the wage bill. If the money rate was lower than the natural rate, the ensuing ability to obtain a net return could induce longer periods of production. But soon a point would be reached where the subsistence fund was depleted before the capital goods projects that had been undertaken were fully transformed into consumer goods. The outcome was an economic crisis. This stemmed from the misleading economic calculations supported by the illusory gains of a monetary expansion. Projects could not be sustained because there was actually an inadequate supply of real capital. We were now at the theory of economic collapse later advanced by Hayek.[356]

This theory may be classified, as Haberler does, with the monetary over-investment group.[357] The critical expansion of credit, said Mises, was caused by the banking system and provided encouragement to the sanguine expectations of the businessman. Such an expansion not unexpectedly was supported by the central banks, who reflected the optimistic thinking of the business community. Without this, individual banks could not undertake to provide the necessary wherewithal, for they would soon be pressing on their reserves. But no problem arose when the entire system acted in concert. If, however, said Mises, the central banks were stripped of their power to issue notes, and if this right were returned to the individual banks so that genuine competition might once more prevail, weak bankers would be eliminated and the expansion of credit placed on a more cautionary basis. Oblivious of the notorious history of American state banking, Mises insisted that what he wanted was "free banking." [358] Those who questioned the value and effectiveness of operating a nation's banking system in this fashion were merely "bigoted étatists." [359] The gold standard was the natural basis for a money and banking structure and "all those intent upon sabotaging the evolution toward welfare, peace, freedom and democracy [must have] loathed the gold standard. . . ." [360]

To return to the theory of economic collapse, Mises remarked that a boom did not create capital in a real sense, a somewhat unlikely conclusion in the light of recent economic history. Basically, he was a fantastic deflationist, even more so than the most conservative of hard money economists. Said he:

Prices of the factors of production . . . must come down before business can become profitable again. The entrepreneurs enlarge their cash holdings because they abstain from buying goods and hiring workers as long as the structure of prices and wages is not adjusted to the real state of the market data. . . . Thus, any attempt of the government or the labor unions to prevent or to delay this adjustment merely prolongs the stagnation.[361]

This may also be described as the blood-letting theory of economic cycles. In fact, said Mises, as his economics acquired a true Alice-in-Wonderland quality, a boom was retrogression and a depression progress, for the quality and quantity of goods improved in the latter phase.[362] While a boom wasted resources through investment, a depression, on the other hand, " . . . is the way back to a state of affairs in which all the factors of production are employed for the best possible satisfaction of the most urgent needs of the consumers." [363] Moreover, a boom made people despondent and dispirited while a depression encouraged new saving for the accumulation of new capital goods. Mises forgot to say where the income would come from to provide such "new saving" in a depression.

That Mises would express little but jaundiced views on labor was to be expected, and that he would distort historical evidence to prove a point was also to be anticipated.[364] Thus, under early capitalism, said he, job seekers had thronged to the plants for jobs so that they could join the scramble for products. (Did the products come first, or the jobs?) "The benefits which the masses derived from the capitalist system," said Mises, "were so obvious that no entrepreneur considered it necessary to harangue the workers with pro-capitalist propaganda." [365] This, despite the vast literature demonstrating the devastating impact of the factory sysem.[366] As Cole and Postgate have observed, ". . . it is more than possible that after 1815 there was an actual worsening of conditions in the rapidly developing factory towns, where houses were being run up wholesale by contractors intent chiefly on cheapness. . . ." [367]

Mises would relegate the workingman to a life of perpetual, unremitting labor, whose fate was to struggle for all time with the disutility of work.[368] If the workingman fell prey to such noxious ideologies as trade unionism or

Marxism, he would become unbalanced. Wages, governed by supply and demand, reflected labor's contribution to the wealth of the nation. While on the one hand, wages were paid for specific skills, on the other, all laborers competed together. The employer could not establish monopolistic practices in the labor market because that would have implied a monopoly of demand, a concept which to Mises didn't mean much, despite all the discussion of monopsony in the texts.[369] Mises also insisted that employers were in no position to exert pressures in the labor market; fortunately, most businessmen are a good deal more astute than their arch apologist. Even more preposterous was his notion that workers were at no special disadvantage, because they were better able to wait than the employer. The very condition of unemployment demonstrated this for otherwise they would take jobs at lower wages![370] That is to say, unemployment was always voluntary and consequently represented a catallactic illusion. Poverty, however, was not a praxeological problem, for these matters were "beyond the frame of a theory of human action which refers only to the provision of the means required for consumption, not to the ways in which these means are consumed."[371] Of course, if there were no means, there was no problem.

At no time in his career did Mises adequately demonstrate why his version of the theory of choice was superior to others. He merely asserted its higher powers and let it go at that. Why the rejection of *a priorism* should lead to absurdities was never clear, either. The simple fact of the matter was that Mises failed to prove that his way of arriving at the truth was better than others, while there was ample evidence that it was a good deal worse. His intransigent dogmatism and his penchant for the easy insult to his intellectual opponents, as in his *Theory and History* and the various political tracts, made him more a special pleader than a scholar. Methodologically, he was unable to proceed from *a priori* principles to *a posteriori* experience and to use one to qualify the other. His kind of action seemed synonymous with the rational only on his terms. Moreover, he suggested that what were essentially empirical statements regarding exchange and value could be derived from purely analytic propositions, so that the derivatives of his *a priori* laws were required to fulfill what were tantamount to institutional conditions. This, as Fritz Kaufmann has clearly shown, is impermissable.[372]

Evidently Mises had certain norms in mind and one might be less prone to quarrel with him had he not disguised them so much and advertised his obviously double standard as a single one. His own criteria of action were arbitrary and limited, and any violation according to his lights would bring forth blasts of anger and self-righteousness. He was especially wrathful at those who suggested the need at times for intervention in economic processes. Yet his demand for complete abstention would have resulted in precisely the sort of market distortion that he abhorred, for a free market inevitably destroyed itself.[373] Based on the automatic pricing mechanism enforced by supply and demand, for example, labor was given a price. But labor was a peculiar commodity; it could be neither stored nor separated from its carrier, the human person. The logic of the market economy, however, pressed to its cruel conclusion, would have required that labor be dealt with as the merchant dealt with corn. There was bound to be protest against an inhuman theory that would convert people into mere adjuncts of the loom and steam engine. The barbarous demands of an unrestrained price economy were rejected. Furthermore, capitalists themselves had discovered that the highly technical apparatus, necessitated by modern mass production, could not function along free market lines. They had to be assured that price would recover current outlay and investment. Thus they had begun to exercise control over price and, Mises notwithstanding, had abolished effectively the free market. Prices now were determined long before commodities reached the consumer, who often had to be persuaded that his welfare would be enhanced were he to buy those things the admen said would impart virtue, power, and a glistening smile.[374]

vi

Friedrich von Hayek: The Austrian Tradition Refined

In many ways more subtle and tougher minded than Mises, Friedrich A. von Hayek (1899-   ) has most ably continued the Austrian tradition. A graduate of the University of Vienna, Hayek specialized in law and economics. After spending several years in the Austrian civil service and as director of the Austrian Institute for Economic Research, he went to the London School of Economics in 1931 where he stayed until 1949. Currently at the University of Chicago, Hayek has authored numerous articles, many subsequently published in book form, and has also written one very technical treatise, a fantastically popular but slight book on political theory, a study in theoretical psychology, and a huge tome on conservative political philosophy.[375] His lectures and writings, however, suffer from a curiously dense style, which demands a considerable effort to extract his essential meaning. This is rather disconcerting to one who follows all of Hayek's literary output, for as an historian of economic thought he has been top rank. His *John Stuart Mill and Harriet Taylor,* his essays on Menger and von Wieser, and his study of the origin of the doctrine of forced saving illustrate just how good Hayek can be in this branch of the subject.[376]

But, unfortunately, the economic and political writings have been less happy products. Generally quite abstruse, their central theme is individualism, the price system, and the related "real" structure of capital. Much of this stemmed from Knut Wicksell as well as Böhm-Bawerk and Mises. Wicksell had tried to construct a theory of long-term price changes, and, in doing so, he abstracted from cyclical movement in order to allow for a period of sufficient length to permit averaging economic data. Mises pursued this line of analysis by observing that a credit expansion often resulted in a displacement of income which then moved across the economy in an irregular way, affecting various groups quite differently, while the price level as a whole began to move upward. Hayek's self-appointed task was to analyse this same process of income displacement in the short run. As one commentator has observed, the logical sequence of the three writers was the reverse of their historical appearance.[377]

Interestingly enough, Hayek's psychological studies make the best starting point for a review of his contribution to contemporary economics. These studies, incorporated in the somewhat opaque *The Sensory Order,* have revealed in striking fashion the preconceptions and ideological bias which Hayek has exhibited. As a student, he had thought to specialize in psychology. But his thinking in this field was quite unaffected by behaviorism, Gestalt or Freudian psychology, and has been limited to the influences of Hermann von Helmholtz and Ernst Mach. Hayek's excursion into psychology was like his economics—theoretical and philosophical, with little concern or interest in empirical material.

Once a subject perceived an object, said Hayek, he engaged in taxonomy, for perception was related to the properties of other objects and consequently was only a mode of interpretation. In fact, the properties of the perceived objects did not actually reside in them, but were really actions of the subject mind which had created the classifications. Properties of objects, therefore, became relations of perception created by an individual nervous system. Thus, said Hayek, perception was reduced to a mere mental construct, an abstraction which might be modified by something called experience. Meaning and significance stemmed from the process of ordering perceptions, which in turn was based on a body of keyed responses rooted in earlier perceptions. Each response was related to the whole collection of past responses which had been accumulated in the course of individual growth.

This was precisely the sort of idealistic philosophy to which Hayek's economics could affiliate itself. Mind became an order of events taking place within an organism which was quite unrelated to the events of the physical environment. Thus one could never really know objective reality.

But just how the ordering was to be done, Hayek never made clear. His description was so mystical that it took on the aura of a superphenomenology. Objectivity merely implied that an order of events might be built on a level different from what our sensations tell us is the situation.[378] But in that case the known object became irrelevant and objectivity in the social sciences was reduced to non-sense. A complete description of social reality was actually impossible according to Hayek's analysis, for all one could do was to search for new relationships between mental constructs. To try to build a sociology of knowledge in which an effort was made to explain how the views of people were related to external circumstance at certain periods in history would be erroneous, he insisted. For mind, which accomplished the ordering of events, could itself not be penetrated. It was to be known only through experience.[379]

Of course, such a philosophy was most useful in justifying the sort of atomistic society that Hayek advocated. He seemed to say that while we could understand relationships between events we could not control them. But what he quite patently had omitted from his philosophic framework were the basic connecting elements relating the world of the external to the world of mental impressions.[380] These elements are prior to any set of coherent, comprehensible sentences which describe the kind of relationships that Hayek spoke of. In his system the principle of connectibility had been broken, and the definition of a thing divorced from the sense impressions to which it was to be related. This did not allow for a genuinely vital description of the economic order, which in Hayek's view was little more than a collection of distinct, unrelated economic men.

Hayek was able to separate the world of things from the world of men because he rejected the application of the methods and laws of science to society. To him, scientism was a fatal philosophy which employed materialistic principles to discover the nature of human action. All who sought to explore this approach came within reach of his wrath.[381] Scientism, he insisted, sought real or physical facts when these were essentially subjective perceptions. While an objective fact was a relation between physical things, relations between humans were not to be viewed in the same way. Therefore, said Hayek, we had to reject such notions as "society" and "capitalism," for these were not amenable to analytic treatment; the only genuine material at our disposal was to be found in the set of relationships between individuals. Models could be built, after the fashion of the physical sciences, to represent these relationships. Yet these were doomed to frustration, for no model could ever hope to encompass the full complexity of existing relationships.

Only mental constructs, said Hayek, properly belonged to the social sciences, for they were based on sense perceptions. How this relationship between the mental construct and social science was to be established however, was never made clear. Yet it would seem essential that the connection between the mental and the social would have to be established irrefutably in order to validate the theory itself. But Hayek refused to take this step, since it would have suggested that his later concept of the atomistic economy could be called into question. Time and again, he approached the problem, only to veer away from the principle of connectibility. At best, he would concede that people behaved in the same way because they had learned to classify things alike. No attempt was made, however, to explore the genesis of this common pattern of behavior. The mental, he insisted, was no subject for science, for it dealt ". . . not with relations between things, but with the relations between man and things, or the relations between man and man. [The moral sciences] are concerned with man's actions, and their aim is to explain the unintended and undesigned results of the actions of many men." [382] Here, seemingly, was the start of social inquiry. But Hayek was not really interested, for his focus was the set of actions of a single individual. The facts to be dealt with were merely opinions. These were the data of the social and moral sciences. Thus, even more sharply than in the case of Menger, social science was reduced to an individualistic level. Knowledge was no suitable guide for action, since it existed only in a dispersed and incomplete form in the minds of many people; consequently, knowledge could be neither consistent nor coherent. Solipsism reigned supreme.[383]

According to Hayek, the only connection one had with others rested in the belief that they would act as he would in similar circumstances. Crime and punishment, accordingly, could not be classified as objective facts. This would have made the yellow star that Jews under Hitler were forced to display not an "objective" fact, even though the consequences were hardly subjective ones.[384] Admittedly, the beliefs of people are relevant and will motivate action: why should these not be objective *social* facts? Let us grant to Hayek the argument that prices and crimes and the twentieth-century hell of Treblinka are rooted in beliefs. But how shall we account for the action that flowed from them? Here Hayek refused to proceed from his philosophy of sensationalism to the level where connections between individual sense impressions are established. For him, social reality was purely a matter of mind.[385] "The individuals are merely the *foci* in the network of relationships and it is the various attitudes of the individuals towards each other . . . which form the recurrent recognizable and familiar elements of the [social] structure." [386] The social role, however, was acted out only in the individual mind. Consequently, "society," "collective," "economic system," "capitalism" became terms without genuine meaning; they were not social facts in Hayek's sense.[387] What more effective way was there to reaffirm Adam Smith's divine unseen hand, since the individual actions of people unconsciously produced an order which was no part of their individual action? [388]

The assumption was made that understanding was created by the simple existence of minds in addition to our own and that social categories could be developed on such a basis. It never occurred to Hayek that since reality consisted solely in what was in our minds, we could not possibly know others unless connectibility had been established. Thus, in his view one would have to reject such "objective" categories as cost and the idea of production. On this basis the entire corpus of Hayek's economics is to be questioned, since his analysis was generally carried on in "real" terms. This would suggest that the relationship of input to output and his own requirement of a constant income flow were merely imaginary propositions.

Hayek's preconceptions were based on his refusal to acknowledge that ideas are in many ways functions of social involvement, rooted in the principle of connectibility. Only on such a level is it possible to investigate the relationship between an idea and the situation in which it reveals itself. Frequently these are the very collectivities against which Hayek has often fulminated. However, these are not artificial constructs, but rather the settings in which ideas are to be transferred and conveyed to others.[389] And this can be accomplished not because we merely hope there are minds available similar to ours; we can communicate ideas, aspirations, and fears because we do operate in a social context. To be sure, collectivities such as the "nation" or the "market" are not directly perceived by the senses, but we can comprehend them because social and psychological ties do exist between men. This by no means suggests that collectivities have a reality above and beyond the relationships that give them meaning. What we assert, simply enough, is that man is a political and a social animal and that social science must explore the very relationships that make him this complex being. Quite simply, mental processes do have a social dimension, and a useful social science should endeavor to discover what this is. However, Hayek explicitly abdicated this task. For him, economic theory consisted of a set of propositions derived in tautological fashion from *a priori* concepts; monopoly, macroeconomics, and even statistical inferences were to be considered as dubious ventures.[390] Those who asserted that categories on the social level of analysis were essential analytic tools were worse than mere fools, intimated Hayek; they were dangerous men, for they invariably passed from a discussion of the nature of the collective to the proposition that the coherence of the larger entity required subjection to the conscious control of an individual mind. Thus only the individualist was prepared to sound the tocsin, for only he saw the fearful prospect of a new road to serfdom.[391]

Yet Hayek seldom acknowledged that the collectivities he abhorred have been evolving manifestations over the centuries of a changing political and social structure. The problem we face today is how to control existing collectivities in order to protect the very "reason" he cherished so highly.[392] It is no longer a matter of introducing new collectivities, as Hayek feared, but one of comprehending existing ones. Meaning is a social concept and cannot be torn out of the context of connectibility, which is itself established with the very formation of a community. An analysis devoid of this concept, as was the case with Hayek's, became a mere "groping within the solipsistic realm of appearances." The dual nature of meaning—individualistic and social—made such abstractions as institutions, capitalism, and the state genuine realities. It was possible to grasp the concepts of interdependence, division of labor, and income, and to employ them for further analysis without recourse to the psychological patterns of single workers or bosses. Models could be constructed without establishing the particular role of each individual involved in the situation. Capitalism became a framework in which people performed certain sociological and economic acts: references to capitalism implied a structural pattern which illuminated, conditioned, and governed the behavior of individuals.[393]

With this backdrop, we can well understand Hayek's contention that economic propositions were to be concerned solely with the acquisition of knowledge. Economic analysis had meaning for him only insofar as one spoke of the behavior of a single person; the accumulation of information, which involved the whole area of foresight and uncertainty, was the function of the individual.[394] From these assumptions, which we need belabor no longer, Hayek passed to the concept of equilibrium, which again he asserted to have meaning solely in individual terms. Plans of action were evaluated on the basis of the pure logic of choice. Equilibrium for an individual implied perfect foresight. This could not be said to exist for a group, since it would suggest virtually the same plans and set of circumstances for all the participants, an unlikely happenstance.[395]

Hayek then moved on to the definition of a market. The textbook version was rejected; only the Pure Logic of Choice existed (an undefined notion which appeared to be rooted in nothing more than Austrian utility), functioning in a context of regularity and predictability. This, together with the idea of the common quality of different minds, established the relevant knowledge needed to work out market solutions. While such knowledge was partial and incomplete, said Hayek, economics had come closer than any of the social sciences in showing how the process operated.[396] But this analysis was frightfully vague, and he had to appeal to the analogy with other minds to account for the transmission of knowledge because the propositions of economics could in no sensible way be verified by reference to external fact. Since such facts in any of the social sciences were in the realm of the group, no empirical test was possible. Consequently, social science was reduced to a sort of methodology for handling the relationships of thoughts in men's minds.

Few of the basic propositions in ordinary economics were deemed to be valid by Hayek. For example, perfect competition in the traditional sense was rejected on the ground that if it did work it would result, through the effects of perfect elasticity of demand, in the destruction of competition.[397] Perfect competition suggested a timeless concept, whereas the actions of individuals really succeeded each other through time. The basic problem was to discover how plans in the minds of different persons were adjusted to the objective facts of their environment.[398] A competitive theory, he argued, must explain the process whereby new data were adapted to old. Competition was a dynamic process which must be accounted for as such. The criterion of perfect knowledge—an old mainstay of the theory of competition—could not be considered seriously, said Hayek, for each market participant acting with absolute foresight could behave in a way that would effectively eliminate competition. The classical competitive problem, therefore, was not to be considered a genuine one; since knowledge was distributed unevenly, the real question was how to create the institutional arrangements that would impel those with the best knowledge to do the necessary economic job. This, averred Hayek, was the real purpose of the market. Its function precisely was to spread information so that buyers and sellers could react and establish a price. The latter was not the starting point for analysis as in classical theory but the final objective.[399]

Since it excluded movement, perfect competition was not really a good description of market events. In a realistic sense, competitive theory should tell who can serve us; yet it excluded the personal relations and good will that compensated for the inadequate knowledge that buyers and sellers possessed.[400] The fact was that beliefs differed; it was this which caused competition. Hayek here offered nothing less than the theory of monopolistic competition, for he suggested that each product was by definition different from every other. Realistically, what we faced, he said, was a continuous range of close substitutes or a situation where no two producers created exactly the same product. He granted that although ideally there should be agreement between price and marginal cost, this occurred only in a situation of infinite elasticity. But, in a practical sense, to compare this with the kind of competition that existed was otiose. The proper comparison, he said, leading to a not unexpected attack on "statism," was between his kind of competition and a situation in which a central authority dictated the conditions of the market. In the latter case, those who knew how to produce would be prevented from doing so, and prices and costs would not come anywhere within hailing distance of each other.

In the final analysis, the basic element was the character of human response: what was important was the constant struggle for competitive advantage.[401] The imperfect market, said Hayek, was in reality a more intense area of competition than other markets, emphasizing again that one had to think in terms of what actually existed. Competition was ultimately a way of forming opinion: by spreading information it effectuated coherence and unity. It was a way of telling people what was best and cheapest, and, in this sense, was a process of changing data. What we had to worry about, urged Hayek, was the suppression of such information.[402]

This set forth the philosophic and institutional framework for Hayek's economics. His more technical theory was embodied in his magnum opus, *The Pure Theory of Capital,* and in published lectures and articles reprinted, in the main, in *Prices and Production, Monetary Theory and the Trade Cycle,* and *Profit, Interest and Investment.* A heated debate has raged through the years over his leading ideas. Frequently, the complaint was voiced that much of it was unintelligible. The theories themselves were abstruse enough, but they were made even more inaccessible by a heavy, almost turgid style. When Hayek came to Britain he received quite a buffeting. Piero Sraffa attacked his *Prices and Production* with no little venom, and Keynes called it a frightful muddle which was interesting because it was such an extraordinary example of how one could, starting with a mistake, end up in bedlam.

Central to Hayek's economic theory was the notion of "neutral money." This purportedly was a kind of money that had no effect on relative prices, production or interest. On close examination it seemed evident that money was entirely outside the analytical model that Hayek wanted to construct. Although one might have expected some comparison with an actual money economy, Hayek was interested only in sketching the outlines of a system with a constant supply of money which presumably would permit "voluntary" saving to be carried on. Any other policy, he insisted, would result in distortion of the structure of production or the proportionate distribution of revenues between producers' goods and consumers' goods industries. Not only was "voluntary" saving the desired policy; it was in reality the natural one. Of course, Hayek did not take into account the patent fact that such voluntary saving might not have desirable effects, that it could lessen demand, enforce a cutback in sales, and actually reduce investment. The inducement to invest was dependent in large part on a lower rate of interest which could be interpreted as Keynes did, as a function of money and liquidity preference rather than saving. Thus in seeking to postulate a concept of neutral money, Hayek ignored its basic characteristics as both a medium of exchange and a store of value. Since these played little or no role in his theory, the relationships which were altered by shifts in relative prices seemed utterly obscured: contract prices and debts were virtually eliminated. Neutral money was, in effect, no money.

His saving concept was indeed unusual. This was defined as the total flow of resources going to the producers' goods industries in contrast to what went into consumers' goods. Of course, such a definition was based on gross income rather than net, which was the more common starting point for an analysis of capital formation. In Hayek's view, consumers gave their savings to producers who then employed these resources to lengthen the period of production. In this way capital accumulation was built up. It ceased when consumers stopped saving. The same quantity of labor now utilized a larger quantity of capital, so that output was increased and a new level of production achieved. Now, the same results could be attained, at least momentarily, through "forced" saving, a process which was engendered when the banking system injected new credit into the economy. Initially, the effects were identical with those stemming from voluntary saving, with the important exception that inflationary pressure on prices was added to the expansionary movement. Hayek insisted that ultimately this proved to be harmful; for, as soon as forced saving halted, consumers, in an effort to restore their earlier level of consumption, performed acts of cannibalism on the new capital and restored the *status quo ante:* they consumed all the added capital! But why this should happen Hayek failed to specify. This situation suggested that somehow consumers had access to the capital with which they had already parted, enabling them to consume it once their freedom of action had been restored. It suggested further that capital would be in some sort of fluid shape to allow for direct consumption, a thought quite in conflict with Hayek's basic notion of capital as concrete goods. It suggested above all that there might be a conflict of interests over economic issues between different social classes, a quaint semi-Marxian notion for such an avowed opponent of socialist theory. Yet the fundamental contradiction seemed self-evident: if money was neutral, why should the expansion of credit through the banking system have such a deleterious impact?

The structure of production played a very significant role in Hayekian theory. This was defined in a curiously abstruse fashion as the relationship between the demand for producers' goods and the demand for consumers' goods. That is to say, the various stages were so organized and proportioned as to yield a certain output. Any structural changes that might take place were related to shifts in demand, which required a delicate concatenation of output to consumer spending. Alterations in the underlying relationships were bound to have widespread ramifications since so many industries were essentially complementary. Equilibrium was maintained when money was so distributed as not to upset the balance: that is, money was neutral. (The circularity of the concept was also quite patent). But the structure of production was an impermanent one, for with shifts in relative prices there were bound to develop new conditions for profitability.[403] Now, with voluntary saving, the changes were permanent, for in these circumstances expenditures for consumption goods were reduced for all time, and money income going to the original factors of production, land, and labor, was curtailed. The prices of consumer goods would fall faster than the income going to labor, resulting in an irreversible shift in the distribution of goods and resources.[404] In the case of a credit expansion, however, the pressure on consumption expenditures was relaxed; and it was this very effect which led to difficulties, for the financing of additional producers' goods was imposed on consumers through inflation.[405] Consumers suffered a "forced saving" because they were now unable to purchase as many goods: commodities sold at higher prices while income remained the same. If consumers did secure more money income, they would attempt to increase their expenditure to the earlier level. This, in effect, would mean a return to the former proportions existing between the producers' goods and consumers' goods industries, with the sad result that projects under way would have to be suspended for lack of sufficient resources. A crisis, said Hayek, would be the result.[406] Now, one cogent question occurs in examining this analysis. Why should not consumer income expand together with the producers' goods industries? Surely, the experience of the last twenty years has supplied enough evidence to suggest this as a possibility. One can speak of a lag in the growth of consumer income as compared with the growth in producers' goods, but this does not preclude some expansion. There seems no special reason why consumers' goods industries need remain static: it appears entirely possible for the producers' goods industries to move to new levels, followed by the other sectors of the economy.

For Hayek, equilibrium implied an equality of certain basic economic ratios, so that the demand for goods, the money required to sustain this demand, and the supply of goods would all be proportionate to each other. Only under these circumstances would resources be fully employed. Deviations from whatever the norm might be would have to work themselves out until an identity of supply and demand was established.[407] But this process of adjustment, which suggested that use would be made of resources that were unprofitable in previous stages, seemed a violation of Hayek's own rules: unused resources could be employed profitably only by altering the input mix or production function, whereas the theory had it that the same ratios of goods in process, money, and consumers' goods were to be maintained.[408] The equilibrium concept affected also the period of production, for the latter was not only related to a given structure of relative prices but was such that the flow of finished goods onto the market had to balance the demand for consumption goods. When expenditure for consumer goods bore the correct proportion to available resources, then, and only then, would existing productive equipment maintain a proper flow of goods.

This was a terribly complicated way of saying that equilibrium is what it is and must necessarily be equilibrium, especially in the long run. It is evident that today this is hardly a useful theory of capital, despite some interesting insights. Granted that capital structures are complex and have an extensive time dimension, it is unlikely that businessmen are so intently concerned with events in an unknown distant future. More important are the relations of expected returns and anticipations in the short run, with the rate of interest influenced more by relative desires for liquidity positions. And it is no longer possible to assert that interest plays the predominant role in capital investment decisions.

Also implicit in Hayek's involved theory was the notion of a surplus, albeit a Bawerkian rather than a Marxian one. As raw materials moved along the production line and were converted into specific goods, the price margins at the various stages of production were greater than the mere value added by labor and material. This, said Hayek, was to be absorbed mainly by interest.[409] But such a surplus could be generated only so long as the required voluntary saving was provided. Any shift in the ratio of saving to capital would upset the delicate balance between the price margin and interest and cause a regrettable change in the structure of production.[410] Interest, of course, was deemed to be more than a passive element, although thus far this has not appeared to be the case. In a moneyless economy, said Hayek, interest regulated the proportional development of the consumers' goods and producers' goods sectors and assured that production would not outrun the supply of voluntary saving.[411] To name this concept, Hayek borrowed the term "natural rate of interest" from Wicksell, defining it, however, as the totality of price margins in the economy.[412] The latter was one in which there were no unemployed resources, no monetary upsets, and no forced saving. Goods moved easily along the production line toward the consumer and exchanged for the available neutral money in equal intervals corresponding to periods of production. Changes in the structure of production were to be accounted for only by future needs. The rate of interest from the latter standpoint was that which equated the present value of a good in a particular stage of production to the value of a completed good after some time lapse. But as Keynes pointed out in his *General Theory,* this made the rate of interest equivalent to the marginal efficiency of capital, or the prospective rate of return on capital, so that profit and interest became virtual identities.[413] In Hayek's view, (as with Mises) a fall in the ratio of consumer goods prices to those set for producers' goods was tantamount to a fall in the rate of interest and therefore good for investment. The thing to do, if growth was to be encouraged, was to increase voluntary saving and cause consumer prices to fall. But since this meant also a fall in the marginal efficiency of capital, investment in reality would be discouraged. The outcome was a grand mish-mash of theoretical analysis.

Hayek contended that it was the unwarranted action of the banking system that created a divergence of the actual rate of interest from the natural one.[414] But economists not of the Hayekian persuasion have pointed out that even without the banks it is quite possible for market rates to deviate from a supposed theoretical equilibrium. Hayek also contended that efforts to maintain a going money rate of interest during periods of expanding production would cause prices to fall and that a steady price level would require a low interest rate. But aside from a sudden concern with the general price level, which conflicted with an earlier emphasis on relative prices, there was considerable confusion on other counts in Hayek's concept. The market rate was identified with the money rate, while the equilibrium rate was the natural one. But if there were as many rates of interest as there were markets for capital, there would be as many natural rates as there would be goods. Certainly the latter notion was reinforced by Hayek's basic definition of capital in terms of specific commodities. The result of a shift in the supply and demand of consumption goods ought to be the same for either a neutral money economy or one in which money did have an impact; both would result in price changes and a possible realignment of the structure of production.

Hayek's major contribution to contemporary economics was incorporated in his treatise, *The Pure Theory of Capital*, a heavy-going exploration of the nature of capital. It represented an important advance over previous works in the Austrian tradition and, in fact, altered the argument in some ways. As had been the case with his earlier concepts, the main elements stemmed from Jevons, Böhm-Bawerk, and Wicksell. Hayek wanted to develop a sound general theoretical base for his analysis of business cycles, and he felt that it would have to be deeply rooted in a proper notion of capital and interest. As it was, he produced a ponderous and frequently tedious tome which failed to give even the satisfaction that one might have in working out mathematical equations.

Austrian theory, it will be recalled, had reduced capital goods to land and labor, thus implying the need to call upon the past to define the true nature of capital. Further, it seemed that a significant aspect of capital was its prospective return, so that the period of actual investment was intimately related to expectations. These beginnings provided Hayek with the raw material for his theory. He would have little to do with the version of capital developed in Britain or the United States. The Anglo-Americans tended to stress the importance of *fixed* capital and thought of it in terms of durable goods. Hayek, however, wanted to emphasize circulating capital which "arises out of the duration of the process of production." He conceived capital to be essentially nonpermanent so that attention might be called to the need for continuous reproduction. For the Americans, capital replacement was a discontinuous business, attendant upon the wearing out of equipment. For Hayek, the decisive element became the time span that ostensibly elapsed before the final services, to which capital contributed, would mature. Thus, it was the position of capital in the "time structure" of production that was significant. Further, the supply of available capital, he insisted, determined the choice of a particular technology, in contrast to the Western view of a more or less fixed production function. That is to say, additional units of capital would supposedly induce shifts in techniques of production rather than serve as mere increments to the existing stock. Finally, since there were bound to be changes in the relative demand for producers' and consumers' goods, there would be correlative changes in available capital. As in the earlier statements, the demand for capital varied inversely with the demand for consumer goods.[415]

Hayek was quite firm in rejecting the notion of capital as a fund. For him capital was a stock of particular items requiring maintenance: social overhead items, such as tunnels and docks, were not to be considered capital since they did not require upkeep.[416] It must be conceded though that Hayek's arguments against the idea of capital as a fund were quite forceful. The fund idea suggested a kind of simultaneity in production and consumption which seemed warranted only in the static long run, not in a dynamic economy. Automatic replacement of capital, in other words, was to be considered a most dubious proposition. Yet some aspects of Hayek's own concept exhibited as many mystical features as the fund theory. His contention that a lengthened period of production would increase output *in general* rather than being related to specific goods was quite strange in the light of his basic definition of capital, and the insistence that intermediate goods need not be specific revealed an almost fatal concession to the fund notion. The contradictory turns in Hayek's thinking were underscored when he rigidly defined capital in a way as to exclude any movement whatsoever. New capital was never the same as old capital, he insisted, despite the patent fact that this was but partly true.[417] There would appear to be many instances of circulating capital in which the forms and the types are identical.

For some years a furious debate raged over these concepts, spurred by Frank H. Knight's articles during the early 1930's.[418] Knight questioned the legitimacy of the investment period and was in turn answered by Hayek and Fritz Machlup as well.[419] The highly technical literature became vast enough to fill many volumes, and was frequently tedious in an almost medievalist fashion. Of course, neither disputant convinced the other. While Hayek was content to repeat the salient points of his capital theory, Knight, who had been trained originally in technical philosophy, made so many philosophical asides in leveling his objections that the main purpose was almost lost entirely. Knight's view of production as a process creating generalized values had to be contrasted with Hayek's physical conception in which a certain input mix was combined to obtain a particular output. The latter was prior to valuation and consequently had to be set in a time framework. The value approach made synchronization a conceptual possibility in J. B. Clark's meaning, while an average period of production, based on some sort of dating procedure, made equal sense if the physical approach was adopted. Certainly, the concept of a period of production could pose problems. The technical methods employed would have to be spelled out rather carefully, for otherwise the concept of roundaboutness would remain quite vague. At the very least, one would arrive at some measure of the capital-labor ratio utilized in production. But this was an index which conceivably might be computed in some way other than the period of production. Of course, not only was dating of the inputs required, but one had to consider the problem of weights and the reduction to some common measurement. The latter, of course, could be achieved only through a valuation procedure. Thus, there would appear to be merit in both approaches, if one were to seek a rounded view of economic reality.

Much of Hayek's approach to these questions was later summarized in his *Pure Theory of Capital,* as systematic a treatment of the modern Austrian version of capital theory as could be found. Although his concern centered about a kind of moving equilibrium, the period of production still played a central role. Interest was related to both marginal productivity and time preference, while real forces were separated from monetary ones. The central problem of capital was visualized as follows: how do nonpermanent resources enable production to be maintained at a high level to yield permanently a constant flow of income?[420] The definition of capital was implicit in the mere statement of the problem: we must be concerned with the total supply of nonpermanent resources used in roundabout methods of production. Since these were "wasting assets," capital was to be restricted entirely to circulating capital.[421] They would provide an income for a limited period, thus permitting investment of permanent resources in more time-consuming processes in order to raise productivtiy. Although Hayek insisted that this was not a restatement of Böhm-Bawerk, it was difficult to accept the disclaimer.[422] The analysis was then pursued in terms of a simple economy governed by central command as contrasted with a competitive price economy. While Hayek never developed any sets of equilibrium equations as did Walras, he did insist that his system was just as determinate. Said he: "The members of the society must distribute their total resources between use for present and use for future consumption in such a way as to make the relative values of the different types of resources exactly proportional to their relative costs of production. . . ."[423] There seemed no doubt in his mind but that this was the way in which the economy functioned.

A feature of the book was an attempt to study the relationships between the organization of production and the size of the product. The input-output relationship was defined in various ways, with a "continuous input-point output" situation at one end of the spectrum and a "point input-continuous output" case at the other. The formal nature of the various possibilities was then explored in great detail.[424] All this was preliminary to a study of a particular investment structure. Hayek's initial assumption was that any stock of capital represented "contributions" to some future income. The time element suggested that the fruit of any set of inputs would spread itself over all future periods so that yield eventually would peter out. Although Hayek would not specifically say so, this was clearly nothing more than diminishing returns extended into the future. An elaborate analysis of input and output curves then followed.[425] The result of the analysis was the statement that as "we move further into the future the rate at which products of given units of input mature will decrease more rapidly than the rate at which given units of output mature." [426] One can hardly think of a more laborious way of saying that resources are used up in production. The structure of production admittedly underwent change because the replacement of durable goods was done discontinuously.[427] Here durable goods acquired new meaning, although one of his earlier precepts had denied their significance for the capital problem. Another contradiction occurred when Hayek limited the flow of demand from consumers' goods to producers' goods industries, thus seemingly placing a barrier between them. Yet when prices affected costs there was the most intimate of relationships between the two sectors.

The problem of dating equipment and the relation that this had to the various stages of production made capital analysis quite complex, said Hayek. In fact, the stress on complexity was so strong that one wondered if he were not expressing a philosophic bias. Hayek seemed to be suggesting that reality could not be ordered in the various ways necessary to satisfy all the demands of economic analysis. It almost appeared as if he were trying, with inadequate analytical tools, to translate an engineering problem into economic terminology. The solution of many of Hayek's problems really had to await the development of such powerful techniques as linear programming.[428] Much of his difficulty was due to a penchant for frequent shifting between value and real concepts in a most disconcerting way and to the employment of such curious notions as the perpetual investment of interest. It simply never occurred to him that interest might be consumed.[429] The desire for a constant income stream was never demonstrated; this was a mere assumption, for it would be rather hard to find the economic man who behaved this way.

One way of assuring a constant income stream would be to arrange production so that the rate of increase in output would be the same for all units of input over the given time period.[430] This was a kind of equi-marginal principle adapted to a time span. Hayek asserted that in attributing output to a specific input the ". . . values of these quantities must bear a relationship to one another corresponding to a compound rate of interest which is uniform throughout the system." [431] Where the situation would be complicated by the inability to identify a given output with a specific input, as seems most likely in modern industry, Hayek tried to solve the problem by resorting to the old Austrian tool of imputation from a marginal product.[432]

The major problems in an individual economy stemmed from unforeseen changes. The basic data were the varieties of wants and the distribution pattern of resources, which were in large part, it was conceded, under the control of a small sector of the population.[433] Although this was a virtual admission that the entire theory was geared to the theoretical requirements of a particular class, this was done, as it were, *en passant*. Again, the central argument was the need for consumers to engage in voluntary saving if the structure of production was to be moved to higher levels. In the main, the thesis of the earlier works was resumed and restated in even more subtle ways. Indeed, one could not escape from the concept of the period of production, for it pervaded everything Hayek did. In his study of the business cycle, *Monetary Theory and the Trade Cycle,* the concept again was utilized as a central feature of the argument.

Hayek's business cycle analysis was, as might be expected, a monetary one, with emphasis on the phenomenon of overinvestment—a theory which exerted considerable attraction for such writers as Fritz Machlup, Wilhelm Röpke, and Lionel Robbins. The key to economic upset, he said, was monetary expansion through the banking system. For these purposes money was to be defined in the broadest conceivable manner, including such substitutes as certificates of exchange. There is no need to repeat here his analysis of the effect of a money influx on the structure of production: it was the "forced saving" argument all over again leading to a top-heavy expansion and the ultimate collapse of work in progress. Why did the boom collapse? The proximate cause was the unwillingness of the banks to extend credit any further. Everyone was caught in a dilemma, because the completion of the newer projects required a continuous flow of capital over the entire period of construction. The shortage of investible funds could not be corrected through the injection of new money for this merely postponed the day of reckoning. Furthermore, the proportionate division of resources between the producers' goods and consumers' goods industries no longer corresponded to the flow of voluntary savings. Although money could be injected, the problem stemmed from the fact that the authorities could not control spending without imposing strict and rigid controls. The best solution rested in a diminished level of consumption and the stimulation of voluntary saving to help lengthen the period of production and to facilitate the completion of works in progress that had been forced to be held in suspense.

However, recent investigations have suggested that investments which are previously committed are unlikely to be influenced by monetary restrictions. It seems that the availability of funds, interest rates, and the like have little impact on actual equipment outlays, which characteristically lag behind decisions to invest. It is rather the latter which react to changes in the money market. Once the decision has been made to undertake a particular project, it takes a significant shift in finances to alter investment plans. After a while, when costs have been built up, it pays to continue, despite increased interest charges, rather than to cancel the project. If this is the case, then an important keystone in Hayek's structure begins to sag.[434] Had he meant to say that overinvestment discouraged *plans* for expansion, he would have been on stronger ground. Although a rising price level can depress expectations, this is a far cry from the assertion that present commitments would be cancelled.

According to Hayek, the final "accounting" ensued because the amount of capital necessary to produce a consumer good declined as prosperity continued.[435] This contradictory situation was due to Hayek's version of the Ricardo effect. When this part of the theory was proposed, Nicholas Kaldor dubbed it the "concertina effect," on the ground that Hayek was now trying to explain cyclical movements through underinvestment as well as overinvestment.[436] Yet this was really no new position: Hayek simply was looking at his kind of economic reality through both ends of the telescope. Ricardo had argued that the ratio of capital to labor varied directly with real wages. Hayek took up this proposition, saying that when the latter fell, a substitution of labor for capital ensued, leading to a shortened or less roundabout period of production. Presumably this discouraged investment because it became more profitable to substitute labor for machinery. What happened, said Hayek, was that real wages fell relative to the cost of machinery as a result of the more rapid rise in consumer prices as compared with wages. Here Hayek simply ignored the evidence, for real wages tend to rise rapidly in the latter stages of a boom.[437] This version of the Ricardo effect seemed quite wrong, for, as has been demonstrated recently by Seymour Melman, it is the relation of *money* wages and machine cost that determines the substitution of one for the other.[438]

Hayek's theory suggested an extraordinary ability to shift resources about in the short run. He quite evidently was trying to supplement Böhm-Bawerk's analysis with a detailed short-run theory. In his view the crisis was one in which the producers' goods industries were disturbed by over-expansion of demand in the consumers' goods industries. The culprits were the banking system, the trade unions, and taxes.[439] Hidden assumptions, however, vitiated the entire argument, for Hayek was saying that production functions—the technical relations of input to output—were really not fixed in the short run. But the patent fact is that producers cannot move their resources about as easily as Hayek thought. As Kaldor has remarked, the concertina effect, in which periods of production became longer or shorter depending on shifts in the production function, simply didn't exist. Hayek insisted that things would have been much better with a constant supply of money, so that prices would fall with increases in productivity.[440] The basic cause of cycles, said he, was the "elasticity of the volume of circulating media": the mechanism was a shifting in output and capital formation through changes in relative prices.[441] But if monetary expansion is contingent on increased profit expectations, one may well wonder whether Hayek's system may not be awry. He was unable to account satisfactorily for responses to stimulation that might take place in conditions of underutilized resources. Further, how a reduction in the prices of consumer goods would enhance profitability in the producers' goods industries was rather hard to comprehend. The solution for the crisis was almost as strange as the theory itself: it may be summed up as decreased consumption, deflation, and lower wages. If some economists have called the Hayekian school "sadistic deflationists," they have not been too far wrong.

The entire doctrine, which suggested that voluntary saving could be restored only by depressing consumption, was well received by the business community, for it provided a seemingly forceful rationale for some of the more curious economic policies in western nations in the 1930's. Wage cuts and enhanced saving were thought to be the only ways to solve the riddle of the depression.

Obviously, said Hayek, investment can be legitimated only through voluntary saving. Now, the bulk of saving is done by the upper income strata of the population. It would not be too far amiss to suggest that his scheme would redistribute income in the direction of the savers even more sharply than is now the case. This would indeed stimulate voluntary saving. And the tax structure might be modified to encourage this tendency. But the greatest fillip would be the restoration of profit margins.[442]

While Hayek's theory suggested a breakdown of investment, some net investment has occurred even in the worst of depressions. Capital shortage was certainly not a significant factor in the three post-war recessions: the basic element seemed to be a failure of effective demand to keep pace with capital expansion. The injection of purchasing power would seemingly have had the effect of stimulating rather than dampening investment, for if consumers goods' prices would have risen relative to producers' good prices it would appear that the marginal efficiency of capital would be heightened. And in a condition of unemployed resources, the notion of capital shortage seems highly questionable.

Hayek's assertion that the withdrawal of monetary stimulation would merely restore the old proportions bore but a superficial resemblance to Wicksell, who had made it quite clear that money was a secondary factor and that changes in real factors were the important ones.[443] Hayek was simply overstressing monetary elements, for both theoretically and empirically his baneful developments could not take place. The experience of the early New Deal, when no amount of monetary manipulation was then able to revive the economy, has supplied ample evidence of that. And if output increases in consonance with the expansion of money there seems to be little justification for Hayek's concern. The notion that everything hinges on differential rates of growth in the various sectors of the economy was much too imprecise to make the theory genuinely useful. Yet there was some value in Hayek's emphasis on structural distortion, assuming that one would grant him the premise of fully employed resources. There was merit to his argument that, under conditions of maximum use, increased competition for input factors could cause prices to rise. But why this should affect only consumer goods industries was not clear. Nor did he specify whether the kind of distortion he had in mind was a horizontal one, traceable to shifts in consumer demand, as in the case of the growth of the automobile industry, or merely overinvestment in individual industries in a vertical sense.

Implicit in this sort of economics was not only a defense of individualism but an attack on the supposed trend to collectivism and socialism. Hayek insisted that the extension of the powers of the state would lead to the suppression of intellectual and cultural freedom. He argued that,

Comprehensive economic planning, which is regarded as necessary to organize economic activity on more rational and efficient lines, presupposes a much more complete agreement on the relative importance of the different social ends than actually exists, and that in consequence, in order to be able to plan, the planning authority must impose upon the people the detailed code of values that is lacking.[444]

The apogee of his attack on the trend toward statism was set forth in both *The Road to Serfdom* and *The Constitution of Liberty,* in which he warned that the Western world would follow the frightful path to totalitarianism unless the economic habits of the eighteenth century were restored. Hayek took the liberalism of a century and a half ago and placed it squarely into the center of contemporary economic life with little qualification or alteration. Only the unhampered operation of the free market, said he, could assure our basic liberties. So long as the state tampered with spontaneous economic forces, so long were we to witness continuous encroachments on freedom. "Good" planning was possible only in a laissez faire context, while the sort of planning now advanced destroyed the individual.

A new coherence was given to this hoary argument by Hayek. But although his statements had the appearance of axiomatic truth and the elegance of rigid logic, they were revealed, when subjected to historic test, as mere political prejudice.[445] Planning was described as a demand for release from the rigorous compulsions enforced by a limited environment. This was a good generalized formula, for such compulsions do injure personality, and intelligent planning would seem to be an important corrective. But Hayek rejected group or social action: he could counsel only resignation to market forces and advise that in the end all would be well, for only free competition would be able to effectively coordinate economic decisions.

In *The Constitution of Liberty* Hayek defined freedom as the absence of coercion.[446] Of course, he was quite free to do this; but without some specification of coercion, it was difficult to grasp the meaning of its opposite, liberty. Aware of this, he proposed to define coercion in terms of arbitrary power, and urged that this should be monopolized by the government and then kept to a minimum, so that only taxation and certain limited public aims might be pursued. This raised doubts as to Hayek's orthodoxy among some of the other libertarians who under no circumstances would accept even the rigidly restricted areas which he had found admissible for government action—unemployment relief and old age care. However, their fears were unfounded, for Hayek would in no case admit that social security or public education or rent control were proper functions for government. These he condemned as either "administrative despotism" or excessive power over the minds of little children. Yet the sort of coercion that Hayek overlooked oftentimes has been more oppressive than the highest of progressive taxes. Monopolistic markets, price rigging, and the right to fire employees at will have been forms of coercion that have needed some counterweights. And these coercive pressures could not be dismissed lightly. Precisely for these reasons government and unions have intervened in the economic process. Surely they have provided more freedom in the modern industrial context rather than less.

The idea of the market had derived its inspiration from eighteenth-century natural law doctrines. A hundred and fifty years ago that philosophy had been a powerful ideological weapon in the struggle against the divine right of kings. An expanding capitalism had demanded theoretical justification for commercial enterprise. The means of production were widely distributed and the pursuit of self-interest was identifiable with social interest. Yet such competition resulted all too frequently in frightful spectacles: the history of the factory system has offered ample evidence of human degradation.[447] Social legislation, therefore, became part of the economic tradition. Today the economic structure is so complex that its healthy functioning is a proper concern for the state.[448] Yet Hayek preferred submission to the kindly "unseen hand" of an abstract market. To accomplish this we should have to retrace the steps of the last century and a half and create a world of small independent units, *sans* monopoly and *sans* large aggregations of capital. But even more disturbing was the patent fact that this doctrine became an ideological justification and shrewd rationalization of unbridled private economic power. The problem of planning and control was not the central question: it was, rather, who shall impose the plans—a private power élite or society in general?[449] This was the final pass to which Austrian doctrine had brought itself.[450]

vii

The Marginalist Debate
Today

One of Austrian marginalism's chief virtues was its underscoring of the element of interdependence. Even if this notion had been not nearly so well put as in Walras, it at least had suggested a way that could lead to some fruitful results. The classicists had thought in terms of cause and effect, but with marginalist doctrine there began the tradition of studying the interrelationships of the various elements in a way that was basic to partial as well as to general equilibrium. Some of the deficiencies of the older approach were highlighted, as in the case of the statement of the laws of return which Anglo-Saxon doctrine had limited to argiculture. Marginalism, however, developed it into a general statement applicable to any of the factors of production, thus providing a useful insight into the basic unity of production and distribution. This was especially evident in Jevons and J. B. Clark, in whose hands the marginal productivity theory became direct and distinct from any entanglements with the realm of utility. If labor, for example, commanded a given wage, that automatically set the level of employment. Price and income were identical. In more sophisticated versions, matters became a bit more complex. The return to a given factor was studied under conditions of pure competition with *ceteris paribus* techniques. All factors but one were fixed, so that the effect of changes in the variable factor might be carefully examined. This permitted the derivation of industry demand curves and market demand curves and the exploration of all kinds of subtleties.[451]

In this way marginalism had developed a fairly clear exposition of business action. With technological elements summarized in the single expression of the production function, it was even possible to postpone discussion of the problem of returns to scale. But this was tacit recognition of the short-run character of marginalist analysis. In addition, modern industrial processes, with joint and multiple product outputs, have raised doubts about the general applicability of marginalism. Yet efforts were continually being made to test the marginalist propositions by empirical studies. One such notable attempt was Henry Schultz' *Theory and Measurement of Demand* which not only sought to evaluate the available statistical techniques, but actually made demand studies of over a dozen agricultural products, particularly with respect to complementarity and cross-elasticities.[452] Another relevant example was Paul H. Douglas' *The Theory of Wages* which sought an answer to the question: are there laws of production?[453] Although Douglas was fully aware of the close relationship of production and value theory, he felt that an independent study of the former was quite feasible. He recognized the limitations of the marginalist assumptions: the latter implied that producers were able to measure added productivity; that competition was free and labor knew its own marginalist position; that workers competed keenly for jobs; that full employment existed; that labor and capital were fluid; and that labor's bargaining powers were equal to those of capital. Nevertheless, he felt that these assumptions contained a limited validity, at least enough to make a statistical study possible.[454] The least useful assumptions were those which ascribed more power to labor than was actually the case, but those concerning knowledge of productiveness and mobility were, he felt, largely correct. The empirical data, drawn from American, Australian, and South African experience, sought to test a production function devised by Douglas and his colleague, Charles E. Cobb, an Amherst mathematician. The function, and the various studies as well, suggested that labor's share of output was in the neighborhood of three-fourths of the product. Douglas concluded that "taken in the large, there is an almost precise degree of agreement between the actual share received by labor and that which, according to the theory of marginal productivity, we should expect labor to obtain."[455] Yet, despite the statistical ingenuity and the richness of Douglas' work, the marginalist aspect seemed to have been dragged in by the heels. Even if it were severed from the empirical content, Douglas' contribution would still be a useful one.

Nevertheless, Douglas' approach was subjected to some rather sharp criticism. Objection was made to the exclusion of land from the analysis on the ground that in the long run the supply of land was not constant, thus making the assumption of constant returns a dubious one. Moreover, critics argued that the approach had excluded technical progress, particularly at the turn of the century, the period to which the study applied. Further, since Douglas had used physical rather than value data, the effects of changes in relative prices were obscured. There was some question too about the underlying statistical methods: fitting a line of regression to the data overlooked the possibility of other solutions. At best, it was said, the results measured only relationships in historical rates of change between the product and the factors, but not marginal productivity.[456]

In short, marginal productivity could not explain how distributive shares were shaped: it could show only how a firm might hire input factors once the latter's prices were known. Since it was really a theory of demand for factors, and only at the level of the firm, it had little to say in a macroeconomic sense. The problem was no longer one of shifting about doses of land, labor, or capital, but of establishing a highly complicated distribution process dominated by a fairly inflexible structural organization in which change was almost always discontinuous. To reply that in the long run everything was variable was hardly a satisfactory answer, for in the long run the marginalist analysis collapsed. In short, the suspicion grew that this approach did not really tell us much about the process of decision-making in the field of economics.

For example, there has never been full agreement that the objective of the businessman is to maximize profit.[457] General experience has indicated that businessmen will seek maximum sales, not profits, as the primary goal. Naturally, profit considerations are taken into account, but there is great reluctance to cut back on revenue. The pricing technique generally employed is a reasonable or customary markup on full average cost. Whether this be correct or not, it is the way the businessman behaves. That this has made him the despair of economic theorists is undeniable. He is frankly unaware of his marginal costs and is unable to estimate the elasticity of demand for his product. Does he try to think marginally? Is it possible for him to evaluate alternative courses of action in the cold, deliberate way the theory suggests when the underlying data change so rapidly? Actually, the character of economic change is obscured in marginalist doctrine, since each shift must be examined by itself. Only with great difficulty are elements of inter-dependence effectively delineated. Since cost and revenue are deemed to be functions of output, alterations in the cost of inputs, quality, or technology result merely in a shift of the relevant curves. Changes take place only along the curve. In practice, businessmen seem to rely on trial-and-error methods: markups may be varied, or standard costing practices shifted about to provide a more advantageous prospect for certain items, just so long as the product can be kept on the move.

Nor is it entirely unwarranted to ask that marginalist curves have an objective manifestation.[458] This certainly would be essential if their adequacy is to be tested.[459] Any considerations of the objective aspect of marginalism would have to admit nonpecuniary motives. But quite simply, it is perfectly possible that maximum profit may not be the final aim; as Robert A. Gordon says, "satisfactory" profits may be deemed sufficient. If this be so, then the average concept rather than the marginal one may be appropriate. But even on this, the received theory may be awry, for in one study at least, it seemed that most average cost curves, as defined by businessmen, were not at all as set forth in the texts, that is, falling toward a least cost point and then sharply rising. The least cost point appeared to be located somewhere near capacity! [460] Moreover, marginal computations in a multi-process plant are difficult, if not impossible, so that price determination on the basis of average total cost for some normal or usual output may be a more useful procedure.[461]

In such plants, production is frequently discontinuous; the smooth change implied by the marginalist calculus appears unrealistic, unless one wishes to resort to the use of difference rather than differential equations.[462]

One of the major difficulties in marginalism has been its inability to deal with such macroeconomic questions as employment or income.[463] A survey of businessmen's decision processes revealed that the ratio of labor to total cost had little effect on decreasing unit costs, a not unreasonable surmise in situations where direct labor costs were a small portion of total cost. Evidently, businessmen do not make adjustments to market conditions through price, but rather through product changes or simply by altering their methods. Knowledge of the shape of their demand curves seems unknown to businessmen; moreover, they often can not make the quick price changes that an ordinary demand curve would suggest. What businessmen are concerned with is the element of uncertainty that suffuses and dominates their decision-making. This would require that economic analysis introduce time as a factor, a complication which has been met with but varying degrees of success. At any rate, the thinking of businessmen apparently has had little in common with the propositions of marginal economics.

It has been argued, notably by Fritz Machlup, that the description of businessmen's thinking is not pertinent to theoretical discourse, since they do not employ the modes of analysis utilized by economists.[464] Empirical investigations into the nature of the decision-making process in no way have upset marginalist theories, Machlup has said, for businessmen, without knowing it, frequently act in accordance with marginal ideas. This has been done intuitively and unconsciously, so that in the end the "laws" of economics are obeyed. But this argument has suggested merely a broad interpretation of marginalism: it has remained unproven and as such has been merely an expression of faith very much like certain ontological arguments in theology. For true believers it has sufficed, but for the study of human behavior such statements have been as useful as affinity and phlogiston in explanations of chemical change. At best, it has become a rather roundabout way of saying that a business would increase its income as much as it could.[465]

Although unschooled in the marginal ritual the businessman sometimes does achieve a fair approximation to profit maximization. But if the marginalist wants to develop his theories on the basis of his own hunches and not on what the businessman thinks, then he can say nothing about the underlying motivations of economic behavior. The psychological underpinning, at least on the consumption side, has been equally faulty. By employing utility as it did, it has assumed that the intensity of desire for an object reflected the commodity's want-satisfying power. An illegitimate transfer from utility to desire had been accomplished, suggesting ordinary hedonism. There has been little recognition that people do not compare units of pleasure derivable from successive units of a good or from different goods. Buying is a complex of unconscious drives, irrational impulses, fashion, habit, custom, and actions stimulated by the hidden persuaders of the advertising world. And the attempt to assert the validity of some of the curves of the marginalist's tool box without recourse to psychology has not been convincing.[466] There seemed to be sufficient empirical exceptions to raise serious questions regarding the uses to which marginalism has been put as a *general* theory of behavior.[467]

In short, marginalism has emerged as a merely formal way of developing the implications of certain propositions about human actions which in themselves have possessed but limited validity. As such, it is a pure system, with little operational usefulness. As Goran Ohlin has said, marginalism, supported in academic and other circles mainly by faith, was rooted in the desire for a theory that could supply incontestable criteria with which to judge economic efficiency. The marginalist wanted to know whether the correct amounts are being produced according to his special vision of a rational universe. But if a theory is to provide a framework for research and investigation, it ought to be prepared to accept empirical evidence, even if the latter calls for some alteration in the theory itself. However, it is to be feared that some marginalists will continue to clutch the theory to their breasts, even though it be a mere figment they hold.[468]

5

Equilibrium Economics

and the Unification

of Theory

Léon Walras: The Greatest
Economist?

ESCRIBED AS THE greatest of the "pure theorists," Léon Walras (1834-1910) set economics on a path from which it has not yet departed.[1] The mathematical mode of analysis which he developed has been compared to the achievements of theoretical physics, and while now admittedly outdated, it nevertheless has provided the foundation on which a good deal of theoretical economics is currently based. The use of mathematics in economics grew at a remarkable pace in the latter part of the nineteenth and early twentieth century. Of course, attempts to employ figures had been frequent, going back at least to William Petty and continuing on through Ricardo and Marx. But the utilization of mathematical reasoning to formulate results into systems of equations was quite another matter. Such a procedure, while seemingly quantitative in form, was not necessarily numerical. The mathematical method meant resorting to the entire apparatus of algebra and the calculus. It meant expressing economic relationships as functions, variables, derivatives, and today as problems in set theory and matrix algebra.[2] Purportedly, the advantage of this approach lay in its restatement of economics in precise form, capable of rigorous proof. The theory of the Austrians, who had rejected the use of mathematics, could be recast, for example, in a way that would sharpen basic concepts. As Schumpeter has said, value theory seemed to move inevitably toward the calculus.

The tradition in which Walras worked appeared destined to culminate in the vast mathematical structure that he created. It was mainly French in origin with inspirations that went back to Condillac and Quesnay, continuing on to Cournot and Auguste Walras, Léon's father. The elder Walras, a professor of philosophy, had written a book on wealth and value that was to provide Léon with many of the ideas he was to develop later. Walras was born in Evreaux, France, into a cultivated and highly moral home, conducive to the pursuit of intellectual endeavor.[3] He at first studied the classics, receiving a degree in literature at the age of seventeen and one in science a year afterward. Evidently his mathematical training had not been adequate, for he twice failed to gain admission to the Polytechnic Institute. He was finally allowed to enter the School of Mines, but he manifested little interest in problems of technology and engineering, preferring to spend his time with literature and philosophy. After he had published a novel in 1858, which proved to be a sad failure, he began to drift, and it was economics that finally rescued him.

At the urging of his father, Walras turned to economic study. In 1860 he published a polemic against Proudhon and, in the same year, took part in an essay competition staged by the Swiss Canton of Vaud, participating at the same time in an international tax congress at Lausanne, Vaud's chief city. The strong impression he made then was to bear fruit a decade later. Certainly Walras' paper, for which he had the help of his father, was remarkable for so young and inexperienced a man. And his daring in suggesting that taxes be based on the principle of equity seemed to impress his listeners. Ironically, the first prize winner was Proudhon![4] Walras now sought to have his scientific papers published in the professional journals, but they were all rejected. He then worked for the railroads, participated in the cooperative movement, a life-long interest, tried journalism, was employed by a bank for cooperatives, and was finally able to settle down when he was appointed to the newly created chair of political economy at Lausanne in 1871. The offer was made through the intervention of several persons who had heard his paper ten years earlier. One of them, Louis Ruchonnet, the director of public education for Vaud, became a close friend of Walras', exerting no small influence on him. Evidently, the opposition to Walras' appointment had stemmed from several persons who thought he was too liberal and objected to his avowed intention to introduce mathematical methods into economics courses. However, they were overruled.[5]

At Lausanne, where he remained until 1892, Walras developed the details of his theory of general equilibrium, which encompassed the fields of exchange, production, capital, and money in a unified formulation. And while at first given but scant attention, Walras gradually attained a world-wide reputation. Upon his retirement (he was succeeded by Vilfredo Pareto), Walras turned to the study of practical issues where his contributions in this area were incorporated in two collections of essays, *Études d'Économie Sociale* (1896) and *Études d'Économie Politique Appliquée* (1898). Unfortunately, most economists have been uninterested in these volumes.[6] Yet they are important because they do reflect more adequately Walras' social outlook. He was a prolific writer, especially of letters, keeping not only those he received, but copies of his own correspondence with Jevons, Böhm-Bawerk, Marshall, Clark, Wicksell, and Schumpeter, in many of which he went to great pains to clarify obscure points in his pure theory. But in his own country, Walras was a prophet without honor. Despite his many friends, French schools would have nothing to do with mathematical techniques in economics, a fact that had caused him much pain.[7]

Auguste Walras, a noted economist in his own right, had been the major influence on Léon, who frequently remarked that his ideas could have been found in the writings of his father.[8] Indeed, the theories of value, production, property, and wealth all could be traced to the elder Walras' thinking, and attributing his inspiration to his father was not simply a matter of filial loyalty. The connection was as direct as it could have been. But there was also the influence of Cournot, whose *Mathematical Principles of the Theory of Wealth* (1838) introduced Walras to the mathematical approach. Léon Walras, whose philosophic bias had predisposed him toward the notion of interdependence, felt that all social phenomena—religion, politics, economics and intellectual life—were related one to the other in intimate ways.

In the main, the general outlook expressed in his less technical writings was a reflection of the spirit of 1848. Society, he knew, was an association of all men, not merely a device to facilitate the exploitation of some by others. He also knew of the intense disparities that had accompanied economic development. Wages then were as depressed in France as they had been in Britain during the industrial revolution; the distress of the working class was plain for all to see; housing and working conditions were deplorable; and the socialists had ample reason to grumble. The outcome of this exacerbating situation had been the inevitable explosion of 1848.[9] Although the irrepressible faith in progress which overthrew Louis Philippe appeared perfectly sound to Walras, he abhorred revolution. Change, he thought, should be slow and scientific. Men ought to search carefully for the correct social ideal and, when this was discovered, should advance toward it steadily and without fear. Science at all times, said Walras, would have to be the guide to practice.

Thus, the "social question" was for Walras quite a serious matter. And he was determined to cut through the morass of accumulated opinion to find his own way. Yet his aim—to reconcile the scientific laws of economics with the basic principles of social justice and ethics—was a noble purpose that he was never to attain. The first attempt was made in his polemic against Proudhon, *L'Économique politique et la Justice,* in which absolute equality of opportunity was deemed to be the remedy for injustice. Progress, he said, was inherent in social development, for society grew and advanced along logical lines, albeit not those of the Hegelian dialectic. Consequently, economics ought to view the process of change dispassionately. To be certain that this would be done, it was best to study social problems with quantitative, mathematical techniques. This, said Walras, would assure the application of scientific method in the solution of the problems of poverty.

Implicit in these conceptions was the idea of natural order as well as progress. And the abstract individual who inhabited this realm was none other than the economic man of the classicists, the perfect expression of nineteenth-century liberalism who gave voice and justification to the principle of unremitting production. Private interests naturally, and in themselves, met the requirements of the general welfare, so that it was most inappropriate and even harmful for government to interfere with individual effort. Left to itself private endeavor would effect the proper proportions among the various components of the economy. Thus, said Walras, what seemed to be confusion was really order.[10]

Yet a dichotomy appeared in Walras' own thinking, for while laissez faire might seem to work satisfactorily in the production of wealth, there was undeniable distortion in the realm of distribution. Production reflected the practical application of economic law. In the case of distribution, the principle of justice would have to displace utility as an organizing force.[11] By advancing such a precept, Walras believed that he was following John Stuart Mill and in fact, in his autobiography, he called himself a social economist after the style of the great British writer. Pure economics and social economics he placed into separate compartments, despite his ambitious desire for a truly general theory. The socialist solution, however, was rejected: Walras considered Louis Blanc and Proudhon to be ignorant of fundamental economic principles. Moreover, they wanted to turn things topsy-turvy when what was called for was the application of science and a careful search for correct solutions.

Comtean positivism was also a major philosophical influence in France during Walras' lifetime. Comte had set forth the view that a definite order governed the evolution of society. His *Cours de philosophie positive* expressed certain laws by which the human mind evolved. According to Comte, history unfolded itself in three stages: the theological, metaphysical, and positive. The first two stages were concerned with the search for absolute criteria, while the positive stage, abandoning absolutes, was to explore the relative human relationships existing in society. Although many were repelled by Comte's penchant for blueprinting his new utopias, there appeared to be some merit in his insistence on analysing human behavior through an inter-related body of social science. While Walras was not directly influenced by Comte's philosophy, he could not have failed to absorb its emphasis on progress and the strength of ideas as a force in human action. Moreover, the stress on man's central role in history struck in him a sympathetic chord. However, Walras could not accept the proposition that there was but one science of society. Economics, he insisted, was indeed a proper field for independent study.

In his social philosophy Walras was somewhat in the middle of the road, yet frequently closer to socialist thinking than were the other theorists of his time. For example, land nationalization seemed to him essential for establishing equality of opportunity, for then ground rent would provide all the revenue the government needed. Clearly this was a radical proposal. But while he understood the moral fervor that impelled socialists to their peculiar stance, he considered their proposals to eliminate social evils to be in violation of economic law. Scientific economics, said he, would have to oppose socialism because it had to oppose ignorance. Marxism particularly was in grievous error because it rested on the untenable assumptions that labor was the sole source of value, that normal value was derived from em-bodied labor, and that different skills could be reduced to a common factor. These ideas, stemming from Adam Smith, had been developed to their ultimate degree by Karl Marx. But they were still errors, said Walras. The new economics, on the other hand, revealed that value was a derivative of utility and scarcity and was proportional to the "intensities of the last needs satisfied," that is, to their marginal utilities. The same principle could be ap-plied to land and capital as well as labor. No one factor was reducible to the other, each deriving their values from the economic laws of scarcity and utility.[12]

Walras started from a position of economic equilibrium in which the total product of society was comprised of a series of goods offered at certain prices. A correlative series of demands was expressed by consumers who guided themselves by the principle of utility. Now it was possible, he said, that the demands would not equal the offers made, that is, equilibrium would not be in effect. Thus Marxism had failed to show how equilibrium was attained, for only under such conditions could value be established. But this seemingly powerful argument failed to recognize that Marx had been asking questions of quite a different character. His purpose had been not to establish the price of a single good in a free competitive market, but rather to show how the flow of surplus value moved under capitalism. In short, his interest had been the nature of capitalist motion.

Similarly, Walras could not abide Bastiat's platitudes of economic harmony, which sacrificed scientific economics on the altar of sentimentalism. Not even classical theory, in which conflict was assuredly present, was able to demonstrate perpetual harmony. Bastiat's thinking, said Walras, was little more than a grand tautology and therefore could not be considered as a serious answer to the economic problem. He opposed Bastiat on practical grounds as well, for he knew that pure laissez faire was illusory. The state, he averred, had definite responsibilities—to insure the stability of money, to provide for security, to establish a system of education, to control speculation, to strengthen the position of the worker through social legislation, and generally to insure a proper environment for effective competition. It was evident that in these views Walras was expressing the viewpoint of a reformer, who occasionally was willing to describe himself as a mild sort of socialist. But pure theory would have to be the first step toward the attainment of these meliorative goals.

In the light of his earlier experience, Walras was naturally well disposed toward the cooperative movement. He believed that it was an excellent school for teaching the basic principles of political economy in a way that would lend a genuinely moral and democratic tone to the capitalist mode of doing things. Yet insofar as socialism was an expression of a deep rooted desire to enhance the status and position of the individual, he believed himself to be a socialist, despite the fact that he could not abide official party doctrine.[13] One of his major reform proposals was for the revision of land holdings along single tax lines. Such measures would presumably reconcile individual and social needs.[14]

There was really no pure individualist, said Walras, for man lives in society. The state, therefore, had to provide the conditions under which the individual satisfied his requirements. Thus, while resources for individual needs could be provided by capital and labor, the state ought to obtain its own resources from land rent. This basic reform, Walras suggested, might start with the state buying land, using government bonds as the purchase price. The rents that would accrue to the government would then be used to liquidate the bonds and pay the interest. Eventually, the state would own all land outright. With the price based on the capitalization of income, future land values automatically would be included in the exchange, thereby eliminating speculative activity. In actuality, said Walras, the state would gain, since, as a result of improved technology, surplus values on land would increase faster than present owners thought possible.

Thus, in his social philosophy Walras sought to determine the respective roles of the individual and the state. The main problem was that of order, so that both freedom and equality might be established. While man as an individual was endowed with certain rights, the state nevertheless would have to exercise a measure of authority to preserve balanced social conditions. Between man and man there might be situations of inequality; between man and state, all persons were to be equal. In Walras' words, the total situation was encompassed by the slogan, equality of conditions, inequality of positions.[15] This was his solution for the problem of justice and order. For him, it had the attributes of a mathematical formula which effected a positive reconciliation of the disparate rights and desires of men *qua* individuals and members of a social structure. The principle of voluntarism was to be carried out insofar as the individual sought to guide his own destiny. But the state was obligated to provide the security and legal environment in which individuals could pursue their chosen mode of work and life. For this reason Walras rejected Bastiat and Say's brand of laissez faire; it was the specific function of the state to insure the effective operation of the competitive system, not merely to stand by and do nothing. Consumer satisfaction would have to be enhanced and producers encouraged to make useful and beneficial goods. Consequently, the state had the right to intervene on occasion in the economic process. Aware that entrepreneurs had a virtually innate propensity toward monopoly, Walras strongly rejected Manchesterian free enterprise. Railroad regulation, control of hours of work, intervention in the money market were all legitimate functions of government. Compared to the intransigence of the latter-day libertarians such views seem indeed refreshing.

At Lausanne, Walras bent all his energies toward the construction of the theoretical edifice on which his renown was to be based. His pure economics quickly overshadowed all his other thoughts. He believed that since economic law could not be stated with sufficient rigor in ordinary language, mathematical expression was a *sine qua non* for economic science. There was no other way, for example, to show that value was an increasing function of utility and a decreasing function of quantity. This approach, of course, was not new and Walras generously acknowledged his predecessors. When he learned that Jevons had been doing work along similar lines, he conceded the latter's priority in developing the theorem of maximum utility in exchange.[16] In fact, a considerable tradition had stressed the centrality of utility on which Walras was able to build. The idea of general equilibrium had been implicit in Quesnay's work more than a century earlier. And the importance of the entrepreneur had been sketched by J. B. Say in 1803. That value stemmed from scarcity rather than cost of production was the core of this newer economics. And gradually a school of subjective economics grew up, enthusiastic over the possibilities for a scientific economics.[17] Not that there were no opponents: indeed, many thought Walrasian mathematics a hindrance to economic research. Nevertheless, Walras insisted that his method permitted a more exacting and complete analysis, clearer and more rapid than ordinary methods. It was a unique approach, he believed, which would enable man to conquer nature. At first, only the Italians, especially Enrico Barone and Maffeo Pantaleoni, took up the lead provided by Walras, while in the United States Irving Fisher and H. L. Moore viewed the mathematical method as worthwhile. And today there is no question but that Walras has won out, for virtually every economist must be adept at counting equations and manipulating the calculus.

Walras' intention to produce three distinct volumes in economics, one each in pure theory, applied theory, and social economy, was never fulfilled. The books in the latter two fields were little more than collections of disparate essays. Yet they demonstrated rather forcefully that his thinking was not limited to the purely theoretical; nor were these essays uninteresting, as John R. Hicks would have us believe.[18] Nevertheless, the total corpus of Walras' work in political economy has revealed a peculiar compartmentalization. One is never certain that the theoretical work, as unified as it is, could fit comfortably into the rather moderate social theory that he advanced. The somewhat artificial distinction between pure and applied theory was something that Walras never overcame. Pure economics remained the area in which basic laws were to be unravelled: akin to Kant's forms of a priori knowledge, pure theory was to be based ostensibly on facts given by experience, and by studying these facts, independent of moral or utilitarian objectives, one would be able to discover what their internal operations really were. They were to yield pure, rational, empirical laws. Applied economics, on the other hand, was to be considered as an exercise of man's will,[19] further divisible into morals—which would study the relations between people—and technology, which would study the relationship between man and nature.[20]

To Walras, mathematics seemed to be the only logical and sensible way of demonstrating the validity of a theory.[21] Proof in pure economics stemmed from the realm of exchange and required a double condition for equilibrium: each party in an exchange necessarily secured maximum utility and for each good the aggregate demand had to equal aggregate supply. Marginal utility was of course a mathematical concept. In fact, Walras may be considered as one of the discoverers of this central idea. Labeled by him as rareté, it was a decreasing function of the quantity consumed, and was proportional to the price paid. Marginal utility was attained when the last units of expenditure in the consumer's scale of preferences (given the available income) yielded equivalent satisfactions at the point of equilibrium. Utility was maximized when these conditions prevailed. Mathematically, it was measured by the derivative of total utility, thus tying together not only the quantity of a good and its utility but also indicating the rate of change in utility for each unit of the good.

There was also in Walras' concept a suggestion of interpersonal comparisons of utility, although Walras' eminent translator, William Jaffé, doubts that this was so.[22] Rather, said Jaffé, Walras anticipated one of the propositions of welfare economics, in which the utility of one person could not be increased without decreasing utility for someone else. Be that as it may, such disquisitions have illustrated the kind of obscurities which may be found throughout the *Éléments*. Marginal utility in Walras' system suggested that all consumers had an equal vote in the market. But the pattern of income distribution has belied such a conclusion, for with differences in income there would also be differences in marginal satisfactions. From a welfare standpoint, maximizing total social utility would imply a redistribution of income and its consequent equalization of marginal utilities. Undoubtedly the theory would have had more relevance for an egalitarian society than for the kind that Walras knew. *Rareté* was also the cause of value, making the consumer the final arbiter in the decision-making process which ultimately guided the economy. Since the utility analysis was introduced by Walras *after* his discussion of exchange, it appeared as something of an afterthought; yet without *rareté* the analysis could have no satisfactory psychological basis.[23]

The virtue of the method lay in its extension to production and capital. From the initial equations that Walras constructed for exchange, others could be built to develop a system of general equilibrium that would encompass the entire economy. The number of equations were to equal the number of unknowns, but the solution was not to be attained in simultaneous fashion. Rather, there was a movement toward equilibrium through a process of groping, or *tâtonnement,* until the correct balance was struck. With this theory, Walras made economics virtually identical with the mathematical method. "Pure economics," he said, "is also the theory of *social wealth.*"[24] That this did not jibe with his more general discussions of applied doctrine seemed patent. The result was that the preoccupation with mathematics had confused form with substance. While it certainly could be a useful tool in the economist's kit, it hardly could be said to have comprised the whole subject matter of the science, as Walras himself must have known. Yet he could not explain the content of economics without a plentiful supply of equations. The result was so high a level of abstraction that even his translator, Jaffé, had to go to great lengths to rework some of the formulas.[25]

The basic assumption could be nothing else but free competition. This was not, however, a smooth and even process, for equilibrium was like the surface of a lake on a calm day. Suddenly, disturbances took place and everything was agitated. Thus it was possible, said Walras, for prices to be above costs for extended periods of time, creating considerable upset.[26] Nevertheless, for theoretical purposes it was essential to assume free competition, fixed coefficients, and a timeless process of production. All but the bare essentials were to be eliminated in the early stages of theory building, even though the results might have little in common with economic reality. Another key concept was value in exchange, defined as the property of a thing "being bought and sold," so that in every transaction there was a double purchase and a double sale.[27] Pareto objected rather strenuously to this notion on the ground that it defined an unknown value in terms of an unknown property. At any rate, it did appear that Walras' exchange ratio was not clearly defined.

Walras' system was a closed one, with no impact from the outside. Consumers sold their services and bought the output of firms, while the latter bought factor services and raw materials to make products for sale to both consumers and other firms. Within this general framework, the major problem was to determine the conditions of equilibrium for the entire economy, for it was only then that the prices of products, factor services, output, and costs could be established. These were the basic elements in the economic flow, which was guided at its center by the entrepreneur. The factors of production with which he dealt were the usual ones—land, labor, and capital. But the entrepreneur was concerned with the *services* rendered by the various factors. Consequently, Walras found it necessary to distinguish between fixed capital, which provided more than one service, and circulating capital, which was capable of but a single use.[28] In one sense, land was also capital, but of an imperishable type. The entrepreneur bought services in one market and sold products in another. Goods were to be exchanged in terms of the *numéraire,* a commodity that served as a unit of account. Although the *numéraire* served as a standard for all other goods, it also had its own marginal utility. Transactions were to take place by a process of "crying out" bids and offers, after the fashion of a gigantic auction, until equilibrium was attained in both product and service markets. In this way, the equations were to be solved as though the different markets were computing machines. When bids and offers were initially cried, demand conceivably could be in excess of supply. Prices rose, and more offers were cried, until at last equilibrium was reached. Implicitly, it was the law of large numbers that permitted the market to function in this manner, thereby giving the system a sense of stability. A solution was arrived at empirically through free competition.[29] However, it was not clear how the process of groping in one market would affect equilibrium in the others.[30]

Although Walras conceded that his system was an ideal one in the Weberian sense, he felt that it described the normal state toward which the economy spontaneously moved under free competition.[31] Should surplus gains develop in one product area, there would be a flow of capital in its direction. Losses would occasion an outward flow. This implied that in equilibrium there were no profits other than normal. This concept was subjected to some criticism, but within the context of the general Walrasian theory, it does seem reasonable enough.[32] It remained a theoretical idea of remarkable simplicity. But while satisfying the requirements of the theory of competitive price, it nevertheless reduced the entrepreneur to a passive buyer of services and seller of goods, making no room for the kind of innovative drives described by Schumpeter.

Pricing occurred in each sector of the economy—consumer goods, factor services, land, and capital goods. But the major concern was with the flow of services or income stemming from assets. There were at least thirteen different kinds of assets in Walras' catalogue: [33] landed capital, personal capital, capital goods, all yielding consumer services; three like categories yielding productive services; new capital goods, temporarily unable to provide income; stocks of income goods held by consumers; raw materials; new income goods; cash holdings; and savings.[34] All these comprised the elements of a complex economic tableau which depicted the flow of income in a closed system. The process of "crying out" represented tentative bids and offers, so that producers and consumers could withdraw from the market if they so wished.

As a description of the economic process, this was certainly an heroic abstraction, issuing in a complicated structure of mathematical analysis. Four problems were evident: services, products, and capital goods had to be priced in terms of the *numéraire,* and there was, of course, the *numéraire* itself. The equilibrium process was not only stable, but could be upset only by some external shock. By itself, it moved irresistibly toward that price which would clear the market. The system was described by several sets of equations. There were the demand equations which expressed consumer bids not only as functions of the price of the goods in question, but of all other consumer goods as well. Then came the cost equations, and on the assumption that prices varied directly with costs, one could obtain a series of equations in which price was equal to the outlays for productive services. Quantity equations then described the relation between the stock of available productive services and the quantity utilized for each good. The prices of the productive services also established the technical coefficients, or the production function, so that the lowest cost combinations would be employed in working up a firm's output. Further, the use of productive services was dependent on the prices of goods as well as on the prices of services. Thus, there were x goods; $x-1$ prices (not counting the *numéraire*); y productive services; y prices of productive services; xy coefficients; $x-1$ demand equations; x cost equations; y quantity equations for the productive services; and y supply equations. An interdependent economic model was consequently constructed in which demand, cost, productive services, and production functions were closely related one to the other. The quantities of available goods were matched by the demand equations, prices were matched by costs, and productive services by their quantity equations. The whole apparatus, extended also to intermediate goods, became the basis for all subsequent work in general equilibrium analysis.

That it was genuinely applicable to problems of modern industry was another matter. The logic of the system stemmed from the logic of simultaneous equations, suggesting that a set of given conditions would inevitably determine its consequences. The construction exhibited an "as if" character, and implied that not only did consumers know their demand functions when they entered the market, but that supply functions, technical coefficients, and all other required data as well were equally available. The solution was worked out in virtually automatic fashion in a lively auction by atomistic economic units operating under conditions of free competition. From the way in which Walras developed the theory, it was evident that factors were deemed to be continuously divisible and that perfectly fluid movement was to be attributed to them. The purity of the model required abstraction from its institutional setting, yet there was no denying the relevancy of information stemming from the latter. For example, the total stock of a good could affect its market supply; the distribution of wealth and income clearly could influence the amount of productive services that would find its way to the market; and the desire for leisure could influence the flow of labor services offered for sale. All this, however, was separate and apart from the inherent logic of the Walrasian equations. They appeared in a separate compartment, lest the quality of pure economics be disturbed.

In reality, a good case could be made for the argument that the data entering into the equilibrium equations were not independent of the underlying institutional forces. And the abstract quality of the system could not help but be revealed in rather strong outline when contrasted with Walras' applied and social economics. While he had intended his pure theory to be a set of statements regarding the basic movements in an economy, it unfortunately took on the coloration of a prescription; for it did lead to the conclusion that the methods of price determination it set forth would maximize satisfactions and welfare. The Walrasian apparatus could be described also as a neutral one, able to describe price determination in any economy. Ironically, in spite of its deficiencies, non-Marxian socialist theory has made effective use of just the sort of economics Walras developed.

The theory of exchange, first presented in terms of two commodities,[35] was the basis for Walras' formal structure. Implicit in it was the assumption that the consumer would always seek maximum utility. Walras' formulation of marginal utility may certainly be said to have been more precise than Jevons', and, though introduced after the discussion of exchange, was actually the foundation for the general equilibrium theory. Not only was marginal utility virtually self-evident, but it was measurable as well. Theorists after Walras, however, troubled by the notion of comparability and measurability, simply avoided the question as not really essential to analysis, although in recent years measurability has been reintroduced, notably in game theory.[36] That cardinal utility was difficult to defend did not trouble Walras. The analysis was modified so that all that was required was to *order* utilities within a given range of preferences without necessarily measuring them.[37]

While Lesson 9 of the *Éléments* presented the possibilities for equilibrium with two goods, the case of general equilibrium for several commodities was developed in Lessons 11 to 14. There were the equations for individuals: there were also market equations, in which the quantities exchanged also had to be equal. Since the last market equation was not independent, it had to be removed from the system. With the number of equations now equal to the number of unknowns, a solution could be obtained simultaneously. It might be noted that Gustav Cassel, the Swedish economist, described a similar apparatus.[38] But while Walras employed utility functions from which he obtained his market equations, Cassel assumed the market equations as given. He did this on the ground that utility was not a measurable concept: only price and quantity, he argued, could provide a basis for measurement.

Since the market process implied the existence of reservation prices, it was also possible that no solution would be available.[39] There was only a tendency toward market equilibrium, and in the market for productive services this was carried on through the *tâtonnement*. Here Walras introduced an additional device, the *bons* or chits, which entrepreneurs used as provisional contracts in buying and selling goods and services. The *bons* were made final only if prices were actually at equilibrium. Otherwise, they would not be redeemed and a process of recontracting would occur.[40] The device was rather ingenious, for it obviated the need to trace the path along which market prices might move in the search for equilibrium.[41] When viewed together with the *tâtonnement,* the chits became nothing more than a technique for carrying through trial-and-error price setting. One might be tempted to say that Walras was on the verge of introducing dynamic economics into his static analysis. Yet the whole business had a remarkable air of fantasy and unreality. The *bons* were imaginary figments that added little if anything to the analytical apparatus. Moreover, it has been argued that Walras did not really prove that his system of equations had a unique solution. It was mathematically possible that there might be several solutions or even none at all. That is to say, an imbalance in the economy might not be rectified by a return to the original state of grace.[42] It was left to others, notably Vilfredo Pareto, to attempt a tracing of the path of equilibrium through variations in the successive static states.

On the other hand, Walras anticipated much of contemporary theory when he came to capital and capital formation. He was concerned with establishing the rate at which the capital value of a flow of income was determined, and this, of course, depended on the rate of capital formation. The latter was also the basis for interest and was conditioned by the prices of capital goods. Said Walras: "Values of capital goods are rigorously proportioned to their net incomes." The theory of capital had to make room for depreciation and a premium for insurance.[43] Presumably, these were set by certain fixed technical relations. Since capital goods were subject to price determination, there had to be a market for them. Walras generally utilized the three standard categories for factor analysis, but in the case of capital he spoke of landed capital used as consumer goods, or residential land; personal capital employed in consumption, as with servants; capital per se, or housing; land in production; personal capital applied to production, that is, labor; and capital itself employed in production, that is, factories and equipment.[44] Net saving, in Walras' construction, was equal to investment, since saving was simply the demand for capital goods. But the equilibrium condition was not this identity: it was, rather, the equality of saving to the costs of producing capital goods. If this relation did not hold at any given time, a movement would ensue toward expansion or curtailment of output.

Since the value of capital goods was proportional to their net incomes, all capital goods were essentially alike, thus enabling Walras to reduce the whole complex to a single price from which a perpetual net income could be secured.[45] In effect, this apportioned the demand for new capital goods among the various industries so that the net value of their output was equal to the costs of the products. The theory, applied to both consumer and producer durables, was based on the drive toward maximum want-satisfaction by those who supplied the savings and those who demanded the services of new capital goods. There were limits, of course, imposed by depreciation charges and insurance.[46] Thus, a theory of capital goods prices was developed which encompassed all types of capital. Interest was also included, even though its movements were but occasional: interest reacted to changes in the values of capital goods, so that again it was the price mechanism that motivated entrepreneurial behavior. The rate of interest was somewhat passive and almost disappeared.

At certain key points, the capital theory was patently weak. Wicksell later argued that raw materials and goods in process were as much a form of capital as fixed equipment. Advances by entrepreneurs to workers and landowners also could be considered as forms of capital. Thus Walras' theory, since it was applied only to fixed capital,[47] seemed incomplete. Equilibrium ought to require the rate of net income to be equal for all types of capital, for prices in all cases had to be equal to their costs. Further, as Enrico Barone pointed out to Walras, interest was important by virtue of the entrepreneur's need for a quantity of *numéraire*.[48]

The services of land, labor, and capital had to be allocated, and the description of how this was done stemmed from the theory of production.[49] Since the productive services were called into action via the price mechanism, the analysis could be nothing more than one of price determination. Again, Walras employed his general equilibrium model, with bids and offers "cried out," supplemented by the devices of *tâtonnement* and *bons*. In order to establish the principle of equilibrium, the element of time was at first excluded.[50] Of course, this came dangerously close to making capital goods

and their services synonymous. At any rate, given the demands of consumers, entrepreneurs presumably sought to obtain certain services in order
to meet these demands. With fixed resources, there was no waste, for any goods
that were not utilized could be taken over by the producers themselves.[51]
This simplified the problem of relating the equational system stemming from
the production sector to the demands of consumers. The mathematical construction was quite the same as in the theory of exchange: the entrepreneur
was a buyer of productive services and seller of goods; he merely had to follow the applicable technical coefficients. There were no lags or bottlenecks in
production. Only the solution of a new set of simultaneous equations was
necessary. With equilibrium, consumers, having offered their services, were
satisfied with their earnings, for the prices of productive services were determined coterminously with the prices of commodities. Just as demand was
the function of all prices, so the price of a productive service was a function
of the prices of all goods and other services. In this way it was possible to
derive aggregate demand and aggregate supply functions.[52]

The technical coefficients, or production functions, affected the price and
cost equations. By virtue of their impact on price, they implicitly entered
into all the other equations as well. In Walras' formulation, they were linear
homogeneous, or of the first degree, so that a proportionate increase in
productive services would yield an equally proportionate increase in output.
This meant an economy of constant returns, for otherwise equilibrium could
be upset when one entrepreneur pushed ahead of the others. And this could
destroy perfect competition, since the more aggressive firms would develop
advantages over the others and establish monopolistic conditions. Fixed coefficients of production, however, overlooked the fact that productive services
were often limited or that it was possible to substitute one factor for another
and so alter the economy's productivity. Pareto, on the other hand, visualized
a variety of possibilities; coefficients which varied with output or changes in
other coefficients, as well as fixed coefficients, were deemed possible. For
Walras, however, variations from the norms set by the fixed coefficients would
be rectified rather quickly. Increased demand would draw in more producers, while increased costs would curtail demand. The economy could
not depart from equilibrium for long.

All this was developed in full mathematical dress, but in a way that evidently does not fully satisfy contemporary mathematical economists. Logical
difficulties kept cropping up in Walras' formulas. It could be asked whether
production does exhibit the instantaneous responses implied in the theory. Not
only does the real market have no *bons* or "cries," but there is frequently a
good deal of ordinary guesswork based on all sorts of expectations. Somewhat dissatisfied with the notion of fixed coefficients, Walras later sought, not
very successfully, to convert them into variables. The points of equilibrium
still remained a series of static positions.

Variations in the technical coefficients, however, became the basis for Walras' version of marginal productivity. In fact, he may be said to have been one of the co-discoverers of this theorem. Adjustments of total demand to supply at first could be made only by altering the number of firms, which were theoretically the same size and possessed the ability to move easily from one industry to the next. But with capital formation and economic growth, such a proposition no longer could be tolerated in the theory, and a new production function was required so that firms might substitute one factor for another. Marginal productivity then became a device to determine the size of the variable coefficients. Two propositions comprised marginal productivity: first, that cost of production would be at a minimum under conditions of free competition; and second, that the prices of the productive services were proportional to their marginal productivities in equilibrium, with marginal productivity defined mathematically as the partial derivative of the production function.[53] This was a notable refinement of the problem of equilibrium, with prices for the firm now essentially a parameter.

Walras did not develop the marginal productivity theory until the fourth edition of the *Éléments* and only after he had discussed his ideas with Barone and indulged in polemics with Wicksteed. But the theory exhibited no genuine dynamic quality, again appearing as a series of static states. Coefficients were altered and a new equilibrium established only when capital and population increased. The presentation was quite obscure, and it has continued to puzzle commentators down to the present.[54] As finally unraveled by Jaffé, the marginal productivity theorem revealed that the total cost of producing a given output was at a minimum when the production function was so set that marginal productivity would be proportional to the prices of productive services.[55] If this meant that the prices of factor services were established by marginal productivity, a common interpretation, then what Walras had done was to create a theory of distribution. While he insisted that distribution of income depended ultimately on the distribution of wealth, it was evident that in his view, at least theoretically, the total product would be divided among the factors in accordance with their prices. This was the theorem of product exhaustion. Proportionality of marginal productivity to prices held for any output and was not connected with producers' efforts to maximize profit. Achieving minimum costs was to be attained by the usual process of groping, *tâtonnement*. Progress, therefore, had become a matter of reducing the marginal utilities of consumer goods consonant with increases in population. This meant simply a greater quantity of capital goods, assuming at the same time that such increases would be larger than those in population growth. Patently, this was not a satisfactory theory of growth, for it had failed to demonstrate what ratios of capital accumulation to total product were required for expansion, nor did it explore the impact of such elements as uncertainty. It was, at best, superficial.

When he came to rent theory, Walras demurred rather strongly from the views promulgated by Ricardo, asserting that the latter's theory made sense only on the assumptions that wages and interest were constant and "predetermined." [56] Classical analysis, said Walras, failed to compare rents over different intervals of time, nor did it explain variations in rent in a changing economy. At best, it merely accounted for differential rent at a given moment, taking into account alternative possibilities for capital. Moreover, even marginal lands commanded a price by virtue of the fact of ownership and so had to enter into the prices of productive services. Rent, therefore, was more than a differential payment, for it underlay differences in the quality of resources, thus affecting price quite as much as did wages. The only problem was that these resources were fixed in supply, said Walras. This approach, however, which exhibited some features of the older theory of absolute rent, failed to make much impression, and the Ricardian version was to prevail.[57]

Nor was Walras' interest theory as well worked out as it might have been. This form of income arose in situations of capital accumulation, since entrepreneurs in an expanding economy had to borrow money in order to finance their ventures. Consequently, the capital and credit market had to be introduced into the model of general equilibrium, with interest defined as the price of savings. Since price and cost were to be equated, interest as well as depreciation had to be included in the prices of producers' and consumers' goods. Quite naturally, the setting for the expanded model was a progressive economy with uninterrupted growth in capital accumulation.[58] New capital goods were to be exchanged against net savings, so that the conditions of equality between the value of net capital accumulation and net savings would yield the equation for determining the rate of growth and the prices of capital equipment. The quantity equations were similarly derived. The possibility of disinvestment was excluded.[59] Wicksell was the first to question this formulation, contending that even in a stationary economy interest would appear, especially with regard to circulating capital. In Walras' scheme, capital values were proportional to net revenues at a given rate of interest, which was defined as the ratio of perpetual net income to the value of capital. Thus the exchanges that took place in the capital market were between the contending perpetual net incomes. Interest, in a sense, became a source for investment. With free consumer choice, it was the demand equation which ultimately determined the types of capital equipment that would be produced. Interest was then proportional to the demand for consumer goods and proportional as well to the demand for productive services. Therefore, it provided for saving as well as serving as a capital rationing device.

The first edition of the *Élements,* published in 1877, contained several chapters on money, and was followed by the *Theory of Money* in 1886. The latter, revised in 1898, was then included in the *Theory of Applied Political Economy.* Walras further revised his exposition for the fourth edition of the

Élements, so that what appears in Lessons 29 and 30 is his final statement on the theory of money. The earliest versions began with a money function which stressed the consumer's concern with the goods he sought on the market. The marginal utility of money referred to its uses as a commodity with purchasing power. Later formulations, however, were based on a kind of cash balance approach, analogous to that developed in Britain. The theory was applied to money *qua* money, so that the marginal utility analysis now seemed unnecessary. The equations involving the "price" of money brought interest into the picture, and the usual process of groping toward equilibrium was employed. By the time of the fourth edition marginal utility was reintroduced in more explicit fashion, so that monetary theory once more was fused to the general equilibrium analysis. The equation of money was now

. . . deduced rationally from the equation of exchange and maximum satisfaction as well as from the equations showing equality between the demand and offer of circulating capital goods. In this way, the *theory of circulation and money,* like the *theories of exchange, production, capital formation, and credit,* not only posits, but solves the relevant system of equations.[60]

The need for cash balances arose when it was no longer assumed that consumers had to wait for goods, for with supplies immediately available there was a need to have cash on hand. But since consumers might be aware of delivery dates, it was not clear why cash balances should be required. Certainty would seem to have eliminated the need to hold cash. As was pointed out by some commentators, Walras' explanation of cash balances seemed somewhat inadequate. At any rate, the displacement of the *numéraire* by money per se did not presumably upset the system's stability. Money holdings could be related to marginal utility and became an important element of the circulatory process. As goods moved forward, cash flowed backward. With credit, circulatory capital, and repayments the equilibrium model became even more complex. But at least all elements of the economy were now coordinated. With a demand for money, there was also a market for money. It was just another productive service for which an equilibrium price had to be established. Since the "price" of money affected all other equations and therefore all quantities, money had become an active element in the economy, for the desire to hold cash depended on the totality of transactions.[61] Walras' theory was certainly not based on barter, but was integrated quite effectively into his general system.[62] The relationships that he finally worked out made prices the results of money-flows, so that receipts and expenditures could be expressed in money. Sales proceeds flowed through entrepreneurs toward the factors of production and became income to be spent once again on products. It was an extraordinary tableau, of infinite complexity, exhibiting a fine and delicate capacity for relating the various sectors of the economy to each other.[63]

Certainly Walras' performance was a remarkable intellectual accomplishment. It underscored the notion of mutual interdependence, going so far as to depict how such interdependence was achieved and sustained. But it failed to show how the economy grew, or how fundamental social and economic relationships were altered. It was a system devoid of human beings functioning in a complex social matrix. The factors of production remained what they had been throughout all such systems—abstract categories unmoved by the forces that give an economy its characteristic motion.

Time, uncertainty, growth, innovation, liquidity-preference, accretions to investment, taste, advertising, and the business cycle were nowhere to be found in such a system.[64] Economics thus became a science of exchange, buttressed by a mechanical technique of maximizing satisfactions. As Milton Friedman has said, the Walrasian model was a form of analysis without much substance. Indeed, the bare framework seemed hardly enough to provide a viable economic science; something would have to be said about the content of the relationships which Walras had described.[65] In Walras' system, for example, each good and productive service was to have its own equation, so that with 10,000 goods and 1,000 factors there would have to be 21,999 equations. For the whole economy the number of equations would be immense: empirical research, consequently, would have to group data in order to make economic investigation manageable. Nor was it really possible to say much about marginal utility: the shift to the ordinal approach seemed inevitable. Even more important was the fact that the analysis had little to say about joint and multiple products, an almost fatal defect.[66] It may very well be that the institutionalists are right: perhaps more psychology and history and sociology are necessary if we are to grasp the true nature of the human animal. Mathematics, queen of the sciences, was shown to need some additional workers.

Moreover, any theory of free competition in the modern context does exhibit strange normative overtones, even though it may seek to establish a straightforward positive quality. By doing so, it becomes merely another variant of utopianism, for the economic world is no longer one comprised of innumerable small units. Although writers of the equilibrium persuasion are reluctant to admit it, overhead costs, large-scale production, administered pricing, and the dominance of the corporations are the realities, and a useful economic theory ought to take cognizance of these new and often puzzling conditions. As a guide to policy, equilibrium under free competition remains less than adequate. While the institutionalists may have resembled Leacock's horseman, riding off in all directions at once, they were at least aware that a fire was raging somewhere. Equilibrium economists, on the other hand, enamored as they are with the delicate concatenation of economic categories, seem unwilling to raise questions of immediate pertinence. Like all pure systems, Walras' economics is not genuinely operational: the conditions that would uphold his equations no longer exist. In the words of John Kenneth

Galbraith, many parts of the economic order are in virtual disequilibrium. Walras' failure to ask questions which were genuinely pertinent for *political* economy can explain in large measure the schizoid gap that existed between his pure and practical economics. While in the latter realm he was a mild sort of socialist, this had little to do with his elaborate mathematical constructions. Equilibrium theory of the Walrasian type, which has been the basis for a good deal of theoretical work in modern economics, has not considered how a balanced economy might be attained in a system where technology is complex and changing and where the corporation, with its oligopolistic habits, predominates. These problems, which raise virtually all the major economic questions of the day, can find little place in such a theory.

ii

Vilfredo Pareto: Science as Sermon

The tradition initiated by bourgeois liberal Léon Walras was continued in very capable fashion by aristocrat Vilfredo Pareto (1848-1923). No two individuals could have exhibited more disparate outlooks: Walras, something of a congenital optimist in his social thinking, proposed measures that were direct reflections of nineteenth-century ideas of perpetual and even progress, while Pareto more and more despaired of the possibilities of a rational society. Walras' social ideals stemmed from utilitarianism: Pareto went beyond laissez faire to suggest the purest form of individualism. He too had imbibed the heady drink of liberal doctrine flowing from Spencer and Darwin, but the overwhelming tide of governmental interference in the affairs of men had converted him into the dour pessimist and Machiavellian devotée who composed the immense and dark sociological tract, *Trattato di sociologia generale*,[67] in which men were either cunning foxes or brutal lions.

The details of Pareto's life are known but in the rough. Few intimate word portraits are available and the occasional studies suffer from a paucity of biographical data.[68] Born in Paris of French and Italian parentage, his father had been a *marchese* whose espousal of Mazzini's political views kept him in exile for many years. The followers of Mazzini had been humanitarian democrats—believers in progress and social harmony and in the perfectability of man—a philosophy that Pareto was to reject violently. When the liberal democrats were caught between the grinders of government politics and left-wing opposition, many of them, disillusioned, simply had adapted themselves to life under the monarchy. This left Pareto with a hatred for all their works and a disgust that permeated all of his writing. The family was permitted to return to Italy in 1858 where Pareto received his education. Trained as a mathematician and engineer, he worked for a number of years for the Italian railroads, and when the government nationalized the rail lines his hostility to the elder Pareto's ideology was heightened. He caustically described the government as a "pluto-democracy." Following his post on the railroads, Pareto was employed by an iron and steel concern, which he served in the capacity of director. He was able to travel extensively over the Continent, and quickly acquired a solid grounding in the practical side of economic affairs. Early in his career, Pareto tried political activity but was beaten in his first campaign. Thereafter, he saw the government reject all efforts to institute a policy of economic liberalism. A parliamentary majority was maintained by the usual tactics of corruption and log-rolling. Pareto first attacked protectionist policies, then the government, and finally its leading politicians: they retaliated by prohibiting his lectures and denying him a university post. There was relief on both sides when he finally left Italy in 1893.

Pareto's interests were quite broad, covering the fields of ancient history, philosophy, sociology, linguistics, and religion as well as mathematics and economics. His erudition, reflected in virtually all his writings, revealed a powerful affinity for the kind of liberalism that was later so characteristic of a Mises or Hayek. Economic liberalism was an attractive doctrine in Italy during the 1870's and 1880's. But the influence of the German historical writers was also visible, especially in the work of Maffeo Pantaleoni, who had encouraged both Pareto and Enrico Barone to pursue the study of economics. In fact, it was Pantaleoni who had recommended Pareto to Walras when the latter was searching for a successor at Lausanne. In 1890, Pareto inherited a sizable fortune and retired from business to follow his own interests. When Walras invited him to take over his chair of political economy in 1893, Pareto was happy to leave the detested Italian parliamentary system behind.[69] The struggle for unification in the 1860's had left the country spiritually exhausted, and Italy seemed to him an intellectual desert. Moreover, he had been unable to find an academic post in his own country, and the political disturbances that were to plague Italy after 1893 were events he was glad to escape.[70]

Walras and Pareto, however, were never friendly. Walras was a middle-class reformer by temperament, while Pareto was an embittered nobleman to whom democracy and corruption were synonymous. Such a violent reaction against the democratic aspects of the Mazzini movement clearly stemmed from his revolt against parental influences. Humanitarians for Pareto were "animal pests," and special scorn was reserved for demagogues and others who profited from democratic forms of government. His interest in economics had been exhibited as early as 1877 when he lectured on economic logic, and his views on economic policy were strong and bluntly stated. With his aristocratic background, he found it difficult to accommodate himself to the institutions of the middle class. An alienated soul, he was, nevertheless, like Veblen and Marx, a product of the civilization he despised, even though his reactions were markedly different from theirs.[71] The Lausanne appointment started Pareto on a second career, that of economic theorist. Following Walras' pattern, he lectured on pure economics one semester and on applied economics the next. A heart condition enforced his retirement in 1906, and for seventeen years he worked at his estate near Celigny on Lake Geneva developing his system of sociology. Although the quality of mind that he had developed in his early training as an engineer stayed with him and was fully evident in both his economics and sociology, he was not particularly successful as an empirical researcher. He could never completely shed Spencer, and most of his facts came out of the books in his large and copious library. Field investigation was beyond him, so that Paretian sociology can be described as essentially speculative.[72] He became the "lone thinker of Celigny," looking out upon a world he despised, composing acerb thoughts disguised as science. So far as Pareto was concerned, civilization was in utter decay. He was a Cassandra to whom no one would listen; he finally came to feel that he was merely an objective bystander expressing impartial judgments on both men and society.

In his old age, with full beard, wearing a flowing cloak and surrounded by at least two dozen cats, Pareto maintained a lonely existence at his villa in Celigny. Like his pets, he was "independent, feline and proud," a lover of form and capable of showing his teeth when displeased. A congenital rebel, he welcomed those who were in conflict with their government. His imagined enemies were numerous: democrats, Pan-Germans, temperance ladies, prudes, and those of his countrymen who treated his works with silence. And so he continued to work away at his theory of society, putting examples of cat behavior into his sociology and living with aristocratic disdain for the world from which he had come.

He was made a Senator by Mussolini and though the Italian Fascists drew some inspiration from his theory of the élite, it is unlikely that Pareto cared much for them. This was probably because he disliked ideologues. Yet, in the final analysis his social science, both economics and sociology, was as much ideological as any other. Paretian economics exerted no small influence, especially in Italy, and his sociology enjoyed a temporary vogue in the United States in the 1920's and 1930's. Some of Pareto's economic techniques have found their way even into standard textbooks, notably the indifference curve analysis which he adapted from Francis Y. Edgeworth, the British mathematical economist. If these had been his only contributions, Pareto would still deserve notice; but added to them was the more highly refined version of general equilibrium analysis which provided one of the major points of departure for modern economic thinking. It was this that made him a major figure in the development of the science.

In celebrating the twenty-fifth anniversary of his Lausanne professorship, Pareto remarked that his attempt to go beyond pure economics stemmed from a feeling that the theory of mutual interdependence had not successfully isolated the various genres of social phenomena. Economics had come to an impasse, for many of its conclusions, he admitted, could not be verified by experience. It was this lack of correspondence that had impelled him to undertake further inquiry and to move from the realm of pure economic theory to that of sociology.[73] This sense of failure was buttressed by the collapse of economic liberalism which Pareto had espoused with such passionate force. For, despite the dire prediction of all the free trade liberals, Italy's protectionist policies did not seem to harm the country. Logically, pure economics and the programs it had suggested appeared irrefutable. Yet something must have been omitted, said Pareto. The gap could be filled he decided, only by sociological investigations, for the nonliberal actions were patently nonlogical—residues or sentiments, expressing the fears, phobias, and myths of mankind. Having classified all the logical categories of behavior in his pure economics, it only remained for him to uncover the nature of nonlogical action.[74]

Many of the ideas for Pareto's sociology grew out of his earlier critiques of socialism and Marxism. In essence, his *Les Systèmes Socialistes* represented a bridge between his pure economics and sociology.[75] The demolition of Marxism as economics and social theory was a great intellectual pastime in the latter part of the nineteenth century, and Pareto engaged in it with much relish and with greater skill than most. As he fired away at socialist theory from the positivist heights built by Spencer and Comte, his brilliant polemic was pointed enough to give official Marxists good cause for worry. Yet the Paretian critique failed to encompass a complete analysis of the Marxian system. In fact, it was possible to conclude from Pareto's economics that socialism was logically feasible, since it could provide for maximum utility in virtually the same way as any competitive system. Moreover, by virtue of its ability to cover fixed costs through general taxation, it was possible to regard socialism as even more effective than capitalism.[76] Nevertheless, argued Pareto, socialists failed to take into account the problem of resource allocation, and, insofar as they failed to do so, they were merely behaving as utopians. The allocation of economic resources required a market and pricing mechanism, argued Pareto, and without it socialists would have to engage in centralized decision-making.

This was not Pareto's first involvement in socialist theory. In 1893, the year he went to Lausanne, he had written a critical introduction to an abridged version of *Das Kapital* prepared by Marx's son-in-law, Paul Lafargue. The two-volume attack came eight years later. He dismissed any claim to scientific validity in Marxism. But while its logic was worthless, said Pareto, Marxism was important because it issued from genuinely important social situations. In effect, this was the start of Pareto's sociology in which he saw social reality as composed of a host of myths, sentiments, and beliefs that were themselves frequently untrue and irrational. Yet, said Pareto, there was a kernel of truth in Marx, particularly in his sociology of class conflict, which had the virtue of inspiring practical courses of action.[77] This, it seemed to Pareto, offered the beginning of a viable social theory, despite its vagueness. Nevertheless, Pareto claimed, Marxism misled the vulgar by its passion and seduced the learned by its supposed logic. It was moral fervor alone that made Marx so attractive. At any rate, Pareto conceded that the materialist interpretation of history exhibited some attributes of a scientific theory.[78] But, said he, giving his interpretation an odd twist, this view of history had only a sentimental attachment to socialist ideas. The class struggle was an objective historical fact independent of the special coloration given to it by socialists. Marxian ideology might be necessary to the socialist as religion to a peasant, he said, but it had precious little to do with the fact of social tension and conflict.[79]

The struggle that Pareto visualized was not between "proletariat and bourgeoisie," but between new élites, persons of superior ability determined to win power for themselves, and old entrenched élites. The mass of people were like the "proles" of George Orwell's *1984*—dumb beasts doing the fighting for different masters. Slogans of justice and humanity were useful devices for moving the masses, and no doubt they believed in them deeply. But the fundamental struggle was for power to be exercised by an élite.[80] Even a collectivist society would be witness to social struggles: the Marxist notion of a peaceful classless state was an illusion.[81] Certainly, later history upheld Pareto on at least this point: the Soviet Union has supplied ample evidence of conflict in a collectivist state. Nor did he see socialism as an inevitable successor to capitalism, for like Veblen, Pareto believed that historical possibilities were infinite. Thus, as Stuart Hughes has said, Marx was stood on his head [82] and historical materialism given a conservative bias quite to the liking of Mussolini's intellectual apologists.

In the realm of sociology and political theory, Pareto was a direct descendant of Machiavelli.[83] The Machiavellian quality in his thought derived from an unshakeable belief in the division between peoples and rulers, in his depiction of coercion and fraud as essential bedfellows to government, and in the prediction that all political institutions were bound to flounder. In many ways Pareto's views became a more generalized version of Sorel's theory of social myth. Sentiments and irrational beliefs were considered the prime movers of human action. Since the élites, which contended with each other for superior positions, were innately better than the rest of the populace, it was to be expected that they would want to attain power. Political activity came mainly from small interested groups while, even in popular government, the mass of people remained passive.

The theory became a general one, describing in effect all human behavior. Residues, the virtually instinctive motives of action, and derivations, the non-logical rationalizations that men constructed to justify the residues, were applied to the totality of man's life, including wars and religion as well as statecraft. Although the rationalizations might seem more important and more interesting, it was the constant and unchanging residues, Pareto urged, that were basic. He supported his theory with a flood of illustrations gathered through an enormous appetite for reading, a pastime to which he resorted to fill long waking hours induced by insomnia.

While the residues were constant, the derivations changed rapidly and differed from era to era and nation to nation. Thus the common factors in human experience were the residues. But these were sociological categories, rather than psychological or biological ones. Yet, by forcing his attention on sentiments and residues, Pareto could not help but underscore the psychological aspects of business behavior. Pareto listed six main groups of residues: combinations of residues or sentiments thought to be efficacious; persisting relations of men to men and men to things; residues of expression, such as religion; residues of sociability, of which self-sacrifice was an example; residues concerned with preserving the integrity of the individual; and sexual residues. These then were the nonlogical patterns of human behavior. The derivations, on the other hand, expressed man's desire to think and to justify the residues. Sometimes logical, although often unscientific, they related one residue to the others as devices for establishing sanctions. Of the derivations there were four: assertions; appeals to authority; conversion of sentiments into principles; and verbal proofs, which were often based on emotive expressions and the employment of ambiguities. But the derivatives were not the organs of social change; this was the function of the residues.

Although Pareto's sociology enjoyed a limited popularity after World War I, and while some of its self-evident truths are generally acknowledged, few persons today take it seriously as a systematic theory. It was nevertheless a remarkable performance—at an age when most men have just enough energy to tend their gardens, Pareto had set out to explore a new body of ideas. Said he:

The main objective of my studies was always to apply to social science, of which economics is but a part, the experimental method which has given such brilliant results in the natural sciences. . . . Human activity is comprised of two principal branches: that of sentiment and that of experimental research. One cannot exaggerate the importance of the first. It is sentiment which gives impetus to action, establishes rules of morality, devotion and religion in all their varying and complex forms. Human society subsists and progresses by the aspirations of ideals. But the second branch is also essential for society; it furnishes the material that sets the first to work. We derive from it the knowledge that makes efficacious the action and usefulness of sentiment, which itself adapts slowly to the environment.[84]

Nevertheless, Pareto failed to probe the structure of sentiments and residues; the sort of inquiry developed by Freud was alien to him.[85] Similarly, the concept of *Verstehen,* which underpinned much of German sociology, was unknown to him; he probably would have rejected it anyway, for such a notion implied a concern with value systems. As a result, the residues were neither fish nor fowl. At times they appeared as instincts rooted in biology; at other times they were little more than forms of action. The six residues were really abstract taxonomies, with illustrative material arbitrarily assigned to each. They were imposed on the data, rather than developed out of Pareto's vast conglomerate of historical facts. The theory, consequently, became merely formal social mechanics.[86] Pareto's assertion that his sociology was based on analogical thinking was not convincing, for at no time did he really examine the character of his residues, as might have been done with a genetic method. The assortment of facts, as Stuart Hughes has remarked, simply were illustrations of Pareto's own prejudices.

The admission that ritualistic behavior performed a useful role suggested some awareness of the centrality of value. Moreover, the residues and derivations acquired genuine meaning only when placed in a political context. In fact, his whole system of sociology and economics, addressed in the final analysis to political questions, demonstrated a complete lack of the neutrality which Pareto had hoped to attain. As an objective exercise in social theory, his sociology was simply not successful. It did contain some useful insights: the residues drew attention to the irrational quality of behavior, and the derivations suggested that ideology was a large component of man's thinking. But none of this was really new. Only as a critic of social forms did Pareto stand out. Fundamentally, his theory was "a political manifesto in scientific guise" with an irresistible appeal to authoritarian groups. Italian Fascists were not remiss in grasping the point.[87]

When the residues were finally reduced to their two basic categories, one arrived at Machiavelli's symbols of the fox and the lion. The fox, typified by "combinations of residues," ruled by cunning. The lion, on the other hand, exhibiting the "persistence of aggregates—" as did all idealists, revolutionists, and zealots—ruled by force. Out of this contrast came a cyclical theory of social change.[88] When the foxes ruled, the concern was with immediate ends. But as the residues that sustained them were weakened, a condition of social disequilibrium set in. Then new élites with the attributes of lions began to seek power. On the economic level, struggle ensued between rentiers and entrepreneurs. Social conflict affected the intellectual superstructure, with skepticism predominant among the foxes and faith motivating the lions. In Pareto's view, it was high time for some new lions to come upon the scene to overthrow the foxes of plutocratic democracy.

The movement of history was reflected in the movement of élites.[89] New élites were always desirable, for they were courageous and forceful and quickly disposed of the chicanery of the old. The tragedy was that eventually they too would rule by the cunning of the fox. Thus force, struggle, and revolution were the prime movers of society.[90] The theory of the circulation of the élites was, in effect, a theory of change, of society's growth and decay, in the same pattern as the theories of Spengler and Toynbee—just the sort of myth that could serve a Mussolini.[91] When applied to society as a whole, Pareto's theory became one of social utility or welfare. Individuals were required to conform to certain standards set by particular derivations. Moral philosophy became a series of connected derivations which assured social equilibrium. Whenever the latter was threatened, forces were called into play to restore the balance.[92] Pareto did not observe that such balances were perpetually upset by the circulation of élites. Nor did he successfully apply mathematics to these social concepts. The hope that the methods of physics would yield equally good results in social science was not fulfilled.

The economic equilibrium which Pareto developed was but one facet of the more general equilibrium which was admittedly conditioned by political and sociological factors. A complete social science, therefore, would need postulates and data of historical and statistical character. But since sentiments pervaded everything, one could not rely solely on pure economics if the ultimate truth were to be discovered. The inference in Pareto's system was clear: only a complete study of society could satisfactorily solve problems of monopoly, trade unions, and other power blocs. The similarity to Comte's positive theory of society was obvious. By studying sentiments one could remove theology and metaphysics from economics and discover the nature of economic law. Once, when Gustav Schmoller challenged Pareto, saying that there were no economic laws, Pareto politely asked if there were any restaurants where one might eat for nothing. Schmoller disdainfully replied that one always had to pay something. That, retorted Pareto, was natural economic law.[93]

Turning to Pareto's economics, one finds that in its early formulation, it was merely a restatement of Walras, despite the fact that his outlook and philosophy were utterly different. The similarity is plainly evident in the *Cours d'économie politique*[94] and in the *Manuale d'economia politica*.[95] Of course, the basic similarity between the two was to be found in the theory of general equilibrium and in their espousal of the mathematical method. While the indifference curve technique created a new mode in economic analysis, the Paretian conception was that of a static general economic equilibrium which brought together all elements of the economic situation and solved all problems simultaneously. The solution was attained by opposing wants or tastes and obstacles or resources. Equilibrium exhibited the quality of a tableau, with time virtually absent. The exclusion of the time factor may have been deliberate, for Pareto felt that the study of static equilibrium was a necessary prelude to the study of all economic forces. The functions that related wants and resources had meaning only at equilibrium. Hopefully, the model might be made a dynamic one when time was introduced. But whatever dynamics there was in Pareto represented merely a succession of static states, and were largely appendages of historical and sociological material. In fact, when Pareto defined time periods in his economic relationships as being of very short duration, he unwittingly disposed of all dynamics. Such an analysis would compel one to resort to empirical statements outside the realm of pure economic doctrine, and in Pareto's hands these became abstractions derived from historical averages.[96] The concept of an unstable equilibrium and of continuous vibrations was suggestive of the closed-cycle, feed-back systems developed more recently by A. Tustin.[97] The relationships in Pareto's system, however, were to be interpreted subjectively as the actions of individuals, rather than as results arising from objective behavior. They were complex enough to require mathematical treatment, but the notion of the individual was always in the forefront. For example, with revenue and income curves as subjective concepts, the contrast of such notions in *ex ante* and *ex post* terms simply never occurred.

Unlike Walras' *Élements,* the *Cours* put mathematics into notes, allowing the argument to be followed without recourse to symbols and equations. The mathematics demonstrated that economic problems might be solved and that they were determinate. Accordingly, the Paretian method implied a rejection of Walras' *tâtonnements,* since the latter had failed to emphasize a single, unique point of equilibrium. The organization of the *Cours* was somewhat chaotic, with the theory of equilibrium preceded by a long discussion of methodology and then followed by several unrelated chapters on applied economics. It contained frequent *obiter dicta* on social and political questions which seemed quite out of place in the light of Pareto's desire to develop a purely neutral theory. In fact, many of his observations had a distinctly normative character which provided the seeds of his subsequent sociology. Society, said Pareto, was ruled by two sets of forces, one coercive and the other automatic: progress consisted in suppressing the first and advancing the second. It was all too easy for him to identify the coercive elements with the actions of parliamentary governments.

Dissatisfied with the word "utility," Pareto introduced the seemingly neutral term *ophélimité*—which meant simply the desirability of a good. And marginal utility became *ophélimité élémentaire.* Why the new term should have been so much better than the older was not clear. Pareto's main point seemed to be that marginal utility did not depend solely on the quantity of the good in question, but, in accordance with the general principle of interdependence, was related also to the total stock of all other goods. With the total utility of all goods presented as a function of the total supply of all goods, marginal utility could be more effectively related to an additional unit of the good in question. In this way, Pareto was beginning to establish an equilibrium system in the broadest possible sense. But, as Schumpeter showed, this conception of marginal utility was difficult to translate into appropriate mathematical terms, for this meant dealing with partial derivatives, thus unnecessarily complicating the whole analysis.[98] Pareto insisted, however, that by assuming the fact of choice and employing mathematical logic, one could establish a truly general theory of economics. One could then deduce . . .

the special theories which are valid for communities where there is free competition, which are monopolistic and where collective property is established, etc. In short, imagine any economic order applied to society: there will always be a first set of problems related to finding out whether such an order can, in practice, be created and what are its relations to law, morality, etc. And then there will be another problem, which is to investigate the economic effects of the order in question. Now, our general theory has nothing to say as to the first set of problems (it being entirely outside the slice of phenomenon that we are studying); but the said theory enables us entirely to solve the second problem.[99]

The notion that maximum utility was obtainable only under a régime of free competition received rather sharp criticism from Wicksell.[100] The Swedish writer had argued that not only was it necessary to take prevailing prices into account, but that the standards of free competition did not preclude workers, for example, from improving their positions through concerted action, despite the fact that free competition might provide a maximum wage compatible with a given level of interest. That is, workers might be able to circumvent the strictures imposed by a freely competitive market. Pareto would go only so far as to assert that workers could enhance their situation by a refusal to work with certain equipment, thus in effect altering the production coefficient.[101]

Benedetto Croce, although not an economist, also attacked the utility notion.[102] To Croce, it was self-evident that economic facts and economic propositions were not neutral, since statements concerning economic behavior carried with them connotations of appraisal and approval. Therefore, said Croce, it was important to make thoroughly explicit the ethical elements in economics. Furthermore, choice itself was not the pure, colorless concept Pareto thought it to be, for, in any scale of preferences, the selection of a particular point rendered all the others "non-values." They no longer could be considered as part of the situation once a decision had been made; the concept of the alternative simply had no genuine meaning. Each choice created a new condition, and it was a fact that human activity was always preceded by other logical acts. That is to say, a genetic chain of events could be employed to explain economic acts. Pareto's response was at best weak: he asserted that he was interested in only a small slice of human action and that pure theory was the best method for examining these problems. The definition he gave to choice was most efficient, he insisted; like Occam's razor it dispensed with such extraneous matters as hedonic valuations. The important thing for him was whether the consequences of his theory were able to fit the facts as they were. But as in his sociology, the facts were ultimately selected to fit the theory. Croce went even further, dismissing all of Pareto's social theory as an extravaganza of positivist philosophy.[103] Its logic was not only impossible, he said, but it was inadmissible to treat spiritual actions as though they were external to the human being. Nor was Pareto clear in his use of the so-called logical categories: at times they seemed to refer to economic or utilitarian acts, while at others they merely suggested coherence in behavior. Pareto's social science, said Croce, was merely a translation of ordinary truth into mathematical language, illustrated with anecdotes from ancient history and current newspapers and presented with the explosive temper of a pessimistic moralist whose hatred for all philosophers from Plato to Kant led him into incessant attacks on all who would improve public morals. The only thing Pareto understood was the potency of force in history.

The mathematical method in economics was, of course, a *sine qua non* for the scientific investigation of equilibrium. It was simply a matter of constructing a theory for which someday there would be enough data to allow actual computation. Eventually, Pareto abandoned this hope. But he insisted that interdependence demanded the special logic of mathematics. The numerous mutual relationships, he said, could be dealt with only by employing the powerful tools of the calculus. This implied that the relationships between the variables were reversible, that they were continuous in character, and that the factors which the variables represented were fluid and highly mobile. Yet Pareto recognized that for the individual continuous variation was not quite correct and that economic units were themselves discrete. The bridge between actuality and theory was the law of large numbers which would reduce differences to negligible proportions. Unfortunately, this was an inadequate construction which threatened to collapse in the face of critical winds, for the law of large numbers did not dispose of the individual, discrete nature of single units in a statistical universe. The averages or central tendencies obtained from manipulating the data for a large group did not always apply to the behavior of individual members, particularly at the extremes, and Pareto's economics was nothing if not individual.

Pareto's conception of equilibrium, while derived from Walras, exhibited its own peculiar qualities which deserve notice. For him the economic order was a kind of Cartesian field in which the co-ordinates represented quantities of various goods, with the position of the consumer defined by points moved about by certain forces and restrained by others. Wants represented the moving forces, while limited resources were the constraints enforced by the need to transform raw materials into finished goods. Thus, tastes or wants and obstacles represented by limited resources became the balancing weights which ultimately defined equilibrium. When variations in one set of conditions called forth countervailing variations in the others, equilibrium was established. The theory was supposed to provide an analysis of how this balance was achieved in simultaneous fashion. In contrast to Walras, however, Pareto did not deal with the path along which equilibrium was to be achieved. Still, his examination of the problem was somewhat broader in scope, encompassing free competition with constant and variable prices, as well as several types of monopolistic markets. He even thought that the theory might apply to a collectivist society, taking into account both fluctuating prices and varying coefficients of production. In fact, his comments on the economics of collectivism undoubtedly provided the foundation for a rational socialist economic theory.[104]

While Walras hoped that equilibrium theory might one day be made amenable to computation, Pareto, after contemplating the question, threw up his hands. If his theory, said he, were to apply to only 100 individuals exchanging 700 goods, 70,699 equations would have to be solved.[105] So far as he was concerned, this was impossible in the current state of knowledge. And, further, the millions of equations that would be requisite for a total economy would require the rounding-off of numbers in ways that would reduce the results to nonsense. Ironically enough, this in no way upset his assumption that individuals in the market do carry through the calculations necessary to make the theory cohesive. A solution was available, however: by combining the variables into common groups it could become possible to establish an overall system that would be amenable to computation. This approach is the underlying concept in modern input-output analysis. Such a possibility, however, did not occur to Pareto.[106]

Pareto began to formulate the proposition that economic equilibrium was quite independent of marginal utility around 1900 in the *Manuale*.[107] Utility notions implied the kind of interpersonal comparisons of utility which would have to be eliminated if the theory was to be made completely neutral. To Pareto, utility meant ethics and psychology, and these had no place in a scientific economics. His shift from cardinal to ordinal utility presaged in large measure modern developments under R. G. D. Allen and John R. Hicks.[108] Cardinal utility, implied, of course, a real function of the quantity of available goods. With ordinal utility, it was necessary to show only the individual's scale of preferences for combinations of certain goods. The individual consumer presumably knew what pleasure or *ophélimité* he received from one combination as compared with others.[109] But magnitudes of utility really could not be compared: the only thing left was ordinal "measurement." That is to say, the consumer was interested in the existence of the pleasure he derived from goods rather than in rates of change. Thus, the marginal utility concept was inapplicable, and attention was to be paid rather to the total utility to be derived from consuming a given quantity of goods.

Pareto's technique for establishing ordinal comparisons was the now famous indifference curve analysis. The quantities of goods were to be measured along two coordinates, while a third coordinate indicated the total utility to be derived from various combinations of the two goods concerned. The result was a utility surface shaped somewhat like a smooth dome. The indifference curves were the contour lines of equal height on the surface which might be obtained by cutting planes parallel to the two goods ordinates: each point on a plane had the same total utility, although each represented different combinations of the goods in question. Each combination on the same indifference curve was equally satisfying, while moving to a higher curve implied greater satisfactions. The indifference surface was a "hill of pleasure." If one looked at the curves as if on a map, they would all appear convex to the origin. In developing the theory, Pareto at first replaced utility with index functions which were mathematical expressions of preference, but the indifference curves seemed to suggest a purer theory of choice.[110] There was now no need to know whether or not utility was measurable. Preference was simply taken as a fact of experience.

Pareto thus inverted the usual theoretical approach. By starting with choice, he was able to compare different combinations of goods to which the consumer was ostensibly indifferent; by altering the various combinations he was able to trace the lines of utility which indicated an individual's equilibrium. Since the indifference curves were "empirically" determined, economics became a positive science. The economic principle was established merely by observing the selections of goods that were made to satisfy a want. The analysis was applied with marked subtlety to the conflict of tastes and obstacles. "Hills of pleasure" were contrasted with "hills of returns." Barter curves joined points of equilibrium on each of the indifference curves. The whole affair was quite elegant and quite arid.

It also became possible to apply notions of continuous change along the paths of the indifference curves themselves. The rate of change in *ophélimité* could be measured by the inclination of the indifference curve at any point. However, the analysis failed to say which choice would be made, for this depended on relative prices. Since preferences would depend, consequently, on what the consumer would have to pay for each good, the problem became more a question of trading in the market than one of consumer behavior.[111] Although the whole analysis was based presumably on pure choice, it was questionable that it did indeed escape utility. In fact, Pareto continued to employ some of Edgeworth's terms which smacked of the older ideas. Moreover, a note of rather rigid formalism was introduced with a precision that was essentially deceptive. While the indifference curves seemed capable of setting the stage for the determination of value, they were so neutral that they abstracted entirely from the individual, disregarding both income levels and the state of satiety. These facts would have appeared to be relevant if one had said something about the nature of choice. But this would have brought interpersonal comparisons back into the analysis, for to give meaning to a preference schedule, psychic satisfactions would have to be employed. And what was this but hedonism? Choice without measures of satisfaction seemed a bloodless concept. Nor did the theory integrate such extra-economic problems as advertising, despite the fact that demand and choice were deeply rooted in it. All of which illustrated the curious character of the new economic man as sketched by Pareto's social science.

From an over-all view, maximum *ophélimité* was attained when one could move from a given position in a way that would not alter the utility of other individuals. This was the basic proposition of the so-called new welfare economics, of which Pareto may be said to have been the founder. Such a maximum was attained best under conditions of free competition.[112] On this point, Pareto agreed with Walras. And, like Walras, he would have little to do with the optimism of a Bastiat, dismissing the latter's version of laissez faire as so much dogma. Welfare, the problem now to be defined, would have to be dealt with as scientifically as individual exchange. If the action of a society were to be such that the *ophélimité* would be increased for some and decreased for others, then a maximum position could not be reached. But the welfare of a community required that the pattern of distribution be established first. Since this bordered on the realm of sociology, it was evident that for Pareto the economic problem was concerned primarily with production. Welfare was enhanced only if all the members of a community gained. If a movement away from some initial position brought gains to some but none to others, then welfare could decrease. True, theoretically it was possible to make transfer payments to those who were injured, particularly when the gains exceeded the values set for the losses. This suggestion, made years later by N. Kaldor, would at least have allowed something to be done. Yet this did not remedy the situation, for the basic difficulty still remained: the marginal utility of money was assumed to be alike for all concerned, and the hidden premise of interpersonal comparisons of utility was not eradicated.[113] Moreover, it did not occur to Pareto that a position of equilibrium under conditions of free competition might not be the most satisfactory one from society's standpoint.[114] And if an individual altered his preferences while the shift from a given point was being contemplated, then, of course, all bets were off. The restrictive conditions suggested by the Paretian optimum were rather difficult to come by. In short, welfare became essentially a matter of value judgments, and, despite Pareto's desire to create a neutral standard, he had not been able to avoid ethical overtones.

The presentation of the problem in his *Mind and Society* did little to further the analysis, although he conceded that it was possible to have maximum *ophélimité* at more than one point.[115]

A distinction was also made between maximum utility *of* a community, which might lead to a state of wealth with unequal incomes, and maximum utility *for* a community, which might lead to equal incomes but less wealth; thus, the concept *for* a community stressed the impact on the group as a whole, while *of* a community emphasized the interest of the individual. The language describing welfare and its distinction was certainly cumbersome, but one thing Pareto was certain of—the conditions and criteria for welfare would differ in each of the two situations, and would be governed by prevailing sentiments and residues.[116]

One of Pareto's more important contributions concerned the problem of income distribution. Employing extensive statistical materials drawn from nineteenth-century Prussia, Saxony, and Britain, Renaissance Florence, eighteenth-century Peru, and sixteenth-century Augsburg, and other sources, he arrived at the conclusion that the pattern of income distribution was basically the same in different countries and for different times.[117] As cumulative frequency distributions were constructed for each case, their structural similarity made it possible to express the income relationships in a single formula, merely by applying different values to the constants. This relationship, frequently described as "Pareto's Law," was derived by charting the logs of income size against the logs of a distribution of persons. Thus a straight-line curve was obtained which suggested a certain rigidity in income distribution. The political implications were obvious: socialist efforts to secure a redistribution of income would necessarily founder on the hard rocks of statistical certainty. A natural economic law existed which would establish always the shape of income distribution. The trend of income distribution among the population was such, said Pareto, that a change in one part of the curve would change all other parts; society thus would return to its normal form "just as a solution of a given salt always gives similar crystals." [118]

Inequality could be reduced only by expanding income and production faster than population. Pareto thought that the regularity of his law had demonstrated beyond question the universality of unequal human capacities— a none too surprising conclusion for one who bordered on the misanthropic. The connection of this theory with his notion of the circulation of élites was obvious. But he was unable to demonstrate a correlation between capacity and income. Moreover, it has been contended, with no little justice, that income distribution patterns are closely related to certain powerful underlying institutional factors, which are themselves subject to modification.[119]

The "law" was subjected to considerable criticism. Pareto had based his observations on a mass of disparate income-tax data, which in themselves suffered from serious limitations. Moreover, there seemed to be some confusion in his handling of the concepts of income and consumption. Most statisticians now feel that a single mathematical statement describing the entire range of income distribution is impossible since the income curve itself changes its shape over time.[120] That such shifts can take place at all has cast doubt on the Paretian contention that only increased production can alter income distribution.

A rather important debate developed around Pareto's conception of marginal productivity. Pareto had criticized the standard version of the theory on the ground that it did not apply in cases where technical limitations prevented the product from being wholly distributed among the cooperating factors. Doubling the factors of production, he argued, would not necessarily double the product; moreover, certain factors exhibit peculiar technical relationships, that is, some coefficients were fixed, some variable, so that increasing a factor could not always be compensated by a decrease in others. The idea of variable coefficients was not new with Pareto; Walras had introduced them in his later work and it had been taken note of by Wicksteed. But Pareto's reservations approached a complete abandonment of marginal productivity theory, an implication which aroused the anger of many a later economist. George Stigler, for example, argued that Pareto would have been more accurate had he viewed technically related factors as a single datum to which returns might be attributed as a unit.[121] This, however, appears to evade the rather complex issue that Pareto had raised. Henry Schultz' argument that Pareto tried to bring the theory nearer to reality does seem more to the point.[122] Moreover, Stigler's assertion that propositions concerning a variable product stemming from a stated fixed factor would be valid even if they fit the facts but a third of the time is a poor reason for validating a so-called scientific theory. Apparently Pareto had touched upon a rather sore point in his criticism of marginal productivity, to which as yet there has been no completely satisfactory response.

The general character of Pareto's economics was strengthened by its extension to monopolistic market situations. Whereas firms under free competition were price takers, adjusting themselves to given conditions, private and government monopolies were conceived as price makers.[123] Private monopoly established its own price by estimating the future demand for its product. The analysis visualized such firms moving along a line of maximum profits, superimposed on an array of revenue curves, which had the same slope as the total cost curve. Various intersections were established by the marginal cost curve and all the possible marginal revenue curves.[124] Thus, suggested Pareto, the monopoly problem could be solved by the indifference curve technique: the total revenue curve would have to be tangent to the highest indifference curve for profit. The analysis, however, was cumbersome and was complicated by the device of treating many buyers and sellers as though they were one.[125]

While earlier literature had touched on the monopoly problem, it was to Pareto's credit that he underscored it in a way that was to lead to a highly refined development in later years. He acknowledged the role of product differentiation and unique services rendered by the seller, and appears to have been one of the earliest writers in the modern period to attempt an integration of this phenomenon into general equilibrium theory. Yet he found no place in his model for oligopoly—market domination by a few sellers—on the grounds that its solution was indeterminate.[126] This stemmed from his assertion that product differentiation eliminated oligopoly elements, for, with so many possibilities for market reactions, the oligopolist probably would leave things alone. The variables were so many and so complex that the situation could not be handled solely by economic analysis. Thus there were no unique solutions for oligopoly, he argued, but rather an infinity of solutions. Yet when two oligopolists dealing in slightly differentiated products were considered, a solution was suddenly opened up by treating each as a distinct monopolist. Although this was hardly a satisfactory answer to the oligopoly problem, the inclusion of these situations tended to make the Paretian equilibrium system more comprehensive than the Walrasian. The monopolist was not isolated from the rest of the system, but clearly became an integral element.[127]

Although Pareto did not overlook such problems as economic crisis, interest, rent, and money, his remarks on these subjects have left much to be desired. Crisis was initiated by psychic movements which were indigenous to the economy.[128] Since a large portion of production was devoted to goods in process, an internal limiting factor to continued growth was built up. Thus crises were not a matter of accident. The analysis, however, had a tentative character with many of its strands left hanging in the air.

Rent was said to be a surplus derived from the numerous obstacles to optimum resource allocation. Strictly speaking, this could apply to any factor of production. But to Pareto this phenomenon was caused by changing, dynamic situations or transitional stages between one point of static equilibrium to the next. Since it took time to transform savings into capital, older pre-existing capital was able to enjoy a temporary advantage which gave rise to rent. While this was most evident in the case of land, the concept was applicable to all forms of capital. By generalizing rent in this way, Pareto came close to Marshall's position. Capital became a secondary concept, related solely to matters of accounting: it was virtually generalized out of existence. This was, of course, not unrelated to the exclusion of the time factor in Pareto's model. Consequently, the search for a cause of interest seemed fruitless to him. In fact, that capital should yield interest was too obvious to require investigation. He would have nothing to do with anything like Böhm-Bawerk's concern with proving the validity of capital productivity. The rate of interest, being just another price among many, was determined through the process of general price equilibrium, a notion which played a central role in Gustav Cassel's analysis. Again, the absence of a time concept explained this somewhat cavalier approach.

Nor was Pareto much interested in money; he paid virtually no attention to its theoretical aspects. The marginal utility of money was the marginal utility of the commodity employed as a *numéraire,* and that was that. While an extreme liberal, he saw some values in protective tariffs so long as they helped to facilitate the circulation of élites. In the theory of international trade, he introduced some modification in the doctrine of comparative costs by calling attention to the indirect costs of exports: these were the opportunity costs occasioned by shifting resources to the production of goods for export.[129]

This, then, was the social science constructed by Pareto. Its influence was especially marked in Italy, where a kind of Paretian school of economics grew up, with numerous devotees drawing inspiration from both his economics and sociology. But it was not the positive science he had thought it to be: the policy implications were too obvious. The fulminations against the "pluto-democracies" found in the noneconomic writings were clearly tied to his economics. Throughout his work, Pareto's standards were completely normative: as Schumpeter once remarked, he had been preaching a sermon.

iii

John R. Hicks and the Logic
of the Consumer

Equilibrium economics continued to fascinate those economists for whom elegance and precision were the main objectives of theoretical discourse. One of the best paradigms in contemporary thinking has been the self-contained system developed by John R. Hicks (1904-   ), professor at Oxford. Hicks has had a standard academic career: educated at Oxford, he was successively lecturer at the London School of Economics, a fellow at Cambridge, professor at Manchester, and presently holds the Drummond Chair in Political Economy at Oxford. In addition to his contribution to the field of economic theory, he has written on international trade and has co-authored several volumes on British tax systems with his wife, Ursula K. Hicks, a well-known economist in her own right.[130]

Hicks' theory represents a highly refined development of current doctrine, especially in the fields of utility and equilibrium analysis. Thoroughly adept in handling the most abstruse of mathematical formulations (most of which are happily relegated to appendices), he has not hesitated from time to time to tackle issues of policy.[131] Yet no one could accuse Hicks of the Ricardian sin: his theory can by no means be said to carry an undue burden of prescriptive implication. Hicks takes his theory quite seriously and he expects his readers to do the same. But so much of it is imbedded in a rigid writing style and relentless line of logic that it frequently leaves one far behind. Unrelieved by the sort of light touch that makes Sir Dennis Robertson a delight, Hicks makes little effort to present the argument by easy stages. It is as if he were saying, this is my theory, take it or leave it. Characteristically, many have preferred to leave it.

Perhaps the major work of Hicks' career has been his *Value and Capital*,[132] described as one of the genuinely important books in modern economics. To Hicks, the version of utility found in neoclassical doctrine had appeared as little more than a simple restatement of Gossen's Law. In the older theory, marginal utilities had been presumed to be proportional to prices, given the pattern of a consumer's tastes and his level of income. This, of course, had implied that utility could be measured: it was the cardinal concept all over again. And this was intolerable. By utilizing Pareto's indifference curves, Hicks thought that a substantial improvement in theory could be made, insofar as it enabled one to dispense with the notion of measurability. All one would have to do was to talk of preference positions. Yet to many, this seemed something less than a revolutionary change: subjective utility was still the keystone of theoretical analysis. Marshallian notions merely appeared to have been put into new dress: the marginal rate of substitution displaced marginal utility; the price line and its tangency position were substituted for the proportionality of marginal utility to prices; and the declining marginal rate of substitution took the place of diminishing marginal utility itself. Fundamentally, not much had been altered.

Erik Lundberg once expressed the skepticism which many now have adopted toward *Value and Capital*. Said he, rather sharply: "Its sterile problems and its dead logic have already bored to tears ten generations of students and a generation of teachers." [133] Yet the importance of the work, and of Hicks' contribution generally, cannot be dismissed so easily, for the approach it exemplifies now has become the major challenge to Marshall's partial equilibrium analysis, and in some quarters has displaced it entirely. *Value and Capital*, indeed a direct descendant of Walras' *Éléments* and Pareto's *Cours*, sought to amplify the latters' general equilibrium theory and to extend it to problems stemming from capital and interest. There was also a promise to extend the analysis into dynamics, but this did not turn out as well as Hicks might have hoped, for the main corpus of the theory remained rigidly static. The genuinely dynamic elements had already been outlined by Lord Keynes. In fact, when Hicks came to the question of business cycles, he had to resort to the whole panoply of Keynesian ideas, abandoning Walrasian notions almost *in toto*.[134]

In general, Hicks started with the theory of subjective value and wants. But his original goal—to provide a theoretical basis for statistical studies of demand—was soon forgotten, and the entire structure became an exercise in pure theory. A theory of general equilibrium was developed which avoided the task of counting equations. The dynamic theory then followed, permeated with the basic assumption of perfect competition: problems of imperfect competition simply were omitted and virtually no reference was made to the whole battery of institutional factors in value theory.[135] In short, Hicks had built a logical analysis of an economic system rooted in the practices of eighteenth-century free enterprise. Static theory occupied two-thirds of the book, while the ostensibly dynamic portions became little more than a sequence of static equilibria. For, in fact, time was not part of the analysis, and without time there could be no dynamics worthy of the name.

According to Hicks, static theory could work only with homogeneous goods, although this violated the patent fact that consumers dealt mainly with unique items. If but for this reason, one may seriously question the indifference apparatus that Hicks employed with such skill. Another presupposition in the analysis was that consumers were able to choose between long lists of goods in various combinations. This assumption, necessary in order to make ordinal evaluations possible, resulted, however, in the indifference curve presupposing that consumers really were able to make choices between quantities of a good—a rather dubious concept at best. Indeed, it was questionable whether the indifference curve apparatus really could be distilled from the actual behavior of consumers; the theory proceeded rather on assumptions made by the theorist via introspection and was constructed along pathways which he thought consumers followed. But little empirical evidence substantiated the underlying hypothesis.

Like Pareto, Hicks believed that it was impossible to measure utility and that the best one could do was to arrange preferences in a certain order. But it is doubtful that this represented an advance over the older hedonic approach. At best, ordinalism *seemed* less hedonic than cardinalism.[136] A great debate developed over this issue, much of it frightfully arid and of little import for a realistic economic theory.[137] But so far as Hicks was concerned, he was determined to apply Occam's razor and to dispense with the cardinalist method, for in his view the latter was totally unnecessary for the development of a theory of value and demand.[138] By starting with a utility surface, he was able to plot consumers' reactions to two goods and their related total utility. When the surface was converted into a "contour map," one had a system of indifference curves which measured the total utility derived from varying combinations of the two goods. Movements along an indifference curve, which if drawn on a plane diagram would slope down toward the right and also be convex to the origin, indicated compensating shifts in the various combinations. Since such movements also affected the marginal utilities of the goods, a greater supply of a good meant a lower level of marginal utility: the slope of the curves diminished as the axes were approached. Implicit in these formulations were the concepts of consistency in consumer preferences and the insatiability of wants. Consistency meant an invariant sequence of preferred choices (the property of transitivity) while insatiability suggested a continuing hunger for goods. Cross-effects were also possible, since an increased supply of one good affected the marginal utility of the other, as well as its own.

By superimposing a price line, one obtained a point of tangency with an indifference curve which represented the highest utility for the given situation; movement away from that point on the price line would bring the consumer to a lower indifference curve. Thus the amounts that would be purchased and the best combination of goods could be "read off" without reference to the amount of utility obtained. The height of the utility surface was no longer relevant. The tangency point was equivalent to the older theory's notion of the proportionality of marginal utility to prices. Certain assumptions were thereby discarded; the operation with Occam's razor was declared a success. Thus cardinalism was overthrown, preempted by the idea of a marginal rate of substitution. Important now was that the increased quantity of a good would compensate the consumer for the loss of a quantity of another and that the marginal rate of substitution between the two goods had to equal the ratio of their prices in order for the consumers' equilibrium to be established.

Hicks believed that he had laid the foundations for a truly scientific theory of demand. He had demonstrated, he thought, how consumers reacted to changes in market conditions and how this fictive, lightning calculator of a consumer moved from one equilibrium point to the next. There were no kinks between equilibrium points; one might move about quite smoothly along the paths of wants and desires. Yet, obviously, not all consumer expenditures could be fitted into the rigid Hicksian apparatus. Granted the well-known variation in consumer expenditures, a large proportion nevertheless represent fixed commitments, at least in the short run. Such items as housing, fuel, light and refrigeration, insurance, taxes, and transportation are subject to little if any choice; yet they may be as much as 40 or 50 per cent of the total household budget. It may be seriously questioned whether such expenditures involve a search for utility within the Hicksian meaning.[139] Add to these quasi-automatic outlays, those indulged in as a matter of habit, and what realistically, is left for indifference analysis? The fundamental fact appears to be that a calculating consumer is rare: habit and the patent inability or unwillingness to work out preferences simply do not fit Hicks' model, yet these elements seem to dominate consumer behavior.[140] True, the elimination of these factors provided a generalized concept of the consumer, but once that had been done all genuine meaning had been squeezed out of the theory.

But to continue: a line connecting all points of tangency, tying together the different equilibrium positions, yielded a curve which related shifts in income to consumption patterns. This was the income-consumption curve, corresponding to all possible sets of prices.[141] Sloping upward to the right, and cutting an indifference curve but once, it suggested a positive correlation between income and consumption. If the price of one of the goods was altered upwards a new curve connecting the tangency points could be formed. This was the price-consumption curve, which geometrically was to the right of the income-consumption curve as one moved to higher indifference contours. A fall in price, on the other hand, had a double effect: by increasing *real* income it was analogous to higher income, and, by altering relative prices, it created a substitution effect. There were therefore two possibilities: the income effect and the substitution effect, and insofar as Hicks successfully defined these concepts, he helped to clarify the nature of responses to price and income changes. The income and substitution effects might occur at the same time, for alterations in demand that stemmed from price line shifts comprised elements of both. Yet such movements might depend largely on the "terms of trade" between the two goods. If these were omitted in the analysis, then the consumer actually would not know how to establish his preferences.

Thus utility theory was reduced to pure concepts of choice, expressing the logical implications of consumer behavior in accordance with a preference scale which itself did not change. Those who pursued Hicks' line of analysis spoke of pure behaviorism, concealed indifference, or revealed preference. The whole affair became extremely complex. Much energy was expended in demonstrating mathematically that a fall in price would, *ceteris paribus*, lead to an increase in demand.[142] Yet, as Sir Dennis Robertson has demonstrated, the ordinalists actually found it difficult to avoid committing the sin of cardinalism.[143] Marginal utility must be based somehow on want intensities; if preferences were to be ordered, asked Robertson, must something not be said about the spaces between the ordered points, and did this not drag in concepts of addition and subtraction? In their delight at having discovered Occam's razor, the mathematical economists had evidently done just a bit too much cutting. Nevertheless, cardinalism enjoyed an underground existence, for, once it was admitted that consumers wished to maximize their utilities, some resort to measurability was necessary. Moreover, the utility functions could be said to have been historically conditioned, for wants clearly were culturally determined; a study of how they shifted seemed to be more than the simple question of how they moved along certain curves.[144]

Hicks dealt with this problem by redefining the nature of his goods from one hypothetical week to the next. But this was a formal trick. Irrational elements in behavior were ignored; only the fact of choice was allowed since irrationality was understood to be merely inconsistent choice. "Internal" and "external" economies in consumption were explored, but the new economics investigated these problems, which were really problems of psychology, with mathematical tools and hypothetical models that in the end contributed little to an understanding of consumer behavior. It was seldom recognized that wants are flexible and constantly modify each other. Essentially, the indifference curve system was a short, short-run phenomenon, not subject to change and uninfluenced by extra-theoretical considerations.

A cultural analysis would have revealed that the consumer is hardly the sovereign being that Hicks' theory had made him. And there was no reason to assert that one way of dealing with wants was so much superior and rational than another. As Hobson demonstrated, it could in fact be quite uneconomic to be a rational economic man, since the cost involved in minutely calculating alternatives could far exceed the gain in utility. Conceivably large items, consumers' durables, or what the retailer describes as "big ticket goods," may be carefully weighed in the consumer's mind, yet here too irrational factors are significant, as indicated by the contemporary American auto. Frequently purchased goods, such as food and small household items, may be priced more carefully and low-income families may seek higher preference points. But none of this entered Hicks' theory of demand. If the backward art of spending money were counteracted by training and education, we might create an individual who would conform to the theorists' image, but this clearly is not yet the case. Choice, in the final analysis, is but a matter of conditioning, rather than calculation.[145] Moreover, as Ruby T. Norris has demonstrated, wants are seldom one-dimensional; they are clustered about related goods and reflect a complex of desires for different goods.[146] At best, the push toward equilibrium by the consumer emerges as a dubious concept.

In the past, Marshall's theory of consumers' surplus as the excess of anticipated payment over actual price had come under severe attack. The idea of a consumers' surplus was dismissed as a utilitarian error.[147] But the indifference approach suggested that the notion might be rescued for economic analysis since the newer technique dispensed entirely with utilitarian preconceptions.[148] Marshall's critics had objected to his suggestion that the surplus be conceived in absolute terms. Hicks' reformulation made it completely subjective and relative, thereby meeting the peculiar bias of modern economics. The demand curve was reinterpreted subjectively and to it was added the substitution and income affects. At the same time, the idea of the constancy of the marginal utility of money was rescued by asserting that since the consumer spent but a small part of his income on the commodity in question, price changes had a small impact on total income.

Hicks adopted the view that indifference and preference emanated not from introspection but were actually forms of behavior, hence the appellation "behaviorist ordinalism." [149] Yet in the theory, choice was choice, so that one really did not know the extent of indifference, if it existed at all. It was questionable that indifference really avoided psychological presuppositions for while the notion of the measureability of utility was rejected, the supposition remained that preferences in some way could be evaluated.[150] The Hicksian method—an exercise in mathematical logic and quite sterile—had assumed a kind of behaviorism that most psychologists have long since rejected. As Robertson has said, the effort was mainly to formalize in non-mental terms the action of beings where mind was the chief characteristic. As no real human beings behaved the way Hicks said they did, the whole affair became a crashing bore. In fact, one could interpret the utility debate in ideological terms. Ordinal utility theory, especially in its welfare application, could be related to an extreme individualist position, whereas cardinalism, at least in its later versions, had appeared to stress the need for more social and economic equality. The deep concern that Robertson and Pigou had had for broad social problems seemed to be a direct reflection of their flexible and more humane economics. The ordinalist could be accused of wanting to preserve the *status quo,* for in his view it was virtually impossible to move the consumer from his given position without upsetting the apple cart of equilibrium.

Complementarity and substitution were also key items in the Hicksian apparatus. Dealt with to some extent by Edgeworth and Pareto, they were defined more sharply by Hicks. Obviously, it was possible that in a complex of commodities, two or more of them might be positively related. Allegedly the definitions of both complementarity and substitution were made more precise by introducing the concept of the marginal rate of substitution for money: a good became a substitute if its marginal rate of substitution for money decreased when another good was substituted for money in a way that left the consumer where he had been before. Similarly, it became a complementary good if its marginal rate of substitution for money increased when the second good was substituted for money. Perfect substitution would imply a straight-line indifference curve, the relation between the two goods being unchanged. Absolute complementarity would mean right-angle indifference curves; a limited supply of one good would restrict the benefits to be gained from increased items of the second good. These were the extreme ends of the range: between them fell most other goods, exhibiting declining marginal rates of substitution, so that a good that was relatively scarce became generally more desirable. This was a rather complicated way of setting forth some elementary relationships, in which the more intense use of one good might occasion use of another or where greater utilization of a commodity might displace the use of some other good. These concepts were also related to income effects since a high degree of complementarity would be able to drown out income effects. Or in cases of mild substitution, the income and substitution effects might cancel each other.

Hicks' discussion of these aspects was completely taxonomic, and assumed that the consumer knew his preferences and was thoroughly consistent in behavior. The individual became a calculator of extraordinary speed who never, never resorted to impulse buying. It would be hard to visualize a more unrealistic and otiose theory. All the elements of consumer behavior of which Veblen spoke, the genuinely powerful ones in our society, were deemed to be mere trifles. It was a kind of economics which, as Lionel Robbins admitted, had no bearing on practice. "No politician will alter his line of policy, no business executive will change his programme, because of some improvement in the presentation of preference systems or in the definition of indifference in choice." [151]

Yet Hicks was undaunted, and in his *A Revision of Demand Theory* [152] he offered a still more refined version of consumer behavior. For two decades prior a fearsome debate had been generated, especially on the theory's application to economic welfare. Not only were there cardinalists and ordinalists, but sub-species were evolved, depending on whether behaviorism or introspection was deemed to be the correct approach. [153] The behaviorists believed that they could derive their theory through observation; the introspectionists looked into their own souls. Hicks himself became an introspective ordinalist: admittedly his theory could not be verified by direct observation, but presumably the implications of the theory were verifiable. He now felt that the theory required some modification. At about the same time, Paul Samuelson arrived at his theory of "revealed preference." [154] Here the emphasis had been only on "observable data." In the meantime, economists discovered the mathematical theory of sets, with its concepts of strong and weak ordering of related points. [155] The stage now was set for eliminating entirely the slightest hint of psychology in economics.

In his new work, Hicks reiterated his rejection of cardinalism on the ground that utilities were independent of each other and therefore incomparable. One had to start with the "preference hypothesis" in order to separate current price effects from the complex matrix of forces that influenced consumer behavior. The objective was to note how the consumer reacted when only prices and incomes were taken into account. Nothing else really mattered, nor was it necessary to prove the validity of the "preference hypothesis," since its usefulness was entirely pragmatic: one was interested solely in the richness of the deductions it yielded.[156] Consequently, demand theory became nothing more than the "economic application of the logical theory of ordering." The consumer became a more skilled mathematician than ever. Distinctions were made between "strong ordering," whereby each item had a definite place in a sequence of events, and "weak ordering," which implied a clustering of preferences, with no unit enjoying a special advantage over the others.[157] The latter was said to be characteristic of the indifference curve system, since all points on a curve had the same strength and were equally desirable. Thus demand theory became an illustration of weak ordering, for a given position did not logically imply preference per se. Hicks then deduced all the propositions he wanted from these apparently even more simplified assumptions.

The nature of demand again was described in terms of income and substitution effects. Much new terminology was introduced: four different types of consumers' surplus were adumbrated and several kinds of income variations were described. These modifications were required because demand theory could be approached either from the standpoint of what quantities would be consumed at certain prices or from the view of the highest price that would be paid for certain quantities. The first was the ordinary case of the free market; the second implied restraints, as in the case of rationing.[158] Consumers' surplus no longer depended on cardinalist notions or on the assumption that the marginal utility of money was constant. The discussion now could be based on concepts of equivalent gains or losses in money incomes. Compensating and equivalent variations replaced the Marshallian concept which had treated the consumers' surplus as the difference between the actual price and the maximum which might have been paid. Thus deductions from income, such that the same quantity could be consumed without altering positions or subsidies to compensate for opportunities foregone, became the technique for evaluating consumers' surpluses.

But the whole discussion threatened to evaporate in a bewildering array of new curves and concepts, none of which appeared to have much advantage over older modes of analysis. Although Hicks sketched numerous subtle relationships, it was debatable whether any of them were either important or relevant. That such indubitable skill in the higher reaches of mathematical logic ever would have any effect on economic policy was doubtful. Occam's razor again seemed to have slashed everything to shreds, and the whole theory became an exercise in deducing the same conclusions as had been suggested, with a few less assumptions, by the cardinalists.

By transferring the indifference technique to goods in general, Hicks was able to develop a system of general equilibrium, thus converting the theory of demand into a theory of exchange. Yet Hicks, like Walras, could not make his theorems genuinely dynamic. His main concern was with stability—the inherent capacity of the system to return to equilibrium—and he presumed that the study of static equilibrium would provide the starting point for the study of instability under dynamic conditions. Yet unstable systems, defined as those which do not rest at a determinate set of prices, he considered inconsequential, although this was perhaps the most crucial problem for economic analysis. Certainly, the work of Harrod and Domar had emphasized this point. But Hicks was more concerned with an examination of the conditions required for stable equilibrium. Instability appeared to stem mainly from distortions in income effects and extreme complementarity. Conversely, complementarity and imperfect substitutability made for rigidity.[159]

Passing on to the theory of the firm, Hicks found that while expectations were generally precise, there was always an element of uncertainty for which allowance was to be made. Under perfect competition, prices could be taken as a parameter without having to account for the entire range of the price schedule. And with relevant data on the production function and the prices of inputs, the firm was in a position to estimate its profits. A key concept here was the transformation of a group of commodities into a "single" one, so long as their prices changed in the same proportion. Thus, a number of variables was reduced to but one, ostensibly attaining a higher level of generality. All goods could be placed on one axis of an indifference diagram, with money on the other. The concept of a period of production also was introduced, defined as the elasticity of the discounted values in relation to interest rate changes. That is, a decline in the rate of interest, usually stemming from a more rapid growth of capital as compared to other required inputs, encouraged producers to adopt plans for a more distant output. There was a tendency to depreciate the present as against the future. In this complex manner, Hicks paid unwilling obeisance to Böhm-Bawerk; but as Samuelson later demonstrated, the Hicks' formula had made the period of production virtually infinite.[160]

Curiously enough, Hicks did concede that the introduction of monopoloid elements would have disastrous consequences for his theory—a virtual admission of the deeper interest in an elegant self-consistent mathematical doctrine than in the realities of a modern market.[161] Perfect competition had to be assumed again and again in order to rescue the Hicksian version of general equilibrium. But not much damage to his theory was done, he asserted, when monopoly, imperfect competition, the role of the state, or the effects of interest were ignored. A good deal of damage was palpably done, however, to meaningful portrayals of economic reality. And it was some time before Hicks would, at least tangentially, concede this point.

Hicks' theory of production was based on four markets, covering products, factors, services, and intermediate goods. Income and substitution effects were reviewed, mainly to elucidate stability conditions. A market was said to be stable if a decline in price resulted in excess demand, even though all other prices adjusted themselves to the new one; it was imperfectly stable if the excess demand appeared only after the other prices were adjusted. That is, stability meant the insulation of price from all other market effects. Imperfect stability implied that the price of a good was stabilized only after the rest of the economy had worked out the necessary movements. Only the income effect seemed to cause instability.[162] The markets for services behaved quite like the product markets, while those for intermediate goods were bound to be stable because of the lack of income effects. Factor markets, however, could be very unstable because both income and substitution effects were present. The whole business, however, seemed quite formalistic and unreal, for it was unlikely that disequilibrium conditions in one market would have no effect on stability in others.[163]

The idea of substitution was applied also to production.[164] In the simple economy, at least, the notion of comparability seemed legitimate. It was thus possible to ask whether production might not be increased by the transfer of resources between alternative uses. Equilibrium, implying the correct combinations of resources, became the condition for optimum output. A substitution curve demonstrated the possibilities in the case of production of two goods, so that a marginal rate of substitution between the commodities could be derived. In equilibrium, the marginal rate of substitution had to be the same for all goods.

Of course, time had to be introduced in order to make the system dynamic. In the static state, the stock of capital did not change, anticipation and realized prices were alike, and money rates of interest and real rates were identical. But in the dynamic state these variables were subject to lags of various kinds and consequently had to be dated, a task Hicks sought to accomplish by introducing the notion of the "week." This, however, seemed quite mechanical, devoid of genuine process, and failed to convert the model into a truly dynamic one. As Baumol described it, the system was merely one of "statics involving time." [165] The "week," defined as that period of time in which price variations could be neglected, was obviously a functional, rather than a calendar definition. As such it made little improvement over the Marshallian approach. During the "week," plans were to be made regarding resource utilization for the following week, but once commitments were made, there could be no alteration in plans. Hicks must have been aware that this was little more than a series of static pictures, yet he pretended that the whole system did allow for dynamical analysis. Said he: "By using the week, we become able to treat a process of change as consisting of a series of temporary equilibrium; this enables us still to use equilibrium analysis in the dynamic field. By using the plan, we become able to bring out the relation between those actions devoted to present ends, and those actions which are directed to the future." [166] According to Hicks, movement would take place from one equilibrium to the next, allowing entrepreneurial plans to unfold. Deviations from equilibrium were not to be countenanced, for this would have destroyed the model's elegance. If, however, expectations could be understood as sets of probability distributions, the "sense of disequilibrium" would not be disturbing, so long as the relevant expectations were within the anticipated range. Disequilibrium was said to arise only when price expectations became inconsistent, when plans did not jibe, or when errors were made in estimates. Of course, these are just the sort of actions one could expect in a dynamic economy. But Hicks could find no room for them.

Equilibrium was to be maintained through the device of forward trading.[167] Here Hicks made a distinction between a "spot" economy and a "futures" economy, so that ultimately it was speculation that provided the stabilizing rudder. The only limitation on forward trading became uncertainty. The existence of a forward market created the phenomenon of interest. Hicks admitted that there were many rates of interest, yet by reducing the various rates for loan transactions to a "standard type" of short term rate, it became theoretically feasible to analyse the forces leading to interest. Fundamentally, interest was but one of many prices in the economy and was determined, like any other price, in a mutually interdependent system. Money was converted into a kind of security: it was merely a more perfect form than other securities, whose character could be grasped by the relative degree of "moneyness" they exhibited. Obviously, this made liquidity the beginning of monetary theory. For the short run, interest became a way of measuring the difficulty of investing funds for the marginal lender, while in the long run it included a payment for risk. Thus, securities might provide interest because they were imperfect money. In essence, interest in the Hicksian system was a payment for waiting, plus a premium for risk. Moreover, it appeared that securities adjusted themselves to the yield on money. Yet it was conceivable that securities might become desirable enough to circulate on a par with money, thus creating a situation in which money would adjust to the yield on securities.[168] Some writers have felt that Hicks' emphasis on liquidity and the money-security relationship was extreme, and have preferred to stress rather the underlying factors of productivity and thrift.[169] All that Hicks had accomplished, it was said, was a demonstration of how securities and money could co-exist, but he had failed to explain why interest was paid.

Returning to the production sphere, one might observe that technological data provided for substitution between inputs or substitution in outputs. The entrepreneur could also make substitutions over time. The purpose of these maneuvers was to reach a state of equilibrium. As soon as all the relevant factors were known, a production plan could be worked out. The "economic horizon" was limited by time beyond the plan, an area toward which it was inadvisable to direct one's energies. In evaluating the flow of total profits for the period of production, the entrepreneur presumably would take into account the discounted value of future profits. That production plan would be selected which would yield the largest discounted profit.[170] Thus it was possible to arrive at the capitalized value of the firm as a whole.

In this framework, the equilibrium conditions were established. The latter were defined by Hicks in a way that required the marginal rate of substitution in the output of two goods to be equal to their prices. The equilibrium conditions for inputs were similarly defined. In the case of compensatory movements of inputs and outputs, equilibrium required that the marginal technical rate of substitution equal the ratio of the prices of the respective inputs and outputs. In each case, the prices were those discounted to the present.[171] As expected price increases would tend to increase output, higher input prices would lead to curtailed production. Since higher interest rates would tend to cause future prices to fall, their immediate effect would be to concentrate output toward the present and restrict future expansion.[172] In Hicks' terms, interest changes could be interpreted as a substitution among anticipated levels of profit. Added to this highly formalistic analysis was the concept of the elasticity of expectations, which sought to relate anticipated prices to present ones. This was defined as the ratio of a proportional rise in future prices to a proportional rise in present prices. Expectations therefore were elastic when prices were expected to change proportionately more in the future than in the present. In this way Hicks tied expectations to production plans.

More recently, Hicks has sought to work out a dynamic growth model based on the concepts adumbrated in *Value and Capital*.[173] Offered in rather tentative fashion, the new model was intended as a replacement for the dynamic sections of the earlier theory, where the system of prices that was evolved admittedly had applied to only a given moment of time. Anticipations, Hicks conceded, were but one of the sets of data, so that movements *over* time had been inadequately reflected. What seemed to be the difficulty was the presumption that perfect efficiency—Pareto's optimal condition—was inherent in the earlier construction. Yet "optimality" continued to attract Hicks, for such a model could be used, said he, ". . . as a standard of reference by which other (doubtless more realistic) models can be judged." [174] Perfect efficiency could operate only with perfect foresight, an unlikely contingency, yet Hicks believed that his argument was not at all circular. What was implied was merely that set of prices which if expected and realized would generate a dynamic movement. Thus, while the *process* was dynamic, the method of analysis could remain static. Hicks was now in command of the best of all possible worlds.

The newer model incorporated assumptions of a single homogeneous good and homogeneous labor. No distinction was made between fixed and circulating capital, thus simplifying the definition of firms and reducing them to a uniform glob of economic endeavor. As money was eliminated from the model, wages and interest were to be computed in terms of the single

good. While it was assumed that saving did not take place, interest nevertheless was to be established by the simple process of imputation, and was to be
determined by borrowing and lending. The consumption plans of the saver,
who suddenly made an appearance out of nowhere, were based on the
current value of his assets plus the current and expected rates of wages and
interest. The firm would choose that plan that would maximize its *assets*.
The model then demonstrated that, with perfect foresight, saving necessarily
would equal the increment in the value of capital stock. The analysis was
done in terms of goods rather than labor units, on the grounds that this
was the way the capitalist thought. An interesting element of the model was
Hicks' disposal of the production function, which now seemed inessential in
the light of recent developments in linear programming. Since it was obviously
difficult to posit a continuous production function, only a list of alternative
possibilities was necessary. One could well ask, what was happening to
marginalism?

Despite Hicks' ingenuity, the description of a firm's effort to maximize
its assets remained static as both process and method. Production possibilities
were represented by points within a frontier curve (analogous to the boundary
of a convex set) and the point selected was to be the one touched by an
indifference curve representing the consumer's preference at a given price.
When preferences changed, a shift in the price structure was to occur with
a subsequent movement in the production frontier. Ultimately, a movement
toward growth, or the accumulation of assets, was to stem from movements
in the rate of interest. Again it was difficult to see that this elaborate apparatus
had said anything more than had been said elsewhere.

For the most part Hicks' theory was little more than a system of classification. Since expectations usually are vague and indefinite, the kind of precision Hicks' theory lent to them would appear to be quite unrealistic. Furthermore, his unwillingness to acknowledge monopoly and other deviations from
free competition has seemed well-nigh disastrous for the whole painfully elucidated formulation. Hicks himself was aware of this when he commented
rather weakly that monopoly would have meant the wreck of his theory.[175]
In effect, the many qualifications and reservations had reduced it to ". . .
nothing but the stalest conclusions about highly idealized cases whose
practical importance is extremely dubious." [176] All Hicks had accomplished
was to pour old wine into new, oddly shaped bottles.

Economists generally have been agreed that the most important phase
of dynamic theory is that concerned with the business cycle. Hicks announced
his interest in this area with several articles and a short chapter on the
subject in *Value and Capital*. However, not until he had published his *A
Contribution to the Theory of the Trade Cycle* [177] did a full statement of his
views become available. The basic idea, that the capitalist economy gave rise
to certain characteristic oscillations, was sketched in a review of Roy

Harrod's *Towards a Dynamic Economy.*[178] The major source for Hicks' trade cycle theory was Keynes' *General Theory,* which had demonstrated its power over the years as the chief seminal work in modern economics. To the consumption-investment-multiplier complex, Hicks attached J. M. Clark's acceleration principle and the striking analysis which Ragnar Frisch had formed between economic motion and the wave impulses studied by physicists. As far back as 1933, Frisch had suggested that economic fluctuations had an innate tendency to wear themselves out, or to dampen. Continued disturbances, however, were apt to persist because of such external shocks as innovation, political upset, and war. These random forces prevented the economy from attaining a state of quiet equilibrium. Each shock, each outside impulse set up its own motion which was reflected in the totality of trade cycle movements. The motion itself was internal, but the initial force came from outside the economy. This rather interesting development suggested the feasibility of constructing models of the economy along the lines of nonlinearity found in electrical engineering. This line of thought had roots as far back as Lord Rayleigh's work on nonlinear vibrations in 1883, but not until the 1930's had economists begun to explore the possibilities of this approach.[179] Later, Paul Samuelson suggested a "billiard table" theory in which cyclical turning points were said to occur when full employment ceilings were hit, impelling the economy to bounce back.[180] Work in this area also was done by M. Kalecki in Britain.

Hicks' trade cycle—a good example of this newer trend of thought—effectively combined the concepts of the accelerator, multiplier, autonomous investment, and lagged linear functions leading to damped or explosive oscillations, all operating in an economy exhibiting a kind of exponential growth pattern. The various nonlinear models generally displayed a so-called "relaxation" feature: that is, they consisted of self-excited oscillations with quasi-discontinuous characteristics.[181] This was the sort of thing that had been found in some television circuits and economists had begun to wonder whether it might not also describe social phenomena. There were two types of nonlinear models: one in which the limiting factor was external to the movements of the cycle, as in Hicks' theory, and another, in which the "relaxation" or waning of economic motion was attributed to the model itself. Essentially, a nonlinear model of the Hicksian type could exhibit kinks or sharp breaks in the line of economic movement which might either explode outward or suddenly dampen. In Hicks' system it was even possible to describe the movement around the consumption function or the savings curve as a closed loop system.[182]

As the Hicksian analysis was in *real* terms, the consumption function expressed the relationship of real consumption to real income. Only toward the end of the book were monetary influences introduced. The basic equations were Keynesian in that consumers' goods plus producers' goods equalled the national income. But Hicks' interest at this point was in the *path* along which one equilibrium moved to the next.[183] Certainly this marked a conceptual advance over his earlier theories. By introducing time lags, he now was able to define consumption as a fixed ratio of the previous period's income, while investment varied over the cycle. Thus, depending on the time period, it could be said that consumption would converge on the increment of investment, according to the particular lag that was stipulated. By distinguishing between fixed and working capital, the accelerator became more precise. Three stages were discernible in the analysis: (1) depletion of working stocks to meet a greater demand but without new capital investment; (2) capital investment to bring the economy up to new demand levels; and (3) the subsequent series of oscillations, of which there were at least four types—convergence, damped fluctuations, steady fluctuations, and explosive oscillations. Excess capital appeared when the downturn occurred because of the unique relationship at given levels of activity between the total stock of capital and investment. New investment tended to be negative in the downturn because inventory and equipment were not replaced. But when total capital was not excessive, investment was necessary in order to maintain the proper proportion between capital and income. Essentially this was how Hicks applied the acceleration principle. When induced investment was introduced in addition to autonomous investment, the oscillations could be dampened. Consumption lags also served to smooth fluctuations.

A top limit to any upward movement was imposed when resources were fully engaged. Thus, at full employment the increase in income was halted by the ceiling of maximum productivity: the outcome was a sudden collapse of investment, although the economy could crawl along the ceiling for a while before turning down.[184] As income dropped, capital again became excessive; the decline in income was bound to continue until all excess capital was eliminated. At some point an optimum relationship again would be established. What distinguished one cycle from the next in Hicks' theory was the number and length of time lags and the values of various functions and coefficients. The central notion, however, was the ceiling and the limits it imposed. There was also a floor in these motions, for disinvestment in capital stock could not exceed depreciation. Yet all the criticisms that had been levelled at Clark's accelerator could be applicable to Hicks' as well: [185] the failure to account for excess capacity at the beginning of an upswing, the inadequate explanation of replacement investment, and the assumption of a fixed ratio between changes in output and changes in the stock of capital, all made the accelerator a much weaker analytical tool than it had seemed at first glance.

Hicks' accelerator failed to explain responses to differential rates of change. There was no reason to suppose that capital would move proportionately as output adjusted to shifts in demand. That is to say, the accelerator reacted solely to technical changes, with the major element comprising a fixed capital-output ratio: however, empirically the latter is false. Hicks sought to evade the problem by making output affect investment beyond the present. The effort was not successful, for a buildup of proposed investment stemming from backorders would wrench the supposedly fixed capital-output ratio out of kilter. Quite simply, bottlenecks, both real and financial, could prevent a proportionate matching of output and investment.

Of course, according to Hicks, the ceiling itself was always moving upward. This was one of the features of a "progressive economy." Nevertheless, it was not clear that an upward movement necessarily would have to hit the ceiling: nothing in the model said that this had to happen.[186] Hitting the ceiling at the upper turning point had overtones of Hayek's formulation, suggesting as it did a shortage of capital. One might very well have questioned whether downturns were to be attributed to such situations.[187] It would have seemed more reasonable to suppose that full employment could lead to labor-saving investment, enabling the ceiling itself to be pushed up, with activity continuing at high levels for considerable lengths of time. Orders then would accumulate and equipment would be used round the clock. And autonomous investment would begin to act like a ratchet, forcing the economy up to higher and higher levels.[188] But perhaps more important, Hicks overlooked certain institutional factors, particularly the growth of population and the high rate of family formation, both characteristics of recent years. Apparently there was much more to the turning point problem than Hicks had been able to uncover.[189]

Monetary factors especially would seem to be more significant than they were in Hicks' model. But, although he was quite aware of the intimate relationships between money and real factors (as evidenced by his essays on the subject) little in his conception differed from the Cambridge tradition. Certainly, the distortions in expectations which are frequently induced by the so-called "money illusion" require explanation. The condition of the profit and loss statement and the balance sheet do have some impact on the movements of the cycle. True, Hicks did consider credit lags and the alleged weaknesses of the banking system, but again these ideas had a distinct Hayekian flavor. And while they were important considerations, it was just quite possible that profits and profit expectations were more meaningful.

Nothing in Hicks' theory was particularly new. The idea that the cycle should be studied as part of an expanding economy could have been found in Schumpeter and Harrod. The multiplier, accelerator, and autonomous investment had been thoroughly explored in the literature. Hicks' work was, in short, simply a clever synthesis. In actuality, his formulation was not really a theory, but another presentation of certain types of cyclical movements, which ought to have been empirically checked to start with. But perhaps a more serious drawback was its mechanistic nature. Turning points were reached in the model not as a result of *human* reactions, but simply because the elements of the system required that they be reached; movements in investment took place whenever the accelerator or multiplier dictated a change. It was a theory of cycles without the major factor—people.

As a final point, let us briefly review Hicks' contribution to wage theory. His *Theory of Wages* was a closely reasoned attempt to validate marginal productivity theory, for it was evident to Hicks that wage determination was but an illustration of the general law of value.[190] In addition, a unique theory of bargaining was attached to the analysis which implied something less than the free competition implicit in marginal productivity. Prior to Hicks' presentation, bargaining notions could have been traced to Edgeworth's bilateral monopoly model of 1881 wherein the principle of indeterminacy was adumbrated. Hicks, however, offered a determinate solution—by drawing an employer's "concession" curve and a union's "resistance" curve. At the point where both curves intersected, one supposedly found the highest wage that could be extracted by skillful negotiation. The two curves were reminiscent of Marshall's scissors, but unlike the latter, suggested formality for its own sake. But there was no reason to assert that a high wage proposal would induce a strike, as was implied by Hicks.[191] Further, as he failed to demonstrate how the parties would reach the point of intersection, nothing really was said about the bargaining process itself. The suggestion that a long resistance curve would permit the unions to extract a higher wage from employers simply did not accord with reality. And there was more than a hint in the analysis that the employers and the unions knew what the other had in mind. If this were so, it could hardly be said that a bargaining process was taking place. Bargaining occurs because neither party really knows what the other wants.[192]

At any rate, the whole process of bargaining appeared self-defeating, implied Hicks, for marginal productivity would have to win out in the end. Payment of wages above the true level would culminate in unemployment: in fact, this appeared as the sole cause of job loss, a situation that few unfortunately were willing to acknowledge, thus placing the blame on the propensity to violate the law of marginal productivity. Income distribution depended entirely on the complex of impersonal market forces.

An elaborate analysis of inventions was offered to show how changing technology might influence wages.[193] According to Hicks, laborsaving devices increased the marginal productivity of capital while capital saving inventions increased the marginal productivity of labor relative to capital. Thus the possibility of substituting capital for labor played a central role in the analysis.[194] "Neutral" inventions would not alter relative shares, said Hicks. On the other hand, laborsaving devices would reduce labor's relative share, although it was possible for its absolute share of income to rise. "Very laborsaving" inventions, however—those profitable in themselves, not merely because the rate of interest fell—could have deleterious effects because then both the absolute and relative share of income received by labor would fall. Hicks' primary concern here was with the way in which relative changes in the rate of return to a factor of production altered the relative quantities employed of that factor. If the same relative quantities were employed, the elasticity of substitution became zero; on the other hand, elasticity would be great if a small drop in wages caused labor to be utilized more extensively than capital. When this happened the share of the national income going to labor would be increased. Such an analysis implied, of course, all the assumptions of free competition plus a fairly quick response to altered situations by both labor and capital. But the assumption of full employment made it dubious that such ease of movement was even theoretically possible. The chief complaint against the theory, however, was that it shifted all too glibly from the level of the individual firm to the entire economy. Such a simple additive technique was clearly in error, for marginal productivity really had little to say about the general level of wages. At the macroeconomic level, the factors that governed distribution stemmed from human actions, not physical ones.[195]

In reviewing this seemingly impressive body of thought, one has the inescapable feeling that not much had been added to older doctrine. Most of Hicks' work has emerged as a series of delicately attuned refinements which did little, if anything, to disturb the basic framework of received economic theory. Moreover, the precision of his theory has been completely misleading, for mathematical models, no matter how many approximations to reality they may embody, can never encompass the full range of economic data. Economic theorems stem from a host of diverse variables, many of which have the upsetting habit of shifting in unknown ways. Quite simply, economic institutions are neither as stable nor as predictable as this sort of theory had made them out to be.

iv

Paul A. Samuelson:
Neo-Classical Synthesis

Operating with powerful conceptual tools, Paul A. Samuelson has, perhaps more successfuly than anyone else, put economics into a mathematical sanctuary. Born in 1915, he has been described as the *wunderkind* of American economics. Moving rapidly up the academic ladder, he became a full professor at the Massachusetts Institute of Technology while still in his twenties. His work has exhibited that characteristic which Schumpeter attributed to all important economists—a pre-analytic vision of the economic order developed early in one's career and then carried through in an endless relation of give and take between factual and theoretical work. For many, Samuelson's contribution has given economics a new lease on life: by grounding it solidly in mathematical method he has been said to have eliminated inherited contradictions and fallacies.

Samuelson has insisted that mathematics is essential if economic thinking is to be refurbished. For him mathematics is a language unique in its abilities to lay bare the fundamental unities of the realms of economic discourse. The *Foundations of Economic Analysis,* one of the most formidable works in recent literature, won for its author the David A. Wells prize at Harvard.[196] The American Economic Association awarded him the first John Bates Clark Medal in 1947 for the most significant contribution made by an economist under the age of forty. An early paper demonstrated the interaction of the multiplier and accelerator in striking fashion. Other articles on the theory of consumer demand threw him into the midst of the debate on choice and preference.[197] Most of these papers presaged the *Foundations,* a work that astonished his confrères, for here virtually everything in economics was translated into high-powered mathematics. Samuelson was not the least bit perturbed about keeping his formulas at the forefront of economic analysis: he viewed his method as essentially simple and he did not intend to bury his mathematics in footnotes as did Alfred Marshall. So far as he was concerned, "the laborious literary working over of essentially simple mathematical concepts such as is characteristic of much of modern economic theory is not only unrewarding from the standpoint of advancing the science, but involves as well mental gymnastics of a peculiarly depraved type." [198] Unfortunately, many readers have considered Samuelson's disclaimers as a case of misplaced modesty.

Increasingly, many are wondering whether rushing economics so forcibly over mathematical rails may not create a depraved absorption with pure technique, for economics does seem to be after all a *social* science. The methods exhibited in input-output analysis and linear programming have appeared as the payoff of the mathematical method; yet, when all is said and done, these are techniques rather than theories. But Samuelson himself has been fully capable of getting down to earth, as demonstrated by frequent *obiter dicta* in his *Foundations,* and especially in his introductory text, *Economics,* one of the most remarkable books of its kind ever written.[199]

Now in its fifth edition, each successive version has been recast to reflect the current emphasis. The first edition, virtually pure Keynesianism, advocated such seemingly outlandish policies as government spending and tax reduction to alleviate depressions. Through the years Samuelson has revised his textbook approach, arriving at what he has described as a "grand neo-classical synthesis," combining modern national income analysis with the time-honored principles enunciated by the founding fathers, Smith, Ricardo, and others. Such a synthesis has had to assume, of course, full employment in the ordinary course of events, for only under these conditions could any measure of validity be accorded to classical doctrine. The basic concept was the Keynesian theory of income determination, which would provide the key to full employment. After that, such classical beliefs as the virtues of thrift could come into their own and all the ancient paradoxes would lose their force.[200] Thus, at long last, microeconomics and macroeconomics were able to establish diplomatic relations. Samuelson's introductory text, which has sold well over 750,000 copies in various editions and translations, is by far the best introduction for the student, as many teachers have testified over the past decade.[201]

More recently, and not unexpectedly, Samuelson has explored the realm of game theory and linear programming. Much of his work in this area has been incorporated in memoranda prepared for the RAND Corporation, culminating in the joint work (with Robert Dorfman and R. M. Solow), *Linear Programming and Economic Analysis*.[202] Here the theme revolved about the identification of equilibrium positions with the theory of maximizing behavior, a thesis which permeates the *Foundations* as well. Thus, in a 1950 RAND memorandum, Samuelson related equilibrium points to the problem of discovering maxima by the particular technique of game theory. Saddle points—game theory's minimum-maximum—could be reached, he said, by a sequence of difference equations in climbing or descending the hill. But while game theory might have relevance for maximizing patterns, Samuelson could see no special advantage in it over the calculus.

Although in a paper presented in 1952 to the American Economic Association, Samuelson appeared to debunk somewhat the use of mathematics in economics, it has been evident that for him there can be no effective economics without this handmaiden of the sciences.[203] Mathematics might be made interchangeable with language, as has been illustrated in the work of John Bates Clark, but, said Samuelson, it was easier to develop the necessary relationships by using symbols. However, the difficulty with the purely mathematical approach which Samuelson has overlooked on occasion, has been its frequent failure to connect the concepts employed with observable data. This was bound to leave open the question of interpretation. Nevertheless, for Samuelson, propositions, no matter how they are formulated, have had to be subject to verification; otherwise they were operationally meaningless. Of course, mathematics itself is no guarantee that false premises can be avoided. It has been the search for rigorous proof that is important, insisted Samuelson; this implied that the mathematical mode of thought, stemming from the conventions of manipulated symbols, can best provide the necessary verification of economic propositions. Yet, he has said, while mathematics is a useful tool, its lack has not hindered useful work. Thus, Samuelson has been in the enviable position of eating his cake while keeping it intact—a trick he has carried off quite well. Note the juxtaposition of his abstruse professional articles and the popular comments he sends in prolific quantities to such journals as the *Financial Times.* Or compare his brilliant essay on wage theory in the otherwise dreary symposium, *The Impact of the Labor Union.*[204]

The *Foundations of Economic Analysis,* greeted as the most important work in the field since Hicks' *Value and Capital,* announced its major theme in the first paragraph: analogies between the main features of various economic theories suggested a more general conception which in effect would bind together the seemingly disparate areas of economic analysis. The special branches of economics, such as taxes, prices and international trade, were but particular expressions of such a general theory, said Samuelson.[205] The task of the economist now was to demonstrate that there were ". . . formally identical *meaningful* theorems in these fields, each derived by an essentially analogous method." [206] The key word here was "meaningful," for Samuelson was concerned with refutable, verifiable propositions, regardless of their significance or triviality. But meaningfulness, of course, would have to lead to a program for research, for the theoretical propositions would have to be given empirical content.[207] With the ultimate scientific objective defined in this way, Samuelson's main purpose was to show that two fundamental hypotheses bolstered virtually all of economic theory—the description of a maximum and the determination of stability conditions.

First, equilibrium implied a maximizing or minimizing problem. Consequently, the features of an economic model could be outlined by establishing the secondary conditions for a maximum, those which indicated movements to or from a maximum point. That is, merely to establish the maximum was not enough, one had to be able to say something about movements away from that critical spot. This question consumed a good part of the *Foundations* and involved a study of maximizing behavior, the theory of costs and production, consumer actions, and welfare economics. Yet once the economic problem had been stated in this fashion, it was, of course, necessary to talk about dynamic change. This was the problem of equilibrium *per se.* In Samuelson's view, equilibrium represented a stable situation in the sense that deviations tended to be self-correcting. Following Keynes, he divorced the notion of equilibrium from normative precepts, since it was possible to have stability with high unemployment.[208]

Equilibrium conditions could be evaluated best by employing the technique of comparative statics. This was rigorously defined as the study of the ways in which the variables in an equilibrium system responded to changes in the parameters; for it was the shifts in the latter that provided the cause of movement in an equilibrium system. The theory of consumer demand and production was then stated in terms of ordinal preferences. Although Samuelson insisted that this did not imply rational behavior in a normative sense, his argument was not convincing. The consumer was presumed to seek a maximum position and was able to make comparisons or to "reveal" his preferences. Long-run demands were visualized as more elastic than those in the short run. The problem of dealing with finite changes was introduced in explicit and direct fashion. Samuelson demonstrated that the assumption of continuous change could be disposed of and that problems of discrete movements could be handled easily. This was an important contribution, for it did provide a way of dealing with kinks and sudden shifts in the relevant curves. Thus, discontinuities became an integral part of the analysis of prices and factors.[209] In fact, argued Samuelson, discontinuities made the task of analysis much easier, for in such instances the optimum point in production was more clearly discernible and less responsive to changes in the prices of inputs. Moreover, such an equilibrium was bound to be very stable, since it would require large shifts in price to upset it.

Having established his technique, Samuelson then dealt with the theory of cost and production. Here the problem was to indicate how the derivation of minimum cost for each level of output might be achieved. Although the same output might be produced in a variety of ways, the prescription for minimum cost made the problem a determinate one. The key question was the relationship of the production function to the cost curves. Samuelson's exploration was thorough, although such matters as the complementarity of inputs were treated less fully than one might have expected. In his view, the exhaustive treatment previously accorded to complementarity had been unmerited, for it was not really that important.[210] Minimum cost was established by the equality of the marginal productivity of the last dollar of input in all uses. This condition was posited as independent of revenue considerations.

The method for cost analysis was analogous to the indifference curves of consumer preference. The entrepreneur was said to seek those factor combinations that would yield the lowest costs. This was done by relating the marginal productivity of a factor to that of others and by substituting for those with the higher marginal productivity to the point where the ratios of the dollar cost to the marginal productivity was equal in all uses. The method provided a system of isoquants, or curves of equal output for different combinations of inputs, on which a set of isocost curves was superimposed so that the point of tangency between the desired output and the lowest isocost line would show the lowest cost for that output. Samuelson then derived a number of theorems to demonstrate how the variables would change with respect to each other.[211] Accordingly, as the price of a factor increased, other prices remaining the same, less would be employed of that factor: minimum total costs for a given output meant that the price of each factor was equal to marginal physical productivity multiplied by marginal cost; and the change in input, as output increased, necessarily equalled the change in marginal cost occasioned by the changing price of the input. With these principles in mind, it was almost self-evident that Euler's theorem for the distribution of the product to the factors must hold—that the product was exhausted in the process of distribution.

In consumer theory, Samuelson rejected both the cardinalist and introspective approach. "Consumers' market behavior is explained in terms of preferences, which are in turn defined only by behavior," he said.[212] Recognizing that this skirted close to the edge of emptiness, Samuelson nevertheless argued that in a technical sense, at least, meaningful theorems could be obtained from the behaviorist, ordinalist view. By placing certain restrictions on the various functions involved, he asserted that such theorems could be verified or refuted under ". . . ideal observational conditions." That such ideal conditions seldom were obtained did not disturb the theory *qua* theory. The approach was essentially the same as Hicks', with indifference concepts employed in order to distinguish between substitution and income effects. Given the level of income and the existing set of prices, the individual consumer was presumed to select the highest point on the preference scale. Despite Samuelson's disclaimer that this in no way implied felt magnitudes, one ran the risk of getting right back to utility. Samuelson's analysis assumed a "strong" ordering of preferences. That is, the consumer had to make a definite commitment before a description of his state of mind was possible.[213] Thus, all that one had to know about the consumer might be learned by observing how he behaved in the market. If his choice was maintained, even though the price of the commodity increased or despite the fact that its price was higher than another, clearly preference was "revealed." Such preferences would have to be transitive, and the indifference curves derived from them would have to be amenable to treatment by the calculus, that is, integrable. On the other hand, the indifference analysis proposed by Hicks had implied "weak" ordering, and this, Samuelson thought, could not provide operationally significant statements. In his view, preference meant a revelation by the consumer of his specific position, thus ruling out any consideration of strategical maneuvers. Consequently, welfare propositions, which stemmed from this analysis, would have to be related to definite and precise courses of action.

Samuelson's chief contribution to the debate was an investigation of the conditions for the displacement of equilibrium. He determined that the relevant demand functions were single-valued. For each set of prices and income there was a specific set of goods, and with equi-proportional changes in prices and income the quantities involved were left unchanged. As for the indifference analysis per se, Samuelson was not convinced that it was as useful as "revealed preference." In fact, he argued, utility theory generally provided few worthwhile theorems, and even these did not seem very important for economics. Not much would be changed, he said, if utility propositions were found to be untrue. Thus, with a few broad strokes, he undermined the whole apparatus of modern consumer demand theory.

That this view would be resisted was to be expected. It was argued, in opposition to Samuelson, that statistical observation could convert the indifference surface into an operational concept.[214] Yet Samuelson's "strong" ordering, which permitted the derivation of welfare propositions from single acts of choice, would seemingly obviate the need for statistical counting, assuming that this was at all possible. It has been argued further that the Samuelson approach tends to minimize substitution effects and leans more toward income effects, thus preventing the development of a genuinely complete theory of demand.[215] Yet in an economy where a rising price level does not seem to alter relative price relationships, it would appear that this stricture does not have much force.[216] Nor did Samuelson have much to say about consumers' surplus, despite Hicks' heroic effort at rehabilitating it. This stemmed from the fact that in ordinal theory little importance could be given to measures of gain resulting from price changes.[217] The concept of surplus moreover was deceptively simple: gains to the consumer were to be derived from a whole complex of services rendered by a modern advanced economy and this clearly weakened the notion of a specific surplus.[218]

The welfare propositions in Samuelson's economics were rooted in the work of Abram Bergson, who in a 1938 article had developed a social welfare function which synthesized much of what had gone before. In contrast to earlier welfare theorists, Bergson explicitly had accepted value judgments. These might be determined, he said, by some higher authority. Indifference curves could be worked up to establish a social welfare function by which to judge whatever economic policy was to be proposed. Of course, the difficulty here was to know what the collectivity really wanted. Further, it was questionable that any ready legislative technique was available to arrive at such group valuations. That they could be distilled from the deliberations of such august bodies as the United States Congress or the respective state legislatures seemed dubious. According to Kenneth Arrow, social decision-making would require consistency in the array of preferences, a consensus without external pressures, a kind of majority rule, and social choice based only on the alternatives presented. In Arrow's view, at least one of these criteria was bound to be violated, as in the case of voting preferences where consistency did not always govern. Thus, a rigorous concept of social choice would seem difficult to attain.[219]

At any rate, Bergson's ordinal social concept seemed much more suggestive and fruitful than the earlier work of Marshall, Pigou, or Pareto. Although some writers have contended that there was no room for value judgments in economics, Samuelson argued that ". . . it is a legitimate exercise of economic analysis to examine the consequences of various value judgments, whether or not they are shared by the theorist." [220] Yet it was evident that many theorems derived in this way would not be technically meaningful, since they emanated from assumptions that could be neither refuted nor verified. In Marshall, for example, the assumption of a constant marginal utility of income seemed to simplify matters considerably. Samuelson asked, however, whether it was possible to develop such a measure at all. What did the concept mean to start with? It could refer to the common value of the ratios of marginal utilities to the prices of various goods when changes in prices and incomes were constant. Theoretically any number of utility functions could describe this situation. The problem was to select one that would be constant for any change in prices or income. But it could be shown that no such function was available. If the problem were refined to mean a constant marginal utility when price but not income changed, some function might be worked out. But since this would imply a unit income elasticity of demand, an unlikely condition, it seemed dubious that a constant utility function could be obtained. Therefore, drawing on Samuelson's argument, any attempt to derive such a statistical measure as the Consumers' Price Index from a utility function was doomed to frustration.

The welfare function itself was ordinally defined, that is, one had to speak of it in terms of better or worse positions, or those to which the social attitude was one of indifference. While a welfare function might not necessarily be able to indicate which of two social situations was the best to select, it presumably could reveal, for a limited set of situations, which would be the better if a choice were at all possible. In examining the content of such theorems, Samuelson found that prices usually were excluded from welfare analysis; that the relevant variables could be applied to either an individual or to a group, such as a family; that assumptions of homogeneity were made; that inputs were assumed to be fluid and transferable; that preferences were rationally established; that preferences were individual in character, thus excluding Veblen's conspicuous consumption; that the assumption of symmetry in the analysis implied conditions of equality; and that welfare all too often was spoken of as the maximization of cardinal utilities. Interpreting welfare as the maximizing of input-output relationships, Samuelson found that only trivial results were forthcoming. The conclusion that more production of a good was desirable, or that the same output could be obtained with less input did not appear very striking. Equality of income distribution, usually put forth as a condition for optimum welfare, also implied that tastes were alike. Moreover, the welfare function could not help but suggest the possibility of interpersonal comparisons.[221] Samuelson's own "possibility" function seemingly contradicted the contention of other theorists that only measures of increases or decreases in welfare were required. It seemed obvious that even in the contemporary limited approach, comparisons were unavoidable. Thus, said Samuelson, the new welfare propositions were really contained in the old.[222] There were as many ethical implications in Hicks and Pareto as in Marshall and Pigou. Samuelson wondered out loud whether a third area of investigation might not be opened up, namely that of "inter-individual" comparison.[223] This would be carrying the already highly refined, tenuous welfare function beyond the stage that it had reached.

The areas of public expenditures and international trade may be taken as two examples of the application of Samuelson's welfare analysis. Theoretical developments in international trade had evidently come to a halt. While neoclassical doctrine still employed a variant of labor cost, other economists were seeking to install subjective analysis via the indifference curve technique, as reflected in the work of Haberler and Leontief. Jacob Viner was still arguing, however, that real cost had to be explained. Indifference curves, it was said, were influenced by income distribution, and this in turn was affected by the flow of trade. Consequently, the problem was how to measure gains derived from international trade. Samuelson put forth the argument that the assumptions employed by the disputants were not required to demonstrate gain.[224] Quite simply, foreign trade implied that a country was in a position to secure more goods while reducing its own production. This certainly represented a gain, argued Samuelson, although it could not be measured. Thus, no matter what restrictions were placed on international trade, some trade was better than none. Moreover, it was quite possible for tariffs to improve the terms of trade and thereby increase welfare for a particular nation.[225] Despite the general view that tariffs could not increase absolute returns to the protected factors of production (the arguments had been made that, at best, tariffs could improve a nation's relative position), Samuelson contended that, in the absence of counterattack, tariffs could increase returns in both a relative and absolute sense.[226] For, in a two-factor model, the shift of resources occasioned by protection would leave one of the factors relatively scarce in certain industries and thus lead to increased income for that factor.

Preference theory was also employed to analyse the nature of government expenditures.[227] Starting from an admittedly extreme position, Samuelson asked what public policy in this realm ought to be, given the existence of a social welfare function, the absence of technological change, stability in tastes, and constant returns to scale. Basically, the only policy necessary was that which would effect a redistribution of income. The financing of certain minimum government expenditures, as in the world of Adam Smith's unseen hand, would be secondary to the redistribution or transfer problem. Where income was not "optimally" distributed, the method of taxation then would be significant, for this would give rise to further redistribution effects. However, once technological change and increasing or decreasing returns were conceded, the situation would alter and ". . . the ordinary private marketing calculus must be non-optimal." [228] If one were to add to these elements a demand for public goods which "enter into many persons' indifference curves," the model of perfect competition would collapse. Nevertheless, argued Samuelson, theoretically one might work out a socially desirable configuration of indifference points definable in terms of some specified welfare function. Such a model would have to show equality between the social marginal rates of substitution for public and private goods and would have to assume a lump-sum redistribution of private goods to the point of "equal marginal social significance." Samuelson did not think that it would be easy to move in such a direction, for some "rational men" would try to surrender fewer private for public goods by engaging in strategical maneuvers. Thus, central to the Samuelson case was his contention that government budgets might properly include subsidies for "transfer" purposes, if social welfare would be enhanced thereby. The problem would be exacerbated, of course, by returns other than constant and by the diversity of goods and services; but it was possible, at least theoretically, to work out a solution.

Samuelson's most significant contribution was the clarification of the concept of economic dynamics. Equilibrium implied a condition in which the variables of a model would tend to return to their original points when displaced. Consequently, in order to compare static positions, it was necessary that the underlying dynamic forces be stable. Samuelson, obviously, was reversing the usual order of things: John Bates Clark had made dynamics dependent on the static; for Samuelson, statics was but a special case of the dynamic. A dynamic system operated in a context of time; the timeless, static model was merely a degenerate special case in which the functional relationships were expressed in relatively simple forms with time held as a constant. In a dynamic system, on the other hand, there was always a functional relationship between the variables and their rates of change. Moreover, a dynamic system would exhibit a kind of internal, self-generating development.[229] Dynamic forms were conceived to be of two types: period analysis, employing the mathematics of difference equations; and continuous flow analysis, utilizing differential equations.

Statics would show how equilibrium was attained, given certain functional relationships and parameters. The relationship of such a static model to the stability conditions required for dynamics was called by Samuelson the "correspondence principle." The application of this principle, central to Samuelson's thought, required that analysis be a two-way street. Said he: "Not only can the investigation of the dynamic stability of a system yield fruitful theorems in statical analysis, but also known properties of a (comparative) statical system can be utilized to derive information concerning the dynamic properties of a system." [230] The rates of change among the variables in a static system would be zero: in a dynamic set-up the problem was to describe the rates of change of the variables over time, utilizing the whole battery of mathematical techniques provided by differential and difference equations. It was in the realm of the dynamic that one ascertained the stability of a particular equilibrium. Thus, the introduction of time lags into a price-supply situation led to the famous cobweb theorem. Samuelson took issue with Hicks' concept of the dynamic, questioning the usefulness of the notion of perfect stability.[231] It seemed erroneous to postulate such stability conditions for dynamic situations, when they more properly belonged to the static model. Hicks, it will be recalled, had reduced the diversity of goods to a single item and then indicated that a dynamic condition existed when supply exceeded demand. But this did not appear to be sufficiently general in character and was in fact an artificial construct. Samuelson's theory seemed by far to provide the more general case.

After developing the analysis for linear systems, Samuelson then went to the more complex issues of nonlinearity. In linear systems the lack of amplitude in economic motion involved a considerable loss of realism. By introducing time lags into the model and utilizing difference equations to analyse nonlinearity, this handicap could be overcome. Samuelson also made careful distinctions among stationary, causal, and historical systems, a classification which seemed quite helpful in recognizing the chief features of different economic models.[232] In a stationary economy the variables were constant over time. In a causal system, behavior depended solely on the initial conditions that were specified and the time which had elapsed. However, the significant feature was the fact that variables in such a system were internal, as it were. While an historical model also described economic motion, the variables did not enter at the different points of time in an "essential" way, that is, the causes of its movement were primarily external and noneconomic in nature. One could thus list these possibilities: static-stationary, static-historical, dynamic-causal, and dynamic-historical, to which one might add stochastic or accidental systems of either causal or historical origin. Now, such a taxonomy could easily be as sterile as the models to which it leads, but Samuelson managed to rescue his exposition with the acknowledgment that it was frequently necessary to draw upon noneconomic factors in one's presentation. "The world rarely fits into the taxonomic classifications of the pedagogues," he conceded.[233] This was an admission that few other mathematical economists had been willing to make.

Dynamic analysis encompassed such problems as the growth of compound interest at discontinuous points of time, the relationship between the growth of capital stock and income flows, the interaction between the multiplier and the accelerator, cobwebs, and other nonlinear systems. Samuelson quite rightly insisted that the study of cycles and growth demanded dynamic methods of analysis. Thus, while the number of possible models was virtually infinite, it was at least essential to make the methodology explicit. This approach emphasized the likelihood of self-generating cycles, so that once a disturbance occurred, the economy provided its own power for movement. Consequently, cycle theory no longer had to have separate and distinct explanations for turning points, as in Hicks' upper ceiling.[234]

One of the best illustrations of Samuelson's use of dynamic analysis was his famous article on the interaction of the multiplier and accelerator.[235] This had its genesis in Alvin Hansen's attempt to explain the 1938 recession, in which a model with perpetual oscillations was developed.[236] However, Samuelson showed that with different values for the marginal propensity to consume and the relation, or accelerator, various cycles were possible. The model required that income be subdivided into government deficit spending, private consumption expenditure induced by earlier public expenditure (here the multiplier was at work), and private spending motivated by the accelerator. Depending then on whatever values were assigned to the multiplier and accelerator, varying oscillatory systems were possible. If only the multiplier was functioning, that is, with the accelerator at zero, a steady injection of investment would lead to an increase in income equal to the value of the injection times the multiplier. Where the value of the marginal propensity to consume was 0.5 (the multiplier being 2) and the accelerator set at one, the oscillations would be damped, moving about the income obtained from the multiplier action alone. With higher values for the marginal propensity to consume and the accelerator, the amplitudes of economic movement would move around an average income equal to what the latter would be with the multiplier alone. With still higher initial values, explosive effects would be obtained, with income approaching a compound interest rate of growth. The analysis suggested that the accelerator was not the decisive factor in movements of national income, but seemed rather to supplement and intensify the effects of the multiplier. Really high values would be necessary to make the accelerator genuinely effective. Yet the accelerator could have important cyclical influences, and in nonlinear models it would be possible to give it varying values at different points of time, thus making for a really complex analysis. The significant point, however, was that with such a theory one searched for the basic causes of movement within the economy itself.

Yet for all these high-powered techniques, the mathematical method does threaten to lead economics into a blind alley. In less skilled hands than Samuelson's, the models can become virtuous for their own sake; all too often they fail to provide avenues for investigation and research, as any good theory should. Frequently, the algebra becomes so involved as to be practically unmanageable. In the world of nonlinear business cycle models, for example, it seems essential that empirical data be introduced, if further investigation is to continue. As Lloyd Metzler once remarked, it may very well be necessary to bring in statistical data from the start, thus by-passing in the main the kind of theory Samuelson has developed.[237]

It was only natural that this high level dynamic theory should lead to an interest in such newer techniques as linear programming. Samuelson's conception of dynamics, concerned as it was with movements away from a maximum and their return to such points, concentrated on what he described as marginal inequalities. Ordinary marginal theory, interested in the maximum position per se, spoke in terms of the equality of marginal revenue and marginal cost, rather than the kind of inequalities created by movements away from equilibrium. Yet a theory based on the latter concept ought to exhibit a greater degree of generality, said Samuelson.[238] A "theory" which dealt with just such matters was linear programming, developed in this country during World War II as a means of handling military stockpiling and supplies. Although we shall postpone a more complete discussion of linear programming, we may observe here that the question of allocating limited resources to different uses—*the* economic problem—can be stated in terms of linear programming. Such decisions can be described as linear in nature, subject to certain nonlinear inequalities. The temptation to deal with such problems could not be resisted, for they posed, in a broader way, the same challenge faced in the *Foundations*. Many economic problems exhibited attributes of inequality—namely, arbitrage, speculation, and rationing—yet they could not always be explained by maximums.[239]

As a discipline, one of the newest, linear programming has had some interesting origins. Among economists the feeling had grown that simply counting unknowns and equations in a general equilibrium model did not provide usable answers. The questions of resource allocation implicit in welfare economics raised additional questions. Then came the game theory of John von Neumann and Oskar Morgenstern in which minimax notions were central. Allocation and equilibrium were also involved in Leontief's input-output scheme. And, Samuelson noted, developments in both statistical decision theory and the mathematics of sets contributed to the growing background of linear programming.[240] In all of these, the goal seemed to be how to handle problems of maxima in new ways, taking account not of equivalences but rather of the inequalities which characterize economic movements. Thus Samuelson successfully reinterpreted virtually everything that was new in economics in terms of his own vision of theoretical objectives. The basic theme—that economic science can be dealt with by means of a kind of unified field theory—was maintained intact.[241]

Yet for all Samuelson's sharp sense of realism, he has remained the pure theorist par excellence. In his 1961 presidential address to the American Economic Association he spoke at length in praise of analytical economics as opposed to political economics. There was a dichotomy, he asserted, between the inner logic of the science and its implications for the man in the street, a dichotomy which he seemed to welcome. In fact, the good political economist was apt to be an indifferent analyst and the good analyst really did not have to bother about the state of the world. So went the argument, supported by a characteristically personal review of Smith, Ricardo, Mill, Marx, and Marshall, which purported to demonstrate what poor analysts they had been, if only because of their abiding concern with the public weal. Yet it was evident that as a leading economic adviser to the United States government Samuelson did not believe that the economist ought not operate in the realm of *political economy*. He merely questioned whether the economists' words of wisdom indeed would always be heeded. And that, he had failed to see, was the essence of politics.

What then ought the economist do? Nothing, said Samuelson, for the world of analytics *was* different from the world of affairs, and economists were well advised to continue to cultivate only the logic and discipline of their field. To escape from frustration, and perhaps public schizophrenia, it was best, Samuelson cautioned, to retire to the lonely towers of Academe and there to work for the only coin worth having—the scholar's self-applause.

v

Wassily Leontief and Input-Output Analysis

Mutual interdependence had a rather long history, antedating both Walras and Pareto. Its roots extended as far back as the eighteenth-century physiocrats in France, one of whose leaders, François Quesnay, had tried to demonstrate with his *Tableau Économique* the way in which goods and money flowed between the different sectors of the economy. Quesnay's objective was to reveal the superiority of the agricultural sector of the economy and to show that only farm activity yielded a social surplus.[242] A similar construction was at the heart of Marx's theory as well, although the emphasis now was shifted to industry. This was particularly evident in the reproduction schema found in the second volume of *Das Kapital*.[243] These "models," however, were broad in scope and sought to present a rough, general picture of the economy. In Marx's case, there were two sectors—producers' goods and consumers' goods—an aggregating device, which despite its all-inclusive character, had served economists well for many a decade.

Credit for the first precise theoretical formulation of interdependence must go, naturally, to Léon Walras. In his system, as we have noted, were utility functions, supply and demand functions, and coefficients of production, such that it was theoretically possible to establish the prices of goods and the amounts that entered upon the market. But this was all pure theory, and Walras doubted that his system would ever exhibit empirical usefulness, for it was unlikely that the necessary statistical data would ever become available. Nor did Pareto or Barone believe that numerical content could be given to general equilibrium theory. For a long time it was questioned whether the Walrasian system could be "solved," that is, that there was a unique and determined equilibrium. Not until the 1930's did the noted mathematician, Abraham Wald, demonstrate the feasibility of such a solution.[244] Despite Walras' *tâtonnements,* there was no assurance in his model that equilibrium would be restored after a disturbance. As Wald indicated, only one path of equilibrium at best existed in Walras' theory. Pareto's analysis was somewhat richer in content, in that he sought to employ varying technological coefficients rather than single linear homogeneous production functions. And in Hicks and Samuelson one finds an attempt to have the system respond to changes in the parameters. Another problem in Walras' approach was the presence of an equation for each factor and commodity, so that even for a small "economy" it was necessary to "solve" thousands of equations. The question of aggregation was one that did not occur to him, and, in its absence, any meaningful compilation of empirical data would be beyond human capacity.

Perhaps the first approach toward an effective handling of the empirical content of a system of general equilibrium was made by Wassily W. Leontief (1906-   ). This was done through the "input-output" table, first published in *The Structure of American Economy, 1919-1929.*[245] The basic ideas for input-output had been developed earlier during Leontief's student days in Europe, notably in a paper on the Soviet economic balance published in 1925. However, the article was but a first approach toward a quantitative empirical analysis of an economic system. It was some five years before the technique for applying empirical data to general equilibrium theory was worked out.

Leontief was born in Petrograd, attending the university there before going on to Berlin for his doctorate. He came to the United States in 1931 as a research associate at the National Bureau of Economic Research where he did further work on input-output analysis.[246] Leontief joined the Harvard economics faculty in 1931, where he has been professor since 1946. When the Bureau of Labor Statistics of the United States Department of Labor undertook to build a large input-output table in connection with wartime needs, he acted as a special consultant for that project, terminated unfortunately in 1953 by the incoming administration in Washington. (It can be reported that government research on input-output analysis was reinstituted in 1961. An 80×80 matrix for 1958 will be developed.) Leontief also has directed the Harvard Economic Research Project, set up in 1948 to engage mainly in input-output investigations.

Input-output certainly met Schumpeter's criterion for good theory: it became a program for empirical research in which heroic efforts were made to fill theoretical tool-boxes with content. Clapham's complaints could now be minimized. As more statistical information became available and as theoretical frameworks adaptable to numerical treatment were developed, economics began to move out of the realm of pure thought experiments toward a genuine fusion of fact and theory. The day seemed close when one could no longer say of economists that their thinking was dominated by a belief that ". . . by dividing one fiction of the mind by another one comes out with a reality." [247] With the input-output technique it appeared that the theory of general equilibrium, which for so long remained on the shelf of abstraction where Walras had placed it, might now be studied numerically. The development of high speed electronic computers was also an encouraging sign. It seemed that economists would at long last go beyond the statistics of time series and regression analysis, which had been after all still partial investigations of economic reality. Although Pareto and even Wicksell doubted that much could be done to advance numerical calculations of an equilibrium model, the work of Wald and of John von Neumann indicated real possibilities.[248]

The discussion on this aspect of equilibrium theory harkened back to an observation by Hans Neisser in 1932 that it would have to do more than merely specify prices and production rates in terms of non-negative numbers. Several years later Karl Menger noted that one of the functions of an equilibrium model was to distinguish between free and scarce goods. This was the problem to which Wald had addressed himself in his 1935-1936 papers. But the Neumann model went beyond Wald's static system by introducing several production possibilities, albeit with fixed coefficients. Significantly, goods were visualized as both inputs and outputs, leading to the concept of the circulation of commodities between industries. Consumer demand was included, with labor viewed as the output of households and given sets of consumer goods as inputs. The system was a closed one, with any surpluses utilized for investment. The problem was whether equilibrium could be maintained while the economy grew and expanded. Assuming proportionate rates of growth in all sectors, Neumann demonstrated that at least one such growth rate was governed by the rate of interest. Where a component grew faster than its interest cost, the surplus was deemed to be a free good. There was thus a somewhat limited dynamic character in the Neumann model. These developments, although quite abstract and replete with high-powered mathematics, provided a large part of the inspiration not only for input-output studies but for linear programming as well.[249]

However, the major advance in the numerical specification of economic models was made during the 1940's by Leontief with his input-output concept. Large sets of economic equations now were capable of numerical solution. The speed with which modern electronic equipment could work out a system of 30-some-odd equations with an equal number of unknowns was phenomenal. And no fears were generated when the Bureau of Labor Statistics sought to handle several hundred equations. The input-output venture was certainly justifiable, at least theoretically. As Leontief remarked, there were meaningful connections between automobile sales in New York and the demand for bread in Detroit.[250] In essence, the entire country was visualized as one large accounting system, with each sector having its own "budget" of economic activity. The accounting set-up provided a schematic framework or matrix which showed output flows from one sector to all the others and inputs to the various sectors. Outputs were distributed horizontally across the matrix, with inputs distributed vertically. Each sector thus appeared twice, as a producer of outputs and as a consumer of inputs. Either value or quantity terms could be employed: if the former were used, totals could be computed both horizontally and vertically, yielding equations for total output and total input. For quantities, however, vertical totals were meaningless, since tons could not be added to yards. Moreover, the need to aggregate, required to ease mechanical handling, raised certain questions concerning the definition of an industry or a group of industries and did imply some loss of detail. In many of the actual studies, the matter was short-circuited by using Census definitions.

Theoretically, it was now possible to write out an equation which described how much of a sector's output went to the others. The excess of this sum was presumed to be the final demand, or, as Leontief labeled it, the "bill of goods." The latter might be found in households, government, foreign trade, or for that matter any industry or sector placed in this last category. Such equations were called "balance equations." In his own model, Leontief made certain restrictive assumptions as a kind of first approximation (although he went to some length to provide a logical basis for the limiting premises): any good was supplied by only one sector; there was no joint production of commodities; and the amount of input used by the consuming sector was determined by its own output. The last assumption underpinned Leontief's fixed coefficients of production. He argued that costs were strictly proportional to output: consequently, he could operate with homogeneous linear equations and dispense with marginal productivity theory. Increases in output meant that all cost elements had been augmented. And it was clear that the technical substitution of factors had been rejected as an operational concept.[251]

Given then total output and the coefficients of production (defined as the ratio of a sector's output supplied to another, which was also the latter's output, to the total output of that sector), it became possible to establish the final demands. The analysis could reveal the "typical productive and distributive interrelations which determine the structure of the national economy." [252] A structural equation was obtained when the coefficient equation was solved for its input term. Here was an approach that combined the complexities of general equilibrium with the simplifying assumptions of static analysis.[253] When government and households were looked upon as "industries" or sectors, the model was described as a "closed" one. This was Leontief's original formulation, in which he employed a 45 industry classification for the years 1919 and 1929. Since the inputs that went into final demand could be determined, how much each industry had to produce to meet both direct and indirect demand ultimately became known.

When the system was converted to the "open" form, certain relationships akin to the Keynesian apparatus became visible. Opening the matrix was done by disregarding one of the basic relationships of the closed system so that a unique solution could not be attained.[254] That is, some of the variables were presumed to be independently determined and given for the task at hand: they were external to the model. In such cases the sum of the input coefficients would be less than unity for at least one sector. While any industry could be placed in that position, the most likely candidate was the household, for with attention focused on the amount of labor flowing from it, various output combinations could be computed to ascertain the level for full employment. The open model reversed the analytical procedure: with a predetermined final demand, the required magnitudes consonant with that "bill of goods" could be computed. If the final demand changed, employment or output in the matrix changed. The analogy with Keynesian thinking seemed evident. This became the standard procedure in input-output work, since it seemed more relevant to matters of policy.[255]

Input-output analysis, or interindustry economics as some preferred to call it, offered possibilities for a study of locational problems as well.[256] The spatial distribution of economic activity could be easily incorporated into Leontief's single system of interdependence; it was necessary only to split each sector into its geographic subdivisions and to derive the balance and structural equations for each. Then the production of the same good in the various areas or regions would be considered as different sectors. It was possible now to observe the effects of variations in the final demands in the regions as well as the differences in productive methods. And as the analysis proceeded, it was noted that the total income generated in an economy depended in large measure on the distribution of production between geographic areas.

The system could be "dynamized" as well by introducing income creating forces, alternative production methods, and investment. This presumably provided an empirical "law of change" by noting the shifts in structural characteristics and the effects stemming from income movements and investment.[257] The key factor in Leontief's dynamic model was the output going to capital or inventory. The balance equations now had to include stock increases, and the structural counterparts derived from capital coefficients became stock-flow equations.[258] Thus, if one knew the initial position of an economy, argued Leontief, the development of a dynamic system over a given period of time could be forecast. Of course, excess capacities would have to be accounted for, especially when older capital structures proved to be unsuitable for current production. Thus, depending on the direction that production plans might take, excess capacity could develop at various points in the system.

In actual practice, the dynamic model did not work out as had been hoped. An effort was made to retain fixed coefficients despite the introduction of time. Nonlinear movements, for example, could be ignored, at least analytically, only if the intervals between the dated matrices were small. Choice clearly had to be admitted. But not enough work has been done as yet to make a true dynamic model possible. Consequently, questions of accuracy and the relevance of the data used were bound to arise.[259] Moreover, the actual impact of technological change became highly important. Tests of the predictive capacity of the input-output matrix have not been very conclusive.[260] In some cases investment requirements were overestimated when compared with actual levels.[261] A number of testing devices have been constructed. In one, the input-output estimates were compared with data obtained by assuming that the total output in each sector was a constant multiple of its final demand. This was called the "final demand blow-up" test. Another assumed a constant ratio between a sector output and Gross National Product. Still a third "predicted" each sector's output from a multiple regression of that output on GNP over a given time period. The last method emerged as the most accurate, since, by taking time into account, it allowed for a gradual alteration in both technique and consumer tastes.[262] It should be noted that one can move easily from Gross National Product accounts into an input-output matrix, for the latter simply utilizes the information lost by the "netting-out" procedure employed in GNP computations. In this way, the underlying turbulence of the economy is revealed in striking fashion. Empirical work on input-output analysis has been done in a number of countries.[263] Norway, Denmark, Holland, Italy, Britain, Japan, Canada, Australia and several Latin American nations have undertaken interindustry research. Interest has been aroused, mainly through the efforts of Oskar Lange, even in the Soviet Union and its satellites.[264]

Yet not all economists have been willing to accept input-output analysis as a viable way of studying the economic order. Oriented in orthodox habits of thought, critics have expressed marked resistance to Leontief's attempted revolution. The idea of fixed coefficients seemed especially unpalatable. Yet there was a way of treating the problem of varying production functions, if the Leontief system were modified with some of the later tools of linear programming. In the latter, the various levels of input utilization became variables, and criteria could be set down for selecting one method rather than another, whether these were based on minimum cost or on maximum "welfare." Viewed from this standpoint, the Leontief matrix became a special case in the more general theory of linear programming.[265] The rigidity of the Leontief technique suggested that the rate of output might not be a positive one if inputs were large per unit of output. And in strict logic, with a zero final demand, employment and output also would be zero. If zero foreign investment, for example, were set as the "bill of goods" or final demand, it obviously would be unrealistic to think that output would be zero. Thus, it was evident that supplementary information was necessary to describe the final demand. It was also argued that the impact of investment in one sector on the others was not clear in the input-output schema, since "feed-backs" and circular effects were excluded.[266] The necessary correction would have to be made by installing a multiplier apparatus.

Critics insisted that less restrictive assumptions were needed to make a choice of technique available and to allow for the substitution of inputs and joint production. This would restore to economic analysis the nonlinear concepts that the input-output approach had dispensed with. One had to return to the variability in movements depicted by Hicks and Harrod in order to account for significant discontinuities. Yet the empirical prospects of the Leontief model did make it worthwhile, for it remained one of the few analytical devices amenable to numerical treatment. One might quarrel over the fact that there were no behavior equations in the system and that economic psychology had been entirely excluded, with statistical inference substituted for the analysis of consumer reactions.[267] Yet the open model, in which final demand had to be postulated, did suggest room for the kind of behavior equations that would take it beyond the level of technology and production functions.[268]

The most extreme criticism of input-output tables was that they were little more than convenient classifications of past data.[269] But, as Raymond Goldsmith has remarked, they do seem to provide a reasonable approximation of dynamized Walrasian equations. A major difficulty was the lack of timeliness, for so long as the tables were not available at fairly frequent intervals, they did take on the character of historical artifacts. The objection that one could not define an industry or a sector was without weight.[270] More serious were the fixed coefficients implying constant returns and the lack of choice in technique. But from the theoretical standpoint, this too was not fatal; for, as Samuelson demonstrated, if efficiency were assumed so that the input coffiecients were deemed to be the best ones available, substitution and choice did not have to enter the argument, since an optimum condition would have been attained.[271] Despite this rather ingenious defense—one that employed certain immanent qualities of the input-output apparatus—economists increasingly began to turn to what seemed a more flexible approach, that of linear programming. Perhaps the seeming practicability of the latter and its usefulness for microeconomic work was more attractive than the global problems of input-output. Subtleties of doctrine did not upset them in linear analysis. They were now in possession of both received theory and high-powered mathematical technique.

6

Streams of Tradition

in Britain

Sidgwick, Wicksteed, and
Edgeworth

IN THE LATE NINETEENTH CENTURY, British tradition divided itself into two major currents. The first, starting with certain ideas in Smith and Ricardo and stressing objective value, ethics, and amelioration, culminated in the great works of Marshall, Pigou, and Robertson. The second, beginning with little rivulets in the writing of Longfield, and fed by a powerful stream of ideas from the Continent, stressed subjective value and pure theory as the proper basis for economics.[1] Jevons' development of the idea of utility was paralleled by the work of the Austrians. And continental subjective theory had become so powerful in the writings of Hicks and Robbins that it threatened to submerge completely the Marshallian reconciliation of the Austrian and Ricardian tradition. With this new trend the quality of modern economics was displayed in full panoply. Certainly it was more than a theory of price and production. Abandoning the idea of social conflict and group action implicit in Ricardo, and not entirely absent in Marshall and Pigou, a kind of atomistic theory developed in which the behavior of individual consumers became the leitmotiv of economic thought. A universal theory of value applicable to all forms of society emerged, and economics became a pristine system of mechanics, utterly neutral, with nothing to say about the nature of means and ends.

Yet, concern with ethical values in economics was still in evidence before the turn of the century. Henry Sidgwick (1838-1900) was one writer who did seek to maintain ethical standards. Although most histories have tended to ignore Sidgwick, his work is important, at least as a bridge between the old and the new. Primarily a moral philosopher, he was the last of that great group of British thinkers who could write with equal facility in both economics and philosophy. Sidgwick sought to reformulate the heritage received from John Stuart Mill at a time when it was undergoing severe attack. For him there was still an important relation between the physical and social sciences. And while his economics was largely traditional, it was suffused with a greater emphasis on the role of government than was usual for the time. This clearly stemmed from his utilitarian interest in social amelioration.

Sidgwick, born in Yorkshire, attended Rugby, and in 1855 went to Cambridge where he remained for the rest of his life.[2] An excellent student, he pursued the usual course in classics. And his extensive intellectual interests, including investigations of psychical phenomena, a fashionable pastime in those days, led him to Comte and Spencer, with excursions into Arabic and Hebrew. Appointed a Fellow at the age of twenty-one, he began to lecture on Moral Science, a subject whose scope was virtually as broad as it had been in Adam Smith's time. In 1874 he published *The Methods of Ethics,* the first of several books in philosophy. It was during this time that the individual social sciences began to establish themselves as independent fields of inquiry. History was separated from law, and economics began to toddle along on its own feet.

In 1883, the year he was appointed professor of moral philosophy, Sidgwick published his only book in economics, the *Principles of Political Economy.*[3] As a teacher, Sidgwick was overly concerned with administrative details, with the result that few students came to his classes. However, some notable figures did listen to his lectures, including Bertrand Russell and Lord Balfour. The social ethics implicit in economics was approached with the common sense of English utilitarianism, while in political science Sidgwick added a sense of reality to Bentham, supplemented by the logic of Ricardo. It was in the area of personal relationships that Sidgwick made perhaps his

greatest impact. Alfred Marshall once remarked that Sidgwick had been his
". . . spiritual father and mother: for I went to him for aid when perplexed,
and for comfort when troubled; and I never returned empty. . . ." [4]

Sidgwick tried to give the utilitarian tradition a further push toward
evaluating ethics and morals in a more reasoned manner than he felt had
been done by earlier writers. Psychological hedonism was qualified in several
important ways, particularly by applying evolutionary concepts in the development of moral judgments. The latter, said Sidgwick, were to be rooted
in empirical insights rather than in intuition or *a priori* concepts. A universalistic moral consciousness was alien to human experience, he said; if
valid at all it was only an instinctive need to adjust to the world about us that
made it so. These precepts underpinned his economic thinking also.

How Sidgwick sought to bridge the gap between the older classical economics and the newer modes of thought being explored by Marshall was
effectively illustrated by his *Principles of Political Economy*. Production, distribution, and exchange were primarily restatements of Mill, with numerous
refinements and clarifications, for he was reluctant to break too sharply with
tradition. And the notion of marginal utility, fostered by Jevons and Edgeworth, was conspicuous by its absence. Yet the last third of the book did
include an exhaustive treatment of those areas in which the government
might properly intervene. This, he said, was the realm of "art" in economics.
The distinction between "art" and "science" was possible because of a clear
delineation between "what is" and "what ought to be." The latter implied
value judgments which might have relevance for economics, but these necessarily were to be separated from the objective relationships described in abstract theory. Thus the problems of economic *science* were to be divorced
from the political and ethical questions with which they were frequently
associated if the role of each were to be clearly understood.[5] However, it was
much easier to establish relationships between art and science in the area of
production than in distribution, for ethics did intrude more sharply in the
latter. Ultimately, judgments in matters of distribution would be referred to
whatever standards people would employ to define the greatest good for the
greatest number.[6]

On methodology, Sidgwick was equally broadminded. He could see little
point to the inductive versus deductive controversy. While analysis of production might yield better results by induction, he said, the "art" of economics would have to resort in the main to deductive methods.[7] Qualitative
analysis could bring fruitful results when properly used. Value, production,
and distribution—the perennial problems of economics—were derived from
Mill. As Ricardo's interpretation of "real value" seemed perfectly tenable
to Sidgwick, causes affecting variations in exchange value were reduced to
causes affecting supply.[8] Thus, the older view of cost of production did not
seem to be unreasonable. A discussion of wealth and capital followed, in

which one could detect a flirtation with the idea of utility. Variations in production were related to institutional factors in a way suggestive of the later work of Pigou. However, Sidgwick found it difficult to distinguish between the technical and purely economic aspects of production, although he did recognize that an invention, while technically feasible, might be economically impossible.[9] Building on the classical concepts which related factors of production to each other, Sidgwick observed that there was a certain degree of population density in conjunction with a given set of resources beyond which output per capita might fall.[10] Thus the notion of optimum population was clearly defined.

The older definition of capital as wage goods, raw materials, and instruments of production was clarified by distinguishing between capital as seen by the individual and by the community. In the latter case, Sidgwick argued, capital consisted only of those goods which stemmed from human work. However, he was reluctant to include in his concept wage goods in the form of advances from capital.[11] This was certainly an interesting development, for with this formulation, Sidgwick was approaching the idea of wage payments as a flow from income and not as part of a fund of capital. His idea of capital, going beyond a mere collection of goods, expressed, he said, an aspect that all wealth would exhibit up to the moment of consumption.[12] This represented an important amplification of some of the central ideas of the older classicists.

In distribution theory, Sidgwick stressed the role of national output in ways that foreshadowed Pigou. A theory of distribution, he observed, was in effect a theory of exchange for the services of the factors of production. The parallel with market price impelled him to explore this area first. He was struck by Mill's inadequate handling of the supply side of the market equation, and concluded that the variety of possible shifts in supply was probably the most significant element in price determination. But he was not quite prepared to surrender all of classical doctrine: "The Ricardian theory of the determination of Value by Cost of Production appears to me incontrovertible, at least as applied to modern civilised communities . . . if it is understood merely to affirm that industrial competition is a force constantly acting in the direction of equalizing the remuneration of producers of the same class in different departments of industry. . . ."[13] Cost of production could still be valid if looked at in the broadest possible sense. He was perhaps less ready to follow Mill in sharply dividing production and distribution, and he had no doubt that a more equal distribution of wealth would tend to enhance general "happiness."

Sidgwick departed from earlier views in the greater latitude he gave to government in economic affairs. As with Pigou, divergences between private net product and social net product were too important to be ignored. By imposing his own notions of distributive justice on classical theory, Sidgwick was able to point to fresh avenues for the economist to explore. Given the proper circumstances, he said, it might be well to allow industry to function without interference. Yet with economic advancement, the propositions of laissez faire would have to be qualified. Numerous exceptions stemmed from the disparities between the utility accruing to the individual and those accruing to society. Indeed, it could not be demonstrated that the spontaneous efforts of individuals motivated by self-interest would maximize material welfare.[14] Often a private enterprise occasioned social costs which it shifted to others. Social utility did not always flow from private endeavor,[15] and frequently increased social costs were exacerbated by such developments as monopoly. Thus laissez faire could not be taken as an absolute ideal: it exhibited disadvantages which would have to be cast into the balance. Nevertheless, some risks were involved in government intervention due to the mere increase in the exercise of power or in its use for special interests.[16] Despite this caveat, there were sufficient instances when collective action by the community would be required to guide economic activity. This seemed almost self-evident in cases where a conflict existed between the present use of resources and future needs. The difficulty here, of course, was in measuring the value that might be placed on resources to be used by future generations.[17] However, some estimate is made, for community investment in such social overhead as hospitals, schools, ports, and roads does represent a present estimate of future needs.

The defense of private property on the ground that it was a sacred institution did not meet Sidgwick's approval, for when injustices developed, he remarked, they simply would be perpetuated.[18] It was necessary, he said, to study private property as it functioned in society. Nor was the defense of freedom an acceptable argument for private property, since for most people freedom had little relation to property. Private property and free contract often failed to obtain for the worker the wage he deserved. And insofar as laissez faire did not succeed in giving equality of opportunity, government had a justifiable role to perform. The only proviso that Sidgwick set down was that intervention should not reduce output. In sum, he was prepared to accept a gradual movement toward the welfare state. When he questioned socialism, it was not in terms of distributive justice, but rather on grounds of productive efficiency. As he put it, one must pass from the ". . . tribunal of abstract justice to one where utilitarian . . . or 'economic' considerations are taken as decisive." [19] But each question as it developed was to be met on an empirical basis. General *a priori* principles were not acceptable. Policy decisions were to be founded on practical issues with ample scope for empirical evidence. For these reasons Sidgwick was extremely dubious about evaluating all economic matters with abstract criteria.

In contrast to Sidgwick, Philip H. Wicksteed (1884-1927) was one of the chief proponents of the newer subjective approach. A theologian of note whose Unitarian sermons were quite unorthodox, he entered economics as an ardent devotee of W. Stanley Jevons. Like Sidgwick, he too provided a bridge between the old and the new, but with much greater emphasis on the novel ideas Jevons had developed. The emphasis on a unifying psychological principle and the unitary nature of social life reflected the influence also of Auguste Comte. Wicksteed's conviction that the science of wealth was governed by certain general principles of social science clearly emanated from the positivist outlook.[20] Although Wicksteed never forgot his keen interest in social problems, he did develop a more individualistic conception of economic action after reading Jevons. While he criticized the Fabians for their flirtation with Marxian theory and was successful in weaning them away from it, he remained quite sympathetic to their purposes.[21] Although a follower of Jevons, Wicksteed did make several independent contributions to theoretical work. Especially noteworthy was his attempt to develop a general theory of distribution based upon Euler's theorem and his conception of supply as an aspect of demand.

Wicksteed was a most interesting personality. A medieval scholar as well as a minister, he was also an expert on Dante and Aristotle. As Lionel Robbins, who edited his major works, has said, Wicksteed successfully combined a wide range of intellectual pursuits with marked excellence in each.[22] He was able to hold his own with more specialists on their own ground than any other man in Britain.[23] Wicksteed, born in Leeds, entered the ministry after completing his undergraduate work at University College. Following in his father's footsteps, he took a pulpit at the age of thirty and for the next twenty years was quite active in Unitarian circles. Philosophy brought him to a study of medieval culture, and an interest in sociology led him to economics. His extension courses were eminently successful. In 1897, when his unorthodox theological views compelled him to resign his pulpit, Wicksteed gave full time to teaching and writing.

His initial interest in economics had been aroused by Henry George's *Progress and Poverty,* and after studying that peroration he went on to Jevons. While all his life Wicksteed had sympathized with the idea of land nationalization, he would go no further than the advocacy of public acquisition of certain kinds of landed property. It was rather the subjective economics of Jevons and the Austrians that caught his attention. Despite the coolness that Marshall had expressed for the utility approach, Wicksteed began to orient his thinking along these lines, and in 1888 he published *The Alphabet of Economic Science,* an introduction to the newer economics.[24] A scrupulously detailed exposition of utility concepts, the book displaced Jevons' term "final degree of utility" with the now familiar "marginal utility." It was very well received by professional economists; even Pareto, not one to dispense praise easily, offered his compliments. In 1894 his *Essay on the Co-ordination of the Laws of Distribution* appeared which tackled the problem of the distribution of the product among the various cooperating factors of production. Previously, Ricardo, von Thünen, and the Austrians had attempted solutions with somewhat indifferent success, and J. B. Clark and Wicksell had worked out answers of their own. As with the latter two writers, Wicksteed's formulation was based on marginal productivity: the product would be exhausted if each factor was paid according to its marginal contribution. However, when both Edgeworth and Pareto harshly criticized Wicksteed's presentation, he withdrew it in his *Common Sense of Political Economy*.[25] The latter work, published in 1910, was Wicksteed's most important effort in economics.[26]

As Robbins since has pointed out, *Common Sense* was really not a study of *political* economy, but rather a verbal statement of the technical implications of pure marginalist theory. Wicksteed insisted that his deductions were not original: they had been explicit, he said, in the whole corpus of earlier economics. The *Common Sense,* subtly argued and at times quite persuasive, can be, however, a painful experience to read. Each principle and idea was exhaustively investigated and more than liberally illustrated with dozens of examples. The ultimate logic of every point was so relentlessly pursued that one almost could conclude that Wicksteed must have been terribly garrulous.

Why a "common sense" of economics? This simply meant that the unifying economic principle in modern society was one which guided the administration of resources in general, whether for the housewife or the manufacturer. The equality of price and cost at the margin assured the best possible use of such resources, with cost equalizing payments to the factors of production. This made economics a positive rather than a normative science, one that would deal with the means of satisfying wants rather than with their legitimacy.[27] Wicksteed focused attention on the relative scale of preferences exhibited by marginal units of different commodities, rather than the less complex idea of changes in total utility. That is, he was interested in changes in the rate of movement of total utility. With the latter defined in relative terms, the notion of measurability began to give way to that of an order of preferences. Marginal utility was not a characteristic of the last unit, but merely an incremental concept which emphasized the significance of the last unit of a homogeneous stock of goods. Wicksteed also began to emphasize the simultaneous way in which values were established, at least in theory, thus reflecting continental ideas of interdependence.

His *Alphabet,* a small work, mainly mathematical in content, spent almost a third of its space on the calculus of demand. In it Wicksteed reworked Jevons' basic postulates, demonstrating how value was a function of the quantity of a good held either by an individual or a community. Thus the advantages of satisfactions derived from consumption increased or decreased as the holding of a good changed.[28] Once this was conceded, it became possible to establish curves of functional relationships. Although measurability might be questioned, the fact that it could order preferences in the sense of more or less justified the use of curves.[29] By concentrating on marginal changes, it also became feasible to employ the idea of limits. This technique, said Wicksteed, allowed one to compare satisfactions issuing from different goods, thereby establishing a common mode of measurement [30] which, simply enough, was the comparison of the ratio of desires for different goods of different individuals. Equilibrium in an exchange economy would call for equality between these ratios: the function of exchange was to bring about equilibrium by eliminating divergences in relative desires. Consequently, exchange value became a psychic phenomenon which in equilibrium expressed the equivalence of the marginal utility of a good in terms of the marginal utility of some *numéraire*.[31] This lent a quality of complete generality to the equimarginal principle. Said Wicksteed: "The productive forces of the community . . . will tend to distribute themselves in such a way that a given sum of productive forces will produce utilities at the margin. . . ." [32]

Cost of production, essentially an historical concept, had no influence on value,[33] for it was to be defined solely in terms of foregone alternatives. Wicksteed's formulation was virtually a categorical imperative: marginal valuation was posited as a universal precept in which the ". . . inner core of our life problems . . . obey the same all-permeating law." [34] Adam Smith's providential unseen hand functioned again, as those seeking their own gain were allowed to serve others. Yet opportunity cost as applied to labor did seem a bit doubtful, for few workers were engaged in more than one type of activity. On this point Wicksteed was quite vague. Moreover, the theory assumed almost perfect substitutability among the factors of production. This was developed in such extreme fashion that distinctions virtually were obliterated. While Wicksteed did acknowledge that a machine was not a building, he insisted that "within limits" unlike factors could be substituted for each other "at the margin," thus establishing a common measure of marginal serviceability.[35] Indeed, perfect rationality so pervaded the whole system that the housewife as well as the entrepreneur weighed alternatives down to the last item of expenditure. That this was an idealized portrayal of economic behavior is now evident, for such rationality applies to but a small part of the consumer's budget. Nor does rationality per se exist to the degree that Wicksteed believed.[36] In fact, there is ample evidence to suggest that the consumer today is literally trained to consume, much as the circus seal is trained, thereby destroying conscious choice as a deliberate facet of economic behavior. Unfortunately, economic theory has not yet digested this fascinating aspect of modern culture, and, insofar as it has failed to do so, its conception of consumer reaction remains attenuated.[37] Anticipations also were an integral part of Wicksteed's model, since the marginal changes taken as a basis for calculation were only those that one provisionally might expect to acquire.[38]

Although Wicksteed was a follower of Jevons, he rejected the latter's interest theory on the ground that capital yielded a continuous stream of services.[39] Yet his own theory was far from satisfactory: inordinate space was given over to consumption loans.[40] Generally, interest stemmed from a comparative evaluation of future and present satisfactions, with the principle of marginal adjustment once more the key idea.[41] However, not even the superabundance of illustrations could redeem Wicksteed's interest theory: it simply was quite inadequate. Interest and rent were made virtually identical, with no thought given to the fact that the distinction is usually made because the underlying economic relationships are different. This was certainly implicit in the traditional classical outlook; it reflected, of course, certain significant social issues, which by the end of the nineteenth century, had been merely shunted aside.[42] Yet, in Wicksteed, critical observations were obscured: in fact, interest, as a price determined at the margin, disappeared altogether in his model, at least for a stationary state.[43] Similarly, the laws of return were not set forth in an effective and precise manner. Had Wicksteed done so, he probably would not have been so willing to retract his formulation of the law of distribution. The problem seemed to be due to his failure to distinguish sharply between the firm and the industry, so that he was misled into denying that diminishing returns might apply to certain factors of production. He insisted that there was a sufficient supply of land, rejecting the notion of its limited availability.[44] Evidently, the identification of diminishing returns with historical real cost was much too close to make him feel comfortable.[45]

One of Wicksteed's unique ideas was his conception of the supply curve as an aspect of demand, and his attack on the idea of a supply curve was unusually sharp.[46] To him, the supply curve actually was derived from the reservation prices of those who possessed stocks of goods, so that in the final analysis it was the seller's demand for his own goods that determined supply. But Wicksteed seemed to suggest that sellers were prepared to consume the goods themselves, unless the price was satisfactory. Reservation prices, however, imply nothing more than a withdrawal of supply, to await another opportunity for entering the market. The supply curve did remain a useful analytic tool, despite his severe strictures.

In the *Co-ordination of the Laws of Distribution*,[47] Wicksteed first proposed his solution of the distribution problem. His objective was to examine the shares of the product from the standpoint of a single principle. This could be done most easily by stating the problem as a flow of services, so that marginal efficiency or productivity determined the value of a factor. The formula which indicated the total product was a sum of the amounts of the factors each multiplied by its marginal product. This implied that the sum of the shares would exhaust the product. The solution, related to a theorem developed in the eighteenth century by Euler, the famous mathematician, meant that the production function was linear and homogeneous, that is, that the product increased proportionately to the increase in the use of the factors, and that the marginal product of two factors would equal the marginal product of both factors if added separately. Although Wicksteed's mathematical demonstration of the theorem was subjected to some criticism,[48] the theory did allow him to interpret classical rent theory as a case of marginal productivity and to show by a reversal of procedures what the marginal productivity of capital and labor would be. But, as both Edgeworth and Pareto attacked Wicksteed's formulation, he withdrew it, as has been indicated. Pareto was thinking of possibilities other than constant returns, and Wicksteed's assumption of almost infinite substitutability of the factors could not meet the objections. Part of the difficulty was due to Wicksteed's fuzzy conception of cost of production. With decreasing costs, factor payments conceivably would exceed the total product; a deficit would result when increasing costs were obtained. With a surplus, or excessive profits, new firms would be encouraged to enter the industry and eventually equilibrium would be restored. Of course, Wicksteed's formulation could be made palatable if it were assumed that firms did operate at the minimum point of the unit cost curve. Operating even within "the neighborhood of the minimum" would be sufficient to validate the theorem, it seemed.[49]

The *Common Sense* cannot be said to be a completely satisfying work. After some six hundred pages of detailed illustrations of fundamental notions, short shrift was given to such urgent problems as unemployment, business cycles, housing, and trade unions. And the comments on these questions, while stemming from the underlying premises, are bound to leave the contemporary reader aghast. Minimum standards in housing would multiply the "unhoused"; minimum wages would tend to cause unemployment; and it was only slightly possible that public works might be helpful during depressions. Apparently, Wicksteed had so exhausted himself in building a compendium of examples that he no longer had energy left to apply his theoretical analysis to a study of society. The theory remained what it was, a pure construct, in no way able to illustrate what was happening in the world at large.

The development of pure theory in Britain was further advanced by Francis Y. Edgeworth (1845-1926), a descendant of a noted English family which had established itself in Ireland during the reign of Elizabeth I. Edgeworth, taught by private tutors, later received a thorough classical education at Oxford. After becoming Tooke Professor of Political Economy at Kings College, he succeeded Thorold Rogers to the Drummond chair at Oxford in 1891, remaining there for the rest of his life. But as Edgeworth produced no large works, although he edited the *Economic Journal* for many years, his influence was mainly oral. Yet his *Mathematical Psychics*[50] was an important landmark in the history of mathematical economics, containing as it did the first statement of the indeterminacy of bilateral monopoly. The lack of a major treatise by Edgeworth was filled by the publication in 1925 of his collected papers.[51]

Edgeworth's objective was to apply mathematics to the social or, as he would have said, moral sciences, and in doing this he covered a wide range of subjects, including taxation, railway rates, and international trade. In the latter, he noted a similarity with the theory of distribution, particularly when the flow of demand in international trade was visualized as a demand for factor services rather than for goods as such. His argument suggested that since the factors in different areas were not easily transferable, the situation was akin to the problem of distribution in a closed economy.[52] Edgeworth's papers were related to five main subjects: the measurement of utility; the mathematical determination of equilibrium; probability; statistics; and index numbers. In the last of these areas, his contributions were especially noteworthy. Edgeworth looked upon mathematics as a tool for rigorously defining economic relationships, and he was eminently skilled in mathematical reasoning. But some commentators have complained that his handling of formulas too often was obscure or filled with odd slips and errors.

Edgeworth's interest in economics first was stirred by Jowett, the noted classical scholar. Later he met Marshall, who thought that his *Mathematical Psychics* showed much promise. Like Marshall, Edgeworth approached economics through ethics as well as mathematics, but in his search for logically rigorous theorems his analysis became colder and less humanistic than the older man's. The ethics stemmed from Mill and Sidgwick, while the mathematics was derived from Cournot and Jevons. Yet more than he realized, Edgeworth was completely in the stream of British utilitarianism. With perhaps a more sparkling writing style than Marshall, he nevertheless had a penchant for subtle tangents which took the reader into elusive pathways, whereas Marshall's highly polished prose remained a model of clarity. Edgeworth's early writings on ethics had hinted at the possibility of applying mathematical concepts to utilitarianism, and in *Mathematical Psychics* these ideas were further advanced to develop a calculus of pleasure and pain. Numerical computations seemed unnecessary in this technique. In probability theory, Edgeworth at first advocated the frequency approach, with emphasis upon its physical foundations. But in later years, acknowledging objections to the frequency concept, he began to explore the logical and philosophical bases of probability. Probability situations always exhibited an element of the unknown, he said, but this could be reduced to small enough proportions, so that judgments would remain unaffected. In the field of statistics, he feared that a rejection of the frequency theory might affect general applications: nevertheless, the fact that a large mass of statistical data could satisfy the criteria for validity seemed to him quite sufficient.[53] As Keynes later remarked, this did suggest an unwillingness to reexamine earlier preconceptions: thus, even if utilitarianism was subjected to serious question, marginalism, from which it sprang, could still be validated.

If it were assumed that maximizing satisfactions was the true mainspring of human action for individuals, this should be true also of society as a whole. But this would require perfect competition and Edgeworth knew that the economy was ever moving away from this ideal. The major forces behind the trend toward increasing rigidity were the trade unions and cooperatives, he said—disturbing sign of the times. Under a régime of free competition, maximum satisfaction for society could be enhanced by directing the flow of such satisfactions to those best able to enjoy them—people of wealth, the aristocracy, and man as opposed to woman. But monopoly, stemming from trade union organization, had impeded this process and this was regrettable.

In 1887, the *Mathematical Psychics* was followed by *Metretike,* an unimportant work on probability and utility. When Keynes once asked Edgeworth why he wrote no large treatise, the latter replied that large-scale enterprises, such as texts and marriage, did not interest him.[54] But because of his reluctance to expand his ideas beyond short articles and reviews, his influence did not extend as far as it might have. That he was a poor lecturer and speaker also may have deterred him. Moreover, he wrote what he did not for the public at large but for his fellow economists, with the result that many of his most trenchant thoughts remained inaccessible to the nonprofessional.

Edgeworth, who would not accept Wicksteed's formula for marginal distribution, once remarked wryly, with the assumption of homogeneity in mind: "Justice is a perfect cube, said the ancient sage: and rational conduct is a homogeneous function, adds the modern savant." [55] With his emphasis on indivisibilities, it was clear that Edgeworth had to reject the application of Euler's theorem to distribution theory. Nor did marginal productivity satisfactorily explain to him the nature of pure profit, for this was perforce a residual category. The solution rested, he thought, in the balancing of utilities and disutilities. A profitless stationary state was inconceivable because for even in such an economy the increasing activity of the capitalist entrepreneur would have to be present. Only if the latter's share were interpreted as some form of "wage," would it be possible to employ the theory of marginal productivity.[56] Further, there was no assurance that perfect competition could apply to real conditions: the existence of monopoly and trade unions demanded that the economist use his theories with caution.[57]

Utilitarian ethics inevitably led to a discussion of the measurement of utility. A utilitarian calculus would necessarily require comparisons between utilities,[58] particularly in terms of time, number, and intensity, but just how this might be done was not specified. Although Edgeworth's statements on this score were perhaps as vague and general as those of Hobson, he did observe that economic problems involved the attainment of certain maxima.

More significant was his development of the indifference curve, a technique adopted by Pareto and which is now found in virtually every introductory text. Edgeworth's surface attempted to incorporate utility into the theory of exchange. He insisted, however, that utility was a function not of a single good, but of all items that entered into a person's budget. The indifference apparatus seems to have been suggested by Marshall's *Pure Theory of Foreign Trade and of Domestic Values*,[59] and the curves were drawn not as they are today, but in reverse. Since the price lines started at the origin, the resulting curves showed how much the consumer would surrender of one good in order to obtain more of another, assuming there had been no change in total utility.

The incidence of taxation and the criteria for an equitable tax system also interested Edgeworth.[60] He asserted, in full accord with his utilitarian outlook, that least aggregate sacrifice, a principle which Pigou was to elaborate, was most appropriate. This was a restatement of the principle of greatest happiness which necessarily had to rule, for the absence of bargaining relationships in taxation made it impossible to apply the concept of marginal utility. In no event should anyone lose out when tax schemes were introduced. "The condition that the total net utility procured by taxation should be a maximum then reduces to the condition that the total disutility should be a minimum." [61] Since all this was so strongly suggestive of socialist objectives, there seemed to be some risk in pursuing the utilitarian philosophy. Consequently, Edgeworth finally appealed to common sense, which was at any rate implicit in the proviso that no one should suffer injury.

Edgeworth's admiration for Marshall was unbounded and he followed the latter on many points of theory. Costs were interpreted in a "real" sense, and Jevons' conception of labor was reinterpreted in terms of the equality of the marginal disutility and marginal utility of the product of labor. Like Wicksteed, he did concede labor's inability to move about with any measure of ease, but he thought that in the long run adjustments through education and re-training were possible. But Edgeworth's discussion of this point was not satisfactory for theoretical purposes.[62] Disutilities at the margin could no more be compared than utilities: labor cost defined as pain at the margin was not a fruitful notion. Nor was his attempt to apply the same concept and analysis to the other factors any more successful. However, he did make important contributions to the various concepts of return.[63] The distinction between marginal changes and proportional increases in returns was clarified, and the difference between average and marginal calculations was made explicit. Thus it became possible to define in theory the point up to which expansion could move: this was the now familiar intersection of marginal revenue and marginal cost. The marginal approach seemed most useful because it could facilitate the precise definition of a maximum [64]—although the average concept, he thought, could be helpful in cases of monopoly. Yet since full cost pricing was more easily understood, Edgeworth seemed to hesitate in advocating marginalist ideas too strongly. Diminishing returns was a general principle applicable to all industries, although certain limitations did result from indivisibilities.[65] However, Edgeworth failed to differentiate adequately between the scale of output and increases in plant size.

Edgeworth's solution suggested for bilateral monopoly later became the subject for considerable discussion. In his view, equilibrium under such conditions was indeterminate. Nevertheless, he argued, monopoly pricing did not always culminate in public injury, particularly when discrimination was employed. Cournot, the nineteenth-century French mathematical economist, had worked out a solution for the problem in which the reactions of the monopolists to each other would result in the kind of output adjustments that might typify an auction.[66] An equilibrium point would be reached at which the duopolists would sell equal amounts at some point between the monopoly price and the competitive price. Disequilibrium induced the kind of movements that would restore the balance. But Cournot's solution had not been general, for the duopolists might engage either in collusion or in a cutthroat battle. As indicated, Edgeworth did believe such situations to be essentially indeterminate but only within a bargaining range established by limits beyond which the traders would not go. Within this range a possible series of exchanges existed which defined a contract curve, that is, there was a locus of points which traced the exchanges from which both parties might benefit. But as the exchange ratios themselves were indeterminate along the curve, bargaining strength, in the last analysis, established the point at which the transaction would take place. The argument was developed by superimposing the indifference curves of the bilateral monopolists on each other with the origins at either end of a diagonal. Thus one set of curves became tangent to the second, and the locus of all tangency points became the contract curve. It was the most advantageous set for the indifference curves. Implicit in this model were the limitations imposed by technical plant capacity on the range of reactions exhibited by the duopolists. A producer did not have to fear that all his business would be lost to his rival: the situation was such that he would keep some part of it in any case. Thus, the duopolist would sell only as much as he could handle comfortably. He could feel quite certain that the rival producer would maintain prices within a certain range. While it would be necessary to know something of the other fellow's cost conditions, neither homogeneity nor identical cost conditions were essential. Edgeworth's solution, consequently, oscillated between the competitive and the monopoly price, and factors of strategical price determination were clearly in evidence within the stated limits. This had all the elements of a dynamic solution, but one which impelled Edgeworth to suggest that theory give way to empirical investigation—the kind of advice that modern theorists are not always prone to accept.[67]

ii

Alfred Marshall: The Tradition
Established

It was once the height of fashion to dismiss Alfred Marshall (1842-1924) as a dated Victorian theorist. The impressive system built by the kindly professor from Cambridge was said to be no longer viable. Most of his ideas seemed to crumble under the attack of one or another advanced theory. There was a feeling that Marshall's work lacked the highly refined structure to which we have become accustomed. Moreover, his search for a key to value, it was said, was unnecessary, for this merely led to blind alleys in theoretical investigations that could have been easily avoided.[68] Yet almost the entire corpus of modern economic thought can be traced to some hint or suggestion proposed by Marshall, even where there was a reaction away from him, as with John Maynard Keynes. Both the welfare economist and the more neutral "positive" theorist could find something in his own intellectual genealogy that had its origins in Marshall. Evidently, something in what the former Fellow of Balliol had said did strike permanent roots.

If Marshall's father had had his way, young Alfred, who was born in Clapham, London, would have gone to Oxford to study classics and theology. William Marshall, a cashier in the Bank of England, was something of a tyrant who had forced his son to study Hebrew and had forbidden him the fascinating pursuit of mathematics. Fortunately, an uncle helped Alfred to escape to Cambridge where he was able to follow his own predilections, and in 1865 Marshall turned up as Second Wrangler in Mathematics, when Lord Rayleigh was First, no small feat indeed. Whatever religious scruples Marshall may have evinced as a youth were quickly dispelled by the Darwinian climate of the day, and he was easily converted to agnosticism. It was, however, the philosophical debate between John Stuart Mill and Sir William Hamilton that turned Marshall's attention to philosophy and eventually to economics. This soon became the area in which, as Keynes once remarked, "the full exercise of man's higher faculties could be displayed." While reading Mill's *Political Economy,* Marshall explored urban slums, and quickly came to feel that the amelioration of these dreadful conditions must be a major priority. Then in 1868, he went to Germany so that he might learn to read Kant in the original, and the two years he spent overseas brought him into fairly close touch both with Hegelian ideas and the historical economists. It was this background that made Marshall a prototype of the sort of man described by G. L. S. Shackle, who once observed that an economist must be ". . . a mathematician, a philosopher, a psychologist, an anthropologist, an historian, a geographer and a student of politics; a master of prose exposition; and a man of the world with experience of practical business and finance, an understanding of the problem of administration and a good knowledge of four or five languages." [69]

As a professor, Marshall's objective was to take economics out of the hands of the popularizers and amateurs who had reduced it to a set of comfortable aphorisms, and to develop a truly scientific approach.[70] During the 1870's he worked closely with Henry Sidgwick and Henry Fawcett to establish economics as an academic subject worthy of independent study. In 1879 he and his wife, Mary Paley, whom he had married two years earlier, published a slim volume, *Economics of Industry,* which he was to dislike rather intensely in later years. Nevertheless, the book did outline the direction toward which Marshall's future thinking would turn.

Now that he needed a larger income, Marshall began to look for a suitable post, ending up as Principal at the University College of Bristol. Always something of a hypochondriac, Marshall's health began to trouble him, and 1881 he resigned his principalship to spend a year on the Continent to recuperate. A persistent concern with his health was to stay with Marshall for the remainder of his long life. Keynes, in a brilliant biographical essay,[71] has written that Marshall was easily upset by exertion, excitement, or controversy and that he found continuous concentration on work difficult. In 1885, after a short stay at Oxford, Marshall moved over to Cambridge to replace Fawcett, who had died the year before. He held this post until his retirement in 1908.

The neurotic sensitivity that beset Marshall often became a serious barrier in getting his ideas into print. Easily upset by criticism, he found it difficult to be fully generous to his intellectual opponents. Yet he was possessed of a philanthropic streak which impelled him toward good deeds. He would even listen to the socialists, but it was only their humanitarian appeal that attracted him: he could sympathize with their motives, but could not accept them intellectually.

At Cambridge, where a genuine center for economic training was created, Marshall drew the greater majority of superior students. The result was the establishment of an oral tradition quite unique in the annals of economics. In addition, Marshall so often testified before investigating commissions that much of his economic thinking is deeply imbedded in official papers.[72] All of it reflected his deep conviction that a close study of economics would lend a tone of amelioration in facing the problems of poverty and would facilitate the introduction of noble sentiments into the counting house. Thus, Cambridge would make men who could lead the world to a life worthy of the best in mankind. Implicit in this outlook was an obvious concern with pragmatic issues, for Marshall looked forward to the time when the advance of economic "chivalry" would enhance social improvement.[73] And while he might oppose such measures as minimum wage legislation, he nevertheless did urge businessmen to be scrupulously fair to their employees, for otherwise the encouragement of trade unions would be unavoidable. Certainly this was in sharp contrast to his master Mill, who had expressed the view that only through the working class would social problems be solved.

Marshall, who had started to work in the field of economics as far back as 1867, at the age of twenty-five, had by 1883 fully developed his main ideas. But they did not see print until the publication of the *Principles of Economics* in 1890. His thinking in the area of money and credit was not publicly available until 1923, with the result that when Marshallian economics at long last was fully displayed across the printed page, it all seemed archaic. That Marshall's originality was not immediately conceded clearly was due to his own failings. The theoretical structure had been worked out, at least in rough form, by 1870; but instead of publishing his ideas at once, as had Jevons, he preferred to recast, rebuild, and rewrite. Wanting to be certain that everyone understood him, he relegated novelties and difficulties to appendices and footnotes. This, he felt, would not impede the even flow of his prose. But continental writers, unaware that Marshall had developed the notion of marginal utility some twenty years before the *Principles* appeared, wondered why it was hailed as the greatest book of its time.

The initial point at which to start in economics, suggested Marshall, was David Ricardo, according to the gospel of John Stuart Mill. In this comfortable structure, value had been based on the relationship of competition to the cost of production. Wages, rent, and profit were not determined by the same factors, but were influenced respectively by population growth, differential land fertility, and a vague psychological notion called "abstinence." That is, distribution was worked out through a process of residual sharing. Hedonism and utilitarianism were major motive forces. A dark Malthusian future awaited the workers, while the landowners were to be the inevitable victors in the struggle for the lion's share of the national dividend. This was the outline of the then current political economy, and Marshall's attempt to translate these verbalizations into mathematical form stemmed from a deep rooted feeling that it had not been precise enough.

Still, Ricardo and Mill remained the unchallenged paradigms of economic analysis. Although Marx's *Das Kapital*, at least Volume I, had been around since 1868, and Cournot's mathematical economics since 1838, neither had made much impression on professional economists. Marx was to be rejected, said Marshall, because he had underestimated the supreme difficulty of altering economic and social institutions. Moreover, the elimination of poverty could be attained within the framework of a progressive capitalism. Yet, curiously enough, Marshall did admit that socialists often were more aware of the mainsprings of human knowledge than were most academicians. He knew that a precisely logical treatment of economic problems might be an invitation to avoid the difficulties of economic discourse, and for this the humanitarian drive of the socialists was a suitable antidote.

However, the Ricardian doctrine was then about to enter a cultural decline. Marx had been utilizing it for subversive purposes; Mill had rejected the notion of the wages fund; subjective factors were being introduced into value theory; and the German historical economists were hacking away with unabashed glee at the very foundations of the Ricardian system. Darwin had pointed the way to an exciting new evolutionary approach in the social sciences, while the trade unions were blithely ignoring the view that they could do little to hike wages because all had been preordained by Adam Smith. As the hard facts of reality accumulated, the faith in the economists was deeply shaken. Nevertheless, practitioners of the "dismal science" continued to insist that mankind would be doomed to live forever in the stationary state.

Marshall, however, cannot be charged with the hard-heartedness of the traditionalists. While the utilitarians might have argued that sound principles were more urgent than charity, Marshall would have assuredly tempered such harshness with a stress on goodwill.[74] Thus poverty in old age was excusable if it were the outcome of the disbursement of revenues on the rearing and education of children. Certainly, Marshall was no pure Benthamite, for he had received his utilitarianism diluted from Mill. However, despite the concession that habit and irrational behavior do underlie much of human action,[75] Marshall was true to the Benthamite tradition in that his constructs presupposed a concept of man as a deliberate, calculating animal. Thus, the exercise of care ought to be a major factor in economic consumption, and this, in turn, implied that maximum efficiency and higher living standards could be improved only if the workingman pursued precisely those moral precepts suggested to him.[76]

The supply and demand curve apparatus seems to have been derived from Cournot and Fleeming Jenkins, while the marginal analysis in Marshall stemmed from von Thünen. It is probable that Jevons and Walras were less well known to him than they should have been. Schumpeter has insisted, interestingly enough, that there was a closer affinity between Marshall, Jevons, and Walras than Marshall was willing to admit:[77] he argued that the only trouble with the Cambridge master was that he had allowed his theory to become unnecessarily cluttered with Ricardian notions. Schumpeter, of course, was trying to assign priority in the development of certain economic doctrines to his favorite, Walras. Yet he did admit that Marshall was no mere eclectic, for he had worked out the contours of his theory by himself and had not simply borrowed it.[78]

Marshall also had a certain amount of familiarity with the German historical school, especially Wilhelm Roscher. But he was not wholly satisfied with the latter's view of economic matters. He did concede that the perpetually changing character of the subject demanded more attention than he could afford. His main concern, however, was the development of theory and he rejected rather sharply the historical school's attack upon it.[79] Theoretical analysis was the closest thing to the scientific procedure employed by the physicists, he suggested, for one can learn from facts only when "they are examined and interpreted by reason." [80]

Nevertheless, Marshall was one of the first of modern traditionalists fully and consciously aware that economics was something of an evolutionary science, as evidenced by his frequent resort to the biologic concepts of growth and decay.[81] For him economic development was to be explained in terms of "organic" growth. The long-run demand and supply curves were evidently intended to provide a preliminary approach, but they could not be employed in any sensible way to predict how value and production would react in some future dynamic situation. Tastes, technology, and consumer patterns were necessarily subject to change, while old firms were always liable to attack and displacement by new ones. And in this milieu, man's outlook and psychology were always subject to alteration. This implied, of course, a sense of history, and Marshall was an excellent historian. Quite often he would illuminate an analytical proposition with empirical insights drawn from historical sources. As Schumpeter once remarked, Marshall's skill as an historian was not realized by those who had been reared on watered-down neoclassicism. Yet he was genuinely reluctant to enter fully into historical discourse, which may have been traceable to the rather sharp attack launched on the *Principles* by William Cunningham, the noted economic historian.

In its more technical aspects, the development of Marshall's ideas was solidly rooted in Ricardianism.[82] As Marshall examined the doctrine of his predecessors, he observed that the variations of marginal cost with output made both price and output elements in value determination. Yet there was only one equation in the Ricardian system, implying thereby a gap in the theory of value. Furthermore, Ricardian doctrine could be said to have viewed factor proportions as essentially fixed. But realistically, this was hardly the case, for another equation would have to be added to bring factor combinations into some relationship with price and output. Inevitably this led to the problem of distribution. Whereas Ricardo had believed that in the long run wages would settle down to a kind of normal "iron law," Marshall knew that account would have to be taken of the very palpable rise in real wages. This meant that eventually the factor of aggregate demand would have to be introduced into economic analysis, as was done years later by Lord Keynes.

The success of the *Principles of Economics* was virtually instantaneous. To many readers it heralded a new emphasis on the welfare aspects of economic theory—a welcome contrast to the rugged individualism of earlier views. Furthermore, the *Principles* seemed to settle the heated controversy regarding the relative roles of demand and cost of production in the determination of value. The latter was made the product of both, and the beginning of a rigorously scientific theory of distribution seemed to have been established through the concept of substitution at the margin. Thus a concern with national income was made central to economic theory: distribution became but one aspect of value theory and therefore subject to the identical influences of supply and demand. The introduction of time, via the concepts of the long and short periods, permitted an analysis of normal value, a distinction between external and internal economies, and a clear differentiation between prime and supplementary, or as we should say, overhead costs. Normal profit then was sketched through the quasi-rent notion and the fiction of the representative firm.

The *Principles* was a typical example of the British habit of understatement. Its prose flowed so smoothly that even the uninitiated could feel that an intimate knowledge of the subject had been painlessly acquired. This was precisely what Marshall had hoped for. The well-balanced distribution of weight between ethics and economics seemingly made the subject come alive, and, as Keynes once remarked, the reader could wade through economics without really getting his feet wet. No wonder the *Principles* became one of the greatest texts ever written. In the fifty years after publication, it sold over 60,000 copies, with more than half of the sales after World War I.[83]

Not until 1919 did Marshall publish another major work. This was the quite different *Industry and Trade,* a descriptive and historical study of the rise of western industrialism which lacked, unfortunately, the cohesive quality and clarity of the *Principles.* Again, there were many insights and hints for future degree candidates and again, its urbanity and gloss were deceptive. Perhaps the best description of Marshall's writing was the following: "The reader who pierces the highly polished surface, on which everything seems to be reduced to commonplace, is first of all struck by the tremendously skilled taskmaster to whom it never seems to have occurred that nothing will make a book more difficult than the attempt to make it easy." [84]

For a long time economics in Britain and the United States was a matter of regurgitating a well-digested Marshall. He was interpreted, discussed, explicated, dissected, and rebutted. The *Principles* became a kind of Bible for students to gloss and annotate. Even Marshall himself performed in like fashion as he brought out successive editions, each a little different and a bit more perfect than the previous. C. W. Guillebaud wrote that a careful comparison of the various editions of the *Principles* failed to reveal any substantial changes in the development of Marshall's ideas.[85] The many years spent in polishing and revising, said Guillebaud, might have been more fruitfully given to other unwritten volumes.

While Marshall defined economics as the study of mankind going about the ordinary business of life, he did say that only such action was to be examined as was connected with the "material requisites of well-being." In this way he was able to define the content and limits of the subject. Although he did concede that human behavior was influenced by religious as well as economic factors, he thought that the latter were decisive in setting the character of existing institutions. Yet because the social institutions with which Marshall contended were always undergoing change, it was difficult to make specific generalizations about man in society. Harboring no illusions about the general, timeless validity of economic propositions, his aim was an eminently practical one: to arrive at a solution of social problems.[86] The questions he asked were: how is the production, distribution, and consumption of wealth determined? how is industry organized? what is the impact of foreign trade and the money market? how does increased wealth add to well-being? how real and broad is economic freedom? how is the condition of the worker influenced by economic change? Not only were these practical questions, but *welfare* questions as well. And the answers that one gave to them determined the character of the economic theory that was to be advanced.

Free enterprise rather than competition was declared to be the basic institution. The former concept was preferable, for it seemed to suggest independence and choice rather than the rivalry implicit in the notion of competition. Interestingly enough, Marshall was fully aware that no system of economic harmonies existed. In *Industry and Trade,* he said: "There is no general economic principle which supports the notion that industry will necessarily flourish best or that life will be happiest and healthiest when each man is allowed to manage his own concerns as he thinks best." [87] Nevertheless, Marshall's free enterprise was firmly founded on competition, for the basis was a market of many small business units, none of which was able through its own efforts to influence total demand or market price. Free enterprise in this sense differed from monopoly by degree rather than kind because it was but one end of a spectrum of market forms. That is to say, an inescapable element of monopoly existed in all competitive business: thus the basis was laid for the later theory of monopolistic competition.[88] Yet Marshall himself was either unwilling or unable to make the transition to such a theory. Although the tools were close at hand, the whole range of market structure lying between pure competition and monopoly was left uncultivated. It very well may have been that he really felt that the determination of value under imperfect competition was too imprecise to be handled in any satisfactory theoretical way.

Marshall's analytical method could be best described as partial equilibrium. All the elements but one in a given situation were held constant, while the effects of variation in that single element were carefully observed. It has been argued that this approach is subject to the limitations imposed by general equilibrium analysis, in the sense that the former is essentially a special case of the latter. Evidently Marshall was aware of this methodological problem when he recognized that shifts in the factors to be held constant would inevitably effect the variable one as well. This seemed clear from the discussion of joint products, composite demand, and complementarity.[89] But he was unable to develop a cohesive picture of general interdependence. It was easy to construct a simple set of equations representing demand and supply on the assumption of a single commodity in isolation, while all other prices were held constant. For once the respective schedules of supply and demand were made available, it was not difficult to derive value as the point of equilibrium of these two forces. But this ignored the impact of changes in consumption on price resulting from changes in income. These were put to one side as "second order" changes. The problem became even more complex when the method was applied to distribution, for then it became necessary to assume that the supply of the factors of production was relatively fixed and not immediately responsive to market changes.

Nevertheless, insofar as partial equilibrium could be employed at all, Marshall did succeed. The practical problems of the individual industry and firm were adequately revealed, and such elements as prime cost and quasi-rent became useful tools of analysis, for they could be employed to throw light on some of the general relationships in an economy of interdependence. As Schumpeter has said, partial analysis appealed to common sense, since for limited purposes it was not necessary to study all the ramifications of economic change. But the method remained restricted and did not permit a sufficiently broad range of investigation.

Viewed from another standpoint, Marshall's approach may be called static. Not that he was unaware of historical change, but he was interested in uncovering the regularities of economic life, and for this purpose it was understandable that he should resort to the method of *ceteris paribus*.[90] Since representative firms had to be observed in action, no marked change could be granted in productive technique, population, or consumer taste. All this, of course, demanded certain assumptions: free enterprise, stable property rights, gradual changes in population and capital, economic action stemming only from the motive of profit, and full information for all the participants in the game of economics. Such a model evaded the question of growth and accumulation, for it was seldom clear, for example, whether supply price concerned a given stock of capital or some rate of net accumulation. Although the concept of waiting was close at hand to permit the development of a dynamic thrust, it was on the more static assumptions that Marshall built his system of value and distribution and his world of Victorian normality.

Yet this was not the thoroughgoing static system of John Bates Clark. Marshall's invention of time periods did enable him to forge a link between short-run static situations and the long run in which changes did take place. Such changes, however, were little more than tendencies toward the "normal," and one came away from these parts of Marshall with the feeling that, after all, he had been standing still.[91] The fact is, as even Hicks admitted,[92] that while the static analysis was but a limiting case of the more general dynamic approach, ultimately such a theory was little more than an evasion—a dynamic society required a dynamic theory.

Whereas mathematics had not been used too often in ordinary economic discourse prior to Marshall, today virtually every volume and article on economic theory displays a surfeit of mathematical formulas. Marshall, though quite expert at it, took special pains to wrap his mathematical statements in the swaddling clothes of literary formulations for fear that some readers of the *Principles* would think that they understood everything when in reality such was not the case.[93] He deliberately avoided an excessive use of formulas on the ground that they would not throw as much light as might be desirable on the complexities of an economic relationship. In a letter to the noted statistician, A. L. Bowley, he remarked that a good mathematical statement on economics might be good mathematics but was apt to be poor economics.[94] He made it quite clear that use of mathematics was merely a kind of shorthand which always had to be translated into English. If the proposition were still not clear, he said, one should burn the mathematical statement; and if that didn't clarify matters, one should throw out the translation. Basically, he averred, mathematical economic analysis was too mechanical, and unlike organic, biological concepts, failed to convey the idea that economics was essentially a process.

Economics had to have facts, Marshall insisted, for these were the bricks out of which knowledge was built. True, statistics provided some, but they would have to be supplemented by other facts as well. Actually, he thought that there was small chance of going astray if statistics and mathematics were subordinated to a more general framework. The limited usefulness of mathematics in economics was not only due to the complexity of problems, but to the as yet insufficient number of variables which might be made amenable to theoretical treatment. Furthermore, the inability to provide for controlled experiments and the presence of the personal equation in economic investigations made the field a bit different from the physical sciences. Thus a narrative treatment might be more realistic and more flexible than a mathematical one, in which the complexities arising from historical and sociological elements could not be absorbed. But Marshall was not unaware, of course, of the prodigious feats that modern mathematical economics could perform.

He contended that meaningful observations of social and economic phenomena derived not from totals and aggregates but from the units or increments that accounted for changes in these very same aggregates. That is, the demand for a product could be viewed as a continuous function in which the demand for the marginal unit was to be balanced against the cost of its production. Once he had made this discovery, Marshal quickly developed the diagrammatic method of analysis. Although others had also made use of diagrams, Marshall made them truly powerful analytical devices. But he buried them in footnotes and appendices, for he did not want to convert economics into a kind of mathematical application of the *felicific calculus*. Economic analysis was complex enough as it was, and mathematics did not necessarily enhance its viability. Above all, economics had to be practical, and to be practical it had to be understood.[95]

The one attribute of the modern economy that gave rise to measurable quantities was, of course, money. It was the center, said Marshall, around which virtually all human action clustered. He granted that there were motives other than those which stemmed from money, but it was the latter that primarily interested him. For one thing, the measurability of the motives related to money made it possible to characterize economics as a scientific discipline. At least in this respect, it was ahead of the other social sciences.

There has been much debate on just what Marshall meant when he set forth these views. Did he mean that money directly measured the motives for action, or did he mean that it merely measured the *force* of the motive?[96] If he meant the latter, pecuniary phenomena would seem to be rooted in certain deeper "real" factors over which money merely threw a curtain that had to be drawn apart if the truth was to be discovered. On the other hand, money as a direct measure would suggest that it was itself the object with which men were concerned and that satisfactions and desires might be related directly to money income and outgo.[97] Thus in distributing resources the basic principle to be followed would be the equality in all lines of the marginal utilities of expenditure. Money, in this sense, was the focus for a complex of elements and the point from which action was initiated. Yet there was no denying the fact that the *Principles* frequently gave the impression that "real" forces, rather than monetary elements, governed the economy. Marshall, of course, was fully aware of the centrality of money. The price system was not only intimately related to money, but, by virtue of having been raised to the level of a determining factor in its own right, it had become more than a simple question of ratios between goods.[98]

While Marshall did not publish his ideas until quite late, he nevertheless must be viewed as a seminal mind in the field of money, if the oral tradition at Cambridge is taken into account. His statements before the Royal Commissions and the various articles he wrote on these matters reveal that he antedated many present-day notions.[99] Marshall sought to make the quantity theory of money a part of the general theory of value, and in his treatment he laid the groundwork for the cash balance approach. He successfully established a distinction between the "real" and money rate of interest. Although it is Gustav Cassel's name that is usually connected with the purchasing power parity theory of international exchange, it was Marshall who set forth a basis for this view in 1888. Nor was he averse to working out suggestions for stabilizing long-term contractual obligations through such a device as the Tabular Standard.[100]

The latter shows the importance that Marshall attributed to the role of the price system. Within this rubric were all the relations and interactions that determined what goods were to be produced and what rewards were to go to those who helped produce them. It constituted a kind of unified theory for economics, since through the price system a single basic analysis was to be developed to account for both value and distribution. Marshall was influenced by the nineteenth century's search for order and regularity, and when he had worked out his general theory he thought that he had at the same time discovered normality. This he defined, however, not as something fixed, but as a condition which might be expected under the circumstances of the moment. But he seemed quite oblivious of the fact that differences in income levels make the price system mean different things to different people. In his own terms, the marginal utility of money varied from rich to poor, and the number of dollars that each person could bring into the market made it something to be distinguished from the common meeting place that a Hayek or Mises insisted it was.[101]

When it came to the analysis of utility which underpinned the theory of money and prices, Marshall was skating on thin ice with his implication that desires and satisfactions could be measured. Pigou has suggested that Marshall was merely hinting that perhaps some day science would be able to do just that.[102] At any rate, he did want to go behind the observable behavior of the market and to explore the way in which satisfactions and non-satisfactions were balanced. By measuring the underlying motives of behavior, economic theory could attain, he believed, the broadest degree of generality. For example, if interpersonal comparisons of economic satisfaction made it possible to show whether or not consumers gained or lost by government intervention, it would then be possible to pass judgment on what it was that government was trying to do. To Marshall, there was nothing hedonic in this approach, yet it could be said that he never quite fully escaped the hedonic mode. While he was working on these rather abstruse notions, Jevons published the *Theory of Political Economy,* in which he introduced the idea of marginal utility, or as he called it, final utility. Jevons' rush to get his thoughts into print irritated Marshall, who felt that they were somewhat halfbaked and incomplete, and when Marshall reviewed the Jevons volume [103] he was quite cool toward it, pointing to several instances of supposed error. There was little in the new marginal writings for Marshall to draw upon. He had evidently worked out the theory of marginal utility on his own, inspired more by Cournot, von Thünen, and Ricardo than anyone else.

The consumers' surplus idea, of which Marshall made much, was basically a way of measuring utility. Marshal remarked that if total utility was equivalent to the area under an individual demand curve (from zero to the quantity purchased), the consumers' surplus obviously was the difference between the total area and the area under the price line. The individual obtained a surplus because he was able to take advantage of opportunities afforded by the environment. It was not clear, however, whether Marshall meant to say that a surplus was an absolute quantity or merely stemmed from relative price changes.[104] In fact, both ideas were commingled in his discussion, with the consumers' surplus set side by side with "workers" and "savers" surplus. Analytically, the problem could be quite confusing, for while the product was absorbed by factor payments at the margin, each factor nevertheless could obtain a surplus. One way out of the dilemma was to reduce the concept to a matter of psychology, but this implied discarding the absolute interpretation and looking at surpluses solely in a relative sense. The idea was poorly received because its application to economic analysis seemed rather limited. In fact, Frank Knight leveled such an attack on the idea of the surplus that not even the heroic effort of John R. Hicks could restore it.[105] What appeared to be more useful was the doctrine that the equilibrium of supply and demand would result in a maximum of satisfaction.[106]

Central to the *Principles* was the theory of value. Everything that preceded Book V was a prelude to this main theme. The discussion of wealth and wants and the factors of production led up to the business of value determination. Distribution was but an application of the theory of value to the various classes in society, whose returns also were subject to the laws of supply and demand. Value expressed the ratios of exchange between goods. The money system caused these values to be transferred into prices, which were basically reflections of the forces of supply and demand. The latter tended to impel prices toward an equilibrium which ultimately coincided with the cost of production. Any deviation from this norm would set corrective forces into motion. Thus, it was only in the light of the ultimate long run that value could be explained at all. Underlying the law of demand was diminishing utility which asserted that an increase in the stock of a good decreased the utility of the marginal or final unit. This enabled the economist to construct a schedule of demand which was then matched against a schedule of supply. Thus, as in the case of a pair of scissors, two blades were necessary to cut. Utility became the major factor in the short run, while real costs of production were predominant in the long run. A failure to recapture costs would enforce a contraction of supply until a new equilibrium was established: excessive profits would entice new entries into the industry. Interestingly, Marshall refused to extend marginal utility to create a *social* marginal utility. After all, a similar approach in the hands of John Bates Clark had become a powerful weapon to justify the *status quo*. But here Marshall was exercising a greater sense of realism than had his American confrère.

In analysing demand, Marshall did make one great contribution to economic analysis—the explicit use of the concept of elasticity.[107] Of course, the basic idea of elasticity could be traced as far back as Cournot. Marshall tried to show the relationship between a small change in price and a consequent small change in the quantity demanded. More technically, he was concerned with a relative change in quantity divided by a relative change in price.[108] The problem could be illustrated, he said, by comparing the wants of the middle class and the rich. For the latter, wants were generally inelastic; that is, there was no tendency to change demand in response to price shifts. On the other hand, the demand of the middle class was certainly responsive to price changes in goods it considered to be luxuries. The working class, he thought, was limited to an inelastic demand for essentials. However, Marshall's presentation of elasticity was restricted to small variations only, thus making it difficult to speak of discrete movements along the demand curve. Yet while this was the notion of point elasticity, it did suggest other kinds—arc, cross, and all the elasticities of cost functions and substitution. However, since adjustments in supply would require time and perhaps additional capital investment, Marshall was reluctant to extend the concept to that side of the price equation. Later writers did not exhibit such restraint.

A good part of Marshall's investigation of economic phenomena was devoted to the study of supply. This enabled him to escape the tacky question of wants and desires and satisfactions and to get on to the more solid ground of production costs. The problem was quite capable of solution. In the "market" situation, supply was simply a given stock of goods, and demand was the active factor; by merely adjusting price, enough demand could be created to remove the currently available supply from the market. However, once the time element was introduced, supply as stock became transformed into supply as flow. This created some rather ticklish problems which Marshall proceeded to solve with his ingenious elaboration of time periods: the short period in which productive capacity was unalterable; the long, where adjustments in output were deemed possible, permitting the entry of new productive factors; and the very long, which allowed for changes in population, capital, consumer tastes, technology, and the like. Of course, time here was economic time; that is, concepts were defined in terms of functional adjustments. In the *Principles,* Marshall paid primary attention to the second of these situations, for this was the period when normal price was established by cost of production. In the long run, price tended to gyrate about cost as the forces of supply and demand played out their skein. In the short run, prices would not fall below prime costs; in the long run, both prime and overhead, or supplementary, costs would have to be covered. That is, the significant cost items in the short run were variable, while overhead items, stemming as they did from fixed factors of production, were essentially related to quasi-rents. The latter concept, said Marshall, was applicable to any factor of production. It was a short-run, price-determined income flowing from the fixed nature of a factor and could make its appearance as a surplus over normal interest or as extraordinary large earnings for exceptional people. Stated in this manner, however, quasi-rent seemed to be outside the circle of distribution. It became entirely fortuitous, depending on certain market situations which permitted a more than normal return to some factors. Perhaps, because of this extra-theoretical aspect, few theoreticians since Marshall have used the idea.

Costs, as many an economist has learned to his grief, can be a tricky affair. Marshall got around the problem rather cleverly by postulating a "representative firm" which was normally efficient and whose costs affected the determination of normal price in the long run. It was these costs, as Jacob Viner pointed out,[109] that were supposed to provide the key to trends for the entire industry. But Marshall failed to say how the "representative firm" was to be discovered, beyond the proposition that it was the one whose cost, including normal profit, equaled price. This suggested that he was guilty of circular reasoning, for price was being analysed in terms of the cost of a firm which could be pinpointed only by equating its cost to price! Moreover, if disparities in efficiency for land and labor were to be adjusted through competition, why should this not be the case for the entrepreneur? As Lionel Robbins once asked, why different theories for the different factors? [110]

The equilibrium that Marshall developed on the basis of the foregoing was, of course, a stable one. If price went up, demand came down and there was a return to normal. There was a mutuality of influence between price, demand, and supply that he was at pains to elaborate. While all this may appear terribly unrealistic today, one wonders whether in the world of Victorian England it was really so fanciful to suggest that slow adjustments of these elements, one to the other, was the normal way in which the economy unfolded.

A number of side issues, relating to joint supply, prime costs, and internal economies, issued from the problem of supply. Realistically, the demand for many goods was intimately related to the demand for complementary items. This was also the case with supply and, in fact, was considered by Marshall important enough to be accorded special chapters in the *Principles*[111] where it was acknowledged that the pricing of joint products might be determined by the requirements of the market. But this was a short-run problem: what then happened to supply in the long run? Some commentators have felt that the latter simply disappeared and the long run became nothing more than a series of little short runs. If this is a valid criticism, it may very well be charged that the entire Marshallian time analysis has fallen to the ground.

Internal and external economies were the logical bases for the decline in average costs which took place as the size of plant increased. These changes were related either to alterations in technology or to shifts in the input-output package—what is known as the production function. Such movements were the causes of internal economies or cost reductions stemming from improvements within the firm. Where savings resulted from improved transportation or perhaps better availability of one of the factors of production, such as labor, the firm might benefit from external economies. Marshall suggested that internal economies were less significant than external ones,[112] for as a firm expanded not only did it develop savings but it also began to incur certain internal "diseconomies." Thus, it seemed unlikely that industrial giantism would be able to develop simply from the process of growth, or from capital accumulation, since an economy always would be balanced by a diseconomy. Of course, Marshall was evading the issue; a truly rigorous evaluation of the idea of internal economies in the long run surely would have led to a realistic theory of monopoly.

Not surprisingly, the treatment of external economies was harshly criticized by later writers.[113] For Marshall, these economies were due to advantages of location, which included the growth of supporting industries and available pools of skilled labor. Conceptual difficulties arose, however, when the notion of external economies was applied to a stationary state; for then it would be necessary to extend the gains to all industries rather than to a few. As critics have argued, this limited Marshall's analysis to those situations in which economies were external to the firm, but internal to the industry. But if this particular notion of Marshall's did not satisfy the requirements of pure theory, it certainly did illuminate the process of economic growth. It was perhaps too dynamic a concept to be readily employed by static theory.

Such shifts in costs as were implied in these ideas were not unrelated to the notion of the laws of return. Throughout the nineteenth century, economists had held to the idea that agriculture was subject to diminishing returns while manufacturing provided increasing returns. Despite the fact that industrialization was expanding rapidly, Marshall retained these somewhat quaint views,[114] and he failed to make clear, as did his contemporary, J. B. Clark, that "returns" were basically a question of proportionality. As he barely hinted at the problem of excess capacity, he overlooked the fact that under such conditions increased output might very well be accompanied by a situation approximating constant cost. On the other hand, when internal economies and increasing returns were admitted, it was perfectly logical to proceed to the question of excess capacity and cutthroat competition (a not uncommon situation prior to World War II) and to assert that there was a genuine tendency for competition to be replaced by monopoly as firms exerted all possible effort to protect sunk costs over the long run.

In order to keep costs as low as possible, the rational producer would search out the most efficient combination of the factors of production. These would be substituted for each other at the margin until it became simply a matter of indifference as to whether an increment of one factor or another would be employed. Factors, therefore, would be valued in accordance with the contribution to production made by the last or marginal unit. Thus, Marshall came very close to a marginal productivity theory wherein distributive shares tend to equal the value of the product of the marginal unit. But productivity at the margin did not cause value, for it was merely the point at which the forces that determine value might be studied.[115] One cannot escape the feeling that, at bottom, Marshall preferred to remain a Ricardian.

But if the long-run price depends on the cost of production and the latter is a compound of prices, then economic analysis has been running around in a circle. Here Marshall had to resort to his "real forces"—the desire for goods and the disutility incurred in working to get them. The reader was now back once again to the mainsprings of human action and the very hedonic calculus that Marshall had sought to avoid. While he doubted that it would be possible to relate money cost directly to real cost, he nevertheless felt that it was basically the latter which influenced the suppy of factor services. Supply and demand in turn affected factor payments. In the case of labor, for example, work was undertaken up to the point where the marginal disutility of labor equaled the marginal utility of earnings, thus making disutility an important factor in setting the wage rate. But it was doubtful that the use of these "real forces" had enabled Marshall to escape the charge of circular reasoning: the argument was not quite convincing. Furthermore, the attempt to employ subtle psychological elements introduced the concept of waiting. Whereas for Ricardo, labor had been a creative factor and the cost of a good had been rooted in the act of creative work, for Marshall all this was transformed into subjective sacrifices. But the latter was an entirely different inquiry—a study of microcosmic states of mind in which it was thought possible to relate mathematically small increments of a good to small increments in price. How realistic or practical such an inquiry might be was quite another matter.

Marshall's theory of distribution was simply an application of his theory of value. In general terms, it was an examination of the condition of supply and demand whereby the normal price of each of the factors of production was established. Land, labor, and capital received what they commanded in the market place. To this famous trinity Marshall added Organization, so that corresponding to the respective factors one could speak of the various revenues—rent, wages, interest, and profit. Together these comprised the national dividend. The purpose of distribution theory, therefore, was to discover the forces that influenced the supply and demand for each factor. The entrepreneur established the demand for the factors in accordance with the services they were able to render in the process of production. Where the supply was fixed, as in the short run, demand set the price; in the long run, the cost of supplying the additional factors governed. Thus we come once again to the condition of normality with the actual prices of factors gravitating somewhat irregularly about a center of long-run equilibrium.

Marshall was particularly insistent in rejecting marginal productivity as a basis for wage theory.[116] He did not accept the notion that one could measure the net product of a marginal unit, and he thought it even more unlikely that marginal productivity could be utilized as a tool for dealing with the problem of the general wage level. Yet, despite his disclaimers, there was little doubt that he had come quite close to the marginal productivity position. But he would have been confused by what today are described as macroeconomic and microeconomic questions: it was obvious that marginal productivity could not be used to answer the sort of broad, sweeping problems posed by Ricardo and Marx. Apparently, Marshall again had fallen into something of a logical quandary which he tried to solve by applying the famous analogy of the scissors and by making wages subject to supply and demand.[117] Consequently, it was perfectly reasonable for him to suggest that no such concept as a general wage level existed: there were rather a number of grades of labor each of which had its own set of supply and demand forces. Again, demand was dominant in the short run and wages took on the character of a "quasi-rent." Yet it was admitted that there were other elements in the wage question: population growth, educational attainments, mobility, foresight, and the like. In addition, Marshall did not evade the issue of poverty: he recognized that in the case of labor's income, economic relationships were manifestly complex. Here, perhaps more than anywhere else, he exhibited a genuine, sympathetic concern for the welfare of mankind.

But he could not escape the requirements of his theory, for in the long run each grade of labor had its own normal wage rate. Thus, with an adjustable supply, a wage theory might be couched, without too much difficulty, in terms of the notorious "iron law," thereby obtaining a wage doctrine fully appropriate to the stationary state. Some relationship between high wages and efficiency was recognized and increasing the scarcity of the lower grades was suggested as an effective means of raising wages. While the expected appeal was made to economic chivalry, no specific suggestions were forthcoming for such ameliorative measures as social insurance or old-age pensions. It might be proper for government to concern itself with housing, he said, but there would always be the question of bureaucracy.[118] Yet the impression could not be avoided that Marshall's view on these matters was basically eleemosynary.

Land, however, was clearly a factor in fixed supply. Rent was defined as the income from land, including such improvements as were imbedded in the soil. The uses to which land would be put were determined by profit opportunities in the market, where demand became the active element. At this point, however, differential considerations of a somewhat Ricardian character entered the analysis. Since the value of crops on superior lands exceeded the value on inferior parcels and all costs were paid for, the difference between the incomes of the other factors and the value of the crops represented a surplus due to the quality of the land itself. Moreover, the surplus was not subject to long-run adjustments, for land was fixed in supply. Land was therefore the one factor of production whose value was based not on the cost of production but on a capitalization of the values of the annual surpluses.

Of course, from the owner's viewpoint, land so resembled ordinary capital that rent seemed to be a cost. From the social standpoint, however, rent could not be considered a cost since it was fundamentally a surplus arising from a social process of valuation. That such a theory did not serve the purposes of the individual cultivator was obvious. But by permittting a distinction between social and entrepreneurial aspects, Marshall was able to counteract the hostile criticisms of Ricardian rent doctrine that had started with T. E. Cliffe Leslie. Differentiating land from capital further strengthened Marshall's insistence on categorizing land as an economic factor separate and apart from capital.

Marshall's analysis of capital started with an historical review.[119] In the more primitive economic stages, there had been less need to supplement labor with capital equipment; but as wants expanded with the accumulation of wealth, there was an increasing need for produced means of production. This was history as seen by a nineteenth-century Englishman: as population grew the ability to save increased, and this in turn was enhanced by assuring the security of one's investment. Should the rate of interest fall, saving would be discouraged and the required capital accumulation inhibited.

Interest was simply a payment for the use of capital which had to be made because gains were obtained from its utilization. An element of scarcity was also involved in this somewhat crude doctrine: capital required a payment because of the undeniable preference for present over future applications, making it necessary that an owner of capital be remunerated for his willingness to surrender present enjoyments. Consequently, the demand for capital was derived from its productivity while its supply stemmed from saving. However, in the short period, it was possible for interest to be quite unrelated to the earnings of capital, suggesting a probable divergence between rates of interest and real earnings. In fact, once again a factor return took on the character of a "quasi-rent," for, in this same short period, the amount of capital was fixed, thus placing the major burden of price determination on the demand side of the market equation. In the long run, however, the money rate of interest and the real rate tended to converge.[120] Related to this notion was Marshall's contention that the rate of interest on short loans oscillated around the rate of return on fixed investments.[121]

The rate of interest also performed the function of balancing the supply and demand for investment. However, this idea was not very enlightening since any new investment would depend in large measure on the availability of real income, which in turn could be traced to the level of employment of men and resources. Thus the contention that Marshall's analysis was acceptable as a long-run statement of tendency was not convincing, for it was evident that in his view interest was the fulcrum for equilibrium in the short run as well.[122]

Profit was dissolved by Marshall into the wages of management, interest on capital, and payment for risk. To explain the latter component and to make it also part of the theory of distribution, Marshall invented his new factor of production—Organization—behind which stood the institutional superstructure of society. With the growth of corporations and the subsequent dispersion of stock ownership, management came to rest in the hands of a professional class. In these circumstances, remuneration to the businessman was subject to the same laws of distribution as governed labor—that is, payment had to be sufficient to call forth the required service. Anything above this assumed the character of a "quasi-rent." Inherent in this was an element of "opportunity value," [123] which could easily be wiped out in a competitive situation. Consequently, under perfect competition, profits might decline to zero and organization as a factor of production might be reduced to the status of a special kind of labor. While in the short run the "quasi-rent" aspect might persist, in the long run returns were to be separated into normal prices sufficient to call forth the factors of production and rent stemming from a fixed supply. Profits in the pure sense of the term had no place in the model.

Although Marshall felt that competitive forces dominated the economic system, he did not overlook entirely the pressure of monopoly. Through his graphical analysis he was able to show how a monopolist could limit supply and so set the price of a good. But he wondered whether some monopolists might not consider an increase in consumers' surplus just as desirable as a monopoly profit! [124] This implied that instances might occur where it would pay for monopolists to sell at prices lower than their market position could permit them to dictate. It thus might be reasonable for a railroad to build up a community with a view toward future business. This was not a matter of altruism; it was merely foresight. Furthermore, greediness might generate public hostility and legal action. But, on the whole, Marshall tended to minimize the question of monopoly. While he recognized that increasing returns might facilitate business concentration, he nevertheless felt that some organizational benefits might be forthcoming.[125] At any rate, monopolistic pressures were not deemed to be overly severe. In the discussion of the proportion of overhead to prime costs in certain industries, he did approach the idea of monopolistic competition but he did not really spell out this notion, leaving it for his successors to make the theoretical refinements.[126]

It was not surprising, therefore, that the problem of economic crises, which occupied so many economists in the decades after the publication of the *Principles*, did not loom overly large in Marshall's system. As he viewed it, whatever upsets occurred to disturb the even tenor of the competitive economy were rooted in commercial and psychological factors. A pyramiding of credit and an increase in costs might, he said, impose stringent conditions and cause a narrowing of profit margins. But once confidence had been regained, the crisis would recede. He did not discuss the problem in a context of savings and investment; this was a matter for the future. Yet he did admit that economic fluctuations could become a problem in industries with large amounts of fixed capital. Beyond these confident remarks, little in the *Principles* indicated that Marshall was deeply concerned with questions of depression and economic crisis. Most of his ideas on these matters were contained in his answers to the Royal Commission on Depression in Trade and Industry (1886), an article on remedies for business fluctuations which dealt mainly with the question of constant purchasing power, and statements made to the Gold and Silver Commission in 1887-88.

Marshallian theory was basically a theory of prices under competitive conditions. Yet the implications of mutual interdependence were nowhere worked out in such precise detail as they were by Walras. As Marshall himself put it,[127] the *Principles* attempted to develop the basis for equilibrium in different periods of economic time in a way that would establish a fundamental unity between the material and human factors of production. In one sense, this was quite the same problem to which Ricardo and Marx had addressed themselves, for they too were concerned with the distribution of value amongst the classes of society. But this was a big question which, as Joan Robinson has said, Marshall turned into a little one. He worried himself over the question of why an egg might be more costly than a cup of tea. The answer to this required much time and much mathematics and it kept his disciples busy for many years. In short, Alfred Marshall represented the kind of Victorian liberal who gave vague support to measures that would ameliorate the harsh conditions of life. But should the necessary corrective measures imply injury to any one, then care and caution were to become the watchword. Obviously, the central part of his economic doctrine was static in character, for the key element of capitalist motion, the accumulation of capital, played but a minor role. All that was necessary to keep society on an even keel was the maintenance of normality over the long run; who was to gainsay that this was not a feature of the Age of Victoria?

Still, Marshall's influence on economic theory has been important: he affected modes of thought as have few other economists. Despite the criticisms that were often levelled at the notions of utility, equilibrium, real forces, normality, and economic time, a good deal of contemporary theory still stems from the ideas which he elaborated. And after seventy years, economic literature is still replete with developments that were first hinted at in the *Principles*. The theory of monopolistic competition is a case in point. Often associated with Piero Sraffa's famous 1926 article, "The Laws of Return of Competitive Conditions," [128] in which Marshallian long-run analysis was shown to be inadequate to account for external and internal economies, this development actually had its roots in Marshall's concern with returns to different types of industry [129] and in the observation that most firms were able to develop special markets for their products.[130]

As was the case with few other economists, Marshall, through his teaching and personal influence, created a genuine national school of economics which dominated the field, at least in the Anglo-Saxon countries. A line can be traced from Marshall through his successor, A. C. Pigou, to Sir Dennis Robertson and even Keynes, who had a deeper connection with Cambridge doctrine than he was willing to admit.

Yet today, the Marshallian system has an archaic quality. Its treatment of monopoly is almost cavalier, and matters relating to the crucial problems of modern industrialism are conspicuous by their absence. Perhaps Marshall felt that under monopoly price would be indeterminate; this would have violated his sense of order and perfection. Further, for contemporary man money is more than just a *numéraire,* an accounting device; it is the focus of economic existence. Despite his protestations, the accounting approach does seem to have been the way in which money was understood by Marshall. While all this may have been satisfactory for the pre-World War I period, Marshallian economics is admittedly incomplete when the critical problems of output, investment, and employment are taken in hand.

iii

A. C. Pigou and Welfare Economics

When Alfred Marshall retired from Cambridge in 1908, he left Anglo-Saxon economics in the capable hands of Arthur C. Pigou (1877-1959). The latter, often described as Marshall's favorite pupil, had studied mathematics and history as an undergraduate, thus securing a sound foundation for work in theoretical economics. Marshall encouraged the younger man to investigate such practical matters as industrial disputes in order to strengthen his awareness of real problems. His elevation to Marshall's post had been opposed by some academicians on the ground that he was too cloistered a scholar and lacked sufficient practical experience. Perhaps for this reason, Pigou, at the end of his long academic career, urged students to go into shops and mills where economic events actually took place.[131] For thirty-five years, Pigou held the chair of political economy at Cambridge, retiring in 1943. His well-organized lectures on economic principles were somewhat stereotyped in character, but this did not trouble him in the least, for he preferred to bend his main energies toward a thoroughgoing exploration of one branch of economics after the other. In 1912, aged thirty-five, he produced his *Wealth and Welfare,* a book that suggested some new areas of investigation for economists. Later revised and expanded into the *Economics of Welfare,* it not only appeared in several editions, but was to spawn numerous other volumes in diverse branches of the science.

Pigou was soon acknowledged as the true inheritor of Marshall's mantle, and it was unquestionably due to his efforts that the Cambridge tradition became so firmly entrenched. He had other interests too, from participating in many community and academic discussions on philosophy, art, and social welfare, to writing papers on Theism and Browning.[132] A good platform speaker, his characteristically British appearance made an excellent impression on audiences who gave him their confidence, despite the fact that his rugged physique was often untidily clothed. Although Pigou did not mingle with his fellow economists and was seldom seen at conferences and despite a withdrawn personality, he could be quite generous, especially to those many years younger. Further, he wrote frequent letters to the newspapers on issues of the day and willingly gave his services to public causes: he was a member of the Cunliffe Currency Committee in 1918, The Royal Commission on Income Taxes in 1919, and the Chamberlain Committee on Currency in 1924. It was the latter's report that led to the restoration of the gold standard, an action later subjected to heavy criticism. As a teacher, Pigou offered little beyond pure Marshall, yet in his own thinking he went beyond the master, searching for new ways to apply abstract principles to economic action. His brilliant inquiry into how the state might justifiably intervene in economic affairs illustrated his abiding concern with practical matters. In this sense at least, Pigou did offer an important departure from received doctrine.[133]

Many of Pigou's books were, in fact, detailed explorations of some aspect of his welfare economics. In later life he produced a number of slim volumes, usually based on popular lectures, which attempted to explain the more technical features of his theory. These works—*Income, Income Revisited* and *Lapses from Full Employment*—comprise an excellent introduction to the main body of his work, as set forth in the *Economics of Welfare, The Economics of Stationary States, Employment and Equilibrium, Industrial Fluctuations,* and *A Study in Public Finance.* Pigou was not exempt from occasional sharp criticism: at times he was charged with failure to relate real phenomena adequately to theoretical categories; and his concept of national income, central to his theory, raised many questions of definition.[134] Yet though the system did exhibit certain weaknesses and had an aura of an all too quiet Victorianism, it has remained an important landmark in the history of economic thought.

Pigou's writing was suffused with the spirit of utilitarianism and uplift, and his basic philosophic postulate was the greatest good for the greatest number, after the fashion of Henry Sidgwick. The determination of welfare was to be located in the mutual relationship of satisfaction and dissatisfaction: while these psychic states were not really measurable, they were at least "comparable." In an essay on economic chivalry, Pigou looked with favor on the paternalistic programs indulged in by some employers. Yet the role of the patron missed the point, said Pigou, for "the better way is to enlist the workpeople as active partners in the improvements being made, not as mere passive beneficiaries. So far as may be, the control of such social institutions as are set up in the works should be vested in them. For it is through comradeship, not through autocracy, that the good life grows." [135]

Marshall's influence on Pigou was obvious. In *Alfred Marshall and Current Thought,*[136] he paid his respects to the older man by asking how Marshall might have viewed contemporary questions. Moreover, the master's admonition to bury mathematics in footnotes despite the mathematical character of many economic formulations struck him as sound. Excessive mathematics, said Pigou, tended to emphasize mechanical rather than biological analogies.[137] He also accepted the neoclassical stress on the role of interest rates, although many economists were beginning to feel that with industrial integration and the rise of the corporation interest had lost its force. In one respect, however, Pigou parted company from Marshall. This was in the use of the consumers' surplus notion. He preferred rather to study how economic welfare was affected by private and social gains and how variations in output might influence welfare. This enabled him to incorporate into his theory all the frictions that once had been treated as exceptions. Divergences between what he called marginal private net product and marginal social net product became the center of attention. With the elimination of special cases, a general theory of welfare could be constructed, he thought, in which maximum output was attained when both types of net product were equal. Although the Pigovian models were usually based on the assumption of free competition, in which the marginal utility of money was considered to be constant, Pigou did not ignore elements of monopoly or imperfect competition, and strove mightily to incorporate them into his theory. He was less concerned than Marshall in developing a theory of value: social problems, as reflected in questions of the size and distribution of the national dividend, seemed much more fundamental. In this way, Pigou sharply underscored the ameliorative objectives of economic science.

A second influence, having its roots in continental general equilibrium writers, could also be discerned in Pigou's writings.[138] Anglo-Saxon economists had preferred Marshall's partial equilibrium approach. But while Walras had based his theory of maximum satisfactions on the subjective notions derived from the Austrians and the French mathematical economists, he had not fully displaced real cost, particularly when factor supply was related to factor prices. This must have been somewhat attractive to Pigou, for he was still rooted in the Ricardian heritage of real elements. Pigou's definition of national dividend could be equated easily to the Ricardian concept of physical net revenue. And Edgeworth's marginal utility was simply Ricardo's surplus made psychic. Consequently, Pigou's concept of the ideal output exhibited elements not only of the British objective analysis but of the continental subjective approach as well. Fundamentally, welfare as a "real" category was the objective expression of maximum satisfactions as revealed in the content of the national dividend, which itself was defined as a flow of goods and services, after providing for the maintenance of capital.[139]

Pigou's *Economics of Welfare* was in many ways an extraordinary book. A worthy successor to Marshall's *Principles,* it sought to survey the entire range of economic problems and reflected Pigou's firm belief that a study of economics could lead to an improvement in man's condition. Said he: ". . . the social enthusiasm which revolts from the sordidness of mean streets and the joylessness of withered lives, . . . is the beginning of economic science."[140] Yet, by 1939, Pigou had become less sanguine about ameliorative prospects. And he now wondered whether the world's statesmen were really interested in what the economists had to tell them.[141] Nevertheless, the Pigovian emphasis was a far cry from the concern with pure resource allocation that motivated most other writers. To Pigou this was a subordinate aim because economics, said he, was a science of what is and tends to be, not a science of what ought to be.[142] In short, he was much more interested in the world of experience. For such an economist it was inevitable that his attention would be centered on the size of real income and its distribution. This was long before the development of national income analysis in the 1930's.

According to Pigou, real income was related to resources, capital, knowledge, the quality of people, government, and, for a nation such as Britain, foreign trade. Distribution, on the other hand, involved wages, methods of worker compensation, and the whole complex of problems created by unemployment. It was Pigou's contention that a more even distribution of income would enhance welfare. And, as the business cycle raised the question of distribution over time, the question of government intervention flowed logically from this problem and introduced such matters as taxation and fiscal policy. Thus it might be said that a single thread could be traced in Pigou's economics, winding from the problems of the national dividend to every corner of the modern economy.[143]

Yet Pigou was not a pure empiricist: theoretical generalizations were distilled from a vast welter of raw data so that proper guide lines could be formulated. Quantitative statements were essential for studying economic relationships and this was especially necessary since repetitive experiments in social behavior were not possible. Thus he did not dismiss pure theory as useless, as did the German historicists. Some British historians, however, were wont to support the latter: Sir John Clapham, the noted economic historian, loosed a savage attack on theory, especially Pigou's, in his article, "Of Empty Economic Boxes." [144] Clapham charged that the theorists were unable to fit empirical data into their laws of decreasing or increasing returns. Nor did he find their abstract concept of an industry very helpful, either. Grand Analytics, said Clapham, was simply a collection of empty boxes. Pigou retorted angrily that the major function of theory was to pursue the implications of a given set of propositions.[145] This inevitably necessitated abstracting from the mass of things so that the general characteristics of commodities could be embodied in a single concept applicable to all varieties of goods. The so-called empty boxes, said Pigou, were important elements of the intellectual machinery of modern economics. The objective, he continued, was to build better boxes and to see how they might be filled. Clapham, of course, had no alternative to offer, and it remained for such theorists as Piero Sraffa, Joan Robinson, and others to construct a better theoretical tool-kit.

Welfare, said Pigou, referred to the goodness of a man's state of mind or to the satisfactions embodied in it.[146] The basis of welfare, therefore, was necessarily the extent to which one's desires were met. While admittedly these were not directly measurable, an indirect method was available, since the amount of money that one was willing to pay could be used to provide an index. Satisfactions were comparable, both intrapersonally and interpersonally.[147] Any other approach would mean the end of welfare economics as Pigou had defined it. Obviously, this set of assumptions underpinned the proposition that transfers of income could enhance aggregate satisfactions.[148] It was not without justice therefore that Pigou's economics was described as essentially moral.[149] In the final analysis, it did become a study in ethical behavior which served to popularize the use of the word "welfare" and made economics precisely the kind of science he wanted it to be.

Welfare, then, was a state of consciousness which could be measured in terms of greater or less.[150] But in economics only that part of welfare subject to the measuring rod of money was to be studied. Economic welfare, said Pigou, was by no means an index of total welfare, for many other elements in the latter—the quality of work, one's environment, human relationships, status, housing and public security—were absent from the first. Nevertheless, he insisted, there was a strong presumption, in advanced countries at least, that economic and general welfare were roughly correlated. Few propositions have reflected more strongly both the material basis of Pigou's economic theory and the way in which his ethics were related to it.

Economic welfare and the national dividend were essentially "coordinate."[151] Of course, problems would arise in measuring the national dividend. Here Pigou took up many of the questions dealt with today in national income analysis, such as the decrease in national income occasioned by marrying one's housekeeper. In a more serious vein, he was disturbed that desecration of the countryside by mining should leave the national dividend undisturbed. He finally developed a fairly broad definition which included everything purchased with money plus the services provided by home ownership.[152] Problems of transfer payments, depreciation, and double counting were acknowledged. A key question was "maintaining capital intact." In addressing himself to this point, Pigou developed a capital concept which embodied elements from both Böhm-Bawerk and John Bates Clark. He recognized the specificity of capital, yet he saw it also as a fund, ever depleted, ever renewed. But with his emphasis on "real" elements, he was less interested in the constancy of the money value of capital.[153] It was sufficient to provide for depreciation allowances in a real sense in order to avoid contraction in the stock of capital.

With welfare so intimately related to the size of the national dividend it became important for him to make comparisons in successive periods. This was more difficult than it seemed, for it was now necessary to evaluate changes in the real components of the national dividend. Pigou's solution was as follows: given the same tastes and income distribution, an increase in the national dividend would represent a genuine change when more money was offered to conserve the items added than would be offered for those that were deleted.[154] Such conditions also implied that satisfactions and money demand would be greater. Naturally, this raised the difficult and exacerbating problem of index numbers, something that Pigou discussed at great length. The approach excluded enhanced national dividend brought on by scarcity induced price increases. Much more important, he felt, was the need to balance increases in the real national dividend against the disutilities of work.[155] Pigou contended that the national dividend would be increased in most cases even though the disutility of work might also increase. Thus it could be fairly said that the national dividend was as much a measure of physical production as it was of welfare.

Since income transfers conceivably might affect the proportions in which goods were produced, the distribution of the national dividend was a matter of no small importance. Generally, income transfers from the rich to the poor would improve welfare, provided the national dividend itself was not reduced. Such transfers, said Pigou, would mean much less to the wealthy than to the poor, whose economic position thereby would be raised.[156] The crude Malthusian contention that higher wages would stimulate procreation and lead to overpopulation was refuted with a masterful presentation of empirical data. Like most utilitarians, he did not accept the argument that poverty was the fault of the poor: poverty, rather, was related to "bad environment." Nor did Pigou hesitate to resort to sociological material: his handling of the evidence was a model that many other economists might have done well to imitate.

Concern with equality was a common interest of economists at the time. The democratic ethos urged that an equal chance to enjoy life should be made available to everyone and it was thought that greater equality of wealth would enhance such opportunities. Yet the Pigovian argument that economic equality maximized welfare has been sharply rejected in recent years, especially by those anxious to create a scientific, nonnormative discipline. Pigou had argued that with income subject to diminishing marginal utility, transfers of income from the rich to the poor would enhance total welfare by increasing the latter's satisfactions more than the former's would be damaged. But question was raised whether diminishing marginal utility was an appropriate concept to apply to total income. Further, Pigou's position clearly implied interpersonal comparisons of utility—a notion that was anathema to latter-day utility theorists. Such criticisms, however, overlooked the palpable fact that increments of income do seem to bring greater satisfactions or utility to lower income groups than they do to those with a surfeit of goods. And there was always the problem of power, which Pigou's critics were generally reluctant to consider on the specious grounds that this was not an *economic* question.

This was the backdrop against which one had to evaluate the allocation of resources. The central question was the relationship of individual economic interests to those of the community. In Pigovian technical terms, it was the connection that one might establish between the value of the marginal private net product and the value of the marginal social net product that indicated the direction in which economic study was to move. The latter was defined somewhat cumbersomely as the total net product attributable to the marginal increment of resources applied to any use, with both private and social gains, and social costs, included in the evaluation. Thus, whereas smoke damage from a private factory implied a social loss, external economies flowing from a particular enterprise might lead to reduced social costs. Marginal private net product was that part of the total product which accrued to the person responsible for investment. The value of a marginal net product was simply its price in market terms. Now, the national dividend, said Pigou, would attain a maximum when the values of the social net product were equal in all possible uses; for when resources in a given application yielded less than they might elsewhere, it was patent that the national dividend could be improved by resource transfers to more fruitful modes of production. Pigou did not insist on absolute maximums, but rather on relatively superior positions, since even a point near the absolute maximum would be better than others.[157]

How was it possible to reach these desirable points? By self-interest, he said, unhampered by ignorance or other rigidities: it was the royal road to those equilibria where private and social marginal net products were equated.[158] Pigou was aware, of course, that certain business practices tended to foster rigidities and that units of capital and labor exhibited just the sort of indivisibilities which made the theory somewhat questionable. But these simply created divergences between the two types of marginal net product— divergences which could be widened by variations in demand, shifts in tastes, cyclical fluctuations, the rise of new industries, and war. These were the problems that captured Pigou's attention, for they would have to be susceptible to some solution if the ideal output, described by the equality of the private and social net product, was to be attained. Clearly self-interest alone could not do the job. Therefore, interference in the economic process seemed justified.[159]

Divergences occurred because products and resources flowed in different directions and through different persons. In agriculture, for example, the separation of function between tenant and landlord was responsible for one set of divergences. Others occurred when transportation increased nearby land values or when factories dumped soot and smoke on the community. In the former, the marginal social net product was enhanced; in the latter, private gain exceeded the social product. This was one of Pigou's keenest observations, and it was to his credit that he sought to bring it into the realm of economic analysis, even though the concepts were somewhat imprecise. The approach suggested that some innovations might involve certain social costs by displacing older forms of production. Improved technology might create painful adjustments for those who were its victims. Not unexpectedly, Pigou believed that the use of subsidies and other social control measures could be employed fruitfully to counteract increases in social costs stemming from innovation and thus close the gap between private and social marginal net product.

The idea of applying taxes and bounties came from Marshall,[160] and Pigou simply adapted it as a way of eliminating divergences. Later economists, such as Sir Dennis Robertson, Lindley Fraser, G. F. Shove and R. F. Kahn, all demurred from the subsidy and tax proposal.[161] Robertson feared that it might lead to a complete subsidy of plants in decreasing cost situations; Shove argued that expanded production in such industries could reduce rent sufficiently to counterbalance increases in consumers' surplus; Fraser asserted that the shifting of the tax and its ultimate incidence would make increases in welfare unlikely; while Kahn thought that it would be necessary to rank industries according to their competitive characteristics before Pigou's tax could be applied.

The question of bounties inevitably led to the problem of socialism.[162] Implicit in Pigou's analysis, as in Marshall's, was a kind of socialist imperative, for maximum welfare, it was suggested, could be attained through greater equality of incomes. The main reservations that Pigou expressed were the possible checks this might exert on capital accumulation and productive energy.[163] Nevertheless, some sympathy was expressed for at least a moderate form of socialism under which the very urgent needs of society would be met.[164] A socialist society, said Pigou, could deal more effectively with unemployment and also would be more efficient technically.[165] In any case, he was convinced that capitalism required some modification, but this, he urged, would have to be done gradually so as to mould and transform and not uproot society.

Divergences were exacerbated and made even more complex by monopolistic competition. In fact, when rivalry under these conditions led to alliances and virtual monopoly, Pigou had grave doubt that positive values for the social net product would be forthcoming. Neither would bilateral monopoly yield positive gains.[166] Significant divergences occurred depending on whether costs were increasing, decreasing, or constant. (Pigou, however, preferred to translate these concepts into decreasing, increasing, and constant supply price.) Under competitive conditions, supply price equalled both marginal and average cost in the long run. While this could be viewed from the standpoint of either the industry or the community, it was the effect on the latter which interested Pigou. It was evident that Marshall's external economies underpinned the notion of decreasing supply price. External diseconomies led to an increased supply price for the community.[167] This situation could originate from increases in the prices of inputs and in one sense such increased costs might be interpreted as a transfer of income, especially if the actual flow of goods was in no way increased. From the industry standpoint such a situation would appear to stem from the higher cost of obtaining satisfactions. Ultimately, this would bear down heavily on the consumer.

Marginal private net product was greater than, equal to, or less than the social product depending on whether conditions of increasing, constant, or decreasing supply price obtained. Thus, if decreasing supply price existed, the marginal social net product would be greater; if increasing supply price were the rule, it would be less.[168] This suggested that bounties or taxes could be applied to producers in order to equalize net products. Where prices were too high ". . . the direct expense of a bounty sufficient to call forth a greatly increased supply at a much lower price, would be much less than the consequent increase of consumers' surplus." [169] Such was the extent of intervention favored by Pigou: its purpose was to correct divergences between net products. Yet it was evident that in situations of oligopoly or imperfect competition, divergences would be even more widespread. In such cases, nationalization, or at least regulation, appeared a necessary tool. Industries with decreasing supply price were more apt to wind up in monopoly, since marginal cost could be less than average cost over a fairly wide range of output, thus strengthening Pigou's argument for limited intervention. He agreed that some approach to ideal output was possible were the monopolist allowed to install price discrimination, but this too would require social control.

In this theoretical framework, Pigou studied a variety of particular problems, the most notable of which was the case of railroad rates. A long section, in many ways a model of its kind, applied the theory to the impact of labor on the national dividend. These were always related to the basic question of equating marginal private net product and marginal social net product, and the governing principle was the enhancement of the real national dividend. Indeed, the whole performance was that of a virtuoso: its logic was carefully spelled out and the tools of marginal analysis were employed with marked refinement, always exploring discrepancies between private action and social results. Divergences, Pigou said, were usually caused by various economic rigidities as well as monopoly, and it was evident to him, if not to others, that subsidies and taxes were effective ways to make private effort and social purpose coincide. In this way Pigou's theory provided a convenient bridge from Marshall to the more realistic insights into monopolistic and imperfect competition out of which even more precise theoretical formulations were to come.

Pigou further demonstrated his facility with abstruse theory in his *Economics of Stationary States*.[170] In this slow-moving and sometimes ponderous work, he set down economic preconditions as they might appear in a Robinson Crusoe economy and then successively developed the requirements of equilibrium in single and multiple commodity markets. It was an attempt to

study the basic forces that might apply to both the static and dynamic economy. The driving motives were essentially states of mind or "schemes of
preference and indifference." [171] Since absolute desires could not be measured
nor satisfactions maximized without orders of preference, it seemed that
Pigou was now entering the realm of positive economics. The technique for
this exploration was comparative statics in the long run.[172] The stationary
state was defined in the usual way as one in which change occurred at a
constant rate. There were at least three degrees of stationariness: a stationary
system with its industries in motion; a stationary industry with its enterprises in motion; and both industry and firms in a stationary condition. Pigou
was most interested in the third type, which he characterized as a thoroughgoing stationary state, one in which the rate of profit was equal to the supply
price of waiting.

In this model, an ever expanding economic universe was not possible
because the supply of land was limited, enforcing diminishing returns. The
latter eventually affected all other factors as well and so equilibrium finally
was reached. The key problem was to determine whether there would be
perpetual oscillations about equilibrium and whether, in fact, equilibrium
could be attained. Pigou had no doubts about this, for with a large stock
of capital and constant demand, adjustments could be worked out via decreasing increments of change. While increases in capital would tend to curtail
profit and reduce stocks, decreases would have an opposite effect. In a practical sense, however, the adjustment period might be quite long, sufficient, in
fact, to prevent a return to equilibrium. The stationary state meant that population would renew itself within each group at a constant rate and that the
annual rate of consumption for each class of capital would be constant. In
this way, the model avoided the problem of capital replacement, since it was
assumed that capital would be conserved in the same forms as in the past.[173]
This put the question of obsolescence to one side, and it was necessary to
account only for depreciation and depletion.

The basic Crusoe model was motivated by the principle of maximum
satisfaction. There were no frictions; fixed capital was freely available; no
working capital was required, since goods emerged when wanted; and there
was no storage problem because everything was immediately consumed. In this
rarefied system, work was carried to the point at which its disutility equalled
the desire for the net marginal product. All this was related to a productivity
function which was itself subject to diminishing returns. Where several products were sought, the equi-marginal principle applied. In studying what
"Robinson's" reactions might be, Pigou accepted the *ceteris paribus* approach,
varying the different elements of his equations one at a time to examine their
effects. The model was completed with the introduction of elasticity.[174] If
desire and production increased, and the disutility of work fell, more goods
would be obtained, particularly if there was high elasticity in the conditions

of desire and work. On the other hand, if the disutility of work was elastic and desire inelastic, less would be obtained. The same principles apparently held for a multiproduct economy, where the elasticities of desire differed and an improvement in production tended to direct energies into luxury output.

Pigou then introduced time, working capital, and the discounting of future satisfactions. With the length and nature of the production period defined, with given tastes, and a given rate of discounting, the quantity of working capital was established. Similar conditions could be set down for fixed capital and finished goods held as "liquid" capital. The rate of interest would be equal to the rate at which future satisfactions were discounted; this was the rate at which the stock of capital could be maintained intact.[175] Thus, Pigou rejected the Schumpeterian contention that zero interest was characteristic of the stationary state. A low rate of interest merely implied that the stock of capital and real income was large. Improved methods which made the existing stock of capital more productive could have a depressing effect on interest.

The complexities of the model were painstakingly developed. Yet Pigou was unable to deal satisfactorily with the problem of indivisible units and his handling of the matter was weak. From this he passed to a colony of Crusoes and to the area of exchange and cooperation. Economic interaction, he said, could be enforced by government, force, or through voluntary effort. Money was required to make such a system function satisfactorily. But in the stationary state money transactions were shadows of real ones.[176] There were no capital transactions, only income transactions; since the stock of money was constant as was its rate of flow, the numerical relations were also constant. Consequently, money income was some multiple of the money stock. And if the intervals between receipts and expenditures were alike, money incomes in each period would be the same. Yet Pigou knew that money was no passive element.[177] It influenced expectations and thereby profoundly affected economic affairs, but it was in the main a "highway for commerce" which permitted division of labor and markets to be developed to an extraordinarily high pitch.

Pigou then went on to define the concepts of markets and exchange. These, stemming chiefly from Jevons, described homogeneous goods in which transport costs were zero. A single good might appear in several markets at the same time and, in the. absence of transport costs, tariffs, and the like, price uniformity would prevail. Without ideal conditions monopoly, in all probability, would be the outcome.[178] This raised the famous question of duopoly price, which for Pigou was clearly determinate so long as the beliefs of both parties were stated as part of the problem. If it was thought that shifts in output would not affect the "terms of trade," there was no reason why the price problem was not soluble. Yet it was conceded that when both parties behaved as monopolists, the solution was bound to evaporate, since sellers often were guided by mere hunch and intuition. Determinancy was, of course, increased as the number of participants grew larger.

Where one factor differed in quality, as in the case of land, argued Pigou, the proportions of the other factors were apt to differ also.[179] Since the entrepreneur was the residual recipient in the distribution of the product, it was quite possible for the whole product not to be distributed in accordance with Euler's theorem.[180] Yet production and distribution were essentially the same economic process, so that the whole product could be fully distributed, provided that the factors were paid according to their private marginal productivity. Euler's theorem, it will be recalled, had assumed that there were no economies or diseconomies of scale.[181] Since this was unlikely, Pigou seemingly had reached an impasse. Thus, in order to escape the dilemma, he resorted to the "divergences." Diseconomies were clearly present, he said, whenever the private product exceeded collective results.

The demand for the several factors was an interdependent one, and was related to a "maintenance" function, which described the price necessary to keep a factor engaged. In the case of labor, this became extremely complex, for it depended on the length of the working day, the capacity for work, and the number of available workers. Theoretically, the backward bending supply curve for labor was possible, but unlikely.[182] The principle of interrelationship meant that both the demand and supply curves would have to "fit together" if equilibrium in the stationary state was to be attained. The rate of pay for the factor had to equal the maintenance price of putting it to work. When monopoly and shifts were introduced in the conditions of "maintenance," the model became increasingly complex, so that remuneration to the factors was quite varied.

With the introduction of many commodities, it was obvious that the model was becoming almost unmanageable. Maintenance prices now depended on tastes and on the purchasing power of the persons in control of the factors. By now only the Marshallian partial analysis could be used. With a multiplicity of products, new variables were introduced, and internal and external economies had to be brought in explicitly. Monopoly behavior became more likely, for producers had to take account of the effect of their own behavior on price. Equal proportionate changes in demand no longer ruled. The presence of transport costs allowed several monopolistic sellers to coexist in a determinate situation. Under monopoly, output would be less than in competitive conditions and the entrepreneur would be in a position to exploit the other factors.[183] Moreover, there would be a tendency for factor movements to become more rigid. A public monopolist, on the other hand, would be able to take a broader view and equate demand price to "marginal social supply price," thus creating a more flexible output policy than would be the case for private monopolists.

All this was frightfully static. Yet Pigou was realistic enough to declare:

"Transition rules always: stationariness never; the long run never comes." [184] The real world, he knew, was one of perpetual disequilibrium in which the fundamental problems revealed by the static model were intensified and the frequency of adjustment increased. Pigou conceded that questions stemming from adjustment between equilibria were by far the most important. But the discussion of these problems was left for other works. Unfortunately, much of the analysis in the *Economics of Stationary States* resembled a verbal translation of mathematical equations. These, in turn, were qualified by so many involutions of language that the exposition became exasperatingly dense.

Variations in the national dividend brought into focus the problem of the business cycle. Previously, Pigou had discussed cyclical movements in the first edition of his *Economics of Welfare,* but dissatisfied with the treatment, he deleted it in subsequent editions, and a more extensive analysis was prepared which appeared as his *Industrial Fluctuations.*[185] Here the causes of economic cycles were classified as impulses which initiated certain movements that were themselves conditioned by the nature of the economy's reaction.[186] Pigou, however, offered only a short-run analysis, for he was interested more in fluctuations of that part of society's income-getting power which was actually at work.[187] Limited data restricted him to the area of employment as the basic measure of fluctuation. But, despite the lack of empirical information, it was evident that the capital goods industries did exhibit much sharper variability than the consumers' goods industries.[188] Again Pigou sought to translate the analysis into real terms: the proximate causes for cyclical changes were ascribed to variations in the real demand schedule for labor. By positing a kind of general wage goods unit, he was able to combine schedules so that shifts might be studied in the aggregate. In the Pigovian view, the basic forces underlying the schedules were expectations regarding prospective yields. Change occurred because either attitudes or the size of the income flow were altered.[189] In this way psychological factors were sharply underscored: investment elements, such as emphasized by Tugan-Baranovsky, were rejected. But Pigou quite clearly misunderstood what the Russian economist was saying, for it was not at all true that in a condition of underemployment expansion could stem from lower prices. It was this view that led Keynes to attack the Pigovian analysis, for quite patently it had overlooked the significant role of effective demand.

According to Pigou, changes in expectations were due to changes in industrial conditions, psychological effects, and monetary factors. And since the importance of the first lay in its impact on the thinking of businessmen, Pigou's business cycle theory, in the last analysis, could be described as entirely psychological in character. True, such real elements as crop variations, technological improvements, new mineral deposits, industrial disputes, and shifts in consumer taste were important, but their impact was transmitted solely through the behavior of businessmen. In some respects, this resembled Schumpeter's innovation theory, but the greater stress that Pigou placed on "optimism" and "pessimism" made his approach something quite different. He refused to acknowledge that direct economic effects were possible through what is now called the multiplier, so that the psychological and "real" elements of business fluctuations were not blended nearly so well as in Keynesian and post-Keynesian doctrine. Only psychology and errors in estimations appeared as the basic causes of cycles. Errors took place because the facts of industrial life changed or simply because there was insufficient information available to make suitable forecasts. Perhaps most significant was the lack of simultaneity in production and sales. Gaps in these flows could easily cause overestimates or underestimates and thereby influence business decisions. But while Pigou acknowledged the existence of the self-fulfilling prophecy, he was reluctant to add this to his armory of psychological forces.[190] At best, there was a kind of interdependence in decision-making which caused the economy to move inexorably from highly optimistic to depressed business emotions. As errors of optimism spread, business ground to a halt. Liquidation became rapid enough to create new errors—this time, those of pessimism. "This new error is born, not an infant, but a giant." [191] When the wave of pessimism had been overdone, businessmen were wont to uncover new possibilities and the wave would move upward again to repeat the disheartening repetitive cycle.[192]

In Pigou's analysis, the consumption goods industries were the main loci of industrial fluctuations. That is, he stressed the role of the accelerator as against that of the multiplier. He rejected the proposition that investment, especially of the autonomous variety, played a genuine role in the business cycle. Certainly this was his viewpoint in the first edition of the *Economics of Welfare,* although by the time he published *Industrial Fluctuations,* he was somewhat defensive about these views, hinting that cycles might at times originate in the "instrumental industries." [193] He granted that fluctuations in producers' goods industries were by far the more violent and that the turning point there preceded that for consumers' goods. But this, he insisted, was traceable to a slower rate of change in the demand for consumers' goods.[194]

In a somewhat obscure chapter of the *Industrial Fluctuations,* Pigou attempted to trace the relationship of real wages to new capital.[195] It seemed to him that real wages grew more rapidly than fresh investment. This effect, akin to that noted by Wicksell, was to be traced to business exhilaration and its consequent impact on the demand for labor. Such variations then were tied to the elasticity of supply of new capital, so that movements in labor demand would be greater than business expectations.[196] New capital could be obtained from either of three sources: by an increased flow of consumers' goods; by reduced consumption of either workers or entrepreneurs; or by a depletion of existing stocks. An increased flow of consumers' goods was unlikely when new capital was converted into equipment. Of course, bank credits could make the supply of new capital more elastic. Pigou tried to show by this analysis how new capital was drawn into the producers' goods industries, thereby sustaining business optimism.[197] The process could become cumulative, but with periodicity as its main feature. Not only were the wave movements reinforced by replacement effects, but the initial impulses too could be rhythmic. Yet the main driving force was psychological: ". . . anything which improves the fortunes of businessmen constitutes a spur to optimistic error, just as anything which worsens their fortunes constitutes a spur to pessimistic error." [198] Thus, something like windfall profits could generate good feelings, and businessmen, feeding on them, would tend to enter a state of economic exhilaration.

Foreshadowing his theory of wages and employment, Pigou contended that an elastic supply of labor resulting from workers' determination to maintain wage rates could make economic fluctuations more intense.[199] One of the keys to a solution of cycles, said he, was flexibility in wage rates, whereas resistance to this principle would simply bring gains to one group of workers at the expense of others. This solution was, of course, quite in the classical tradition, but its avoidance of the problem of effective demand later impelled Keynes to level one of his sharpest attacks on this sort of theory. Pigou did acknowledge, however, that wage reductions in but part of the economy would not meet the requirements of his model.[200] Wage rigidities, therefore, as well as monetary policies and industrial price policies, became important adjuncts to the basic psychological drives of businessmen. All together, these elements could markedly influence the amplitude of cyclical movements. Yet, said Pigou, banking policies or price policies could not alter the fundamental factor of human error and its consequences, for an expansion ". . . carries within itself the seeds of its own reversal, and when once reversal has taken place, this of itself tends to shift men's minds towards pessimism, and so to start a cumulative process making for industrial depression." [201]

What remedies then were available? Fluctuations were serious matters for society since they entailed a reduction of real income as contrasted with what might have been produced under stable conditions. Should the government introduce corrective measures? Pigou's response was not the easy one given today, since the problem for him was the delicate balance between community and private welfare. He doubted, for example, that social control of innovation and invention was practicable. Monetary policy might be useful if it sought to adjust price movements to income trends per capita, rather than to attempt price stablization in an absolute sense. Flexible wage rates might be useful also, provided they were not brought too low for human welfare. There was a further suggestion that government efforts to restore effective demand could be helpful, for the marginal private net product of attempts to raise demand would be less than the marginal social net product. That is, self-interest could not do the job.[202] It evidently appeared that Pigou's cycle policy was ambivalent: anxious to maintain his loyalty to classicism, he was nevertheless aware that something more than what tradition called for was needed to alleviate the strains of the business cycle.

In his theory of employment, Pigou combined marginal productivity notions with some aspects of wages fund. The amount of employment depended on real wages and the real demand for labor, while wage goods were the basis for comparing wages with other variables. The quantity of labor demanded, given the real wage rate, would be determined by the equality of the value of the marginal net product to the real wage rate, plus employers' contributions for such fringe items as unemployment insurance. The aggregate quantity of labor demanded ultimately would vary with the quantity of wage goods devoted to actual wage payments. This was typically classical in spirit and brought the charge that Pigou would cure depressions by cutting wages. And, despite his disclaimers, the reader has the inescapable feeling that perhaps this really was his recommendation and that it was not until the Keynesian revolution exploded that he began to waver.[203]

Employment and Equilibrium, a highly technical work, attempted to rescue the remains of classical employment theory. It was not, however, fully successful.[204] In this book, Pigou adapted some Keynesian concepts to his own use, as in the definition of savings and investment, and much was made of what has come to be known as the Pigou effect. This latter was simply the increased consumption, stemming from a given real income as a result of price declines, together with the increased real value of money balances.[205] But the price decline necessary to create increased consumption and an upturn in the economy clearly was more than society could bear. Obviously, some institutional considerations would have been in order to clarify the analysis. However, Pigou's central problem at this point was to discover how equilibrium might be attained over a period long enough to assure constant values for income, savings, investment, and employment. In essence, the Pigou effect sought to demonstrate the possibility of maintaining demand by virtue of an automatic flexibility in prices, wages, and money supply. He was concerned primarily with a "flow" equilibrium which would permit him to study the movements of the relevant variables. It was no longer market equilibrium that was at issue, but rather movement and rates of change. There were six fundamental quantities in this new model: labor employed in consumption industries; labor employed in producers' goods industries; the rate of interest; the money wage rate; the stock of money; and the income velocity of money. Money income was simply the product of the last two items. Seven functional relationships were then developed: employment to output in the consumers' goods industries; employment to output in the producers' goods industries; elasticity of real demand in consumers' goods industries; elasticity of demand in producers' goods industries; the relation of the demand for labor in producers' goods industries to the interest rate; the relation of labor supply to interest; and the relation of money income to interest. Introducing money wages brought the discounting process into the model and connected the quantity of labor demanded to the rate of interest.[206] The presumption was that with a lower interest rate in terms of consumption goods, the demand for labor in producers' goods industries was apt to be greater.

More specifically, these quantities and functional relations provided Pigou with three equations which postulated the equality of savings and investment, savings and producers' goods output, and total output and money income. Implicit in the system was a functional relationship between output and money wages that was itself dependent on the elasticities of cost and demand. But there were four unknowns present—employment in the consumers' goods industries, employment in the producers' goods industries, the rate of interest, and the money wage rate—and thus an additional equation was required in order to make the system determinate. This could be handled easily enough, said Pigou, by making money wages an independent variable or asserting the level of employment to be constant. In the latter case, the money wage seemingly could be ignored, yet where employment was deemed to be the key variable the situation was somewhat more complex, for then the relationships among savings, investment, and employment would have to account for the mutual effects of the rate of interest and money wage rates. That is to say, shifts in employment stemming from changes in wage rates might properly be related to changes in interest rates which were themselves influenced by changes in money wages.

Pigou gave a much greater role to the rate of interest than is the custom today. He made interest a tool for stimulating saving and investment, although it would seem in the modern context that investment opportunity per se was the really significant factor in moving the system. The neoclassical theory, as reflected in Pigou's work, insisted that money income was in the last analysis influenced by banking policy. This avoided the Keynesian conception of income determination, and suggested that the level of output was effected primarily by money income and wages. The implication was that a reduction in money wages would increase employment because money then would become plentiful, interest rates fall, and investment be stimulated. Unconvincingly, Pigou attempted to validate the argument by showing how employment had been stabilized prior to World War I. But it might just as well have been foreign investment or new industries rather than monetary policy which acted as the stabilizing mechanism.[207]

The employment model which Pigou constructed might be described as a more generalized version of Marshall's market with some Walrasian overtones. Although this led to some ambiguities in its structural properties, it nevertheless was evident that the main feature comprised several varieties of business confidence so that the psychological basis of economic change remained intact.[208] Another interesting feature of Pigou's study of employment was his use of the multiplier concept, set forth in both money and employment terms.[209] The influence of Keynes apparently was beginning to affect even those who had at first opposed him.[210] Still *Employment and Equilibrium* did not escape some harsh criticism, particularly on its definition of stability conditions. But, Pigou maintained his original position: employment, he contended, was a function of the real demand for labor which ultimately would be related to the rate of interest.

In two further areas of economic theory Pigou's work was notable: money and taxation. Although he was known primarily for the "real" analysis of economic flows, it cannot be said that in his view money was solely a "veil." He was fully aware of its importance for its own sake.[211] True, he thought of income as a collection of commodities, and in his stationary state it was the movement of goods that was basic. Since satisfactions stemmed from goods, it seemed to Pigou that money was inessential. Yet he recognized that money institutions did contribute to welfare and that many transactions could not be completed in the absence of money. It was a kind of lubricant, but of secondary importance, nevertheless, since the number of units of money really made no difference to the flow of real income.

In the analysis of money, which had its roots in Marshall's cash balance approach, Pigou demonstrated that there was no real conflict between the British view and Irving Fisher's transactions equation.[212] In the latter, the hoarding of money reduced velocity and consequently caused prices to fall. In the cash balance approach, emphasis was put on the increased demand for money as against goods, so that again prices fell. Pigou claimed superiority for his view because it focused attention on the proportion of resources that people wished to hold in the form of money.[213] This allowed one to concentrate on the relation of the value of money to the subjective attitudes of individuals. The value of money would fall, or prices increase, when its supply increased or demand for it declined. In these circumstances, it could be said that goods were preferred to money. Demand was therefore translated into terms of the amount of purchasing power an individual wanted to hold. Influential factors were the volume of trade and the length of the transaction period. This tied the cash balance approach to the Fisherine velocity of circulation, for it was, simply enough, its reciprocal. If money was held for one month, its velocity was clearly twelve. The transactions period was small, said Pigou, where financial institutions were well developed, receipts and disbursements close in time, and incomes regular.

Once it was conceded that government might properly intervene in order to raise welfare, it was necessary to talk of taxation and public finance. This involved certain principles of compensation, in which the concept of equity was to play an important part. Here one had to distinguish between pure transfers which merely redistributed income and those government expenditures which actually put resources to work. The sources of tax funds to be used for creative government spending were therefore quite important. Basically, resources taken by government from persons in similar circumstances should be equal, said Pigou.[214] This would assure fulfillment of the equimarginal principle.

Pigou defined his basic tax principle as that of least aggregate sacrifice, which had to be subjected to measurement just as satisfaction was measured. Again Pigou asserted the notion of comparability, and least aggregate sacrifice became the theoretical justification for a progressive tax system.[215] He rejected the idea of equal sacrifice on grounds of ambiguity: moreover, since equal sacrifice was deducible from the more general principle of least aggregate sacrifice it was merely additional and unneeded lumber.[216] Least sacrifice was to be understood in a relative sense, for it was contingent upon the particular tax formula worked out by the government.[217] The importance which higher income groups, for example, ascribed to marginal increments would depend not only on the absolute size of their income, but on what was done to other members of their group as well. That is, sacrifice was relative to the status of the individuals affected. The difficulty with this concept of Pigou's, however, was that it removed the individual from the total income scale, thus obscuring his relation to the whole society. Yet it was the latter that was the important consideration in progressive taxation.

The basic principle underlying Pigou's thought was the equality of marginal sacrifices for all members of the community. Therefore, relative positions as well as places in the total scale of income seemed important. He was fearful lest any tax scheme, by its pressure on present rather than future sacrifices, press on savings and capital accumulation. Consequently, he felt that neither the rich nor the poor were good subjects for taxation.[218] The argument obviously assumed an equality of the marginal utility of money—a questionable notion when income was distributed in lopsided fashion. This criticism, of course, looks upon income *qua* income, without regard to source, whereas Pigou believed that it was necessary to distinguish between different kinds of income.[219] For this reason he insisted that a tax should impel work to expand or at least to contract less than it would otherwise. While for a community of equal incomes, a poll tax would be most efficient, it was evident that in modern societies the progressive tax had ample justification. Yet the least sacrifice principle demanded that size of family and type of income be taken into account.[220]

When John Maynard Keynes attacked the classical tradition in his *General Theory,* he singled out Pigou, his old teacher, as its leading representative.[221] It was Keynes' theory of income determination—with its emphasis on the consumption function and the role of investment—that obliterated the Pigovian vision of economics. Unemployment, said Keynes, was not due to inflexible wage rates, but rather to insufficient effective demand. Keynes agreed that the real wage was related to the marginal product, but the level of employment, he said, which fixed the marginal product, was derived from the level of demand. The key issue was the money wage, not the real one. Workers accepted employment, argued Keynes, at a given wage, even though it might mean a reduced real wage, and if money wages fell it was bound to affect seriously the level of effective demand. A flexible wage policy seemed futile and could simply produce price instability and social turmoil.[222] Keynes ignored Pigou's contention that lower prices could stimulate consumption by enhancing the real value of asset holdings: the so-called Pigou effect had no merit for him. Changes in consumption came about through changes in income, not prices. The Pigovian theorem might work in the long run, said Keynes, but few today would be alive then. The fact was that a general wage cut would reduce demand all around and do little to solve a depressed situation.

Pigou replied to Keynes in a bitter review of the latter's *General Theory*,[223] and charged that his position had been misstated. Nevertheless, he reiterated his flexible wage argument and virtually dismissed the theory of income determination on the ground that savings and investment were practically coterminous. Despite some other criticisms voiced by Pigou, it was evident that he was already on the defensive. In the meantime, the Keynesian revolution was turning economics on its head. Even opponents had begun to talk in Keynes' language and attempts at rebuttal had to be couched in his terms. When Pigou commented on Keynes in a series of lectures at Cambridge in 1949, he too, reluctantly, joined the fold.[224] Yet he insisted that Keynes' argument was solely for the short run: the final equilibrium would have to be dealt with by other devices. Pigou also refused to treat economic categories in monetary terms: a life-long habit of thought impelled him to translate the Keynesian categories into "real" concepts.[225] There was a grudging acceptance of Keynes' equations, to which Pigou added his own functional relationship of the quantity of labor and wage payments.[226] But the force of Keynes' argument could not be denied, and Pigou finally admitted that less employment could be associated with reduced wage rates.[227] Thrift no longer seemed the great virtue that it had been in classical theory.[228] Although Pigou arduously tried to hold on to his own doctrine, he had to admit that it was his distinguished pupil who had pointed the way toward a proper analysis of the economy. Said he finally: "Those of us who disagreed in part with [Keynes'] analysis have, nevertheless, undoubtedly been affected by it in our own thinking; and it is very hard to remember exactly where we stood before. . . ." [229] It seemed as though the classical tradition, as advanced and modified by both Marshall and Pigou, had reached an impasse.

iv

Sir Dennis Robertson: Money and Industrial Fluctuation

A Fellow at Trinity College since 1914, Sir Dennis H. Robertson (1890-   ), studied under Pigou, became a reader in economics in 1930, and succeeded to Pigou's chair in 1944. His entire career has been spent at Cambridge, except for the years 1939 to 1944, when he was professor of economics at the University of London. A brilliant writer, and unafraid to "entertain as well as instruct," Robertson possessed an acerb style that frequently left his opponents helpless. Although he ranged over the whole of economic theory, his major contribution was in monetary matters. His books in this field, particularly *Money* and *Banking Policy and the Price Level,* are works of major importance.[230] Yet from the first he knew that economic movement involved more than money changes, as was demonstrated so well in his early *Study of Industrial Fluctuation.*[231] His collections of essays, *Economic Fragments, Essays in Monetary Theory, Utility and All That,* and *Economic Commentaries,*[232] were capped by a delightfully written three-volume *Lectures on Economic Principles.*[233]

In economic theory, Robertson was mainly a follower of Marshall and Pigou, although he developed his own language and special concepts which many economists have found quite attractive. One of his notable intellectual exploits was a rear-guard action fought against the Keynesian onslaught, but this was to no avail. Robertson was a sharp critic of Keynes and while he found many of the latter's ideas in the *Treatise on Money* very useful, he insisted that the business cycle was not a purely monetary phenomenon, a charge he put squarely at Keynes' doorstep. Shifts in certain types of demand were equally important, said Robertson, and if some change in output was deemed desirable, it would be necessary to allow the price level to move also. Absolute price stability had no virtues for him. To prove his point, he went into a highly detailed technical analysis of banking practice. Keynes, however, remained unconvinced and was certain that a much simpler explanation could be put forth. Yet the two men were quite friendly and worked together in the British Treasury; Robertson himself took an important part in the discussions leading up to the Bretton Woods agreement, while Keynes played a major role in the actual negotiations.

Robertson was basically a traditionalist. In problems of demand he subscribed to what one commentator has called introspective cardinalism. With Marshall, he believed that economic man reacted in terms of measurable quantities of marginal utility which were discerned both independently of other relationships as well as absolutely. And like Marshall, he believed that marginal utility was, in the last analysis, measurable in money. Responding to modern attacks on cardinalism stemming from Pareto and Hicks, he insisted that this approach was not at all absurd.[234] He had little doubt that introspection would show the law of diminishing returns to be a reality, and that the desire for things tended to be proportionate to the utility one expected to obtain from goods. Since both total utility and its increments were intrinsically measurable, the notion of a consumers' surplus was perfectly reasonable. However, variations in taste and in the power to enjoy things, as well as income differentials, made it evident that the same quantity of money implied different reactions for different people. The ordinal approach to demand theory was not very helpful, said Robertson, for by merely implying measurability it became little more than a highbrow refinement of cardinalism.[235] Robertson's delightful essay, "Utility and All That," reiterated the neoclassical position that a concern with welfare necessarily rooted economics in utility propositions.[236] The "normal" consumer tried to maximize something, he argued, and that something could easily be described as satisfaction, welfare, or utility. Therefore, Hicks' marginal rate of substitution was not a useful replacement for diminishing marginal utility, nor was Samuelson's "revealed preference" any better. The fact was, argued Robertson, that ordinality permitted only a comparison of absolute positions while cardinality allowed for comparisons of changes in consumer positions.[237]

Thus, despite all protests to the contrary, measurement was inescapable in ordinal concepts of demand, just as utility was present in the "behaviorist" apparatus. Robertson observed that some ordinalists not only arranged preferences in a given sequence but tried to measure the intervals between successive alternatives as well. It was discovered, said Robertson with great glee, that distances between pairs of magnitudes of utility could be subjected to something called relational addition and, by black magic, that measurability could be brought back into demand.[238] In the light of these observations, it was evident to Robertson that Hicks, Knight, Samuelson, and their followers had accomplished something less than a revolution in economics. In fact, he noted, they had been so busy firing at each other that the main objective of the discipline was lost to sight. Quite simply, the basic issue was to determine whether any genuine relationship existed between economic welfare and changes in real income.[239] This at least would enable an economist to say something about the consequences for happiness of economic change.[240] It was quite possible, he insisted, to handle this problem in the old way, rough and ready as it might be. To repudiate cardinal utility meant giving up the argument that the consumer could compare differences among various situations in which he found himself.[241] And that was too much to ask of a traditionalist. Said Robertson: ". . . it still seems to me to accord better with what we know about ourselves and other people to suppose that the consumer goes about equipped with a law of diminishing absolute marginal utility from individual commodities and from real income in general than to suppose that he goes about clad in a ready-made network of innumerable marginal rates of substitution." [242] Ordinal hypotheses might be more complex in a psychological sense and perhaps more logical, but that was no assurance that they were closer to the truth. The final outcome was Robertson's insistence upon the validity of consumers' surplus on the ground that it was both a useful comment on the ends and aims of economic activity and offered some sanction against interferences with human taste and aspiration.[243]

All this went as far back as Jevons, who had successfully eliminated the word *political* from political economy and turned economics into a study of the behavior of atomistic individuals rather than of the behavior of society at large. Yet Robertson, like Pigou, was unable to escape broader issues, for he knew that individual judgments did have a profound bearing on human welfare and that many of these actions did occur in the political sphere.[244] The definition of economics proposed by his contemporary, Lionel Robbins, by which the economist merely had to study the allocation of scarce resources to alternative uses, was rejected as much too limited. For such a definition would exclude numerous problems which were proper fields of study, such as industrial organization. Passing to the nature of law in social science, Robertson remarked that these were not commands but statements of general tendencies: an economic law, he said, was one concerned with a mode of behavior in which the strength of human motives could be measured by money prices.[245]

All the usual concepts were brought into the Robertsonian purview: diminishing utility, diminishing returns, increasing cost, consumers' surplus, equi-marginal returns, and the Jevonian notion of free capital—all operating in a framework of private property, division of labor, and the money economy. The analysis of supply, demand, and competitive price was thoroughgoing Marshall and Pigou, with but minor deviations. In 1924, Robertson injected himself into the debate between Clapham and Pigou, questioning the latter's application of long-run supply price because it had not adequately explained discontinuities and lumpiness in investment.[246] Increased gains, Robertson suggested, did not always stem from external economies: many could be traced to internal elements, so that increased output over time might be explained more simply by decreased cost per unit. In the case of increasing supply price, the mere fact that resources yielded ever decreasing returns was a sufficient explanation, making all the Pigovian social implications somewhat otiose. In later life, Robertson confessed to some modification of these views, noting that since the long-run cost curve took time to reveal itself, it was likely that considerations other than those stemming from internal economies would prevent a firm from gaining a monopoly advantage. This confirmed his faith in the knockdown, dragout process of competition.

As with most economists, marginal productivity was the basis of Robertson's conception of distribution, although the inherent difficulties of the theory impelled him to give it a rather loose interpretation. Cassel's vigorous attack on marginal productivity was countered with the argument that it was but a broad tendency which had to work itself out over the long haul. Only if one's perspective were wide could it be asserted that the proportions of employed factors were "indefinitely variable" and that marginal productivity and the value of each factor were determinate.[247] Marginal productivity in the short run, Robertson conceded, should be viewed "with some suspicion." But if one were to suggest that the long run was merely a series of short runs, the whole theory could be called into question. Robertson was reluctant to take this drastic step. He wanted to see what the effect on the distribution of real national income would be when the use of a single factor was increased, and for this marginal productivity seemed essential. He noted that the greater substitutability of a factor for others would increase its share of real income. Important also was the factor's elasticity of substitution, defined as the ratio of the proportionate change in the factor in relation to the proportionate change in the other factors to the resulting change in the ratio of its marginal productivity to that of the other factors. When such elasticity was high, that is, greater than one, the tendency would be for the factor to increase its share of income. Yet when one recalled that the factors themselves were really complex entities, the "practical usefulness" of the theory was damaged considerably.[248]

Robertson's treatment of the various categories of return was again traditional, except for his unusual presentation of rent as a cost.[249] He questioned the need for economic rent in its pure sense, asserting that there was no economic necessity to give this part of real national income to individuals. There was ". . . a prima facie case for the diversion into public hands of such future increments of rent as may be expected to arise from general or local increases in the supply of the other factors of production." [250] This, of course, calls to mind the Hobsonian argument: it was clear that Robertson too looked upon rent as a social increment which might very well be earmarked for public use. The other concepts in distribution theory were fairly straightforward. His analysis of interest was quite detailed and extensive, as might be expected from a monetary specialist. The existence of interest was taken for granted: unlike Böhm-Bawerk, he did not feel impelled to develop a theory justifying its payment, but proceeded from the start to examine its functioning.

The demand for labor was related to its marginal productivity, but Robertson carefully defined the marginal man, not as the least effective one, but rather as the one who worked with the smallest supply of the other factors. This made it possible to establish wage payments in relation to efficiency and to broadly equate wages to the marginal product of the labor employed. However, the connection was quite loose and hardly reflected the precision of a mathematical equation. By applying elasticity of subsitution, there was a palpable tendency for nonlabor factors to be employed whenever wages became "excessive." The analysis, of course, assumed perfect competition. In actual situations, combinations of buyers and sellers were possible, so that bargaining rules would necessarily prevail. Since the employer was apt to have the stronger bargaining position, the function of unions became clearly one of securing for the worker his full marginal product of value.[251] That is to say, unions tended to make the supply curve of labor more elastic and thus "synthetically" created the conditions of competition and increased employment. Social efficiency was enhanced by pressure on inefficient producers: operations improved as a result of trade union activity. Robertson also commented that the unequal strength of unions in different industries might hamper the efficient distribution of labor among them, thus requiring a certain measure of intervention in the unorganized sectors. The relative level of "white collar" wages in the United States suggests no little validity to this argument.

Robertson's forté, however, was monetary theory, and his works in this field have attained the stature of modern classics. The basic ideas were closely intertwined with problems of industrial fluctuations, more so perhaps than was the case with other economists. In cycle theory per se, Robertson's analysis was set in "real" terms, in that cyclical change could be traced fundamentally to shifts in the amount of effort that people were willing to exert in order to obtain satisfactions.[252] Thus psychological as well as institutional factors played significant roles in Robertson's model.[253] Since movements in the economy were discontinuous, he argued, resulting mainly from shifts in demands and costs, it seemed inevitable that the general level of prices would be unstable. He defined "appropriate" changes as those which responded adequately to underlying conditions, while "inappropriate" changes were those which overstated shifts. A reduction in real costs could lead to greater output, but this in itself necessarily had to be related to conditions of demand and producers' preference for more income as against more leisure.[254] Secondary effects also were quite important, for a shifting demand pattern might require changes in the scale of output for producers' goods.[255] Robertson noted too that entrepreneurs reacted more sharply to altered conditions than did workers, if only because the former's income response was more elastic. This assumed unequal bargaining positions, a situation valid for a freely competitive system. This assumption has since been criticized on the grounds that bargaining today is more equal than Robertson allowed and that decision-making is more complex.[256] At any rate, Robertson did introduce flexibility through producers' reactions rather than through wages. This permitted a direct tie to monetary policy, for with decisions based so frequently on the "money illusion," what the banking system did became quite important. In fact, allowing prices to rise might be a most suitable approach to "equilibrium." [257] Least effective would be to insist on a constant supply of money. The relevance of these arguments to contemporary debate should be obvious.

Monetary policy, said Robertson, ought to aim at controlling the kind of excessive exhilaration that was caused by "inappropriate" responses. The latter occurred simply because investment was lumpy so that overinvestment was a continual danger.[258] The theory was certainly a suggestive one, yet it seemed rooted in an economy of small business. The counterargument might have been made that large corporations, too, will frequently overshoot the mark along the lines described in Robertson's theory. Yet the fact is that today the kind of monetary policy which stemmed from his model seems largely ineffective, for many large corporations are able to function completely outside the banking system.[259]

The analysis of cyclical movement led to problems of savings and capital formation. Here Robertson focused attention on the process of creating capital—a process described as "lacking." When an individual's consumption was less than the value of his current output, that person was "lacking," a consequence which created capital.[260] As saving took place when consumption was less than disposable income, a careful distinction had to be made between saving and lacking. At this point Robertson began to make use of his concept of a "day," a notion that brought lags into his analysis and permitted him to say that disposable income was that caused by the previous day's output. The "day" was a homogeneous unit of time, a purely analytical concept. It was an important device and criticisms that it was unrealistic could only come to nought once it was admitted that outlays could differ from income.[261] These ideas emphasized that lacking and saving were independent processes: one could take place without the other.

Now, an individual might decide to spend his entire income. But since he would be competing with others for a given quantity of goods, prices would be forced up, making it impossible for him to obtain everything he desired. He was therefore "lacking" to that extent. Contrariwise, a fall in prices due to a contraction of buying by others would lead to savings, but no lacking. Hoarding, on the other hand, was an attempt to raise the proportion of money holdings to disposable income. The usefulness of this apparatus, as strange and complicated as it was, rested in its ability to underscore the differences between the savings and investment processes. When excessive thrift seemed evident, the monetary authorities might overcome it with new money. Robertson insisted that his definitions were truer of the way people behaved, and avoided the early Keynesian definition of saving as stemming from a contraction of consumption to match the contraction of income.[262] For Robertson, saving and investment were not necessarily equal: it was on the differences between them that prices depended. Written in 1933, these ideas must have exerted a strong influence on Keynes' later formulations.

To Robertson, capital exhibited the character of both fund and goods.[263] Circulating capital was no longer the Jevonian stock of goods available for maintaining workers, but merely the sum of goods in process, goods which at any moment were ". . . on their journey through the process of production." [264] Circulating capital was provided by the lacking process, but this was "short" lacking.[265] However, this notion approached Jevons' concept, since short lacking provided, at least in part, consumable goods for those engaged in slow, indirect productive processes. Long lacking provided fixed capital. As was suggested, lacking could be either voluntary or forced. The stinting process imposed by rising prices caused forced lacking. Price increases reduced the real value of money stocks so that "induced" lacking resulted. But the latter occurred only if real values then were restored by higher cash balances. Unless saving did lead to capital formation, it could be dissipated through lower prices. The complex of these actions redistributed economic output and diverted resources to those who were in a position to deal directly with the banks.[266] Thus, Robertson was able to relate capital formation, money claims, and price movements to each other in a suggestive and fruitful manner.

The analysis of money was a integral element of this model. The stock of money was related to its flow, and the idea of the income velocity of money was contrasted with Fisher's transaction concept. Robertson defined velocity as the number of times a unit of money was spent in a given time span to purchase goods and services which were part of real income.[267] The value of money, which could be thought of in terms of consumption, transactions, or income, expressed the power to command goods. This was, of course, nothing more than the index number problem: Robertson concluded, perhaps rightly so, that neither in theory nor in practice was it possible to measure accurately the value of money.[268] In essence, he preferred to center his attention on money "on the wing" rather than money "sitting." Money in motion seemed closer to the way in which prices actually tended to change, although he did admit that an analysis of why people held on to cash balances might effectively reveal underlying psychological motivations. A final element in the analytical apparatus was the average period of production —the speed with which goods were prepared for the consumer.[269] Such periods differed, naturally enough, for different types of goods. Money circulation and the average period of production affected not only circulating capital, but also savings and price changes as well. Thrift was transferred by the banks to those in need of circulating capital, so that with certain limiting assumptions, it could be asserted that circulating capital equalled total bank deposits.[270] When a part of saving went into fixed capital, an excessive demand for circulating capital could force prices to move upward. With a long period of production, the strain might be fairly severe: banks seeking to meet the full needs of trade could engender no small amount of disequilibrium.[271] Here was more than a suggestion that prices responded to the annual flow of money out of the banking system rather than to changes in the stock of money. Consequently, when productivity increased, it was quite reasonable to have the banks make more circulating capital available, but at a rate proportionate to the increase in productivity. Similarly, population increases, said Robertson, might require proportionate increases in the flow of money.

Saving necessarily involved the problem of interest, for the postponement of present satisfactions brought the elements of time and risk into the analysis. This was as far as Robertson went in providing the usual genuflections toward justifying interest payments. Postponement of satisfactions, or waiting, was itself connected with time and in a certain sense was locked up in the goods-in-process part of the economy. Robertson wanted to determine the size of this locked-up-goods-in-process.[272] One prong of the demand for waiting obviously stemmed from the demand for circulating capital, which itself was fixed by the output of each "day" multiplied by the average period of production. The demand for fixed capital was due to a "widening" process, as a result of population growth, and "deepening" through technological improvement and change. Yet implicit in the concept of waiting was the old notion of abstinence about which so much had been written in the nineteenth century. At best it was a dubious idea and in no way described the realities of saving and accumulation.[273] Moreover, Robertson's attempt to sustain both the fund nature of capital and its specificity seemed to encounter some difficulties. One would have to visualize the capital problem in terms of a perpetual rate of return as well as a finite series of yields from embodied capital. He sought to answer the question by establishing a schedule of the marginal efficiency of investible funds which was related to the marginal productivity of a stock of fixed goods. That is, one would go from thrift to productivity to the demand for funds.[274] With a growing stock of capital, the rate of interest would have to be below marginal productivity or, as Robertson preferred to say, below the return on the replacement cost required to maintain the stock of capital intact.

The supply of capital stemmed from waiting, or capital accumulation. A distinction then was made between capital already gathered—"waiting outstanding at any time"—and the stream of new waiting, with the latter viewed as the more important of the two. Waiting, from the supply side, depended on the ability to save and on opportunities for safe investment. Futurity was also an important consideration, for the desire to improve living standards or to provide for old age might influence the behavior of "waiters." Robertson did admit that a host of psychological factors not influenced by prospective rewards could complicate the situation. Nevertheless, his implication that everyone in the economy did some saving is questionable. True, capital formation does demand some form of abstinence, but this is a social process, carried on by a government or a class which is itself not in the least involved in abstaining. Historically, this has been the usual mode of accumulation, as Marx so well demonstrated. There has been little individual psychological cost in accumulation, and the taxation, rationing, inflation, or outright expropriation implied by accumulation bore most heavily on the mass of the population. Rewards or time preference therefore may justifiably be called into question. In modern society, the bulk of saving is provided by upper income groups and corporations, and how much waiting do they suffer? [275] Robertson did say that corporate saving was significant, but to suggest that such entities are motivated in much the same way as individuals is to approach the fallacy of composition. Saving by a managerial class is due to other factors, and these cannot always be related to the rate of interest.

Yet Robertson, true to his Cantabrigian heritage, had to relate the supply of saving to the rate of interest. Generally speaking, the supply curve of saving was forward-rising, although it might on occasion bend backward.[276] This was based on "real" factors, namely the balance of the marginal utilities of consumption and saving, a balance that had to take into account the marginal utility of the interest to be earned, which was itself subject to time discounting. Equilibrium was established in the usual manner, at the juncture of the supply and demand curves. Presumably, in a progressive economy the demand curve would be pushed to the left, while increases in saving would move the supply curve to the right for any given rate of interest. Robertson argued that the supply curve would move more slowly than the demand curve on the ground that the wealthy would tend to save proportionately less as income increased.[277] The tendency, at any rate, would then be for the rate of interest to fall, although it could not drop below a certain level, for then the stock of capital would begin to be consumed. This stemmed from Cassel's argument on the effect of the length of life on interest rates.[278] With the demand for saving derived from population growth and industrial expansion and with supply coming from saving, the history of the rate of interest, said Robertson, became ". . . a tussle between Fecundity and Invention on the one hand and Affluence and Thrift on the other." [279]

This was precisely the view that Keynes attacked in his *General Theory*. To Keynes, the rate of interest was related to liquidity preference, or at least to that part of it concerned with speculative motives.[280] This relationship, exhibiting a high degree of elasticity, was a function not only of liquidity preference but of the money supply as well. Thus the rate of interest was a monetary phenomenon.[281] Keynes suggested that there was a certain indefiniteness in the orthodox Cambridge viewpoint, since the supply of saving would shift with changes in real income. The rate of interest would not be known until income was known; but interest was itself a determinant of income via investment and the multiplier. Of course, it was possible to detect a similar indeterminancy in Keynes, especially if liquidity preference were to be related to income. The Robertsonian relation of savings to disposable income was subject to the same charge. Yet by adding investment and the consumption function, it became possible to develop a coherent theory of interest.[282]

Robertson contended on the other hand that Keynes' theory was time-bound, for it was framed when action on the short-run supply of investible funds was necessary, while little was done about demand itself.[283] It appeared preferable to enhance the demand for loans by improving investment opportunities. Yet this was certainly what Keynes had emphasized. (Curiously, such a favorable environment did not develop until all the nations began to shoot at each other at the beginning of the 1940's.) Robertson also asserted the superiority of his period analysis over Keynesian interest rate determination at a point of time, for it was, he said, part of the supply of loanable funds.[284] Moreover, continued Robertson, the short-run character of Keynes' theory tended to obscure productivity and thrift. But this too has long since been remedied by the neo-Keynesians.[285] While Keynes admittedly touched upon genuine fundamentals by directly stressing psychological elements in his interest theory, this would have had to be checked, averred Robertson, by reference to what was taking place in the capital market itself.[286] A further charge was that Keynes had overlooked the relation between short and long rates.[287] The gap between the two presumably was to be accounted for by the extra inconvenience of renewing short loans and by the greater maneuverability inherent in them. But this would make the short rate a volatile one and, as Robertson agreed, quite the same as Keynes' speculative one. Essentially, for Robertson, the rate of interest was a price, the same as other prices in other markets: it was but a special case of the general theory of price.

The debate between Robertson and Keynes was no mere quibble over terms and definitions. On the face of it, either one or the other had to have the correct explanation. Robertson's loanable fund approach was couched in terms of a flow over time, while Keynes' theory stressed cash balances or stocks. By contrast with the latter, the supply and demand for securities seemed more important, and, consequently, saving, investment, the supply of money, and hoarding appeared more significant than liquidity preference. But if the Robertson "day" were to be sufficiently short, it would appear that the theories were not entirely irreconcilable. At any rate, in the short-run there would appear to be less disparity between the two theories than was at first apparent, since a "flow" in a really short "day" could be viewed, from other aspects, as a kind of Keynesian stock.[288]

Yet the Robertson model did not seem to completely integrate money into economic analysis. The backward glance at "real" factors and the search for utilities and satisfactions made one suspect that behind the analytic apparatus lurked the spectre of a barter economy. A model in which money was fully integrated would be, as Abba Lerner has suggested, one in which liquidity was viewed in the same light as any other good and where cash balances would enjoy the same status as any other asset. The economy would be a money-economy and wealth would encompass both assets and income.[289]

A concern with real factors rather than monetary effects also motivated Robertson's conception of the business cycle. His analysis, first presented in *A Study of Industrial Fluctuation,* drew its inspiration from Pigou in that it selected changes in real national income as the primary object for investigation. Central to Robertson's business cycle thesis was the impact of crops and inventions on economic activity. The analysis of money influences was to come later. The search for real causes made Robertson receptive to propositions which dealt with turning points occasioned by shortages of consumer goods and excess fixed capital. This was suggestive of the neo-Austrian theory of shortages of savings, but in Robertson's approach a temporary excess of capital, or "instrumental goods," represented the primary stress. In this way he was able to emphasize the restriction in the output of consumer goods and thus to combine elements of both undersaving and underconsumption theories.[290] Excess saving during a depression was identified with inventory accumulation, so that some basis for expansion appeared when the upturn arrived. In his early formulation, at any rate, this cast some doubt on the usefulness of public works as a stimulant, and since inventories appeared closely related to banking policy, it now seemed possible to integrate money with cycle theory. Yet since excess cash balances were not always necessary counterparts to stock, it became possible that inventory accumulation might come to nought. Clearly, the business cycle was a complex phenomenon, said Robertson, for which no single explanation could serve.[291] Yet each phase of the cycle bore the seeds of its own dissolution, as margins, profits, and the ratio of profits to invested capital shifted with the fortunes of business.

In Robertson's study of fluctuations, remarkably sophisticated and detailed for a young man of twenty-five, theoretical formulations were illuminated with a host of statistical data culled from a variety of sources. The first part of *Industrial Fluctuation* analysed supply and demand phenomena in particular industries, thus providing a suitable background for general trade movements. On the supply side, both fluctuations in costs and temptations to overinvest exerted powerful influences. Overinvestment was conditioned by the period of gestation of fixed capital, or the period of time it took to build the instruments of production.[292] Thus, the larger the quantity of fixed capital, the more serious might fluctuations be; in certain industries, however, such as cotton-spinning, the peculiarities of circulating capital might engender rather violent gyrations. Nevertheless, fixed capital appeared as the more significant factor in most modern industries. Robertson argued that the imperfect divisibility of equipment often impelled an expansion beyond what the immediate situation called for. Furthermore, there was the problem of the ratio of variable costs to fixed costs; for with a large ratio of variable costs, it conceivably might pay to close down a plant in trying to weather an economic storm.[293] On the other hand, a high proportion of fixed capital could make cessation of operations a serious matter.

On the demand side, the important elements were fashion and taste, wars, and trade barriers. But perhaps most important, at least so it seemed to Robertson at the time, was the direct influence of changes in crop output. Although much less is made of crop effects today, in 1915 it was evident that ". . . the influence of Argentine harvests upon the British constructional trades through the medium of the psychology of the British investor is of importance as well as their influence through the medium of the purchasing power of the Argentine farmer. . . ." This was a condition confirmed by the facts of trade.[294] Robertson's analysis made much of the difference in elasticities of demand for various crops and the effects that followed in income and demand, particularly for "constructional" goods.[295] Movement in any direction could become inflammatory,[296] for the cyclical process was a cumulative one. Windfall profits might accrue to some entrepreneurs as the period of gestation lengthened and prices rose. A greater demand in consumers' goods industries communicated itself to the producers' goods industries. This seemed to approximate the acceleration principle, for it was suggested that a larger proportionate increase in the demand for producers' goods could result. Yet Robertson did not accept acceleration as a driving force: factors other than consumer demand, he noted, could stimulate action in producers' goods. Furthermore, where such an industry was dependent on a number of consumers' goods output, increased demand in any single sector would not be sufficient to create a general and overall movement. The accelerator effect, he argued, would work only if all the consumers' goods industries were so interrelated that a stirring of one caused all the others to move almost at once. This was unlikely, for again the lumpiness and irregularity of investment were bound to prevent a smooth and quick transmission of effects from one sector of the economy to the other. And the presence of excess capacity was bound to modify the impact of acceleration.[297]

Thus, revival simply would be due to the greater attractiveness of investment per se. What seemed to take place, said Robertson, was a heightened anticipation of more want-satisfying power in certain goods: estimates presumably were made of the marginal utility of producers' goods based upon expected future marginal productivities. Since these estimates varied, output itself was subject to variation, and this was the key to industrial fluctuation.[298] Here Robertson was down to his basic real factors. The economic exhilaration characteristic of a boom quite simply meant "real" overinvestment. Such situations could be traced to an exceptional crop, heavy replacement expenditures occasioned by sudden obsolescence, or a new invention. (By the latter, Robertson probably meant innovation, after the fashion of Schumpeter. His illustration of the electrical boom of the 1890's clearly suggests this interpretation, for what he was talking about were applications of new devices in fruitful economic ways.) The collapse was caused by a scarcity of real capital available for investment, a notion quite similar to that developed by Hayek. The evidence Robertson brought to bear on his theory emphasized the depletion of working capital and an excessive absorption of real capital so that in the end an actual capital shortage resulted.[299] The ensuing misdirection of resources was facilitated by easy credit supplied by the banks. Years later, Robertson qualified his theory with the admission that capital shortages were not always responsible for a collapse.[300]

How might this parlous state of affairs be remedied? The suggestions Robertson offered were not very striking: more information to reduce temptations leading to overinvestment; a somewhat more centralized investment policy; improved banking methods; and perhaps some way of smoothing the application of invention. Yet, for a world emerging from the quiet dusk of the Victorian era, even these must have appeared daring enough. In his lectures, published in the 1950's, Robertson supplemented the early policy recommendations: he now approved of monetary expansion as a means of reducing interest rates, for this could put idle resources to work without raising prices. Public works, raw material stockpiling, tax rebates, and a flexible fiscal policy were also included in the new armory of economic measures to control the cycle.[301] The curious point about these policy proposals was the revelation that Robertson was not disturbed about the possibility of stagnation. The chief difference between Robertson and the Keynesians was his unshaken belief that, in the long run, investment opportunities would give rise to a greater demand for loans.

While these suggestions all reflected a keen sense of the practical, on wage policy in a depression Robertson opted for the Pigovian approach. He argued that with rigid money wages, unemployment was bound to increase. Moreover, he said, any fall in money income would sooner or later be checked by an increase in the real value of balances—the Pigou effect—thus stimulating money outlays. And with lower money wages, entrepreneurs would be encouraged to undertake investment. But the fact of the matter was that in a serious decline, such as was experienced in the 1930's, money incomes fell much too rapidly to induce consumer expenditures through the Pigou effect: the collapse of effective demand was too catastrophic. Robertson's argument could be subjected to the same strictures as was Pigou's.

This anti-Keynesian posture was carried also into cycle analysis where issue was taken with the stagnation thesis which had been developed on the basis of Keynes' *General Theory*. Yet Robertson's discussion, no more than a restatement of his objections to Keynes' theory of interest, actually failed to address itself to the stagnation argument.[302] He sought instead to restate the Keynes-Hansen proposition in money terms in a way that would support his own rebuttal of the newer interest theory. The stagnation thesis, developed mainly by Alvin Hansen, had been bound to stir up the ire of traditionalists, because it questioned whether economic fluctuations could be corrected so easily by monetary means. And while Robertson's views did encompass more than money measures, he still could not abide anything which deviated too far from received doctrine. The stagnationists had insisted that an active government policy was needed to haul an economy out of a deep rut—a prophetic point when one recalls that in recent experience it has required hot and cold wars to move the economic system.[303]

Stability in Robertson's view required a condition known as monetary equilibrium. When the economy was experiencing steady and smooth growth, with no change in tastes and techniques, and with all factors growing proportionately, it was the duty of the monetary authorities to assure a supply of money that would grow in the same ratio.[304] This would provide monetary neutrality, preserve a "normal" rate of profit, and maintain equilibrium in the thrift market. An excess flow of money, on the other hand, would tend to shift production toward fixed capital through "forced saving." Monetary equilibrium was difficult to maintain, said Robertson, when capital rose faster than population, since the relative marginal productivities for labor and capital could be changed. If the proportion of the product flowing to input factors were unchanged—that is, if the elasticity of substitution between labor and saving was unity—then the flow of money need not be disturbed. If an increase in capital had the effect of increasing its share of the total product, then total money flows would have to rise just a bit, with prices falling less than in proportion to the increased output.[305] Generally speaking, advised Robertson, prices ought to move inversely with productivity: "price stabilization," he said, was not the issue but rather the "price of productive power." [306] Thus the banking system had a double role to perform: to provide the proper amount of circulating capital and, at the same time, sufficient currency for the public, if prices were to be adjusted to changes in output.

Looking back on Sir Dennis' life work, one observes a refreshing synthesis of monetary elements with both real and psychological factors employed in economic analysis. The development in his thinking was a continuous one: the early empirical and historical analysis—buttressed by theoretical discussions of inventions, crop conditions, and gestation periods—easily absorbed the later propositions on money. And much of the analysis is still germane, at least in the sense that the questions asked are pertinent. Technology was utilized to explain spurts in economic activity and there was a concern with the way in which the composition of aggregates affected the size of the aggregates.[307] Shifts in real costs and demand might require fundamental structural changes, for a decline in costs and prices in one part of the economy could induce output alterations elsewhere. Nevertheless, Robertson failed to escape entirely a certain static flavor in his theory. The dynamic elements, which were admittedly potent, stemmed from the effort to deal with the process of change. At least one can interpret the differences between savings and investment, and their consequences for income in this manner.[308] Yet the barter economy, in which demand was related to the supposed existence of marginal utility and satisfactions, remained the prime mover in economic change; while the sense of general interdependence, which Pigou had sought to approximate, was lost when resort was had to *ceteris paribus*. The model of the wage system likewise was a good deal less realistic than was warranted: labor and waiting were hardly enough to reveal all the crosscurrents in wage patterns and income distribution. And it may be doubted that prices do respond to money supply with all the ease that the Robertsonian model required. The brilliant analytical scheme, inspired by Marshall, Wicksell, and the Austrians, was essentially an amalgam, for Robertson was a true eclectic. But this may have been the only way he could approach economic reality, for he knew, better than most, how complex and diverse it truly was.

v

Sir Ralph Hawtrey: Economics of Traders

When Sir Ralph Hawtrey (1879-   ) made only nineteenth wrangler in mathematics at Trinity College, his sponsor felt rather disappointed, saying that Hawtrey had spent too much time on other activities. This tendency to disperse his energies over several fields was to characterize Hawtrey's work in economics also, yet he still exerted a remarkable influence not only on theoretical developments but on practical affairs as well. With some twenty volumes to his credit, Hawtrey has been one of the most prolific of writers in modern economics.[309] During the 1920's his banking theories were employed to justify the policies of the Federal Reserve System in the United States. The outlook of the Britsh Treasury was shaped in large measure by Hawtrey; and when it was said that credit expansion was necessary to counteract unemployment and that public works alone were insufficient, it was Hawtrey's views that were being expounded. Not until the later days of the Great Depression was the sole use of monetary measures for moving an economy out of the doldrums seriously questioned. By this time Keynes' theory of income determination had been acknowledged as the more suitable policy guide.[310]

Nevertheless, Keynes had a high regard for Hawtrey's ideas, at least in the days before the *General Theory*. Indeed, Hawtrey had been one of the few persons to whom Keynes turned for advice when writing his great work, and their voluminous correspondence continued even after the book was published. But, much as they tried, neither could convert the other and Keynes came away rather disappointed that his friend had remained unconvinced.[311]

Hawtrey, after completing his education, entered the British Civil Service in 1903. He went to the Treasury a year later where he remained until 1945. In 1928 he spent a year at Harvard as guest lecturer and in 1947 was appointed professor of international economics at Chatham House, retiring in 1952. Although many of Hawtrey's theories could be traced to Marshall, he did give them an independent turn quite his own. These fundamental ideas, essentially the same throughout his many books, often were modified in important respects as time went on. Exhibiting both a rapid-fire style and a rather involute sentence structure, Hawtrey's prose was neither as graceful as that of Robertson, nor as smooth as Marshall's. The masterful phrasemaking of Keynes was also lacking. Reading Hawtrey is, in fact, no easy task. Yet his work has been important enough to make the effort worthwhile. One striking feature was his willingness to shift ground under the pressure of actual historical events. Thus, the certainty of *Good and Bad Trade*, issued in 1913, was clearly shaken by the time *Capital and Employment* was published in 1937. Hawtrey often spoke cogently on taxation, labor, collectivism, tariffs, international trade and the uses of economic power, but at almost all times his major emphasis was on money. And although he understood how complex economic affairs could be, he remained the monetary economist par excellence.

Despite the emphasis on the role of money, however, which many have termed excessive, Hawtrey was astute enough to relate economics to the political framework in which it functioned. The economic life of a community, he said, was directed by institutions which had been conditioned and shaped by the political process.[312] Nor could economic action limit itself, as Lionel Robbins had suggested, to matters of pure choice, for such action involved a much broader area of work, done mainly, but not entirely, for material reward. Something of the Hobsonian viewpoint clearly intruded itself in Hawtrey's thinking. Admittedly, market and price were central to economic analysis, and this inevitably gave rise to the idea of wealth as something measureable. But this in no way relegated economics to a merely positive science, unable to offer prescriptions for policy. Nor could economics be disassociated from ethics. The individualist, for example, insisted that absolute free preference yielded maximum welfare. Hawtrey, who did not quarrel with this viewpoint too strongly, nevertheless urged that wide inequalities of wealth and income were sufficient reason to question the pragmatic value of the individualist outlook. When seen as a whole, said Hawtrey, the ordinary theoretical system was deficient in several respects. It had no adequate theory of profit; it failed to integrate money into general theory in a genuinely effective manner; it gave inadequate consideration to accumulation; and it took no account of power as a continuing objective of economic policy. Certainly this was strong condemnation from a major figure; quite simply, Hawtrey was more interested in *political* economy than had been the case for many a year in British economic circles.

The economic problem, said Hawtrey, was to organize society in a way that would impel the individual to contribute toward "real ends" without his necessarily being aware of it.[313] In his *The Economic Problem,* a long discussion of organization in primitive society, reflecting Hawtrey's broad interests, culminated in a statement that the ideal economic solution was that which utilized man's capacity for joint action. Of course, several ways for achieving this solution were possible, as recent history has so forcefully demonstrated. But Hawtrey's interest focused on the one evolved by Western capitalism, one in which everyone did what he deemed proper for himself, while the total results presumably worked out in the best interest for the commonweal. Economic action, he said, was conscious action. A man came to the market place for the express purpose of making money, which was desired for its own sake. As in Wesley Mitchell's analysis, money became the center of economic behavior. It gave freedom of choice in buying, represented security as opposed to risk, and was the source of power over productive resources. There was nothing irrational in this search for monetary dominion, nor was money simply a veil over so-called real transactions.[314] There was no effective way, said Hawtrey, in which this supposed veil could be torn aside. Economic activity took place in a money economy which set the limiting conditions or restraints.[315] Hawtrey made it clear, however, that he was not depreciating the significance of goods, for marketable items were part of the economic matrix and as such represented wealth. But money, nevertheless, was to be the primary focus. The Jevonian concept of utility was adopted as the basis for wealth as a meaningful economic category. Presumably it was utility that was to be maximized, but interpersonal comparisons, Hawtrey agreed, were questionable.[316] What remained was the psychological fact of choice, so that welfare, admittedly an important ethical component in economic analysis, was not really measurable, in the Pigovian sense.[317] However, he insisted, this did not mean that the economist could not comment on the ends of economic conduct.

Hawtrey defined two classes of consumer goods: defensive goods, those intended to remedy pain or injury; and creative goods, those whose purpose was to provide satisfactions. These were not necessarily exclusive. People with high incomes did tend to concentrate on the latter, and concern with them reflected an important aspect of civilized existence. Certainly the economist would need to include them in his data, averred Hawtrey.[318] Once again, the influence of Hobson was evident: the long discussion of art and intellectual products and their impact on the consumer was more than merely reminiscent of the latter's acerb comments on contemporary economics. Hawtrey inevitably came to the conclusion that consumers' preferences had but a slight relationship to the genuine worth of the things chosen and that market value ". . . is so far from being a true measure of ethical value that it is hardly even a first approximation to it." [319] The notion that welfare could be measured by market value simply would have to be surrendered. Man's incompetence and inability to seek real satisfactions had made the results of the market a dubious measuring rod.[320]

The basic concept in Hawtrey's system was the drive for profit. Profit stemmed from selling power, or the ability to dispose of goods. It was the selling strength of the superior trader that enabled him to obtain a larger share of the market, thus leading to inequality. And selling power also determined the magnitude of a particular enterprise. But although the notion of selling power, essentially a qualitative aspect of economic analysis, seemed quite vague and not entirely capable of being placed into a model, Hawtrey, like Hobson, did not hesitate to make use of it. Certainly, it was not meaningless, for it embodied certain key notions in the decision-making process which directed firms toward capturing as substantial a part of the market as they could. In fact, modern analysis has made effective use of the idea, as recently demonstrated by William J. Baumol.[321] It does seem, after all, that the businessman's primary concern is ". . . sales maximization subject to a minimum profit constraint." [322] Output which maximizes sales is determined at the point where marginal revenue is zero, Baumol has said. A profit maximizing output, therefore, is necessarily less than a sales maximizing output. Thus with the latter as the major motivation, a larger share of the market does become the primary objective. Furthermore, profit constraints do assure firms of enough latitude to handle higher costs. Since maximum profit is not reached, alteration in output levels becomes a relatively simple business of shifting such burdens as income taxes to others. In effect, a *minimum* profit constraint is the regulator of sales and output. Once this view was adopted, the failures of ordinary theory were exposed, for profit then stemmed from principles other than those which presumably governed payments to the factors of production. Profit became a residual income, and insofar as this was true, the factor which it rewarded became clearly distinct from all others.

Dealers or traders—the business units that Hawtrey had in mind when he developed his analysis—measured their income as a function of the rate of profit and the volume of business. Enlargement of the mass of profit was attained through turnover. This consequently led to working capital as a basic requirement for market operations, so that it became necessary to introduce the capital market as an important instrumentality. Since the primary function of the capital market was to equalize the supply and demand for investible funds, money thus became the hub of economic action. With profit defined in Ricardian rent terms, that is, stemming from differential advantages of location, resources, and the like, it was evident that differences in economic rent would occasion differences in profit.[323] In other words, rent and profit were opposed to each other in strict classical manner. Hawtrey conceded that some portion of profit at times might be described as the "rent of ability," but this seemingly existed only where profit was more than normal.[324] And like Schumpeter, Hawtrey observed that profit devolved chiefly upon ". . . the inner circle of fully qualified profit makers, who of set purpose seek out selling opportunities, and who are both competent to exploit them and able to command the requisite financial resources." [325] Interest was to be carefully distinguished from profit, for the former was remuneration for the use of capital. Hence, unlike Frank Knight, he preferred to separate the factors of production and their returns into clearly discernible categories.[326] The yield from capital included a premium for risk in addition to "mere interest," said Hawtrey.[327] His rent theory, very similar to Robertson's, stressed economic and social arrangements in which the landowner had no part.

Yet through all these notions ran the current of monetary policy. In wage issues, for example, Hawtrey argued that money policies and the attitudes of society toward profit-making were fundamental in determining employment as well as prices. It was evident to him that the "wealth-value" of the monetary unit affected not only economic activity generally but wage settlements in particular.[328] He thought that wage determination worked poorly in a free market, since custom and resistance to change were bound to keep wages within rather strict limits. Wage concessions depended on prospective profitability, and this, in turn, on monetary policy. It was quite possible for a restrictive credit program to injure wage earners and cause unemployment.[329] In Hawtrey's view, monetary policy had to be neither restrictive nor unduly expansive: a high wage policy ought to lead to a proportionately larger flow of money and proportionately higher profits and prices. Wage determination and monetary policy had to be closely related to each other, for only thus could monetary equilibrium and stability in wages and prices be assured. Yet left to itself, he said, the labor market would exhibit lagging wages behind prices and profit, and working people would be always at a disadvantage.[330] That there was a need for more equal bargaining powers was patent to Hawtrey, but he wondered whether status relationships might not be hardened by trade unionism. While these fears may have been unfounded, Hawtrey's comments did reveal a deeper concern with institutional complexities than was evident among other economists of the day.

Except for its concentration on the "dealer" rather than the producer, Hawtrey's description of the market did not depart from standard analysis. The market not only cleared supply and demand, but was the site at which dealers, wholesale and retail, carried on trading functions and moved goods. The consumer himself was utterly passive: he seldom originated anything and usually took whatever the market offered. It was rather dealer activity that dominated the market: searching for new commodities, estimating how much consumers might take, transporting and storing merchandise, it was the dealer who "cleared the market." All of this required a flow of credit, for, without it, dealers would be forced to enter into factoring relations with each other. Here the banking system entered the analysis. Hawtrey was one of the leading experts in this area and his analysis of banking and credit operations, particularly in *Currency and Credit,* clearly has been of major importance.[331] His detailed description of the way in which banks create credit stressed changes in bank rates as the chief instrument of monetary control, for whenever excesses or deficiencies in inventory holdings occurred, credit rates could be employed as a countervailing device.

Hawtrey achieved a fusion of the cash balance and income approach by relating credit to consumer demand. Since general demand was always defined in money terms, output and price effects could be traced more readily. This suggested some modification of the quantity theory of money.[332] Individual estimates of cash holdings, said Hawtrey, were based on the flow of receipts and expenditures. This represented the demand for money and was bound to be affected by current market values. Cash holdings necessarily would have to be equal to "unspent margins" if the supply of money was to equal its demand. Given the total number of money units, there was some level of prices at which the demand for money would be satisfied, leaving enough to equate the unspent margin to cash holdings. That is, the supply of money available for unspent margins was independent of the total amount. This represented Hawtrey's qualification of the quantity theory; in it, the wealth-value of the money unit was inversely proportionate to the unspent margin. His criticisms of Irving Fisher's formulation seemed quite cogent, especially when the simplistic conception of transactions was noted.[333] Standard quantity theory, charged Hawtrey, was merely a truism and could not indicate causal elements. If, on the other hand, the theory were interpreted as indicating intentions to hold cash and if this were related, in terms of demand functions, to a hypothetical range of prices, it would be possible to ascribe definite meaning to the quantity equation. One then might say that for all prospective price movements, the proper cash holdings would be in certain ratios to those prices, so that the "wealth-value" of the cash holdings themselves would not be altered.

Hawtrey was not averse to employing the concept of the period of production in his analyses.[334] As might be expected, this was related to working capital and inventories. Part of the production period comprised the time devoted to the process of material alterations. An important factor here became the length of time that working capital items were held in stock. When additional elements of time were added to account for the use of capital instruments, the period of production was completed. Hawtrey rejected Knight's contention that there was no average durability of goods and that the production process was of infinite duration.[335] Some of the technical ideas of the Austrians were utilized by Hawtrey but he refined them in significant ways, so that a standard period of production appropriate to current methods could be worked out. Thus, he argued, it was possible to assign a particular production period to every item in current output. The weighted average of these individual periods made up the standard.[336] Cost, therefore, was not to be defined historically, but rather in terms of replacement. And for each structure of production, there was a given standard period, for if capital-labor ratios were altered, it was evident that the time pattern would be changed as well.

While theories relating consumer income and expenditure to business cycles are now commonplace, Hawtrey's version must be given primacy of place among twentieth-century economists. The credit system was an integral part of his model because it was the flow of money out of banks to meet the needs of traders that led to increased incomes, given enough time to allow the process to work through the economy. And from this there stemmed consumer income and outlay, including net investment.[337] Traders' income was derived from business transactions and, ultimately, from profit. But the major impetus to the circular flow of income, he said, was to be traced to increases in consumer outlays.[338] This was a cumulative process, all reflected in a rising price level. Downward movements, on the other hand, could be explained by simply reversing the various phases. However, while the upper turning point of a cycle could be explained easily enough by Hawtrey, there seemed no adequate basis to describe movements out of a recession. During the days of the gold standard, one could appeal to international gold flows as an explanatory mechanism. When the inflow of gold expanded credit internally, a country moving ahead of others would find eventually that the terms of trade were becoming unfavorable. Business would be lost to competitor nations. The cash drain out of banks during the expansion would bring reverses and credit would have to be limited, adding additional pressures to those due to trade relationships. With equilibrium restored, it would be possible presumably for the economy to prepare for another surge of activity. But just how this was to come about Hawtrey never fully explained.

Yet, given the relevance of monetary factors, Hawtrey's theory did make good sense. At least it had the virtue of integrating his quantity theory with price level movements in a really effective way. Nevertheless, the cycle he described was a short-run inventory one which was at best but tenuously connected with deep-rooted factors of investment. The latter were taken into account only by splitting consumers' outlay into direct outlay and market investment in instrumental goods.[339] Disposals, or goods taken off the market, were the sum of direct outlay and traders' capital outlay. And while demand might result in disposals, it actually preceded the latter and was not the same thing, for part of demand moved into working capital, representing goods still on the market. This interesting set of relationships was presented by Hawtrey as a series of money flows, so that the whole theory evolved as a monetary analysis of the significant features of a modern economy.[340]

Consideration was given to nonmonetary elements only insofar as changes in the structure of capital might take place. The accumulation of wealth was equal at any time to the saving of that period. Insufficient saving meant excessive consumption and ultimately a reduction in working capital. Oversaving caused a deficiency in disposals and an accumulation of inventory in the hands of traders. The investment process itself—really a footnote to this complicated analysis—might, through the widening of capital or through the extension of capacity, be altered without any change in the ratio of capital to labor. A deepening of capital, on the other hand, implied a change in the capital-labor ratio. Some industries consequently might become "thicker" in the sense that they developed a heavy investment in equipment. The widening of capital stemmed from the expectations of normal profits, and in fact represented a process by which competition equalized profits in the various industries. Deepening, on the other hand, stemmed from innovations which altered the structure of industry. But all of this, to many other economists the essence of economic change and growth, seemed essentially subsidiary to the main line of Hawtrey's analysis, for only a part of disposals moved in this direction.[341]

Even from the monetary standpoint it has seemed legitimate to ask how total demand could sustain the economic system without making further inquiry into the direction of consumer spending.[342] Furthermore, it now seems evident that nonmonetary elements do play a greater role than Hawtrey was willing to admit. His picture of the way in which traders and consumers functioned seemed more relevant for a thoroughgoing commercial economy than for one in which large industrial corporations have sufficient savings of their own to avoid going to the banks everytime they undertake a particular venture.

Economic upsets, then, were caused by shifts in money flows, said Hawtrey, rather than in distortions in the sequence of production. They were to be attributed to the cumulative change stimulated by the credit system. Thus, easy credit extended by the banking system became the locus of responsibility for business cycles. The major relationships were not to be found in the producers' goods industries but in the way that bank rates affected the inventory holdings of traders, especially those engaged in wholesale and retail activities. An increase in money incomes drew cash away from the banks, compelling them to raise their rates and thus to close off the boom. For Hawtrey, this was conclusive proof that monetary manipulation was sufficient to control the business cycle.[343] Perhaps for the sort of cycle with which he was concerned money really was the central feature,[344] but it was not the kind that afflicted capitalism prior to 1940. Then, structural defects were the major question. Yet for Hawtrey, gluts in capital goods seemed unlikely because the ". . . investment market will succeed in finding an outlet in capital outlay for all the resources it receives. . . ."[345] This optimism was supported by the contention that depressions could not occur so long as general demand was maintained. Of course, that was the rub: few today will accept monetary dislocations as an adequate explanation of what does happen in a depression.[346] Theoretical constructions today generally run in terms of income determination, investment, and other nonmonetary categories.

Hawtrey's emphasis on the trades seemed more appropriate to pre-World War I conditions. It is now questionable that businessmen react with such readiness to bank rate movements. Furthermore, with the rate of interest moving together with the general price level, it would appear that more basic controls must be sought. Yet Hawtrey's analysis cannot be dismissed too lightly, for it has done much to teach us how banking operations affect our daily economic activities. If it did not exist, it most certainly would have had to be invented.

vi

Lord Robbins: The Logic
of Choice

In intellectual temperament, mode of argumentation, and polemical style, Lionel C. Robbins (1898-   ) bears a marked resemblance to Friedrich A. von Hayek. As a young man he had been a devotee of some form of functional socialism compounded with a provisional utilitarianism. After serving in World War I, Robbins turned to a serious study of economics. He thereafter arrived at the conviction that collectivism in any shape or form was no answer to the economic problem of the day. At first he was attracted by Pigou's suggestion that public policy be employed to balance gains and losses. and by Edwin Cannan's notion that value theory might be used to demonstrate the harmfulness of inequality. But it was not long before any connection between economics and politics struck him as scientifically unwarranted. For one thing, the whole approach through utility seemed unsatisfactory and invalid because interpersonal comparisons could not be sustained in logic. It was important, said Robbins, to first clear the ground of all the utilitarian lumber and to dispose of "philosophical squabbles" so that the normative and positive elements in economics might be distinguished clearly.[347]

After his World War I service, Robbins became lecturer at New College, and since 1929, he has been a professor of economics at the University of London. In 1930 he participated in the Prime Minister's study of economic conditions, taking a position opposed to Keynes, who had begun to move toward protectionist views. A confirmed internationalist in economic matters, Robbins looked upon any form of restriction in trade as a violation of ancient principles.[348] His attempt to issue a minority report resulted in some acrimony between the two economists, although later, during World War II, they worked well together. During the war, Robbins was director of the economic section of the war cabinet, rendering distinguished service. These experiences resulted in a mellowing of Robbins' somewhat rigid prewar attitude, enough to cause chagrin among some latter-day libertarians of the Mises-Hayek school.[349] Perhaps it was his participation in post-war planning that upset them, but it was evident that Britain had need for his talents. As a member of the British team at Bretton Woods, Robbins performed notably, smoothing ruffled tempers with "grave and well-reasoned fluency." [350]

In 1959, he was made a life peer, taking the title of Baron Robbins of Clare Market. Like his distinguished contemporary, Keynes, Robbins' interests were broad: he has served as a trustee for the National and Tate Galleries and as director of the Royal Opera House.

Robbins' major work, *An Essay on the Nature and Significance of Economic Science*,[351] was a challenging study on methodology, but was entirely within the continental tradition which limited the scope and function of economics to choice—seen as the only valid unifying principle in economics. Robbins believed that material welfare was much too vague to serve as a useful criterion. But he did admit that the eighteenth-century economists had been quite correct when they had expressed a concern with material gains, for at that time productive capacity was the key problem.[352] At this point, we might note that his exposition of the materialist interpretation of history was completely in error, for he reduced it to a history of technology or tools, just the sort of distortion that Marx would have rejected.[353]

The central concern of economics, argued Robbins, was the allocation of scarce resources among alternative ends. Scarcity, a ubiquitous condition of human existence, made economics a study of the relations between men and things. Unfortunately, this view abdicated the important area of relations between men and men, and perhaps explains the rigid attitude that economists of this persuasion frequently manifested. Economics certainly does include within its ken the human problems stemming from employer-employee, or buyer-seller relations, but Robbins' view demanded that these be cast in terms of commodities first and men second. Yet Ricardo, Marx, and Marshall had been keenly aware that scarcity was more than a matter of choice and allocation; it penetrated deeply into the human psyche and this too was the proper province of the economist. It was not enough to let the sociologist take over the realm of human relationships. But the economics of scarcity never raised questions of this character: it was not permitted to do so by the nature of its inner logic.[354] Robbins may have felt that the market accurately did reflect values, but his theory could in no way comment on valuations which stemmed from economic coercion because it assumed a scarcity of many small buyers and sellers. Resource allocation based on power did not enter into the individualist analysis. One could not help but wonder whether the proper questions were being asked in the first place.

Thus for Robbins, economics was completely neutral as to ends; it could discourse only on means. Consequently, any discussions of economic satisfaction were illegitimate, and for the economist *qua* economist, moral judgments had no bearing on his analysis. This was the realm of the philosopher, at the edges of which the economist was to place his own "no trespass" sign. This view explained in large measure why money was a veil: since economic relationships were those established by men and goods, one had to tear away the cover of money to get at real transactions. It also explained why economists were supposed to accept the technical arrangements of production simply as data; anything beyond that belonged to the province of the engineer. Today, of course, this concept might be troublesome, for such advanced methods as linear programming do apply choice to alternative techniques. Obviously, technical factors cannot be relegated merely to assumptions, for given the objective sought, the question of choice is seriously affected by the technical as well as social environment.[355] But theoretical investigation, according to Robbins, was a study only of the formal properties expressed by the man-goods equation. Supply and demand and the flow of goods were important because they affected price and income structures; nowhere, however, did the distribution of economic power enter the analysis. Moreover, the formal propositions derived by this carefully restricted economics did not have to exhibit any empirical content. The factual story belonged to the economic historian, not the theoretician. Thus, all the urgent problems caused by mass production, economies of scale, and economic crisis were threatened by a pallid theoretical figment, according to which, valuation was a matter of pure mind. Nevertheless, psychology was not to be allowed to enter the economists' garden. Economic behavior was to be studied without any need to grasp the psychological and motivational needs of man. From this standpoint it was not difficult to understand Robbins' gratuitous attack on Wesley Mitchell and the institutionalists.[356] Yet, Robbins was able to say little at this stage about the crucial substantive issues in economics beyond the Mises-Hayek position.

For Robbins, economic quantities were so relative that one could discuss such a problem as the index number after the fashion of Mises, that is, cast it out entirely. This extreme relativity permitted the economist to evade questions such as the distribution of income and allowed him to assert that high incomes were due to the existence of the rich.[357] Yet while relativity pervaded economic quantities, the generalizations that one derived from them were presumed to possess a universal character. The best that might be said about Robbins' methodological presentation was to point to it as a rigorous exercise in economic formalism but one which necessarily prevented the economist from talking about important problems. Choice became an abstract act of behavior: genuine judgment was impossible because no comment was allowed on how choice was conditioned. As Launcelot Hogben once remarked, rational judgment on choice would require far more knowledge than economists were willing to admit. Perhaps that was why they defined choice as choice.[358] The outcome was so general a formulation of economic science that equilibrium was simply a balance of forces.[359] And economics became a peculiarly depraved kind of scholasticism, a "barren dialectic of scarcity," utterly devoid of substantive content. In short, Robbins wanted to create an economics so precise in definition and shape, so formalistic, that its very claim to scientific status was threatened.

An economic proposition ought be verifiable if it is to possess operational meaning. And while empirical tests may not be available at all times, at the very least the conditions under which truthfulness or error can be determined should be indicated.[360] But in the sort of economics that Robbins espoused, truthfulness was distinguished from empirical content. Formal statements of relationships were deemed to be independent of statements of fact. Thus, theoretical statements on costs merely expressed certain relations without any reflection on whether or not costs actually did behave that way. Similarly, the assumption of profit maximization was simply a matter of convenience. Other assumptions, such as sales maximization, would give a different kind of theory, as has been demonstrated so cogently by William Baumol.[361] Theory became a game in which concepts were manipulated in accordance with the rules set forth in the premises and did not become, as Schumpeter urged, a program for research. The best Robbins' theory could achieve was to help spell out the implications that flowed from some empirical statements. But, to compound the confusion, many theorists all too frequently have given the impression that their pure statements are empirical propositions leading to rigorous economic laws which do not admit exceptions or deviations from the norm. As Terence Hutchison has shown, an unwillingness by theoreticians to discuss how political power might affect distribution vitiates the meaning of economic law in the ordinary sense.[362] Ultimately, such law possesses no operational or causal meaning, and certainly manifests no predictive value. To assume that rational behavior means maximization is to posit a definition in advance. The maximizing man cannot be certain that he has achieved his goal, and, if he is in possession of perfect foresight, then the economic problem as described by Robbins has been tossed out the window with both bath-water and baby. Choice and the decision-making process have no meaning under conditions of perfect knowledge and foresight, and the whole apparatus of equilibrium must be called into question.

As might be expected, Robbins subscribed to the ordinalist view of utility. While the measurement of satisfactions was not possible, he said, one still could pass judgment on preferences simply by the order in which they were arranged. Yet, as was the case with all ordinal theorists, measurement seemed to sneak in the rear door. The Pigovian suggestion that redistribution of income might increase utility was unacceptable to him on the grounds that this too implied interpersonal comparisons. And, for the same reason, such concepts as consumers' surplus were inadmissible. Hence, the justification of any welfare policy was an ethical one rather than economic, for arguments based on economic considerations would require unanimous acceptance of the redistribution program. Nevertheless, admitted Robbins, the pragmatic character of a redistribution plan could allow one to act as if interpersonal comparisons were feasible.[363]

Robbins, perhaps rightly so, wanted to introduce anticipations into the analysis of utility. Consequently, he rejected the behaviorist interpretation as much as he did cardinalism. Economic statements, he argued, need not be limited to observed behavior, but could utilize assumed estimates and calculations.[364] But these would have to be set within a framework of ordered preferences. The evaluation of a Holbein or Rembrandt could be done only by a simple ordering procedure, and this was enough to indicate one's judgment of differences. The theory of value, he insisted, required only such decisions on different types of goods: there was no need for measurement. Moreover, in contrast to Robertson, who had sought to distinguish between economic welfare and general welfare, Robbins could think only of states of mind conditioned by economic elements. This was as far as he would go. The study of wants and the way in which their shape and patterns was changed was no business of the economist. In fact, there was no intimate relationship between economics and psychology, and no propositions that the former might unfold could depend on such a relationship.[365] This restricted economic statements to purely technical matters such as cost, value, and rent.

It did not occur to Robbins that psychological preconceptions were implicit in his formalistic presentation: willy-nilly, a picture of the nature of man could be extracted from it. But the picture was one which was eternally fixed, and, if only for that reason, would have to be rejected by those who were aware that only man's plasticity was eternal. Robbins' persuasive arguments to the contrary, economics cannot exist without a concept of man, without a psychology. Down to the present, this remains one of the persistent problems of economic science. Man does not act consciously or rationally at all times in the market: even if he knows what he is doing, he may be guided by habit and impulse. Enough has been learned of the nature of behavior to suggest that what is irrational is the belief that man is rational.[366] Robbins' theory failed because it did acknowledge that inconsistent and therefore irrational behavior need not necessarily conflict with observed preferences. Certainly it may be doubted that a viable theory can exist without psychology.

It was these preconceptions that led Robbins away from the mainstream of Anglo-Saxon economics. Patently, he was more comfortable with the Austrian and continental viewpoints. Marshall's "representative firm" was roughly handled because it implied governing principles for "enterprise" which differed from those adumbrated for land and labor.[367] In a dynamic situation, said Robbins, when equilibrium kept shifting about, it was possible that the representative firm would cease being one.[368] His main objection was based on the heterogeneous nature of management, a feature that Marshall should have taken into account. In his theory of cost, Robbins moved even closer to the continental outlook. Cost became a displaced alternative stated in terms of the values of the goods displaced.[369] And this was more than a technical displacement, as Knight and Haberler had suggested. It was the "resistances" that were encountered in production which had to be emphasized. These resistances were in the nature of psychic phenomena in which anticipations played an important role. Only a general equilibrium analysis, said Robbins, could accomplish this task: Marshall's time concepts were inadequate because they were merely different sections of the same process.

In the main, Robbins adopted the Hayekian theory of business cycles.[370] If depressions were short, he said, then cost-cutting and severe liquidations were justifiable, since such policies would quickly restore business prospects.[371] Little wonder that devotees of this theory were accused of being "sadistic deflationists." The presumption of a flexible economy was completely untenable: little credence was given to increasing rigidities and overhead costs, all of which created a ratchet-like upward effect.[372] Nor, on the other hand, was the collapse of general demand during the 1930's given much serious attention. Moreover, liquidations do not always eliminate marginal firms, since frequently it has been against government policy to allow the bleeding process to continue without applying a tourniquet. Robbins, following Hayek, argued that a collapse came about because of shortages in savings: the fruits of prosperity were plucked before they really ripened.[373] In an economy of roundabout production, he contended, price movements were apt to cause distortions in the structure of production, and new spending power flowing into producers' goods industries was bound to affect the consumers' goods industries. This would react on the producers' goods sector by drawing resources away from them and by further forcing prices upward. An inability to obtain additional financing of construction projects provided the basis for a collapse. And meanwhile, prices in the consumption sector continued to rise, exacerbating the situation. The outcome was a misdirection and wastage of resources. At no time, argued Robbins, was a deficiency in consumption and demand a cause of crisis. So long as prices moved together with costs, profitability was not undermined. It was disparities in these movements, said Robbins, that caused all the difficulty. The simplistic nature of this view was sharply demonstrated by the experience of the Great Depression. Costs were also incomes, and a downward movement on all fronts meant a decline in demand. Given the stickiness of prices, gluts were bound to crop up. Theoretically, it was the differential movement of costs and prices which had to be accounted for.

Robbins' wartime experiences evidently had a sharp impact on his views. In time, he conceded that the tradition he once supported had ignored deepseated upsets and had led to a superficial analysis of the economy. The theories of Keynes and Robertson awakened him from "dogmatic slumbers." [374] The result was a decided modification of his views, at least as judged by his writings after the war. The emphasis on individualism was still in evidence, but there was at the same time a recognition of the relevance of state action in certain situations. For example, the price system did not allo·

cate resources effectively during wartime, since the distribution of income was uneven to start with.[375] The need to provide certain goods and services through public channels was admitted. Free choice in the market was still desirable, and ignorance and fraud were deplored. Robbins, however, was not yet prepared to admit the pervasiveness of the latter. The market, he insisted, still could do its job, despite the stresses it underwent because of taxation, subsidies, and regulations of all sorts.[376] This, however, was a far cry from the days when he had viewed all interference as anathema. "Now it is very clear that, even from the point of view of relative allocation, the price and private enterprise system is open to grave strictures—at any rate if no deliberate attempt is made to curb its aberrations." [377] Although Robbins by no means was prepared to accept even the mild collectivism of an Abba Lerner, fearful that personal liberty would be jeopardized under such a system, he now was willing to experiment so long as the free play of private effort was not called into question. Perhaps, said he, the patent laws ought to be modified, prohibitions against restraint of trade strengthened, and new fiscal controls to stabilize demand introduced, in order to supplement the price system. He discovered too that the classicists were not the pure laissez faire proponents that history made them to be.[378] He found in them a social vision close to the modern temper. To revise one's ideas in this way was certainly no easy task, and it testifies to the strength of Robbins' intelligence that, under the pressures of events, he was able to move away from the rigidities of his early conceptions.

vii

G. L. S. Shackle: Expectations, Time, and Decisions

Genuinely new developments in economic theory have been sparse in the last few decades. One almost feels as Stephen Leacock, who, when asked by a colleague at McGill University why he preferred humor to economics, replied: "When I run across a new idea, I'll write about it." However, one of the more interesting developments in recent years has been the theory of expectations propounded by G. L. S. Shackle (1903-   ), professor at the University of Liverpool. Fundamentally, his theory has sought to define and explore the psychological process undergone by a businessman as he contemplates an action in which he is about to engage. The theory has explored entirely new concepts and ostensibly opened fresh vistas for economic investigation. Moreover, Shackle is a superb writer, with an uncommonly graceful and lucid style that makes even the mathematical sections of his work pleasurable to read.

Shackle, who studied at London University and Oxford, worked during the war as a statistical assistant to Winston Churchill. Since 1941, he has been at Liverpool. His *Expectations, Investment and Income,* published in 1938, was followed by the rather striking *Expectations in Economics* in 1949. But the slim volume of lectures, *Time in Economics,* given at the Institute of Social Studies in Holland in 1957, is perhaps the best introduction to Shackle's thinking, and may be supplemented by the excellent collection of essays, *Uncertainty in Economics,* published in 1955. Two symposiums, *Uncertainty and Business Decisions* (1954) and a special issue of *Metroeconomica* (April-August, 1959), have illustrated the keen interest aroused by this new approach.

In Shackle's system, the concept of time was the central focus. Each time-moment, he wrote, was an unique event, and human beings contemplate only the moment-in-being as the center of sensory experience.[379] The moment-in-being, while ephemeral and solitary, expressed a peculiar individuality which was to be distinguished from those historical sequences in which experience was gathered from outside the person. For present moments, the contemplation of future events existed only in the individual's imagination. But from this contemplation a chain of imagined events could be constructed with supposed consequences attached to them, and even dated. This was the essence of the theory of expectation.[380] Past events, said Shackle, can exert their influence only insofar as they exist in memory in the present. Furthermore, he added, since the uniqueness of a moment makes it doubtful that comparisons of actuality at different calendar dates are genuinely possible, the older utility theory could be put to one side as not especially relevant. With such a precise definition of the element of time, Shackle was able to work out a new concept of economic behavior.

The unique quality of the moment lent to expectation a sense of uncertainty. Of course, it was possible to ask, as did the Swedish economists, whether an expectation matched the feelings created by memory. Now, both enjoyable and disturbing expectations could be given specific calendar dates, and, when a decision was made in the present, a relationship between the moment-in-being and a projected date could be established. There was no need, said Shackle, to raise questions of rationality or irrationality in this analysis. Action was simply action, for who was to say that a wrong choice had been made? Normal feelings that painful consequences would suggest error or irrational behavior did not enter into the situation, he said, for if the contemplated decision encompassed both pleasurable and painful outcomes one could not ascribe the results to improper behavior. An unhappy resolution simply reflected one aspect of the expectations of a single set of choices.

If certainty was a feature of human action, said Shackle, decision-making merely would be a matter of outlining formal solutions for formal problems. Uncertainty was introduced because the entrepreneur exercised his faculty of imagination, and it was those acts of inspiration which flowed through a time continuum that gave economics its dynamic quality. But since no one possesses knowledge of the future, economics cannot be a prescriptive science. A dynamic theory, Shackle insisted, was essentially introspective and imaginative, and there was no reason why self-perception through knowledge of the moment-in-being could not be scientific.[381] However, Shackle's argument was difficult to accept, for, if this were so, there could be no way of developing public criteria of action. It was akin to Hayek's theory of knowledge and, like the Austrian's, it necessarily foundered on the lack of any principle of connectability between individuals. Self-perceptions frequently are delusory and it is this that greatly contributes to uncertainty. Shackle's rejection of a public dynamics on mechanical grounds in which a sense of time can be acquired through external observation of moments did not seem weighty enough. A public dynamics can, in fact, be based on common experiences and shared knowledge without which an ordered social and economic system would be difficult to conceive. Implicit in the latter view, of course, is the idea of a relationship between human beings—a missing element in Shackle's approach. It fact, his theory, as fascinating as it was, could be charged with exhibiting only formal properties abstracted from all those influences of a public nature which impinge on the decision-making process.

The sense of time secured through external observations of events hardly can be described as mechanical. Moreover, it is the capacity to make such observations that allow one to establish cause and effect relationships, especially if the whole process is to be conceived as one of genetic change and growth. In fact, Shackle could be chided for having confused two levels of analysis: one can accept for analytic purposes the atomistic self-perception of the moment-in-being without necessarily destroying the validity and usefulness of public, externally observed reality. As Kenneth Boulding remarked, we can function in terms of objective reality because we have a definite image of what it is, and on this our behavior depends.[382] The images, or the perceptions, that we hold do stem from external reality; it was precisely this central concept, on quite another level of analysis, that Shackle overlooked. Information constantly is brought to the individual, affecting both his perceptions and expectations, and it would not be an overstatement to say that objective reality can be known. In more mundane terms, this is precisely what entrepreneurs seek to accomplish through crop reports, market research, and consumer surveys. The entrepreneur need not be an electronic computer, but even today these frightening devices can tell him a good deal about the milieu in which he operates.

Much of Shackle's argument hinged on the issue of free will, in the sense that the entrepreneur was free to make any decision he wished. It would be pointless to enter into this hoary debate, aside from commenting that free will usually functions within a particular environment, and complete freedom, as Marx once said, is the recognition of its limits. Anticipations may be the spark in decision-making, yet it cannot be denied that there is an important relationship between environment and the formation of anticipations. The consequences of the latter are always confirmed or rejected by the environment; but in Shackle's system, such interactions appeared as mere data. The moment-in-being can be only the start of a theory of expectations, but the analysis turns out even more complex than Shackle made it.[383] For example, time clearly exhibits a texture of duration; but to define it as accumulated intensity, as he did, is not only vague but utterly fails to give the moment-in-being the sense of density which duration implies. Nor would Shackle accept the proposition that anticipations of future events were necessarily less intense, by virtue of distance, than anticipations of events close at hand. It was possible, he urged, to conceive of distant events as creating more intense feelings for the moment-in-being. Cumulation over time was useful only insofar as it contributed to feelings now.[384]

In order to thoroughly clear the way for his own theory, Shackle had to dispose of the idea of numerical probability, which, he claimed, involved serious logical difficulties when applied to expectations. The orthodox approach assigned a numerical value or fraction to each possibility in a given set such that the sum of the values added to unity. This implied both a uniform pattern of conditions in the series of experiments that might be undertaken to ascertain probability and, of course, the capacity to repeat experiments. But many experiments, said Shackle, are unique. What, he asked, is the numerical probability of a single throw of a die? Once-and-for-all commitments of capital are individual events, the outcome of which cannot be given a numerical probability.[385] It would be accurate, perhaps, to label the outcome in terms of credibility or possibility. Once action is undertaken, Shackle argued, the only results are success or failure, which can be measured by what he called "potential surprise." That is, he was seeking a measure of acceptance or belief in order to give equal status to a possible outcome and its opposite.[386] But since such measures would be independent of each other, a probability of one-half could not be assigned to them, nor was it necessary for them to add to unity. To do so would be fallacious, the argument continued, since even after the results were in, one could not say whether the probability distribution had been correct. Uncertainty necessarily involved ". . . an irreducible core of ignorance concerning the outcome of a virtually isolated act." [387] Again, difficulties arose with Shackle's last statement. Are the acts of entrepreneurs isolated? Is social behavior simply a sum of isolated acts? Is numerical estimation the only approach to questions of statistical probability? Does not probability imply a measure of degrees of belief? All that numerical probability seems to suggest is that such degrees of belief have to be consistent. One might very well wonder whether Shackle had proved his case.

Probability distributions in an *ex ante* case were considered by Shackle as bogus. All that the theorist could do, he said, was to describe an individual's state of mind regarding the outcome of a single isolated trial. Consequently, any effort to distinguish between the reliability of a distribution for different ventures was meaningless. [388] Numerical valuations of an expectation could be reduced to a single pair of numbers, one of which represented the favorable outcome, the other the unfavorable one. Such numbers represented genuine psychological states, for they measured outcomes which created intense feelings in the present. They could not be manipulated or added; they stressed the unique quality of experience inherent in expectations. The entrepreneur actually reacted to single situations or, at most, to a small number of situations. Uncertainty was not eliminated, for it was precisely that which ". . . allows [the entrepreneur], and only uncertainty which can allow him, to entertain as possibilities his highest levels of imagined success." [389]

Consequently, Shackle wanted a theory that would explain "originative" acts of mind involving degrees of belief and doubt. Such a theory clearly would cross the lines between logic, philosophy, psychology, and economics. The very definition which he gave to the notion of expectations made this necessary. Hypotheses would have to be formulated which could be subjected to some kind of measurement so that degrees of belief might be established. Beginning then with a kind of wishful thinking, it was possible to imagine the consequences of future actions as either highly successful or catastrophic. [390] This was much more interesting to the entrepreneur than those actions of which the outcomes were known. Of course, all the results of a range of investment opportunities would not have the same power to surprise the businessman. Many possibilities would occasion little surprise, and in this range the likelihood was that the gains or losses would be small. Logically, the entrepreneur ought to focus upon those prospects with a high potential surprise, that is, interest would be heightened by the best and the worst hypotheses. At some point, potential surprise would exceed the relevant increase in gain, and it was this point, said Shackle, that would command the attention of the entrepreneur.

It now was necessary to describe the separate movements of the variables, rather than their net effects. Of course, the entrepreneur's viewpoint would shift as he moved from one calendar date to the next, and for each date a new set of circumstances would arise. Decisions would be based on the greatest enjoyment offered by anticipation of outcomes. The circumstances were unique, for they might not appear again as time moved on. But immediately the question arose regarding recurring decisions, which are frequent in production. Not necessarily habitual in character, they nevertheless do demand commitments of a short-term nature. The suspicion arose that Shackle's once-and-for-all analysis did not meet the requirements of regularly recurring actions, which frequently involved the past much more than he would allow. Uniqueness threatened to become chaos and evidently would not permit the development of trends.[391] As social and political elements disappeared entirely, the individual once again became the calculating automaton of the classicists. Now, however, surprise rather than utility became the measurable quantity. But it is doubtful that businessmen really do think in terms of potential surprise, that they always seek the pleasure of the greatest possible gain. Game theory, for example, suggests rather that they seek reasonable outcomes.[392]

In Shackle's theory, certainty meant a high degree of belief. This implied great surprise when the expected result was not fulfilled. Thus, potential surprise could be viewed as a measure of the degree of belief. If one accepted the proposition that there could be varying levels of potential surprise, a continuous variable could be set forth, amenable to mathematical manipulation. The degree Y of potential surprise, associated with a continuous variable X, was itself a continuous function, so that the potential surprise function could be stated as $Y=Y(X)$. Thus, the entrepreneur, now an expert mathematician, was in a position to measure possible satisfactions. Again, the rejection of probability seemed premature, for Shackle's function described only atomistic behavior. It had nothing to say about group or social action. An airplane crash can be finality itself, yet air flight remains one of the safest modes of public transportation.

With the attention-getting power of an hypothesis put at the center of the theory, outcomes could be arranged in a sequence of increasing or decreasing desirability. The central range of the possibilities seemingly would have certainty: they consequently appeared uninteresting. The entrepreneur would prefer to concentrate rather on the most desirable and the degree of hurtfulness of the most hurtful outcome.[393] From this argument, Shackle derived a diagram which looked like the cross-section of a wash basin, with the bottom representing the inner, less interesting possibilities and the sides moving toward the points of high potential surprise. A surface was then constructed—the contour lines of which represented "attention-getting power"—and by relating the potential surprise curve to the surface, he obtained "standardized" focus values which were required to compare different situations. The argument was quite subtle and, given the premises, almost persuasive. It assumed that perfect knowledge was impossible and that entrepreneurs seldom knew that they would achieve the gains they sought. This seemed especially so in the case of investment.[394] The technique involved the selection of a point on the surface from which an indifference curve could be extended to link equal combinations of surprise and gain. A whole family of such curves could be drawn, each representing equal combinations of surprise and gain or surprise and loss. These indifference curves and the potential surprise curve were then superimposed on one another to obtain the points of "focus-outcome." Presumably, this simplified the analysis of uncertainty. A decision would be made, said Shackle, at the point of tangency of the potential surprise curve and one of the "attention getting" contour lines. Here the highest bids would be made for a particular project.[395] These were the focus points at which uncertainty situations were reduced to a kind of bet where only two possible outcomes were considered. The idea of focus outcomes led to the notion of an indifference map of uncertainties. Given the standardized focus gains and focus losses of any two possibilities, each one unique, the indifference map would indicate entrepreneurial preference. This was derived from a "gambler" indifference map, the lines of which depicted the relation between focus losses and gains. That investment project would be selected whose standardized focus-outcome was on the highest indifference curve. The lines would become steeper toward the left, since, with a greater focus loss, a larger focus gain would be required to compensate for increases in the former.[396] Different types of indifference systems could be constructed, depending on the temperament of the individual concerned.[397]

According to Shackle, his theory might be applied to several areas, one of which was the field of investment.[398] Since the value of a plant stemmed from its ability to yield future services, it was evident that the latter would have to exceed the anticipated outlays for construction. If the plant were to be sold, its value to the entrepreneur would depend on what he expected to obtain for it from the hopeful buyer. The worthwhileness of a project might then be analyzed in terms of the pairs of focus values assigned to different alternatives. Since the plant would include design and location as well as future values, both objective and subjective elements would have to be introduced. As time passed, judgments would be affected by new information and shifts in the relevant data. Factors of liquidity would also enter the analysis as potential gains and losses were continually compared.[399] Thus decisions to commit or not to commit cash, or even whether to borrow, always would be subject to change. At all times, the key was the subjective attractiveness of the investment. Psychological enjoyment by anticipation was always present as the entrepreneur looked forward to pleasurable feelings and experiences. Deceleration of the investment process might occur through delay; or a sense of exhilaration might let loose a host of investment decisions. With the former, liquidity would take preference over specific commitments. But, observed Shackle, there was a certain asymmetry in this area, for either a decrease in gains or an increase in losses could have the same effect. Taking into account the nature of entrepreneurial reactions, it was likely that stoppages in investment would be more abrupt than additions.

The foregoing suggested an approach to a theory of business cycles. But in Shackle's purely psychological framework, it would necessarily have to abstract from production periods, uneven income distribution, money and credit, lags between costs and prices, flows between the producers' goods and consumers' goods sectors, and above all, government influences on the economy. It might be argued, as did Pigou, that the psychology of the businessman was predominant in cyclical movements; yet in the light of the many complex elements required for an understanding of business cycles, expectation and uncertainty alone clearly were insufficient. A further difficulty in Shackle's approach to investment decisions lay in the theory's limited applicability: only two assets or two investment possibilities were deemed possible. Yet it was clear that investors frequently were concerned with a portfolio of assets. It has remained for other writers to assay an extension of Shackle's theory to such contingencies.[400]

Thus far, the analysis omitted taxation. It was obvious that an investment would not be consummated unless the appropriate gambler-indifference curve after taxes would be high enough.[401] The entrepreneur necessarily looked upon a tax as a cost, for it clearly reduced his focus gain. The net effect of taxation, said Shackle, was to reduce the flow of investment. What kind of tax system, then, ought to be installed? In his view, any gain due to luck ought to be taxed, rather than gains derived from imagination and knowledge. But, aside from the patent introduction of contradictory elements into the theory, how would the authorities distinguish between luck and foresight? Would not entrepreneurs always announce the superiority of their imaginative skills? One way out of the dilemma would be to tax at high rates gains far in excess of expectations and at low rates gains that were close to what was anticipated. Entrepreneurs, suggested Shackle, should be required to declare in advance what the "primary focus value of untaxed gains" would be. That is, the businessman should tell the government what rate of profit he expected to earn, and deviations from this would be subject to taxation.[402]

Profit became not a reward for entrepreneurial services, but a net yield flow stemming from the unpredictability of human affairs.[403] It was the power and desire of men to change their environment which gave rise to profit, and, as such, it represented a reward for success and compensation for carrying the burden of uncertainty. Profit as an *ex ante* notion was related to the anticipatory feeling of gain. As an *ex post* concept it clearly affected future courses of action. Thus, there were two meanings in the word "profit" which had to be kept clearly apart. To Shackle, the *ex ante* version was more meaningful because it directly influenced the decision-making process. Yet it was doubtful that such a sharp line could be drawn between them, for *ex ante* events became *ex post* and moved again into *ex ante* forms. There was a perpetual relationship between past, present, and future that Shackle did not successfully integrate into his theory.[404]

Shackle tried to bring interest into his uncertainty theory also, but his formulation made it rather difficult to differentiate interest from profit. The function of interest was to allocate capital among alternative uses up to the point at which degrees of uncertainty were equalized in various endeavors. While liquidity preference might be an element in the determination of interest, the basic consideration was uncertainty. That is, the entrepreneur would relate the cost of borrowing to his anticipated profit, with the latter dependent upon the value of his particular focus point. But expected net yields would seemingly affect only the demand for funds. The lender, who would also face conditions of uncertainty, might very well be in a better position to spread his risks. The likelihood seemed that the lender could apply probability calculations, so that for him interest would represent a payment for a calculable risk.[405] Insofar as Shackle's theory was concerned, it appeared restricted solely to the demand side of interest determination.

The analysis, however, was peculiarly adaptable to the bargaining process.[406] All exchange transactions exhibited elements of uncertainty, since each bargainer developed a set of hypotheses about price offers. There were four price points in the situation: an announced or gambit price; an absolute minimum price; an effective minimum price, or one which a given policy would permit; and the agreed upon price. The bargaining plan could be defined in terms of focus gains and losses, so that the solution became a determinate one if the gambler-indifference system of each bargainer were known. Consequently, the notion of indeterminacy in bilateral monopoly was cast aside. In Shackle's theory, the movement was from the gambit price to the agreed price, with the difference between them called the "descent." This was positive for the seller and negative for the buyer. Limits were set by the respective minimum prices. A slight descent might suggest a fear of loss of prestige; any descent within the given limits would indicate a "loss of face" policy; or there might be combinations of both approaches. Action in this model, therefore, required a decision on bargaining policy, a statement of the gambit price, and establishment of the relevant limits. A gambit price would be selected for which the potential gain was highest, so that action depended in the last analysis on focus gains and focus losses. The various strategies which might be adopted could be described by relating their potential surprise to the gambit prices and to the degree of descent. With the gambler-indifference map known, it then was possible to compare all prospective decisions and to determine the most favorable course of action. But since this implied that all bargaining plans were developed in advance, the only actions which could be explained were those conforming to the plan.[407] Further, certain elements in the bargaining process did not enter into Shackle's theory—namely, bluffing, sudden attacks, and collusion. Coercion and market power also were considerations necessary for a realistic theory of bargaining. Had these omissions been considered, as in game theory, the description of bargaining might have been broadened to include more than ordinary higgling between two parties over a single good.[408] Shackle's bargaining theory suffered from a self-imposed limitation to a few highly restricted conditions. Covering but a small part of economic activity, it thus lacked sufficient generality.

Indeed, the entire theory of uncertainty did raise pertinent questions regarding the logic and psychology of business behavior. Yet, by ignoring recurring actions, a large and important area was overlooked. Moreover, Shackle's premises were insufficient to include the full range of economic activity. Monopolistic tendencies and the significance of overhead costs were not explored. The modern economy is predominantly a corporate one, not a society of atomistic, independent actors, each living in a world of which he knows little. The corporations, which know a good deal about their environment and always seek to discover more, seldom function in utter ignorance. Thus one is tempted to conclude that Shackle's theory was simply another in the long chain of formalistic economic exercises. With so large a bloc of economic behavior subject to constant repetition, it would seem patent that probability cannot be replaced by potential surprise.[409] And, as others have noted, potential surprise appears simply as a more sophisticated version of ordinary utilitarianism, especially since it harps so much on anticipated pleasures and pains.[410] The application of continuous functions in entrepreneurial behavior also may be questioned.[411] It is quite reasonable to suppose that businessmen do not behave like calculus equations and that a description of what they do might require a mathematics of discontinuities. Above all, Shackle was entirely remiss in failing to introduce the political framework and the concept of business goals into his theory.[412] Perhaps the sharpest criticism was voiced by L. M. Lachmann, who charged that the theory was completely static. "It tells us nothing about market processes and nothing about exchange and the transmission of knowledge," said he.[413] The analysis of how expectations were changed and altered was purely formal.

At best, the theory could be applied to those infrequent cases in which once-and-for-all decisions were to be made. Although Shackle did concede that the past was encompassed in the moment-in-being, he preferred to stress the imaginative effort to look into the future. But such decisions, particularly in corporations, are often conditioned by what may have occurred in the very recent past. Boards of directors often hold views in common which establish time-spans of varying duration guiding the decision-making process.[414] The key problem therefore would seem to be one of relating expectations to particular business policies, such as sales rather than profit maximization, and to establish a much broader spectrum of possibilities than Shackle was able to develop, all functioning in a realistic framework of economic action.[415]

.

Part THREE

T*he Thrust Toward Technique*

.

7

The Swedish

Contribution

The Economics of
Knut Wicksell

F OR A NUMBER OF YEARS the Swedish tradition was hidden behind the barrier of language. But as the works from this small but vigorous nation were increasingly made available to American readers, it became evident that here was a remarkable group of economists, quite unafraid to fuse policy pronouncements with theoretical discourse. Stemming from the earlier work of Knut Wicksell, Gustav Cassel, and David Davidson, their diagnosis of what ailed the economic order covered the broad fields of production, prices, money, and fiscal policy. Even at close range, one is compelled to describe the work of the Swedish school as the most remarkably sustained intellectual performance in any of the social sciences in recent decades.

The Swedish economists have had, of course, distinguished forebears,

539

the most important of whom was Knut Wicksell (1851-1926)—a genuinely exceptional personality whose career might have been a model for an Ibsen drama. Wicksell came to economic science at an age later than usual for eminent theorists. Although a contemporary of Menger, Böhm-Bawerk, Marshall, and Walras, intellectually he was their descendant. He first studied mathematics and physics for a decade, giving vent to his radical impulses by pondering such social questions as population, celibacy, and prostitution. Then in the 1870's, an emotional crisis, not unlike the one described in John Stuart Mill's *Autobiography,*[1] impelled Wicksell to reject Christianity, for which he substituted utilitarianism as a more sensible doctrine in an industrial era. Transmuted into the new liberalism of the later nineteenth century, utilitarianism asserted the right of the lower middle class and growing proletariat to a hand in decisions affecting their own fate: the general welfare was meant to include them as well as other classes. This radicalism came to Scandinavia through Georg Brandes in Denmark, Henrik Ibsen in Norway, and August Strindberg in Sweden. The movement was abetted by an economic revolution in these countries in which middle-class rebels were increasingly disturbed by the growing inequality and its accompanying vulgarities. In the 1870's Sweden's agricultural base was altered by an ever-expanding demand for iron and timber. The usual evils of the factory system appeared: child labor, long hours, and unsanitary conditions repeated the experience of the industrial revolution in Britain. Swedish society, nevertheless, remained authoritarian and anti-rationalistic. This was the milieu in which Wicksell came to intellectual maturity.[2]

Knut Wicksell, born in Stockholm, was the youngest child of a small grocer. He grew up in an atmosphere of petty trade, although his father was to become a fairly successful entrepreneur. Shrewd investments in real property and a thriving business provided a good livelihood for the Wicksells, whose associations nevertheless were chiefly workingclass. The family grocery was in a worker's neighborhood; the tenants mainly clerks and craftsmen. It was not unusual that in later life Wicksell should prefer to address workers' audiences in Stockholm rather than make the lecture circuit around the country. When he was fifteen, Wicksell lost both his parents, but with the help of his brother and sisters, he was able to continue his education, entering Uppsala University in 1869. His work was brilliant and he completed a degree in mathematics in half the required time. But emotional problems, religious doubts, and an inordinate concern with student activity absorbed more and more of his energies. By 1885 he had earned another degree, this time in physics. He now considered himself a free thinker and wrote poetry expressing the perennial concern of the lovelorn with the realities of human experience.[3]

In 1880 Wicksell delivered a talk on alcoholism in which he asserted that excessive drink was a social disease, ending this rather innocuous lecture with a mild plea for limitations of family size through birth control. It pre-cipitated the first of the famous Wicksellian scandals, all of which now appear as somewhat comic adventures in middle-class radicalism. In that day, how-ever, people were genuinely outraged. The lecture was an instantaneous suc-cess and several thousand copies of the reprint were sold.[4] Wicksell now became the center of discussion. However, the debate with his critics, espe-cially with David Davidson, convinced him that he needed to know more about social and economic problems. In 1884, he left Uppsala after an extraordinarily long career as a student to study the social sciences else-where. It was in economics that he would at last find room to combine his first interest, mathematics, with an enduring and deep concern for social questions.

For the next five years Wicksell travelled in England, Germany, Austria, and France, carefully studying the works of all the great economists of the past. As he came to know Karl Kautsky and attended Fabian meetings in London, his new attitude was marked by the observation that the theory of the free labor market was absurd, since wage earners were entirely lacking in power.[5] However, he was certain that only mathematical techniques could give economics a solid foundation. To this end, he read Walras, Sidgwick, and Jevons as well as the classicists, but evinced little interest in historicism, then popular in Germany. Wicksell was affected most by Böhm-Bawerk, whose *Positive Theory of Capital* he was destined to extend and modify in rather important ways.

As he was completing his continental studies, Wicksell met Anna Bagge, a Norwegian school teacher. They were anxious to be married, but Wicksell would have nothing to do with religious ritual, and since civil ceremonies were as yet unknown, the two young free thinkers simply entered into a contractual arrangement to be man and wife. It seems likely that this some-what unusual relationship, as well as his radical outlook, accounted for the long delay in securing an adequate academic post. Wicksell was a "dangerous" person who had offended the religious sensibilities of his countrymen. He was not, however, a socialist, although he did know Hjalmar Branting, one of the stalwarts of Swedish social democracy. Wicksell preferred the utilitarian philosophy he had so painfully worked out and this made him something of a stranger to the socialists. As a Malthusian, he felt that even a socialist society would have to impose limits on population growth. Persistent social injustices, he said, stemmed mainly from an excess of people relative to re-sources, and the socialists erred in blaming institutions when in reality it was nature and passion that would have to be controlled.[6] A complete break oc-curred between Wicksell and the Social Democrats in a dispute over the length of the working day. He had taken the position that a shorter day did not necessarily mean an improved situation for the workers: shorter hours, said Wicksell, might increase marginal productivity, but they would also enforce higher wage rates, thereby increasing costs and, indirectly, unemployment. This strict classical position ended whatever popularity Wicksell may have developed among the Social Democrats.[7]

His first serious work in economic theory was an article on interest and wages in Conrad's *Jahrbucher für Nationalökonomie und Statistik* in 1892 and his book, *Value, Capital and Rent,* published the following year.[8] Three years later came his remarkable work on taxation, *Finanztheoretische Untersuchungen nebst Darstellung und Kritik des Steuersystems Schwedens,* which included his doctoral thesis.[9] But since economics was taught in the faculties of law, Wicksell had to obtain still another degree in law before he could qualify for a university position. The academic ritual could not be evaded despite his increasing fame. Böhm-Bawerk hailed *Value, Capital and Rent* as a first-rate contribution, and Walras declared that with it Wicksell had to be reckoned with as a major mathematical economist. He was now working on his *Interest and Prices,*[10] and when he visited Johannes Conrad at Halle in 1896 he had the pleasant experience of hearing the latter tell his students to stand in his honor.[11] But the authorities wanted the law degree. By 1899 this too was done and finally, in 1900, at the age of fifty, Wicksell was appointed an assistant professor in economics and law at Lund University. Considering his independence of mind, his insistence on the truth as he saw it, and his free-thinking notoriety, it is remarkable that he was able to obtain a post at all.

His only serious rival for the job was Gustav Cassel, fifteen years his junior. The latter had been doing work in economics for only a few years, but was supported by conservative elements unwilling to let Wicksell have the post. Cassel, who wanted the matter settled on scientific grounds, was embarrassed by the attacks on Wicksell and withdrew his application. But this by no means settled the differences between them. Cassel began a long campaign against Austrian theory and other variants of marginalism, while Wicksell considered his erstwhile rival as an incompetent. Although a reconciliation was almost effected, Cassel broke completely when Wicksell criticized his work as a "farrago." [12] For the next sixteen years Wicksell taught a variety of courses, always insisting that the equipment of a well-trained economist had to include a thorough grounding in Malthus. But he was still an *enfant terrible.* He defended Russia, a most unpopular act, and refused to employ the proper tone of obeisance when addressing himself to authority. During the course of a lecture at socialist headquarters in 1908, Wicksell made some ironical remarks about the Immaculate Conception, and for this act of blasphemy he was imprisoned for two months—a punishment taken with remarkable fortitude by a man close to sixty years of age. After his retirement from Lund, Wicksell went to Stockholm, where he participated in meetings of the Economics Society and quietly worked at home. Although his sympathies were with the workers' movement, he was critical of their official theory. Yet he supported the Social Democrats when they came to power in 1921. In 1926, Wicksell died suddenly at the age of seventy-four, ending a life that was surely exciting and hardly cloistered.[13]

Wicksell's rigorous training in mathematics largely explains his terse, somewhat formal, yet lucid style. He felt that the empiricism of the German historicists could not yield any fruitful results, nor did he believe that either the Marxists or the Classical Harmony economists had the right answer. The methodological position to which he subscribed was set down clearly in his lecture, "Ends and Means in Economics." [14] Economics, he observed, was the one science in which a particular doctrine always seemed to call forth an opposing view. Controversies appeared to be so persistent that the lasting truths one might explore often seemed to be non-existent. That this reflected the realm of value judgments did not escape Wicksell: he recognized that different conceptions of economic and social aims did color the treatment of theoretical matters, thus seeming to lend substance to the historicists' contention that economic theories were bounded by time and place. This might in some measure be true, but, he insisted, the latter's conclusion that the deductive method therefore was not to be relied upon was false. Although Wicksell was quite generous in his estimation of the historical school, he felt that their one-sided approach simply had hindered economic thought in Germany.[15]

The abstract method, said Wicksell, was merely one way of apprehending reality, especially that part of it that could not be reached by direct observation. The purpose of the deductive method, rooted in experience, was always a comparison with reality, or *verification*.[16] To some degree, even experiments might be conducted, as with monetary matters: the experimenter in this case was the legislator. The Austrian government's success in controlling the supply of paper money seemed to Wicksell dramatic substantiation of his argument. The purpose of theoretical discourse, he continued, was to formulate proper questions: history and statistics were useful adjuncts, of course, but used alone they created only arid monographs. Wicksell wondered aloud whether the political climate of the German Empire had made its scholars abjure theory and question-raising.[17] On the other hand, Bastiat and the Harmony writers were mere dilettantes whose sole function was to sweep away all difficulties as nonexistent or irrelevant. They went Ricardo one better, he said, by making the capitalist the deserving recipient of the labor of his ancestors. By proving so much they proved nothing.[18]

Wicksell adopted the technique of approximation which had been employed with such marked success by Walras. Thus, a theoretical model was constructed in which only the significant and the meaningful were reflected. Useful propositions could be worked out which might then be tested with empirical data as a means of guiding policy. Wicksell's central interest, however, was pure theory, although he did take up such practical matters as taxation and index numbers.[19] His ability to handle the tools of theoretical analysis was revealed with uncommon skill in *Value, Capital and Rent,* where he was able to fuse the apparently disparate elements of the Walrasian and Bawerkian systems in a way that could arouse only genuine admiration.

The differences between the classicists and the Austrians had been apparent when Wicksell came to economics. Jevons and Menger had already published their works rejecting cost as a basis for value, which was now said to stem from the utility of the last unit of a good. The new theory solved the ancient paradox of high value for goods of little use and low value for those of great usefulness. Furthermore, it now was possible to relate the value of the means of production to the value of their output through the process known as imputation. Although he entered the debate rather late, Wicksell made an unusual stir with his quasi-mathematical presentation of the new doctrine in *Value, Capital and Rent.*[20] The argument that value was not a constant objective magnitude, but one which altered with each person's perception of the exchange situation, became the foundation of his interpretation.[21] While scarcity was conceded to be a significant element, it was marginal utility that was deemed crucial. No longer was there need to feel that what one party gained in an exchange, the other lost: both were winners. Wicksell did admit some relationship between value and cost, but this was essentially peripheral. Utility was defined in its strictest sense as a mathematical function of the quantity of a good, with *marginal* utility as the first derivative of total utility. Marginal utility, therefore, was a measure of the rate of change in total utility. Of course, such measurements were conceptually feasible only so long as comparisons could be made with substitutes of the same good in altered circumstances. The analysis then went on to the problem of different uses of the same good, from which the allocation theorem was derived. While the exchange problem was also treated mathematically, Jevons' trading bodies were avoided, resulting generally in a more elegant treatment. Exchange became a maximization problem, since each party in a direct transaction was presumed to be in search of the greatest gain in utility at the given price.[22] Wicksell conceded, however, that indirect exchange involving credit and money was the more realistic and complex version of the matter. But even in these circumstances it was possible to show that exchange was ruled by the principle that the different marginal utilities would be in the same proportion to each other as the prices of the goods involved in the transaction.

Wicksell's equally perceptive analysis of supply and demand allowed him to go over to the theory of production, for potential supply—or that portion of the stock not yet offered for sale—became an element as important as market conditions themselves. In this way, the analysis was able to get back to the factors of production. There seemed to be an imputation process connecting commodities and factors, and it appeared that the same valuation technique could apply to land, labor, and capital. However, Wicksell demonstrated that this was too simple, for the element of time had been omitted. Production was a series of exchanges performed at different moments yet covering the whole period during which it took place. Without this concept it would be rather difficult to explain interest and productivity.[23] Moreover, the standard approach to marginal utility would have to be qualified by the existence of indivisibilities—a factor which made it questionable whether individuals really knew anything of their marginal utilities in any sense other than mere preference. Wicksell also was aware that complementarity and substitutability made the problem even more complex.

However, it was the recognition of imperfect competition that dominated his analysis. Competition and monopoly were not separate and distinct market realms, he said, but represented rather the extremes of a spectrum.[24] Yet it was evident that the existence of price makers—firms able to set their own prices by manipulating production or demand—made it unlikely that marginal utility would be proportional to prices. Wicksell thus acknowledged that the competitive market was meaningful only where economies of scale were unimportant and where constant returns prevailed. He added to the discussion of duopoly, advocating the solution advanced by Cournot, to wit, that it was possible to attain a determinate equilibrium position in such markets. Retailing was noted as an example of imperfect competition. Prices in this area appeared to diverge from the usual theory of cost because of joint supply. Retailing was also characterized by differentiation on the basis of location, a factor frequently harmful to consumers, who all too often were ignorant of product qualities or were at the mercy of the retail merchant. Bilateral monopoly was also discussed. The analysis in *Value, Capital and Rent* appeared similar to Edgeworth's, in the sense that the solution in such situations was indeterminate within the limits of the contract curve. In a later essay on mathematical economics, Wicksell retreated somewhat from this position, holding that equilibrium was possible for the monopolist who was concerned with output.[25] Although he accepted the new theory, Wicksell was much too astute not to reject its ethical implications. He did not for a moment believe that perfect competition could achieve maximum satisfactions, for he knew that such a result would require a more equitable distribution of wealth and income than currently existed. Only if income were "optimally" distributed would there be optimal exchange.[26]

By the turn of the century, marginal productivity theory—which seemed to have gone off in several directions at once—required consolidation and restatement. Disparities had cropped up in the writings of Jevons, Böhm-Bawerk, and Wicksteed. Consequently, it was Wicksell's task to reformulate this branch of marginalism so that, at least, it would be consistent. Although the basic theory was the same for the Austrians and the British, there were substantial differences in their treatment of capital and distribution. Wicksell took the marginal utility of Jevons, fused it with the capital theory of Böhm-Bawerk, and set both into a Walrasian equilibrium framework, thus enabling everybody to live under the same theoretical roof. Again, the approach was mathematical. If the proceeds of production, said he, were to be conceived as functions of the participating factors, the economic principle would require that ". . . each factor shall be employed in such quantities that the falling out of a small portion of this quantity would diminish the result of the production by an amount equal to the share in the proceeds which belong to this quantity." [27] This suggested that the product would be exhausted by its distribution to the cooperating input factors. Functional distribution, essentially, was determined by imputing to the input factors their shares on the basis of marginal productivity. The theory was developed by Wicksell to a rather high pitch, and he was generous enough to credit Wicksteed with the initial discovery of the product exhaustion theorem.[28]

But when the Austrians and Pareto dealt with this problem, they allowed ethical overtones to penetrate the analytical structure. And, in the case of the American, John Bates Clark, the ethics became little more than explicit apologetics. For these writers, marginal productivity represented the best of all possible worlds within the context of general equilibrium. Consumers' utility was maximized, and the equality of minimum average and marginal cost with price became the organizing principle for the sphere of production. Wicksell, however, would have nothing to do with normative positions, going so far as to blame the Manchesterians for this unscientific intrusion and even to chide Pareto for expressing similar views.[29] Wicksell's major objection to the ethical interpretation stemmed from the fact that comparison of utility between different people was not a sound psychological concept.[30] Furthermore, this position failed to take account of the uneven distribution of income and wealth. Wicksell then argued that it was possible to devise a system of uniform prices which might yield more utility than was theoretically obtained through competitive prices, suggesting in this way that a planned economy might be superior to an unplanned one.[31] However, he preferred to identify himself with the competitive-liberal view. But at no time did he confound normative with positive propositions, as was so common with his forebears.

The technical portion of the productivity analysis began with production in the absence of capital; that is to say, attention was first focused on situations involving only labor and land.[32] Considering the landowner as an entrepreneur, the wage of the worker was to be determined by his marginal productivity in a purely technical sense, while rent was to be considered the residual portion of the product. On the other hand, wages would be a residual if the worker became his own entrepreneur. Increasing cost, or diminishing returns, also was incorporated in the analysis, for otherwise small firms would always be absorbed by large ones.[33] The point here was that the scale on which an enterprise operated did affect the average product. Thus variation in proportions was an integral part of the Wicksellian scheme, although at times the application of the marginal and average concepts was somewhat obscure. With respect to rent, no special theory was required.[34]

Inventions and improvements in technology could alter the ratios in which land and labor were employed, but Wicksell insisted that labor could not be injured through the increased application of machinery. The analysis would have to look at what the situation was at the margin, not at production as a whole. In modern terminology, this implied that the distribution of the product as between capital and labor was determined by their marginal rates of substitution. But the logic of this formulation seemed somewhat circular, for such marginal substitution rates, which determined how the product was to be shared, could not be ascertained unless wages and profits were known in advance. At any rate, said Wicksell, returning to his Malthusian origins, labor's inability to make advances stemmed entirely from its excessive numbers.[35] This more than anything else, he said, prevented labor from sharing in increased output. He also remarked rather wryly, that a reduction in the portion of total output going to labor as a result of some technical invention illustrated ". . . the serious error of those who see in free competition a sufficient means for the maximum satisfaction of the needs or desires of all members of society." [36] He berated Cassel for accepting the classical view of the free-price mechanism on moral grounds.[37] There was no economic providence which gave to individuals their allotted and just share of the product. In fact, Wicksell reminded his rival, the lower classes do not have genuine free choice in consumption, for they are offered only the cheapest brands and the worst goods. A decent rationing system certainly would improve their condition!

Although Wicksell was quite aware of the impact of change, more so perhaps than some of his followers, his analysis was cast in a static framework. In his treatment of the effect of technological improvements, he was concerned with the ratios that input factors bore one to the other. As accumulation of capital proceeded through time, he said, the marginal productivity of capital tended to decline, and although its share, in absolute terms, might increase, its share in total output became proportionately less than what rent and wages would be able to obtain. (The relation that this bears to Keynes' marginal efficiency of capital seems self-evident.) Long-term investments, however, could increase capital's profitability, and therefore, the supposed injury done by inventions could be overcome in the long run, so long as accumulation continued—unless, of course, labor continued to multiply itself.[38]

Given full employment, he argued, capital accumulation could take place theoretically only if saving increased faster than the work force. But willynilly competition for resources tended to increase wage rates and other factor payments, so that some portion of saving was absorbed by increased wages, stated in "real" terms. This described what has come to be known as the "Wicksell effect." [39] Under conditions of perfect foresight, it was presumed that the entrepreneur could anticipate this effect and make appropriate adjustments. But where uncertainty prevailed, there seemed little question but that there would be a "partial absorption of real saving." To Wicksell, this had serious implications for the analysis of capital and interest because it was arguable from this that the marginal productivity of capital was not the powerful force in interest determination that others had made it. Hayek later attempted to rescue the latter by suggesting that entrepreneurs might previously accumulate wage goods to meet such a contingency.[40] But this meant a kind of planning and foresight unlikely in a dynamic economy. The "Wicksell effect" seemed realistic enough, especially if it were to be interpreted as a long-run trend [41] in which it would be possible to accommodate structural changes to the gradual increase in real wages. Wicksell's argument was put as follows: an increase in real capital is equivalent to the marginal productivity of capital for society as a whole. Dividing this by saving gives the rate of productivity of real capital. While, according to older views, this ought to have been the same as the rate of interest, it was actually smaller by the extent to which wages were absorbed as part of real capital. When formulated in this manner, Wicksell's approach underscored problems caused by changes in capital formation and the effect that this might have on output, income distribution, saving, and consumption.

What strikes the reader about Wicksell's use of marginal productivity is not only his skillful fusion of the sometimes disparate elements in Walras, Jevons, and Böhm-Bawerk, but the ease with which the mathematical and literary modes of presentation were handled. Although he acknowledged that marginalism raised some questions, criticism based on discontinuities of economic events was at first rejected. His answer, however, was not fully convincing. Economic friction does exist to a much greater degree than Wicksell would admit. He finally had to concede that certain noneconomic elements such as altruism might overwhelm the purely economic ones. And when it came to products in joint supply—a not inconsiderable part of the output spectrum—the marginalist analysis seemed to disappear in a maze of complexities.

Marginal productivity led naturally to the theory of capital. Wicksell's ideas on capital represented a genuine contribution to economic analysis. Although the basic notions rested squarely on Böhm-Bawerk, the refinements and improvements were such as to constitute virtually a new theory.[42] The focus was now on capital accumulation and its effect on distribution. What Wicksell did simply enough was to introduce land and variable factor proportions into the system and then to generalize the whole structure into one that would encompass a number of different goods. Böhm-Bawerk's first ground, that interest is paid because of differences in the ability to provide goods at various times, was rejected as essentially uninimportant. However, the notion that there was a tendency to underestimate the future was considered more meaningful. Böhm's third argument, that present goods have a greater technical superiority over future goods in yielding marginal utility, was related to the concept of productivity more sharply than Böhm-Bawerk probably would have cared for.[43] Wicksell also handled the value aspects of capital productivity more effectively than his predecessors. What established the connection between the value and technical aspects, he said, was the concept of time. Once this was done, it was possible to look at capital as a ". . . single coherent mass of saved up labour and saved up land, which is accumulated in the course of years." [44] It thus appeared that Wicksell had created a unified concept of capital superior to that developed by Böhm-Bawerk, for Wicksell had included all means of subsistence for workers whereas Böhm had limited this to private capital.

The next step in the theory was an analysis of capital with regard to time strata, which led to the argument that the marginal productivities of stored-up labor and land were larger than those of current resources. Thus Wicksell provided for the restoration of used-up capital and "something more," which was nothing else but interest.[45] Time became the central concept as well as *the* variable dimension in capital while interest was converted into the marginal productivity of waiting.[46] Not expectedly, several changes were made in Wicksell's capital concept between *Value, Capital and Rent* and the *Lectures;* the version in the latter seems to be the preferable one, since it could be employed to show the effect of capital accumulation on annual output and distribution. Technically, the capital composition for any society was defined as the total number of units of saved-up labor and land, multiplied by the time period during which such units were invested. This formula stressed the notion that capital had both height and width and that it could be measured by the length of the average period of production required by the amount of capital employed. However, this notion later was replaced by the concept of an average investment period covering the time between the application of inputs and the sale of the finished goods. Since several input applications might be necessary in successive stages, Wicksell thought that the investments would have to be weighted by the rate of interest. This would make it possible to relate the investment process more directly to changes in capital. But there was one seemingly obscure point: in his early work, Wicksell had relegated durable goods to the category of landed property, so that railways, buildings, and roads became merely secondary phenomena, the net return from which was a kind of rent determined simply by the value of their useful services.[47] In other words, these capital forms were essentially social overhead items which entered production but indirectly. Interpreted in this way, Wicksell's definition remains meaningful, despite some questions about it.[48]

The yield from long-period investments would have to be greater than the sum of the yields obtained from short ones. Otherwise the commitment of capital would be limited to short but safer time spans.[49] That is, it seemed possible for less roundabout methods of production to develop. Consequently, the exchange relationships between the present and future would hinge on the difference between the value of total output and what the factors would obtain in a single time period, say a year. This suggested that capital was not merely another factor, but lent a new dimension to the other inputs and received a return that was quite its own. Total product could be reduced to wages plus interest on borrowed capital. That capital, in its free form, made advances to the other factors brought the notion quite close to the wages-fund theory. How these advances would be distributed depended, of course, on the respective marginal productivities of the co-operating factors.[50]

The elements of "height" and "width" in capital were revealed more clearly under dynamic conditions. Only then did the stratification of capital through time become visible. Height referred to the length of time that it took for various items of capital to mature; width, to the proportion of input services required to replace used-up capital goods. Expanded width, therefore, meant a proportionate increase in the kind of capital which was already in existence, while a growth in height implied a shift to different forms of capital. Wicksell thought that the most common development was first a growth in width, which depressed the marginal productivity of capital and the rate of interest. But since a differential pattern did tend to develop as between capital goods of short and long maturities, with the marginal productivity of the former falling more rapidly, a "higher" capital structure could be emphasized.[51]

Wicksell's awareness of the role of capital accumulation further illustrated his sense of the dynamic. Capital, he said, was hardly limited, since it could be increased through saving. Hence, a theory of saving was needed to complete the description of how the economy worked. This led him to the analysis of the motives for saving and to the aside that multimillionaires might not add necessarily to the general welfare by their saving. He did admit that the relation of the rate of interest to capital accumulation was obscure, the general presumption being that there would be some response to changes in interest rates. Wicksell also remarked that a collective society might bring about more effectively the required capital accumulation than an individualistic one.[52] This could be done through a united effort, said Wicksell, but he did not explore the fact that enforced accumulation could create severe social and political strain, as was later demonstrated in Russia.

For Wicksell the modern economy operated on a basis of borrowing, with the whole credit structure geared to facilitating the purchase of goods for sale. Consequently, transactions were carried on in money terms, although the objective was to obtain control over goods.[53] Loans were secured in order to get mobile capital and then to sell the latter or its product at a profit. The purpose might be to convert fluid capital into fixed forms, but the goal of greater profit was not undermined thereby. However, money and capital were not identical, for one gave rise to a money rate of interest and the other to a "real" rate. While interest manifested itself as a surplus value within a monetary framework, it was through the maturing, or seasoning of resources, leading to a greater marginal productivity, that a larger yield was made possible, as in the case of wine.[54] It was the time difference, a Bawerkian notion, that established the connection between the technical and value aspects of capital and that ultimately created the basis for interest as a form of income. While the rate of interest itself was governed ostensibly by the supply and demand for real capital, the demand for capital was increased as a result of technical advances. Supply, made more ample through savings, prosperity, and foresight, was reduced, in true Malthusian fashion, by increases in population. Total interest income then would be distributed according to the marginal productivities of the various sets of real capital. The real rate of interest stemmed from real capital. However, as stored-up resources in a money economy were exchanged for money prices, there came about the money rate of interest, which conceivably could diverge from the real rate.

A considerable exegetical literature has been built up since as to the question of what Wicksell really meant by his "real" rate of interest. Some have called it a "natural" rate, or one that would exist if the economy could function without money. Presumably, when the money rate conformed to the natural rate, one obtained the "normal" rate of interest. The significant divergences, therefore, were those existing between the normal and money rate of interest.[55] Whatever the relationship between the two rates, interest emerged as a return based on the difference in productivity between current land and labor and stored-up resources, with the latter having a higher marginal productivity because it presumably would be less abundant. But in order to assure a constant flow of saving, interest in any time period would have to be the same in all enterprises and in all uses, with the ratio for future land to present land equal to the ratio of future labor to present labor. Any shift in these relationships would change the value of capital and alter the connection between capital goods industries and consumer goods industries.

Assuming an economy of two products, wages, rent, and interest during the production of both goods would have to be equal; interest would be at a maximum at the attained level of rent and wages; existing capital would be adequate for the number of workers and units of land; and the two goods would be so distributed that the ratio of the marginal utilities of what would be consumed equaled the ratio of exchange of the goods concerned.[56] This was a generalized Walrasian equilibrium set-up. But here Wicksell's irrepressible sense of reality got the better of him. The problem was complicated, he conceded, by the existence of hundreds of commodities; land and labor were not homogeneous masses; the type of capital utilized had to be taken into account, nor could such capital really be considered as part of land; commodity production was a complex process in which many firms shared; and the supply of labor was not a fixed factor, but varied rather with certain economic and demographic forces.

Wicksell's monetary theory can be understood best against the background of the great money controversy of the 1890's in Europe and elsewhere, which presaged developments in this area up to the 1930's. Eventually, Swedish views did reach the outside world and were reflected, albeit tangentially, even in Keynes' work. But at the turn of the century, the gold standard had been at the center of discussion. After it had been generally accepted as the best of the standards, falling wholesale prices had stimulated a demand for bimetallism, the gold and silver standard. This now became the focus of attention of both politicians and theoretical experts. In the meantime, the quantity theory of money had been discredited, and the advocates of credit control through banking operations had won out over their opponents, the so-called currency school. Yet Wicksell was not satisfied. It seemed to him that the proponents of the currency school had posed a legitimate question when they stressed excessive note issue as an inflationary factor. Wicksell, interested in achieving a stable price level, thought that interest rate policy could be the means to this end. The effect of interest on economic activity and thus on prices was traced through his noted "cumulative process." This established the impact of banking practice on the price level and provided what was tantamount to a supplementary quantity theory of money, for now the expansion of bank credit played a key role.[57] Previously, changes in individual prices had appeared somewhat unrelated to the general price level, with the result that any connection between money and price theory seemed rather tenuous. But from Wicksell's initial position, it was now possible to set up equations for the supply of producers' goods and consumers' goods as well as for consumption and saving. And this was exactly what was done by Wicksell's followers, such as Erik Lindahl, permitting the development of insights beyond those afforded by the quantity theory. Thus, Wicksell's theoretical structure began to move out of the realm of statics into dynamical analysis.

However, after World War I, Wicksell began to shift ground somewhat.[58] He now thought it possible for a reduction in the money rate of interest to act as a depressant on the real rate, so that the supposed stimulating effects would not occur. Also he began to doubt that maintaining equilibrium between the money rate and the real rate would necessarily stabilize prices. When the argument was made during the war that profit was too great to make the rate of interest an effective control device, one of the pillars of Wicksell's system began to sag. In the ensuing debate, it was repeated again and again that under these circumstances shifts in the money rate of interest could not immediately affect profit, although the corollary argument—that in a situation of plentiful funds outside the banking system an increased rate would have equally little impact—was overlooked. The latter effect, at least in the United States, was not revealed until the late 1930's.

Gradually the view was developed that an expansion of purchasing power, stemming from a rise in price, supplied its own ability to meet these self-same higher prices. There now appeared an intimate relationship between costs and income. Should such a movement begin to cumulate, any rise in the rate of interest might not be able to exert sufficient pressure to control the expansion. The inflationary factors were visible in increased demand for money and in an expectation of even higher prices. Changes in output or perhaps the imposition of sumptuary taxes would not alter the basic drives. Contemporary events have emphasized the cogency of Wicksell's analysis. The cumulative process of price change, either upward or downward, could be traced to a divergence between the real and money rate of interest. Expansion stemmed from a real rate higher than the money rate. Theoretically, all that needed to be done to control the cumulative process was to bring the money rate up to the real one. While this might not restore prices to their original levels, there nevertheless would be a new equilibrium, assuming that stability in the supply and demand for savings could also be achieved at that point. This seemed to come quite close to Keynes' later notion of equilibrium at different heights of economic activity.

Wicksell's monetary theory included not unexpectedly the cash balance approach with some stress on the problem of velocity. There was a close connection between his views and Ricardo's analysis of the relation of the rate of interest to the profitability of borrowing.[59] Wicksell was able to show quite clearly how a rise in commodity prices plus an unchanged supply of money induced either a reduction in demand or a larger supply of goods—the means whereby adjustments in cash balances were effected. Ultimately, Wicksell was concerned with the quantity of money and its exchange value in equilibrium. That is, money was not unlike other commodities, since an increase in its supply varied inversely with value, and moreover in a proportionate way.[60] Like the Austrians, Wicksell viewed money primarily as a medium of exchange, although there were hints that money as a store of value also had some analytic virtues. Certainly this concept seemed to be implicit in the cash balance approach to money.

The major objective was to provide a theoretical underpinning for policy decisions, and, in this sense, Wicksell was pursuing an eminently practical course. Monetary factors, he said, were at the root of changes in the general price level; relative price changes were caused by other elements.

In this sense, the quantity theory touched upon basic truths when it said that close relations did exist between money and the supply and demand for goods. It was the *ceteris paribus* assumptions that introduced doubts into the discussion, for it was clear that production and trade were affected by changes in other parts of the equation. The quantity theory merely needed a bit of filling out, as it were, to make it a useful tool. Aggregate demand and aggregate supply provided the necessary modifications. Price rises resulted, consequently, from excess general demand.[61] Thus money was viewed in both a quantity and turnover sense, with the latter concept related to the desire to hold cash balances. Credit itself helped increase velocity. Nor could money as a store of value be ignored, since this was the basis for holding cash balances. At a given level of prices, the need to hold a certain amount of money per se was not to be overlooked.[62] The desired policy objective was a stable price level, which presumably would show up as general economic equilibrium. But this presupposed that at current prices and wages the total supply of goods and services would equal total demand. That is to say, there would be full employment of resources.[63] Disequilibrium would reveal itself as either excessive demand or a surplus of materials and labor. These shifts might be made more or less permanent by changes in costs or technical input coefficients. That these relationships could be recast into Keynesian terminology now seems self-evident.[64] Wicksell also would have strengthened the institution of monetary control, including open market operations as well as the discount rate. He questioned the need for the gold standard, pointing to the success of the Austrian government with a paper money system. And he suggested that international trade transactions could be settled through clearing arrangements, an idea that found expression years later in the International Monetary Fund. But his constant search for stability and flexibility was something that many students have felt to be unattainable.

Whatever the subtleties worked out by commentators, however, Wicksell's fundamental meaning was clear: the money rate of interest depended in the final analysis on the supply and demand for real capital, and was regulated therefore by profits derived from the use of capital, rather than by the amount of money in circulation. Successful business transactions stimulated the demand for loans which were repaid out of proceeds. But there was also in the latter a "surplus value" corresponding roughly to the loan rate of interest. Interest, therefore, said Wicksell, stemmed not so much from the use of fixed capital, but rather from the free, mobile variety of goods ready to be moved further along the economic line, either into consumption or for more processing. The normal or natural rate was the one at which the demand for loans and the supply of savings corresponded to the expected yield of new capital. Should the expected yield increase, the demand for loan capital would be stimulated. Rates would rise and act as a depressant on further activity. Undoubtedly, Wicksell's analysis was a marked advance over earlier conceptions, for here, at least, was an effective system that combined the theory of price and the theory of money.

The first major criticism of Wicksell's approach came from his friend, David Davidson. While Wicksell had been urging a policy of stable prices to be achieved via the rate of interest, Davidson, on the other hand, suggested that stability might be attained if prices fell in proportion to the increased output stemming from technical advances. If this were to be the normal situation, said Davidson, the money rate of interest and the real rate could remain in their accustomed relations to each other. A reduction in the money rate, he said, might start an inflationary cycle. Wicksell contended, however, that businessmen reacted on the basis of current prices. They might feel, he said, that existing prices would continue in the immediate future, and, under conditions of technological change and exhilarated activity, they actually might find prices rising unless controls were instituted through the interest rate. Any other view, such as Davidson's, assumed that the supply of capital increased with a larger output. Although the debate between the two writers became somewhat confused, it did lead to some clarification of the role of expectations, for it was demonstrated that actions often do depend on what businessmen think will happen to prices. Wicksell's restatement of the idea of the natural rate of interest approached a theory of marginal productivity in a moneyless economy. He insisted that a reduction in the price of technologically improved goods would be counterbalanced by an increased demand for other goods. A permanent reduction in the price level could not be achieved through technological means, he argued, for this was an erratic phenomenon.

The debate on inflation—the actual core of the argument—was reopened by Gustav Åkerman, a pupil of Wicksell's, in 1921. Åkerman expanded the capital theory to include durable items as well as circulating ones.[65] He contended that inflation was impossible if the market and real rate were identical. Saving might reduce the real rate through capital accumulation, said Åkerman, but if the government were to appropriate savings and use them for unproductive purposes as with, say, the issuance of fiat money, then savings will have been sterilized and separated from the private economy. However, an accumulation of cash in the banks could force the money rate of interest to decline while the real rate remained unchanged, creating a situation of forced inflation as distinguished from voluntary inflation caused by reduced bank reserves. Wicksell, however, did not think much of the terms "forced inflation" and "subjective inflation," while Davidson thought that Åkerman's cases were special ones, implying that government borrowing from the central bank would be repaid with new money. Clearly, Åkerman's assumptions were somewhat extreme: the government's need was limited to total saving: new money did not enter the sphere of production; and the issuance of additional money was not balanced by withdrawal of old money. Wicksell's analysis still seemed the better one, for it set forth more clearly than other formulations the notion that monetary policy offered a chance to deliberately institute programs that would benefit everyone and that the economy was not a device which responded automatically to the unconscious needs of just one class—the businessman.[66]

Wicksell's theory, however, was not without its severe critics. In addition to the technical yet friendly strictures of Davidson, others claimed that the concept of the real rate was vague, and that, since it was developed for a natural economy, its applicability was limited. Moreover, the assumptions were said to be basically static. The answer to these charges was that Wicksell was making a first approximation to a money economy. Nevertheless, his opponents insisted that the continued use of the real rate in a money economy never got him away from the "natural" state of affairs. Even for a natural economy a single rate seemed unrealistic, for there were many goods and each ought to have attributed to it its own rate of interest. But this should have created no insuperable logical difficulties, since one of the goods could be made to act as a medium of exchange. In this way, the natural economy was transformed into a money system.

As has been suggested, Wicksell's monetary system was the basis of his "cumulative process." Decreases in the money rate of interest enhanced profitability through a reduction in costs. Expectations of additional gains arose and investment plans were increased, stimulating the demand for factors of production. This increased wages and rent payments, causing a greater demand for consumption goods and compensating for any losses occasioned by higher prices for factor inputs. The whole business, said Wicksell, began mainly in the capital markets.[67] From this area the effects passed over to the consumption goods sector. As one transaction infected another in rapid succession, presumably the upward swing could go on indefinitely. Wicksell, however, made virtually no mention of the turning point, although it is fairly evident that he was aware that the expansion could not be perpetual. Continuously rising prices would require continuously expanding credit, eventually causing heavy pressure on bank reserves and enforcing an increase in interest rates.[68] Furthermore, limitation of available resources would provide its own ceiling on expansion. The system was not by any means an explosive one, for equilibrium would be restored, albeit at another level. However, it was left to others in the Swedish group to work out the sequence in greater detail, as in Erik Lindahl's noted contribution.[69] Wicksell, though, did bring the disequilibrium problem into the center of economic discussion, and, as rough-hewn as it may appear in spots, it was certainly preferable to the older, completely static notions.

Yet when it came to business cycle theory, Wicksell's ideas were not exclusively monetary. In fact, he anticipated Spiethoff's views, asserting that the ultimate cause of an economic crisis rested in real factors.[70] Technical improvements were such, he said, that they did not permit material advances to be as smooth as the expansion of needs. And while he could not deny that the interest rate might play a critical role, he would have rejected the Mises-Hayek contention that egregious credit policies were the sole cause of booms and depressions. Monetary elements were part of the picture only insofar as the money rate of interest was such as to establish a cost of reproduction of capital less than the value of existing capital.[71] But the fact was that the real rate did shift more easily than the money rate, for bankers seldom undertook new courses of action unless impelled to do so by strong outside circumstances. Technology and population growth enforced a more rapid shifting of the real rate, with quick impact on such capital goods industries as steel, railroads, and the like.[72] Again, this was virtually a Keynesian statement of the problem.

Wicksell gave a particularly good presentation of his position on economic crisis in a lecture delivered in 1907 to the Political Economy Club in Oslo.[73] Here he remarked that one could discover the causes of crisis not only in certain external factors but in those internal elements which stemmed from the time it took for these changes to affect business expectations. Overproduction in the sense of a deficiency of effective demand was, he said, a reflection of bad times, not a cause. He questioned whether it were really possible for production to exceed the capacity to consume, for consumption and income grew as well as output. However, he was compelled to admit that there might be lags in these important flows which could lead to upset. Excessive output characterized the downturn and prepared the economy for a recovery by making free mobile capital ready for conversion into the fixed capital forms necessary for expansion. Of special interest in these comments is Wicksell's confession that theory had to be checked by statistical inquiry. Yet he felt that the basic dichotomy was between population growth, which increased consumer demand smoothly and regularly, and technical progress which exhibited marked accelerations and decelerations.[74] Even if production were not subject to diminishing returns, he said, allowance would have to be made for the sporadic impact of new discoveries and inventions. At a meeting in 1924, Wicksell said:

In my opinion there is one particular fact in the human economy which by necessity must produce a disturbance in it. It cannot produce evenly from one year to another so long as there is an increase in population. The increase in population, which goes on all the time, does not only require that the new men get employed like the old, nor is it enough that capital accumulation goes on at the same rate as the increase in population, but it requires in addition—because the large factor nature is unchanged—that there are all the time introduced new methods of production, that is, technical progress goes on. The question then is if this technical progress can proceed according to a curve that increases as smoothly as the curve of the increasing population. It is difficult to escape the conclusion that here must be a certain lack of harmony. . . . The difference between technical progress and human wants causes a jerk in the organism and the jerk is transformed into a wave proceeding in a certain rhythm, because of the structure of the human society itself.[75]

If there were insufficient savings during the upswing, the prosperity phase would be weak, unless outside capital were made available. Oddly enough, Wicksell contended that inventions were depleted during an upswing and accumulated in downward movements, a notion quite contrary to actual business behavior. But this was related to his belief that disposable or mobile forms of capital were accumulated during quiet periods and then converted into fixed forms in more active times. Again, the concept of turning points was defined rather vaguely.[76] The best formulation he could give to this crucial feature was that an insufficiency of credit would cause a collapse of incompleted projects. This might then engender a lack of confidence in the money market and lead to a serious break. Getting out of a depression required making capital available to those engaged in preparing mobile capital for proper conversion into fixed forms.

Despite some curious details, Wicksell's contribution to business cycle theory was profound, for it was an effort to relate investment to the role of money in the economic order. All that it needed were the multiplier and the consumption function to make it a completely useful explanation of what did happen when the economy was in motion. One of the first modern conceptions of how the economic system really worked, it was remarkably insightful. Yet beneath it all was a neo-Malthusian feeling that population increase could very easily outdistance the growth of resources. This was, of course, a serious blind-spot, for it suggested that an expanded or more intensive use of resources was unlikely. Nevertheless, Wicksell felt that given a stable population it still would be necessary to increase the public sector of the economy in order to make the private areas more workable—an idea which most recently has emerged in John Kenneth Galbraith's *The Affluent Society*.[77]

Monopolies, Wicksell thought, should be operated for the public benefit, especially those which exhibited a "natural" character. This might be done, he said, through a combination of a suitable tax program and pricing policies based on marginal unit cost. Prices could be adjusted through trial and error and output expanded in accordance with whatever the elasticity conditions happened to be, up to the point where marginal revenue equalled marginal cost. Deficits could be met through general taxation. These propositions—precisely those set down by Lerner, Lange, Taylor, and others for a socialist economy—indicated that in Wicksell's view the operation of public enterprise for profit was senseless.[78] The present tendency to charge fees covering the full cost of operation in certain public ventures, as in turnpikes and bridges, would have met Wicksell's scorn. Public enterprises, he suggested, should be a means of achieving a better allocation of resources, not to institute indirect taxation. Marginal pricing would increase the use of services so much that a good deal of the basic cost would be covered—clearly a powerful argument for government ownership of such enterprises as railroads and utilities.

Why should the public realm be expanded? Aside from the need for complements to private production there was also the need to provide services for those unable to buy them directly from income. Wicksell had no difficulty in visualizing a situation in which total output would be sufficient, but labor's marginal productivity low. In such circumstances some way would have to be worked out to transfer additional income from rent and interest.[79] In practical terms, this meant more adequate education and scholarships and a genuine social security program.[80]

The regressive character of the tax system in Sweden aroused Wicksell's ire. He urged progressive rates for personal incomes, estates and business, rather than sumptuary taxes, which were, in effect, rationing devices. But he knew that the basis for a better tax structure would have to stem from more democratic political institutions: hence he supported universal suffrage and, while not a socialist, advocated a strong labor movement as essential to a broader democracy.[81] That his ideas would mean the use of tax policies to alter some of the existing property relations did not frighten Wicksell. He saw no reason why monopoly, unearned increments, and inheritance of property could not be dispensed with. Particularly he insisted that the unearned increment on land values should be subject to a special tax.[82] He saw indirect taxation as a device whereby the propertied escaped their just burden, and he spoke out sharply against "capitalistic bolshevism"—the whole set of evil practices which allowed rentiers and entrepreneurs to increase their wealth via inflationary devices. Marginalist analysis could provide adequate guides to a sensible tax program: by comparing the utility of the proposed services with the tax burden that would be incurred, a sound judgment could be worked out. The tax burden itself was related to the marginal utility of income.[83] If the new service were for the general benefit, as in the case of roads, harbors, and other items of social overhead, said Wicksell, it should be supported through taxation derived from "ability-to-pay" sources. If the benefits accrued to but a special segment of the population, the "benefit" principle should rule. Generally, however, he preferred the benefit approach and gave it primacy of position. He felt that there was a greater *quid pro quo* in such a tax philosophy and that it would avoid creating social tension. Moreover, he urged the necessity of planning public expenditures simultaneously with the determination of the means for covering their cost. Wicksell wanted maximum unanimity on tax matters, and he felt that a close linkage of planned expenditures and planned revenues would facilitate agreement. This, of course, was essentially a political problem, for it called for the best possible communication between the various tax interests and the legislature. This meant that there would have to be a just distribution of the burden, since there could hardly be anything like a "just part in an unjust whole." Above all, Wicksell was concerned with the protection of minorities through the utilization of a "qualified majority" in legislative actions. With these arguments he emerged as an advocate of a mixed economy in which society, while moving toward a better use of resources, more equal distribution of income, and higher living standards, would still safeguard the rights of the individual.

Although it may be said justifiably that Wicksell placed too much faith in the efficacy of the money mechanism, there is little doubt that he deserves a place in the pantheon of the truly great creative economists of the modern world. A theoretical master with a touch of genius, his works are continually exerting their profound influence on economists in England, Germany, Italy, Japan, and the United States. His analysis of interest and investment, for example, was an important source for Keynes' own system. In price theory he brought to a high order of elegance ideas that had been making the academic rounds for decades. Marginal productivity theory, which he perfected, was brought into line with capital and price analysis.[84] His Lectures, an incisive treatise for the professional, perhaps a bit abstruse for the student, have been a veritable mine of ideas for the teacher. In monetary theory he anticipated a whole generation of specialists.[85] He was always quick to point to his predecessors, even though his own work was a marked advance over theirs, a trait contrasting vividly with that of Cassel. There was boldness and originality in his books, which are now as important to the economist's tool-kit as those of Alfred Marshall. Although trained in the liberal tradition, he never hesitated to suggest strong government measures if that would raise the level of living just another notch. Much of his analysis was cast in mathematics, but he was quite capable of presenting his ideas in straight verbal form, so that the nonmathematician could see what he was up to. His easy prose was not unrelated to his youthful efforts at verse and drama. Never doctrinaire, he was always receptive to new ideas, examining them most critically in an anxious effort to advance the cause of economic science. For this reason, perhaps, he never felt that his was the definitive answer: the year before he died he confessed that post-war price fluctuations were quite puzzling and hoped that someone would come forward with an authoritative explanation. Honors finally came to him at the age of seventy when a volume of economic studies in homage to him was published in Davidson's journal, Ekonomisk Tidskrift. He was also a recipient of an honorary degree from Oslo and was granted an honorary membership in the American Economic Association.

As might be expected, Wicksell's influence on the Scandinavians was enormous. By the 1930's it was freely acknowledged that he had anticipated much of the modern theory of money, interest, and value, and that his concepts, which could inspire such antipathetic writers as Keynes and Mises, exhibited that rare quality described as seminal. As Schumpeter remarked, in his day there was no finer intellect that graced the field of economics: ". . . he always thought of the subject only and never of himself and what could serve his own best. . . . We trace the vivid flash of constructive imagination, we see the original formulations, the difficulties and doubts such as they presented themselves . . . he gives us more than the actual result; he teaches research itself and points in every line beyond himself." [86]

From the start Wicksell had set a tradition that looked at economic problems in the round. He was interested in total and aggregates and developed theories that provided a basis for macro-analytics. He was concerned with total interest, total consumption, and total investment, and against these magnitudes he set total production and total money and prices. The outcome was a theory in which prices, income, money, and business cycles were effectively integrated.[87] Debates ensued over his details and objectives, but on fundamentals of theory one can only say that Wicksell's work was a remarkable achievement. Only in the area of practical application did Wicksell betray a weakness: his lack of historical sense made it difficult for him to avoid the purely abstract. Yet, by 1921, he felt that those starting to study economics were at a greater advantage, for they now had at their command a collection of factual data with which to work. And his advice to the young economist was to ground himself thoroughly in history.

ii

Gustav Cassel: Economics as Pure Price

The reputation of Gustav Cassel (1886-1944), which was world wide, stemmed from his extensive writing and participation in public affairs. Starting as an engineering student, he later took a degree in mathematics at Uppsala in 1895 and then went on to economics. He worked as a school master before obtaining a post at Stockholm and then produced a book on "labor's right to the product." Ostensibly a criticism of Marxism, it was a vigorous attack on all economics, presaging the maverick of later years who would conduct a life-long campaign against marginalism. Although he lacked the legal qualifications for a professional post, he was advanced as a rival to Wicksell by those who feared the latter's radicalism. As we have noted, they were not successful.[88]

Several years after the incident in connection with the Lund position, Cassel was appointed to Stockholm, despite his lack of a proper university background in economics, and remained there until 1933. Cassel invariably took positions opposed to Wicksell's. He argued, for example, against the latter's views on population, asserting that a nation whose demographic trends were on the decline would be overrun by its neighbors. This, among other things, emphasized Cassel's nationalistic bent. During World War I, he wished for a German victory. It was plain that Wicksell cared for him neither as a person nor as an economist. Davidson's effort to effect a reconciliation came to naught, and an unremitting antipathy continued between them. Cassel did attend a few meetings of the Economists' Club in which Wicksell was quite active, but when the latter attacked him in *Economisk Tidskrift,* that was the end. So far as Wicksell was concerned, Cassel's economics was a thoroughgoing failure. Nor did he think his views on politics or religion any better.[89] Unfortunately, Cassel invited these attacks by his careless scholarship and indiscriminate praise of his own virtues. Such arrogance was not well received in Swedish academic circles, and to such genuine thinkers as Wicksell and Eli F. Heckscher, the noted historian, Cassel seemed but a poseur. Yet the latter did have a keen mind and frequently displayed an enviable facility with factual data. After World War I, he was to be hailed as a leading expert on international money. He exerted a remarkable influence not only on Sweden's monetary policy, but on that of other nations as well. A long flow of articles, reviews, speeches, pamphlets, and commentary came from his pen, most of them appearing in the Swedish newspaper, *Svenska Dagebladt.* He wrote reports for the League of Nations, toured the United States lecturing on money, and offered his views to the House of Representative's Committee on Banking. Many years were spent in fighting for the restoration of the gold standard. Yet with the coming of the depression and the rise of the new economics, Cassel was soon eclipsed. At his death in 1944, his influence was virtually nonexistent. His economics, with its insufferable dogmatisms and self-esteem, simply had not met the requirements of the day.

Cassel's major interests were value theory, money, cycles, and the criticism of socialist doctrine, the latter an activity which he discharged with great relish. His philosophic roots seemed to stem from the Neo-Kantianism of Hermann Cohen and Ernst Cassirer, who had asserted that the purpose of philosophy was to investigate the relationship between logical statements and experience. Thus the logic of relations between scientific statements became all important to inquiry, so that in economics one could dispense with disputations over utility and concentrate on price, which is exactly what Cassel did. In his first major work, *The Nature and Necessity of Interest,*[90]

—a miniature imitation of Böhm-Bawerk—the main theoretical ideas were derived from Walras, to whom he gave but grudging acknowledgment and then only in his early publications, notably the *Elementary Theory of Prices* (1899). Cassel's main opus was the widely read *Theory of Social Economy,*[91] the theoretical content of which was later restated in *Fundamental Thoughts in Economics* and *On Quantitative Thinking in Economics,* two little books which though quite readable added little to his reputation.[92] Terribly anxious to be known as an original thinker, he did influence many, although this was due more to his skill as a teacher and economic journalist than as a theoretician.

Cassel believed that he was placing economics on an entirely new foundation. The science, he stated, must deal only with measurable quantities. But simply to apply mathematics would be foolish, for it was essential first to clarify underlying concepts.[93] Certain rules were necessary to accomplish this: making a scientific analysis prior to defining one's terms; moving slowly from the elementary and simple to the advanced and complex; establishing universal rather than restricted conclusions; emphasizing economic rather than technical problems; analysing the "social" rather than the private economy; and creating a fixed measure of economic activity, that is, a stable monetary unit. By "social," Cassel meant the whole economic order in which production could be visualized as a continuous process. He implied that the economist had much to learn from the practical businessman (although present-day writers assert that the reverse is more essential.)[94] Yet economists, admitted Cassel, were more apt to seek an overview of the entire economy, something for which the average businessman had neither time nor predilection. Only the total view permitted exploration beyond the external form, frequently the only one visible to a busy practical man of affairs.

At times Cassel seemed to feel that economic activity functioned in a world of its own, distinct from the organizations and institutions that comprised its framework. This was evident in his assertion that the job of economics was to examine the degree to which its course could be distinguished from its noneconomic background. He was certain that this would enable him to reach generally valid conclusions for all "social economies" without regard to the external structure of society.[95] Unfortunately, the formulation was so vague, that the method that Cassel intended to use in his analysis had to be displayed in the equations he *talked* about, rather than set forth in any precise way. He deplored the use of political power as a way of effecting social change. Presumably, he felt that growth would take place by slow accretion. Such *obiter dicta* were patently useless in a time when the only major social and economic changes accomplished were through the exercise of political power.

Despite his self-deception, Cassel's method was no different from the traditional one. Beginning with a static analysis he followed this with the notion of a uniformly progressive system which would, by virtue of its very motion, transform itself into a dynamic one. Deduction was employed in the static and uniformly progressive states, whereas induction based on empirical material was needed for trends, deviations, and lags. One of the supposed virtues of this quite stale procedure was to make interest not an agio on transactions between present and future goods, but a "regulator of the continual social economy standing in closest connection with the rates of progress of that economy and serving both to maintain a certain degree of saving and to limit the demand for the available savings." [96]

Cassel's rejection of the notions of value and utility was complete and thoroughgoing. Even marginalist analysis was derided as misleading—a rather surprising statement for one trained in mathematics. So far as he was concerned, money was the only genuine standard of value, and, since utility made no room for it, the latter would have to be discarded. Money was the center of economic activity, said Cassel, and any theory about man's activity that might be constructed would have to stand four square on this fact. A special theory of value was redundant. All that was necessary was price: this had added virtues in that it simplified the analysis, anyway.[97] The significant fact being explored, said Cassel, was the relationship of one good to the next, or relative price.[98] The true basis for economic science, therefore, was a general theory of *price,* not value. Marginal changes in utility were particularly puzzling and ultimately unreal, he continued, since comparability of feelings and psychological satisfactions were impossible to establish. It was also impossible to define utility. Although Wicksell thought this objection well grounded, Cassel's other comments on marginalism only made the older man furious. The "principle of scarcity," which to Cassel was an instrumental concept, asserted, after the fashion of Walras, that demand was set once the whole system of prices could be established.[99] This structure had no need for utility or value, insisted Cassel, especially since the marginal utility of a good did not necessarily equate itself to price. The degree of utility, on the other hand, depended on the nature of demand and its intensity. But the most telling point was Cassel's charge of circular reasoning, for prices were being employed to measure marginal utility, he said, when the very aim of the theory was to uncover the way in which price was formed.[100]

There was, however, a hint of the theory of imputation in Cassel, although it was not developed in any sharp degree. As might be expected, he rejected marginal productivity just as sharply as utility, again on the grounds of tautological reasoning.[101] Marginal productivity, he said, could not be considered a factor in pricing or distribution because the relative quantities used in a given productive process were in a very deep sense functions of the price structure. Properly visualized, both price and production were the unknowns to be determined by analysis, hence marginal productivity was also an unknown. Furthermore, the idea of marginal productivity made sense only in a situation where there was continuous employment of input factors, that is, where discontinuities were entirely absent. Said Cassel: ". . . marginal productivity can be constructed only in those cases where the amount of a factor of production can be varied continually and where the product itself may be regarded as a continuous function of this variable factor." [102] Such conditions were most unlikely, he said, not without justice. Also, how did one apply the concept to complex processes, when its logic, such as it was, had meaning only for the production of a single good? [103] It goes without saying that for Cassel marginalism had no application in distribution any more than it did in the realm of price. The "scarcity principle" established how the product would be shared among the input factors: the relative scarcity of inputs in proportion to the indirect demand determined distribution—a rather long-winded way of saying that scarcity determined the prices of the factors of production. This position, repeated in the discussion of wages, was restated even more forcefully in his *On Quantitative Thinking in Economics*.[104]

The wages fund concept, continued Cassel, illustrated what was wrong with traditional economics. Based as it was on the experience of a single entrepreneur (to whom it might easily appear that his capital was really providing sustenance for the labor he hired), it failed to explain the broad social-economic aspect of the problem. The fact was, said Cassel, that total production supported everybody in society. Thus, the period of production was an "impossible" concept, for the satisfaction of a want required a whole series of productive efforts spread over many time periods. That is to say, production was a continuous process with no beginning and no end. It remained unchanged, with a steady output of goods which might be subject, however, to variation in quantity.[105] This was the only proper abstraction in economic analysis. A specific time period, therefore, had little meaning for the study of economic movement. Cost of production also had no meaning for Cassel, any more than the idea of an average period of production, which, he argued, attempted to compare different items—overlooking the fact that his own price theory should have provided a basis for conversion to common measurement. Indeed, some of his concepts bordered on the mystical, as when he insisted that from the social standpoint real capital was an "external" phenomenon: once invested it was forever committed. To analyse capital properly, he insisted, one had to compute the ratio of capital to income,[106] and it was more than likely that it would be constant.

Although Cassel's concept of continuous production might have suggested that time was a significant factor, the whole matter was dropped after paying the notion some lip service. As a result neither capital nor interest was related to time factors, as the Austrians had attempted to do, and the exchange features of the economy were introduced *de nuovo,* without much tie to the process of production. Monetary features were easily tacked on to the edifice by making one good the medium of exchange.[107] Suddenly the whole focus on capital shifted to the concept of a sum of money which, for the *time being,* was incorporated in concrete capital, but which might assume another form through sales on the market. Cassel then ventured on a long disquisition on capital which culminated in the distinction between formal and abstract capital. Obviously, he was struggling to clarify the notion of capital as fluid fund and as a collection of embodied goods. In this regard, he was midpoint between the Austrian and the American economists and could enjoy the best of both worlds.

Insofar as income was concerned, said Cassel, the distinction between it and capital was not a sharp one. Of course, this view was entirely understandable when production was deemed to be a continuous business, for only the human need to break this process into artificial periods made it necessary to create an income concept. Yet even Cassel could not deny the usefulness of the idea. Normally, he implied, production adjusted itself to the division of income between saving and consumption. He objected, however, to use of the word *investment,* alleging that the action it described was already implicit in the income concept and in the behavior of banks which gathered the saving of many persons and put them to work in industry.[108] He acknowledged the importance of the division between consumption and saving, however, for changes in their proportions did have profound effects on the structure of production. At this point one might think that Cassel would have pursued real factors, but this was not the case. He resorted instead to monetary causation, attributing virtually all changes in the savings pattern to changes in the rate of interest and to the reaction that central banks might have to altered circumstances.

Cassel's "monetary" definition of income was at best cumbersome. It included the total value of goods used in consumption plus any net additions to capital. This led to the proposition that total income just sufficed to pay for total real consumption and the "surplus value" of land and capital. Income stemmed from the remuneration of the factors of production, and so was equal to the total remuneration of the cooperating input factors. This must be sufficient to purchase the total product and, in fact, to exhaust it.[109] As a consequence of this perfect circular system, saving could not have a really constricting effect. The truth of this proposition could be seen, said Cassel, if consumption and saving, as well as production, were visualized as continuous, everlasting processes. If really long periods were taken into account, increases in income proportionate to increases in capital would promote stability. In connection with this discussion, Cassel arrived at his famous statement that capital grew 3 per cent a year.[110] Later on, he used his income and capital concept to counteract Keynesian thinking, which, of course, was quite false in his lexicon. Saving did not render any part of purchasing power inoperative, he exclaimed, for nothing in the economic structure would reduce purchasing power in relation to total production. (While this comment preceded automation, Cassel was not unfamiliar with rationalization; but then he believed that technological improvements would always create more jobs.) Keynesian theory, he averred, confused the means of payment with real purchasing power; the depression was simply a monetary phenomenon, hence the English economist's concern with effective demand was misleading! [111] (This, incidentally, was not unrelated to the Hayek-Mises position.) Yet all the manipulation of the early New Deal in the United States should have indicated to Cassel that monetary factors were insufficient. After 1940 real factors stemming from war production went to work in such a way as to suggest that it was Keynes who had been right after all.

Cassel, who had decided quite early in his career that only price was important, set forth this view in his first important book and later reiterated it in virtually everything he published.[112] He was almost bitterly determined to do away with value theory and cast economics into a new mold. Value, he claimed, referred to undefined psychological processes which for a scientist interested in precision were not very helpful. Economics could dispense with it easily.[113] In fact, some benefit might emerge from such drastic surgery, he said, for now it would be possible to integrate monetary theory with price. Value anyway was nothing more than a hypothetical price. Economics thus would become a science ". . . dealing with quantities and their relations to one another and with conditions of equilibrium between forces that must be conceived quantitatively." [114] In one sense, Cassel was applying a sort of Occam's razor. The theory of value itself was ambiguous. Was it utility or relative exchange or command over goods? If utility, then the units of measurements were indefinite. For Cassel this demonstrated with virtual certainty that one should start and end discussions in economics with price without deviating from this precise guide, for it was literally imbedded in the exchange economy. When starting with a theory of value, one simply betrayed an unconscious desire to return to some initial point in a natural, moneyless economy. Money, he insisted, had always existed: all societies have had some medium of exchange. "There has never existed in the history of human life a society normally dependent upon the exchange of goods without the use of money," said he firmly.[115] Analysis must simply start with a fixed and invariable unit of exchange which would logically and inevitably lead to a theory of price—there was no other way to develop the quantitative approach. He was careful, however, to avoid offering pure mathematics as a panacea; in fact, he implied that the mathematical approach might be a handicap in hands less skillful than his. Primarily, he was concerned with stating concepts clearly, and he would have preferred to do without such notions as Ricardo's cost of production, Marx's surplus value, and Böhm-Bawerk's agio.

What was Cassell's price principle? The ". . . price fixing process," said he, "is determined by the conditions which apply to it, and all the prices are then fixed, and fixed simultaneously. The social-economic work of this general price fixing process is. . . the realization of the general economic principle in the exchange economy." [116] Since what one buys is a function of price, Cassel posited the theory that demand was not determined until the prices of all goods had been established. To all intents and purposes, this was a literal translation from Walras, yet not once in the *Social Economy* did Cassel so much as mention his illustrious predecessor. In the *Quantitative Thinking* he virtually claimed personal credit for the "discovery" of the idea of general equilibrium.[117] Wicksell, of course, was not one to let this oversight slip by, and he took his rival to task for it.

Imbedded in Cassel's price theory was the notion of the "scarcity principle," one of his pet phrases, which was intended to reveal how the limited supply of goods coupled with insatiable wants made it essential that demand be restricted in some way. Here price began to play a central role, for its major task was to limit demand until equilibrium with supply had been achieved. In the case of capital, this rationing function was carried out by the rate of interest which imposed a balance between the demand for capital and scarcity. When men act in consonance with this principle, said Cassel, they follow a proper economic course without resort to any ethical precepts. This was the key to economic behavior.[118] What Cassel had done was to proceed from price to supply and demand. Price for him was an organizing principle rather than the outcome of market forces. In fact, it was an active force itself: ". . . it is the object of prices to restrict the demand for any particular article [so] that the supply shall be adequate to the demand." [119]

There was also a concept of demand elasticity in Cassel's system, but it lacked the precision found in most good textbooks today. Yet he knew that elasticity of demand, the way in which demand shifted as a result of price change, was important, especially in such situations as public utility rate determination. The "scarcity principle," which he imagined a great contribution to economic science, was, however, more important. By it, economic activity per se was stressed as being central to the social economy: that scarcity and the fact of exchange was all the economist needed to know. All the other great problems—value and distribution—were not so much avoided as simply done away with.

The scarcity principle, however, did not seem to cover all situations. And even Cassel recognized that as it lacked true generality, it became necessary to add supplementary ones. The first, the differential principle, explained variations in price when a good was produced by several firms not in the same cost situation, with the result that some might earn a "differential" profit. This was formulated in a way reminiscent of Ricardo's differential rent. Cassel still had to employ classical ideas in spite of his self-proclaimed determination to be original. The second of the supplementary rules concerned falling average cost and suggested that when increased output reduced average cost, price would have to follow suit. The third, the principle of substitution, advised that of several alternative methods of production, the one with the lowest cost ought to be employed. All of this involute discussion, consequently, reduced itself to little more than an attempt to relate the pricing mechanism to the cost of production. Cassel did not realize how closely he was approaching the British classicists whom earlier he had so disdainfully dismissed. As one reviews these concepts one cannot help but feel that Wicksell's criticism was fully justified.[120] The substitution idea appeared salvageable only if one could assume a measure of fluidity in the factors of production. Such a notion underlies the theory of linear programming, the recent mathematical technique which calculates just how factor proportions might be combined to obtain the highest output at the lowest cost in a given productive effort.[121]

Cassel's analysis was not only cumbersome, but frequently imprecise. Cost of production remained a significant part, while contradictions were many. He noted that a firm could stay in business even if it merely recaptured prime costs.[122] Yet, as we have already indicated, the structure was essentially Walrasian. After postulating the need for a set of simultaneous equations, Cassel proceeded to conditions of variable supply. Production functions, or "technical coefficients," were fixed. Now, the principle of scarcity required that there be a price for each factor input as well as for finished articles. The equations followed from the definitions: the demand for each good was a function of its price and all other prices. Supply, on the other hand, was a function not only of price but of quantity as well. If knowledge of the means of production was substituted into the production function, it became possible to establish a single relationship between supply and the prices of the factors themselves. The interrelationships of the various equational systems thus made it possible not only to solve the pricing problem but to establish that factor returns were income as well as costs and represented the source from which the demand for goods stemmed.[123] That is to say, the price of each good equaled the sum of the prices of the input factors employed in its production, and the total supply of the factors equaled the total quantity used in production. The prices of finished goods were related to the prices of factors. At each price there was a certain supply of factors and a certain demand for goods as well as for input factors. One of the price combinations was at equilibrium. There was, in other words, a unitary theory of production and distribution that could be made available in this way, for with prices established at a given level, the pattern of distribution was also set. At the center of this complex sat the entrepreneur who bought the inputs, sold the outputs, and coordinated everything.

Wicksell complained that Cassel's construction had omitted the savings-investment problem, and that the whole business consequently was static. The flow of income was in no way related to investment, nor were leakages from income taken into account. Further, by not considering capital as a factor of production in its own right, so that the demand for it could be made part of the analytical apparatus, Cassel overlooked the relation between expected yield and current cost. The outcome was to make interest merely the price for available capital.[124] Other criticisms pointed out that Cassel confused accounting prices with money prices. Consequently, the commodity equations in the early sections of the first parts of the *Social Economy* could not be fully valid for the concrete economic order to which Cassel later referred.[125]

Cassel's concern with problems of interest and capital had been evinced early in his career with the publication of his book *The Nature and Necessity of Interest*. Beginning with a long introductory discourse on doctrinal history, quite in the central European tradition, predecessors were chided for having followed the path of error, and Böhm-Bawerk especially came in for heavy attack. The agio concept was dismissed as essentially ambiguous and for having added little by its stress on the idea of an exchange between present and future.[126] Cassel was convinced that interest was simply a price paid for a certain object or service. Only in this way, he contended, was it at all possible to reveal the supply and demand aspect of interest; Böhm-Bawerk's "three grounds" were incapable of doing this. But Cassel himself did not get very far with his statement that interest was a price paid for "waiting" or the use of capital, with the latter defined as the "independent and elementary" factor of production [127]—a rather primitive concept. Moreover, when he said that interest merely expressed actual economic conditions and that it was therefore unnecessary to know what it should be, he reduced the whole affair to a simple matter of the supply and demand for loans. This was tied to the problem of waiting for the services which durable goods were able to provide.[128] Waiting was said to be an essential economic element, for production in the technical sense involved the expenditure of time. It was, in effect, synonymous with capital and therefore a factor of production. To measure waiting we need but multiply a certain sum of money by time. But all this appeared to be little more than verbal display, for Cassel still was skipping along the surface of economic reality. The absence of subtlety and genuine insight was fairly patent. Böhm-Bawerk, for all his prolixity, clearly had been the superior thinker.

As population increased, the demand for "waiting" was met by normal capital growth.[129] Captial saving devices reduced the demand for waiting. Generally, however, there was a continuous upward movement in capital demand, said Cassel, which could be further stimulated by a low rate of interest.[130] An important distinction was made between capital saved at rates higher than 3 per cent and that saved at lower rates. The argument was that changes in low rates could cause sharp reactions in the amount of capital to be saved. Saving with high rates was ostensibly conditioned by existing resources, but as the rate of interest declined, the capitalist would save less and the middle class more.[131] The former was concerned with an even stream of income, so that a lower rate would stimulate capital consumption. However, the assertion that increased saving by the middle class would counterbalance the decreased saving of the capitalists did not appear realistic.

At this point Cassel introduced an interesting problem seldom explored—the relation of saving to the length of life. The shortness of human life allegedly placed a limit on low interest rates, for this obviated the need to save too long to maintain a constant income stream.[132] It was thus unlikely that the rate of interest would fall much below 3 per cent, since this would only stimulate the consumption of capital. This implied that savings under a 3 per cent rate were elastic in response to changes in the rate of interest, while they tended to be inelastic above that. The fall in the rate of interest below 3 per cent allowed security holders to increase their money revenues by converting investments into annuities. This was another way of saying that a reduction in interest rates led to capital consumption as a way of maintaining a given level of money expenditure which in turn could reduce the supply of capital.[133] Such tendencies were reinforced at a time when a large quantity of capital was held by older persons. A longer period of life would counteract this influence and make more capital available. But where the largest proportion of capital is held by institutions and corporations with an indefinite length of life, the argument would seem to collapse. Further, the major concern of individual savers may be prompted not so much by the urge for a steady income as by a desire to give their children a start in life. Such motives do not appear to be related to the rate of interest.

Nevertheless, for Cassel saving was the source of capital or of waiting. Among the older economists, he said, the notion that saving was a deduction from income, including wage income, had tended to create the impression that there was a wage fund advanced by the capitalist. But, continued Cassel, there was no such thing in a continuously functioning economy. There existed rather a steady stream of goods, some partly finished, some completed. Savers had a claim against a portion of this stream: this was interest. Workers also had a claim in the form of wages. Both together comprised consumption. It seemed that Cassel was fumbling here toward a flow analysis, only to bog down in some rather turgid prose. Suddenly real capital was not the significant factor, but rather capital disposal. Yet despite the shifting of terms and definitions, the entire analysis remained little more than an ordinary supply and demand description.

Cassel's long discussion of rent added little to the development of this phase of distribution theory. He opposed Ricardo's formulation with the contention that rent was really part of the cost of production.[134] But considerable confusion arose in his handling of the distinction between rent as contractual payment and as analytic concept. The rule of scarcity, the central principle of the whole structure, determined rent, which so far as he could see, was merely the price for the services of land. Of course, this statement was virtually self-evident, as Wicksell had conceded; [135] but the assertion that Ricardo had failed to account for differences in capital and labor on different parcels of land was simply wrong. Further, the suggestion that the value of the product could be increased by reducing the quantity of land in operation revealed a compromise between the ideas of increasing and decreasing returns.

Wage theories were characterized as either pessimistic or optimistic, and, as might be expected, Cassel rejected the former, illustrated mainly by Ricardian theory. Their basic error was revealed by the continual rise in both wages and the standard of living.[136] The wages fund was attacked, as indicated above, because in addition to other shortcomings, it suggested a periodicity in economic life, which in reality was nonexistent. Marginal productivity, admittedly an "optimistic" type of theory, was also false, since the marginalist principle was not an objective element in the price equation.[137] As was the case with the other factors of production, wages were simply a a price determined by relative scarcity. The latter was to be viewed from the standpoint of the demand for a factor and this in turn depended on the quantity of work to be done. Now, while labor was a major factor in production, the other being waiting, there were many different types of labor. This complicated matters considerably and required that labor as a factor of production be viewed as command over a certain kind of ability during a given time period.[138] The price for this power or disposal over work was wages, averred Cassel. Again, this was little more than ordinary supply and demand, and, as such, was quite confused, for the income of the worker, said Cassel, included something in addition to "wages." Just what this was he did not specify, but wages and income were deemed to be different magnitudes.[139] This, of course, would be true if the worker held stocks and other securities, but Cassel did not seem to have this in mind.

Low wages, then, could be explained by the presence of surplus labor. In the second edition of the *Social Economy,* Cassel expressed his support of rationalization in industry and regretted that union monopolies, tariffs, and government aid to the unemployed were setting barriers to efficiency.[140] His conservative bias was further illustrated by the assertion that supplementing low wages was not as good as encouraging self-reliance.[141] He hoped that labor could become a more fluid factor of production by urging free movement across borders. Cassel was quite right on this point, at least in a general sense, as was later emphasized by Gunnar Myrdal.[142] But not unexpectedly, he apportioned the major blame to the trade unions which were seeking to create "monopolies" within their own borders. This was a basic cause of unemployment, since the high wage objectives of the trade unions made demand fall below supply, leading in virtually automatic fashion to unemployment. Cassel's solution was to put more workers into agriculture and to depress the wages of the industrial worker. He did not seem to realize that the latter would have to be done by fiat, since in market terms the two devices appear clearly contradictory. The only legitimate reason for limiting migration would be the ". . . natural desire to protect a good and pure race from being mixed up with elements which, even if good in themselves, would have a pernicious influence on the future of the race." [143]

The scarcity principle also determined the value of money through the relative lack of valid means of payment. But this concept was just as static as the rest of Cassel's system. The basic monetary unit was fixed and invariable, and, in a sense, merely existed so that prices could be determined by the set of general equilibrium equations. Cassel thought this represented an integration of monetary and price theory; but if this were so, it was only mechanical. The monetary side was essentially a restatement of the quantity theory in which general prices were affected by the volume of money in circulation. But it was never clear whether Cassel wanted to relate the value of money to banking policy or to base it on the relation of total currency in circulation to the underlying gold unit and the degree of convertibility.

Cassel did achieve a measure of fame by his study of the quantitative relation of gold to the price level. After comparing wholesale prices between 1850 and 1910 with the stocks of gold, he asserted that the level of prices was about the same at both dates. This was said to have been due to a regular and steady increase in gold stocks at an annual rate of 2.8 per cent. When prices rose, this was occasioned by an excessive increase in gold, as in the period 1896 to 1914; the downward movement of 1873 to 1896 was caused by gold shortages. Price stability, therefore, might be assured by a positive relationship of gold to economic growth. Unless this were done, Cassel asserted, it would be difficult to maintain the price level on an even keel.[144] If this relationship did not develop, it would be necessary to have recourse to central bank reserves. However, Cassel overlooked the known fact that for a good part of the nineteenth century silver had been more important than gold. In addition, the periods he chose to illustrate his argument seem to have been special ones, for these were particularly the years in which the use of gold had increased. Cassel's case was weakened further by the situation in retail prices where there was a good deal less stability at the time than in wholesale prices. It was also possible to argue that the causal relation had been from prices to gold production rather than the other way around.[145]

Cassel also sought to connect gold and monetary policy to interest and saving. The scarcity principle, that is, the way demand adjusted to price, made the idea of an insufficiency of income for saving purposes illogical. The exhaustion of investment was deemed inconceivable, for savers would simply have to supply the necessary capital. If there was to be any hoarding, monetary policy, including the creation of new money, could rectify matters. The obvious contradictions in these views did not trouble Cassel. Monetary manipulation and changes in bank rates would cure the world's ills. Even a free paper standard could be made to yield salutary effects; but the best measure of all, after World War I, would have been to return to the gold standard. Redolent of Victorianism, the disastrous impact of such a policy was forcefully exposed by Keynes in the 1920's. Cassel could only assert that gold remonetization had failed because the rate of exchange did not correspond to the internal purchasing power of the various countries—a problem more severe than the sticky flow of capital in international trade.

But if many of Cassel's ideas were questionable, a large part of his business cycle analysis did seem fairly useful. Quite early in his career he had noted the periodicity of commercial crises and wondered how such movements could be distinguished in the light of political upsets, monetary disturbances, tariffs, government intervention, and the growth of monopolies. The economic system, he thought, would not exhibit any disturbances were it not for such extreme factors. Yet he did acknowledge that upsets could stem from technical change and from the situations engendered by a shift from primitive or feudal economies to a more complex order. The influence of Arthur Spiethoff and Tugan-Baranovsky seemed evident when he pointed to iron output and coal production as important measures of cycles. Said he: "A period of advance is one of special increase in the production of fixed capital; a period of decline, or a depression, is one in which this production falls below the point it had reached." [146] A bit later he added: ". . . change from periods of advance to periods of decline is in its innermost nature a variation in the production of fixed capital, but is not directly connected with the rate of production." [147] The demand for additional workers occasioned by increased output was met from the pool of the unemployed, which frequently was drawn from an excess of agricultural workers. Such a movement in the work force reflected the changing structure of the economy.[148] The boom phase, a period of growth, hastened the shift of labor from agriculture to industry, and also hastened the development of the capital goods industries. During such times the rate of growth was frequently above the "normal rate," an idea that was to be developed in the post-Keynesian era by Roy Harrod and Evsey Domar. The notion of the accelerator also was implicit in Cassel's discussion, particularly in his assertion that a drop in consumer demand would cause a decline in the output of consumer goods and an eventual halt in the producers' goods industries dependent on them. In analyzing the British shipbuilding industry, for example, he remarked that,

". . . slight deviations from the steady proportional rise are enough to cause grave disturbances in the shipbuilding industry. There seems, therefore, to be little prospect of attaining a perfectly regular activity not exposed to any [cyclical change] in the sphere of the capital-producing industries." [149]

The boom's turning point came with an increased scarcity of capital, which was reflected back on the rate of interest. Now, at certain yields a low rate of interest would suggest a high capital value. As the demand for capital rose there ensued upward pressure on interest rates, which in turn caused the value of capital to fall. As the yield fell below the rate of interest, an inhibiting effect on the production of fixed capital was created. The boom was converted into a depression. However, Cassel was vague as to which was the initial cause—the change in the rate of interest or the alterations in the value of fixed capital. He did insist that there was no capital saturation at the upper turning point. Investment opportunities, he contended, were always ample, so that a decline in the prospective yield of capital was not the major consideration. The doubts and hesitations of the moment were caused rather by increases in interest rates. What this meant was not overproduction but a shortage of capital and, naturally, of savings, all reflected in the inability to complete projects already undertaken.[150] Such capital shortages were always obscured by the way in which the banking system increased the supply of money during the prosperous upswing. That is to say, there was a discrepancy between money flows and production.

The business cycle, said Cassel, did not peter out, but continually repeated itself because that was the price we had to pay for progress. No other way existed to secure the new technologies, new industries, and new resources which spelled a progressive economy. These supplied the external shocks, without which the cyclical movements would slowly disappear. In its internal mechanism, consequently, there was nothing in capitalism to cause the boom and prosperity sequence. It all was due to external nudges. As Alvin Hansen has observed, there was almost an econometric character to the theory. Inventions, economic expansion of new regions, and population growth led to bursts of fresh investment, causing capital goods prices to rise above initial costs. New capitalization at higher rates of interest developed later, leading to a decline in the value of fixed capital. Consonant with this, there might be a rise in the cost of fixed capital, reducing the margin between the value and cost of equipment. All this, accompanied by various lags in the responses of businessmen, accounted in large measure for the recurrent upswings and downturns. Cassel's analysis, unfortunately, was seldom clear: if new opportunities were always present why didn't growth simply continue? Also, how inducements to invest died out was somewhat fuzzy. Was the rate of interest really so potent? Were external shocks the sole source of economic motion? Despite the numerous statistics and the occasional insightful perceptions, the whole analytic structure collapsed in vast indecision.

Another area in which Cassel exerted considerable influence was in international trade theory. Here too he was basically a nineteenth-century thinker. In a 1934 lecture, he saw the world's ills stemming from protectionist policies, although he insisted that he was not a dogmatic free trader.[151] Monetary disequilibrium was a major contributing factor to these ills, for it prevented the natural processes of recovery from accomplishing their full effects. The "deflation" which had manifested itself in the United States beginning in 1928 had caused a halt to capital export and imposed credit restrictions on domestic trade. This forced prices to decline and led to widespread debt liquidation. The ensuing protectionist policies which attempted to build defensive Chinese walls were of no avail as the economic disease spread from country to country. In fact, quotas, control measures, and restrictions merely intensified the depression. The increase in autarchy destroyed the international division of labor and reduced world production. The gold standard, which had worked so well through the principle of purchasing power parity, was abandoned. Wage rates could no longer adjust themselves to the inflow and outflow of currency between nations. Protectionist policies entangled the government in private affairs and inevitably led to a planned economy. But this was bound to create even more problems, for such an economy could not allocate incomes between saving and consumption with any degree of efficiency. As socialist ideas gained ground, faith in the automatic functioning of the economy was forever lost.

Cassel had a solution for this urgent problem: the establishment of "normal" rates of exchange, so that prices, wages, and costs could adjust themselves to these rates and thus represent the true purchasing power parity of currency. Only in this way would a reliable basis for international economic equilibrium be attained. Although the purchasing power parity notion was no new invention, Cassel's effective publicist activity on its behalf did make it appear as his. But the theory dated back to John Wheatley who had offered a fairly clear exposition in 1803. As early as 1916 Cassel had advocated a theory of international economic relationships based upon a quantitative tie between the average price levels of the nations involved. He argued that under conditions of normal trade, a rate of exchange was established which reflected the relationships of the purchasing power of the respective currencies. Where prices advanced in one country, the adjustment in the rate of exchange would be such as would make the new rate equal to the old one multiplied by the quotient between the "degrees of inflation" of the countries concerned. That is, the ratio of the purchasing power of the different countries set the new rate of exchange. Cassel developed the theory mainly in terms of paper money and suggested that stable exchange rates might be maintained by influencing the internal price levels through credit and monetary policies. With purchasing power parity in effect, no one country would have an advantage over others. If a nation possessed few resources, there still would be some rate of exchange at which it could trade.[152] Such inequalities could be strong enough to overcome transportation costs, for it was these differences, said Cassel, based on variations in the primary factors of production, production functions, and demand that make up the motive drive for international trade. The objective of trade was to equalize differences.[153] Purchasing power parity became, in effect, a causal statement as well as a description of relationship. Exchange rates were determined by relative price levels and ultimately, of course, by the omnipresent principle of scarcity.

The theory, however, ought to have applied to the gold standard as well as to paper currencies. Granted that the range of movement would be restricted by the gold points, there should have been sufficient area for the relative demands of two countries for each other's goods to alter price levels.[154] But this criticism, which revealed the limited nature of the theory, did not shake Cassel: he sought to rescue it by talking of *general* price levels and goods in international trade abstracted from transportation and tariffs. This, of course, reduced the whole proposition to a useless truism. The only relationship required in international trade became that between the prices of the various goods which actually did enter into trade channels. In seeking to buy other currencies, we do not obtain a generalized purchasing power, but one for specific goods. The general price level is not relevant to this problem. Further, not only must transport costs and tariffs be taken into account, but the possibility of monetary conversion into other currencies as well. The fact of the matter was simple enough: there was no need for the internal purchasing power of a nation to equal its external purchasing power.[155]

With so much of his writing quickly dated, one wonders why Cassel need be considered important. Yet, he did have a widespread influence, particularly after World War I. But he also had numerous critics. It was charged that far from destroying value theory, his rejection of it had been merely a verbalism that utterly failed to exorcise this personal devil.[156] His attempt to price the factors of production was in essence a matter of imputation, despite his heroic fight against the Austrian doctrine. In large measure quite unoriginal, he was given to hasty judgments, as in his misreading of Ricardo. Spiritually he was in full harmony with nineteenth century British liberalism. An empiricist and an individualist in philosophy,[157] this more than anything else exposed his inability to escape the problem of value. Had he been willing to listen to someone other than himself he might have come to appreciate this failing.

It was Cassel's interpretations of economic affairs that earned him a large following. His frequent reports and articles in the Swedish press brought him a reputation as a realist. And in many ways this did direct Swedish students to practical applications of economic analysis and helped them to avoid entanglements with theoretical scholasticism. If Cassel was far from being as careful and scholarly as some of his contemporaries, his influence nevertheless was as far-reaching.

iii

David Davidson: Swedish Ricardian

The third of the founders of Swedish economics, David Davidson (1854-1942), was truly a cloistered scholar. Entering Uppsala at the age of seventeen, he remained there until his death, aged eighty-eight. In his youth he travelled on the Continent for awhile, mainly to study, and for a short time lived in Stockholm, but aside from these brief wanderings, Davidson's life was rooted in the University. His family, a large one, was of German-Jewish ancestry. The father had built a modest fortune based upon trade, but between parents and son there seems to have been little in common. Once he had left for the University, Davidson seldom returned home. Yet, his father had been no simple merchant: an accomplished Biblical scholar, he taught himself Hebrew and conducted a world-wide correspondence with rabbis and other Bible students.[158]

Davidson soon revealed a penchant for economic theory, demonstrating a remarkable ability to follow an abstract line of reasoning to whatever conclusion it might lead—a trait that both Walter Bagehot and Alfred Marshall thought to be especially characteristic of Jews.[159] Davidson's well-known admiration for Ricardo grew slowly but not until his later work did he come to acknowledge the Englishman as a master. Unfortunately, little of Davidson's output has been published outside Sweden, which may have been due to his primary concern with purely national problems. Indeed, he showed little interest in an international exchange of ideas, an attitude which he may have acquired from Uppsala where foreign affairs received but small attention.

Davidson taught economics at the law faculty, a common arrangement in Sweden. No stranger to the legal profession, he had been trained in it, taught civil law, and for a short time served as a magistrate. This experience sharpened his interest in public finance and it was not long before he became Sweden's leading scholar in this field. Lecturer at the age of twenty-five, acting professor a year later, and full professor by the time he was thirty-five, his progress up the academic ladder was rapid. Up to 1901, when Wicksell finally received his appointment at Lund, Davidson was the only economics professor in Sweden. Not until 1919 did he retire from active teaching.

Davidson's first book, *Laws of Capital Accumulation* (1878), a short work on capital formation, attracted no little attention in international circles and, in the strictest sense, made him the founder of Swedish economics. This little volume anticipated some of Böhm-Bawerk's ideas on capital and interest. As was the case with so many nineteenth-century writers, he had to demonstrate his knowledge of the tradition, so that the approach was mainly historical. Although British writers were not excluded, major attention was given to the Germans—Menger, Kniès, Mangoldt, and even Marx—revealing how much closer the Swedes felt themselves to continental writers than to the English classicists. However, his general theoretical viewpoint manifested little influence of marginalism, as in the case of Wicksell. The only utility economist discussed was Menger and his basic ideas were treated briefly, chiefly in relation to the period of investment. Jevons and the Walrasian equilibrium concept were not touched upon at all.

In the beginning, Davidson had not been sure that economics merited treatment as a separate field of study. When he visited Germany in 1879, he felt that the fundamental propositions in economics were uncertain, even inaccurate, and that it might better suit the purpose of scientific knowledge to merge them into sociology. This concern was reflected in his *Contribution to the History of the Theory of Rent* (1880), which was a good deal more sociological than the rest of Davidson's output. Not only were there traces here of John K. Ingraham but of Karl Rodbertus as well, whose contributions to rent analysis Davidson thought to be especially valuable. Rodbertus' overproduction theory seemed to him quite useful and the latter's open lack of interest in social democracy and the labor movement struck a sympathetic chord. He began to examine Ricardo more carefully than he had done previously, but still he did not accept the common belief that Ricardo was the fountainhead of the labor theory of value.[160]

Davidson now was beginning to sharpen his critical faculties. In the 1880's he published a number of articles on taxation, expressing some sympathy with the view that expenditure rather than income ought to be the tax base. After this period all of Davidson's work appeared in the form of articles, which were published mainly in *Economisk Tidskrift,* a journal he founded and edited from 1899 to 1938. Davidson did virtually all the editorial work on this magazine alone. Not that he was unable to find assistance; he simply was reluctant to let others share in its affairs. He was not only the sole editor, but wrote well over 250 articles for it himself. The journal's scope was broad, accepting contributions from statisticians, businessmen, and other cognate fields. Articles on practical as well as theoretical issues were to be found in its pages. After the first World War, however, its interest shifted to more theoretical work, especially in connection with the problem of exchange rates and monetary disequilibrium.[161] Led by Wicksell, who frequently helped Davidson with the magazine, some of Sweden's best economists wrote for it. Davidson himself finally came around to the view that theoretical discourse might be of help at arriving at economic truth.

Wicksell and Davidson were close friends, despite the latter's negative reaction to neo-Malthusianism. Davidson, who felt that there had been no sound theoretical grounding for the famous lecture on birth control, did chide his noted friend for being so indelicate as to raise the question to a mixed audience. He also urged Wicksell to obtain a law degree, without which he knew he could not teach. But despite these reservations on Davidson's part, they remained friends, and were brought even closer by a common antipathy to Gustav Cassel. Certainly a good deal of Wicksell's work was inspired by Davidson, and he benefited much from the latter's critical perception. Davidson, even more sharply than Wicksell, subjected Cassel to merciless examination, exposing contradictions and unsound chains of reasoning without pity. Cassel's enviable skill at popularization and simplification represented to Davidson a tampering with the truth. For him, nothing was easy and the proof of a statement had to be absolutely rigorous. All problems were bound to be complex and difficult. Consequently, he found the outgoing, arrogant, and practical Cassel more than he could abide comfortably and made his feelings on the matter quite plain. Cassel, for his part, treated Wicksell and Davidson with complete disdain and continually called attention to his own work as vastly superior.

As time went on Davidson kept returning to the classicists, especially to Ricardo—a passion stemming from his early work on rent theory. Interpretations of what Ricardo really meant became, in fact, central to Davidson's handling of economic problems. Yet his approach was never cohesively developed in his writing: his comments on theoretical and practical questions were scattered over forty years of articles in the *Economisk Tidskrift,* many being discussions of taxation and monetary policy, as well as of prices, business cycles, foreign exchange, and the like. Unlike Wicksell, Davidson did not construct a coherent body of economic ideas; he had no system, no integrated view of how the economic order functioned. Even in his interpretations of Ricardo, he related his ideas to a sequence of specific questions rather than to the Englishman's vision of income flow and the problems it created. Quite simply, Davidson had a distaste for synthesis: he much preferred a series of analytical exercises. Yet he knew Ricardo so thoroughly that he was able both to correct such luminaries as Keynes and Myrdal and to show that the purchasing power parity theory had not started with the English classicists. In a real sense, Davidson was completely independent of any economic school. His criticisms were aimed at laissez faire doctrinaires as much as to those who saw state intervention as the panacea for all social ills.

However, this discrete, piecemeal approach did not always bring fruitful results. The history of Swedish central banking in Davidson's writing became a series of technical problems without any perceptible relation to external affairs. Accepting social legislation as necessary for some situations, he had no objection to government action in cases of monopoly. However, he did feel that large-scale organization and even monopoly control might be effective instruments for avoiding overproduction and economic crisis. A favorite theoretical problem became the question as to whether, under certain conditions, it might be possible for saving to raise wages without generating capital formation, and, conversely, whether a wage reduction might increase real capital without requiring new saving. The first instance seemed possible during a depression when real wages tended to increase, while the second could develop in a boom when real wages lagged. Such movements might be related to shifts in the value of money. In discussing these problems, Davidson emphasized the need to distinguish clearly between the wages fund and real capital.

But his most important work was in monetary theory. Here too he was influenced by Ricardo. The experience of the post-Napoleonic era had offered some striking parallels for World War I. Inflation and excessive issues of paper currency had plagued both periods, and the discussion among Ricardo, Horner, Bosanquet, and others did seem especially appropriate to the early decades of the twentieth century. Generally, Davidson accepted Wicksell's distinction between the real and money rate of interest. The height of the money rate, said Davidson, in relation to the real rate of interest, was at the root of all changes in the value of money. This too was the mechanism for price level changes, for shifts in the basic relationships would inevitably lead to changes in the quantity of money in circulation and thereby influence prices. Davidson also discussed the possibility of employing the rate of interest as a counterinflationary device.

However, there was no full and genuine agreement between the two leading economists in Sweden. Davidson, markedly influenced by Ricardo, sought an "objective" basis for value. He did not, therefore, accept the concept that the value of money and goods would vary inversely, and said so in his review of Wicksell's *Interest and Prices* in 1899. Evidently, he meant to say that the value of goods and money had to be determined not only in relation to each other but in relation to the measure of scarcity that obtained for each as well. That is, the value of a good shifted with changes in inputs and productivity. Consequently, Davidson did not feel that Wicksell's desire for a stable average level of prices was wise, for this failed to consider changes in productivity. An increase in production coupled with correlative price reductions would itself, he said, maintain the real level of wages and assure a constant flow of real income. But if production was to increase while prices were constant, a rise in wages and profit would ensue and the value of capital would fall. Davidson expressed preference for a policy that would vary the average price level inversely with productivity, together with stability in the payments made to input factors. Workers and entrepreneurs would have the same money income, but it would be worth more—a view which seems to have had some impact on Swedish monetary policy.[162] It also seems to have been intended as an ethical objective; Davidson plainly meant to say that the fruits of greater productivity should be shared equitably, and this was his way of showing how it might be done.

Although Wicksell replied that changes in productivity were too small to make much difference, Davidson countered with the comment that monetary management had to take into account future changes in productivity.[163] He was thinking of progress in agriculture, and, in addition, argued that increased productivity with an unchanged price level would make Wicksell's natural rate of interest a good deal higher than the money rate. Equilibrium could be attained either by raising the money rate or by reducing the price level. But if the money rate were raised it would lead to a fall in prices; hence, Davidson concluded, equilibrium did require this inverse relationship.

The argument was based on the contention that the objective value of a good was increased by a greater degree of scarcity and that when this affected all goods the character of the changed value was quite different from changes that stemmed from alterations in the relationship between goods and money. The fact was, said Davidson, that the relation between one part of a stock of goods to all goods differed from the parallel relation in the case of money. Each good in a stock possessed value stemming from its individuality as a good: a monetary unit derived value only because it was part of money. Increase the total supply of money and each unit would lose value. Where the value of the total supply of money was related to goods turnover, the value of a single unit was related to the totality of money itself. The value of goods and the rate of turnover could not be controlled; but this did not hold for money, for the latter was subject to management. Thus, it was possible to manage money so as to make the prices of goods correspond to their objective, albeit variable, values. Price level changes in World War I were said to be due to four causes: increases in the quantity of money; a shrinkage in the quantity of goods; tax policies; and monopoly practices. Only the first might be dealt with via monetary policy. Strictly speaking, said Davidson, only this category was inflationary. Consequently, changes involved in the other groups were matters of justice. Unless gains in productivity and output were passed on in the form of lower prices, the relations between creditors and debtors would be altered just as surely as under conditions of monetary inflation, since the former would not gain anything from the increased ability of the economy to produce, the entire advantage going to debtors. On the other hand, a fall in productivity with prices remaining unchanged would injure debtors. Consequently, the best policy would be that which enabled prices to move in opposite fashion to productivity. That stable prices were not really an effective cyclical policy was the obvious implication, for under such circumstances an increase in real income or increases in productivity presumably would place a strain on the economy and possibly lead to speculative action and collapse.

Davidson's influence remained almost entirely limited to Sweden. He was so devout a student of Ricardo that his comments were tantamount to a reconstruction of the classical theory of value. But although this part of his work does seem somewhat antiquarian, it did not weaken the monetary analysis. Justifiably concerned with the redistribution effects of price level changes, he was beginning to move in the direction of showing that these could stimulate other movements. The contemporary economists who made the most of these observations were Hayek and Mises. But the great, and more salutary, impact of Davidson's work was to be found in the analyses developed by the younger Swedish writers, Gunnar Myrdal, Erik Lindahl, and others.

In a country such as Sweden, so deeply concerned with import-export problems, the question of increased import prices and a worsening of the terms of trade with consequent higher costs of production per unit and reduced efficiency, was quite important, said Davidson. All this was familiar enough during wartime, but it had meaning for peacetime as well. If general prices were to remain the same internally, higher import costs would have to be counterbalanced by lower ones for other goods. Otherwise, the general price level would not be stable. Yet reduced internal costs might generate deflationary movements. With sticky wages, profits might be adversely affected, with unfortunate results for the job market. However, were prices to increase proportionately to the fall in output, equilibrium might be maintained, for higher costs then could be recaptured without upsetting the demand for labor and other input factors. The other side of the coin suggested that constant prices under conditions of increased productivity would mean further inducements to investment and output as a result of higher profit. The ensuing greater demand for factor services could mean inflation. The new demand would be supported by additional bank credit, leading to further wage and price increases. The argument does have a curiously contemporary flavor, but one suitable to the more conservative view.

As Davidson developed these ideas, he moved away from his concern with distributive ethics and sought to justify the case for the inverse relation of prices to productivity on purely analytical grounds. He now wanted to define the problem of stabilization of the value of money. Again, this was an attempt to bring Ricardo up to date. While his essays contained suggestions for practical problems, the emphasis on the primary importance of productivity revealed an attempt to relate the question to some sort of objective value element in commodities. This emphasis, approaching pure Ricardian theory, involved him in a complicated and obscure debate with Wicksell. The latter pointed out that unanticipated changes do have a serious effect on price stability. In other words, uncertainty considerably weakened the Davidson position. But Davidson continued to argue his point of view right up to 1934. He insisted on his distinction between price changes occasioned in the goods sector and those which originated in purely monetary elements. Yet he did acknowledge some relationships of a quantity-theory character as valid. During the first World War he had thought that interest rate manipulations could be useful, but after 1919 he returned to his original position. The value of money was said to be determined by the value of the stock of goods and the latter, in turn, purportedly was rooted in productivity. The price of goods, he insisted, should be varied in the same degree and direction as the absolute amount of their "objective value changes." [164]

Much of Davidson's other work concerned itself with questions of money. He analysed problems related to the supply of gold, opposed Fisher's managed currency idea, and wrote often on Swedish currency. A fixed high price for gold was creating high prices in Sweden, he said, for the central bank was required to accept all the gold offered to it—an analysis which had a profound effect on Swedish banking and later led to a "blocking" policy. After World War I, Davidson opposed Cassel's view on the gold standard, expressing some skepticism about its restoration. He was hopeful that American experience in central banking would demonstrate once and for all how to control the price level and gold movements. But the disaster of 1929 blasted these hopes.

However, the seeds sowed by Wicksell and Davidson did bear fruit in one of the most remarkable groups of economists ever developed in any one country. By the 1930's it became evident that the Swedish economists were dealing with critical and fundamental problems in profound ways. Bertil Ohlin, Gunnar Myrdal, Erik Lindahl, Johan Åkerman, Dag Hammarskjold, and Erik Lundberg, who comprised the core of this group, demonstrated an extraordinary ability to deal with matters of practical import, yet in a manner that did not ignore basic theoretical concepts. Clearly these writers were meeting the needs of their time: the Great Depression may have called for immediate measures, but theoretical insights also were necessary if the true causes of the deepening social catastrophe were to be discovered. Some of them met in Stockholm to study particular problems and to discuss possible solutions for the crisis, and from these sessions emerged the "Stockholm School." Actually, the work of the group had begun in 1927 with Myrdal's dissertation on pricing, a book which introduced the factors of risk and expectations and which, by emphasizing elements of chance, allowed a new kind of dynamics to enter economic discussion. It heralded a complete rejection of the earlier static analysis; only the new approach, which more accurately reflected the reality of the case, seemed to be a suitable way out of the impasse into which economics had gotten itself.

A Rockefeller Foundation grant helped the Swedish scholars to develop their statistical techniques. They also worked closely on a number of government investigating committees that were set up between 1927 and 1935 to study unemployment and related problems. Much fruitful debate took place over such questions as monetary policy, business cycles, public works, fiscal programs, and the like; and it was all to the good, for there was always a conscious effort to fuse theory with practice. The 1931 unemployment commission produced several notable monographs which explored the basic problem of unused resources and sought to establish useful criteria for corrective measures. Most notable were Hammarskjold's *Spread of Business Cycles* and Johansson's *Wage Development and Unemployment.*[165] The roots of these studies were the same: Wicksell's cumulative process and Cassel's hostility to orthodox price theory. The discussion continued with undiminished vigor through the war years, shifting to the new problem of inflation, and the debates on this question were particularly intense and very learned. But as soon as the war ended, most of these men turned to practical affairs. Myrdal became Minister of Commerce in the Social Democratic government of 1945, and later moved to the post of Executive Secretary of the United Nations Economic Commission for Europe. Ohlin, expressing no fear of the thought of government intervention in economic activity, moved over to the Liberal party. In 1944 he became head of the Liberals and for a time served as Cabinet member. Sune Carlson, a brilliant young theoretician, joined the United Nations staff; Dag Hammarskjold became the United Nations Secretary General; and Ingvar Svennilson, author of a notable economic study on Europe [166] directed an important research bureau.

While these writers did not all agree with one another, there were some common features which do permit a close grouping. Interested in movements of the entire economy and in the interrelations of aggregate output and aggregate demand, monetary theory was for them, even more so than in Keynes' case, an integral part of general economic theory. Central to their thinking was the emphasis placed on the distinction between planned and realized activities—the *ex ante, ex post* concepts. Much of this was set in a framework of period or sequence analysis in which simplified yet rigorous models of the economic order were made to carry the burden of their logic. Myrdal especially was influential in this development. With his *ex ante-ex post* ideas he was able to focus attention on anticipations and expectations of both entrepreneurs who were incurring costs and on the input factors to whom the payments meant income. Monetary policy became central to the thinking of the Swedes. Yet it was clear that the bank discount rate in a depression was not very helpful; it was almost self-evident that at both upper and lower turning points of the cycle the interest rate was not an effective tool. Nevertheless, it seemed essential to maintain confidence in the monetary system.[167] The arguments this school developed in the early 1930's were extremely powerful and did much to counteract the rather widespread but false belief that an economy had to pattern its behavior along the lines of the prudent individual and that budgets must be balanced. The notion then was being bruited about that the recession was due primarily to an insufficiency of saving. The crisis, it was said, came from overinvestment or perhaps misdirected investment, and these errors simply would have to be purged from the system. The implication was that depressions were necessary and should not be interfered with.[168] However, the Stockholm economists advocated public works as a means of hauling an economy out of a depression. The argument was not complicated: such projects at a time when resources were unemployed did not really cost anything in real terms. The Swedes were prepared to deal with a depression just as they were prepared for Keynesian doctrine. So well had the founders done their work that government intervention did not shock them as it did the rest of the world.[169] Indeed, the tradition for theoretical analysis tempered by practical needs bore very interesting fruit in the Swedish environment.

The ideas of the Swedish economists perhaps were more important in helping to formulate their goverment's policy than in other countries. Adapting their theories to the objectives of policy, the allegedly naive concepts of a quantity theory of money and a general price equilibrium were displaced by a *disequilibrium* system. Swedish theory was expressed in terms of periods and sequences and was directed toward the problem of purchasing power. Some argued that production and sales could be stabilized if uncertainty were eliminated and the price-income relationship made constant. Practical considerations, however, were directed more frequently to factor earnings than to monetary elements. Classical ideas now were relegated to the classroom, for policy makers were not interested in supply and demand curves for their own sake. They knew that the price system could be nudged and moved in ways that pure theorists had thought impossible: in fact, private entrepreneurs had been doing just that for many years. It all depended on the direction in which one wanted to push the price system. Free competition and automatism became legends. The distortions and errors of the economy could be corrected by the action of the state.[170] Economics now was once again *political* economy. It was infused with an inescapable political content, and such matters as the level of purchasing power became determined by considerations beyond the market itself.

Therefore, it was no accident that the Swedish economists began to stress policy as well as theory. The very fact that they were now in high position and closely involved in decision-making insured a fusion of idea and action. The major emphasis in Swedish discussions was on price movement.[171] The wartime increase in prices seemed a natural consequence of commodity scarcity, and with the postwar recovery it appeared that prices should fall so that the gain in productivity would be distributed among all the factors of production.

This was the Davidson position. But matters did not work out quite in the way he had prescribed. Production and prices and factor income all went up. Why was this so? Evidently the original theory had overlooked the pressures of effective demand which enforced new and higher levels of economic activity. The cumulative process appeared to have been a better description than the inverse relation of prices and productivity.

iv

Bertil Ohlin: Trade and Factor Prices

Bertil Ohlin (1899-   ) started as a pupil of Cassel's and in his *Theory of Trade* (1924) made extensive use of the idea of general price equilibrium. However, he went far beyond Cassel in that he extended the idea of interdependence to price formation between nations. This new theory explaining how international trade was possible permeated the well-known *Interregional and International Trade*,[172] a book now standard in its field.

Ohlin first came to the attention of economists as a result of his dispute with Keynes over German reparations and the transfer problem, in which he insisted that equilibrium could be sustained despite the international movements of money. When Keynes published his *General Theory* in 1936, the Swedish writers looked at it as something of a curiosity, despite the fact that they all were talking about similar problems. Between 1936 and 1937 Davidson leveled no less than four attacks on Keynes in the *Economisk Tidskrift,* and it was not entirely unexpected when Cassel rejected the new British theory.[173] Yet the younger economists, including Ohlin, were not entirely unsympathetic. They thought only that Keynes should have employed the *ex ante, ex post* distinction, for, they said, it was only *ex post* that investment equaled saving. It was quite possible for these aggregates to differ in terms of expectations, and, in fact, dynamic economic movements were deemed to stem from these divergences. But the Swedish view had its own problems, for an *ex ante* notion of total saving was difficult to sustain. Ohlin himself felt that economic events depended on certain actions and that it was these phenomena that required investigation. This meant an analysis in terms of revenue, cost, depreciation, and similar categories so that net and gross income as well as saving and consumption might be defined more rigorously. The result was a definition of capital as comprising "old savings made available." If current saving were added to these quantities, one would obtain total capital, or what Cassel had called "waiting."

Yet the important phenomena were *ex ante* ones. This made the analysis something of an exercise in psychology: expectations and plans were said to determine the course of economic affairs. There was an implicit assumption in all of this of a set of alternatives available to businessmen. However, this appeared dubious for most except the largest concerns. In the main, the range of alternatives was severely limited by immediate *ex post* experiences. Clearly defined alternatives also seemed questionable for consumers, who did not often think in terms of varying possibilities. But the emphasis on hopes for certain levels of profitability did seem sound enough, for it was known that such expectations do influence decisions for expansion and the like. Ohlin, however, suggested that the expectations of many future periods might exercise an influence on economic action. This was rather far-fetched. He was saying, in effect, that a long look into the future could bring about an expectation concerning the realization of plans in the next period. But this did not seem to face up to the prospect of plan failures in the immediate future.

Stressing the significance of time lags, Ohlin suggested that variations in psychological reactions might be more important than monetary or bank rate policies. He was especially concerned with the reaction speed of buyers and sellers, emphasizing this as the most significant element in the whole host of economic equations.[174] He rejected the Hayek-Mises contention that expansion was always financed by new money. Furthermore, the use of *ex ante* and *ex post* concepts eliminated the possibility of employing the rate of interest as an equilibrating device, for whatever the rate of interest might be, saving and investment became identities anyway. The fact is that interest was merely a price for credit, and in that way was able to exert a limited influence on investment. And as shifts in interest rates might redirect the course of economic development, the notion of a "normal" rate did not seem especially useful. If one wanted to talk of a normal rate, it was rather that which appeared comparable with a given pace of economic development.[175] But it could be charged that Ohlin at this point was dodging the issue posed by both Wicksell and Keynes. Where borrowing was a significant element, the relation of anticipated profits to the cost of borrowing did become important.

Ohlin objected to this position, asserting that it was really a complex of rates with which businessmen were concerned. Bond yields, for example, bore no relation to banking rates, yet they had to be considered part of the interest rate complex. Insofar as employment was concerned, Ohlin agreed that the neoclassicist's appeal for a reduction in wage rates was more harmful than helpful, nor did he accept the argument that technological unemployment was merely temporary. While labor-saving devices did make available more productive power, there was no assurance that new jobs would be created automatically for the displaced workers. To the contrary, said Ohlin, wage increases might create a larger output and increased employment.

Work on interest theory was continued by Ohlin with the volume *The Capital Market and Interest Rate Policy* (1941). He had been quite critical of the government's handling of interest rates, and, in this book, looked at the problem from his own theoretical standpoint. Ohlin's views met with a respectful reception.[176] His main objective, however, was to develop a theory of the capital market. There was a good deal of discussion of loan rates, yields, and monetary effects, but nothing in the book was of particular import for the so-called Stockholm theory. Psychological explanations were not in evidence and some earlier views appeared to have been altered. The purpose of interest rate policy still was price stabilization and economic development of the kind deemed desirable by the authorities. Interest still was a price determined by supply and demand. The banking system was criticized for its failure to issue short-term securities during the war, a necessary step to develop a modicum of flexibility. A more liquid market would have made it possible to float long-term issues at lower rates. Ohlin finally came to the conclusion that a 3 per cent rate would have been appropriate. Later on, his main objective, a flexible capital market, was accepted as a desirable criterion.[177]

One of Ohlin's more striking conclusions urged that money played a minor role in economic activity. Rejecting the notion that the quantity of money was basic to price movements, he related the problem rather to government borrowing, fiscal control, and budget deficits. The *ex ante-ex post* analysis showed that it was not the quantities of money but conditions in the capital market which were critical. Involved in this analysis was the whole set of psychological reactions regarding liquidity, interest rates, and the like. This meant that attention had to be paid to acting individuals, not to money and its circulation. "It is not money that makes purchases," he said, "but men who buy with the help of money or credit." [178] Monetary theory, to be truly viable, would have to contribute to the analysis of a process in time. There was no other way to explain changes in income adequately. The number of concepts required to do this was considerably greater than the quantity theory could make available.

Ohlin's awareness of the complexity of economic life was revealed in his treatment of the unemployment problem. A wide variety of policies was necessary, he said, to deal with this exacerbating question. Easy money combined with an appropriate foreign trade policy might increase demand, but the needs of trade at times conflicted with easy money. For example, a lower interest rate might stimulate construction, but this itself could encourage high prices for building materials. Exchange depreciation might seem to be a satisfactory approach at first, but this could encourage retaliation. Also, poor timing of public works could be harmful.

Ohlin's forte was foreign trade. In his *Interregional and International Trade* he employed Cassel's interdependence theory of prices as the basis for his analysis. He was reacting from the classical views in this area, which he described as a labor value approach to trade. Moreover, international trade had to be closely related to location problems, if account was to be taken of the influence of such factors as transportation costs. Against this background, Ohlin discussed both the movements of the factors of production and international capital movements, coming eventually to Cassel's purchasing power parity theory. He started with a restatement of Cassel's equilibrium proposition to which he added elements of time and space. The latter was especially intriguing to him, for he felt, with a good deal of reason, that earlier price theory had been based upon the notion of a single rather than several markets. It was entirely possible, he said, for the factors of production to face more than one market at a time with the result that "prices of commodities, as well as productive factors, will be different from what they are under the one market assumption. Commodities move with more or less difficulty, chiefly because of the costs of transport, another element of fundamental importance for the space aspects of pricing. . . ." [179] The element of space was important in international trade and in domestic economies as well. It was differences in ability and resources, said Ohlin, which underlay the desire to exchange. That is, a country exported goods which it could produce more cheaply and imported those which cost less elsewhere. The relative costs of production depended on the relative prices of the input factors, on the technical production functions, as well as on the internal and external demand for goods. But the major factor was relative prices of the factors of production. This involved the element of scarcity, for where certain factors of production were plentiful, money costs presumably would be low.

While the cause of trade could be traced to cost differentials, the real problem was to discover what was behind such inequalities. This led Ohlin to a statement of supply and demand conditions which were expressed in terms of consumer wants, ownership of the factors of production, the available supply of factors, and the physical conditions of production. Of course, these were demand relationships which were affected by the prices of goods in both countries as well as by the prices of input factors. Consequently, prices in all regions were said to affect the prices and trade of each. Not only supply, but demand as well, governed the conditions of international trade. This was Ohlin's system of mutual interdependence. He argued that the immediate effects of trade were that "commodity prices everywhere are made to tally." [180] That is, abstracting from transport costs and other barriers, all goods would command the same price in all regions. This stemmed from the fact that trade allowed industrial activity to adapt itself locally to the situation existing in the particular factor's area. Industries requiring certain input factors tended to migrate to a place where they were readily available. Ohlin did concede that too smooth an adjustment of this sort would eliminate trade, hence adaptations were rough and usually incomplete, mainly because of joint demand.[181] However, the mobility of goods compensated for the lack of factor mobility. There were also other frictions: prices could deviate from underlying costs; the ensuing variations might not be counterbalancing, but could move in one or another direction; there might be serious unused capacities; and capital not only was fixed in certain forms, but lacked divisibility. In the main, Ohlin was successful in introducing these elements into his analysis. Attempting to explain the differences in the quality of the production factors and in technical processes, account also had to be taken of the different stages of development in large-scale production. Yet he could not help but return to what he considered as basic—supply and demand. Despite his awareness of all the complexities, he was convinced that in the final analysis only actual conditions in the respective markets, functioning through the apparatus of mutual interdependence, could explain the nature of trade. One had to rely after all on the effect of *ex post* conditions on present and future social habits, psychological elements, and institutional patterns to know what the economic outcome would be.[182]

As Ohlin himself admitted, his theory of international trade was a variant of location theory, a kind of *internationale standortslehre,*[183] highlighted by the desire to connect resource location and large-scale production to transportation and to the problems of regional trade. For example, he believed large-scale production to be concentrated at the best transfer points— a conception which has been sharply criticized as being too static. Insufficient attention was paid to the spatial shifts of input factors, which might have revealed the conditions of mobility and the speed of factor adjustments.[184] On the transfer mechanism, Ohlin stressed the equilibrating effect of shifts in money incomes on trade balances so that relative price changes tended to become less important. In the case of reparation payments, for example, he believed that transfers had less impact on relative prices than most writers thought to be the case. He maintained this position despite a sharp counterargument by Keynes, who rejected the idea that a tendency toward equilibrium would come about with the transfer of monies.[185] Ohlin's case rested patently on the purchasing power parity theory which insisted that the transfer of the means of payment could result in a shift in demand resulting in a restoration of equilibrium. He also argued that the terms of trade might turn against a borrowing country by virtue of idle resources. The doctrine of comparative costs, the classical theorists' basis for their conception of foreign trade, was vigorously rejected.[186] Indeed, Ohlin tried to be true to the Casselian heritage at almost all cost.

v

Erik Lindahl: Money and
Capital

One of Wicksell's more noted pupils, Erik R. Lindahl (1891-1960), started his work in the field of public finance. His analysis was rooted in marginalist principles leading to a value-of-service theory. In all important essentials he followed the tax doctrine sketched by Wicksell. These views were developed in his *Die Berechtigkeit der Besteurung,* a doctoral dissertation published in 1919. In it, Lindahl took the position that government activity was necessary to satisfy man's needs and that taxes were a means of converting private into public property.[187] He insisted, however, in contrast to the adherents of the organismic theory, that the state was not a metaphysical construction but, rather, a community of citizens, so that it was entirely feasible to assess the value that public services might possess for the individual. Since state services do bring satisfaction to people, the sole argument against the individualist approach could be only that these satisfactions were difficult to measure. Nevertheless, Lindahl felt that this was possible with the use of marginalist techniques.

Justice in taxation inextricably was linked with justice in the distribution of property, for the tax burden was distributed quite the same way as property. The price to be paid for public services was to be determined in the way price was set in a private market. Lindahl's model was analogous to the case of joint products, with the supply schedule of public services considered a function of the cost of services and the share of those costs which others were willing to assume. Supply and costs then were determined by an analysis reminiscent of Marshall in which ability to pay was reflected by the different contributions made according to income. The benefit principle was fulfilled because payments were made on the basis of personal valuations by equating marginal rates of substitution between private and social goods with their price ratios.

The value of material benefits was directly measurable by the impact on the marginal productivity of property: but subjective benefits also were possible as in the case of art galleries or parks. Lindahl's formulation of this problem, however, did appear somewhat vague: the valuation of public services was said to rest partly on the individual's direct interest and partly on economic capacity with the valuation directly proportional to capacity.[188] Yet in all likelihood lower income groups are apt to place greater emphasis on public education and parks than the wealthy. Finally, Lindahl had to concede that ". . . people do not carefully assess the marginal utility of each outlay, but act on some sort of general feeling of what they can afford [which] rests on considerations concerning the amount of benefit in each case." [189] This was hardly a neat argument. Nor was the assertion that in the absence of coercion the tax burden would be distributed proportionately to income any the more convincing. And Lindahl had to admit that a more realistic approach would view tax distribution in political terms.[190]

It was evident that in the area of taxation Lindahl was anxious to vindicate the Wicksellian posture. By relating justice to property distribution, it was possible to reemphasize the role of benefit and in fact to make it central to the theory. By further reducing the impact of public services to predominantly subjective elements, the ability-to-pay concept was converted into a variant of the benefit principle.[191] Presumably, the latter would allow an integration of fiscal and value theory. It even seemed more democratic, for it was assumed that no one would be required to pay for public services which he thought were not of his concern or to his interest. The lack of practical realism here was obvious, since the kind of voluntarism implied by the theory would make it possible for individuals to contribute nothing at all toward the maintenance of public services.

However, the major area of interest for Lindahl was monetary theory and policy. Here his views sought to modify those of both Wicksell and Davidson; in his *Scope and Means of Monetary Policy* (1929), he took the position that the aim of any program should be to reduce risk and upset stemming from unexpected conditions. Still, the Wicksellian influence was marked, especially in the collection of essays gathered in his *Studies in the Theory of Money and Capital*.[192] Another of Lindahl's important contributions to contemporary economic theory was the development of the concept of income, a notion destined to play an important role in modern studies of gross national product, particularly in Sweden. He gave this work a theoretical setting, suggesting alternatives for estimating various components. Much of this found its way into the first part of *Money and Capital,* an essay on economic dynamics which contained a striking discussion of the algebra of national income. This important contribution to the literature carefully analysed microeconomic and macroeconomic quantities involved in national income accounting. Lindahl recognized that double counting posed a serious problem. Later on he did acknowledge his system to be incomplete in some respects, especially in its treatment of government activity.[193] Indirect taxes, for example, were omitted on the ground that they could have been considered as included in the private sector's expenditures for production and consumption and in the government sector's income from "sales."

Lindahl also addressed himself to problems of methodology. The first essay in *Money and Capital,* concerned with the nature of economic dynamics, was in a sense an exploration of the predictive quality of economic analysis. In it, Lindahl wanted to explain both present and future phenomena. Causal elements had to be unraveled and for this a kind of "immanent" analysis was required. Beginning in terms of the conditions obtaining in a preceding situation, he developed the consequences in the light of whatever the conditions might be. The purpose of economic theory, said Lindahl, was ". . . to provide a theoretical structure showing how certain given initial conditions give rise to certain developments." [194] This could be eminently practical, for it was possible to provide in this way the essential materials for the treatment of concrete economic problems. Pure theory, consequently, had to be based four square on data and on information relevant to the particular problems at hand. This implied the need for a theory that was sufficiently general to be applicable to both open and closed systems, to socialist as well as capitalist economies. While the technique was simply the time-honored approach to real economic conditions through successive approximations, in Lindahl's hands it did contain a fresh quality. The problem of socialist economics, for example, touched on in a short note, dealt with the Lerner-Lange model in a very interesting way.[195] Where production and consumption were to be determined by a single authority, only one plan was required. However, in a decentralized socialism, said Lindahl, where free consumer choice was the rule, the authority had but to set prices that would equate supply to demand and then make certain that the value of total output at the established prices could not be increased by some other use of inputs. If these conditions would be met, satisfactions in the entire society could be maximized. Surpluses or deficits would be occasions for modified production plans. However, the important point was that the analysis flowing from these concepts was essentially the same as in a dynamic capitalist society. Still, Lindahl did concede that the character and flavor of a particular economic analysis was conditioned by the institutions of an epoch.

Throughout this treatment there ran a basic theoretical thread—the concept of time. When time was taken into account, a static situation could be only a special case of the more general dynamic approach. In fact, it was an awareness of this which made the static analysis sensible at all: in any case, dynamics was clearly at the center of theoretical discourse,[196] and the basic problem was to discover how individuals went about fulfilling their plans. This, of course, introduced the whole question of expectations. While Lindahl rightly emphasized the latter, he by no means overlooked the influence of past events. He did concede that individuals do not always have the clearest ideas concerning an expected course of action. Habit and ingrained tendencies might displace calculated motivations, but one also would have to acknowledge the possibility of alterations in plans. Revisions might be frequent and entirely lacking in logical consistency. Lindahl's view of the matter—a refreshing concession to its complexity—suggested an awareness of the fact that economic problems could not be reduced at all times to ordinary psychology. While it might be necessary to make some simplifying assumptions about behavior in the market place, it was also good to recognize that these were but initial hypotheses.

Sometimes contractual obligations and fixed commitments were enough to set a pattern of behavior for future periods. Lindahl's insistence, however, that a general solution was available by supposing the existence of a set of probability values for given expectations which could be subjected to calculation did not seem really adequate. Be that as it may, he did seek to compress probabilities into a time period structure which might connect past occurrences and future plans. The various kinds of plans that economic subjects were apt to make were categorized and classified: Lindahl contrasted non-economic versus economic events and immediately relevant changes versus more remote changes. From this taxonomy, he concluded that economic behavior concerned itself with that which was immediately relevant, leading to shifts or changes in expectations. The plans themselves could be on different levels—private individuals, business firms, or public bodies. But a truly general theory of economics could be derived only from an analysis of these plans and of their relevance for the future.

The definition of time periods did become a matter of some dispute in Swedish economics.[197] And a somewhat heated debate ensued as to whether the point between time periods was more meaningful than the period itself. The argument was offered that decisions were made in the interstices between periods; activity during the period was based allegedly on commitments. However, the discussion of these methodological tactics became a bit dreary, and the whole business tended to bog down in a terminological morass. As for Lindahl, his basic contention was that economic movement could be described as a series of disequilibrium positions. In the case of price, for example, neither the equality of supply and demand nor the idea of a continuously changing price was deemed to be correct.[198] Price decisions are made, said Lindahl, at a given moment of time: this implied that movements per se did not take place during the period *qua* period, for the relationships were supposedly fixed by prior commitments. This impelled Lindahl to divide the economic process into very short periods, making it possible for decisions to take place at the interstices or at points of transition. During the period, transactions were carried out at given prices and production and consumption were considered to be continuous. But this converted the dynamic process into a series of static positions or intertemporal equilibria which could be justified as Lindahl did only on grounds of convenience and malleability.

The method was illustrated by an ingenious presentation of the various algebraic relationships implicit in investment-savings-consumption equations.

A series of microeconomic statements were developed which Lindahl contended were valid for both *ex ante* and *ex post* values. The initial equation made sales and receipts from financial capital equal to factor or productive purchases, consumption, taxes, net lending, and increases in cash holdings. An income equation then was derived from this relation (income from factors equalled sales less factor purchases and real investment). As anticipations, changes in productivity, and subjective elements were introduced, the analysis became more and more complex. The same technique then was applied to macroeconomic phenomena, with the result that various ways of estimating national income were developed, the choice of the method depending on available statistics. Although the enormous quantity of research in the last decade and a half in Western countries has superseded a good deal of Lindahl's theory, certainly he still must be counted as one of the great pioneers in the field of national income analysis.[199]

The combination of the various equations revealed that differences were possible between plans and expectations: it was at these points that disequilibrium occurred, since any gap between plans and expectations had to be reflected in a similar gap between future and past values. The method was applied also to government budgets and national accounting.[200] A beginning was made with estimates of production and consumption as a basis for deciding where to best exert budgetary influences. Most important, the assumption of disequilibrium as a built-in feature of the economy was made quite explicit.

An interesting question raised by Lindahl was whether saving or investment was the primary phenomenon in the income equation. In his view, the answer depended on the relative strength of the different components: in a long period, savings might have to be adapted to the level of required investment, making the latter the primary factor.[201] Ordinarily, for the single short period, saving was the significant item, for planned investment, said Lindahl, depended on the rates of interest, and the latter could be altered by the banking system in order to make investment conform to the given level of saving.

Implicit in Lindahl's theory, as in most of Swedish theory, was a firm belief in the potency of the rate of interest.[202] This was defined in his equational system as a net gain on the capital values of economic resources stemming from the element of time. With the banking authorities drawn into the system, the objective then became one of employing the rate of interest in a way that would permit some exercise of control over the price level. Little impact on prices could be engineered in situations of perfect foresight, since all events were fully and correctly anticipated. All contingencies presumably were taken into account in outlining one's production and consumption plans. In these circumstances, monetary policy was described as passive. However, where foresight was less than perfect and where probability judgments regarding the future played a part in decision-making, the monetary authorities did have a decided role in influencing the price level.

Lindahl placed no small stress on the proposition that marked influence on business expectations could be affected by announcements of the monetary authorities as to what steps they planned to take. For example, if a tendency toward increased prices was revealed, the central bank's declaration of intent to adjust the rate of interest could exert a salutary influence, so that a shortage of consumer goods would not develop, and there would be no drain of resources from consumers' goods to producers' goods. This might be supported by an increase in the short term as contrasted with the long-term rate of interest. Changes in the rate of interest were said to affect the proportion of income that could be saved, although Lindahl did acknowledge that the size and distribution of the national income, as well as the general outlook of specific classes in society, could have more profound impacts on the savings ratio. The analysis of changes in the rate of interest was actually an effort to trace out in detail Wicksell's cumulative process. Lindahl felt that Wicksell had not completely explored the problem of turning points in the business cycle. If resources were to shift from consumer goods to producer goods industries, the ensuing shortage of consumer goods should cause higher prices and in turn further stimulate producer goods industries. Without restraining forces, the expansion might continue indefinitely. Saving would be adjusted to investment as a result of the redistribution of income, for as entrepreneurs increased their profit they would be disposed to expand further by applying their saving to investment purposes. The causal factor in this process, Lindahl noted, was the redistribution of income.[203] Even in the case of unused resources, prices would tend to rise with expansion. The turning point would occur when the ". . . supply of capital has been increased until it corresponds to the new rate of interest." [204]

This whole process presumably was initiated by a lower rate of interest. An increase in the interest rate would have similar but opposing effects: a decline in capital values affected the heavy industries; the position of lenders was improved; money wages must fall if full employment was to be maintained; there was a return to shorter investment periods; and the prices of consumption goods dropped. All the signs of a marked downswing in the economy were manifested. But while Lindahl did observe that changes in short-term interest rates worked more rapidly if with less permanence, he gave no consideration to those institutional changes which permitted corporations to rely on their own accumulated resources or to turn to nonbanking financial sources. The direct impact of the rate of interest in such cases evidently has been considerably weakened. Assuming that the short-term rate still had some meaning, its increase over the long-term rate would enhance producer's goods output and so place the economy in a position to provide more goods while moving to a new situation. At this point much of Lindahl's analysis concerned itself with the relation of productivity to price changes, after the fashion of Davidson; in fact, the latter's criterion for policy was accepted implicitly.[205] Rejecting Wicksell's real or normal rate in favor of a complex of rates for different goods, the analysis of capital followed the Cassel-Walras general equilibrium tradition, although Lindahl did prefer A. O. Bowley's notation.[206] Time was introduced as an important element, for without it the concept of capital could have no genuine meaning. Yet even where capitalistic production did not prevail, interest, said Lindahl, was an important factor.[207] Impulses away from general equilibrium were attributed to external shocks; again, foresight could mitigate the impact.[208] Consequently, the main purpose of his theory was to explore ways in which risks and unanticipated events might be reduced to a minimum. Once a particular tendency was observable, it presumably became a simple matter to work out the appropriate countervailing monetary policy.

Despite a number of obscurities, Lindahl's analysis does merit close attention, for it is in the best tradition of economic analysis. Calling for an understanding of basic concepts as essential to an investigation of economic plans, his theory, in effect, was a kind of guide to further research, the end product of which would be an economic policy that would insure confidence and regularity. This could be attained, he insisted, if the differences between a planned program and its realization were reduced to a minimum. Although in general, the Davidson criteria were accepted, Lindahl's own emphasis was more directly on constant incomes. In this way, the needs of both equity and science were met in the same theory.

vi

Erik Lundberg: Sequence Analysis

One of the few really modern works mentioned by Schumpeter in his stupendous *History,* the *Studies in the Theory of Economic Expansion* [209] by Erik Lundberg (1895-   ), merits a permanent place in the literature of economic analysis. Essentially a study of cyclical change, Lundberg attempted to work out the dynamic problems of economic growth by employing the Stockholm school's technique as the basis for a series of so-called model sequences. These revealed a number of possibilities for different growth lines. Exploring their consequences, he showed that all the models were connected by variations in the assumptions regarding shifts in data. After dealing with numerous leads and lags, he then arrived at an extraordinarily many-sided description of business cycle change along completely macroeconomic lines. In fact, Lundberg rejected anything but macroeconomic analysis. Since, he argued, the data were always changing, a static microeconomic theory was in no position to explain shifts in the underlying material. And there also was an early use of difference equations in analysing lags between variables.

This methodological approach was necessary to validate Lundberg's conception of economic theory as a study of change through time. The latter could not be disregarded, for, without it, adaptation and adjustments to change would be unthinkable. The objective of theoretical analysis was to reveal change as part of the system's internal mechanism: if change was to be explained solely by outside influences beyond the economy itself which merely impressed themselves like cosmic forces on human events, all one could obtain, said Lundberg, would be a series of moving equilibria.[210] A "sequence analysis," on the other hand, would examine developments within a time span as events moved from one point to the next. Thus, situations in one period could be explained wholly in terms of preceding events. Such a framework, he remarked, made it quite feasible to establish an integrated theory of price and money.

An economic movement can be in one direction only, he said, for once commitments have been made there can be no reversibility, as was illustrated in the case of the cobweb theorem.[211] Money was made part of the analysis, for to identify production and exchange with a barter economy, as was once done, even as a first approximation, simply removed the economy from the realm of the real.[212] Money was not a neutral factor, but a vital element exercising a pervasive influence on all the other parts of the system. Although Lundberg did utilize the technique of partial equilibrium in his sequences merely as a convenient device, he did not rule out the idea of general equilibrium. But he found the lack of any tendency toward it to be a fact of no little significance, for in any sequential phase the motive drives always stemmed from the failure to achieve equilibrium. This was a kind of homeostasis, a perpetual effort to regain a position of balance. It was this conception that impelled Lundberg to question the approach of Böhm-Bawerk and particularly Keynes. A special complaint regarding the English economist was that the multiplier concept, which related levels of income to investment impulses, was itself a variable that called for investigation. Keynes, who operated with the multiplier as though it were constant, was seen to have ignored the fact that one of the fundamental tasks of the economic theorist would be to explain how its values might change.[213] This implied that genuine insights into change and growth in the economy could be revealed best through the sequence approach.

The key problems in constructing a sequential phase were the choice of variables, the nature of the reactions by the participants, and timing. There was no such thing as simultaneous adjustments in Lundberg's sequences. Variations did not occur the same way, in the same places, and at the same time for all factors: there were numerous leads and lags in the system; and unit periods had to be carefully selected, although these could be defined as fairly short ones, since the economic process did move more or less continuously. However, the unit period had to be long enough to make the analysis meaningful in terms of the various plans involved. This made it an operational concept, quite unrelated to clock time.

Once these basic notions were defined, Lundberg then was able to review the work of Wicksell, Keynes, Robertson, and other writers [214] with fresh and perceptive insights. He observed that most of the theories, interpreted as forms of sequence analysis, had omitted variations in saving and fixed capital investment. Since working capital, the more fluid portion of total investment, generally had been utilized as the element subject to change, an unconscious habit had developed of applying the conclusions stemming from working capital to that for fixed capital. Thus, the central problem became the matter of instability, which stemmed mainly from time discrepancies between payments viewed as cost and as purchasing power. The result was that costs incurred to produce goods consumed in a given period were not identical with the incomes used to buy these goods. Cyclical movements appeared rooted in these crucial differences.[215] In fact, given a relatively short unit period, these payments could be quite independent of one another.

Lundberg then developed his analysis through a series of unusual and ingenious geometrical devices to show how the stability of the economy depended upon the fraction of purchasing power in any given period that was derived from those costs which were incurred to produce goods consumed in the same period. The formula, however, providing as it did for an index of instability, in the sense that movement was motivated by the relation of net profit to costs, did not appear to be substantially different from Keynes' marginal efficiency of capital. While Lundberg did insist that his index was not the same as Keynes' marginal efficiency, certainly it was conceptually similar, and like Keynes' device, had the virtue of being an integral element of the model itself. It also provided some measure for evaluating the extent to which the system was self-reinforcing.

Naturally, money had to be included in the system, but Lundberg would not accept the notion of a transaction or income period. The velocity of circulation of money, he said, could not be usefully related to the element of time. Payments by firms at particular moments of time were merely matters of convenience, with no special economic significance. Further, he insisted that changes in the flow of payments did not necessarily affect the model sequence. On the other hand, saving was viewed as more than just a passive element, for, once time was introduced into the equations, saving could be made to play an active role. An increase in income, for example, could temporarily increase saving, at least until consumption standards had shifted enough to absorb the added income.[216] This illustration pointed the way in which Lundberg emphasized each element in his model sequences. The ultimate purpose was to investigate how a private economy might move toward stability. Saving and investment, he said, depended not merely on total incomes but on its distribution as well.

Certain costs were deemed to be income generating. Wages, interest, dividends, and purchases created income, whereas depreciation, interest, and dividends on new capital did not, at least in the given period. On this basis a system of equations could be constructed, but one in which the possibility of discrepancies was clearly demonstrable. Current investments were the sources for income which filled the gaps caused by saving and non-income generating costs.[217] The final structure evolved by Lundberg, his model sequences, made it possible to include numerous factors—Spiethoff's capital goods materials, Wicksell's real rate of interest, and Keynes' multiplier, among other things. Although this may suggest mere eclecticism, such was not the case, for to Lundberg, all these various elements were genuinely significant parts of the whole. Cyclical change simply encompassed a multiplicity of conditions. One could also detect a similarity in the model sequences to the later Harrod-Domar models,[218] for what Lundberg was asking was whether growth in production, consumption, income, investment, and saving could continue at a steady and regular pace or whether built-in mechanisms, internal to the economy, could make the whole thing grind to a halt.[219] In this way, he was exploring in a genuinely fundamental sense the formal relationships set up in the Wicksellian and Keynesian models. Even if no changes did occur in prices or costs or in the proportion of capital goods, expansion still would require constant additions to capital: saving would have to match or rise faster than investment. And the relationships between these two elements, implied Lundberg, would require an exponential function in the rates of change in income, saving, capital, and the like in order to achieve a dynamic balance. "The amount of new investments must be sufficiently large," said he, "to balance the amount of savings forthcoming at that level of employment and income, which ensures full utilization of the new capital at remunerative (in this case constant) prices." [220]

Nor was the production of consumer goods a passive factor, as was so often implicit in post-Keynesian writing. Lundberg noted that increases in consumer spending could have fairly meaningful repercussions: in fact, one of his model sequences took this situation as a direct assumption.[221] With no change in the producers' goods industry, an expansion in consumers' goods output could generate income just as well as growth in other sectors of the economy. Taking into account the inhibiting influence of the existing stock of capital goods, he acknowledged that overcapacity in a depression would result in effects quite different from a full employment economy. From this example Lundberg went on to consider a "sequence" in which the major investments were in working capital. While this model did contain built-in discrepancies, its outstanding characteristic was the slackening of any self-reinforcing elements. How components of the national product moved when investment in residential housing and other building activity was dominant also was examined. Shifts in the rate of interest and saving as well as "rationalization" were made part of the analysis. And although all the model sequences were quite complex, they did show the movements of the different factors in a way frequently superior to that of other analytical models. In the housing model, for example, income was generated not only through outlays on labor and direct materials, but also on the resources behind them. Yet there was always the prospect that an upward movement would exhaust itself, for new investment could not always rise in a way that would permit enhanced receipts and increased demand for housing to be large enough to make investments worth while.[222]

The changes that caused crises were shown to start many periods prior to the time of trouble, for the discrepancies between saving and investment began early in the model. Additions to purchasing power diminished steadily up to the point where total investment fell below total saving. Of special interest was Lundberg's "rationalization" model in which the use of labor-saving machinery was assumed. In this case, although the costs involved were not income generating, there still was a possibility for quick expansion of surplus income so that economic growth could continue. However, equilibrium demanded that the pace of expansion be continued: investment had to increase at a fast tempo if industrial capacity was to be brought into full play. The system resembled a man on a treadmill.

Lundberg was quite modest about the whole model sequence structure, conceding that they contained gaps, exceptions, and even errors. Admittedly, the reaction patterns of consumers and producers were not necessarily the same as those assumed in the models, and the relationships could be altered in significant ways. But this only underscored the complexity of the economic order. The theory itself was an excellent guide to research: filling it with empirical content would help to select new variables and even to modify the analysis. While no simple theory, no one factor was sufficient to explain why and how change did take place, it was evident that the expansion process did carry the seeds of its own breakdown. Two types of crises were involved in Lundberg's models: in one, the break in consumer outlay could be attributed to excessive saving and a lack of sufficient purchasing power; in the other, there was not enough saving to match new investment. At last, Keynes and Hayek were met on common ground.[223]

While Lundberg's first book was quite technical and addressed mainly to his professional colleagues, the second major work, *Business Cycles and Economic Policy,* commanded a wider audience.[224] Published originally in Sweden in 1953 as part of a larger research project, the *Business Cycles* stemmed in great measure from Lundberg's skepticism on the supposed accuracy of national income data. The book was important for all economists, despite its localized concern with Swedish economic policy. It began as an empirical investigation of business behavior, with the initial data gathered through questionnaires. This part of the study was omitted in the English version, although it did provide considerable interesting and useful material.[225] Full of numerous insightful comments on business cycle policy, the book gave Lundberg an opportunity to express his own views separate from the official reports of the Economic Research Institute.

Somewhat reminiscent of Schumpeter's life-long attempt to fuse statistical, historical, and theoretical material, the book also employed some Keynesian concepts, such as the multiplier, the 45° consumption line, as well as the idea of acceleration. Lundberg made his political bias quite clear: he was unalterably opposed to government regulation of economic activity in peacetime.[226] Although he did try to relate this position to a general philosophic stance regarding the aims of economic policy, this unfortunately was a bit vague.[227] He seemed to grope for some justification of the economist's participation in public affairs. With so much activity going on about him, he wondered whether the public role was a proper one for the economist. Recognizing that economics was able to appraise a given policy by taking into account a wide range of alternatives, he knew that this would have to fit within the confines of legislative programs and institutional limits.

Two viewpoints developed out of these concerns with ends and means. One might deal with economic problems either through fiscal or monetary policy. Lundberg himself favored the latter: he did not believe that changes in discount rates were ineffective, arguing that this might be a suitable operation at the turning points of the cycle.[228] He agreed with Lindahl that a statement of the central bank's intentions would be helpful in stabilizing delicate situations. However, he was disturbed over the possibility that a thoroughgoing and many-sided attack on cyclical upsets would make it somewhat difficult to distinguish between the effects of interest rate changes and the quantity impact of pure monetary policy. But once the complexity of the real world was acknowledged, attempts at such fine distinctions would most likely fail in any case. If interest were used as a rationing device, an increase in the rate might imply a reduction in the supply of money. Higher rates, Lundberg argued, would reduce both the desire to borrow and the willingness to lend. A more rigorous climate for credit could develop, although the reactions and behavior sequences were quite complicated and were not often fully encompassed in either a quantity or interest rate theory.[229]

At this point, Lundberg's analysis suggested that there was a large element of imprecision in monetary policy. However, there would appear to be some need for such imprecise methods, for while the aims of monetary policy should be clearly stated and while all persons ought to know that the objective of the banking system is to help maintain a stable price level, the ways in which this might be done were usually surrounded by ". . . an atmosphere of uncertainty and perhaps even mysticism. . . ." [230] The purpose seemed to be to raise the ill-understood symbolism of the national currency to the level of a mystery so that the banking authorities could easily command the behavior they deemed desirable. Lundberg had some doubts about this sort of legerdemain. Was such an approach really suitable for a full employment economy in which movement and change had to be rooted in certain knowledge of circumstance? If monetary policy was to be based on psychological shock or obeisance to symbols, would the criteria associated with sureness have to be abandoned? Lundberg's innate skepticism as to the impact of deliberate action suffused his entire approach: he insisted that not enough was known about the effects of fiscal and monetary policy to warrant anything other than a program of groping. Recent American experience has suggested that this Swedish writer was on sound ground.

Lundberg also questioned the use of national budgets as either a device for explaining disequilibrium via the inflationary gap or as a method for reestablishing economic balance.[231] One of his major reservations stemmed from the uncertainty of the statistical data employed. In fact, said he, the standard gap analysis, familiar to so many post-Keynesians, might be more useful to a controlled economy than to one free of central constraints. These analytical techniques, as well as many other tools in the kit-box, were thought to be more helpful as pedagogic devices, for the complexities of the real world cast doubt on their usefulness in global decision-making. Theoretically, ". . . one can visualize a perfectly rational fiscal policy, with the Finance Minister at the controls of a highly complicated economic regulator; by manipulating the appropriate switches he produces the desired marginal effects on income, demand, prices and creates and maintains perfect economic balance. Mathematical constructions along such lines are doubtless formally possible, but the satisfaction and usefulness will certainly be confined largely to the instructor himself." [232] Formulas of a mathematical nature do appear otiose when we cannot really foretell how people react to economic change. For this reason, Lundberg preferred a cautionary approach to monetary policy.

Policy aims in real life were not directed toward equilibrium, he correctly argued, but to secure a particular objective. It was for this reason that policy was so elusive and why it was more urgent than ever to develop "good theory" in economics.[233] Existing theories, which included multipliers, accelerators, inflationary gaps, and the like, were concerned with the transmission of economic impulses. And Lundberg, seemingly disturbed by the failure of these macroeconomic theories to show how change was diffused over the system, began to move somewhat closer to the position of the National Bureau of Economic Research of making detailed empirical studies before sketching a theory.[234] The problem was to "disaggregate" and to collect details. The "good theory" suddenly disappeared into a welter of facts.

Reaction to Lundberg's views was rather sharp.[235] Some thought that he had dismissed much too lightly the aggregation problem; others felt that fiscal policy techniques had more to them than Lundberg would admit; still others were certain that a postwar inflation was unavoidable and that government decision-makers had been assigned too much blame. Lundberg's reply was that he had intended no new theory, but merely a test of existing ones, and that he had found these wanting. At this juncture it is difficult to say who has been right.

vii

Gunnar Myrdal: Values in Theory

The best known of the present group of Swedish economists, Gunnar K. Myrdal (1898-   ), has been ". . . successively university professor, government adviser, member of parliament, director of a study of the Negro in American life, cabinet minister, bank director, chairman of a planning commission, and international civil servant. . . ."[236] It was perhaps this broad-gauged experience that made him so predisposed toward a philosophic and sociological examination of the preconceptions one finds in economics. Myrdal, however, manifested these interests quite early in his career, as evidenced in his work, *The Political Element in the Development of Economic Theory*.[237] Here the philosophy of economic doctrine was examined more carefully than anywhere else in Swedish economics. Myrdal wanted to place social science in a proper context: the outcome was a body of ideas thoroughly impregnated with methodological observations. He questioned the wisdom of setting down purely theoretical welfare propositions without a statement of goals, for the division between science and politics only became confused when modern writers refused to make their value judgments explicit. These judgments were precisely those that comprised the essential political elements in economic thought. It was an illusion, said Myrdal, to assert that political attitudes could be excluded or subordinated to a set of putative "first principles." These would have to be introduced explicitly and made part of the analysis.[238]

The central problem for the social sciences was to prevent bias and class interest from influencing the search for truth. Toward this end it was necessary to acknowledge the rationalistic and relativistic nature of the social sciences. But this, said Myrdal, was seldom done. Despite their adoption of a positive stance, the theorists' use of value, utility, and welfare did reveal an unconscious normative bias. Even in Walras and Cassel, Myrdal charged, the concept of what ought to be was not entirely submerged. Further, such subterfuges were obscured by an unwarranted claim for having established rules of "what really is." Certainly, the history of economic thought supplied ample evidence to support this charge. Most economists were never merely theorists. Their inspiration, said Myrdal, came as much from the urge to improve society as from scientific curiosity.[239] The current situation has only brought about a polarization of attitudes: on the one hand, conservatives appealed to a supposedly fixed human nature as the basis for social analysis, while, on the other hand, radicals urged changes in institutions as the way to improve society. Ultimately, the radicals won out. Still, the conservative yen for an allegedly tough-minded realism acted as a warning against the excesses of enthusiasm. Only the trend to bigness in industry and government and the avowedly open attempts to plan had underscored the limitations of the traditional view. Economics could not remain "pure" and hope to contribute anything of lasting value, said Myrdal. The great economists always had made policy recommendations, and this had been true for Malthus, Ricardo, Marx, and Keynes.

Thus, it was necessary to make value perceptions part of the theoretical structure of economics. But, said Myrdal:

Value premises should be introduced openly. They should be explicitly stated and not kept hidden as tacit assumptions. They should be used not only as premises for our policy conclusions but also to determine the direction of our positive research. . . . This is our only protection against bias in research, for bias implies being directed by unacknowledged valuations. The value premises should be formulated as specifically and concretely as possible. They cannot be *a priori* self-evident or generally valid. They should be chosen, but not arbitrarily, for the choice must meet the criteria of relevance and significance to the society in which we live.[240]

The influence of Max Weber and Karl Mannheim seemed fairly evident.

When Myrdal met with the latter-day institutionalists in the United States, his feeling about the problem of value was strengthened. The Americans' concern with pure fact appalled him: their belief that empiricism was the be all and end all of economic science seemed fatuous. As a young man Myrdal had thought that once the metaphysic buried in economics was removed it then would be quite a simple matter to solve social problems by merely adding to factual knowledge what one knew of value judgments. But in later years he was less certain that this mechanical approach could be successful. Mere observation was hardly sufficient, for it still was necessary to have a theoretical framework and this always implied value judgments.[241] This approach was found in virtually all of Myrdal's later work. In *An American Dilemma,* the value system, known as the American creed, was contrasted in the sharpest possible manner with the known deed. In his two books on underdeveloped nations, *An International Economy* [242] and *Economic Theory and Under-Developed Regions,*[243] the value premises that lie at the roots of the problem were shown to be equality of opportunity and the advancement of democracy. Value premises were essential in any kind of research work, said Myrdal, and no study could be free of it.[244] But always they would have to be made explicit parts of the argument.

In one of Myrdal's best methodological discussions, found in an essay on "Ends and Means in Political Economy," written in 1933,[245] he pointed out that the ends-means problem was plainly visible in any sort of economic planning. In an advanced society, planning was the central principle by which knowledge was organized. Yet, in no way was it possible to assert that ends could be objectively determined, for they always meant judgment and ultimate recourse to value systems. Nor was it possible to say that means were ethically neutral. Thus, a ". . . political value judgment refers not only to the end but to every component in all possible alternative sequences which are to be compared." [246] Social science procedures then were essentially relativistic and excluded the notion that values might be ordered into a logical hierarchy. The findings of disciplines other than economics were essential to analysis, particularly psychology. These could help to determine the proper causal sequences; in fact, value premises, said Myrdal, were obtained from a study of the psychology of attitudes—a fact which made the economist something of an artist, and demanded of him the "empathy of the poet." Once a coherent set of judgments was worked out, many of them admittedly political, it then would become possible to order social data more effectively than might be done now and to impart to theoretical research a direction corresponding to the important practical problems of the day.[247]

The question of program and prediction was related to this problem. The former was a proposed or intended plan of action, the latter a forecast. A program, said Myrdal, was a policy decision, and insofar as an effort was made to carry it out, it had a built-in prediction which was virtually self-fulfilling.[248] Yet this could be distorted by value judgments, for value did affect the content of a program and involved such problems as rationalization and distortion. Judgments implied selection of problem areas, thus restricting social and economic inquiry in ways that allowed only a limited experience to be revealed. In this sense, Marxian and Keynesian theory might be said to be but short-run protests against the conditions of a given period. Still, value judgments did frame our vision of economic society and were in fact expressions of personality. They could not be deduced from abstract principles, nor were they given for all time, for they were subject to perpetual drift. There was a continuous interaction between values, programs, and predictions. Therefore, no possibility existed for establishing separate areas for ends and means, said Myrdal, something once thought possible. But how does one work out a given set of values? Primarily, this became a psychological problem for which the criteria of economy or relevance, terms of which Myrdal made much use, were conceivably insufficient.

Another key concept in Myrdal's analytical system was the idea of cumulation. Introduced in opposition to the notion of equilibrium, in which the relevant forces always were purportedly returning to a state of rest, the principle of cumulation placed emphasis on a process which, once begun, fed on its own effects. The final outcome, said Myrdal, might be quite out of proportion to the initial push. Further, these forces all tended to move in the same direction. The variables were ". . . assumed to be interlocked in such a causal mechanism that a change of any one causes the other to change in the same direction, with a secondary effect upon the first variable, and so on." [249] There was never any question of balance or equilibrium. What needed to be studied, Myrdal insisted, were processes moving in one direction or another, always subject to impulses stemming from one place or another. As in the case of *An American Dilemma,* the method implied a kind of taxonomy together with some measuring device to indicate the strength of the various social forces. The central idea in cumulation was the existence of multiple factors, all interdependent.[250]

In essence, Myrdal was, as Paul Streeten has remarked, a kind of cheerful pessimist. Wanting a world of free men and open opportunity, he did not hesitate to warn that the industrial nations were making it difficult for the underdeveloped nations to attain a satisfactory level of growth. While he could trace his intellectual roots to nineteenth-century liberalism and socialism, he did not subscribe to their notions of continuous, unabated progress. Myrdal emphasized ". . . the need for the scientific analysis of society and on the presence and positive function of value clashes that [was] reminiscent of Marx, with a faith in a better society whose shape the imagination of free men can design, that recalls the Utopian Socialists." [251]

We come now to Myrdal's more technical theory, reflected mainly in his *Monetary Equilibrium.* Published originally in 1932[252] and cast in the form of an "immanent" criticism of Wicksell, the book met with harsh reception by some of Myrdal's colleagues. They were indignant that his position should have shifted so markedly between the original Swedish edition in 1932 and the English version seven years later.[253] Objection was made to the imprecise way in which Myrdal defined his economic periods, a concept to which the Swedish writers were quite addicted. Myrdal, in fact, did prefer a kind of instantaneous analysis, arguing that to simplify the concept required the adoption of a point in time. On the other hand, his critics, prone to converting the analysis into a flow, were forgetting that both conceptions had their uses.

Myrdal's position pointed to the need for a multiplication factor to transform relative prices into absolute ones if the idea of equilibrium was to become a vehicle for economic perception. This, of course, was taken from his teacher, Cassel.[254] Traditionally, this effect had been provided by the quantity theory, but there the causal relation was never clarified, for the value of money always was determined by the very condition that the theory sought to explain; namely, the price level. However, the latter was not a genuinely clear concept: incapable of being defined precisely, it was complicated also by the existence of credit transactions which were themselves related to the element of time. Yet price formation necessarily excluded credit, for price was explained as an event at a given moment. The result was that ordinary theory could not explain such problems as business cycles. The latter became a separate compartment in economics and the theorists were in the position of arranging their observations, ". . . according to a more or less complete aggregate of hypotheses which [were] openly admitted to be unsatisfactory." [255] Wesley C. Mitchell's work was declared to be an excellent example of this sort of fruitless procedure.

The analysis began with a review of the ways in which supply and demand equilibrium might be disturbed. The fact that upset was possible led to notions of either underconsumption or overproduction. In Wicksell's theory the rate of interest was the fulcrum about which disequilibrium could move, thus initiating the famous cumulative process. Myrdal only wanted to add the concept of anticipation, for, without it, useful definitions of investment, saving, and consumptions were not possible, he said, since future actions were conditioned by the immediate past. Thus he introduced the *ex ante* and *ex post* concepts which were to play so large a part in the development of economics in Sweden. Monetary equilibrium in the commodity markets was said to be quite a different matter from equilibrium in the area of productivity and capital.

There was considerable methodological discussion in Myrdal, particularly with regard to period analysis. He insisted that time in economics had to be modified to a "point," a concept derived from the simple business of setting up very short periods. Certain flows such as saving and income implied time periods; these were easily calculated for the past when the balance was obvious. This was the *ex post* situation. But if anticipation and plans were the focus of concern, it became possible to say that saving might increase without any investment offsets.[256] Wicksell's equilibrium in the sphere of production was replaced with the concept of "exchange value productivity," so that credit and the money rate of interest might be incorporated in the definition of the natural rate of interest. Myrdal came to the conclusion that it was expectations with regard to the absolute level of money prices that determined productive relations rather than anticipations based on relative prices.[257] It was, in fact, the *ex ante* or expected yield of capital that became significant, for while rough probabilities might be taken into account, even these were based on the hoped-for ratio of net return to capital values. All this comprised a complex pattern of business reaction, entirely lacking in precision or elegance. The equation of yield, gross revenue minus output costs, had to be multiplied by all the probabilities. The vagueness in these formulations was almost self-evident. Myrdal himself confessed that a single money rate of interest was purely conceptual, for in reality there were numerous rates. Nor was it possible to give genuine empirical meaning to the notion of yield since there were many different types of capital. What Myrdal had accomplished then was a restatement of the idea of the natural rate of interest in a way that brought it quite close to Keynes' later concept of the marginal efficiency of capital. The conditions for equilibrium in the area of production were recast in terms of the *reproduction* of real captial. *Ex ante* and *ex post* concepts were tied by making real capital the sum of anticipations discounted to a given point in time.[258]

Myrdal argued that equilibrium in the capital market was a precondition for equilibrium in production, a seemingly reasonable argument for a monetary economy. How did this come about? The natural rate of interest had to be redefined to show that money and credit were part of the analytical system. This meant making the natural rate a rate of profitability. Clearly this was an *ex ante* concept; it was the yield of planned investments. The difference between this rate and the money rate could equal the value and cost of production of planned real investment. For practical reasons, the last proposition might be restated as the relation between actual capital value and the cost of reproduction of capital goods. Redefined in this way, the analysis provided for different profit margins in different parts of the economy. For the whole economy, it was possible to weigh the concepts by the various elasticities of investment. Monetary equilibrium was achieved when equilibrium in the capital market led to investment in the sphere of production. In the last analysis, gross real investment had to equal saving plus anticipated changes in capital value.[259]

Yet the fact remained, said Myrdal, that there was an inherent tendency toward disequilibrium between real investment and free capital disposal. The description of the process is by now a familiar one: profit margins increase real investment while savings tend to decrease relatively. That is, the latter may not increase as fast as income. This, however, was but one of several causes for disturbance. Myrdal then analysed the impact of shifts in the rate of interest and movements in real investment in *ex ante* terms.[260]

An effort was made to show how successes or failures in anticipations caused cumulative movements in the economy. In an upward movement, for example, a large unanticipated saving might eliminate the discrepancy between investment and available free capital. The situation, of course, could become quite complex. Expectations by different parties about the same economic category might differ; the estimate on the outcome of production or the yield of input factors could turn out to be incorrect, causing major disparities. It might be quite impossible to balance these disparities with actual occurrences. And the further we proceed, the more does the analysis seem to come apart into numerous details, each appearing quite distinct from all others.

Myrdal then entered into the Wicksell-Davidson debate and arrived at the notion that monetary equilibrium required a stable price level weighted according to the significance of certain "sticky" prices and the importance that these had for investment. He admitted that this did not necessarily mean stabilization of the general price level.[261] Some realism was introduced when Myrdal conceded that monopoly might have something to do with sticky prices. Yet monetary equilibrium was important as a means of reducing the effects of the business cycle. At this point, normative elements and value judgments entered economic analysis. After weighing the effect of alternative approaches, Myrdal concluded that a basic dichotomy did exist between price stabilization and monetary equilibrium. Said he: "Maintenance of monetary equilibrium in the presence of changes in the primary factors determining prices is not the same as the economic development which is most free of risks for the capitalists. Monetary equilibrium involves a balancing of gains and losses only on actual current investment. This is something quite different from the balancing of gains and losses on existing real capital as well." [262]

There are quite a number of Swedish economists whose writings merit attention. In addition to those whose work we have already reviewed, there are Dag Hammarskjold, late Secretary General of the United Nations, Bent Hansen of the Swedish Economic Research Institute, Sune Carlson, Ingvar Svennilson, and many others. All their publications have testified to the extraordinarily high quality of work in economics produced in that nation.[263]

While we cannot examine all of these fascinating studies, we may take as illustrative those written by Bent Hansen, whose highly technical and difficult The Theory of Inflation [264] is an important landmark in recent economic writing. The inflation problem, quite intense in Sweden, especially in the immediate postwar period, aroused a public discussion that often was highly theoretical, as in Hansen's case. His analysis described two types of inflationary situations—repressed and open inflation. In the former, prices and wages might be under government control, yet the characteristics of an inflationary gap could make their appearance in either commodity or factor markets, or perhaps both. Those who watched the market situation in the United States during World War II can testify to the validity of such a distinction.[265] Hansen made effective use of Walras' general equilibrium approach in constructing his models, particularly with regard to "open" inflation.[266] Lindahl's *ex post* and *ex ante* equations also were employed, with aggregate supply and demand functions attached to them. In this way Hansen sought to bridge the gap between ordinary equilibrium theory and his inflation models. The analysis proceeded in terms of excess demand in either factor or goods markets. Equilibrium presupposed the elimination of these gaps. The pure saving-investment analysis was rejected on the ground that it was too clumsy for a study of inflation. Hansen's own approach was in effect a disequilibrium one which sought to explore ways and means of closing the gaps between aggregate supply and demand in the various markets.

The *Economic Theory of Fiscal Policy*, Hansen's second book, gives additional evidence of the theoretical vigor of the Swedish school.[267] Prepared originally as part of a series of government reports on the problem of maintaining stable money values with full employment, the book is a paradigm of what a thoroughgoing analysis is able to produce. Hansen begins with a somewhat abstract discussion of the means-ends problems, a question which is found to arise when alternative choices are available for reaching different economic objectives. This was a meaningful problem in the framework of the particular report with which Hansen was concerned, for the goals of full employment and a constant money value might conceivably be contradictory. Under such circumstances it seemed necessary to develop the appropriate measures which a central bank and government might employ. Much of the analysis developed by Hansen was similar to the argument worked out by Jan Tinbergen, the noted Dutch economist.[268]

The first part of Hansen's work investigated the impact of taxes on microeconomic units. The behavior of households and firms, assuming profit maximization, was examined. The Stockholm notions of *ex ante* and *ex post* were applied to government budgets insofar as they might affect private industry. The assumption here was that budgetary changes were possible so that actual results conceivably could diverge from expectations. The government, however, had less need to concern itself with expectations, for it controlled many more factors than did the individual. Should one approach fail to yield the desired results, others could be utilized.

An extremely interesting and suggestive chapter on "Organization and Fiscal Policy" was regrettably too slim to yield substantial results, yet it is important to take note of the problem it raised.[269] Hansen observed that decisions once made by households, firms, and individuals now had been transferred to organizations. In his own language, the parameters of action for the latter are different than for microeconomic units: administered price action and wage determination through trade unions were cited as classic examples. The principles of behavior for these are patently unlike that which classical economic theory had described. It might be possible, Hansen thought, to develop economic models for organizations, but, in fact, the area of action was no longer purely economic. To assume that these social units would behave exactly in the way as individuals was unwarranted. Organizations do have political objectives and political ties, and their motivation shifts about depending upon the pressures generated within their own structures. They have a logic of their own quite distinct from that of the open market. In a world comprised of such bodies, economics very well may be displaced from the center of social analysis, leaving the stage entirely to politics and sociology.

8

The American
Dichotomy

i

The Young Radicals: Ely,
Patten, Seligman, Carver

P RIOR TO THE twentieth century, American economic thought exhibited certain attributes that gave it a tone markedly divergent from the dominant chords of Anglo-Saxon theory. The latter had stressed free trade and the conflict of classes, although in France, Jean Baptiste Say and Frederic Bastiat advanced the notion of economic harmony. In addition, the Germans, seeking to hasten industrial development, ardently espoused protectionist policies. American writers, adopting many of these views, then added several features which made their outlook pragmatic and parochial. A new nation spreading across an unbounded continent filled with virtually all the resources necessary for everlasting prosperity could not be expected to receive favorably the cold logic and gloomy prospects of diminish-

614

ing returns. Economists on this side of the Atlantic, like the industrialists, gave vent to a buoyancy quite alien to the more restricted economy of Great Britain, where the struggle over the national dividend had been quickly noted by David Ricardo. The American spirit was an ebullient one, stemming as it did from a fervent belief in harmony: the latter was almost preordained, expressing a manifest destiny that neither desert nor Indian could resist, and it explained in great measure the optimistic and curiously exceptionalist nature of nineteenth-century American economic thinking. America was a chosen nation and it would remain so, given the Lord's beneficence and the protective tariff. This optimism reflected in the main a belief in unbridled competition: Adam Smith's unseen Providence and Herbert Spencer's Social Darwinism joined hands to justify whatever it was the business community might want to accomplish.

Nevertheless, not all economists were prepared to accept the conservative bias of nineteenth-century thought. The institutionalist group, Thorstein Veblen and John R. Commons, and later, Wesley C. Mitchell and John Maurice Clark, while stressing different facets of theory, were all sharply critical of the dominant schools of thought. As a cohesive type of thinking, institutionalism is now unfortunately all but extinct, except for an occasional economist-cum-sociologist. There was also, at the turn of the century, a group of bright young economists, who, having tasted the heady wine of European scholarship, returned to these shores determined to move economics in a new direction. When these young men—Richard T. Ely, E. R. A. Seligman, and others—formed the American Economic Association in 1885 they clearly were rebelling against the self-satisfied domination of orthodox doctrine.[1] Ely and Seligman felt they could model themselves after the German historicists who had created the *Verein für Sozialpolitik* to discuss and promulgate new views. In fact, the German historical economists had given the American rebels most of their arguments against orthodoxy. The writings of Cliffe Leslie and John K. Ingram also were popular reading for the Americans. In the 1880's more than two thousand American students had gone to European universities. Of 116 economists who were asked in 1908 where they had studied, 59 had taken graduate work in Germany.[2] Among them were H. C. Adams, Simon N. Patten, Richard T. Ely, F. W. Taussig, A. T. Hadley, and E. R. A. Seligman, all attracted by such scholars as Knies, Roscher, and Schmoller.

Upon their return to America, many of these younger economists wanted a platform from which to declare to the profession and to the public that collective action was the most efficient way to utilize the nation's resources and to advance individual potentialities.[3] They found the labor issue especially disturbing and urged that capitalists and trade unionists settle their differences amicably. Grants-in-aid for education, they said, should be given to the states; social regulation was necessary for a decent transportation system;

and only the Federal government, they further asserted, could really sponsor and support economic growth. These thoughts were, of course, utterly heretical. But Ely, for one, pressed the attack on orthodoxy. Laissez faire, he argued, was unsound in economics, politics, and morals. The deductive method inhibited the scientific gathering of facts. It was time for a fresh approach in economics and the other social sciences.

The original manifesto of the American Economic Association was so sharply worded that many of the more moderate economists were taken aback, to say nothing of the reaction from the conservative side of the profession. After wiser heads prevailed upon Ely to modify his statement, the criticism of laissez faire was converted into a rather lukewarm assertion of general principles with which individualists could live. When Francis A. Walker, the grand old man of American economics, accepted the first presidency, the Association became respectable upon birth. Even so, its members, who thought of themselves as the "new school" in American economics, did not gain immunity from attack. Simon Newcomb sneered at them as a gang of socialists, reserving special venom for Ely. A dispute ensued which almost took on the disheartening features of the European *Methodenstreit*.[4] The conservatives pointed to Seligman's flirtation with income taxes, Ely's interest in European socialism, and Adams' advocacy of railroad rate control. Even Taussig, conservative that he was, suffered from guilt by association. But anxious to attract as many younger members of the conservative group as possible, the American Economic Association modulated its statement of principles still more in 1887, and, within a few years, it became a polite enough organization for everyone to join.

The interest in historicism was short-lived. The dominant mood in the country was, after all, laissez faire, and it was not long before most economists, including the Young Turks, began to move back toward classicism and deductive technique. When Ely and Seligman wrote their famous texts, one could discern a palpable drift to the Anglo-Saxon and Austrian systems of economics. Although these books did begin with historical outlines and sought to depict stages of economic development, the substantive content was a blend of marginal utiltiy and cost of production. As time went on, only a few economists incorporated the empirical stress of the German historical school into their work. Moreover, traditionalism obtained important support from the marginalist doctrines advanced by John Bates Clark. Soon there were no prophets crying in the wilderness. Only the Jeremiad of a Thorstein Veblen was to ruffle the placidity of received economics.

Perhaps the best known and most active of the younger rebels was Richard T. Ely (1854-1943). Born in Ripley, New York, Ely studied at Columbia and then spent three years in Germany on a scholarship subjecting himself to the rigors of Kantian and Hegelian philosophy. More important to his future development, however, was the contact with the German historical economists, an influence that was to last a long time. In 1881 he joined the faculty of Johns Hopkins, combining teaching with a variety of off-campus activities, including journalism and tax collection. He wrote profusely for newspapers and magazines, calling unceasingly for sundry reforms. In economics, he urged more investigation and empirical research on specific problems. As a Christian Socialist, he believed that the Church should become involved in all crucial social issues, and it was not surprising that he should express sympathy for labor and consumer cooperatives. Employers, Ely felt, were all too often arrogant in their attitudes towards workers: the class struggle would be lessened quite markedly if only labor's rights were acknowledged. Ely's writing was incisive and he did not obscure his meaning. Such forthright statements did much to arouse interest in what the "new school" of economists had to say.

Ely's *Introduction to Political Economy* (1889) became one of the first of the new textbooks. His later *Outlines of Economics,*[5] subsequent editions of which drew in Allyn A. Young, T. S. Adams and Max O. Lorenz as collaborators, became a best-seller. The *Outlines* was notable for its stress on historical forces and exhibited a marked ethical tone, clearly explained by Ely's Christian Socialist background. While sharply criticising what he conceived to be John Stuart Mill's rigid conception of man, Ely expressed admiration for the latter's treatment of the problem of distribution. Classical rent theory, for example, was defended as a valid analysis. However, Ely failed to realize that Mill had employed the economic man concept of the classicists merely to indicate the pursuit of wealth as one facet of man's condition and that for him economic law was historically conditioned.

From Johns Hopkins, where he met Commons, Ely went in 1892 to the University of Wisconsin as professor and director of the School of Economics, Political Science, and History. Not restricting his career to the campus, he gave considerable time to public activities, serving on numerous federal and state commissions. But as the years passed Ely became more and more conservative. His career typified the way in which the "younger" economists were absorbed into the mainstream of orthodox thinking. As the Marshallian amalgam of marginal utility and cost of production became palatable, many of the social problems which Ely and others once had thought to be their proper concern were handed over by default to the more tender mercies of the sociologist. Ely's *Outlines* adopted the marginalist analysis in its later editions. Although at first a Ricardian in rent theory, Ely later rejected the belief that economic rent should be taxed, and finally accepted J. B. Clark's virtual identification of land with capital. He denied in no uncertain terms that he was a socialist, at least of the Marxian variety. However, the *Outlines* continued to exhibit an eclectic merger of historical, Marshallian, and Austrian ideas. Its treatment of economic evolution, value theory, distribution, and production united theories that ordinarily had seemed far apart. Natural laws were merely an expression of general economic tendencies; objective value was a ratio between utilities; and normal value was the long-run device by which a marriage between marginal utility and cost was achieved.

Ely's speciality became land economics and he founded a scholarly journal to deal with the subject.[6] This provided him with a medium for an extended discussion on conservation, in which he continually called for some means of public control over the disposition of natural resources. Property was described as a series of rights, but nevertheless subject to modifications.[7] An interesting suggestion for dealing with depressions was his proposal for a peacetime industrial army, an idea drawn from William James' *Moral Equivalent of War*. Such an army could be engaged, said Ely, in such useful projects as reforestation and land development. And in the midst of the ravaging depression of the thirties, Ely's notion bore fruit in the Civilian Conservation Corps, established in 1933, in which over 2,500,000 young men planted trees, built fish ponds, dug ditches, fought plant disease, and improved recreation spots.[8]

Not all of the younger economists subscribed to the internationalist spirit implicit in classical theory. Simon Nelson Patten (1852-1922), was one who preferred to stress nationalist sentiments in his version of the "new" economics. Born in Illinois and educated at Northwestern University, Patten was something of a romanticist for whom the economic laws applicable to the United States, with its great wealth and resources, were bound to differ from those stemming from European economies. In 1878 he obtained a doctorate from Halle, where he became familiar with the work of the historical economists, although he was no stranger to Austrian doctrine. The German historicists, he thought, offered a new platform from which to examine the economic system. Society, rather than the individual, became the center of interest and productive power stemmed mainly from social organization.

Unable to obtain a college post upon his return to America, he spent ten years in farming and teaching in the public schools. Finally, in 1889, he was appointed to the Wharton School. The influence of Austrian doctrine was much more visible in his theory than was the case for some of his contemporaries. Yet at the same time, he was an ardent protectionist. Free trade, he argued, encouraged cash cropping rather than variety in agriculture and this in turn contributed to monopoly. Similarly, he rejected Malthusian pessimism, describing the economics of the classicists as more suitable to a deficit rather than a surplus economy, such as was found in the United States. Here resources were abundant enough to provide a social surplus for public needs; nature was not niggardly, but rather so generous that her gifts simply waited to be used. For such an environment, diminishing returns was an alien concept, and with the growth of industry, the new age would be a cooperative, not a competitive one. Variety in agriculture and industry, stimulated by protective tariffs, would bring forth the civilizing forces which the nation needed.

Although Patten's ideas had strong roots in Austrian theory, his inferences and conclusions were markedly different. In his view, consumption was central to economic theory.[9] In order to raise consumption to new heights, he urged the wealthy to open their art collections to the public, for such actions would increase community satisfactions without incurring any greater cost. Education and parks ought to be supported through higher taxes, he said, and in order to achieve freedom in its true sense, workers and the public generally ought to be accorded the rights once held by landowners.[10] To attain these rights it was essential to expand the social surplus and to give the worker the best of conditions. He had a right to leisure and comfort and clean surroundings. Urban growth, observed Patten, actually inhibited the ability to produce and prevented the development of a cohesive economy. Society ought to step in whenever individuals could not sustain themselves. Certainly these were broad and even radical views for the time, yet Patten was quite vague as to how his high objectives were to be attained. Legislative action, aside from tariffs, seemed to him rather dubious.[11]

Like Veblen, the conflict between pecuniary and industrial employment and its effect on the future of the economy was of great interest to Patten. The clash between the pecuniary and the industrial stemmed, he said, from a failure to adjust psychologically to new ways. True, the vested interests often did resist change, but there was hope that they would learn from the irresistible struggle. Patten was much more optimistic about the outcome than Veblen: to him, the conflict was pluralistic rather than dual in nature. Eventually, the various contending groups would accept the values of cooperation. Ultimate economic salvation would be reached by the acceptance, not the rejection, of modern industrial methods.

At times it was rather difficult to follow the thread of Patten's argument. Confusing the factors of production with the services that flowed from them, he then complicated matters by employing a language all his own. Terms from other disciplines were borrowed indiscriminately and used in new ways. Yet his ideas were so passionately presented that many of his students were influenced to enter such areas as social work and reform activity. Perhaps he was a better interpreter of American culture than he was a technical theorist. Affected by emerging philosophic trends, as reflected in his concept of economic pluralism, Patten sought to examine society in the round. Social problems were not merely the sum of individual concerns, for society was something more than the sum of its parts. Certainly, the study of history was an important tool for grasping and comprehending this basic idea.[12] Economics would have to be pragmatic and functional, he urged, since a single set of principles never could be said to govern all societies. Thus the economist should utilize abstractions moderately, exploring the realities

of economic life. Preferring induction and statistics to deductive generalizations,[13] he found the scholasticism of ordinary theory distasteful, describing
it as a "hybrid product of bookworm and hair splitters." [14] Yet added to this
strange and heady mixture of sociology and utopianism was a strong dose
of classical doctrine. Patten could not dispose completely of his heritage.

The economic laws, said Patten, which governed rent, profits, and wages
did not stem from some remote province of nature. Such laws had historical
origins and their validity depended upon their relationship to a particular
historical situation. Economists, therefore, ought to explore the beginnings
of institutions as well as the culture of their time. Economic behavior was
time-bound and historically conditioned.[15] Some social institutions were rooted
in predatory habits, others in useful patterns of work. Although biological
drives were significant elements in the creation of institutions, cultural conditioning was more important. Specifically, a good deal of labor did not enter
into cost, said Patten, because of its pleasurable aspects. If all work were
pleasurable, cost would disappear entirely. But since exchange still would
continue, the value of goods would not be diminished. Exchange, in fact,
was founded on the continued reproduction of capital, and it was this that
gave it a broad social character, a notion that evidently came from J. B.
Clark. Patten's curious concatenation of ideas reflected the outlook of a
welfare economist, an applied historian, a subjective theorist, and an incorrigible optimist. As a thinker he was more than a simple electic: he was
seeking a synthetic fusion of ideas which unfortunately was too brittle to
be sustained for long.

A sounder, if less dramatic economist, was Edwin R. A. Seligman (1861-
1939), scion of a famous American banking family. Seligman, born in New
York City and educated at Columbia, preferred the world of scholarship to
the family business and like others of his generation made the grand tour
of European universities, visiting Germany, Geneva, and Paris. His was a
distinguished career, with heavy emphasis on public finance, which he raised
to the front rank of economic specialities, contributing many still useful
studies on income taxes, and on the problem of shifting and incidence.
Seligman's interests also extended to the history of economic thought to
which he made important contributions. He built an enormous library in
economics which is now housed at Columbia University, and capped his life
work with the chief editorship of the *Encyclopaedia of the Social Sciences,*
a fifteen-volume monument yet to be matched in the literature.

Seligman was perhaps better read in other social sciences than most
economists of his day, and with his broad, catholic taste he usually could
find something worthwhile in all writers. An effective lecturer, he never
failed to present his class materials in an orderly and systematic fashion.
His writing was always lucid, and as a teacher he was considered among the
best. Quite early in his career Seligman exhibited an interest in the plight

of the worker and urged that the concept of a living wage would raise competition to higher levels. But his chief field of interest was taxation. In his major works, *Progressive Taxation in Theory and Practice* and *The Shifting and Incidence of Taxation*,[16] he advocated the ability-to-pay criterion. By relating this to problems of production and distribution he was able to broaden the area of tax theory. Although he developed a persuasive theoretical justification for progressive income taxes, he did urge caution by starting first with proportionate rates and then instituting elements of progression.

Less radical than Ely, he did not think, in the debates on the American Economic Association, that there was as yet sufficient evidence to support as much government intervention as the former thought necessary. The *Economic Interpretation of History*,[17] which went through several editions, traced the origins of materialistic ideas to pre-Marxian writers. And he revealed in it a much firmer grasp of Marx's philosophic intentions than did most writers of the day. *The Principles of Economics* [18] was thoroughly saturated with the historical point of view, with a heavy emphasis on stages of economic development and American economic growth. In his versions of value and distribution theory, Seligman displayed the influence of J. B. Clark and the Austrians: like the other writers of his day, he did not mind a bit of eclecticism. He deviated from classical notions only in his advocacy of protective tariffs as a way of building up nascent industries. The exposition of marginal utility was thought by Europeans to be quite accurate, but Seligman was less disposed toward utilizing Robinson Crusoe illustrations than were his predecessors. His discussion of the social implications of economics clearly stemmed from Bücher and other German historicists. The *Principles* was an excellent piece of pedagogy, its theory well sprayed with facts, tables, and diagrams. Curiously enough, F. W. Taussig thought it a poor performance, perhaps because Seligman went beyond the old masters. Böhm-Bawerk's marginal pairs of buyers and sellers were expanded into social groups which came onto the market. Demand, consequently, depended upon the social situation of the buying public, while supply was conditioned by the existing technique of production. Since, in the short run, demand was the predominant side of the market equation, the purchasing power of the marginal social class became the really crucial factor. The implications stemming from this formulation were more than the conservative economists could bear. Nevertheless, Seligman's approach did suggest a way of investigating social reality which seemed to escape the pure marginalists.

While basically a follower of classical-Austrian doctrine, Seligman was sympathetic to the aspirations of the trade unions. He advocated a certain measure of social legislation to modify the rigors of the competitive system. So far as he could see, taxation was a burden only so long as entrepreneurs failed to increase output. In tax theory, he made an important distinction between incidence—where the tax finally settled—and the incidental burden which accompanied the process of shifting.[19] The study of incidence was extremely important, he said, for it revealed the ultimate effects of a tax. He also noted capitalization and transformation as ways of escaping tax burdens. The latter reflected changes in the method of production enforced by a tax, that is, increases in efficiency which permitted the tax to be absorbed without further shifting. Not all taxes, consequently, were shifted to the consumer, said he.

If the inheritance tax did lessen the desire to accumulate, this at best was but an indirect effect. Certainly, it had no immediate impact on prices, said Seligman. Thus despite the existence of an economic relationship between the taxpayer and others, it was not always possible to shift the burden of taxation. If a monopolist, for example, sought to shed his entire tax burden, he might decrease his sales more than if the tax were absorbed. Ultimately, Seligman recognized, it was the varying elasticity of demand and supply which determined the extent of shiftability, a view not shared by all economists today. An integrated tax system, Seligman went on to say, should employ a variety of imposts. And he knew that government expenditures were a function of expanded activities. As Joseph Dorfman has said, these were the views of the enlightened sector of the business community. But like most members of that sector, Seligman did not expect that the stock market collapse of 1929 would move into a depression. Nevertheless, he did not hesitate to urge public works as an ameliorative step once it was realized that the worst was yet to come.

Thomas Nixon Carver (1865-1961), a colleague of Taussig's at Harvard, also sought to loosen the bonds of orthodox doctrine. Carver was born in Iowa, studied at the University of Southern California, and did graduate work with Ely at Johns Hopkins. While Ely's influence was revealed in Carver's espousal of sociological formulations, he was not averse to employing abstraction when necessary, a skill at which he was quite adept. For Carver, economic activity rather than commodities was the true subject for economists to study. Valuation was a case in point, for in this process "psychical" phenomena were pre-eminent. While less disposed toward the historical approach than others of his generation, he did assert that economic policy had to be adapted to particular circumstances: there were no firm theoretical rules that could be applied at all times.[20] Prosperity, a problem to which Carver gave much attention, depended primarily on the conversion of purchasing power into goods which yielded an income. The classical cost of production doctrine was not the sole element in value, and, as with Clark, the law of diminishing returns was applied to all factors of production.[21] However, he did make a clear distinction between the factors, and insisted that land could not be converted into a kind of capital, as other economists were attempting to do. Rent and interest, therefore, had to be carefully differentiated, for the relationships expressed by these payments were different.

Fetter, particularly, opposed Carver on this point, insisting that land was a much more flexible factor than Carver construed it to be. Although Carver did accept the marginal productivity theory to explain distribution, he was astute enough to observe that such a theory failed to explain the pattern of personal distribution of income, with the result that marginal productivity could be employed unjustifiably as an ethically correct proposition. By making interest the price which measured marginal productivity and marginal sacrifice, he was able to fuse various seemingly disparate elements.

For Carver, prosperity required a certain economic balance for which the factors of production would have to be employed in a way that would render maximum results. Welfare was enhanced when a harmonious relationship existed between lowest cost and highest productivity. This meant that natural resources were to be carefully utilized. Yet, noted Carver, American experience in this area revealed that little thought was being given to the idea of a proper economic and social balance. Were this done, some knowledge of ultimate goals necessarily would be required, for in the absence of such knowledge, only waste could ensue. (As applied to wages, the notion of balance was little more than the classical theory of an equilibrium wage.) One way out of the dilemma, said Carver, was by economic expansion and industrial growth; and for underdeveloped areas it was especially important that the inflow of foreign capital be supported by real internal growth and improvements in the quality of the work force. In the light of modern writings on underdeveloped nations, this was certainly a remarkable bit of foresight. Although Carver did not develop a cohesive system as was attempted by Clark and Fetter, his various books did offer many suggestive ideas.[22]

ii

Frank W. Taussig: American Traditionalist

Frank W. Taussig (1859-1940) offered perhaps the most rounded system of economic thought developed by any of the early members of the American Economic Association. By no means as "radical" as Ely, Taussig was, in fact, quite conservative. As first of the so-called "old" school to join the American Economic Association, he gave it the kind of respectability it needed to succeed. A descendant of an energetic line of Czechoslovaks,

Taussig's father had migrated to the United States in the 1840's, where he had a remarkable career as physician, judge, banker, and industrialist. Taussig was reared in a cultured family, and given an excellent education, including study on the violin, a love for which remained with him throughout a long and active career. At Harvard he majored in economics and history, and then came the traditional European tour. Like other students who visited Germany, he familiarized himself with the historical economists and their reform ideology. Upon his return to the United States, he was appointed secretary to President Eliot of Harvard. Despite a rather full work schedule, Taussig was able to program studies for the doctorate degree. With tariffs as his speciality, he combined institutional insights with theoretical analysis in a unique manner. Specific problems were looked at in their sociological setting, and while the traditional free trade policy seemed the essence of logic and good sense, Taussig could see some merit in the infant industry argument.

Active in public affairs, Taussig served on various governmental bodies, and, when the Tariff Commission was created in 1916, he became its first chairman, giving it the initial direction it needed to succeed. After World War I, he served on the Advisory Committee on the Peace at Versailles. As editor of the *Quarterly Journal of Economics* for many years, he showed enough broadmindedness to print articles he personally disliked, such as Henry L. Moore's contributions in mathematical economics and even Thorstein Veblen's acerb comments on current customs and theories. For Taussig, economic theory was an investigative tool to be used primarily for exploring real problems. An excellent teacher, he exerted no small influence on the next generation of economists, including such outstanding figures as Jacob Viner, John H. Williams, James W. Angell, and Frank D. Graham. And his book on principles, one of the best pedagogic works of its kind, went through numerous editions.[23] Like most texts, it was organized along traditional lines, covering the realms of production, distribution, and value quite thoroughly. The reader was taken in easy stages from the simplest propositions to the most complex formulations. Taussig did not hesitate to use mathematics whenever he thought it necessary. Value theory was developed in the orthodox way. However, Taussig's most important books were in his special field, tariffs and international trade, *The Tariff History of the United States* and *International Trade*.[24] After retirement in 1935, he spent the remaining years rewriting his *Principles*. As Joseph Schumpeter once remarked, Taussig indeed had been the American Marshall.[25]

The validity of the classical system was never questioned by Taussig. The verities of Ricardo and Mill formed the substructure of his economic thinking, although occasionally he did accept ideas from Böhm-Bawerk and Marshall. *Wages and Capital,* for example, his chief work of pure theory, was essentially a defense on the wages fund notion, which Mill himself had abandoned in

1869.[26] Taussig insisted that wages were in the last analysis an income stemming from a fund of consumer goods which could not be expanded in the short run. Labor services exhibited elements of futurity which bore fruit not in the present, yet present goods had to be surrendered for those services. What might be advanced in the way of wage goods depended on past productivity. The general level of wages was related to that portion of an entrepreneur's fund that was intended to enhance profitability, that is, wages were the result of the impact of circulating capital against the supply of labor. Taussig did grant that the rigid form given to the doctrine by the classicists had been an overstatement, but, essentially, he argued, it had been correct.[27] Even if wages were defined as a flow or stream, its source acquired the characteristics of a fund because of the lack of expandibility. It was this situation that prevented a general rise in wages.[28] He suggested that wage levels could be raised only if conditions of demand were improved. But behind demand stood all the "intricate problems of value as well as of production and distribution." [29] By this, Taussig meant to underscore the significance of variable production functions and the relationship between the flow of goods and the time structure of capital equipment. Thus the availability of wage goods was no longer a simple function of circulating capital. The main point, however, was that wages did not stem from its own product and that the attack on the wages fund theory had not been completely justified. Wages were set under competition by the "discounted marginal product of labor," an argument similar to that advanced by J. B. Clark. But Taussig would not go so far as Clark in asserting that marginal productivity gave the worker just what he merited. Such judgments, said Taussig, were outside the purview of the economist. Yet, as he could not reply satisfactorily to the criticism that wage advances came from the most recent product, he gradually, under repeated attacks, gave up the term "wages fund." [30] Such theories underscored Taussig's basically conservative attitude. He did not believe, for example, that social legislation would be very helpful, although he was astute enough to assign responsibility for many labor disputes to the capitalist, as in his sharp criticism of Henry Clay Frick in the Homestead affair.

During World War I, Taussig, as a member of the Price Fixing Committee of the War Industrial Board, helped to develop the idea of "bulk line" prices. The bulk line was defined as the required amount of goods of a particular type needed for the war effort. Bulk line cost was the unit cost to the marginal firm whose output was essential. Thus the price that was established had to cover the costs of all the producers whose output had to be taken by the government. Inefficient operators and those whose production was inessential were thereby excluded. This was a patent if somewhat crude attempt to apply marginalist concepts. Presumably, taxation would recapture the excess profits of the very efficient. However, as a method of wartime pricing, it was not successful and merely generated adverse criticism.[31]

Yet Taussig's experience during those turbulent days did lead to a certain modification of his purely classical outlook. While he was still cautious and conservative, he now permitted himself to give somewhat fuller expression to his innate humanitarian feelings and he urged a better distribution of the fruits of economic advance. The thrust toward the accumulation of capital was still a powerful incentive, but whatever evils might stem from it could be lessened by progressive taxation. Situations other than purely theoretical models now seemed worth studying, for there were many deviations from market price in which equilibrium was seldom, if ever, established. There was a region of indeterminateness, he said, a "penumbra," which merited investigation. He even agreed with the British historian, Clapham, that many empty economic boxes still were to be filled.[32] Insofar as labor unions were concerned, Taussig remained hesitant, for to him a competitive labor market still appeared workable.

His explanation of economic crises was not very advanced. A distinction was made between an industrial depression and a purely financial crisis.[33] The larger oscillations of a depression were attributed to the structure of capitalist production, that is, to the division of labor, and, in part, to psychological causes. Since production was divided into various stages, erroneous adjustments became quite likely: this was the proximate cause of a depression, especially when rapid changes were taking place. While heavy fixed investment was bound to exacerbate the condition, poor adjustments in one sector would tend to spill over into others, generating a sense of pessimism and hesitancy. And, of course, the credit system always could lead to more pronounced movements.

Although Taussig never questioned the efficacy of purely deductive methods, he could not help but engage in fact gathering while developing his analysis of trade and tariffs. This was not simply a matter of illustrating general principles with statistics and historical examples, but rather a genuine integration of theoretical and empirical data. Ultimately, it was *The Tariff History of the United States* which provided the factual basis for his *International Trade*. Taussig began his analysis with Mill, and, although he introduced any number of modifications, he never really departed far from the classical master. His teaching had a powerful influence, for with Viner, Williams, and Angell, considerable impetus was given to empirical research in international trade. Little advance had been made in theory since Mill, so that one could easily begin with Taussig's contributions.[34] It represented a coordinated theory of international trade, comparative costs, and the effects of money and credit. There had been some difficulty in the classical version because of its dependence on comparative labor costs or some variant of labor theory. One way out of this dilemma was to speak of money costs; Taussig pursued this avenue, emphasizing the effect of wage differences and the differences in the ratios of capital costs to totals costs for different industries in the nations concerned. He felt that over the long run, a money cost interpretation would conform fairly closely to the labor cost version. His argument was based on the contention that the structure of wages in the different countries was roughly alike and that differences in interest, a small part of total cost anyway, were not substantial. Trade, he argued, would not be affected appreciably if the disproportion in money costs and labor costs were approximately the same between nations. As Viner has pointed out, the argument might have been strengthened if Taussig had included in his analysis the effects of land-use costs on money costs and if income distribution and changes in demand had not been altered in any marked degree.[35]

One of Taussig's more striking performances was his analysis of trade under paper money conditions.[36] He began with the assumptions that commodity trade was a significant factor prior to any situation of disequilibrium and that depreciation of paper currency was measured by the premium on specie. Taussig then showed how a large loan flowing from, say, Britain to the United States, would make imports in this country available at lower prices in terms of dollars and cause a drop in exports to Britain. This was the mechanism for restoring equilibrium. The adjustment would be the same as under the gold standard, although money prices would tend to move somewhat differently.[37] Significantly, the substitution of foreign goods for domestic ones would lead to a fall in the prices of the latter, an important conclusion. But there seemed no reason to assume that costs of production or the flow of money income would not be affected. The notion of the income elasticity of demand was barely approached by Taussig. It is interesting to note that Viner, perhaps Taussig's leading pupil, has raised this question as well.[38]

The concept of a "gross barter terms of trade," another interesting point raised by Taussig, was intended to take account of one-way flows, such as immigrant remittances, by including them in the definition of barter terms. That is, total flows were to be considered in evaluating the terms of trade.[39] Taussig also studied the relation of wages in the export industries to the movement of exports and imports and the effect that these might have on the national income. In his view, the impact stemmed from the export industries to other fields. He also argued that specialization in international trade did not necessarily have to agree with the principle of comparative advantage, for differences in wages in different occupations might conceivably cause relative prices to deviate from the underlying labor costs.[40] He believed further that trade balances tended to adjust themselves to capital movements. But again, as Viner has demonstrated, it may be possible for adjustments to move in either direction: after World War I, shifts in Canadian trade balances stemmed from borrowings abroad, while in New Zealand the reverse seemed to be the case.[41]

These were the ways then in which Taussig sought to amplify the classical system. But aside from his own speciality, international trade, it remained largely the same deductive body of thought which had made advances only by fusing Austrian subjectivism onto Anglo-Saxon tradition. It was conservative and safe and well-received, despite an occasional guilty glance in the direction of the exacerbating social questions raised by the conflict of capital and labor.

iii

Pecuniary Economics: Fetter
and Davenport

By now virtually all major American economists had become specialists of one sort or another. Ely was concerned with land economics, Seligman with taxation, Taussig with tariffs. Yet a number of scholars, such as Frank A. Fetter and Herbert J. Davenport, continued to direct their main efforts toward a purification of theory. Frank Fetter (1863-1949), who like the others of his generation had gone through the German academic mill, remained a pure theorist with a more systematic development of doctrine than was evident, for example, in Patten. His major contribution was an emphasis on "pecuniary logic," with a new psychological twist applied to Austrian theory. By refining both concepts and language, Fetter sought to adapt marginalist arguments to the American business scene.

Fetter, born in Peru, Indiana, attended the State University at Bloomington where he obtained an excellent grounding in the philosophic bases of economic thought. Unable to complete his senior year, Fetter went into business, operating a bookstore, which supplied him with ample reading material for after hours. Eight years passed before he was able to return to school. Jeremiah Jenks encouraged him to make the usual European trip, and, upon his return to the United States, Fetter taught successively at Cornell, Indiana, Stanford, and Princeton. He was a popular teacher, especially stimulating to social work and engineering students.[42]

Although Patten and Clark seemed to him the best advocates of the new marginalist analysis. Fetter felt that much still remained to be done, for the absolute standard of labor appeared to lurk behind the more recent theories, and this would have to be exorcised. At first, Fetter thought the hedonic approach sufficient. The object of economic action was to achieve maximum pleasure at the least cost, and, since value stemmed from the pleasure provided by a good, one could proceed from this to the marginal analysis without any reservations. But in the second edition of his *Economic Principles* [43] Fetter shifted ground. Realizing that straightforward utilitarianism could not provide a logically satisfactory base for economics, he now appealed to a "volitional" psychology in which the mere act of choice seemed sufficient to explain the phenomenon of value. Like Pareto and others on the Continent, he proposed to abandon the older view as inadequate and, in fact, erroneous. Many theorists were discovering that they could no longer accept the hedonic formulations in the light of new biological and psychological findings. Thorstein Veblen had quite thoroughly demolished utilitarian presuppositions, and his vitriolic attack was followed by one from Henry W. Stuart, a former student, who exposed the hedonic assumptions in economic theory even more starkly.[44]

With the intellectual climate changing in such dramatic fashion, Fetter was determined to restructure economic theory rather than to merely bring J. S. Mill up-to-date. The first five sections of *Economic Principles* dealt with the personal acquisitive aspects of value—the prices of immediate consumables, prices of intermediate goods, valuation of human services, interest and time-preference, and entrepreneurial profits. This was followed by a discussion of population, land, technology, and saving. The organizing principle throughout was the theory of value, a derivative of human desire, with the prices of all the agents of production reflected back from the prices of their products. In his effort to avoid merely modernizing Mill, Fetter was not averse to employing new terms or using old words in new ways. But as laudable as this was, the desire to clarify economic concepts through semantic devices created no little amount of difficulty.

Psychic income was defined as desirable feelings generated by goods. The mainspring of economic action, therefore, became anticipated psychic income. Fetter, however, was not prepared to make the leap into a theory of price after the fashion of Cassel. He still was interested in value theory per se, for choice, the prime volitional act in economics, necessarily implied value as the basis for choosing.[45] Instead of talking about utility, one simply had to refer to gratification and marginal valuation. Value was the quality of importance which things possessed when they were objects of choice.[46] Yet Fetter knew that in comparing commodities, there were manifold influences stemming from man and nature which affected choice. Value, therefore, was not an intrinsic quality, but one which fluctuated as the intensity of desire shifted with extreme pressures. The logical sequence, insisted Fetter, was from choice, through an act of valuation, to value. This enabled him to introduce impulsive actions and did not require any pleasure-pain calculations prior to making a choice. Thus volitional psychology pictured behavior in terms of choice alone, without direction from sensations of pleasure. Economic behavior did not need reflection as a guide. The danger with this approach lay in its limitation of economics to a study of wants and market satisfactions. Actually, Fetter was not willing to go so far. Yet he did feel that this approach had cast new light on value theory.

Upon close examination, however, the substance of the large body of theoretical propositions offered by earlier writers was not much altered by Fetter's supposedly new analysis. It merely presented another in the long chain of explanations for the variety of actions that provided the arena in which supply and demand were fixed. Whether the psychology involved was phrased as utility or choice, it was still the same basic theory. One could substitute the terms for each other and still arrive at the same place.[47] The disheartening conclusion could very well be that psychology was unnecessary for the economist: one need start only with the fact of supply and demand, and go on from there, as Lionel Robbins and Gustav Cassel had done. But this still evaded the basic question: what is the nature of economic man and why does he behave as he does? By presenting an old answer in a new shape, Fetter, like so many economists after him, revealed that he was not really interested in the problem. It was enough that man behaved and that the actions manifested could be classified as economic.

This did not mean that Fetter arrived at the same specific theories as did other economists. For example, while he recognized time preference, his interest notions were different from Fisher's in some respects. Future satisfactions, agreed Fetter, were not as important as present ones, so that a discounting process was involved. He described his version as "capitalization," but one which so strongly stressed psychological aspects that even Böhm-Bawerk was taken aback.[48] Time was Fetter's central concept, and the capitalization of psychic income became the mode of establishing the value of a good. He granted that discounting was bound to vary between persons, but generally there was a predisposition toward the present. Time discounting was antecedent to interest: it was the palpable fact that present goods were able to command future surpluses that made interest possible. The contractual rate of interest, argued Fetter, was a market reflection of the rate of capitalization involved in the prices of goods.[49] Price, depending on the capitalization process which involved the discounting of future uses, was prior to contractual interest. First came choice in terms of time, then value and price in terms of capitalization, and, finally, interest. This model was used to explain in psychological terms the emergence of a surplus when goods reached maturity. Time became the connecting link between the emerging surplus and present goods, and, in effect, unified production and consumption. Since it was an average of time preferences which determined interest, explanations that resorted to waiting or impatience seemed incomplete. Fetter, however, might have chosen a better illustration than the case of workers for whom the promise of higher earnings in the future was insufficient to induce them to invest in education and training. In fact, he simply omitted, in this case at least, the *ability* to "invest," exemplifying the emptiness of a theory which did not rest on a sound institutional base.

Nor did it appear that Fetter had escaped fully from a productivity theory of interest, although he did reject such a characterization. When goods manifested a capacity to provide a surplus in the future sufficient to remunerate the undertaker for risk and to pay contract interest, there seemingly would be an element of expanded productivity. But for Fetter productivity was only one fact in a total situation in which time preference was predominant. Moreover, he argued, increased physical output could lead to a decline in interest rates since this would cut the rate at which the future was discounted. Further, since under conditions of abundance, present wants became less urgent, the time discount would be lower and the value of the future services of the goods less. In a relative sense, present goods would cost more and there would be a lower margin of profit in their utilization, thus depressing the rate of interest. The key factor was the present rate of discount which emerged from the sets of individual demand and supply schedules for future goods. The rate of interest, therefore, was an index of the ratio implicit in the equilibrium of psychological forces expressed through time preference. While the businessman might not be conscious of these forces, said Fetter, he who best anticipated the future would be the most successful.

These concepts explained Fetter's desire to abolish the traditional tripartite division of the factors of production. Wealth ought to be classified, he urged, in terms of scarcity, duration, and reproducibility. Together with the capitalization theory, these ideas offered the soundest means for constructing a unified economics.[50] Rent, wages, and profit were redefined as aspects of psychic income. Rent was the price paid for the services of a durable good for a given time limit; wages, as a service payment, were affected by worker efficiency, risks, and the worker's own psychic income; and profit, while residual and noncontractual, could be accounted for by the entrepreneur's contribution to the conduct of business.

Economic growth and advancement demanded businessmen who could foresee the future and supervise the vast conglomeration which comprised modern industry. Corporations by themselves could not accomplish all this, for management skills still were essential.[51] The best setting for growth was a competitive system in which prices and wages were governed by market forces. Fetter deplored the way in which the competitive norm was disturbed by such extraneous humanitarian questions as minimum wages and adequate living standards. Obviously this deep concern with the competitive model explained his zeal for neo-Malthusian population measures and eugenics programs. Improved standards could be attained only by lessening the pressures of population on resources.

Fetter also wrote rather extensively on monopoly problems, setting forth a rather strong antimonopoly attitude in both *Modern Economic Problems* and *The Masquerade of Monopoly*.[52] In the 1923 Federal Trade Commission hearings on steel pricing methods, he argued that the basing point method utilizing f.o.b. Pittsburgh prices to establish charges to customers elsewhere was unfair and inhibited competition. His analysis of market areas and market boundaries was notable in that it underscored the impossibility of a pure competitive condition in all markets. That is, the concepts of competition and monopoly had to be drawn closer, for markets exhibited features of each in varying degrees. The elimination of price discrimination, cross hauling, and freight absorption required a straight f.o.b. pricing technique, he said. Competition could develop only between mills which shared a market or at the borders of two markets.[53] Making similar points in the Temporary National Economic Committee hearings of 1939, Fetter also commented that the chief evil of monopoly was the "longtime steady effect in limiting production and increasing its prices." He did not believe that monopoly contributed to the inception of the economic crisis, but certainly it was important in "aggravating and prolonging industrial depression." [54] These views reflected a lifelong philosophy of individualism which went back to an oration given as a student in which he had exclaimed that the self and nothing but the self was the "axiom of evolution, the postulate of political economy." [55]

It was Herbert J. Davenport (1861-1931) who really carried the "pecuniary logic" to its highest pitch. Davenport was one of the greatest teachers in American economics. In the classroom he would pit one student against another and then subject them to a rigorous cross-examination. His students were expected to solve problems for themselves and to develop orderly thought habits. He was harsh, but like all good teachers, he was unafraid to express his own ideas in a straightforward and frequently blunt manner. Davenport was born in Vermont, the descendant of a long line of Puritan stock. He entered Harvard Law School at the age of twenty-two, but, as a special student, was not given a degree. He then went into the real estate business in South Dakota. However, unable to resist the world of intellect, he departed for Leipzig and Paris in 1890 to pursue further study. Obtaining the doctorate from Chicago in 1898, he joined the faculty there after a short stint as a high-school teacher. In 1908 he was at the University of Missouri and in 1916 went to Cornell, where he remained for the rest of his life.

At Chicago, Davenport studied with Veblen and later they became close friends. He thought that Veblen had no peer in those areas of economics which bordered on philosophy and sociology.[56] Many of the latter's acerb remarks on American capitalism were unconsciously reflected in Davenport's later descriptions of individualistic economics. Accepting the latter as a fact, he was determined to describe it as accurately as he could: often his paragraphs were even more abrasive than the most sardonic of Veblenian passages. Davenport authored numerous articles and books, including the *Outlines of Economic Theory*, a highly theoretical college text; *Value and Distribution,* a critical history of economic theory; *Economics of Enterprise,* an exposition of his own views; and the posthumous *Economics of Alfred Marshall,* a criticism of classical doctrine.[57] While in some ways the classical line of reasoning persisted in Davenport's thinking, particularly in the concept of value as a ratio and in the centrality of the entrepreneur, he was frequently a sharp critic of received doctrine. Many classical ideas had no place, he would argue, in a genuinely scientific pecuniary economics. He meant especially such notions as labor time, real costs, marginal pricing, the tripartite classification of factors, and the belief in a social organism. On marginalism, for example, he asserted that this idea, so fundamental to orthodox theory, was essentially relative to the individual, so that only utter confusion could occur when speaking of the marginal character of an instrument of production.[58] Neither marginal utility nor total utility could be measured by market price, since the latter merely equated total demand and total supply.[59] And from the pecuniary standpoint, land was quite like capital, with cost a simple business calculation.

Certainly these were refreshing and challenging ideas. As with Cassel, Davenport found it unnecessary to talk about value. Since economics was a science that dealt with the industrial and commercial activities of man, the central focus of discussion should be price. In no way did the ethical aspects of economic activity upset Davenport's rigorous logic. Burglar's tools were the thief's capital: it was not for the economist to question whether men were evil or foolish. His task was simply to analyze how economic man functioned. Fact was to be distinguished from appraisal. Yet as one reads Davenport, especially the latter sections of the *Economics of Enterprise,* his prose does take on an inescapable tongue-in-cheek quality.[60] "All gainful activities are productive," he said, "in the sole sense of the term appropriate to the competitive economic order, and . . . all objective bases of continuing income to the individual possessor are capital, no matter what may be their social significance." [61] Davenport referred, of course, only to an economy based on price, competition, and money. In other societies, with other institutions, a different emphasis would be called for. The inherent logic of capitalism was spun out more sharply by Davenport than was the case for most of his colleagues, who found its implications distasteful. The simple fact of the matter, the argument went on, was that men in our society were motivated by selfish gain: this was the fundamental starting point of a pecuniary economics. Consequently, productive labor was anything which yielded an income. Patents, royalties, tribute rights, legislative authority to pass special interest laws such as tariffs—these were all forms of capital providing income to someone.[62]

This suggested an economics in which utilitarian and ethical inferences were to be discarded. With marginal utility recast into relative concepts, ethical tests simply became irrelevant.[63] "Peruna, Hop Bitters, obscene literature, indecent paintings, picture hats and corsets are wealth, irrespective of any ethical or conventional test to which they may or may not conform. Being marketable, price-bearing, they are wealth." [64] Grass-cutting, the slave trade, pocket-picking, drug adulteration, and product manipulation were all productive occupations. The idea of productivity was to be applied to all instruments, for productivity found its test only in price. Stated in a tone of scientific neutrality and presented as a coldly objective description of the pecuniary system, it was, however, as Dorfman has so well observed, suffused with the Veblenian idiom.[65] How else was one to take seriously the huge heap of machines, burglars' tools, poison, murder weapons, patents, monopoly, cheating, lying, factories—anything that was productive by the supreme test of private gain? Davenport knew, of course, that institutions were subject to change, but his interest was in the present. Although he thought of himself as something of a traditionalist, merely trying to refine the older theory, he had come closer to the Veblenian heresy than he knew. The reaction to Davenport's analysis could not be very friendly. He was accused of extreme statements and of engaging in unwarranted attacks on the existing system: he was said to be a radical.[67]

Davenport granted that the economic theorist might start with utilities as the basis for a consumer's evaluation of goods. These were the bases on which offers were made for goods on the market. Similarly, sellers had an idea of what they wanted for their merchandise. These judgments underpinned the demand and supply schedules from which the phenomenon of price was derived. Yet the economist did not have to know anything about utilities; actually, he could know very little about them. The whole business of price determination stemmed from individual action and there was nothing "social" about it. Hence, social utility or social time discounts were not meaningful concepts. Utility, if it was an analytical device at all, could apply only to the individual, with no logical possibility of interpersonal comparisons being made.[68] Price offers consequently were merely expressions of relative marginal utility.

The notion of a "social organism" was sharply rejected, for in no way did it fit the facts of a competitive economy. Did private exchange transactions really reflect a collective action or organic unity, asked Davenport, when a football coach was accorded a salary of $1000 a month and an instructor of economics $1000 a year, or when a robber obtained $200 for ten minutes of daring and a ditch digger $2 for 600 minutes of boredom? Surely, he remarked wryly, the social organism ought to be put into a social insane asylum.

To return to Davenport's market analysis, there was more involved, said he, than the schedule of utilities for particular goods. There was also the utility of the purchasing power to be considered, which could be expressed in terms of the utilities of all the other goods available. Similarly with supply, for the price which might be accepted depended on the prices of all other goods. This implied, of course, the concept of opportunity cost, which Davenport did so much to advance. In his view, the operation of supply and demand involved a displacement of alternatives, a ". . . sacrifice of some second thing in the process of getting some particular thing. . . " [69] The idea of interdependence, which this suggested, actually might not be in the mind of the businessman, since it did not seem possible to reduce money cost to other denominations. Yet it was evident that cost of production was not the ultimate explanation of price, for it was necessary to take account of opportunity cost.[70] The economist was to carry the analysis beyond money cost, back to those forces which conditioned entrepreneurial activity. But did not Davenport here contradict his earlier concepts of the scope and limits of economics? The ultimate forces behind price were, after all, human desires: these provided the motives for exchange and production.[71] Thus, while suggesting that the exploration of such factors might be a proper task for the economist, Davenport himself was unwilling to go beyond price. The problem floundered in a condition that was not "intellectually satisfying." [72]

With the entrepreneur at the center of the productive and distributive process, the justification of the division of the product on the basis of the specific productivity theory seemed undeniable to most economists. Under free competition, the sharing of output presumably represented an accurate equivalent of the contributions made by the different factors. But, said Davenport, this was not necessarily the case, for there really was no method by which specific productivity could be measured. The theorist could accept such a formulation only in the broadest sense and then only so far as both product and proceeds were identical.[73] The logic of specific productivity suggested a perfect ethics: in the world of reality it was nonexistent. If the product was the same as proceeds, then all that could be said for a pecuniary economy was that differential advantages or a producers' surplus would emerge, a notion not unlike Marshall's quasi-rent. This, of course, made sense once the tripartite division of productive factors was dropped.

Interest was deemed to be a purely monetary phenomenon, representing a payment for the loan of funds.[74] In Davenport's common sense version, interest gave command over future purchasing power, and was closely related to the function of the banking system. Abstinence had little to do with interest: in the light of a sensible analysis of the workings of credit and banking, such a theory was little short of grotesque, said Davenport. As an ethical rationalization, abstinence was irrelevant and there certainly was no pain in abstaining.[75] Quite simply, interest was a premium for present dollars over future ones, and the determination of its rate was merely a pricing problem. The loan fund, stemming as it did from monetary roots, did not depend on the supply of production goods or other concrete wealth. It was the business of the banking system to create it and lend it.[76]

Given a rate of discount applied to a stream of services, capital emerged from the process of capitalization. As the value of a good was related to the flow of services it might render, present prices were tied to future services. With but a single outlay, the buyer of a good was able to obtain the right to a series of benefits. But this seemingly contradicted cost theory, since cost affected price through rents. Davenport tried to reconcile the two concepts by considering them essentially complementary. Cost led to supply which affected rents, and rents, through the capitalization process, determined price-demand.[77] Thus demand prices were derived from future earning powers and then were transformed by capitalization into immediate "paying dispositions." More important to Davenport perhaps was the contention that capitalization also affected reservation prices. Actually, capitalization had nothing to do with price-fixing or the determination of interest on loan-funds. The process of capitalization was a method for bringing a psychological future into a psychological present: it was not therefore a universal phenomenon, but had meaning only when a future stream of income or services was expected. Interest, therefore, represented an exchange between present and future, in which the sum now was the discounted price of the sum months or years from now.[78] As a consequence, wherever deferred payments were involved, capitalization, interest, and capital were all involved.

Davenport also commented briefly on economic crises. These seemed to him traceable primarily to financial causes, since there was a tendency for currency to expand more rapidly than business activity.[79] At the root of the difficulty lay the credit system, which, despite its great advantages, brought great risks. At the peak of a cycle, for example, business arrangements were such that credit could no longer be absorbed easily. The solution seemed to be not only a more effective banking system, but a flexible currency as well, so that the unfavorable effects of credit might be reduced. Once a depression was under way, difficulties were compounded. Various dislocations occurred; prices moved unevenly; debts became burdensome; and wage rigidities prevented a flexible adjustment to new levels.[80] Davenport recognized that falling prices would not stimulate consumption: there was a hint here of the role of effective demand in the Keynesian sense.[81] Although somewhat conservative in his policy views, Davenport did concede that there was a good case for public works during a depression.

Generally then, Davenport may be described as one of the more interesting economists of recent decades. His biting, savage analysis of individualistic economics and pecuniary values was more than just a scientific series of biopsies. It was in many ways an almost cruel examination of business mores that could have been motivated only by the highest of ethical standards.

iv

Irving Fisher: Capital, Interest, and Income

Pecuniary logic, to use Dorfman's phrase, was developed in other directions by Irving Fisher (1867-1947). A mathematician, statistician, businessman, reformer, and teacher, Fisher was indeed a man of many pursuits. As an inventor, he made a small fortune with a visible card index file system. Yet his passionate concern with eugenics, health fads, and temperance caused the general public to view him as something of a curiosity, and among economists his intellectual gadgeteering with compensated dollars and 100 per cent money tended to overshadow his genuinely important theoretical work. Only in later years did his ideas on capital, income, interest, and money begin to command the serious attention they merited. Fisher's contributions to statistics were especially important, particularly in the field of index numbers. And, by applying mathematical methods to economics he sought to unify theory and quantitative techniques. A prodigious writer, with twenty-eight books to his credit, eighteen of which were on economics, he also contributed numerous articles to the professional and popular journals.[82] But while there was a noticeably consistent thread in Fisher's work, his theory was not constructed in a cohesive way as was Marshall's or Walras'. Much too involved with a variety of reform movements to attempt that, he virtually eschewed teaching entirely in the last phase of his academic career.

Fisher was born in Saugerties, New York, the third child of a Congregational minister. Family illnesses and a three-year bout with tuberculosis in his early thirties made him a life-long health faddist. Fresh air became a compulsive creed, and all sorts of schemers and quacks were given quick and attentive audiences. As Fisher's father died in 1884, the year he entered Yale, he had to support the family while at school. Nevertheless, he did achieve a top academic ranking, taking a number of prizes, especially in mathematics. He was deeply influenced by Willard Gibbs, the noted physicist, under whom he studied mathematics, and particularly by William Graham Sumner, who taught him economics and suggested a combination of the two fields. During this time Fisher read Cournot, Auspitz and Lieben, Walras, Jevons, Edgeworth, and the Austrians. The outcome was his doctoral dissertation on the mathematics of value and price, a still useful work in the field. In 1893, he went to Europe to study higher mathematics with Frobenius and Poincaré. Upon his return, he began to teach mathematics at Yale, moving to the economics department in 1895. In 1898 he was elevated to a full professorship, just ten years after completing his undergraduate work.

Fisher's contribution to the field of statistics was especially important. He noted, for example, that the effect of a disturbance on an economic variable should be distributed, since the impact is generally carried beyond the variable itself. This observation demonstrated that statistics was for him more than a handy tool, but rather an integral aspect of economic analysis. In his *The Making of Index Numbers*,[83] he studied and classified hundreds of formulas, subjecting them to a variety of tests. Virtually all modern work on index numbers has stemmed from this genuinely monumental analysis. Fisher compared the various formulas by plotting different curves for the same set of data for the years 1913 to 1918. Thus able empirically to study weights, biases, and the like, he found, by a process of elimination, 47 formulas which agreed with each other; these were reduced to a group of 13, then 8, and finally he arrived at an "ideal" formula. Fisher did not suggest that this was the only one to use: it merely seemed to have less bias and distortion than the others.

In Fisher's doctoral thesis, well received by both Edgeworth and Pareto, no small honor, he developed an interesting and terse version of the Walrasian schemata, illustrated with mechanical models. He tried to depart from the notion of utility as a measurable quantity: seeking to connect utility with objective commodity relations, his analysis virtually became a pure logic of choice. Still there was some hesitancy at this stage, for while a theory of choice was deemed to be central, Fisher felt that some room might yet be made for measurement. The latter ideas, while developed in the classroom, were not published until 1927.[84] The suggestions for utility measurement were based on the now standard indifference curve approach, but Fisher quickly realized that once the utility surface was turned into an indifference map, only the logic of choice would remain. Moreover, this implied that the assertion which made the utility of a good depend solely on the quantity of that good would have to be abandoned: utility now was related to the quantity of all goods. That is to say, no problem arose when utilities were independent, for a utility schedule could be constructed easily enough. But with a generalized utility function, in which many goods affected each other, the formerly independent utility curve assumed quite a different form.

Thus while it might be helpful to attempt to measure utility, it was best, Fisher thought, to avoid the entanglements with ethics, psychology, and metaphysics that this would entail. Since the goal of the economist was to study the "mechanical interactions" implicit in the exchange process, it was sufficient to begin with the objective facts of price. There was no need to search for a theory of psychology. But this clearly meant that the market would have to be large enough to prevent any single person from influencing price; that rates of production and consumption were identical; that complete knowledge of market conditions was available to all concerned; that factors and products were continuously divisible; and that the law of diminishing marginal utility was universally applicable. In short, classical perfect competition always would have to prevail. By limiting the analysis to given periods of time, said Fisher, deviations from equilibrium could be put aside. At any rate, fluctuations were presumed to be self-correcting, so that in equilibrium the marginal utilities of each dollar of expenditure in various uses were equal. The marginal utilities of all goods were proportional to the marginal utilities of the same goods for other consumers. While in this way Fisher approached the idea of interdependence, he felt that a partial analysis would be more helpful, at least pedagogically. His "utility" was not hedonistic, he insisted: it merely indicated "desiredness," a notion devoid of ethical or value judgments. Clearly this was the beginning of the whole apparatus of modern economic analysis, with its concepts of complementarity, substitution, price lines, and income effects. Had he not cluttered his presentation with so many cumbersome mechanical illustrations, Fisher might have been given more credit for originality.

Defining capital as the stock of wealth at any given moment, the concept included both the physical and fund aspects, with perhaps greater emphasis on the former. Accounting definitions, deployed with rare skill, were effectively used to clarify economic ideas. In some ways, Fisher's distinctions between capital and income were similar to those advanced by the French economist, Adolphe Landry, in 1904. The capital-income relation had not been too much in evidence in the *Mathematical Investigations*. But when Fisher studied the problem more closely in preparing his *Nature of Capital and Income,* he was impressed by the way in which accountants were wont to approach the whole question. A mere differentiation between one kind of wealth and another did not seem adequate, for it was now important to delineate clearly the difference between stocks and flows. These notions were further advanced in the *Rate of Interest* wherein interest rates were made dependent on the size, composition, and distribution over time of the income stream. The discussion in *Capital and Income* also sought to clarify the nature of wealth, property, claims to property, services, and utility. This, said Fisher, was especially important in order to avoid double counting when computing total wealth.[85] Aggregating wealth might be done in one of two ways—by the method of "balances" or by the method of "couples." The first comprised the totality of personal values, showing the capital of individuals; the second was the addition of the capital values of specific goods. One reflected ownership, the other, things owned: both were mutually exclusive, being essentially ways of summing social wealth.[86] Similar methods were employed to sum income flows, so that in modern parlance, one became a kind of "value added" and the other a final product concept.[87] To clarify matters still further, Fisher dropped the term productive services and substituted for it the word "interactions" as a more satisfactory way of describing changes in wealth which were occasioned by production, transportation, and selling. These interactions stemmed from the fact that many of the services rendered in production were preparatory to other services. Yet ultimately they all wound up in the psychic income of the individual.[88]

Capital was meaningful only insofar as it yielded an income. The connection between physical capital and the value of capital was established both through income and the rate of interest. By capitalizing income at the current rate of interest, the tie to capital as a fund was made: value was determined by a process of discounting to the present. There was thus a need to relate physical to value concepts while at the same time stock and flows were kept clearly in view. Four basic ratios were set down: physical productivity, or the ratio of the quantity of services to the quantity of capital; value productivity, the ratio of the value of services to the quantity of capital; physical return, the ratio of the quantity of services to the value of capital; and, most important of all, value return, the ratio of the value of services to the value of capital.[89] This was simply the present worth of a future income derived from a particular item of capital,[90] and it revealed, Fisher insisted, that no genuine differentiation could be made between interest, rent, or other flow categories.

The latter thesis permeated Fisher's early essay, "Appreciation and Interest," [91] which embodied the ideas of time discount, or impatience, and investment opportunity, or the marginal rate of return over cost—notions that Fisher was to develop at greater length in subsequent works. Interest was not a separate flow, but rather an aspect of all incomes, be they wages, rents, or profit. The whole structure rested on the idea of choice between alternative income streams. Interest was the link between capital and income, and it was to be computed as a per cent of premium paid on money at one date in terms of money available at a later date. Since time was inherent in the whole process, discounting became the method for translating the future into the present.[92] Interest entered into all economic relations and permeated all prices. The influences which impinged upon it were admittedly unstable and rooted in a variety of causes, some of which were not economic in nature.

In the *Theory of Interest,* Fisher brought these concepts into sharp focus, and "investment opportunity" was matched with impatience as the keystone of the model. Capital gains, however, as mere capitalizations of future yields, were not considered to be present income.[93] The factors which determined interest were approached through a series of approximations in which the first stage represented impatience or preferences for present goods; the second, productivity; and the third, elements of risk and uncertainty. It was necessary that the rates of marginal time preference, or impatience, and "marginal return over cost," or productivity, be equal in order to establish a rate of interest.[94] The analysis was developed on three levels—narrative, geometric, and algebraic. Fisher's charts relating present to future income could be interpreted as preference curves on which interest lines were superimposed so that movement toward a point of tangency represented an approach toward the maximum value of an income stream. Equilibrium meant equality of the marginal rate of return over cost, the rate of interest, and the marginal rate of time preference.[95] Fisher's productivity concept seemed quite similar to what Keynes was to call the marginal efficiency of capital. In fact, the latter, who was quite familiar with Fisher's writings, believed the two concepts to be alike.[96] However, as A. A. Alchian has shown, they really were not the same,[97] for Fisher's notion involved a comparison of alternative possibilities, rather than the discounting of just one investment option. The rate of return over cost depended on the extent to which an income stream might be shifted by changes in capital utilization.[98] Moreover, Fisher, at this point at least, had not yet introduced uncertainty, an element central to the Keynesian theory.

Fisher's "impatience" was perhaps more closely related to Böhm-Bawerk's "second Ground," or underestimation of future requirements, while the idea of investment opportunity appeared not unlike the latter's notion of present technical superiority. In Fisher's system, however, the stress was put on preferences for goods today, so that the primary motivation for interest became an unwillingness to wait. This was not necessarily short-sightedness, but rather an urgent desire for present enjoyment. As against the Austrian view, Fisher argued that without time preference it was conceivable that a product would increase indefinitely, making present value infinite. Consequently, technical superiority alone could not explain the difference in the value of present and future goods. Only time preference could account for interest, said Fisher, for where one was indifferent as to the present and future, interest could not arise. The Austrians, on the other hand, suggested that technical superiority, or roundabout production, could provide an independent explanation for interest. Of course, Fisher did not ignore the factor of productivity, for this was indubitably a significant influence on the supply of goods. But time preference still was the major element: technical superiority was not independent of impatience.[99]

Yet Fisher's insistence that interest was not simply a factor return like rent or wages, but the foundation of all incomes, was virtually an Austrian conception. The fact was, he said, that interest stemmed from a time discount applied to all productive services. Interest was a way of studying all income flows, and when these were capitalized at a given rate, capital value was obtained.[100] This aspect also suggested Frank Knight's conception of capital.[101] With Knight, however, the idea of capital as physical goods played an even smaller role than it did in Fisher's analysis. While the latter at least did begin with real goods, Knight stressed in a most extreme fashion the notion of capital as a fund. The difficulty with the fund idea was that it obscured the underlying social relations, and, while logically susceptible to mathematical handling, the sociological implications were completely submerged. In this sense, Marx's emphasis upon capital as a relation between men would appear to have much merit. And, in Ricardo, income flows had reflected a given social and class structure. But in theories such as those propounded by Fisher and Knight, regardless of the differences in detail between them, all this was irretrievably lost. The aura of apologetics was unmistakable. Moreover, Fisher refused to answer the question, *why* does interest exist? This he evaded by asserting that any analysis of *how* interest was determined was sufficient.[102] Yet the determination of the size or speed of a given flow hardly begins to explain its origin. It would seem that function and aetiology had been hopelessly confounded.

Fisher held that interest, as a price paid for money, could very well be interpreted in terms of purchasing power. Since interest rates varied inversely with bank reserves, there seemed to be a tendency for them to move directly with the supply of money. And as low reserves and high rates of interest indicated rising income and increasing prosperity, bank rates under these conditions reflected accelerated income flows. This led to the idea of a real rate of interest, which could be established without much difficulty by using index numbers.[103] Expectations of declining prices would depress the rate of interest in money terms. Fisher buttressed his description of these movements with a good deal of empirical data.[104] But the difficulty with the real rate was obvious to him, for it became essentially a multiplicity of rates: "There are as many rates of interest expressed in terms of goods as there are goods diverging from one another in value." [105]

Despite the seemingly impregnable logic of the theory, sharp criticism ensued. It was alleged that the analysis was much too general and that it failed to show adequately how the banking system affected interest rates. The concept of impatience was said to be misleading in that its stress was almost entirely on the consumer sector. Expectations of high future returns could very well stimulate investment despite upward moving rates. Others argued that capitalization was not always a true guide to values, for while rental returns on poor neighborhood properties, for example, might suggest one level of values at capitalized rates, in actuality the open market would bring a much lower price. That is, in many instances, there were divergences between rental markets and resale markets. Moreover, Fisher, it appeared, did not quite break through the circle of capitalization. Value was derived from income by capitalizing the latter at prevailing interest rates. But value multiplied by the rate equaled the original income which was the basis for interest. Thus, there seemed to be a need to reach for more basic causes.

When Veblen leveled his usual acerb criticisms, Fisher responded that he had been misunderstood and that his analysis was really closer in spirit to the *Theory of Business Enterprise* than Veblen himself realized.[106] One of Veblen's chief points was that the hedonic element had not been completely eradicated by Fisher's formulation. His theory, therefore, was not sufficiently pecuniary in character. Fisher's refusal to separate intangibles from their underlying real properties and to accord them a distinct treatment was said to reflect a failure to recognize the purely pecuniary structure of modern capitalism. Furthermore, Veblen remarked, the capitalization theory of interest, with its notions of impatience and investment opportunity, was not universal, but historically time-bound. Intangibles in our society, argued Veblen, have acquired a value quite separate from goods: it was this clue to the aetiology of interest that had escaped Fisher, for interest ". . . can emerge only on the basis afforded by the *mature* development of the institution of property." [107]

Fisher's concern with problems of stability impelled him to undertake a detailed study of money and its purchasing power. His work restored the ancient quantity theory to a position of preeminence, and his well-known formula, $MV + M'V' = PT,$ found its way into all the textbooks. His insistence that the equation held true under certain conditions virtually made it an economic law, one that seemed difficult to rebut, suffused as it was with historical and empirical data. But in the *Purchasing Power of Money,* the impression was created, perhaps unfortunately, that the whole question was really a simple one. Complicating factors were treated so lightly that Fisher's position became indefensible. It may very well have been, as Schumpeter once remarked, that Fisher allowed his crusading ardor to get away from him. So important and urgent did economic stability seem to him that almost all exceptions were put aside.

An important contribution, however, was the expansion of the idea of a monetary stock to include instruments of credit, particularly bank deposits. The level of prices was said to be proportional to the total quantity of money, including such deposits. Other things being equal, twice the quantity of money would double prices; or cut T in half and prices would double. That is, prices were proportional to total spending and this in turn was proportional to money stocks. An important question which Fisher did not clarify too satisfactorily was how money stocks were fixed. A lack of proportionality between prices and money was acknowledged only for the so-called "transition" periods, when the economy was moving from one level of equilibrium to another. But it was precisely these deviations that were more common than Fisher was willing to admit. And it was such situations that made the terms of the quantity equation interconnected rather than independent. A rapid expansion of money could raise prices more than proportionately, as in a runaway inflation; or price controls might reduce rather sharply the velocity of money; or in a depression an injection of money might increase trade and output long before prices were affected. The typical Fisherine formula did not take these variations and lags into account and to that extent failed to explain shifts in cash balances. And from an empirical standpoint, bank deposit velocity was not only lower than Fisher estimated but was subject to broad seasonal changes.[108]

Thus Fisher's exposition appeared fairly rigid, despite his heroic efforts to relate it to various sets of originating causes. Certainly the presentation in the early parts of the *Purchasing Power of Money* was quite mechanistic. Yet, though the quantity equation was attacked as a mere identity, it was possible to defend it as a kind of equilibrium statement, with price determined by the interplay of money, velocity, and production. At any rate, variations in the relationships of the four basic elements did appear during "transitions." Fisher postulated a definite relationship between cash and deposits and between bank reserves and deposits. And since deposits depended on the quantity of primary money, limiting or expanding the latter presumably would make for a really effective control device. But Fisher's treatment of "transition" effects seemed much too perfunctory, for in dynamic situations it was precisely these indirect influences which were significant. Causal factors displayed themselves most forcibly during "transitions": the concept of velocity, for example, might be most usefully decomposed at a time when the economy seemed to be shifting from one level to the next.

The indirect influences were classified in terms of resources, the division of labor, productive techniques, capital accumulation, wants, the banking system—in fact, the whole roster of forces that moved the capitalist economy was listed by Fisher. The end product of economic motion was a given level of purchasing power.[109] These categories provided a useful framework for empirical investigation, as was later attempted by Milton Friedman and his co-workers.[110] Yet the admission that the quantity relations did not hold for transition periods seemed to be fatal.[111] The theory's rigidity again was revealed when velocity was said to affect prices rather than money or production. It appeared, nevertheless, that changes in velocity could affect money holdings. In essence, Fisher's brave attempt to work up a theory of value without resorting to the standard supply and demand apparatus was not very successful. To assert that prices were a passive end product seemed to place economic analysis into a straightjacket.

Like many of Fisher's other books, *The Purchasing Power of Money* was a prolegomenon to reform. His favorite device, the "compensated dollar," was to be based upon the gold exchange standard with the gold content of the dollar altered in accordance with an official price index, so that the dollar would represent a constant amount of purchasing power. Monetary individualism, said Fisher, had damaged the economy, with an excessive stock of money creating waste. The compensated dollar would correct the effects of purchasing power fluctuations, provided there were agreements on international exchange. Fisher then organized a variety of public campaigns to further his monetary reform ideas and in many ways helped to foster a climate of opinion in which change was possible.[112] Yet while interest in the compensated dollar was keen, most professional economists felt that it would not work in practice. Moreover, it was pointed out, the continued use of credit would sharply curtail the ability of the compensated dollar to affect the price level.

Fisher's main concern—to stabilize debtor-creditor relationships, rather than production and employment—was pursued in subsequent works, such as *Stabilizing the Dollar* (1920) and *100% Money*,[113] in which Fisher supported the plan proposed by Henry C. Simons of the University of Chicago. The latter would have required the banks to maintain full 100 per cent reserves against deposits, and, in effect, would have prevented them from expanding check currency unless supported by cash reserves. Cash would be substituted for part of the security holdings of the banks. Since such new cash would be held in reserve, the money stock would not be increased. Thereafter, check deposits would have to be limited to the amount of cash in the banks. Any loss in income as a result of the decline in earning assets would be compensated by service charges to the customers. The plan presumably would eliminate bank failures and allow for a more stringent control over the quantity of money in the economy. With the stock of money growing at a slow pace, a stringent limit on credit expansion would ensue, since bank loans would have to be fully supported by existing money supplies. Only if the central bank intervened could credit be expanded in any significant manner. Yet the banks would still be able to call in outstanding loans, so that the possibility of deflationary actions would not have been eliminated. Moreover, there would be no way of restraining a rapid turnover of money in circulation. That is, velocity movements would still operate independently of the full reserve plan. Another difficulty lay in initiating such a program, for the imposition of a 100 per cent reserve requirement would unquestionably mean a severe deflation. The impact on business practices seemed much too upsetting to make the plan palatable.[114]

The more rapid movement of credit as compared to the stock of money, said Fisher, was at the root of crisis and depression. This explained the peculiar behavior of the rate of interest during transition periods.[115] Here was Fisher's theory of business cycles in a nutshell. It did not occur to him that as resources might be idle, price movements could provide an important stimulus for a staggering economy. For him, depressions were only "dances of the dollar." To conceive of cycles as a self-generating phenomenon was a fiction. The only corrective device necessary was a little "reflation." While the causes of disequilibrium were manifold, the major ones stemmed from indebtedness and debt liquidation. That is to say, the cycle was simply a matter of debtor-creditor relationships. The upper turning point could be traced to the overwhelming pressure to liquidate obligations, a process that might move so rapidly as to increase the purchasing power of remaining debts—a rather oblique way of saying that prices would fall quickly. All that was necessary to halt a decline, suggested Fisher, would be fast action by the central banks.

Early in his career, Fisher had deplored the extension of government regulation, for he felt that corporate controls and such measures as workmen's compensation would move the nation along the road toward socialism. One class would come to dominate another, power would be abused, and society become corrupt. Amelioration of recognized abuses demanded, rather, that voluntary societies teach the lower classes how to further their own interests. However, in his later years, Fisher did acknowledge the need for a more equitable distribution of income and opposed pure laissez faire as a guide to public policy. Inheritance taxation was no instrument of oppression, but rather a way of broadening economic democracy. This was also true of the growing dispersion of corporate ownership. Although the problem of ownership and control escaped him, he was beginning to approach the idea of a mixed economy.

Despite Fisher's curious penchant for leaping on Leacock's horse and riding off in all directions at once, he did do heroic work in focussing public attention on the exacerbating problems of prices and inflation. It is clearly evident that those who now are so much more sophisticated about these questions than he was are standing firmly upon his shoulders.

v

Frank H. Knight and Abstractionism

In the hands of Frank H. Knight (1885-   ), economic theory became a grand exercise in rarefied abstractions. Possessed of a remarkable background in philosophy and theology as well as the social sciences, Knight was able to bring some rather interesting perceptions to bear upon the perennial problems of economics. Yet there has always been a peculiar bifurcation in his writing: on the one hand, economic theory was a pure discipline concerned with drawing inferences from a certain set of *a priori* statements and therefore devoid of history or normative implications, while on the other, economic behavior was conditioned by custom, institutions, and the legal framework. Somehow, the two positions were never reconciled, and, in fact, it was the former that has dominated Knight's whole system of thought.

Born in McLean County, Illinois, Knight did not enter college until the age of twenty. His early student career was spent at two theologically-minded Tennessee institutions, American University and Milligan College, where in addition to the regular courses he studied Bible history and cognate subjects. He met expenses by teaching sciences, languages, bookkeeping, and short-hand. In 1913, after receiving a B.S. in science and an M.A. in German, he went to Cornell for his Ph.D. in philosophy, with a minor in eco-nomics under Alvin Johnson. Endowed ". . . with dyspepsia and a graven expression of pessimism . . ." Knight soon ran into trouble. His philosophy teachers, thinking him much too skeptical a person to trust with young persons, were only too happy to turn him over to Johnson and economics.[116] When Johnson left Cornell in 1914, Knight continued to work with Allyn A. Young. After a short stay at Cornell, where he came to know Herbert J. Davenport, Knight went to Chicago as an instructor; and there rewrote his doctoral thesis on business profits as the winning essay in the Hart, Schaffner, and Marx contest. This study, published in 1921 under the rubric *Risk, Uncertainty and Profit,*[117] established him as one of the more important econo-mists on the American scene. A nine-year stay at the University of Iowa was followed by an appointment to the University of Chicago in 1928 as successor to John Maurice Clark. The recipient of the American Economic Association Walker medal in 1957, Knight is now the Hull Distinguished Service Pro-fessor, Emeritus, of Social Science and Philosophy at the University of Chicago.

The most explicit statement of Knight's economic method may be found in the 1949 debate he staged with the noted anthropologist, Melville J. Herskovits.[118] Knight's blistering review of the latter's book, *The Economic Life of Primitive Peoples* (1940), rejected any definition of economics which included technology and other empirical details. Economics, he insisted, was not a descriptive science, and therefore could not deal with these matters. It employed rather certain highly generalized notions to explain how the econ-omy functioned which in turn exhibited a kind of universality in no way con-nected with culturally relative concepts. The idea of maximizing results was the sort of general principle Knight had in mind: the only possible normative implication in it was the thought that there ought to be a desire to operate efficiently and that social policy should be guided by this precept. Here, of course, Knight trod the thin line between consistency and contradiction, for judgments on how the economy actually worked always suggest alternative systems, and these Knight in no way was prepared to accept. His caution repeatedly turned him back to first principles, so that in the end these were all that were left to him. The inherent fallacy in his approach was revealed wher he asserted that while "cost of living" might be a useful economic category, the notion of a "standard of living" was not admissible into economics because it was essentially an "aesthetic" idea.

Economics, Knight argued, necessarily had to be abstract, since it utilized inferences drawn from certain premises and always had to have recourse to *intuitive* knowledge. But just how economic truth was to be secured through intuition was not made clear.[119] While induction from observation is an accepted procedure, it is difficult to conceive that any proposition in economics may be characterized as *a priori*. Such assertions were precisely the kind of statements that gave Knight the free-swinging latitude he wanted and made him one of the most difficult of theorists to pin down. With any platform available to him, all sorts of philosophic points could be scored against less well prepared opponents. Thus rationality, according to his own definition, became an *a priori* premise in pure theory. Yet Knight knew well enough that it was impossible to extend plans for rational action into an indefinite future. He knew that *a priori* statements should not be taken literally. Yet by straddling both sides of the methodological fence, he could be both a rip-roaring institutionalist with a straightforward orthodox theorist and a determined defender of received doctrine with a follower of Veblen.[120]

Intuitively perceived economic principles suggested that they were pure concepts inaccessible to verification and therefore nonoperational. When Knight insisted that such facts as were necessary to expound basic principles did not have to be facts in the sense of actual reality, but merely "realistically illustrative," he certainly emphasized this point.[121] He could hardly complain with any measure of justice about the attacks of other social scientists upon his type of theory when all they found was a fictional "as if" philosophy. As Herskovits replied in his rejoinder, such fictions could be bad scholarship and even worse pedagogy.[122] It was difficult to determine, with Knight's sharp dichotomy between inference and empirical verification, how advances in social science might be made. About the only thing to do would be to refine almost beyond redemption the sundry niceties of theoretical discourse.[123] So far as Knight was concerned all economic theory was abstract, formal, and without content. Price economics was really Robinson Crusoe economics and provided universal laws valid only as to form, but not as to content.[124]

Curiously enough, it presumably was possible to draw policy implications from these principles: they were intended ". . . to explain the working of our modern economic organization and also to criticize and suggest changes." [125] Thus one was never sure whether Knight wanted a positive or normative economics, whether pure theory only was desirable, or whether a *political* economy in his terms was really feasible. Yet the latter did seem implicit in many of his statements, for he often wrote of the importance of the institutional aspects of social and economic existence. He knew that man was often irrational, combative, and self-seeking, yet all this had no place in basic principles. To relate cultural norms to economic behavior merely revealed a political bias! (Yet many writers have discovered a hidden bias in the very assertion of a pristine neutrality in economics.) And to suggest, according to Knight, that it was possible to discuss alternatives to the free enterprise system was revelatory of political romanticism. Given such a set of preconceptions, it was difficult, for example, for him to deal dispassionately with economic planning: his invariable response was that a planned economy was a well-managed penitentiary.[126] Though he rejected on occasion the extremism of the Mises-Hayek position, his own philosophy nevertheless brought him quite close to the latter.

The roots of such an inordinate formalism could be traced in part to the *Wissenschaftslehre* of Max Weber, who, in his essay on objectivity in social science, stressed the relationships between intellectual problems as against the material relation between things.[127] Weber's objective had been to heighten the formal nature of theoretical work. But in the hands of such economists as Knight and Lionel Robbins, this goal was converted into an intransigent formalism. It was certainly helpful to provide concepts and ideas which allowed for a better arrangement of intellectual materials. But not even Weber went so far as did Knight. Complete ethical neutrality did not seem valid to Weber, much of whose work consisted precisely of an investigation of the influence of noneconomic elements on economic life.[128] General concepts were much more closely related to ultimate reality in Weber's system than it was possible to discern in Knight's.

Though Knight sometimes described himself as an institutionalist of sorts, he saw much more value in pure theory on the ground that men economize and seek efficiency.[129] Any rejection of the universality of economic principles was simply a display of emotional bias. Yet he knew that the kind of want-satisfying organization prevalent in the West was neither so general nor covered the greater part of human conduct.[130] He did concede that it was essential to go beyond the basic ideas expressed by the initial set of principles: problems of specialization, historical beginnings, and change were all important, but they were not the proper realm of study for the theoretical economist. Once economics began to discuss ideals, it became political, encompassing statistical analysis, the study of motivation, analysis of symbols, social objectives, and the use of economic power.[131] But all this, he insisted, did not supply an adequate theory of social organization. From the theoretical standpoint, social organization in economics meant a study of free enterprise, just as political science was a study of democratic institutions.[132] Economics, said Knight, provided laws which explained the consequences of intelligent rational action.[133] Basically, he was no institutionalist of any kind: the use of occasional sociological and historical data did not convince him that economics might fruitfully study relationships between people.[134]

Knight by no means accepted the precepts of the British classicists, either.

Much closer in spirit to John Bates Clark, he found the subjective approach to be a good deal more useful than the real cost doctrine of Ricardo.[135] Value, he argued, was a matter of choice, defined in a relative sense, while economizing was a problem of securing maximum returns by equalizing the increments of return from a continued application of increments of resources. The classicists had erred too in defining production as the creation of wealth rather than of services. According to Knight these two fallacies, real cost and wealth creation, had led to the notion that labor was the basis of wealth and prevented the older writers from seeing that social-economic life was rooted in the exchange of services. The classicists also failed to recognize that causality was not a sequence, but a relation between variables. Thus, the theory of distribution, based upon the concept of imputation, had to await other hands. And without these ideas, the notion of maximizing values remained dormant. Finally, Knight chided the classicists for establishing separate categories for rent, wages, interest, and profits, which to him were all essentially the same. For without a single flow of services one could not adequately measure the value of a productive plant by its anticipated income.

An important distinction was made between statics and dynamics.[136] The underlying ideas in statics, thought Knight, had been borrowed from theoretical mechanics, but in economics these were transmuted into those forces that tended toward equilibrium. But this quickly passed over into motion and movement and into the realm of dynamics. Such an approach to change made it possible for economics to become a study of historical analytics, after the fashion of some modern econometricians. Knight asserted that his interest too was in equilibrium not as a state of rest, but as a process.[137] But one had to start with a static state in which there were certain wants and resources for satisfying them and a particular pattern of distribution set within a given framework of government. In the static economy, consumers and producers exhausted the supplies of the commodities that were produced as well as the available productive sources. The main dynamic impulses seemed to stem from saving and investment, a process that allowed increases in the supply of productive services. All this was set within a rather pointless and often dreary search for economic concepts analogous to force, momentum, inertia, space, and other mechanical ideas. Knight's singular definition of capital as a homogeneous fund was brought into the analysis, thus raising issues of the rate of interest and the demand for capital. The latter were in many ways central to his system, and he never failed to iterate again and again his version of capital theory. In sum, he concluded that there was no overall tendency toward economic equilibrium: the idea of progress as a "unitary" process was of but limited application. Here Knight's rude sense of the institutionalist viewpoint came to the fore: business, he found, did not comply with the theoretical behavior of economic man, for there was ". . . evolution in the nature of capitalism." [138] The notion of price equilibrium did not seem to apply to the realities of economic change!

Exchange relations in Knight's system comprised the center of social organization. Here again there seemed to be an approach to a broad institutional meaning, almost akin to Commons' transactions. Exchange established markets which coordinated the work of the economy. But these were impersonal relationships, a characterization that seemed to conflict with the description Knight often gave to the exchange process as a game, the motivations of which stemmed from a desire to undertake risks for their own sake. [139] Interestingly enough, modern theory does admit game elements, but for that very reason suggests that businessmen exercise more caution than Knight was aware of. [140] Yet he did not quite attain the level of analysis required to describe human relationships in their economic context: work and wages, for example, were never a matter of employer-employee tensions and bargaining was but an impersonal expression of a flow of disembodied services. The closest he was able to get to economics as a study of the significant ties between men and groups was his functional analysis of the entrepreneur and business manager. Social organization, consequently, was little more than the market structure and a mechanism to provide for growth. [141] This was certainly an extraordinarily narrow frame for the whole complex of modern economic relationships. Fundamentally, it represented an artificial identification of the economy with market forms only.

At best, Knight would concede that ours was an enterprise economy with production carried on by abstract units distinct from the persons who comprised them. [142] Individuals, he insisted, did not exchange goods but sold services to enterprises, the proceeds of which were used to purchase goods. In early societies exchange may have been a complex process of specialization. But under the price system and free enterprise, the search for certain goods and services guided individuals toward an automatic control of production and distribution. This, of course, was little more than the orthodox theory of the exchange mechanism in which mutual interest was inherent in the business of seeking individual gain. Competition was the lubricant of the whole operation. In this imaginary society, ostensibly constructed for analytic purposes, people acted rationally and were fully aware of the consequences of their acts. Each individual was the final and absolute judge of his own welfare, while complete mobility of resources and plans and full knowledge of market conditions were assumed. Organization was atomistic, consisting of small economic units, and no one indulged in fraud or deceit [143]—the most perfect of perfect economic models.

Again Knight seemed to hesitate in pursuing the implications of his analysis. He recognized its limitations, its severity and abstract quality, and its search for maximum satisfactions under dubious conditions without regard to the distribution of economic power. Complete rationality did seem doubtful, for, he noted, when these abstractions were clothed with facts, the results appeared far from ideal.[144] But these damaging admissions did not daunt him; he was to return again and again to the system of free enterprise as the acme of economic wisdom.

Demand theory suggested that the aim of economic action was want satisfaction. But the underlying ideas in demand were not amenable to analysis in such a quantifying science as economics, said Knight. The notion of economizing was grasped intuitively and implied diminishing utility. But while added units of a good might be valued, Knight could not see how this procedure was to be applied to extra units of satisfaction. Still the law of diminishing utility, when properly stated, was useful for a psychologically valid interpretation of consumer choice.[145] If this were not done, only objective behavioristic statements remained. Thus, no explanation of behavior was possible, a proposition that seemingly destroyed whatever psychological underpinnings economics might have. Knight thus applied Occam's Razor with relish and abandon. The ordinal approach, Knight argued, was a compromise, and in any case could not avoid some judgment on the degrees of difference between units in the scale. Nor did the indifference curve method seem to provide any better quantification. It was really a hypothetical experiment, he implied, and one might just as well go back to the ordinary demand curve.[146] Again, Knight qualified his pure theory by acknowledging changes in the value of money, errors in behavior, and all the complexities of human motivation.

More specifically, Knight preferred to limit the term "demand" to the amount that "would be taken" off the market rather than the amount actually taken, on the ground that such a definition stressed price causation.[147] While utility and other motivations were elements of demand, analysis could proceed on the basis of consumer estimations, money income and its distribution, the prices of available substitutes, and complementary goods. Thus high prices for complementary goods tended to lower demand. This analysis could be extended to the various productive services, for they too were related as either substitutes or complementary factors. The major relationship in demand was to price, that is, to elasticity, although Knight preferred to employ the expression "responsiveness of consumption." This, he thought, would stress the fact that the causal relationship was from price to the amount sold, as in the case of brand name items. He also observed that advertising could be used to vary demand, even though price and quantity were fixed, as in monopolistic competition. Elasticity, certainly an important bit of information, played an important role in taxation as well as monopoly.

Whereas demand was a function of price in Knight's analysis, supply referred only to the quantity of a product that flowed to the market. As price was not one of its determinants, it was quite possible for lags to develop between price and supply. Disequilibrium therefore was conceivable, particularly in the short run, since supply did not always equal the consumption of a good or service. The difference, said Knight, was made up by stocks on hand and by surplus capacity. This, of course, was entirely a short-run view, for in the long run, he insisted, production and consumption were in fact simultaneous processes. Viewed from the latter standpoint, supply was the rate of output, assuming that all resources were fully employed. Within this framework marginal productivity was the rule, with resources allocated according to the time-honored principle of equi-marginal returns. Although the differential rate at which resources were used complicated matters, Knight argued that they would move easily from industry to industry under the compulsion of shifting demand. This seemed a gross overestimation of the ability of capital to be transferred in response to the call of profit. It was a conception of capital as pure fund, a notion that Knight defended with great eloquence. Moreover, it was doubtful that the absorption of idle capacity did illustrate how mobile capital was. In one sense, fluidity was an aspect of foresight, something very much in short supply, as indeed Knight was the first to admit.

Even for the long run, Knight rejected the idea of supply as a function of price, for with constant costs price could easily adjust to shifts in demand.[148] With decreasing cost, monopoly would tend to rear its ugly head and again output would be independent of price. Nor was supply the obverse of demand, as in the theory of reservation prices, since production was undertaken for sale; and even when the goods could not be stored or moved to another market, producers were in no position to consume their own output.[149] The supply curve was essentially a cost of production curve, showing cost as a function of output. Such a long period analysis, said Knight, would suggest to producers that with decreasing costs less output would be forthcoming at higher prices than at lower ones.[150] This paradox proved to Knight that decreasing cost as a long-run tendency was impossible under competitive conditions, for, given the latter, costs would be quickly adjusted for all producers.[151] Knight assumed, of course, a large number of producing units, each operating at its most efficient size. Consequently, changes in output meant only a change in the number of units without any change in scale. Any economies stemming from large-scale operations could be accomplished only by reducing the number of units and by increasing their sizes: there would be no increase in industry output.[152] And a trend toward large-scale production meant inevitable monopoly. Long-run marginal cost too was meaningless, for under competition all costs had to be the same for all enterprises. The upshot of this involved argument was the dissipation of any distinction between short-run and long-run changes in production.[153] Marshall and his followers were simply in error when they sought to distinguish between cost and supply conditions for different periods of time. Excess capacity was not much of a problem, averred Knight, for it merely indicated that output could without difficulty move to the point for which the plant had been designed, and in any case excess capacity was only a temporary problem! Written in 1921, these words now have a strange sound. Excess capacity is not by any means to be dismissed with such glibness. Moreover, the argument that capital and labor exhibited an effective *physical* mobility sufficient to afford a close adjustment of production to demand was utterly unrealistic.[154] Knight's sole objective was to demonstrate that large-scale production was vastly overrated. The validity of this argument needs no comment.[155]

In a long-standing effort to simplify distribution as well as price theory, Knight repeatedly called for the abolition of the venerable tripartite separation of the factors of production. Considering the notions of land, labor, and capital as distinct categories useless and superfluous, he pursued this viewpoint with such rare doggedness that the case was overstated.[156] Knight argued that there was no substantive difference between permanent and non-permanent resources.[157] The former, meaning land and other gifts of nature, required as much maintenance as the nonpermanent variety in order to obtain a flow of services from them. If one wanted to have a "factor of production," it was capital; for this, Knight insisted, was at least theoretically all-inclusive. That is, capital was not a group of things, but a generic term for *all* productive services. Consequently, any separation between natural and artificial or permanent and nonpermanent resources was otiose.[158] With our price- and exchange-centered social-economic organization, the argument remorselessly continued, one could talk only of productive services and a distribution of the product in terms of competitive valuation. Class or group identification had nothing to do with the problem, for one so-called factor was an easy substitute for another.

Fearful that he had gone a bit too far, Knight did concede that it might be necessary to postulate a large variety of factors. Yet even in such a case it hardly can be said that one factor is a simple substitute for another. Evidently, here was a confusion of no mean proportions between physical and value concepts. Quite simply, productive agents are limited in their degree of substitutability, which depends upon a variety of cost, price, and technological elements, unless, of course, one wants to accept at face value Knight's reduction of all economic factors to "one vast homogeneous fund." [159] If this were done, all productive resources would have to be remunerated in the same way. But if supply were more directly involved in price determination, a difference between the factors would arise. It appeared that only from the standpoint of demand did the factors look alike; from the supply side, considerable differences were observable. Fundamentally, the fusion of one factor into another obscured the quality and basic character of economics. There still was some usefulness in indicating the relatively fixed nature of original resources, and labor still was something different from the relationships inherent in the term "capital." To convert all three factors into a single stream was bound to lead up a blind alley.[160]

Knight's general approach impelled him to attack certain facets of Austrian theory, engendering a heated controversy that continued for some five years.[161] The debate was mainly with Hayek and Fritz Machlup, although a number of other economists, such as Nicholas Kaldor and Kenneth Boulding, joined in from time to time. It cannot be said that Knight prevailed in the dispute. Fighting heroically, his views were given respectful attention, but the outcome was not favorable to his side. The tripartite separation of factors has continued in the literature, attesting to its broad usefulness in analysis, while a good many writers, accepting the Keynesian view, look upon interest primarily as a monetary phenomenon. Perhaps it was Knight's remarkable dexterity in economic logic that was self-defeating. Certainly the arguments and numerous corollaries which he developed in great profusion tended to obscure the main points, while his penchant for paradox created the impression that his theory could be all things to all men.

Marginal productivity, said Knight, underscored the fact that the traditional separation of the factors was unnecessary, since the entrepreneur was interested only in productive agents, each of which tended to be remunerated according to its specific contribution to output. Accordingly, all productive services were simply different forms of capital or productive capacity expressed in an abstract quantitative way and transferable from one use to another by virtue of changes in form.[162] Measurement of such productive capacity was simply a question of valuation. Yet neither valuation nor borrowing or lending gave capital its importance: this stemmed rather from the process of investment. Certain limits, however, were acknowledged: human beings could not be considered capital; intangibles sometimes had to be distinguished from corporeal property; some services were used up immediately, while others continued over time; durable goods might be utilized by the owner directly or leased to others. The durability of an agent was also important because this affected mobility and the application of capital to alternative uses.

But in the main, productive agents were similar: land had to be developed and maintained at a cost, and its value necessarily had to be compared with the values of other forms of capital. Consequently, argued Knight, no genuine distinction existed between rent and interest. The only differences were legal and contractual. The view that these payments reflected different economic relationships between people who performed disparate functions was dismissed as totally unwarranted. Even for workers no real distinction existed, for wages were simply a return for services rendered; and the fact that chattel slavery no longer existed simply reflected a different institutional background. The return to the worker was essentially like a return to capital: in fact, labor was a form of capital! Theoretically, the meaning of capital and its yield was the same regardless of the kind of society one was talking about, said Knight.

So severe an abstraction, so intense a search for generality could result only in obfuscation. The implications that flow from the various relationships which underpin particular types of factor returns do have an important bearing on the analysis of an economic system. While Knight may have delegated the responsibility for investigating them to the other social sciences, they still are economic in nature. Without them economics becomes an exercise in pure logic, an empty formalistic discipline without much relevance to the human condition.

Knight charged that the Austrians had virtually adopted the classical agricultural cycle in their capital theory by asserting fixed proportions between capital and labor and by converting the former into a linear function of a variable production period. This assumed a false cooperation between capital and labor, since in fact, he contended, the relationship between the two factors was essentially coordinate and simultaneous.[163] There was, therefore, no production period: services were consumed as they were produced, in a continuous stream. Consumption and services rendered did have a time dimension, it was true, but since they were involved in transactions they became "objectified" and acquired values through the market, even though they were time flows. It was this theoretical relationship that led to the concept of wealth: conceived as discrete units in flow, wealth was really a product of income and time. Dimensionally, it was a kind of compressed income, though it was held as a stock. All the confusion over these concepts had arisen, said Knight, because the activities of creating wealth and of making it yield an income were carried on by different persons. The older views became invalid once capital was recognized as a process and as a fund which grew. That there might be some lags between production and consumption was deemed to be a "vague" idea: at any rate, when it did occur, its cause was "abstinence." The instantaneous character of production and consumption made wealth as permanent as capitalism itself. Any replacements of capital items were mere technical details in the process of maintenance, while the yield from investment flowed in perpetuity.

Yet Knight could not deny that there was an occasional retrogression, especially during depressions. And despite his concern with values, he never quite clarified the pecuniary nature of capital in his sense of the word. Had he done so, the assertion that durability was a matter of indifference to investors would not have been made.[164] This might be so for speculators, but there are other classes of investors whose behavior calls for quite a different description. There may be fluidity in securities, but not all entrepreneurs utilize the stock market to effect a transfer of capital, and to that extent durability appears to be of some importance. Moreover, the argument that the liquidation of a going concern was simply a return of assets to the general stream of capital was meaningless without an analysis of the impact of such shifts upon pecuniary values. Knight wrote as though he had never heard of bankruptcy and the sudden deflation of asset values. It was a case of forgetting the trees for the sake of the forest.

With a production period that had no beginning and no end and a stream of capital that was "inherently immortal," the concept of an average durability of capital was without real meaning, wrote Knight.[165] Since wealth goes on producing forever, one could only speak of an increment of perpetual income. There was no connection between time and the stream of capital. From this vantage point, Knight leveled broadsides at the Austrian theory of roundabout production.[166] Hayek, for example, had argued that larger amounts of capital implied a lengthening of the structure of production. But so far as Knight could see, there was no ". . . production process of determinate length, other than zero, or 'all history.' " [167] It all depended on what was being added: if the new units were the same kind of goods or equipment that had existed previously, there could be no effect, and if different, one still could not predict the outcome. The notion of a production period, Knight continued with vigor, was based upon the false assumption that capital was consumed at a fixed rate and that a precise correspondence existed between the quantity of capital and a period of production. Averaging the life of individual units of capital to derive an average construction period was an erroneous approach. Capital, he insisted, was an integrated, organic conception in which no particular unit could be recognized. Aside from repairs and maintenance, it went on into an infinite future. Problems of forced sale, liquidations, obsolescence, salvage, and depressions were all treated rather lightly as being of no great consequence.[168] Pieces of equipment could be dated, but this had significance only for determining turnover. Liquidation was really a problem of the theory of money, and, in a depression, it was the momentary maladjustment that prevented capital from being as mobile as it might be. One need be sure only that the "real" rate of return on an investment was such that the rate of amortization would equal the yield.

Yet given a certain time spread for investments, it was possible to visualize a period of production with certain finite limits. And quite clearly, this was in accordance with ordinary business practice. Knight's view of the matter bordered on the metaphysical, and failed to answer the question how different rates of return on different investments were equalized. These limitations in his analysis, observed by a number of other economists, revealed how devoid of operational meaning his theory was.[169] As Machlup later remarked, it proved only that a society which maintained its capital maintained its capital. In the absence of a period of production, it was difficult to sustain the notion of net investment or disinvestment, countered Machlup. The simultaneity of production and consumption had meaning only as a time slice. Above all, it was apparent that beyond the theoretical stationary state these were disparate processes, and that the differences in their time rate of movement was a subject for economic analysis. Capital replacement, output, and the way in which capital was used were different flows, and the time interval between input and output indeed could be crucial for a study of certain problems of changes. Moreover, added Machlup, the valuation of capital in perpetuity was unrealistic and seldom done that way. Here theory ought to look to actual practice, for capitalization was always applied to a limited series of returns.[170] What was of concern was present investment, not an historical process extending forward and backward into infinity at both extremes.

Was it possible to define an investment or production period? Nicholas Kaldor suggested that the degree of roundaboutness could be measured by the ratio of the initial cost of an investment to its annual maintenance.[171] Variations in the rate at which maintenance expenditures were undertaken and variations in initial construction did meet the conditions of roundaboutness, for this was nothing more than relating the stock of capital to other factors. The major difficulty was establishing an average period because the stock of capital was essentially heterogeneous. Further, said Kaldor, capital could be set off from other productive agents by virtue of its "augmentability."[172] The rate of interest, therefore, had to be rooted in the nature of production functions, since some factors could not be augmented significantly. A fall in the rate of interest tended to lead to a fall in the yield of capital and a rise in noncapital returns: hence, said Kaldor, there was still room for differentiating between rent and interest. A good deal of the weakness in Knight's theory stemmed from his refusal to accept a distinction between constant and increasing cost. Yet these did reflect different kinds of resource conditions. Why should one want to shift to some other line of endeavor if only constant costs existed?

A further weakness in Knight's analysis of capital and production was his unwillingness to acknowledge the latter as a *physical* process which was antecedent to value determination. While Knight preferred to measure production solely in terms of dollars, he forgot that it was also a flow of material goods which could be expressed as an average and then translated into values through the pricing mechanism. As Kenneth Boulding has said, there was a confusion in Knight's thinking between value and things which exhibited value.[173] Capital, said Boulding with telling force, was a bridge between input and output, so that the total capital required would depend upon revenue and the period of production.[174] Capital as a perpetual fund abstracted far too much from reality, submerging stocks, flows, and periods of transition while converting the whole theory into a dimensionless piece of metaphysics, with value a mere derivative of the capital fund.

Together with Knight's notion of everlasting capital came that of a perpetual uniform income achieved by borrowing in the present and investing in the future.[175] It then was a simple matter to derive the rate of interest, for the latter became the ratio of an enlarged income to investment. The rate of discounting was equal to the rate of accumulation. However, it would have appeared more useful to relate the discounting process to some definite time span, for projections into an indefinite future seemed utterly vague and unlikely to motivate most people. But in Knight's formulation the rate of interest was equal to the rent on capital goods less perpetual maintenance. The cost elements involved were related to abstinence since this involved foregone alternatives on which the rate of interest was similar. The supply of capital presumably was equal to the demand for savings and was also elastic because capital goods could be indefinitely produced at constant cost. The demand for capital was equal to the amount of saving which was inelastic because of certain undefined institutional reasons. This seemed to turn ordinary theory on its head; yet in a dynamic context it was evident that the supply of saving was a good deal less than inelastic.

Interest as a payment for the use of capital, said Knight, arose from specialization, particularly of the entrepreneurial function. Since there were people who had capital in their possession but did not want the bother of applying it to productive use, this required that capital be converted into a generalized form so that it might be lent easily. That is, capital was value and the yield from its use in this form was identical with the rental yield from a specific type of capital. Whatever differences arose between rent and interest could be explained by those portions of the income stream which flowed to entrepreneurs in the shape of profit. Interest, then, was simply a form of income, and time preference played no role in its determination, for, Knight insisted, consumers distributed their desires evenly over time. Post-mortem prestige, a concern for survivors, or "ideal sentiments" might account for accumulation or savings, but these were institutional factors. Men borrowed because they could put capital to work, and its ability to yield services, its productivity, became the basis for interest, the rate of which was defined as the "anticipated specific productivity ratio." [176] That is, the rate of interest was the expected productivity of the net unit of capital investment at a particular time. However, the notion of an even distribution of desires over time was completely false. Different time horizons do exist for different people and preferences do depend on that. Young persons exhibit preferences for the present, while the middle aged begin to think of the future. Family status as well as age, and, indeed, the capacity to provide for the future do exert subtle and important influences on time preference. They exist even in the productive process. But all this, Knight ignored.

The major elements in Knight's interest theory were productivity and cost.[177] The rejection of time preference allowed no room for psychological elements. Cost entered the analysis because the wherewithal that it took to produce new assets determined the rate of return at which future yields on all other assets were to be set.[178] Cost also permitted one to break out of the circularity implicit in time preference since the amount of capital could be determined separately from the yield of current capital. Yet the quantity of capital was not especially germane, said Knight, since the rate of interest was merely an expression of the relationship between the rate of investment and the rate of potential growth. By defining interest in terms of rates of change, there was no need to go back to physical elements: interest was placed in a complete marginal productivity setting—an extremely abstract argument which in a fully stationary state made interest identical with rent. One invested not a quantity of capital but rather a stream of consumption income of a certain intensity and duration. And the objective of an even level of returns over time could be attained simply enough by investing and disinvesting as the occasion required.[179] This meant the application of the equi-marginal principle over time to the yield of current satisfactions and future investments. Borrowing would take place up to the point where its cost would equal what might be expected from a new investment. One possible interpretation was that the marginal productivity of capital determined the rate of yield and the interest rate. With the introduction of historical factors and accumulation, it seemed that Knight's concept came close to what Keynes was to call the marginal efficiency of capital.

Yet Knight no doubt would reject such a characterization of his theory, for he did not believe that it was possible for capital to reach a saturation point.[180] There was, in fact, no reason to try to draw a supply curve for capital. The rate of interest had no connection with the total supply of capital, and there was no basis for establishing an equilibrium rate apart from the market rate. Ordinary equilibrium theory did not apply to the capital market because it spoke only of the case in which goods came to the market at a steady rate.[181] But here too there was no small amount of confusion. On the one hand, cost did affect future yields, so that the quantity of capital did have some relationship to the rate of interest; on the other, interest per se was unrelated to the supply of capital. The difficulty stemmed from a comparison of stationary price determination with movements in the capital market over time. Such time periods as Knight was concerned with were very long, virtually in perpetuity, permitting an absolute adaptability of productive services. Yet in another sense, his conception suggested an instantaneous rate of return without reference to investment or time preference. The theory foundered because Knight failed to mark the limits between the two situations.

Knight believed the concept of abstinence to be sufficient to explain the origin of interest.[182] The advantage of the abstinence theory, he argued, was that it became a theory of supply.[183] This was so especially when demand was infinitely elastic. Abstinence was the sacrifice continuously incurred by an owner of capital in not consuming the marginal unit already saved. Knight went to great pains to distinguish this from the sacrifice involved in creating additional capital, offering an elaborate analysis of the motives underlying abstinence. Yet for the modern temper all this was frightfully unreal, for in a corporate milieu abstinence has little genuine meaning.[184] Nor was Knight's occasional appeal to institutional factors helpful: he continued to conceive of interest theory as but another exercise in economic formalism. Had he pursued a thoroughgoing institutional analysis, the fallacy of his own position would have been revealed. Abstinence, Knight insisted, was a necessary explanation because without it there would be too many other unknowns to be accounted for. All the complexities were avoided simply by calling for an analysis of the supply and demand for consumer goods, proceeding next to the supply and demand of indirect goods, and ultimately to the supply and demand for capital. Thus, all issues were subsumed once more within the problem of capital. Nothing else was of real consequence.

The outcome of the furious debate between Knight and the adherents of a theory of real capital has been, in the main, a victory for the latter. For one thing, it was evident that the element of time would have to be spelled out clearly, something that Hayek, Machlup, Kaldor, Boulding, and others tried to do, though disagreeing frequently on details. At any rate, the existence of a quantity of output in the immediate past did become relevant for the direction and pace at which the economy could move in the future. Moreover, a study of capital in terms of specific goods did make it possible to offer a structural analysis—a virtual impossibility with Knight's concepts. It was certainly conceivable that the relationship of one capital sector to another was an important consideration in grasping how the economy moved. A concern with these matters had been patently common even to such disparate theorists as Marx and Hayek. The problem had an ancient and honorable history that could not be shunted aside by philosophic disputation, for it was at the very root of so many economic disturbances.

Knight's early reputation was founded upon his theory of uncertainty and profit—essentially a further development of Mill's concept of risk.[185] A similar theory of entrepreneurial function had been developed also by Maurice Dobb in Britain in the 1920's.[186] Both stressed the way in which the decision-making process was expressed through the entrepreneur.[187] Yet such theories, and especially Knight's, frequently bore the burden of apologetics, and, as Joseph A. Schumpeter remarked, they were bound to be met by hostile views.[188] In strict logic, this was the difficulty with any "functional" analysis, an attribute which has characterized virtually all of Knight's work. In his view, the unique nature of profit meant that capital gains were not part of the picture. So global was his theory that profits were matched against losses with the former entirely disappearing from the economy. This was a profit-and-loss system, he said, a statement that might have had some meaning from a macroeconomic standpoint. But many other theorists preferred to talk about profit in a positive sense because they remained at the same level of analysis without shifting from the microeconomic to the macroeconomic at their own convenience.

True profit, said Knight, stemmed from uncertainty. Windfalls and speculative gains were won because of this element. If the future were really known in advance, the market would discount any shortages, so that profit could not be obtained. High returns from risky undertakings were simply a premium for unmeasurable risk or uncertainty. If losses did exceed gains, those who assumed the burden of carrying risks would have to pay to the suppliers of productive services more than they actually took in. The risk-carriers were too optimistic. When gains outweighed losses, the productive services would obtain less than they would have if the future had been more accurately estimated by them. Thus, from an over-all view, a portion of profits represented payments for services rendered by risk-carriers. Profit was accordingly a deduction from other payments and was really a part of what went to the productive services.[189] It was not a factor return in itself and was due solely to uncertainty as to the future.[190]

Every income, therefore, contained an element of profit, which could not always be segregated because of the difficulty in establishing the equilibrium price of a factor payment. Analytically, profit explained the results of deviations of actual from theoretical conditions. In a sense, it was an explanation of market imperfections and was to be centered on the attempt to identify the unique service rendered by the entrepreneur not already included in his normal "wages of management." This was the service of risk-bearing. By this Knight meant not those risks covered by insurance, but rather the unmeasurable, the uncertain kind. Thus his theory became a description of business judgment and decision-making, with profit an important element in dynamic change. Knight believed that this approach was a significant supplement to ordinary price theory for it stressed the great role that losses played in a free enterprise economy. That business profits over the long run have been quite ample made no impression upon him.[191]

One of the purposes of uncertainty was to adapt men to particular occupations, thus providing for specialization within the entrepreneurial group.[192] As the outcome presumably was a greater measure of responsibility and control in business, Knight's description became a panegyric to the entrepreneurs whose function was said to be so vital as to constitute an ". . . enormous saving to society, vastly increasing the efficiency of economic production." [193] Yet his proposition that corporate life exhibits a kind of economic democracy is completely unacceptable in the light of what really goes on in these institutions, where professional managers select Boards of Directors which the stockholders promptly elect so that the Boards can appoint "with an equally solemn ritual" the managements that selected them.[194] With losses included in the profit concept, Knight had to resort to such noneconomic motives as the game spirit and gambling in order to make entrepreneurial activity meaningful. To him, that was at least as important as efficiency. But the drive for profit could not be eliminated entirely, for without it efficiency and the game spirit would be useless concepts. A conflict existed too between ethical behavior and the notion of efficiency which Knight clearly recognized, but since these were different areas for investigation, he had no answer for all the ensuing dilemmas.[195]

Although Knight never felt monopoly to be a serious problem, he did admit that it was an evil when it developed. Monopoly was merely interference with the operations of free competition.[196] In short, monopoly was monopoly —hardly an enlightening definition. Yet, for Knight monopoly could be productive in a mechanistic sense, especially if it originated better ways of getting things done, as sometimes did happen. But essentially, Knight said, monopoly was not very significant because there still was marked substitutability between services. A rather extraordinary view, even for 1921, it is even less helpful in understanding economic reality today. The control that large-scale organizations exercised over resources and services was supposedly "crude and imperfect," and, moreover, such control had to be nearly complete to be effective. Yet price leadership and collusion were common around World War I, and had Knight but taken more account of empirical data than was his wont, his views on monopoly might have assumed another shape. He insisted that the monopoly power of private producers had been greatly exaggerated and that the public had a ". . . gross misconception of the nature of the real evils of monopoly." [197] In fact, criticisms of monopoly were expressions of prejudice. Public efforts to limit private economic power were merely attempts to exorcise an evil by "liquidating somebody."

Similarly, imperfect or monopolistic competition resulted from imperfect behavior.[198] That is, limited knowledge explained why it was possible for producers to differentiate their products from like items sold by others and why advertising was such a great industry. In effect, Knight minimized the significance of the whole new body of theoretical analysis developed by Joan Robinson and Edward H. Chamberlin.[199] It was little wonder that Chamberlin was so furious with Knight and his followers.[200] In the latter's lexicon, economics was to be limited only to the highly restricted assumption of a free enterprise market, with real situations merely a reflection of mechanistic imperfections.[201]

In Knight's system, the theory of business cycles was equally limited.[202] Causes were attributed chiefly to disequilibrium starting in one of the speculative markets. Although money was not part of his basic theory, it nevertheless did rear its head in the explanation of cycles. Knight had long objected to the Keynesian view that money was a central feature of modern capitalism, especially when it was said to be an independent force with its value stemming in part from liquidity preference. And as this seriously clashed with Knight's pure theory, it could not be accepted. The notion that the rate of interest might be a payment for giving up money holdings was anathema. Only at the turning points could liquidity preference play a role, he said.[203] So long as money performed its fundamental role as a medium of exchange and payments were made for services rendered, velocity would be fairly stable. Oscillations occurred when money was employed as a store of value, for then velocity was changeable, causing prices to fluctuate. The really important elements in cycles, argued Knight after the fashion of Pigou, were psychological. Oversaving was impossible since a proper monetary policy could effectively put surplus funds to work. Several types of oscillatory movements were noted, among them cumulative price movements in a speculative market with fixed supply and variations stemming from the response of supply to price. Although Knight dismissed J. M. Clark's acceleration principle as confusing, his rebuttal fell far short of being persuasive.[204] In the main, the business cycle, according to Knight, was a phenomenon involving speculative holdings of money. While monetary policy conceivably might affect the course of interest rates, this was at best nominal, indicating changes in the unit of measure and not any difference in the real rate of yield on loans. More important were prospective price changes in the investment process itself. But once Knight went into a description of the cycle, one could detect sundry elements taken from Keynes and Hayek.[205] The theory, far from being cohesive, seemed in fact to have been tacked on by Knight as an afterthought.

Not unexpectedly, Knight's attitude toward labor was hostile, with accusations of monopoly and other sins levelled against unions. As early as his book on risk and profit, he had attributed low wages to the disposition of workers to gamble recklessly with life and limb as well as income. This supposedly explained why in a free enterprise system their condition was so poor.[206] Society, therefore, had to step in with all sorts of social legislation to make up the losses the worker sustained due to his own recklessness. As was the case with many general theorists, Knight's analysis of labor questions left much to be desired. Even at so late a date as 1959 he could view the complex problems of labor in modern society only against the backdrop of a putative free market.[207] The anomaly was indeed disturbing. Even more extraordinary was his assertion that real markets conformed more closely to theoretical norms than free enterprise detractors alleged. It then was a simple matter to belabor the unions for their violation of market principles. Like Edward H. Chamberlin and a number of other writers of similar ideological persuasion, Knight objected to collective bargaining beyond the enterprise or plant level. But he went the others one better by arguing that bargaining in any case was monopoly price-setting. The capacity of major enterprises to administer the prices of their output was not mentioned. That such enterprises continued to operate under conditions of open competition was elevating a fable to the status of a fact. Those familiar with industrial relations and its history would find it most unlikely that the employer was handicapped because ". . . he cannot afford high-handed action toward an employee; other workers will know about it, and productive efficiency requires worker morale." [208] Quite patently, Professor Knight knew or cared little for the facts of industrial history. To understand the role of unions today one must necessarily leave the general theorist to his ratiocinations and examine the studies of labor historians and labor specialists.[209]

By now it was clear that Knight's political views, insofar as they could be identified, were on the conservative side.[210] Deploring the clamor for change and modification of traditional economic institutions, he bitterly attacked Roosevelt's New Deal as a program of planned scarcity, and he could find only harsh words for social legislation such as the wages and hours law. The free market, he insisted, while perhaps not perfect in all respects, was still better than anything we had because it allowed people to cooperate without any prior agreement on objectives. The mixed economy we were then experiencing was much to be regretted.[211] Curiously enough, while Knight was imploring economists not to predict or make judgments, his own pure theory contained the most egregious judgment of all—that this was the best of all possible worlds.

In the 1933 preface to the reissue of his *Risk, Uncertainty and Profit,* Knight thought it poor taste for economists to descend to the "public's level of thinking" in order to exert some influence on policy. There was an odd sort of snobbery in this remark, for he was patently referring to those economists who had left the campus to go to Washington. They should have stayed home, Knight intimated, to engage exclusively in problem-solving. But, surely, discovering a way out of the Great Depression was a meaningful problem. To Knight, however, those economists who believed the administrative tasks of government to possess their own worthwhile intellectual excitement were merely pandering to the tastes of the crowd.[212] This was bad, he said, because crowd-thinking was romantic and not given to impartial analysis. Yet, in virtually the same breath, he could say with complete equanimity that relevance in economics was tied up with institutional factors. Evidently bad things or actions were only those for which he had a marked personal distaste.

Thus pure formalism was merged with political bias to create the narrowest body of economic thought in modern times. Despite all his protestations to the contrary, Knight was more of a traditionalist than he knew.[213]

vi

Alvin H. Hansen and the
Mature Economy

The interventionist philosophy of the New Deal was, of course, anathema to economic libertarians. And writers such as Alvin H. Hansen of Harvard (1887-   ), to whom problem-solving was not a matter of spinning out the web of abstract theory but an application of economic analysis to practical policy, were bitterly attacked. The views expressed by Hansen and other New Deal economists were derided as "academic apologetics" for the Roosevelt administration and a justification of "reckless collectivism." [214] Hansen himself was accused of wanting a perpetually rising public debt.[215] Virtually all of these savage onslaughts were levelled from the standpoint of the libertarian outlook, to which the maintenance of a framework for laissez faire was deemed more urgent than solving pressing problems of wide-scale unemployment and of an economy that was stagnating in the slough of despondency and depression.

Yet Hansen, often described as the "American Keynes," had begun his career as a somewhat conservative and cautious economist, quite in the mainstream of orthodox thinking. Born on the family farm in South Dakota, he was graduated from Yankton College in 1910. And after teaching in the high schools for three years, he entered Wisconsin to complete his graduate studies in 1918. Hansen manifested a keen interest in business cycles right from the start. A comparative analysis of cyclical behavior in the United States, Britain, and Germany, which comprised his 1921 doctoral thesis, concluded that monetary phenomena stemming from bank credit extensions were the major factors in causing cycles. This was followed by *Business Cycle Theory,*[216] in which Hansen found the cycle to be much more complex. His analysis now became more institutional in character, with technology, the legal structure, and business organization all related to the fluctuations that afflicted the contemporary economy. Uneven income distribution, uncertainty, inventory stock piling, and lags in the flow of goods from one sector to another all contributed to the modern business cycle. Disruptions seemed to occur most frequently when anticipated profits deviated from the rate of interest. Such deviations, Hansen found, might stem from new inventions, technological change, shifts in consumer habits or crops, and wars. More important, he now recognized that expansion or contraction exhibited cumulative effects, restricted only by a limited labor supply, industrial capacity, and available savings.

This was the beginning of Hansen's economics which culminated in a body of thought that exerted a profound influence on contemporary affairs. As a teacher and writer he always infused theoretical investigation with a realistic and tough-minded analysis of policy requirements. Although at first somewhat critical of the newer approach advocated by John Maynard Keynes, he became, after the middle 1930's, the leading American exponent of the latter's theory of income determination. With a sharp grasp of the nature of social institutions, Hansen was tireless in developing some of the more fruitful applications of Keynesian theory to practical matters. A whole generation of economists in this country has learned from Hansen what it is that makes the capitalist economy move. Perhaps the most striking illustration of the kind of genuinely creative work done by his students and followers may be seen in the collection of essays written in honor of his sixtieth birthday, *Income, Employment and Public Policy*.[217]

In a 1932 work, *Economic Stabilization in an Unbalanced World*,[218] Hansen still was not prepared to accept government intervention in economic affairs. He did acknowledge that high long-term interest rates in the absence of adequate profit prospects impeded recovery. Unless long-term rates were reduced, he feared that stagnation would develop. Thus the seeds of his stagnation theory began to sprout. There seemed little opportunity for any further rationalization of industry, and his European trip in 1928 suggested that a decline in the rate of population growth would have a depressing effect. Yet there seemed to be some virtues in these tendencies, for with a slowing down in population growth, less emphasis would be placed on producers' goods industries and more attention paid to expanding consumers' goods. Like Schumpeter, he believed that a depression could lay the ground work for new improvements and higher standards through "creative destruction." [219]

In the main, Hansen's early views were diametrically opposed to those he would later espouse with such great vigor. In 1933, he thought that government deficits and public works would inhibit savings necessary for private investment. Government spending, he said, could depress business confidence, and, like Hayek, he thought that federal programs to relieve the depression would only harm the capital market. Public works were deemed a stop-gap.[220] Yet by the late 1930's, when Keynes' *General Theory* began to exert its remarkable influence on both economists and the public, Hansen had shifted ground. He now recognized that the savings-investment approach to income determination, utilizing the notion of aggregate output and employment, represented an important departure from older theory. In fact, the latter now had become but a special case of Keynes' *General Theory*. The determining causes of prosperity and depression were to be located in such factors as investment and consumer expectations, and these in turn were rooted in the institutions of society.

Not that Hansen was blind to the astounding performance of Western economics after World War II.[221] Yet in his over-all view, he has continued to argue persuasively that strong stagnationist forces were at work in the interwar years. Moreover, public policy did not meet the challenge posed by stagnationist tendencies: the pessimistic outlook which pervaded the atmosphere between the wars was not solely psychological but due rather to deep-rooted factors which only a defense program seems to have lessened. While, prior to the war, high capital accumulation was a decidely positive element, there were nevertheless at work such forces as a declining rate of population growth and increasing industrial rationalization which reduced the ratio of capital to output. These, together with a relatively low propensity to consume, led to the phenomenon of underemployment equilibrium. Secular unemployment was superimposed on cyclical unemployment.[222] Yet the older economic views prevailed, Hansen noted, so that deflationist policies were justified on the basis of cost-price relationships rather than in terms of aggregate demand, employment, and economic growth. As a result, underemployment in the advanced nations grew apace as their economies moved along at "low pressure" rates.

For Hansen, the older "liberalism" was *passé*. In the interwar years Western nations had begun to move toward a welfare state based upon a mixture of public and private enterprise. And while the older market economy had not yet been entirely displaced, it had been markedly altered by a variety of social controls intended to correct distortions in the underlying supply and demand conditions inherited from World War I.[223] State intervention was essential to speed the transition to the kind of system that would more effectively achieve stability and yet maintain progress.[224] This, said Hansen, was attained by income transfers and various forms of social saving without in anyway impeding capital accumulation. Western economies were transformed into high employment, "high pressure" systems. Hansen did concede that all this might very well have been an accident of history, stemming from the Cold War, yet it demonstrated as little else could that a "high pressure" economy required government participation. The postwar experience of Western Europe especially demonstrated the essential validity of his argument, Hansen contended. "The answer to stagnation is not the dogma of automatic adjustment. The answer is the vastly enlarged role of democratic governments —the assumption of responsibility for the maintenance of full employment." [225]

Hansen's economics has been said to be depression rooted—and so it is. The Great Depression of the 1930's was certainly unique in the annals of the American economy. Perhaps no other event in American history, other than the Civil War, had seared the American consciousness so deeply and harshly. Unemployment raged over the land like hurricanes storming the shoreline, and those who did have jobs lived in fear that tomorrow there would be none. No one was exempt from the nameless terror, and it was in desperation that America turned to a New Deal to do something, anything that would mitigate the worst economic setback the nation had suffered.[226] In this milieu, Hansen was determined to find out what was happening. What sort of business cycle was this, really? The major factors associated with these fluctuations, thought Hansen, were shifts in real investment, that is, changes in the output of producers' goods, inventories, and housing. These were the crucial elements.[227] Hansen's analysis of cycles was indeed an informed one, noting the differences between major and minor movements, with the latter often characterized by inventory changes.[228] In addition, building cycles exerted important influences, with longer wavelike movements frequently superimposed on the major cyclical fluctuations. In building cycles, lags in both factor and product markets seemed to explain their longer length.[229] When, however, the downturn of a major cycle coincided with a building collapse, as in the early 1930's, a major depression was bound to occur. The housing saturation of the late 1920's had contributed in a significant way to later difficulties. Hansen now felt monetary factors to be secondary: the main cause of long cyclical movements were to be sought in technological change and innovations which affected real investment.[230]

Clearly the static circular flow model was an unsatisfactory explanation of what was actually happening. In fact, argued Hansen, in such a dynamic system, where progress was being generated by innovation and discoveries and the opening of new territories, investment could by no manner of means be considered a function of consumption. Ordinarily, with full employment, the distribution of output tended to be skewed toward profit, thus creating disequilibrium. Continuous investment was required to keep the economy moving forward, so that a high level of consumption was dependent upon high net investment. In the absence of private investment, therefore, it was essential that government expenditure be substituted which, together with a whole battery of fiscal and tax policies, could be directed toward building an adequate consumer base. Hansen did agree that price flexibility was helpful in facilitating the full use of resources. But still the problem of administered prices and the consequent tendency to make adjustments through production remained. A forcible reduction of prices, Hansen warned, given these circumstances, could intensify the effects of a downturn. Moreover, there was little prospect that the "Pigou effect," stimulation of the economy through real income changes, would come about in any deflationary movement unless it really were massive. Much more important, said Hansen, was "structural" price flexibility, the capacity of prices to adjust to changes in unit costs.

With each new pronouncement, the Keynesian character of Hansen's analysis became more evident. Many of the British writer's implications were amplified and documented.[231] Beginning with a close study of national income,

Hansen developed the concepts of savings and investment along what now are considered traditional Keynesian lines. The factors which determined the level of net investment included Keynes' marginal efficiency of capital, innovations, technological skills, expectations, and the like. The consumption function, multiplier, and even the accelerator became part and parcel of the now familiar analytical apparatus.

The most striking and most controversial portion of Hansen's contribution was his exploration of the problem of economic maturity and secular stagnation. This much maligned theory had considerable merit, and, if one could attribute the remarkable behavior of the postwar economy to extraordinary defense budgets, it comes out a good deal less time-bound and depression-rooted than its critics were wont to charge.[232] Analysing with keen insight the complex factors tending toward stagnation, his policy suggestions were offered to modify such eventualities. And, in effect, the Cold War and the population explosion have refuted Hansen's critics and vindicated his position. Certainly, those who today find it fashionable to deride the Hansen thesis cannot prove that heavy government investment was not responsible for making the economy more viable.[233] Quite simply, Hansen argued that nineteenth-century automatism could not overcome the drift toward a stationary state. Libertarian and business economists who tried to shout Hansen down recognized that his prescriptive analysis was a serious challenge, for it questioned the putative efficiency of a pure free enterprise economy. It was indeed unfortunate that Hansen's role as a government advisor in the Roosevelt administration should have called forth cries of "politics." For quite in the Keynesian mode, Hansen had suggested only that capitalism could be made to function effectively with proper governmental policies: prosperity had to be made available to everyone, including the capitalists.[234] Interestingly, the policies stemming from the theory were identical with those adopted by most Western nations as important tools in their armory dealing with recalcitrant economic problems.

In Hansen's model, the level of output could be expressed as the product of investment and the particular multiplier appropriate to the community. When investment was decomposed, that is, split into its component elements, one obtained induced investment as a function of output over time, autonomous invesment as a function of the rate of population growth, resource utilization and technology, and government investment. The multiplier would have to account for the relation of savings to output with taxes defined as a kind of leakage. Thus output or national income was affected by the marginal propensity to save and by the tax system. Growth was impeded when either or both of these were high. As induced investment depended on national income, with the latter relatively stable, there was little likelihood that induced investment would expand. The key element, therefore, was autonomous investment.

During the 1920's and 1930's it was evident, argued Hansen, that the American economy was losing its dynamism: population growth was declining, the frontier had long since disappeared, and firms were economizing in their use of capital. It was inevitable that output should fall, especially with government investment a small and negligible factor. Yet the stock of resources and the labor force did display some growth potential. Even in such circumstances, it seemed that some upward push was possible. Nevertheless, a widening gap had developed between actual and feasible growth. Secular stagnation loomed over the horizon as autonomous investment lagged. Such an analysis virtually suggested its own corrective measures: increased government investment was a *sine qua non* for a viable economy. The problem, however, was made more complicated because the pattern of autonomous investment kept shifting, so that the ratio of capital use to labor moved in the direction of capital-saving devices. Conceivably, this would intensify the drift to stagnation, particularly in the absence of any great new innovations. Hansen urged that such tendencies were reinforced by institutionalized savings, a situation in which large corporations found it possible to accumulate sufficient reserves of their own and to by-pass normal financing channels. Moreover, the growth of insurance schemes and pension plans had so swelled the volume of savings that ever more investment offsets were needed to keep the economy going. Consumption though rose concomitant with investment, for at higher income levels families did move toward higher spending habits. Thus the noninstitutionalized, noncontractual position of total savings was continually squeezed. This, Hansen contended, was what had happened prior to 1935.[235]

With these relationships, it was entirely possible for underemployment to ensue, especially when autonomous investment waned. Essentially, Hansen was exposing the gap between actuality and potentiality. The population explosion of recent years and the need for a defense program has had a powerful retardation effect upon these tendencies. And governments throughout the West have undertaken measures which have narrowed the Hansen gap. But none of these disprove the validity of his theory, for the latter merely underscored what could happen in the absence of suitable countervailing measures. Clearly, an important relationship does exist between population growth and investment, while equally important is the relation between the labor force and capital accumulation, particularly as it affects productivity. During the nineteenth century, as much as half of new capital could be accounted for by housing, transportation, and other investment forms rooted in population growth. Further, as every market researcher knows, the rate of family formation and the age structure of the population have had important effects on consumer demand. Clearly, population growth cannot be overlooked in any dynamic analysis of economic change. In the past, lagging population growth was compensated by high resource use, inward migration, and technological advance, so that internal markets were able to expand. And as the frontier pressed westward, capital and labor moved into the new areas, in no way depressing investment in older regions.[236] It was evident too that expanded consumption alone was insufficient to stimulate growth, for replacement investment stemming from an increased propensity to consume merely provided an even level of sustenance. And in the current context of affairs, spontaneously generated investment seemed unlikely to offer the full stimulus necessary for an expanding economy.[237]

Thus Hansen in one sense reversed the classical problem: whereas Ricardo and Malthus had been troubled by the possibility of excessive population growth in relation to available resources, he felt that a more rapid population growth was necessary to attain a high level-high pressure economy. This is precisely what has happened. Hansen's employment of Keynesian analytics to demonstrate how rapid growth might stem from the population and resource factors was a dramatic and creative application of the new economics. And if later writers offered a more elegant presentation, it was mainly in matters of detail. Hansen recognized the need for change and policy reform long before economists of his generation would concede that these were required. Only when the economy had been functioning at fairly high levels for some time, as in the 1950's, was it asserted that both Hansen and Keynes were outmoded and that the ancient verities of the classical system had reasserted themselves.[238] Yet it seems evident that the American economy operated as well as it did during the postwar period because government investment was high, because there were the so-called "built-in stabilizers," because social legislation was more highly advanced than in the halcyon days of the Twenties, and because the creaking "progressive" tax system we possess did its job with some modicum of satisfactory performance.[239] It can hardly be said that Hansen's theories were rooted in pessimism: in fact, the inferences one draws from them are wholly optimistic, for they suggest that the American economy can readily devote more resources for housing, education, medical care, roads, and all the other public needs that have been so long unattended. Only those afflicted by the "conventional wisdom" have failed to appreciate this.[240]

vii

Milton Friedman: Theory as Ideology

The viewpoint represented by Alvin Hansen was not at all well received in certain academic circles. This has been especially so at the University of Chicago where Frank Knight, Jacob Viner, Henry Simons, Lloyd Mints, George Stigler, and Milton Friedman have built with great vigor and forcefulness a tradition emphasizing the virtues of pure competition and the belief that ". . . the less economic theory has to do with the economic world we live in, the better" it will be.[241] One of the sharpest exponents of this outlook has been Milton Friedman (1912-   ), whose methodological and substantive essays offer well-reasoned defenses of the new traditionalism. A protegé of Arthur Burns' at Rutgers, he did his graduate work at Chicago and Columbia, and is now perhaps the most vigorous proponent of neo-orthodoxy and a strong advocate of the modern version of the quantity theory of money.[242] A severe critic of the Federal Reserve System and of most existing monetary institutions, his policy recommendations have been directed, after the fashion of Henry C. Simons, toward the installation of so-called "automatic" devices which would erase government intervention for all time. This, in the main, has reflected an innate distrust of the abilities and capacities of public administrators and of virtually all government in general.

As in the case of Knight, one may fruitfully start by reviewing Friedman's methodological approach. He has very carefully distinguished lines of demarcation between positive and normative economics, asserting that the former can be as objectively scientific as any of the physical sciences.[243] He has deplored the tendency to reject the conclusions of positive propositions because they clash with normative standards. Nor does he believe that values are necessary to any positive analysis of economic questions. Yet as Gunnar Myrdal has demonstrated, a belief in the existence of scientific knowledge in social science independent of value systems does reflect a rather naive empiricism. Facts, Myrdal has told us, are organized through concepts which are fundamentally expressions of human interest and particular points of view: these can be described only as valuations.[244] Nor are such value systems arbitrary, for they stem from the society in which we live and work. Of course, since it is possible for several schemes of valuation to co-exist in a single society, intellectual conflict does arise. But it seems fallacious to assume that values can be suppressed: in fact, the various models emanating out of Chicago reflected certain well-defined values when they urged that free, unbridled competition was worthwhile because it ensured individual freedom. The difficulty was that the character of such freedom generally remained an abstraction: rarely were its attributes and limitations adumbrated. Consequently, Friedman's contention that progress might be made only on the basis of a positive analysis collapsed, for policy decisions clearly do require some consensus in the area of normative standards.[245]

The validity of an hypothesis, Friedman contended, had to be judged solely by its predictive powers. Conversely, if a prediction were not contradicted by subsequent events, the initial hypothesis was fully acceptable. That is, direct verification was not essential. Thus, any consideration of the "realism" of one's assumptions in economic theory became irrelevant.[246] The argument was indeed ingenious: there is no need to examine one's assumptions because in any theory which abstracts from a complex reality they will be so far removed from real conditions that little information about them will be forthcoming. Yet it would appear reasonable to suggest that evidence should be brought to bear on any point in an economic theory, including its premises.[247] It was certainly a scientific oddity to suggest absolution for one's preconceptions and premises. A search for "congruence with reality," to employ Stigler's phrase, is essentially an attempt to explore the relevance of a set of assumptions for the problem at hand.[248] The marginalist approach, for example, provided an elegant and self-consistent theory, but it stemmed from certain self-limiting assumptions whose realism could be questioned for lack of broad relevance. Marginalists, of course, have been quite adept in meeting alleged exceptions: in the case of increasing marginal utility of certain goods, they simply have asserted a change in the whole utility function.[249] Friedman's approach merely insisted that a theory is a theory. Yet he could not escape the impulse to check his assumptions, for an hypothesis, he remarked, had to be consistent with the evidence at hand.[250] Certainly, if one's assumptions facilitated even an indirect test of a theory, there was room for judging the relevance of premises.

Friedman then sought to substantiate his argument by analogy with physical science in which "laws" were derived from certain given conditions. But in economics such conditions are essentially fictional and exist only in "as if" situations, with the result that their predictive powers are constrained and limited. It would have been good to say that neo-orthodoxy has extended and revised its specifications, but it is difficult to find much of this being done. For example, it is relevant to ask whether the variable which businessmen seek to maximize is profit or sales. Further, how does standard costing practice and the desire for certain profit ratios affect theoretical formulations? And is it, perhaps, the relationship of assets to other balance sheet items, as Kenneth Boulding has suggested, that motivates business behavior? [251] It is precisely these matters that justify raising the question of realism and relevance.

Some of the problems with which neo-orthodoxy concerned itself, such as utility and choice, were hardy perennials. Friedman entered the debate with an analysis of utility under conditions of risk.[252] He noted that with diminishing marginal utility and risk, ordinary maximizing principles were not applicable, since some additional payment to compensate for the extra factor of risk would be required. This was quite in the tradition of Alfred Marshall, who also had rejected utility as an explanation of choice plus risk situations. While it might be possible to apply the indifference curve technique and ordinal analysis, said Friedman, this too did away with diminishing marginal utility, since utility comparisons were not part of the apparatus.[253] However, by adopting the Morgenstern-Neumann game theory format, it did seem possible to devise a way to measure utility-risk situations; for so long as numerical properties were available, they could be employed to explain choice involving risk. Decisions involving risk were classified as those with little risk and known returns, moderate risk without extreme gains or losses, and great risk but with high returns or losses. It then was necessary to assume that an economic unit had a consistent set of preferences which could be described by some function giving numerical values to alternatives.

The objective, of course, was to maximize utility. By an elaborate analysis of the logic of choice, Friedman and his collaborator, J. L. Savage, constructed a formula which permitted them to insert numerical values. Thus the utility attached to any set of outcomes was subject to computation. Not unexpectedly, total utility increased with the size of money income. Seemingly contradictory, yet simultaneous behavior reactions, involving gambles with all sorts of possibilities and alternatives, were made part of a generalized utility function. While it was acknowledged that people did not consciously follow the behavior patterns of the formula, pursuing difficult chains of mathematical logic, all this was brushed aside with the contention that it was only necessary to suppose that such actions, comparisons of utility and knowledge of odds, did exist.[254] One interesting if minor observation which came out of all this legerdemain was: increased income which improved the position of the economic unit yet failed to move it out of its particular class reflected diminishing marginal utility, while increases which shifted a unit to a new class revealed increasing marginal utility. Thus, a gamble on a new job, the income from which could raise one to a higher status, reflected higher utility. But Friedman then reversed his logic with the assertion that people of low incomes would be unwilling to assume added risks, for with falling marginal utility a premium would have to be paid to induce action. On the other hand, moderate income groups were conceivably greater risk-takers. All this demonstrated how the shape of a utility curve could indicate varying economic positions. It was like saying that those who survived were the fittest.

The significance of Friedman's utility conception was more clearly revealed when he sought to relate it to the problem of income distribution.[255] An effort was made to establish a bridge between functional and personal income distribution. The former, of course, was to be explained by market operations and the pricing of input factors; whereas personal distribution was to be attributed to chance, accident, natural ability, inheritance, in fact anything but the uneven distribution of wealth. The latter never reared its disturbing head in Friedman's analysis. The major factor of his model was risk and the reactions that people had to it. An economy or a community which disliked to undertake risks would prefer insurance to lotteries and progressive taxation to regressive levies. It would have more transfers built into it, so that income would be more equally distributed.[256] All this was based on Friedman's notion of utility: each Robinson of a society of Crusoe's would select a particular utility curve to guide allocation decisions. The outcome was that choice underpinned any inequality of wealth or income that developed: that is, inequality was entirely voluntary. Transfers between the Crusoes were, of course, possible. If the marginal utility of wealth was diminishing, that is, if the society preferred not to undertake risks, egalitarianism would ensue. Therefore, inequality was bound to develop where risk was predominant: it stemmed mainly from tastes or preferences and not from such ordinary and less subtle factors as lack of opportunity or initial wealth distribution. But for all the ingenuity involved in such an argument, the reader remained utterly unconvinced. Its implications, that poverty was simply a matter of choice made by the poor, were so outlandish in the light of contemporary sociological knowledge, that it had to be rejected out of hand.

Friedman's work on the consumption function may be taken more seriously.[257] The consumption function, a central idea in modern economics which had been employed by Keynes, suggested that there was a relationship between income and consumption such that the latter, while increasing as income increased, did not rise as rapidly.[258] Keynes' formulation aroused an enormous amount of empirical and theoretical research.[259] Some of the studies did presuppose that Keynes was correct, but the work of Simon Kuznets, Raymond Goldsmith, and others suggested a more stable relationship between consumption and income than Keynes had imagined. A conflict then developed between the budgetary cross-section analysis on which the earlier concept was based and the time-series data initiated by Kuznets. As a result of further work done by James Tobin, Dorothy Brady, Rose Friedman, James Duesenberry, and Franco Modigliani, the absolute income interpretation stemming from Keynes was modified to allow elements other than current income to be introduced. It was suggested that consumption depended in large measure on the position of the consumer in the income scale: that is, the relative income status of a consumer appeared more significant than did his absolute income level. Thus, as in Duesenberry's interesting work, Veblen's conspicuous consumption was allowed to penetrate formal economic analysis.[260]

To this rather interesting debate Friedman added a new concept—the permanent income hypothesis—whose antecedents could be traced to Fisher and particularly, to Knight. Dissatisfied with the ordinary Keynesian approach, Friedman argued that the predictive usefulness of a consumption function based on income was limited, for in his view real investment had no multiplier effect on real consumption. The latter was determined by its own long-term trend.[261] There was a tendency, said Friedman, for an economic unit to seek a particular level of consumption over time by modifying its current income through lending or borrowing. In a sense, one's income was related to one's capital position.

There were two parts to both consumption and income, one permanent and the other transitory.[262] Permanent income, the flow a person expected to receive over the long haul, depended largely on one's time horizon and foresightedness,[263] and was affected by environment, occupation, and capital holdings. The transitory elements were unexpected additions and subtractions. Friedman conceded that it would be rather difficult to ascertain the size of the permanent component through direct observation, but he nevertheless felt that some inferences might be drawn if certain assumptions were made regarding the relationship between permanency and transitoriness. Such a relation would have to depend on the rate of interest, the ratio of income to wealth, and consumer tastes. But since there was no correlation between the transitory parts of consumption and income, total consumption depended only on permanent income. This meant that a consumer maintained his spending plans over time regardless of whether income movements were more or less than anticipated outlays.

This rather rigid framework was not completely convincing.[264] Studies by the Federal Reserve Board and Survey Center of the University of Michigan have suggested a much larger measure of consumer flexibility than Friedman would allow.[265] Moreover, his approach stressed a certain symmetry of buying intentions over time which could be sustained only by assuming complete certainty, an unlikely prospect for the average consumer. As in Frank Knight's system, time preference was virtually eliminated, with the economic unit operating into infinity. And if there really were a desire for a permanent income flow, the inability to borrow or lend could wreak havoc with one's intentions. Such difficulties appear fairly common among low income and middle income groups. But a major drawback in Friedman's theory was the sheer statistical inability to uncover the permanent portion of "measured" or total income. Available data relate obviously only to the latter, so that the crucial relationships of the consumption function may be set forth solely in terms of total income and total consumption. However, in the Friedman model, total consumption varied with total income only to the degree that changes in total income stemmed from the permanent component. A good deal of empirical material of a rather intricate nature was brought to bear on the theory, yet none of it was sufficiently probative to sustain the notion of "permanent income." In Friedman's view, of course, the theory was not disproven. But as H. S. Houthakker has shown, much of the data employed were spotty and Friedman's statistical coefficients demonstrated virtually nothing.[266] In fact, Houthakker offered an alternative analysis utilizing the Bureau of Labor Statistics' data which clearly placed Friedman's hypothesis under a cloud of doubt. It could be imagined too that transitory income might have a greater impact on consumption than Friedman supposed, or that liquid assets do affect spending possibilities.[267] The curious nature of the theory was emphasized when its assumption of a rigid consumer horizon was employed in other contexts to attack minimum wage legislation. The argument was offered that an increase in minimums would not flow into the stream of spending, but rather would be saved. That is to say, upward adjustments of minimums would not create "high velocity" dollars, but in fact would be deflationary, since consumption levels already had been established. The validity of such a construction for individuals earning less than a dollar an hour, as in large sectors of the retail trades, was very much in question. At any rate, the value of Friedman's hypothesis on consumption was its suggestion of the need for further research on the matter, something few would deny.

One of the topics still considered important at Chicago has been the quantity theory of money. Here Henry Simons, Lloyd Mints, as well as Friedman have sought to integrate it more effectively with general price theory than it was in the past. Certainly, it has been worthwhile to emphasize the importance of money in the modern economy, but then this is precisely what the Keynesians had been saying. The upshot of the Friedman approach though has been to argue the need for a stable economy in the short run and a stable price level in the long run if free enterprise is to survive.[268] The quantity theory of money now was heading the counterrevolution against Keynes, Friedman once told a Congressional Committee, without however indicating to them that neoclassical propositions manifested some measure of validity only under conditions of relatively full employment. The ostensible applicability of classical theory in recent years has emhasized as little else could their special nature within the more general Keynesian framework. But Friedman would have none of this. For him the depression had been a monetary phenomenon as evidenced by the fall in the stock of money during the 1930's. Moreover, said Friedman, Keynes was quite wrong in the way he looked at effective demand, for he had failed to take account of increased real income stemming from a fall in prices. Yet one may very well wonder where or when this "Pigou-effect" went to work during the Great Depression: historical records are fairly clear in demonstrating that it took a massive defense program to reawaken the American economy.

But to the neo-orthodox economists, unemployment suggested no special flaw in the economic system: it was rather certain rigidities and monetary changes that were at fault. Therefore the key to an explanation of how the modern economy functions became the quantity theory, at least in its newer form as presented by Friedman. This version was expressed as $MV = Py$, where M was the stock of money, V the velocity of income, and y the rate or flow of real income. The emphasis in this formula was on the demand for money.[269] For consumers, money was one way of holding wealth; for producers, it was a form of capital. Thus, money demand could be subsumed either into a theory of choice or a theory of capital. Money holdings consequently could be explained by a general theory of apportioning wealth among alternative uses, the objective of which was to maximize utility. For enterprises, the amount of money holdings depended on the yield of alternative productive services as compared with the cost of holding money. This, of course, involved the production function, since it was the latter which determined yield. The volume of transactions was not included in Friedman's formulation,[270] for technical and cost conditions seemed more fundamental. Similarly, velocity became a subsidiary factor in the equation. The empirically important elements were the rate of interest, expected price changes, the ratio of wealth to income, consumer tastes and preference, and the relevant production function.

Essentially, this procedure decomposed the elements of the quantity equation after the fashion of Irving Fisher. The concept of "active" and "idle" balances, as well as the various Keynesian "motives" for holding cash, were discarded. Changes in cash balances over the short period were deemed to be less volatile than the volume of transactions.[271] Friedman denied that the secular increase in the ratio of transactions to income was sufficient to explain the growth in the ratio of money balances to income. If there was a precautionary motive at work, as in Keynes' model, it could be explained only as a reflection of the permanent income hypothesis. Consequently, under conditions of stable demand, total income would be fairly sensitive to changes in the stock of money. That is, only an increase in the stock of money could sustain rising money income. Thus, given the stock of money and its income velocity, the level of money income was established. It was necessary, of course, to determine how income velocity was fixed and what variables went into income determination. The conclusion was that the demand for money was stable, though not numerically fixed over time. There were, of course, certain factors influencing the supply of money which were not directly related to its demand, such as the political climate, the banking system, and government monetary policy.

Friedman did concede that the basic equation said little of the effects of changes in the stock of money. Conceivably, there were various possibilities: increased money could be absorbed by sluggish velocity with no changes in prices and output, or, conversely, prices might turn out to be the sponge. But whatever happened, said Friedman, the causal relationships were monetary. Yet these absorption effects made the theory less useful, as Friedman acknowledged. The main point was that control of the stock of money was beyond individual capacities, for this crucial power had been long ago turned over to the Federal Reserve System. An individual attempt to reduce cash holdings simply increased velocity, caused a rise in income, reduced the ratio of cash balances to income, and depressed the real value of money holdings. Adjustments necessarily had to take place if the public wanted to maintain the same real balances. The major considerations affecting the latter were the cost of holding money and the level of living. The former depended on the rate of interest on alternative assets and the "expected rate of change in prices." With higher prices, the cost of cash holdings would rise, requiring a reduction in balances. Despite Friedman's admission that such effects could result only in a prolonged inflation and that the impact of the rate of interest was "not large in magnitude," he still insisted that all this explained why the ratio of the stock of money to income was declining.[272] Monetary policy, Friedman argued, required close supervision of the stock of money in relation to prices and output. Yet he recognized that it was difficult to ascertain the correct relationship in the short run. The only proper policy then was to let the stock of money grow in roughly equal proportion to the rate of growth in output. This, of course, was completely mechanistic, for the supply of money was to be increased regardless of whatever else might take place in the economy. In addition to this advice, tantamount to having the government do nothing, the basic needs were thrift, initiative, competition, and free trade. Hortative expostulation suddenly replaced economic analysis.

Senator Paul Douglas once questioned Friedman's theoretical explanation by pointing to a 3 per cent increase in demand deposits between 1954 and 1957 while gross national product went up some 12 per cent. This, in Friedman's terms, should have suggested a price rise of about 8 per cent, yet the increase in prices was only about half of this. Friedman's reply was that increased income velocity would have to be taken into account. However, the major destabilizing influence, he insisted, came from the Federal Reserve, which increased money stocks during booms and contracted it in recessions. This stemmed mainly from lags in policy pronouncements and their effective implementaton, for time was needed to carry out open market operations and changes in discount and reserve requirements. Credit controls were, of course, anathema to Friedman. He insisted that the stock of money had been a good deal more stable before 1914 and that the Great Depression could have been ended in 1931 had not the Federal Reserve System contracted the stock of money.

Similarly, he viewed the role of the government in the monetary sphere with great suspicion. From his standpoint, that of a nineteenth-century liberal,[273] all economic activity was more properly carried on in the free market. Admittedly some government overview was needed to enforce contracts, but the fiduciary nature of the money system implied elements of monopoly and there was danger in turning this over to the government. Presumably, the nineteenth century's wildcat banking system, a clear expression of a free market economy, was to be preferred.[274] Blaming the government for economic instability, which he saw as basically monetary instability, Friedman insisted that the evidence of history would support his analysis.[275] Yet a fair reading of the record would reveal that the causes of monetary disturbance cannot be assessed so easily. Different kinds of money have been involved at different historical periods and so complex have been the institutional elements that the aetiology of upset would have be traced far beyond the money factor. A complete and thoroughgoing review of the record of past money movements would offer little basis for confidence in Friedman's quantity theory interpretation of history.[276]

For the present, Friedman insisted, no controls other than open market operations were needed, and all other measures, including credit regulations, should be dispersed or abolished.[277] In fact, anything the government undertook was bad, even if the action might merit some commendation. For example, deposit insurance was good because it improved economic stability, but its value was questionable because the benefits were accorded only to certain sectors of the populace.[278] The only major change Friedman would recommend was the rather curious 100 per cent reserve system and the elimination of fractional reserve requirements. In effect, he would return the banking business entirely to private hands. Only such a program, he insisted, could meet his policy standard of correlating the stock of money with the growth in output.[279]

The neo-orthodox criterion of a competitive market dominated Friedman's economic thinking. Only under free enterprise, we are told again and again, can the objectives of political freedom, economic efficiency, and equality of economic power be achieved.[280] His positive program included the 100 per cent reserve scheme, in order to curtail discretionary control of money stocks; a level of government expenditure based on the "community's desire, need, and willingness to pay for public services"; a fixed set of transfer payments unresponsive to cyclical fluctuations; and a tax system based upon an invariable rate structure for progressive levies. Somehow the elements of this fantastically rigid set of ideas would "fluctuate countercyclically." Deficits in a recession might be financed by fiat currency which then would become permanent additions to the stock of money. Allegedly, these fixed standards would offer automatic adjustments of government outlays whenever aggregate demand faltered. The argument suggested that when national income and tax receipts were high, a surplus would pull money out of the income stream and thus correct the excessive level of total demand. Conversely, at low income levels, relatively high transfer payments would provide the necessary stimulus. Presumably, prices and wages would be flexible. But aside from the patent fact that the amplitude of change would have to be enormous if the model were to work effectively, Friedman blithely overlooked elements of rigidity in both prices and wages. The institutional alterations necessary to make this new "laissez faire" model work, even at low pressure levels, would be far too great. The proposals could best be described as interesting but dubious exercises in economic logic. It was unlikely that any government would surrender the freedom of movement implied in Friedman's program. With such rigid stabilizers, fiscal and monetary policy would be helpless to influence investment decisions. And even if it were thought advisable to stimulate consumption, this would be impossible. It was evident that Friedman simply didn't trust the public authorities to follow prescribed rules of procedure.[281]

His objection to government intervention issued from a laudable concern for individual freedom.[282] As a value criterion, freedom was expressed in absolute terms and given priority over standards of equity, morality, or justice. In fact, anything impinging on individual freedom was to be deplored. But such abstract discussions are difficult to deal with, for they take no account of the numerous limitations on freedom that any functioning system must impose. Any consideration of these limitations which stem from the nature of a society and its industrial organization, needs to be a good deal more specific.[283] How, for example, would one evaluate smoke control and other industrial nuisances from the Friedman standpoint? Further, the libertarian position evades the question of concentrated economic power: its refusal to discuss seriously the theory of monopolistic competition is a case in point.[284] Government intervention was admissible only in instances of natural monopoly, market imperfections, the presence of "neighborhood" effects, and where children and other irresponsibles were involved.[285] Yet, given these criteria, precious little area was left in which the philosophy of the free market might find open expression. Neighborhood effects pervade all economic actions and monopoly and imperfections are to be found everywhere. Individual behavior does not express itself in a vacuum: no one is a Robinson Crusoe, however useful that much exploited figure may have been in formal economic models. And it is at least possible that group decisions may be more helpful in meeting critical economic problems than the actions of an isolated individual. Since the libertarians have not yet disproven this proposition, it still may be valid.

Friedman, whose economics often has served to bolster his own bias, seldom has approached political and sociological problems in other than black and white terms.[286] Going so far as to apply the requirements of legislated laissez faire to public education by limiting the government's role to financing and by eliminating compulsory aspects wherever possible, he would have the law of the market rule even here. Parents would be permitted to select their own schools,[287] and in no case would vocational training be provided by the authorities. Public education was to be limited solely to citizenship, whatever that meant. Just how this would enhance freedom was not clear. And ironically, every piece of social legislation attacked by Friedman, including education, public housing, and group medical practice, could be validated by his so-called permissive standards and neighborhood effects.

In the final analysis, the version of neo-orthodoxy built by Friedman emerged as a highly sophisticated but still fallacious collection of arguments upholding all the ancient economic verities, including the nefarious nature of modern trade unions.[288] Despite the unquestionable subtlety of the argument and its high powered statistical apparatus, most of it disintegrated when tossed upon the hard bedrock of historical and sociological evidence. The excessive stress on the role of the stock of money excluded a variety of other economic factors. Oligopoly, price leadership, artificially stimulated wants—all were too easily dismissed. And quite simply, most of Friedman's proposals lacked political relevance. Aside from their interest as theoretical curiosities, they had no meaning for the existing processes of a legislative democracy. Such considerations were brushed aside with a commendable although unrealistic display of academic absolutism.

viii

Kenneth E. Boulding: The Economics of Organization

Although born in Liverpool, England, Kenneth E. Boulding (1910-   ) has done virtually all his work in the United States. The recipient of several scholarships, he studied at Oxford, Chicago, and Harvard, and, after a short stint at the University of Edinburgh, returned to the United States as an instructor at Colgate University. A short stay with the League of Nations Economic and Finance Section led to his *The Economics of Peace*.[289] After a series of teaching posts at Fisk, Iowa State, and McGill, he joined the faculty at the University of Michigan, where he is now professor of economics. Boulding's first major work, *Economic Analysis*,[290] perhaps the most thorough text in the field of analytics, offered an amazingly complete exploration of the subject. Boulding, who has written extensively, has been unafraid to embark upon new paths in economic theory. And while his ideas have, on occasion, called forth, as he himself once put it, "hoots and catcalls," their very freshness has been eloquent testimony of their author's willingness to probe areas ignored by others.[291] Something of a minor poet and a deeply religious man, Boulding has been quite active in disarmament circles as well as in the Federal Council of the Churches of Christ. In recognition of his contributions to economic theory, he was awarded the John Bates Clark medal by the American Economic Association in 1949.[292]

An early article in the *American Economic Review* signaled Boulding's sense of discomfort with the contemporary theory of the firm.[293] He recognized the great advances made by Joan Robinson and Edward H. Chamberlin, but observed that the element of time had been neglected. The firm, said Boulding, was not merely a repository for inputs and outputs, but actually a kind of account in which each item was a flow with a date attached. And it also was possible that the firms might want to maximize some variable other than net revenue, since the latter was not unique, but subject rather to a range of probability values. But the standard theory of the firm spoke solely of revenue and cost curves of certain shapes which were either maximized or minimized, even though the necessary data were not always available. Boulding urged that a proper theory ought to be related to actual decisions and "to the environment which surrounds these decisions." [294] In fact, said he, a firm was a going operation with a balance sheet, liquidity problems, budgets, and an investment program. It had expenditures which might be rather tenuously related to maximizing net revenue. Further, the latter, as a description of behavior, was quite dubious, for in reality firms knew little if anything about their marginal costs and marginal revenues.

The information system [of the firm] reveals average costs, it reveals sales, production, inventory, debt and other figures in the balance sheet and income statements. It does not, however, generally reveal marginal costs and still less does it reveal marginal revenues. If the firm cannot know when it is not maximizing profits, therefore, there is no reason to suppose that it maximizes them.[295]

Marginalist conditions also failed to recognize the possibility of more than one "maximum" or of the sort of discontinuities that might make a sales curve resemble a staircase. It was evident that in too many instances profit was not the variable to be maximized.[296]

Standard distribution theory was equally unsatisfactory, said Boulding. Marginal productivity did not offer an effective alternative to either classical or Marxian theory. The latter's predictive powers admittedly had failed despite their "magnificent dynamics," yet modern economics had provided no useful substitute.[297] Marginal productivity could not explain discontinuities and its maximizing assumptions were unreal.[298] Boulding's major objection, however, was to the theory's exclusive recourse to income or flow variables which turned the firm into a curiously "bloodless creature" devoid of assets, debts, or liquidity problems, unable to express preferences for certain combinations of resources, equipment, and claims. Banking theory, he remarked rather pointedly, was based on assets and liabilities, but these strangely enough were not to be found in the private firm. Income flows, Boulding argued, were essentially incidental to the maintenance of stocks, while consumption too was derived from a stock.

In ordinary theory, the link between functional and personal distribution had been established through property holdings, with the former rooted in price determination. But this attempt to explain the demand for the factors of production had failed to account for the effect of the price system on that demand. This required analysis at a level not reached by marginal productivity. A suitable theory of distribution would have to display a kind of equilibrium system in which the appropriate aggregates would be reflected by relevant identities together with a sufficient number of behavior equations equal to the number of unknowns. But the behavior equations would have to express relationships revealing some facet of human action in such way that if the relationships were not satisfied by the variables of the system, some movement would be initiated to alter the variables involved. Essentially, this meant that variables had to be homogeneous and that the behavior equations had to indicate a meaningful pattern of social action.

Now, an approach had been made toward genuine macroeconomic theory by Lord Keynes, although some of the aggregates were not homogeneous enough and the consumption function, particularly, was unstable. But marginal productivity was in an even worse condition, Boulding charged: aside from the fallacy of composition continuously committed in its name when transitions were made from the individual firm to the larger society, the behavior equations which it implied were utterly fallacious. For example, a decline in real wages did not raise employment, and individual decisions on money did have effects quite different from decisions stemming from government. In fact, declining employment usually was accompanied by falling prices as well as by declining wages.[299] Consequently, microeconomic analysis was not suited for the broader problems stemming from distribution.

Boulding might have been expected to turn to Keynesian doctrine for an answer to his question. He felt, however, that it first was necessary to clarify some of the confusion he had detected in Keynes' theory, particularly that related to the process of money payments as well as in the theory of accumulation. For example, spending frequently was equated with consumption, he noted, leading to a clash between the concepts of income and receipts and to an identification of gross national product in its real and money aspects. Boulding preferred to define consumption as a "wearing down" of a stock of goods.[300] Production added to the stockpile, while accumulation was the difference between the processes of adding and wearing down. Of course, these could be stated as rates of change. The advantage of stressing fundamental economic theorems in this way stemmed from the light it threw on capitalism's basic problem: fixed capital could be accumulated to the point where its advantages were dissipated, for as the stock of goods grew, the rate of accumulation declined. This could be corrected only by increasing consumption or by reducing production. With a large stock, the rate of consumption would have to be fairly substantial to stave off stagnation.[301] Keynesians, said Boulding, had tended to ignore these real changes and overlooked the fact that "expenditure" was merely a shifting of assets. A clear-cut distinction between the real and value approach made it easier, for example, to study the impact of changes in the velocity of money.[302] Moreover, one might more readily recognize how consumers' capital was constituted and then move in a more direct fashion from consumer asset preferences to inventories to production, rather than via the more complex chain of income, expenditures, profits, interest rates, expectations, and prices. When speaking of the multiplier, said Boulding, one had to indicate clearly whether the real or monetary multiplier was meant, for while the former was useful in describing physical processes and employment changes, it was much less helpful in understanding the circulation of money.

Yet Boulding was not uninfluenced by Keynesian modes of thought. The policy recommendations in *The Economics of Peace,* quite Keynesian in character, did include such notions as variable tax rates for reaching the same objectives as a budget deficit, but with perhaps greater speed. Similarly, his theory of distribution, described below, bears the stamp of Keynesian doctrine. And one may note the sharp and effective yet Keynesian-like criticism of the "hang-over" theory of depression, according to which depressions serve a useful function by correcting maladjustments of the preceding boom.[303]

Boulding's catholicity, demonstrated by a unique willingness to explore other schools of thought, included varieties of underground theory such as institutionalism. In his intensive search for a body of doctrine that would escape the formal aridity of received systems, he in no way underestimated the power of dissent: underconsumption had subsisted on the edge of economics for a hundred years before Keynes had pulled it into the mainstream of economic thought. But Boulding's own thorough grounding in standard theory made him hesitate, even though he did acknowledge the validity of some of the complaints voiced by Veblen, Mitchell, and Commons. The latter's demand for a dynamic theory in which psychological and sociological elements would play important roles struck a responsive chord in him. He knew that the propositions of comparative statics were "at about the level of household wisdom." [304]

Of the great dissenters, Boulding had the least regard for Veblen and perhaps the highest for Commons. While Veblen had pointed the way to an integrated social science, it was, said Boulding, a "ramshackle affair." Commons was attractive because his generalizations—transactions, going concerns, and working rules—could be equated to exchange, firms, and behavior patterns. All this was even more significant than it might appear at first glance because it suggested a theory of organization, something that Boulding was to develop to a high pitch. The institutionalist concern for more meaningful empirical data was admittedly important. Unfortunately, Boulding's attitude toward Veblen exhibited something of an *ad hominem* nature, looking more at quirks of character than at quality of thought. Yet this concern with dissenting streams of theory was interesting, for in many ways Boulding himself has become an important dissenter from received economic theory.

There was no effective way, said Boulding, to separate economics from politics, especially when one examined society as a whole. Nor was it possible to consider the government as a *deus ex machina,* for it was indubitably part of the total situation.[305] In reality, it was essential that an ecological point of view motivate social inquiry, for there was necessarily a balance among the diverse elements that comprised an economic system. Here Boulding employed a number of highly suggestive biological analogies. He began with "ecosystems" which contained a number of populations, each consisting of more or less homogeneous individuals. The equilibrium size of each population in an ecosystem was a function of the size of the other populations. The extent of competitiveness or cooperation explained shifts in the ecosystem's equilibrium. Thus the concept of a population became an important analytical tool, for it could be applied to changes in the stock of such goods as automobiles and so became an influential element in capital theory. Such notions, reflecting at least partly an institutionalist philosophy, were evidently motivated by the observation that pure economics was interested in commodities rather than men.[306] The fact that Boulding then went on to develop a theory of organization revealed his thoroughgoing awareness of the limitations of standard economics.[307] Somewhat more of an institutionalist than he was prepared to admit, Boulding once wrote: "The economist cannot afford to be totally indifferent to the behavior of men and of organizations, even if his prime interest is in the behavior of commodities." [308]

The *Reconstruction of Economics,* containing Boulding's major technical contributions, unfortunately has not received the attention it merits. And the failure of others to follow up its many fruitful suggestions merely indicates a sad reluctance to pursue new lines of theoretical investigation. Boulding's basic contention was that economic relationships may be expressed more powerfully as changes in balance sheet items and that flows become more meaningful when seen as alterations in stocks. Certainly, this viewpoint does appear valid when one realizes that in bookkeeping the "nominal" accounts of the profit and loss statement merely stem from shifts in the "real" balance sheet items. Consumers or, for that matter, firms, argued Boulding, do not seek to maximize satisfactions emanating from a flow of goods over time, but desire a preferred position as described by their asset holdings and obligations. That is, preferences relate to some set of asset ratios. Such an approach made it possible to deal with genuinely observable configurations—quantities, prices, and the relationships among them. Thus prices affected asset holdings directly through both exchange and use and, together with quantities, entered explicitly into economic analysis. It now was possible to give specific reasons for a shift in tastes and to explore more thoroughly the forces behind supply and demand in terms of asset preferences, resources, exchange, and technical transformations.[309]

By relating relative preferences for goods to those for money, market demand equations could be derived from the total of individual equations to show that prices would rise when the quantity of money increased or the quantity of goods declined or the preferred liquidity ratio dropped. If the latter were zero, prices would rise infinitely, as in a runaway inflation. Thus when liquidity preferences were high, prices were affected more by changes in the stock of goods than in the supply of money. Boulding did concede that this had more than a speaking acquaintanceship with Fisher's equation.[310] Yet he insisted that his approach stressed movements in stocks rather than flows and could describe the component elements in historical terms. Moreover, the theory did provide a more general framework for price analysis: the explanation of interest, for example, became a special case, operating through the impact of asset preferences on the prices of securities.

Against this background Boulding developed his concept of the firm as part of the general theory of organization which he found emerging in the works of W. B. Cannon, Chester Barnard, and Norbert Wiener. In fact, organization theory now does promise to become an important area for investigating the nature of the firm, particularly when it is conceived as a field of action.[311] The basic notion in Boulding's formulation was that of homeostasis, a self-functioning device by which variables were stabilized within certain limits.[312] This idea, originally a physiological concept, described how an organism was built and renewed by materials coming from outside itself. Equilibrium or constancy of conditions was maintained by countervailing compensations within the organism or in its environment. In organization, it seemed to Boulding, there were governing mechanisms operating through feedbacks to maintain relative equilibrium: in a firm, the balance sheet provided the data necessary for a good first approximation to homeostasis. As sales flowed out drawing down inventories, the firm was impelled to undertake purchases or production in order to restore the desired balance. The theory would have to investigate the nature of an ideal balance sheet: only at this point, Boulding remarked, did profit maximization become relevant. Yet even then it was possible that liquidity might be preferable, as in instances of extreme uncertainty or a belief in such uncertainty: the classic case was Montgomery Ward under the régime of Sewell Avery. The limits of the firm's decisions were circumscribed to a considerable extent by the rigidity and inflexibility of certain of its assets.[313] Asset preferences were frequently a function of the nature of the firm. Actual or potential behavior shifts necessarily were conditioned by such uncontrollable elements as market imperfections or invariance in the transformation or production function.[314]

Accordingly, firms do tend to relate themselves to certain asset preference ratios rather than to the time-honored but somewhat unrealistic principle of profit maximization. Boulding employed indifference curves to explore how such preferences operated in guiding decision-making. Money stocks and goods were associated on an indifference diagram such that a convex curve connecting the respective axes reflected various combinations of money and goods attainable through the production process. This was the production line: its slope represented the marginal cost of output. An exchange line could be superimposed which in a perfect market would be straight, since total revenue would increase at a constant rate. The good would be exchanged for money up to the point where the exchange line was tangent to the highest production line, thereby indicating the best output, sales, and inventory.[315] This suggested a fairly effective integration of preference systems, production, sales, and inventory plans. In the case of imperfect markets, that is, where price itself was a variable, the amount of production became a variable as well. In essence, profit-making was a process ". . . by which the net worth of an organization is increased through successive asset transformations and revaluations." [316]

Boulding urged with considerable justification that his theory was more realistic than ordinary marginalism and offered wider scope for empirical research.[317] Marginalist doctrine was an appendage to the standard analysis of supply and demand, and could be dispensed with if necessary. And preference theories, said Boulding, would be more meaningful if they substituted the maximizing of "utility" for the maximizing of profit. This would yield a more dynamic theory of the firm by centering attention on asset ratio preferences expressed within the context of the firm as an organization.[318] Obviously, preferences impinged significantly on the demand for input factors, and they could provide an instantaneous picture of the firm as well as the mechanism required for a process analysis. Moreover, in studying supply and demand movements, the past could be easily distinguished from the future by tying existing money and goods to desired asset ratios.

This emphasis led to a view of consumption quite at odds with standard theory. Consumption, said Boulding, was not the end of economic activity, for, in order to maintain some level of real assets, it was necessary to economize: the basic principle was minimum rather than maximum consumption.[319] Satisfaction stemmed from the effective use of goods, not from their destruction. Certainly, this was a striking concept which demanded a marked shift in one's point of view. Saving became a net addition to the stock of goods while hoarding was simply a monetary phenomenon. True, a portion of assets was always being consumed, but the major activity was to add to them through exchange or production. This was the theoretical basis for an equilibrium system expressed in terms of the kind of preference function described by Boulding.[320] The model was certainly quite complex; it was necessary to take account of price changes as well as the accumulation or "wearing down" of stocks. Elements of complementarity and rivalry between goods also were introduced into the analysis. Once all the diverse factors were considered, it became difficult to distinguish between the theory of the firm and the general theory of consumption.[321]

Boulding's concern with real and monetary aspects of economic stocks provided one of the more realistic and genuinely satisfactory capital theories in recent literature. Capital was viewed as a kind of population with a certain age structure that sharply revealed its salient features. The idea of an age structure was important not only for production and consumption, but in business cycle theory as well. With age groupings, survivals, and net "births" or additions, it seemed possible to predict the history, number, and age distribution of a stock of capital goods. Depending on the assumption one adopted regarding the functional relationships, different growth patterns could be evolved. Boulding acknowledged that there was more than a close connection between his concepts and Austrian capital theory, for in the latter the time structure of capital became the significant factor in establishing a given ratio of capital to income.

Capital, said Boulding, was a heterogeneous collection of physical items which were subjected continuously to a process of valuation.[322] It was by no means the mythical homogeneous fund described by Frank Knight. The valuation process itself necessarily was related to the age structure of capital, a point all too often obscured by others. Consequently, the idea of a period of production was not at all so far-fetched, since it was possible to work out the relationship of stocks of goods to annual production, consumption, and the average length of life of capital. Now, disturbances in the age structure pattern conceivably could lead to disequilibrium. Burgeoning and hollow age classes can occur in a population of physical items as well as in humans. One thinks, for example, of the wartime shortage of automobiles and the consequences this had for postwar production, or of the high auto output in 1955 and the effect this has had on the present age distribution of the auto population.

The problem of functional distribution, like many of the other areas of economic discussion, also was approached through the balance sheet concept. Boulding sought to demonstrate that the distribution of the national product was determined, in the last analysis, by decisions affecting the accumulation of real assets and the whole complex of actions revolving about liquidity preferences.[323] Neither wage bargaining nor managerial efficiency was as important as these factors. Beginning with a "fundamental" balance sheet identity, in which income meant net additions to asset holdings or increases in net worth, the question was to determine how such increases were distributed as between profits and wages. This was the central problem of distribution theory, not the division of "profit" into interest, rent, and some residual portion. The latter were historically determined by contractual obligations.[324] This was virtually the same theme that had been set forth by Marx!

A long series of identities were postulated with the basic economic units described as either a business or a household. While it was possible to introduce government as another unit, this was not essential. By a process of aggregation and by eliminating "contra" claims between households and businesses, it became possible to derive a total business net worth identity which equaled money holdings, the value of goods held, and net receivables from households. If one added interest and dividends, the total of the distributive share other than wages was obtained. The important point that Boulding sought to stress was the independence of the components in his final identity. This reflected a search for meaningful behavior equations that would realistically describe the decisions made by businesses and households. Net changes in money holdings, real assets, and net receivables, argued Boulding, moved independently of each other. Undistributed profits, or business savings, generally were not determined by business decisions to save but by numerous other actions. Consequently, when a business decided on what it wished to save through its dividend policy, it was in effect determining its profit level.[325] With net worth determined independently, dividend distributions became a kind of "widow's cruse," for the increase in such distribution by one firm enlarged the profits of others and ". . . an increase in the distributions of all firms swells the profits of all." [326] Among households, net worth was equal to the total quantity of money plus the total value of the stocks of real assets. Household savings, consequently, were equal to the net increase in these items, and ultimately equal to total savings of the community. But household savings also equaled income less consumption with income comprising wages, dividends, and business savings. Wages consisted of consumption and the net increase in consumer stocks, less any changes in cash holdings, net receivables, and dividends. Profits then were equal to increases in the value of business assets plus the net change in cash holdings, net receivables, and dividends. In this way the output of society was distributed as between profits and wages.

But all this, expressed in algebraic identities, clearly was not enough. The usefulness of such "truisms" depended on whether their components varied with shifts in human behavior. The model was intended to demonstrate how the cumulative processes of population growth, capital, and knowledge affected society. The implications of his distribution theory were more clearly spelled out by Boulding in a version which preceded that given in *The Reconstruction of Economics*.[327] While population growth did stimulate investment and consumption, the continuous expansion of capital could restrict profit opportunities, unless new knowledge opened fresh vistas for investment. With an increase in consumption there was conceivably a long-run tendency for wages to grow *vis-à-vis* profits. Therefore, there was just a possibility that a "day of judgment" might arrive ". . . in which accumulation is so great that all investment ceases, in which profits fall to zero and in which consumption is not adequate to absorb the full employment output, so that the system perishes in a slough of unemployment and profitlessness." [328] Such a bleak conclusion, Boulding remarked, stemmed, however, from certain behavior assumptions which were by no means rigid. The historical movement of relative shares was determined by human action, not by any predetermined iron laws. If there was a relationship between the direction of income distribution and economic growth, the solution essentially was one of attaining higher production levels. Man is not helpless, said Boulding, for his behavior can be analysed, dissected, and, in the final analysis, influenced.

It was this firm belief in the malleability of man that suffused Boulding's theory of organization. Goods, prices, and assets did not move by themselves; they were animated always by men. In this way he sought to escape the curious commodity fetishism which has pervaded modern economic theory. It was the kind of preconception that made economics a behavioral science in which the most realistic models were those describing an organization.[329] A theory of this kind would start with a physical balance sheet, a "statement of position," through which the organization could function along homeostatic lines. All organizations, said Boulding, assume certain characteristic forms, with periods of expansion, maturity, and decay inevitably following each other.[330] But their daily functioning required mechanisms for distinguishing between actual and ideal values of the variables with which they dealt: data communicators, executives to interpret reports and information, transmitters of directives and orders, devices to receive orders, and devices to pass them on to the environment—all were necessary to the organization. Such a system could function only so long as the direction and magnitude of change was judged with some measure of accuracy. Information lags merely induced oscillations, as in the cobweb theorem. While the heart of the system was the flow of information, economics, Boulding observed, had remained singularly laggard in its development of an information theory.[331]

The transmission of knowledge and information in an organization required a kind of *gestalt,* in which the past and present were employed to evaluate the future. Here again "balance sheet" data provided the link, for past experience could be related to expected or desired ratios among the various items comprising the statement of condition. However applied, organizational theory in economics would necessarily have to cross the boundaries of the other social sciences, for ". . . most of the basic phenomena of the empirical world are to be found in *all* sciences—behavior, interaction, growth, decay." [332] Boulding also recognized that investigating a social problem was much more difficult than in the physical sciences, not only for the lack of controlled experiments, but because the social scientist by the very act of investigation could alter the problem as well as himself. All too often the self-fulfilling prophecy worked with a vengeance. Obviously, there was need for a closer rapprochement between economics, psychology, and sociology, and Boulding had no hesitation in urging this upon his fellow economists. While the economist might describe oligopoly behavior by means of curves, such situations did contain aspects of conflict which would have to be examined with the eye of the sociologist and political scientist. [333] With such an approach Boulding finally came face to face in spirit, if not in technique, with those institutionalists whom he once had thought merited little attention.

9

From Realism

to Technique

i

Joseph A. Schumpeter and

His Innovator

WHEN AN ECONOMIC theory successfully fuses into one vast system the ideas that an economy continuously reproduces itself without altering levels of production or consumption, that perfect balancing of economic forces is attainable, that the prime movers in economic development are adventurous entrepreneurs whose perpetual search for profit induces such change, and that capitalism will fail simply because it is too successful, there is little doubt that it will be described as an intriguing and even startling doctrine. Such was the system constructed by one of the truly great economists of our time, Joseph A. Schumpeter (1883-1950), professor at Harvard from 1932 until his death.[1]

Born in the Austrian province of Moravia, Schumpeter received a thoroughgoing middle-European education, including Greek and Latin.[2] In 1901, he entered the University of Vienna, receiving the degree of doctor of law five years later. Then, after practicing law for a brief period in Cairo, Schumpeter decided to devote full time to economics. As a student he had paid a good deal of attention to economic problems, particularly in seminars on statistics and economic theory. His teachers had included such luminaries as Wieser, Philippovich, and Böhm-Bawerk. And among the students at Vienna who took part in these seminars were Mises, Felix Somary, and the brilliant young socialists, Otto Bauer and Rudolph Hilferding. There seems little doubt that Schumpeter's life-long interest in socialism stemmed from these sessions. In 1909 he took a post at the provincial University of Czernowicz and then moved to Gras in 1911. As the only economist on the faculty, he gave courses ranging over the entire field, including some related problems in sociology. It was evident that his masterful grasp of so many branches of economics and the polymathic quality so often revealed in his work had its roots in these early experiences. In 1913, Schumpeter spent a year at Columbia University as an exchange professor, returning to Europe just before the war broke. Blunt in his pro-Western sympathies (he had visited Cambridge and Oxford in 1906 and was married to the daughter of a Church of England dignitary), he was wont to call the conflict a "bloody madness."

When the Austrian republic was established in 1919, the coalition Catholic-Social Democratic government called upon Schumpeter to take the post of Finance Minister (evidently at the behest of Otto Bauer).[3] The situation was, of course, little short of utter chaos: inflation seemed unavoidable. And as a conservative who had been recommended by a socialist, Schumpeter's position was not especially enviable. Within seven months he was forced to resign having had no real opportunity to put into effect his ideas on controlling inflation.[4] He wanted a strong and united government that would be able to impose a capital levy to support the foreign loans that were so essential for reconstruction and he wanted a balanced budget. Moreover, his perfectly sensible statement that "a crown is a crown" did not sit well with thousands of Austrian burghers who were seeing their assets disappear. Two years after leaving the government, Schumpeter became head of a small bank, which was to collapse in 1924. Having tasted of both politics and business, he decided to return to the relative quiet of the Academy. After a guest professorship in Japan, he accepted a chair in public finance at Bonn where his general seminars provided broad channels to deflect the historicist stream that still flooded German economics. In 1932 Schumpeter accepted a post at Harvard (he had lectured there in 1927 and 1930) where he remained for the balance of his life.

Schumpeter's literary output was enormous. And many of his early articles still are worth close study.[5] Yet while he was in many ways a lineal descendant of the Austrians, the major influence in his thinking was Walras, whom he considered the greatest of modern economists. So far as he was concerned, anyone who did not study and comprehend Walras' general equilibrium was unlikely to become a good theorist.[6] In addition to Walras, however, one could detect the effect of Irving Fisher and John Bates Clark on Schumpeter's early vision of the capitalist process. Although he thought the former's effort to employ accounting notions in economic analysis especially useful, he rejected Fisher's concept of capital in favor of Clark's fund notion— an idea that was to play a central role in his own *Theory of Economic Development*.[7] Moreover, Clark's scattered remarks on dynamic theory seemed to have provided Schumpeter with the inspiration needed to compose his pioneer study of economic development. Inevitably, an important influence stemmed from Böhm-Bawerk, whom Schumpeter held in high esteem. Von Wieser's concepts could be detected in the 1909 essay on social value.[8] And the notions of the order of goods, imputation, opportunity costs, and marginal productivity all came from Vienna.[9] Where Schumpeter differed from the Austrians was in his contention that the circular flow represented an economy that was without profit or interest. Profit was but a temporary phenomenon induced by development, with interest a monetary payment flowing from entrepreneurs to capitalists via the money market, and, consequently was nothing more than "tax upon profit." [10] Nor did he accept the idea of a smooth and continuous accumulation of capital, for development came erratically and in bunches.[11] Above all, he preferred by far the broadness of scope and predilection for sociological implication which he found in Marx to the somewhat restricted models of a Böhm-Bawerk.

Schumpeter's system, however, was not an eclectic collection of con- glomerate notions. Indeed, out of his cohesive theory of the origin, func- tioning, and decline of capitalism was built an imposing set of hypotheses on business cycles, money, interest, and prices. Many of Schumpeter's ideas had been fixed when he was still a young man. In 1908, at the age of twenty-five, he published a work on theoretical economics that touched on virtually all of the problems of the field and even suggested the solutions at which in later life he would arrive. By the time he was thirty, he had written a short history of economics which was to be expanded decades later into the posthumous and fantastically huge *magnum opus,* the *History of Economic Analysis.*[12] Yet, questioning the more recent developments in monopolistic competition and Keynesian doctrine, he did remain basically a kind of old-fashioned economist.[13] Despite his acknowledgment of the importance of advertising and product differentiation, his own doctrinal system was based essentially on "pure" competition. His rejection of the Keynesian message was even sharper, stemming from a distaste for the implication that an economy could be tinkered with to make it work. His own ideas were based on a kind of prime-mover notion: once capitalism started it should be permitted to keep going under its own sealed-in, self-lubricating power. In pure theory, it would be necessary to reject all political, philosophical, and ethical considerations.

The initial model with which Schumpeter was concerned dealt with the behavior of single business units in an environment over which they exercised but little control. It was, in the main traditional, and he sought to reformulate it in terms of simultaneity and interdependence. Implicit always in this structure was the notion of marginal utility, which never quite avoided the accusation of making economic man a dextrous balancer of pleasure and pains.

In an early work, *Das Wesen und der Hauptinhalt der Theoretischen Nationalökonomie,*[14] Schumpeter insisted that economic analysis could be freed of hedonism and that theory should not be used to rationalize the existing pattern of income distribution. This was a particularly important point to stress, for, more and more, economists at the turn of the century either were consciously or unconsciously employing marginal utility and productivity theory to justify this as the best of all possible economies. At this point Schumpeter's model was still static. Equilibrium existed between the variables and one could determine how the elements of the system would react when a single variable was shifted. The relationships were purely formal and rooted, as in Austrian theory, in marginal utility. But this model was not confounded with actuality, for, as Schumpeter knew, economic life was essentially dynamic and ever changing, the nature of which was to be explored in the later theory of development.

As a theorist, Schumpeter exhibited an unusual generosity. An avowed conservative, he still did not hesitate to recognize Marx as a brilliant economist. What mattered to him was the quality of a man's work and what Schumpeter liked to describe as "vision." By this he meant a "preanalytic cognitive act" that supplied the raw material for scientific investigation.[15] This was a perception into economic problems that would enable one to ask really meaningful questions. Given, therefore, the ideological biases, there was no reason to condemn a man's intellectual output simply because one disagreed with it. Ever willing to listen to his adversary, Schumpeter was never satisfied until he had viewed reality from the standpoint of the other—an extraordinary desire in a field where the most innocent inquiry could elicit an hour-long exposition of some personal belief.

While Schumpeter did acknowledge mathematics as an important tool in economics,[16] it could never replace, he felt, the exercise of intuitive insight. Such intuition led to the art of building useful abstractions, an art in which Ricardo, Marx, and Walras were supreme. This, thought Schumpeter, was the real core of economic method. Doubtlessly, he had imbibed a good deal of this thinking during his student days at Vienna, and assuredly must have had to demonstrate sharp wit in debates with Bauer and Hilferding.

Despite his predilection for the precise, he was something of a romantic among economists. Capitalism, he averred, should be an exciting, glamorous adventure. In his advocacy of the use of mathematics he did not preclude an appeal to historical evidence. In 1950, the last year of his life, he conceded that mathematical models in business cycle studies had not been as fruitful as he had hoped and that as between the theoretical, statistical, and historical methods, the third was the most important. Yet in his own vast research, he seldom failed to employ all three—an ability stemming from his own great knowledge of scientific method. He who doubts this has only to read the introductory chapters of the *History,* where Schumpeter demonstrated a grasp of the philosophical and sociological interrelations in economics which is indeed rare.[17]

No method, insisted Schumpeter, possesses so general a validity that it can claim to be superior to all others. Each has its specific application: while the historical method might be appropriate for an examination of economic organization, price theory might demand abstraction and model building. Yet both, he pointed out, "often converge and become indistinguishable." Of all the social sciences, he argued, only economics came close to the natural sciences and this only because it dealt with phenomena capable of being "quantified." In fact, measurement of much economic data did not have to be superimposed, as in physics, for they presented themselves to observation as quantities made numerical by life itself. Once this proposition was grasped, there was no need to resort to a study of motives or mainsprings of human behavior. It was the failure to realize this that led the classicists astray, since associationist psychology, hedonism, and comparisons of utility were all irrelevant to the basic technique of economic quantification. But measurement and statistics were not sufficient for comprehending the *relationships* between economic facts. For this, theoretical economics was required. Either one had to put trust in bold and perhaps unsafe mental experiments or else give up all hope.[18]

He conceded that these experiments might not partake of the reality we knew, but, while they were arbitrary constructs, they were created with the facts in mind. This gave to economic theory its system and rigor, while at the same time shaping it by the phenomena it purported to study. Within this methodological framework, equilibrium theory became for Schumpeter a static system in which the long-run effects of small and continuous changes in basic data were observed. While there might not be any practical relevance in this, Schumpeter nevertheless felt that variations in static conditions could yield significant answers for some economic problems such as tariffs and taxation. Where changes were large and discontinuous, dynamic methods were called for. First setting forth a dynamic model in his *Theory of Economic Development,* Schumpeter later elaborated it in his book on *Business Cycles.* Starting with static analysis as presented in his doctrine of the circular flow, he noted how breaks in the flow, such as the introduction of new goods, new methods of production, and the opening of new industrial organizations, made the economy dynamic. These were the forces that created "development." [19]

At this point, it may be well to pause and survey briefly the conceptual bases of Schumpeter's thinking.[20] What strikes the historian is its remarkable consistency. And it does accord with the remark which he once made that a man's ideas are fairly well set by the time he reaches the age of thirty; for the rest of his life a man's work is merely a development of the original underlying themes. This was virtually an autobiographic description.

The root problem of an economic system, said Schumpeter, was the attainment and maintenance of equilibrium. But he rejected the Marshallian partial approach and, true to his heritage, utilized as the major tool for analysis the more general concept advanced by Walras. In Schumpeter's initial model, economic activity was simply repetitive, so that the theory described a kind of circular flow. All firms were in perfect equilibrium, with costs equal to income. Profits and interest were zero, prices were set by average costs, and there was full utilization of economic resources. Into this model was injected a new production function, that is, a new relationship of input and output. This was generally carried out by an Innovator searching for greater profit than was available through normal channels. He had the remarkable ability, found only in a capitalist society, of visualizing new opportunities and then being able to take advantage of them. But to accomplish this he needed to obtain new credit, with the result that the banker ultimately became the one who permitted the Innovator to operate.[21]

With the new purchasing power obtained from the banks, the Innovator moved into the market to outbid the older, more lethargic entrepreneur for available factors of production. The flow of producers' goods increased, while consumers' goods declined. The first of these innovating adventurers made the path smooth for those who followed, but soon investment opportunities petered out. Borrowing was lessened, bank loans were repaid, and deflation set in as new firms competed with old. Values were revised while some firms passed away entirely. A new circular flow was established. However, there could be no going back to the old equilibrium. Output was at a new level and the very composition of the commodity package produced by society was altered. There were no errors and no speculation in this first approximation to economic reality. The length of time it took for the process of expansion and contraction to work out was indefinite, depending on the specific innovation that broke into the closed circle. The institutional elements in the situation also were rigidly defined, so that the kind of capitalism that the model was intended to illustrate became historically fixed.

It was presumed that the Innovator would have to obtain grants of credit from the banking system in order acquire the economic strength to break out of the circular flow. This introduced a whole range of perplexing problems concerned with money, capital, and interest. The Walrasian character of his model, impelling Schumpeter to visualize money as a flow of spending that moved in one direction while goods flowed in the other, offered an analytical framework in which money could become a useful vehicle for studying the economic process. It became the link between economic events and was also "claim ticket and receipt voucher" tying together production and income going to the cooperating factors.[22] Yet money exhibited no power of its own, for its movement was conditioned ultimately by entrepreneurial decisions.[23] In fact, the intervention of money was but a technical matter in the model, since the circular flow still could function even if money did not intervene. Schumpeter knew full well that it was necessary to distinguish the money role of a *numéraire* from its use as physical material. All the problems that arose in the analysis were expounded with remarkable clarity, including such questions as the marginal utility of money, its value, velocity of circulation, as well as legal aspects. His 1917 essay on the subject is still one of the more incisive discussions in the literature.[24]

The notion of flow dominated Schumpeter's concept of capital as well. For him, capital was not to be identified with concrete goods, but was an independent agent partaking of the nature of a fund of purchasing power, not unlike that found in the J. B. Clark-Frank Knight version of capital theory. In this respect Schumpeter departed from Austrian economics, especially as developed by Böhm-Bawerk and later on by Hayek.[25] Capital was employed to purchase goods and was replenished through sales. Interestingly enough, by seeking to express an important economic relationship in this way, Schumpeter brought a concern with men as well as things into his system. Capital, however, became significant only when development took place: there was nothing in the circular flow to which it corresponded.[26] It was therefore an aspect of dynamic analysis which explained why interest, as an income flow, arose only when growth and development occurred. In the static state, or the circular flow, the whole product went to wages and rent, and interest did not arise. It was a price paid for the acquisition of new productive services and emerged out of profit stemming from the adoption of innovations. Interest in Schumpeter's view, consequently, was a "loanable funds" phenomenon. It arose only in the money market, which itself was a creature of development.[27]

It has been argued that this description cannot be valid even in the circular flow, since without any yield for capital there would be no incentive to maintain it even at the level required for a static economy.[28] However, the circular flow assumed complete certainty with no time horizon to talk about. With zero interest and a given even flow of income and utility always expressed as the same function of income, there was no special advantage in substituting future for present satisfactions. Thus, a model without interest did seem logically possible.[29]

As is common in analytical economics, a pure model may be modified by relaxing assumptions and by introducing more complex elements so that the conceptual structure might be brought closer to reality. In Schumpeter's economics this was done by introducing the effects of an innovational wave with all the fluctuations and imperfections that were induced by it. The addition of plant and equipment to the existing capital structure was accompanied by increased consumer spending. Some entrepreneurs expanded their facilities with the hope that conditions would continue to be promising, thus introducing speculative factors. Account now had to be taken of mistakes and rosy views gone wrong. The total picture became a mixed one; prosperity and boom began to reveal pockets of weakness. When the break did occur, it became possible for an actual depression to displace what appeared in the earlier model to be a new equilibrium. Perfectly good economic positions deteriorated as the liquidation of previous values accumulated. Only the effort to attain a new balance made a revival possible.

In his version of cyclical change, Schumpeter depicted the well-known phases of prosperity, recession, depression, and recovery, but he refused to impose any uniform pattern on the various cycles in capitalist history. Each was a unique phenomenon, with its own specific features. Marking off cycles from peak to peak or trough to trough was an artificial procedure that obscured the specific character of capitalist development. While it was possible to study cyclical change without reference to its effects on economic growth— and this was what was done when cycles were compared as to amplitude and length—the reverse made no sense, said Schumpeter. Economic growth was deeply rooted in the turbulence of cyclical movement: one need but study the problem of investment and accumulation to realize the importance of this proposition. A simple illustration was to be found in the nature of induced investment which was related to the initial expansion of income stemming from innovation. Thus, increased output in one part of the economy could impel activity elsewhere: in fact, this was a central feature of revival.[30]

When Schumpeter began to work out the details of his version of economic change, he offered a schematic picture of an admittedly complex cyclical pattern. All development stemmed from innovation. Different innovations required different lengths of time in order to be fully absorbed, while some, as in the history of railroad construction and automobiles, might exhibit similarities. And to complicate matters even more, some innovations might be viewed as interdependent in character, being part of a larger, more basic outburst in economic growth.

Thus, Schumpeter's analysis suggested the possibility of several simultaneous movements rather than a congeries of fluctuations which would keep succeeding each other through time.[31] The resulting multicycle theory was rooted, of course, in the belief that the economic system had to be described in terms of general equilibrium. After some experimentation, Schumpeter fixed on a 3-cycle apparatus as the most practical way of describing what was happening under capitalism. Naming these after the economists, N. D. Kondratieff, Clement Juglar, and Joseph Kitchin, each cycle was set at respectively fifty-five years, ten years, and two years, four months in length. These were not independent movements, but bore certain definable relationships to each other. When one examined the recovery phase of a Kondratieff, said Schumpeter, one observed a fairly close approximation to general equilibrium, for at this point there seemed to be a conjuncture among the three movements. On other occasions what appeared to be a Juglar prosperity or depression might be part of another movement which modified the nature of the Juglar itself. Thus, each Kondratieff contained a number of Juglars, each Juglar some Kitchins, so that ". . . the sweep of each longer wave supplies neighborhoods of equilibrium for the wave of the next order." [32] With this imposing structure Schumpeter sought to establish a conceptual framework within which the necessary empirical material might be fitted and so give substance to the theory of economic change.

Schumpeter's economic theory exhibited a kind of internal drive that had nothing to do with either a great man or devil theory of history. Economic change was caused by "innovation," a catch-all word for breaks in the circular flow. Innovation was, of course, a broad social process in which many individuals took part, making change a pervasive aspect of the economy. Granting that the economic system was affected by wars, revolutions, crop variations, and taxes, Schumpeter characterized these as "external" factors. He did not deny their importance, but like Marx he wanted to discover the "internal" laws of capitalist motion. He wanted to know what elements within the economy impelled shifts in activity. These, he thought, were the important things—changes in taste, in ways of making things, and in methods of supplying goods. It was evident that the last was the most significant, for nowhere else did innovation exert greater force.

Clearly, Innovation was not the same thing as Invention. The latter was a technological fact, while the former was an economic and sociological process.[33] Innovation, Schumpeter insisted, was a matter of business behavior in that it turned existing productive forces to new uses. Technically, Innovation set up a new "production function" which was associated always with the rise of new business leadership. New way of making things did not take place in old businesses. So-called old firms which survived the rigors of economic change were able to do so, said Schumpeter, because they were fundamentally transformed under the impact of Innovation: they no longer were able to display the attributes of conservatism.[34]

Innovation did not proceed smoothly: it came in clusters and spasmodic movements. As one industrial leader overcame technological and financial impediments and opened a new path to profit, others followed with a rush. But toward the end of such prosperous periods the entire economy became upset and further gains were uncertain. Errors and miscalculations forced some firms into bankruptcy. There were adjustments, of both the sharp and rolling variety, with concomitant destruction of values. And as realizations no longer met expectations, a depression ensued in which everyone waited for new facts to be discovered before economic calculations once more could be balanced. This Schumpeter called the process of "creative destruction." This was capitalism's essential fact.[35]

Nevertheless, capitalism was able to produce increasingly greater quantities of goods. According to Schumpeter, the major criterion for an economy's success was its ability to expand production: capitalism, he argued, had unquestionably measured up to this index.[36] While Innovation might cause a painful disarrangement of previous economic relationships, in the long run it resulted in social gain. Set in this context, large-scale industry, often criticized as monopolistic, had a special function to perform. In actuality, rigid prices, limited output, and patent control kept capitalism on an even keel, thus serving as a desirable counterbalance to Innovation.[37]

Yet while capitalism has operated admirably, said Schumpeter, it cannot continue to do so. The causes of capitalism's breakdown, however, were not to be sought in the realm of the economic, but in the habits of thought which comprised its cultural superstructure. Capitalist thought, he said, was initially rational and logical; the very nature of economic calculation impelled the businessman to clear thinking. Antiheroic, basically pacifist, it was apt to insist on the application of private morals to international relations. Moreover, it provided the social arena for a new bourgeoisie which produced, on the basis of a strong, powerful, and Puritanical individualism, ". . . not only the modern mechanized plant and the volume of output that pours from it, not only modern technology and economic organization, but all the features and achievements of modern civilization." [38] From the purely technological standpoint, insisted Schumpeter, capitalism could certainly function at high levels. The depression-inspired argument that opportunity had shrivelled did not seem valid to him. Nor was he convinced that Innovation was becoming capital-saving or that the closing of the frontier could have permanent effects.[39]

Yet, declared Schumpeter, the superb engine called capitalism will fall apart.[40] In its early stages when capitalism had been essentially an adventure, the individual businessman might have undertaken risks for the anticipated return, but he also had been motivated by the implicit challenge to his industrial and commercial ability. But today, said Schumpeter, as progress has been mechanized, the function of the entrepreneur, to apply new innovations, has atrophied and is being reduced to mere routine. The romance of earlier commercial adventures is eroding; bureau and committee work now have displaced individual action. All this, the inevitable outcome of the capitalist process, tends to convert the bourgeoisie into a superfluous class. Thus, the very success of capitalist enterprise paradoxically has impaired the status of the class primarily associated with it.

This displacement eliminates the small businessman; private property and freedom of contract become archaic legal instruments; millions of absentee stockholders take the place of active participants in the capitalist process; the economic order eventually fails to evoke the loyalty and emotional response required to sustain it. The people begin to turn away from capitalism, said Schumpeter, in spite of its effectiveness as a producing machine. And as the great mass of people are unable to express their loss of faith, their disappointments and dissatisfactions must be articulated by those alienated intellectuals who have acquired a vested interest in unrest. Intellectuals sooner or later become detached from the dominant order. Overproduced and given no financial stake in capitalism, they are driven to stimulating, verbalizing, and organizing discontent in a system that fails to provide them with a satisfying role. And as the social atmosphere becomes hostile, people will refuse on principle to take account of the requirements of capitalist production and in this way seriously impede its effective functioning. Since capitalism can operate well, the explanation of its final collapse lies in the destructive action of noneconomic-minded individuals.[41] Said Schumpeter:

Capitalism, whilst economically stable, and even gaining in stability, creates, by rationalizing the human mind, a mentality and a style of life incompatible with its own fundamental conditions, motives and social institutions, and will be changed, although not by economic necessity and probably even at some sacrifice of economic welfare, into an order of things which it will be merely matter of taste and terminology to call Socialism or not.[42]

It almost appeared that Schumpeter would agree with Marx: capitalism, in the long run, tended to stumble over its own inner contradictions. Perhaps this similarity of vision made Marx so attractive to him. Not that he was uncritical: there seemed little left of the technical aspects of the Marxian structure after he had finished with it, especially in the *History*.[43] Schumpeter placed little stock in Marx's political aims, his Hegelian metaphysics, or his materialistic sociology. And while he did acknowledge the remarkable precision with which Marx had formulated the economic interpretation of history, Schumpeter felt that it inhibited the construction of more generalized theories. Nevertheless, Marx was four-square in the classical tradition: in his *Economic Doctrine and Method,* Schumpeter made clear that the scientific core of Marxism was traceable to Ricardo and his forebears.[44] Above all else, said Schumpeter, Marx had been a very learned and extremely capable economist. He also described him as a prophet, sociologist, and teacher.[45] The point was that despite the special Marxian bias there was an interest in economic problems in their own terms: there was a primary concern, said Schumpeter, with "sharpening the tools of analysis proffered by the science of [the] day, with straightening out logical difficulties and with building . . . a theory that in nature and intent was truly scientific whatever its shortcomings may have been." [46] Only because Marx based himself on Ricardian value did he fail to break out of the intellectual limits of the time, said Schumpeter. Both Ricardo and Marx had argued that the value of a commodity was proportional to the quantity of labor embodied in it (with Marx it was socially necessary labor) and both had measured this by resorting to labor time as a standard. Both had encountered the same difficulties with the theory, difficulties that led Schumpeter to pronounce it not merely wrong, but dead and buried. However, Marx's ability to distinguish between the quantity of labor and labor power, the ability to create embodied value, did represent a marked and even ingenious analytical advance over Ricardo. What had complicated the problem for Marx was the recognition of the divergence of prices from values. Marx's problem was to show how absolute values were shifted about so that, in the end, commodities, while still retaining their values, were not sold at relative prices proportional to such values. In other words, price deviations did not alter values but only redistributed them. [47]

Marx's greatness as an economist, admitted Schumpeter, stemmed from his realization that capitalism could not be attacked with merely ethical slogans. Marx sought to prove that exploitation was inherent in the logic of capitalism and that no single industrialist could be assessed with personal responsibility for what the system did. This was done with the theory of surplus value, one of the most facile and, for that reason, most powerful inventions of economic discourse. Yet, while Schumpeter did a respectable job in refuting Marxian value theory in its own terms, he was not averse to employing on occasion a kind of *ad hominem* argument. At one point he remarked that the exploitation theory was a rationalization of ancient slogans expressing the resentment of the lower classes against the upper strata living on the fruits of their labor. This eventually, he said, became synonymous with exploitation.

However, it was Marx's emphasis on capitalist change that attracted Schumpeter. Marx's recognition that capitalism was not and cannot be stationary, that it was altered continually by internal forces, came close to his own system, Schumpeter felt. [48] It will be recalled, however, that Schumpeter derived the motive power for his dynamic changes from the breakthrough in the circular flow that an Innovator achieved. In the circular flow stage, which was static, all the factors of production and all the consuming power required for normal circulation were present. But the Innovator, securing new credit from the banking system, was able to divert factors of production from existing channels, thus initiating a dynamic phase. In other words, the economy required the *deus ex machina* of an innovating break in order to achieve significant changes. Thus, Schumpeter did not quite succeed in making economic development completely dependent on elements internal to the economy itself. In this regard, Marx's theory does seem superior. For, by emphasizing the problems of accumulation of capital, the flow of economic resources through simple and extended reproduction, productivity, and the tendency of the rate of profit to fall, he sought to demonstrate that what made capitalism move were forces generated from within. Whatever one may have to say about its details the very conception of the Marxian system was breathtaking.

Yet the first approximation developed by Marx and Schumpeter—simple reproduction and the circular flow—were amazingly alike. Both were static models: one had no accumulation, the other no innovator, and surpluses did not appear until growth began to push the economy beyond the limits established by the initial formulation. And it was not impossible for the dynamic thrust of one model to infuse the other. Marx and Schumpeter also recognized that the entrepreneur was becoming increasingly obsolescent. Marx, in his chapter on credit, pointed out that the functioning capitalist was being transformed by the spread of corporate organization into an administrator of other people's money, with the owner turning into a mere lender of capital. Furthermore, said Marx, the centralization of capital, facilitated by the growth of corporations, enforced a rationalization of productive processes. In this sense, corporate growth might be interpreted as a stabilizing factor, a notion akin to Schumpeter's defense of large-scale enterprise. The similarity here is too striking to go unobserved. But these are similarities in detail only, for one thing that Schumpeter surely did not savor was the change in the whole apparatus of organizational and political control that stemmed from Marx's theory.

Perhaps the major difference between Marx and Schumpeter might be described as follows: Marx always analysed his economic factors in a successive chain of causation, calculating the relationship in an arithmetical manner and deducing thereby the information he wanted about the unknowns that interested him: Schumpeter, on the other hand, sought to discover how the various elements in an economic situation affected each other simultaneously and, for this, the more powerful tools of algebra and calculus were required. Not that Marx had been unaware of the interdependence of economic factors: attention need only be called to his analysis of the way in which the organic composition of capital depended on the rate of surplus value. Yet, in the main, he had held to the causal technique and this placed him at a decided analytical disadvantage, for it was difficult to express clearly in this way the mutually interdependent character of economic relationships.

In the *History,* Schumpeter defended the Marxian system, despite alleged errors and inconsistencies, on the ground that it was analytical and logical, comprised as it was of statements of relations between social facts. Weighed down by class ideology, influenced by heated value judgments, and overladen with questionable sociology, Marxian economics still possessed an undeniable methodological meaning. And although Marx had wrestled with every fact and argument that came his way, often to the detriment of his main point, he was, said Schumpeter, ". . . a born analyst, a man who felt impelled to do analytic work, whether he wanted to or not." [49] Whatever inconsistencies existed in Marxian economics, were in details, not in vision.

As the theory of imperialism had become an important facet of Marxian analysis, it was not unexpected that Schumpeter also would deal with the matter. His own essay on the subject, *The Sociology of Imperialisms*,[50] he considered among the most important he had written. His thesis diverged sharply from that propounded by the Marxists. The latter utilized class and accumulation theories to account for the complex maze of international economic relations and the resulting politics. The inherent logic of capitalist development, according to Marxism, explained loans, tariffs, and aggressive wars. But although history could supply enough evidence to support the Marxist doctrine, Schumpeter argued that the historical facts in the matter were never made clear. Moreover, he said, Marxists failed to integrate adequately their theory of imperialism with their general doctrine: the heyday of imperialism had occurred during capitalism's youth; class conflict was lessened by imperialism; and businessmen followed the flag, not the other way round. In actuality, said Schumpeter, capitalists tended to be anti-imperialist and quite rational about business problems, while imperialism was wrapped in nationalistic sentiment. However, the entire construction seemed somewhat dubious and Schumpeter's refutation was not fully convincing.[51]

It is well to observe in these days, when Marx is so often dismissed as unworthy of scholarly attention, that Schumpeter advised: "There is no point whatever in perusing selected bits of Marx's writings or even in perusing the first volume of *Das Kapital* alone. Any economist who wishes to study Marx at all must resign himself to reading carefully the whole of the three volumes—and the *Theorien über den Mehrwert*." [52] Schumpeter also cautioned that careful preparation was required for Marx: understanding him demanded a knowledge of the economics of his time and especially of Ricardo.

Yet Schumpeter could not abide the Ricardian approach. He thought as much of Ricardo's theory as he did of his policy suggestions. So repelled was he by the latter that he charged Ricardo with a lack of insight ". . . into the motive power of the social process and in addition [a lack of] historical sense." [53] One has but to glance at Schumpeter's famous description of the Ricardian method to really savor the antipathy. Ricardo was not concerned with a broad vision of the economic system, said he, but with rewriting Adam

Smith, for out of the Ricardian criticism of the *Wealth of Nations* had come the *Principles of Political Economy*. The major purpose—to obtain results of practical significance—was described by Schumpeter as the Ricardian vice. This was done by freezing all the variables but one, so that economic relationships might be deduced in rather simple logical fashion. But this method led to error, insisted Schumpeter, as in the argument that profit depended on the price of corn, for all other factors in the situation were taken by Ricardo as given. And tacked on to this questionable theoretical structure, he continued, were unjustifiably confident solutions of practical problems.

But more important, Schumpeter felt that the Ricardian analysis had been little more than a detour in the history of economic thought. True, the Ricardian analytical machine did have much in it that could be admired. It exhibited some characteristics of a general purpose apparatus, and for this alone might have merited Ricardo a place in doctrinal history. And insofar as it did represent an advance in technical skill, one would have to say that Ricardo had made some contribution. Obviously, Schumpeter was not terribly generous in his estimation of Ricardo. Further, he tended to overlook functional distribution, the major problem to which Ricardo had faced. The chief question in political economy, said Ricardo, was to discover how the revenue of society was proportioned among the classes. In this process, he had argued, an irreconcilable antagonism existed between the landlords, on the one hand, and industrialists and workers, on the other. Quite patently, Ricardo had sympathized with the latter. Furthermore, he successfully highlighted the ideas of social interrelationship and interdependence. And a not inconsiderable contribution to this intellectual development was made by his stress on cause and effect in economic behavior. What Schumpeter objected to was the fact that Ricardo had sought to make economics not merely a matter of theory but one of practice as well. But this revealed more about Schumpeter than Ricardo.[54]

Schumpeter's great intellectual hero was Léon Walras. In the *History,* he said:

So far as pure theory is concerned, Walras is in my opinion the greatest of all economists. His system of economic equilibrium, uniting as it does the quality of revolutionary creativeness with the quality of classical synthesis, is the only work by an economist that will stand comparison with the achievements of theoretical physics. . . . It is the oustanding landmark on the road that economics travels toward the status of a rigorous or exact science and, though outmoded by now, still stands at the back of much of the best theoretical work of our time.[55]

Schumpeter thought Walras so important because he found exact forms for phenomena whose interdependence was attested to by actualities; he derived these forms from each other; he did it in a new field without the accumulated experience of prior work; and he achieved favorable results despite great difficulties.

Yet Walras' theory was simply a refined and precise statement of how supply and demand determined price. As Schumpeter said, Walras tried to show that while in actuality traders in a market might not be the lightning calculators the theory seemingly suggested, that nevertheless, they did arrive empirically at roughly the same thing. People entering a competitive market with a good and an approximate idea of what they wanted to sell it for were met by others who were bound to make offers. Somewhere along the line a balance was struck. Walras was saying the same thing with greater precision.[56]

Walras' approach, however, abandoned the problem of price causation. Any connection between price and value seemed irrelevant. No longer would economists have to search for the source of value: they now had a formal theory of interdependence in which economic relations were stated in the neutral language of functional equations. For this purpose mathematics proved an invaluable asset. The system, also, was a determinate one because the the number of equations was equal to the number of unknowns. However, the entire structure seemed to possess but dubious practicality, dealing as it did with idealized cases. One thing was certain: the increasing neutrality and formal rigidity removed such economic theory from the realm of political applicability. In fact, some economists have been able to make this theory so neutral that it can be used, they aver, for a socialist as well as a capitalist society. Walrasian economics, in this sense, resembled a huge research program, said Schumpeter, which had not yet been able to supply all the answers. As a starting point it provided for the clear formulation of all possible premises and the inclusion of all important elements. And, insofar as this was true, it had its usefulness.

Interestingly enough, Schumpeter's long and detailed discussion omitted Walras' theory of applied and social economics. This was no doubt due to the fact that Schumpeter visualized his *History* as one of analysis rather than of economic thought in general. In other words, Schumpeter was interested in efforts to describe and explain economic facts and in attempts to provide logical tools for doing so. Policy questions, to which legislators might address themselves, were excluded from major consideration. He was concerned only with the so-called scientific aspects of economic thinking. However, it is doubtful that this was a completely defensible approach, for it can be argued that the particular outlook of a theorist in the social sciences is bound to impart a special coloration even to the most formal parts of his system. Failing to acknowledge this was to dodge the task of evaluation. Schumpeter did admit that ideas often glorified the interest of the class which was in a position to assert itself. This very well could result in a theory that did not match the truth, but he still felt that it might be possible to recognize ideological influences and that a detached intelligence could "enjoy the privilege of being exempt." [57] Some doctrines, then, could develop a quality of universality which would make them adaptable to varying social atmospheres. This was the case with the Walrasian system, whose author, it must be remembered, had been something of a socialist.

As much as Schumpeter admired Walras, so did he abhor Keynes.[58] The late English economist had enjoyed, of course, a fantastic success: his great work, *The General Theory of Employment, Interest and Money,* had set the tone of public discussion on economic matters for almost two decades and, perhaps even more important, reflected the temper of his time in a way that Schumpeter could never approach, even if he had wanted to. It was precisely this that Schumpeter rejected in Keynes. The latter's applied economics could not be separated from the theoretical framework and this Schumpeter could not abide. Keynes, he argued, merely had built a conceptual vehicle for an ideology which posited that the cause of capitalism's collapse was within itself. In it, the alienation of the intellectual and the obsolescence of a class did not count as significant factors: capitalism simply stumbled over its own feet. In Keynesian doctrine noneconomic causes were irrelevant.

Keynes, like most Englishmen, viewed theory as a program of action. Schumpeter, on the other hand, was wary of such approaches. Keynes was the utilitarian who believed that the State would have to establish rules for economic behavior, especially when things went awry. But Schumpeter, who did not understand Keynes' "enlightened conservatism," thought that a legislature, in order to serve the masses, would only introduce basically anticapitalist measures, whereas the solution of capitalism's ailments lay rather in a continuation of the past rate of increase in total output. And as Keynes' system avoided time sequences and dealt with short-term problems, Schumpeter described it as a depression-ridden doctrine, lacking in the kind of generality that a good theory should have. However, Schumpeter's own theory suffered from certain weaknesses that might have been overcome with a touch of Keynesianism. Schumpeter's interest theory, for example, which postulated its occurrence only in a dynamic society, was related to the possibility of profit in new ventures. It was thus a monetary phenomenon linked to innovation and, in this sense, bore certain similarities to Keynesian doctrine. However, Schumpeter emphasized only the demand side and said little about the supply of loanable funds. Whereas Keynes connected the supply of funds not only to conditions in the money market but to the level of savings as well, Schumpeter always denied that savings could be related functionally to income. In fact, he argued that persons in the upper income brackets saved less, relatively and often absolutely, than did lower income groups and that the bulk of savings was done with some investment goal in mind. Such a theory did not begin to approach the incisiveness of the Keynesian analysis.

Nor was Schumpeter willing to accept the idea that oversaving and overinvestment might become chronic. So far as he was concerned, Walrasian equilibrium was attainable at the end of every cycle. But Keynes clearly showed that persistent deflation might be an unwelcome accompaniment of such equilibrium. This was obviously important for any theory of economic development. Perhaps Schumpeter ought not to have rejected the Keynesian system as he did, for the absorption of some features from the latter might have enhanced his own. The bunching of investment in Schumpeter's analysis stemmed from a sudden rush to imitate innovators who had demonstrated the profitability of a new mode of technology. Yet the Keynesian multiplier and the relationship between investment and output could have illuminated the innovation process.

Schumpeter's contention that Keynes' doctrine could lead to radicalism was unwarranted. What Keynes had attempted was to give the British liberal tradition a new *political* economy. But essentially conservative, rejecting the Labor party because it was a class party, he himself had preferred to remain with the bourgeoisie. And, despite his proposals for government participation in the economy, he had opposed collectivism in any form. He thought Marxism erroneous and was puzzled that it could exert an enduring influence on men's minds. In this regard he differed from Schumpeter, who, as we have already noted, believed Marx a great thinker, as indeed he was.

By contrast, Schumpeter was allergic to any doctrine that suggested the feasibility of policy participation by the economist. Throughout the *History*, for example, he showed a persistent preference for pure theory, the "positive" features of doctrinal history, rather than for so-called "normative" propositions. Implicit in this approach was a belief that scientific knowledge was possible in the social sciences independent of value judgments. This, of course, was little more than naiveté. Facts do not order themselves without concepts, and the latter, insofar as they are expression of our interest in the world about us, are essentially value judgments. Thus, at the very inception of social inquiry, at the point where facts are put together for the purpose of drawing generalizations, "normative" propositions are involved. What is important is to set forth clearly such value judgments as may be implied in particular doctrines. For example, it would be very helpful if the hedonistic presuppositions of much contemporary theory, especially in that branch described as "welfare" economics, were admitted beforehand. Value judgments cannot be discarded; they must be meaningful for the particular society which any theory purports to describe. They should be related to the interests of groups in that society and should be expressed in terms of current social and economic change.

Schumpeter's predilection for the general and abstract was itself an expression of inverted interest. During the last few years of his life he turned away from political events; he had believed Germany not unjustified in seeking to rectify the injustices of Versailles. The sharp reaction this incurred, together with what he thought to be an appalling increase in government intervention in economic affairs, impelled him to turn to purely "scientific" interests. While he had an extraordinary grasp of the methods, views, and limitations of virtually all theories, his expressed preference was for those that sought an everlasting universality.

An intellectual descendent of the Austrian school of economics, it was unavoidable that Schumpeter in his historical and sociological views should assume what was essentially the attitude of the Middle European intelligentsia. This was perhaps best exemplified in his analysis of the political role of the bourgeoisie, who he insisted was incapable of managing the long-run interests of society. As a result, political affairs became the province of the upper strata of the bourgeoisie and former aristocrats. This, perhaps, more than anything else, demonstrated the weakness of his sociological apparatus; it explained also his somewhat arrogant insistence that sociology might be regarded as the proper occupation of a tired economist. Although of middle-class origin, Schumpeter early had adopted the tastes and habits of a Viennese aristocrat. At Harvard he would sometimes describe himself as the last representative of true European culture. He was repelled by much of Alfred Marshall's writing because of the tone of Victorian morality he sensed in it. Yet he did admire England; its aristocracy knew how to rule

Unquestionably, Schumpeter is important not only as an economist but as a social scientist. He advanced a striking and forceful theory of economic development: he achieved at many points a remarkable integration of theory and history; he emphasized, in the main, the dynamic aspects of economic problems; he studied, with a broadness of vision comparable only to Marx, the origin, functioning, and decline of capitalism; he sought to employ not only theory and statistics, but historical, sociological, and even psychological data; and he was concerned, despite the details of economic analysis, with the over-all functioning of the capitalist economy, a problem that most academic economists preferred not to discuss.

Although he exerted great attraction as a teacher and theorist, there really are no Schumpeterian followers as there are Marxists or Keynesians. This was due not only to the extremely involute presentation of his doctrines but also to the obvious fact that in a time of crisis, the critique of policy is usually more attractive. Devoid of the passion that possessed Marx, unable to construct a seemingly simple system as did Keynes, Schumpeter hid his virtues, such as they were, in niceties of logical distinctions and in a phraseology so complex that it might have been lifted from his native German. He could not give his readers what they wanted; he was not a reformer. So intent was he with being "scientific," that he ran the risk, in an era when politics and economics once again are being fused, of finding himself without an audience.

ii

Sraffa and the Collapse of Competitive Theory

When economists took a second look at Marshall's system during the 1920's, they discovered that he had left behind some rather untidy concepts. Certain functional relationships seemed to delay movement toward equilibrium or in fact to shift equilibrium completely away from the original location. Even more significant was the presence of a variety of frictions which suggested entirely new market relationships. Normal price in the free market became something of a will o' the wisp. More and more, Marshall's time periods, his representative firm, the external economies, and increasing returns were criticized as ambiguous. Despite the patent fact that monopoly was rapidly becoming a predominant feature of the real-life market, Marshall's analysis appeared as but an afterthought. Empirical studies of industrial organization emphasized that economic theory had not kept pace with a changing environment. Neoclassical doctrine was a poor explanation of what actually was happening in modern capitalism.

Not that Marshall was unaware of these problems: numerous remarks in his work do indicate a clear recognition of frictions and exceptions, but he tended to slight these matters in favor of a cohesive and evenly flowing theory of the free competitive market. Increasing returns, for example, did hint that cutthroat competition would wind up in monopoly. This indicated, as Mrs. Joan Robinson once remarked, a conflict between static analysis and dynamic conclusions, yet ". . . somehow we managed to swallow it all." [59] In the meantime, John Maurice Clark was demonstrating how overhead introduced doubt and ambiguity into the computation of unit costs.[60] Harold Hotelling at Columbia wrote an important article on location theory relating price strategy to spatial equilibrium.[61] And in Denmark, F. Zeuthen (1888-1959), professor at the University of Copenhagen, showed in his *Problems of Monopoly and Economic Warfare* [62] that the ordinary theory of value was unsuited for noncompetitive markets. Economic analysis would have to deal with oligopoly, bilateral monopoly, and bargaining between economic *groups.*

The space between the extremes of absolute monopoly and unhindered competition would have to be filled by a new kind of theory.[63] Conditions were varied, argued Zeuthen, and prices were most typically set in a composite market which involved both spatial and price relationships. By utilizing the Marshallian "area" technique, Zeuthen offered some rather interesting insights to his fellow economists. Moreover, pieces of a theory of imperfect competition could be found in Pareto, whose occasional references to incomplete or limited competition were generally overlooked.[64] In effect, a rather broad theoretical movement developed among writers in many countries which viewed the economy in a fresh light: even in Germany, where the heritage of the historicists still was felt, Erich Schneider and Heinrich von Stackelberg were able to make important contributions to the new theory.

The task of clearing away the debris of the older view was carried out by Piero Sraffa, a young Italian economist transplanted to Cambridge. In 1925, he published some critical ideas in an Italian journal, *Annali di Economia,* in which he insisted that each producer tended to develop his own private market and that this was most significant for the theory of profit. The following year his path-breaking essay, "The Laws of Return under Competitive Conditions," printed in the *Economic Journal,*[65] showed that, given the competitive conditions of classical theory, an industry could not be in equilibrium if external economies governed its flow of output. With such economies, the assumptions of the older theory were "illegitimate," for with increasing returns the particular industry as well as others would be affected.[66] Equilibrium seemed possible only in the relatively small number of cases where input factors were used entirely by the industry or where economies, though external to the firm, were internal to the industry. The only way to solve the problem, said Sraffa, was to drop the assumption of free competition and to move in the direction of an analysis of monopoly.[67]

Many industries could be found to operate within the spectrum of market forms between competition and monopoly. Moreover, the conditions that fragmented the competitive market were more than mere "frictions"; they were ". . . active forces which produce permanent and even cumulative effects." [68] The relevant range for economic analysis was patently that which would encompass diminishing rather than increasing costs. And within this range the central question related not to production but to the demand or sales curve which was so shaped that a larger quantity could not be sold without reducing the price or incurring "marketing expenses." This implied that buyers by no means were indifferent as to the sellers from whom they purchased their goods. Personal acquaintance, custom, credit facilities, location, tradition, special designs, and packaging—all destroyed the alleged indifference of the customer. Consequently, one could no longer speak of a single market: there were now a series of special markets, each enclosed and sustained by the peculiarities of buyers' preferences. And it was of no import to the theory whether these preferences were rational or not; they simply existed. For a firm to crash through another market meant heavy advertising costs and investment in goodwill, while in its own area it enjoyed protected advantages. Obviously, the only equilibrium in such an economy was a monopolistic one in which influences were manifested by the elasticity of demand for the enclosed product. Faced with a less than perfectly elastic demand, a curve which was not geometrically infinite, the seller necessarily had to keep in mind that an increase in his price might occasion some loss of custom. This, of course, was conditioned by the degree to which acceptable substitutes were available to buyers.[69] Where the firms were somewhat similar, this could issue in a monopoly price. And where "monopoly" profits were not too high, the costs of entering the industry could establish effective barriers against newcomers.

Sraffa's article came just at the right time. It blew the older theory virtually to bits. A flood of articles by Dennis Robertson, G. F. Shove, Roy Harrod, Lionel Robbins, and Joan Robinson followed, notably in the *Economic Journal*.[70] Here in the United States, Jacob Viner helped to clarify many of the concepts involved in a famous 1931 article on cost and supply curves.[71] Thus, when Joan Robinson and Edward H. Chamberlin published their classic works at practically the same time in 1933, the economics profession was well prepared for this minor revolution—and a revolution it was, thought not as explosive as that initiated by Keynes.[72] Economists now felt that they possessed a superior tool-kit which at long last could be filled with real content. The new theories, particularly those of Robinson and Chamberlin, were enthusiastically received, for they effectively brought monopolistic models to a high level of development. For years afterward, students and scholars were to add more ornaments which, however, did not change the basic product. Chamberlin, whose entire career has been devoted mainly to this area, has noted that up to 1956 almost 1500 articles have appeared in the professional journals on monopolistic and imperfect competition.[73] The effect was to give Marshall's partial equilibrium analysis a fresh lease on life, while the brief excursions into the area by Cournot, Pareto, and Edgeworth were displaced by a cohesive and integrated theory of the ground between competition and monopoly. Marginal concepts were sharpened as they seldom had been before, especially by Mrs. Robinson. And, perhaps even more significantly, advertising costs and selling efforts were brought by Chamberlin right into the center of economic analysis.

iii

A World of Monopolies: Joan Robinson and E. H. Chamberlin; Stackelberg and Triffin

Joan Robinson (1903-   ) entered Cambridge in 1922 when Marshall's economics was still supreme—an influence that was shed in the next decade and a half. Indeed, her own remarkable contribution to the economics of a noncompetitive world helped to shatter the Marshallian inheritance. Within a few years Keynes' *General Theory* pointed the way to a much more important problem than relative prices and equilibrium, namely, income determination and employment. Keynes' influence became quite important in Mrs. Robinson's thinking, and she worked toward extending the *General Theory* from the short-run analysis it was to a long-run explanation of accumulation and growth. One had but to peruse her *Introduction to the Theory of Employment*[74]—a gem of expository writing—and her *Essays in the Theory of Employment*,[75] to see how completely captivated she was by the new economics. However, another interesting development in her thought soon manifested itself—a serious concern with Marxian theory. Mrs. Robinson has been one of the few contemporary writers to take pains to read Marx himself. An early article on John Strachey's *Nature of the Capitalist Crisis,* in which Marxian theory was central, was followed by the superb *Essay on Marxian Economics.*[76] Here the essence of Marx's analysis was recognized to be the problem of capitalist circulation and accumulation rather than the labor theory of value. And, when Mrs. Robinson came to her own profound study of accumulation in *The Accumulation of Capital,*[77] it was evident that Marx's stress on technological aspects had deeply affected her approach to the question.

Mrs. Robinson acknowledged a greater affinity between Marx and Keynes than many were ready to admit.[78] Accumulation as a process rooted in profitability stemmed from both; one could readily discover in their work the notion that a chronic conflict between the ability to produce and the power to consume was the basic cause of crises. Her interest in accumulation sent Mrs. Robinson to Rosa Luxemburg, for whose translation she wrote a critical yet appreciative forward. Here she remarked that for all its confusions, Luxemburg's book ". . . shows more prescience than any orthodox contemporary could claim." [79] Always generous in her acknowledgments, Mrs. Robinson has expressed her obligation to M. Kalecki for his theory of expectations, Roy Harrod for his concept of natural and potential growth, and, in her study of imperfect competition, to Theodore Yntema and others for the marginal revenue concept. But in no way should this suggest a resort to mere eclecticism: Mrs. Robinson's works bear the stamp of originality and are thoroughly integrated analyses of some of the really fundamental problems of modern capitalism.

Mrs. Robinson was attracted not only to Marshall's partial equilibrium analysis but also to those scattered elements in the master's system that suggested a more dynamic concept of development and economic growth. But first a new level of statical analysis would have to be reached; this she accomplished in the *Economics of Imperfect Competition,* a work that ploughed through relatively fresh ground. The coincidence of its publication at about the same time as Chamberlin's book was extraordinary and demonstrated that the climate of opinion indeed was ready for a new theory of value determination. Mrs. Robinson, however, looked upon the economic landscape from the standpoint of monopoly. She began by saying that ". . . no sooner had Mr. Sraffa released the analysis of monopoly from its uncomfortable pen in a chapter in the middle of the book than it immediately swallowed up the competitive analysis without the smallest effort." [80] This observation is crucial, for as one reads the *Imperfect Competition,* there is a clear impression that this is precisely what happened in Mrs. Robinson's economics. The difficult and troublesome problem of the impact of rivals' behavior and of a seller's reaction to what he thought they would do—the question of oligopoly —was conspicuous by its absence. The spectrum of markets that one found in Chamberlin's analysis was lacking in her exposition, yet both had arrived at virtually the same place. Mrs. Robinson argued that once rival producers were seen as producing distinctive articles, so that each had a monopoly of his own output, it was inevitable that competitive theory would be put aside.[81] The free market involved also questions of entry, mobility, and the absence of uncertainty. In Chamberlin's definition these attributes added to the homogeneity of the product with numerous sellers creating perfect as compared with pure competition.[82] But this, implying a fair degree of knowledge of market conditions on the part of both producers and consumers, was at best an ambiguous assumption: if universal knowledge of prices and costs was meant, clearly it was unrealistic. And, if a firm was supposed to know its own cost and demand functions, even this was questionable. The basic proposition now, however, was that the demand curve of the individual firm in an imperfect market sloped downward.[83] This was in sharp contrast to the infinitely elastic demand curve under competition.[84] While the downward sloping demand curve had not been unknown in economics, the Robinsonian emphasis suggested that it was a good deal more prevalent than had been supposed.

The technique itself was rooted in partial equilibrium: all firms in an industry but one were deemed to be in equilibrium, and it was its movements that were isolated for study. According to the marginalist analysis, production would be undertaken up to the point where marginal cost equaled marginal revenue. Under perfect competition the producer, unaffected by external economies (for individual output could not affect price), would expand his scale of operations to the point where marginal cost and price were equal.[85] But price was also average revenue. On the other hand, in imperfect competition, each producer was a kind of monopolist subject only to the possibility of consumers substituting rival products for his own. Of course, the demand curve in such situations was affected by the degree of elasticity, for if the latter was less than unity at the point of contemplated output, marginal revenue would be zero or less.[86] Were this the case, it would pay to contract operations. Market activity, therefore, required an elasticity of demand of one or more. With a shift in demand, there would be a change in elasticity and the relevant marginal cost also would be affected. Given the change in marginal cost, the direction of price movements would depend on the elasticity of the new demand curve. Underlying these formal changes were such factors as increases in the number of buyers, greater income, the elimination of rivals, and higher costs for possible substitutes. All these would affect total demand and their impact would be different for different producers.[87] The next step was to analyse costs. In the short run only variable costs governed, since the fixed unit cost curve described a rectangular hyperbole and could not influence short-run marginal costs. One then moved to long-run cost analysis and the way in which the scale of operations was affected.

Whatever the details of the formal analysis, it was evident that economic theory now had to acknowledge the patently observable fact that consumers did take into account more than price. Quality, transport costs, location, service, credit—even inertia and ignorance—impelled consumers to make distinctions between sellers. And while Mrs. Robinson did not discuss "product differentiation" per se, it was obvious that this phenomenon pervaded her analysis.[88] The sort of competition that ensued made the perfect market a fiction, for the very intensity of the rivalry tended to break up the market in a way that would require more than a small price advantage to encourage someone to foresake a particular source of supply.[89] Under perfect competition, a firm would produce up to the point at which its average cost was a minimum. Beyond this point, production would mean high profits: competition would depress the average revenue curve (identical with marginal revenue) to where it would be tangent to the average cost curve. Thus, ease of entry was related to the level of profits. Under imperfect competition, equilibrium for both the firm and the industry required that average revenue be tangent to average cost, thus implying that the latter was falling at that point. Consequently, normal profit under imperfect competition meant that firms would be less than optimum in size.

The analysis also was extended to input factors. With a perfectly elastic supply and no economies of scale, an increase in demand would move price to the point at which it was equal to marginal cost. Expansion under conditions of limited supply would force up the prices of input factors. If a choice were available as between relatively scarce and relatively plentiful factors, increased costs would bring about the possibility of substituting one for the other, provided technique permitted such a shift. Still, economies of large-scale production could counterbalance any increases in cost stemming from the use of scarce inputs.[90] Moreover, imperfect competition tended to provide a protective umbrella, and encouraged a measure of specialization which enhanced such economies. A comparison of costs under perfect and imperfect competition suggested that in the latter there was a tendency for output to be less.[91] The degree of difference depended, of course, on the shape of the supply and demand curves. A concave demand curve would tend to reduce monopoly output, while a concave supply curve would tend to increase it. And, as output was restricted, there was a decided tendency for price to rise.[92] If entries by potential rivals into the industry were easy, some pressures could be exerted against price increases. But in a real sense, this depended not only on capital requirements, but on the degree of differentiation, something that Mrs. Robinson did not explore to any great degree.[93]

In the case of buyers—the situation of monopsony—there was a patent ambiguity in the statement that the value of input factors tended to equate to their marginal net product; for this could refer either to the value of the marginal physical product or to the marginal total value attributable to the employment of an additional input. This problem, both Mrs. Robinson and Chamberlin recognized, but with quite different conclusions. Under perfect competition, these two marginal concepts were equal; but when noncompetitive conditions prevailed, the latter was less than the value of the marginal physical product and the return to the factor was based on that. To Mrs. Robinson, this suggested exploitation. With rising supply price, a firm could construct a marginal expenditure curve for the input factor: the quantity purchased then would be set by the intersection of the marginal expenditure and marginal total value curves. But at that point the marginal physical product was greater than marginal total value. The factor received its marginal total value, with the difference between that and marginal physical product going to the monopsonist.[94] Now, said Mrs. Robinson, where labor was the input factor it was quite evident that minimum wage legislation and trade unions did impose an equality of the two marginal measures, thereby simulating the conditions of perfect competition and fostering a better utilization of economic resources.[95] According to her, exploitation stemmed from an absence of perfect elasticity in the supply of labor, which, in effect, unions could enforce.[96] The rationalizing monopsonist, Mrs. Robinson concluded, was perhaps ". . . the best pilot to find a channel between the Scylla of competitive inefficiency and the Charybdis of monopolistic exploitation. . . ." [97] With costs falling over a given range, "monopolies" did seem to perform a useful function. But what were the causes of monopoly? In a 1953 essay, Mrs. Robinson clarified this point by emphasizing that competition itself and unfavorable shifts in demand caused firms to reinforce prices through extra-market behavior.[98] But, more significantly, one could ask why these reactions ensued. And here, it would seem that the pervading pressures of overhead costs had an important role to play.

Despite some lacunae, as in the case of oligopoly behavior and its essential interdependence, and despite a less than full treatment of product differentiation, Mrs. Robinson's book does remain one of the great landmarks in the history of economic analysis. The *Imperfect Competition* and Chamberlin's *Monopolistic Competition* shook economists out of their lethargy. And, in part, the new theory was well received because it was couched in the kind of language the profession best understood, the language of marginalism. In Mrs. Robinson's version, the emphasis was on monopoly, with perfect competition set as a special case, useful as a standard of comparison, as in monopsonistic exploitation.[99] It was also evident that in a world of monopolies, the distribution of income could be altered quite radically. And the larger the business unit, the more likely were input factors to be exploited.[100] The world of laissez faire could be defended, if at all, only on certain curious ethical grounds. Positive economic theory now demonstrated that laissez faire was dead, and that the only way in which its conditions could be approximated was through conscious intervention. Price-fixing, for example, was theoretically justifiable because it was the only way to establish an elastic supply curve. The free market could be sustained only by economic planning! This, of course, was thoroughly Marshallian in spirit, as well as in method, for the urge to trace the ameliorative implications of an economic theory was too deeply rooted in Britsh tradition not to have had its impact on Mrs. Robinson's analysis.[101]

Professor Chamberlin has always insisted that his was a different theory.[102] His objective was to achieve a blend of monopoly and competition in one over-all theory. While Mrs. Robinson argued that control over supply was established through the industry, Chamberlin felt certain that he had successfully achieved his blend by emphasizing product differentiation and selling costs. Thus, whereas Chamberlin stressed the product and the way in which a firm's decision-making might influence the behavior of rivals, Mrs. Robinson was primarily concerned with points of equilibrium and profit maximizing. She excluded selling costs through the simple device of deducting such items from the demand curve. Yet, as Robert Triffin has demonstrated by parallel citations, the two theories did deal with identical substantive issues.[103] While Chamberlin preferred to analyse monopoloid situations through the medium of large and small groups, Mrs. Robinson focused her attention on industry on the ground that this was the area in which the firm operated.[104] Still, Chamberlin has waged a persistent campaign to differentiate his theory from that of Mrs. Robinson's, although economists have continued to lump them together. Stating that there was no connection between his thinking and development in Britain which led to the new theory, he has testified that his own ideas went back to 1921 and had been fully worked out by 1927. Yet, observing this part of the debate, one has the feeling that Chamberlin has been overly concerned to establish a priority claim: be that as it may, the indisputable historical fact is that both theories grew up in a climate of utter dissatisfaction with the doctrine of the competitive market.

Edward H. Chamberlin (1899-   ) studied at Iowa, Michigan, and Harvard, where, since receiving his doctorate in 1927, he has been teaching. The objective in developing his version of the theory was to provide a general framework for a broad spectrum of problems.[105] He always stressed the point that competition and monopoly are not exclusive categories but ". . . contributing elements to a total situation in that they are both involved and interact upon each other." [106] The area to be explored, that between monopoly and competition, included product heterogeneity and oligopoly. This described an economy quite different from what was found in ordinary theory. Nor could the mixture of market forms be explained merely by recourse to consumer ignorance, as some economists were wont to do.[107] A theory that would perform the task set forth by Chamberlin would deal not only with mixed market situations and heterogeneous productions, but also would be able to explain the functioning of markets with few or many sellers, advertising and selling costs, product variation, differences in location, and the application of the full-cost pricing principle.

Although price determination in Chamberlin's competitive case was not unlike that in Mrs. Robinson's theory, the behavior of the individual seller was made more explicit. When the analysis shifted from the total market, in which equilibrium was described by the intersection of the supply and demand curves, to that of the single seller, that point was converted into an infinitely elastic demand to which costs were related. The firm's optimum output was attained when marginal cost equaled marginal revenue (which, under competitive conditions, was the same as average revenue). In the broader context of monopolistic competition, equilibrium was affected not only by optimum output, but by product variation and selling costs as well.[108] The inclusion of the latter, a decided advance over Mrs. Robinson's version, was certainly a closer approximation to real market situations. Thus, elasticity of demand could be applied to the product as a variable, creating the concept of "product elasticity." [109] Intense rivalry between sellers could culminate in quality changes and improvements which in turn affected costs. It was evident that quality competition was an additional market force which conceivably might inhibit price competition. The difficulties of reducing these factors to measurable quantities did not strike Chamberlin as serious. [110] The basic problems seemed to be custom and community standards, categories that were mainly institutional in nature. Variations in product would necessarily involve changes in the relevant cost curves, since a shift in the production function was required. Analytically, the use of a single diagram appeared inordinately difficult, yet the meaning of equilibrium was not altered, for the concept still implied that profit could be increased by changing elements within the firm's control. [111]

An important ingredient of Chamberlin's discussion was his explicit consideration of oligopoly. [112] Mrs. Robinson, on the other hand, found it difficult to incorporate oligopoly into her system because of a "fuzzy handling" of the demand curve. [113] But to Chamberlin, oligopolistic behavior was of no small importance. There was a clear and discernible pattern of interaction between oligopolists. The tendency, he argued, was for price in such situations not only to be determinate, but stable, for ". . . no one will cut from the monopoly figure because he would force others to follow him, and thereby work his own undoing." [114] Stability was lessened when numbers in the industry increased. This raised the whole question of "free entry," an assumption that Chamberlin explicitly introduced into his analysis. It was used to explain market inefficiency and the proliferation of small producers, as in the case of retailing and the needle trades. Yet the existence of product differentiation did imply some barriers to entry, particularly when a less than infinitely elastic demand curve was supported by product variation and selling costs. The free entry assumption necessarily weakened as the analysis moved toward industries in which capital investment requirements were not insignificant. And the changing nature of retail operations today, with its large chain-stores, super-supermarkets, and the increasing trend toward one-stop shopping, more than ever makes the free entry premise dubious. It seemed that Chamberlin had far more faith in ease of entry than was warranted.

Yet such a belief allowed him to construct a market with a substantial number of sellers, each independent and each selling a product for which some buyers had special preferences stemming from either singular quality, trade marks, packaging, special services, reputation, location, and the like. Similar products were less perfect substitutes. [115] Thus a good was more or less "monopolized," and, to the extent that the substitution of rival items played a role, competition became part of the picture as well. Consequently, Chamberlin was able to claim that he had successfully fused competition and monopoly. Equilibrium involved that of the firm, analogous to pure monopoly, and that of the group, in which the competing "monopolists" had to adjust to each other. While the presence of substitution made the demand of one commodity sensitive to price changes in others, price reductions would not succeed in pulling away all of a rival's customers simply because of the attachment created by differentiation. The demand curve, as in Mrs. Robinson's analysis, would decline as output increased. Product variation and selling effort also would influence sales volume. With output set at the point of intersection of marginal cost and marginal revenue, profit was defined as the difference between average revenue and average total cost multiplied by the number of units sold. If profits were to be defined as some necessary minimum required to induce entrepreneurs to provide services, the average revenue curve would be tangent to the average cost curve.[116] The free entry assumption strengthened this "tangency solution," for excessive profits would call up new rivals. Equilibrium via tangency also permitted introduction of the full-cost pricing principle.[117] In any case, the effect of monopolistic competition was to make price higher and output less than under mere competition.

The concept of industry equilibrium, however, created some theoretical difficulties. Chamberlin did recognize that different production functions, demand curves, and elasticities among the firms could mean considerable variation, yet he introduced an "heroic assumption" which posited a uniformity of demand and cost curves. Preferences supposedly were distributed evenly within the complex of differentiated commodities, and sharp discrepancies in costs were assumed as nonexistent. Certainly this was questionable, for it was to be doubted that adjustments would distribute themselves evenly over all the rivals in a market.[118] It was much more likely that individual elasticities and demands would be influenced in different ways: Chamberlin later conceded the point when he quoted Jan Tinbergen to the effect that more "parameters of conduct" were needed to analyse the industry.[119] The mere assertion that uniformity in no way implied pure competition was not a satisfactory response to objections that were raised.[120] And Chamberlin's "large group" threatened to dissolve into an ordinary Marshallian industry. However, a way out did suggest itself, namely, the existence of sub-classes within the large group, to which firms, with their indivisible factors and economies of scale, could relate themselves despite the presence of a certain amount of overlapping. At any rate, the uniformity assumption together with free entry clearly did weaken the analysis.

A decided tendency for excess capacity to occur in an industry when the régime of privately controlled prices developed led to what Chamberlin called the wastes of monopoly.[121] Price maintenance, however, did not necessarily mean collusion, said he, for such uniform practices came about simply as a corollary of profit maximization under noncompetitive conditions. His suggestion that excess capacity might be overcome by producing multiple products was not very persuasive, for joint production is attempted only if technically and economically feasible. And easy entry, as in the needle trades, often does create excess capacity. Nor do enterprises tend to distribute themselves over market space, as Chamberlin suggested: successful supermarkets frequently will attract rivals to the same block or area.[122] Moreover, excess capacity hardly can be attributed to consumer desire for variety. Actually, consumers can say little on such matters, for they simply react to the particular undertaking *ex post facto*. Consumer responsibility merely introduced the competitive market through the rear door.[123]

The question of consumer reaction could be related more effectively to the phenomenon of selling costs, since the purpose of the latter was to create a psychological attachment to a specific product. Here Chamberlin made a most important contribution to modern theory by translating selling outlays into cost curves, which then were superimposed onto production costs. References to the role of selling costs could be found in the writings of other economists— notably Thorstein Veblen—but in Chamberlin's work they were given greater analytic precision. Ordinary theory was unable to utilize the selling cost concept, for it was assumed that the entire output of a firm could be sold at infinite market demands. On the other hand, the purpose of selling cost was to alter the position or shape of the demand curve. Chamberlin's analysis, however, related only to costs: the impact of these expenditures on the demand curve had to be sketched in institutional terms. It was presumed that the elimination of rivals as a result of advertising and the like would increase the sales volume of the remaining producers. But how such outlays would affect the shape or slope of the sales curve had to be handled in descriptive rather than analytic terms.[124] By increasing demand, advertising could move the sales curve toward the right, but whether such shifts were proportional to, or more than, or less than in proportion to the increase in selling costs seemed difficult to ascertain. All that could be said was that a general benefit did stem from advertising,[125] since the so-called "institutional" variety conceivably increased elasticity. On the other hand, an emphasis on brand names tended to create inelasticity of demand.[126] That is to say, selling costs were incurred in order to adjust demand to the product.

Chamberlin introduced the ideas of diminishing and increasing returns into the study of selling cost outlays, with major emphasis on how output shifted in response to combined sales and production expenditures. Different results were obtained when selling costs were of the lump-sum variety as contrasted with uniform unit selling costs. The objective was the same in both cases—the attainment of the largest net return. A uniform or fixed selling cost per unit did alter the shape of the total cost curve, although the minimum point was moved to the right, thus indicating that output could expand when a sales effort was added to production.[127] It was also evident that with a sharper differentiation of products occasioned by selling efforts, including advertising, dealer discounts, and demonstration as well as salesmen's salaries, competition and rivalry meant higher, not lower, prices. Thus, a considerable portion of the economy's resources were applied to cajoling consumers into buying something that was ostensibly unique, and, for this dubious privilege, larger inroads were made into their budgets.

Monopolistic competition theory was replete with distasteful implications. Chamberlin solved the problem of structural rigidity, for example, by assuming ease of entry; higher prices and less production called for no corrective steps (in contrast to Mrs. Robinson's analysis); advertising was, on balance, beneficial; and in no way did a condition of monopsony mean exploitation of input factors. In the latter case, Chamberlin noted the divergence between the value of the marginal product and the marginal revenue product, showing quite clearly that any degree of monopsony would reduce factor payments below the value of their marginal product. Obviously, the monopsonist was interested only in the marginal revenue product.[128] But where Mrs. Robinson looked upon such situations as matters of exploitation, Chamberlin did not; for in equilibrium, only the minimum profit required to call forth entrepreneurial services was involved. The factor produced more than it received, yet the product was exhausted according to the law of marginal productivity. Further, Chamberlin argued that where monopoly advantages were found, price adjustments should be made in favor of the consumer, not the input factor, particularly if the latter were labor.[129] Something evidently was awry at this point. In fact, in later years Chamberlin fostered a myth of powerful labor in which the horrendous domination of industry by unions became a frightful prospect. Labor, said he, was high up in the income scale, an assertion in no way supported by evidence. Indeed, it is curious that while the monopolistic implications of his general theory were evaded, empty *obiter dicta* on labor were offered without the slightest hesitation. Although monopoly in product markets was merely part of the rules of the capitalist game, in factor markets, such as labor supply, it was downright heinous. Such a double standard could have little useful to say about so difficult and specialized an area as labor relations and trade unionism.

Overton Taylor tells us that Chamberlin visualized his analysis as simply a more detailed and more realistic presentation of market behavior.[130] No reform, no process of amelioration was necessary. But as Mrs. Robinson once remarked, "every economic doctrine that is not trivial contains political judgments," [131] and monopolistic and imperfect competition certainly was not trivial. But so determined was Chamberlin to make the whole theory scientific that even the most obvious policy conclusions were dispensed with. And whereas Mrs. Robinson did make a distinct effort to delineate the results stemming from a world of monopolies, Chamberlin persistently has evaded critical social issues in his pure theory.[132] By no means could he be accused of having committed the Ricardian sin.

Before reviewing some recent reactions to theories of noncompetitive markets, let us examine briefly the work of Heinrich von Stackelberg (1905-1946), a German economist whose contribution to this area generally is deemed to be important. Stackelberg was born in Russia of a German father and Argentine mother, but the family had moved to Cologne shortly after the October Revolution. Stackelberg's doctoral thesis covered the pure theory of costs, and, in 1934, he published his major opus, *Marktform und Gleichgewicht,* a study of oligopoly and duopoly.[133] After teaching at the University of Berlin, he accepted a post as guest professor at Madrid in 1943, where he wrote his *Grundlagen der Theoretischen Volkswirtschaftslehre,* translated in 1952 as *The Theory of the Market Economy.*[134] While Stackelberg's main interest was focused on market forms, he wrote also on such topics as international trade theory.[135] His thinking was shaped by Walras, Pareto, and the neo-Austrians despite the fact that such influences were still suspect in Germany during the 1920's. Undaunted, Stackelberg argued forcefully in favor of mathematical methods, asserting that they made economic ideas more precise and imposed self-discipline on theorists.[136]

His technical apparatus was quite the same as that described above: in pure competition, equilibrium was established by the intersection of the supply and demand curves, with lags explained by cobweb movements around the point of equilibrium. In monopoly, the assumption of price independence was dropped, since "action parameters" had to be employed to work out the point of maximum net revenue. And the divergence of marginal revenue from average revenue could be measured by dividing price by the elasticity of demand, a relationship that described monopoly price.[137] These conditions clearly indicated higher prices and smaller output under monopoly than would be the case in a competitive market. In monopsony, the factors were not paid the full value of their marginal product, and in an economy of large market units, considerable conflict could ensue. From this observation, Stackelberg drew the inference that monopoly markets could not achieve social balance and order. And, so far as he could see, state intervention was necessary, a rather comfortable doctrine for the Nazi regime with which Stackelberg identified himself.[138]

Oligopoly was viewed as an unstable market form in which certain reaction functions expressed profit maximizing behavior in terms of variables ascribed to market rivals. Stackelberg's analytical technique utilized indifference curves which related the variables of a firm and its rival, thus leading to profit curves rather than to those describing revenues and costs. Various reaction patterns were developed, enough to suggest considerable disequilibrium. For example, in the case of two or a few large firms there would be perpetual striving for leadership positions in the market. In fact, some firms might prefer to be followers, as in the case where a seller might adjust his price and profit maximizing policy to the behavior of his rival. Or, a firm, conjecturing that this was precisely the way his rival would react, consequently might go about his business behaving as though he were the leader. Or, as both might have guessed wrong, the market might wind up in a "follower" equilibrium. And if both wanted to be leaders, disequilibrium and struggle would ensue which could last for a long time.[139] The struggle for leadership therefore might result in any one of the large numbers of possible outcomes.

Stackelberg's purpose was to reveal the nature of market forms in the absence of collusion. But the exclusion of overt agreement between sellers was rather mechanical and overlooked some important possibilities.[140] Nor did the element of leadership, central to Stackelberg's analysis, necessarily eliminate collusion. Indeed, all sorts of quasi-agreements could persist that would facilitate joint profit maximizing behavior. And such a development could bring about market stability even though the leadership phenomenon was absent. The virtue of Stackelberg's formulation, however, rested in its emphasis on strategical behavior, suggesting some of the features of game theory. These considerations, noted by Bowley,[141] were later explored more fully by Ragnar Frisch,[142] who remarked: "Any study of polypolistic situations must first take account of the considerable diversity in the modes of strategy which can be exploited." Frisch's market classes, which were set forth in terms of parametric action, adaptation, and negotiation, could be assimilated easily enough to Stackelberg's leader-follower framework. Consequently, Triffin's strictures are not well taken, since bluff and strategical pressures may very well be precisely the policy pursued by a firm.[143]

Similar concepts were applied by Stackelberg to the realm of imperfect competition,[144] with advertising, sales organization, and the like adding new action parameters. To Stackelberg, the imperfect market merely comprised a number of individual markets which resembled oligopoly. It was in disequilibrium because the individual partial markets of which it was comprised were themselves unstable.[145] Stackelberg thus placed greater stress on the interdependence of firms than did Mrs. Robinson or Chamberlin. But, as oligopoly characteristics remained central to his system, the analysis moved from duopoly to oligopoly to imperfect competition with interdependence making the final results rather indeterminate. Equilibrium in the Robinson-Chamberlin sense was rejected.

Although these models of noncompetitive markets did bring economic theory somewhat closer to real situations, they still were static. Containing no genuine dynamic analysis, they all too often overlooked movements on the supply side. Changes in asset holdings, such as inventories, were excluded as indeed were such factors as collusion between ostensible rivals. The institutions described were changeless and the participants presumed to be completely rational. Certainly the market conditions that were described were more varied, with product differentiation, changes in elasticity, and nonprice competition providing a more viable and more promising theoretical framework. Yet, lacunae were revealed when it was discovered that institutional descriptions were necessary to complete the analysis, as in the case of demand reaction to selling costs. Not unexpectedly, some efforts have been made to overcome the gaps. But, at least in the theories' own terms, they have not been convincing.[146] Further, it was not always clear whether the demand curve represented expectations or actual market situations: this distinction was not unimportant, for different effects could flow from *ex ante* and *ex post* patterns.[147] To suggest, as was sometimes done, that the market itself would eliminate any discrepancies between anticipations and actual outcomes was more than the theory could bear. Chamberlin's symmetry conditions for the group had brought him much too close to Marshall's industry: in fact, only the concepts of chain relationships and degrees of substitution enabled him to escape the charge of having produced little that was new. Robert Triffin's way out of the dilemma was to try to deal solely with firms and commodities, dispensing entirely with the analysis of groups. Yet even he found it necessary to classify certain market situations.[148] Triffin's major contribution to the discussion was his attempt to provide a general equilibrium framework through the use of cross-elasticities which presumably measured the change in a firm's sales caused by movements in its rival's price. But this was a rather difficult concept to pin down, since, in a general equilibrium system, the value of the measure of cross-elasticities would be affected not only by the rival, but by other firms as well. Even if the cross-elasticities of all the firms were obtained, Triffin's model appeared as little more than a formal description of market structure; it did not contain sufficient information to allow for a reasonably good description of market *behavior*. Triffin's main point, however, that market forms are more varied than was suggested by the theory, was well taken. It now became possible to speak of moderately concentrated oligopolies, with or without easy entry, with or without product differentiation, or highly concentrated oligopolies with similar cross-classifications.[149] The types of markets that could be explored empirically became much more complex than the theory initially had supposed.

One might have thought that for all its alleged deficiencies so striking a set of tools would have been welcomed by all economic theorists. But such was not the case. Neotraditionalists, centered mainly at the University of Chicago and appropriately named by Chamberlin, "The Chicago School," became the source of a sharp counterattack against noncompetitive theories.[150] Starting with Frank Knight's contention that the only economic theory worthy of the name was that which dealt solely with the competitive economy, the latter-day traditionalists rejected any analysis whose message was the inadequacy of laissez faire models. Monopolistic competition theory, they said, was unsystematic, and, if market imperfections did exist, they could be attributed to consumer ignorance. They were quick to take up the apparent contradiction between product differentiation and the uniformity assumption.[151] Chamberlin replied that the symmetry argument was merely a preliminary analytical device, which in no way could be considered fatal, and, that even if the uniformity assumption was replaced by a representative firm, monopolistic elements still would be revealed.[152] But what has been interesting in the Chicago School's attack was a determined effort to preserve its own special variety of competitive theory: no real attempt was made to test noncompetitive theory on the empirical front. Perhaps the pudding would have tasted better in the eating.

Still the fact does remain that noncompetitive market theory has been one of the few genuine advances in the present century. Those who prefer to solve theoretical problems might have been expected to work on refinements of concepts, rather than to seek a return to the simplicity of free competition. For, when all is said and done, this is a world of monopolies, and the economist searching for a meaningful conceptual framework could do no worse than to plough these fields. No longer is the idea of a providential order in society useful. And the relationship of a monopolistic economic structure to accumulation and economic growth are problems that do demand further exploration. Yet these urgent matters have not received nearly as much attention as the distillation of elegant mathematical refinements of pricing and factor returns. This frame of mind seems to have affected the noncompetitive theorists as well. Chamberlin really has not gone beyond his original theory, and the literature is filled with minute investigations of points of equilibrium. Yet, product differentiation and quality control are not historically new phenomena: such practices could be found in medieval guilds.[153] The need today would seem to be for more empirical work so that the kind of "conduct parameters" necessary for a macroeconomics of monopoly might be made available. It also might be asked how these models can be applied to the area of public services. It may very well be necessary to go beyond mathematics to grasp the nature of this problem.[154]

But while there has been a reluctance to introduce extra-market factors into theoretical models, their influence has been inescapable. And it is not impossible to do this, as Mrs. Robinson's discussion of exploitation has proved. If different theoretical tools are necessary to accomplish this aim, they must be developed: otherwise we shall not be able to account for coercion, violence, strategy, and irrationality.[155] The political climate, the basic drives and aims of a society are too complex to be entirely compressed into mathematical equations and marginal curves: the ultimate understanding of a changing economy may very well require the modern theorist to resort to detailed institutionalist analysis, much as he may not want to do so.

iv

The New Economics of
John Maynard Keynes

There have been few occasions when so abstruse a discipline as theoretical economics has entered into general currency.[156] Adam Smith's unseen hand and Marx's surplus value were the two main examples up to the present in which recondite notions were absorbed into popular ideology. In this way an economic theory frequently has been employed as an elaborate rationalization of what was thought to be desirable social action. This particularly has been the case in times of crisis, when the demand for getting something done is persistent. And the theorist who has been able to supply the answers often has been accorded the role of hero.

Such was the pleasant fate of John Maynard Keynes (1883-1946), whose impact on popular thinking has been the greatest since Smith, Ricardo, and Marx. New Dealers grasped at his theories to justify what it was they were doing. Keynes himself had a rather happy facility for recognizing history as it moved, and he was not averse to suggesting that its motion was essentially Keynesian. In 1935 he wrote to George Bernard Shaw: "I believe myself to be writing a book on economic theory which will largely revolutionise . . . the way the world thinks about economic problems." And, of course, he was right.

His major work, *The General Theory of Employment, Interest and Money,* whose influence has been matched only by *Das Kapital* and the *Wealth of Nations,* showed that governmental action was just what was necessary to meet the psychological and economic needs of the day.[157] It was his ability to frame a set of popular ideas within a resplendent border of principles that made Keynes so well received an economist.

Born of a Cambridge family (his father, J. N. Keynes, who outlived him, was a noted logician and economist in his own right), Keynes' background was traditionally unexciting. The intellectual climate of his day was characterized by a calm Victorian utilitarianism in which reform was conceived to be the instrumentality of progress and intelligent discussion the primary basis for attaining the ultimate goal of social prefectability. Keynes never surrendered his belief in the idea of progress; when world war and a depression undermined his original preconceptions, he sought new ones in order to sustain his faith that society always can be improved.

A short stay in the British India Office in 1906 drove Keynes to take a post at Cambridge, where Alfred Marshall's *Principles* ruled the realm of economics. Here he began as an avowed Marshallian for whom basic principles were well established; only the discovery of practical rules of application remained. This gave to economic study a condition of serenity that it was never to recapture. At this time, Keynes ignored much contemporary theorizing, which was perhaps an advantage, since he later was able to devise a system of his own without too much concern for its relationship to other doctrines.[158] At Cambridge, Keynes was held in high esteem for both his scholarship and business achievements.[159] Put in charge of the finances of Kings College, he increased its income substantially by careful investments. Nor did he ignore his own fortunes: speculating shrewdly in foreign currencies, his profits were sufficient to provide a fair sized personal estate. Then, when World War I shattered the placidity of capitalist society, Keynes went to work for the Treasury. At Versailles, he acted as advisor to the British delegation, but disgusted by the machinations of the world's politicians, he left Paris before the Treaty was signed, exclaiming that the Peace was outrageous. His anguish was poured into *The Economic Consequences of the Peace,* a devastating polemic and bitter portrayal of "insensate folly leading to tragedy." [160]

There was enough in Keynes' career to fill a half-dozen lives. A close friend of the famed "Bloomsbury Circle," which included such literary figures as Virginia and Leonard Woolf and Lytton Strachey, he was at the same time a successful banker, mathematician, college bursar, don, writer of fascinating polemical pamphlets and profound essays on probability, and patron of the arts. He possessed a razor-edged mind which explored paradox for its own value. While he abhorred the nationalist spirit, he literally gave his life in the service of his country. Suffering from a coronary ailment, he drove himself at a furious pace through Bretton Woods and all the postwar monetary negotiations. The heavy burden took its toll in 1946.

Early in his career Keynes had accepted the proposition that the interests of the various groups in society were harmoniously balanced. Whatever suggestions there were in Ricardo of dire social conflict had been dismissed by the classicists to a fiery subterranean existence in the pages of Marx's *Das Kapital.* The English utilitarians, who had accepted some forms of government intervention, found the theory of harmony not incompatible with their scruples, for it was possible to justify at least a minimum of government action as a means of preserving the balanced state. On these grounds, Keynesian theory, even as later developed, could be made to support utilitarianism: if unequal distribution of income, for example, was the cause of economic imbalance, measures to attain a better distribution could increase social happiness (or, as the economist would prefer, economic welfare). Years later Keynes came to feel that "effective demand" was the prime mover in the attainment of this balance: if government actions were needed to make the economy operate properly, he was willing to go along. Above all else, he wanted to make capitalism work. Here he was no different from Marshall or Mill or Say.

Keynes, however, countered traditional long-run equilibrium theory with an incisive short-run analysis that led him directly to the theory of employment. Despite its seemingly static framework, Keynesian theory lent itself quite easily to a study of economic motion. Once such elements as time periods, lags, and anticipations were introduced, it was not difficult to pass on to dynamic analysis.[161] With such an approach, growth and accumulation became questions of major importance. Classical theory had placed income distribution at the center of economic theory, and, as a result, said Keynes, it had become overly concerned with the way the national income was divided and was inattentive to the problems of size. It assumed that the level of activity which set the amount of the national income was already fixed, and, moreover, fixed at full employment levels. This Keynes argued, was a gratuitous assumption. He attacked the cardinal capitalist appeal to unremitting thrift by demonstrating that to husband resources during a depression was harmful. His argument that cutting money wages was no cure for economic imbalance upset traditional habits of thought, although he did say that a reduction in real wages might turn the trick. But above all he was concerned with the flow of income, and here he began to see more clearly than most that money was no mere veil for transactions but the source of the energy that made the capitalist economy tick. With this new vision, Keynes believed that he was leaving the classical system behind.

But in the early work, *Indian Currency and Finance,*[162] Keynes still was a classically oriented economist, despite a plea for a managed currency. What he urged in this book was a gold exchange standard with a central bank that would conserve gold reserves and avoid the unusual drains on Indian gold. Yet, as his biographer Roy Harrod has said, he appeared even this early as a man of expediency.[163] That is, he was always advocating some practical course of action. As he continued to observe the economic scene, he felt more and more that satisfactory price levels and full employment would have to be created by tinkering, by deliberate policy. All his early writings emphasized the practical. But, by the time Keynes went to work on his *Treatise on Money,*[164] some suggestion of a developing theoretical synthesis, later to flower into the structure of the *General Theory,* became visible. Yet, no sooner had the *Treatise* been published than Keynes expressed dissatisfaction with its line of argument and began to pursue a markedly different analytical approach.

In the years after the first World War, Keynes concerned himself mainly with the problem of price "stability." This was to be his major objective, and it did not trouble him in the least that it might mean the destruction of the gold standard. Would this not result in continuously rising prices or, even worse, wildcat inflation, asked his opponents? Unperturbed, Keynes answered that rising prices were fine, for that would stimulate investment and business activity. Furthermore, such a condition would weaken the *rentiers* who were an inactive class anyway, their desire for high interest rates being a serious impediment to Keynesian aims. Thus, monetary manipulation seemed to him the most effective way of solving economic ills. Setting forth these views in a *A Tract for Monetary Reform*,[165] Keynes suggested that a managed paper currency be substituted for the gold standard. Stable prices could be assured only through the mechanism of Central Bank discount rates and a conscious control of the stock of money. The key device was to be an official index based upon a standard composite commodity whose price would be maintained within certain limits. Further, the price of gold was to be regulated in order to keep exchange rates stable as well. The reaction to this was somewhat fearful and hesitant. Keynes then returned to the fray with his *The End of Laissez-Faire*,[166] in which he announced the passing of pure individualism. The inequality of wealth, unemployment, and general uncertainty to which individualism gave rise could be cured only by deliberate control of currency and credit. In this way society could express its collective intelligence in order to counteract the effects of individual caprice on general economic movements. It was this attitude that led some persons to call him a congenital inflationist.

Yet, the Keynesian conception of inflation did not mean simply an increase in the amount of money in circulation.[167] During the 1930's, for example, monetary supply had increased, yet no one would suggest that inflation had existed at that time. Nor could such a situation be described merely as an increase in income and spending. Increased demand for money in relation to available goods does force prices upward. If this situation is anticipated, however, it is possible to make adjustments that will circumvent "inflationary" effects. It is rather the unexpected, unanticipated events that are important. When unforeseen increases in the price level permit demand to exceed supply, true inflation develops with troublesome social impact; there is a loss of real income, maladjustments ensue between creditor and debtor, and distortions in the use of resources upset accustomed economic equilibrium.

This definition of inflation, however, does reveal a basic bias in the Keynesian approach. Neo-Keynesians conceded that what they wanted was to achieve "stability" through a steadily rising price system.[168] Suggesting that inflation in the ordinary sense was no longer the heinous affair that the conservative mood made it out to be, they insisted that a secular rise in prices could be a pleasant and respectable experience. This implied that if the main purpose of economic policy was to attain full employment through "balanced" government spending, the accompanying cost of a price rise would not be too disturbing. All this was to be accomplished by economic gadgetry; a low tax structure, low interest rates, and government deficits. Should the situation get out of hand, a mere reversal of policy could impose down-draft dampers.

Yet when prices begin to surge upward, certain goods become more desirable. And, as people want to hedge against unknown contingencies, they begin to purchase durable commodities, real estate, and even old postage stamps. Soon, holders of such assets acquire a vested interest in inflation. A speculative psychology comes to the forefront, and people become more concerned with rising values per se than with more basic productive processes. A feeling that it is better to make money through price changes begins to motivate social behavior, as evidenced by the relatively more rapid movement of stock prices than is the case with other indices. Inflation becomes respectable, for it maintains purchasing power. It reduces strain between groups and softens social conflict. Ultimately, it becomes the economic ideology of mass society.

This may seem to contradict the general understanding of Keynesian analysis, which, in the Thirties, had set forth a theory of capitalist stagnation. According to this thesis, capitalism would continue to suffer a depressed economy because of the decline of the rate of population growth, the passing of the frontier, the exhaustion of natural resources, and the drop in the rate of profit. Now, all this does appear old-fashioned, for, it is argued, all the indices of industrial production and economic activity have made these propositions invalid. Yet, what actually has happened is that a vast government intervention has altered the situation without in the least undermining the older notions. Stagnation has been replaced by a permanent war economy. The anticipated beneficent price rise has been attained largely through the needs of a growing military élite. In reality, say the Keynesians in implicit fashion, there is no conflict between capitalist stagnation and the theory of gently rising prices. One is merely the cure of the other; it is as patently improper to accuse them of inconsistency as it is improper to charge a man with inconsistency when he wears an overcoat in winter and Bermuda shorts in summer.

To place Keynesian economics in the main stream of economic thought requires a review of the so-called "real" versus monetary analysis. In the former, economic propositions are derived solely from decisions based on the relations between men and goods. Money, it is argued, enters into a system of economic equations only as an accounting device or as a means of facilitating transactions. Normally, the monetary factor has no effect on economic situations since the modern economy is nothing more than a extension of a barter system. Thus, money becomes an opaque veil which must be withdrawn if we are to learn the actual ratios of exchange that lie behind money prices. Income is defined as the flow of goods and services in exchange for labor, while saving is the actual accumulation of productive factors and their conversion into physical equipment. Real analysis emphasizes the nonmonetary aspects of economic behavior.

This approach accounted for Say's famous Law of Markets, in which every supply was supposed to create its own demand, making general overproduction a logical impossibility.[169] Say admitted that specific commodities might be overproduced, but a general glut in the sense of a general depression was unthinkable, for the very process of production created the required effective demand necessary to absorb total output. There was an implied faith that the total amount of the national income always would be predetermined at full employment levels. This revealed a lack of understanding of demand as a flow of income which might have breaks and leakages, so that some part of output would conceivably fail to be taken up. Say's Law implied, simply enough, a kind of flexibility that was not apparent in real life. There was no assurance that a fall in prices would enhance real balances sufficiently to provide a thrust toward the reestablishment of equilibrium. It was particularly Pigou's version of Say's Law that Keynes subjected to harsh attack. Institutional rigidities, he argued, would have to be introduced into any realistic theory of money movements. In fact, said he, money income was related to demand and workers markedly resisted downward pressures on wage rates.[170] An understanding of these conditions required an analysis that explicitly would make money a significant factor in the economic system.

Monetary analysis, on the other hand, denies that money is an illusion. It insists rather that it is the central feature of economic behavior. A laborer works for money wages; a capitalist seeks money profits; and our society has developed money institutions in which the art of making more money has become basic. In fact, the economic system has developed a set of counting-house attitudes which are extremely important elements in the drives that dominate contemporary behavior. Money is not only the measure of economic activity but also the very force that gives rise to the phenomenon that it purports to measure. And, as both Wesley Mitchell and Joseph Schumpeter acknowledged, it is a rationalizing device which establishes behavior patterns in a specific and historically conditioned manner.

Such an analysis emphasizes that money is the compass by which individuals must steer. As mathematical economists are wont to say, it is a parameter that provides the matrix in which specific economic forms take shape. Simply enough, this means that economic life under capitalism is a matter of making and spending money and that it is possible to derive from this proposition all that need be said about ways and means for increasing the national welfare. But since money is the only credential required to obtain consumer goods, there is no guarantee that people will be rewarded according to the time-honored theory of marginal productivity. The use of money becomes complex and irrational: it even may be used as an instrument of coercion. Above all, it is never the neutral phenomenon that so-called real analysis says it is. The relationships between men and goods that are expressed in monetary form acquire a life and importance of their own which cannot be obscured by considering it a mere veil, as did the classical economists.[171]

One of the important results of the monetary approach was the growth of the so-called macroeconomic technique. The realization that money is significant enabled economists to reduce a complex image of the economic system to a few social aggregates—income, saving, investment, and consumption. These, in turn, became homogeneous concepts, easy to handle in an analytical scheme, as was evident in the doctrinal system constructed by Keynes. Here, he tried to relate the behavior of individuals and firms to such aggregates through a number of recondite concepts: these were the now famous "marginal propensity to consume," "liquidity preference," and "the marginal efficiency of capital."

Keynes then went on to analyze the motives for holding money. These were basic to the idea of liquidity preference, an important component in his system. Money, he said, was held to facilitate transactions, to engage in speculation, or for precautionary reasons. The first arises from the fact that income receipts are discontinuous while expenditures are continuous, thus creating a need for holding some cash in order to meet obligations. The transactions motive itself was divided into demand created by consumers, which, in turn, depended on the average interval between pay periods and the size of the national income, and on business requirements for the payment of wages and purchase of raw materials. The precautionary motive was merely a matter of saving for the proverbial rainy day. The speculative motive, described by Keynes at great length, was considered by him to be very important in an advanced capitalist economy. And, since Keynes was so preoccupied with speculation, his emphasis was understandable.

With money so institutionalized, manipulation to compensate for disturbances became quite possible, said Keynes. Drawing the implication that accumulation and thrift could lead to impoverishment—an implication which his critics termed outrageous—he further suggested that "socialized" investment might be the vehicle for attaining a high level of employment. This, too, might be done through monetary stimulation. However, it does seem especially germane to inquire whether the permanent war economy which has been so important in recent years is not an embodiment in a refined form of "socialized investment." For by what means other than a massive defense program does the state so thoroughly organize investment? The corollary drawn by some writers does not seem unreasonable: Keynesian theory can work as well in a totalitarian society as in a democratic one, for this system of economics is by itself entirely neutral. While it did combine policy with economics, Keynesianism failed to create a true political economy. And, by employing aggregate thinking almost exclusively, it ran the risk of creating a merely mechanical theory which would suggest that some kind of socialized gadgetry would be sufficient to attain economic change, whether in depression or prosperity. Unfortunately, society does not function that way. For political economy in the proper sense must account for irrationality and errors in human judgment and movements in underlying components.

Basic to the Keynesian system was the concern with effective demand. Keynes was interested in the problem of how much people intended to spend, since it was this that determined the level of consumption and investment. Intentions to spend were translated into aggregate demand, a psychological rather than a technological factor. Should aggregate demand, said Keynes, fall below what businessmen expect and thereby fail to cover costs of production, there will be cutbacks, resulting in unemployment. On the other hand, should aggregate demand exceed expectations, production will be stimulated. That level of aggregate demand which led to an equilibrium was the effective balance. This had two facets: it represented actual consumer expenditure and it also was income to the factors of production. In other words, it was the national income when seen from Keynes' view which was the determining factor in the creation of employment.

Keynes then went on to analyze that aspect of effective demand which he described as the propensity to consume.[172] He started with a simple proposition: consumption bore a certain relationship to income, changing in clearly defined ways as income itself changed. What this relationship would be depended not only on the amount of money earned but also on price levels, consumer tastes, tax policies, corporate depreciation plans, and the like. These objective factors were suffused by numerous subjective ones. True, the description of psychological motives here did bring to economic thinking a freshness that was long overdue. But Keynes, unfortunately, concerned himself only with short-run situations. He analyzed only those ". . . psychological characteristics of human nature and those social practices and institutions which, though not unalterable, are unlikely to undergo a material change over a short period of time. . . ." [173] Long-run alterations he left to others.

The relation of consumption to income was described as follows: consumption increases as income increases, but not as rapidly. This implied, among other things, that while spending habits are fairly stable, saving is done by upper income groups, a not unreasonable surmise. From this was derived the schedule of the propensity to consume, a purely mental construct which tabulated the quantities that persons would buy at certain prices. Such a schedule, of course, would have to exhibit multidimensional features, for consumption habits are determined not by income alone. To Keynes, however, consumer behavior was stable in the short run, and shifts in spending patterns stemmed from changes in the national income. Thus, consumers were mere passive reactors to external economic influences. And the mere matter of choice which was involved in such a schedule suggested the problem of comparability, something that most psychologists doubt is possible. Furthermore, some economists have questioned the statement that the proportion of consumption declines as income increases, contending that a constant share of income is consumed at all levels; or, conversely, the argument has been made that consumption is resistant to declines in income. Others have said that saving habits are independent of income. All this has represented some fairly rough shoals for Keynesian theory to traverse, yet it has come through without too much damage.[174] Interestingly enough, a fantastic amount of empirical research was stimulated in an effort to discover in just what ways consumption did depend on income.[175] Factors of time and place were introduced in order to ascertain which income patterns were meaningful. Yet most of these studies continued to show the age-old lop-sided distribution.[176]

The connection of income to employment was inescapable. Classical theory had described wages as the price paid for labor, and, like all prices, it was subject to ordinary market influences. When such a price failed to move with the freedom assured it by Smith's unseen hand, failure was due, it was thought, to frictions, immobility, or even trade unions. Rapid adjustment to market change was the desired goal, since this was the way in which unemployment could be eliminated. That this suggested wage cutting and less income did not occur to the theorists. Keynes rejected the whole approach out of hand. It was, he intimated, more a mode of ancestral worship than economic analysis.

To understand the situation, he argued, we must begin with an over-all view of the entire economy. Total employment is created by expected total proceeds from forthcoming production. This was aggregate demand. The cost of producing total output was called aggregate supply. Now, it should be clear that if production is to occur, total expected proceeds must cover costs. Since employment is derived from output, each supply price will give rise to a particular level of employment. This suggested that economic equilibrium was entirely possible even under conditions of mass unemployment. When employment does increase, costs conceivably can match receipts at levels below full employment. This occurs whenever anticipated receipts are insufficient to call forth a large enough output. Keynes then focused his sights on the demand side of this relationship, feeling that it required greater attention. Supply was basically a technical matter dependent on available resources, machines, and manpower skills. Only in inflationary conditions, as in wartime, did interest center on the supply side, for then balance could be maintained only by breaking through bottlenecks.

To this apparatus, Keynes added the notion of the multiplier, an idea borrowed from R. F. Kahn, who had traced the effect of an increase in investment on employment.[177] Keynes converted this into an income multiplier designed to show the relationship of a small increase of investment to increases in income. The total increase in income resulting from an initial expenditure would be far greater, he said, than ordinarily would be supposed, since a snow-balling effect would ensue.[178] The multiplier mechanism suggested that heavy spending—by government, business, or consumers—would have a salutary impact on the national income.

However, it did have an outer limit set by several leakages in the system, such as debt cancellation, hoarding, taxes, and imports (since the latter do not provide domestic employment). Also, there was a relationship between the multiplier and consumption, or more precisely, the "marginal propensity to consume" (defined as that part of added income which is consumed rather than saved) which assumed a certain stability in consumer behavior, a notion denied by some economists. They have argued that while resistance to cutting consumption is often evinced in an economic downturn, the upswing phase of the business cycle generally has shown an evenly proportionate variation between income and consumption. The conclusion then is that the economy does not necessarily stumble over its own feet: causes external to the system must be sought for explanations of cyclical change. However, the implication that overall spending patterns are the same for all income groups must be rejected. A more cogent criticism was that Keynes' consumption-income relation failed to account for corporate income, the earning and spending of which bear no visible relationship to the psychological habits of consumers. Furthermore, it was possible that the character of the multiplier was itself a variable, the values of which shifted with the cycle. If this were so, it no longer would be possible to consider it a causal factor.

Despite these strictures, the multiplier concept did successfully call attention to investment as the major dynamic element in the economy. Not only did it indicate the direct creation of employment, it revealed that income was generated throughout the system like a stone causing ripples in a lake. In this context, investment could mean only newly constructed physical assets, not the mere purchase of securities. But such investment is undertaken under capitalism only if it yields a profit equal to at least the next best alternative. If the capitalist must go to the money market for funds, it is clear that earnings on new capital cannot fall below the going interest rate on loans.[179] The prospective net yield resulting from this relationship was called the marginal efficiency of capital. In a more exact sense, it was the rate of discounting that made the present value of a series of future returns equal to the replacement cost of capital.[180]

The main drift of the argument here, that prospective yield became the decisive factor in influencing the rate of investment, introduced a broad range of questions raised by the theory of expectations and anticipations. Estimations of profitability, however, may be related not to the actual embodied historical cost of assets but to their replacement cost, a notion which is largely of an "iffy" character. In this way the marginal efficiency of capital brought psychology to the forefront of economic theory.[181] The strength of businessmen's convictions about the future became crucial. Keynes observed that these reactions had been quite unstable in the past, inducing rather violent fluctuations in the demand for investment goods. Business gyrations had arisen too from the fact that the largest part of investment was made by a small group which did not absorb the bulk of consumer goods. The most fruitful answer to the question of how capitalism functioned seemed to lie in this disparity.

Keynes made much of the argument that there was a tendency for profitability to decline as the market for any given capital good filled up. In this, his "declining marginal efficiency of capital," he was referring to nothing less than the familiar falling rate of profit, a proposition that economists from Adam Smith to Marx had acknowledged as important. Keynes' conception, which attributed this tendency to an excessive supply of capital, was in many respects fairly close to the Marxian idea. Increases in investment brought forth new capital goods which competed with old equipment, while expanded output forced prices down, thus reducing anticipated yields. This could continue so long as the rate of interest remained below the marginal efficiency of capital. In fact, should interest rates fall to zero, a point might be reached where capital would continue to be created until it was no longer "scarce." However, increases in population, expansion of territory, and technological improvements could prevent such a gloomy outcome.

During the first five decades of the twentieth century, geographic expansion and population growth slowed down, while technology emphasized capital-saving devices. The result was a number of short, sudden spurts of capital formation which failed to take into account long-run social needs. The implication that society could ill afford to allow private expectations to determine the required investment level was drawn by Keynes as well as by his chief American disciple, Alvin Hansen. In 1938 Keynes thought that there should be a Board of Public Investment which would influence the course of the business cycle by its decisions. But he did not want government domination. Insisting that there still would be a place in such a setup for private capitalists to seek unexplored avenues, the board merely would specify the total amount of investment without directly allocating resources. His thinking here, though, seemed somewhat woolly; it is an interesting question how such "socialized" investment policies could operate without a certain amount of central direction.[182]

Keynes' original conception of the dynamics of capitalist motion placed a good deal of emphasis on the rate of interest. The relationship between the marginal efficiency of capital and interest underscored that idea. Since interest was a "price," the critical determinants were supply and demand, as in the case of all prices. Considerable debate arose over Keynes' liquidity theory of interest as contrasted with the usual loanable funds explanation.[183] But where ordinary theory spoke of the balance of capital productivity and capital supply, Keynes related the demand element to the desire for cash (liquidity preference) and supply to the stock of money. The theory now seemed complete, with all the required equations at hand. Investment was a function of the marginal efficiency of capital and the rate of interest; employment stemmed from income and investment; the marginal efficiency of capital was related to expectations and capital cost; and the rate of interest was based on liquidity preference and the stock of money. Consequently, if liquidity preference fell, the rate of interest would drop, encouraging businessmen to undertake investment, while income would be enhanced by virtue of the multiplier. And the multiplier itself could be derived from the consumption function. So facile a system could not help but attract adherents.[184]

Keynes' interest theory, however, failed to account for investment made by corporations out of accumulated reserves, a situation in which the rate of interest is at best but a fictional yardstick. Furthermore, the reasoning at this point seemed somewhat dubious, since relating the rate of interest to liquidity preference overlooked the fact that the latter itself depended in large measure on income. Some circularity resulted: interest affected investment which in turn determined income. Yet, curiously enough, elimination of the rate of interest as a significant factor in no way upset the logic of the Keynesian system. It still was quite possible to study the capitalist economy along the lines suggested by Keynes without paying too much attention to the rate of interest, just as it was possible to follow Marx's analysis of circulation without recourse to the labor theory of value.[185]

But, of course, the Keynesian system did not go unchallenged. Arthur F. Burns, in one of his rare theoretical moments, has leveled severe attacks on it.[186] He has questioned whether Keynes really provided enough information to enable governments to deal with cyclical situations. Such a feeling might be ascribed to Burns' inordinate passion for facts and his sharp rejection of theory. Burns also objected to the aggregate approach on the ground that not all firms act alike; windfall profits, he insisted, would upset the Keynesian equilibrium; the consumption function does not assume the shape ascribed to it in the *General Theory;* there was no guarantee that spending would always revive dormant economic life; and the trouble with Keynesian economic thought, concluded Burns, was that it employed a mechanical approach that failed utterly to comprehend the real turbulence of the business world. But these objections merely revealed a thoroughgoing misunderstanding of the aims of theoretical discourse; Burns would have quarrelled as much with Ricardo or Marshall as he did with Keynes.

A more serious criticism was the contention that Keynes did not really advance much beyond classical theory. It has been demonstrated that the latter's picture of a pleasant economic equilibrium is applicable only to periods of full employment, and since such a condition has been more or less attained, classical analysis became just as useful as any other. Keynesian theory, continued the argument, was but a special instance of the more general Marshallian version, with no particular relevance for current prosperity conditions. As one commentator remarked, Keynes merely had established diplomatic relations between standard theory and the business cycle.

Keynes also was charged with having arbitrarily selected his variables and constants which are the really critical elements in any theory. Had he chosen, for example, to cast his analysis in terms of the propensity to save rather than consumption, he might not have acquired so many followers. Formulating the *General Theory* along the lines that he did allowed him to adapt his thinking to contemporary political and social changes. His formula permitted economists to hold on to their notions while taking a new look at the way capitalism really functioned. This was a most comfortable procedure and many of his co-workers were very grateful. But they all failed to recognize that the mores of our society have created a dichotomy between peacetime full employment and the system of free enterprise. Full employment is possible only where government spending reaches astronomic magnitudes. There was a certain amount of doubt in some quarters that free enterprise per se could establish the necessary requirements for maximum utilization of economic resources without resorting to the stimulus of a cold war.

It was Marx, of course, who had contended that capitalism could not possibly function without periodically grinding its gears. The gap between standard theory and Marx always has seemed unbridgeable. Marx, who viewed capitalism as a passing phase in history, sought to expose its failings; classical doctrine insisted that capitalism was solid and permanent. Marx said that interest and profits were merely divisions of exploitative spoils; the classicists called them rewards for astuteness and abstinence. Yet the modifications that Keynes introduced into received economics revealed common roots in both doctrines. Keynes showed that it was possible to discuss economic problems with labor as the major or even sole factor of production. He thought that capitalism, unless revived, would founder entirely, and, when a neo-Keynesian remarks that the tragedy of investment is that it leads to crises that are themselves useful, he comes dangerously close to the Marxian conception. Keynes' rejection of Say's theory of markets and his underscoring of the lack of automatism in economics also may be found in Marx. In fact, with but a few shifts in definition and some alteration in variables, it is possible to bring Marxian theory quite close to Keynes. For example, the concept of the declining rate of profit may be visualized as the objective manifestation of the declining marginal efficiency of capital. Moreover, if the theory of prices adumbrated by Marx in Volume III of *Das Kapital* were modified after the fashion of von Bortkiewicz,[187] not too much adjustment would be needed to incorporate it into the main body of economic theory. Difficulties arose when Marx analyzed the total supply of capital and its rate of profit. Here Marx's objective definition of capital appeared at odds with Keynes' monetary motivation. But Keynes did emphasize the fact that accumulation depended not on saving alone but was an active, sometime creative, sometime disturbing, process penetrating all aspects of the economy.

Perhaps the closest affinity in the two systems was to be found in the theory of capitalist circulation which Marx discussed so profoundly in his second volume of *Das Kapital*. The Keynesian version saw breakdown caused by variations in the inducement to invest. Since the latter depended on profits, the actual limit to investment ultimately became the saving-consumption relation. In Marx, it was the rate of saving out of surplus value that governed investment: the pace was set by the competitive urge to beat down all rivals. And, as effective demand as a consideration in determining investment patterns did not enter the Marxian system at all, unemployment and crises were due basically to an insufficiency of accumulation. In Marx, the depression had to await further acquisition of capital before renewed activity could take place. This is what economists today describe as structural unemployment, a quite different kind from that which occurs when there is merely a failure in demand. The latter is what happened in the Thirties, and it is the likeliest type of unemployment in modern capitalism. Yet, high levels of activity accompanied by high unemployment do suggest structural defects.

The most striking parallel is both writers' contention that breakdown results from internal insufficiencies.[188] At this point, Keynes and Marx differed only in their use of aggregates. Marx employed the categories of producers' and consumers' goods with a three-fold division of value into constant, variable, and surplus cutting across both groups. This made it possible for a table of values to be distributed among producer and consumer industries. Each value portion thus represented not only a certain type of good but a cost and demand item as well. From this construction it was possible to work out a circular flow which then could be converted without much logical hazard into Keynesian categories.[189]

It can be argued that this procedure would demonstrate only formal similarities. For whereas Marxians insist that the variables employed in their economic theorizing are implicit in the system itself, Keynes' basic elements are derived from noneconomic psychological factors. Yet, it is extraordinary that, despite an antipathetic outlook, Keynes was able to develop a vision of capitalism the mechanics of which approximated Marx's. When Marx spoke of the excess of surplus value over capitalists' consumption as being limited by the expenditure for new producers' goods and foreign investment, he did approach the Keynesian view, for here investment was seen as a purchase without a sale and saving as a sale without purchase. That is to say, in neither system were automatic adjustments a reality. While he ignored "monetary" analysis, Marx did concede that the amount of money in circulation was affected by business habits as well as by prices. As for interest rates,

Marx attached much less importance to them than did Keynes: interest was nothing more than that part of surplus value subject to bargaining between capitalists. In the Keynesian system, interest was important where borrowing was involved. Otherwise, it was quite possible to omit it. For both, productive techniques were quite significant: to Keynes, long-run investment decisions depended on productivity, a notion not entirely alien to Marx. Both also recognized that the contradiction, to employ the Marxian term, between consumption and production lay at the root of economic crises. Consumption was limited by the kind of income distribution a society developed. This restricted profitability and investment. Counterbalancing factors were the growth of new industries and the compulsion to expand outwardly. An additional countervailing element that both writers would surely have acknowledged is the permanent war economy.[190]

But Marx wanted to go beyond the technical economic variables to what he conceived to be underlying social relations. Searching for the forces that led to the creation of value, he was compelled to conclude that the crucial relationships could be expressed quantitatively through commodity exchange. Yet, in this search, one of the most exciting in the history of economic thought, he overlooked the patent fact that such commodity transactions acquired an independent reality. The failure to recognize this made the Marxian model essentially a classical one with an unexpected moral twist, one that was rejected by later economists. Furthermore, Marx made his schema so involved and abstract that all too often his most trenchant insights were lost.

The Keynesian aggregate analysis, on the other hand, exhibiting a simple neutrality, successfully evaded the charge of moralizing. The chief characteristic of Keynes' major idea, the national income, is the fact that its basic analytical techniques are applicable to all sorts of economic systems. When Keynes pointed out that investment implied payments to the factors of production without necessarily bringing goods to market, he was offering an operational as well as an empirical concept. The drawback in the original version as presented in the *General Theory* was his failure to take aftereffects into account, so that it became possible for him to offer, half in jest, pyramid building as a prescription for depression.

Despite its seemingly static character, the Keynesian system does lend itself to all sorts of dynamical modification. It can be made quite complex without damaging its inherent logic. The Marxian aggregates, on the other hand, lacking operational character, do not lend themselves easily to empirical verification. In a sense, they are pure concepts and, like the Ricardian categories from which they derived much of their form, they are not measurable.

Objection has been voiced to Keynes' use of net national income as the fundamental idea in economic analysis. The argument has been made, not without some justification, that a net concept does not tell the entire story of total income flows, since it reveals only the final outcome without explaining what has happened in the meantime. Keynes consequently could be charged with looking upon the economic process as just a process and nothing more: his followers, taking these strictures to heart, have made valiant efforts to achieve a more detailed approach.[191] Marx's study of the relationships among constant capital, variable capital, and surplus value was meant to answer just this question: it sought to determine how income was distributed among the various classes as a gross rather than a net flow, and, in this respect, Marx was analytically superior to Keynes.

Despite Keynes' rejection of neoclassicism, his system was deeply rooted in it. Marshall's individual demand was a disaggregated image of Keynes' total demand. Aggregate supply was an extension of the optimum output of the firm. And, in both, the short run predominated, in which equilibrium was the central problem for economic analysis. However, while in Marshall, investment stemmed automatically from saving, in Keynes, no necessary connection existed between them simply because the two processes were traceable to different groups of people. Marshall's basic assumption, as in virtually all of economic theory up to then, was full employment, so that one started from that position as a given element in the economy. This was precisely what Keynes rejected: in his system, employment was a variable, and the object of economics was to discover the many ways in which it moved. If Marshall's capitalism was one of peace and prosperity, to Keynes, this happy outcome could be brought about only by conscious intervention.[192]

There is no denying the fact that the influence of the *General Theory* has been enormous. All contemporary economic discourse, even that of Keynes' critics, is cast in its terms. His most intransigent opponents began to think as he did. And although Alvin Hansen and Arthur Pigou, Keynes' teacher, greeted the *General Theory* with anger and disdain, it was not long before Hansen became the first apostle, while Pigou later conceded that his star pupil had been right after all. A school, in the true sociological sense, was formed: there was an inner core of expert exegetes surrounded by an outer layer of popularizers. The experts—Harrod, Lerner, Hansen, Robinson —kept themselves busy filling in gaps and "dynamizing" the system like engineers tinkering with a strange new motor.[193] Beyond these, there grew up a large body of sympathizers who spoke the language of the master with wonderful glibness. As Schumpeter once remarked, this had happened before only to the Physiocrats and to Marx.

It was understandable that Keynes' ideas should have a striking influence on opinion concerning inherent tendencies in capitalism. These effects were especially noticeable in the United States during the early Thirties. While in England, knowledge of the sources of Keynes' ideas seemed to dull their brilliance, in this country the extraordinary unemployment in the midst of an astounding natural resource potential made almost everyone ready to accept Keynesian theory as the last word in economics, for it pointed to the behavior of people as the motivating force in the economic process. It was the action of people, it seemed to say, rather than brutish, impersonal market drives that created the "stocks and flows" of economic analysis. The explanation of income and its movement could be framed in terms of persons, and, with such an approach, it even was suggested that it might be possible to exercise the kind of control that would dispose of the disheartening cyclical variations to which capitalism so often gave rise. If this belief were correct, economic relationships could be defined as the outcome of interpersonal and group relationships; governmental action could be effectively utilized to modify and influence the behavior of the important economic groups—certain businessmen, trade unions, and even consumers. The social groups, in other words, might be the proper vehicle for the operation of all the Keynesian "propensities."

Keynesian economics thus represented an attempt to create an acceptable political economy at a time when people wanted action as well as analysis. This lent to the *General Theory* an irresistible attraction. In a depression, the need to do things pointed to questions of policy: and as this was the direction in which Keynes moved, he was able to give intellectual expression to both despair and hopefulness, while his use of aggregates and global figures seemed to make everything disarmingly simple. But this was a mechanical simplicity in which talk about the kind of "built-in stabilizers" that would absolve all of us of ultimate responsibility replaced the need to comprehend and grasp the complex, vibrant, and all too often turbulent realities of economic activity. The simple fact of the matter was that Keynes' economics failed to achieve the status of a true political economy. As was suggested above, it simply embodied too much gadgetry, too much "engineering," with no concern for the underlying social realities of economic tension. The entire system was so "neutral" that it could easily serve as a convenient theoretical justification (particularly as it related to the social control of investment) for a totalitarian movement seeking to extend the *status quo* by state action.

Such a use of this theory could happen only because the human and the political did not penetrate the economic in Keynes' thinking. For all his consideration of cash balances, liquidity preferences, multiplier effects, and consumption functions, one did not always have the feeling that these were categories of human behavior. All too often, the social groups that were *implied* by Keynesian economics merely comprised a number of individuals who reacted in the economy as a result of certain none-too-well defined expectations or because of speculative moods or as a result of some action undertaken by the central bank. Moreover, none of these groups ever seemed to exhibit any identifiable social interest beyond the course of action prescribed for them by the theory. Like the aggregates, they had meaning only in the *mass*. And the major concern, as with the classicists, was always with economic equilibrium. This ultimately focused attention on the level of economic values and their flows rather than on origins and consequently led to an overweaning interest in the mere mechanics of the economy. It was little wonder that unimaginative applications of Keynesian concepts by postwar forecasters led to disastrous results. Human behavior was much more volatile than had been expected. Had Keynes acknowledged the appropriateness of the political and social, for example, he might have been less hasty to suggest that a constant rise in prices would achieve the millennium, and he would not have fostered the view that social engineering can dispense with the need for a truly rigorous re-evaluation of capitalist society.

This, in the final analysis, revealed Keynes as essentially a conservative thinker.[194] While his social philosophy was grounded in a belief in unremitting economic endeavor, leadership was for him a function of the chosen few. Yet he did not reject reform: social evils were an abomination not to be tolerated in his England. Change could best be attained by careful study and a program of gradualism. Improving the lot of the poor simply was something that all Englishmen should advocate because they were English. National income ought to be distributed in a way that would provide for the unfortunate, but absolute equality was completely undesirable. Although the profit motive might have sordid implications, state enterprise was most impractical. There is little doubt that when we get down to the root of the matter Keynes firmly sustained the principle of private enterprise. Perhaps that is why he became a social tinkerer and a man of principled expediency.

v

Neo-Keynesianism:
Some Theories of Growth

With the coming of the new realism, economists began to inquire whether it was possible for Western nations to continue their seemingly miraculous ability to put more people to work, make more goods, and add to the national income.[195] Back in the 1930's, when the major concern had been depression and instability, the economy was headed downward in what seemed to be a never-ending plunge. The rate of population growth had dropped rapidly and nineteenth-century chatter about race suicide revived.

The limits of our territorial frontiers had long been reached. And, as national output moved sluggishly, the unemployed huddled with puzzled brows around makeshift fires and apple boxes. Then came the war and a burgeoning need for men in newly created jobs. But, with expanded income and overtime pay, there were fewer goods available than might have been expected. This was the anomaly of inflation, and economists had on their hands a new though not unfamiliar problem. And it stayed with them even after the war.

Then, as international politics began to intrude into an already complex situation, economists took a long look at the so-called "underdeveloped" countries, and, lo!, they discovered a fresh center of interest. They became aware of "growth": they learned that the "underdeveloped" nations, once contemptuously dismissed as backward, might be able to use modern technolgy as well as the West. They observed an insistent pressure in these areas for quick economic advancement which revealed itself with startling force as country after country sought political independence and economic self-sufficiency. But how would such economies grow? How could they accumulate the capital needed to enable them to take a proud place among the family of full-grown political economies? No longer could one tell these nations that they must be resigned forever to supply raw material for the West, for there was always the example of totalitarian Russia, employing Draconian devices to build its industry. There, material advance was stressed as a religious imperative: this was a tempting paradigm. Western economists had to search for ways in which growth might be instituted without the horrible nightmare of the Soviet crash program.

But, despite this new interest, the theory of economic growth remained on the periphery of the main body of economic doctrine. True, there had been some discussion in Adam Smith and David Ricardo of what might be characterized as growth theory: they had talked about the "stationary state" and diminishing returns. And there was Marx's "law of capitalist motion." But nowhere was there a unified explanation in the literature to show, for example, why Great Britain had beat out everyone else in the industrial race, or why the rate of American growth had been more rapid during the nineteenth century than in the twentieth.

To the classicists, the basic theme in economic growth was an unhalting drive toward the stationary state.[196] The latter did not mean a stagnant economy, but merely one in which population, capital, and technology underwent no change. The classical theory of economic development, compounded of elements of Malthusian population, Ricardian wage and rent doctrine, the law of diminishing returns, value based on cost of production, and saving through abstinence, said that growth depended primarily on capital accumulation. But, in order to obtain more capital, the economy had to be able to provide enough profit to encourage businessmen to assume risks. As capital accumulation went on, wages (derived from a special wage fund) tended to rise and, according to Malthusian beliefs, thereby encouraged population increases. The consequences were greater pressures on less fertile land and the depressing spectre of diminishing returns. Productivity fell and the major part of subsequent price increases were appropriated by the landed aristocracy. If wage rates rose in an effort to keep pace with higher prices, profit margins had to decline. One, therefore, was faced with the bleak outcome that capital accumulation did induce a falling rate of profit. In time, the inducement to save and invest disappeared, as the economy ground down to the repetitive cycle of the stationary state. Population just about maintained itself; natural resources were constant; the various forms of capital did not change; consumers kept buying pretty much the same sort of goods; and saving merely was enough to keep capital equipment from wearing out. Thus, the economic system reproduced itself at a constant, changeless rate and all untoward events were fully anticipated in errorless fashion. The economic system could not falter: in the words of Schumpeter, it was "hitchless."

But in reality, as Keynes so clearly demonstrated, there were, indeed, numerous "hitches." Stability under capitalism seemed almost a contradiction in terms, for fluctuations and even sudden collapse appeared as a built-in feature of capitalist growth. Certainly, the problem was a most challenging one, and post-Keynesian writers have not been averse to facing up to it. There were enough suggestions in the *General Theory* on which Roy Harrod, Evsey Domar, Joan Robinson, and others could build. Aware that while the original Keynesian apparatus was in a formal sense comparative statics, they believed nevertheless that it was applicable to an examination of an economy undergoing change. For example, consumer anticipations and supplier reactions to investment expenditures could be studied as time rates of change.[197] Similarly, the outlay lag in the multiplier was a dynamic process. And, once lagged variables were introduced, it was evident that dynamics had entered into economic analysis.

While post-Keynesians did observe that lags in income could be corrected by increased investment, they frequently overlooked the fact that such investment invariably increased total productive capacity even more than had been the case previously. Some writers felt that since this was a problem for "long-run analysis" it could be safely ignored in short-term predictions. It was Sir Roy F. Harrod (1900-   ), Keynes' biographer, and a leading British theorist in his own right, who first called attention, in 1939, to this problem of augmented industrial capacity.[198] Harrod, who was educated at Oxford and began his academic career as a lecturer in 1922, served during the war with the statistical office of the Prime Minister. Also a frequent advisor to governmental and international agencies, his works include, in addition to the highly important studies on economic growth, books on international trade, business cycles, and monetary questions.[199] In problems of growth, the basic question, said Harrod, was the rate of growth in income required to ensure the full use of an ever *increasing* quantity of capital. Furthermore, can such a rate of growth sustain itself or must it sooner or later break down? Will deviations from the required rate of growth stimulate any corrective forces? How is this rate related to the needs of full employment? Suppose actual growth falls short of full employment? What steps are necessary to bring growth up to full employment levels? Or must the economy first fall on its face? Will explosive inflationary conditions set in should the actual growth rate exceed what is required for full employment? None of these questions is easy to answer, and much technical ingenuity has been expended in constructing elegantly erudite solutions. But it is generally agreed that the effort has been worthwhile: its purpose has been ". . . to perceive in precise terms the relations between the long run forces of economic growth and the forces inducing instability in the growth of income such as has characterized the development of capitalism." [200]

Another cogent presentation of the problem was that made by Evsey Domar (1914-   ).[201] Domar, whose education began in Harbin, Manchuria, has studied at the University of California, Michigan, and Harvard. Addressing his essays to the problem of determining what rate of growth in national income would maintain full employment, Domar has observed that investment exhibits a *dual* character in that it not only generates income but also increases productive capacity. The Keynesian proposition that savings equals investment and that income paid out must return to the productive process are formulations that merely maintain the *status quo*. A more realistic conception, said Domar, would make room for added capital formation and the subsequent increase in the ability to produce.[202]

Now, such new capital might either be unused, merely put to one side, or employed at the expense of earlier, older capital, or possibly substituted for labor and other factors. While the first instance represents a simple waste of resources, the others are changes that always take place in a dynamic economy. Yet such problems are seldom, if at all, set forth in standard Keynesian doctrine, argued Domar, for in the latter employment is a relatively uncomplicated function of income. More technically, the problem is to ascertain the magnitude of investment required to make the increase in income equal to the increase in productive capacity. This suggests that employment ought to be visualized as a function of the ratio of income to productive capacity. The difficulty, of course, is the definition of productive capacity; but this may be stated as output at full employment. Thus the problem was reduced by Domar to an equation in which the required ratio of growth was established by setting the rate of increase in productive capacity equal to the rate of increase in income. In analytical terms, this meant that continuous full employment could be attained only if investment and income grew at constant annual percentage rates which were equal to the product of the marginal propensity to save and to the average propensity of investment.[203] This was a technical way of saying that simple offsets to saving were insufficient to maintain full employment, that, in fact, investment must always exceed saving, and that there must be a continuous growth in income to provide the additional saving. Increases in capacity were related to investment, while increases in total demand were connected with the rate of growth in investment. Consequently, stability required that both income and investment be somewhat like the Einsteinian universe, always expanding at an accelerated rate.

Of course, the likelihood of investment increasing *all* the time is at best moot. Yet, if investment did not satisfy the conditions of required growth set forth by these relationships, excess capacity would set in and inhibit further investment. As Domar has said, the presence of unemployed capital can be dangerous because it inhibits new investment.[204] In situations engendered by a monopolistic economy, such excess capacity clearly would be a threat to continued growth and expansion. In fact, it was Domar's view that a capitalist society exhibited inherent deflationist tendencies which could be counteracted, but not necessarily eliminated, by technological advances.[205]

Harrod, on the other hand, argued that the economy can develop a rate of growth, consonant with full capacity operation.[206] While Harrod employed a rather high degree of abstraction, his model was dynamic in that he assumed productive technique to be improving. Now, the "warranted" rate was that which insured a continuation of investment at levels that met the profit expectations of the businessman. Unexpected, unanticipated results in output were due entirely to changes in investment plans. However, limitations on "warranted" growth were set by the size of the labor force and by the current state of technology. "Warranted" growth was, therefore, a ceiling rate set by existing economic conditions. In one important sense, this notion was really nothing more than "potential" growth, and, if this exceeded *actual* growth, stagnation could be the outcome. That is to say, the economic system seemingly failed to meet its promise. In the reverse conditions, one in which actual growth was greater than what appeared to be inherent in the current economic situation, a state of perpetual exhilaration was created in which facilities expanded and inflationary pressures accumulated.

Another cornerstone of Harrod's model was the "acceleration" factor, which posited a fixed relationship between the quantity of a flow and the size of stock from which it came. To illustrate, a definite relation was said to exist between purchases, inventories, and sales. As shifts in the rate of sales might lead to more than a proportionate change on the rate of purchases, the final effect would be magnified. Now, when sales declined, there was a tendency to cut back on investment. Should this react particularly on consumer goods industries, net investment could very well become a negative quantity coupled with the nightmare of excess capacity. Similarly, an increase in sales might be a harbinger of economic exhilaration. And, while "acceleration" might have little influence in the early stages of a cyclical upswing because of existing excess capacities, it could have a choking effect as the upper limits of the cycle were attained. Then the usual bottlenecks and shortages would begin to plague the economy. The businessman, however, was generally satisfied if income increased fast enough to justify the outlay on new capital. Thus, the higher the income, the higher the investment, and again higher the income, on in continuing leapfrog fashion, with the economy running ever-faster as though on a giant treadmill.

Further analysis of growth required that a distinction be made between different kinds of investment. Harrod separated "autonomous" from "induced" investment. The former, which resulted from innovation and was therefore independent of sales and current output, did not need the stimulus of income expansion to get going: only an adventurous spirit and the unremitting search for profit were required. The latter kind of investment, however, was directly connected with output and, consequently, depended on "acceleration." If sales in the immediate past were brisk and future prospects good enough to create a real sense of certainty, induced investment was given a considerable fillip. Should prosperity be extended, profits might very well become extraordinary. In fact, conditions could be so good that it might become difficult to distinguish between autonomous and induced investment. However, in such a situation, the growth of income would have to be more rapid than ever, for there would have to be enough investment created to absorb the savings generated by both types. What could very well ensue was a condition of sustained periods of economic exhilaration alternating with long periods of stagnation.

Yet, it does seem unlikely that growth would be continuous. Some firms expand while others go out of existence. And, a smooth growth configuration cannot be derived from innovation, for this comes in spurts and clusters, creating all sorts of turbulences. Furthermore, existing firms are hardly the ones that introduce innovation. They usually stand pat so that new ways of doing business or new ways of making things require an "adventurous" spirit. Monopoly, cartels, a fear of excess capacity, the rise of the professional manager—all may exert dampening effects on any tendency for unceasing expansion.

With an increasing labor force each year, there is a need for a growth pattern that will absorb new workers. In the absence of such absorptive capacity, the increased supply of man-hours coupled with increased labor productivity can lead only to a "labor reserve," a condition, it will be recalled, predicted by Marx. To overcome this, it would seem to be necessary for income to rise directly with labor supply and productivity. Yet, all too often, growth has been discussed solely in terms of the increase in capital. It is quite possible that the full use of capital equipment will not lead to full employment of labor, particularly in an economy where the use of capital is directed toward labor-saving devices, as with automation. Further, it is conceivable that the growth rate of capital might exceed "full employment" growth, so that the tendency toward excessive capital accumulation will be reinforced, eventually leading to a depressing effect. On the other hand, in underdeveloped countries, a tendency for "full employment" growth to exceed capital growth results in what economists call "involuntary unemployment." Perhaps this can be overcome by resorting to the kind of investment that stems from innovations rather than from sources internal to the economy itself. But innovation does not have a strong effect where there is a considerable backlog of idle capacity. Consequently, it is in the interplay of factors such as these that makes for secular stagnation, and it apparently takes the strength of a garrison economy's innovative impact to dispel the drag of idle capacity.

Yet, for a number of years now, the situation has been hardly like this at all. We have experienced in the main a condition of secular exhilaration, one probably due to an overabundance of the innovative, autonomous kind of investment. In such a milieu, investments exhibit a self-generating character, since extremely favorable profit margins can encourage the introduction of new devices and gadgets, while at the same time creating relatively high income levels by an atmosphere of receptivity to change. Further, at levels of high economic activity, people may place more stress on consumption than on saving. This may weaken the role of the induced type of investment, from which is derived the purely internal growth drives. As a result, autonomous investment may displace induced investment during prosperous times. Suppose now that the profitability of autonomous investment begins to wear out: it is evident that in such circumstances the sense of exhilaration may quickly evaporate as economic growth grinds to a painful halt.

According to this theory, an upward movement in perpetuity is a moot question.[207] Distortions in the physical structure of production may ensue, which in turn might affect markedly the growth line. Differences in rates of growth in various parts of the economy may require a redirection of output, perhaps from capital goods industries to consumer goods. Such a contingency could cause idle capacity to appear in some sectors and so break the circular flow of income. (In fact, a problem of this sort may very well be at the root of the difficulties faced by the Soviet economy, for it is conceivable that an absolute imperative toward capital goods production has been built into Russian industry, thus making it by now a superhuman task to supply an adequate flow of consumer goods.) As Adolph Lowe once said, the way in which the different sectors of the economy are structured can have a significant impact on growth.[208] In most instances, the process of growing is carried on by only a few major sectors of the economy. These may be based on new technology, as in British textiles in the eighteenth century, or American transportation in the nineteenth, or on political motivations. Such changes may set in motion a host of corollary lines, as with the automobile industry. But historical evidence suggests that major growth patterns do not involve the entire economic system. As a result, it is entirely possible to draw fairly pessimistic inferences should the impetus toward expansion collapse in the major sectors.

It is patently clear that growth is an extremely complex phenomenon. Any adequate theory would have to include natural resources, political institutions, legal structures, and a host of psychological and sociological factors. But to work out an all-encompassing theoretical framework seems an almost impossible task. Hence, theoreticians necessarily have had to select those features which seem to them to be most relevant. It was to Domar's credit that he focused attention on capacity as a significant element in growth theory. The problem then could be stated as follows: given a condition of equilibrium for output and capacity, what is the rate of growth in each that must be exhibited to avoid both inflation and unemployment?[209] Recently, Paul Samuelson and Robert Solow have given a somewhat pessimistic answer to this question. Expansion, they have suggested is bound to bring price rises, while a "low pressure" economy is likely to generate unemployment.[210] These are indeed gloomy conclusions.

But William Fellner, successor to the late Irving Fisher at Yale, has rejected such a dark outlook.[211] Employing, in the main, the same general techniques as Harrod and Domar, Fellner has arrived at quite different conclusions. He has acknowledged that in a growing economy investment must keep pace with total savings but, said he, if the economy is enjoying a condition of exhilaration, there will be inevitably an adequate supply of savings to match investment. While the "matching" problem might be basic, it cannot become a really serious matter so long as there are enough technological improvements to provide investment outlets.

An approach such as Fellner's, which placed stress on the relationship of technological advances to available resources, was fundamentally an effort to expose the "structural" problem. He contended that the essential requirement was to heighten productivity in order to encourage investment. By doing so, the economy would be able to overcome the insufficiency of "planned investment," a condition that in the past has led to a slowing down of growth. This led Fellner into some rather odd pathways: growth became a purely "psychic" phenomena, and idle capacity was of no great importance so long as entrepreneurs did not consider the total stock of capital as excessive. This suggested, too, that unemployment and growth were not really incompatible. However, it was not made clear whether businessmen's plans for expansion could be long sustained in the face of declining purchasing power.

Making much of the problem of what he considered to be a correct time sequence, Fellner feared that too much variation from a smooth growth path would upset the entire apple cart and cause either uncontrolled inflation or stagnation. The limits of tolerance were quite small: in the final analysis, steady growth demanded that net capital formation always equal net savings at a stable general price level. This was indeed a tall order; and it was precisely the difficulty of achieving such stability that was underscored by Harrod. But Fellner was undismayed, for, said he, a smooth pattern could be worked out through the effective control of money. In addition, capital always must be more abundant than labor (so that the old devil of diminishing returns might be exorcised) and structural shifts would have to be gradual so that bottlenecks and distortions arising from the improper application of resources might be avoided.

Yet Fellner's views were not entirely clear: while sometimes perturbed by divergences from smooth growth rates, he insisted at others that the possibility of instability had been exaggerated. Planned investment usually was set in a *range* of magnitudes, he said, and so long as what was actually attained fell within the anticipated limits, no great harm would be done by straying slightly from the mark. A divergence from what was necessary for upward growth has generally been temporary in any case, and, should economic conditions worsen, a point would be reached eventually where the need for some goods and some investment would set things going again. But this was precisely the sort of analysis of economic change that had been offered twenty-five years ago, and it seems just about as helpful now as it was then. What Fellner suggested basically was that growth depended on the compatibility of expectations and the plans stemming from them. Since we know that expectations and results do not always jibe, said he, continuous little adjustments would have to be made to avoid mal-investment, and the best place to effect such numerous adjustments was, of course, the free market!

Methodologically, growth theories such as those just described, cannot help but reveal their roots in static analysis. While the latter has described economic forces in terms of equilibrium and its stability, much of modern development theory speaks in terms of constant rates of growth and a moving equilibrium. The objective has been to reveal certain points of equilibrium over time which are consistent with the various dynamic pressures which impinge on the economy. What is interesting is the concession that such a movement can be quite unstable and even explosive with wide amplitudes revealed about the path of growth. Thus, the elimination of structural disproportions in the economy would not necessarily give an easy solution to violent and sharp changes. Nor would such adjustments ever be quick enough to overcome the strains of growth: raw materials and labor cannot be moved about like chess pieces, and it is impossible to convert factories quickly to alternative uses. Nor can fluctuations be dampened or eliminated by the correction of structural disproportions, for the fundamental relationships between saving, investment, and income would continue to operate even if all segments of the economy were affected in the same way.

Thus, the problem of growth is complicated by the fact that investment and consumption are always going on at different rates of speed in different parts of the economy. While this is happening, the production functions are undergoing change so that different recipes for mixing economic ingredients—capital and labor—are required. This sets limits to both the rate and extent of growth. Also, there are other limits: availability of finance, existing industrial capacity, and, for countries with a high foreign trade component, the balance of payments itself. Mrs. Joan Robinson has argued that growth can take place only if there is ". . . a technical surplus available above subsistence," and, within that limit, only if there is a ". . . surplus above the level of real wages that the workers are willing to accept . . . ," and, within that limit, only if the entrepreneurs energetically carry out the business of accumulation.[212] That is to say, growth ultimately depends on the totality of savings that an economy can set aside.

In recent years, Mrs. Robinson has given much attention to growth questions, stemming from her efforts to develop a long-run version of Keynesian theory.[213] The problem was not dissimilar from that posed by Domar: what, she asked, is the relation between the rate of output and the growth in the stock of capital over time? Generally, she observed, capitalism could grow if the proper conditions were present.[214] These were an expansion of effective demand at the same pace as output, the ability of capital in both the producers' and consumers' sectors to adapt to new techniques with replacement investment a constant proportion of the stock of capital, and the continuous investment of depreciation reserves. It was evident that it would be difficult for all of these conditions to operate simultaneously: often depreciation charges were far greater than capital replacements so that it would appear that excessive savings were possible.[215] The point was self-evident: savings are essential, but if not used, they become dangerous to the health of the economy. At any rate, Mrs. Robinson felt certain that a reasonably useful model could be built to demonstrate how capitalism might become viable. Such a model, exhibiting a harmonious concatenation of what a community wanted to accumulate, the actual possiblities, and the initial conditions of growth, could be employed to show what happened when balances were upset. Yet the real description of capitalistic growth has revealed an erratic framework: the existing stock of capital has a history that frequently has made it difficult to establish the required coordination with demand, while the level of profits necessary to sustain investment levels has not always been forthcoming. Accumulation, as Mrs. Robinson said, would have to occur against a background of cyclical change.

The problem of growth was tackled by Mrs. Robinson in her *The Ac-*

cumulation of Capital, a most perceptive theoretical treatise. The models and arguments, albeit quite rarefied and exuding a markedly high degree of abstraction, did provide useful insights into the nature of capitalist motion. That is to say, her model was not one that exhibited equilibrium characteristics.[216]

There were three economic classes in the Robinsonian model: workers, who spent all their income on consumption; entrepreneurs, who received wages of management plus a share of profit together with rentier income in the form of some interest and dividends; and rentiers, who lived on rent, interest, and dividends. Total value then came to wages, profit, rentier expenditure, and rentier saving. The last three terms could be labelled quasi-rent. The terms also were separated into a consumption and production sector, so that total value in the former exceeded its wage bill, since consumer goods would have to be supplied to other workers and other classes. The quasi-rents (from another view, gross margins) in the consumption sector were necessary to cover the consumption of rentiers and wages in the investment sector. The basic questions in such a model were the relation of wages to profit, of the stock of capital to the labor force, and the effect of the particular technique or production function selected. The larger investment expenditures or rentier outlays became, the smaller wages would be in the consumption sector. At some point, an increasing ratio of investment and rentier outlays would lead to pressures for higher money wages, so that conflict could develop between the desire to invest and between the levels of wages that would have to be consonant with such investment.[217] Accumulation was necessarily the basis for profit, and, conversely, without profit there could be no accumulation. Total profit was equal to the expenditures of rentiers plus wages in the investment or producers' goods sector. Thus, the excess of profit over investment stemmed from rentier spending, and the excess value of investment over borrowing (from rentiers in the model) was equal to retained profit. It then could be demonstrated that the equality of aggregate saving and investment operated through the flow of profit. If output merely equaled wages, no profit would be forthcoming; and, if only enough labor were employed to just maintain capital intact, no excess over quasi-rent could arise; and, hence, no accumulation was possible. Thus satiety in the sense of overinvestment, or technical poverty, could lead to a condition of stagnation. The significant point was that workers had to produce a surplus if profits were to be extracted.

Assuming a single technique and no consumption by the entrepreneur, capital accumulation was limited by the available surplus over subsistence; and, within that limit, by the level of real wages, the energy and activity of entrepreneurs, and the growth of the labor force. If accumulation failed to match the rate of growth in the labor force, unemployment was bound to occur. This entire problem was similar to that posed by Wicksell in his analysis of the relation of the stock of capital to the level of real wages.[218] Wicksell had been concerned with the degree to which capital growth might be absorbed by rising real wages, the noted "Wicksell effect." This was certainly an important question, for, as real wages increased, the rate of profit would tend to fall. To Mrs. Robinson, a basic question was the effect this might have on the value of capital and on investment decisions. Where labor increased more slowly than capital accumulation, money wage rates conceivably might rise, until the upper limit of the inflation barrier was reached. Employment could be stable only when capacity grew at the same rate as per capita output together with a constant rise in real wages and profit.[219] The situation, however, became considerably more complex when shifts in productivity were taken into account, for then the relationships between money, labor, output, and capital were altered. Smooth economic growth then required that the stock of capital expand consonant with the increase in output per man. Demand could be maintained only if real wages kept up the same pace. Yet the supply of capital would have to be adjusted to the growth in the labor force.

This was a precarious balance: progress and growth could become uneven when the rate of technical progress changed and accumulation did not move evenly with increases in productivity. Ordinarily, it might be expected that real wages would rise with increases in output per person, but if there was a greater stress on the producers' goods industries, wages could not maintain the necessary pace. Thus, with uneven technical progress, booms developed in some areas, slumps in others,[220] progress slowed down, and real demand was depressed. Underconsumption reared its ugly head, counterbalanced only by armament expenditures.[221] In such situations, the only recourse was to trade union pressure for higher money wages; for, in an economy with sticky prices and monopolistic behavior, such actions would help increase real wages. Unions consequently saved the situation by enforcing as rapid a rise in real wages as in output per capita.

The kind of technique that entrepreneurs would select depended on the rate of output, degree of mechanization, and labor cost. The objective was not merely higher output, but one that would yield the highest rate of profit at the prevailing rate of wages. Thus a technique which utilized relatively less labor still might be preferred to others, provided its profitability were greater. Mechanization was no virtue to be pursued for its own sake. From another viewpoint, the wage rate could be considered the determining factor, for the choice of technique would be based on the equality of wages to the marginal product of the labor employed. The selection of technique could be restricted by a lack of finance, enforcing a technical level that would provide a lower rate of profit. Thus, where accumulation was insufficient to allow the adoption of the best possible rate of technical progress, unemployment conceivably could develop. The best conditions under capitalism were an expanding supply of capital with a limited labor force, leading to an increase in real wages.

Mrs. Robinson's basic model sought to demonstrate that an expansion of output at a constant rate of profit depended on the rate of technical progress and the rate of increase in the labor force. Potentially, the rate of increase in output each year was equal to the percentage rates of growth in employment plus the percentage rates of growth in per capita output. The ideal condition—Mrs. Robinson's "Golden Age"—revealed a steady rate of growth, neutral technical progress, and a constant rate of profit as well as a constant ratio of capital to employment. There might be a tendency toward demechanization if the latter ratio, the real capital ratio, were to fall. Yet it was possible, argued Mrs. Robinson, for a rapid growth in capacity to be associated with a tendency to demechanize. Thus, the "Golden Age" became the stationary society, the state of bliss, in which a constant proportion of capital was replaced each year. The growth ratio was defined as the highest rate of accumulation of capital that could be sustained at a constant rate of profit. A higher rate of accumulation would increase the degree of mechanization, and, over the long run, induce a lower rate of profit. Consequently, changes in the growth ratio made the attainment of the Golden Age a virtual impossibility.[222]

Thus, while capitalism can show progress, it bears within itself seeds of destruction. The system could maintain itself if real wages kept pace with output per capita, that is, if technical change did not upset the balance between these key distributive shares. Moreover, accumulation must keep the stock of capital expanding together with output per capita. The entrepreneurial spirit must not flag, Mrs. Robinson warned, for the enemy was not thrift, but a slackening of capitalist drives. Profit underpinned accumulation, yet real wages had to be maintained at adequate levels. The complex balance required for the successful conduct of a capitalist economy seemed quite difficult to attain, for as the various ratios altered, all sorts of problems arose—falling real wages, unemployment, shifting profits, and inflation. A variety of paradoxes developed, and all too often the rules of the capitalist game became unplayable.

Yet these "rules" in a sense could apply to a socialist society as well, and could become equally unplayable. There are certain relationships between population growth, capital stock, and technique that any viable industrialized nation must display regardless of its political structure. The connection between social income and social surplus is as important under socialism as it is under capitalism, and the rate of accumulation is something that a planning authority can ignore only at its peril. Thus, Mrs. Robinson's analysis exhibited a certain quality of universality and yet was rooted in several of Marx's fundamental concepts. The relation between her quasi-rent and wages paralleled the latter's surplus value and variable capital, and the accumulation process was reminiscent of the reproduction schema found in *Das Kapital*. Certainly, her description of the motive power of capitalism and the competitive drive toward accumulation was, at the very least, Marxian in spirit, if not in detail. Once again Mrs. Robinson demonstrated ways in which Marxian categories could be usefully employed.

Nevertheless, these theories of growth were inspired mainly by Keynesian modes of thought. It was patent that the stagnation of the Thirties and fears of a recurring recession after the war impelled Harrod, Domar, Robinson, Fellner, and others to take a close look at how the economy moved over time. In Domar's system stress was placed on the role of new capacity, so that it was necessary to relate investment to increments in income in a way that would absorb the additional capacity. In Harrod's formulation, the emphasis was on changes in demand, particularly as it affected current output and net capital investment. This allowed him to distinguish between autonomous and induced investment and, by basing the latter on the level of income, enabled him to investigate its relationship to full capacity economic growth. Mrs. Robinson's model was even more emphatically based on technological factors, in that mechanization, real wages, and the rate of profit were intimately related. Despite their somewhat formalistic character, all of these models easily could absorb such factors as population growth, accumulation of human knowledge, adaptability to technological potentials, and political and social relations between national states. Not unrelated to the last item were such questions as: must smaller nations always employ drastic measures of self help in order to secure the savings necessary for growth? Or will they have to seek the kind of aid that merely makes them victims of large empires? Another critical question: does the kind of forced economic growth imposed by the Soviets on their own peoples distort the economic structure in such a way that totalitarian forces are inevitably strengthened? If so, will the underdeveloped nations want to pursue such a course? It is when questions like these are raised that the usefulness of theoretical models comes to the fore. Moreover, it must be asked whether growth, particularly in certain "underdeveloped" areas, is really a desirable social objective. At least, the British economist, W. A. Lewis, now head of the University College of the West Indies, began by asking this fundamental question in his *Theory of Economic Growth*.[223]

Certain costs, he said, are engendered by the painful process of development, and not everyone may believe that rapid economic change is a satisfactory way of reaching social goals. Some people may prefer the habits of a stable society. Nevertheless, continued Lewis, the range of human choice does increase with the extended control over environment which is implied by growth. Growth banishes famine, lessens infant mortality, eliminates disease. It creates more goods and services and provides time for the pursuit of mental endeavors, and, where human aspirations exceed available resources, it helps to reduce social tensions.

But the cost of these advances must be recognized, said Lewis. As acquisitiveness becomes ascendant and the commercial spirit is given full sway, tension is generated at both social and individual levels; social responsibilities may be side-tracked while individual needs are being met. Things become big for their own sake: corporate monopoly enters into the price paid for growth. To all of this must be added the maddening discipline of the clock and the excesses of rapid urbanization. Yet it might be asked whether these are not the costs of hasty industrialization rather than of growth. If urban life were carefully planned and nurtured, need it exhibit the blight it now manifests? A more optimistic view would suggest that man's aspirations can harness the materialism of economic growth with reasoned and directed effort. This much Lewis did admit.

Growth, he continued, stems from three basic causes: first, by the effort to economize and create more goods; second, by the increase of knowledge and its application to material techniques; third, by the increase of capital per head of population. Yet, analysis of these elements alone will not tell us enough about the way in which an economy grows. How, for example, does a society's system of values effect this process? Does a caste-dominated, religion-centered social order inhibit the accumulation of goods? Does equality as a social value facilitate expansion? Do those habits of thought that facilitate growth have accumulative effects, or is some point reached at which they begin to fetter development?

Lewis then asked: just how much does capital contribute to the growth process? Studies by Simon Kuznets and Colin Clark, the noted Australian statistician, have shown that in the advanced nations a net investment of 10 per cent of annual output yields a 3 per cent increase in income.[224] This evidently exceeds what the underdeveloped countries are able to accomplish. In the former, a higher ratio of capital to income means a greater ability to produce heavy equipment and thereby a greater stream of goods. For the underdeveloped areas, the root of the difficulty lies in their lack of skills and knowledge, so that the production of an output similar to that of the more developed nations demands an even greater investment. Thus, if India were to maintain a net investment ratio of a mere 4 or 5 per cent, the gap between it and the United States would continue to widen.

This raises a crucial question for the analysis of growth: how fast can capital be accumulated without undue strain on the populace? To judge by the experience of prewar Japan and Germany, it can be quite rapid. Yet, there are limits, for buildings cannot be put up without the requisite complement of bricklayers, carpenters, and masons. Moreover, expansion at a steady rate can proceed only if certain "social overhead" items are provided, such as utilities, docks, water supply, and means of communication. While these do not immediately produce goods, they are, nevertheless, essential to high production. Even in countries where only a modest endowment of natural resources exists, such as Denmark or Switzerland, the existing social overhead provides a basis for a relatively high level of production. In fact, some nations with a rich supply of resources, lacking such social overhead, cannot begin to match the latter in productivity: Brazil seems a case in point.

Such notions suggest that effective growth is dependent upon a delicate balance of the numerous elements required for economic development. Ragnar Nurske, one of the major proponents of this viewpoint, set forth the analysis in his *Problems of Capital Formation in Underdeveloped Countries*.[225] Calling for investment in a number of. different industries at the same time, he argued that low income stemmed mainly from a deficiency of capital, which in turn resulted from a lack of saving. Moreover, any inducement to invest was circumscribed by the smallness of the market and this was kept in bounds by a low level of productivity. Thus, one vicious circle was superimposed on another. Individual investment cannot establish conditions for a breakthrough, said Nurske, since what is required are huge jumps in the rate of output, which can be attained only by synchronized investment over a wide range of different industries. These can support each other ". . . in the sense that the people engaged in each project, now working with more real capital per head and with greater efficiency in terms of output per man-hour, will provide an enlarged market for the products of the new enterprises in other industries." [226] Such a theory opposed policies of gradualism in economic development, especially for nations caught in a trap of "low-level equilibrium." [227] The discontinuities in the process of growth demand at the very least a "big push" to overcome centuries of inbred inertia. A massive effort, it was said, would give rise to "external economies," from which the entire economy gained. Thus, the necessary social overhead as well as the complementary industries could be provided without which long-range growth for most firms would be impossible.[228]

Underlying these notions was the belief that some minimum effort or "take-off" was required for sustained growth and expansion, a thesis implicit in W. W. Rostow's, *The Stages of Economic Growth*.[229] Rostow posited three conditions for the take-off: (1) a rise in investment to more than 10 per cent of national income; (2) a rapid development of one or more manufacturing sectors; and (3) the emergence of a political, social, and institutional framework which would permit the exploitation of impulses to growth.[230] These are, of course, quite complex arrangements, but once achieved, Rostow said, societies could reach economic maturity within sixty years. However, so mechanistic was the formulation of this process that Rostow seemed to be saying that all economies, regardless of their political character, would wind up at the same place. Hence, the intense pressures of totalitarian methods were unnecessary. But whether the underdeveloped areas can reach maturity in such a space of time and yet escape the human costs of early capitalist development or the terrors of totalitarian methods is at best moot.[231]

The problem of the minimum effort was more carefully explored by Harvey Leibenstein, particularly in his excellent treatise, *Economic Backwardness and Economic Growth*.[232] A backward economy, said Leibenstein, exhibits either equilibrium or quasi-equilibrium features. Utilizing per capita output as a measure, various states of low-level equilibrium were suggested.[233] Some of these low-level economies might even display growth in such variables as capital and labor, yet the interaction between these variables and others in the system might be such as to keep per capita income close to the subsistence level. That is, there could be depressants present which were too powerful for ordinary investment efforts to overcome. Per capita income might be kept at low-level equilibrium, even though some of the variables manifested no such tendencies.[234] An economy of growth would not be in equilibrium. It would demonstrate continual increases in capital, population, labor, technology, and per capita output. The backward areas, on the other hand, revealed conditions of "quasi-stable subsistence equilibrium," for, without some big push, some critical minimum effort, they tended almost always to relapse into a subsistence state despite all hopes to the contrary. Thus, small efforts usually meant equilibrium, while large ones generated disequilibrium and growth. This implied that in most underdeveloped nations there was some critical level of per capita income and growth above which disequilibrium provided the necessary surge for expansion and development. In the absence of this critical minimum effort, the income-depressing forces would dissipate whatever investment was undertaken.

The minimum effort required an environment in which certain forces, described by Leibenstein as "growth agents," would expand at rates sufficiently large to counteract income-depressing factors. Such growth agents included entrepreneurship, innovations, the supply of skills and knowledge, savings, and the like.[235] A significant question on which Leibenstein was able to cast much light was the attitude of entrepreneurs in a low-level economy. It was not that this factor was lacking in underdeveloped areas, but rather that the attitudes they manifest and the incentives available inclined them to undertake activities which were not income creating for the community. Purely commercial activities or land holdings were profitable for individuals, but did not necessarily mean economic growth. In other words, these were "zero-sum" endeavors.[236] Positive-sum activities, on the other hand, were those that contributed to growth, and the environment had to be such as would allow the anticipation of profits to be fulfilled. On balance then, the inhibiting forces of zero-sum entrepreneurial activity, resistance to change and new ideas, nonproductive consumption, and relatively excessive population growth could be counterbalanced by adequate incentives for growth stemming from previously successful ventures, a continuous expansion of per capita income, strengthening of the appropriate growth factors, increased comprehension of the general situation to overcome traditional mind sets, and increased mobility and specialization of work.

The implications of "balanced growth" in these theories has been harshly challenged on several occasions, most notably by Albert O. Hirschman, professor at Yale and formerly economic advisor to the Republic of Colombia. In his *The Strategy of Economic Development*,[237] he has argued that these notions essentially combine a defeatest attitude toward what the underdeveloped nations can do with unrealistic expectations of their creative abilities.[238] There is sufficient evidence at hand, argued Hirschman, to demonstrate that an underdeveloped economy can be penetrated in piecemeal fashion. There is no need to assume that growth can be attained only by massive investment on all fronts at once, or that all the abilities and skills found in industrialized nations must be displayed in full panoply by backward economies as well. Simultaneous multiple development, with its innate pessimism and ultimate dependence on governmental intervention, is unnecessary, said Hirschman, if it is recognized that uneven development, but development nevertheless, is possible in different sectors of an economy and that this can generate native investment activity. The fact is that every area does have a previous history of growth which may have culminated in certain useful investment activities. And, while no balance from the overall view may exist, these projects do provide a good starting point. That is, imbalances may provide precisely the sort of impetus necessary for speedy development.[239] This stems from such factors as complementarity and the need to fill the gaps in earlier economic experience. Actually, an economy never really does complete its requirement for complementary activities: recognition of this as a process provided Hirschman with his theory of deliberate imbalance and his *strategy* of economic development. This implied that certain sectors should be selected for a "big push," so that growth can be transmitted from leading industries to followers, from one firm to another.[240] The implications were clear: a strategical selection of growth points could minimize the need for government intervention and excessive investment in social overhead.

The objective of selecting a proper strategy of growth was to encourage the decision-making process itself. Beyond that, projects should be chosen that would stimulate investment both "fore and aft," that is, those investments with ties to subsequent as well as earlier stages of production would be bound to be most fruitful. How to discover the largest number of linkages of this kind would require empirical input-output studies, noted Hirschman.[241] A further characteristic of the linkage idea was its revelation that the underdeveloped areas were weakest in this sort of interdependence. Thus, agriculture has no backward linkage effects, while the forward linkages are tenuous and weak. Similarly, enterprises dominated by foreign nations, "enclaves" in Hirschman's terminology, have links which slip out of the country with little impact on internal development. Imports, on the other hand, do exhibit useful internal effects, so that assistance to industries that would replace imports can be justified. In short, the economy can be supplied with the proper thrust by developing, as it were, a comparative advantage in imported goods.[242]

While Hirschman had no objection to rapid expansion when necessary, a theory such as he propounded, did question, in the main, whether people would take easily to a régimen of rapid accumulation and growth. While growth would be quickly visible if investment went into drainage and irrigation, thus increasing agricultural output, there would be less to show in the early years should investment go into schools and "social overhead." For this reason, resistance might easily arise unless there was a dictatorial political régime to impose forcibly such policies. Yet some writers have argued that rapid development might shock the underdeveloped countries into a sustained rate of growth—that these nations would overleap the boundaries of tradition and thus uproot their static habits. Disease, poor diet, lack of sanitation, and inadequate housing—all require large capital outlays as a remedy, so large in fact that they frequently demand state intervention. Proponents of this view, who find voice mainly in United Nations publications, express distrust for such notions as consumer sovereignty and have no faith in the viability of the free price system. Abjuring the ruthlessness of Soviet techniques, they nevertheless have felt that the "big jump" into modern industrialism can be made, provided the richer nations will help, thus avoiding the totalitarian approach. And, as Gunnar Myrdal has pointed out in his *An International Economy,* there is a strong emotional drive in the underdeveloped nations which has sharply reinforced this urge for rapid economic growth.[243]

The alternative is for a more gradual approach, one that would allow new ways to be absorbed into society without tumult and upset. It is argued that unless there is a strong domestic base, stagnation will be apt to set in again as soon as foreign aid ceases. The fundamental nature of a society cannot be altered from without, say the gradualists, but must itself respond to internal needs. It does little good, for example, to institute improved health measures without also providing for the kind of economy that can sustain the inevitable increase in population. Events in Egypt in recent decades have illustrated the problem. There, a sharply declining death rate merely has increased the pressure on arable land, already limited, and exacerbated poverty-stricken conditions. A more lasting solution, therefore, say the gradualists, is the slow but persistent accumulation of capital which will move underdeveloped societies in the direction of permanent change. Ragnar Nurske, for example, stressed the view that growth in the last analysis must stem from domestic savings.[244] While foreign investment, may be helpful, he said, the basic force must be the sweat and effort of the people themselves.

A gradualist approach does allow for the introduction of cultural and sociological elements into one's model in a genuinely effective manner. Unfortunately, most efforts in this direction have been somewhat piecemeal.[245] The most incisive analysis of these crucial elements has been made by Bert F. Hoselitz (1913-   ), whose work at the Research Center in Economic Development and Cultural Change at the University of Chicago has contributed much to an understanding of the issues involved.[246] Of course, the effort to develop a general theory of cultural and economic change was beset with many pitfalls. Yet it is important that any analysis of economic movement take account of the way in which social relationships are altered.[247] To accomplish his task, Hoselitz made effective use of Talcott Parsons' "pattern variables" in which economic action could be related to general behavioral typologies.[248] Thus, a social system might place greater value on custom or kinship relations than on individual achievement, and status might be powerful enough to prevent mobility of labor and the development of specialization, thus impeding the possibility of higher levels of productivity. True, primitive societies do have specialized tasks assigned to particular individuals, but invariably these are intended to sustain traditional behavior patterns.[249] These elements explain why programs for development in some instances have failed, for account has been omitted precisely of those cultural norms which manifest an income-depressing tendency. Economic change must necessarily be associated, Hoselitz has insisted, with the transformation of forms of social behavior as well as increases in per capita income. Development must shift behavior from status to achievement; from ritual exchange to a bargaining mechanism based on economic values; from a caste structure to genuine mobility; from undifferentiated economic roles to division of labor.

How were these changes to be accomplished? Here Hoselitz applied his theory of social deviance, a notion related to Schumpeter's theory of innovation.[250] The early entrepreneurs and financiers were seen as social deviants whose behavior had contributed in no small measure to the break up of the rigidly structured feudal society. They had become vehicles of growth, accumulating capital and effecting innovation through a complex of factors comprising personality conflicts, cultural attitudes, technological possibilities, and the use of available resources. The entrepreneur's major service had been to mobilize savings and apply the resulting financial capital to the problem of increasing productivity.[251] In colonial America, for example, entrepreneurs had discovered an extraordinarily low man-land ratio and an unbelievable opportunity for increasing returns on their investment. As a result, a premium had been placed on devices that would save man-hours. In addition, the relative absence of old world rigidities had favored entrepreneurial activity and in time the adventurous businessman was no longer viewed as quite the social deviant that aristocratic values had made him out to be. And, as the entrepreneur became a common phenomenon, he lent leadership to the new communities on this side of the ocean. In many small towns in the eighteenth and early nineteenth centuries, as William Cochran has noted, the general store became the focus of business and social life and the owner a figure of community power. Capital accumulation kept pace with business expansion, banks became permanent parts of the economic landscape, government helped out with patent laws, rights of way, and land grants, and American culture became an entrepreneurial culture. Of course, there had been many miscalculations and failures, many entries and exits: managerial skill ". . . was learned at the expense of empty-handed creditors."

But in the twentieth century, the functions of the entrepreneur have been bureaucratized. The entrepreneur has been made obsolescent through the rise of the professional executive, the growing importance of the financier, and the clamping down of government regulation. Even his area of operation has been restricted: highways, bridges, and power facilities are now the special province of government investment, and, with the coming of the garrison economy, the private entrepreneur's scope is even more limited. Thus the entrepreneur has successfully worked himself out of a job: his role in capital formation and economic growth is now a dubious one. There are serious implications in this analysis, for it leads to the startling thought that even "growth" itself has become bureaucratized. And, in fact, those who point to the fantastic abilities of modern corporations to finance investment out of their own resources would doubtlessly lend support to this view. Progress is no longer an adventure, but a calculated, carefully weighed proposition packaged in the corporate conference room.

Under these conditions, economic growth is a precarious affair. The savings and investment process may break down for any number of reasons, among which are a shift in the technological substructure of industry, an increase in the number of monopolistic situations, or a rise in productivity without any commensurate change in investment. The problem may be intensified when there is a lack of sufficient capital, as is illustrated by the comparison of the growth experience of the United States and other nations. Among the latter, low income and low productivity stem from an inadequacy in both the amount and the utilization of capital. The suggestion that they should acquire more equipment merely underscores the dilemma in which they find themselves, for the accumulation of capital presumes a sufficiency of income and a high enough level of productivity to provide the wherewithal.

In the meantime, the advanced nations, which form a small part of the world's peoples, not only keep getting richer, but have a common expectation that in the future they will be able to provide more economic opportunity for their citizens and even higher consumption standards. They anticipate all this despite the fact that international relations have been beset in the last forty years by numerous calamities which should have impeded the course of economic growth. But these frequent crises and wars merely have intensified the concern with the state of *national* economies, while at the same time international economic relations, so essential to the well-being of the less fortunate nations, have continued to deteriorate. As Gunnar Myrdal has argued, growth is a matter of concern for all nations, not only the West.[252] But, unfortunately, the retreat to economic nationalism and the ensuing damage to international growth has continued unabated. Myrdal saw evidence of this in the drastic decline in the movements of capital and labor: virtually all nations sealed their borders against intruders from other labor markets, while the flow of international capital, which could help stimulate growth in Latin America or Southern Asia, practically ceased except for the re-investment of profits or some new investment in colonial areas whose economy could be controlled from metropolitan centers. With attention focused only on internal economies, import barriers in most countries arose. Together with currency and payment restrictions, these practices progressed from being mere symptoms of economic dislocation to becoming root causes.

The problem of economic growth was sharpened when the disparities in capital resources, labor productivity and skills, and, consequently, living standards between the advanced and underdeveloped nations were exhibited to full view. The latter, determined to do away with their "have not" status, are breaking away from old traditions. That this sometimes assumes the form of violent nationalism or a flirtation with communism is not unexpected. Drives for economic growth often are converted into ambitious political programs for the adoption of modern industrial techniques. But while the underdeveloped nations do want to skip the stage of capital accumulation, they lack at the same time the international capital market which eased the rigours of growth in the West. The idea of economic growth and the high standard of living it brought in its wake—based on decades of capital accumulation—has gone forth from the Western countries to the underdeveloped nations who now have the advice, but not the capital.

Myrdal argued that the underdeveloped areas need a deliberate population policy which will help reduce pressure on resources. He has insisted that governments will have to play a more significant role than they did when the Western economies were in their growing stages. Certain reforms will have to be instituted. But the basic approach is a program of self-help intended to stimulate savings at high levels and to do all this when consumption levels are low, with little or no capital imports and widely fluctuating prices for export commodities. The underdeveloped nations will have to search for a greater diversity of products in their output, while all available foreign exchange is used to acquire producers goods. But Myrdal was not sanguine about prospects; ". . . short of a number of near miracles," said he, "few underdeveloped countries will succeed in attaining their essential goals." Yet, only when these underprivileged nations, with their vast numbers of humans of different colors, religions, and cultures, have attained equality of opportunity will the full potentials of economic growth be reached. This, Myrdal's basic concept, is one that we can ill afford to shunt aside. The problem is not merely economic or political—it is essentially a moral question. For, asked Myrdal, can the Western nations, whose prospect for continued growth remains undiminished, continue to look inwardly and build only a nationalistic parochial paradise while multitudes in Asia, Africa, and Latin America strive for just a little more sustenance? Moreover, can we afford to let them follow willy-nilly the totalitarian way to industrialization?

Clearly, this was a frame of mind that took planning for granted. As Myrdal demonstrated in his *Beyond the Welfare State*,[253] planning exists in a way that most conservative writers refuse to acknowledge, despite the fact that the interests for which they frequently speak have not been known especially for an altruistic rejection of tariffs, land grants, or other government subsidies. In fact, national economies more and more have been regulated and literally planned to an extent quite unthinkable a hundred years ago. Consequently, the whole heated discussion on planning has had an element of fantasy about it, for the fact is that government activity now is crucial for a viable economy and will continue to be so. Once again Myrdal has touched a raw nerve in American life: the split between creed and deed is as marked in economics as in race relations.

Paradoxically, planning has been unplanned. It emerged gradually under the pressures of objective needs. The pure market economy conceived of man —or rather labor power—as a commodity, yet was unable to separate man from his ability to work. The dreadful conditions that this dilemma engendered during the Industrial Revolution were fully documented by Engels, Marx, Toynbee, and the Hammonds. Yet the evil brought its own cure in the beginnings of state intervention. True, all this was at first *ad hoc,* limited to the protection of women in factories; but the idea of state intervention to meet needs that private industry ignored was bound to spread. Wars and depressions accelerated the process; the gold standard, that myth of pristine automatism, was discarded; and businessmen, oppressed by an evergrowing burden of overhead and fixed investment, learned that they could not entrust the fate of their enterprises to the vagaries of a free market. Control and planning at enterprise, industry, and national levels, became the dominant mode of answering economic questions.

The most striking aspect of this development, said Myrdal, has been the change in people's outlook. Old norms are losing their hold, and more and more there is a desire to apply rational methods to recurrent problems. No longer do we hesitate to make private contract subordinate to public requirement, and we have adopted bargaining between groups as the organizing principle for social action. New personality types have been thrown up by changing economic forces. A whole psychology has been altered: the significant point, said Myrdal, is that this is a nonreversible process.

What has been happening, then, is a thrust toward a welfare state through "cumulative causation," a secular increase in state intervention occasioned by international crisis, increasing rationality, broader political participation, and the growth of large-scale organization in all sectors of political and economic activity. Adopting a wide historical perspective (America "is still so young"), Myrdal is hopeful that we shall move from ordinary intervention centered in narrow interests to meaningful planning. The usual techniques and objectives are all there: fiscal devices, maximizing opportunities, better education, progressive taxation, and full employment, all culminating in a "created harmony."

Drawing upon his experience with the Swedish welfare state, Myrdal has insisted that this is what people want. They feel freer, not less free, in such an environment. A high degree of civic education and responsibility, with participation reaching deep into the political "infrastructure," has enabled the Swedes to meet their problems head-on. We here have been all too ready to discover deficiencies in this evolving society, but there are a good many more virtues in it, we are told, than can be found in our own political economy. And once the new rules of a "welfare culture" have been established, decentralization through a balanced growth of interest groups within the infrastructure can mean an actual decline of state intervention.

All this, Myrdal has admitted, is a Utopia. And, like all painters of Utopia, he has deliberately drawn the picture with broad, hopeful strokes so as to highlight its genuine possibilities. We still are plagued by bureaucracy, a proliferation of legalistic rules, and separatist tensions. Nowhere is this more evident than in the United States, where state intervention is rising only because the kind of inchoate planning we have has not yet caught up with "the need for coordination and simplification." Perhaps the major drawback in the kind of planning now going on is that it has intensified rather than lessened the parochial, nationalist sentiment which plagues all countries, large and small.

Myrdal has argued that planning as it is practiced today has served to widen the economic gap between the West and the "underdeveloped" nations. International economic disintegration has not been halted despite the heroic efforts after World War II; and, with the collapse of colonialism and the coming of the Cold War, there seems little likelihood that the Asian and African nations will soon catch up. In Myrdal's terms, global planning means a world without boundaries and without the kind of discrimination that sets off one nation from the next. Unwilling to admit that the cause of internationalism is hopeless, he has urged that the only real prospect for man is to internationalize those very measures for integration which are pursued in building a national welfare state. There is no alternative except to build the Welfare World.

Is this possible? Myrdal says yes, despite the sorry start made in the United Nations and its satellite agencies.[254] As he has observed with no little acerbity, the International Trade Organization was stillborn, the Economic and Social Council has mirrored the debating propensities of the General Assembly, the FAO draws blueprints which remain on paper, and the ILO was outmoded forty years ago. Yet he feels that these sad failures do represent stumbling beginnings toward a genuine international community. Myrdal's optimism has been boundless. His views have been a rather heady draught for those afflicted with a dyspeptic view of world affairs. Yet, so long as one harbors the slightest hope of a genuine international community, his arguments necessarily do bear a strong measure of validity.

vi

The Ultimate in Technique:
Game Theory and Linear
Programming

Although much of traditional theory sought to highlight the notion of economic harmony, the presence of conflict as observed by Ricardo, Marx, Joan Robinson, and others could not be suppressed entirely. Conflict, as a vehicle of change and even progress, was a theme that pervaded a good deal of social thinking in the past.[255] True, many theorists, in their concern with the subtleties of price and capital, simply ignored economic and social conflict. This was much too broad a question and was perhaps the proper province of the sociologist: interest in economics was to be focused on much narrower issues. Yet, a good deal of the foregoing discussions of innovation, oligopoly, and economic growth did treat ultimately of conflict and opposing interests. The problem, particularly in such matters as price determination or investment, could not be evaded. Decisions in the latter area especially had to be based on more than what one thought the size of an asset should be, for often the hard facts of economic conflict intruded.[256]

Contemporary theorists have been concerned, if not with harmony in the nineteenth-century sense, at least with adjustment and the attainment of equilibrium. The central assumption has been the universal character of economic forms, and theory in many ways has sought to delineate their modes of efficient operation. Yet, the existence of conflict and tension was undeniable and it was bound to turn up in the writings of some of the more perceptive social scientists. In fact, it was possible to assert, as did Georg Simmel, the noted nineteenth-century philosopher and sociologist, that conflict was a form of socialization.[257] In economics, one could trace the seeds of a theory of conflict, in part at least, to Daniel Bernoulli's work on probability in gambling. Bernoulli, member of a famous eighteenth-century Swiss family of mathematicians and scientists, had studied the so-called St. Petersburg paradox in order to elucidate some rules for guiding payments for a play in a game. Bernoulli's solution rested not on the absolute sums involved, but on their relative worth to the participants, a notion that later was to shore up the utility concept in game theory.[258]

These ideas, however, remained forgotten and, in fact, most economists made not the slightest use of them. The development of a viable theory of conflict, amenable perhaps to numerical treatment, lagged far behind other branches of economics. First rumbles were heard in 1928 when John von Neumann (1903-1956), a young mathematician, presented a striking paper on the theory of games before the Mathematics Society at Göttingen. Not much more was forthcoming until 1944 when Neumann, in collaboration with Princeton economist, Oskar Morgenstern (1902-   ), published the now famous *Theory of Games and Economic Behavior*.[259] Some of the concepts of game theory had been suggested in the early 1920's by Émile Borel, a French mathematician, but certain critical points, such as the minimax solution, had escaped him.[260] Neumann, who was born in Budapest, studied at the University of Berlin and the Institute of Technology in Zurich. After obtaining his doctorate at Budapest in 1926, he taught in Germany for four years. In 1930, he came to Princeton, where he later began to work with Morgenstern on game theory. It is said that Neumann got the idea for his theory by watching a poker game and that the whole structure was built around the poker tables at Princeton. Neumann was a scientist of many parts: in addition to his mathematical contributions, he did basic work in quantum theory on which many existing concepts of nuclear energy rest and was one of the major participants in the development of the high speed computer. A member of the Atomic Energy Commission, he was the recipient of several scientific awards. His untimely death at the age of fifty-three was a great loss to both the natural and social sciences. Oskar Morgenstern, a native of Germany, first visited the United States in 1925 and then returned thirteen years later to begin his career at Princeton. In an early work, *The Limits of Economics,* he sought to explore the proper role of theory in relation to policy, taking the position that economic analysis must be free of ideology.[261] His later *On the Accuracy of Economic Observations* [262] was a brilliant critique of certain types of statistics used in economic discourse.

The Neumann-Morgenstern book on game theory raised high hopes among economists, for it now seemed possible to find answers to all the problems created by monopoly, economic coalitions, and other deviations from the orthodox doctrine of free markets, questions that received theory had failed to treat in a satisfactory way. The new approach was thoroughly mathematical. Of course, mathematics had been no stranger to economics, but, up to this point, major reliance had been placed on the infinitesimal calculus. More and more it appeared questionable whether the calculus could be employed to say anything really meaningful about economic behavior. And the use of simultaneous equations to provide equilibrium statements to describe an economy that was never in equilibrium seemed a quite dubious procedure. Moreover, the existing tools were ill-suited to the exploration of the problems stemming from a contest between countervailing groups in society.

Game theory ventured into a relatively new realm of mathematics in order to illuminate economic problems and to fuse both theory and reality. It was a kind of mathematics seldom seen in economics, with concepts drawn from set theory, group theory, and mathematical logic. Yet all of it was essential to formulate the theory rigorously. The objective was to specify a theory of games of strategy in which opposing or similar interests, the availability of information, and the presence of rational choice or perhaps chance determined the course of action to be pursued. The parallel with economic and sociological problems seemed obvious. These were the questions that confronted people in both games and economics. And, in contrast to Robinson Crusoe theory, it seemed that the game was the only suitable vehicle for developing a theory for a social economy. This rather novel approach appeared as useful in political science and military affairs as it did in economics: in fact, it has been in those areas that game theory has had its most fruitful application.[263]

Despite the high-powered mathematics, it was possible for a nonmathematical reader to ". . . absorb the motivation, the reasoning and conclusions of the theory." [264] The book was hailed by many mathematicians and not a few social scientists as truly path-breaking. Jacob Marschak wrote: "Ten more such books and the progress of economics is assured." [265] G. T. Guilbaud, a French economist called it a monumental achievement,[266] and Leonid Hurwicz remarked that the theory's ". . . potentialities seem tremendous . . . and may lead to enriching in realism a good deal of economic theory." [267] One of the areas that benefited was statistical decision theory, particularly through the work of A. Wald. And, as the literature grew rapidly with studies in mathematics and economics comprising an ever expanding list of books and papers,[268] it seemed that all the basic problems would now be solved. But this has not been the case: most game theory investigations have been highly theoretical with but few empirical applications. But the hope does remain that the future will fill the gap. This by no means denigrates Neumann and Morgenstern's achievement: their model, while abstract, is in many ways clearer than those which followed, and, while much additional work on game theory has been done, it has been patterned in most instances on their fundamental study, with virtually all of their concepts employed as the core of the newer versions.

In essence, game theory attempted a mathematically exact description of certain unsettled questions of economic behavior. The basic assumptions were those of an individual who sought to maximize gains and minimize losses, just as he might in playing chess or poker. But something other than ordinary maximization was involved, for without this new element the theory would not have differed very much from the older hedonic approach. In game theory, the individual existed in a "social" economy: he was no Robinson Crusoe. Basically, transactions in the newer theory depended not only on what one wanted to do but on what others sought to accomplish as well. As Neumann and Morgenstern put it, each participant in a game sought to maximize a function of which he did not control all the variables. This was not the maximizing problem of earlier theory, but a mixture of several maximum problems in which the guiding principles, or strategies, of the individuals varied from one to the other.

The theory asserted that the outcome of a game, or its "payoff," could be specified. Thus the different but nevertheless consistent preferences of the participants became crucial. This suggested that the players were intelligent and rational: of course, a stupid play might be made, but this would not advance the theory in any sensible way. The rationality assumption was essential, though neither such behavior nor the knowledge of probabilities required for some aspects of the theory were likely to be found in real life. With the introduction of some measure of uncertainty, the consistency of preferences was used to set forth a utility function.[269] While this was not quite the same utility that was found in older theory, it still persisted as a psychological measure of satisfaction. The cardinality involved, it was argued, had little in common with the absolute concept of the classicists. It was more like the ordinalist's marginal rates of substitution, since it dealt with reactions to increments of probabilities. There was no measurement of the intensity of wants, for the purpose of game utility was to enable one to determine which of several strategies might be chosen. Once the minimum or maximum nature of preferences were known, applying probabilities to them permitted the calculation of the choice. Game utility thus was derived in part from the concept of expected wins in situations of risk involvement. In the case of the latter, probabilities were to be determined and a decision to act reformulated in such terms.

Game theory, then, assumed that satisfaction did exist and that it was possible to apply measurement to it. But with the utility function defined as the mathematical relation between the objective gain or payoff and satisfaction, it appeared nevertheless that economic theory was back at the old cardinal stand. If utilities were not comparable, as most economists agreed, game theory was in trouble right at the start, for in its basic form, the two-person zero-sum game, the fundamental postulate was that losses washed out gains.[270] However, if one were to be concerned only with the ratios of the difference in pairs of utilities derived from some ordering process, one could arrive at a scale of intervals, as in the measurement of temperature.[271] The starting point and the size of the unit did not matter. Fahrenheit and Centigrade scales are quite different, yet both do the job of "measuring" degrees of heat. The important point is that the ratio of the difference between them is invariant, so that by applying a linear transformation they can be compared. Similarily with utilities, for so long as the utilities of the players were defined as proportional to the payoffs involved, there was no problem. Utility functions could be established, provided the ordering of preferences was consistent; the notion of expected values under uncertainty became a useful concept for game theory.[272] Utility stemmed from preference and was not related to the payoff in any objective manner. The debate over this notion has been extensive, but game theorists generally have found it acceptable despite the implication of transitivity, or ordered successive preferences which in reality might not exist.[273]

Neumann and Morgenstern started with a one-person game which could be viewed as an analogue for a rigidly created communist society in which the pattern of distribution could not be disputed. Here, the interests of society were presumed identical with the interests of its individual members. The pattern of distribution therefore was invariable. The two-person game, however, was much more interesting: it became the basis for all subsequent developments not only in game theory but in such areas as statistical decision functions and linear programming. And, as Luce and Raiffa have observed, it served to attract mathematicians to the study of economic and social problems.[274] The theory came up with its own careful definitions of game elements: thus, moves were a player's decision from a set of possibilities; the choice, the possibility actually selected; the play, a sequence of choices; and a game tree, a connected chart showing all the plays. The rules of the game specified the tree itself, with its partitioned sets indicating which player took what moves. The rules also indicated the probabilities in such chance moves as existed and the outcome for the plays and the game itself. At each end point there was a payoff function derived from the utility concept. This was the extensive form of the game, in which full knowledge of the rules and payoff functions were known to all the players.

In a normal game each player would seek to maximize his payoff, but the outcome depended not only on his choice but on his opponent's as well, and this, in turn, depended on what he thought the first player would do. Thus the players had opposing interests. The game was labelled "zero-sum," since what one gained the other lost: the game merely resulted in a redistribution of total values. All information was made available when the game was specified in a matrix form. Assuming that the first player knew his opponent's strategy, or which row of the matrix he would choose, he then could select that column of the matrix which would bring the highest return of the row. The second player, in anticipation of such thinking, might select quite a different row, one that would draw him to the least highest point. On the other hand, if the first player suspected that his strategy was known, he would advisedly choose the column whose lowest payoff was as high as he could possibly make it. In substance, the first player would be seeking the highest minimum payoff—the maximin—and the second would search for the lowest maximum—the minimax. Obviously, this was the ultimate in cautious, conservative play, for recklessness could incur a good deal of damage. When both strategies coincided, that is, when both the maximin and the minimax were found in the same cell or element of the matrix, a "saddle point" or equilibrium had been achieved. This was really a form of defensive play rather than aggressive action.[275] But it was the kind of game in which the elements of pure strategy were revealed. In fact, the complete strategies could be given to a referee before the start of the game, describing what would be done in all conceivable situations, and the referee then could announce the winner. That is, a pure strategy prescribed what was to be done over the entire course of the game.

The element of chance, of course, was lacking in pure strategy. With chance, the outcome no longer depended solely on the choice of a strategy, and the whole theory became somewhat shaky. But if the matrix was based upon anticipated payoffs, probabilities could be utilized, with strategies employing the principle of randomization. The mixture of strategies in effect withheld information and heightened the security aspects of the game.[276] Moreover, a correctly mixed strategy could manifest all the properties of the minimax-maximin theorem. If both players randomized their strategies, the lowest long-run expected payoffs could be maximized. This was now a unified theory, at least for the two-person zero-sum game, and its value could be defined as the final agreed-upon utility.[277]

Game theory then went on to analyse noncooperative, nonzero sum games as well as coalition and cooperation. The former was illustrated by the Prisoners' Dilemma in which two prisoners who are kept apart try to decide whether or not to confess.[278] But what was true for zero-sum games no longer held, since an apparently good payoff might not be acceptable to one of the players. The pattern of strategical plays would be revealed by repeated tries over time. Should one player seek a quick gain, he could be subjected to harassment by the other. Of course, some pre-game discussion by the participants was admissible, but one then entered the realm of cooperative games. This was the sort of game that began to approach the character of an economic situation, as in labor relations or oligopoly. Yet game theory has not been completely successful in attacking these problems, despite the heroic efforts of such writers as Martin Shubik.[279] But at least the point has been emphasized, one that has not always been obvious to economists, that maximization is not necessarily the essence of economic existence. Lacking control of all the variables that affect a payoff, players may be satisfied with more modest results. This certainly is in sharp contrast to traditional theory in which it has been assumed that economic units exercise complete control over all the factors influencing transactions. Once this assumption was dropped, it was discovered that reality was not at all as simple as theory had made it.

In the cooperative game, for example, side payments could be made by one participant to another simply as part of the strategy. (One thinks of the recent price-fixing adventure in the electrical equipment industry as a case in point.) In these situations, pre-play communication, binding agreements, and known utility functions were made part of the rules. Consequently, coalitions were made and unmade as economic units jockeyed about for an optimum position. In Shubik's analysis there was the virtue, even if it did not always depart from traditional modes, of drawing in such variables as a firm's asset structure, the need to either protect or extend it, ease of entry into an industry, and the availability of information. In oligopoly or bilateral monopoly, it was possible to demonstrate through game theory analysis, that price might vary more sharply than in traditional doctrine because of such things as discounts and premiums.[280] Negotiation consequently became an integral element of the theory, involving all facets of bargaining. The question was the attainment of a "game theoretic" solution, regardless of any issues of justice. (This has been the common goal of most arbitrators and conciliators.) [281] Thus, one of the great achievements of game theory has been an approach to a precise analysis of the conditions of coalition creation—indeed an important contribution to economic and social theory. Whereas traditional analysis merely had postulated economic coalitions without really investigating how they were formed, game theory tried to show in precise mathematical form how collaborative action took place, consequently approaching reality more clearly than the older formulations. As Neumann and Morgenstern demonstrated, the decisive exchanges in a market might not be among the many atomistic units, but rather between coalitions.[282] The role that trade unions, oligopolies, and political associations play in modern economic life underscores the significance of a theory which can describe the behavior of these groups.

Coalitions seemed possible even in a two-person game, provided the total gain for both was a variable quantity. In that case, both players could agree upon a joint strategy that would enhance the payoff. No coalition was possible, however, if the total gain was constant. In a game of three or more persons, coalitions were possible even with constant sums. This could become quite a complicated situation, since the participants could act either independently or as members of three possible two-person coalitions. But whatever the final outcome, it would reflect certain social and psychological standards, and, to the extent that this was the case, it indicated a degree of correspondence between the concepts of game theory and social organization.[283] It was this that underpinned the notion of stability in a game, for where there was more than one possible imputation, or distribution of the payoff, the "solution" was attained when no imputation was considered superior to any other, that is, when a set of imputations was reached the units of which did not dominate each other.[284] But these imputations would have to come from the set of socially acceptable patterns, for one which did not reflect desired standards would soon be put to one side. In this sense, the Neumann-Morgenstern analysis was a stable one.

Although considerable research has been undertaken since game theory was first offered as a useful approach to social and economic analysis, it is today by no means a completed structure. In addition to the two-person zero-sum game and the variety of solutions and models proposed for the three-or-more person games, there are the problems which stem from situations in which the rules are not fully specified and, of course, dynamic games.[285] The case of the incomplete rules, or games against "nature," involve even more uncertainty than those mentioned earlier, for here a strategy needs to be selected against an unknown opponent who has his own unknown strategy. In one sense, the problem is akin to that posed by Shackle's notion of potential surprise,[286] or to that faced by a farmer when he approaches the sowing season. Here the maximin strategy might be entirely inadequate, for, by examining possibilities other than those dictated by a conservative equilibrium, one could gain a good deal more. One would have to assign equal probabilities to "nature's" strategies and select the one whose payoff was highest. However, if "nature's" probabilities are known as a matter of experience, as is often the case, the selection of a strategy can be a matter of indifference.[287] Nevertheless, a good deal of work remains to be done.

While game theory has unquestionably enriched the corpus of economic concepts, it has not been without its critics. Some writers have expressed impatience with its essentially static framework, while others have argued that insufficient weight has been given to commitments which reflect interdependence and mutual accommodation.[288] Others have rejected the philosophy of extreme caution implied by the minimax theorem, arguing that the possibilities of great pains can induce a pattern of adjustment quite as rational as the behavior described by Neumann and Morgenstern.[289] However, the process of accommodation and commitment can be handled by setting forth new games. It seems that this sort of maneuvering can be readily absorbed into the theory.[290] And the criticism which asks why go for zero when something can be won, that is, why play at all, has been answered with the comment that many of us are unwilling players. Yet, it is true that game theory does need to account more effectively for the sort of communication which itself alters the condition of play: this is the dynamic problem. Perhaps the greatest weakness in game theory, from a technical standpoint, is its basic assumption that a utility scale can be constructed. This more than anything else has threatened the applicability of its logic to the analysis of human conflict. But even more significant has been the extreme formalism of the theory, tending to give it an aura of aridity. It has threatened to become mere mathematical dexterity and technique. Game theorists have not yet been able to place their analysis into a broader framework. As Lewis Coser has shown so well, conflict does perform certain social functions, such as providing a safety valve for tensions or even acting as a kind of binder in certain group situations. Structurally, conflict needs to be analysed in terms of existing relationships both within and between groups. Thus, an important proposition offered by Coser stresses the impact of conflict on the structure of a group and the internal reactions that are bound to follow.[291] Game theory, on the other hand, has been able thus far to discuss conflict only in terms of payoff without being able to say much about the underlying impulses that drive toward conflict, coalition formation, and maneuvering. Clearly, this is an area in which the economist, insofar as he is really interested, must seek interdisciplinary cooperation. Yet there is little doubt that game theory has been useful and that it will continue to be so: its development has been a challenge to all social scientists, and, if some situations are not fully amenable to its present mode of analysis, new techniques will have to be discovered, as its founders readily have conceded. But one wonders whether these will make any greater effort to employ institutional factors than is presently the case.

A remarkable illustration of the enthusiasm with which some economists have turned to technique is afforded by the rapid spread of linear, or more accurately, mathematical programming and its direct descendant, operations research. This may very well be a reflection of the frustration suffered as a result of the inability of ordinary theory to supply computational methods. Something simply had to be done, and, when it was discovered that certain practical problems could be solved by linear programming, its future in the profession was assured.[292] Curiously enough, most of those working in this highly specialized area have been engineers, mathematicians, and statisticians, with economists supplying only questions.[293] Certainly the problems posed have been important, concerned as they are with choice and alternatives in production, cost, transportation, and the like. But most economists have remained aloof and even skeptical about the advantages of programming techniques, while proponents of the newer methods have deplored their colleagues' lack of interest on the ground that the specific and concrete applications of theoretical concepts afforded by programming should command the attention of the nonmathematical theorist.[294] Even if the computations stemming from programming might be wide of the mark, its widespread use would affect the behavior of firms sufficiently to require close study.

Linear programming was mainly a postwar development. The techniques and tools it provided have seemed clearly enough to be of substantial usefulness to individual firms. But whether it has provided new insights into the theory of an economy is as yet moot. The specific formulation of the linear programming technique had its roots in G. B. Dantzig's work for the Air Force during the war, when the question arose on how to schedule related activities for a large organization concerned with such matters as stockpiling, production, and inventory maintenance, all subject to certain alternatives and limitations.[295] However, the roots of the problem have been traced back to the early 1930's when Hans Neisser and Heinrich von Stackelberg investigated certain properties of the Walrasian system. Similar questions were studied also by the Soviet mathematician, L. V. Kantorovich, whose 1939 article on production planning recently has been rediscovered.[296] Kantorovich sought to provide a method for selecting one of several possible ways to produce a good so that its output would be maximized—the classic linear programming problem. Further, the challenge that Mises and Hayek hurled at socialists of all kinds led their opponents to the idea that the price system, no matter how established, could act as a kind of parameter to make resource allocation a rational and feasible affair in a centralized economy. This too could be interpreted as a linear programming problem. Added to these were the developments in input-output analysis and game theory, both providing additional inspiration to the linear programmers.[297]

The formal solution required a mathematical technique that would enable the analyst to maximize a linear function of a set of variables subject to certain constraints. Most of the problems treated thus far have been linear, that is, proportionality was presumed to exist between inputs and outputs, a condition which the economist interprets as constant returns. More recently, attempts have been made to construct nonlinear models, but the emphasis on extracting numerical answers for practical purposes has stressed the linear solution.[298] Most striking, however, has been the omission of institutional elements. The technique became a completely abstract analysis of the requirements for the most efficient least cost allocation of resources at microeconomic levels. The procedures then could be deemed suitable for capitalist firms and socialist economies, in fact for any organization in which the decision-making process was centralized. Presumably, the institutional framework was to be added later.[299] Of course, the necessary computations could by no means be worked out with pencil and paper: electronic computers would have to do the work even for an individual firm, but at least the formal properties of programming were to be made available before enveloping the theory in institutional descriptions.

Linear programming was concerned essentially with the age-old economic problem—the allocation of limited resources in order to maximize a product or minimize its cost. It became a highly refined mathematical restatement of the maximizing-minimizing condition. The mathematical techniques involved were drawn from set theory and the theory of linear vector spaces.[300] While ordinary mathematical economics was based on systems of equations, linear programming utilized systems of inequalities. Of course, for economic purposes the numerical values had to be nonnegative. Moreover, linear programming dealt not with a production function such as is found in most textbooks but rather with a finite number of processes or "activities." Whereas the focus in the traditional approach was on the relation between flows of inputs and outputs,[301] the programmer broke production into concrete, detailed steps. Formulating the analysis in terms of the specific equipment, labor, and techniques available to the firm or plant, the "activity," defined as a specific method for doing a particular task, thus captured the center of the stage.[302] With linear constraints or limitations set forth, the available resources were not a limitless flow, but rather those factors which specified what the firm actually could accomplish. In fact, according to the programmer, it seemed that a production function in the traditional sense could not be formulated until the particular programming problem applicable to the firm was solved first.[303] That is, the domain of the variables was bounded: only compact convex sets could be considered. Linear programming, like marginal analysis, specified a goal in terms of the relation of inputs to outputs, but it sought to provide a computational basis for decision-making about goods and activities and assumed that these were finite, and, for analytical purposes, homogeneous as well.[304]

A favorite illustration found in the literature was the case of an automobile company attempting to establish the level of production it ought to set for automobile and truck assembly, given the capacity limits of its metal stamping and engine assembly departments. Other typical problems were the construction of a least cost diet containing a specified quantity of food elements (this was solved by George Stigler in 1945 without linear programming).[305] The blending of gasoline in a refinery was another linear programming problem. The shipment of a standardized product from several warehouses to different locations, or shipping newsprint from different mills to various customers posed questions that were amenable to the programming treatment; and, as an extension of these problems, even international trade and comparative advantage were analysed along linear lines.[306] It was evident that linear programming could be applied to specific industry matters. In the case of the simplified auto factory, for example, the question at hand was to work out that combination of auto and truck assembly, subject to departmental capacity restraints, which would maximize net revenue. The graphic solution was as follows: with the x-axis set for truck output and the y-axis for automobiles, perpendiculars to both axes indicated maximum output of each. Lines then were superimposed to indicate the capacities of the engine assembly and metal stamping departments showing the maximum possibilities in producing combinations of each product. An area of feasible production then was clearly defined, bounded by the line segments specified by the capacity restrictions. Mathematically, this was a convex set of non-negative values for the outputs,[307] that is, a set of points such that a line connecting any two points in the set was contained in the set. When isoprofit or net revenue lines were drawn, the maximum net gain would be shown by the point in the area of feasibility which coincided with the highest iso-profit line, a kind of indifference curve. The boundary of the convex set could be described as a production opportunity curve. It was not smooth, but rather a polygonal line with the important points located where it bent, at the vertices. Thus the profit-maximizing point was to be found at a corner of the feasibility set, at a vertex.[308] It may be seen that the constraints or limiting factors were central in this approach. Maximum revenue was not found at the usual tangent; in fact, tangency was unlikely since what was involved was the corner of a convex set where the price line or the indifference curve sloped more sharply than the slope of the feasibility boundary to the left of the crucial point and less than the boundary to the right of that point.

As indicated, the assumption of linearity was equivalent to the assumption of constant returns or a strict proportionality between inputs and outputs. The argument has been made that this has some empirical basis and that such an assumption at least offers a standard of measurement for the activity or process involved.[309] Another important linear programming axiom was that an optimal solution could be discovered if the number of inequalities with positive values did not exceed the number of constraints. That is, an optimal feasible program could be found if the number of activities or processes at nonzero levels equaled the number of restrictions. Further, the activities included in the program had to be such that no excluded activity was more profitable than any of the included ones. Suggesting the possibility of utilizing successive or iterative procedures, as in the simplex method worked up by Dantzig, these propositions had important implications for some of the solution methods that were devised.[310] A simplex is the n-dimensional analogue of a triangle: the method then consisted of an iterative investigation of the adjacent vertices of the simplex. The operation utilized continual revisions of the proposed feasible set of activities by making small changes in order to reach as few processes or activities as possible at positive levels. Each step required a recomputation, and the final point was reached when there were no more "justifiable" processes available.[311] The computation involved was quite formidable, and, as Dantzig remarked, would require large-scale computers.[312]

Associated with every maximizing problem in linear programming was the "dual" minimizing problem. Maximum production had to be done at minimum cost and this involved the imputation of values to the inputs employed. The "dual" problem in a sense set forth the amounts necessary to distribute values to the inputs. The maximizing variable, let us say profit, was subject, of course, to certain constraints, but there were also corresponding minimum cost variables, with the requirement that all values were to be distributed. Thus resource allocation in linear programming was one aspect of the pricing problem, and the solution of one was the solution of the other.[313] Technically, with the programming problem solved, the dual became merely a matter of linear equations. In Koopmans' words, each optimum activity had at least one system of prices compatible with the technology.[314] The "dual" indicated the ". . . imputed prices that minimize the total imputed value of the available primary commodities . . . under the restraint that no process in the technology shall be profitable." [315]

In essence, linear programming became a vindication of the theory of economic equilibrium under competitive conditions. Now, it is evident that it has been a useful tool for individual managements, as in the oil industry. But, insofar as general theory is concerned, programming, aside from a clarification of concepts, does not seem to have added anything new. One almost commits the fallacy of composition by leaping to the conclusion that programming techniques are analogues for the economy as a whole. The theorists appear to have forgotten institutional limitations, and as yet developments in nonlinear programming have not provided theorems that are operationally useful for the total economy. Theoretical conclusions for a *political* economy must be held in abeyance.

Illustrative of this lack is the application of linear programming to welfare economics.[316] This clearly was motivated by the central role of efficiency in both welfare theory and mathematical programming. Solutions in the latter provided points of efficiency, so that the competitive determination of prices for goods and input factors would in effect be the efficient ones.[317] This concept provided the connection between competitive theory and linear programming. Programming was merely a computational technique for discovering the relevant points of efficiency, an objective of the free market as well.[318] Moreover, it was argued, programming did not have to distinguish between individual firms, for under constant cost conditions for everyone, the problem was expressed for the entire economy. But like the older theory, this was an ideal statement and suffered similarly from the same limitations. Once dynamic elements and conditions of monopoly were introduced, other questions and doubts arose. Linear programming had to be well spiced with reservations. To take but one situation, activities that were influenced by diminishing returns were not handled satisfactorily at all. And increasing returns could virtually nullify a linear solution which recommended a process or activity less concentrated than was desirable.[319]

Upon close examination, there was little fundamentally startling about linear programming insofar as the substance of economic theory was concerned. Its theorems have supplied newer, more elegant "proofs" of standard theory, but, as Baumol remarked, the revolution has been more in methodology than in content.[320] Moreover, the primary emphasis has been placed on developing instructions to discover new solutions. Only when the whole economy is viewed as a firm, as in a socialist system, does linear programming offer important possibilities for achieving a social balance between production, technology, and prices. But the technique then would have to be advanced far beyond present developments in order to encompass the infinitely more complex conditions of a total society.[321]

Concluding Remarks

WHAT THEN is the image of man offered in all of these disparate theories of economics? Clearly, the simplistic notion of *homo oeconomicus* is no longer a useful conception. In today's complex civilization, man is neither as rational nor as mercenary as the classicists made him, nor is he the lightning calculator of Milton Friedman's billiard player. The ability to predict a particular course of action from an ideal pattern of behavior is severely limited because men are men and all too often will confound the most ingenious of mathematical formulas. Yet, even though the arena for action is stringently bounded, the search for "ideal types" in economics continues apace.

Thus recent theory has supplied us with minimax man, simulating man, potential surprise man, sequential decision-making man, satisficing man, and heroic man, as well as attempting from time to time to resuscitate self-centered, greedy economic man. Minimax man, whom we have already met, is a worrier, not overly aggressive, preferring the safe and sane way, very much like executives in the middling reaches of the corporate milieu.[1] Simulating man, completely undecided as to what to do, feeds information into a digital computer to help make up his mind.[2] The sequential decision-maker, equally uncertain, equally cautious, addresses himself to the unknown contingencies of nature and society with a slide rule in order to see whether he can continue the even tenor of his ways before making good on some colossal error. Potential-surprise man is willing to gamble on a single throw of the dice in the hope of making a fat killing. Satisficing man isn't interested in optimal behavior at all. Something of a second cousin to minimax man, he is content merely with satisfactory results.[3] Most challenging of all is Boulding's heroic man whose ethic is an expression of those noneconomic drives that give meaning to existence. Like Schumpeter's Innovator, he is both a destroyer of equilibrium and a creator of the kind of dynamic thrust which makes society embark on new adventures of the soul.[4]

None of these characterizations is real by itself, yet taken together they do say something about the nature of man. For, reflecting upon the complexity of his environment, man is all of these images, and more. In an ever changing, ever evolving society, neither firm nor household, neither capitalist nor worker are today what they were two decades ago. Man once may have been an adventurous innovator; today he is an institutionalized manager for whom a table of organization is a categorical imperative. Yet, in his anxiety to be as "scientific" as possible, the economist has evaded the fundamental principle of complexity. Converting economics into a discipline unto itself, its practitioners no longer remember that economics is a *social* science, that the economist must be a philosopher, psychologist, anthropologist, historian, geographer, and political scientist as well as a student of mathematics.[5]

Economics may be said to be but one way of looking at the total complex of social behavior. In this sense, it is a branch of a general theory of social systems.[6] Economics becomes a study of those processes which are specifically economic and of those forms of behavior which stem from them. Traditionally, attention has been focused upon the areas of production and distribution. But goods and services are not mere commodities and performances; they are significantly related to the human actors who control them or who in turn are controlled. Above all, the relationships which the actors establish between themselves are also economic.[7] Only in such an analytic framework can economists escape the overwhelming commodity fetishism which has enveloped them for almost a century. By taking account of what they now deem to be merely sociological phenomena, by including these as data, their models would contain the goals that people pursue as well as modes of adaptation to changing circumstance and urges toward homeostasis. It is reasonable to suggest that these models then would provide more malleable behavior equations. Utility surfaces and welfare propositions would not be based upon assumptions of isolated preferences, for it would be recognized that analytic concepts are rooted in social experiences. Nor would there be any warrant for asserting the validity and independence of the individual want of an individual consuming unit—an abstraction as bloodless as Boulding's bloodless firm.

The assertion that such strictures as applied to contemporary economic thought indicate a misapprehension of the purpose of model building itself betrays an abdication of the role of economist *qua* social scientist. A purchase and sale is not only a movement of goods and money in opposing directions, but also a measure of interpersonal relationships which, in the case of such factors as labor, may even involve class and group interests. In recent years, economists have refused to discuss the *economic* theory of these relationships, turning the job over to sociologists, social psychologists, and labor relations experts. The result is that as "generalists" they have had little to say on matters which are really important.[8] All this is a repeat performance of what went on in the field of demography, which the economist handed over to the statistician and sociologist. Yet the rare economist who did pay attention to population studies, such as Joseph J. Spengler, made significant contributions. Economists, I would hope, do have something to say about urgent social questions. They possess a subject matter not too difficult to define and a heritage of analytical methods which can be sharpened by broadening rather than narrowing their field of vision.

Economists, someone once remarked, can be "blockheads who make financial plasters to cover the sores of the body politic. They do not even know that a nation can have a sick soul." The usual response is that economists do specify ends as well as means—security, justice, welfare, freedom, growth. And indeed they do, yet these goals seldom inform the esoteric analysis that has been constructed with such consummate care and skill. The ultimate aims of social behavior are not often specified, and when an effort is made to do so, there is just enough vagueness in it to disguise a mephitic ideology. How unfortunate it is that economic theory finds it difficult to comment on such urgent problems as urban strangulation, the phenomenon of suburbia, the meaninglessness of work today, and the drift to companies with the best pension schemes. These questions, infused as they are with *economic* content, now must be left to sociologists and such perceptive writers and critics of the contemporary scene as Harvey Swados, Daniel Bell, Richard Chase, Paul Goodman, and William Whyte, Jr. Would it not be proper to suggest that economics re-establish diplomatic relations with the other social and humanistic sciences, if indeed it is to remain a culturally relevant discipline?

Economics is a subset of a larger set of social problems, and, at the same time, many of its elements intersect with the elements of other subsets. If this concept were employed operationally, it would become inappropriate to describe the underlying motivation in economic behavior as rationality and self-interest. True, these are values ingrained in large sectors of the populace, internalized and institutionalized, but by no means are they so universal that the economist may be permitted to take them as *the* economic assumption. Other forms of motivation may be just as useful. Since economic behavior is set in a noneconomic context, it is the latter which is the parameter of all human action.[9]

For example, the significance and immanent meaning of economic theory can be studied fruitfully by relating it to practical policy.[10] This suggests an interest and concern with the quality of *political* economy inherent in doctrinal developments. It is not unrealistic to argue that economic thought does emerge as pro and con statements in movements of social reform or in periods of crisis. In this context, verbal meaning and practical goals are anterior to logical validity and analytical elegance. Moreover, if economics is a science of fact rooted in the human condition, one will have to check theory against real events. No simple correspondence exists, of course, for economic facts all too often are squeezed and pushed through the grinder of political policy and social turmoil. The problem of relevance with which the economist must necessarily be concerned here is that which makes the theory itself a way of perceiving reality. Unless this perception is made available, theory cannot perform its primary function—that of guiding empirical inquiry. Although Keynes once remarked that a theory was a method and not a doctrine, this must be taken with a grain of salt. For there is no escaping the fact that most methods in that sense also issue in normative propositions and thereby involve doctrinal statements. Certainly, a theorist may seek to construct his analysis in such guise that it will purport to deal only with means, but it is doubtful that he can entirely escape penetrating the quality of the ends sought. This is doctrine as well as method. Certainly, it is difficult to disentangle pure theory from normative statements, even though it may be methodologically desirable. Such difficulties demonstrate the virtual impossibility of establishing a "scientific" economics without reference to value judgments. For, at the very point where economic inquiry begins, where facts are ordered, there is an inescapable resort to evaluate notions. Indeed, the whole theory of the competitive economy, curious model that it is, has been turned into little more than a value judgment.

Of what use, it may be asked, are all the intricate models in economics? Presumably they provide an opportunity for prediction, for marking out paths of development and economic motion. Contemporary writers, pointing to the Marxian or Schumpeterian models, often say that their predictive capacity is severely limited. And so they are, yet present-day model builders have fared no better, as witness the postwar national income guessing-game debacle.

Clearly, the assumptions and postulated relationships of these models were defective: the considerable uncertainty of the world at large makes prediction a hazardous affair. But many modern models essentially are nothing more than mechanistic constructions utilizing highly restricted premises and developing even fewer operational concepts. Such principles as are developed are expected to function in the same way under all circumstances, an unlikely contingency in the real world.[11] One difficulty stems from the utilization of homogeneous factors. As a preliminary analytical device, this very well may be a necessary evil. But once labor and capital are postulated as homogeneous units, the analyst frequently forgets his own *caveat* and treats economic affairs only in such terms. At times taxonomy is confused with analysis, as in some recent studies of economic growth.[12] Or it is asserted that the internal consistency of a model is sufficient to establish its validity. More and more, theorists have limited themselves to tracing the implications of a set of premises to arrive at conclusions which are tautologies to start with. Verification has become a secondary matter and, to some writers, of no interest at all. There has been no urge to construct a theory relevant to practical issues. The assertion that this parallels what happened in physics is at best a curious defense. For those concerned only with "problem-solving," one may suppose the issue of policy to be a matter of taste. But in the arena of decision-making, whether at micro- or macroeconomic levels, theory surely must be more than just a "sequence of models." [13]

As matters now stand, economics is not a science when it is economics and not economics when it is a science.[14] As description, it is a branch of history, and as a system of analysis, a heavy borrower from mathematics. At best, economics, as John A. Hobson emphasized, is an art, very much like the practice of medicine, utilizing techniques taken from other fields and employing them in interesting and useful ways, but with no sure principles of its own which would allow it to be a predictive science as, say, is astronomy. The economist may very well have an abiding faith in the predictive worthwhileness of his model of the firm, but how frustrated he becomes when he tries to tell the very practical businessman that he ought to behave according to the dictates of the theory. When rebuffed, the economist consoles himself with the fiction that his theory indeed possesses validity because all he, the theorist, need do is to suppose that businessmen behave in marginalist ways. This is poor consolation for a society deeply in need of comprehending the behavior of corporations, trade unions, chambers of commerce, and government regulative bodies. As Broadus Mitchell once remarked, the models dwell reluctantly in the body of collectivism.[15] Moreover, they frequently dwell together in an atmosphere of conflict, rather than harmony, as some writers have supposed.

Economics can clarify issues and problems; this is primarily a practical task. And, within the great tradition of economic thought—from Smith to Ricardo, from Marx to Keynes—the great economists have always responded to issues that disturbed the minds of men. Today, all too many theorists are enamored of their empty tool boxes which they build and rebuild, describing them in virtually incomprehensible language, the language of symbols and formulas whose conclusions add little more to what a "literary" economist might have to say. Model building is said to be a way of setting forth hypotheses regarding a particular problem. At this point, both literary and symbol-manipulating economists are doing the same job, each in his own way. But once the logic of the hypothesis and its implications have been elaborated, there is a need for empirical testing. Without this step, the tool kits cannot be filled and the theory remains sterile. While mathematics may help to state a problem in a precise form, mathematics does not *ipso facto* make a better economist of its user. One still needs insight, perception, and wisdom to reach to the heart of a problem. The manipulation of symbols does not mean that the skills of the economist as economist have been improved. However, the mathematical technique has arrived and cannot be displaced, even if some would want to do so. Yet its application needs to be more sure-footed than it is.[16] Beyond that, it would be good if the mathematicians among economists ceased writing for themselves and offered verbal formulations for all to ponder. This very well might irrigate the field of "literary" economics. But more important, it might help all theorists to focus attention on really urgent questions rather than on such small things as the price of a cup of tea.

Whatever the method employed—verbal, mathematical, statistical, historical, econometric—the crucial matter is the choice of the problem. Do we really know what questions to ask? A meaningful theory ought to address itself to a meaningful issue. It is at this juncture that the message of the institutionalist still may be worthwhile. Focusing his attention on economic relationships in their social context, the institutionalist has cast doubt on *a priori* techniques and abstractions which promised to simulate reality but never did. Institutionalism, defined in the broadest possible way, sought for explanations of economic movement in a manner not immediately available to the pure model builder. While it might have lacked the finesse and refinement of recent analytics and while the institutionalist has tended to become a kind of applied economist, he nevertheless was able to pose questions such as seldom occurred to those who dealt exclusively in preference orderings and indifference curves.

Only a few present-day theorists, however, have explored issues of policy. Most of them, interestingly enough, are Europeans. Rarely has the example of Jan Tinbergen in Holland, or of the Swedish economists, been paralleled on this side of the Atlantic.[17] Perhaps this stems from the fact that European writers generally have been more involved in government economic planning than has been the case here. But it does demonstrate that the fusion of theory and practice is not impossible. The striking feature in Tinbergen's work is the effort to elucidate among the known data of his equations institutions and economic policies. The data include physical and psychological characteristics and the operations of institutions which may be expressed either quantitatively or qualitatively. And, while one may question Tinbergen's use of a social utility or welfare function based on the notion of equality, this does give his model a scope and fullness that others lack.

For example, Tinbergen makes two important observations on an "optimum régime": not only will it be different under different conditions, but also it is unlikely to be an extreme one. That is, it is apt to include both a private and public sector and will be neither completely centralized nor decentralized. In Tinbergen one discovers that a seemingly cold analytical model can be given political and social meaning. But, in the main, the extraordinary concentration on formalistic techniques characteristic of much of the field today has offered few guide lines for policy. There is one small consolation in this strange situation—often in a time of crisis someone does come along with a theory relevant for practice. But ought we wait for that?

Notes

Chapter I
Protest from the Historicists

1. Cf. H. Stuart Hughes, *Consciousness and Society*, New York, 1958.
2. W. C. Mitchell, *Lectures on Current Types of Economic Theory*, mimeographed, New York, 1935, II, 540.
3. Cf. Herbert Marcuse, *Reason and Revolution: Hegel and the Rise of Social Theory*, New York, 1941.
4. Cf. Crane Brinton, *Ideas and Men*, New York, 1950, pp. 423ff.
5. For a trenchant criticism of this view, cf. Karl Popper, *The Poverty of Historicism*, Boston, 1957.
6. Cf. G. P. Gooch, *History and Historians in the Nineteenth Century*, 2nd ed., London, 1952, pp. 72ff.
7. Cf. R. G. Collingwood, *The Idea of History*, New York, 1946, p. 173 and Hughes, *op. cit.*, p. 195.
8. Cf. Hughes, *ibid.*, p. 199.
9. Cf. Joseph A. Schumpeter, *Economic Doctrine and Method*, 1912, translated London, 1954, p. 161.
10. Cf. Walter S. Buckingham, Jr., *Theoretical Economic Systems*, New York, 1958, p. 67.
11. Mitchell, *op. cit.*, p. 543.
12. *Schmoller's Jahrbuch*, 1883, "Zur Methodologie der Staats und Sozialwissenschaften," p. 978.
13. See p. 273 below.
14. Cf. also *On the History of German Small Industry in the Nineteenth Century*, Halle, 1870, and *Social and Industrial History*, Leipzig, 1890.
15. Cf. Walter Abraham and Herbert Weisgast, *The Economics of Gustav Schmoller*, mimeographed,

New York, 1942. This is a useful summary of the first sections of the *Grundriss.*

16. See p. 129ff. below.

17. Mitchell, *op. cit.*, p. 549.

18. A useful introduction to Schmoller is Carl Brinkmann, *Gustav Schmoller und die Volkswirtschaftslehre*, Stuttgart, 1937. Another helpful introduction to Schmoller is the synthetic essay, "The Historical Development of the Enterprise," in *Enterprise and Secular Change: Readings in Economic History*, ed. F. C. Lane and J. C. Riemersma, Homewood, 1953, pp. 3ff.

19. Cf. especially, Books III and IV of Smith's *Wealth of Nations,* Modern Library ed., New York, 1937, pp. 356ff, for a famous analysis of the rise of towns and of the mercantilist system, an analysis with which Schmoller was quite familiar.

20. Cf. Richard Jones, *An Essay on the Distribution of Wealth and the Sources of Taxation*, 1831, reprinted, New York, 1956. Jones, who succeeded Malthus at Hailesbury, disliked Ricardian deductive logic as much as did the Germans. He advocated patient research which would yield generalizations that could be used to describe the economic system.

21. Cf. Schmoller's *Über einige Grundfragen des Rechts und der Volkswirtschaft,* Jena, 1875.

22. F. A. Hayek in his *Counter-Revolution of Science*, Chicago, 1952, pp. 198ff, implies that Schmoller was inspired by Comte. This is erroneous. Cf., for example, Joseph A. Schumpeter, *History of Economic Analysis*, New York, 1954, p. 812.

23. Veblen chided Schmoller for praising skilled workers while attacking socialists, pointing out that most of the skilled workers of Schmoller's day were socialists. Cf. T. Veblen, "Gustav Schmoller's Economics," in *The Place of Science in Modern Civilization*, New York, 1919, pp. 273-276.

24. Torsten Gårdlund, *The Life of Knut Wicksell*, Stockholm, 1958, p. 108.

25. *Socialism and Social Movements*, London, 1909; *Friedrich Engels*, Berlin, 1895; *Life Work of Karl Marx*, Jena, 1909.

26. Cf. Leo Rogin, "Werner Sombart and the Uses of Transcendentalism," *American Economic Review*, September, 1941, p. 494.

27. Some of Sombart's chief works were: *Der Bourgeois*, Munich, 1913; translated as *The Quintessence of Capitalism*, London, 1915; *Der Moderne Kapitalismus*, Leipzig, 1902; *Händler und Helden*, Munich, 1915; *German Economy in the Nineteenth Century*, Berlin, 1921; *Die Drei National ökonomien*, Munich, 1930. Other works are cited below.

28. Cf. B. F. Hoselitz in Introduction to Sombart's *The Jews and Modern Capitalism*, translated 1913, reprinted, New York, 1951, p. xx. Cf. also M. J. Plotnik, *Werner Sombart and His Type of Economics*, New York, 1937.

29. Hoselitz, *op. cit.*, p. xvii.

30. Cf. Frederick L. Nussbaum, *Economic Institutions of Modern Europe*, New York, 1933.

31. W. Sombart, "Capitalism," in *The Encyclopaedia of the Social Sciences*, New York, 1930, III, 196.

32. *Der Moderne Kapitalismus.*

33. *Encyclopaedia of the Social Sciences*, III, 200.

34. *Ibid.*, p. 201.

35. *Ibid.*, p. 202.

36. Sombart divided the history of capitalism into three parts: early, high, and late phases. In *Der Moderne Kapitalismus* he placed the first period between the thirteenth and middle nineteenth centuries. High capitalism supposedly started in Britain in the eighteenth century and lasted until 1914. For a useful discussion of this aspect of Sombart's analysis, cf. Abram Harris, *Economics and Social Reform*, New York, 1958, pp. 276ff.

37. *The Jews and Modern Capitalism.*

38. Cf. Harris, *op. cit.*, p. 282.
39. Cf. G. G. Scholem, "Jewish Mysticism and Kabbala," and A. Steinberg, "Jewish Religious Thought," in *The Jewish People: Past and Present*, New York, 1946, I, 308ff. and 273ff.
40. *Jews and Modern Capitalism*, p. xxiv.
41. Miriam Beard, *History of the Business Man*, New York, 1938, pp. 118ff.
42. *Ibid.*, p. 122. Cf. also Henri Pirenne, *Economic and Social History of Medieval Europe*, 1937, reprinted, New York, 1957, pp. 131ff.
43. Sombart, *op. cit.*, p. 29. Cf. also Oliver C. Cox, *Foundations of Capitalism*, New York, 1959, pp. 168, 180, 196, 239. Cox says: "The Jew lived in capitalist society without being instrumental in the formation of its constitution . . . As a group [they] virtually had no integral role in the founding of the Dutch Republic."
44. Sombart, *op. cit.*, p. 54.
45. Cf. M. F. Ashley-Montagu, "Race Theory in the Light of Modern Science," in *The Jewish People: Past and Present*, Vol. 1.
46. Cf. Salo W. Baron, "Modern Capitalism and Jewish Fate," Menorah Journal, Summer, 1942; Max Weber, *General Economic History*, reprinted, New York, 1950, p. 358; and numerous references cited by Amintore Fanfani, *Catholicism, Protestantism and Capitalism*, New York, 1935, p. 16.
47. Cf. Bede Jarrett, *Social Theories of the Middle Ages*, Westminster, 1942.
48. Cf. Maurice Dobb, *Studies in the Development of Capitalism*, New York, 1947, pp. 9ff.
49. Rogin, *op. cit.*, p. 502.
50. *Deutscher Sozialismus*, Charlottenburg, 1934; translated as *A New Social Philosophy*, Princeton, 1937.
51. Cf. Karl Mannheim, "Conservative Thought," in *Essays on Sociology and Social Psychology*, New York, 1953, pp. 80, 82.
52. Some of Weber's major works are: *Roman Agrarian History*, 1891; *Protestant Ethic and the Spirit of Capitalism*, 1904, reprinted New York, 1958, the famous work in which it was argued that the Reformation created the kind of outlook and spirit that led to the capitalist spirit and to capitalism itself. Weber sought to prove this thesis with a series of brilliant studies of the sociology of religion. Cf. also *Ancient Judaism*, 1917, translated, New York, 1952; *General Economic History. Economy and Society*, Part III of the *Grundriss der Sozialökonomik*, a huge work edited by Weber and in which Wieser's *Social Economy* also appeared. A large part of *Economy and Society* has been translated in H. Gerth and C. Wright Mills, *From Max Weber*, New York, 1946, and Talcott Parsons, ed. and translator, *Theory of Social and Economic Organization*, New York, 1947. For a useful if somewhat unimaginative introduction to Weber, cf. Reinhard Bendix, *Max Weber, An Intellectual Portrait*, New York, 1960.
53. The aetiology of his ailment was unquestionably rooted in Weber's relations to his father and mother. The first breakdown came within a few weeks after a violent scene with his father. Cf. Hughes, *op. cit.*, p. 296 and Gerth and Mills, *op. cit.*, p. 29.
54. Gerth and Mills, p. 17.
55. Published originally in *Schmoller's Jahrbuch*, 1903-06 as "Roscher and Knies und die Logischen Probleme der Historischen Nationalökonomie."
56. Parsons, *op. cit.*, p. 11.
57. Cf. Raymond Aron, *German Sociology*, London, 1957, pp. 101ff.
58. Cf. Weber, *The Methodology of the Social Sciences*, New York, 1949. This volume reprints Weber's essays on ethical neutrality and objectivity in the social sciences— all important contributions to general methodological theory in the social sciences.
59. Gerth and Mills, *op. cit.*, p. 47.

60. Hughes, *op. cit.*, p. 317.
61. Cf. Parsons, *op. cit.*, pp. 158ff.
62. See p. 104 below.
63. Cf. Parsons, *op. cit.*, pp. 254ff.
64. *Ibid.*, pp. 275ff.
65. *Ibid.*, pp. 319ff.
66. Cf. Gerth and Mills, *op. cit.*, p. 302.
67. *Protestant Ethic*, pp. 95ff. Cf. also J. Bronowski and J. Mazlish, *The Western Intellectual Tradition*, New York, 1960, pp. 96-97.
68. Gerth and Mills, *op. cit.*, p. 63.
69. Cf. William H. Whyte, Jr., *The Organization Man*, New York, 1956. This is a remarkably perceptive study of the bureaucratization of modern man.
70. Cf. Gerth and Mills, *op. cit.*, pp. 295ff.
71. Cf. Weber, *General Economic History*, p. 358.
72. *Ibid.*, p. 369.
73. Cf. R. H. Tawney, *Religion and the Rise of Capitalism*, New York, 1926, pp. 79ff., especially pp. 90-91. Tawney comments that Luther's theory of society was even more medieval than Middle Age thinkers would have demanded, since it dismissed the commercial growth of the previous two-hundred years as paganism.
74. Cf. Beard, *op. cit.*, p. 348.
75. *Ibid.*, p. 350.
76. Cf. his *Aspects of the Rise of Economic Individualism*, Cambridge, 1935. Cf. also R. H. Tawney in his Introduction to the *Protestant Ethic*, p. 7.
77. Some of his chief works were *Labor Guilds of the Present*, Leipzig, 1871; *Economic Man in History*, Leipzig, 1923; *Economic Development of England*, Jena, 1927; *Development of Value Theory*, Munich, 1908; *Origin of Modern Capitalism*, Jena, 1916.
78. *Industrial Evolution*, New York, 1901.
79. *Ibid.*, p. 143.
80. Cf. John R. Commons *et al.*, *History of Labor in the United States*, New York, 1918, I, 26ff.
81. Knapp, *State Theory of Money*, translated, London, 1924.
82. Ludwig von Mises carried on a furious polemic against Knapp's theory, Cf. Mises' *Theory of Money and Credit*, 1912, translated, London, 1934, pp. 463ff.
83. A substantial portion of his *Krisen*, first published in the *Handworterbuch der Staatswissenschaften*, 1923, was reprinted under the title, "Business Cycles," in *International Economic Papers*, No. 3, London, 1953, pp. 76ff.
84. *Ibid.*, p. 76.
85. Spiethoff, "The Historical Character of Economic Theories," *Journal of Economic History*, Spring, 1952, p. 132. Cf. also his article, "Die Allgemeine Volkswirtschaftslehre als Geschichtliche Theorie" in *Schmoller's Jahrbuch*, 1932, p. 891.
86. Cf. Leo Rogin, *The Meaning and Validity of Economic Theory*, New York, 1956, pp. 1ff. This is precisely the thesis of Rogin's interesting and useful work. Cf. also my review of Rogin in the *New Leader*, Oct. 8, 1956.
87. Cf. his synthetic article, "Pure Theory and Economic Gestalt Theory," in *Enterprise and Secular Change*.
88. Cf. p. 94 below.
89. Spiethoff, "Crisis Theory of M. V. Tugan-Baronovsky and L. Pohle," in *Schmoller's Jahrbuch*, 1903.
90. "Business Cycles," *International Economic Papers, ibid.*, pp. 80-81.
91. *Ibid.*, p. 101.
92. *Ibid.*, p. 147.
93. *Ibid.*, p. 148.
94. *Ibid.*, p. 153.
95. Cf. William Baumol, *Economic Dynamics*, New York, 1951, p. 108 and R. G. D. Allen, *Mathematical Economics*, London, 1956, pp. 1ff.
96. Spiethoff, *op. cit.*, p. 158.
97. "Overproduction," *Encyclopaedia of the Social Sciences*, II, 513.
98. *International Economic Papers, op. cit.*, p. 171.
99. His data were utilized by Paul H. Douglas in the latter's *The Theory of Wages*, 1934, reprinted, New York, 1957.
100. Cf. F. Simiand, *Le Salaire: l'evolu-*

tion sociale et la monnaie, Paris, 1932.

101. J. K. Ingram, *History of Political Economy*, London, 1915.

102. Arnold Toynbee, *Lectures on the Industrial Revolution in England*, 1884, reprinted, Boston, 1956.

103. *Ibid.*, p. 2.

104. *Ibid.*, p. 5.

105. William Cunningham, *The Growth of English Industry and Commerce in Modern Times*, Cambridge, 1882.

106. Cf. obituary notices by H. S. Foxwell and L. Knowles, *Economic Journal*, September, 1919, pp. 382ff., 390ff.

107. Cunningham, *op. cit.*, pp. 680ff.

108. Cunningham, *Politics and Economics*, London, 1885, p. 238.

109. Cf. B. Semmel, *Imperialism and Social Reform*, Cambridge, 1960, pp. 188ff.

110. William Ashley, *Introduction to Economic History and Theory*, 4th ed., London, 1914-23.

111. For biographic data, Cf. Anne Ashley, *William James Ashley: A Life*, London, 1932.

112. Semmel, *op. cit.*, p. 206.

113. R. H. Tawney, *Religion and the Rise of Capitalism*, New York, 1926.

114. *Equality*, London, 1931; *The Acquisitive Society*, New York, 1920.

115. Bede Jarrett, *op. cit.*, and Tawney, *Religion and the Rise of Capitalism*, p. 17.

116. Tawney, *ibid.*, pp. 84-85.

117. *Ibid.*, p. 101.

118. *Ibid.*, pp. 110-111.

119. *Ibid.*, p. 118.

120. *Ibid.*, p. 180.

121. *Ibid.*, p. 230.

122. *Ibid.*, p. 253.

123. R. Williams, *Culture and Society*, New York, 1958, p. 219.

Chapter 2
The Socialist Attack

1. Kenneth E. Boulding, "A New Look at Institutionalism," *American Economic Association Proceedings*, May, 1957, p. 1.

2. Joseph A. Schumpeter, *History of Economic Analysis*, New York, 1954, pp. 386ff.

3. Joan Robinson, *On Re-reading Marx* (pamphlet), Cambridge, 1953.

4. Joseph A. Schumpeter, *Capitalism, Socialism and Democracy*, New York, 1942, p. 21.

5. Cf. Paul A. Samuelson, "Marxian Economic Models," *American Economic Review*, December, 1957, pp. 884ff., in which a contrary view is offered.

6. Joan Robinson, *Marx, Marshall and Keynes* (pamphlet), Delhi, 1955; reprinted in *Collected Economic Papers*, Oxford, 1960, II, 1.

7. Joan Robinson, *An Essay on Marxian Economics*, London, 1942.

8. See p. 749 below.

9. C. A. Landauer, *European Socialism*, Berkeley, 1959, I, 137ff.

10. Cf. *ibid.*, pp. 140ff.

11. Cf. T. B. Bottomore and M. Rubel, *Karl Marx: Selected Writings in Sociology and Social Philosophy*, London, 1956.

12. Cf. Robinson, *Essay*, Chap. V, *et seq.*

13. Schumpeter calls attention to this implication of Marx's discussion of this point in his *History*, p. 628; Cf. also *Theorien über den Mehrwert* in the Terence McCarthy translation, New York, 1952, pp. 194ff.

14. Ladislaus von Bortkiewicz, "Value

and Prices in the Marxian System," reprinted in *International Economic Papers*, No. 2, London, 1952, p. 5.

15. Orthodox Marxists such as Ronald Meek of the University of Glasgow still feel that the labor theory is good science and that there have been striking developments in it since 1894. It is not clear whether Meek has in mind the puerile discussions under Stalin. See Meek's *Studies in the Labour Theory of Value*, London, 1956.

16. Cf. *Das Kapital*, Vol. II, Chaps. 18-21, Kerr ed. A good discussion of this is to be found in Leo Rogin, *Meaning and Validity of Economic Theory*, New York, 1956, Chap. 9, pp. 332ff. Cf. also Benjamin Higgins, *Economic Development*, New York, 1959, pp. 107ff., for an excellent schematic presentation of the Marxian model. Cf. also I. Edelman, *Theories of Economic Growth and Development*, Stanford, 1961, pp. 60ff.

17. J. Steindl, *Maturity and Stagnation in American Capitalism*, Oxford, 1952, pp. 228ff.

18. S. Kuznets, *National Income and Its Composition, 1918-1938*, New York, 1941. For an interesting analysis of nineteenth-century wage trends in the United States, cf. S. Lebergott, "Wage Trends, 1800-1900," in *Trends in the American Economy in the Nineteenth Century*, National Bureau of Economic Research, Princeton, 1960, pp. 449ff.

19. Cf. John Strachey, *Contemporary Capitalism*, New York, 1956, pp. 118ff.

20. Joan Robinson's *Essay* has an excellent treatment of the law of profit, Chap. V, pp. 41ff.

21. David Weintraub, *Effects of Current and Prospective Technological Developments upon Capital Formation*, Philadelphia, 1939.

22. Karl Marx, *Das Kapital*, III, 568, Kerr ed.

23. Rogin, *op. cit.*, pp. 399-400.

24. Higgins, *op. cit.*, p. 120.

25. Cf. Schumpeter, *History*, p. 392. Only a failure to read Marx carefully would impel one to characterize him as a minor post-Ricardian. Cf. Samuelson, *op. cit.* A large part of the foregoing was drawn from my article, "Marxian Economics Revisited," *Dissent*, Autumn, 1958, p. 342.

26. "The Marxian Theory of Value," reprinted in Wicksteed's *Commonsense of Political Economy*, London, 1950, II, 705.

27. *Ibid.*, p. 713, italics in original.

28. *Ibid.*, p. 723.

29. Eugen von Böhm-Bawerk, *Karl Marx and the Close of His System*, ed. P. M. Sweezy, New York, 1949, p. 79.

30. Paul M. Sweezy, *The Theory of Capitalist Development*, New York, 1942, p. 115.

31. Böhm-Bawerk, *op. cit.*, pp. 28ff.

32. *Ibid.*, p. 30.

33. *Ibid.*, pp. 32ff.

34. *Ibid.*, pp. 58ff.

35. *Das Kapital*, I, 12.

36. Böhm-Bawerk, *op. cit.*, p. 88.

37. Pareto, *Les Systèmes Socialistes*, 2 vols., Paris, 1902-03.

38. *Ibid.*, p. 64.

39. *Ibid.*, II, 369.

40. Rudolf Hilferding, *Böhm-Bawerk's Criticism of Marx*, reprinted together with Böhm-Bawerk, *Karl Marx . . .* in the vol. ed. Sweezy, pp. 121ff.

41. *Ibid.*, p. 133.

42. *Ibid.*, p. 134, italics in original.

43. *Ibid.*, p. 146.

44. *Ibid.*, p. 192.

45. *Marx-Engels Correspondence*, New York, 1934, p. 245.

46. *Ibid.*, pp. 527ff., cf. also *Das Kapital*, III, 196, 211, 244.

47. *Das Kapital*, III, 37ff.

48. *Ibid.*, III, 233.

49. *Ibid.*, III, 206. Cf. also Meek, *op. cit.*, pp. 189ff.

50. Meek, *ibid.*, p. 191.

51. Cf. Schumpeter, *History*, pp. 851ff.

52. The largest part of Bortkiewicz' essays on Marxian value theory are available in English. See "Value and Price Calculation in the Marxian System" in *Interna-*

tional *Economic Papers*, No. 2, London, 1952 and "The Correction of Marx's Fundamental Theoretical Construction in Capital, Volume III," reprinted in the Sweezy edited volume on Böhm-Bawerk cited above.

53. Cf. also J. Winternitz in *Economic Journal*, June 1948, pp. 276ff. in which a similar solution is offered, but with less awkwardness.

54. Cf. Bortkiewicz in *International Economic Papers, op. cit.*, p. 54.

55. Cf. Sweezy, *Theory of Capitalist Development*, p. 129.

56. Cf. Maurice Dobb, *On Economic Theory and Socialism*, London, 1955, pp. 273ff.; F. Seton, "The Transformation Problem," *Review of Economic Studies*, June, 1957, pp. 149ff.; R. Meek, "Some Notes on the Transformation Problem," *Economic Journal*, March, 1956, pp. 94ff.

57. Seton, *op. cit.*, p. 149.

58. Joan Robinson, *Collected Economic Papers*, London, 1951, I, 146ff.; cf. also Samuelson, *op. cit.* The latter is a devastating attack on the Marxian system, in which values once more are discarded and the entire presentation developed in price terms. Samuelson calls the transformation problem pointless and then finally dismisses Marx as a minor post-Ricardian! Unfortunately, Samuelson resorts to some rather unfair arguments; on p. 907, for example, he would deny to Marx the advantages of a simple model with restrictive assumptions. Had he said that Marx seldom relaxed these assumptions, he would have been on safer grounds. Further, it appears that Samuelson based himself on Sweezy rather than a reading of Marx.

59. Cf. Arthur Rosenberg, *Democracy and Socialism*, New York, 1939, pp. 225ff.

60. G. D. H. Cole, *A History of Socialist Thought*, London, 1956, Vol. III, Part 1, pp. 3ff.

61. *Ibid.*, pp. 35ff.

62. Peter Gay, *The Dilemma of Democratic Socialism*, New York, 1952.

63. Cf. Landauer, *op. cit.*, I, 311ff.

64. Cf. Schumpeter, *Capitalism, Socialism and Democracy*, pp. 344ff.

65. The best history of revisionism and Bernstein's role in it is Gay's *op. cit.*; cf. also Cole, *op. cit.*, Vol. III, Part 1, pp. 271ff.

66. Eduard Bernstein, *Evolutionary Socialism*, reprinted, New York, 1961, preface, p. xiff.

67. Herbert Marcuse, *Reason and Revolution*, New York, 1954, pp. 399ff.

68. Gay, *op. cit.*, pp. 151ff.

69. Cf. *Evolutionary Socialism*, pp. 34-38. The orthodox Marxist reply to Bernstein's argument is given in Meek, *op. cit.*, pp. 214ff., where it is alleged that the purpose of a theory is precisely to be abstract. A more telling objection to the elimination of a theory of value is that we can then no longer develop a theory of distribution in which it is sought to explain not only how the various incomes are apportioned but which factors account for the relative size and the direction of income flow. That this was the key task to which Marx addressed himself seems to have escaped most of the parties to the Revisionist debate.

70. *Ibid.*, pp. 59ff.

71. *Ibid.*, pp. 79ff.

72. Cf. Gay, *op. cit.*, Chap. VII, pp. 157ff.

73. Karl Kautsky, *Economic Doctrines of Karl Marx*, published in 1887 and translated into English in 1925.

74. Cf. Paul Frölich, *Rosa Luxemburg: Her Life and Work*, London, 1940.

75. Rosa Luxemburg, *Sozialreform oder Revolution*, Berlin, 1925.

76. Cf. Theodore Draper, *The Roots of American Communism*, New York, 1957, pp. 57ff.

77. Louis Boudin, *The Theoretical System of Karl Marx*, Chicago, 1907.

78. *Ibid.*, p. 108.

79. *Ibid.*, p. 211.

80. *Essays in Political and Moral*

Philosophy, p. 227, quoted by M. Beer, *History of British Socialism*, London, 1940, p. 234.

81. Sir Alexander Gray, in his *The Socialist Tradition*, London, 1946, remarks that the Fabians had no Marxism to react against. However, Sir Alexander would have had to explain away the careful reading the Fabians gave to *Das Kapital* and such oddities as George Bernard Shaw's conversion from Marx to Jevons.

82. Gray, *ibid.*, p. 384. For a lively if somewhat racy study of the Fabians, cf. Anne Fremantle, *This Little Band of Prophets*, New York, 1960.

83. Cole, *op. cit.*, Vol. III, Part 1, p. 190.

84. B. Semmel, *Imperialism and Social Reform*, Cambridge, 1960, p. 128ff.

85. Edward Pease, *History of the Fabian Society*, New York, 1916, p. 269.

86. Cole, *op. cit.*, Vol. III, Part 1, p. 118.

87. Beer, *op. cit.*, II, 287.

88. The more important of these are the Webb's *Industrial Democracy* (1897), *Works Manager Today* (1917), *Cooperative Movement in Great Britain* (1891), *Problems of Modern Industry* (1898), *History of Trade Unionism* (1894, revised 1920), *The Cooperative Movement* (1914), *Decay of Capitalist Civilization* (1923), *Soviet Communism: A New Civilization?* (1935); also E. R. Pease, *History of the Fabian Society* (1916); George Bernard Shaw, *Essays in Fabian Socialism* (1932); and Beatrice Webb, *My Apprenticeship* (1926), *Our Partnership* (1948).

89. Cole, *op. cit.*, Vol. III, Part 1, pp. 120, 206. For a more sympathetic view, cf. R. H. Tawney, "The Webbs and Their Work," in H. W. Spiegel, *The Development of Economic Thought*, New York, 1952, p. 341.

90. G. D. H. Cole, *Self-Government in Industry*, London, 1917, p. 321.

91. Cf. Gray, *op. cit.*, pp. 436ff.

92. Cole, *History*, III, 246. Cf. also C. J. Ratzlaff, *The Theory of Free Competition*, Philadelphia, 1936, pp. 254ff.

93. Cole, *The World of Labour*, London, 1913, pp. 286ff.

94. Cf. his *Essays in Social Theory*, London, 1952, p. 29 and his *History of Socialist Thought*, III, 247.

95. Several charming memorials to Cole may be found in *Essays in Labour History*, ed. A. Briggs and J. Saville, London, 1960.

96. Cf. Gray's criticism of the Guild Socialists, *op. cit.*, p. 453.

97. Cf. Landauer, *op. cit.*, I, 337; II, 1605.

98. Rudolf Hilferding, *Das Finanzkapital*, Vienna, 1920. I am grateful to Morris Watnick for the loan of materials relating to Hilferding.

99. *Ibid.*, Chap. V, pp. 80ff.

100. *Ibid.*, Chap. VI, pp. 107ff.

101. Cf. Chap. XII, p. 265.

102. Cf. Chap. X, p. 218ff. See also p. 59 above on the transformation problem.

103. Cf. F. Lundberg, *America's Sixty Families*, New York, 1937, pp. 447ff., for a latter-day version of this thesis.

104. Hilferding, *op. cit.*, Chap. XIV, pp. 298ff.

105. The disproportion argument is akin to Tugan-Baranovsky's thesis. See p. 94 below.

106. Cf. E. M. Winslow, *The Pattern of Imperialism*, New York, 1948, p. 164.

107. Cf. Hilferding, *op. cit.*, Part V, pp. 400ff.

108. Cf. Frölich, *op. cit.*, pp. 67ff.

109. *Gewerkschaftskampf und Massenstreik*, ed. P. Frölich, Berlin, 1931.

110. Cf. Cole's discussion in his *History*, Vol. III, Part 2, pp. 315ff. and Frölich, *op. cit.*, pp. 156ff.

111. The second volume was a sustained polemic against her critics. Volume I is available in translation, New Haven, 1951.

112. Cf. her pamphlet, *The Russian Revolution*, reprinted, New York, 1940. Translation and introduction by Bertram D. Wolfe.

113. *Ibid.*, p. iv, Wolfe's Introduction.
114. *Ibid.*, pp. 47-48.
115. Luxemburg, *Accumulation,* p. 125.
116. *Ibid.*, pp. 132ff.
117. *Ibid.*, pp. 329ff.
118. *Ibid.*, p. 352.
119. *Ibid.*, p. 428.
120. Cf. Sweezy, *Theory of Capitalist Development,* p. 205.
121. Cf. Landauer, *op. cit.*, II, 1579ff.
122. Fritz Sternberg, *Der Imperialismus,* Berlin, 1926.
123. *Ibid.*, p. 106.
124. *Ibid.*, pp. 69ff.
125. Fritz Sternberg, *The Coming Crisis,* New York, 1947; *Capitalism and Socialism on Trial,* New York, 1950. Some of the arguments in these books stemmed from his earlier *Decline of German Capitalism,* Berlin, 1932. Some of the paragraphs below are taken from my article, "Is The Depression Inevitable?" *Commentary,* September, 1947, p. 281.
126. Cf. Maurice Dobb, *Political Economy and Capitalism,* London, 1937; *idem, On Economic Theory and Socialism,* London, 1955.
127. Cf. Lewis Corey, *The Decline of American Capitalism,* New York, 1934; *idem, The Crisis of the Middle Class,* New York, 1935; *idem, The Unfinished Task,* New York, 1942; and files of *The Marxist Quarterly,* a short-lived journal of 1937. For a perceptive portrait of Corey and an understanding brief biography see Draper, *The Roots of American Communism.*
128. John Strachey, *The Coming Struggle for Power,* New York, 1933; *idem, The Nature of the Capitalist Crisis,* New York, 1935.
129. Strachey, *Contemporary Capitalism,* New York, 1956; *idem, The End of Empire,* London, 1959.
130. Henryk Grossmann, *Accumulation and Breakdown of the Capitalist System,* Leipzig, 1929.
131. His best-known works were *Essays on the History of Political Economy and Socialism,* St. Petersburg, 1905; *Modern Socialism in its Historical Development,* London,

1910; *Theoretical Foundations of Marxism,* Leipzig, 1905; and particularly *Les Crises Industrielles en Angleterre* (1894), translated Paris, 1913.
132. Alvin H. Hansen, *Business Cycles and National Income,* New York, 1951, p. 226.
133. J. M. Keynes, *A Treatise on Money,* New York, 1930, II, 101.
134. Official Marxism disavowed itself from the implication in Tugan-Baranovsky that production could develop unheedful of what took place in consumption. Kautsky, Hilferding, and Luxemburg attacked him for his seeming audacity in challenging official theory. But then Tugan was no Marxist. For a summary of the debate see Sweezy, *op. cit.*, pp. 169ff. Sweezy himself objects to Tugan's analysis on the grounds that its suggestion of the posible elimination of proportionality is quite un-Marxlike. But all Sweezy does is to sneer at Tugan's work as superficial (p. 166) and then turns to a demonstration of the underconsumption thesis as the major factor in economic collapse. But, in fact, the separation of production from consumption which Tugan-Baranovsky spoke of and which Sweezy calls an error may be precisely what has happened through the years in the Soviet Union! Sweezy has simply ignored Tugan's emphasis on investment as the driving force, rather than consumption. Nor did Tugan suggest that capitalism would solve its basic economic problem. On the contrary, he thought the situation would be increasingly exacerbated. By 1905, Tugan had moved close to the Bernstein position. He saw "class struggle" as a fatal error which had nothing to do with either economic analysis or the economic interpretation of history. The labor theory of value, the concept of exploitation, and the doctrine of increasing misery were all deemed to be untenable in the light of known social fact. This

obviously explains the antipathy of neo-Marxists to Tugan's views. Cf. E. R. A. Seligman, *The Economic Interpretation of History*, New York, 1907, p. 111.

135. Cf. Alexander Kornilov, *Modern Russian History*, New York, 1917, reprinted 1943, I, 282.

136. S. M. Schwarz, "Populism and Early Russian Marxism on Ways of Economic Development in Russia: 1880's-1890's," in *Continuity and Change in Russian and Soviet Thought*, ed. E. J. Simmons, Cambridge, 1955, pp. 40ff.

137. M. Tugan-Baranovsky, *Russian Factory in Past and Present*, St. Petersburg, 1898.

138. *Selected Works*, I, 221ff. This is a grossly truncated version, but illustrates Lenin's method in economics.

139. The major Leninist works are included in the *Selected Works*, New York, 1935-39. An important study of the corpus of Leninist ideology is Alfred G. Meyer, *Leninism*, Cambridge, 1957.

140. Cf. Barrington Moore, Jr., *Soviet Politics: The Dilemma of Power*, Cambridge, 1951, pp. 46-47. This volume is by far the best study of its kind.

141. Cf. *Selected Works*, III, 279 and XII, *passim*.

142. Edmund Wilson, *To the Finland Station*, New York, 1940, reprint, 1953, p. 383.

143. *Ibid.*, p. 383.

144. Cf. *Imperialism* in *Selected Works*, V, 81ff. Also cf. N. Bukharin, *Imperialism and World Economy*, New York, 1929, and Landauer, *op. cit.*, II, 1596ff.

145. Cf. Meyer, *ibid.*, p. 244.

146. Cf. Thomas T. Hammond, *Lenin on Trade Unions and Revolution, 1893-1917*, New York, 1957, pp. 15ff.

147. Cf. "What Is To Be Done?" in *Selected Works*, II, 51ff.

148. *Selected Works*, VII, 44ff.

149. Moore, *op. cit.*, pp. 40ff.

150. *Ibid.*, p. 43.

151. Schwarz, *op. cit.*, p. 42. Cf. also, Peter I. Lyaschenko, *History of the National Economy of Russia*

to the 1917 Revolution, New York, 1949, pp. 669ff.

152. Cf. Landauer, *op. cit.*, I, 205, 1062.

153. Cf. B. E. Lippincott, ed., *On the Economic Theory of Socialism*, Minneapolis, 1938, pp. 130ff.

154. *Marx-Engels Correspondence*, p. 246.

155. Cf. *Das Kapital*, Vol. III, Parts IV-V, for indications of Marx's awareness of the allocation problem.

156. Cf. the extensive debate on the uses of marginalist analysis in the *American Economic Review*, March 1946, September 1946, March 1947, June 1947, September 1947, particularly articles by Richard A. Lester and Fritz Machlup.

157. Fritz Machlup, *The Economics of Sellers' Competition*, Baltimore, 1952, p. 28.

158. Despite Machlup's insistence, however, most businessmen do not think as precisely as the marginal concept supposes they do. Empirical investigations suggest that at best a kind of tentative, rough-and-ready approach is made to marginalist analysis. Cf. George Katona, *Psychological Analysis of Economic Behavior*, New York, 1951, Chap. 10, pp. 214ff., and W. J. Eiteman, *Price Determination—Business Practice versus Economic Theory*, Ann Arbor, 1949. Eiteman rejects marginalism entirely.

159. Cf. E. von Böhm-Bawerk, *Karl Marx and the Close of His System*, and Rudolf Hilferding, *Böhm-Bawerk's Criticism of Karl Marx* in the Sweezy edited volume cited.

160. Cf. Hilferding, *op. cit.*

161. Cf. Friedrich von Wieser, *Natural Value*, New York, 1956, (Reprint), Book IV, pp. 215ff.

162. Von Wieser, *Social Economics*, New York, 1927, p. 185.

163. The Pierson article, first published in the Dutch *Economist*, was reprinted in *Collectivist Economic Planning*, ed. F. A. von Hayek, London, 1935.

164. Cf. his *Omnipotent Government*,

New Haven, 1944 and my review of it in the *New Leader*, July 29, 1944. Cf. also Mises' *Human Action*, London, 1949, pp. 694ff.

165. *Idem, Socialism*, 2nd ed., New Haven, 1951.
166. Cf. *Collectivist Economic Planning*.
167. *Ibid.*, p. 6.
168. Cf. F. A. von Hayek, *Individualism and Economic Order*, Chicago, 1948, especially Chap. IV, "The Use of Knowledge in Society," pp. 77ff.
169. Cf. my article, "Dice, Dr. Hayek and the Consumer," in *Commentary*, March, 1946.
170. *Collectivist Economic Planning*, pp. 207-8.
171. *Ibid.*, p. 90.
172. *Ibid.*, p. 91.
173. *Ibid.*, p. 103.
174. Vilfredo Pareto, *Les Systèmes Socialistes*, 2 vols., Paris, 1902-03.
175. Pareto's discussion of socialist economics in the sense discussed here was contained in the second volume of his *Cours d'Economie Politique*, Lausanne, 1896-97, and the *Manuel d'Economie Politique*, Paris, 1907. The latter was reprinted in 1927.
176. Paul A. Samuelson points out in his *Foundations of Economic Analysis*, Cambridge, 1947, p. 212, that the implications of continuous smooth change in Pareto's use of the infinitesimal calculus was considered objectionable by some economists who saw reflected in economic reality a pattern of discontinuous, discrete movement. Analytically, Pareto's equilibrium analysis does not really define a unique point, says Samuelson, for if income transfers are arbitrarily imposed, new optimum conditions must be defined.
177. Luigi Einaudi, "Fifty Years of Italian Economic Thought: 1896-1946, Reminiscences," reprinted in *International Economic Papers*, No. 5, London, 1955.
178. Reprinted in *Collectivist Economic Planning*, p. 245.
179. Samuelson, *op. cit.*, p. 217.
180. Hayek, *op. cit.*, p. 287. On the use

of computers, cf. O. Morgenstern, *Economic Activity Analysis*, New York, 1954, pp. 484ff.

181. An interesting variation of Barone's thesis was developed by Herbert Zassenhaus, a German economist who left his native country in the early thirties and has been in the United States since 1937. His article, "On The Theory of Economic Planning," written in 1934, is reprinted in *International Economic Papers*, No. 6, London, 1956. Zassenhaus employs the basic Barone solution for a socialist society in which the Ministry of Production would have to guide itself along marginalist principles. While the initial income distribution would be established by the Ministry, it would be very much influenced by the different interest groups in society whose rivalry would relay information to the central planners regarding their respective positions of strength. That is, Zassenhaus begins his analysis on the political level, although he turns quickly to the economic when he suggests that the various interest groups would exchange their "income" for the goods produced by the Ministry, thus initiating the movement toward equilibrium. Zassenhaus quite explicitly applies the marginal productivity concept, yet arrives at the conclusion that economic calculation under socialism is entirely feasible.
182. Cf. Hayek, *Individualism and Economic Order*, especially pp. 181ff.
183. *Ibid.*, p. 192.
184. Reprinted as "The Guidance of Production in a Socialist State" in Lippicott, *op. cit.*
185. *Ibid.*, p. 54.
186. *Ibid.*, pp. 57ff.
187. Joseph Berliner, *Factory and Manager in the USSR*, Cambridge, 1957.
188. Cf. H. D. Dickinson, *Economics of Socialism*, London, 1939.
189. See p. 477 below.
190. Later, in the 1940's, Lerner came to doubt that even Marx's *Theor-*

ien über den Mehrwert was worth translating.

191. A. P. Lerner, *Essays in Economic Analysis*, London, 1953, pp. 38ff.
192. *Idem., Economics of Control*, New York, 1944.
193. *Ibid.*, p. 67.
194. Cf. Samuelson, *Foundations of Economic Analysis*, pp. 219ff.
195. I. M. D. Little, *A Critique of Welfare Economics*, London, 1952.
196. *Ibid.*, p. 119.
197. *Ibid.*, p. 160.
198. Cf. his *Marginal Cost Price—Output Control*, New York, 1955, and *Economic Theory of a Socialist Economy*, Stanford, 1949.
199. Cf. his *Economic Theory of a Socialist Economy* with its numerous instructions to all levels of administration.
200. *Ibid.*, p. 78.
201. E. F. M. Durbin, *Problems of Economic Planning*, London, 1949. This extremely useful volume by the British Labor Party's late economist contains many useful observations on administrative aspects. Cf. also W. A. Lewis, *Principles of Economic Planning*, London, 1950, and J. E. Meade, *Planning and the Price Mechanism*, New York, 1949.
202. Durbin, *op. cit.*, p. 151.
203. *Ibid.*, p. 89.
204. Cf. his *Economics of Welfare*, London, 4th ed., 1932, and *Socialism versus Capitalism*, London, 1937.
205. Pigou, *Socialism versus Capitalism*, p. 119.
206. Additional remarks by Pigou on planning may be found in his *Essays in Economics*, London, 1952, p. 201.
207. Cf. Joseph A. Schumpeter, *Capitalism, Socialism and Democracy*, New York, 1942, pp. 167ff.
208. *Ibid.*, p. 167.
209. *Ibid.*, p. 172.
210. *Ibid.*, p. 174.
211. *Ibid.*, p. 177.
212. Cf. C. Northcote Parkinson, *Parkinson's Law*, New York, 1957. "Parkinson's Law" is the growth of manpower in inverse proportion to the amount of work done.

213. Schumpeter, *op. cit.*, p. 195.
214. *Ibid.*
215. Cf. his *On Economic Theory and Socialism*, London, 1955, p. 38.
216. *Ibid.*, p. 40.
217. Cf. his essay on economic planning in *Survey of Contemporary Economics*, Homewood, 1952, II, 355ff.
218. *Ibid.*, p. 384.
219. Cf. his *Political Economy and Capitalism*, London, 1937, p. 273.
220. Abba P. Lerner, "Economic Theory and the Problems of a Socialist Economy," *Review of Economic Studies*, October, 1934, p. 58.
221. Dobb, *op. cit.*, p. 319.
222. Dobb, *On Economic Theory and Socialism*, pp. 153 and 76ff., where the author's preference for a highly centralized economy is especially emphasized.
223. Cf. Dobb, *An Essay on Economic Growth and Planning*, New York, 1960.
224. *Ibid.*, pp. 77ff.
225. *Ibid.*, p. 5.
226. *On Economic Theory and Socialism*, pp. 89ff.
227. The best analysis of this debate may be found in Gregory Grossman's article, "Scarce Capital and Soviet Democracy," *Quarterly Journal of Economics*, August, 1953, pp. 31ff. Cf. also, Dobb, *Essay*, pp. 23ff.
228. Cf. R. W. Campbell, *Soviet Economic Power*, Cambridge, 1960, pp. 83ff.
229. Cf. Grossman, *op. cit.*
230. Alfred Zauberman, "Law of Value and Price Formation," in *Value and Plan*, ed. Gregory Grossman, Berkeley, 1960. This symposium by a group of knowledgeable Soviet experts is one of the best of its kind.
231. Grossman, "The 'Time Factor' in Soviet Economics," *Problems of Communism*, Washington, May-June, 1959, p. 6.
232. Their major papers were translated in *International Economic Papers*: cf. No. 1, 1951, p. 160 for Strumilin's essay, "The Time Factor in Capital Investment Projects," and No. 6, 1956, "On

Choosing Between Investment Projects," p. 66. Cf. also T. S. Khachaturov, "Economic Effectiveness of Capital Investments in the USSR," *Proceedings, American Economic Association*, May, 1958, p. 368.

233. *International Economic Papers*, No. 6, p. 69.

234. *Ibid.*, p. 163.

235. For an interesting, if pathetic, example of Stalinist fawning, see Oskar Lange, "The Economic Laws of Socialistic Society in the Light of Joseph Stalin's Last Work," reprinted in *International Economic Papers*, No. 4, 1954. This was written after Lange's return to Poland. Lange is now able to do more serious work, cf. his *Essays on Economic Planning*, Calcutta, 1960.

236. Alec Nove, *Soviet Survey*, November-December, 1957.

237. *New York Times*, 4 January 1959, p. 22. Cf. also E. M. Fels, "Some Soviet Statistical Books of 1957," *Journal of American Statistical Association*, March, 1959, pp. 16ff.

238. Grossman, *op. cit., P. O. C.*, p. 7. Cf. also his article "Suggestions for a Theory of Soviet Investment Planning," in' *Investment Criteria and Economic Growth*, New York, 1961, pp. 95ff.

239. *International Economic Papers*, No. 7, London, 1957, p. 125. Cf. also for other post-Stalin discussions of Soviet and satellite economic theory, Oskar Lange, "A Reconversion Plan for the Polish Economy," *ibid.*, p. 145; R. Janakieff, "On the Use of the Gross Production Index," *ibid.*, No. 8, London, 1958, p. 179; and S.

Varga, "Money in Socialism," *ibid.*, p. 201. Current Soviet articles on the subject are being made available in translations from *Problems of Economics*, the official economics journal of the Soviet Union. For a discussion of Polish economics, cf. J. M. Montias, "Producer Prices in a Centrally Planned Economy," in *Value and Plan*, pp. 47ff., and B. Cazes, "Rationality and Doctrine in Economic Thought," in *Problems of Communism*, March-April, 1960, p. 9. Cf. also, A. Nove, *The Soviet Economy*, New York, 1961, especially Parts II and III, pp. 145, 251ff.; and F. D. Holzman, ed., *Readings on the Soviet Economy*, Chicago, 1962.

240. W. Leontief, "The Decline and Rise of Soviet Economic Science," *Foreign Affairs*, January 1960, pp. 261ff.; *New York Times*, 19 April 1958, p. 5.

241. *New York Times*, 24 May 1959, p. 1.

242. Cf. also Campbell, *op. cit.*, pp. 110ff.; and B. Ward, "Kantorovich on Economic Calculation" in Holzman, *op. cit.*

243. Cf. W. Leontief, "Problems of Quality and Quantity in Economics," *Daedalus*, Vol. 88, No. 4, 1959, p. 622.

244. *New York Times*, 12 June 1960. Cf. also the excellent summary of the debate by J. M. Montias, *Problems of Communism*, May-June, 1960, pp. 61ff.

245. *New York Times*, 29 May 1959, p. 3.

246. Alec Nove, "Politics of Economic Rationality," *Social Research*, Summer, 1958, pp. 127ff.

Chapter 3
Institutionalism and
the Dissenting Spirit

1. William Jaffé, *Les Théories Économiques et Sociales de Thorstein Veblen*, Paris, 1924; Joseph Dorfman, *Thorstein Veblen and His America*, New York, 1934; David Riesman, *Thorstein Veblen; A Critical Interpretation*, New York, 1952; Lev E. Dobriansky, *Veblenism, a New Critique*, Washington, 1957. Cf. also, Bernard Rosenberg, *The Values of Veblen*, Washington, 1956. Other useful studies are S. M. Daugert, *The Philosophy of Thorstein Veblen*, New York, 1950; Louis Schneider, *Freudian Psychology and Veblen's Social Theory*, New York, 1948; and Douglas F. Dowd, editor, *Thorstein Veblen, a Critical Reappraisal*, Ithaca, 1958. Good shorter essays may be found in Alfred Kazin, *On Native Grounds*, New York, 1942; Daniel Aaron, *Men of Good Hope*, New York, 1951; Morton White, *Social Thought in America*, New York, 1947; Allan G. Gruchy, *Modern Economic Thought: The American Contribution*, New York, 1947; and A. L. Harris, *Economics and Social Reform*, New York, 1958.
2. Cf. John Chamberlain, *Farewell to Reform*, New York, 1932.
3. Cf. John R. Commons *et al.*, *History of Labor in the United States*, Vol. IV, New York, 1935 and Philip Taft, *The AFL in the Time of Gompers*, New York, 1957.
4. Cf. A. Lindsay, *The Pullman Strike*, Chicago, 1942.
5. Richard Hofstadter, *The Age of Reform*, New York, 1955.

6. Cf. Joseph Dorfman, *The Economic Mind in American Civilization*, New York, 1949, III, 217ff.
7. Cf. Stow Persons, *American Minds*, New York, 1958, pp. 221ff.
8. William Miller, *A History of the United States*, New York, 1958, pp. 317ff.
9. Chamberlain, *op. cit.*, pp. 119ff. Cf. also A. and L. Weinberg, eds., *The Muckrakers*, New York, 1961.
10. Dorfman, *Veblen*, p. 16. Cf. also his *Economic Mind*, III, 215-237, 309-358, for an excellent overview of the economic and social problems in the thirty year period from 1890 to 1920.
11. Dorfman, *Veblen*, pp. 7ff.
12. Thorstein Veblen, *Essays in Our Changing Order*, New York, 1943, pp. 219ff.
13. Virtually all commentators from Wesley Mitchell to Alfred Kazin to Bernard Rosenberg have noted that this essay, written originally for a Zionist journal, was a sketch for a self-portrait.
14. Cf. Richard Hofstadter, *Social Darwinism in American Thought*, 1944, revised Boston, 1955, pp. 51ff.
15. Cf. Joseph J. Spengler, "Evolutionism in American Economics," in Stow Persons, ed., *Evolutionary Thought in America*, New Haven, 1950, pp. 212ff.
16. Dorfman, *Veblen*, pp. 73ff.
17. Veblen, *Theory of the Leisure Class*, New York, 1899.
18. Veblen, *Place of Science in Modern Civilization*, New York, 1919, p. 70.

19. Cf. R. L. Duffus, *The Innocents at Cedro*, New York, 1944.
20. W. C. Mitchell, *What Veblen Taught*, New York, 1936, p. xviii.
21. Dowd, *op. cit.*, p. 23.
22. Lucy Sprague Mitchell, *Two Lives: The Story of Wesley Clair Mitchell and Myself*, New York, 1953, p. 86.
23. Veblen, *The Place of Science in Modern Civilization*, New York, 1919; *idem., Essays in our Changing Order*, New York, 1943.
24. Veblen, *The Theory of Business Enterprise*, New York, 1904.
25. *Leisure Class*, p. 188.
26. Cf. White, *op. cit.*
27. The major criticisms are to be found in the extraordinary set of three essays entitled, "The Preconceptions of Economic Science," included in *Place of Science in Modern Civilization*, pp. 82ff. Several other essays in this volume amplify the theme.
28. *Place of Science*, p. 70.
29. Cf. also Morris Raphael Cohen, *A Preface to Logic*, New York, 1944, p. x.
30. *Place of Science*, p. 175. Veblen did admit that Marshall sought to work out principles of continuity, but, he added, his technique was regrettably static.
31. *Ibid.*, p. 32.
32. *Ibid.*, p. 241.
33. *Ibid.*, p. 123.
34. *Ibid.*, p. 111.
35. Cf. with the Hayek-Knight debate p. 657 below.
36. Cf. Veblen, *op. cit.*, pp. 70ff.
37. *Ibid.*, pp. 201ff.
38. *Ibid.*, p. 73.
39. Veblen, *The Instinct of Workmanship*, New York, 1914, p. 39.
40. "Professor Clark's Economics," *Place of Science*, pp. 180ff.
41. See discussion on Clark, p. 312 below.
42. "Gustav Schmoller's Economics," *Place of Science*, p. 252.
43. Cf. Veblen, *Absentee Ownership and Business Enterprise in Recent Times*, New York, 1924, pp. 62ff.
44. *Place of Science*, p. 421.
45. John S. Gambs, *Beyond Supply and Demand*, New York, 1946, pp. 6ff.
46. For an interesting comparison between Keynes and Veblen, cf. Allan G. Gruchy in C. L. Christenson, ed. *Economic Theory in Review*, Bloomington, 1949, pp. 96ff.
47. Cf. Dorfman, *Veblen*, p. 451.
48. Cf. especially Paul M. Sweezy, "Veblen's Critique of the American Economy," *Proceedings of the American Economic Association*, May, 1958, pp. 21ff.
49. *Place of Science*, pp. 409ff.
50. *Ibid.*, p. 141.
51. *Ibid.*, p. 426.
52. *Ibid.*, p. 32.
53. Cf. Sidney Hook, *The Hero in History*, New York, 1943.
54. *Place of Science*, p. 61. Cf. also on the principle of social cumulation, Gunnar Myrdal, *Value in Social Theory*, London, 1958, pp. 198ff. Myrdal also spoke of cumulative economic causation as a dynamic force in his *Monetary Equilibrium*, London, 1939, pp. 24ff., and in his massive study of the Negro problem, *An American Dilemma*, New York, 1944, pp. 1065ff.
55. *Place of Science*, p. 44.
56. *Ibid.*, p. 326.
57. On the economic basis for the rise of the priestly class, cf. Paul Radin, *Primitive Religion*, New York, 1937, pp. 40ff. Said Radin: "No great insight or vast accumulation of information was required to recognize the role of the economic determinants in the simpler civilizations and the specific and intimate connexion there of the method of food production with every phase of the struggle for wealth and power."
58. *Instinct of Workmanship*, p. 160.
59. *Ibid.*, p. 285.
60. On this point see Hannah Arendt's interesting and perceptive analysis in her *The Human Condition*, Chicago, 1958.
61. *Theory of Business Enterprise*, p. 27. For a useful description of capitalist economic change, cf.

also O. C. Cox, *The Foundations of Capitalism*, New York, 1959. Cf. also Commons *et. al.*, *op. cit.*, I, 31ff.

62. Cf. Gardner Murphy, *Experimental Social Psychology*, New York, 1931.
63. Cf. Rosenberg, *op. cit.*, p. 45.
64. *Instinct of Workmanship*, p. 41.
65. *Ibid.*, p. 39.
66. *Ibid.*, p. 1.
67. *Place of Science*, pp. 8ff.
68. *Instinct of Workmanship*, p. 31.
69. *Place of Science*, p. 241.
70. *Leisure Class*, p. 190.
71. *Ibid.*, p. 11. Cf. also Schneider, *op. cit.*, for a critical study.
72. Cf. Dorfman, *Veblen*, p. 324.
73. Dowd, *op. cit.*, p. 35.
74. Schneider, *op. cit.*, p. 76.
75. Cf. Herbert Marcuse, *Eros and Civilization*, Boston, 1955.
76. Cf. "The Beginnings of Ownership," *Essays in Our Changing Order*, New York, 1943, pp. 32ff.
77. *Leisure Class*, p. 193.
78. *Place of Science*, p. 71.
79. *Leisure Class*, p. 98.
80. *Ibid.*, p. 1.
81. *Place of Science*, p. 441.
82. *Absentee Ownership*, pp. 82ff.
83. *Ibid.*, p. 107.
84. *Ibid.*, p. 118.
85. *Ibid.*, p. 124.
86. *Ibid.*, pp. 319ff.
87. Dorfman, *Veblen*, p. 485.
88. Cf. A. A. Berle ˙ and Gardiner Means, *The Modern Corporation and Private Property*, New York, 1933.
89. Mitchell, *What Veblen Taught*, p. 41.
90. Veblen, *Business Enterprise*, p. 290.
91. *Ibid.*, pp. 26ff.
92. *Ibid.*, p. 296.
93. *Ibid.*, p. 139.
94. *Ibid.*, p. 119.
95. *Vested Interests*, p. 160.
96. *Business Enterprise*, p. 94.
97. Cf. *ibid.*, pp. 199ff.
98. *Essays in Our Changing Order*, p. 111.
99. *Business Enterprise*, p. 113.
100. *Ibid.*, p. 183.
101. *Ibid.*, p. 224.

102. Cf. J. M. Keynes, *The General Theory of Employment, Interest and Money*, New York, 1936, p. 315.
103. Veblen, *Engineers and the Price System*, New York, 1921, p. 90.
104. For a modern version of this theory, cf. C. Wright Mills, *The Causes of World War III*, New York, 1958.
105. *Business Enterprise*, pp. 294ff.
106. *Ibid.*, pp. 391ff.
107. *Absentee Ownership*, p. 425.
108. *Engineers and the Price System*, *passim*.
109. *Ibid.*, pp. 166ff.
110. *Absentee Ownership*, p. 445.
111. A host of recent writings, from *The Organization Man* of William Whyte, Jr. to Vance Packard's *The Status Seekers*, testifies to the potency of the Veblenian vision on this score. Cf. William H. Whyte, Jr., *The Organization Man*, New York, 1956; Louis Kronenberger, *Company Manners*, New York, 1955; John Keats, *Crack in the Picture Window*, Boston, 1957; idem, *The Insolent Chariots*, New York, 1958; Vance Packard, *The Hidden Persuaders*, Philadelphia, 1957; idem, *The Status Seekers*, Philadelphia, 1959; and A. C. Spectorsky, *The Exurbanites*, New York, 1955. This genre of sociological writing has done much to expose the flaccid quality of contemporary culture and in this respect its lineage may be traced to Thorstein Veblen. Cf. also, in a more literary vein, Richard Chase, *The Democratic Vista*, New York, 1958.
112. Rosenberg, *op. cit.*, pp. 9ff.
113. Cf. Veblen, *The Higher Learning in America*, New York, 1918, *passim*, and C. Wright Mills, *White Collar*, New York, 1951, pp. 129ff.
114. *Higher Learning*, p. 88.
115. *Ibid.*, p. 156.
116. Riesman, *op. cit.*, defends the universities against the Veblenian animus, for, he insists, they had to be practical in their ways. But we must observe that of all

the works on Veblen, Riesman's, which ascribes most of Veblen's theory to a deep rooted hostility to his father, is the least useful. Riesman convinces himself that he knew Veblen better than anyone— including Veblen himself.

117. *Place of Science*, p. 241.
118. The first use of the term, institutionalist, according to Joseph Dorfman, was made by Walton H. Hamilton in an essay on Robert F. Hoxie in 1916. Cf. Dorfman, *Economic Mind*, IV, p. 353.
119. C. E. Ayres, *The Theory of Economic Progress*, Chapel Hill, 1944. Cf. also Joseph Dorfman, "The Source and Impact of Veblen's Thought," in Dowd, *op. cit.*, p. 8ff.
120. Cf. Spengler in Stow Persons, *op. cit.*, pp. 252ff.
121. John R. Commons, *Myself*, New York, 1934, p. 11. This charming autobiography is essential reading for an understanding of Commons' personality.
122. J. R. Commons, *Social Reform in The Church*, New York, 1894, with an introduction by Richard T. Ely.
123. Dorfman, *Economic Mind*, III, 285.
124. J. R. Commons, *Distribution of Wealth*, New York, 1893.
125. *Myself*, p. 58.
126. *Ibid.*, pp. 65-67.
127. W. C. Mitchell, *The Backward Art of Spending Money*, New York, 1937, p. 316.
128. Commons, *Documentary History of Industrial Society*, Cleveland, 1910-11.
129. Commons, *History of Labor in the United States*, 4 vols., New York, 1918-1935.
130. New York, 1924 and New York, 1934. Commons was a prodigious writer. The bibliography in the posthumous *Economics of Collective Action*, New York, 1950, lists over thirty pages of articles, reviews, and books ranging over a fantastic variety of social and economic fields. The major works in addition to those cited are *Proportional Representation*, New York, 1907; *Trade Unionism and Labor*

Problems, New York, 1905; *Races and Immigrants in America*, New York, 1908; *Labor and Administration*, New York, 1913; and *Principles of Labor Legislation* (with John B. Andrews), New York, 1916.
131. *Myself*, p. 3.
132. *Ibid.*, p. 18; *Collective Action*, pp. 25ff.
133. For a sympathetic statement of the Peirce philosophy, cf. Philip P. Weiner, "Introduction," to Charles S. Peirce, *Values in a Universe of Chance: Selected Writings*, New York, 1958.
134. *Myself*, p. 10.
135. *Ibid.*, p. 87.
136. *Ibid.*, p. 124.
137. Cf. Dorfman, *Economic Mind*, IV, 393ff.
138. *Distribution*, p. 14.
139. *Ibid.*, p. 67.
140. *Ibid.*, p. 223.
141. *Ibid.*, p. 249.
142. *Myself*, p. 63. Cf. also Wicksell, p. 539 below.
143. For an excellent summary of Commons' monetary views, cf. Dorfman, *Economic Mind*, IV, 383ff.
144. *Institutional Economics*, p. 3.
145. *Ibid.*, p. 5.
146. *Ibid.*, p. 8.
147. *Ibid.*, p. 16.
148. *Ibid.*, p. 25.
149. *Ibid.*, p. 43.
150. *Ibid.*, pp. 45ff.
151. *Ibid.*, p. 704.
152. *Ibid.*, p. 378.
153. *Ibid.*, pp. 390ff.
154. Cf. *Legal Foundations*, p. viii.
155. *Institutional Economics*, p. 103.
156. *Ibid.*, p. 107.
157. *Ibid.*, p. 723.
158. *Ibid.*, p. 709.
159. Cf. *Documentary History*, III, 18; *Institutional Economics*, pp. 763ff.; and *Collective Action*, p. 61.
160. *Documentary History*, III, 61ff.
161. *Institutional Economics*, p. 771.
162. *Ibid.*, p. 773. Cf. also the chart of economic stages, p. 764.
163. *Ibid.*, p. 511.
164. *Ibid.*, p. 889.
165. *Ibid.*, p. 898.
166. Cf. Henry C. Simons, *A Positive*

Program for Laissez-Faire, Chicago, 1934, *idem, Economic Policy for a Free Society,* Chicago, 1948. While Simons might have accepted this inference from the Commons argument, it is questionable whether he would have flirted with anything else that Commons wrote about.

167. Gruchy, *op. cit.,* p. 154.
168. Cf. Harris, *op. cit.,* pp. 226ff. But Harris could be chided with having read his own neo-conservative bias into the various decisions.
169. *Legal Foundations,* pp. 143ff.
170. *Ibid.,* pp. 182ff.; also cf. *Institutional Economics,* p. 620.
171. *Institutional Economics,* p. 634. It is regrettable that contemporary organization theory has ignored Commons. Cf. J. G. March and H. A. Simon, *Organizations,* New York, 1958, pp. 83ff. These authors have analysed the structure of organization in terms of the participation of individuals as they function within the organization. Their concepts of withdrawal and acceptance in terms of bargaining relationships seems to have a striking kinship to Commons, especially when they consider the question of conflict over alternative patterns with elements of uncertainty as significant factors in the situation. Commons' view can be fairly described as one in which the designs, purposes, and activities of humans lead to organization. This is the way in which economic relations are established. Cf. Kenneth Parsons, "John R. Commons' Point of View," Appendix iii, in *Economics of Collective Action,* p. 341, reprinted from *Journal of Land and Public Utility Economics,* August, 1942.
172. *Collective Action,* p. 11.
173. *Ibid.,* p. 27.
174. *Ibid.,* p. 29. The similarity to game theory is striking. Cf. my article "Games Theory and Collective Bargaining," *Labor and Nation,* August 1952, p. 50.
175. Cf. John K. Galbraith, *American Capitalism,* Boston, 1952.
176. *Collective Action,* p. 38.

177. *Institutional Economics,* p. 55.
178. *Ibid.,* p. 58.
179. Cf. on this point, Kenneth E. Boulding, *A Reconstruction of Economics,* New York, 1950. Boulding attempts in this work to deal with the firm from the point of view of capital accounts, inventory changes, cash position, and the like. These are all asset-liability concepts and, as in Commons' approach, make the balance sheet the central focus of economic concern. Cf. p. 683 below.
180. *Collective Action,* p. 46.
181. *Institutional Economics,* p. 684.
182. *Collective Action,* pp. 77, 81.
183. *Institutional Economics,* p. 718.
184. *Ibid.,* pp. 737-38.
185. *Collective Action,* p. 98.
186. *Institutional Economics,* p. 256.
187. *Collective Action,* pp. 94ff.
188. *Institutional Economics,* p. 423.
189. *Collective Action,* p. 104.
190. *Institutional Economics,* pp. 390ff.
191. Cf. *Ibid.,* p. 429.
192. *Myself,* p. 155.
193. *Ibid.,* p. 156
194. *Institutional Economics,* p. 682.
195. *Ibid.,* p. 683.
196. *Collective Action,* p. 145; *Legal Foundations,* p. 379.
197. *Collective Action,* pp. 152-153.
198. *Ibid.,* p. 159.
199. *Legal Foundations,* p. 380.
200. *Myself,* pp. 84ff.
201. *Ibid.,* p. 87.
202. *Documentary History,* III, 18ff.; VII, 19ff.; and IX, 19.
203. *Ibid.,* V, 23ff.
204. Cf. *Labor and Administration,* p. 261.
205. *Ibid.,* pp. 49ff.
206. *History of Labor,* I, 5, 9ff.
207. Cf. *Industrial Goodwill,* New York, 1919, p. 185.
208. *Myself,* p. 73.
209. Cf. Harvey Swados, "The Myth of the Powerful Worker," *The Nation,* June 28, July 5, 1958. These articles demonstrated how a politically dominated National Labor Relations Board could be something less than the impartial adjudicators that the Commons' view would call for.
210. Mills, *White Collar.*

211. Cf. Harvey Swados, "The Myth of the Happy Worker," *The Nation*, August 17, 1957.
212. Cf. Dorfman, *Economic Mind*, IV, 361.
213. The best source for biographic facts on Mitchell is the superb book by his wife, Lucy Sprague Mitchell, *op. cit.*
214. *Ibid.*, p. 16.
215. *Ibid.*, pp. 83-84.
216. Letter to John Maurice Clark, August 9, 1928, reprinted in latter's *Preface to Social Economics*, New York, 1936, pp. 410ff.; also in A. F. Burns, ed., *Wesley Clair Mitchell: The Economic Scientist*, New York, 1952, pp. 93ff.
217. Burns, *ibid.*, p. 95.
218. Cf. Paul T. Homan, *Contemporary Economic Thought*, New York, 1928, p. 409.
219. John Dewey, *Human Nature and Conduct*, New York, 1922, p. 84.
220. *Two Lives*, p. 85.
221. Dorfman, *Economic Mind*, III, 272.
222. *History of the Greenbacks*, Chicago, 1903.
223. *Two Lives*, p. 92.
224. *Greenbacks*, p. 207.
225. From an address on statistical method, quoted by Dorfman, *op. cit.*, III, 459.
226. *Economic Scientist*, p. 16.
227. Letter to Lucy Sprague Mitchell, October 18, 1911, cited in *Economic Scientist*, p. 66.
228. *Two Lives*, p. 171.
229. *Gold, Prices and Wages Under the Greenback Standard*, Berkeley, 1908, p. 281.
230. *Two Lives*, p. 173. For a recent history of economic thought along these lines, cf. Leo Rogin, *The Meaning and Validity of Economic Theory*, New York, 1956.
231. *Two Lives*, p. 176.
232. *Ibid.*, p. 187.
233. *Ibid.*, p. 290.
234. *Ibid.*, p. 485.
235. *Ibid.*, p. 246.
236. Cf. *The Backward Art of Spending Money*, especially the essays on Bentham and Ricardo, pp. 177ff. and 203ff.
237. *Two Lives*, pp. 294ff.
238. *Ibid.*, p. 302.
239. *Ibid.*, pp. 342-43.
240. Some of these studies were Mitchell, King, Macaulay, and Knauth, *Income in the United States*, New York, 1921; Simon Kuznets, *National Income and Capital Formation, 1919-1935*, New York, 1937; idem, *National Income and Its Composition, 1919-1938*, New York, 1941; idem, *National Product in Wartime*, New York, 1945. For a complete bibliography of the Bureau's publications, see its thirty-eighth Annual Report, *Investing in Economic Knowledge*, May 1958, pp. 101ff.
241. Burns, *op. cit.*, p. 51.
242. The description of his last ailment is related with sadness and affection by his wife, cf. *Two Lives*, pp. 517ff.
243. This is currently available in a paperback edition, Berkeley, 1959.
244. *Ibid.*, p. vii.
245. Burns, *op. cit.*, p. 24.
246. Wesley C. Mitchell, *Business Cycles*, Part III, reprint ed., p. x.
247. *Ibid.*, p. 2.
248. *Ibid.*, p. 5.
249. *Ibid.*, p. 13.
250. *Ibid.*, p. 17.
251. *Ibid.*, p. 23.
242. *Ibid.*, p. 25.
253. *Ibid.*, p. 53.
254. Hansen's essay in the Burns edited volume, p. 304.
255. Alvin H. Hansen, *Business Cycles and National Income*, New York, 1951, pp. 404ff.
256. Cf. Mitchell, *Business Cycles*, pp. 64ff.
257. *Ibid.*, p. 123.
258. *Ibid.*, p. 135.
259. *Ibid.*, p. 139.
260. *Ibid.*, pp. 144-45.
261. *Ibid.*, p. 166.
262. *Ibid.*, p. 168.
263. *Ibid.*, p. 171.
264. *Ibid.*, p. 173.
265. Cf. Joseph Dorfman in the Burns edited volume, p. 130.
266. *Business Cycles*, p. 191.
267. Cf. Hansen, *op. cit.*, p. 406.
268. Cf. Burns, *op. cit.*, p. 26.
269. M. Friedman, "Wesley C. Mitchell as an Economic Theorist," *Journal*

of *Political Economy*, December, 1950, reprinted in Burns, *ibid.*, p. 237.

270. *Ibid.*, p. 271.

271. For an interesting discussion of the relation of economic change to cycles in the Mitchell sense, cf. Simon Kuznets, *Economic Change*, New York, 1953, p. 125.

272. Cf. C. Wright Mills, *The Sociological Imagination*, New York, 1959, pp. 85ff.

273. *Two Lives*, p. 516.

274. *Business Cycles: The Problem and Its Setting*, pp. 61ff.

275. "Human Behavior and Economics," *Quarterly Journal of Economics*, November, 1914, p. 1.

276. *Ibid.*, p. 11.

277. *Backward Art of Spending Money*, p. 30.

278. *Business Cycles: Problem and Its Setting*, p. 106.

279. *Backward Art*, p. 150.

280. *Ibid.*, p. 160.

281. *Ibid.*, p. 171.

282. This first appeared in the *American Economic Review*, June, 1912. It was reprinted in the book of the same title, New York, 1937.

283. *Ibid.*, p. 16.

284. "Making Goods and Making Money," in *Backward Art*, p. 142.

285. *Ibid.*, p. 143.

286. "Role of Money in Economic Institutions," *Journal of Economic History*, Supplement IV, December 1944, pp. 64ff.

287. *Backward Art*, p. 256.

288. *Ibid.*

289. *Ibid.*, p. 371.

290. *Ibid.*, p. 20.

291. Cf. Dorfman, *Economic Mind*, IV, 362.

292. Mills, *op. cit.*, p. 20.

293. *Backward Art*, p. 177. Jacob Viner, who has been characterized as a twentieth-century Ricardian, demurs from Mitchell's demolition of Bentham's felicific calculus, suggesting that it was but an early version of econometrics. Cf. Viner's essay, "Bentham and J. S. Mill: The Utilitarian Background," in his *The Long View and the Short*, New York, 1958, pp. 315-16.

294. Homan, *op. cit.*, p. 433.

295. Cf. Gruchy, "Keynes and the Institutionalists," in *Economic Theory in Review*, pp. 104ff. Cf. also H. R. Bowen and G. M. Meier, "Institutional Aspects of Economic Fluctuations," in K. K. Kurihara, ed., *Post-Keynesian Economics*, New Brunswick, 1954, pp. 155ff.

296. Cf. Morris A. Copeland, *Fact and Theory in Economics*, Ithaca, 1958, p. 62.

297. Mitchell, *Lectures on Types of Economic Theory*, mimeographed, New York, 1935.

298. Allan Gruchy, *Modern Economic Thought*, New York, 1947, p. 249.

299. *Lectures*, I, 1.

300. *Two Lives*, pp. 363ff.

301. *Ibid.*, p. 368.

302. *Ibid.*, pp. 373ff.

303. *Ibid.*, p. 380.

304. *Backward Art*, p. 91.

305. *Two Lives*, p. 523.

306. *Backward Art*, p. 127.

307. Cf. Dorfman, *Economic Mind*, V, 667.

308. Cf. F. G. Hill, "Wesley Mitchell's Theory of Planning," *Political Science Quarterly*, March 1957, pp. 100ff.

309. Robert S. Lynd, *Knowledge for What?* Princeton, 1939.

310. *Ibid.*, pp. 74ff.

311. *Ibid.*, p. 121.

312. Cf. *Two Lives*, p. 553.

313. *Ibid.*, p. 562.

314. *Backward Art*, p. 78.

315. Cf. especially Mitchell's essay, "Facts and Values in Economics," *Journal of Philosophy*, April 13, 1944, in which the issues are stated with admirable clarity, yet does not achieve a fusion of social science objectives. Mitchell's views at this point began to approach the mechanistic.

316. Burns and Mitchell, *Measuring Business Cycles*, New York, 1946, p. 96.

317. A. F. Burns, "New Facts on Business Cycles," in *The Frontiers of Economic Knowledge*, Princeton, 1954, p. 107.

318. *Ibid.*, p. 114.

319. *Measuring Business Cycles*, p. 448.

320. G. H. Moore, *Statistical Indicators*

of Cyclical Revivals and Recessions, Occasional Paper, No. 31, New York, 1950; *idem,* ed. *Business Cycle Indicators,* 2 vols., Princeton, 1961.

321. Hansen, *Business Cycles and National Income,* p. 589.

322. Joseph A. Schumpeter, "Mitchell's Business Cycles," in *Quarterly Journal of Economics,* November, 1930, p. 150.

323. *Ibid.,* p. 160.

324. *Ibid.,* p. 166.

325. Edward Ames, "A Theoretical and Statistical Dilemma in the Contributions of Burns, Mitchell and Frickey to Business Cycle Theory," *Econometrics,* October, 1948, p. 347; T. C. Koopmans, "Measurement Without Theory," *Review of Economic Statistics,* August, 1947, p. 161 and comments in *Review of Economics and Statistics,* May 1949, p. 27.

326. Cf. *Measuring Business Cycles,* pp. 466ff.

327. Koopmans, *op. cit.,* p. 164.

328. *Ibid.,* p. 167.

329. For a devastating attack on formalistic methods in social science, cf. Mills, *op. cit.,* pp. 50ff.; cf. also Copeland, *op. cit.,* "Institutional Economics and Model Analysis," pp. 54ff.

330. Dorfman, *Economic Mind,* V, 438.

331. *Ibid.,* p. 439.

332. J. M. Clark, *Demobilization of Wartime Economic Controls,* New York, 1944.

333. *Ibid.,* p. 440.

334. Cf. Clark, *Economic Institutions and Human Welfare,* New York, 1957, p. 68.

Cf. also J. M. Clark, *Competition as a Dynamic Process,* Washington, 1961, Chap. 9, especially pp. 230ff., in which the limited capacities of the consumer to judge prices and qualities are thoroughly explored. On consumer sovereignty as usually described in theoretical economics, Clark was quite dubious. For one thing, he seriously questioned the habit of taking as given the whole range of consumer problems by applying the rubric of "taste." Some things,

such as education, safety, and health, did demand measures of social control and therefore required analysis. The fact was, said Clark, that the capacities and facilities of the consumer were ". . . most sketchy relative to the requirements of their exacting task as purchasers," *ibid.,* p. 232. To improve the position of the consumer, Clark urged product testing and education in consumer economics. *Competition as a Dynamic Process,* the latest of his works, which he published at the age of seventy-seven, came to hand after my manuscript had been completed and sent to the printer. However, an effort has been made to incorporate the major points of this most remarkable book from the pen of America's dean of the economics profession.

335. Clark, *Preface to Social Economics,* New York, 1936, p. 113.

336. *Ibid.,* p. 118.

337. *Ibid.,* p. 3.

338. *Ibid.,* p. 9.

339. On this point, cf. the cogent analysis in Hannah Arendt, *The Human Condition,* Chicago, 1959. Dr. Arendt's study of the distinction between work and labor is one of the most incisive analyses yet made on this question.

340. *Social Economics,* p. 38. On this point Clark may have been somewhat premature.

341. *Ibid.,* p. 49.

342. *Ibid.,* p. 59.

343. *Ibid.,* p. 94.

344. *Ibid.,* p. 97.

345. *Ibid.,* p. 99.

346. *Ibid.,* p. 104.

347. *Ibid.,* p. 105.

348. *Ibid.,* p. 111.

349. *Ibid.,* pp. 123-34.

350. *Ibid.,* p. 141.

351. *Ibid.,* p. 146.

352. *Ibid.,* p. 207.

353. J. M. Clark, *Alternatives to Serfdom,* New York, 1948.

354. *Ibid.,* p. 27.

355. *Ibid.,* p. 29.

356. *Ibid.,* p. 39.

357. *Ibid.,* p. 59.

358. Cf. p. 318 below on J. B. Clark.

359. *Social Economics*, p. 226. Cf. also *Competition as a Dynamic Process*, pp. 55ff., in which a greater stress is placed on dynamic factors.
360. *Social Economics*, p. 211.
361. For a good discussion of these types of investment, cf. Daniel Hamberg, *Business Cycles*, New York, 1951, pp. 101ff.
362. *Social Economics*, p. 335. Cf. also Clark, *Strategic Factors in Business Cycles*, New York, 1934, p. 76.
363. Cf. G. Haberler, *Prosperity and Depression*, revised ed., Geneva, 1940, p. 88.
364. *Social Economics*, p. 348.
365. *Strategic Factors*, pp. 18, 20.
366. Cf. *Ibid.*, p. 21.
367. *Ibid.*, p. 38.
368. *Ibid.*, p. 52.
369. *Ibid.*, p. 154.
370. *Ibid.*, p. 85.
371. *Ibid.*, p. 147.
372. Cf. John P. Lewis, *Business Conditions Analysis*, New York, 1959, pp. 338-39.
373. R. Frisch, "Interrelation between Capital Production and Consumer Taking," *Journal of Political Economy*, October 1931, p. 646.
374. This was similar to the position taken by Nicholas Kaldor in his article, "A Model of Economic Growth," *Economic Journal*, December, 1957, reprinted in his *Essays on Economic Stability and Growth*, New York, 1960, p. 259. Kaldor argued that the ratio of capital to output is constant in the long run. This is, of course, a moot question. Cf., for example, J. W. Kendrick, *Productivity Trends in the United States*, Princeton, 1961, pp. 164ff. and S. Kuznets, *Capital in the American Economy*, Princeton, 1961, p. 218.
375. Haberler, *op. cit.*, p. 99.
376. Cf. Lewis, *op. cit.*, p. 205.
377. *Strategic Factors*, pp. 192-93.
378. J. M. Clark, *Studies in the Economics of Overhead Costs*, Chicago, 1923.
379. *Ibid.*, p. 9.
380. *Ibid.*, p. 11. For Clark's latest views on market structure and behavior in relation to costs, cf.

Competition as a Dynamic Process, especially Chaps. 5, 6, 12, 14.
381. *Overhead Costs*, p. 29.
382. *Ibid.*, p. 60.
383. *Ibid.*, p. 87.
384. *Ibid.*, p. 215.
385. *Ibid.*, p. 147.
386. Cf. Joe S. Bain, *Barriers to New Competition*, Cambridge, 1956, for a cogent study of this problem. Bain found that barriers to entry were based on absolute cost advantages of the established firms, an advantage which stemmed from control of production techniques, market imperfections, or a preferential position in the money market. These conditions supplement Clark's factor of size.
387. *Overhead Costs*, p. 386.
388. *Ibid.*, p. 401.
389. *Ibid.*, p. 415.
390. *Ibid.*, p. 416.
391. For Clark's latest views on price discrimination, cf. *Competition as a Dynamic Process*, pp. 344ff. Also cf. L. Walras, *Elements of Pure Economics*, translated by William Jaffé, London, 1954, pp. 440ff. For a good analytic presentation, cf. George Stigler, *Theory of Price*, New York, 1947, pp. 223ff.
392. J. Robinson, *Economics of Imperfect Competition*, London, 1933; A. C. Pigou, *Economics of Welfare*, 4th ed., London, 1932, pp. 275ff. Clark's system of market classification was criticized as being too all-inclusive in that the criteria employed related only to the number of sellers, neglecting such factors as the number of buyers, durability of product, and the problem of ease of entry into an industry. Cf. J. S. Bain, "Price and Production Policies," in *Survey of Contemporary Economics*, Philadelphia, 1948, I, 161.
393. Dorfman, *op. cit.*, V, 453.
394. *Overhead Costs*, p. 361.
395. *Ibid.*, p. 372.
396. *Ibid.*, p. 377.
397. *Ibid.*, p. 384.
398. J. M. Clark, *Social Control of Business*, Chicago, 1926, 2nd ed., New York, 1939.
399. A cogent argument in support of

this position was made by Erich Kahler in his *The Tower and the Abyss*, New York, 1957. On the requirements for a balanced economic community, cf. *Competition as a Dynamic Process*, Chaps. 17, 19.

400. *Social Control*, pp. 149ff.
401. Cf. Clark, *Alternatives to Serfdom*.
402. Clark, *Economic Institutions and Human Welfare*, New York, 1957, p. 101.
403. The theme of social responsibility implicit in these views was reiterated by Clark in his essay, "Financing High Level Employment," in *Financing American Prosperity*, ed. P. T. Homan and F. Machlup, New York, 1935, and in "Criteria of Social Wage Adjustment," in *The Impact of the Labor Union*, ed. D. M. Wright, New York, 1951. Unfortunately, most of the other contributors to the latter symposium did not exhibit the same sense of balance as did Clark. Cf. my review of the book in *The New Leader*, November 12, 1951.
404. Cf. James Bonar, *Philosophy and Political Economy*, London, 1893; cf. also Joseph A. Schumpeter, *Economic Doctrine and Method*, translated London, 1954, pp. 13ff.
405. *Economic Institutions*, p. 59.
406. *Ibid.*, p. 29.
407. On the present role of intellect in modern society, cf. Jacques Barzun, *The House of Intellect*, New York, 1959.
408. *Economic Journal*, September 1913, p. 39.
409. Keynes, *op. cit.*, pp. 365ff.
410. Cf. G. D. H. Cole, *History of Socialist Thought*, London, 1956, III; 194.
411. J. A. Hobson, *Confessions of an Economic Heretic*, London, 1938, p. 15.
412. *Ibid.*, p. 26.
413. *Ibid.*, p. 29.
414. *Ibid.*, p. 30.
415. J. A. Hobson and A. F. Mummery, *The Physiology of Industry*, reprinted, New York, 1956.
416. *Confessions*, p. 30. Cf. also, T. W.

Hutchison, *Review of Economic Doctrines*, London, 1953, pp. 118ff.
417. If Hobson seemed somewhat acerb about academicians, there was ample reason. Hobson's attitude ought not to be so puzzling as it is to E. E. Nemmers. Cf. the latter's *Hobson and Underconsumption*, Amsterdam, 1956.
418. For a complete bibliography, cf. Nemmers, *ibid.*, pp. 144ff.
419. J. A. Hobson, *Evolution of Modern Capitalism*, London, 1894, 3rd ed., reprinted 1949.
420. J. A. Hobson, *Imperialism*, London, 1902, 3rd ed., 1938.
421. *Confessions*, p. 61.
422. *Ibid.*, p. 58.
423. J. A. Hobson, *Work and Wealth*, London, 1914, p. 9.
424. *Confessions*, p. 39.
425. *Ibid.*, p. 42.
426. *Ibid.*, p. 77.
427. J. A. Hobson, *Free Thought in the Social Sciences*, London, 1926.
428. *Confessions*, p. 80.
429. Cf. Nemmers, *op. cit.*, p. 26.
430. *Physiology*, p. iv.
431. Cf. Nemmers, *op. cit.*, pp. 5ff., and Hansen, *Business Cycles and National Income*, pp. 229ff.
432. Keynes, *op. cit.*, pp. 368ff.
433. *Physiology*, p. 25.
434. Cf. p. 749 below.
435. Cf. J. A. Hobson, *The Industrial System*, London, 1910, pp. 40ff.
436. *Physiology*, pp. 121-22.
437. *Ibid.*, p. 87.
438. *Industrial System*, pp. vii, 62.
439. *Physiology*, p. 55.
440. Hutchison suggests that Hobson and Mummery did not break entirely with Say's Law. Hutchison's interpretation is not clear, however, for the very concept of underconsumption is the antithesis of Say's ebullient optimism. Cf. Hutchison, *op. cit.*, p. 120.
441. *Physiology*, p. 70.
442. *Ibid.*, p. 90.
443. *Ibid.*, p. 98.
444. *Ibid.*, p. 111.
445. *Ibid.*, p. 117.
446. *Evolution of Modern Capitalism*. p. 286. On the stickiness of consumer habits, cf. James S. Duesenberry, *Income, Saving and the*

Theory of Consumer Behavior, Cambridge, 1952.

447. J. A. Hobson, *Economics of Unemployment*, New York, 1922, p. 51.

448. *Physiology*, p. 162.

449. J. A. Hobson, *Problem of the Unemployed*, London, 1896.

450. *Industrial System*, p. 90.

451. Cf. V. I. Lenin, "Imperialism," in *Selected Works*, V, New York, 1935-39.

452. This by no means is intended to denigrate the work of Bauer, Hilferding, Kautsky, and Luxemburg. Cf. also, E. M. Winslow, *The Pattern of Imperialism*, New York, 1948.

453. Hobson, *Imperialism*, p. 4.

454. J. A. Hobson, *International Trade*, London, 1904; idem, *An Economic Interpretation of Investment*, London, 1911.

455. *Imperialism*, p. vi.

456. *Ibid.*, p. viii.

457. *Ibid.*, p. xxi.

458. Nemmers criticizes Hobson's imperialism thesis on the ground that greater profit opportunities, rather than excess savings and overproduction, were the major attraction for overseas expansion. This is quite unconvincing. Cf. Nemmers, *op. cit.*, p. 41. Cf. also Joseph A. Schumpeter's, "The Sociology of Imperialism," (1919) reprinted in *Imperialism and Social Classes*, New York, 1951. Schumpeter argued that imperialism was a feature of capitalism's youth and that in fact class conflict was reduced by imperialist ventures. Businessmen, he argued, follow the flag, not the other way around, and in fact, they tend to be anti-imperialist. That is to say, imperialism was a kind of atavistic policy that had no place in a rational capitalism. It would seem that Hobson had the better of the argument here.

459. John Strachey, *The End of Empire*, London, 1959, p. 117.

460. *Industrial System*, p. vii.

461. *Ibid.*, pp. 9-10.

462. Cf. *ibid*, Chap. 2, pp. 11ff.

463. *Ibid.*, p. 29.

464. *Ibid.*, p. 32.

465. *Ibid.*, p. 48.

466. Cf. *ibid.*, Chap. 4, pp. 56ff.

467. *Ibid.*, p. 60.

468. *Ibid.*, p. 62.

469. *Ibid.*, pp. 65, 68.

470. Homan argues that in Hobson's analysis all payments were reduced to rent, thus suggesting that he took over the marginal concept of the classicists *in toto*. This is clearly a misreading of Hobson. Cf. Paul Homan, *Contemporary Economic Thought*, New York, 1928, pp. 308ff.

471. *Industrial System*, p. 95. Classical theory held that marginal land was "no rent" land. Cf. David Ricardo, *Works and Correspondence*, ed. Piero Sraffa, London, 1951, I, 70ff.

472. *Industrial System*, p. 99.

473. *Ibid.*, p. 115.

474. *Ibid.*, p. 152.

475. *Free Thought in the Social Sciences*, Chap. III, pp. 112ff.

476. *Industrial System*, p. 118.

477. *Ibid.*, p. 123.

478. *Ibid.*, pp. 126-127.

479. Cf. *Work and Wealth*, Chap. XI, pp. 146ff.

480. *Industrial System*, pp. 294ff.

481. *Ibid.*, p. 307.

482. *Free Thought in the Social Sciences*, p. 2.

483. On this point, cf. Karl Mannheim, "Conservative Thought," in *Essays in Sociology and Social Psychology*, London, 1953, pp. 74ff. Mannheim pointed out that unattached intellectuals, whose own social position did not bind them to any special cause, were able to find arguments for any trend they happened to serve.

484. *Free Thought*, pp. 61ff.

485. *Ibid.*, p. 71.

486. *Ibid.*, p. 108.

487. *Ibid.*, p. 82.

488. *Work and Wealth*, p. 70.

489. *Ibid.*, p. 112.

490. *Ibid.*, p. 139.

491. *Ibid.*, p. 158.

492. Cf. *Free Thought*, p. 133 and *Industrial System*, p. 320.

493. Hobson, *Work and Wealth; idem, Economics and Ethics*, New York, 1929. The latter was published in

Britain under the title of *Wealth and Life.*

494. *Economics and Ethics*, p. xviii.
495. *Ibid.*, p. 21.
496. *Ibid.*, p. 40.
497. *Work and Wealth*, p. 293.
498. Cf. Homan, *op. cit.*, p. 374, and J. M. Clark, *Economic Institutions and Human Welfare*, p. 59.
499. C. E. Ayres, *Theory of Economic Progress*, Chapel Hill, 1944.
500. *Ibid.*, p. 85.
501. C. E. Ayres, *Divine Right of Capital*, Boston, 1946. This was a popularization of the ideas of the earlier book.
502. Robert F. Hoxie, *Trade Unions in the United States*, New York, 1917.
503. Alvin Johnson, *Pioneer's Progress*, New York, 1952, pp. 205ff.
504. The best analysis of Perlman's career is in *Labor Union Theories in America*, Evanston, 1958, pp. 190ff., written by his son, Mark Perlman.
505. Selig Perlman, *A Theory of the Labor Movement*, New York, 1928.
506. Cf. Philip Taft, *The A. F. of L.*, New York, 1959, Vol. II, Chaps. 11-15, pp. 140ff.
507. Cf. Gruchy, *op. cit.*, pp. 473ff.
508. A. A. Berle and Gardiner Means, *The Modern Corporation and Private Property*, New York, 1933.
509. Means, "Collective Capitalism and Economic Theory," in *Science*, August 16, 1957, pp. 287ff.
510. *Ibid.*, p. 288.
511. Cf. on this point, William J. Baumol, *Business Behavior, Value and Growth*, New York, 1959. Baumol offers the thesis that oligopolies are concerned with *sales* maximization, subject to certain profit constraints. This observation is one of the most important made in recent years, with serious implications for economic theory.
512. Means, *op. cit.*, p. 289.
513. *Ibid.*, p. 290.
514. *Ibid.*, p. 291.
515. A. A. Berle, *The Twentieth Century Capitalist Revolution*, New York, 1955.
516. Cf. Gruchy, *op. cit.*, pp. 496-97.

517. Means, "Collective Capitalism . . . ," p. 293.
518. For an excellent summary of these developments, cf. Dorfman, *op. cit.*, Vol. V, Chap. XX, pp. 589ff.
519. This was similar to the problem of repressed inflation discussed in more technical ways by Bent Hansen, *The Theory of Inflation*, London, 1951; H. K. Charlesworth, *Economics of Repressed Inflation*, London, 1956; cf. also A. J. Brown, *The Great Inflation*, London, 1955.
520. *A Theory of Price Control*, Cambridge, 1952.
521. *Ibid.*, pp. 22ff.
522. J. K. Galbraith, *American Capitalism: The Concept of Countervailing Power*, Boston, 1952.
523. Joan Robinson, *Economics of Imperfect Competition*, London, 1933, and E. H. Chamberlin, *Theory of Monopolistic Competition*, Cambridge, 1932. Cf. also George Stigler, *Five Lectures on Economic Problems*, London, 1949, especially Lecture 2, p. 12.
524. Galbraith, *op. cit.*, p. 51.
525. *Ibid.*, p. 93.
526. Cf. Daniel Hamberg, statement to the Joint Economic Committee, *Hearings on Employment, Growth and Price Levels*, Part VII, Washington, 1959, pp. 2337ff.; *idem, Principles of a Growing Economy*, New York, 1961, p. 689; *idem*, "Less Noise, More Research," *Challenge*, May, 1961, p. 18.
527. Galbraith, *op. cit.*, p. 118.
528. Cf. F. Y. Sutton, S. E. Harris, C. Kaysen, and J. Tobin, *The American Business Creed*, Cambridge, 1956.
529. J. K. Galbraith, *The Affluent Society*, Boston, 1958. For an attack and defense of Galbraith's position, cf. E. van den Haag, "Affluence, Galbraith, The Democrats," *Commentary*, September, 1960, and L. A. Coser and B. B. Seligman, "Affluence," *ibid.*, January, 1961.
530. Cf. Galbraith, *ibid.*, Chap. VII, pp. 78ff. Galbraith's data, however, rather blandly overlooked the fact

that in 1957 half the consumer units had incomes of less than $4200. per annum. Cf. *Federal Reserve Bulletin*, September 1958.

531. Galbraith, *op. cit.*, p. 116.
532. *Ibid.*, Chap. X, pp. 139ff.
533. Cf. *Ibid.*, pp. 150-51. On the latter point Galbraith quotes Keynes,

Essays in Persuasion, London, 1931.

534. Cf. Galbraith, "On Criticism in The Open Society." Address at Annamalai University, 12 October 1961, in which he said: "All open societies employ criticism as an instrument of change."

Chapter 4

From Marginalism

to Libertarianism

1. That there were earlier signs of the subjectivist approach was made evident by E. R. A. Seligman in his famous essay, "On Some Neglected British Economists," in *Essays in Economics*, New York, 1925, pp. 65ff.
2. Cf. Maurice Dobb, *Political Economy and Capitalism*, London, 1937, p. 139.
3. Harvey W. Peck, *Economic Theory and Its Institutional Background*, New York, 1935, p. 196. For an early Marxian attack on marginalism, cf. N. Bukharin, *Economic Theory of the Leisure Class*, 1919, translated New York, 1927.
4. Cf. C. Wright Mills, *The Power Elite*, New York, 1956.
5. Cf. *Letters and Journal of W. Stanley Jevons*, ed Mrs. W. S. Jevons, London, 1886, p. 101.
6. Appendix III, in W. S. Jevons, *Theory of Political Economy*, London, 1871, reprinted, New York, 1957, pp. 303ff.
7. Cf. the essay on Jevons by J. M. Keynes published originally in the *Journal of the Royal Statistical Society*, 1936, and reprinted in H. W. Spiegel, *The Development of Economic Thought*, New York, 1952, pp. 490ff. The comment referred to above is on pp. 515-16. For additional biographic notes,

cf. P. H. Wicksteed, *Common Sense of Political Economy*, London, 1933, II, 801.
8. Keynes, *op. cit.*, p. 491.
9. Cf. *ibid.*, p. 525.
10. *Letters*, p. 329.
11. *Ibid.*, p. 331.
12. Jevons, *Theory of Political Economy*, pp. 3ff.
13. *Ibid.*, p. 95.
14. Cf. Knut Wicksell, *Value, Capital and Rent*, 1893, (English translation, London, 1954) p. 18.
15. Jevons, *op. cit.*, p. 165.
16. Cf. Dobb, *op. cit.*, p. 163.
17. Jevons, *op. cit.*, pp. 183ff.
18. *Ibid.*, p. 93.
19. *Ibid.*, p. 32.
20. Cf. the essay on Bentham by W. C. Mitchell in *The Backward Art of Spending Money and other Essays*, New York, 1937, p. 177.
21. Jevons, *op. cit.*, p. 27.
22. Cf. C. Reinold Noyes, *Economic Man*, 2 vols, New York, 1948, pp. 452ff. and 1303.
23. Jevons, *op. cit.*, p. 16.
24. Dobb, *op. cit.*, p. 164.
25. Cf. Jevons, *op. cit.*, pp. 223, 263.
26. Cf. Jevons, *State in Relation to Labour*, London, 1882, p. 96.
27. Jevons, *Theory*, Appendix II, "Fragment on Capital," p. 295.
28. On this point one must agree with Wesley C. Mitchell who argues

this view in his essay, "The Role of Money in Economic Theory," in *The Backward Art of Spending Money*, pp. 152ff. Arthur W. Marget dissents strenuously in his *Theory of Prices*, New York, 1942, II, 54ff.

29. Published, London, 1909. This is actually a collection of essays including studies of the value of gold, the London money market and the sun-spot theory.

30. Cf. Marget, *op. cit.*, pp. 55ff.

31. Jevons, *Theory*, p. 168.

32. *Ibid.*, pp. 170ff. Cf. especially diagram p. 173.

33. Cf. Jevons, *Methods of Social Reform*, London, 1883, p. 186.

34. *Ibid.*, pp. 141ff.

35. Cf. Joseph Dorfman, *The Economic Mind in American Civilization*, New York, 1949, III, 101ff., for a discussion of this type of wage theory as popularized by the American economist, Francis A. Walker.

36. Jevons, *Theory*, p. 270.

37. Cf. *Investigations*, Chaps. VII and VIII, pp. 18 and 201.

38. *Ibid.*, p. 1.

39. Keynes, *op. cit.*, pp. 498-99.

40. W. C. Mitchell, *Business Cycles: The Problem and Its Setting*, New York, 1927, p. 194.

41. Jevons, *Investigations*, p. 184. The suggestion of disproportionate investment appears on p. 28.

42. *Letters*, p. 393.

43. Keynes speaks of Jevons as a manysided personality, but the circumscribed nature of his interests would suggest otherwise. Cf. Keynes, *op. cit.*, p. 516. For Jevons on Cantillon, cf. his essay in Henry Higgs edition of Cantillon's *Essai sur la Nature du Commerce en Génerale*, London, 1931, p. 363.

44. Jevons refers to the change of name in his Preface to the Second Edition, in which he stresses his concern with formal relations. pp. xivff.

45. Cf. M. Dobb, *Introduction to Economics*, London, 1932, pp. 109ff.

46. Jevons, *Theory*, p. 15.

47. Cf. F. v. Wieser, *Natural Value*, reprint, New York, 1956, Chap.

VII, p. 64; J. M. Clark, essay on John Bates Clark in Spiegel, *ibid.*, p. 610; Philip Wicksteed, *Common Sense of Political Economy*, London, 1910, reprinted 1933, II, 792.

48. Carl Brinkman, "Nationalism," in *Encyclopaedia of the Social Sciences*, New York, 1930, I, 166.

49. Jevons, *Social Reform*, p. 205.

50. Cf. George F. Stigler, *Production and Distribution Theories*, New York, 1941, pp. 13ff.

51. *Social Reform*, p. 108.

52. Cf. essay on Gossen by Léon Walras, reprinted in Spiegel, *op. cit.*, p. 474.

53. Jevons, *Letters*, p. 387.

54. Cf. pp. 272ff. below.

55. Translated as *Principles of Economics* by James Dingwall and Bert F. Hoselitz, New York, 1950.

56. "Geld" in the *Handworterbuch der Staatswissenschaften*, Jena, 1909, IV, 555.

57. Cf. Seligman, "On Some Neglected British Economists," pp. 65ff.

58. Joseph A. Schumpeter, *Ten Great Economists*, New York, 1951, p. 80.

59. Cf. F. A. von Hayek's essay on Menger in Spiegel, *op. cit.*, pp. 549ff.

60. Leo Rogin, *The Meaning and Validity of Economic Thought*, New York, 1956, p. 482.

61. Cf. Joseph A. Schumpeter, *History of Economic Analysis*, New York, 1954, pp. 300ff.

62. Cf. Appendices F and G in *Principles*, pp. 305ff. of the Dingwall-Hoselitz translation, the edition referred to here.

63. Hayek, *op. cit.*, p. 531.

64. Cf. p. 343 below.

65. Cf. Schumpeter, *op. cit.*, p. 814.

66. Cf. Karl Polanyi, *The Great Transformation*, New York, 1944, especially Part II, pp. 130ff.

67. Cf. *International Economic Papers*, No. 5, London, 1955, the first five papers of which clearly demonstrate the character of this influence.

68. Schumpeter, *op. cit.*, p. 827.

69. Cf. Noyes, *op. cit.*, pp. 29ff., and Kenneth E. Boulding, *The Skills of The Economist*, Cleveland,

1958, pp. 70ff. The notion of homeostasis forms a central part of Boulding's theory. Cf. also his *A Reconstruction of Economics,* New York, 1950.

70. *Principles,* p. 58.
71. *Ibid.,* p. 52.
72. *Ibid.,* p. 59.
73. *Ibid.,* p. 63.
74. *Ibid.,* p. 65.
75. *Ibid.,* pp. 77ff.
76. *Ibid.,* pp. 94ff.
77. *Ibid.,* pp. 106ff.
78. *Ibid.,* p. 126.
79. Cf. Stigler, *op. cit.,* p. 145.
80. Cf. p. 284 below.
81. Cf. Knut Wicksell, *Selected Papers on Economic Theory,* London, 1958, p. 197.
82. Menger, *op. cit.,* p. 165.
83. Cf. Joan Robinson, "Euler's Theorem and the Problem of Distribution," in *Collected Economic Papers,* London, 1951, I, pp. 1ff. Mrs. Robinson emphasizes the numerous difficulties inherent in this solution of the allocation problem.
84. Menger, *op. cit.,* p. 180.
85. *Ibid.,* pp. 191ff.
86. *Ibid.,* p. 187.
87. Wicksell, *op. cit.,* p. 199.
88. Menger, *op. cit.,* p. 131.
89. *Ibid.,* pp. 149-50.
90. *Ibid.,* p. 162.
91. Cf. Wicksell, *op. cit.,* p. 189.
92. Cf. Menger, *op. cit.,* pp. 257ff.
93. *Ibid.,* p. 87.
94. Cf. p. 284 below.
95. Cf. Menger, *op. cit.,* pp. 78ff.
96. *Ibid.,* pp. 115ff.
97. *Ibid.,* p. 112.
98. Originally published as *Theorie der Gesellschaftlichen Wirtschaft,* translated by A. F. Hinrichs, New York, 1927, with forward by Wesley C. Mitchell.
99. Cf. essay on Wieser by Friedrich von Hayek in Spiegel, *op. cit.,* p. 559.
100. Weiser, *Natural Value.*
101. This statement seems much closer to John Bates Clark's version than to Jevons' or Menger's. Cf. Dorfman, *op. cit.,* Vol. III, Appendix, p. iii, New York, 1949.
102. Wieser, *op. cit.,* p. 172.
103. *Ibid.,* p. 11.

104. *Ibid.,* p. 15.
105. *Ibid.,* p. 43.
106. *Ibid.,* p. 49.
107. *Ibid.,* p. 52.
108. *Ibid.,* p. 56.
109. This may also explain why some writers, such as George Stigler, consider him unimportant. Cf. Stigler, *op. cit.,* p. 158.
110. Wieser, *op. cit.,* p. 58.
111. *Ibid.,* p. 59.
112. *Ibid.,* p. 81.
113. *Ibid.,* p. 86.
114. Cf. Stigler, *op. cit.,* p. 164.
115. Wicksell, *Value, Capital and Rent,* p. 24.
116. Wieser, *op. cit.,* p. 92.
117. *Ibid.,* p. 125.
118. Cf. *Social Economics,* p. 38 and *Natural Value,* p. 167.
119. *Natural Value,* p. 200.
120. *Ibid.,* p. 161.
121. Cf. Stigler, *op. cit.,* pp. 170ff.
122. *Ibid.,* pp., 181ff.
123. Published originally in 1912 as *Epochen der Dogmen und Methodengeschichte,* translated, London, 1954.
124. *Social Economics,* p. 19.
125. *Ibid.,* p. 160.
126. *Ibid.,* p. 115.
127. *Ibid.,* pp. 149ff.
128. *Ibid.,* p. 151.
129. Cf. *ibid.,* p. 156.
130. *Ibid.,* p. 185.
131. *Ibid.,* p. 187.
132. *Ibid.,* p. 189.
133. *Ibid.,* p. 209.
134. *Ibid.,* p. 217.
135. See p. 716 below.
136. *Social Economics,* p. 378.
137. *Ibid.,* p. 379.
138. Cf. D. Mc. Wright, ed., *The Impact of the Labor Union,* New York, 1951, and my review of it in the *New Leader,* Nov. 12, 1951, p. 23. The Wright volume was a presentation of a symposium on labor unions by a number of economic theorists, which for sheer hostility and theoretical irrelevance would be hard to match. Seldom have so many biases been elevated to the realm of putative scientific truth with so much disregard for fact as in this volume. A noted Harvard economist once remarked to the

writer that the book should have been suppressed.

139. *Social Economics*. pp. 396ff.
140. Cf. p. 111 above.
141. *Ibid.*, pp. 456ff.
142. Cf. Stigler, *op cit.*, p. 168.
143. Cf. p. 403 below.
144. Cf. p. 60 above.
145. Cf. Schumpeter, *Ten Great Economists*, pp. 143ff.
146. *Ibid.*, p. 145.
147. Schumpeter, *History*, p. 844.
148. Cf. John Rae, *Sociological Theory of Capital*, reprint, New York, 1905, pp. 19, 132.
149. Subtitled, *A Critical History of Economical Theory*, trans. William Smart, London, 1890.
150. Böhm-Bawerk, *Rechte und Verhaltnisse*, Innsbruck, 1881.
151. Schumpeter, *op. cit.*, p. 161.
152. Cf. Böhm-Bawerk, *The Positive Theory of Capital*, London, 1891, p. 396.
153. Cf. Theo. Suranyi-Unger, *Economics in the Twentieth Century*, New York, 1931, pp. 89ff.
154. Cf. *Positive Theory*, p. 229.
155. *Ibid.*, p. 209.
156. *Ibid.*, p. 226.
157. *Ibid.*, p. 203.
158. *Ibid.*, p. 79. This was a notion that went back as far as Sir William Petty.
159. *Ibid.*, p. 234.
160. *Ibid.*, pp. 170ff.
161. *Ibid.*, p. 100.
162. *Ibid.*, p. 104.
163. *Ibid.*, p. 20.
164. *Ibid.*, pp. 71ff.
165. Cf. Wicksell, *op. cit.*, p. 100, and Veblen's essay, "Böhm-Bawerk's Definition of Capital," in *Essays in Our Changing Order*, New York, 1934, p. 134. Veblen argued that wages paid out are a claim on the stock of social rather than private capital.
166. Cf. comments by Stigler, *op. cit.*, pp. 194ff., who is quite harsh with Böhm-Bawerk, chiding him for the vagueness of his key concepts.
167. Cf. *Capital and Interest*, p. 423.
168. *Positive Theory*, pp. 83ff.
169. Cf. Schumpeter, *History*, p. 904n.
170. Cf. *ibid.*, pp. 906ff. Böhm-Bawerk was attacked on this point by

Irving Fisher, J. B. Clark, Knut Wicksell, L. von Bortkiewicz, and more recently, Frank Knight.
171. Cf. *Positive Theory*, pp. 88ff.
172. Cf. Jevons, *Political Economy*, pp. 224ff.
173. Schumpeter argued that Böhm-Bawerk converted the period of production from a technological datum into a variable, and thus successfully made it part of his theory. In his view, the existing stock of consumer goods influenced this as a variable by affecting the length of the period of production, for it would be through the claims on the total supply of consumer goods that these influences would exert themselves. And it was by virtue of the functioning of a period of production that wages, rent, and all the other significant variables are established. But even in Schumpeter's more skillful hands, the theory remains unconvincing; he too fails to bring interest into the production sphere, for it continues to be fixed in the area of exchange. Cf. Schumpeter's essay on Böhm-Bawerk in Spiegel, *op. cit.*, pp. 577ff. originally published in *Neue Oesterreichische Biographie*, Vienna, 1925.
174. Schumpeter, in Spiegel, *ibid.*, p. 574.
175. *Capital and Interest*, pp. 111ff.
176. See p. 281 above.
177. *Capital and Interest*, p. 286.
178. *Ibid.*, pp. 275ff.
179. Cf. *ibid.*, pp. 259, 345ff.
180. Cf. *Positive Theory*, pp. 249ff.
181. *Ibid.*, p. 286.
182. *Ibid.*, pp. 253ff.
183. *Ibid.*, p. 281.
184. Wicksell, *op. cit.*, pp. 110ff.
185. On this point, cf. Wicksell, *Selected Papers*, pp. 180ff.
186. A similar point is made by Hayek. Cf. the latter's *Pure Theory of Capital*, Chicago, 1941, pp. 171ff.
187. *Positive Theory*, p. 382.
188. *Ibid.*, p. 386.
189. *Ibid.*, p. 448.
190. In one of his later essays, *Power and Economic Law*, Böhm-Bawerk discussed the question of the trade union's ability to raise wages suf-

ficiently to depress interest below its natural level. This could be done, he said, only if efficiency were increased. However, he thought that increases in prices would nullify the action of the trade unions. In the long run, said he, unions must increase their share of the national product at the expense of other workers.

191. *Positive Theory*, p. 457.
192. *Ibid.*, pp. 401ff.
193. *Ibid.*, p. 410.
194. *Ibid.*, pp. 419ff.
195. Cf. William Smart's introduction to *Capital and Interest*, p. viii. Smart insists that the capitalists secure a just return.
196. Schumpeter, *History*, p. 846.
197. Schumpeter, in Spiegel, *op. cit.*, p. 575.
198. Cf. Seligman, *op. cit.*, pp. 64ff.
199. Cf. Wicksell's, *Value, Capital and Rent*, and Erik Lindahl's introduction to Wicksell's *Selected Papers*. Lindahl remarks that Wicksell felt the *Positive Theory* to be a "revelation."
200. Cf. essay on J. B. Clark by his son, J. M. Clark in Spiegel, *op. cit.*, p. 593.
201. *Philosophy of Wealth*, Boston, 1887; *Distribution of Wealth*, New York, 1899, reprinted 1956.
202. J. M. Clark in Spiegel, *op. cit.*, pp. 597.
203. *Philosophy*, p. 18.
204. *Ibid.*, p., 20.
205. Dorfman, *op. cit.*, III, 188ff.
206. Clark, *op. cit.*, pp. 10ff.
207. *Ibid.*, p. 13.
208. *Ibid.*, p. 35.
209. Cf. *ibid.*, p. 37.
210. *Ibid.*, p. 44.
211. *Ibid.*, p. 47.
212. *Ibid.*, p. 56.
213. *Ibid.*, p. 62.
214. *Ibid.*, pp. 78, 80.
215. *Ibid.*, p. 96.
216. *Ibid.*, pp. 108-9.
217. *Ibid.*, pp. 111, 113.
218. *Distribution of Wealth*, pp. viii, 84-5.
219. *Philosophy*, pp. 131-32.
220. *Ibid.*, pp. 135-37.
221. *Ibid.*, p. 157.

222. *Ibid.*, p. 179.
223. *Ibid.*, p. 190.
224. *Ibid.*, p. 196.
225. In *Work and Wages*, Nov. 1886, quoted by Dorfman, *op. cit.*, p. 194.
226. John Bates Clark, *Essentials of Economic Theory*, New York, 1909.
227. *Distribution of Wealth*, p. 13.
228. *Ibid.*, p. 21.
229. *Ibid.*, p. 3.
230. *Ibid.*, p. 3.
231. *Ibid.*, Preface, p. vii.
232. *Ibid.*, p. 29.
233. Cf. *ibid.*, pp. 27-8.
234. *Ibid.*, p. 48.
235. *Ibid.*, p. 56.
236. *Ibid.*, pp. 30ff.
237. *Ibid.*, p. 33.
238. *Ibid.*, pp. 59, p. 400.
239. *Ibid.*, p. 60.
240. *Ibid.*, p. 178.
241. *Ibid.*, p. 404.
242. Thorstein Veblen, *The Place of Science in Modern Civilization*, New York, 1919, p. 190.
243. A few odd references by Clark to economic crises are mentioned by T. W. Hutchison in his *Review of Economic Doctrines*, London, 1953, p. 260.
244. Cf. *Distribution*, pp. 432ff.
245. *Ibid.*, pp. 210ff. and *Essentials*, p. 225.
246. Cf. Veblen's criticism, *op. cit.*, pp. 188ff.
247. *Distribution*, p. 46.
248. *Ibid.*, pp. 53, 54, 94.
249. Veblen, *op. cit.*, p. 203.
250. *Distribution*, p. 102.
251. *Ibid.*, p. 108.
252. The optimum implied by all this was firmly rejected by John A. Hobson who contended that the level of wages, as the outcome of social conflict, was actually depressed below marginal productivity. Cf. p. 232 above.
253. *Distribution*, pp. 376ff.
254. *Ibid.*, p. 230.
255. *Ibid.*, p. 218.
256. *Ibid.*, p. 243.
257. *Ibid.*, p. 377.
258. Quoted in Dorfman, *op. cit.*, Vol. III, Appendix iii.

259. Cf. Menger, *Principles*, pp. 126ff. Cf. also Eraldo Fossati, *The Theory of General Static Equilibrium*, London, 1957, pp. 48ff.
260. *Distribution*, pp. 116ff.
261. *Ibid.*, p. 117.
262. *Ibid.*, p. 121.
263. *Ibid.*, p. 123.
264. *Ibid.*, p. 125.
265. *Ibid.*, p. 136.
266. *Ibid.*, p. 142.
267. Cf. p. 264 above, and *ibid.*, p. 151.
268. Cf. comment by Hayek, *op. cit.*, p. 93, in which the concept of capital as a fund is labeled "pure mysticism."
269. *Distribution*, pp. 63ff.
270. *Ibid.*, pp. 158ff.
271. *Ibid.*, p. 165.
272. *Ibid.*, p. 171.
273. See p. 657 below.
274. The best summary of the Clark-Böhm-Bawerk debate may be found in Rogin, *op. cit.*, pp. 543ff. Cf. also Suranyi-Ungar, *op. cit.*, p. 293.
275. Veblen, "On the Nature of Capital," *op. cit.*, pp. 324ff.
276. *Distribution*, pp. 191ff.
277. *Ibid.*, p. 341.
278. *Ibid.*, p. 345.
279. *Ibid.*, pp. 198-99.
280. *Ibid.*, p. 335.
281. *Ibid.*, pp. 256-57.
282. *Ibid.*, p. 180.
283. *Ibid.*, p. 325.
284. Cf. Stigler, *op. cit.*, pp. 297-98. Other contemporary economists have also employed marginal productivity in curiously apologetic ways. They have contended, for example, that changes in money wages have had little or no effect on relative wage shares and that collective bargaining has been of no consequence in altering income distribution. All this has been done with the full weight of the marginalist apparatus behind it. Nevertheless, the experience of most trade unions has been quite to the contrary. Cf. H. M. Levinson, *Unionism, Wage Trends, and Income Distribution*, Ann Arbor, 1951, pp. 114ff.; Sidney Weintraub, *An Approach to the Theory of Income Distribution*, Philadelphia, 1958, pp. 53ff.; Melvin W. Reder, "Alternative Theories of Labor's Share," in *The Allocation of Economic Resources*, ed. Moses Abramovitz, Stanford, 1959, pp. 180ff. The extreme version of this position may be found in Milton Friedman, "Some Comments on the Significance of Labor Unions for Economic Policy," in *The Impact of The Labor Union*, pp. 204ff. An excellent antidote to these views is Robert Ozanne, "Impact of Unions on Wage Levels and Income Distribution," *Quarterly Journal of Economics*, May, 1959, p. 177ff.
285. *Essentials*, pp. 35ff.
286. *Ibid.*, viii.
287. *Ibid.*, p. 195.
288. Cf. Dorfman, *op. cit.*, p. 202.
289. Clark authored two little books on monopoly but they were not particularly enlightening works. These were *The Control of Trusts*, New York, 1901, and *The Problem of Monopoly*, New York, 1904.
290. *Essentials*, p. 374.
291. Cf. Joseph Dorfman, *Thorstein Veblen and His America*, New York, 1934, pp. 208ff.
292. *Essentials*, p. 454.
293. *Ibid.*, p. 480.
294. Mises' main works are *The Theory of Money and Credit*, 1912, translated 1934, revised, London, 1953; *Socialism*, 1922, translated 1936, enlarged, London, 1951; *Omnipotent Government*, New Haven, 1944; *The Anti-Capitalist Mentality*, Princeton, 1956; *Theory and History*, New Haven, 1957; *Epistemological Problems of Economics*, 1933, translated Princeton, 1960.
295. *Theory and History*, p. 4. An alternative definition of discursive is "digressive and desultory." In many ways this is an apt description of some of his notions.
296. *Human Action*, p. 32.
297. *Ibid.*, p. 199. Cf. also I. M. Kirzner, *The Economic Point of View*, Princeton, 1960, p. 162.
298. *Human Action*, p. 14. This was

clearly the same as Menger's notion of unsatisfied desires. Cf. p. 275 above.

299. Cf. *Ibid.*, pp. 21, 224.
300. *Ibid.*, p. 407.
301. *Ibid.*, p. 88.
302. *Ibid.*, p. 122.
303. *Ibid.*, p. 141.
304. *Ibid.*, p. 164.
305. *Ibid.*, p. 188.
306. *Ibid.*, p. 193.
307. *Omnipotent Government*, p. 83.
308. *The Anti-Capitalist Mentality*, p. 107.
309. *Human Action*, p. 118.
310. *Ibid.*, p. 347.
311. *Ibid.*, p. 350. Mises evidently had in mind the pioneering work of the late Henry Schultz. Cf. the latter's *Theory and Measurement of Demand*, Chicago, 1938.
312. *Human Action*, p. 572.
313. Cf. Irving Fisher, *The Making of Index Numbers*, Boston, 1922; "Index Numbers" in *Encyclopaedia of the Social Sciences*, VII, 652.
314. *Human Action*, p. 223.
315. *Theory of Money and Credit*, pp. 172, 176.
316. Cf. *Human Action*, pp. 706ff.; also p. 104 above.
317. *Ibid.*, pp. 374ff.
318. *Ibid.*, pp. 245ff.
319. *Ibid.*, p. 237.
320. *Ibid.*, p. 248.
321. *Ibid.*, p. 259.
322. For the technique of convincing consumers to demand certain products they might in a more rational state not want, cf. Vance Packard, *The Hidden Persuaders*, New York (Cardinal ed.), 1958.
323. *Human Action*, p. 205.
324. *Ibid.*
325. *Ibid.*, p. 324.
326. Cf. discussion regarding market socialism, p. 100 above; see also section on Hayek, p. 342 below.
327. *Human Action*, p. 211, italics supplied.
328. *Ibid.*, p. 390.
329. *Ibid.*, p. 521.
330. *Ibid.*, p. 391.
331. *Ibid.*, p. 279.
332. *Ibid.*, p. 497.
333. *Ibid.*, p. 285.

334. Cf. Francis V. Sutton, S. E. Harris, Carl Kaysen, and James Tobin, *The American Business Creed*, Cambridge, 1956, and my review of it in *Dissent*, Autumn, 1957, p. 372.
335. *Human Action*, p. 309.
336. *Theory of Money and Capital*, p. 90.
337. *Human Action*, p. 264.
338. *Ibid.*, p. 507.
339. Cf. discussion of Hayek-Knight debate, p. 657 below.
340. *Human Action*, p. 488.
341. *Ibid.*, p. 494.
342. *Ibid.*, p. 478.
343. For a cogent analysis of utilitarianism, cf. Hannah Arendt, *The Human Condition*, Chicago, 1958, pp. 153ff., also Elie Halévy, *The Growth of Philosophic Radicalism*, reprint, New York, 1949.
344. Cf. *The Theory of Money and Credit*, p. 130 for a long discussion of the relation of the quantity of money to the forces of supply and demand for it.
345. *Human Action*, p. 415.
346. Cf. discussion of Keynes, p. 730 below.
347. *Human Action*, p. 427.
348. Cf. *Money and Credit*, introduction by Lionel Robbins, p. 12.
349. *Ibid.*, pp. 48ff.
350. *Ibid.*, p. 103.
351. *Ibid.*, p. 139.
352. *Ibid.*, p. 205.
353. *Human Action*, p. 521.
354. *Money and Credit*, p. 347.
355. *Ibid.*, p. 352.
356. See p. 358 below.
357. Cf. Gottfried von Haberler, *Prosperity and Depression*, Geneva, 1940, p. 65.
358. *Human Action*, p. 437.
359. *Ibid.*, p. 438. Cf. also Mises' essay, "The Nationalization of Credit," in *Essays in European Economic Thought*, ed. L. Sommer, Princeton, 1960, pp. 106ff.
360. *Human Action*, p. 470.
361. *Ibid.*, p. 566.
362. *Ibid.*, p. 573.
363. *Ibid.*, p. 573.
364. For an analysis of Mises' penchant for distorting history see my review

of his *Omnipotent Government* in the *New Leader*, July 29, 1944.

365. *Human Action*, p. 587.

366. Cf. for example, J. L. and Barbara Hammond, *The Rise of Modern Industry*, London, 7th ed.; 1947; *idem. The Village Labourer*, London, reprint, 1948; *idem. The Town Labourer*, London, reprint, 1949; G. M. Trevelyan, *English Social History*, New York, 1942, Chaps. XV and XVI, pp. 463ff.; Henry Hamilton, *England: A History of the Homeland*, New York, 1948; G. D. H. Cole and Raymond Postgate, *The British Common People 1746-1938*, New York, 1939, pp. 118ff.

367. Cole and Postgate, *op. cit.*, p. 127.

368. Cf. *Human Action*, Chap. XXI, pp. 584ff.

369. Cf. for example, Fritz Machlup, *The Economics of Seller's Competition*, Baltimore, 1952, pp. 126ff.; Sidney Weintraub, *Price Theory*, New York, 1949, Chap. 11, pp. 247ff.

370. *Human Action*, p. 595.

371. *Ibid.*, p. 600.

372. Cf. F. Kaufmann, *Methodology of the Social Sciences*, New York, 1944, pp. 224ff.

373. Cf. Karl Polanyi, *The Great Transformation*, New York, 1944.

374. Cf. John Kenneth Galbraith, *The Affluent Society*, Boston, 1958, Chap. XI, pp. 152ff. It is of some minor interest to note that Mises has associated himself with the John Birch Society, an authoritarian right-wing political group. Cf. Alan F. Westin, "The John Birch Society," *Commentary*, August, 1961, p. 99.

375. Hayek's published books include, *Prices and Production*, London, 1931; *Monetary Theory and Trade Cycle*, New York, 1933; *Collectivist Economic Planning*, London, 1935; *Monetary Nationalism and International Stability*, London, 1937; *Profit, Interest and Investment*, London, 1939; *The Pure Theory of Capital*, Chicago, 1941; *The Road to Serfdom*, Chicago, 1944; *Individualism and the Eco-nomic Order*, Chicago, 1948; *John Stuart Mill and Harriet Taylor*, Chicago, 1951; *The Counter-Revolution of Science*, New York, 1952; *The Sensory Order*, London, 1952; and *The Constitution of Liberty*, Chicago, 1960.

376. The latter is "A Note on the Development of the Doctrine of Forced Saving," *Quarterly Journal of Economics*, November, 1932, reprinted in *Profits, Interest and Investment*.

377. B. J. Dempsey, *Interest and Usury*, Washington, 1943, p. 58.

378. Cf. *The Sensory Order*, p. 173.

379. *Ibid.*, p. 194.

380. Richard von Mises, *Positivism*, Cambridge, 1951, pp. 61ff.

381. Cf. *The Counter-Revolution of Science*, Part Two, pp. 103ff., in which Hayek attributed this erroneous view to Saint-Simon, Comte, Hegel, and, by implication, Schmoller.

382. *Ibid.*, p. 25.

383. *Ibid.*, p. 30.

384. Cf. *Ibid.*, p. 209, n. 23.

385. *Ibid.*, pp. 46-47.

386. *Ibid.*, p. 34.

387. *Ibid.*, p. 37.

388. *Ibid.*, p. 40.

389. Cf. *ibid.*, p. 54.

390. *Ibid.*, pp. 59, 61, 75.

391. *Ibid.*, p. 86.

392. For a cogent and incisive discussion of the problem of collectivities, cf. Erich Kahler, *The Tower and The Abyss*, New York, 1957.

393. Cf. Karl Mannheim, *Essays on the Sociology of Culture*, London, 1956.

394. Cf. the essays, "Economics and Knowledge" and "The Uses of Knowledge in Society," in *Individualism and the Economic Order*, pp. 33 and 77 respectively.

395. Again, one detected a contradiction here, for Hayek conceded that subjective agreements were brought about by external fact, while at the same time he refused to deduce equilibrium from anything but subjective conditions.

396. *Individualism and the Economic Order*, p. 54. In another essay,

"The Facts of the Social Sciences," economic concepts again were reduced to mental constructs.

397. "Meaning of Competition," *ibid.*, p. 92.
398. *Ibid.*, p. 93.
399. A proper view of classical doctrine would reveal that once again Hayek had constructed a straw man. In ordinary theory, price is the ultimate objective, for what happens is that buyers and sellers move toward price through their respective schedules!
400. *Individualism and the Social Order*, p. 97.
401. *Ibid.*, p. 103.
402. *Ibid.*, p. 106.
403. *Prices and Production*, pp. 48ff. Hayek, however, did not want to include expectations in his theory, a view which generated a debate with Charles O. Hardy. Cf. the latter's *Risk and Risk Bearing*, Chicago, 1931.
404. Cf. Raymond J. Saulnier, *Contemporary Monetary Theory*, New York, 1938, p. 235.
405. Hayek, *Prices and Production*, p. 58.
406. *Ibid.*, pp. 57ff.
407. *Monetary Theory and the Trade Cycle*, p. 97.
408. *Prices and Production*, p. 78.
409. *Ibid.*, p. 73.
410. *Monetary Theory*, pp. 212ff.
411. *Ibid.*, p. 203.
412. *Ibid.*, p. 210.
413. John Maynard Keynes, *General Theory of Employment, Interest and Money*, New York, 1936, pp. 192-93.
414. *Prices and Production*, pp. 20ff.
415. *Pure Theory of Capital*, pp. 47ff.
416. *Ibid.*, pp. 89ff. How long a tunnel would provide service without maintenance is an interesting question to which Hayek did not address himself. Cf. also his article, "The Mythology of Capital," from *Quarterly Journal of Economics*, Feb. 1936, reprinted in *Readings in the Theory of Income Distribution*, Philadelphia, 1946, pp. 355ff.
417. *Readings, ibid.*, p. 371.
418. Cf. especially Knight's, "Capital, Production, Time and the Rate of Return," in *Economic Essays in Honour of Gustav Cassel*, London, 1933, pp. 327ff., and "Professor Hayek and the Theory of Investment" in *Economic Journal*, March 1935, pp. 77ff. Cf. also Chap. 8 below, p. 656, for a discussion of Knight's views.
419. F. Machlup, "Professor Knight and the Period of Production," *Journal of Political Economy*, October, 1935, p. 577.
420. *Pure Theory*, p. 54.
421. *Ibid.*, p. 330.
422. *Ibid.*, p. 59.
423. *Ibid.*, p. 264.
424. *Ibid.*, pp. 66ff.
425. *Ibid.*, pp. 103ff.
426. *Ibid.*, p. 109.
427. *Ibid.*, p. 129.
428. Cf. R. Dorfman, P. A. Samuelson, and R. M. Solow, *Linear Programming and Economic Analysis*, New York, 1958, for a treatment of input-output relationships in the modern temper.
429. *Pure Theory*, p. 144.
430. *Ibid.*, p. 170.
431. *Ibid.*, p. 193.
432. *Ibid.*, pp. 205ff.
433. *Ibid.*, p. 250.
434. Cf. F. Gehrels and S. Wiggins, "Interest Rates and Manufacturers' Fixed Investment," *American Economic Review*, March, 1957, pp. 79ff.
435. *Profits, Interest and Investment*, pp. 8ff.
436. Cf. Hayek, "The Ricardo Effect," in *Individualism*, pp. 220ff.; N. Kaldor, "Professor Hayek and the Concertina Effect," *Economica*, Nov. 1942, p. 360.
437. Lorie Tarshis, "Changes in Real and Money Wages," *Economic Journal*, Vol. 44, 1939, reprinted in *Readings in the Theory of Income Distribution*, p. 330.
438. Seymour Melman, *Dynamic Factors in Industrial Productivity*, Oxford, 1956.
439. *Prices and Production*, p. 128.
440. *Monetary Theory*, pp. 112ff.
441. *Ibid.*, pp. 176ff.
442. Cf. *Prices and Production*, p. 128. Hayek's views were paralleled by some of the Swedish economists in

the 1930's, notably Johan Akerman. Cf. Erik Lundberg, *Business Cycles and Economic Policy*, London, 1957, pp. 114ff.

443. Knut Wicksell, *Interest and Prices*, London, 1936, p. 167.

444. *Freedom and the Economic System*, Chicago, 1939, p. 7. This was a pamphlet written in a slightly more popular vein than his *The Road to Serfdom*.

445. Cf. the definitive reply to Hayek, Herman Finer's, *Road to Reaction*, Boston, 1945. Cf. also E. F. M. Durbin, "Professor Hayek on Economic Planning," *Problems of Economic Planning*, London, 1949, p. 91, and Raymond Williams, *The Long Revolution*, London, 1961, pp. 96ff.

446. *Constitution of Liberty*, pp. 19ff.

447. Cf. Hayek, ed. *Capitalism and the Historians*, Chicago, 1954, a volume intended to prove that the growth of capitalism was not accompanied by the evil of low wages, child labor, unsanitary conditions, and sheer degradation.

448. Cf. Polanyi, *op. cit.*

449. Cf. Mills, *op cit.*

450. While Mises and Hayek were the major representatives of Austrian-marginalist-libertarian views, other writers of stature subscribed to similar doctrines. Among them were Jacques Rueff (1896-), active in French economic affairs, and Wilhelm Röpke (1899-), a German economics professor, long resident in Switzerland. The latter's works are in a sense an even more extreme statement of the libertarian position than those of Mises', expressing as they do an unabashed hostility toward urbanization and other forms of modern existence. Röpke prefers not merely decentralization, but the small economic unit of pre-eighteenth century days. Cf. his *A Humane Economy*, Chicago, 1960, and *The Social Crisis of our Time*, Chicago, 1950. A good illustration of Rueff's views may be found in his "A Letter to The Advocates of a Controlled Economy" in Sommer, *op. cit.*, pp. 133ff.

451. Cf. Weintraub, *op. cit.*, pp. 2ff.

452. Henry Schultz, *Theory and Measurement of Demand*, Chicago, 1938.

453. Paul H. Douglas, *The Theory of Wages*, 1934, reprinted New York, 1957.

454. *Ibid.*, pp. 76ff.

455. Douglas, "Are There Laws of Production?" *American Economic Review*, March, 1948, p. 41. A study by Stefan Valavanis, however, cited by Benjamin Higgins, *Economic Development*, New York, 1959, p. 379, reverses the Douglas figures, giving a labor coefficient of 0.2 and a capital coefficient of 0.7. An elegant mathematical statement of the laws of return may be found in Karl Menger, "The Logic of the Laws of Return," in *Economic Activity Analysis*, ed. O. Morgenstern, New York, 1954, pp. 419ff. Menger analyses diminishing returns and the production function by utilizing the tools of symbolic logic. A distinction is made between decreasing marginal product and decreasing average product, and the impact of large outlays and small outlays are carefully reviewed. The laws of return, Menger notes, are capable of being subdivided into numerous substatements which describe the manifold relationships of changes in output to changes in the factor inputs. Menger's essay, a virtuoso performance, should be examined carefully. For other references to recent work in this area see, H. S. Ellis, ed. *A Survey of Contemporary Economics*, Philadelphia, 1948, especially articles by B. F. Haley, p. 1, and W. Leontief, p. 388.

456. Cf. D. Durand, "Some Thoughts on Marginal Productivity," *Journal of Political Economy*, Dec., 1937, p. 740; Horst Mendershausen, "On The Significance of Professor Douglas' Production Function," *Econometrica*, April, 1938, p. 145; E. H. Phelps-Brown, "The Meaning of the Fitted Cobb-Douglas Function," *Quarterly Journal of Economics*, Nov., 1957, pp. 546ff.

457. Cf. R. A. Gordon, "Short Period Price Determination in Theory and Practice," *American Economic Review*, June, 1948, pp. 265ff., and Richard A. Lester, "Shortcomings of Marginal Analysis for Wages-Employment Problems," *American Economic Review*, March, 1946, p. 63.

458. Fritz Machlup in his article, "Marginal Analysis and Empirical Research," *American Economic Review*, Sept., 1946, pp. 519ff., has argued for the pure subjectivist view, a position restated in his *The Economics of Sellers' Competition*. Gordon, in his *American Economic Review* article cited above, opposes Machlup. It would seem that Gordon and Lester have the better of the argument.

459. Gordon, *op. cit.*, p. 269.

460. Cf. W. J. Eiteman and G. E. Guthrie, "The Shape of the Average Cost Curve," *American Economic Review*, December, 1952, pp. 632ff.

461. Gordon, *op. cit.*, p. 275.

462. Cf. R. G. D. Allen, *Mathematical Economics*, London, 1956, Chap. 6, p. 176, and Paul A. Samuelson, *Foundations of Economic Analysis*, Cambridge, 1947, Appendix B, p. 380.

463. Cf. Lester, *op. cit.*, p. 63.

464. Machlup, *op. cit.*, *American Economic Review*, p. 537.

465. Cf. H. M. Oliver, Jr., "Marginal Theory and Business Behavior," *American Economic Review*, June, 1947, p. 376. Cf. also, W. J. Baumol, "Marginalism and Operations Research," *Review of Economics and Statistics*, October, 1958, pp. 210-11. Baumol says that it is possible to have businessmen employ marginal notions, at least in broad, rough and ready ways. The elimination of an unprofitable line of merchandise, as he says, may be a marginalist act, but it still does not exhibit the elegance of a textbook curve.

466. Cf. Jacob Viner, "The Utility Concept in Value Theory and Its Critics," *Journal of Political Economy*, 1925, reprinted in *idem, The Long View and the Short*, New York, 1958, pp. 182ff.

467. A complex mathematical effort in this direction was Ragnar Frisch, *New Methods of Measuring Marginal Utility*, Tübingen, 1932. Frisch proceeded on the basis of Irving Fisher's work and sought to apply empirical testing as well. But it is doubtful that marginal utility can be made to depend on the annual consumption of a good. Cf. *ibid.*, p. 8.

468. Cf. George Stigler in *American Economic Review*, March, 1947, p. 154.

Chapter 5

Equilibrium Economics and the Unification of Theory

1. Joseph A. Schumpeter, *History of Economic Analysis*, New York, 1954, p. 827.

2. Cf. such works as R. G. D. Allen, *Mathematical Economics*, London, 1956, and J. G. Kemeny, J. L. Snell, and G. L. Thompson, *Introduction to Finite Mathematics*, Englewood Cliffs, 1956.

3. The major source of biographic data is the autobiography which was written at different times and edited by Walras' daughter, Aline. Cf. William Jaffé, "Unpublished

Papers and Letters of Léon Walras," *Journal of Political Economy*, April, 1935, pp. 187ff.; and Marcel Boson, *Léon Walras, Fondateur de la Politique Économique Scientifique*, Paris, 1951. Jaffé is also preparing what promises to be the definitive study of the life and works of Walras.

4. Cf. Boson, *op. cit.*, p. 80.
5. *Ibid.*, p. 95.
6. Cf. Schumpeter, *op. cit.*, p. 828, and J. R. Hicks' essay on Walras in H. W. Spiegel, ed. *The Development of Economic Thought*, New York, 1952, pp. 581ff.
7. Boson, *op. cit.*, p. 24.
8. *Ibid.*, p. 41.
9. *Ibid.*, pp. 48ff. For a good description of the social background, Cf. J. M. Thompson, *Louis Napoleon and the Second Empire*, New York, 1955, pp. 78ff.
10. Boson, *op. cit.*, p. 68.
11. This point was expressed most forcefully in Lesson 42, Taxation, of Walras' major work, *Elements of Pure Economics*, translated by William Jaffé, London, 1954, p. 447. This translation was based on the 1926 definitive edition.
12. Boson, *op. cit.*, pp. 138ff.
13. *Ibid.*, pp. 313ff.
14. Cf. *Études d'économique Sociale*.
15. Boson, *op. cit.*, p. 194.
16. *Elements*, p. 37.
17. Cf. citations in Boson, *op. cit.*, p. 103.
18. Hicks, essay on Walras, reprinted in Spiegel, *op. cit.*, pp. 581ff.
19. Boson, *op. cit.*, p. 189.
20. Cf. *Elements*, Lesson 2 and 3, pp. 58ff.
21. *Ibid.*, p. 43.
22. *Ibid.*, p. 511.
23. *Ibid.*, Lesson 8, pp. 115ff.
24. *Ibid.*, p. 40. Italics in original.
25. Cf. *Ibid.*, Translator's Notes, *passim*. Cf. also George Stigler, "The Mathematical Method in Economics," in *Five Lectures on Economic Problems*, London, 1949, pp. 37ff. Stigler rightfully raises grave questions regarding the exclusive use of mathematics in economic analysis.
26. *Elements*, p. 380.

27. *Ibid.*, p. 83.
28. *Ibid.*, p. 212.
29. *Ibid.*, p. 162.
30. For an incisive analysis of this point, cf. Don Patinkin, *Money, Interest and Prices*, Evanston, 1956, p. 380.
31. *Elements*, p. 224.
32. Cf. Leo Rogin, *The Meaning and Validity of Economic Theory*, New York, 1956, p. 432.
33. *Elements*, p. 227.
34. *Ibid.*, pp. 218-19.
35. *Ibid.*, p. 83.
36. Cf. R. D. Luce and H. Raiffa, *Games and Decisions*, New York, 1957, pp. 12ff. and 371ff.
37. For a history of the development of these notions, cf. Schumpeter, *op. cit.*, pp. 1060ff.
38. Cf. p. 568 below.
39. *Elements*, p. 185.
40. *Ibid.*, p. 242.
41. Cf. Jaffé's note, *ibid.*, p. 529.
42. Cf. Judith B. Balderston, "General Economic Equilibrium," in *Economic Activity Analysis*, ed. O. Morgenstern, New York, 1954, pp. 15ff.
43. *Elements*, p. 268.
44. *Ibid.*, pp. 218ff.
45. *Ibid.*, p. 274.
46. *Ibid.*, p. 296.
47. Knut Wicksell, *Value, Capital and Rent*, (1893) translated, London, 1954, p. 167.
48. Cf. George J. Stigler, *Production and Distribution Theories*, New York, 1941, p. 253.
49. *Elements*, pp. 243ff.
50. *Ibid.*, p. 242.
51. As Schumpeter says, this was heroic theorizing. Cf. his *History*, p. 1010n. Implicit also was some sort of alternative cost theory. Cf. M. Friedman, "Walras and His Economic System," *American Economic Review*, Dec. 1955, pp. 900ff.
52. *Elements*, pp. 214ff.
53. *Ibid.*, p. 385.
54. Cf. *Ibid.*, Jaffé's note, p. 550, and J. R. Hicks, *Theory of Wages*, London, 1932, p. 234.
55. *Elements*, p. 552.
56. *Ibid.*, p. 415.
57. Cf. Schumpeter, *op. cit.*, p. 934.

58. *Elements*, p. 269.
59. Cf. *ibid.*, Jaffé's note, pp. 531-33.
60. *Ibid.*, p. 38.
61. *Ibid.*, pp. 333-34.
62. Cf. A. W. Marget, *The Theory of Prices*, New York, 1942, II, 70ff.
63. Don Patinkin has argued to the contrary, asserting that in Walras' model equilibrium was first established in the commodity market, and then in the money market, without disturbing the former, a rather unlikely situation. Cf. Patinkin, *op. cit.*, pp. 401-403.
64. Cf. G. L. S. Shackle, *Time in Economics*, Amsterdam, 1957, p. 93. Shackle accedes that general interdependence is nevertheless essential for an understanding of dynamic movements.
65. Friedman, *op. cit.*, p. 908.
66. H. L. Moore sought to overcome many of the difficulties of the Walrasian system by starting with empirical curves of demand and supply, thereby including elements of monopoly as well as free competition. Cf. his *Synthetic Economics*, New York, 1929, pp. 109ff.
67. Vilfredo Pareto, *Trattato di sociologia generale*, Paris, 1919, translated as *Mind and Society*, 4 vols., New York, 1935.
68. A charming sketch, "Pareto As I Knew Him," by Marian Einaudi, daughter of the Italian economist and later president of the Italian Republic, may be found in the *Atlantic Monthly*, Sept. 1935, pp. 336ff. Cf. also G. H. Bousquet, *Vilfredo Pareto, Sa Vie et son oevre*, Paris, 1928, which is a useful summary of his life and works.
69. Cf. T. W. Hutchison, *Review of Economic Doctrines*, Oxford, 1953, p. 217.
70. H. Stuart Hughes, *Consciousness and Society*, New York, 1958, p. 63.
71. Cf. Schumpeter, *op. cit.*, p. 860.
72. Hughes, *op. cit.*, p. 260.
73. Quoted by George C. Homans and Charles P. Curtis, Jr., *An Introduction to Pareto*, New York, 1934, pp. 295ff.
74. Cf. Talcott Parsons, *Structure of Social Action*, Glencoe, 1949.
75. Pareto, *Les Systèmes Socialistes*, 2 vols. 1902, 2nd ed., Paris, 1926.
76. *Manuel d'économie politique*, Paris, 1909, p. 363.
77. *Les Systèmes socialistes*, II, 338.
78. *Ibid.*, p. 402.
79. *Ibid.*, p. 413.
80. Cf. Karl Mannheim, *Ideology and Utopia*, New York, 1936, (paperback ed.) p. 138.
81. Pareto, *op. cit.*, p. 430.
82. Hughes, *op. cit.*, p. 79.
83. Cf. James Burnham, *The Machiavellians*, New York, 1943.
84. Quoted by Homans and Curtis, *op. cit.*, Appendix, p. 291, translation, B. B. S.
85. Cf. Hughes, *op. cit.*, p. 262.
86. Cf. Mannheim, *op. cit.*, p. 138.
87. Cf. Franz Borkenau, *Pareto*, London, 1936, p. 169.
88. *Mind and Society*, para. 2174.
89. Cf. Burnham, *op. cit.*, p. 206.
90. *Mind and Society*, para. 1531.
91. Cf. Burnham, *op. cit.*, p. 219, which suggests tacit approval of the Paretian thesis.
92. *Mind and Society*, para. 2068.
93. Quoted by Theo Suranyi-Ungar, *Economics in the Twentieth Century*, New York, 1931, p. 128.
94. Pareto, *Cours d'économie politique*, 2 vols., Lausanne, 1896-97.
95. Pareto, *Manuale d'economia politica*, Milan, 1906. This work expanded Edgeworth's indifference curve analysis.
96. Cf. G. Demaria in Spiegel, *op. cit.*, p. 645.
97. Cf. *Cours* I, 18, and A. Tustin, *Mechanisms of Economic Systems*, London, 1953.
98. J. A. Schumpeter, *Ten Great Economists*, New York, 1951, pp. 127-28.
99. Pareto, "On the Economic Phenomenon," *International Economic Papers*, No. 3, London, 1953, p. 184. This was part of an exchange with Benedetto Croce, published originally in *Giornale degli Economisti* in 1900.
100. Knut Wicksell, *Selected Papers on Economic Theory*, London, 1958, pp. 142ff.

101. *Cours*, II, 100.
102. Cf. the Croce-Pareto debate reprinted in *International Economic Papers*, No. 3, pp. 172ff.
103. "The Validity of Pareto's Theories," *Saturday Review of Literature*, May 25, 1935, p. 12.
104. Cf. p. 100 above.
105. *Manuel*, p. 227.
106. Cf. O. Morgenstern, "Experiment and Large Scale Computation in Economics," in *Economic Activity Analysis*, pp. 484ff.
107. Cf. Schumpeter, *History*, p. 1062.
108. Cf. R. G. D. Allen and J. R. Hicks, "A Reconsideration of the Theory of Value," *Economica*, February, 1934, pp. 52ff. and May, 1934, pp. 196ff. Cf. also, J. R. Hicks, *Value and Capital*, London, 1939.
109. *Manuale*, p. 264.
110. Cf. his article, "Mathematical Economics," written originally for the *Encyclopedia des Sciences Mathématiques* and reprinted in *International Economic Papers*, No. 5, pp. 58ff.
111. Cf. C. R. Noyes, *Economic Man*, New York, 1948, II, 1327.
112. *Cours*, I, 28.
113. Cf. N. Kaldor, *Essays on Value and Distribution*, London, 1960, pp. 147-48.
114. Cf. Knut Wicksell, *Lectures on Political Economy*, translated, London, 1934, I, 83. The Pareto optimum suggested that point rationing was superior to goods rationing, since it allowed a consumer to work out his own adjustment. Cf. W. J. Baumol, *Economic Theory and Operations Analysis*, Englewood Cliffs, 1961, p. 263.
115. *Mind and Society*, para. 2128.
116. Homans and Curtis, *op. cit.*, p. 279ff.
117. *Cours*, II, 299ff.
118. *Manuel*, p. 393.
119. Cf. Oskar Lange, *Introduction to Econometrics*, Warsaw, 1959, pp. 199-200.
120. Cf. for example the data in *Income Distribution in the United States, 1953*, United States Department of Commerce. Cf. also F. R. Macauley, "Pareto's Law," in *Income in the United States*,

Vol. II., National Bureau of Economic Research, New York, 1922.
121. Stigler, *op. cit.*, p. 367.
122. Cf. the debate between Schultz and John R. Hicks in *Economica*, February, 1932, p. 79, and August, 1932, p. 285.
123. Cf. *International Economic Papers*, No. 5, p. 86; *Manuel*, p. 288.
124. *Manuel*, p. 187.
125. *Ibid.*, p. 189.
126. *Ibid.*, p. 601ff.
127. Cf. *ibid.*, pp. 613ff.
128. *Cours*, II, p. 278.
129. *Cours*, II, 210.
130. Some of these are: *Taxation of War Wealth*, Oxford, 1941 (with L. Rostas); *Standards of Local Expenditure*, Cambridge, 1943; and *Incidence of Local Rates*, London, 1945. Mrs. Hicks has authored works of her own in the area of public finance.
131. Cf. especially Hicks' *Essays in World Economics*, London, 1959.
132. Hicks, *Value and Capital*, Oxford, 1939.
133. "The Stability of Economic Growth," *International Economic Papers*, No. 8, London, 1958, p. 55.
134. *Value and Capital*, p. 4; cf. Hicks, *A Contribution to the Theory of the Trade Cycle*, Oxford, 1950.
135. *Value and Capital*, p. 7.
136. Cf. Ruby T. Norris, *The Theory of Consumers' Demand*, New Haven, 1941, p. 51.
137. Cf. Tapas Majumdar, *The Measurement of Utility*, London, 1958; Sir Dennis Robertson, *Utility and All That*, London, 1952.
138. *Value and Capital*, p. 18.
139. Cf. Norris, *op. cit.*, pp. 98ff.
140. *Ibid.*, p. 54.
141. *Value and Capital*, p. 27.
142. Cf. Paul A. Samuelson, "Consumption Theorems in Terms of Overcompensation rather than Indifference Comparisons," *Economica*, February, 1953, p. 1.
143. Sir Dennis Robertson, "Utility and All What?," *Economic Journal*, December, 1954, p. 665.
144. Norris, *op. cit.*, pp. 63ff.
145. *Ibid.*, p. 74.
146. *Ibid.*, p. 140.

147. Cf. Frank H. Knight, *Risk, Uncertainty and Profit*, Boston, 1921, pp. 69ff.
148. J. R. Hicks, "Rehabilitation of Consumers' Surplus," *Review of Economic Studies*, February, 1941, pp. 10ff.
149. Cf. Hicks and Allen, "A Reconsideration of the Theory of Value," *Economica*, February and May, 1934, pp. 52ff. 196ff.
150. Cf. J. M. Clark, "Realism and Relevance in the Theory of Demand," *Journal of Political Economy*, August, 1946, pp. 347ff.
151. Lionel Robbins in "Foreword" to Majumdar, *op. cit.*, p. ix.
152. J. R. Hicks, *A Revision of Demand Theory*, Oxford, 1956.
153. Cf. Måjumdar, *op. cit., passim*.
154. Samuelson, "Consumption Theory in Terms of Revealed Preference," *Economica*, 1948, pp. 243ff.
155. Cf. T. C. Koopmans, *Three Essays on the State of Economic Science*, New York, 1957, p. 18ff.
156. *Revision of Demand Theory*, pp. 17-18.
157. On ordering theory, cf. K. Arrow, *Social Choice and Individual Value*, New York, 1951, pp. 9ff. Cf. also J. Rothenberg, *The Measurement of Social Welfare*, Englewood Cliffs, 1961, *passim*.
158. *Revision*, pp. 84ff.
159. *Value and Capital*, p. 76.
160. Cf. *ibid.*, pp. 216ff. Also, cf. Samuelson, *Foundations*, p. 188. The Hicks' formulation became a mathematical justification of Frank Knight's philosophical predisposition for infinite production periods.
161. *Value and Capital*, p. 83.
162. *Ibid.*, pp. 67ff.
163. Cf. Paul A. Samuelson, "The Stability of Equilibrium: Comparative Statics and Dynamics," *Econometrica*, April, 1941, pp. 111ff.
164. Cf. J. R. Hicks, "Foundations of Welfare Economics," *Economic Journal*, December, 1939, pp. 696ff.
165. W. Baumol, *Economic Dynamics*, New York, 1951, p. 3.
166. *Value and Capital*, p. 127.
167. *Ibid.*, p. 135.
168. Cf. Paul A. Samuelson, *Foundations of Economic Analysis*, Cambridge, 1947, pp. 123ff.
169. Cf. Patinkin, *op. cit.*, pp. 83-84.
170. *Value and Capital*, p. 195.
171. *Ibid.*, p. 197.
172. *Ibid.*, p. 215.
173. "A 'Value and Capital' Growth Model," in *Review of Economic Studies*, June, 1959, pp. 159ff.
174. *Ibid.*, p. 160.
175. *Value and Capital*, p. 84.
176. Eric Roll, *A History of Economic Thought*, New York, 1942, p. 512.
177. Hicks, *A Contribution to the Theory of the Trade Cycle*.
178. Reprinted from *Economica*, May, 1949, in *Readings in Business Cycles and National Income*, ed. Alvin H. Hansen and R. V. Clemence, London, 1953, p. 249.
179. Cf. Sinichi Ichimura, "Toward a General Non-Linear Macrodynamic Theory of Economic Fluctuations," in *Post-Keynesian Economics*, ed. K. K. Kurihara, New Brunswick, 1954, pp. 192ff.
180. Cf. Samuelson, *Foundations*, p. 340.
181. Cf. S. Ichimura, *Historical Development of Economic Dynamics*, Tokyo, 1955.
182. *Trade Cycle*, pp. 29ff.; cf. also W. J. Baumol, *Economic Dynamics*, 2nd ed., New York, 1959, p. 268.
183. *Trade Cycle*, p. 17.
184. *Ibid.*, pp. 95ff.
185. Cf. J. M. Clark, p. 211 above.
186. Cf. Daniel Hamberg's interpretation in his *Economic Growth and Stability*, New York, 1956, p. 285.
187. Cf. p. 357 above.
188. Hamberg, *op. cit.*, p. 291.
189. Cf. W. W. Rostow, "Some Notes on Mr. Hicks and History," *American Economic Review*, June, 1951, pp. 316ff. Rostow argued that the type of investment had profound effects on the level of the "ceiling."
190. *The Theory of Wages*, London, 1932.
191. For a sharp criticism of the Hicksian formulation, cf. G. L. S. Shackle, "The Nature of the Bargaining Process," in *The Theory of Wage Determination*, ed. John

T. Dunlop, London, 1957, pp. 299ff.

192. Cf. *Theory of Wages,* pp. 140ff.
193. *Ibid.,* pp. 121ff.
194. *Ibid.,* pp. 115ff.
195. Cf. Kenneth E. Boulding, "Wages as a Share in the National Income," in *Impact of the Labor Unions,* New York, 1951, p. 132.
196. Paul A. Samuelson, *Foundations of Economic Analysis,* Cambridge, 1947.
197. These comprised a series of articles in *Economica:* "Notes on the Pure Theory of Consumer Behavior" (1938), "Consumption Theorems in Terms of Revealed Preference" (1948), and "Consumption Theorems in Terms of Overcompensation Rather than Indifference Comparisons" (1953), as well as an article in the *Review of Economic Studies,* "Numerical Representation of Ordered Classification and the Concept of Utility" (1938).
198. *Foundations,* p. 6.
199. Paul A. Samuelson, *Economics,* 1st ed., New York, 1948; 4th ed. 1958.
200. An early example of Samuelson's skillful handling of Keynesian propositions may be found in his Hansen volume essay, "The Simple Mathematics of Income Determination," *Income, Employment and Public Policy, Essays in Honor of Alvin H. Hansen,* New York, 1948, pp. 133ff. An example of the application of statistical techniques to the measurement of the consumption function may be found in Samuelson's appendix to Chap. XI of Alvin Hansen, *Fiscal Policy and Business Cycles,* New York, 1941, pp. 250ff., a remarkable performance for a young man of twenty-five.
201. Yet even Samuelson has not carried through the synthesis completely, as witness the sharp break between his treatment of the theory of the firm and the problems of monopoly. It may be that this is an impossible task and suggests that not all the classical verities can be used. Cf. *Economics,* 4th

ed., Chaps. 24 and 25, pp. 453ff.
202. Samuelson *et al. Linear Programming and Economic Analysis,* New York, 1958. Some of the RAND Corporation memoranda were "Equilibrium Points in Game Theory" (1950), "Notes on the Dynamic Approach to Saddlepoints and Extremum Points" (1951), and "Linear Programming and Economic Theory" (1955). On game theory and linear programming see p. 771 below.
203. "Economic Theory and Mathematics, An Appraisal," *Papers and Proceedings of the American Economic Association,* May, 1952, pp. 56ff.
204. *The Impact of the Labor Union,* ed. D. M. Wright, New York, 1951.
205. *Foundations,* p. 3.
206. *Ibid.*
207. Cf. A. G. Papandreau, *Economics as a Science,* New York, 1958, p. 11.
208. *Foundations,* p. 5.
209. *Ibid.,* pp. 70ff.
210. *Ibid.,* p. 183.
211. *Ibid.,* pp. 63ff.
212. *Ibid.,* p. 91.
213. Cf. Robertson, *Utility and All That,* p. 21.
214. Majumdar, *The Measurement of Utility,* p. 83.
215. *Ibid.,* pp. 84-95.
216. Cf. H. Wolozin, "Inflation and the Price Mechanism," *Journal of Political Economy,* October, 1959, pp. 463ff.
217. *Foundations,* p. 198.
218. Cf. Samuelson, *Economics,* p. 445. For a criticism of this point, cf. I. D. M. Little, *A Critique of Welfare Economics,* 2nd ed., Oxford, 1957, pp. 180ff.
219. A. Bergson, "A Reformulation of Certain Aspects of Welfare Economics," *Quarterly Journal of Economics,* February, 1938, pp. 310ff. Cf. also Arrow, *op. cit.* Arrow's criteria, however, were too restrictive in that they suggested the irrelevance of third parties in politics. But cf. the role of the Liberal Party in New York. Moreover,

Arrow considered only rank orders of preferences, so that the intensity of preferences leading to a consensus was excluded. Cf. Baumol, *op. cit.*, pp. 271ff; and Rothenberg, *op. cit.*, Chap. 2, pp. 17ff.

220. *Foundations*, p. 220.
221. *Ibid.*, p. 244.
222. *Ibid.*, p. 246.
223. Cf. his "Further Commentary on Welfare Economics," *American Economic Review*, September, 1943, p. 605.
224. "The Gains from International Trade," *Canadian Journal of Economics and Political Science*, May, 1939, pp. 195ff.
225. "Welfare Economics and International Trade," *American Economic Review*, June, 1938, pp. 261ff.
226. Samuelson and W. Stolper, "Protection and Real Wages," *Review of Economics and Statistics*, November, 1941, pp. 58ff.
227. The main ideas in this area were presented in several articles appearing in the *Review of Economics and Statistics:* "The Pure Theory of Public Expenditures," November, 1954, pp. 387ff.; "A Diagrammatic Exposition of a Theory of Public Expenditures," November, 1955, pp. 350ff.; and "Aspects of Public Expenditure Theory," November, 1958, pp. 332ff.
228. *Review of Economics and Statistics*, November, 1958, p. 334.
229. Cf. Samuelson's essay "Dynamic Process Analysis," in *A Survey of Contemporary Economics*, Vol. I, ed. H. S. Ellis, Philadelphia, 1948, p. 352.
230. *Foundations*, p. 284.
231. *Ibid.*, pp. 270ff.
232. *Ibid.*, pp. 313ff.
233. *Ibid.*, p. 320.
234. Cf. "Dynamic Process Analysis," p. 376.
235. "The Interaction between the Multiplier Analysis and the Principle of Acceleration," *Review of Economics and Statistics*, May, 1939, reprinted in *Readings in Business Cycle Theory*, Philadelphia, 1944, pp. 261ff.

236. Alvin H. Hansen, *Fiscal Policy and Business Cycles*, New York, 1941, pp. 261ff. Cf. also Samuelson, "Alvin Hansen and the Interaction between the Multiplier Analysis and the Principle of Acceleration," *Review of Economics and Statistics*, May, 1959, pp. 183ff.
237. In his review of Samuelson's *Foundations*, *American Economic Review*, December, 1948, p. 910.
238. "Spatial Price Equilibrium and Linear Programming," *American Economic Review*, June, 1952, pp. 213ff.
239. Samuelson in a RAND Corporation memorandum, "Linear Programming and Economic Theory," May, 1955, p. 4.
240. *Ibid.*, p. 4.
241. Of course, more work of importance may be expected from Samuelson. He undoubtedly will continue to apply his high-powered mathematical tool-kit to a variety of economic problems, both past and future. Witness his recent applications of modern analysis to the work of Ricardo and Marx: "Wages and Interest: Marxian Economic Models," *American Economic Review*, December, 1957, pp. 884ff., and "A Modern Treatment of the Ricardian Economy," *Quarterly Journal of Economics*, February, 1959, pp. 1ff.
242. Cf. E. Whittaker, *Schools and Streams of Economic Thought*, Chicago, 1960, pp. 85ff.; Schumpeter, *History*, p. 240. Schumpeter credits the idea of the *Tableau* to Richard Cantillon, an eighteenth century banker-economist. Cf. Cantillon, *Essay on the Nature of Trade* (1755), reissue, London, 1959, p. 45.
243. *Das Kapital*, Vol. II., Kerr ed., Chicago, 1909, Part III., pp. 404ff. Cf. also S. Tsuru, Appendix A, in Paul Sweezy's *Theory of Capitalist Development*, New York, 1942, p. 365.
244. "On Some Systems of Equations in Mathematical Economics," *Econometrica*, October, 1951, pp. 368ff. This was a translation from an

earlier German article. Wald's mathematics were quite formidable. For a lucid version of his formulaton, cf. R. Dorfman, P. A. Samuelson, and R. M. Solow, *Linear Programming and Economic Analysis*, pp. 366ff.

245. Wassily W. Leontief, *The Structure of American Economy, 1919-1929*, Cambridge, 1941.

246. Oskar Lange asserts that Leontief's concept stemmed from Marx's reproduction scheme. Cf. Lange, *op. cit.*, p. 223. This may have been an attempt to legitimate input-output analysis for Soviet use. Leontief's work had no relation to Soviet sources, according to correspondence with me, December, 1960.

247. K. M. Savosnick, quoted by H. Brems, *Output, Employment, Capital and Growth*, New York, 1959, p. 6.

248. Cf. Oskar Morgenstern, ed. *Economic Activity Analysis*, New York, 1954, pp. 493ff.

249. Cf. Lionel McKenzie, "On The Existence of a General Equilibrium for a Competitive Market," *Econometrica*, January, 1959. Another source was the famous Mises-Hayek-Lange-Lerner debate on the possibility of socialist calculation. Cf. p. 100 above.

250. *Structure of American Economy*, p. 3.

251. *Ibid.*, p. 39.

252. *Ibid.*, p. 23.

253. *Ibid.*, p. 35.

254. Leontief, "Recent Developments in the Study of Interindustrial Relationships," *American Economic Association Proceedings, May, 1949*, p. 214.

255. Cf. Leontief, "Output, Employment, Consumption and Investment," *Quarterly Journal of Economics*, February, 1944, pp. 290ff. and "Exports, Imports, Domestic Output and Employment," *QJE*, February, 1946, pp. 171ff. Cf. also C. P. Modlin and G. Rosenbluth, "Treatment of Foreign and Domestic Trade and Transportation Charges in the Leontief Input-Out-put Table," in Morgenstern, *op. cit.*, pp. 129ff.

256. Leontief *et al., Studies in the Structure of the American Economy*, New York, 1953, pp. 93ff.

257. *Ibid.*, pp. 53ff.

258. *Ibid.*, p. 57. For an interesting, if somewhat mechanistic application of the technique to economic adjustments to disarmament, cf. W. W. Leontief and M. Hoffenberg, "The Economic Effects of Disarmament," *Scientific American*, April, 1961, p. 47.

259. Cf. National Bureau of Economic Research, *Input-Output Analysis: An Appraisal*, Princeton, 1955, especially Carl F. Christ, "A Review of Input-Output Analysis," pp. 137ff.

260. Cf. H. B. Chenery and P. G. Clark, *Interindustry Economics*, New York, 1959, p. 79; pp. 164ff.

261. *Ibid.*, p. 157.

262. Koopmans, *op. cit.*, p. 191. Koopmans suggests that these may not be fair tests, since they were done for peace-time years while the major input-output tables available were intended for a wartime economy.

263. Chenery and Clark, *op. cit.*, pp. 186ff.

264. Cf. Leontief, "The Decline and Rise of Soviet Economic Science," *Foreign Affairs*, January, 1960, pp. 261ff.; cf. also Lange, *Essays in Economic Planning*, Calcutta, 1960 p. 40ff.; R. W. Campbell, *Soviet 1960, Economic Power*, Cambridge, 1960, p. 99; Alec Nove, *The Soviet Economy*, New York, 1961, p. 208; B. Ward, "Kantorovich on Economic Calculation," *Journal of Political Economy*, December, 1960, p. 545ff.

265. Koopmans, *op. cit.*, p. 102.

266. H. M. Smith, "Leontief's Open Input-Output Models," in T. C. Koopmans, ed. *Activity Analysis of Production and Allocation*, New York, 1951, pp. 136-37.

267. Cf. Leontief, *Studies in the Structure of the American Economy*, p. 15.

268. Cf. Christ, *op. cit.*, p. 139.

269. Cf. R. W. Goldsmith in NBER, *op. cit.*, p. 4; cf. also comments in the same volume by Rutledge Vining, pp. 31ff.

270. Vining, *op. cit.*, p. 42.

271. Paul A. Samuelson, "Abstract of a Theorem Concerning Substitutability in Open Leontief Models," in Koopmans, ed. *Activity Analysis*, pp. 142ff.

Chapter 6
Streams of Tradition in Britain

1. On Longfield, cf. E. R. A. Seligman, "On Some Neglected British Economists," in *Essays in Economics*, New York, 1925, pp. 65ff.

2. For the chief facts on Sidgwick's life, cf. *Henry Sidgwick: A Memoir*, London, 1906.

3. Henry Sidgwick, *Principles of Political Economy*, London, 1883.

4. Quoted by John Maynard Keynes, *Essays in Biography*, London, 1933, p. 161.

5. *Political Economy*, p. 24.

6. As Schumpeter argued, this was rather difficult to accomplish, but British utilitarians often expressed an unshakeable faith in progress. Cf. J. A. Schumpeter, *History of Economic Analysis*, New York, 1954, p. 806.

7. *Political Economy*, pp. 34ff.

8. *Ibid.*, pp. 60-61.

9. *Ibid.*, p. 124.

10. *Ibid.*, p. 150.

11. *Ibid.*, p. 131.

12. *Ibid.*, p. 139.

13. *Ibid.*, p. 208.

14. *Ibid.*, p. 408.

15. *Ibid.*, p. 414.

16. *Ibid.*, p. 419.

17. Cf. Hla Myint, *Theories of Welfare Economics*, Cambridge, 1948, p. 131.

18. *Political Economy*, p. 500.

19. *Ibid.*, p. 516.

20. Cf. Wicksteed, *Common Sense of Political Economy*, London, 1933, II, p. 771.

21. *Ibid.*, p. 705.

22. *Ibid.*, I, p. v.

23. H. W. Spiegel, ed., *The Development of Economic Thought*, New York, 1952, p. 700.

24. Philip H. Wicksteed, *The Alphabet of Economic Science*, reprinted, New York, 1955.

25. Wicksteed, *Common Sense of Political Economy*, Vol. I, p. 373. Both Robbins and Stigler suggest in their comments that the retraction was purely verbal and applied only to Wicksteed's particular mathematical version. Cf. Robbins' forward in *Common Sense*, p. xi, and *Stigler, Production and Distribution Theories*, New York, 1941, p. 333. Cf. also J. R. Hicks' *Theory of Wages*, London, 1932, p. 236. Hicks has argued that Wicksteed's formulation would be quite valid if the assumption of constant returns is made. Edgeworth's and Pareto's strictures appear well grounded, however, since constant returns as a universal attribute is a dubious proposition. Wicksell's solution was more elegant: he suggested that Euler's theorem was validated when a firm operated at the minimum point of the marginal cost curve, for there returns were constant.

26. The Robbins edition, a superb example of scholarly editing, includes some of Wicksteed's important papers, such as his first essay on Marxism and his Presidential Address to Section F of the British Association on the scope and method of economics (1913).

27. Cf. *Alphabet*, p. 8.
28. *Ibid.*, p. 7.
29. *Ibid.*, p. 15.
30. *Ibid.*, p. 53.
31. *Ibid.*, p. 93.
32. *Ibid.*, p. 111.
33. *Common Sense*, I, p. 380.
34. *Ibid.*, II, p. 776.
35. *Ibid.*, I, p. 361.
36. Cf. George Katona, *The Powerful Consumer*, New York, 1960, pp. 138ff.
37. Cf. Randall Jarrell, "A Sad Heart at the Supermarket," *Daedalus*, Spring, 1960, p. 362.
38. *Common Sense*, I, 82.
39. *Ibid.*, II, 753.
40. *Ibid.*, I, 107ff.
41. *Ibid.*, p. 114.
42. Cf. M. Blaug, *Ricardian Economics: A Historical Study*, New Haven, 1958.
43. Cf. Stigler, *op. cit.*, p. 59.
44. *Common Sense*, II, 533.
45. *Ibid.*, p. 540.
46. *Ibid.*, pp. 506 and 785.
47. Wicksteed, *Co-ordination of the Laws of Distribution*, London, 1894, reprinted, 1932.
48. Cf. Stigler, *op. cit.*, p. 328.
49. Cf. Knut Wicksell, *Lectures on Political Economy*, London, 1934, I, 129, and Hicks, *op. cit.*, p. 238.
50. Francis Y. Edgeworth, *Mathematical Psychics*, London, 1881.
51. *Papers Relating to Political Economy*, 3 vols., London, 1925.
52. *Papers*, II, p. 5.
53. J. M. Keynes, *Essays in Biography*, London, 1933, p. 282.
54. *Ibid.*, p. 285.
55. *Papers*, I., p. 31.
56. *Ibid.*, pp. 26ff.
57. *Ibid.*, p. 55.
58. *Mathematical Psychics*, p. 7.
59. Marshall, *Pure Theory of Foreign Trade and Pure Theory of Domestic Values*, London, 1879, reprinted, 1949.
60. Cf. his "Pure Theory of Taxation" reprinted in *Classics in the Theory of Public Finance*, ed. R. A. Musgrave and A. T. Peacock, London, 1958, p. 119.
61. *Ibid.*, p. 121.
62. Cf. *Papers*, II, 475.
63. *Ibid.*, I, 61ff.
64. *Ibid.*, p. 66.
65. *Ibid.*, I, 79ff.
66. Cf. Augustin Cournot, *Researches into the Mathematical Principles of the Theory of Wealth*, 1897, ed. reprinted, New York, 1960, p. 79ff.
67. *Papers*, I., 111ff.
68. Cf. Gustav Cassel, *On Quantitative Thinking in Economics*, London, 1935, and his *Theory of Social Economy*, New York, 1924.
69. G. L. S. Shackle, *Uncertainty in Economics*, Cambridge, 1955, p. 241.
70. Cf. Marshall's essay, "Present Position of Economics," in *Memorials of Alfred Marshall*, ed. A. C. Pigou, London, 1925, p. 152.
71. Keynes, *Essays in Biography*, p. 150. The same essay is to be found in the *Memorials*.
72. Cf. *Official Papers of Alfred Marshall*, London, 1936.
73. *Memorials*, pp. 323ff. The notion of economic chivalry implied, of course, the practice of philanthropy as the major instrumentality for advance and progress.
74. Cf. Jacob Viner, "Marshall's Economics: The Man and his Times," *American Economic Review*, June, 1951, p. 228.
75. *Principles of Economics*, London, 8th ed., 1920, p. 20. The reader may want to consult the recently issued variorum edition of the *Principles* which indicates changes of language and substance since the first edition and reproduces other related materials as well. Cf. *Principles of Economics*, ninth (variorum) edition, 2 volumes, ed. by C. W. Guillebaud, London, 1961.
76. Cf. W. A. Weiskopf, *The Psychology of Economics*, London, 1956, pp. 161ff. Weiskopf seeks to convert Marshall into something of a preacher. While there is a strong element of moralizing in the *Principles*, Weiskopf overstates his argument. Cf. *Principles*, p. 70. Cf. also G. F. Shove, "The Place of Marshall's *Principles* in the Development of Economic Theory," *Economic Journal*, December, 1942, reprinted in *Essays on Eco-*

nomic Thought, ed. J. J. Spengler and W. R. Allen, Chicago, 1960, pp. 762ff.
77. Schumpeter, op. cit., p. 837.
78. Terence W. Hutchison wonders in his A Review of Economic Doctrines, 1870-1929, Oxford, 1953, p. 64, whether Marshall may not have derived a large part of his mathematical apparatus from William Whewell whose obscure essays on mathematical economics appeared between 1833 and 1850 in the Transactions of the Cambridge Philosophical Society.
79. Memorials, pp. 165ff.
80. Ibid., p. 168.
81. Principles, pp. 723ff. George Stigler expresses the view that Marshall overdid the evolutionary viewpoint to the detriment of the concept of a stationary economy. Yet there was enough of the latter in Marshall to make the most static of theorists happy. Cf. Stigler, op. cit., pp. 62-63.
82. Cf. Shove, op. cit., p. 713.
83. Economic Journal, December, 1942, p. 293.
84. Schumpeter, op. cit., p. 835.
85. Economic Journal, op. cit., p. 349.
86. Principles, p. 42.
87. Industry and Trade, London, 1919, p. 736.
88. Ibid., p. 397.
89. Principles, pp. 381ff.
90. For a recent attack on this method, cf. Sidney Schoeffler, The Failures of Economics, Cambridge, 1955.
91. Cf. Leo Rogin, The Meaning and Validity of Economic Theory, New York, 1956, pp. 576-77, 612. Joan Robinson makes the same point in a lecture given at Oxford in 1953. Cf. her On Re-reading Marx, Cambridge, 1953, p. 14.
92. J. R. Hicks, Value and Capital, Oxford, 1939, p. 117.
93. Cf. his Pure Theory which became a point of departure for many later mathematical economists.
94. Cf. Memorials, pp. 419, 417.
95. Principles, p. 459n.
96. Marshall spoke of money as "the center around which economic science clusters." See ibid., p. 22.

97. See discussion of the real versus monetary approach in chapter on Keynes below, p. 735.
98. Don Patinkin in his Money, Interest and Prices, Evanston, 1956, argues that Marshall failed to construct a successful monetary theory in the sense that the stability conditions of value were not adequately transferred to monetary analysis. He feels that there is a certain confusion in the Marshallian analysis of the value of money which not even the famous diagrams were able to clarify. Of course, all Marshall did was to demonstrate how the value of money could be established by the ordinary supply and demand curves. This was quite evident in Marshall's version of the quantity equation (known as the cash-balance equation) which formed part of the oral tradition at Cambridge. The liquidity ratio, or desired cash holdings, in Marshall's M-kPT was a function of both real income and the rate of interest. The ratio M to P was the supply of real balances, while kT became the demand for such balances which could be divided into a demand on account of transactions or as a precaution against contingencies in the future. Cf. Marshall, Money Credit and Commerce, London, 1923, pp. 44ff., and Sir Dennis Robertson, Money, 1922, reprinted Chicago, 1959, pp. 23ff.
99. Cf. Official Papers, pp. 3ff.
100. Ibid., pp. 17ff. Marshall proposed a tabular standard to maintain purchasing power of long term contracts. The government would publish tables showing changes in the purchasing power of gold so that long term contracts might be made in units of fixed purchasing power. This, Marshall, suggested, could apply to loans, interest, rent, and even wages. The idea was first broached in 1885.
101. See p. 333 above.
102. A. C. Pigou, Alfred Marshall and Current Thought, London, 1953, pp. 37ff.

103. *Memorials*, pp. 93ff.
104. Cf. *Principles*, pp. 126ff.; also p. 830, Appendix K.
105. Cf. F. H. Knight, *Risk, Uncertainty and Profit*, Boston, 1921, reprinted, 1948, pp. 69ff.; Hicks, "Rehabilitation of Consumer's Surplus," *Review of Economic Studies*, February, 1941, pp. 108ff.
106. *Principles*, pp. 470ff.
107. *Ibid.*, pp. 102ff.
108. For an excellent modern discussion of the mathematics of this notion see Kenneth E. Boulding, *Economic Analysis*, New York, 1941, Revised ed.; p. 137.
109. Jacob Viner, "Costs," *Encyclopaedia of the Social Sciences*, New York, 1931, IV, 472.
110. Lionel Robbins, "The Representative Firm," *Economic Journal*, September, 1928, pp. 387ff.
111. *Principles*, Book V, Chaps. 6 and 7, pp. 381ff.
112. *Ibid.*, p. 441.
113. Cf. Frank H. Knight, "Fallacies in the Interpretation of Social Cost," *The Ethics of Competition*, New York, 1935, pp. 229ff; Piero Sraffa, "The Laws of Return under Competitive Conditions," *Economic Journal*, 1926, reprinted in *Readings in Price Theory*, ed. G. J. Stigler and K. E. Boulding, Homewood, 1952, pp. 180ff.
114. *Principles*, pp. 150, 318.
115. *Ibid.*, p. 410.
116. *Ibid.*, p. 518.
117. *Ibid.*, p. 532. N. Kaldor has argued that Marshall's distribution theory, such as it was, applied only to the short run, since with profits considered as a kind of "quasi-rent" set by the difference between marginal and average prime costs with prices equal to marginal prime costs, only short run considerations became meaningful, for the relevant prices of labor and capital are those of the immediate past. Cf. N. Kaldor, "Alternative Theories of Distribution," *Review of Economic Studies*, 1955-56, reprinted in Kaldor's *Essays on Value and Distribution*, New York, 1960, pp. 209ff.
118. *Principles*, pp. 717ff.
119. *Ibid.*, p. 220.
120. *Ibid.*, p. 594.
121. *Official Papers*, p. 272.
122. Pigou, *op. cit.*, p. 31.
123. *Principles*, p. 625.
124. *Ibid.*, p. 487.
125. *Memorials*, pp. 256ff.
126. *Principles*, pp. 455ff.
127. *Ibid.*, p. 660.
128. *Economic Journal*, Vol. 36, 1926, reprinted in *Readings in Price Theory*.
129. *Principles*, pp. 458-59.
130. *Industry and Trade*, p. 182.
131. Colin Clark in Spiegel, *op. cit.*, p. 781.
132. Roy F. Harrod, *The Life of John Maynard Keynes*, New York, 1951. p. 144.
133. Cf. his article, "Some Aspects of Welfare Economics," *American Economic Review*, June, 1951, p. 287.
134. Cf. C. J. Ratzlaff, *The Theory of Free Competition*, Philadelphia, 1936, pp. 181ff.
135. *Essays in Applied Economics*, London, 1923, p. 23.
136. Pigou, *Alfred Marshall and Current Thought*.
137. *Ibid.*, p. 10.
138. On this point, cf. Hla Myint, *op. cit.*
139. Cf. *ibid.*, pp. 173ff.
140. A. C. Pigou, *Economics of Welfare*, 4th ed., London, 1932, p. 5.
141. Hutchison, *op. cit.*, p. 284.
142. *Welfare*, p. 5.
143. A good general statement of Pigou's system may be found in his article, "One Way of Looking at Economics," *Essays in Economics*, London, 1952, p. 66.
144. *Economic Journal*, 1922, reprinted in *Readings in Price Theory*, pp. 119ff.
145. *Ibid.*, p. 132.
146. "Some Aspects of Welfare Economics," *American Economic Review*, June, 1951, p. 288.
147. *Ibid.*, p. 293.
148. *Alfred Marshall and Current Thought*, pp. 49ff.
149. Cf. I. D. M. Little, *A Critique of Welfare Economics*, London, 1950, p. 9.
150. *Economics of Welfare*, p. 10.

151. *Ibid.,* p. 31.
152. *Ibid.,* p. 34.
153. *Ibid.,* p. 44.
154. *Ibid.,* p. 54.
155. *Ibid.,* p. 85.
156. *Ibid.,* p. 96.
157. *Ibid.,* p. 140.
158. *Ibid.,* p. 143.
159. *Ibid.,* p. 172. J. E. Meade has suggested a way of measuring divergences based on the ratio of the difference between the value of the marginal social net product and marginal cost of the factor to the marginal cost of the factor. This Meade calls the rate of divergence, which cumulates as products pass from the original factor to the consumer. Cf. Meade's *Trade and Welfare,* London, 1955, pp. 24ff.
160. Cf. Marshall's *Principles,* pp. 472ff.
161. Cf. summary of this debate in B. P. Beckwith, *Marginal-Cost Price-Output Control,* New York, 1955, pp. 45ff.
162. Pigou, *Socialism versus Capitalism,* London, 1937, pp. 42ff.
163. *Marshall and Current Thought,* p. 54.
164. *Socialism versus Capitalism,* p. 21.
165. *Ibid.,* p. 84.
166. *Welfare,* p. 200.
167. *Ibid.,* p. 220.
168. *Ibid.,* pp. 222ff.
169. Marshall's, *Principles,* p. 472.
170. Pigou, *Economics of Stationary States,* London, 1935.
171. *Ibid.,* p. 3.
172. *Ibid.,* p. 6.
173. *Ibid.,* p. 21.
174. *Ibid.,* p. 43.
175. *Ibid.,* p. 54.
176. *Ibid.,* p. 72.
177. Cf. his *Veil of Money,* London, 1950.
178. *Stationary States,* pp. 86ff.
179. *Ibid.,* p. 136.
180. *Ibid.,* p. 139.
181. *Ibid.,* p. 147.
182. *Ibid.,* p. 168.
183. *Ibid.,* p. 229.
184. *Ibid.,* p. 264.
185. Pigou, *Industrial Fluctuations,* 2nd ed., London, 1929.
186. *Ibid.,* p. 8.
187. *Ibid.,* p. 10.
188. *Ibid.,* p. 15.
189. *Ibid.,* p. 26.
190. *Ibid.,* p. 84.
191. *Ibid.,* p. 92.
192. Pigou did not deny the force of monetary factors, but these were seen as conditions on which the primary psychological forces acted. Cf. *Ibid.,* pp. 102-103.
193. *Ibid.,* p. 104.
194. *Ibid.,* p. 110.
195. *Ibid.,* Chap. X, pp. 114ff.
196. *Ibid.,* p. 125.
197. *Ibid.,* p. 137.
198. *Ibid.,* p. 180.
199. *Ibid.,* p. 193.
200. *Ibid.,* p. 201.
201. *Ibid.,* p. 231. Pigou sought to apply his psychological theory to the economic history of post-war Britain. Cf. his *Aspects of British Economic History, 1918-1925,* London, 1947, pp. 169ff.
202. *Industrial Fluctuations,* p. 321.
203. Cf. Alvin Hansen, *Business Cycles and National Income,* New York, 1951, p. 519.
204. Pigou, *Employment and Equilibrium,* London, 1941, 2nd ed. 1952.
205. A more recent attempt to validate the "Pigou effect" was developed by Don Patinkin, *op. cit.*
206. *Employment and Equilibrium,* p. 56.
207. *Ibid.,* p. 97. Cf. also Paul A. Samuelson, *American Economic Review,* September, 1941, p. 551.
208. *Employment and Equilibrium,* p. 222.
209. Cf. A. P. Lerner, *Essays in Economic Analysis,* London, 1953, pp. 256-57, for criticism of Pigou's multiplier concepts.
210. *Employment and Equilibrium,* pp. 181ff.
211. Cf. *The Veil of Money,* pp. 18ff.
212. Cf. "The Exchange Value of Legal Tender Money," in *Essays in Applied Economics,* London, 1923, p. 176.
213. *Ibid.,* p. 178.
214. *A Study in Public Finance,* 1928, 3rd ed., London, 1949, p. 6.
215. *Ibid.,* p. 43.
216. Roy F. Harrod, on the other hand,

took the position that equal sacrifice was the preferable approach. His argument was based on the concept of absolute sacrifice and the notion that the utility of the marginal income was equal to the disutility of marginal effort. This implied that the richer one became, the less work one did. Such psychological assumptions were dubious, leaving Pigou's more subtle relative concept of least aggregate sacrifice undisturbed. Cf. summary of the debate in E. D. Fagan, "Recent and Contemporary Theories of Progressive Taxation," *Journal of Political Economy*, 1938, reprinted in *Readings in the Economics of Taxation*, ed. R. A. Musgrave and Carl S. Shoup, Homewood, 1959, p. 27ff.
217. *Public Finance*, p. 51.
218. *Ibid.*, p. 61.
219. Cf. Richard A. Musgrave, *The Theory of Public Finance*, New York, 1959, p. 95.
220. Pigou, *Public Finance*, p. 81.
221. J. M. Keynes, *The General Theory of Employment, Interest and Money*, New York, 1936, p. 272.
222. *Ibid.*, p. 270.
223. *Economica*, May, 1936, p. 115.
224. Pigou, *Keynes' General Theory*, London, 1951.
225. *Ibid.*, p. 10.
226. *Ibid.*, p. 21.
227. *Ibid.*, p. 55.
228. *Ibid.*, pp. 40-41.
229. Memoir, *John Maynard Keynes, 1883-1946, Fellow and Bursar*, Cambridge, 1949, p. 22.
230. Dennis H. Robertson, *Money*, New York, 1922, new ed., Chicago, 1959; *Banking Policy and the Price Level*, London, 1926.
231. Robertson, *A Study of Industrial Fluctuation*, London, 1915, reprinted 1948.
232. Robertson, *Economic Fragments*, London, 1931; *Essays in Monetary Theory*, London, 1940; *Utility and All That*, London, 1952; *Economic Commentaries*, London, 1956.
233. Robertson, *Lectures on Economic Principles*, 3 vols., London, 1957-59.
234. *Lectures*, I, 72.

235. *Ibid.*, p. 85.
236. *Utility And All That*, p. 14.
237. *Ibid.*, p. 25.
238. *Economic Commentaries*, pp. 46-47.
239. *Utility And All That*, p. 35.
240. *Economic Commentaries*, p. 57.
241. *Ibid.*, p. 45.
242. *Ibid.*, p. 48.
243. *Lectures*, I, 92.
244. *Ibid.*, p. 17.
245. *Ibid.*, p. 27.
246. "Those Empty Boxes," in *Readings in Price Theory*, pp. 143ff.
247. *Lectures*, II, 27.
248. *Ibid.*, p. 33.
249. *Ibid.*, p. 42.
250. *Ibid.*, p. 45.
251. *Lectures*, II, 119.
252. *Banking Policy and the Price Level*, passim.
253. Cf. *A Study of Industrial Fluctuation*, passim.
254. *Banking Policy*, p. 9.
255. *Ibid.*, p. 14; also *Industrial Fluctuation*, passim.
256. R. L. Saulnier, *Contemporary Monetary Theory*, New York, 1938, pp. 122-25.
257. *Banking Policy*, pp. 22ff.
258. *Ibid.*, pp. 39, 45.
259. Cf. Daniel Bell, "The Subversion of Collective Bargaining," *Commentary*, March, 1960, p. 186, particularly the comments on the decline of external financing in the modern corporate set-up.
260. Cf. *Banking Policy*, p. 41, and *Essays in Monetary Theory*, p. 66.
261. Cf. Saulnier, *op. cit.*, p. 144. Lloyd Metzler questioned the validity of Robertson's "day" for lack of empirical verification. Cf. Metzler's "Three Lags in the Circular Flow of Income," in *Income, Employment and Public Policy: Essays in Honor of Alvin H. Hansen*, New York, 1948, pp. 11ff.
262. *Essays*, p. 79.
263. *Lectures*, II, 53.
264. *Economic Essays and Addresses*, London, 1931, p. 42.
265. *Banking Policy*, p. 43.
266. *Economic Essays*, p. 100.
267. *Money*, p. 27.
268. *Ibid.*, p. 22.

269. *Ibid.*, p. 85.
270. *Ibid.*, p. 87.
271. *Ibid.*, pp. 88-89.
272. Cf. *Lectures*, II, 54.
273. Cf. for example, B. S. Kierstead, *Capital, Interest and Profits*, Oxford, 1959.
274. Cf. *Utility And All That*, p. 98.
275. Cf. Kierstead, *op. cit.*, pp. 12ff.
276. *Lectures*, II, 77.
277. *Ibid.*, p. 82.
278. Cf. p. 571 below.
279. *Lectures*, II, 87.
280. Keynes, *General Theory*, p. 197.
281. Cf. Keynes, "The General Theory of Employment," *Quarterly Journal of Economics*, February, 1937, reprinted in *The New Economics*, ed. S. E. Harris, New York, 1947, pp. 181ff.
282. Cf. Alvin H. Hansen, *A Guide to Keynes*, New York, 1953, pp. 146-47.
283. *Utility And All That*, p. 114.
284. *Essays*, p. 7.
285. Cf. Hansen, *op. cit.*
286. *Lectures*, III, 161.
287. *Ibid.*, p. 77.
288. Cf. for detailed analysis of the two types of theories and their possible reconciliation, J. W. Conard, *Introduction to the Theory of Interest*, Berkeley, 1959, pp. 203ff.
289. Cf. Abba P. Lerner, "On Generalizing the General Theory," *American Economic Review*, March, 1960, p. 136.
290. *Industrial Fluctuation*, 1948 ed., p. xiv.
291. *Ibid.*, p. 2.
292. *Ibid.*, p. 13.
293. *Ibid.*, p. 32.
294. *Ibid.*, p. 87.
295. *Ibid.*, pp. 91ff.
296. *Lectures*, III, 98.
297. Cf. *ibid.*, pp. 109ff., and p. above, for a discussion of J. M. Clark on the accelerator.
298. *Industrial Fluctuation*, p. 157.
299. *Ibid.*, p. 174.
300. *Lectures*, III, 98.
301. *Ibid.*, pp. 113ff; on flexible tax rates, cf. Kenneth E. Boulding, *The Economics of Peace*, New York, 1945, pp. 161ff.
302. Cf. *Lectures*, III, 59ff.
303. For a discussion of the stagnation argument, cf. Alvin H. Hansen, *Full Recovery or Stagnation?*, New York, 1938; *Fiscal Policy and Business Cycles*, New York, 1941. Cf. also Benjamin Higgins, *Economic Development*, New York, 1959, pp. 167ff., for a discussion of the continuing validity of Hansen's argument and William Fellner, "The Robertsonian Evolution," *American Economic Review*, June, 1952, p. 268.
304. *Lectures*, III, 31.
305. *Ibid.*, p. 39.
306. *Ibid.*, p. 42.
307. Cf. Fellner, *op. cit.*, p. 279.
308. Cf. *Ibid.*, p. 269.
309. Hawtrey began with *Good and Bad Trade*, London, 1913, and completed his long writing career with *Cross Purposes in Wage Policy*, London, 1955. Among the more important books are *Currency and Credit*, London, 1919, 4th ed., 1950; *The Economic Problem*, London, 1926; *Trade and Credit*, London, 1928; *The Art of Central Banking*, London, 1932; *Capital and Employment*, London, 1937; 2nd ed., 1952; and *Economic Destiny*, London, 1944.
310. Cf. Harrod, *Life of Keynes*, p. 352.
311. For a close critical analysis of Keynes by Hawtrey, cf. *Capital and Employment*, Chap. VII, pp. 157ff.
312. *Economic Destiny*, p. 2.
313. *Economic Problem*, p. 3.
314. Cf. *ibid.*, pp. 141ff.
315. *Trade and Credit*, pp. 105ff.
316. *Economic Problem*, pp. 181-82.
317. *Ibid.*, p. 185.
318. *Ibid.*, pp. 190ff.
319. *Ibid.*, p. 225.
320. These arguments were repeated with slight modifications in *Economic Destiny*, pp. 202ff.
321. Cf. W. J. Baumol, *Business Behavior, Value and Growth*, New York, 1959, especially Chap. 6, pp. 45ff. Cf. also E. T. Penrose, *Theory of the Growth of the Firm*, Oxford, 1959, pp. 116ff.
322. Baumol, *op. cit.*, p. 49.
323. Cf. *Economic Problem*, p. 80.

324. *Ibid.*, p. 80.
325. *Economic Destiny*, p. 41.
326. Cf. F. H. Knight, "Capitalistic Production, Time and the Rate of Return," *Economic Essays in Honour of Gustav Cassel*, London, 1933, pp. 327ff. Cf. also p. below.
327. *Economic Destiny*, p. 35.
328. Cf. *Cross Purposes in Wage Policy*, London, 1955.
329. *Ibid.*, p. 118.
330. *Economic Destiny*, p. 61.
331. Cf. *Currency and Credit*, London, 1919, 4th ed., 1950; also *Economic Destiny*, pp. 75ff.
332. Cf. *Currency and Credit*, pp. 29ff.
333. *Ibid.*, pp. 34-35.
334. Cf. *Capital and Employment*, pp. 7ff.
335. *Ibid.*, p. 18.
336. *Ibid.*, p. 21.
337. *Currency and Credit*, p. 52.
338. *Ibid.*, p. 55.
339. *Ibid.*, p. 63.
340. Cf. *Economic Destiny*, pp. 78ff.
341. Cf. *Capital and Employment*, p. 30.
342. Cf. Saulnier, *op. cit.*, p. 43.
343. *Monetary Reconstruction*, p. 134.
344. Cf. *Trade and Credit*, p. 98.
345. *Capital and Employment*, p. 99.
346. Cf. Hawtrey's view on the Great Depression in *Art of Central Banking*, pp. 41ff.
347. Cf. his "Interpersonal Comparisons of Utility," *Economic Journal*, December, 1938, p. 635.
348. Cf. Harrod, *Life of Keynes*, p. 427.
349. Cf. *On Freedom and Free Enterprise*, ed. Mary Sennholz, New York, 1956, p. 253. In this symposium, M. N. Rothbard commented that when Robbins depicted the British classicists as qualified defenders of laissez faire, he thereby abandoned his earlier "praxeological" approach. Cf. also Robbins, *The Theory of Economic Policy in English Classical Political Economy*, London, 1953.
350. Harrod, *op. cit.*, p. 555.
351. Lionel C. Robbins, *An Essay on the Nature and Significance of Economic Science*, London, 1932, 2nd ed., 1935.
352. Cf. Robbins "Production" in *Encyclopaedia of the Social Sciences*, XII, 462; also cf. *An Essay*, p. 10.
353. Cf. *An Essay*, pp. 42-44.
354. Cf. *ibid.*, p. 17.
355. Cf. *Ibid.*, p. 38.
356. *Ibid.*, pp. 112-13.
357. Cf. *ibid.*, p. 58.
358. Cf. L. Hogben, *Retreat from Reason*, New York, 1937, p. 10.
359. Cf. *An Essay*, p. 143.
360. Cf. T. W. Hutchison, *The Significance and Basic Postulates of Economic Theory*, London, 1938, p. 9.
361. Baumol, *op. cit.*, passim.
362. Hutchison, *op. cit.*, pp. 61-62.
363. "Interpersonal Comparisons of Utility," *Economic Journal*, December, 1938.
364. "Robertson on Utility and Scope," *Economica*, May, 1953, p. 99.
365. "Remarks on the Relationship between Economics and Psychology," *Manchester School*, 1934, p. 89.
366. There is an enormous body of literature on behavior which cannot be reviewed here. Not only are there the works of Sigmund Freud, but those of his followers and critics. Reference, however, may be made particularly to Hans Gerth and C. Wright Mills, *Character and Social Structure*, New York, 1953, and Erich Fromm, *Escape From Freedom*, New York, 1941.
367. See p. 469 above.
368. *Economic Journal*, September, 1928, p. 398.
369. "Remarks Upon Certain Aspects of the Theory of Cost," *Economic Journal*, March, 1934, p. 1.
370. Cf. Robbins, *The Great Depression*, London, 1934.
371. *Ibid.*, p. 55.
372. Cf. Charles Schultze, *Recent Inflation in the United States*, Study Paper No. 1, Joint Economic Committee, Washington, 1959.
373. "Consumption and the Trade Cycle," *Economica*, November, 1932, p. 427.
374. *The Economic Problem in Peace and War*, London, 1950, p. 68.
375. *Ibid.*, p. 6.
376. *Ibid.*, p. 22.
377. *Ibid.*, p. 75.

378. *Theory of Economic Policy in English Classical Political Economy, passim.*
379. *Time in Economics,* Amsterdam, 1957, p. 13.
380. *Ibid.,* p. 15.
381. *Ibid.,* p. 24.
382. Cf. K. E. Boulding, *The Image,* Ann Arbor, 1956, p. 6.
383. Cf. Penrose, *op. cit.*
384. *Time in Economics,* p. 33.
385. *Expectations in Economics,* Cambridge, 1949, 2nd ed. 1952, pp. 110ff.
386. *Ibid.,* p. 114.
387. *Ibid.,* p. 118.
388. *Ibid.,* p. 122.
389. *Ibid.,* p. 127.
390. *Ibid.,* p. 2.
391. Kenneth Arrow makes the cogent point that a theory of uncertainty must permit the study of sequential decision-making. Cf. K. J. Arrow, "Functions of a Theory of Behavior Under Uncertainty," *Metroeconomica,* April-August, 1959, p. 16.
392. Cf. R. D. Luce and H. Raiffa, *Games and Decisions,* New York, 1957.
393. *Time in Economics,* p. 47.
394. Cf. *Uncertainty in Economics,* p. 18.
395. *Ibid.,* p. 46.
396. *Ibid.,* p. 50.
397. For an analysis of the different varieties of such systems, cf. R. A. D. Egerton, *Investment Decisions Under Uncertainty,* Liverpool, 1960.
398. *Expectations in Economics,* pp. 59ff.
399. *Ibid.,* p. 67.
400. Cf. Egerton, *op. cit.,* especially pp. 73ff.
401. *Expectations in Economics,* p. 95.
402. For a critical analysis of Shackle's views on taxation, cf. C. S. Shoup, "Some Implications for Public Finance in Shackle's Expectation Analysis," *Metroeconomica,* op. cit., pp. 89ff.
403. *Uncertainty in Economics,* p. 92.
404. Cf. Kierstead, *op. cit.,* pp. 28ff.
405. Cf. *ibid.,* pp. 51-52.
406. *Expectations in Economics,* pp. 101ff.

407. Cf. on this point J. Pen, *Wage Rates Under Collective Bargaining,* Cambridge, 1959, p. 192.
408. For the rich possibilities of game theory, cf. Luce and Raiffa, *op. cit.,* and Martin Shubik, *Strategy and Market Structure,* New York, 1959.
409. Cf. Musgrave, *op. cit.,* p. 331. Musgrave argues that an individual investor, while undergoing a unique experience, can learn from the large number of attempts made by others. This would permit the application of the probability approach, and, in fact, seems to be the way most businessmen think.
410. Cf. D. J. O'Connor in *Uncertainty and Business Decisions,* p. 18.
411. *Ibid.,* p. 40.
412. *Ibid.,* p. 87.
413. L. M. Lachmann, *Capital and Its Structure,* London, 1956, p. 27.
414. Cf. Kierstead, *op. cit.,* p. 31.
415. Cf. Johan Åkerman, "Shackle's System and Theories of Business Cycles," *Metroeconomica,* op. cit., p. 4-5. Attention must be called to Shackle's newest book, *Decision. Order and Time,* Cambridge, 1961, which arrived too late for a detailed discussion. However, we may note that Shackle now carries his theory one step further in that decision-making is completely divorced from knowledge of the past and related exclusively to desired experience by anticipation. Yet he cannot avoid the admission that individual decision-making is conditioned by circumstances "visible to others as well as himself." Conceivably, some of these circumstances may have roots in the past. Shackle's new work also contains some interesting replies to his critics. In essence, Shackle contends that decision-making precludes rigid laws of historical cause and effect. He does concede that there are constraints on what can happen, so that uncertainty, to be meaningful, must be visualized as being "bounded." cf. *op. cit.* p. 271. There is an interesting parallel in these concepts with those de-

veloped by Marx in his younger years. cf. George Lichtheim, *Marxism: An Historical and Critical Study*, London, 1961, *passim*. But whereas Marx spoke of human action in a social context, Shackle insists in describing a type of behavior which can be characterized only as atomism *in extremis*. It

it difficult to see how he leaps from a definition of economic theory as a systematization of a part of psychological law to the assertion that theory accounts for the "orderliness of society in its business," unless economics is to be converted solely into a study of psychology.

Chapter 7
The Swedish Contribution

1. John Stuart Mill, *Autobiography*, reprinted New York, 1924, Chap. 5, p. 93. The best source for biographic details on Wicksell is Torsten Gårdlund, *Life of Knut Wicksell*, Stockholm, 1958.
2. Gårdlund, *ibid.*, p. 15.
3. *Ibid.*, p. 42.
4. Erik Lindahl, "Wicksell's Life and Works," introduction to Wicksell, *Selected Papers on Economic Theory*, London, 1958, p. 10.
5. Gårdlund, *op. cit.*, p. 105.
6. *Ibid.*, p. 85.
7. *Ibid.*, p. 136.
8. Knut Wicksell, *Value, Capital and Rent*, translated, London, 1954.
9. Wicksell, *Finanztheoretische Untersuchungen nebst Darstellung und Kritik des Steuersystems Schwedens*, Jena, 1896.
10. Wicksell, *Interest and Prices*, Jena, 1898, translated, London, 1936.
11. Gårdlund, *op. cit.*, p. 171.
12. Cf. *Ibid.*, p. 184; Lindahl, *op. cit.*, pp. 22, 23 footnote. For Wicksell's review of Cassel's *Theory of Social Economy*, see the former's *Lectures on Political Economy*, translated London, 1934, Vol. I, Appendix 1, p. 219. The review was originally published in 1919.
13. Joseph Schumpeter, who should have known better, described Wicksell as having led the life of a quiet and retired scholar. Cf.

Schumpeter's *History of Economic Analysis*, New York, 1954, p. 863.
14. *Selected Papers on Economic Theory*, pp. 51ff.
15. *Ibid.*, p. 57.
16. *Ibid.*, p. 58.
17. *Ibid.*, p. 62.
18. *Ibid.*, p. 64; *Value, Capital and Rent*, pp. 41ff.
19. Cf. *Interest and Prices*, Chap. 2, and *Lectures*, II, 132.
20. Cf. Gårdlund, *op. cit.*, p. 195.
21. *Value, Capital and Rent*, p. 47.
22. *Ibid.*, p. 75.
23. *Ibid.*, p. 94.
24. *Lectures*, I, 96. Cf. also Carl G. Uhr, *Economic Doctrines of Knut Wicksell*, Berkeley, 1960, pp. 38ff. This is by far the definitive study of Wicksell's theories.
25. Cf. *Value, Capital and Rent*, p. 69, and *Selected Papers*, p. 204. The latter was a review of A. L. Bowley's *Mathematical Groundwork of Economics*, Oxford, 1924, reprinted, 1960.
26. *Lectures*, I, 80-81.
27. *Value, Capital and Rent*, p. 25.
28. This proposition was developed not only in *Value, Capital and Rent* but in the *Lectures*, I, 101ff., as well as in several articles on the subject. Cf. *Selected Papers*, pp. 93, 121ff. The problem also is discussed at great length by George J. Stigler, *Production and Distri-*

bution Theories, New York, 1941, Chap. XII, pp. 320ff., as well as by Joan Robinson, *Collected Economic Papers,* Oxford, 1951, I, 1ff. Mrs. Robinson argues that under conditions of imperfect competition, entrepreneurs receive more than the value of their marginal physical product. In other words, they are in a position to "exploit" the other factors of production and to extract from the distributive process more than their "fair share."

29. *Lectures,* I, 73.
30. *Ibid.,* p. 77.
31. *Ibid.,* p. 80.
32. *Lectures,* I, 108; *Selected Papers,* p. 94.
33. *Selected Papers,* pp. 98ff.
34. *Lectures* I, 132.
35. *Selected Papers,* p. 105.
36. *Lectures,* I, 141.
37. *Lectures,* Appendix, I, 219.
38. *Lectures,* I, 164. Cf. also John R. Hicks, *The Theory of Wages,* London, 1932, pp. 121ff., for an analysis of the impact of inventions on wages.
39. Cf. C. G. Uhr, *op. cit.,* pp. 120ff.; *idem,* "Knut Wicksell: A Centennial Evaluation," *American Economic Review,* December, 1951, pp. 850ff.; also Wicksell, *Lectures,* I, 177ff.; Stigler, *op. cit.,* p. 287.
40. F. A. Hayek, *Pure Theory of Capital,* Chicago, 1941, p. 273. An interesting problem was suggested by Uhr in the relationship of forced saving in Hayek's sense to capital absorption by wages. Uhr felt that forced saving could be the more dominant factor. Cf. Uhr, *op. cit.,* 852. On the "Wicksell effect," Cf. also Joan Robinson, *Collected Economic Papers,* II, 185.
41. Uhr, *Economic Doctrines of Knut Wicksell,* pp. 140ff.
42. Cf. *Value, Capital and Rent,* pp. 97ff., where it was presented for the first time.
43. *Ibid.,* pp. 108-10.
44. *Lectures,* I, 150. Cf. also *Selected Papers,* p. 108.
45. *Selected Papers,* p. 110; *Lectures,* I, 154. These parts of the *Lectures* are virtually the same as the earlier

papers reprinted in the first volume cited.
46. *Lectures,* I, 177.
47. *Value, Capital and Rent,* p. 119.
48. Stigler considers Wicksell's classification unreal. Cf. Stigler, *op. cit.,* pp. 274-75.
49. *Selected Papers,* p. 114. Cf. also *Lectures,* I, 202, and Ragnar Frisch's essay on Wicksell in H. W. Spiegel, *Development of Economic Thought,* New York, 1952, pp. 653ff.
50. *Value, Capital and Rent,* p. 145; *Lectures,* I, 193.
51. Uhr, *op. cit.,* pp. 99ff.
52. *Lectures,* I, 212.
53. *Lectures,* II, 191.
54. *Lectures,* I, 153.
55. Cf. B. J. Dempsey, *Interest and Usury,* Washington, 1942, pp. 12ff.
56. Cf. *Value, Capital and Rent,* p. 160.
57. *Lectures,* II, 168, 194; *Interest and Prices,* pp. 87ff., pp. 136ff.; for a delineation of the cumulative model, cf. Uhr, *op. cit.,* pp. 235ff.
58. Cf. Bertil Ohlin's "Introduction" to *Interest and Prices.*
59. Cf. *Interest and Prices,* p. 39. On Ricardo cf. *Works and Correspondence of David Ricardo,* ed. Piero Sraffa, London, 1951, *Principles,* I, 364. Cf. also Wicksell, *Lectures,* II, 172ff.; for a cogent presentation of Wicksell's monetary theory, Cf. Uhr, *op. cit.,* pp. 198ff.
60. For a similar interpretation, cf. Don Patinkin, *Money, Interest and Prices,* Evanston, 1956, p. 422.
61. Wicksell, *Lectures,* II, 159ff.
62. *Lectures,* I, 224.
63. *Lectures,* II, 195.
64. Cf. Erik Lundberg, *Business Cycles and Economic Policy,* London, 1957, pp. 155ff.
65. Cf. Wicksell, *Lectures,* I, 258; Uhr, *op. cit.,* pp. 266ff.
66. Cf. *Interest and Prices,* p. 4, where the objective of a stable price level is set forth; and *Lectures,* II, 3, wherein the possibility of social control is expressed. With regard to money ". . . everything is determined by human beings themselves. . . ."
67. *Interest and Prices,* p. 144.

68. *Ibid.*, pp. 135, 143.
69. *Studies in the Theory of Money and Capital*, London, 1939.
70. *Lectures*, II, 209.
71. *Interest and Prices*, p. 134.
72. *Lectures*, II, 195.
73. Reprinted in *International Economic Papers*, London, 1953, No. 3, pp. 58ff.
74. *Ibid.*, p. 66.
75. Quoted by Ragnar Frisch in Spiegel, *op. cit.*, p. 698. As Frisch points out, this is virtually a complete description of what contemporary theory describes as erratic shocks. Cf. also *Lectures*, II, 211ff., although here changes in the purchasing power of money were deemed to be a significant factor.
76. *International Economic Papers, op. cit.*, p. 68.
77. J. K. Galbraith, *The Affluent Society*, Boston, 1958.
78. Cf. p. 113 above.
79. *Lectures*, I, 143.
80. For an excellent review of Wicksell's social program, cf. Uhr, *American Economic Review*, December, 1951, pp. 385ff., and *idem*, Note, *American Economic Review*, June, 1953, p. 366.
81. Wicksell's tax ideas also are discussed by Gunnar Myrdal, *The Political Element in the Development of Economic Theory*, London, 1954, pp. 176ff.
82. Wicksell, "A New Principle of Just Taxation," in R. A. Musgrave and A. T. Peacock, ed., *Classics in The Theory of Public Finance*, London, 1958, p. 114.
83. *Ibid.*, p. 102. For a good discussion of Wicksell's tax ideas, cf. Uhr, *Economic Doctrines of Knut Wicksell*, pp. 158ff.
84. Cf. Stigler, *op. cit.*, p. 261.
85. Gårdlund, *op. cit.*, p. 17.
86. Quoted by Frisch in Spiegel, *op. cit.*, p. 653.
87. Cf. Lundberg, *op. cit.*, p. 108.
88. Cf. p. 542 above.
89. Cf. Wicksell's devastating review of Cassel's *Theory of Social Economy* in former's *Lectures*, I, 219ff.
90. Gustav Cassel, *The Nature and Necessity of Interest*, 1903, reprinted, New York, 1957.
91. Cassel, *Theory of Social Economy*, 1918, translated, New York, 1924. This translation was so poor that it had to be redone (London, 1932). The latter is clearly preferable for consultation purposes.
92. Cassel, *Fundamental Thoughts in Economics*, New York, 1925; *On Quantitative Thinking in Economics*, London, 1935.
93. *On Quantitative Thinking*, p. 6.
94. *Fundamental Thoughts*, p. 13.
95. *Ibid.*, p. 24.
96. *Ibid.*, p. 32.
97. *Social Economy*, pp. 50ff. Most references here are to the 1924 translation.
98. *Quantitative Thinking*, p. 30.
99. *Social Economy*, p. 80.
100. *Ibid.*, p. 84.
101. *Ibid.*, p. 109.
102. *Quantitative Thinking*, p. 123.
103. *Ibid.*, p. 173.
104. *Quantitative Thinking*, pp. 122ff. Paul Douglas was chided for attempting an empirical test of marginal productivity in the latter's *Theory of Wages*, 1934, reprinted, New York, 1957. Cassel charged that the basic formula employed by Douglas was in error on the ground that the exponents in the production function could not be assumed as constant. In effect, Cassel was asserting that statistical data would not justify the kind of rigid mathematics that Douglas employed. Further, the Douglas approach was limited, said Cassel, by confining the study to manufacturing industries, and, in that framework, to fixed capital. Cf. Cassel, *ibid.*, p. 135.
105. *Social Economy*, p. 24.
106. *Quantitative Thinking*, p. 22.
107. *Social Economy*, p. 49.
108. *Quantitative Thinking*, pp. 80ff.
109. Cf. p. 448 above.
110. *Social Economy*, pp. 61ff.
111. *Quantitative Thinking*, p. 63. This, incidentally, was not unrelated to the Hayek-Mises position.
112. Cf. *Nature and Necessity of Interest*, p. 68.
113. *Social Economy*, p. 2.

114. *Quantitative Thinking*, p. 1.
115. *Fundamental Thoughts*, p. 55.
116. *Social Economy*, p. 89.
117. *Quantitative Thinking*, p. 153.
118. *Social Economy*, p. 75.
119. *Ibid.*, p. 76.
120. Wicksell, *Lectures*, I, 230.
121. Cf. R. Dorfman, P. A. Samuelson, and R. M. Solow, *Linear Programming and Economic Analysis*, New York, 1958.
122. *Social Economy*, p. 118.
123. *Ibid.*, p. 147.
124. Cf. Wicksell, *Lectures*, I, 225ff.
125. Patinkin, *op. cit.*, pp. 445ff.
126. *Interest*, p. 61.
127. *Ibid.*, p. 67.
128. *Ibid.*, p. 87.
129. *Ibid.*, p. 99.
130. *Ibid.*, p. 128.
131. *Ibid.*, p. 145.
132. *Ibid.*, p. 155.
133. *Social Economy*, p. 245.
134. See especially the 2nd ed. of *Social Economy* in the 1932 translation, p. 264.
135. Cf. Wicksell, *Lectures*, I, 243.
136. *Social Economy*, p. 296.
137. *Ibid.*, p. 301.
138. *Ibid.*, p. 307.
139. *Ibid.*, p. 308.
140. Cf. 2nd ed. of *Social Economy*, pp. 342ff.
141. *Ibid.*, p. 337.
142. Cf. his *An International Economy*, New York, 1956, especially Chap. VII, pp. 89ff.
143. Cassel, *Recent Monopolistic Tendencies*, Geneva, 1927, p. 12.
144. *Social Economy*, p. 472.
145. Cassel's statistical methods were sharply criticized by J. T. Phinney, "Gold Production and the Price Level," *Quarterly Journal of Economics*, August, 1933, pp. 647ff.
146. *Social Economy*, p. 521.
147. *Ibid.*, p. 523.
148. *Ibid.*, p. 545.
149. *Ibid.*, p. 571.
150. Cf. Hayek on this point, p. 357 above.
151. "From Protectionism t h r o u g h Planned Economy to Dictatorship," *International Conciliation*, New York, October, 1934, p. 307.
152. *Social Economy*, pp. 658ff.
153. *Ibid.*, p. 665.

154. Cf. Jacob Viner, *Studies in the Theory of International Trade*, New York, 1937, p. 381.
155. For other criticisms, see A. C. Pigou, *Essays in Applied Economics*, London, 1930, and J. M. Keynes, *Treatise on Money*, London, 1930, I, 72ff.
156. Cf. Gunnar Myrdal, *Value in Social Theory*, London, 1958, p. 238.
157. Edgeworth was one of the first to note the similarity. Cf. the latter's "Professor Cassel's Treatise," *Economic Journal*, Vol. 30, 1920, p. 533.
158. The facts on Davidson's background are drawn from Eli F. Heckscher's excellent article in *International Economic Papers*, No. 2, London, 1952, pp. 111ff. Cf. also, Uhr, *op. cit.*, pp. 255, 279, 292.
159. Walter Bagehot, *Economic Studies*, 1891, reprinted Stamford, 1953, p. 168.
160. On this point, cf. George Stigler, "Ricardo and the 93% Labor Theory of Value," *American Economic Review*, June, 1958, p. 357.
161. K. G. Landgren, *Economics in Modern Sweden*, Washington, 1957, p. 96.
162. Cf. Dag Hammarskjold, "Swedish Discussion on Aims of Monetary Policy," *International Economic Papers*, No. 5, London, 1955, p. 146.
163. Cf. Brinley Thomas, "The Monetary Doctrines of Professor Davidson," *Economic Journal*, March, 1935, pp. 35ff. Cf. Uhr, *op. cit.*, pp. 270ff., for a good summary of the Wicksell-Davidson debate.
164. Hammarskjold, *op. cit.*, p. 149.
165. For a detailed description of this phase of Swedish economics, cf., Landgren, *op. cit.*
166. Ingvar Svennilson, *Growth and Stagnation in the European Economy*, Geneva, 1954.
167. Lundberg, *op. cit.*, p. 112.
168. Gustav Cassel, as quoted by Lundberg, *op. cit.*, p. 114. Cassel, for example, feared that government efforts to mitigate a crisis would cripple private enterprise. That

this has not occurred at any time in the last twenty-five years testifies to the inadequacy of Cassel's views.

169. Myrdal, *Value in Social Theory*, p. 240.

170. Lundberg, *op. cit.*, p. 93. Cf. also B. Ohlin, "Some Notes on the Stockholm Theory of Savings and Investment," *Readings in Business Cycle Theory*, ed. G. Haberler, Philadelphia, 1944, pp. 87ff.

171. Lundberg, "Business Cycle Experience in Sweden," in *The Business Cycle in the Post War World*, London, 1955, pp. 60ff.

172. Bertil Ohlin, *Interregional and International Trade*, Cambridge, 1933. For a discussion of Ohlin's international trade theory, cf., R. E. Caves, *Trade and Economic Structure*, Cambridge, 1960.

173. Landgren, *op. cit.*, p. 27.

174. "The Stockholm Theory," *Business Cycle Readings*, p. 105.

175. *Ibid.*, p. 109.

176. Landgren, *op. cit.*, pp. 51ff.

177. *Ibid.*, p. 55.

178. Ohlin, "The Stockholm School versus the Quantity Theory," *Economisk Tidskrift*, 1943, reprinted in *International Economic Papers*, No. 10, London, 1960, p. 132.

179. *Interregional and International Trade*, p. 4.

180. *Ibid.*, p. 35.

181. *Ibid.*, p. 38.

182. *Ibid.*, p. 130.

183. *Ibid.*, p. 589.

184. Landgren, *op. cit.*, p. 26.

185. J. M. Keynes in *Economic Journal*, 1929, cited by Viner, *op. cit.*, p. 307ff.

186. Ohlin, *op. cit.*, Appendix III, pp. 571ff.

187. Cf. the extracts from the *Gerechtigkeit* published in *Classics in the Theory of Public Finance*, pp. 168ff. Also his reply to his critics, *ibid.*, p. 214. Cf. also Uhr, *op. cit.*, pp. 188ff., for a brief statement of part of Lindahl's tax theory.

188. *Ibid.*, p. 217.

189. *Ibid.*, p. 219.

190. *Ibid.*, p. 225.

191. *Ibid.*, p. 228. Cf. also, Lindahl's last paper, "Tax Principles and Tax Policy," *International Economic Papers, op. cit.*, p. 9.

192. Erik Lindahl, *Studies in the Theory of Money and Capital*, London, 1939. Cf. also Uhr, *op. cit.*, pp. 298ff.

193. Lindahl, "Basic Concepts of National Accounting," 1954, reprinted in *International Economic Papers*, No. 7, London, 1957, p. 73. Cf. also Ingvar Ohlsson, *On National Accounting*, Stockholm, 1953, pp. 251ff., in which the gaps in Lindahl's system are pointed up.

194. *Money and Capital*, p. 23.

195. *Ibid.*, pp. 69ff.

196. *Ibid.*, p. 33.

197. Cf. Tord Palandar, "On the Concepts and Methods of the Stockholm School," 1941, reprinted in *International Economic Papers*, No. 3, London, 1953, pp. 8ff.

198. Lindahl, *op. cit.*, p. 60. The method has been used as a basis for analyzing the impact of inflation. Cf. Bent Hansen, *A Study in the Theory of Inflation*, London, 1951, pp. 26ff. Cf. also, J. K. Galbraith, *A Theory of Price Control*, Cambridge, 1952, and Uhr, *op. cit.*, pp. 307ff.

199. Cf. Ohlsson, *op. cit.*, Lindahl, "Basic Concepts of National Accounting," IEP, No. 7; National Bureau of Economic Research, *A Critique of the United States Income and Product Accounts*, Princeton, 1958, especially George Jaszi, "The Conceptual Basis of the Accounts," p. 15ff., for a summary of the American situation; and Paul Studenski, *The National Income*, New York, 1958.

200. Cf. Ohlsson, *op. cit.*, and Bent Hansen, *The Economic Theory of Fiscal Policy*, London, 1958, pp. 41ff.

201. *Money and Capital*, pp. 132ff.

202. The effectiveness of the rate of interest as a regulatory device was questioned by Mordecai Ezekiel, "Saving, Consumption and Investment," *American Economic Review*, March, June, 1942, pp. 281-93. Ezekiel argued that the events of the immediate past were most meaningful to businessmen, whose

reactions could best be related to the ratio of profit to investment. He could find no empirical evidence for a relationship of interest to investment.

203. Lindahl, *op. cit.*, p. 175.
204. *Ibid.*, p. 181.
205. *Ibid.*, p. 231. At one point Lindahl suggested that a lower short term rate of interest can allow production for stockpiling in cases where a labor dispute reduces the output of capital goods. A cogent question, and one that underscores the institutional weaknesses of this sort of theory, is who, in such a situation, would do the producing? Unless, of course, the employment of scabs is allowed.
206. A. L. Bowley, *Mathematical Groundwork of Economics*, Oxford, 1924.
207. Lindahl, *op. cit.*, pp. 288ff.
208. *Ibid.*, p. 331.
209. Erik Lundberg, *Studies in the Theory of Economic Expansion*, 1937, reprinted New York, 1954.
210. *Ibid.*, p. 2.
211. For analyses which posit different directions of movement in the cobweb theorem with curious results, cf. William J. Baumol, *Economic Dynamics*, New York, 1951, pp. 108ff., and R. G. D. Allen, *Mathematical Economics*, London, 1956.
212. Lundberg, *op. cit.*, p. 29.
213. *Ibid.*, p. 37.
214. *Ibid.*, Chap. 3, pp. 51-88.
215. *Ibid.*, p. 89.
216. *Ibid.*, p. 131.
217. *Ibid.*, p. 168.
218. See p. 751 below.
219. Lundberg, *op. cit.*, p. 183.
220. *Ibid.*, p. 185.
221. *Ibid.*, pp. 194ff.
222. *Ibid.*, p. 211.
223. Cf. *ibid.*, p. 255.
224. Lundberg, *Business Cycles and Economic Policy*, London, 1957.
225. Cf. Landgren, *op. cit.*, p. 85.
226. Lundberg, *Business Cycles*, p. 334.
227. *Ibid.*, p. 85.
228. *Ibid.*, p. 111.
229. *Ibid.*, pp. 160ff.
230. *Ibid.*, p. 163.

231. *Ibid.*, p. 201.
232. *Ibid.*, p. 221.
233. *Ibid.*, p. 298.
234. *Ibid.*, p. 299.
235. Cf. Landgren, *op. cit.*, p. 89.
236. Paul Streeten in "Introduction" to Myrdal, *Value in Social Theory*, p. ix. In addition to the works cited, Myrdal was chief author of the pathbreaking study on the American Negro, *An American Dilemma*, New York, 1944.
237. Gunnar Myrdal, *The Political Element in the Development of Economic Theory*, 1930, translated, Cambridge, 1954.
238. Cf. *ibid.*, pp. 20ff.
239. Cf. Leo Rogin, *The Meaning and Validity of Economic Theory*, New York, 1956.
240. *Value in Social Theory*, p. 52.
241. *Ibid.*, p. 254.
242. Myrdal, *An International Economy*, New York, 1956.
243. Myrdal, *Economic Theory and Under-Developed Regions*, London,, 1957.
244. *Ibid.*, *Social Theory*, p. 261.
245. *Ibid.*, p. 206.
246. *Ibid.*, p. 211.
247. Cf. Ralph Barton Perry, *Realms of Value*, Cambridge, 1954, especially the discussion of value as related to the concept of interest, Chaps. 3, 5, 10, and 15.
248. Cf. Robert K. Merton, "The Self-Fulfilling Prophesy," *Social Theory and Social Structure*, Glencoe, 1957, p. 421.
249. *Social Theory*, p. 201.
250. *Ibid.*, p. 205.
251. Streeten, "Introduction," *Social Theory*, p. xiv.
252. Myrdal, *Monetary Equilibrium*, London, 1939.
253. Cf. Polandar, *op. cit.*, pp. 5ff. For a good exposition of Myrdal's equilibrium concept, cf. Uhr, *op. cit.*, pp. 313ff.
254. *Monetary Equilibrium*, p. 11.
255. *Ibid.*, p. 19.
256. *Ibid.*, p. 46.
257. *Ibid.*, p. 53.
258. *Ibid.*, p. 71.
259. *Ibid.*, p. 96.

260. *Ibid.*, pp. 116ff.
261. *Ibid.*, p. 137.
262. *Ibid.*, p. 200.
263. A good survey is presented in Landgren, *op. cit.* also *International Economic Papers*, No. 9, London, 1959, pp. 172ff., for selected book reviews of Swedish works.
264. Bent Hansen, *The Theory of Inflation*, London, 1951.
265. Cf. also H. K. Charlesworth, *The Economics of Repressed Inflation*, London, 1956, and John K. Galbraith, *A Theory of Price Control*, Cambridge, 1952.
266. *Theory of Inflation*, pp. 189ff.
267. Hansen, *Economic Theory of Fiscal Policy*, London, 1958.
268. *Ibid.*, p. 28. Cf. also Jan Tinbergen, *Economic Policy: Principles and Design*, Amsterdam, 1956; *idem, On the Theory of Economic Policy*, Amsterdam, 1955; *idem, Centralization and Decentralization in Economic Policy*, Amsterdam, 1954.
269. *Fiscal Policy*, p. 208.

Chapter 8
The American Dichotomy

1. Indispensable to a detailed study of the growth of American economic thinking is Joseph Dorfman's painstaking five volume work, *The Economic Mind in American Civilization*, New York, 1946-1959, the essential source for material on American economics. A huge, sprawling, and encyclopedic treatise, it reviews not only texts and analytical publications but pamphlets, legislation, and correspondence as well. I have continually consulted the Dorfman volumes in dealing with the American scene. For a good short essay on the quality of American economic thought, cf. P. A. Samuelson, "American Economics," in *Postwar Economic Trends in the United States*, ed. R. E. Freeman, New York, 1960, p. 31. Cf. also A. W. Coats, "The First Two Decades of the American Economic Association," *American Economic Review*, September, 1960, pp. 555ff.
2. W. C. Mitchell, *Lectures on Current Types of Economic Theory,* New York, 1935, mimeographed, II, 466.
3. Dorfman, *op. cit.*, III, 205.
4. Cf. Mitchell, *op. cit.*, II, 467-68.
5. Richard T. Ely, *Outlines of Economics*, New York, 1893; 4th ed., 1923.
6. Dorfman, *op. cit.*, IV, 212.
7. *Property and Contract*, New York, 1914.
8. Cf. Arthur M. Schlesinger, Jr., *The Coming of the New Deal*, Boston, 1958, pp. 338ff.
9. Cf. his *Consumption of Wealth*, Philadelphia, 1889; also J. L. Boswell, *The Economics of Simon Nelson Patten*, Philadelphia, 1933, p. 32.
10. Cf. *Theory of Prosperity*, New York, 1902.
11. Cf. Dorfman, *op. cit.*, III, 186.
12. Cf. his *Essays in Economic Theory*, ed. R. G. Tugwell, New York, 1924, p. 277.
13. *Reconstruction of Economic Theory*, Philadelphia, 1912.
14. *Essays*, p. 243.
15. Cf. his *New Basis of Civilization*, New York, 1912, pp. 32ff.

16. E. R. A. Seligman, *Progressive Taxation in Theory and Practice*, Princeton, 1908; *The Shifting and Incidence of Taxation*, New York, 1921, 4th ed.
17. Seligman, *Economic Interpretation of History*, New York, 1902.
18. Seligman, *Principles of Economics*, New York, 1905.
19. *Shifting and Incidence*, p. 11.
20. Cf. Dorfman, *op. cit.*, III, 354.
21. *Distribution of Wealth*, New York, 1904.
22. Other books by Carver were *Principles of Political Economy*, Boston, 1919; *Economy of Human Energy*, New York, 1924; *Principles of National Economy*, Boston, 1921; and *Essays in Social Justice*, Cambridge, 1915.
23. *Principles of Economics*, 2 vols., New York, 1911.
24. Frank W. Taussig, *The Tariff History of the United States*, New York, 1888; 8th ed., 1931; *International Trade*, New York, 1927.
25. Schumpeter, *Ten Great Economists*, New York, 1951, p. 220.
26. *Wages and Capital*, New York, 1915. Mill recanted on the wages fund doctrine in a review of Thornton in the *Fortnightly Review*, May, 1869.
27. *Wages and Capital*, p. 19.
28. *Ibid.*, p. 104.
29. *Ibid.*, p. 108.
30. Cf. summary of this discussion in Theo. Suranyi-Unger, *Economics in the Twentieth Century*, New York, 1931, pp. 301ff. Cf. also Joseph A. Schumpeter, "Professor Taussig on Wages and Capital," reprinted in *Essays*, Cambridge, 1951, pp. 143ff.
31. Dorfman, *op. cit.*, III, 480.
32. Cf. p. 480 above.
33. *Principles*, 3rd ed., 1923, pp.388ff.
34. Cf. Jacob Viner, *International Economics*, New York, 1951, pp. 151-52.
35. *Ibid.*, p. 156.
36. "International Trade under Depreciated Paper," *Quarterly Journal of Economics*, May, 1917, pp. 380ff.
37. Cf. *International Trade*, p. 337ff.
38. Viner, *op. cit.*

39. Both Viner and Haberler have suggested that unilateral flows should be treated separately. Cf. Viner, *Studies in the Theory of International Trade*, p. 563, and G. Haberler, *Theory of International Trade*, London, 3rd impression, 1950, p. 164.
40. *Principles*, I, 467ff.
41. Viner, *op. cit.*, pp. 364ff.
42. Dorfman, *op. cit.*, III, 361.
43. Frank Fetter, *Economic Principles*, New York, 1915.
44. Cf. Dorfman, *op. cit.*, III, p. 443ff.
45. *Economic Principles*, p. 18.
46. *Ibid.*, p. 19.
47. Cf. Mitchell, *op. cit.*, II, 488ff.
48. Cf. Böhm-Bawerk, *Capital and Interest*, translated by G. D. Honke and H. F. Sennholz, South Holland, 1959, p. 476.
49. "Interest Theories, Old and New," *American Economic Review*, March, 1914, pp. 68ff.
50. Cf. Dorfman, *op. cit.*, V, 465.
51. Cf. *Economic Principles*, pp. 27ff.
52. Fetter, *Modern Economic Problems*, New York, 1916; *The Masquerade of Monopoly*, 1931.
53. Fetter's testimony, 1923 FTC Hearings, cited by Dorfman, *op. cit.*, V, 560.
54. TNEC Hearings, 76th Cong. First Session, Part 5, *Monopolistic Practices in Industry*, pp. 1672, 1913ff.
55. Cited by Dorfman, *op. cit.*, III, 365.
56. Dorfman, *Thorstein Veblen and His America*, New York, 1935, p. 256.
57. Herbert J. Davenport, *Outlines of Economic Theory*, New York, 1896; *Value and Distribution*, Chicago, 1908; *Economics of Enterprise*, New York, 1913; *Economics of Alfred Marshall*, Ithaca, 1935.
58. *Economics of Enterprise*, p. 81.
59. *Ibid.*, p. 84.
60. *Ibid.*, p. 504.
61. *Ibid.*, p. 502.
62. *Ibid.*, p. 519.
63. *Ibid.*, p. 97.
64. *Ibid.*, p. 126.
65. Dorfman, *Economic Mind*, III, 382.
66. Cf. Davenport, *op. cit.*, p. 131.

67. Cf. Dorfman, *op. cit.*, III, 385-86.
68. Davenport, *op. cit.*, p. 97.
69. *Ibid.*, p. 60.
70. *Ibid.*, p. 117.
71. Cf. *Ibid.*, pp. 143ff., where Davenport concedes the point.
72. Mitchell, *op. cit.*, II, 520. Mitchell's criticism of Davenport here was quite sharp.
73. Davenport, *op. cit.*, p. 150.
74. *Ibid.*, pp. 332ff.
75. For a forceful modern version of this argument, cf. B. S. Kierstead, *Capital, Interest and Profits*, Oxford, 1959.
76. Davenport, *op. cit.*, p. 353.
77. *Ibid.*, p. 212.
78. *Ibid.*, p. 234.
79. *Ibid.*, p. 282.
80. Cf. *Ibid.*, pp. 295ff.
81. *Ibid.*, p. 303.
82. Fisher's important works in economics were *Mathematical Investigations in the Theory of.Value and Price*, New Haven, 1891, his doctoral dissertation; *The Nature of Capital and Income*, New York, 1906; *The Rate of Interest*, New York, 1907; *Elementary Principles of Economics*, New York, 1910; *The Purchasing Power of Money*, New York, 1910; *The Making of Index Numbers*, New York, 1922; *The Theory of Interest*, New York, 1930, reprint, 1954; *Booms and Depressions*, New York, 1932.
83. Fisher, *The Making of Index Numbers*.
84. Cf. "A Statistical Method for Measuring 'Marginal Utility,'" in *Economic Essays in Honor of John Bates Clark*, New York, 1927.
85. *Capital and Income*, p. 39.
86. *Ibid.*, p. 98. Cf. also *Elementary Principles*, pp. 51ff.
87. *Capital and Income*, p. 157.
88. *Theory of Interest*, p. 5.
89. *Capital and Income*, pp. 185ff.
90. *Ibid.*, p. 202.
91. *Publications of the American Economic Association*, August, 1896.
92. *Theory of Interest*, p. 14.
93. *Ibid.*, p. 25.
94. *Ibid.*, p. 182.
95. Cf. *ibid.*, pp. 231ff.
96. Cf. Keynes, *General Theory*, pp.

140-41. Keynes also agreed with Fisher that the gold standard was a poor basis for a monetary system. Cf. Keynes, *Tract on Monetary Reform*, London, 1923.
97. A. A. Alchian, "The Rate of Interest, Fisher's Rate of Return over Costs and Keynes' Internal Rate of Return," *American Economic Review*, December, 1955, p. 938.
98. *Theory of Interest*, p. 183.
99. *Ibid.*, pp. 473ff. Fisher's first salvo at Böhm-Bawerk was hurled in the *Rate of Interest*, which brought a quick reply. Cf. Böhm-Bawerk, *Further Essays on Capital and Interest*, reprinted, South Holland, 1959, pp. 162ff.
100. Cf. *Theory of Interest*, pp. 331ff.
101. Cf. Frank H. Knight, "Capital and Interest," in *Readings in the Theory of Income Distribution*, eds. W. Fellner and B. F. Haley, Philadelphia, 1946, pp. 384ff.
102. *Theory of Interest*, p. 13.
103. *Ibid.*, p. 42.
104. *Ibid.*, p. 411.
105. *Ibid.*, p. 42.
106. Cf. Dorfman, *Thorstein Veblen and His America*, p. 285.
107. Veblen, *Essays in Our Changing Order*, p. 142. Italics mine.
108. Cf. Dorfman, *Economic Mind*, IV, 203.
109. Cf. *Purchasing Power*, p. 150.
110. M. Friedman, ed., *Studies in the Quantity Theory of Money*, Chicago, 1956.
111. *Purchasing Power*, p. 161.
112. Cf. Dorfman, *op. cit.*, p. 289.
113. Fisher, *100% Money*, New York, 1935.
114. Cf. Albert G. Hart, "The 'Chicago Plan' of Banking Reform," *Review of Economic Studies*, 1935, reprinted in *Readings in Monetary Theory*, eds. F. A. Lutz and L. W. Mints, Homewood, 1951, pp. 437ff.
115. *Purchasing Power*, p. 56.
116. Alvin Johnson, *Pioneer's Progress*, New York, 1942, p. 227-28.
117. Frank H. Knight, *Risk, Uncertainty and Profit*, reprinted London, 1933, 7th impression, 1948.
118. *Journal of Political Economy*, April, 1941, reprinted in M. J. Herskovits, *Economic Anthropol-*

ogy, New York, 1952, pp. 507ff.

119. Cf. *ibid.*, pp. 511-12.

120. This, by his own admission in his *Intelligence and Democratic Action*, Cambridge, 1960, p. 82.

121. Herskovits, *op. cit.*, p. 516.

122. *Ibid.*, pp. 526-27.

123. Cf. *Risk, Uncertainty and Profit*, p. xi.

124. Cf. *Ibid.*, p. xii; also *The Ethics of Competition and Other Essays*, London, 1935, pp. 135, 281.

125. Herskovits, *op. cit.*, p. 510.

126. *Ibid.*, p. 515.

127. Max Weber, *The Methodology of the Social Sciences*, New York, 1949, pp. 49ff.

128. Cf. *ibid.*, pp. 1ff.

129. *American Economic Association Proceedings*, May, 1957, p. 18.

130. *Risk, Uncertainty and Profit*, p. 9.

131. *Ibid.*, pp. xviff.

132. *Ethics*, p. 295.

133. *On the History and Method of Economics*, Chicago, 1956, pp. 127, 145.

134. Cf. "Institutionalism and Empiricism in Economics," *American Economic Association Proceedings*, May, 1952, p. 45.

135. "The Ricardian Theory of Production and Distribution," *Canadian Journal of Economics and Political Science*, 1935, reprinted in *History and Method*, pp. 37ff.

136. Cf. "Statics and Dynamics," reprinted in *Ethics of Competition*, p. 161.

137. *Ibid.*, p. 169.

138. *Ibid.*, p. 184.

139. Cf. *Risk, Uncertainty and Profit*, p. 53.

140. Cf. *Ethics of Competition*, pp. 62ff., and R. D. Luce and H. Raiffa, *Games and Decisions*, New York, 1957.

141. *Risk, Uncertainty and Profit*, pp. 57ff.

142. This, of course, abstracted from the decision-making process, which is entirely an affair of human beings. Cf. E. T. Penrose, *Theory of Growth of the Firm*, Oxford, 1959.

143. *Risk, Uncertainty and Profit*, p. 76.

144. *The Economic Organization*, New York, 1951, p. 35.

145. Knight's Introduction to Carl Menger, *Principles of Economics*, Glencoe, 1950, p. 20.

146. Cf. "Realism and Relevance in the Theory of Demand," *Journal of Political Economy*, December, 1944, p. 298.

147. *Encyclopaedia of the Social Sciences*, V, 69.

148. *Risk, Uncertainty and Profit*, p. 98.

149. *Encyclopaedia of the Social Sciences*, XIV, 470.

150. *Ethics of Competition*, p. 197.

151. "A Suggestion for Simplifying the General Theory of Price," *Journal of Political Economy*, June, 1928, pp. 353ff.

152. *Ethics of Competition*, p. 199.

153. *Ibid.*, p. 204.

154. Cf. *ibid.*, p. 215.

155. Robert Triffin reports that in later years Knight modified his position, acknowledging that specialization and the stickiness of invested resources could lead to increasing costs. Cf. R. Triffin, *Monopolistic Competition and General Equilibrium Theory*, Cambridge, 1940, p. 147; *American Economic Association Proceedings*, May, 1956, p. 101.

156. Cf. Knight, *op. cit.*, passim, *Journal of Political Economy*, June, 1928, and *History and Method*, pp. 55ff.

157. *Risk, Uncertainty and Profit*, p. 160.

158. *History and Method*, p. 57.

159. *Risk, Uncertainty and Profit*, pp. 124ff.

160. For a devastating critique of Knight's argument, cf. N. Kaldor, "The Recent Controversy on the Theory of Capital," *Econometrica*, July, 1937, pp. 220ff. It should be noted that Kaldor recently modified his defense of neoclassical capital theory by rejecting the application of marginal productivity to society as a whole. Cf. F. A. Lutz and D. C. Hague, eds., *The Theory of Capital*, London, 1961, p. 294.

161. The debate started with Knight's articles, "Capitalistic Production, Time and the Rate of Return," in *Economic Essays in Honour of*

Gustav Cassel, London, 1933, pp. 327ff., and "Capital, Time and the Interest Rate," *Economica*, August, 1934.

162. "Capital and Interest," *Readings in the Theory of Income Distribution*, p. 389. Cf. also *Risk, Uncertainty and Profit*, p. xxiv.

163. "Capitalistic Production . . . ," in *Cassel Essays*, and "The Quantity of Capital and Rates of Interest," *Journal of Political Economy*, August, 1936, p. 453.

164. *Ibid.*, *Journal of Political Economy*, p. 460.

165. *Op. cit.*, *Cassel Essays*, p. 338.

166. Cf. "Professor Hayek and the Theory of Investment," *Economic Journal*, March, 1935, pp. 77ff.

167. *Ibid.*, p. 78.

168. *Ibid.*, p. 89.

169. Cf. F. Machlup, "Professor Knight and the 'Period of Production,'" *Journal of Political Economy*, October, 1935, p. 577; cf. also K. E. Boulding, "Time and Investment," *Economica*, May, 1936, p. 196.

170. Machlup, *op. cit.*, p. 584.

171. Kaldor, *Econometrica*, July, 1937, p. 213.

172. N. Kaldor, "On the Theory of Capital," *Econometrica*, April, 1938, p. 171.

173. Cf. K. E. Boulding, "Professor Knight's Capital Theory," *Quarterly Journal of Economics*, May, 1936, p. 527.

174. *Ibid.*, p. 528.

175. *Op. cit.*, in *Cassel Essays*.

176. "Neglected Factors in the Problem of Normal Interest," *Quarterly Journal of Economics*, February, 1916, p. 298.

177. Cf. his article "The Quantity of Capital and the Rate of Interest," *Journal of Political Economy*, August-October, 1936, pp. 433, 612.

178. Cf. E. Rolph, "The Discounted Marginal Productivity Doctrine," *Journal of Political Economy*, 1939, reprinted in *Readings in Income Distribution*, p. 291.

179. *Op. cit.*, *Income Readings*, p. 394.

180. *Op. cit.*, *Journal of Political Economy*, October, 1936, pp. 614ff.

181. *Ibid.*, p. 614.

182. *Encyclopaedia of the Social Sciences*, I, 382.

183. *Op. cit.*, *Journal of Political Economy*, October, 1936, p. 631.

184. Cf. B. S. Kierstead, *Capital, Interest and Profits*, pp. 42ff.

185. Cf. *Risk, Uncertainty and Profit*, p. 20.

186. M. Dobb, *Capital Enterprise and Social Progress*, London, 1925.

187. Cf. *Risk, Uncertainty and Profit*, p. 268.

188. Schumpeter, *History*, p. 895.

189. *Risk, Uncertainty and Profit*, p. 329.

190. *Ibid.*, pp. 38, 232.

191. Cf. "Profit," in *Encyclopaedia of the Social Sciences*, XII, 480.

192. *Risk, Uncertainty and Profit*, p. 270.

193. *Ibid.*, p. 278.

194. As wittily expressed by John Galbraith in *The Liberal Hour*, Boston, 1960, p. 30.

195. Cf. *Ethics of Competition*, p. 75.

196. *Risk, Uncertainty and Profit*, p. 185.

197. *History and Method*, p. 520.

198. Cf. "Immutable Law in Economics," *American Economic Association Proceedings*, May, 1956, p. 103.

199. Cf. *The Economic Organization*, p. 90.

200. Cf. E. H. Chamberlin, "The Chicago School," in his *Towards a More General Theory of Value*, New York, 1957, pp. 296ff.

201. Cf. Chamberlin's remarks in *American Economic Association Proceedings*, May, 1956, pp. 139ff.

202. Cf. *History and Method*, pp. 202ff.

203. "Capital and Interest," *Readings in the Theory of Income Distribution*, p. 406.

204. Cf. *ibid.*, p. 209.

205. Cf. *ibid.*, p. 214.

206. *Risk, Uncertainty and Profit*, p. 301.

207. Cf. his essay, "Wages and Labor Union Action in the Light of Economic Analysis," in *The Public Stake in Union Power*, ed. P. D. Bradley, Charlottesville, 1959, pp. 21ff. The paper was replete with fallacies of composition.

208. *Ibid.*, p. 38.
209. The remarkable inability of general theory in this area was revealed by Knight's comments on the impact of minimum wage legislation. More relevant are the empirical studies such as those conducted by the United States Department of Labor. For Knight's remarks, cf. *The Impact of the Labor Union,* ed. D. Mc. Wright, New York, 1951, pp. 104-05.
210. For Knight's social and political outlook, cf. *Freedom and Reform,* New York, 1947, and *Intelligence and Democratic Action,* Cambridge, 1960.
211. *The Economic Organization* p. 27.
212. *Risk, Uncertainty and Profit,* pp. xxvi, 13.
213. Cf. *Risk, Uncertainty and Profit,* p. lii.
214. H. C. Simons, "Hansen on Fiscal Policy," *Journal of Political Economy,* April, 1942, pp. 161ff.
215. Cf. H. G. Moulton, *The New Philosophy of Public Debt,* Washington, 1943, and Hansen's rejoinder, Appendix A, in Hansen and H. S. Perloff, *State and Local Finance in the National Economy,* New York, 1944.
216. Alvin H. Hansen, *Business Cycle Theory,* Boston, 1927.
217. Hansen, *Income, Employment and Public Policy,* New York, 1948.
218. Hansen, *Economic Stabilization in an Unbalanced World,* New York, 1932. Other works by Hansen were: *Full Recovery on Stagnation,* New York, 1938; *Fiscal Policy and Business Cycles,* New York, 1941; *Economic Policy and Full Employment,* New York, 1947; *Business Cycles and National Income,* New York, 1951; *Monetary Theory and Fiscal Policy,* New York, 1949; *A Guide to Keynes,* New York, 1953; *The American Economy,* New York, 1957; and *Economic Issues of The 1960s,* New York, 1960.
219. Cf. Dorfman, *op. cit.,* V, 725.
220. Lawrence Klein, *The Keynesian Revolution,* New York, 1947, p. 48. Klein cites Hansen's surveys of business cycle theory in *Econometrica,* 1933, and in *The Review of Economic Statistics,* 1936.
221. Cf. *The American Economy,* pp. 3-4.
222. *Ibid.*, p. 7.
223. Cf. Gunnar Myrdal, *Beyond the Welfare State,* New York, 1960. Myrdal demonstrates quite conclusively that the debate over planning is fruitless. The problem rather is the kind of planning needed to make national economies viable.
224. Hansen, *American Economy,* p. 11.
225. *Ibid.*, p. 23.
226. For a dramatic description of these events, cf. Arthur M. Schlesinger, Jr., *The Crisis of the Old Order,* Boston, 1957; *idem, The Coming of the New Deal,* Boston, 1958. Cf. also, J. K. Galbraith, *The Liberal Hour,* pp. 80ff.
227. *Fiscal Policy and Business Cycles,* p. 16.
228. *Business Cycles and National Income,* p. 20.
229. *Fiscal Policy and Business Cycles,* p. 21.
230. *Ibid.*, p. 38.
231. Cf., for example, *Business Cycles and National Income,* Part II, pp. 93ff.
232. Cf. Hansen's "Economic Progress and Declining Population Growth," *American Economic Association Proceedings,* March, 1939, reprinted in *Readings in Business Cycle Theory,* Philadelphia, 1944, p. 366; G. Terborgh, *The Bogey of Economic Maturity,* Chicago, 1945; Hansen's reply to Terborgh in *Economic Policy and Full Employment,* pp. 298ff.
233. William Fellner, who believes that Hansen was wrong, concedes that this argument cannot be refuted. Cf. his *Modern Economic Analysis,* New York, 1960, p. 289.
234. Cf. Joan Robinson, *Collected Economic Papers,* Oxford, 1960, II 105.
235. Cf. *Fiscal Policy and Business Cycles,* pp. 225ff.; *Business Cycles and National Income,* pp. 145ff. For an early statement of Hansen's

views, cf. *Temporary National Economic Committee Hearings,* Part 9, 76th Cong. pp. 3495, 3538, 3837.

236. Cf. B. Higgins, *Economic Development,* New York, 1959, p. 188.

237. Cf. D. Mc. Wright, "The Prospects for Capitalism," *Survey of Contemporary Economics,* Philadelphia, 1948, pp. 457ff.; on the role of government, cf. my article, "Can the U.S. Reconvert to Peace?," *Dissent,* Winter, 1960, pp. 12ff.

238. Cf. Milton Friedman, *Joint Economic Committee Hearings,* 86th Cong., *Employment, Growth and Price Levels,* Part 4, pp. 605ff.

239. For a vivid description of the economy's performance in the 1950's, cf. J. P. Lewis, *Business Conditions Analysis,* New York, 1959, pp. 318ff.

240. Cf. J. K. Galbraith, *The Affluent Society;* Alan Sweezy, "Secular Stagnation," in *Postwar Economic Problems,* ed. S. E. Harris, New York, 1943, p. 81.

241. E. H. Chamberlin, *Towards a More General Theory of Value,* New York, 1957, p. 298; cf. also M. Bronfenbrenner, "Contemporary American Economic Thought," *American Journal of Economics and Sociology,* July, 1950, p. 487.

242. Friedman was the recipient of American Economic Association's Clark medal in 1951.

243. Cf. "The Methodology of Positive Economics," in his *Essays in Positive Economics,* Chicago, 1953, pp. 3ff.

244. Cf. G. Myrdal, *The Political Element in the Development of Economic Theory,* Cambridge, 1954, p. vii.

245. Cf. Friedman, *op. cit.,* p. 6.

246. *Ibid.,* p. 14. On this point one might contrast George Stigler's view in "The Development of Utility Theory," *Journal of Political Economy,* August, October, 1950, reprinted in *Essays in Economic Thought,* ed. J. J. Spengler and W. R. Allen, Chicago, 1960, pp. 644-45.

247. Cf. T. W. Hutchison, *The Significance and Basic Postulates of Economic Theory,* reprint ed., New York, 1960, p. xiii.

248. Cf. J. J. Spengler, "The Problem of Order in Economic Affairs," *Southern Economic Journal,* July, 1948, reprinted in Spengler and Allen, *op. cit.,* p. 8, wherein Spengler points out that a theoretical subrealm in the social sciences must accurately represent its corresponding real subrealm.

249. Cf. Stigler, *op. cit.,* p. 645.

250. Friedman, *op. cit.,* p. 13.

251. Cf. K. E. Boulding, *A Reconstruction of Economics,* New York, 1950.

252. "The Utility Analysis of Choices Involving Risk" (with J. L. Savage), *Journal of Political Economy,* August, 1948, pp. 279ff.

253. *Ibid.,* p. 281.

254. *Ibid.,* p. 298.

255. "Choice, Chance, and the Personal Distribution of Income," *Journal of Political Economy,* August, 1953, pp. 277ff.

256. *Ibid.,* p. 278..

257. M. Friedman, *A Theory of the Consumption Function,* Princeton, 1957.

258. Keynes, *General Theory,* p. 96.

259. For a bibliography of this development, cf. Friedman, *op. cit.,* pp. 3-6.

260. J. S. Duesenberry, *Income, Saving and the Theory of Consumer Behavior,* Cambridge, 1949. It might be observed that consumption theory is usually predicated on the assumption of insatiability and, in Kenneth Arrow's words, on the absence of points of bliss. Yet this very well may be questioned, as Saul Engelbourg does in "Reckoning Your Bliss Point," *Columbia University Forum,* Fall, 1960, pp. 27ff. Expansible wants in our culture seem to stem from Veblen's conspicuous consumption, so that the utility of such goods, usually luxuries, is a function of the utility of goods consumed by others. Where increments of utility are essentially independent of other

utility functions, one deals with necessities. As Engelbourg suggests, this makes it possible to locate points of maximum utility with independent origins: the state of bliss can be found, and the assumption of insatiability falls by the wayside.

261. "A Statistical Illusion in Judging Keynesian Models" (with G. S. Becker), *Journal of Political Economy*, February, 1957, pp. 64ff.

262. *Consumption Function*, pp. 20ff, pp. 220ff.

263. *Ibid.*, p. 93.

264. Cf. comments by James Tobin, Theodore Morgan, Irwin Friend, and G. H. Orcutt in *Consumer Behavior*, ed. L. H. Clark, New York, 1958, pp. 447ff.

265. Cf. "Consumer Buying Intentions," *Federal Reserve Bulletin*, September, 1960, pp. 973ff., and George Katona, *The Powerful Consumer*, New York, 1960.

266. Cf. H. S. Houthakker, "The Permanent Income Hypothesis," *American Economic Review*, June, 1958, p. 400. Houthakker's sharp comments generated a debate on what statistical techniques were appropriate. Cf. R. Eisner, "Comment," *American Economic Review*, December, 1958, p. 972.

267. Cf. Friedman, "Savings and the Balance Sheet," *Bulletin, Oxford Institute of Statistics*, May, 1957, in which the role of liquid assets was acknowledged.

268. For Friedman's monetary views, cf. "The Quantity Theory of Money—A Restatement," in *Studies in the Quantity Theory of Money*, ed. Friedman, Chicago, 1956; *idem, A Program for Monetary Stability*, New York, 1960; and his testimony before the Congressional Joint Economic Committee, *Hearings on Employment, Growth and Price Levels*, May 25, 1959.

269. *Studies in the Quantity Theory of Money*, p. 4.

270. *Ibid.*, p. 12.

271. Friedman, "The Demand for Money: Some Theoretical and Empirical Results," *Journal of Political Economy*, August, 1959, pp. 1ff.

272. When a group of Soviet economists visited the United States, Friedman admitted in a discussion with them that inflation was not a serious problem. Cf. *Committee for Economic Development Memorandum*, March 18, 1960, p. 23. The foregoing description of Friedman's view on money stems largely from his testimony before the *Joint Economic Committee*, May, 1959.

273. Cf. his *A Program for Monetary Stability*.

274. For a brief history of American experience in banking under a régime of free enterprise, cf. E. C. Kirkland, *A History of American Economic Life*, New York, 1933, pp. 246ff. Cf. also F. A. Bradford, *Money and Banking*, 4th ed., New York, 1940, pp. 274ff.

275. Cf. Friedman, "Prices, Income and Monetary Changes in Three Wartime Periods," *American Economic Association Proceedings*, May, 1952, pp. 612ff.; *Program for Monetary Stability*, pp. 9ff.

276. Cf. C. R. Whittlesey, *American Economic Association Proceedings*, May, 1952, p. 642.

277. Cf. his attack on consumer credit regulation, "Consumer Credit Control as an Instrument of Stabilization Policy," in *Consumer Installment Credit, Conference on Regulation*, Part II, Vol. II, Washington, 1957, p. 73, in which Friedman argued that consumer credit control was a poor stabilization instrument; that it was arbitrary as between different consumers; that it distorted resource allocation; and that it interfered with the free market. The latter, of course, is what consumer credit regulation is intended for, especially during wartime and inflation.

278. *Monetary Stability*, pp. 21, 38.

279. Cf. Friedman, "The Supply of Money and Changes in Prices and Output," *Compendium on the Relationship of Prices to Economic*

Stability and Growth, Joint Economic Committee, 85th Cong., Washington, 1958, pp. 241ff.

280. *Positive Economics,* pp. 133ff.

281. Cf. his reply to Philip Neff, *American Economic Review,* September, 1949, p. 950.

282. Friedman's political philosophy was most clearly set forth in "Liberalism, Old Style," *Colliers Year Book,* New York, 1955, pp. 360ff.; his statement for the Committee for Economic Development in the latter's *Problems of United States Economic Development,* New York, 1958, p. 86; and in "What Price Inflation," *Proceedings, American Petroleum Institute,* Vol. 38, 1958, p. 18. In substance, his views in this area are identical with the libertarianism of Mises and Hayek.

283. Cf. K. E. Boulding, *Principles of Economic Policy,* New York, 1958, pp. 110ff.; on the conservative view of society, cf. William J. Newman, *The Futilitarian Society,* New York, 1961.

284. Cf. *Positive Economics,* p. 38; also, cf. Chamberlin, *op. cit.,* pp. 296ff.

285. Friedman, "The Role of Government in Education," in *Economics and the Public Interest,* ed. R. A. Solo, New Brunswick, 1955. p. 124.

286. Cf. comments by R. C. Turner in *Consumer Installment Credit,* p. 106.

287. "Role of Government in Education," *op. cit.,* p. 129.

288. "Some Comments on the Significance of Labor Unions for Economic Policy," in *The Impact of the Labor Union,* ed. D. Mc. Wright, New York, 1951, pp. 204ff.

289. Kenneth E. Boulding, *The Economics of Peace,* New York, 1945.

290. Boulding, *Economic Analysis,* New York, 1941; 3rd ed., 1955.

291. For a representative illustration of the profession's reactions to Boulding's new ideas, cf. *The Impact of the Labor Union,* pp. 149ff.

292. Boulding's books include in addition to the above, *A Reconstruction of Economics,* New York, 1950; *The Organizational Revolution,* New York, 1953; *The Image: Knowledge in Life and Society,* Ann Arbor, 1956; *The Skills of the Economist,* Cleveland, 1958; *Principles of Economic Policy,* New York, 1958; and *Conflict and Defense,* New York, 1962. Together with George Stigler, he edited *Readings in Price Theory,* Homewood, 1952.

293. "The Theory of the Firm in the Last Ten Years," *American Economic Review,* December, 1942, pp. 791ff.

294. *Ibid.,* p. 802.

295. "Implications for General Economics of More Realistic Theories of the Firm," *American Economic Association Proceedings,* May, 1952, p. 36.

296. *Skills,* pp. 42ff.; on this point, cf. also W. J. Baumol, *Business Behavior, Value and Growth,* New York, 1959.

297. "The Fruits of Progress and the Dynamics of Distribution," *American Economic Association Proceedings,* May, 1953, p. 473.

298. "Professor Tarshis and the State of Economics," *American Economic Review,* March, 1948, p. 93.

299. Cf. *Reconstruction,* pp. 172-73.

300. The Consumption Concept in Economic Theory," *American Economic Association Proceedings,* May, 1945, p. 2.

301. *Op. cit., American Economic Review,* March, 1948, p. 100.

302. *Op. cit., American Economic Association Proceedings,* May, 1945, p. 8.

303. Cf. *The Economics of Peace,* pp. 171ff.

304. "A New Look at Institutionalism," *American Economic Association Proceedings,* May, 1957, p. 9.

305. *Reconstruction,* p. 4.

306. Cf. Boulding's "Welfare Economics," *Survey of Contemporary Economics,* Homewood, 1952, II, 3-4.

307. Cf. *Skills of the Economist,* p. 32.

308. *Ibid.,* p. 67.

309. Cf. Boulding, "A Liquidity Preference Theory of Market Prices,"

Economica, May, 1944, reprinted in *Readings in Price Theory*, Homewood, 1952, pp. 53ff.

310. *Ibid.*, p. 320.
311. Cf. A. G. Papandreou, "Some Basic Problems in the Theory of the Firm," *Survey of Contemporary Economics*, II, 185ff.; J. G. March and H. A. Simon, *Organizations*, New York, 1958; Mason Haire, ed., *Modern Organization Theory*, New York, 1959; H. Leibenstein, *Economic Theory and Organizational Analysis*, New York, 1960. Much of the literature concerned with organizations and their structure stresses the need for harmonious relations among the component members. This has implied manipulation and subtle controls to maintain the hierarchical structure deemed to be essential for business viability. Cf. C. Z. Wilson, "Organization Theory: A Survey of Three Views," *Quarterly Review of Economics and Business*, August 1961, pp. 53ff. An alternative view is expressed by S. Krupp who, in his *Pattern in Organization Analysis*, Philadelphia, 1961, justifiably argues that much of contemporary organization theory ignores conflict and consequently has little to say about power struggles within the organization. Yet resource allocation and income distribution may be deeply affected by such struggles. Any theory of organization, says Krupp quite rightly, should include analyses of authority, conflict, and power. The role of the social scientist in organizations is trenchantly reviewed by L. Baritz, *The Servants of Power*, Middletown, 1960. Boulding has also dealt with the problem of conflict, but in a broader context than that of the organization. Cf. his recent *Conflict and Defense*, which arrived too late for discussion here. Con-

flict is properly viewed by Boulding as part of the social process: insofar as this is true, Krupp's thesis seems validated.

312. Cf. C. R. Noyes, *Economic Man*, New York, 1948, I, 29ff., and *passim*.
313. Cf. *Reconstruction*, pp. 26ff.
314. *Skills of the Economist*, p. 57.
315. *Reconstruction*, pp. 95ff.
316. *Skills*, p. 51.
317. *Op. cit.*, *American Economic Association Proceedings*, May, 1952, p. 41.
318. Cf. also *Reconstruction*, pp. 35ff.
319. *Ibid.*, p. 135.
320. *Ibid.*, p. 147.
321. *Ibid.*, p. 153.
322. *Ibid.*, p. 195.
323. *Ibid.*, p. 174.
324. *Ibid.*, p. 246.
325. *Ibid.*, p. 249.
326. *Ibid.*, p. 250.
327. *Op. cit.*, *American Economic Association Proceedings*, May, 1953, p. 478.
328. *Ibid.*, p. 480.
329. *Skills*, p. 69.
330. *Ibid.*, pp. 78ff. Cf. also Penrose, *op. cit.* Mrs. Penrose makes the argument that there is no limit to the growth of firms. The main factor accounting for growth, she says, is an excessive supply of managerial skill, and, while there is no limit to size, the rate at which a firm can grow is restricted only by the time it takes for managerial personnel to learn to work together.
331. In one sense, information could be visualized as a sequence of images. Cf. Boulding, *The Image*, pp. 7, 19ff.
332. *Skills*, p. 133.
333. An interesting application of the feedback principle to oligopoly problems may be found in Tun Thin, *Theory of Markets*, Cambridge, 1960, pp. 94ff.

Chapter 9
From Realism to Technique

1. A large part of the following section is drawn from my articles "The Economics of Joseph Schumpeter," *Dissent*, Autumn, 1954, pp. 370ff., and "Is the Depression Inevitable?" *Commentary*, September, 1947, pp. 282ff.
2. For a fairly complete biographic sketch, cf. Gottfried Haberler's essay in *Schumpeter, Social Scientist*, ed. Seymour E. Harris, Cambridge, 1951, pp. 24ff.
3. *Ibid.*, p. 31.
4. These ideas had been set forth in a 1918 lecture, "The Crisis of the Tax State," reprinted in *International Economic Papers*, No. 4, London, 1954, pp. 5ff. In the first part of the lecture, Schumpeter set forth an erudite and, in many ways, fascinating history of modern taxation, discussing therein the limits to which certain taxes might be pushed. In the second part, he discussed the problem of postwar reconstruction and suggested reliance upon a capital levy as a means of eliminating the war debt. This was the policy he sought to pursue as Austrian finance minister.
5. In addition to the article on taxation in *I. E. P., op. cit.*, there is available in translation the article on "Money and the Social Product," in *I. E. P.*, No. 6, London, 1956, p. 148. Most of the important early articles were gathered together by Erich Schneider and Arthur Spiethoff (who had been Schumpeter's colleague at Bonn) in the volume *Aufsätze zur Ökonomischen Theorie*, Tübingen, 1952. This includes the famous essays on distribution and imputation theory and the debate with Böhm-Bawerk over interest theory.
6. Erich Schneider, in Harris, *op. cit.*, p. 54.
7. Joseph A. Schumpeter, *Theory of Economic Development*, Leipzig, 1912, translated, Cambridge, 1934, pp. 119ff.
8. "On the Concept of Social Value," *Quarterly Journal of Economics*, 1909, reprinted in *Essays*, Cambridge, 1951, pp. 1ff.
9. Cf. especially, *Economic Development*, pp. 24ff.
10. *Ibid.*, p. 175.
11. *Ibid.*, p. 216.
12. Schumpeter, *History of Economic Analysis*, New York, 1954.
13. For Schumpeter's views on monopoly and oligopoly, cf. his essay "The Instability of Capitalism," *Essays*, pp. 47ff. His famous defense of monopoly was presented in his *Capitalism, Socialism and Democracy*, 2nd ed., New York, 1947, pp. 87ff.
14. Schumpeter, *Das Wesen und der Hauptinhalt der Theoretischen Nationalökonomie*, Leipzig, 1908.
15. *History of Economic Analysis*, p. 42.
16. *Ibid.*, p. 955.
17. *Ibid.*, especially, Chaps. 2, 3, 4.
18. Cf., for example, the introductory chapters of *Business Cycles*, 2 vols., New York, 1939, especially Chap. II, pp. 30ff., which is an excellent statement of Schumpeter's basic theoretical model. On Schumpeter's views on measurement, cf. *Essays*, pp. 100ff.
19. *Economic Development*, pp. 66ff.
20. A useful summary is available in R. V. Clemence and F. S. Doody, *The Schumpeterian System*, Cambridge, 1950.
21. This enabled Schumpeter to relate interest rates to profits. Cf. also

Business Cycles, Vol. I, Chap. III, pp. 72ff.

22. Cf. "Money and the Social Product," *International Economic Papers,* No. 6, pp. 150ff.

23. A. W. Marget broadens this concept to include all economic units. Cf. his essay on Schumpeter in *Schumpeter, Social Scientist,* p. 63.

24. *International Economic Papers, op. cit.*

25. *Economic Development,* pp. 115ff.

26. *Ibid.,* p. 122.

27. *Ibid.,* p. 124.

28. Cf. Clemence and Doody, *op. cit.,* p. 28.

29. Cf. *ibid.,* pp. 28ff.; Haberler in *Schumpeter, Social Scientist,* pp. 72ff.; and J. W. Conard, *Introduction to the Theory of Interest,* Berkeley, 1959, pp. 89ff.

30. *Business Cycles,* Chap. IV, pp. 130ff.

31. *Ibid.,* pp. 161ff.

32. *Ibid.,* p. 173; also cf. *Essays,* pp. 134ff.

33. *Business Cycles,* I, 85.

34. *Ibid.,* pp. 94ff. Cf. also, J. Schmookler, "Invention, Innovation and Business Cycles," in *Variability of Private Investment,* Part II, Joint Economic Committee, Washington, 1962, pp. 45ff.

35. *Capitalism, Socialism and Democracy,* p. 83.

36. *Ibid.,* pp. 63ff.

37. *Ibid.,* p. 87.

38. *Ibid.,* p. 125.

39. Cf. *ibid.,* pp. 111ff.; also *Essays,* pp. 174ff.; *Business Cycles,* II, 1032ff.

40. *Capitalism, Socialism and Democracy,* p. 139.

41. Cf. *ibid.,* especially Chaps. XIII and XIV.

42. *Essays,* pp. 71-72.

43. *History,* pp. 588ff.; pp. 647ff.; pp. 651ff.; cf. also *Capitalism, Socialism and Democracy,* Chap. III, pp. 21ff.; *Essays,* p. 160.

44. Originally published in 1912; translated, London, 1954; pp. 119ff.

45. *Capitalism, Socialism and Democracy,* Part I, pp. 5ff.

46. *Ibid.,* p. 21.

47. *History,* p. 597.

48. *Essays,* p. 160.

49. *History,* p. 387.

50. Reprinted in *Imperialism and Social Classes,* New York, 1951.

51. Cf. an interesting debate on this question in *Social Research,* June-December, 1952.

52. *History,* p. 392. It is indeed refreshing to note such comments as contrasted with the views of Paul Samuelson in the *American Economic Review,* December, 1957, pp. 884ff., or those of N. Georgescu-Roegen in *Econometrics,* April, 1960, pp. 225ff.

53. *History,* p. 472.

54. For a more sympathetic attitude toward Ricardo in this context, cf. Jacob Viner's review of Schumpeter's *History,* reprinted in Viner's *The Long View and the Short,* Glencoe, 1958, pp. 357ff.

55. *History,* p. 827.

56. Schumpeter's discussion of Walras, like much else in the *History,* has a rugged quality which at times becomes disturbing. A good deal of this can be attributed to the incomplete state of the book. While elaborate in design and execution —it weaves together many threads in economic theory, philosophy, sociology, history, money, business cycles, and public finance—there are numerous gaps in it. The discussion of Keynes, for example, is sketchy, being no more than notes, while American institutionalism is entirely lacking. When Schumpeter died in 1950 he had not completed any part in final form and his widow, Elizabeth Boody Schumpeter, who edited the manuscript, had to put it together from material found in at least three different places. The editorial task was made more difficult by Schumpeter's habit of keeping early notes and later drafts together with more polished versions.

57. In his presidential address at the American Economic Association in 1948, Schumpeter set forth an opposite view, feeling that there was no escaping ideological influence. Ideologies, he then said, stem from the same source as "vision," and while progress might be slowed

by ideology, it would be impossible without it. Reprinted in *Essays*, pp. 267ff.

58. Cf. *Essays*, pp. 153ff.

59. Joan Robinson, *Collected Economic Papers*, Oxford, 1951, I, vii.

60. J. M. Clark, *Economics of Overhead Costs*, Chicago, 1923.

61. H. Hotelling, "Stability in Competition," *Economic Journal*, 1929, reprinted in George J. Stigler and Kenneth E. Boulding, eds., *Readings in Price Theory*, Homewood, 1952, pp. 467ff.

62. F. Zeuthen, *Problems of Monopoly and Economic Warfare*, London, 1930.

63. *Ibid.*, p. 1.

64. For a discussion of Pareto's rather sketchy approach, cf. Robert Triffin, *Monopolistic Competition and General Equilibrium Theory*, Cambridge, 1940, *passim*.

65. Reprinted in *Readings in Price Theory*, pp. 180ff.

66. *Ibid.*, p. 184.

67. *Ibid.*, p. 187.

68. *Ibid.*, p. 188.

69. *Ibid.*, p. 193.

70. For a bibliography of this discussion, cf. Triffin, *op. cit.*, pp. 8-9.

71. Reprinted in J. Viner, *op. cit.*, pp. 50ff.

72. Cf. Joan Robinson, *The Economics of Imperfect Competition*, London, 1933; E. H. Chamberlin, *The Theory of Monopolistic Competition*, Cambridge, 1933. References to the latter are to the 3rd ed., issued in 1938. Chamberlin states that he had been working on his version of the new theory since 1921, when he was a student at Michigan. Cf. Schumpeter, *History*, p. 1150.

73. E. H. Chamberlin, *Towards a More General Theory of Value*, New York, 1957, pp. 8-9.

74. Joan Robinson, *Introduction to the Theory of Employment*, London, 1937.

75. Robinson, *Essays in the Theory of Employment*, 2nd ed., Oxford, 1947.

76. *Ibid.*, pp. 183ff.; Robinson, *Essay on Marxian Economics*, London, 1942.

77. Robinson, *The Accumulation of Capital*, London, 1956. A description of this aspect of her economics is given below, p. 756.

78. Cf. Chap. 8, especially, of *Marxian Economics*, pp. 75ff.

79. Introduction to Rosa Luxemburg, *The Accumulation of Capital*, New Haven, 1951, p. 28.

80. *Imperfect Competition*, p. 4.

81. *Ibid.*, p. 5.

82. Chamberlin, *Monopolistic Competition*, p. 8; Robinson, *Essays*, I, 21.

83. *Imperfect Competition*, p. 50.

84. Mrs. Robinson employed the marginal technique rather than the "area" method utilized by F. Zeuthen, *op. cit.* Her geometrical method was perhaps the most lucid presentation of the relevant curves yet developed. It was little wonder that within five years or so of its publication, the diagrams of the *Imperfect Competition*, gems of pedagogy, found their way into almost all the standard textbooks. While refinements have been made by others, the basic analysis has remained virtually the same since 1933. Cf. *Imperfect Competition*, Bk. I, Chap. 2, pp. 26ff.

85. *Papers*, I, 30-31.

86. *Imperfect Competition*, p. 53.

87. *Ibid.*, p. 88.

88. *Ibid.*, p. 89; cf. also *Papers*, II, 228.

89. *Imperfect Competition*, p. 90.

90. *Ibid.*, p. 127.

91. *Ibid.*, pp. 143ff.

92. Monopoly output could exceed competitive output, Mrs. Robinson observed, only in the rare situation in which the full "quasi-rent" was not paid to an input factor and where large-scale economies were present. Cf. *Ibid.*, pp. 153-54.

93. Cf. *Papers*, II, 227; the best contemporary discussion on problems of entry may be found in J. Bain, *Barriers to New Competition*, Cambridge, 1956.

94. *Imperfect Competition*, pp. 236ff.

95. *Ibid.*, p. 282.

96. *Ibid.*, p. 281; *Papers*, II, 243.

97. *Papers*, II, 224.

98. *Ibid.*, p. 236.

99. *Imperfect Competition*, p. 307.
100. *Ibid.*, p. 313.
101. As might be expected, the one economist who demurred from this impulse to spell out the social implications of a theory was Schumpeter, for whom this was the "Ricardian sin," an appellation he applied to all who transgressed the limits of pure scientific inquiry. Cf. Schumpeter's *Essays*, p. 132.
102. Cf. *More General Theory*, p. 65.
103. Triffin, *op. cit.*, pp. 38ff. Cf. also, N. Kaldor, *Essays on Value and Distribution*, London, 1960, pp. 81ff.
104. Robinson, *Papers*, II, 223.
105. *More General Theory*, p. 3.
106. *Ibid.*, p. 4; cf. also *Monopolistic Competition*, p. 3.
107. *More General Theory*, p. 17.
108. *Monopolistic Competition*, Chap. 5, pp. 71ff.; Chap. 7, pp. 130ff.
109. Cf. *More General Theory*, pp. 105ff.
110. *Ibid.*, p. 113; cf. also Hans Brems, *Product Equilibrium under Monopolistic Competition*, Cambridge, 1951; L. Abbott, *Quality and Competition*, New York, 1955.
111. *Monopolistic Competition*, p. 79.
112. O. H. Taylor credits Chamberlin with the invention of this weird term. Cf. Taylor's *History of Economic Thought*, New York, 1960, p. 456. Chamberlin himself, however, acknowledged that the word was used in the same sense by Karl Schlesinger, the German banker-theorist, in 1914, and, in fact that it could be found in Sir Thomas More's *Utopia*, published in 1518. Cf. *More General Theory*, p. 34.
113. Cf. *Imperfect Competition*, p. 21, and Mrs. Robinson's later comment in her *Papers*, II, 228.
114. *Monopolistic Competition*, p. 49.
115. *Ibid.*, p. 63.
116. *Ibid.*, pp. 76-77.
117. R. F. Harrod has argued the importance of full-cost pricing. Cf. his "Theory of Imperfect Competition Revised," *Economic Essays*, New York, 1952, pp. 139ff. Chamberlin has insisted that his

approach does allow for full-cost pricing. Cf. the latter's *More General Theory*, pp. 272ff.; pp. 280ff.; and *Monopolistic Competition*, p. 165.
118. Cf. N. Kaldor, "Market Imperfection and Excess Capacity," *Readings in Price Theory*, p. 389.
119. *More General Theory*, p. 9.
120. Cf. George J. Stigler, *Five Lectures on Economic Problems*, London, 1949, pp. 16ff.
121. *Monopolistic Competition*, p. 109. Some debate over excess capacity did occur in which some theorists sought to demonstrate that this did not necessarily have to develop. Cf. Kaldor, *op. cit.*; Harrod, *op. cit.*, pp. 140ff. The latter's argument did appear convincing enough to upset Chamberlin's thesis.
122. Cf. *More General Theory*, p. 290.
123. This argument of consumer responsibility is advanced by Taylor, *op. cit.*, p. 461.
124. *Monopolistic Competition*, Chap. 6, pp. 117ff.
125. *More General Theory*, pp. 149ff.
126. *Monopolistic Competition*, p. 118.
127. Cf. *Ibid.*, p. 144.
128. *Ibid.*, p. 179.
129. Nothing revealed Chamberlin's conservative bias so much as his essays on labor and trade unionism. Cf. his "Monopoly Power of Labor," in *Impact of the Labor Unions*, pp. 168ff.; his pamphlet, *The Economic Analysis of Labor Union Power*, Washington, 1958; and testimony given to the Senate Committee on Labor, May 21, 1958.
130. Taylor, *op. cit.*, p. 467.
131. *Papers*, II, 6.
132. Cf. the sharp criticism of Chamberlin by M. Shubik, *Strategy and Market Structure*, New York, 1959, pp. 27-8.
133. Heinrich von Stackelberg, *Marktform und Gleichgewicht*, Berlin and Vienna, 1934.
134. Stackelberg, *The Theory of the Market Economy*, London, 1952. Unfortunately, *Marktform und Gleichgewicht* has not yet found a translator. Readers without access to this book may consult

William Fellner's discussion in *Competition Among the Few*, New York, 1949, pp. 98ff.; W. Leontief, "Stackelberg and Monopolistic Competition," *Journal of Political Economy*, August, 1936, pp. 554ff.; Triffin, *op. cit., passim;* and Alan T. Peacock's useful introduction to his translation of the *Grundlagen.* For a mathematical summary, cf. Tun Thin, *Theory of Markets,* Cambridge, 1960, p. 51.

135. Cf. "The Theory of Foreign Exchanges under Perfect Competition," *International Economic Papers*, No. 1, London, 1951, pp. 104ff.

136. *Market Economy,* p. xiii.

137. *Ibid.,* p. 175.

138. J. K. Galbraith, "Monopoly and the Concentration of Economic Power," *Survey of Contemporary Economics*, I, 110. Cf. also Stackelberg, *op. cit.,* pp. 182, 213.

139. Cf. Fellner, *op. cit.,* p. 100.

140. *Ibid.,* p. 116.

141. A. L. Bowley, *Mathematical Groundwork of Economics,* Oxford, 1924.

142. R. Frisch, "Monopoly—Polypoly—The Concept of Force in the Economy," *International Economic Papers*, No. 1, pp. 21ff.

143. Cf. Triffin, *op. cit.,* p. 74.

144. Stackelberg, *Market Economy,* p. 207.

145. *Ibid.,* p. 208.

146. Cf. Chamberlin, "Advertising Costs and Equilibrium," *More General Theory*, pp. 149ff.

147. Cf. Triffin, *op. cit.,* p. 63.

148. Cf. *ibid.,* Chap. 3, pp. 97ff.

149. Cf. J. Bain, *Industrial Organization,* New York, 1959, p. 34.

150. Cf. Chamberlin, *More General Theory*, pp. 296ff.

151. Cf. Stigler, *op. cit.,* p. 16.

152. Chamberlin, *op. cit.,* p. 301.

153. Cf. Max Weber, *General Economic History,* Glencoe, 1950, Chap. IX, pp. 136ff.

154. Cf. J. K. Galbraith, *The Affluent Society,* Boston, 1958.

155. Cf. E. R. Walker, *From Economic Theory to Policy,* Chicago, 1943, Chap. VI, pp. 100ff.

156. The following section appeared originally in a slightly different form in *Dissent*, Winter, 1956.

157. Cf. *General Theory of Employment, Interest and Money,* New York, 1936. It would be quite wrong, however, to call Keynes the father of the New Deal, as seems to be the fashion in some quarters. While Keynes' interest in the use of public works to counteract unemployment does go back to 1924, when Lloyd George began to advocate this device, the final shape of his theories came after the New Deal was initiated. The Rooseveltian program had both reform and recovery aspects, but Keynes was interested primarily in the latter. The New Deal itself was evolved in a purely *ad hoc* fashion and by men who eschewed economic theory.

158. Keynes did acknowledge that Wicksell sought to explore similar problems, namely those relating investment to the rate of interest. Cf. *Treatise on Money,* London, 1930, I, 198.

159. The major source for biographic facts on Keynes is the brilliant book by Sir Roy F. Harrod, *The Life of John Maynard Keynes,* New York, 1951.

160. John Maynard Keynes, *The Economic Consequences of the Peace,* London, 1920.

161. Cf. Alvin H. Hansen, *A Guide to Keynes,* New York, 1953, pp. 47ff.

162. Keynes, *Indian Currency and Finance,* London, 1913.

163. Harrod, *op. cit.,* p. 163.

164. Cf. especially Bks. III and VI, *Treatise.*

165. Keynes, *A Tract for Monetary Reform,* London, 1923.

166. Keynes, *The End of Laissez-Faire,* London, 1926.

167. Cf., for example, Abba P. Lerner, "The Inflationary Process—Some Theoretical Aspects," *Essays in Economic Analysis,* London, 1953, pp. 328ff.

168. Cf. *Post-Keynesian Economics,* ed. K. K. Kurihara, New Brunswick, 1954.

169. Cf. William Fellner, *Emergence and Content of Modern Economic*

Analysis, New York, 1960, pp. 80ff.

170. *General Theory,* pp. 8ff.
171. A further advantage accrues from this approach in that it enables one to bring together sociological and psychological as well as economic criteria in analyzing a given situation.
172. Much has been written on this concept: a considerable technical literature now exists with which we cannot concern ourselves here. Cf. bibliography and references in *The New Economics,* ed. Seymour E. Harris, New York, 1947.
173. *General Theory,* p. 91.
174. Cf. p. 676 above.
175. A particular incisive study is James J. Duesenberry, *Income, Saving and the Theory of Consumer Behavior,* Cambridge, 1952.
176. It is frequently contended that the pattern of income distribution assumes a diamond shape, thus proving that there are fewer rich, fewer poor, and many more middle-class people. The latter are supposedly in the $4,000-$10,000 bulge. But all such statistics are based on *family* income; it is sometimes admitted that most of the families in the lower range of this bulge have more than one wage earner. Should such families revert to a single wage earner status, they would drop into the below-$4,000 class. Thus, while family income is a useful market research tool, it fails to reveal the entire story. Since marginal productivity theory presupposes single units of capital and labor, it would not be remiss for economists to consider the suggestion that a better picture of income distribution might be secured with the individual as a basis. The pertinent data are instructive: in 1941 there were 17.8 million families with an extra wage earner and another 10.9 million families with two or more. In 1953 the numbers were 21.5 million and 17.1 million, respectively.
177. *General Theory,* pp. 113ff.
178. However, this was not an espe-

cially new idea: it could be found in the writings of the famous Russian economist, Tugan-Baranovsky, as well as in Knut Wicksell. Cf. pp. 95 and 553 above.
179. Alvin Hansen has noted that this idea can be found in Veblen. Cf. the latter's *Theory of Business Enterprise,* pp. 89ff.
180. *General Theory,* p. 135.
181. Cf. *General Theory,* pp. 162-63.
182. Both Barbara Wootton and Lord Beveridge quickly discovered that economic planning for investment necessitated control from a center. See Beveridge's *Full Employment in a Free Society,* New York, 1945, and Wootton's *Plan or No Plan,* New York, 1934.
183. Cf. Hansen, *op. cit.,* pp. 140ff.; Conard, *op. cit.,* pp. 203ff.
184. For an incisive mathematical translation of the Keynesian equation, cf. R. G. D. Allen, *Mathematical Economics,* London, 1956, Chap. 2, pp. 31ff.
185. Cf. Joan Robinson, *An Essay on Marxian Economics,* and Ladislaus von Bortkiewicz, "Value and Price in the Marxian System," reprinted in *International Economic Papers,* No. 2, London, 1952, 5ff.
186. Cf. Arthur F. Burns, *The Frontiers of Economic Knowledge,* New York, 1954.
187. Cf. L. von Bortkiewicz, *op. cit.* Dudley Dillard, a noted Keynes expert, asserts that a greater intellectual kinship exists between Keynes and Proudhon than between Keynes and Marx. Dillard points to the similarities in their social reform program, the monetary approach, attitudes toward the "rentiers," and their general optimism concerning the effectiveness of their respective theories. See *Journal of Economic History,* May, 1942. Cf. also Hans Peter, "A Comparison of Marxian and Keynesian Dynamics," *International Economic Papers,* No. 3, pp. 240ff.
188. Cf. Joan Robinson, *op. cit.,* p. 86.
189. For example, the portion of surplus value used to purchase addi-

tional producers goods can be equated to Keynes' entrepreneurial transactions. Cf. S. Tsuru in *Post Keynesian Economics*, pp. 320ff.

190. In an article on war finance, written in July, 1940, especially for the *New Republic*, Keynes said: "It is, it seems, politically impossible for a capitalist democracy to organize expenditure on the scale necessary to make the grand experiment which would prove my case—except in war conditions. . . . If the United States takes seriously the material and economic side of the defense of civilization and steels itself to a vast dissipation of resources in the preparation of arms, it will learn its strength—and learn it as it can never learn it otherwise; learn a lesson that can be turned to account afterward to reconstruct a world which will understand the first principles governing the production of wealth. . . . War preparations, so far from requiring a sacrifice, will be a stimulus, which neither victory nor defeat of the New Deal could give you, to greater individual consumption and a higher standard of life. . . ."

191. K. K. Kurihara, *op. cit.* However, for a strictly Marxian treatment of Keynes (in a quasi-Stalinoid fashion), see *Science and Society*, Spring, 1955. This article demonstrates to the author's satisfaction that neither Keynes nor Marx would have known what the other was talking about.

192. Cf. Joan Robinson, *Collected Economic Papers*, II, 1ff.

193. Cf. for example, K. K. Kurihara, *Introduction to Keynesian Dynamics*, London, 1956.

194. In the same *New Republic* article mentioned above, Keynes wondered why politics in peacetime impeded the attainment of the kind of prosperous conditions that could be established through wartime production. He urged that partisanship be replaced by moderation. Reformers, he said, ". . . must believe that it is worthwhile

to concede a great deal to preserve the decentralization of decision and of power which is the prime virtue of the old individualism. They must zealously protect the variously woven fabric of society, even when this means that some abuses must be spared."

195. The following section is based in large part on my article, "On the Nature of Economic Growth," *Diogenes*, No. 19, Fall, 1957.

196. For an excellent statement of the classical theory of growth, cf. Benjamin Higgins, *Economic Development*, New York, 1959, pp. 85ff. Cf. also B. F. Hoselitz, ed., *Theories of Economic Growth*, New York, 1960 and I. Adelman, *Theories of Economic Growth and Development*, Stanford, 1961.

197. *General Theory*, p. 124.

198. Cf. "An Essay in Dynamic Theory" and "Supplement on Dynamic Theory," in *Economic Essays*, New York, 1952. The first essay dates back to 1939. Cf. also his *Towards a Dynamic Economics*, London, 1948.

199. Cf. *The Trade Cycle*, Oxford, 1936; *The Dollar*, London, 1953; and *Policy against Inflation*, London, 1958. An interesting book in another area is his *Foundations of Inductive Logic*, New York, 1957, in which he argued, against the skeptical trends in modern philosophy, that it was possible to demonstrate the validity of inductive techniques without recourse to *a priori* statements.

200. Daniel Hamberg, *Economic Growth and Stability*, New York, 1956, p. 25.

201. Cf. his *Essays in the Theory of Economic Growth*, New York, 1957, especially essays Nos. 1, 3, 4, and 5.

202. *Ibid.*, p. 73.

203. *Ibid.*, p. 75.

204. *Ibid.*, p. 79.

205. *Ibid.*, p. 5.

206. *Towards a Dynamic Economics*, *passim*.

207. Cf. Kurihara, *Keynesian Theory of Economic Development*, p. 185.

208. "Structural Analysis of Real Capital Formation," in *Capital Formation and Economic Growth*, National Bureau of Economic Research, Princeton, 1955, pp. 581ff.

209. Domar, *op. cit.*, p. 19.

210. Cf. their "Analytical Aspects of Anti-Inflation Policy," *American Economic Association Proceedings*, May, 1960, pp. 177ff.

211. William Fellner, *Trends and Cycles in Economic Activity*, New York, 1956.

212. Joan Robinson, *The Accumulation of Capital*.

213. Cf. "The Generalization of the General Theory," *Rate of Interest and Other Essays*, London, 1952, pp. 69ff.

214. *Papers*, II, 74.

215. Cf. Domar, *op. cit.*, pp. 154ff.; Robinson, *Papers*, II, 209ff.

216. Robinson, *Accumulation of Capital*, pp. 28, 34, 76, and "Equilibrium Growth Models," *American Economic Review*, June, 1961, p. 361.

217. *Ibid.*, p. 48.

218. Wicksell, *Lectures*, I, 177ff.; Robinson, *Papers*, II, 185ff.

219. *Accumulation of Capital*, p. 88.

220. *Ibid.*, pp. 90-92.

221. *Ibid.*, p. 93.

222. *Ibid.*, p. 175.

223. W. A. Lewis, *The Theory of Economic Growth*, London, 1955.

224. Cf. S. Kuznets, "International Differences in Capital Formation and Financing," *Capital Formation and Economic Growth*, Princeton, 1955, pp. 19ff.; Colin Clark, *The Conditions of Economic Progress*, 3rd ed., London, 1957, Chap. XI, pp. 565ff.

225. Ragnar Nurske, *Problems of Capital Formation in Underdeveloped Countries*, Oxford, 1953, A mathematical argument for balanced growth is presented in R. Dorfman, P. A. Samuelson, and R. M. Solow, *Linear Programming and Economic Analysis*, New York, 1958, p. 329.

226. Nurske, *op. cit.*, p. 13.

227. This is Harvey Leibenstein's term for underdeveloped areas. Cf. his *Economic Backwardness and Economic Growth*, New York, 1957.

228. Cf. P. N. Rosenstein-Rodan, "Problems of Industrialization of Eastern and South Eastern Europe," *Economic Journal*, June, 1943, p. 205.

229. W. W. Rostow, *The Stages of Economic Growth*, Cambridge, 1960. Cf. also Henry Pachter's perceptive review of Rostow's book in *Dissent*, Autumn, 1960, p. 400.

230. Rostow, *op. cit.*, p. 39.

231. Pachter, *op. cit.*

232. Harvey Leibenstein, *Economic Backwardness and Economic Growth*, New York, 1957.

233. *Ibid.*, pp. 15ff.

234. *Ibid.*, pp. 34-35.

235. *Ibid.*, Chap. 9, pp. 111ff.

236. The terminology was borrowed from game theory. Cf. *ibid.*, pp. 113ff.

237. Albert O. Hirschman, *The Strategy of Economic Development*, New Haven, 1958.

238. *Ibid.*, pp. 52ff.

239. *Ibid.*, p. 66.

240. *Ibid.*, p. 62. The concept of strategical selection could be applied also to the question of foreign aid to specific nations. Cf. A. Shonfield, *The Attack on World Poverty*, New York, 1960. Cf. also, Hoselitz, *op. cit.*, p. 257. Historically, it seems evident that growth was a matter of one industry or sector pulling along the rest of the economy.

241. Hirschman, *op. cit.*, pp. 98ff.

242. Cf. Higgins, *op. cit.*, p. 408.

243. Gunnar Myral, *An International Economy*, New York, 1956.

244. R. Nurske, *Problems of Capital Formation in Underdeveloped Countries*.

245. Cf. Higgins, *op. cit.*, pp. 274ff.

246. Cf. especially his *Sociological Aspects of Economic Growth*, New York, 1960, and his article "Tradition and Economic Growth," in *Tradition, Values and Socio-Economic Development*, ed. R. Braibanti and J. J. Spengler, Durham, 1961, pp. 83ff.

247. *Sociological Aspects,* p. 26.
248. Cf. Talcott Parsons, *The Social System,* New York, 1951; cf. also Talcott Parsons and N. J. Smelser, *Economy and Society,* London, 1956.
249. Hoselitz, *op. cit.,* p. 34.
250. *Ibid.,* pp. 61ff.
251. "The Entrepreneur in American Capital Formation," *NBER, op. cit.,* pp. 339ff.
252. *An International Economy,* pp. 48ff.; cf. also Myrdal's *Economic Theory and Underdeveloped Regions,* London, 1957.
253. Gunnar Myrdal, *Beyond the Welfare State,* New York, 1960. Some of the following paragraphs are taken from my review of this book in *Dissent,* Autumn, 1960. p. 404.
254. Cf. on this Shonfield, *op. cit., passim,* who is just as sharp as Myrdal in his criticism of United Nations agencies, particularly of the International Monetary Fund, which he claims has behaved more like a country banker than a developmental agency. For a trenchant discussion of the politics of foreign aid, cf. Henry Pachter, "Paradoxes of Foreign Aid," *Dissent,* Spring, 1960, p. 167.
255. Cf. Lewis A. Coser, *The Functions of Social Conflict,* New York, 1956, pp. 16ff.
256. Cf. the description of inventory problems in the liquor industry in John McDonald, *Strategy in Poker, Business and War,* New York, 1950, pp. 95ff.
257. Cf. Coser, *op. cit.,* p. 31.
258. For a good description of this development, cf. A. Rapoport, *Fights, Games and Debates,* Ann Arbor, 1960, pp. 111ff.; cf. also R. D. Luce and H. Raiffa, *Games and Decisions,* New York, 1957, pp. 20ff.; R. D. Theocharis, *Early Developments in Mathematical Economics,* London, 1961, pp. 15ff.
259. John von Neumann and Oskar Morgenstern, *Theory of Games and Economic Behavior,* Princeton, 1944.
260. Luce and Raiffa, *op. cit.,* p. 2.

261. Morgenstern, *The Limits of Economics,* London, 1937.
262. Morgenstern, *On the Accuracy of Economic Observations,* Princeton, 1950.
263. Cf. C. D. Flagle, W. H. Huggins, and R. N. Roy, eds., *Operations Research and Systems Engineering,* Baltimore, 1960, *passim;* cf. also T. C. Schelling, *The Strategy of Conflict,* Cambridge, 1960.
264. Luce and Raiffa, *op. cit.,* p. 3.
265. Quoted in Dorfman, Samuelson, and Solow, *op. cit.,* p. 417.
266. "The Theory of Games," *International Economic Papers,* No. 1, London, 1951, p. 37.
267. "The Theory of Economic Behavior," *American Economic Review,* 1945, pp. 909ff.
268. Cf. Luce and Raiffa, *op. cit.,* for an extensive bibliography.
269. Cf. Dorfman, Samuelson, and Solow, *op. cit.,* pp. 428ff. and 465ff.
270. *Ibid.,* p. 468.
271. Cf. Rapoport, *op. cit.,* pp. 124ff.
272. Luce and Raiffa, *op. cit.,* p. 21.
273. For a good summary of this aspect of the debate, cf. H. M. Wagner "Advances in Game Theory," *American Economic Review,* June, 1958, pp. 377ff.
274. Luce and Raiffa, *op. cit.,* p. 57.
275. Neumann and Morgenstern, *op. cit.,* pp. 93ff.
276. *Ibid.,* pp. 146ff.; cf. also Luce and Raiffa, *op. cit.,* pp. 75ff.
277. Cf. Wagner, *op. cit.,* p. 379.
278. Cf. Rapoport, *op. cit.,* p. 173.
279. Cf. his *Strategy and Market Structure,* New York, 1959.
280. Cf. *ibid.,* pp. 107ff.
281. Cf. O. Morgenstern, "Oligopoly, Monopolistic Competition and the Theory of Games," *American Economic Association Proceedings,* May, 1958, pp. 10ff.; cf. also my article "Games Theory and Collective Bargaining," *Labor and Nation,* January-March, 1952, pp. 50ff.
282. Neumann and Morgenstern, *op. cit.,* pp. 220ff.
283. *Ibid.,* pp. 43ff.
284. Cf. Morgenstern, *American Eco-*

nomic *Association Proceedings, op. cit.*, p. 15.

285. M. Shubik, "Game Theory as an Approach to the Firm," *American Economic Association Proceedings*, May, 1960, p. 557.

286. Cf. p. 529 above.

287. Cf. E. G. Bennion, *Elementary Mathematics of Linear Programming and Game Theory*, East Lansing, 1960, p. 135.

288. Schelling, *op. cit.*, pp. 83ff.

289. Cf. D. Ellsberg, "The Reluctant Duelist," *American Economic Review*, December, 1956, pp. 909ff. Ellsberg's aggressive duelist is, of course, Shackle's entrepreneur. However, Raiffa in an as yet unpublished study has found that the common behavior pattern in risky undertakings is for a modest but safe return.

290. Cf. Rapoport, *op. cit.*, p. 229.

291. Coser, *op. cit.*, p. 95.

292. A rather large-sized literature has developed in linear programming. The standard work for economists is Dorfman, Samuelson, and Solow, *op. cit.* A basic book is T. C. Koopmans, ed., *Activity Analysis of Production and Allocation*, New York, 1951. The mathematics in both these is at times quite forbidding. A good entrée into the mathematics is J. G. Kemeny, J. L. Snell, and G. L. Thompson, *Introduction to Finite Mathematics*, Englewood Cliffs, 1957. A more advanced text is Samuel Karlin, *Mathematical Methods and Theory in Games, Programming and Economics*, Reading, 1959. Also useful is Bennion, *op. cit.*, and K. E. Boulding and W. A. Spivey *et al*, *Linear Programming and the Theory of the Firm*. Shorter treatments are available in Allen, *Mathematical Economics*, London, 1956; R. Dorfman, "Mathematical or 'Linear' Programming," *AER*, December, 1953, pp 797ff.; *idem*, "Operations Research," *AER*, September, 1960, pp. 575ff.; and W. J. Baumol, "Activity Analysis in One Lesson," *AER*, December, 1958, pp. 837ff. A good brief dis-

cussion may be found also in T. C. Koopmans, *Three Essays on the State of Economic Science*, New York, 1957.

293. Dorfman, "Operations Research," *op. cit.*, p. 577; Samuelson, "Linear Programming and Economic Theory," RAND Corp., May 25, 1955. p. 5.

294. *Ibid.*, p. 6.

295. Cf. M. K. Wood and G. B. Dantzig, "The Programming of Independent Activities," in Koopmans' *Activity Analysis*, pp. 15ff.

296. See pp. 127 and 436 above.

297. Koopmans, *op. cit.*, p. 1.

298. Cf. Dorfman *et al.*, *op. cit.*, Chap. 8, pp. 186ff. A good exposition of nonlinear programming may be found in W. J. Baumol, *Economic Theory and Operations Research*, Englewood Cliffs, 1961, pp. 98ff.

299. Koopmans, *Three Essays*, p. 71.

300. A good summary of the mathematics involved may be found in Boulding and Spivey, *op. cit.*, Chap. 2, pp. 18ff., as well as in the works cited in Note 292 above.

301. Dorfman *et al.*, *op. cit.*, pp. 131, 201.

302. Dorfman, *American Economic Review*, December, 1953, p. 798.

303. Dorfman *et al.*, *op. cit.*, p. 202.

304. This was necessary to allow for the property of additiveness. Cf. Koopmans, *Three Essays*, p. 72.

305. Cf. his "The Cost of Subsistence," *Journal of Farm Economics*, May, 1945, pp. 304ff.

306. Cf. P. A. Samuelson, "Spatial Price Equilibrium and Linear Programming," *American Economic Review*, June, 1952, pp. 283ff.

307. Koopmans, *Three Essays*, p. 81.

308. Cf. Dorfman, *American Economic Review*, December, 1953, pp. 799ff.; Dorfman *et al.*, *op. cit.*, p. 133.

309. Dorfman *et al.*, *op. cit.*, p. 162.

310. Cf. G. B. Dantzig in Koopmans, *Activity Analysis*, pp. 29ff., 359ff.; cf. also Dorfman *et al.*, *op. cit.*, pp. 64ff.

311. Dorfman *et al.*, *op. cit.*, pp. 67ff.

312. Dantzig, *op. cit.*, p. 30.

313. Dorfman *et al.*, *op. cit.*, pp. 39ff.

314. Koopmans, *Three Essays*, p. 88.
315. *Ibid.*, p. 98.
316. Cf. *ibid.*, pp. 390ff.
317. *Ibid.*, p. 404.
318. A good comparison with marginal analysis is given in Boulding and Spivey, *op. cit.*, Chap. 4, pp. 94ff.
319. Baumol, *op. cit.*, pp. 108-109.
320. Baumol, *American Economic Review*, December, 1958, p. 872.
321. The Leontief open matrix which suggests ways of guiding production given certain goals can be handled with linear techniques. Cf. Dorfman *et al.*, *op. cit.*, pp. 281ff.

Concluding Remarks

1. On the corporate life, cf. W. H. Whyte, Jr., *The Organization Man*, New York, 1956. Many of the new types were catalogued by Martin Shubik in *Administrative Science Quarterly*, December, 1958, pp. 284ff.
2. Cf. the symposium on simulation by G. H. Orcutt, M. Shubik, G. P. E. Clarkson, and H. A. Simon in *American Economic Review*, December, 1960.
3. J. G. March and H. A. Simon, *Organizations*, New York, 1958, pp. 140ff.
4. K. E. Boulding, *The Skills of the Economist*, Cleveland, 1958, pp. 178ff.
5. Cf. comments by G. L. S. Shackle, *Uncertainty in Economics*, Cambridge, 1955, p. 241.
6. Cf. T. Parsons and N. J. Smelser, *Economy and Society*, London, 1956.
7. Cf. Bert F. Hoselitz, "Social Structure and Economic Growth," in his *Sociological Aspects of Economic Growth*, Chicago, 1960, pp. 23ff.
8. The classic example of the impotence of the "generalist" is the volume, *The Impact of the Labor Union*, ed. D. Mc. Wright, New York, 1951.
9. Cf. E. R. Walker, *From Economic Thought to Policy*, Chicago, 1943.
10. Cf. L. Rogin, *The Meaning and Validity of Economic Theory*, New York, 1956.
11. Cf. S. Schoeffler, *The Failures of Economics*, Cambridge, 1955.
12. An illustration of this is W. W. Rostow, *The Stages of Economic Growth*, Cambridge, 1960.
13. Cf. T. C. Koopmans, *Three Essays on the Study of Economic Science*, New York, 1957, pp. 142ff.
14. Schoeffler, *op. cit.*, p. 154.
15. Broadus Mitchell, "The Poverty of Economics," *Economics and the Public Interest*, ed. R. A. Solo, New Brunswick, 1955, pp. 23ff.
16. Cf. R. Ruggles, "Methodological Developments," in *A Survey of Contemporary Economics*, Homewood, 1952, II, 414-15.
17. Cf. Jan Tinbergen, *Economic Policy: Principles and Design*, Amsterdam, 1956; idem, *Centralization and Decentralization in Economic Policy*, Amsterdam, 1954; idem, *On the Theory of Economic Policy*, Amsterdam, 1952; and idem, *Selected Papers*, Amsterdam, 1959, especially the essay, "The Theory of the Optimum Regime," pp. 264ff. The fusion of theory and policy has received its best expression in Tinbergen's work.

Index

For Product Safety Concerns and Information please contact our EU representative GPSR@taylorandfrancis.com Taylor & Francis Verlag GmbH, Kaufingerstraße 24, 80331 München, Germany

Printed and bound by CPI Group (UK) Ltd, Croydon, CR0 4YY

02/05/2025

01859993-0001